International Directory of
COMPANY HISTORIES

International Directory of
COMPANY HISTORIES

VOLUME 74

Editor

Tina Grant

ST. JAMES PRESS
An imprint of Thomson Gale, a part of The Thomson Corporation

Detroit • New York • San Francisco • San Diego • New Haven, Conn. • Waterville, Maine • London • Munich

International Directory of Company Histories, Volume 74
Tina Grant, Editor

Project Editor
Miranda H. Ferrara

Editorial
Virgil Burton, Donna Craft, Louise Gagné,
Peggy Geeseman, Julie Gough, Linda Hall,
Sonya Hill, Keith Jones, Lynn Pearce,
Maureen Puhl, Holly Selden,
Justine Ventimiglia

Imaging and Multimedia
Lezlie Light, Michael Logusz

Manufacturing
Rhonda Dover

Product Manager
Gerald L. Sawchuk

LIBRARY OF CONGRESS CATALOG NUMBER 89-190943
ISBN: 1-55862-549-6

BRITISH LIBRARY CATALOGUING IN PUBLICATION DATA
International directory of company histories. Vol. 74
I. Tina Grant
33.87409

Printed in the United States of America
10 9 8 7 6 5 4 3 2 1

CONTENTS

Preface . . . . page vii
List of Abbreviations ix

Company Histories

PREFACE

The St. James Press series *The International Directory of Company Histories (IDCH)* is intended for reference use by students, business people, librarians, historians, economists, investors, job candidates, and others who seek to learn more about the historical development of the world's most important companies. To date, *IDCH* has covered over 7,600 companies in 74 volumes.

Inclusion Criteria

Most companies chosen for inclusion in *IDCH* have achieved a minimum of US$25 million in annual sales and are leading influences in their industries or geographical locations. Companies may be publicly held, private, or nonprofit. State-owned companies that are important in their industries and that may operate much like public or private companies also are included. Wholly owned subsidiaries and divisions are profiled if they meet the requirements for inclusion. Entries on companies that have had major changes since they were last profiled may be selected for updating.

The *IDCH* series highlights 10% private and nonprofit companies, and features updated entries on approximately 50 companies per volume.

Entry Format

Each entry begins with the company's legal name, the address of its headquarters, its telephone, toll-free, and fax numbers, and its web site. A statement of public, private, state, or parent ownership follows. A company with a legal name in both English and the language of its headquarters country is listed by the English name, with the native-language name in parentheses.

The company's founding or earliest incorporation date, the number of employees, and the most recent available sales figures follow. Sales figures are given in local currencies with equivalents in U.S. dollars. For some private companies, sales figures are estimates and indicated by the abbreviation *est.* The entry lists the exchanges on which a company's stock is traded and its ticker symbol, as well as the company's NAIC codes.

Entries generally contain a *Company Perspectives* box which provides a short summary of the company's mission, goals, and ideals, a *Key Dates* box highlighting milestones in the company's history, lists of *Principal Subsidiaries, Principal Divisions, Principal Operating Units, Principal Competitors,* and articles for *Further Reading.*

American spelling is used throughout *IDCH*, and the word "billion" is used in its U.S. sense of one thousand million.

Sources

Entries have been compiled from publicly accessible sources both in print and on the Internet such as general and academic periodicals, books, annual reports, and material supplied by the companies themselves.

Cumulative Indexes

IDCH contains three indexes: the **Index to Companies**, which provides an alphabetical index to companies discussed in the text as well as to companies profiled, the **Index to Industries**, which allows researchers to locate companies by their principal industry, and the **Geographic Index**, which lists companies alphabetically by the country of their headquarters. The indexes are cumulative and specific instructions for using them are found immediately preceding each index.

Suggestions Welcome

Comments and suggestions from users of *IDCH* on any aspect of the product as well as suggestions for companies to be included or updated are cordially invited. Please write:

The Editor
International Directory of Company Histories
St. James Press
27500 Drake Rd.
Farmington Hills, Michigan 48331-3535

AB	Aktiebolag (Finland, Sweden)
AB Oy	Aktiebolag Osakeyhtiot (Finland)
A.E.	Anonimos Eteria (Greece)
AG	Aktiengesellschaft (Austria, Germany, Switzerland, Liechtenstein)
A.O.	Anonim Ortaklari/Ortakligi (Turkey)
ApS	Amparteselskab (Denmark)
A.Š.	Anonim Širketi (Turkey)
A/S	Aksjeselskap (Norway); Aktieselskab (Denmark, Sweden)
Ay	Avoinyhtio (Finland)
B.A.	Buttengewone Aansprakeiijkheid (The Netherlands)
Bhd.	Berhad (Malaysia, Brunei)
B.V.	Besloten Vennootschap (Belgium, The Netherlands)
C.A.	Compania Anonima (Ecuador, Venezuela)
C. de R.L.	Compania de Responsabilidad Limitada (Spain)
Co.	Company
Corp.	Corporation
CRL	Companhia a Responsabilidao Limitida (Portugal, Spain)
C.V.	Commanditaire Vennootschap (The Netherlands, Belgium)
G.I.E.	Groupement d'Interet Economique (France)
GmbH	Gesellschaft mit beschraenkter Haftung (Austria, Germany, Switzerland)
Inc.	Incorporated (United States, Canada)
I/S	Interessentselskab (Denmark); Interesentselskap (Norway)
KG/KGaA	Kommanditgesellschaft/Kommanditgesellschaft auf Aktien (Austria, Germany, Switzerland)
KK	Kabushiki Kaisha (Japan)
K/S	Kommanditselskab (Denmark); Kommandittselskap (Norway)
Lda.	Limitada (Spain)
L.L.C.	Limited Liability Company (United States)
Ltd.	Limited (Various)
Ltda.	Limitada (Brazil, Portugal)
Ltee.	Limitee (Canada, France)
mbH	mit beschraenkter Haftung (Austria, Germany)
N.V.	Naamloze Vennootschap (Belgium, The Netherlands)
OAO	Otkrytoe Aktsionernoe Obshchestve (Russia)
OOO	Obschestvo s Ogranichennoi Otvetstvennostiu (Russia)
Oy	Osakeyhtiö (Finland)
PLC	Public Limited Co. (United Kingdom, Ireland)
Pty.	Proprietary (Australia, South Africa, United Kingdom)
S.A.	Société Anonyme (Belgium, France, Greece, Luxembourg, Switzerland, Arab speaking countries); Sociedad Anónima (Latin America [except Brazil], Spain, Mexico); Sociedades Anônimas (Brazil, Portugal)
SAA	Societe Anonyme Arabienne
S.A.R.L.	Sociedade Anonima de Responsabilidade Limitada (Brazil, Portugal); Société à Responsabilité Limitée (France, Belgium, Luxembourg)
S.A.S.	Societá in Accomandita Semplice (Italy); Societe Anonyme Syrienne (Arab speaking countries)
Sdn. Bhd.	Sendirian Berhad (Malaysia)
S.p.A.	Società per Azioni (Italy)
Sp. z.o.o.	Spólka z ograniczona odpowiedzialnoscia (Poland)
S.R.L.	Società a Responsabilità Limitata (Italy); Sociedad de Responsabilidad Limitada (Spain, Mexico, Latin America [except Brazil])
S.R.O.	Spolecnost s Rucenim Omezenym (Czechoslovakia)
Ste.	Societe (France, Belgium, Luxembourg, Switzerland)
VAG	Verein der Arbeitgeber (Austria, Germany)
YK	Yugen Kaisha (Japan)
ZAO	Zakrytoe Aktsionernoe Obshchestve (Russia)

$	United States dollar	ISK	Icelandic krona
£	United Kingdom pound	ITL	Italian lira
¥	Japanese yen	JMD	Jamaican dollar
AED	Emirati dirham	KPW	North Korean won
ARS	Argentine peso	KRW	South Korean won
ATS	Austrian shilling	KWD	Kuwaiti dinar
AUD	Australian dollar	LUF	Luxembourg franc
BEF	Belgian franc	MUR	Mauritian rupee
BHD	Bahraini dinar	MXN	Mexican peso
BRL	Brazilian real	MYR	Malaysian ringgit
CAD	Canadian dollar	NGN	Nigerian naira
CHF	Swiss franc	NLG	Netherlands guilder
CLP	Chilean peso	NOK	Norwegian krone
CNY	Chinese yuan	NZD	New Zealand dollar
COP	Colombian peso	OMR	Omani rial
CZK	Czech koruna	PHP	Philippine peso
DEM	German deutsche mark	PKR	Pakistani rupee
DKK	Danish krone	PLN	Polish zloty
DZD	Algerian dinar	PTE	Portuguese escudo
EEK	Estonian Kroon	RMB	Chinese renminbi
EGP	Egyptian pound	RUB	Russian ruble
ESP	Spanish peseta	SAR	Saudi riyal
EUR	euro	SEK	Swedish krona
FIM	Finnish markka	SGD	Singapore dollar
FRF	French franc	THB	Thai baht
GRD	Greek drachma	TND	Tunisian dinar
HKD	Hong Kong dollar	TRL	Turkish lira
HUF	Hungarian forint	TWD	new Taiwan dollar
IDR	Indonesian rupiah	VEB	Venezuelan bolivar
IEP	Irish pound	VND	Vietnamese dong
ILS	new Israeli shekel	ZAR	South African rand
INR	Indian rupee	ZMK	Zambian kwacha

International Directory of
COMPANY
HISTORIES

ACCUBUILT

The Leading Manufacturer of Specialty Vehicles

Accubuilt, Inc.

2550 Central Point Parkway
Lima, Ohio, 45804
U.S.A.
Telephone: (419) 224-3910
Fax: (419) 222-4450
Web site: http://www.accubuilt.com

Private Company
Incorporated: 2000
Employees: 200
Sales: $70 million (2004)
NAIC: 336111 Automobile Manufacturing; 336999 All
     Other Transportation Equipment Manufacturing

Accubuilt, Inc., is a manufacturer of specialized vehicles, operating as the largest and oldest maker of funeral coaches. The company's funeral coaches, constructed from chassis made by Ford Motor Co. and General Motors Corp., are manufactured in Lima, Ohio, and sold under the names Superior, Sayers & Scovill, Eureka, and Miller-Meteor. Accubuilt also manufactures wheelchair, shuttle, and limousine vans under the Vartanian name. Accubuilt is controlled by Paladin Capital Partners Fund, L.P. and Hancock Mezzanine Partners III, L.P.

Origins

Accubuilt was a corporate title created at the beginning of the 21st century to represent a number of brands with origins in the 19th century. The process by which the handful of brands came together under one umbrella entity occurred over decades, engendered by acquisitions and mergers during the 1980s and 1990s that ultimately created the largest and oldest manufacturer of funeral coaches in the United States. At the core of the organization that adopted the Accubuilt name in 2000 were two companies, Sayers & Scovill (S&S) and Superior Coach Co., each regarded as pioneers in the business of manufacturing vehicles designed for, as the April 2001 issue of *Automotive Manufacturing & Production* noted, the "last ride."

Of the two main pillars of Accubuilt, S&S was established first, a firm founded by William Sayers and A.R. Scovill in 1876. The founders, who christened their enterprise the Sayers & Scovill Coach Company, began making horse-drawn hearses in the Cincinnati, Ohio, area, starting what became, by the beginning of the 21st century, the oldest continuously operating funeral coach manufacturer in the United States. The company distinguished itself early in its development by demonstrating a high standard of craftsmanship. The carriages, sometimes constructed with glass side panels, bore ornate carvings on supporting wood structures, reflecting the public's desire for elegance and a certain sort of pageantry in a funeral procession. As time passed, preferences with respect to funeral ceremonies and attendant proceedings changed. Funerals became more staid affairs, and funeral coaches correspondingly became more somber in design. As with any business, S&S's longevity depended on its ability to adapt to changing market conditions and emerging trends, something the company would have to do many times during its development. The company's greatest test in this regard occurred during the early 20th century. The invention of the internal combustion engine revolutionized the funeral-carriage trade, making S&S's signature horse-drawn carriages relics of an era gone by. (The first commercially available automobile hearse was introduced in 1909 by another Ohio-based company, Cincinnati's Crane & Breed). S&S successfully adapted to the profound change that swept throughout its industry, becoming one of the few funeral coach companies to make the transition from carriages to motor-powered vehicles without surrendering its standing in the marketplace.

As S&S quickly learned the craft of converting automobiles to hearses, the story of another funeral coach manufacturer was just beginning. In 1909, The Garford Motor Truck Company was established. An Ohio-based company as well, Garford Truck was formed in a small town 30 miles outside Cleveland named Elyria, where it began manufacturing heavy trucks. The company did well, enjoying sufficient demand for its trucks to require a substantially larger manufacturing facility. In 1925, the company moved its operations to Lima, Ohio, where it occupied a new plant housing both its manufacturing operations and its administrative offices. The move to Lima marked a turning point in the company's history, occurring at the same time Garford changed its name to The Superior Body Company and diversified, introducing a line of hearse and ambulance

Company Perspectives:

Accubuilt doesn't just build vehicles. Accubuilt re-invents vehicles. Turning a traditional vehicle into a specialty vehicle is no simple task. The vehicle's structure must be completely modified. At its 168,000-square-foot manufacturing facility, Accubuilt has the extensive capabilities, state-of-the-art technologies and highly skilled workforce necessary to extend and reassemble vehicle structures to exacting and consistent standards.

bodies. (Because they were the only ones with vehicles long enough to carry someone in a recumbent position, funeral homes were often the sole providers of ambulance service). Although the company had built its business on manufacturing heavy trucks, the line of hearses became its mainstay business line not long after the move to Lima, when the Superior brand became one of the most well-regarded names in the funeral coach industry.

Superior, like S&S, was in the business of converting vehicles, not making them. Both companies were involved in producing what later became known as professional cars: hearses, flower cars, rescue cares, service cars, ambulances, limousines, and vehicles built to combine two or more of these functions. Professional cars were custom-bodied vehicles based on passenger car styling, entirely made by hand except for the commercial chassis and front and rear clips. Both Superior and S&S relied on established car manufacturers to provide the framework for their conversion efforts, purchasing chassis that formed the basis of their funeral coaches. Initially, Superior built its hearses and ambulances on the Studebaker chassis, adding chassis built by Pontiac in 1936. The company changed its name to The Superior Coach Company in 1940, inaugurating a decade that would see it build hearses styled on Cadillac, LaSalle, Chrysler, DeSoto, and Dodge chassis. During this period, S&S introduced several distinctive models, bringing back the carved pillars of the late 19th century with the production of the "Art Carved" hearse in 1929. In 1938, the company introduced the industry's first victoria-style hearse, a model equipped with a heavily padded leather roof and a blind quarter panel decorated by S-shaped irons reminiscent of horse-drawn carriages of the late 19th century.

During the post-World War II era, as Superior and S&S affirmed their reputations in the funeral-car industry, both companies were acquired by other companies. Superior became part of the Sheller-Globe Corporation. S&S was purchased by Hess & Eisenhardt Company. The two companies were brought together when an entrepreneur and veteran of the limousine industry, Tom Earnhart, decided to acquire two of the most venerated brands in the business. In 1981, Earnhart acquired Superior from Sheller-Globe and later that year purchased S&S from Hess & Eisenhardt, forming a new company S&S/Superior of Ohio, Inc. to oversee the further development of the two businesses. Manufacturing operations were consolidated at Superior's plant in Lima, which had been expanded 30 years earlier.

The next eventful chapter in the development of Superior and S&S occurred during the 1990s. In 1995, a new plant in

Lima was constructed, becoming the state-of-the-art facility where funeral coaches built on Cadillac, Lincoln, and Ford chassis were constructed. The establishment of the new plant, which blended hand-building and mass-production techniques, represented the modern symbol of a nearly 120-year-old organization, one that began to exhibit a desire to increase its opportunities for growth after it gained new owners. In 1996, PNC Equity Management, a part of the Pittsburgh-based PNC Bank, acquired a controlling stake in S&S/Superior. The combined factors of having a new equity partner and a need to exploit the new manufacturing plant to its fullest led to two important acquisitions several years later, purchases that joined four old rivals in the funeral coach industry.

Expansion in 1999

In 1999, PNC Equity Management, through a subsidiary named Superior Holdings, Inc., acquired certain assets belonging to CCE, Inc. The acquisition added two esteemed names in the funeral coach business, each with rich histories rivaling the legacies of S&S and Superior. The older of the two brands was Eureka, which started business in Rock Falls, Illinois, in 1871 as the Eureka Manufacturing Company. Initially, Eureka manufactured desks, chairs, and church furniture, a line of work the company later abandoned to focus on making horse-drawn vehicles. Like S&S, Eureka had to contend with the invention of the automobile, which prompted the company to apply its woodworking talent and equipment to producing carved wooden bodies for hearses and ambulances. In the early 1920s, the company introduced a style of hearse that became ubiquitous, the limousine, an innovation followed later in the decade with one of the first three-way hearses, which featured a casket table that moved along a Y-shaped track to emerge from either the side or the rear of the coach. Despite the company's solid reputation and its contributions to its industry, Eureka struggled during the post-World War II era, eventually closing its doors in 1964. The brand was resurrected in 1980, when Thomas McPherson used the Eureka name to open his own funeral coach manufacturing company in Toronto, Canada. The brand name enjoyed success during its second life, drawing the attention of a group of investors at the end of the decade. The investors, represented by their company, CCE, Inc., acquired Eureka in 1989 and moved the company to a new manufacturing location in Norwalk, Ohio. Several years later, in 1993, CCE's management followed through on its goal of expanding operations in Norwalk by purchasing another funeral coach firm, the Miller-Meteor Company.

Miller-Meteor began business in 1915 as the Meteor Motor Company. Meteor's first funeral coach, introduced the year of its formation, was built on a Model T chassis and became instant sales success. One year later, the company introduced a combination pallbearer's coach and ambulance, a model that also proved successful, selling more than 200 cars during its first three months on the market. Meteor became the first company to design and build chassis designed specifically for use as a hearse and ambulance. In 1954, after nearly 40 years on its own, the company was acquired by Wayne Works, Inc., a manufacturer of school buses and delivery trucks. In 1956, Wayne Works purchased A.J Miller Company, an enterprise founded in 1917 in Bellfontaine, Ohio, that manufactured complete cars. After purchasing A.J. Miller, Wayne Works's management merged it with Meteor, believing the two companies

Key Dates:

1871: Eureka Manufacturing Company is founded

1876: The Sayers & Scovill Coach Company is founded.

1909: The Garford Motor Truck Company is founded.

1915: Meteor Motor Company is founded.

1917: A.J. Miller Company is founded.

1925: Garford Motor Truck Company changes its name to The Superior Body Company.

1940: The Superior Body Company changes its name to The Superior Coach Company.

1957: Meteor Motor and A.J Miller are merged, creating the Miller-Meteor Company.

1981: Sayers & Scovill and Superior are acquired by an entrepreneur named Tom Earnhart, creating S&S/ Superior of Ohio, Inc.

1995: A new manufacturing plant is built in Lima, Ohio.

1996: PNC Equity Management acquires a controlling interest in S&S/Superior.

1999: The Eureka and Miller-Meteor brands are acquired by PNC Equity Management.

2000: S&S/Superior changes its name to Accubuilt.

2002: Accubuilt acquires Vartanian Industries, Inc.

2004: Paladin Capital Partners Fund, L.P. and Hancock Mezzanine Partners III, L.P. acquire a controlling interest in Accubuilt.

would benefit from the exchange of technical information and shared operations. The decision led to the creation of the Miller-Meteor Company in 1957. For the next two decades, Miller-Meteor operated in the funeral coach business, eventually expanding its product line to include 34 models. Like Eureka, the company struggled financially, however, shuttering its operations in 1979. Also like Eureka, the company's brand name was given a second life when Collins Industries began using the Miller-Meteor name, beginning in 1984, on its line of funeral coaches and limousines. Roughly a decade later, CCE purchased Miller-Meteor, using the company to expand its manufacturing operations in Norwalk.

When PNC Equity Management completed its purchase of certain CCE assets in 1999, its funeral coach business comprised four venerable brands: S&S, Superior, Eureka, and Miller-Meteor. S&S/Superior stood as the oldest and largest maker of funeral coaches in the United States, but its corporate title no longer reflected the breadth of the company. In 2000, the company changed its name to Accubuilt, the new corporate banner that controlled approximately 70 percent of the U.S. market through its four distinguished brands. After the operations were absorbed into the facility at Lima, 200 production workers were employed at the 160,000-square-foot facility, making 1,500 funeral coaches and six-door limousines each year.

Diversification in 2002

During the first years of the 21st century, Accubuilt's expansion efforts continued, creating a larger, more diversified specialized vehicle manufacturer. In 2002, the company added another brand to its portfolio in order to explore other avenues of growth to complement its stalwart market position in the funeral coach business. "We've got 65 to 75 percent of that market," Accubuilt's chief executive officer, Stephen Griffith, explained in a November 6, 2002 interview with the *Blade*, a Toledo, Ohio, newspaper. "It's a fine market," Griffith continued, "but there isn't a lot of growth. If you want to grow you have to look at other opportunities. And mobility products are generally a better-growing market than funeral vehicles." Griffith's statement referred to Accubuilt's August 2002 purchase of Vartanian Industries, Inc., a Brodheadsville, Pennsylvania-based manufacturer of wheelchair, shuttle, and limousine vans. "It's a small acquisition," Griffith said at the time of the purchase in an August 12, 2002 interview with *Knight Ridder/Tribune Business Times*, "but it brings with it significant growth potential." Vartanian's Brodheadsville plant was closed after the acquisition, unable to accommodate new business, and moved to Lima, adding another dimension to Accubuilt's manufacturing activities.

As Accubuilt plotted its future course, further acquisitions were expected, with strong indications of an expansion-minded orientation revealed when control over the company changed hands. In May 2004, PNC Equity Management sold its controlling interest in Accubuilt to Paladin Capital Partners Fund, L.P., a private equity investment company with offices in Atlanta, Georgia, and Washington, D.C., and Hancock Mezzanine Partners III, L.P., an investment fund managed by John Hancock Life Insurance Company. Dominic D. Cuzzocrea, who served as chief executive officer of Accubuilt when the company gained its new backers, commented on the implications of the deal in a May 18, 2004 company press release. "The Accubuilt management team is delighted to partner with Paladin and with Hancock Mezzanine as we continue to grow and serve our markets more effectively," the statement read. "We thank PNC for their guidance and assistance with our growth over the last seven plus years and we are quite confident that Accubuilt will continue to prosper by delivering the best values to our diversified customer base, just as we have always done. Paladin shares Accubuilt management's goal to maintain our dominant position in funeral vehicles while diversifying into growth markets such as our recently acquired commercial van business. We have increased our funeral vehicle market share in 2004 while simultaneously growing our mobility van business into the third largest Ford pool account after less than two years in the industry." In the years ahead, Accubuilt promised to maintain its overwhelming lead in its core market and to broaden its presence in the specialized vehicle market.

Principal Competitors

Federal Coach LLC; Chateau Horse-Drawn Hearses; Eagle Coach Company.

Further Reading

Pakulski, Gary T., "Lima, Ohio, Hearse Builder Branches Out to Wheelchair Vans," *Blade*, November 6, 2002, p. B2.

Rutz, Heather, "Accubuilt, Union Reach 3-Year Agreement," *Lima News*, February 9, 2005, p. A1.

Sabin, Jim, "Lima, Ohio, Limousine Maker Expands Operations," *Knight Ridder/Tribune Business News*, August 17, 2002, p. ITEM022229058.

Whitfield, Kermit, "Building the Last Ride," *Automotive Manufacturing & Production*, April 2001, p. 62.

—Jeffrey L. Covell

AIR PRODUCTS

Air Products and Chemicals, Inc.

7201 Hamilton Boulevard
Allentown, Pennsylvania 18195-1501
U.S.A.
Telephone: (610) 481-4911
Fax: (610) 481-5900
Web site: http://www.airproducts.com

Public Company
Incorporated: 1940 as Industrial Gas Equipment Co.
Employees: 19,900
Sales: $7.41 billion (2004)
Stock Exchanges: New York
Ticker Symbol: APD
NAIC: 325110 Petrochemical Manufacturing; 325120
   Industrial Gas Manufacturing; 325211 Plastics
   Material and Resin Manufacturing

Air Products and Chemicals, Inc., is a leading global producer of industrial, specialty, and medical gases such as oxygen, nitrogen, argon, and hydrogen. Since the late 1990s Air Products has been focused on opportunities in the electronics, energy, and healthcare industries. Another growth platform was the commercialization of nanomaterials. The company also was building filling stations for hydrogen powered vehicles. Air Products has a reputation for both fiscal security and the safety of its workers. Formed around the concept of onsite industrial gases production, the development and growth of Air Products has been characterized by innovation. As former company president Dexter F. Baker noted in *Research Management* magazine in 1986, the company found success through the employment of four fundamental criteria: ''Finding a market that is not being well-satisfied, creating a superior technical solution, commercializing the solution, and acting as an investor in one's own new creative solution.''

Depression Era Origins

Air Products founder Leonard Parker Pool began his career as a teenager selling oxygen to industrial customers, and, by the age of 30, he was district manager for Compressed Industrial Gases. In 1938, when Pool began his work, the oxygen market was dominated by large companies such as Linde AG and the Air Reduction Company, which avoided price wars and did not intrude in each other's sales territory. Oxygen was inexpensive to distill, and the raw material from which it is distilled, air, is free, so the chief costs involved shipping oxygen in heavy containers. Pool's idea was to distill oxygen in the customer's plant; however, the cost of this plan would have been prohibitive unless a cheap oxygen generator could be designed.

Pool, the son of a boiler-maker, had only a high school education, so, to design the generator he needed, he hired a young engineer by the name of Frank Pavlis to work with him. Their design was revolutionary because it used a compressor lubricated with liquid oxygen and graphite. At that time, competitor compressors were lubricated with water due to the fear that the compressed oxygen, in contact with a lubricating oil, would ignite when exposed to the smallest spark. When oxygen was compressed using water, several steps were required to then remove the water from the oxygen. The new generator, however, could skip these steps and, as a result, it was less expensive to build, install, and maintain.

By 1940, Pool and Pavlis had a functioning generator. Pool quit his job, sold his insurance policy, and borrowed all the money that his wife—a schoolteacher—had saved. With this capital, he founded Air Products Inc. and opened shop in a former mortuary. In these last years of the Great Depression, the American business climate was dismal, and Pool had a great deal of difficulty selling his generators.

With the onset of World War II, Air Products began to thrive, manufacturing mobile oxygen generators for the armed services and heavy industry. When the war ended, Air Products lost many of its clients and was forced to aggressively pursue new accounts. Although Air Products could provide oxygen at a cost 25 percent lower than its competitors, customers were slow to take advantage of the new system, which was offered through five- to ten-year leasing agreements, under which Air Products would maintain the generator and teach employees how to operate it. While customers found the idea appealing, many were locked into long-term contracts with a company that shipped oxygen to their plants.

Company Perspectives:

Air Products touches the lives of consumers around the globe in positive ways every day. We serve customers in healthcare, technology, energy, and industrial markets worldwide with a unique portfolio of products, services and solutions, providing atmospheric gases, process and specialty gases, performance materials and chemical intermediates. The company has built leading positions in key growth markets, such as semiconductor materials, refinery hydrogen, home healthcare services, natural gas liquefaction, and advanced coatings and adhesives.

In desperation, Pool traveled to Pittsburgh and used a sales technique called ''door-stepping'' to win a major contract with Weirton Steel. This sales technique involved staying at the customer's plant until the contract was signed. Pool said years later, ''God, we just lived at Weirton Steel when we learned they were interested in our proposition.'' Indeed, Weirton was practically Air Product's only customer at that time.

In need of funds to construct a new plant, Air Products sent out a prospectus to potential investors. Pool acknowledged the company's inexperience, stating that Air Products ''has no background in prewar civil business,'' and that in competing ''by a new method of distribution in a well-established field against experienced competitors who have much greater resources'' Air Products expected ''to operate at a loss following the completion of its government contracts.'' The company's boldness and candor apparently impressed investors, and the necessary $300,000 was raised. Soon, Air Products had installed generators at several chemical companies and had built a huge generator for Weirton Steel, a generator 100 times larger than any that had been built before.

Pool attributed a large part of his company's success to his ''tiger pack,'' a group of aggressive young engineers serving as sales staff at Air Products. Pool maintained a close watch over operations, and, although he became known for his sense of humor and his commitment to his employees, he was also capable of dealing out a tongue-lashing to anyone who misled a customer or lost a sale.

Space Age Spurring New Interest

In the late 1950s, Air Products profited from the launching of the first Soviet Sputnik, which American scientists surmised was powered by liquid hydrogen. When the U.S. defense department wanted liquid hydrogen, Air Products was asked to supply it. As a security precaution, new Air Products Company plants were provided with code names such as ''Baby-Bear'' and ''Project Rover''; one large plant was disguised as the ''Apix Fertilizer Company.''

In addition to the production of liquid hydrogen, Air Products also branched out into new areas of chemistry, like fluorine chemistry and cryogenics (the science of ultra-low temperatures). The company's oxygen business also continued to grow. The company no longer leased generators but built multimillion dollar

operations near major customers, including Ford Motor Co. and U.S. Steel, selling any excess capacity to smaller customers.

Throughout the 1960s, Air Products thrived; sales rose 400 percent, while earnings rose 500 percent. The expansion into merchant gas (gas sold in tanks) proved profitable for the company, although Air Products was a latecomer to the field. Air Products used its late entrance into the field to its advantage by conceding the saturated markets to its well established rivals, Linde and Air Reduction Company, seeking out smaller, more receptive markets instead. In fact, as Air Products saw its fortunes growing, competitors like Linde experienced decreased profits.

During this time, oxygen-fired furnaces became a popular alternative to the hearth-style furnaces used in the steel-making industry, increasing oxygen consumption considerably. Nitrogen, another Air Products specialty, was also in demand as a refrigerant. Air Products also began selling the implements necessary to handling gases, such as welding tools, anesthesia equipment, and cryogenic systems. Gases and gas-related equipment accounted for approximately three-fourths of Air Product's profits during the 1960s; the remainder came from chemicals and engineering services.

The diversification of Air Products into chemicals began in 1962 with the company's purchase of Houdry Chemicals and, later, Air Company, a specialty chemical company. When the Air Company was purchased by Air Products, it was losing money. To achieve a turnaround, Air Products took Air Company's acetylic chemicals and made them into specialty chemicals that fetched a higher price; the plant became profitable almost immediately. In 1969, Air Products purchased Escambia Chemicals, paying a cash price well below its market value. Escambia's attraction lay in a product called DABCO, regarded as the best catalyst for making urethane foam.

Weathering the 1970s and 1980s

Due to the energy crisis and a recession, the 1970s was a difficult period for many chemical companies. Although Air Products could not sustain the phenomenal growth it experienced in the 1960s, its annual sales and profits increased at least 9 percent and sometimes as high as 20 percent. During this time, the company held a strong position in industrial gases both in the United States and abroad, as its gases were used by virtually every major industry. The chemical division performed erratically, however, and, during the recession, its engineering services division, which designed pipelines and plants, yielded disappointing results. Nevertheless, Air Products' industrial gases kept the company afloat.

The energy crisis had both positive and negative effects on Air Products. The industrial gases division, which consumed a large amount of electricity, was sensitive to rising utility rates. As the price of organic fuels rose, however, oxygen became a more popular fuel. The increased production costs of petrochemicals and plastics were offset by higher demand for cryogenic equipment and gases to liquify natural gas. Like many other successful chemical companies, Air Products was thus able to benefit from the high energy prices in some cases.

```
┌─────────────────────────────────────────────────┐
│                                                 │
│               Key Dates:                        │
│                                                 │
│ 1940:  Leonard Parker Pool forms Air Products.  │
│ 1957:  Soviet Union's Sputnik launch spurs U.S. │
│        interest in Air Products' compressed     │
│        hydrogen.                                │
│ 1962:  The company diversifies via acquisitions │
│        of Houdry Chemical and the Air Company.  │
│ 1980:  Air Products joins a synthetic fuel      │
│        venture.                                 │
│ 1985:  A methane recovery plant is acquired.    │
│ 1996:  The company divests most of its          │
│        environmental-energy businesses.         │
│ 2000:  The APD/Air Liquide $11 billion takeover │
│        of British Oxygen is scuttled on         │
│        antitrust grounds.                       │
│ 2002:  American Homecare Supply is acquired.    │
│ 2003:  Air Products acquires the $200 million   │
│        electronic chemicals business of Ashland │
│        Specialty Chemicals.                     │
│                                                 │
└─────────────────────────────────────────────────┘
```

During this time, the OPEC oil embargo convinced company management to invest in synthetic fuels. In 1980, Air Products, Wheelbraton Fry Inc., the state of Kentucky, and the U.S. Department of Energy formed a joint venture to produce a high-energy, low-pollution fuel from coal. Air Products invested $45 million in the project, while the bulk of the money, $748 million, came from the federal government. As none of the various synthetic fuel projects were successful, Air Products' only consolation was the high levels of oxygen consumed in the unsuccessful venture. Still, Air Products remained interested in energy development. In 1985, the company bought a methane recovery plant and accelerated development of a plant that converted garbage to steam and electricity.

A 12-year, $281 million contract to supply liquid hydrogen for the space shuttle bolstered earnings, as did the discovery of expanded uses for industrial gases. For instance, the food industry increased its use of hydrogen for hydrogenating vegetable oils, and flash-freezing, a process that required nitrogen, became an increasingly more popular technique.

In the 1970s and the early 1980s, Air Products, like other highly successful chemical companies of the same size, became concerned with having a product that could be used by a myriad of industries, in order to avoid overdependence on staple products linked to cyclical industries. Toward this end, Air Products focused on marketing oxygen and industrial gases to a wide variety of clients, so that dramatic downturns in an industry—such as steel manufacturing—would not be fatal to the company.

Also during this time, Air Products established a reputation for hiring highly competent, professional engineers, chemists, and business staff. Rather than assuming responsibility for such hirings, company president Edward Donley delegated the job to the vice-presidents and line managers, whom, according to Donley, were better judges of an applicant's potential than professional recruiters. The applicants hired by Air Products sometimes spent up to three years working in different departments of their choice, in order to decide where their skills would be best employed. Air Products also believed the exposure of engineers and chemists to management positions would prove vital to future success.

Air Products also demonstrated a commitment to the health and safety of its workers. In the 1970s, when three employees died from PVC-induced cancer, Air Products periodically tested 492 other workers at two plants for possible exposure, and steps were taken to minimize health risks. In the late 1980s and early 1990s, the company developed ''Responsible Care'' objectives to promote safety, environmentalism, and health at its facilities. At the same time, however, the company initiated a legal challenge to industry regulations, claiming that many were unfeasible to implement.

New Environment-Energy Business for the 1990s

In 1986, Air Products embarked on a ten-year strategic plan that added a third core business, environment-energy, and focused on globalization of the firm. Between 1986 and 1993, the company invested $1 billion in European facilities as part of its strategy to replace older, less efficient plants, add new production capacity, and create new products. Significant investments in Asia resulted in the construction of seven industrial gas plants by 1992. The company also gained access to significant markets by buying mid-sized competitors and entering into joint ventures.

By 1990, investments of $1.2 billion in the environmental-energy systems segment had expanded that division to include: a refuse-fired cogeneration facility; the American REF-FUEL joint venture with Browning-Ferris for building waste-to-energy facilities; a joint venture with Mitsubishi Heavy Industries to market flue gas desulfurization systems; and a methane gas reclamation business for landfills. Air Products' tire recycling program, which was undertaken in 1988, came to fruition in the early 1990s, as the rubber recovered from scrap tires promised to reduce the environmental and health hazards presented by scrap tires and offered cost savings for the production of rubberized asphalt, shoe soles, carpet underlay, and other products. Although Air Products faced well-established competition in the environmental arena, the rapid expansion of that market promised significant returns.

During this time, Air Products' earnings per share increased about 20 percent per year, double the rate of Standard & Poor's industrial index. In 1992, Harold A. Wagner, who had been a key proponent of the strategic plan, replaced Dexter Baker as chairperson and chief executive officer, and Air Products launched a two-year program to consolidate and restructure its $1.1 billion chemical business. The reorganization streamlined the chemicals segment from four to three divisions, realigned its management, and reduced its workforce by 7 to 10 percent, or 1,000 to 1,400 jobs. In 1993, Air Products achieved record cash flows, sold record volumes of industrial gases and chemicals, and ranked as the third largest supplier of industrial gases in the world. The company planned to continue expanding its global investment programs throughout the 1990s.

Refocusing in the Mid-1990s

The second half of the 1990s was a period of intense consolidation in the industrial gases industry. To survive as a public company, Air Products had to keep meeting Wall Street's expectations. Air Products sold its share of the American Ref-Fuel business in 1996 for $400 million. The company was focusing on areas where it was a leader or expected significant growth, while maintaining a commitment to its energy and environmental segment. Industrial gases, however, which with sales of $2.5 billion accounted for 60 percent of total revenues, remained its core business, CEO Harold A. Wagner told *Chemical Week.*

Air Products acquired an intermediates business from Britain's Imperial Chemical Industries in 1997. This was soon supplemented with the purchase of Solkatronic Chemicals and the addition of a methylamines plant in Florida.

Air Products was aiming to grow its business in international markets. Its overseas gases business was built on enduring joint ventures and preferred to deal in higher-value gases such as those used in the electronics industry, which landed a number of key contracts abroad in the mid-1990s. The Asian industrial gas business was up 35 percent in one year, according to *Chemical Week,* and Air Products was preparing to enter the Indian market. Air Products had invested more than $1 billion in Europe since the mid-1980s and was establishing facilities in former Soviet satellites.

An $11 billion deal to acquire British Oxygen in cooperation with Air Liquide was scuttled by the Federal Trade Commission in 2000. According to *Chemical Market Reporter,* this failed takeover helped put a damper on consolidation activity across the entire industry. The industrial gases industry was considered highly consolidated, with five producers controlling two-thirds of the market, according to one consultant. Air Products was then reckoned to be the fourth largest global player, with a 9 percent share.

As noted in *Forbes,* around this time the company's CEO, John P. Jones, steered Air Products' research and development toward the fast-growing areas of energy, electronics, and healthcare, which together accounted for 30 percent of the company's total revenues of $5 billion in 1999. Within five years, these areas would provide half of all revenues.

The company divested slower growing businesses. Air Products exited a large but highly fragmented market in early 2002 when it sold most of its U.S. cylinder gas business to Airgas of Radnor, Pennsylvania for $236 million.

Acquisitions in Europe and America grew the home healthcare business rapidly. In 2002, Air Products acquired the home respiratory business of German rival Messer Griesheim. American Homecare Supply (AHS) was acquired in October 2002. AHS, later renamed Air Products Healthcare, was a leading private supplier of home medical equipment. With this entry into the U.S. market, Air Products was supplying homecare services to more than 275,000 patients from more than 200 sites in 14 countries. It would soon buy several smaller healthcare businesses in the United States.

Air Products was able to complete the acquisition of the $200 million electronic chemicals business of Ashland Specialty Chemicals in August 2003. The deal went through despite a legal challenge by Honeywell.

Air Products and its rivals in the industrial gases industry weathered the recession better than their counterparts devoted to the chemicals business, noted *Chemical Week.* Air Products had a reputation as a strong performer during economic downturns. Most of its contracts were long-term and included provisions for passing on energy costs, noted *Chemical Market Reporter.*

Air Products fared even better as the recession began to ease. After three years of sliding profits, net income rose 18 percent to $604 million on sales of $7.4 billion for the fiscal year ended September 30, 2004. More good results were expected in the future as the lackluster economy improved.

Air Products was conducting considerable research on performance materials, another growth platform. It was in joint ventures with Nanotechnologies Inc. of Texas and Europe's Nanogate to develop materials with new properties. Air Products was at the forefront of applying other new technologies. By 2005, it had 30 filling stations for hydrogen-fueled vehicles up and running.

Principal Subsidiaries

Air Products Asia, Inc. (U.S.A.); Air Products Europe, Inc. (U.S.A.); Air Products Japan, Inc. (Japan).

Principal Divisions

Chemical Intermediates; Performance Materials.

Principal Operating Units

Chemicals; Gases and Equipment.

Principal Competitors

Air Liquide Group; Linde AG; Praxair, Inc.

Further Reading

Butrica, Andrew J., *Out of Thin Air: A History of Air Products and Chemicals, Inc., 1940–1990,* New York: Praeger, 1990.

Freedman, William, "Air Products' Second Wind: Setting the Trim for New Growth," *Chemical Week,* April 24, 1996, pp. 20ff.

Hunter, David, and Natasha Alperowicz, "Industrial Gases: Riding High, Despite Recession," *Chemical Week,* February 20, 2002, pp. 21ff.

Milmo, Sean, "BOC Gases Deal Collapses and Shakes Industry," *Chemical Market Reporter,* May 22, 2000, p. 8.

Nelson, Brett, "Suddenly Sexy," *Forbes,* February 14, 2005, p. 122.

Storck, William J., "Air Products on Course in Ambitious Strategic Plan," *Chemical & Engineering News,* October 5, 1992, pp. 44–46.

Swaim, Will, "Air to the Throne," *World Trade,* February 1993, pp. 66–68.

Teresko, John, "From Confusion to Action," *Industry Week,* September 2005, pp. 56–62.

Tilton, Helga, "In Tough Times, Air Products Plays the Stability Card," *Chemical Market Reporter,* June 16, 2003, p. 18.

—updates: April Dougal Gasbarre;
Frederick C. Ingram

Aluar Aluminio Argentino S.A.I.C.

Marcelo T. de Alvear 590
Buenos Aires, C.F. C1058AAF
Argentina
Telephone: (54) (11) 4313-7593
Fax: (54) (11) 4311-9026
Web site: http://www.aluar.com.ar

Public Company
Incorporated: 1970
Employees: 1,791
Sales: ARS 1.47 billion ($500 million) (2004)
Stock Exchanges: Bolsa de Comercio de Buenos Aires
Ticker Symbol: ALUO
NAIC: 331312 Primary Aluminum Production; 331314
Secondary Smelting and Alloying of Aluminum;
331315 Aluminum Sheet, Plate and Foil Manufacturing;
331316 Aluminum Extruded Product Manufacturing

Aluar Aluminio Argentino S.A.I.C. is Argentina's only producer of aluminum. The company converts alumina (aluminum oxide) to primary aluminum and aluminum products for use in the transport, construction, electrical, medical, water treatment, and packaging industries. More than 80 percent of Aluar's production is exported to other countries.

A Controversial Concession: Aluar in the 1970s

The aluminum plant began as a project of Argentina's military-ruled government, which sought to make the nation self-sufficient in security matters. The planning commission—a ten-member air force body—apparently expected the aluminum to be used by a vigorous local aircraft industry, improving Argentina's trade balance by substituting for imported aluminum. Puerto Madryn, a town of 4,000 to 5,000 people on Patagonia's bleak Atlantic coast, was chosen to be the site because a deepwater port would be needed for import and export and because cheap electricity could be obtained by building a hydroelectric complex in the Andes Mountains, about 320 miles to the west. Although the project required the import of bauxite (aluminum ore) refined into

alumina, Argentina already produced enough petroleum coke, the other main raw material needed.

Aluar was incorporated in 1970 by Fate S.A., which assumed 52 percent of the shares. This company's origins went back to Leiser Madanes, a Polish immigrant who arrived in Buenos Aires in 1912 and began manufacturing and selling rubberized articles, including condoms for the city's flourishing brothels. He made his fortune in the 1930s with a raincoat factory. Taking advantage of the inability of international tire manufacturers to supply the Argentine market during World War II, his sons founded Fate, a tiremaking plant, in 1943. Friction eventually developed between the ambitious Manuel Madanes and his more cautious brother Adolfo. During the 1960s Manuel turned to Jose Gelbard, the head of Argentina's employers' federation and a man with high-ranking connections throughout the world, including places as ideologically disparate as Washington and Havana. According to Maria Seoane, Gelbard's biographer, he supplied the laundered money that enabled Manuel to buy out his brothers Victor and Marco and thereby isolate Adolfo. In return, Gelbard received a one-third share of the family holding company.

Aluar, in 1971, won the concession to build and operate the aluminum plant, aided—according to Seoane—by a $4 million slush fund assembled from the three Italian subcontractors who actually built the plant, and controlled by Gelbard, who distributed half of the money to military men. The Argentine state provided critical infrastructure in the form of a dam, the hydroelectric plant, transmission lines, an auxiliary thermoelectric plant, an aqueduct, the deepwater port, and a connection to a gas pipeline. Fate also benefited from a special rule that allowed it to exempt its shares in Aluar from a tax on earnings. Other large Argentine companies also took a stake in the company, and it began selling shares on the Buenos Aires stock exchange in 1979. For its part, the government took preferred shares paying a fixed dividend and an additional participation in the profits.

There were many critics of this project. Fate's winning bid was attacked as tainted. It was pointed out that the state's investment in the dam and hydroelectric plant alone was double the projected cost of the aluminum plant. A 20-year contract with the Aluminum Co. of America (Alcoa) for alumina from

Key Dates:

1971: Newly formed Aluar wins the concession to produce aluminum in Argentina.

1974: The aluminum plant begins production.

1976: Argentina's former leaders are arrested for their part in the Aluar contract.

1980: Aluar's chief executive returns after four years in exile.

1983: Aluar buys a firm that molds aluminum into various manufactured products.

1995: The company buys a majority share of the hydroelectric plant providing much of its power.

1998: Aluar acquires a company that becomes its division of semimanufactured products.

2003: Booming Aluar's aluminum plant is operating at 99 percent of capacity.

2004: Aluar signs a contract for a transmission line to meet its growing need for power.

two facilities in Australia seemed to contradict the rationale of national self-sufficiency. When another military junta came to power in 1976, it arrested the members of the earlier one on charges of having granted Fate excessive tax exemptions and other concessions. Gelbard, who had risen to become minister of the economy, fled to Washington, where he died soon after. Madanes fled to Canada, where he remained until he was cleared in 1980. Gelbard's heirs eventually recovered his property and sold his stakes in Fate, Aluar, and the family holding company in 1992.

Growing Enterprise: 1974–2000

Aluar's factory began production in 1974, powered by six turbines until 1978, when the Futaleufu hydroelectric plant came on line. The electrolytic process needed to produce aluminum from alumina was supported by anodes constructed in a satellite plant. Petroleum coke initially was imported. Including complementary facilities and living quarters for the 1,100 employees and workers, the cost of construction came to about $223 million. Once the hydroelectric plant was supplying power, Aluar, which produced 49,000 metric tons of aluminum in 1978, was capable of turning out 140,000 metric tons a year. More than three-quarters of the 1978 production was in the form of ingots to be used for the manufacture of electrical conductors, with another 20 percent in the form of bars for the construction and automobile industries. The rest was in the form of sheets of foil used in the food industry.

Aluar was the 47th largest enterprise in Argentina in 1979 and advanced to 30th place in 1980, when it earned ARS 27.21 billion on sales of ARS 535.83 billion (about $280 million). Given that it had accumulated a debt of about $133 million and, within Argentina, not only was required to meet internal demand but to sell there at a price determined by a government formula, the enterprise was anxious to market its goods abroad. By 1982, Aluar, its plant operating at full capacity, was exporting more than 60 percent of its production. Unfortunately, a world recession in this period had resulted in low market prices. The accompanying slump in the Argentine economy was not good news either, and in 1985 Aluar dropped to 42nd place in sales.

By this time Aluar had invested another $61 million on three projects to make its plant more efficient. The first consisted of the installation of an electronic circuit for its electrolytic cells. This permitted an increase in current and a corresponding decrease in energy consumption. The second involved the installation of 16 more electrolytic cells, raising the number to about 400, each of them holding about a ton of molten aluminum each day. These two projects allowed an increase in aluminum production of 8,750 metric tons a year. The third project, based on years of experimentation, allowed the company to put a lid on the cells and capture, for later treatment, the gaseous products of electrolysis.

Aluar was seeking added value from aluminum when it purchased, in 1983, Kicsa Industrial y Comercial S.A. Originally established as a subsidiary of Kaiser Aluminum & Chemical Corp. to manufacture aluminum products, this firm had been sold to local entrepreneurs before being acquired by Aluar, which then spent another $10 million to modernize Kicsa's equipment for molding aluminum into sheets, foil, profiles, and bars of aluminum alloys. Located in La Plata in the province of Buenos Aires, Kicsa was, in 1987, employing 680 people and had annual sales of $55 million, compared with $240 million for Aluar.

Angelo Bertolucci was president and general manager of Aluar in this period, working under Manuel Madanes. After Madanes died at the end of 1988, a power struggle developed between his daughter Monica and his sons Leiser, Miguel, and Pablo. Control of the firm subsequently went to another branch of the family, headed by a relative by marriage, Dolores Quintanilla de Madanes, who owned 40 percent of the shares of the Fate-Aluar group in 1997. She took the position of president in 1992 or 1993 and dropped Monica and her brothers from the board of directors. Her son Javier Madanes Quintanilla first appeared on the board in 1995 and succeeded her as president in 1997. Dolores was reported, in 1999, not to be speaking to her son (or her nephew Daniel Friedenthal, longtime executive vice-president of Aluar) after the 37-year-old Javier married a photographer of whom she disapproved. Family members controlled between 70 and 75 percent of the enterprise at this time.

In 1993 Aluar merged Kicsa with Camea S.A., a manufacturer of aluminum products owned by the Canadian company Alcan Aluminium Holdings Ltd. The two jointly owned the merged company, C&K Aluminio S.A., until 1996, when Aluar purchased Alcan's share of C&K, which then became Aluar's division of manufactured products, located in Abasto in the province of Buenos Aires. In 1995 the Argentine government opened the Futaleufu power plant to private capital. Aluar then purchased 59 percent of the facility for $135.8 million. In order to increase its percentage of sales in added value rather than primary aluminum, Aluar in 1998 acquired Refineria Metales Uboldi y Cia. S.A. for $17.9 million. This company had two plants—one in Puerto Madryn—and was specializing in the manufacture of special alloys and aluminum wire, the latter employed in the production of cables. Uboldi became Aluar's division of semimanufactured products.

Aluar spent another $340 million to expand its Puerto Madryn plant, which in 1999 became capable of turning out 260,000 metric tons of aluminum per year. Only about 75,000 tons were reaching the local market. Interviewed for the business magazine *Mercado,* Madanes Quintanilla indicated that the problem lay with Argentine industry. ''One typical case is the automobile industry,'' he told Mario Benechi. ''In the rest of the world autos have a high composition of aluminum to lighten the weight and thereby lower fuel consumption. [By contrast] Our strongest local customer continues to be the construction industry, which accounts for more than half the sales.'' Madanes foresaw Aluar making 90 percent of its sales in the foreign market.

Aluar in the 21st Century

Madanes also told the magazine that the Fate-Aluar group, along with some overseas partners, would spend $1.5 billion over the next five years to build a new plant in Patagonia for aluminum products that would bring production to more than 500,000 metric tons a year. Such an undertaking, however, would require more electricity. Aluar was consuming, in its Puerto Madryn factory, as much electricity as the city of Cordoba—Argentina's second largest—and 80 percent of all the consumption in Patagonia. Because the region did not belong to the rest of Argentina's national grid and Futaleufu no longer came even close to meeting Aluar's needs for power, the company had been obliged to invest in a backup system in case of a power failure by taking stakes in thermal electricity-generating plants.

Aluar later scaled down its expansion project so that production would rise to 400,000 metric tons. To meet its electricity needs, the company proposed a new 355-kilometer (220-mile) transmission line that would be linked to the national power grid and provide power not only to the smelter but benefit all consumers in northern Patagonia. Aluar proposed to contribute 15 percent of the $70 million investment needed for the line, with another 15 percent from the Futaleufu hydroelectric enterprise and the remaining 70 percent from the federal government. The contract was signed in 2004, with work to be completed by the end of 2005.

Argentina's economic recession, which began in 1998 and worsened until the country defaulted on its debts at the end of 2001, hardly affected Aluar since most of its production was being sold abroad. Indeed, the devaluation of the peso at the end of 2001 made its goods cheaper and thereby more attractive to foreign customers. Operating at 99 percent of capacity, the Puerto Madryn plant produced 227,251 metric tons of primary aluminum in 2004, a record. Aided by the opening of a second plant, the division of semimanufactured products produced 66,838 metric tons of aluminum wire, zinc-aluminum, and ingots of aluminum alloys. The division of manufactured products produced 24,069 metric tons of aluminum sheets and molded products. The total sales volume was 283,435 tons, of which 74 percent was exported. Aluar's profit margin continued to be sizable in 2004; it recorded net income of ARS 335.5 million ($114.12 million) on net sales of ARS 1.47 billion ($500 million). Its long-term debt consisted of ARS 212.72 million ($72.35 million) in loans.

Aluar's extrusion process was producing aluminum bars, tubes, and profiles in a variety of sizes and forms. The profiles, developed for metal carpentry, were available in a series of finishes, such as anodized and painted surfaces. The rolling line was turning out sheet metal and rolls in a wide range of alloys for multiple uses, including foil for applications that included not only home kitchen use, disposable food containers, and weather proofing, but also printed, painted, lacquered, and other forms of foil products used, for the most part, in packaging for the tobacco, pharmaceuticals, food, and other industries.

Principal Subsidiaries

Hidroelectrica Futaleufu S.A. (59%); Infa S.A.

Principal Divisions

Manufactures; Primary; Semimanufactures.

Principal Competitors

Alcan Inc.; Alcoa Inc.; Aluminium Pecheney; Corus Group plc; Kaiser Aluminum Corporation; Noranda Inc.; Rio Tinto plc.

Further Reading

''ALUAR: El aluminio por el mundo,'' *Mercado,* November 1, 1984, p. 42.

''Aluar: Monica Madanes y el estilo suave,'' *Mercado,* September 1991, p. 25.

''Aluar no se detiene,'' *Mercado,* May 20, 1982, pp. 29–30.

''Aluminium from Patagonia,'' *Financial Times,* July 30, 1969, p. 5.

Benechi, Mario, ''La salida es hacia arriba,'' *Mercado,* November 1998, pp. 67–68.

Garcia, Luis F., ''Las ventajas de cotizar,'' *Mercado,* April 5, 1979, pp. 64–67.

''Los herederos,'' *Mercado,* December 1999, p. 36.

Kinch, Diana, ''Argentine Power Project May Spur Aluar Aluminum Smelter Expansion,'' *American Metal Market,* July 23, 2003, p. 6.

Moyano, Julio, ed., *The Argentine Economy,* Buenos Aires: Julio Moyano Comunicaciones, 1997, pp. 536–37.

Onis, Juan de, ''Argentine Right-Wingers Set Back by Court Decision,'' *New York Times,* June 22, 1977, p. A9.

Pellegrinelli, Victoria, ''Aluar, una local que gana de visitante,'' *Apertura,* July 2002, pp. 44–46, 48.

Seoane, Maria, *El burgues maldito,* Buenos Aires: Planeta, 1998.

Sguiglia, Eduardo, *El club de los poderosos,* Buenos Aires: Editorial Planeta Argentina, 1991, pp. 75–78.

Silveti, Edgardo A., ''El caso Aluar,'' *Mercado,* February 20, 1975, pp. 28–34.

——, ''Mas y Mas aluminio,'' *Mercado,* June 25, 1987, pp. 75–77.

Solari Yrigoyen, Hipolito, *El escandolo Aluar,* Buenos Aires: Rafael Cedeno, 1976.

Stamore, K., and B. Pillonel, ''Argentina's Aluminum Industry,'' *Aluminum International Today,* July-August 2004, pp. 31+.

—Robert Halasz

American Coin Merchandising, Inc.

397 South Taylor Ave.
Louisville, Colorado 80027
U.S.A.
Telephone: (303) 444-2559
Fax: (303) 247-0480
Web site: http://www.sugarloaf-usa.com

Wholly Owned Subsidiary of Coinstar, Inc.
Incorporated: 1988
Employees: 1,157 (2003)
Sales: $201.4 million (2003)
NAIC: 45421 Vending Machine Operators; 421920 Toys
   Wholesaling

American Coin Merchandising, Inc., which does business as Sugarloaf Creations, Inc., is the largest business of its kind in the United States. It owns and operates more than 140,000 coin-operated skill-crane machines, bulk vending dispensers, kiddie rides, and video games throughout the United States. The crane machines, called ''Shoppes,'' dispense stuffed animals, plush toys, watches, jewelry, and other items. Bulk vending machines sell gumballs, candy, nuts, and novelties. The company's machines are placed in major supermarkets, mass merchandisers, bowling centers, bingo halls, bars, restaurants, warehouse clubs, and other high-traffic locations, including AMF Bowling Centers, Bonanza Steak Houses, Brunswick Bowling Centers, Cub Foods stores, Denny's restaurants, Flying J Truckstops, Fred Meyer Stores, Kmart stores, Kroger supermarkets, Ponderosa Steak Houses, Safeway/Vons supermarkets, 76 Truckstops, Truckstops of America, and Wal-Mart outlets. The company pays the stores where its machines are located roughly 25 percent of each machine's gross revenue.

Early Growth through Franchising

American Coin Merchandising was formed in Colorado in July 1988 by a group of four businessmen, who among them owned Southwest Coin, Omaha Coin, Colorado Coin, and T.R. Baron & Associates. Under the leadership of Richard Jones and J. Gregory Theisen, the goal of the new company was to support and add to the license, sale, and setup agreements of its predecessor businesses. Shortly thereafter, American Coin began to combine the buying power of its affiliated businesses to purchase products and skill-crane machines at lower prices. By 1990, it was creating its own territories and, in 1994, it hired Jerome M. Lapin, cofounder in 1958 of International House of Pancakes, to be its chief executive officer. It was reincorporated in Delaware in 1995. When Lapin became chairman in 1995, he brought all the companies under one roof and took the company public, raising net proceeds of $10.1 million. To expand operations, the company subsequently purchased substantially all of the inventory, property, and equipment of its original affiliated entities for a purchase price of $9 million.

Skill-crane machines have been in operation since the 1920s in the United States, but the new company sought to invent something different and better: to offer an alternative way to sell retail products, to sell toys instead of time. It incorporated what it considered to be several improvements and refinements into its Shoppes, increasing the size of its machines to enhance their visibility and to display and vend more products; creating bright and distinctive signage to attract customer attention; and improving the exterior and interior lighting of machines to focus customer attention on the products in the Shoppes. In addition, the company upgraded machine operating mechanisms to achieve consistency of play and reliability of performance.

The SugarLoaf Toy Shoppe, in operation since the company's inception, featured a play price of 50 cents and dispensed stuffed animals, plush toys, and other toys. In 1993, the company introduced the SugarLoaf Fun Shoppe, which featured a play price of 25 cents and dispensed small toys, novelties, and candy. The SugarLoaf Treasure Shoppe came along in 1994 and, for a play price of 50 cents, dispensed jewelry, watches, bolo ties, and belt buckles. Between 1994 and 1996, American Coin Merchandising increased the number of machines it owned from 168 to 3,800; it controlled another 3,200 machines operated through franchises. In 1994, total profit for the company was $1.1 million. During 1995, overall revenues totaled $25.7 million on the company's net income of $2.6 million. In that year, approximately six million stuffed toys were dispensed from SugarLoaf machines. The SugarLoaf Treasure Shoppe

Company Perspectives:

The company's business strategy is to differentiate itself from traditional skill-crane operators and to strengthen its position as a leading owner and operator of skill-crane machines in the United States by offering a selected mix of high quality products; maintaining readily identifiable, attractive, well-maintained "Shoppes" marked with the SugarLoaf logo in locations which have a reputation for quality and a high level of foot traffic; controlling product cost; closely monitoring the vend ratio or revenue per product dispensed; providing training and support services to retail accounts, franchisees and managers.

dispensed approximately 250,000 watches and 500,000 bracelets, necklaces, and other items.

As the defining force in its market ("We are the market," Jerry Lapin liked to boast of American Coin Merchandising), the company installed 856 new crane machines and opened seven new offices during the first six months of 1996. Revenues for the first half of 1996 increased 37.8 percent over the same period a year earlier. By the end of the year, that number was up to 50 percent. In the final quarter of 1996, the company gained its first major contract and established itself as Wal-Mart's principal skill-crane supplier, a move that brought another 700 Shoppes on board by November with more installations planned for 1997. This step was only a first in the direction of developing customer accounts in new markets, such as the chain restaurant industry. In 1997, American Coin Merchandising signed a three-year agreement with Safeway that made it the supermarket chain's domestic skill-crane operator and another three-year contract with AMF Bowling, Inc. to service approximately half of the latter's locations.

Buying Back Franchises in the Mid-1990s

At about this point, the company changed its approach, instituting a strategy of buying back the remaining franchise offices around the country so that profits would stay within the company. American Coin Merchandising realized only about three cents on the dollar in the form of franchise royalties, whereas it made about a 29 cent profit per dollar for every machine it owned. The first buyback occurred in January 1996 with the $500,000 purchase of the Indiana-based operations and territory of Hoosier Coin Company, responsible for generating about $1.4 million in revenue in 1995. In July, it added its Utah territory to its operations with the $938,000 purchase of SugarLoaf of Utah, which had 1995 revenue of $1.9 million. In September, for $1.65 million, it acquired SugarLoaf, Inc., which operated 202 machines in Louisiana and Oklahoma and parts of Missouri, Illinois, and Texas. American Coin Merchandising rounded out the year with the December purchase of Creative Coin of Arizona for $1.46 million, bringing its Arizona territory back to the fold.

American Coin Merchandising was now five times larger than its largest competitor, and its vending machine empire continued to grow by the quarter. With just 14 percent of the skill-crane market under its control, the possibilities for its future growth loomed large. By September 1997 the company had added another 2,000 machines to its roster, and its share price had risen to a 52-week high of almost $18. It sold off another one million shares at $15 per share, increasing its outstanding shares to 18 percent, and used the money raised to repay debt, purchase additional skill-crane machines, and fund acquisitions of other companies. *Business Week* named American Coin Merchandising number 54 in its list of Hot Growth Companies for 1997, based on its three-year results in sales growth, earnings, and return on invested capital. *Forbes* ranked American Coin Merchandising number 13 in 1997 in its list of the 200 best small companies, those with sales of at least $5 million but not more than $350 million, based upon its 44.7 percent five-year average return on investment and revenues of $48 million for its latest 12 months.

The company's acquisition trend continued into 1998 with the addition of the Texas-based operations of Tejas Toy Corporation and control of American Coin Merchandising's Texas territory for $2.23 million; R&T Marketing, Inc, with its 370 skill-crane machines in American Coin Merchandising's northern California territory for $2.14 million; and NW Toys Co., Oregon Coin Company, and Suncoast Toys, Inc. for an aggregate purchase price of approximately $30 million. The latter three purchases brought the Washington, Oregon, and central Florida territories of American Coin Merchandising under company control and added another 1,300 skill-crane machines to its inventory. In a move to no longer limit itself to the skill-crane business, American Coin Merchandising also acquired McCathren Vending Corporation, a Colorado-based bulk vending business that operated close to 5,000 pieces of vending equipment in Colorado, Utah, and Wyoming. The company had earlier bought Quality Amusement Corp. and Quality Entertainment in late 1997, part of a natural expansion, since those locations that housed SugarLoaf skill-crane machines often housed bulk vending machines and kiddie rides as well. The new direction came after Wal-Mart stores suggested that American Coin Merchandising put other kinds of machines in its stores. With the number of remaining franchisees down to 16, Jerry Lapin announced in the *Rocky Mountain News* that his company's growth strategy would not depend on its ability to buy out its franchisees; instead, it would go after new markets and its competition.

Related Acquisitions in the Late 1990s

American Coin Merchandising operated more than 10,000 skill-crane machines by the middle of 1998. Its share price was in the upper teens after a setback that analysts regarded as temporary when it missed its earnings projections by a few cents. As a result, its stock tumbled 23 percent from its previous high of almost $23. The company, which earlier had been laughed at by analysts, was receiving high recommendations and experiencing great potential for growth as a result of the expansion of the big national chains with which it was allied. *Business Week* again named it to its list of the Hot Growth Companies, although this time it came in at only number 90. *Forbes* placed it number 60, down from its former ranking as number 13, in its list of the 200 best small companies.

American Coin Merchandising's next purchase enabled it to branch out into the amusement video and simulator game business, an industry with late 1990s revenues in excess of a billion dollars. For a purchase price of $4 million, the company acquired the privately held Chilton Vending Co. in mid-1998, thereby gaining a significant presence in Kansas and Missouri and expertise in the amusement video business. The acquisition added approximately 1,800 simulator and traditional video game machines, as well as some skill-crane and redemption equipment. Chilton, which had installations at Family Golf Centers, Inc., AMF Bowling Centers, and Worlds of Fun Amusement Park, had 1997 revenues of $4.5 million. Randy Chilton, third-generation management of Chilton, came on board with the acquisition to become American Coin Merchandising's new vice-president of Amusement Games Development.

In October 1998, with the acquisition of Plush 4 Play, American Coin Merchandising obtained placement agreements with Shoney's, Inc. and Friendly Ice Cream Corporation. The purchase, which cost American Coin $6.8 million plus a contingent earn-out of up to $2.7 million, was part of its plan to branch further into the restaurant industry. Plush 4 Play also sold prepackaged plush toys and animals to the skill-crane industry.

Planning for Continued Success

As American Coin Merchandising closed out 1998, it claimed about 23 percent of the more than 50,000 skill cranes in retail outlets in the United States, of which it owned 10,671, an increase of about 73 percent from the end of 1997. Since 1995, it had averaged greater than a 50 percent increase in annual revenues. It had completed ten acquisitions since October 1997 and had expanded into complementary vending operations, adding approximately 6,800 other vending and amusement machines at retail operations. Its revenues for the year rose 65.4 percent to a record $97.7 million, although net earnings decreased 12 percent to $3.9 million. This was due in part to higher interest and administrative costs related to the 1998 acquisitions.

As it entered 1999, American Coin Merchandising expected to acquire at least four more companies and had its sights on another ten to 12 related businesses. The immediate aim of the company was to integrate its acquisitions into its national network. Its larger plan was to consolidate the industry as a whole, a goal that management judged to be within its reach.

Fighting the Expansion Blues

In the third quarter of 1998, the road to industry consolidation turned rocky. Although revenues for the quarter increased 87 percent to a record $27.4 million, net earnings for the period fell 9.9 percent to $906,000. The company's stock, which had reached a high of more than $22 per share in May 1998, plummeted more than 73 percent to a year-end low of $5.88. Steven Barnard, senior vice-president at Everen Securities Inc. in Chicago told Carly Schulaka of the Boulder, Colorado, *Daily Camera* (December 31, 1998) that a lack of "standout" merchandise contributed to the slump. "There was no hot item this year. In the past [American Coin Merchandising] had Lion King and Space Jam merchandise, but there was not really a must-have, signature item this year."

Officials at American Coin Merchandising concurred with Barnard's judgment. As the company's downturn continued into 1999, its leadership attributed the drop in earnings to administrative costs incurred as a result of the company's rapid expansion and to a combination of slowing foot traffic in retail outlets and a poor merchandise mix in its vending machines. Senior vice-president of operations Randy Fagundo pointed to an overall slowing of the toy industry as one reason for the company's drop in earnings per machine and indicated that American Coin Merchandising's burst of acquisitions activity in 1998 was a source of lingering expenses. "We did a lot last year and probably put a little stress on the system," he remarked to Vicky Uhland of the *Rocky Mountain News* (February 14, 1999). CEO Jerome Lapin echoed this statement, opining that revenues would "continue to be depressed into 1999." Fagundo noted that its 1998 acquisitions doubled the company's number of skill cranes and employees and created redundancies in accounting and management computing and warehouse operations.

During 1999, American Coin Merchandising addressed these problems, purchasing a new computer system with online accounting report functions, consolidating its warehousing into a 100,000-square-foot facility in Seattle, and turning its attention toward fixing its merchandising weaknesses. The company also pursued the aim of "lobby domination," so that it would own and service every vending machine, ride, and game in its clients' lobbies. Randy Fagundo told Vicky Uhland, "Wal-Mart and other national chain accounts don't want to have two to three vendors coming in to service machines, so they came to us.''

By June 2001, the company's fortunes seemed to be turning around. At the end of the first six months of 2001, revenues reached $69.4 million, and the company's stock held at about $6 per share. American Coin Merchandising estimated that vending revenues for the year would yield between $136 million and $143 million. The company even managed to weather a general economic decline in 2001 without suffering the slowdown that affected other U.S. businesses.

''A Classic Public Orphan''

American Coin Merchandising's performance attracted the attention of Wellspring Capital llc, a leveraged-buyout firm, which partnered with the investment firm Knightsbridge Holdings llc to purchase the company for $125 million, a sum five times its projected cash flow for 2001, plus the assumption of $50 million in debt. Wellspring and Knightsbridge offered shareholders $8.50 per share in cash for their outstanding common stock, about $2.50 above the market price of the shares at the time. The purchase was Wellspring's first public-to-private transaction. William F. Dawson, Jr., a partner at the buyout firm, told a reporter from *Buyouts* in September 2001, adding, ''Right now market conditions are unfavorable in general,'' adding that his company intended to ''double the business to make it much more attractive for an IPO,'' or for sale to an appropriate buyer, by 2006. Dawson noted, ''This company is what I would call a classic public orphan that's too small to be public. It's a quirky business, but they are growing strongly, and we think it has a lot of upside potential.'' American Coin Merchandising's leadership was equally sanguine about the buyout, which they expected to give the company access to new capital to fund expansion, acquisitions, and product development. Because the company's stock had not been liquid enough to attract investors, the stock was undervalued on the market despite American Coin Merchandising's strong cash flow and growth potential. The amount of capital necessary to pursue the company's goals was not forthcoming from the stock market. In addition, going private promised to improve American Coin Merchandising's competitive edge. ''We're the only public company in the industry, so all our competitors and customers know a lot more about our business than we know about them,'' Fagundo told *Buyouts.*

Wellspring's investment paid off far more quickly than projected. In May 2004, Bellevue, Washington-based Coinstar purchased American Coin Merchandising from Wellspring for $235 million in cash, funding the purchase with debt. Even though Coinstar did not assume any of American Coin Merchandising's $100 million existing debt, which was to be paid down with the proceeds of the sale, Wellspring realized nearly two and a half times its original investment of $125 million. Coinstar, which operated 11,000 coin-counting machines that converted change into bills for a fee of 7 percent of the value of coins counted, looked to American Coin Merchandising to bring it additional markets and greater route density in both urban and rural areas. Coinstar hoped that the increased territory would provide new venues for its coin-counting machines, which were located primarily in grocery stores, and bolster its emerging e-payment business, including electronic payroll ser-

vices and prepaid Master Cards, wireless airtime, and long-distance plans. As of March 2004, American Coin Merchandising's revenues totaled $220 million. The company employed 1,150 people and operated 28,000 skill cranes and 112,000 candy and toy vending machines, kiddie rides, and video games in 50 states and Puerto Rico.

Principal Competitors

A & A Global Industries; All Star Vending; Innovative Concepts in Entertainment; Lieberman Companies Inc.; Theisen Vending Company.

Further Reading

''American Coin's Revenues Jump 87% but Earnings Slip,'' *Denver Post*, November 12, 1998, p. C-05.

Barrett, William P., ''Brotherly Love,'' *Forbes*, July 28, 1997, p. 74.

Batsell, Jake, ''Coinstar Banks on Amusement,'' *Seattle Times*, May 25, 2004.

Branaugh, Matt, ''Shareholders Approve Acquisition of American Coin,'' *Daily Camera* (Boulder, Colorado), February 6, 2002.

——, ''Louisville-Colo.-Based Vending Machine Company to Buy New York-Based Outfit,'' *Daily Camera* (Boulder, Colorado), March 18, 2003.

''Coinstar Announces Completion of American Coin Acquisition,'' *Business Wire*, July 7, 2004.

''Coinstar to Acquire American Coin Merchandising Inc.,'' *Business Wire*, May 24, 2004, item 5470.

Draper, Heather, ''American Coin OKs Buyout,'' *Rocky Mountain News* (Denver, Colorado), p. 8B.

Eaton, John, ''Little Cranes, Big Bucks,'' *Denver Post*, October 14, 1998, p. C-01.

Gray, Ellen, ''They're Not Just Playing Games,'' *Colorado Business Magazine*, February 1998, p. 39.

Holman, Kelly, ''Wellspring, Knightsbridge to Buy American Coin,'' *Daily Deal*, September 10, 2001.

——, ''Wellspring Flips American Coin,'' *Daily Deal,* May 25, 2004.

Lewis, Al, ''Toy Dispenser Claws Way to Top,'' *Rocky Mountain News* (Denver, Colorado), June 2, 1998, p. 1B.

Narvaes, Emily, ''Toying with Success,'' *Denver Post*, September 2, 1996, p. F-01.

Paton, James, ''American Coin to be Sold,'' *Rocky Mountain News* (Denver, Colorado), May 25, 2004, p. 2B.

Pearce, Dennis, ''American Coin Merchandising Buys Wichita, Kan.-Based Chilton Vending,'' *Knight-Ridder/Tribune Business News*, June 11, 1998, item OKRB981620E7.

Romero, Christine L., ''Boulder, Colorado-Based American Coin Grabs 'Hot' Listing,'' *Daily Camera* (Boulder, Colorado), June 19, 1998.

Schulaka, Carly, ''Business Analysts Give Colorado's American Coin Merchandising High Marks,'' *Daily Camera* (Boulder, Colorado), June 16, 1997.

——, ''Boulder, Colo.-Based Crane Amusement Firm Continues Slide,'' *Daily Camera* (Boulder, Colorado), December 31, 1998.

Svaldi, Aldo, ''Bellevue, Wash.-Based Coin Machine Operator to Buy Amusement Firm,'' *Denver Post*, May 25, 2004.

Sweeney, Patrick, ''American Coin,'' *Denver Business Journal*, March 10, 2000, p. 15A.

Uhland, Vicky, ''Skill-Crane Firm Hopes Business Picks Up,'' *Rocky Mountain News* (Denver, Colorado), February 14, 1999, p. 3G.

''Wellspring Acquires American Coin,'' *Buyouts*, September 24, 2001, item 1274006.

—Carrie Rothburd
—update: Jennifer Gariepy

American Kennel Club, Inc.

260 Madison Avenue
New York, New York 10016
U.S.A.
Telephone: (212) 696-8200
Web site: http://www.akc.org

Nonprofit Organization
Incorporated: 1908
Employees: 500
Sales: $69.98 million (2004)
NAIC: 115210 Support Activities for Animal Production;
   511130 Book Publishers; 711320 Promoters of
   Performing Arts, Sports, and Similar Events without
   Facilities; 813990 Other Similar Organizations
   (Except Business, Professional, Labor, and Political
   Organizations)

The American Kennel Club, Inc. (AKC) is involved in a wide range of activities relating to purebred dogs. It is best known for its registry of millions of dogs that dates back to before the 20th century. The group also sanctions dog shows and events put on by its 479 independent dog clubs and more than 4,000 affiliates. It has taken to lobbying for owners' rights and has sponsored services such as microchip-aided dog recovery. The AKC has embraced DNA technology as a way to verify pedigrees. It also has sponsored veterinary research into hereditary diseases. The AKC has been producing its *Gazette* magazine for more than 100 years; other publications include *The Complete Dog Book.* Headquartered in New York City, the group has significant operations in Raleigh, North Carolina.

19th-Century Origins

The American Kennel Club (AKC) was formed in 1887 by representatives of a dozen existing dog clubs. The AKC was to oversee a confederation of independent dog clubs. About a month after their initial meeting at the Philadelphia Kennel Club, the delegates adopted a constitution and bylaws when they convened in New York City's Madison Square Garden on October 22, 1884. Major James M. Taylor was named the group's first president.

The AKC was not the first organization of its kind in the world; the British Kennel Club had been launched in 1873. For that matter, the classification of various breeds dates back at least to 1576, when Johannes Caius wrote his *Of Englishe Dogges.*

The British held the first known dog show in Newcastle in 1859; the practice soon spread, however, to Europe and America. The first dog show in the United States is believed to have been held in Mineola, New York in 1874, predating the famous New York City's Westminster Kennel Club show by three years. The first Westminster show boasted 1,201 dogs.

The AKC got its first permanent office in 1887 when one was rented at 44 Broadway in New York City. Around this time, the group was publishing *The American Kennel Club Stud Book,* which had been started by Dr. N. Rowe several years prior to the AKC's formation. A serial, the *Gazette,* was launched in January 1889. It would be published continuously throughout the 20th century and beyond.

The AKC was incorporated in New York State on May 18, 1908 by an act of the legislature. Headquarters were relocated to 221 Fourth Avenue (later Park Avenue) in 1919 and would remain there for 45 years.

A major refinement of the dog judging rules came around 1924, when breeds were separated into five groups: Sporting Dogs, Working Dogs, Terriers, Toy Breeds, and Non-Sporting Breeds. A few years later, Hounds were made a separate group from the other Sporting Dogs. Herding dogs got their own category for judging purposes in 1983.

A long-running publishing venture was launched in 1929 as *Pure Bred Dogs.* It was renamed *The Complete Dog Book* in 1938.

Postwar Popularity

Dog show judging became more professional in the 1940s and 1950s. The Professional Dog Judges Association was formed in the mid-1940s, and a directory of judges was pub-

Key Dates:

1887: The American Kennel Club is formed.
1889: *The Gazette* begins its run as one of the country's longest-lived magazines.
1908: The AKC is incorporated.
1929: The AKC begins publishing *The Complete Dog Book* (originally *Pure Bred Dogs*).
1960: The AKC registers 443,000 dogs; one million people attend 850 AKC dog shows.
1980: American Kennel Club Museum of the Dog is opened.
1987: The AKC's centennial is celebrated with an 8,000-dog show in Philadelphia.
1999: Pedigrees are made available online.
2003: The AKC launches "Responsible Dog Ownership Day."

lished soon afterward. The number of dogs each judge could see per day was limited to 200 in 1951.

The AKC's standards for establishing breeds also were updated in the mid-1950s. The new rules required breeds to have been documented for at least several generations by a domestic or foreign kennel club, with more than 100 members presenting representative dogs. A few more years in a probationary "development" period then followed.

The popularity of purebreds boomed after World War II. The AKC was sponsoring about 1,750 events a year in the mid-1950s, with 300,000 dogs participating, according to the *Atlantic.* The AKC registered 443,000 dogs in 1960, with poodles the top breed in the era of the poodle skirt. About 850 AKC dog shows were held in 1960, drawing as many as 250,000 participants and one million spectators, according to a contemporary *Saturday Evening Post* feature. The AKC, it said, "controls the purebred-dog world the way the Treasury controls the minting of money."

Headquarters were moved to 51 Madison Avenue in 1964. Within a few years, the organization was using computers to store pedigrees of the increasing number of AKC-registered dogs.

Celebration and Scrutiny in the 1980s

The American Kennel Club Museum of the Dog opened in New York in 1980 and moved to St. Louis seven years later. To celebrate its 100th anniversary in 1987, the AKC organized a massive, 8,000-dog show in Philadelphia.

At the end of the 1980s, the AKC had about 450 member clubs. It was sponsoring about 11,000 events a year, with 1.5 million dogs participating. Revenues were about $20 million a year, with most from registrations. The AKC was recognizing 130 breeds at the time. According to the *Atlantic,* 12 million dogs were AKC registered—half of the country's eligible purebred dogs. (Other groups, like the United Kennel Club, together had about five million in their registries. Mutts and nonrecognized breeds accounted for the United States' remaining 28 million or so dogs.)

In spite of its success, Mark Derr reported in the *Atlantic,* the AKC was facing criticism for allegedly harming purebred dogs. By emphasizing appearance above other qualities such as health and ability, the group was encouraging inbreeding, some said. The group also was accused of failing to deal effectively with puppy mills and other pet industry problems.

The AKC was, though, successful in lobbying to prevent communities from banning specific breeds, such as the pit bull, in

"vicious dog" ordinances. The group also was funding research into hereditary disorders.

There also would be allegations of rampant fraud in the AKC registry. According to the *Philadelphia Inquirer,* the AKC had hired its first investigator in 1973. The group would be dogged, however, by allegations that its registries were in large part "worthless," since they relied on the word of the breeders, who stood to profit considerably from AKC designation for their dogs. Several investigators turned whistle-blower in the mid-1990s.

Technical Advances in the 1990s

Revenues were $29 million in 1993. Some of the AKC's functions were moved to Raleigh, North Carolina by 1998, and the headquarters was moved up the street to 260 Madison Avenue. The data center in Raleigh employed about 350 people. By this time, the AKC's 15,000-member licensed and sanctioned events were attracting two million canine participants every year, while more than one million dogs were being registered.

In 1999, the organization made its database of 30 million AKC-registered dogs available on its revamped web site. Pedigrees were available to owners for a small fee. An online store was another main feature of the site. Also in the 1990s the AKC began backing a number of public-minded initiatives, including the Canine Health Foundation, the Canine Good Citizen program, and the Companion Animal Recovery program. The AKC ended the 1990s with revenues of about $50 million a year.

The AKC was turning to DNA testing to assure the accuracy of its registry, as well as sponsoring research into genetic diseases. In other high-tech developments, an affiliated company called Companion Animal Recovery was implanting microchips to aid in dog recovery and identification. The AKC from time to time acknowledged the existence of new breeds. About 250 of the 400 breeds known to man, however, were not counted by the AKC.

Reaching Out After 2000

According to the *Atlanta Journal-Constitution,* a fancier could spend a half-million dollars to campaign to success at

Westminster. The costly sport of showing top dogs was made a little bit more lucrative with the launch of the AKC/Eukanuba National Invitational Championship in 2001. It featured a $50,000 prize for best in show.

In 2002, the group launched a magazine title geared toward the general dog owner called *AKC Family Dog.* It also was reaching outside the world of the fancier in print advertising.

The AKC was reinforcing its communications efforts in an attempt to reverse a several-year decline in membership figures, reported *PR Week.* The group had had poor relations with the media, after being blamed for trends such as overbreeding and puppy mills, a pet columnist told the journal. One initiative to improve public relations was "Responsible Dog Ownership Day" held on the group's September 17, 2003, anniversary.

In 2004, the Labrador retriever was into a 15-year run as the most popular dog in the AKC's annual registrations. The once-supreme poodle was still popular, but had slipped to eighth place.

By 2005, the AKC/Eukanuba National Championship was attracting more than 3,000 dogs, some from as far away as Thailand and Australia. Competitions included the National Obedience Championship and the wildly popular National Agility Championship.

Principal Competitors

American Rare Breed Association; BowTie, Incorporated; International All Breed Canine Association; National Canine Association; United Kennel Club.

Further Reading

"AKC to Offer DNA Certification," *Dog World,* May 1998, p. 8.

"The American Kennel Club's Dogged Pursuit of a More Groomed Image," *PR News,* April 20, 2005.

Coile, D. Caroline, Ph.D., "The AKC and the Gene Pool," *Dog World,* September 2004, pp. 18, 43.

——, "The Other Shows," *Dog World,* June 2004, pp. 32ff.

Dale, Steve, "Meet the AKC's Top Dog," *Dog World,* July 1997, pp. 30ff.

Derr, Mark, "The Politics of Dogs," *Atlantic,* March 1990, pp. 49ff.

Durand, Marcella, "AKC Begins Advertising Campaign to Reach Dog-Lovers," *Dog World,* February 2003, p. 6.

Eckstein, Sandra, "The Road to Westminster," *Atlanta Journal-Constitution,* February 9, 2003, p. LS1.

Hirshberg, Charles, "Barking Up a Different Tree: The Strangest Dogs You've Never Seen Mingle at the American Rare Breed Association's Cherry Blossom Classic," *Life,* July 1, 1999, pp. 58f.

Hively, Suzanne, "Meet the All-American Team of the AKC," *Plain Dealer* (Cleveland), July 9, 2003, p. E10.

"It's a Dog's Life," *Economist,* December 21, 2002.

Jaynes, Gregory, "In Philadelphia: Superdogs," *Time,* December 17, 1984, pp. 12f.

Kuehn, Bridget M., "A Puppy Paternity Test," *Journal of the American Veterinary Medical Association,* April 15, 2004, pp. 1239f.

Lemonick, Michael D., and Ann Blackman, "A Terrible Beauty," *Time,* December 12, 1994, pp. 64ff.

O'Hallaren, Bill, "The Crazy World of Dog Shows," *Saturday Evening Post,* April 1, 1962, pp. 13–13, 85–87.

"Organization Case Study: PR Breeds Knowledge of the American Kennel Club," *PR Week* (US), March 10, 2003, p. 10.

Popiolkowski, Joseph, "Popular Culture Goes to the Dogs: Mathematical Model Shows Breeds Follow Whims of Style," *USA Today,* June 9, 2004.

Ray, Angela G., and Harold E. Gulley, "The Place of the Dog: AKC Breeds in American Culture," *Journal of Cultural Geography,* Fall/Winter 1996, pp. 89ff.

Satchell, Michael, "Should You Buy That Doggie in the Window?," *Parade Magazine,* July 19, 1987.

Smith, Samantha Thompson, "American Kennel Club's New Web Site Features Canine Lore, Pedigrees," *News & Observer* (Raleigh), October 26, 1999.

Stark, Karl, "American Kennel Club Does Little to Verify Lineage of Dogs It Registers As Purebreds," *Knight Ridder/Tribune News Service,* December 30, 1995.

Warren, Ellen, "American Kennel Club Recalls Dog Book Following Ferocious Feedback Over Which Breeds Aren't Kid-Friendly," *Chicago Tribune,* April 8, 1998.

Wood, Fran, "Breeding Trouble at the AKC," *Star-Ledger* (Newark, N.J.), February 11, 2001.

—Frederick C. Ingram

Analex Corporation

5904 Richmond Highway
Alexandria, Virginia 22303
U.S.A.
Telephone: (703) 329-9400
Fax: (703) 329-8187
Web site: http://www.analex.com

Public Company
Incorporated: 1964 as Biorad, Inc.
Employees: 920
Sales: $94.4 million 2004
Stock Exchanges: AMEX
Ticker Symbol: NLX
NAIC: 541519 Other Computer Related Services

Through its subsidiaries and operating units, Alexandria, Virginia-based Analex Corporation offers information technology, systems engineering, security services, and intelligence services in support of homeland security, aerospace, and defense-related projects. Aerospace services are provided to such clients as NASA, the United States Air Force, Lockheed Martin Corporation, Boeing, and the National Reconnaissance Office. These services include control dynamics, failure modes effects and critical analysis, launch integration, mission assurance, stress analysis, and systems integration. Analex's medical services provides software and system engineering services to medical product and device manufacturers. The company's commercial engineering services unit is involved in such areas as software integration, system integration, database design and development, imaging technology, engineering research and design, electromagnetic compatibility, and software development. Wholly owned subsidiary Beta Analytics International, Inc. provides security services to both government and non-government clients, ranging from high-tech information assurance and technology protection to access control at client sites. Another subsidiary, ComGlobal Systems, Inc., primarily serves the Department of Defense, offering information technology for weapons systems and command and control systems. Subsidiary SyCom Services develops software engineering services for use in civilian and military radar systems, signal analysis, and other communication and database systems. Analex is a public company listed on the American Stock Exchange.

Origins in the 1960s

Filings with the Securities and Exchange Commission (SEC) indicate that Analex was incorporated in New York in 1964 as Biorad, Inc. and four years later assumed the name Hadron, Inc. According to the *Washington Post* in a 1986 article, the company was originally involved in the manufacture of industrial laser products, then "shifted gears in the late 1970s to focus on professional services." *Barron's* offered more details in a 1988 article, maintaining that "the outfit emerged in 1979 from the ashes of Xonics, a notorious high-tech fiasco." Members of top management were accused by the SEC of fraud and manipulating the company's stock price in order to use the stock to acquire other companies. "In 1979 Dominic Laiti gathered a group of former Xonic executives and bought Hadron. By 1983, the company was lauded in the press as an 'investment banker's dream.' For the child had, it appeared, inherited the parent's acquisitive streak, snapping up nine companies in just three years." While Laiti led the investor group that owned Hadron, it was Xonic's former president, Dr. Earl Winfrey Brian, who called the shots. He was politically well connected, friend to President Ronald Regan and the head of Regan's Justice Department, Ed Meese, and, if speculations are true, he had a hand in a number of scandals, including the October Surprise of 1980 that supposedly kept the embassy hostages in Iran until Regan was inaugurated as president, the Iran-Contra affair in which a rogue operation traded arms for hostages, and the selling of sensitive crime-tracking software to the intelligence services of foreign governments, an incident in which Hadron supposedly played a bit role.

Brian earned a medical degree from Duke University in 1966, then did postgraduate work at Stanford Medical School. It was here that he met Ned Hutchinson, one of Ronald Reagan's county campaign managers when Reagan was governor of California. Hutchinson was so impressed that he recommended Brian to state health officials, and at the age of 25 he found himself executive secretary for the California State Social Welfare Board. Two years later, he went to Vietnam, where he spent two years as a well-regarded surgeon. After his stint in the service, he returned to California and was soon in charge of the state's entire medical department, a position in which he would work closely with Regan's chief of staff, Ed Meese. In 1974, Brian attempted to become a Republican nominee for the U.S. Senate. Failing that bid, he now joined the University of Southern California as professor of medicine. According to a 1991 article in the *Financial Post*, "It appears Brian gave up the medical game for good in the mid-1970s. He inherited $50,000 from his father, and in 1975 showed up as president of a company called Xonics Inc. But it was Biotech Capital Corporation, the predecessor to Infotech, that would become Brian's main business vehicle." Although biotechnology was his interest at the time, Brian "found a new love—information technology, data management and software engineering." All of Brian's business interests were interconnected in a web difficult to untangle. It was through Infotech that Brian controlled Hadron, despite owning only a modest stake in the company. His interests eventually extended to the mass media as he gained control of both the wire service United Press International and a cable TV channel, FNN (Financial News Network).

According to the *Washington Post*, some of Hadron's acquisitions in the early 1980s failed to pan out: "Buying a company that made computer numerical controllers that speed up automatic knitting machines was a flop. . . . Other acquisition mistakes included a company that aimed to replace draftsmen with computers, and a company that made software for public agencies." What emerged from the flurry of acquisitions in the 1980s was essentially a high-tech consulting firm that primarily served government clients. It was an acquisition Hadron did not make, however, that would became the source of controversy and the subject of litigation in the years to come. This episode centered on the PROMIS (Prosecutor's Management Information System) software, created to manage and track criminal records from start to finish, including details of arrests, investigations, grand jury hearings, trials, prison terms, and paroles. It also had the potential to monitor intelligence cases.

PROMIS was developed by a company called Inslaw, which was founded by Bill Hamilton. Maggie Mahar of *Barron's* wrote in a 1988 article, "As Bill Hamilton tells it, it was April of 1983 . . . when he received the call from Dominic Laiti, chairman of Hadron Inc." Laiti said he wanted to buy Inslaw. Hamilton made it clear he was not interested in selling, but, the *Post* article continued, Laiti kept pushing, and, according to Hamilton, boasted, as he remembers, "We have very good political contacts in the current administration—We can get this kind of business. . . . We have ways of making you sell." Inslaw had a $10 million deal with the Department of Justice to provide PROMIS to the 20 largest U.S. attorneys' offices. Within months, Justice stopped payment on the contract, and in 1985 Inslaw was forced into

Chapter 11 bankruptcy protection. A year later, Hamilton sued Justice for theft of property and soon learned of Brian's connection to Hadron and to Meese in Justice.

According to the *Financial Post*, Hamilton came to believe that "Brian and his old crony, Meese, were behind the attempt to bankrupt and liquidate Inslaw. His theory, based on considerable circumstantial evidence, is that Meese wanted to award Brian a sweetheart computer contract." Others have suggested a more sinister motive. Writing for the *Columbia Journalism Review* in 1991, Phil Linsalata reported that Hamilton met a man named Michael Roiconosciuto, who "claimed advanced skills" in a number of areas that "made him a favorite among intelligence operatives in need of assistance." Roiconosciuto claimed that someone in Justice stole PROMIS and "gave it to American Intelligence operatives for resale in the international intelligence market. He later said he had been hired to alter the software prior to these sales. . . . Riconociuto told Caolaro that the software had been traded for cash, with some of the money going to reward American intelligence figures for services rendered, and the balance going into slush funds for future operations outside the purview of Congress. . . . One of the services rendered was orchestration of the 1980 release of the American hostages in Iran," in which Brian was alleged to have acted as one of the negotiators for the Reagan camp. This backdoor channel would then be used in the weapons sales in the Iran-Contra affair, according to Riconociuto. Hamilton eventually charged that PROMIS "had been illegally distributed to military and intelligence agencies in Iraq, Libya, South Korea, Singapore, Israel, Canada, and other nations."

Brian Indicted in the Mid-1990s

Hamilton won his suit against Justice, which was ordered to pay Inslaw $8 million. Justice lost an appeal but appealed again, until finally, in May 1991, the case was thrown out on a technicality, a judge ruling that the matter should never come before a bankruptcy judge. Brian always denied any connection to the Inslaw matter or any espionage intrigue. While the Inslaw case was relegated to the files of conspiracy theorists, Brian was soon caught up in a more tangible scandal. He was accused by regulators of hiding losses at FNN through false intercompany billings. In this way, he could falsify financial statements, thus giving FNN the opportunity to secure financing. In 1996, he was convicted on ten counts of conspiracy, fraud, and related charges and sentenced to nearly five years in federal prison. Even while he was indicted and undergoing a trial, Brian maintained his connection to Hadron and was paid $4,000 a month as a consultant.

Hadron was not doing well in the early 1990s, a victim of tightened federal budgets. By 1993, the company was on the verge of bankruptcy and being delisted by the NASDAQ. Hadron stayed out of Chapter 11 protection but only temporarily staved off delisting by engineering a ten-for-one reverse stock split to boost the price of the company's stock above the $1 threshold. Revenues dipped to $18.5 million in fiscal 1994, and the company lost more than $4 million. Hadron returned to profitability in fiscal 1996 but continued to lack direction: sales were up one year and down the next. In 1998, Hadron's management pared the company's focus to three areas: trusted/secure systems, computer systems support, and intelligent

```
┌─────────────────────────────────────────────┐
│              Key Dates:                      │
│                                              │
│ 1964:  Company founded as Biorad, Inc.       │
│ 1964:  The company's name is changed to      │
│        Hadron, Inc.                          │
│ 1979:  Former Xonic executives acquire       │
│        Hadron.                               │
│ 1993:  The company delisted by the NASDAQ.   │
│ 2000:  An investment group led by Jon Stout  │
│        acquires the company.                 │
│ 2001:  Analex Corporation is acquired.       │
│ 2002:  Hadron assumes name of Analex         │
│        Corporation.                          │
│ 2004:  Beta Analytics, Inc. is acquired.     │
│ 2005:  ComGlobal Biosystems, Inc. is         │
│        acquired.                             │
└─────────────────────────────────────────────┘
```

weapons systems. In 1999, a bio-defense unit was added to develop medical defenses and treatments for biological warfare toxins, an important step in the company's involvement in homeland security.

New Management and Focus in the 2000s

Not until 2000 would Hadron begin to find itself and evolve into a national security company. It was then that a new investment group, led by Jon M. Stout took charge. Stout was well familiar with the needs of the intelligence community, having previously headed DPC Technologies Inc., a military intelligence company. The *Washington Post* reported in April 2000 that Stout "hadn't even heard of Hadron until a few months ago. . . . It was investment banker J. Richard Knapp—who helped Stout sell DPC to Northrop Grumman, and who also happens to be on Hadron's board—who brought the company and its new CEO together. 'The company should begin to grow very smartly, I think,' Knapp said of Stout's new leadership. For the 53-year-old Stout, this is a move to the higher end of technology and higher level of organization. Stout plans to refocus the company's business on military intelligence work, and appears to prefer the high barriers of entry in the field, with its secret clearances and specialized knowledge requirements." Under Stout, Hadron forged a three-year strategic plan with the goal of being recognized as a major player in signals intelligence, imagery intelligence, electronic intelligence, human intelligence, measurement and signature intelligence, and biological warfare defense research. Stout stepped down as CEO in January 2001, turning over the post to Sterling E. Phillips, Jr., who assumed the chairmanship as well in 2004.

The terrorist attacks against the United States on September 11, 2001, were a milestone event for Hadron, which found itself well positioned to take advantage of increased spending in national security. To improve its position, in November 2001

Hadron acquired a competitor, Analex Corporation, a Littleton, Colorado-based company that provided engineering and program management services to NASA and the U.S. intelligence community. The integration of the acquisition was completed in March 2002, but during the process management came to realize that Analex was a more recognizable brand in the marketplace. Thus, in July 2002 Hadron changed its name to Analex Corporation.

Revenue grew steadily in the early 2000s, increasing from $22 million in 2001 to $59.3 million in 2002, $66.2 million in 2003, and $94.4 million in 2004. To stimulate further growth, Analex completed a pair of strategic acquisitions. The first was the $33.3 million cash and stock purchase of Maryland-based Beta Analytics International Inc., a company with more than 20 years of experience in protecting clients' assets, including personnel, information, operations, facilities, and equipment. In April 2005, Analex completed the $47 million cash purchase of San Diego-based ComGlobal Systems, an information technologies and services company.

Revenues during the first six months of 2005 were greatly improved over the same period the previous year, increasing from $38.8 million to $66.6 million, a clear indication that after 40 years in existence, Analex may have finally begun to find its stride.

Principal Subsidiaries

Beta Analytics, Inc.; ComGlobal Biosystems, Inc.; SyCom Services, Inc.

Principal Competitors

Anteon Internation Corporation; CACI International Inc.; Science Applications International Corporation.

Further Reading

Hinden, Stan, "When the Music Finally Stops, Hadron Won't Look the Same," *Washington Post*, July 31, 1989, p. F35.

Linsalata, Phil, "The Octopus File," *Columbia Journalism Review*, November–December 1991, p. 76.

Mahar, Maggie, "Rogue Justice," *Barron's National Business and Financial Weekly*, April 4, 1988, p. 6.

Musgrove, Mike, "New Leader for Hush-Hush Hadron," *Washington Post*, April 10, 2000, p. F05.

Reguly, Eric, "Questions Grow as 'Big Daddy' Watches His Empire Crumble," *Financial Post*, August 17, 1991, p. 8.

Tucker, Elizabeth, "Hadron Inc.: Stumbling Along," *Washington Post*, November 28, 1988, p. F36.

—Ed Dinger

Archon Corporation

3993 Howard Hughes Parkway, Suite 630
Las Vegas, Nevada 89109-6750
U.S.A.
Telephone: (702) 732-9120
Fax: (702) 658-4302
Web site: http://www.archoncorporation.com

Public Company
Incorporated: 1983 as Public/Hacienda Resorts, Inc.
Employees: 514
Sales: $45.70 million (2004)
Stock Exchanges: Over the Counter
Ticker Symbol: ARHN
NAIC: 721120 Casino Hotels; 713990 All Other
    Amusement and Recreation Industries; 551112 Offices
    of Other Holding Companies

Through its chairman and CEO, Paul W. Lowden, the Archon Corporation holds a more than a 20-year stake in Las Vegas casino history. Formerly known as Santa Fe Corporation and Sahara Gaming Corporation, Archon owned and operated the famous Sahara and Hacienda casino hotels. Those properties were sold in 1995 to former Circus Circus leader William Bennett, but the company remains active in Nevada's casino industry as owner and operator of the Pioneer Hotel and Gambling Hall, located in Laughlin, Nevada. Archon also owns commercial office buildings in Dorchester, Massachusetts, and Gaithersburg, Maryland, and 27 undeveloped acres on Las Vegas Boulevard South.

Rooted in 1950s Vegas

Both the Sahara Hotel & Casino and the Hacienda Resort Hotel and Casino were rooted in the early development of the Las Vegas casino industry in the 1950s. The Sahara, built for $5.5 million by the Del Webb Corporation, was founded by Milton Prell, a Los Angeles jewelry magnate, on the site of the former Club Bingo in 1952. The first high-rise casino in Vegas, and the fifth constructed since Bugsy Siegel's Flamingo, which was also built by Del Webb, the Sahara, and its trademark 100-foot freestanding neon sign, was also the largest at the time,

until the Sands opened two weeks later. The following year, the "Jewel of the Desert," as Prell dubbed the hotel, made the first of many expansions, adding 200 rooms to its hotel. In 1961, Prell sold the Sahara to the Del Webb Corporation, although he continued to run its operations until 1964. Del Webb immediately invested some $12 million in renovations. In 1966, the Sahara added a $50 million, 14-story, 200-room tower, making it the city's tallest building. Two years later, the Sahara built again, adding a 400-room, 24-story skyscraper, expanding its casino, and extending its operations into Vegas's growing convention industry by building a 44,000-square-foot convention center. Del Webb, which had grown to become one of the industry's largest casino operators, continued to manage the Sahara through the 1970s. However, when Del Webb ran into financial problems in the late 1970s and early 1980s, it sold the Sahara to Paul Lowden for $50 million in 1982.

By then, Lowden already owned the Hacienda. That hotel, situated at the far southern end of Las Vegas Boulevard from the Sahara, was built in 1956 for $6 million as part of a California-based chain of low-rise motels owned by Judy and Warren "Doc" Bayley. Problems with the Gaming Control Board delayed the Hacienda's casino licensing, but by 1957 the hotel's casino was up and running. Situated far from the main strip, the Hacienda catered especially to families, locals, and "lowrollers," eventually earning the hotel the nickname of "Hayseed Heaven." Nonetheless, the Hacienda—which was imploded on New Year's Eve 1996, an event that was broadcast to a national television audience—was long a popular fixture on the strip and was also the first Vegas hotel to operate an airplane shuttle service, building a fleet of more than 30 airplanes serving a number of major cities. When the Federal Aviation Administration decreed the fleet an airline, that service was discontinued. Doc Bayley died in 1964; Judy Bayley continued to run the hotel casino until her death in 1971. Lowden purchased 15 percent of the Hacienda the following year and became its entertainment director. In 1977, Lowden took full possession of the Hacienda for $20 million.

Becoming a Vegas Mogul in the 1970s

Lowden was a teenager when, with $7,500 in savings, he journeyed to Nevada in 1961. He joined a band playing in a

Reno casino, then moved to Las Vegas, where he worked through the decade as a keyboardist, accompanying, among others, singer Ann-Margret. By 1970, Lowden had become the musical director of the Flamingo. However, Lowden had already set his ambitions higher.

With no formal business training, Lowden began investing in the stock market. These investments proved successful enough that, in 1972, Lowden and a group of partners raised $250,000, half of which came from the Valley Bank of Nevada, to buy 15 percent of the Hacienda. One of Lowden's partners brought in Allen Glick, a land developer from San Diego, to purchase majority control of the Hacienda. Lowden became the hotel casino's entertainment director. Under Lowden, the Hacienda launched its famous "topless" ice skating revues, which ran in various incarnations until 1993. Lowden expanded his casino holdings in 1975, putting up $500,000 for a share of the Tropicana. By then, a fresh scandal was brewing along the Vegas Strip.

In mid-1976, Lowden walked away from his Tropicana investment, discouraged by Mafia figure Joseph Agosto's control over the hotel casino's operation. Lowden first asked the Tropicana's majority owners to buy out his investment; when they declined, Lowden simply walked away rather than jeopardize his casino owner's license through the Tropicana's Mafia association. Lowden did not begin to regain his investment until 1979, after Agosto had pleaded guilty to skimming charges, and the Tropicana's owners were forced out by the state.

Meanwhile, a similar scandal was brewing at the Hacienda. Glick, who at age 29 controlled two other casino hotels, the Stardust and the Fremont, making him Las Vegas's second-largest casino operator, had come under a separate skimming investigation. Glick would later admit that he had been working as a Mafia front. In 1977, facing these charges and financial problems, Glick agreed to sell the Hacienda to Lowden. Paying $21 million, raised through Valley Bank and the First American National Bank of Nashville, Tennessee, Lowden bought out Glick and the other minority owners and took full control of the Hacienda.

Lowden immediately ran into difficulties. The Gaming Control Board, concerned by Lowden's past association with Glick, recommended against allowing Lowden's purchase of the Hacienda. Nevertheless, the Nevada Gaming Commission overturned the recommendation and cleared Lowden of any connection with Glick, giving Lowden a new license to operate the Hacienda. Lowden was joined by William Raggio as corporate counsel, who served at the time as Republican majority leader in the Nevada state senate and who later joined Lowden's company as a director and officer. One year after buying the Hacienda, Lowden began looking to expand his casino holdings by buying Glick's two remaining casino properties. However, the mortgages to the Stardust and Fremont were held by the reputedly mob-tied Teamsters Central States Pension Fund. Because of this connection, Lowden's investment banker refused to handle the financing for the deal, and Lowden backed off on the purchase.

Building Sahara Gaming in the 1980s

Instead, Lowden concentrated on expanding the Hacienda. In 1980, he spent $30 million on a facelift and expansion of the property, revamping the hotel in the style of Old World Spain and adding a convention center and an 11-story, 300-room tower. The Hacienda proved profitable, as did the institution of a side business, that of selling timeshares in the Hacienda hotel rooms, a first in Vegas. By 1982, Lowden had built up a $25 million timeshare portfolio in that and another hotel in Hawaii. The timeshares mortgages gave Lowden valuable collateral for additional financing, and Lowden began looking for a new casino purchase.

The Del Webb Corporation, which had been suffering losses since the late 1970s, put the Sahara on the block in 1982. Leveraging his assets, Lowden put together $50 million to purchase the famed casino. The following year, the Sahara and Hacienda went public, incorporating as Public/Hacienda Resorts, Inc. With the proceeds from the public offering, the company expanded the Hacienda again, adding 400 rooms and more than doubling the size of its casino, hotel, rooms, and restaurants. Next, the company acquired an additional 22 acres behind the Sahara for the hotel's future expansion plans. In the meantime, the highly leveraged company, burdened by interest payments on more than $30 million in debt, was bleeding. Losses began in 1982 and continued into the next year, when the company lost $2.6 million on $92.6 million in revenues. The following year, with revenues of $94 million, the company lost nearly $2 million. It was not until 1986 that the new corporation, by then renamed Sahara Resorts, recorded its first profit, of $411,500 on $101 million in revenues. Meanwhile, the Sahara, which had not had any large renovations in nearly 20 years, was beginning to show its age.

Lowden hit on an idea to provide financing not only for a Sahara expansion, but also to help the company reduce its debt. In 1987, he formed publicly traded Sahara Casino Partners L.P., a master limited partnership (MLP), which sold 6.2 million units at $9 per share. A first for Las Vegas, the MLP offering was immediately successful (in fact, it was oversubscribed) and generated $63 million for Sahara Resorts, enabling the company to pay down its debt and to finance a new expansion of the Sahara. Sahara Resorts retained 63 percent of Sahara Casino Partners. Under terms of the MLP, which was executed shortly before federal tax restrictions were created to eliminate tax advantages from non-real estate partnerships, Sahara Resorts agreed to a five-year subordination of its own profit distributions until minimum distributions were made to public investors. These investors, in turn, would take no ownership position in the casinos.

After paying off the $30 million Sahara mortgage, Lowden, whose interest in Sahara Resorts remained at 73 percent, began work on the casino hotel's most ambitious renovation and expansion. In 1988, the Sahara added a third tower, this time reaching 26 stories and adding 575 rooms, bringing the Sahara's total to 1,500 rooms. Two years later, Lowden performed a still more ambitious expansion, adding a new 600-room tower to the Sahara and a 400-room tower to the Hacienda, while doubling the Hacienda's casino area, bringing that hotel's total rooms to 1,200 and its gambling space to nearly 40,000 square feet. By then, however, Lowden had already moved to expand his casino holdings.

The Way to Santa Fe in the 1990s

Las Vegas's 1980 gambling boom had spread beyond the city into other areas of the state, and in 1988 Lowden moved to capitalize on the growing casino demand by purchasing the gambling operations at the Pioneer Hotel and Gambling Hall in Laughlin, Nevada. Built in 1982, the Pioneer was designed as an old-west style gambling hall and saloon, complete with dark wood walls, chandeliers, and antique-style slot machines. The Pioneer's River Rick, a large neon sign of a cowboy waving welcome, is a "first cousin" to Las Vegas's Vegas Vic. The complex sits on 12 acres of land along the Colorado River and consists of three hotel buildings with 400 rooms and a casino. The Pioneer casino features over 800 slot machines, nine blackjack tables, two craps tables, and one roulette wheel. The Laughlin area caters to customers different from those at the Las Vegas casinos, drawing in primarily local residents and the drive-in gambling crowd from Southern California and Arizona. After paying $112.5 million for the Pioneer, Lowden raised $116 million to fund the 1990 expansions of the Sahara and Hacienda as well as to build an entirely new hotel casino and entertainment complex, the Santa Fe.

The Santa Fe Casino Hotel, which opened in 1991, features a 200-room hotel, an 85,000-square-foot casino, a 60-lane bowl-

ing center, a National Hockey League regulation-sized ice skating arena with 3,000 seats for spectators, three themed restaurants, and a bingo parlor on its 40-acre site. Located some nine miles north of the main Las Vegas casino strip, the Santa Fe exploited a niche different from that of the company's Strip hotels. Instead of gambling tourists, the Santa Fe, with only 200 rooms, marketed to local residents. Operating without competition for most of the first half of the 1990s, the Santa Fe proved immediately profitable.

Lowden's activity was taking its toll on the company's profits, however. By 1991, the company's debt had soared to $310 million, generating interest payments of some $33 million per year. Despite revenues that reached $179.5 million in 1991 and neared $220 million in 1992, Sahara had returned to the red, posting losses of $9 million and $6.5 million for those years, respectively. These losses would continue through 1995, reaching $15 million in 1994 and $22 million in 1995.

Adding to the company's troubles were its ill-fated attempts to expand its operations beyond Nevada. Gambling fever had been spreading throughout the country in the first years of the 1990s, with more and more states legalizing gambling and a new trend, riverboat casinos, filling the docks of more and more river communities. Sahara's first target was Parkville, Missouri, located near Kansas City. In 1993, the company, now renamed Sahara Gaming Corp. after merging the Sahara Resorts and Sahara Casino Partners operations, purchased the Spirit of America riverboat casino complex for $7.8 million and paid to have it towed to Parkville. That community, meanwhile, was engaged in a drawn-out battle over whether to allow casino operations, a process that required three elections and would not be decided until November 1994. By the time Sahara received the go-ahead for its casino, the Parkville operation was losing money, to the tune of $50 million. A second investment outside of Nevada, into the Treasure Bay riverboat complex near Biloxi, Mississippi, also ground to a halt, costing the company a $12.6 million writeoff charge. By then, too, the Hacienda was faltering, draining the company's revenues. The Laughlin market was also leveling off; meanwhile, the Santa Fe was forced to greet new competition in its area.

In 1995, Lowden retrenched his operations. His first step was to sell off the Hacienda for $80 million to former Circus Circus chairman and CEO William Bennett. By June 1995, Lowden and Bennett had struck a new deal. Bennett bought the Sahara for $193 million; under terms of the deal, Lowden took possession of an undeveloped, 27-acre parcel on the Vegas Strip. By the time Bennett imploded the Hacienda on New Year's Eve 1996, in order to make room for an $800 million hotel-casino megacomplex, Lowden had renamed his company to reflect its new focus. The stripped-down company, now named Santa Fe Gaming Corporation, completed its first year of operations with revenues of $148.4 million. A $40 million gain from the Sahara sale helped the company achieve its first profitable year, with a profit of $9.7 million, of the decade.

Sales were down to $105 million in 1997, primarily because of a drop in casino revenues from the Pioneer, and the company showed a loss of $13 million. The Santa Fe subsidiary Pioneer Finance Corp. had financial troubles in 1998 when it was unable to pay $60 million in principal due on mortgage notes. The subsidiary was forced to reorganize, filing for Chapter 11 bankruptcy in February 1999. Because of this circumstance, Santa Fe had a net loss for 1998 of $62.3 million.

In 1999, Santa Fe's subsidiary Sahara Las Vegas Corp. sold a 40-acre parcel of property in Henderson, Nevada, to Station Casinos, Inc. for $37.25 million. The company's financial outlook improved somewhat in that year, with sales of $125 million and a net loss of only $19.9 million. The year 2000 saw the company sell the Santa Fe Hotel and Casino for $205 million to Station Casinos. Net sales for 2000 were $131 million, with a profit of $12.8 million.

Company Becomes Archon Corporation

On May 11, 2001, Santa Fe Gaming Corporation changed its name to Archon Corporation. That same year the company acquired investment properties in Dorchester, Massachusetts, and Gaithersburg, Maryland, for a total cost of $145 million. The 12-acre Dorchester property consists of several buildings with about 425,000 square feet of commercial office space. The 55-acre Gaithersburg property includes one building with about 342,000 square feet of office space. The buildings on both properties are leased out under long-term agreements.

Sales for 2001 were considerably lower, by almost 63 percent, than for 2000 because of the sale of the Santa Fe Hotel and the resulting loss of its gambling revenues. The $48 million in sales for the year, however, was augmented by the profit from the hotel sale, giving Archon a net profit for the year of $87.2 million. The company showed a loss of $9.3 million in 2002. Much of the loss was due to a decrease in gambling revenues at the Pioneer. Archon management blamed this revenue decline on the growth of Native American casinos in Southern California, Arizona, and New Mexico, which was hurting the Laughlin casino business generally. The year 2003 saw a further decline in revenues to $46.1 million and a net loss of $8.9 million.

In late 2003, the company ceased to operate Duke's Casino in Sparks, Nevada, through its Archon Sparks Management Company subsidiary. That casino's furniture, fixtures, gaming and non-gaming equipment were transferred to the Pioneer. In January 2004, Archon purchased the fee ownership of the Pioneer for $36 million from an affiliate of GE Capital. In this deal, the company purchased outright the Pioneer's real estate, buildings, and equipment. Lowden commented in a press release: "We are excited about this asset acquisition, and we will continue our efforts to provide an entertaining experience to our Pioneer customers."

Sales for 2004 were $45.6 million, down from 2003, with a loss of $3.4 million. Revenues for the Pioneer were down 10 percent from 2003, due to a decrease in the number of casino patrons, according to Archon management. In the first six months of 2005, this decline continued. Revenues from the Pioneer slid 13.8 percent from the same period in 2004, and Archon reported a loss of $2 million.

Despite its losses in the early 2000s, the future looked bright for Archon. In December 2003, the company announced that it planned to develop the 27-acre property on Las Vegas Boulevard acquired during the sale of the Sahara. It also planned to construct the Palace of the Sea hotel and casino on the site. The complex would be Australian-themed with a 3,000-room hotel, high-roller suites designed to look like yachts, and a casino based on the Sydney Opera House. Architect Veldon Simpson would design the hotel, which would include a 600-foot tall observation wheel to lift guests high above the Las Vegas Strip and give them a view of the entire Las Vegas Valley. The company has filed use permits with the city of Las Vegas but still needs to obtain further approvals and permits, and the necessary financing, before the project can begin.

Principal Subsidiaries

Archon Sparks Management Company; Pioneer Hotel Inc.; Sahara Las Vegas Corp.

Principal Operating Units

Pioneer Hotel and Gambling Hall.

Further Reading

"Archon Corporation Reports Fiscal Year End Financial Results," *PR Newswire*, December 28, 2001.

"Archon Corporation Reports Second Fiscal Quarter 2005 Financial Results," *PR Newswire*, May 17, 2005.

Benston, Liz, "Stockholder: Archon Options Unfairly Enrich Owner's Family," *Las Vegas Sun*, June 20, 2005.

Cook, James, "Heads I Win, Tails I Also Win," *Forbes*, July 6, 1992, p. 51.

——, "Rolling the Dice on Gambling and Retail," *Chain Store Age Executive*, May, 1997, p. 106.

Delugach, Al, "Casino Owner Beats the Odds," *Los Angeles Times*, March 13, 1988, Sec. 4, p. 1.

McKee, Jamie, "Analysts: Hacienda Sale a Good First Step for Sahara Gaming," *Las Vegas Business*, February 27, 1995, p. 1.

Moore, Thomas, "When Will Green Valley See Gamblers' Green?" *Las Vegas Business Press*, March 27, 1995, p. 3.

Morrison, Jane Ann, "Implosion Bittersweet for Those Close to Hacienda," *Las Vegas Review-Journal*, January 1, 1997, p. 3A.

Morrissey, John, "Sahara Resorts Markets Unique MLP Offering," *Las Vegas Business Press*, July 1, 1987, p. 12.

Post, Theresa, "Sahara Partners to Expand Hotel Operation in Vegas," *Travel Weekly*, August 16, 1990, p. 20.

"Santa Fe Gaming Corp. and Pioneer Finance Corp. Announce Filing of Involuntary Bankruptcy Petitions in Connection with 13 1/2% First Mortgage Notes," *PR Newswire*, January 18, 1999.

"Santa Fe Gaming Corporation Announces 1997 Fiscal Year End Results," *PR Newswire*, December 24, 1997.

"Santa Fe Gaming Corporation Announces Sale of Henderson Property," *PR Newswire*, November 17, 1999.

Wood, Tara, "Focuses on the Ultimate Jackpot: A Cure," *Quest*, March-April, 2005.

—M.L. Cohen
—update: Thomas Wiloch

BARON DE LEY
Baron de Ley S.A.

Ctra de Lodosa a Mendavia km 5.5
Mendavia E-31587
Spain
Telephone: +34 948 69 43 03
Fax: +34 948 69 43 04
Web site: http://www.barondeley.com

Public Company
Incorporated: 1985
Employees: 106
Sales: EUR 77.36 million ($101 million) (2004)
Stock Exchanges: Bolsa de Madrid
Ticker Symbol: BDL
NAIC: 312130 Wineries

Baron de Ley S.A. is a fast-growing Spanish winery. The Mendavia-based company focuses especially on producing mid- to high-end Rioja wine grades, with an emphasis on Crianza (62 percent of production) and Reserva (25 percent). The company also produces a limited range of premium Gran Reserva (less than 3 percent). The company's wines bear the labels of its two main wineries, Baron de Ley and El Coto de Rioja, as well as fast-growing El Meson. The company also bottles wines under the Maximo label, launched in 2002 to produce varietal wines, chiefly for the international market. Since 2003, the company also has been producing ''modern'' wines at its Finca Museum winery in the Cigales DOC region. Baron de Ley also has been developing the ambitious Los Almendros vineyard and winery, for which it has acquired a total of 235 hectares. Planting at Los Almendros was launched in 2004, with the final phase of planting expected to be completed by 2007. Baron de Ley, led by Eduardo Santos-Ruiz Diaz, is often cited as being a driving force behind the resurrection of Rioja's profile in the international wine market. In an extension into a new market, Baron de Ley has been developing a business producing cured Iberian ham, through subsidiary Dehesa Baron de Ley SL. The company expects production of its hams—said to be an excellent accompaniment for Rioja wines—by 2006. Established in 1985, the company has led the modernization of growing, production, and aging techniques to create superior wines. The company is listed on the Bolsa de Madrid. In 2004, Baron de Ley's sales topped EUR 77 million ($101 million).

Founding a Rioja Dream in the 1980s

Spanish wines, once international favorites—especially popularized by Ernest Hemingway, among others—had begun to fade in the face of growing international competition in the late 1960s. With high-quality wines appearing from the United States, South Africa, Australia, and elsewhere, sales of Spanish wines, and particularly its flagship Rioja wines, entered a long slump. Shifting consumer tastes, favoring the lighter and sweeter wines from the so-called ''new world'' producers, led wine drinkers away from the heavier flavors of the oak-aged Rioja wines. At the same time, Rioja, and Spanish wine in general, became associated with lower quality wines.

In the early 1970s, however, the Spanish government adopted a new DOC system, which established regulations governing Spain's appellations and their grades. In the case of Rioja, for example, the classification required the Gran Reserva wines be aged at least five years, while Reserva wines were to be aged for three years. At the mid-range, Crianza, the aging process was established at two years or more. The new classification system played an important role in restoring the reputation of Spanish wines, and particularly of the country's flagship Rioja appellation.

The promise of a new era for Rioja wines led to the creation of a number of new wineries in the early 1970s. In 1973, for example, a new winery, backed financially by Banco Union, was established in Oyon, Alava, called El Coto de Rioja. The winery, created to produce the full range of Rioja grades, later reached a production capacity of nearly nine million liters, based on some 90 hectares of vineyards. Yet compliance with the new regulations governing the Rioja appellation placed a heavy burden on the region's wineries, with El Coto de Rioja among them.

The new winery slipped into financial trouble soon after its founding. In response, Banco Union brought in Eduardo Santos-

Ruiz Diaz to restructure the company. Santos-Ruiz then hired Julian Diez Blanco and Julio Noain to assist him. By the middle of the 1980s, the trio had succeeded in establishing El Coto de Rioja as one of the region's most prominent, and profitable, wineries. In 1985, therefore, Banco Union exited from its shareholding, selling the winery to expanding British drinks conglomerate Bass PLC.

By then, Santos-Ruiz, who continued to serve as managing director at El Coto de Rioja, and his partners had begun planning a new winery venture based on a new idea—that of emulating the Bordeaux estate wines. Into the mid-1980s, Rioja wines typically represented blends of grapes from a number of farmers and vineyards. Santos-Ruiz's idea, however, was to develop a winery based on the production of a specific vineyard, such as was the case with many of the Bordeaux region's famous labels.

In 1985, Santos-Ruiz and partners purchased a 16th-century Benedictine monastery, as well as the surrounding estate, in Mendavia, Navarre, and established Baron de Ley. The group's choice of location raised some eyebrows, given the arid conditions of the estate and the resulting difficulty of producing a quality Rioja wine from its grapes. Yet the soil and climate proved ideal for Baron de Ley's goal of developing a modernized version of Rioja wine.

Work began on planting the vineyards, including 90 hectares of Tempranillo, the traditional grape variety of Rioja wines. Yet Rioja regulations also permitted the planting of ''experimental'' grape varieties—in Baron de Ley's case, the company planted some 20 hectares of Cabernet Sauvignon, a prominent variety used in Bordeaux and other French wines. Meanwhile, the company converted the former monastery buildings into its headquarters, winery, and winery cellar.

Acquiring Scale in the 1990s

Baron de Ley released its first bottles of Reserva wine in 1990. The company also had begun building up its wine stock, which reached 6.5 million liters in 1991. That year marked an important milestone for the company as well. In 1991, Baron de Ley reached an agreement with Bass to acquire El Coto de Rioja. To raise funding for the acquisition, Baron de Ley turned to an investors consortium led by Mercapital, which then took control of more than 65 percent of the merged companies' shares.

Mercapital proved an important partner for Baron de Ley, providing investment capital, as well as assistance in establishing its international marketing and distribution operations. Backed by Mercapital, Baron de Ley undertook an extensive investment program, upgrading its two wineries and expanding capacity. The company also made the strategic decision of maintaining its two labels as separate entities, handled by different distributors. Baron de Ley's investment program also en-

abled it to shift its focus toward the higher range, increasing its percentage of Reserva and Gran Reserva. By the middle of the 2000s, the company's Reserva production accounted for 25 percent of its total production, while its Gran Reserva neared 3 percent.

Positioning itself toward the upper end enabled the company to build a strong export business. By the late 1990s, Baron de Ley's international sales represented nearly one-third of its total revenues. The company's wines were prized particularly in the northern European markets, especially Sweden, Switzerland, Germany, and the United Kingdom.

Having helped the company develop a strong and growing business, Mercapital decided to exit its shareholding in 1997, listing Baron de Ley on the Bolsa de Madrid that year. The public offering also enabled Baron de Ley to continue its investment in upgrading its facilities, with plans to spend more than $10 million into the end of the century. Part of the group's investment went into expanding its wine stocks. By 1994, the company boasted 16.4 million liters in stock; by 2000, the company's wine stock had expanded past 40 million.

Expansion in the 2000s

At the dawn of the 21st century, Baron de Ley began implementing a new phase in its growth. The company now began seeking to expand beyond its core operations at the Baron de Ley and El Coto de Rioja wineries, to enter a wider range of wine segments.

As part of this effort, the company established a new winery, Museum, to produce wines under the Cigales appellation. For this, the company invested some EUR 9 million, building a winery supported by 104 hectares of vineyards. The Museum winery, completed in 2002, quickly built up production capacity of more than 1.5 million liters, making it one of the largest of the Cigales producers. The company launched sales of the first bottles of Museum wines in 2003.

Baron de Ley also took steps to counter the growing popularity of varietal wines—that is, wines marketed according to the grapes used to produce them, rather than according to the location of the producer—on the international market. In 2002, the company launched its own varietal label, Maximo. The new label proved a success and, by 2004, sales of Maximo wines had reached nearly 25 countries.

In the meantime, Baron de Ley had begun planning a still more ambitious winery project. The company began buying up parcels of vineyards in the Rioja district in the early 2000s. By 2004, the company had succeeded in combining more than 240 plots of land previously held by more than 40 owners to create a single estate of 235 hectares. The company then began construction of a new winery, Los Almendros, and planted its first 40 acres of Tempranillo grapes in 2004.

Planting at Los Almendros continued in 2005; by the end of that year, new vineyards were expected to add another 35 hectares. The planting of 60 more hectares was slated for 2006, and the first harvest was scheduled for 2007. At full planting, the Los Almendros winery was to become the largest single Rioja estate.

Key Dates:

1973: The El Coto de Rioja winery is founded, backed by Union Bank; Eduardo Santos-Ruiz Diaz becomes the winery's managing director.

1985: Santos-Ruiz and partners set up Baron de Ley in order to establish a Bordeaux-style winery in the Rioja region.

1986: El Coto de Rioja is sold to Bass PLC.

1990: The first bottles of Baron de Ley are released.

1991: Backed by Mercapital, Baron de Ley acquires El Coto de Rioja.

1997: Baron de Ley goes public on the Bolsa de Madrid.

1999: The Museum winery is created to produce Cigales wine.

2002: Construction of the Museum winery is completed; the Maximo brand of varietal wines is launched for the international market.

2003: The company releases the first bottles of Museum wines.

2004: Baron de Ley restructures.

Baron de Ley restructured in 2004. As part of a reorganization, the company created a new company, Vinedos Baron de Ley SL, which became the owner of the company's land and vineyards, as well as overseer of its planting and grape production. At the same time, the company created separate companies for each of its wineries. Baron de Ley itself adopted a holding company structure, providing centralized services to its subsidiaries.

By then, the company had launched another subsidiary, taking the group in a new direction. In 2004, the company established Dehesa Baron de Ley, which began developing operations for the production of cured Iberian ham from acorn-fed pigs. The company began building a production facility in 2005, with completion expected for 2006.

Nonetheless, Baron de Ley's focus remained firmly on its wine labels. By 2005, the company had become one of the Rioja region's largest wine producers, with more than 700 hectares of land, including more than 300 hectares of planted land, as well as a new plot of 135 hectares acquired in the Cigales region in 2005. The company also had built up wine stocks of 64 million liters, representing some four years of sales. At the same time, Baron de Ley had established a solid international reputation for the quality of its wines, winning a number of awards, including that of Spanish Wine Producer of the Year at the London International Wine and Spirit Competition.

Principal Subsidiaries

Baron de Ley S.A.; Bodegas El Meson SL; Bodegas Maximo SL; Dehesa Baron de Ley SL; El Coto de Rioja S.A.; Finca Museum SL; Inversiones Coto de Rioja SL; Vinedos Baron de Ley SL.

Principal Competitors

Osborne Compania S.A.; Freixenet S.A; J. Garcia Carrion S.A.; Grupo Codorniu; Gonzalez Byass S.A.; Miguel Torres S.A.; Felix Solis S.A.; Bodegas AGE S.A.; Grupo de Bodegas Vinartis S.A.; Mostos Vinos y Alcoholes S.A.

Further Reading

''Baron de Ley and Anodil (Iberia),'' *Acquisitions Monthly,* November 2002, p. S59.

''Baron de Ley,'' *thewinedoctor.com,* January 2005.

''Baron de Ley Improves,'' *Food and drink.com,* July 29, 2003.

Parry, John N., ''Institutions Get Ready to Lay Down Rioja Shares,'' *The European,* July 10, 1997.

Walker, Larry, ''A Wine Renaissance in Rioja,'' *Wines & Vines,* March 2002.

—M.L. Cohen

Bibliographisches Institut & F.A. Brockhaus AG

Querstraße 18
04103 Leipzig
Germany
Telephone: +(49) (341) 978630
Fax: +(49) (341) 9786560
Web site: http://www.bifab.de

Private Company
Founded: 1805
Employees: 300
Sales: EUR 65.17 million ($88.91 million) (2004)
NAIC: 511130 Book Publishers; 511210 Software
    Publishers; 511199 All Other Publishers

The Bibliographisches Institut & F.A. Brockhaus AG (BIFAB) is the leading publisher of reference books in the German-speaking world. Headquartered in Mannheim, BIFAB's publishing program is based on three of the most respected reference book lines in Germany: the Meyers encyclopedias, including *Meyers Großes Taschenlexikon*; the Brockhaus encyclopedias, including the *Brockhaus Enzyklopädie*; and the Duden catalog of dictionaries, including most notably, *Die deutsche Rechtschreibung,* a book found in virtually every German home and office. The BIFAB editorial staff is based in the firm's historical headquarters in Leipzig, Germany. Administrative and production staff members work out of Mannheim, Germany. Of a total staff of approximately 300, 70 work in the company's Leipzig headquarters, while another 230 are based in Mannheim.

BIFAB AG grew out of the work of three of the most important figures in German publishing history: F.A. Brockhaus, Joseph Meyer, and Konrad Duden. Individually the three men set the standard for the production of reference books in Germany.

Brockhaus Publishes His First Encyclopedia in the Early 1800s

Friedrich Arnold Brockhaus, assisted by Dutch friends, founded the publishing company Rohloff & Co. in Amsterdam in October 1805. The firm made its first significant acquisition a

year later at the Leipzig publishing fair where Brockhaus paid 1,800 Talers for the rights to the *Conversationslexikon mit vorzüglicher Rücksicht auf die gegenwärtigen Zeiten* (Conversational Encyclopedia with Particular Emphasis on Present Times). Until then the encyclopedia had had so little success that its authors had never finished writing it. Brockhaus arranged for its completion and in 1809 published the *Conversations-Lexicon* in eight volumes. The new work offered, in Brockhaus's own words, "the most important information, from science, nature, art and public life, for general education, presented briefly and clearly, in a manner suited to the form, character and needs of the latest times." The work would be the foundation for future Brockhaus as well as various foreign encyclopedias.

By 1817 the enterprise had moved its operations from The Netherlands to Leipzig, Germany, and adopted its owner's name, becoming F.A. Brockhaus. Leipzig at the time was the capital of the German publishing industry, and within four years the company had settled into a headquarters that included its own printing plant, all located in Leipzig's so-called Graphics Quarter. Brockhaus established a financial foundation for his house by including in its publishing program works of general interest from the fields of history, literature, and philosophy, along with other reference works. The company pulled off a coup in 1819 when Arthur Schopenhauer, one of the most popular and influential philosophers of the day, became a Brockhaus author. Three years later Brockhaus published Casanova's *Memoirs* in a bowdlerized German edition. Although the company owned the sole copy of the original manuscript, it did not publish a complete version until 1963.

When F.A. Brockhaus died at the age of 51 in 1823, his sons Friedrich and Heinrich took over the company then at work on a new edition of its *Conversations-Lexicon.* The first *Encyclopedia Americana,* published between 1829 and 1833, was based directly on this Brockhaus edition. Although the firm continued to publish the works of important authors, including Johann Wolfgang von Goethe, reference books constituted the primary focus of its catalog. In 1831 it acquired Verlag Johann Friedrich Gleditsch, the publisher of the *Allgemeine Encyclopädie der Wissenschaften und Künste* (General Encyclopedia of the Arts and Sciences). When it was finally completed in 1889, the 167-

volume work was the largest and most extensive German-language encyclopedia of the time.

Joseph Meyer Producing Encyclopedias for the People in the 1820s

In 1826 Joseph Meyer founded the Bibliographisches Institut, a publishing house that practically from the start would be Brockhaus's primary competitor. Meyer was a canny businessman. He published literary classics at affordable prices in his *Cabinets-Bibliothek der Deutschen Classiker* in print runs of thousands. The project—advertised under the motto "Education for all!"—was a magnet for resentment throughout a German publishing industry that bitterly resisted marketing. Meyer brought other strategies to bear as well. While other German publishers of the day were content to announce their new books by simply having the titles printed in the newspaper, Meyer's advertisements took up several pages. When readers subsequently inquired about his books, booksellers—whatever their feelings for Meyer—were forced to stock them. Meyer used sales representatives from outside the book trade to sell his books in areas with no bookstore or where local book dealers refused to do business with him.

Such innovative techniques (he sold 50,000 copies from his series of classics alone) made Meyer one of the most successful publishers of the 19th century. He created long-term interest in his multivolume geographical reference work *Meyers Universum* by selling volumes on a subscription as they were published. By keeping the price for individual volumes relatively low, he was able to interest customers who otherwise would not have been able to afford an expensive set of reference books. Subscription sales were essential to Meyer's first encyclopedia, *Grossen Conversationslexikon für die gebildeten Stände* (Large Conversational Encyclopedia for the Educated Classes), which he began publishing the same year he founded his publishing house. Publication of the work, which eventually ran to 52 volumes published over a 13-year period, would not have been financially feasible otherwise.

The *Conversationslexikon* proved that in addition to being a visionary businessman, Meyer was also a radical advocate of

Enlightenment values. The purpose of the *Conversationslexikon*, as he saw it, was to open the possibility of culture and education to the developing middle classes. The work was "a tool of intellectual emancipation," he wrote in its preface, which would "overthrow the oppressive monopoly on knowledge" long held by the privileged few.

With the publication of the *Conversationslexikon*, Meyer entered a crowded encyclopedia market, which included Brockhaus's *Konversationslexikon*, the *Allgemeine Encyclopädie der Wissenschaften und Künste*, and the *Encyclopädisches Wörterbuch*. But in Meyer's view, each of these works had disadvantages: The first was targeted at the highly educated, the second was too expensive for the general reader, and the content of the last was outdated. Meyer set his sights high, designing the *Conversationslexikon* to be of interest to specialists as well as the general reader. Completed in 1855 by 120 editors who worked more than 20 years to complete a comprehensive and popular German encyclopedia, its 52 volumes consisted of 66,000 pages and more than 90 million words. It was the first German encyclopedia to include tables and text illustrations. Its subscribers received the entire set in approximately 1,000 individual installments.

Following Joseph Meyer's death in 1856, his son Hermann Julius Meyer took over the Bibliographisches Institut's leadership. He launched a revision of the *Conversationslexikon*, along with an abridgement of the set. Edited down to 15 volumes, the new set was completed in 1860 under the title, *Neues Konversations-Lexikon für alle Stände*. The briefer, more affordable encyclopedia became the most important and popular item in the Bibliographisches Institut's catalog. The third edition sold 130,000 sets, and the fifth edition, completed in 1897, sold 233,000. Meyer took another bold step with the publication of Meyer's *Hand-Lexicon des allgemeinen Wissens*, a single-volume reference work that became known as the *Kleiner Meyer* (the Small Meyer) to distinguish it from the *Grosses Conversationslexikon*, which became known as the *Grosse Meyer*. These books, together with atlases, popular scientific books on animals, and similar titles, made the Meyer name synonymous with reference books in Germany by the end of the 19th century.

Duden Standardizes Orthography in the Late 19th Century

Konrad Duden, a *Gymnasium* teacher inspired by the unification of the diverse German states in the Empire in 1871, set out to unify German orthography as well. Until that time there were no standardized rules governing spelling or punctuation in written German. Every writer, every publisher, every newspaper and magazine, followed its own individual house style. In 1872 Duden first publicized his ideas, which were vetoed by Chancellor Otto von Bismarck himself after the First Conference for the Introduction of Standardization of German Orthography. Duden was not discouraged. He began compiling his *Vollständiges Orthographisches Wörterbuch der deutschen Sprache* (Complete Orthographic Dictionary of the German Language). He based the book on the orthography taught in Prussian schools, recognizing that without Prussian approval his work had no chance of adoption. His fundamental guiding principle was that the written language should be based on the spoken, in order that they be learned as easily as possible.

The dictionary was published in 1880 by the Verlag Bibliographisches Institut, the publisher of the Meyer encyclopedias,

Key Dates:

1805: Verlag Rohloff & Co. is founded in Amsterdam.

1808: F.A. Brockhaus obtains the rights to *Conversations-lexikon mit vorzüglicher Rücksicht auf die gegenwärtigen Zeiten* for 1,800 Talers.

1814: Verlag Rohloff & Co. changes its name to Verlag F.A. Brockhaus.

1817: Brockhaus moves to Leipzig and puts its own printing plant into operation soon thereafter.

1823: F.A. Brockhaus passes away.

1826: Joseph Meyer founds the Bibliographisches Institut.

1832: Brockhaus puts its own book binding plant into operation.

1837: Brockhaus opens a branch in Paris, Brockhaus & Avenarius.

1890: Subsidiary Brockhaus & Efron is opened in St. Petersburg, Russia.

1891: Brockhaus opens a branch in London, England.

1903: Representatives of Germany, Austria, and Switzerland adopt orthographic rules developed by Konrad Duden.

1912: Albert Brockhaus writes "Brockhaus Testament," which codifies the company's accumulated knowledge about reference book publishing.

1923: Brockhaus is authorized to print its own money during Germany's postwar hyperinflation.

1937: Anonymous articles denouncing Brockhaus appear in *Das Schwarze Korps,* an influential Nazi periodical.

1945: Hans Brockhaus is allowed by American occupation forces to open a branch in Wiesbaden.

1948: German Democratic Republic (GDR) nationalizes Bibliographisches Institut as VEB Bibliographisches Institut.

1950: Soviet occupation authorities confiscate all copies of the new 11th edition *Volks-Brockhaus.*

1953: GDR nationalizes the Leipzig Verlag F.A. Brockhaus and renames it VEB F.A. Brockhaus.

1963: GDR Central Committee centralizes the country's travel book publishing in VEB F.A. Brockhaus.

1984: Brockhaus and Bibliographisches Institut merge, forming BIFAB AG.

1985: The BIFAB headquarters are moved to Mannheim, Germany; BIFAB is converted from a public to a private company.

1988: Langenscheidt KG becomes the majority shareholder in BIFAB following a takeover attempt by Robert Maxwell.

1990: VEB Bibliographisches Institut is absorbed by BIFAB AG.

1992: Brockhaus property confiscated by GDR in 1953 is returned to the firm; VEB Verlag Brockhaus is absorbed into BIFAB AG.

1993: BIFAB moves its headquarters to Leipzig; BIFAB introduces its first electronic product, *Die PC-Bibliothek.*

2001: BIFAB acquires Xipolis.NET online databases.

2005: Brockhaus celebrates its 200th anniversary.

which by that time also was based in Leipzig. With approximately 27,000 entries, Duden's book originally was intended primarily for teaching orthography in the schools. Priced at only one mark, however, it quickly spread through wide areas of German society and by the dawn of the 20th century it had gone into six editions, all produced in large part by Konrad Duden himself. Eventually, at the Second Orthographic Conference in January 1903, representatives of three German-speaking nations, Germany, Austria, and Switzerland, agreed to officially adopt the rules Duden had developed. As a result, the Bibliographisches Institut expanded the department working on Duden's dictionary.

When Duden passed away in 1911, he left a nearly completed manuscript of his book's ninth edition, which was published in 1915 under a new title, *Duden – Rechtschreibung der deutschen Sprache und der Fremdwörter.* Since that time the name Duden has been synonymous with German dictionaries, as Webster is with dictionaries of American English. New titles were added systematically to the Duden series, including first a grammar book, a visual dictionary, and a style dictionary, and later volumes on etymology, foreign words and phrases, synonyms, quotations, and pronunciation.

Economic and Political Struggles in the 1920s and 1930s

Work at both Brockhaus and the Bibliographisches Institut for the most part ground to a halt during World War I. Hard times continued in the early 1920s as Germany struggled through political and economic difficulties. The seventh edition of the *Grosser Meyer* was canceled in 1922. As a result of inflation in Germany, which was only just beginning to skyrocket, the cost to produce a single volume would have cost DEM 50 million or more. Publication of the new edition could not take place until 1925 when the economic situation had stabilized.

Brockhaus stayed afloat during the great postwar inflation in part by taking on simple print jobs, turning out calendars, paper doilies for bakeries, gold cardboard picture frames, and advertising matter of every kind. In order to pay its workers, the Weimar government authorized Brockhaus to print its own "emergency currency," which bore the "Brockhaus" signature. Such extraordinary measures enabled the publisher to bring out a modest reference book, the four-volume *Handbuch des Wissens* (Handbook of Knowledge). In 1928 Brockhaus began revising its flagship encyclopedia, by then known simply as the Brockhaus. Its 20 volumes were completed in 1934.

With a new Brockhaus on the market, arch-competitor Meyer was expected to respond with a new edition of the *Grosser Meyer.* By the beginning of the 1930s, however, times had grown difficult again. The Great Depression devastated the German economy. In 1929, some 1.9 million were unemployed—approximately one third of the country's population. By January 1933 the number had swollen to 6.04 million, a grim economic situation that helped bring Hitler and the National Socialists to power. Publishers were soon forced to submit to Nazi censorship, which slowed work on both Meyer's and

Brockhaus books. The influence of Nazi ideology could be seen clearly in the Duden dictionaries; the 11th and 12th editions of the *Rechtschreibung,* published between 1937 and 1943, institutionalized Nazi language, with entries such as *Reichpropagandaleiter* (Head of Propaganda in the Third Reich), *Reichkulturamt* (Reich Office of Culture), and *Reichsfeind* (enemy of the Reich). The revision of the eighth edition of the *Grosser Meyer* dragged out for ten years because of political interference and financial hardship at the Bibliographisches Institut and, in the end, was never completed. Such Nazi influence led to a decline in the publisher's reputation and, in turn, to lower sales both in Germany and abroad.

Brockhaus, on the other hand, suffered because of its resistance to Nazi control. When it did not revise the *Volks-Brockhaus* to conform sufficiently to the prevailing ideology, the company was denounced in 1937 in an influential Nazi magazine. The Brockhaus family only narrowly averted losing their enterprise altogether as a result. Brockhaus also had to contend with physical destruction before the war ended. In December 1943 its Leipzig editorial offices and printing plant were destroyed, in large part, by an Allied air raid. The company was able to continue operations, but on a greatly reduced scale, until the war ended in the spring of 1945.

Rebuilding After 1945

The signing of the capitulation did not automatically signal the resumption of prosperity for Brockhaus and the Bibliographisches Institut. Under the accords signed by the United States, the USSR and Great Britain, Leipzig was to be located in the Soviet zone of occupation. The American army, however, reached Leipzig before the Soviet did. Before they turned the city over to the Russians, they made arrangement for publishing houses that had not had close ties to the Nazis, including F.A. Brockhaus, to establish ''branches'' near Wiesbaden and Frankfurt/Main in the American zone of occupation. As a result, F.A. Brockhaus's great-great-grandson Hans Brockhaus and his son Eberhard were able to relocate their publishing company in Wiesbaden. It operated under the name Verlag Eberhard Brockhaus until 1953 to distinguish it from the Verlag F.A. Brockhaus that continued to operate in Leipzig.

In Leipzig the Soviets set Brockhaus to publishing books in Russian as well as political works by Marx, Engels, Lenin, and Stalin in German. In the years after the German Democratic Republic (GDR) was founded in the Soviet zone in 1948, the Bibliographisches Institut and Brockhaus were both nationalized as ''people's companies,'' and renamed VEB Bibliographisches Institut and VEB F.A. Brockhaus Leipzig, respectively. The control of the GDR government proved to be as thorough as that of the Nazis. It decreed that the Bibliographisches Institut would be the nation's sole reference book publisher. Its publications were saturated with the socialist worldview from behind the Iron Curtain. For decades parallel versions of Meyer encyclopedias and Duden dictionaries were published, one in West Germany and another in East Germany. Ironically, the *Volks-Brockhaus*'s ideological unsoundness was attacked by GDR communists much as it had been by the Nazis 15 years earlier. Eventually the East German Brockhaus firm was limited to publishing ''progressive'' travel books.

The Bibliographisches Institut was able to establish a public corporation in the West German city of Mannheim in 1953. That firm's first publication in 1968 was *Meyers Grosses Handlexikon.* Between 1971 and 1979 it published *Meyers Enzyklopädisches Lexikon,* which with 25 volumes containing approximately 250,000 entries was one of the most extensive German-language encyclopedias of the century. Unfortunately, that encyclopedia, as well as *Meyers Grosses Universal-Lexikon,* were disappointing sellers.

Merger of German Reference Giants in the 1980s

Increasing competition in the reference book market together with the high production costs resulted in an increasingly precarious financial situation for Brockhaus. After a particularly disappointing fiscal year 1982–83, the firm began quietly looking for a partner. After discussions with the *Frankfurter Allgemeine Zeitung* came to naught, it seemed that for lack of capital Brockhaus would be forced to delay work on the new *Brockhaus Enzyclopädie* indefinitely. Out of the blue, however, a merger offer came from a most unexpected source—from Brockhaus's main competitor, the Bibliographisches Institut. It was received with skepticism from one of the four Brockhaus shareholders, who felt the terms favored the Bibliographisches Institut to too great a degree and that Brockhaus would lose its identity and, ultimately, its autonomy. In May 1984, however, the merger became reality and the Bibliographisches Institut und Verlag F.A. Brockhaus, the two giants of German reference book publishing, joined forces. Because of the merger, the two firms saved significant amounts of money by combining their information databases, accounting, and marketing resources. It also—gradually—marked the end to more than a century and a half of fierce competition. The new firm was named Bibliographisches Institut & F.A. Brockhaus AG, abbreviated to BIFAB. In 1985 BIFAB centralized its operations in Mannheim, giving up the Brockhaus facilities in Wiesbaden. A year later the united editorial Brockhaus and Meyer departments launched their first common project, the 19th edition of the *Brockhaus Enzyklopädie,* the 24th volume of which eventually appeared in 1994.

In 1988 Robert Maxwell threatened BIFAB with a hostile takeover. The British media magnate offered to purchase BIFAB stock from shareholders (he targeted members of the Meyer family primarily) at DEM 550 a share, some DEM 150 above the market value. Hubertus Brockhaus, fearing that in Maxwell's media empire BIFAB would become a small piece of a large foreign puzzle, opened secret negotiations with representatives of dictionary publisher Langenscheidt KG to keep the tradition-laden firm in German hands. Langenscheidt was the perfect choice to save BIFAB. It was a German reference book company, which had for years been owned and run by the Langenscheidt family, much like Brockhaus and the Bibliographisches Institut. Within a month an agreement had been reached. Langenscheidt agreed to become BIFAB's majority shareholder. The firm offered to purchase the Meyer family's shares at a price competitive to Maxwell's offer. In May 1988 BIFAB became a Langenscheidt subsidiary. Hubertus Brockhaus remained on its board of directors. Later Langenscheidt bought out the remaining BIFAB shareholder, the Rheinpfalz Verlag. Langenscheidt and the Brockhaus family were the sole remaining shareholders. In 1985 they jointly converted the firm from a public to a privately held company.

Returning Home and Beginning the Digital Era in the 1990s

Further organizational changes continued at BIFAB. In May 1990, six months after the fall of the Berlin Wall, the East German VEB Bibliographisches Institut in Leipzig was absorbed by BIFAB. VEB F.A. Brockhaus followed suit in late 1992. The same year the Brockhaus property seized in 1953 by the GDR government was returned to BIFAB. In 1993 the Brockhaus subsidiary of BIFAB moved its headquarters to its historical home in Leipzig's Graphics Quarter. In June 1995 BIFAB itself moved to Leipzig. Since then BIFAB editorial staff have worked out of Leipzig.

BIFAB entered the digital age in the early 1990s with the development of CD-ROM products such as *Die PC-Bibliothek* (The PC Library), which combined material from Meyer and Brockhaus encyclopedias as well as from Duden dictionaries. Another CD-ROM, *LexiRom,* included standard reference works from Meyer, Brockhaus, and Duden on a single disc, supplemented by animated illustrations, sound documents, and video clips. BIFAB used digital technology to set a new standard for reference books with the release of the 21st edition of the Brockhaus Encyclopedia. The set includes a DVD audio library that contains more than 4,000 sound clips, from animal calls and musical instruments to political speeches and readings from classic literature. In the mid-1990s the firm broadened its product line, adding a series of books for children and young people to its list of reference titles.

In November 1994 representatives of German-speaking countries established new orthographic rules for the German language. The modified rules were designed to confirm more to the dictates of common sense. The new rules, which went into effect in 1998, unleashed a flurry of controversy throughout Germany among language experts. Nonetheless the Duden *Rechtschreibung* dictionary, which codified the new orthography quickly, shot to the top of the German bestseller lists, where it remained for several years. Around the same time, in 1996, because of rapid changes that were under way in the world, including the fall of communism and the rise of digital technologies and the Internet, the 20th edition of the *Brockhaus Enzyklopädie* was begun ahead of schedule. It was completed in a remarkably brief period of time, in part because it was the first version prepared using a computerized editorial system. The 24-volume set hit the market in March 1999 with a price tag of EUR 4,992.

Growth and Acquisitions in the 2000s

In 2002 BIFAB boasted a turnover of EUR 57.1 million, with a profit of EUR 4.52 million. New products in the areas of art, music, nutrition, and law contributed to the positive showing. BIFAB's financial backbone, however, remained its Duden catalog, in particular the bestselling *Rechtschreibung* volume. The traditional Duden popularity was boosted even more in 2002 by a EUR 1 million marketing campaign. That same year, a BIFAB subsidiary, Brockhaus Duden Neue Medien GmbH, acquired Xipolis.net, a reference database developed by Tanto Xipolis GmbH. The web site, which featured online versions of numerous reference books, including the Brockhaus encyclopedia, firmly established a presence for BIFAB in the new media landscape. One year later, in 2003, BIFAB became the majority holder in PAETEC, a publisher of materials for elementary through high school. In January 2004 BIFAB took over the Harenberg Lexikon- und Kalenderverlag of Dortmund. The acquisition made the company the leader in the "knowledge calendar" niche.

The year 2005 marked the 200th anniversary of Brockhaus's founding. It was celebrated in Leipzig, the traditional capital of German publishing, where Brockhaus has long operated. As part of the festival year, the first six volumes of the 21st edition of the *Brockhaus Enzyklopädie* were to be published in the autumn. As planned, the new collection would be the largest German-language encyclopedia, with 30 volumes and some 300,000 entries. It would also include a CD-ROM of the entire set, as well as access to online materials.

Principal Subsidiaries

Bibliographisches Institut GmbH; Brockhaus Duden Neue Medien GmbH; DUDEN PAETEC Schulbuchverlag.

Principal Competitors

Bertelsmann Lexikon Institut; Deutscher Taschenbuch Verlag GmbH & Co. KG; Wissen Media Verlag GmbH; Verlagsgruppe Droemer Knaur GmbH & Co. KG; Goldmann Verlag.

Further Reading

"Brockhaus auf neuen Marketingwegen," *HORIZONT,* October 16, 1997, p. 22.

"Brockhaus," *Financial Times Deutschland,* May 6, 2005, p. 8.

Brockhaus, Heinrich Eduard, *Die Firma F.A. Brockhaus von der Begründung bis zum hundertjährigen Jubiläum, 1805–1905,* Leipzig: Verlag F.A. Brockhaus, 1905.

"Brockhaus, Duden und Meyers mit Umsatzsprung," *News Aktuell Schweiz,* October 7, 2004.

"Brockhaus erweitert Schulsparte," *Stuttgarter Zeitung,* June 4, 2003, p. 13.

"Brockhaus festigt Position auf dem Schulbuchmarkt," *Stuttgarter Zeitung,* May 21, 2004, p. 13.

"Brockhaus und Duden verkleinern ihre Redaktion," *Frankfurter Allgemeine Zeitung,* May 27, 2000, p. 20.

"Brockhaus-Verlag investiert in neue Vertriebswege," *Stuttgarter Zeitung,* May 31, 2005, p. 13.

"Dickes Lob für Brockhaus," *Börsen-Zeitung,* July 16, 1996, p. 21.

Glebe, Bernd, "Duden-Verlag kaempft fuer Rechtschreibreform," *Deutsche Presse-Agentur–Europadienst,* August 2004.

Keiderling, Thomas (editor), *F.A. Brockhaus, 1905–2005,* Mannheim: Verlag F.A. Brockhaus, 2005.

"Mit elektronischen und gedruckten Angeboten in die Zukunft," *Frankfurter Allgemeine Zeitung,* May 25, 2002.

"PAETEC in neuer Partnerschaft mit Duden," *News Aktuell Schweiz,* March 20, 2003.

"Rechtschreibreform hilft Duden-Verlag," *Frankfurter Allgemeine Zeitung,* October 2004, p. 14.

"Rechtschreibreform: Streit belastet Duden-Verlag," *Frankfurter Allgemeine Zeitung,* June 5, 1999, p. 19.

—Gerald E. Brennan

BLYTH

Blyth, Inc.

One East Weaver Street
Greenwich, Connecticut 06831-5118
U.S.A.
Telephone: (203) 661-1926
Fax: (203) 661-1969
Web site: http://www.blyth.com

Public Company
Incorporated: 1977
Employees: 4,900
Sales: $1.6 billion (2005)
Stock Exchanges: New York
Ticker Symbol: BTH
NAIC: 339999 All Other Miscellaneous Manufacturing

Blyth, Inc. is a leading home expressions company. From a $3 million maker of religious and institutional candles, Blyth has grown into an industry powerhouse, with sales exceeding $1.6 billion and operations in 18 countries. Through its subsidiaries, Blyth designs and markets home fragrance products, seasonal decorations, home décor, and household convenience items. The company's direct selling business, PartyLite, shores up nearly half of annual sales, while its Wholesale and Catalog & Internet divisions account for the remaining revenue. In 2005, there were more than 57,000 PartyLite independent sales consultants across the globe. Blyth has expanded over the years through acquisition as well as organic growth.

Marketing 101 in the 1960s and 1970s

As late as the 1970s, it was barely possible to speak of a candlemaking "industry." The candle market was highly fragmented among many small, privately held companies, each of which tended to be limited to producing for a specific market segment. Since the introduction of gas and then electric lighting, candle use had become increasingly marginalized, limited primarily to religious ceremonies or candlelight dinners. Despite an upsurge in candle use during the 1960s, driven by the hippie and "flower power" cultures, estimates suggested that the candle industry was worth barely more than $60 million per

year. The majority of candle sales were in religious and food service/institutional products; the consumer market was, in large part, untapped.

Enter Robert Goergen. When Goergen took over a small candle maker in 1977, he was just 37 years old and already had a varied career behind him. Goergen originally studied to become a nuclear physicist, but after taking a degree in physics from the University of Rochester, he decided he did not like that field. Instead, in 1960, Goergen enrolled in the Wharton School at the University of Pennsylvania, where he earned a master's degree in business, with honors, in only one year. While in school, Goergen had worked for Procter & Gamble, and upon receiving his degree, Procter & Gamble made him a supervisor over a 16-member crew in its manufacturing operations. But Goergen's career goals sought a more rapid rise than would have been available to him at Procter & Gamble. He entered the army, and then left military service after six months to join the McCann-Erickson advertising agency. Toward the middle of the 1960s, Goergen had risen to become a senior account executive, in charge of the Coca-Cola account.

Goergen had long set his ambitions, however, on the business side, and in 1966 he left McCann-Erickson for a position with the McKinsey & Co. consulting firm. With McKinsey, Goergen gained the experience in retail marketing strategy and in mergers and acquisitions of consumer goods industries that would prove crucial to his later success. Yet, after rising to principal partner in less than four years, Goergen made a new career move. As he told *Forbes,* "When I finished my reports for management I was out of the picture and had to start all over again. I got a good salary but I wasn't staying around long enough to reap the big rewards. That's when I decided to get into venture capital."

Goergen was hired by Donaldson, Lufkin & Jenrette (DLJ) in 1973 and named administrative manager of DLJ's Sprout venture capital investment group. Goergen found early success when he convinced his partners to invest $500,000 in start-up Royce Electronics, formed to distribute Japanese-made citizens' band (CB) radios. As the CB craze built in the mid-1970s, Royce's revenues jumped to $40 million per year. In 1975, just before the CB market became overcrowded, and then bust,

---

Company Perspectives:

*Blyth's business strategy is unique in the global home ex-
pressions market in which it competes. As a leading designer
and marketer of home decorative and fragranced products,
we seek to reach consumers across each distribution channel in which they make their purchases, offer a wide variety
of products to satisfy multiple needs and help people express
themselves in their homes.*

Royce was merged into Masco Corp., netting the Sprout partners $7.5 million on their two-year-old investment. Meanwhile,
Goergen's success with DLJ led him to make personal,
"hobby" investments in companies too small to capture DLJ's
interest. One of these investments, made in 1976, was in Candle
Corporation of America, a small, family-owned Brooklyn, New
York, company with about $3 million in sales, primarily to the
religious candle market. But when that company started losing
money, Goergen and three partners each put up $25,000 and
bought the company. Goergen was made chairman.

Building a Better Candle in the 1980s

Goergen explained the leap from investment to management to the *Fairfield County Business Journal* this way: "I had
to personally guarantee company loans, so that really focused
my attention." Goergen's first step was to change the name of
the company, to Blyth Industries, an existing unit of Candle
Corporation of America, telling *Investor's Business Daily,*
"We didn't want to say 'candle' or 'America' in the name,
because we wanted to move toward a broader product line."
Blyth's first move was to expand the company into consumer
sales. To accomplish this, the company acquired four small
candle makers between 1977 and 1981, adding $16 million in
revenues and adding the gift market to Blyth's food service and
religious market base. Each acquisition followed a similar
pattern: The company would tighten the newly acquired company's manufacturing process, strengthen management, develop new distribution channels, and step up new product
development. With the increased revenues, Blyth next turned
to a new acquisition.

By 1982, these acquisitions had helped raise Blyth's sales to
$26 million. Goergen also was learning how to market candles,
explaining to *Forbes,* "This is not a demand product—you
have to push it." The company's marketing push was to create
candles as an "affordable luxury" product. Toward this end,
the company began expanding its product line as well as the
nature of the consumer candle market itself.

Apart from candles made by the tiny artisan shops, candle
manufacturers still produced almost exclusively white,
unscented candles. As a consumer product, candles were most
likely to be found on the dining room table. But Blyth set out to
change the market. Between 1982 and 1985, the company
focused on developing new products, introducing colors (to
match the colors in a consumer's home) and then fragrances to
its candles. The company also introduced its own line of outdoor citronella-scented candles, replacing the standard glass
holder with pails and colorful ceramic pots.

By the mid-1980s, Blyth had achieved strong internal
growth. But, to step up production, the company began to look
outside the company to fuel its expansion. Goergen next directed Blyth's energies toward consolidating the candle industry, creating a critical mass of products and retailers. In 1986
Blyth made its first major acquisition, of Old Harbor Candles,
then a subsidiary of Towle Manufacturing. The following year,
Blyth acquired the Lenox Candle assets, including its Carolina
brand, from Brown-Forman subsidiary Lenox Inc., strengthening Blyth's distribution to the retail and specialty store channels. The Lenox acquisition also placed Blyth in the lead among
major candle manufacturers, ahead of Hallmark and Colonial
Candle of Cape Cod. Both of the new subsidiaries kept their
former management, operating as independent business units.
In 1988, the company introduced a new subsidiary, Atmo-
spherix Ltd., as it expanded its line of fragrance products.

Blyth's next major acquisition came in 1990, with the purchase of former rival Colonial Candle of Cape Cod from General Housewares Corp. Colonial brought Blyth deeper penetration into the department store channel. The purchase also
included Colonial's direct-selling PartyLite Gifts unit. By then,
Goergen had crafted the company's unique industry position as
a single-source supplier of candles, fragrances, and accessories
across the full range of industry distribution channels. Two
years later, Blyth made its next acquisition, of Aromatic Industries, a subsidiary of The Mennen Company. Aromatic, which
was based in California, was one of the country's leading
producers of potpourri and other home fragrance products,
which further complemented the Blyth line of products. By then
Blyth's revenues had reached $87.3 million. Net income for the
year was $3.9 million, continuing the company's unbroken
record of profitability since Goergen assumed its leadership.

Burning Brighter in the 1990s

With the company's wide assortment of candle designs,
colors, and fragrances, and with its variety of accessories ranging from candle holders to potpourri, Blyth helped move candles beyond the living and dining room into the bedroom,
bathroom, and throughout the consumer's home. Aided by its
insect-repelling citronella candles, Blyth also was able to extend
sales from the typical candle buying seasons, Christmas and
Easter, to more year-round revenues. The company also
matched its segmented approach—from the high-end Colonial
brand, to the mid-market Carolina brand, and the low-end Old
Harbor brand—with a commitment to quality, describing the
range of its products, in its first annual report, as "good, better,
best." The company profited as well from the disposable nature
of its products. As Goergen told *Forbes:* "We are in the razor
business, except our razor blades burn."

Having consolidated its position as the leader of the candle
industry, Blyth entered the next phase of the company's development, stepping up the introduction of new products, expanding its distribution channels, and improving its customer service
and production efficiency. The company's sales built quickly, to
$116 million by January 1993 and to $157.5 million by January
1994, producing net incomes of nearly $6 million and more than
$9 million, respectively. To fuel continued growth and to ex-
pand production capacity to meet the growing demand for its

Key Dates:
1977: Robert Goergen and three partners take over the Candle Corporation of America and change its name to Blyth Industries.
1986: Old Harbor Candles is acquired.
1987: Lenox Candle assets, including the Carolina brand, are purchased from Lenox Inc.
1990: Blyth acquires Colonial Candle of Cape Cod.
1992: Aromatic Industries is added to Blyth's holdings.
1994: Blyth goes public.
2000: Sales surpass $1 billion.
2004: Direct selling company Purple Tree is launched.

The company's partnership with Hallmark and its overall strategy appeared to pay off. In 1998, sales climbed 29 percent over the previous year to $687.5 million. Its products were found in more than 50,000 stores across the United States and its independent sales consultant force exceeded 20,000. During that year, Blyth acquired Endar, a manufacturer of environmental home fragrances, and New Idea International, a marketer of fragrance filter products.

During the late 1990s, the company eyed Europe as a crucial market for additional growth. In 1999, it strengthened its foothold in that market with the purchase of Liljeholmens Stearinfabriks AB. The deal secured the company's position as a leader in Sweden, Denmark, Germany, and Switzerland. Blyth also entered Brazil through formation of a joint venture designed to manufacture and market scented candles. In less than one year, its products were found in more than 300 retailers. Sales continued their upward climb in 1999. In fact, over the past five years, the company's compound annual growth rate was 40 percent in net sales, 53 percent in operating profit, and 53 percent in net income.

Blyth entered the new millennium on solid ground. During fiscal 2000, sales surpassed the billion dollar mark. By now, the company had dropped the ''Industries'' from its name and was operating as Blyth Inc. While the company had experienced remarkable growth since its initial public offering in 1994, consumer spending slowed and global economies weakened during 2000 and 2001. As such, Blyth made key adjustments to its business strategy and was determined to remain profitable in the tough business environment. It restructured its business into two main operating segments in 2000—candles and home fragrance products, and nonfragrance products. In 2001, it acquired decorative products company Midwest of Cannon Falls Inc. as part of its plan to grow its nonfragrance business line. Subsidiary PartyLite Gifts entered Mexico that year.

products, Blyth went public in 1994, raising more than $50 million. Goergen retained 42 percent of the company.

By then, the candle industry itself was growing by about 15 percent per year, aided by increases in the home decorating market. With cash raised from its public offering, Blyth added production capacity, building a new plant in Chicago, another in North Carolina, and buying a third in Massachusetts. The company next turned its focus on its international sales, which accounted for only 5 percent of total sales in 1994. To Goergen, the European market was especially promising, since, as he told *Investor's Business Daily,* candles there were ''still white and unscented.'' In 1995, Blyth purchased 25 percent equity investments in two British candle companies, Colony Gift Corporation, Ltd. and Eclipse Candles, Ltd., whose product lines complemented Blyth's domestic product base. On the domestic front, Blyth expanded its product lineup again, buying an 80 percent stake in Tulsa, Oklahoma-based Jeanmarie Creations, a maker of decorative wrapping paper, gift bags, and other accessories.

Through 1995, the company's revenues rose again, from $215 million for the year ending January 1995, to $331 million for the year ending January 1996. Net income also continued to grow, to $13.3 million and to $24 million. By then, the company had made a secondary offering, of 1.5 million shares in October 1995. One month later, Blyth announced a two-for-one stock split. Proceeds from the new offering were earmarked for new capital investments and to make some $150 million in intended new acquisitions over the next several years. Goergen's $25,000 investment was now worth more than $380 million.

In 1996, the company took two new steps to increase its share of the candle market. The first was its introduction of a new line of coordinated candles, potpourri, and home fragrances. Sold under the Ambria brand name, the new line was targeted especially at mass merchandisers such as Wal-Mart, extending the square footage given to Blyth products in such stores. The next step came with the announcement of the company's partnership agreement with Hallmark, with the first shipment of Blyth products to Hallmark stores begun in June 1996. The Hallmark partnership was not yet expected to add greatly to Blyth's revenues, predicted to reach $470 million for the year, for 1996. The full impact of the partnership, which offered the potential of adding Blyth products to more than 5,000 Hallmark Gold Crown stores, would not be known until the end of its 1997 fiscal year.

During this time period, the company exited the citronella candle sector of the market and sold its religious candle business. Those divestitures, coupled with the company's restructuring and weakening consumer demand, forced the closure of its Chicago manufacturing facility in its fiscal year 2002. Over the next several years, the company made key purchases including home décor and gift firms CBK Ltd. L.L.C. and Miles Kimball Company. In 2004, Walter Drake, a marketer of home products via the Internet and through catalogs, was purchased in a $53 million deal. Seasonal decorations designer and marketer, Kaemingk, also was added to the company's growing arsenal. In September of that year, European-based Edelman and Euro-Décor were acquired. Jeanmarie Creations, Blyth's decorative gift bag subsidiary, was sold the following year.

At this time, Blyth reorganized into three major groups: Direct Selling; Wholesale; and Catalog & Internet. Along with its acquisition strategy, Blyth looked to organic growth as a means to expand. On this front, the company launched Purple Tree in 2004 as a direct selling company specializing in craft projects. Over the past ten years, Blyth had evolved into a leading home expressions company with $1.6 billion in sales. By focusing on its candle business as well as the home décor, decorative accessories, and giftware markets, management believed the company's success would continue in the years to come.

Principal Subsidiaries

Aromatic Industries, Inc.; Blyth Home Expressions, Inc.; Blyth Direct Selling Holdings Inc.; Blyth Wholesale Holdings Inc.; Blyth Catalog and Internet Holdings Inc.; Candle Corporation of America; CBK Styles Inc.; Direct Initiatives Inc.; Endar Reserve Inc.; Fabrica de Velas Borinquen Inc.; Fragrance Solutions Inc.; KWA Inc.; Midwest of Cannon Falls Inc.; Miles Kimball Company; New Ideas International Inc.; PartyLite Gifts Inc.; PartyLite Holding Inc.; PartyLite Worldwide Inc.; Purple Tree Inc.; TSG Acquisition Corporation; Two Sisters Gourmet LLC.

Principal Operating Units

Direct Selling; Wholesale; Catalog & Internet.

Principal Competitors

Lancaster Colony Corporation; S.C. Johnson & Son Inc.; The Yankee Candle Company Inc.

Further Reading

"Blyth Inc. Acquires Walter Drake," *PrimeZone Media Network,* January 29, 2004.

"Dealmaker Out in Cold After Drake Deal Sealed," *Gazette,* November 14, 2004.

"Development Banking a la DLJ," *Forbes,* April 15, 1977, p. 56.

Galarza, Pablo, "Blyth Industries, Inc.," *Investor's Daily Business,* July 25, 1994, p. A6.

Gubernick, Lisa, "Razor Blades That Burn," *Forbes,* May 20, 1996, p. 278.

Maio, Patrick J., "Blyth Industries, Inc.," *Investor's Daily Business,* June 19, 1996, p. A4.

——, "Blyth Industries, Inc.," *Investor's Daily Business,* November 30, 1995, p. A6.

McElroy, Camille, "Blyth Industries Expands Across Market Lines," *Fairfield County Business Journal,* November 28, 1994, p. 8.

Mehta, Neil, "Candle Power," *Advocate & Greenwich Time,* April 25, 2004.

Retzlaff, Heather, "Colonial Candle Breaks into Catalogs," *Catalog Age,* December 1, 2004, p. 7.

—M.L. Cohen
—update: Christina M. Stansell

Bols Distilleries NV

2700 AE Zoetermeer
NL-2152 CZ Nieuw-Vennep
Netherlands
Telephone: (+31) 79-3305-305
Fax: (+31) 79-3305-353
Web site: http://www.bols.nl

Wholly Owned Subsidiary of Remy Cointreau SA
Founded: 1575
Sales: $742 million (2004 est.)
NAIC: 312140 Distilleries

Bols Distilleries NV is the leading producer of genever, the Dutch form of gin and the most popular distilled alcoholic beverage in the Netherlands, as well as a variety of other spirits and liqueurs. The company produces a range of genevers, under the Bols and Bokma brands, among others, spanning the range of official genever classifications (grain, old, young, and korenwijn). Together, Bols' brands control some 50 percent of the total Dutch genever market. Internationally, the Bols brand is better known for its range of gin, vodka, and liqueur products. The company markets its gin under the Damrak Amsterdam label. Bols vodkas are available as non-flavored and as Lemon Ice, Forrest Fruits, Mandarin, and Peach. Liqueurs forms one of the largest branches of the Bols brand family. The company's liqueur range includes 24 varieties, ranging from Bols Blue, a blue curacao liqueur and one of the group's oldest liqueurs, to coconut, peppermint, triple sec, banana, and coffee, among others. Since 2000, Bols Distilleries has formed a major part of France's Remy Cointreau group. The addition of Bols helped boost Remy Cointreau into the ranks of the world's leading drinks groups. Distribution of Bols products, especially on the international market, is handled by Maxxium, a joint-venture distribution group set up by Remi Cointreau, the Edrington Group, and Jim Beam at the end of the 1990s that also includes V&S Group, which joined in 2001. Bols Distilleries itself serves as a holding company for several Remy Cointreau drinks units, including Erven Lucas Bols NV, which directly oversees much of the Bols's production, fellow Dutch genever producer Bokma, and Greece's Metaxa.

16th Century Origins of a Dutch National Drink

Since the 16th century, the Bols name has been at the center of the Netherlands' liqueur and spirits industry, specifically with respect to the production of genever, considered by some to be something of the Dutch national drink. Genever itself appeared to have developed from several different origins. Methods for the distillation of alcohol had appeared in Italy and France in the Middle Ages, with these countries' vast vineyards providing the raw materials for the creation of new types of alcoholic beverages. The use of distillation slowly spread into northern Europe, where, due to this region's lack of vineyards, methods were developed for the distillation of alcohol from grains and other sources. The new type of alcohol became known as gin, with the dryer English variant becoming the most internationally known gin type.

Geneva, Switzerland, was purportedly the site of the creation of another, sweeter tasting variant of gin, which became known as genever. Some sources trace the origins of genever to French-speaking Flanders, with the term genever derived from the French word "genièvre." In the meantime, the grain-based distillation had reached the Netherlands, where Dutch distillers developed their own recipe for gin, based on "coorn," a mash of barley malt and other grains, which was then roasted ("branden"), and mixed with water and yeast. The resulting alcohol became known as "korenbrandewijn."

Coornbranders, as the Dutch distillers were originally known, began seeking ways to improve the basic korenbrandewijn recipe. In particular, distillers sought to improve the flavor of the pure distilled alcohol. The Dutch Golden Age and the country's far-flung colonial empire had introduced a wide variety of herbs, spices, fruits, and other products previously unknown to the European continent. Dutch distillers began experimenting with the new ingredients, creating a variety of beverages from the korenbrandwijn recipes.

Sylvius de Bouve, a well-known figure of the 16th century who had served as a professor at the University of Leyden, was among those experimenting with korenbrandwijn recipes. De Bouve, who was a noted pharmacist, chemist, and alchemist, hit upon using juniper berries, which were believed to have medici-

Company Perspectives:

The fact that Lucas Bols understood that growing popularity is based on constant quality becomes evident in the family's coat of arms, which bears the Latin motto ''Semper Idem'' (''Always the Same''). To the master distiller of today this means that he is committed to composing liqueurs, genevers and other spirits of the same high quality every day. His craftsmanship is now backed up by a system of strict quality controls, both techical and organoleptic.

nal benefits, in the korenbrandewijn recipe. By reducing the alcohol content, and adding the flavor of the juniper berries, De Bouve had succeeded in creating a more palatable variation of the drink. As was common during the period, the new alcoholic beverage was meant to serve as a medicine. By 1595, De Bouve had begun selling his juniper-based gin as a remedy for lumbago and associated pain under the name Genova.

The Genova recipe quickly became a popular beverage among Dutch drinkers, who adopted the name genever for the spirit. By this time, other distillers had begun producing their own genevers. Among this group, the Bols family emerged as one of the country's most prominent distillers. The Bols family, led by Lucas Bols, set up its own distillery in a wooden shed next to a small river outside of Amsterdam in 1575. The family called the distillery '' 't Lootsje'' (''the little shed'').

Bols proximity to the bustling Amsterdam port, then one of the busiest in the world, gave him a ready source of the growing variety of exotic spices, fruits, plants, and other foods arriving from the Dutch colonial possessions and elsewhere. In this way, Bols began developing a variety of liqueur recipes, using such ingredients as coffee from South America, cinnamon from Asia, curacao, orange blossoms and other citrus fruits from the Caribbean, the Mediterranean, and elsewhere, and cloves and other ingredients from Africa. A number of the company's long-standing recipes dated from Bols's earliest period, with such liqueurs as Bols Blue curacao remaining strong sellers into the 21st century.

Bols also began producing its own variant of the genever recipe, capturing the attention of the Amsterdam and later Dutch market. By the beginning of the 17th century, the company had become a prominent distiller in the city. In 1612, in order to meet the rising demand for its beverages, the company established a new and larger distillery on one of Amsterdam's most important canals, the Rozengracht. The stone building, which remained owned by the company nearly five centuries later, also became known as 't Lootsje. Its situation on the Rozengracht enabled the company to receive shipments of spices and other ingredients directly by boat.

Diversified Portfolio in the 1980s

The Bols family remained involved in the distillery for more than 250 years. The company's recipes remained strictly guarded, and leadership of the company was passed from father to son. By 1816, however, the direct family line had come to an end. The company and its recipes were sold to owners from outside of the family. Nonetheless, terms of the sale included the condition that the company permanently retain the Bols name. Thus, it became known as Erven Lucas Bols (''Heirs of Lucas Bols'').

The Rozengracht canal was filled in 1889 in order to provide a new major thoroughfare for the city. At the same time, the Rozengracht site lacked the capacity for further expansion for the company. As a result, Bols decided to move out of Amsterdam, setting up a new facility in nearby Nieuw Vennep.

While genever proved more or less an exclusively Dutch pleasure, with the rest of the world preferring the dryer British variant, Bols nonetheless achieved a great deal of success on the international front through sales of its popular liqueur recipes. Former Dutch colonial possessions proved natural markets for the group's products, and by the 1930s the company had begun to expand even further abroad. South America became an important market for the company, and a subsidiary was established in Argentina as early as 1935.

Other international markets followed, with the company's Blue curacao playing a prominent role in the group's growing international success. By the 1970s, Bols had continued its expansion, adding, among other markets, operations in Brazil toward the middle of that decade. By the mid-1980s, Bols's products had reached more than 125 international markets.

Bols was among the first to recognize a coming slowdown in the Dutch and global alcoholic beverages markets. Increasing health consciousness among consumers, including the growing awareness of the negative effects of alcohol consumption, was beginning to impede the growth of the market. A new generation of adult drinkers was increasingly turning away from traditional spirits and liqueurs in favor of other beverages.

Bols recognition of these trends led the group to launch a diversification effort as early as the late 1970s. The company's first move beyond its core, largely Netherlands-focused genever and liqueurs business, came in 1977 with the acquisition of Cynar. That purchase enabled Bols to claim a leading position in the Italian liqueurs market, adding the alcoholic beverages Cynar, an artichoke-based aperitif, and the popular Bianconsarti brand.

Bols sought further expansion at the beginning of the 1980s. The fruit juice and soft drink market became an obvious target for the company. At the same time, the company's strong presence in the Italian market stimulated its interest in further expansion in that country. In 1983, therefore, the company added its first non-alcoholic beverage operations with the acquisition of Terme di Crodo. Based in the Italian Alps, the company produced Crodino, a popular carbonated, orange-flavored, non-alcoholic aperitif.

After paying NLG 90 million for the Crodino acquisition, Bols continued its expansion in the mid-1980s and through the end of the decade, spending more than NLG 300 million. Part of this effort went toward increasing the company's range of soft drinks, notably with the purchase of the popular Oransoda and Lemonsoda brands of carbonated soft drinks. The company also began a large-scale expansion to boost capacity, building a new bottling plant, adding a new production facility in the south of

<table>
<tr><td colspan="2"><h2>Key Dates:</h2></td></tr>
<tr><td>1575:</td><td>Lucas Bols family sets up a distillery in a woodshed outside of Amsterdam, and later begins producing genever, a Dutch variant of gin.</td></tr>
<tr><td>1612:</td><td>Bols opens a larger distillery on Amsterdam's Rozengracht canal.</td></tr>
<tr><td>1816:</td><td>Company ownership by the Bols family ends and the distillery is named Erven Lucas Bols ("Heirs of Lucas Bols").</td></tr>
<tr><td>1889:</td><td>The company moves to a new factory in Nieuw Vennep, outside of Amsterdam.</td></tr>
<tr><td>1977:</td><td>Bols launches its first diversification effort, acquiring Italian aperitif group Cynar.</td></tr>
<tr><td>1983:</td><td>The company diversifies into soft drinks with the purchase of Terme di Crono and its Crodino brand.</td></tr>
<tr><td>1986:</td><td>Oransoda and Lemonsoda brands and genever rival Henkes are acquired; Bols extends into mineral waters with its Swiss Adelboden brand.</td></tr>
<tr><td>1988:</td><td>German korn schnapps leader Strothmann Brennereien GmbH & Co AG is acquired.</td></tr>
<tr><td>1989:</td><td>Bols merges with the GWN unit of Heineken.</td></tr>
<tr><td>1993:</td><td>The company merges with Wessanen, creating Bols Wessanen.</td></tr>
<tr><td>1997:</td><td>The company moves to a new headquarters and production facility in Zoetermeer.</td></tr>
<tr><td>1999:</td><td>CVC backs a management buyout of Bols.</td></tr>
<tr><td>2000:</td><td>Remy Cointreau acquires Bols.</td></tr>
<tr><td>2005:</td><td>Remy Cointreau sells Bols vodka production unit in Poland to Central European Distribution Corporation.</td></tr>
</table>

Italy, and extending its distribution operations in Switzerland. That country served as the site for the company's full-fledged entrance into the mineral water market with the purchase of Adelboden in 1986. Bols boosted its mineral waters division again in 1989 when it acquired a source in Italy as well.

Market Leadership in the 1990s

The beginnings of a great consolidation wave among the global drinks industry in the 1980s led Bols to seek greater scale. Already the leading distiller in the Netherlands, the company launched a new campaign to become the market's dominant player in the mid-1980s. One of the first steps in this effort came in 1986, when Bols acquired rival genever producer Henkes. Based in Rotterdam, Henkes also brought Bols into the world of retailing with its network of liquor stores in the Netherlands.

In order to strengthen its distribution, Bols turned to Germany for its next acquisition. In 1988, the company acquired Strothmann Brennereien GmbH & Co AG. The addition of Strothmann gave Bols control of that company's market-leading position in the German Korn schnapps market, with a 15 percent share. Strothmann also gave Bols a solid distribution network in Germany, as well as a strong production unit. Indeed, following the acquisition of Strothmann, Bols closed down its own, smaller, production unit in Germany.

A major event in Bols's expansion was the company's merger with Gedistilleerd en Wijngroep Nederland (GWN), the wine and distilled beverages unit of Heineken. GWN had been Bols's largest rival in the Netherlands genever market since its purchase in 1971 of the Bokma brand. Through its merger with GWN, Bols attained a market share approaching 50 percent in the Dutch distilled beverages market.

New Owners for the New Century

Bols continued its expansion into the early 1990s. In 1989, for example, the company branched out into wine distribution with the purchase of 85 percent of Consortium Vinicole de Bordeaux (CVBG), formerly part of Douwe Egberts. Bols followed up this purchase with the acquisition of three smaller wine traders in France's Anjou, Cotes du Rhone, and Beaujolais regions. The company also boosted its operations in Italy in 1990, buying up Ottavio Riccadonna, adding that company's Spumante and Ricadonna brands.

Nevertheless, Bols remained a mid-sized player in an increasingly globalized market dominated by far larger competitors. In 1993, the company appeared to have found a way to take itself to the next level when it agreed to merge with Dutch foods group Wessanen. However, the merger of Wessanen's dairy products and Bols alcoholic beverages made little sense. By the end of the decade, the combined company, known as Bols Wessanen, was forced to accept the obvious, and in 1999 Bols was spun off in a management buyout backed by the Australian investment firm of CVC Limited. By then, Bols had already settled into its new main production plant and headquarters, in Zoetermeer, near Rotterdam.

Bols's new independence proved short-lived, however. The crushing competition of the global market forced the company to look for a larger partner in order to ensure its survival. By 2000, the company had agreed to be acquired by France's drinks giant Remy Cointreau for EUR 510 million ($446 million). Bols Distilleries was then established as the holding company for Erven Lucas Bols, as well as the group's distribution operations, which included subsidiaries in Hungary, Poland, and elsewhere, as well as Bokma and the Greek liqueur producer Metaxa.

By 2001, however, Remy Cointreau separated much of Bols's international distribution operations, which were then placed into the Maxximum joint venture set up among Remy Cointreau, the Edrington Group, and Jim Beam in 1999. Remy Cointreau continued to reposition its own distribution business into the mid-2000s. In 2005, for example, the company decided to sell off Bols's vodka production operations in Poland to Central European Distribution Corporation in exchange for a stake in that company. The move gave Remy Cointreau strong access to the Eastern European markets. The Bols brand remained a central feature of the enlarged drinks group portfolio, remaining the dominant Netherlands genever producer, as well as a globally recognized player in the liqueur market.

Principal Subsidiaries

't Lootsje II BV; Bokma Distillateurs BV; Bols Distilleries BV Distribution; Distilleerderijen Erven Lucas Bols BV; Erven

Lucas Bols NV; Gedistilleerd en Wijn Groep Nederland BV; Meekma Distileerderijen BV; Metaxa BV.

Principal Competitors

Diageo plc; Seagram Company Ltd.; Jim Beam Brands Worldwide Inc.; Irish Distillers Group plc; United Distillers and Vintners Ltd.; Allied Distillers Ltd.; Cantrell and Cochrane Group Ltd.

Further Reading

''Bols Unveils a Modern Design,'' *Duty-Free News International*, September 15, 2004, p. 11.

De Vries, Peter Paul, ''Drama Wessanen,'' *Effect*, No. 3, 2003.

''Remy Cointreau and Bols Merge,'' *Corporate Money*, September 6, 2000, p. 4.

''Remy Cointreau to Acquire Bols for $446 million,'' *International Financial Law Review*, October 2000, p. 8.

—M.L. Cohen

Brach's Confections, Inc.

19111 North Dallas Parkway
Dallas, Texas 75287
U.S.A.
Telephone: (972) 930-3600
Toll Free: (800)999-0204
Fax: (972) 930-3612
Web site: http://www.brachs.com

Wholly Owned Subsidiary of Barry Callebaut AG
Incorporated: 1904 as E.J. Brach & Sons; 1906 as Brock
    Candy Company
Employees: 1,600
Sales: $340 million (2003)
NAIC: 311330 Confectionery Manufacturing from
    Purchased Chocolate; 311340 Nonchocolate
    Confectionery Manufacturing

Brach's Confections, Inc., is a leading confections maker in the United States. For more than 100 years, the company has been supplying Americans with hard candies and chocolates. Brach's sells more than 200 varieties of confections, including candy corn, StarBrites Mints, Milk Maid Caramels, Maple Nut Goodies, and Double Dippers. The company operates as a subsidiary of Swiss-based Barry Callebaut AG.

Early History

Both Brach and Brock grew from small, turn-of-the-century storefronts. In 1904, German immigrant Emil J. Brach pulled together $1,000 to open the ''Palace of Sweets,'' an 18- by 65-foot candy shop located on the corner of Chicago's North Avenue and Towne Street. Joined by sons Edwin, and later, Frank, Brach's store featured its own one-kettle candy kitchen. From the start, Brach sought methods for boosting production while reducing labor costs, and early on introduced not only a mechanized kettle-heating element, but also a device for dipping taffy, Brach's initial product. With these devices, Brach could sell his candy for 20 cents per pound, far lower than the typical retailer's price of 50 to 60 cents per pound. Brach soon began to sell his candy to retailers throughout Chicago,

adding four new kettles and producing 3,000 pounds of candy per week.

Expansion in the Early 1900s

By 1906, Brach's customers quickly included almost all of the city's large department stores. He was forced to expand production again, now moving to a larger facility. At the same time, Brach introduced peanut and hard candies to his product line. In the new plant, Brach's production soon passed 12,000 pounds per week, and three years later he was forced to move again to a still larger facility. With this move, Brach added coconut candies and expanded his line of hard candies. Within a year, however, the company had outgrown the new plant. Additional space, doubling the size of the company's production area, was leased in a building next door, and Brach's product line grew to include cream, gum, fudge, and crystallized candies.

One year later, in 1911, with production topping 50,000 pounds per week, Brach expanded yet again, moving his offices to a building down the street and converting the old offices into additional floor space. Brach's candies were reaching farther and farther outside of the city and, because the railroads were still the principal means of distribution, Brach faced new difficulties in transporting growing shipments of his candies. In 1913, Brach moved again, to a larger plant located on the railroad. The addition of chocolate and cream dipping and icing, as well as marshmallow confections, increased production to 250,000 pounds per week. At this point, Brach instituted product testing and quality control measures, creating a Laboratory of Control in the Brach plant.

Brach next moved into chocolate manufacturing, installing machinery to make chocolate from the bean in a second, 60,000-square-foot space. From 1915 to 1918, Brach's capacity grew to 1.1 million pounds per week. Incorporated in 1916, Brach added a third site in 1918, increasing production of his candy line to more than 2 million pounds per week. Four years later, Brach consolidated operations, building a $5 million facility on Chicago's West Side. Brach's sales grew to $7.9 million in 1925, with a net income of more than $1 million.

The onset of the Depression era hit the candy industry hard. Candy sales, which had reached nearly $448 million in 1914, fell to $211 million in 1933. Brach's sales dropped as well, to a low of $1.27 million in 1934. Nonetheless, the company remained profitable, posting a net income of $175,000 for that year. By then, Brach employed more than 1,000 people, making the company one of Chicago's largest employers. Sales climbed slowly through the 1930s, returning to $7.9 million in 1938. The candy industry was tested again by the outbreak of World War II and the resulting shortages of sugar and other raw products. Yet, emerging from the war, Brach's sales had tripled, to $21.5 million in 1945.

Postwar Growth Leading to an Acquisition in 1966

By the end of the next decade, Brach's sales more than doubled, reaching more than $58 million in 1960. Its 23-acre Chicago plant was the largest candy factory in the country. A second, 30-acre site was purchased in New Brunswick, New Jersey in 1959. Brach's line had grown to 250 types of candy, including hard candies, chocolates, fudge, peanut, caramels, cremes, jellies, lozenges, and panned candies, with specialty items for Halloween, Christmas, Easter, and Valentine's Day. Production in the Chicago facility alone topped four million pounds per week, making Brach the country's largest candy producer.

Brach began to attract the interest of larger companies. In 1966, after rejecting a $19 million offer that would have given Consolidated Foods a 17 percent stake in the company, Frank Brach, by then company president and chairman, accepted American Home Products' $136 million offer to acquire the company. In 1977, Frank Brach turned over the presidency to Ned Mitchell, who would lead the company into the 1980s. At the time of American Home's acquisition, Brach's $83 million in sales held about 7 percent of the total candy market. Over the next 20 years, Brach's sales would grow to more than $700 million per year, and Brach would capture as much as two-thirds of the general line and bulk candy market.

Overcoming Challenges in the 1980s

A new trend in the candy industry, however, which began to develop especially in the postwar years, would erode Brach's longtime position as the nation's largest candymaker. Prior to World War II, consumer candy purchases went in large part to the penny candy and individual item variety; after the war, consumers turned more and more to a new type of candy, the candy bar, many of which would become household brand names. Candy bars held an advantage over general line candies such as Brach's, in that sales of candy bars could be made from a far wider variety of selling points, from vending machines to

drugstores to convenience stores, and so on. Brach, especially with its Pick-a-Mix bin candies, was limited, for the most part, to grocery stores. The candy bar supported more successfully the impulse purchases important to the candy industry, and by the early 1980s Brach's share of the overall candy market shriveled, while other giants, particularly Hershey and M&M/Mars, emerged. Meanwhile, Brach's pegboard displays had changed little in the past decades, presenting an outdated look against the more modern packaging and advertising of its competitors. The candy industry also was growing; during the 1980s alone it would nearly double in size, from about $5 billion to nearly $10 billion in 1991. But the 1980s would see Brach's fortunes decline drastically.

In 1987, American Home sold Brach to Jacobs Suchard AG, a Swiss coffee and candymaker with about $3.3 billion in sales in 1987. Run by Klaus Jacobs, Suchard hoped to use Brach to expand its European empire, and especially its Toblerone and Milka brands, into the United States.

Suchard and Brach ran into problems almost immediately. Management styles and goals clashed, and Jacobs quickly fired Brach's top officers and gutted the leadership of its sales, marketing, production, and finance departments as well. Some of these positions were filled with executives from Suchard's European operations; other positions, including a large percentage of Brach's sales and marketing department, were staffed by people with little experience in the candy industry. Under the European management, which failed to recognize many key differences between the U.S. and European candy markets, Brach faltered through a series of poor decisions. One of these involved the scaling back of Brach's line, which had reached 1,700 different candies and packaging types and sizes, to only 300 SKUs. This proved disastrous for Brach, because the bulk of its sales continued to be made at the grocery stores and through other vendors that required the flexibility of Brach's former range to realize the highest profit margins. To make matters worse, the Suchard-led company did not recognize the U.S. candy market's purchase pattern—in that the bulk of sales are made surrounding Valentine's Day, Easter, Halloween, and Christmas—and failed to promote and, at times, even produce the specialized holiday candies. Corporate headquarters were relocated to a Chicago suburb. Finally, Suchard changed Brach's name, which enjoyed recognition by as much as 77 percent of the U.S. candy-buying public, to Jacobs Suchard Inc.

Brach's customers, including major chains such as Walgreens, deserted the company for its competitors. Sales dropped, and the company began posting losses, reaching $50 million in operating losses in 1988, and more than $200 million over the next several years. By 1990, the company had gone through two CEOs in three years. Its new CEO and president, Peter Rogers, formerly with RJR Nabisco, attempted to turn the company around, restoring the Brach name and rebuilding its product line. When Philip Morris paid $3.8 million to acquire a majority stake in Jacobs Suchard AG, however, it refused to take Brach as part of the package. Brach's losses mounted, and the company began a series of massive layoffs that would trim its employee rolls from nearly 3,000 workers to about 1,700. Production dropped to 50 percent capacity. Sales picked up slightly during the early 1990s, to about $430 million in 1993, but Brach continued to lose money.

Key Dates:

1904: German immigrant Emil J. Brach opens the ''Palace of Sweets.''
1906: William E. Brock establishes Brock Candy Company.
1966: Frank Brach accepts American Home Products' $136 million offer to acquire the company.
1987: American Home sells Brach to Jacobs Suchard AG.
1994: Brach acquires Brock in a $140 million deal.
2003: Barry Callebaut AG purchases Brach.

The Brock Purchase: 1994

Rogers was replaced by Kevin Martin, formerly of M&M/Mars and Pillsbury Co. Under Martin, Brach stepped up its new product development and worked to refine its packaging and point-of-sale design. Martin also brought the company's corporate headquarters back into its Chicago plant. By 1994, Brach posted its first operating profit—of about $1 million—since 1987, on sales of an estimated $475 million. In September of that year, Brach announced the acquisition of the Brock Candy Company for $140 million.

Unlike Brach, the Brock Candy Company had remained a privately held, family-run company through most of its history, only going public in 1993. Founded in 1906 by William E. Brock, Brock Candy would not reach the size of Brach, but achieved a strong reputation for the quality of its products.

William E. Brock, born in North Carolina, had been a traveling salesman for R.J. Reynolds Tobacco Co. when, in 1906, he decided to settle down in Chattanooga, Tennessee. Brock bought a small wholesale grocery shop, which also held a candy shop, the Trigg Candy Company. Brock continued the candy-making operation, which consisted of handmade penny and bulk candies, peanut brittle, peppermints, and fudge, changing the company's name to the Brock Candy Company in 1909. Brock's first major expansion came in the early 1920s, when it modernized its factory, installing automatic moguls. Next, Brock eliminated all slab confectionery items, such as peanut brittle and fudge, which were products already produced by many manufacturers, making that area extremely competitive. Instead, Brock concentrated on launching new lines of jelly and marshmallow candies, using its automated moguls equipment. During the 1920s, Brock also began packaging its candies in cellophane bags, making it one of the first to do so. During the 1930s, Brock introduced its Chocolate Covered Cherries, which not only helped the company survive the lean Depression era but would remain one of its biggest sellers for the next 60 years. During World War II, when rationing forced the company to cut back on much of its production, it introduced the Brock Bar, a coated nut roll using the still plentiful ingredients corn syrup and peanuts. William E. Brock went on to a career in the U.S. Senate, and his son, William, Jr., succeeded him to head the company.

Brock's next great expansion came in 1950, when it added 60,000 square feet to its plant, bringing its downtown Chattanooga plant to 180,000 square feet. By the end of that decade,

however, Brock was again ready for further expansion, and it purchased a 30-acre site on the Jersey Pike outside of Chattanooga. In 1964, Brock constructed a 64,000-square-foot distribution warehouse on the new site. By the end of the 1960s, the warehouse was expanded by another 25,000 square feet. The company also made its first acquisition, of Schuler Chocolates in Winona, Minnesota, adding to its seasonal confection capacity.

By the mid-1970s the company was producing more than 30 million pounds of candies per year. It moved to a newly constructed production and office facility on its Jersey Pike site in 1976. By the early 1980s, and led by Pat Brock, son of William Brock, Jr., Brock's sales reached $34 million, and its product line included chocolates, jelly sweets, and hard candies. In 1981, Brock also became the first American producer of European-style gummi candies. Later in the decade, Brock introduced a line of fruit snacks, and then moved into contract and industrial production of its fruit-based products. In 1990, sales passed $72 million, bringing a net income of nearly $2.5 million. Production had grown to 70 million tons per year.

Brock made a second acquisition, of Shelly Brothers, Inc., of Souderton, Pennsylvania, for $600,000, in 1990. That purchase was followed by Brock's first international partnership, when the company bought a 30 percent share in Clara Candy, of Dublin, Ireland in 1993. By then, Brock had gone public, with an initial public offering of 2.3 million shares, for nearly 63 percent of the company's stock. Brock's sales continued to rise, to $102 million in 1993 and $112 million in 1994, for net incomes of $5.3 million and $6.5 million, respectively. In 1994, Brock accepted Brach's $140 million merger offer.

The combined company, renamed Brach and Brock Confections, marked the second attempt for the two companies to join forces. A first deal had been struck in the early 1980s, but American Home, fearing an antitrust suit, forced Brach to back out. The merger of the companies was seen as beneficial to both, offering Brach's strong production facilities, and Brock's strong distribution lines, which included its largest customer, Wal-Mart, accounting for nearly 40 percent of Brock's sales. By 1995, the merger allowed Brach to post its first profit in nearly a decade, with net income estimated to reach $20 million. Brach's troubled past seemed behind it, and for the combined candy companies, the future looked sweet.

Changes in the Late 1990s and Beyond

As the fourth largest candy maker in the United States, Brach and Brock immediately set out to strengthen its hold on the candy industry. One of its main strategies at this time was to gain a stronger foothold in the Gummi candy and fruit snacks segments. In 1997, for example, the company launched Donkey Kong, Batman, and Hi-C-licensed fruit snacks. It planned to tap into the growing $332 million market by promoting its new products via advertising ads in national magazines, through coupons, and by giving away free samples. In 1998, Brach and Brock introduced two additional fruit snacks, Hi-C Juice Fillers and Smucker's Fruit Fillers. An $8 million television advertising campaign touted the new products.

Heightened competition, inconsistent management, and ever-changing consumer demands forced Brach and Brock to embark on a cost-cutting mission in the early years of the new millennium. In order to shore up profits, the company divested certain assets, including chocolate mint subsidiary Andes Candies. In early 2001, it announced plans to shutter its Chicago-based manufacturing facility. As part of the firm's restructuring efforts, it built a new plant in Mexico.

Brach's owner—now known as KJ Jacobs AG—agreed to sell the company to Swiss-based Barry Callebaut AG, the world's largest chocolate manufacturer, in 2003. KJ Jacobs was a majority stakeholder in Barry Callebaut and believed the purchase would strengthen its distribution channels in the lucrative U.S. market. As part of the deal, Barry Callebaut agreed to assume $16 million in debt, fund restructuring efforts over the next five years, and pay a symbolic $1 for the company. Barry Callebaut's CEO remarked on the purchase in a September 2003 *Candy Industry* article claiming, "The acquisition of Brach's allows us to accomplish two strategic objectives at once: First, the substantial expansion of our activities in the United States, the world's largest single consumer market, and second, the creation of an attractive platform to further build our consumer confectionary business, with ultimately a global reach in mind."

As part of Barry Callebaut's arsenal, Brach's Confections, Inc. was well positioned for future growth. The company celebrated its 100th anniversary in 2004 amid strong sales, especially during the Halloween and holiday season. New products, including those made with Splenda artificial sweetener, also experienced strong demand. Brach's CEO Terry O'Brien summed up management's optimism in a 2004 company press release. "Brach's has a 100-year history of satisfying this nation's sweet tooth with fresh, delicious candies—and, with retailers embracing products like our new better-for-you line of our traditional favorites, we're more confident than ever that we'll be filling America's candy bowls in the century to come."

Principal Competitors

The Hershey Company; Mars Inc.; Nestlé S.A.

Further Reading

"Barry Callebaut Finishes Brach's Purchase," *The Deal,* September 18, 2003.

"Barry Callebaut Picks Up Brach's Confections," *Candy Industry,* September 2003.

Klokis, Holly, "The Palace of Sweets: Brach's Then and Now," *Candy Industry,* December 1983, p. 82.

Langley, Alison, "Swiss Maker of Chocolate Will Acquire Brach's Candy," *New York Times,* September 2, 2003.

Lazarus, George, "A Sweet Development at Brach Duo," *Chicago Tribune,* August 31, 1995, p. B3.

——, "Brach Acquiring Competitor To Sweeten Income," *Chicago Tribune,* September 2, 1994, p. B2.

Raffles, Richard, "Brock Candy Move Marks the Dawn of a New Era," *Candy & Snack Industry,* June 1977, p. 79.

Shackleford, Chris, "The Sweet Smell of Success," *Chattanooga Free Press,* September 4, 1994.

Stalter, Nedra, "Believing in a Dream Brought Brock Success," *Candy Industry,* December 1983, p. 152.

Thompson, Stephanie, "Brach Gets Active in Fruit Snacks," *Brandweek,* March 24, 1997.

——, "Brach's Plots $8M Impact on Fruit Snacks," *Brandweek,* November 2, 1998.

Tiffany, Susan, "Brock: Dedicated to 'Sweet Things in Life,'" *Candy Industry,* May 1994, p. 20.

—M.L. Cohen
—update: Christina M. Stansell

Brazil Fast Food Corporation

Rua Voluntarios da Patria 89
Botafogo, Rio de Janeiro CEP 22.270-010
Brazil
Telephone: 55 (21) 2536-7500
Web site: http://www.bobs.com.br

Public Company
Incorporated: 1951 as Falkenburg Sorvetes Ltda.
Employees: 1,681
Sales: BRL 85.38 million ($29.14 million) (2004)
Stock Exchanges: OTB Bulletin Board
Ticker Symbol: BOBS
NAIC: 722211 Limited-Service Restaurants

Brazil Fast Food Corporation operates Bob's, the second largest fast-food chain in Brazil in number of locations and the chief competition for McDonald's, the leader, because of its American-style menu oriented toward hamburgers, hot dogs, french fries, and milkshakes. A strong franchising program has enabled Bob's to become a presence in major cities throughout Brazil, and it is almost ubiquitous in Rio de Janeiro and Sao Paulo. Nevertheless, Brazil Fast Food has had difficulty in turning a profit.

Introducing American-Style Food to Brazil: 1952–96

Active on the tournament circuit in the 1940s and 1950s, Bob Falkenburg was an American tennis player who won the 1948 men's singles title at Wimbledon and was later inducted in the National Lawn Tennis Hall of Fame. While playing in a tournament in Rio de Janeiro, he fell in love with the city and eventually settled there. In 1951 he introduced vanilla ice cream to Brazil, and the following year he opened the first Bob's on the famed Copacabana beachfront. Its prototypical U.S. treats, such as burgers, hot dogs, sundaes, and shakes, were virtually unknown in Brazil, and Bob's was immediately successful. It was followed by a half-dozen more in the better neighborhoods of the metropolitan area. These early Bob's were amply sized eateries whose neon, chrome, and glass represented the era's idea of modernity and attracted the Rio glitterati. There were 13 Bob's fast-food restaurants, all in the Rio area, in 1974, when

Falkenburg sold the business, which was then Bob's Co-mestíveis S.A., to Maine-based food products company Libby McNeill & Libby and returned to the United States.

Libby, which was majority-owned by Nestlé S.A., was merged into Nestlé in 1976. Nestlé opened additional Bob's outlets, broadened the menu, and emphasized the cleanliness of the outlets and the quality of the products. By 1981 Bob's, the largest existing fast-food chain in Brazil, was a 29-unit operation with revenues of $20 million. But for the first time it was facing big-league competition in the form of McDonald's Corporation, which opened the first Brazilian unit of its eponymous chain in 1979. Although Bob's outlets had become counter-service units accommodating mainly teenagers, the new ones, starting in 1980, included table seating to attract family-oriented customers. Nestlé sold the business in 1987 to Bob's Industria e Comercio Ltda., whose affiliate was Vendex International N.V., a Dutch group. By mid-1990 there were 69 Bob's outlets, earning total revenue of $67 million a year.

Ten of these units were franchises, in keeping with a program put into effect by Bob's in 1984, when it still led McDonald's in number of units (but not in annual revenue). Brazil was the third-leading country in the world in franchisers in 1990, after the United States and Canada, and the concept was especially popular in the fast-food field, with franchises offered not only by McDonald's and Bob's but also by the operators of Pizza Hut, Big Boy Restaurants, Domino's Pizza, and Subway. By mid-1993 the total number of Bob's had reached 84. The chain was not performing well, however, and was expected to be sold to Burger King Corporation, a transaction that was never effected.

The Going Getting Tougher: 1996–2003

Bob's remained in Dutch hands until 1996, when it was sold for $19.2 million to Trinity Americas Inc., a U.S.-based company that had been formed in 1992 to invest in Latin America and had, in 1994, made an initial public offering of its equity securities, which raised net proceeds of $9.6 million on the NASDAQ. To raise more money for an expansion program, Trinity then sold about $10 million worth of its shares to new investors in a private transaction. It retained Vendex's Venbo

Comercio de Alimentos Ltda. as its Brazilian subsidiary and changed its own name to Brazil Fast Food Corporation.

One of the new owner's investors was Peter van Voorst Vader, a former Royal Dutch Shell marketing director who became chief executive officer of Brazil Fast Food. He inherited an operation that had been losing money since at least 1994 and continued to lose money in each year through 2003. "We thought it would take three or four years to turn Bob's around," Vader told Jonathan Wheatley of *Business Week* in 2001. "It turns out it's taking a bit longer."

By 1997 the easy profits had been made in fast food, and the competing chains were locked into a kind of arms race that required them to open more branches simply to keep likely locations out of the reach of their rivals. McDonald's, for example, had 340 sites and was planning for almost 800 in the year 2000. The inevitable overcapacity meant that in many cases the chains had to lower their prices and/or expenses to continue competing. Bob's, for example, cut its costs 15 percent by renegotiating its contracts with its suppliers. Even worse, existing branches of a fast-food chain sometimes found themselves competing with new outlets of the same chain. "This is a business that only becomes lucrative for a large chain or small owner-operated enterprises of two or three branches," Vader told Marília Fontoura of the Brazilian business magazine *Exame* in 1997. "Medium-sized businesses have no future." In 1996 Bob's raised its number of outlets from 79 to 127, by means of acquisitions. "We are entering in each new shopping center that opens," he added.

By August 1999 the number of Bob's outlets had reached 173, of which 108 were franchised units. Vader also had the company units refurbished, added new items such as fried-chicken sticks to the menu, and economized by moving company headquarters from Rio's beachfront to a busy highway straddling the city limits and by allowing franchisees to purchase their ingredients directly from local suppliers. He negotiated a deal with Brazil's state-owned oil giant, Petrobras, to open 30 full-menu Bob's restaurants in a chain of convenience stores operated by Petrobras's service-station subsidiary. A Portuguese Bob's opened in 2001. But Brazil Fast Food continued to lose money, hampered by recurrent national economic crises. These problems forced out rivals such as Subway, KFC, and Arby's as MacDonald's continued to steamroller the competition, its number of Brazilian outlets passing 1,000 and its revenues outstripping Bob's by almost ten to one.

Latin Trade correspondent Thierry Ogier took a job at a Bob's in Sao Paulo for one day in 2000 to learn whether Brazilians could find a future in a local burger joint. With the real unemployment rate as high as 20 percent and nearly half the population under 20 years of age, any job looked good to many youngsters "even if it involves wearing a silly red tie, a blue and red baseball cap and an apron that says Bob's." "We make a standard product," he found, "but it takes 12 of us moving in harmony to do it well. . . . The key to the business is slicing tasks into well-defined, bite-sized pieces that just about anybody can master." The manager, only 23 but with seven years of experience at Bob's, was running the third best-selling unit in the chain. At the end of a long day, this outlet had sold nearly 2,000 burgers, taking in more than $4,500.

To keep from being obliterated by McDonald's, Bob's needed more money, which required more investment. In 2002 the Bomeny family, in collaboration with the Forza group, invested BRL 8 million in Brazil Fast Food, tripling their share of the company to about 60 percent. Thirty-three-year-old Ricardo Figueiredo Bomeny succeeded Vader as chief executive officer at the beginning of 2003. He renegotiated contract terms with some 40 suppliers and settled the short-term debt of BRL 8 million. Another BRL 16 million in taxes owed was to be paid over ten years. The arrangement with Petrobras—and a similar one with Shell—served as the model for an agreement with the Bompreço group to open branches in the group's northeastern Brazil supermarkets. Brazil Fast Food also formed a partnership with Blockbuster, Inc. for a joint drive-through location in Sao Paulo. The company even negotiated a deal to place Bob's outlets in the churches of an evangelical Christian group.

Other steps that Brazil Fast Food took in 2003 included promotional pricing outside of peak-traffic hours and training of its workers at a newly created school reminiscent of McDonald's "Hamburger University." Bomeny promised franchisees that, with more branches in existence, the company would be able to spend more money advertising the chain. Its problems continued, however, with Brazil Fast Food recording negative stockholders' equity in 2004 for the second consecutive year. The auditor's report noted that this, and negative working capital, "raises substantial doubt about its ability to continue as a going concern."

In 2004 Brazil Fast Food ended at least ten consecutive years of net losses by earning a small profit. At midyear eight officers and directors of the company owned 56 percent of the common stock. AIG Latin America Equity Partners, Ltda., a unit of American Insurance Group, Inc., owned 21 percent. Just before the end of the year, however, the latter sold about one-fourth of its shares to CCC Empreendimentos e Participaçoes and BigBurger Ltda., companies controlled respectively by Romulo Fonseca and José Ricardo Bousquet Bomeny, the chief executive's father.

Brazil Fast Food's plan for 2005 was to increase its points of sale to 500. Many of these would be compact—no more than 30 square meters (about 350 square feet), because, although these locations accounted for only 15 percent of all Bob's outlets, they were bringing in nearly a third of sales. The company also intended to open a franchised Bob's in Angola and was registering the Bob's name for possible use in Europe, the United States, and the other Mercosur countries of Argentina, Paraguay, and Uruguay.

Status in 2004 and Expectations for the Future

At the end of 2004 Brazil Fast Food had 388 points of sale in 23 states, including 98 kiosks and trailers. Of this number,

Key Dates:

1952: An American tennis player, Bob Falkenburg, opens the first Bob's in Rio de Janeiro.
1974: Falkenburg sells the existing 13 Bob's fast-food restaurants—all in the Rio area.
1981: Bob's consists of 29 units doing $20 million a year in sales.
1984: The company begins to franchise Bob's units.
1987: Bob's owner, Nestlé S.A., sells the chain to a Dutch company.
1990: The 69 Bob's outlets have combined annual sales of $67 million.
1996: Bob's is sold to a company incorporated in the United States.
1999: Of Bob's 173 outlets, 108 are franchised units.
2004: Brazil Fast Food earns a small profit, ending at least a decade of annual net losses.
2004: Some 325 of the company's 388 points of sales are franchised units under the Bob's name.

the company owned and operated 63. The remaining 325 were franchises operated under the ''Bob's'' name. About 58 percent of the points of sale were in Rio de Janeiro and Sao Paulo, with the remainder widely spread throughout major cities in other parts of Brazil, with the exception of the franchised unit in Lisbon.

All Bob's outlets served a uniform menu of hamburgers, chicken burgers, hot dogs, sandwiches, french fries, soft drinks, juices, desserts, ice cream, and milkshakes. Selected points of sale also served coffee and/or beer. Outlets were generally open all year round, seven days a week, for lunch and dinner. Bob's was attempting to maintain the overall cost of its meals at levels competitive with prices offered by popular street snack bars known as ''lanchonetes.''

All restaurants in operation, excluding kiosks and movable trailers, were being built to company specifications as to exterior style and interior decor, and were substantially uniform in design and appearance. They were constructed on freestanding sites ranging from about 1,100 to 7,500 square feet. Most were located in downtown areas or shopping malls and were of a storefront type.

Despite the company's great number of franchised units, Brazil Fast Food's franchise income came to less than 10 percent of net operating revenues in 2004. In addition to royalty fees derived from a percentage on the sales of the stores operated by franchisees, the company received from these operators initial fees due at the signing of a new contract and funds that represented franchise contributions to finance corporate marketing investments. In 2005 Brazil Fast Food expected a potential franchisee to make a minimum investment of BRL 250,000 (about $100,000). The franchise fee was BRL 90,000 (about $35,000). The royalty rate was 5 percent of gross sales and the marketing fee 4 percent of gross sales. The franchising contract was for ten years. Brazil Fast Food provided a four-month training program for franchisees. Construction of the outlet generally began at the same time and took three to six months to complete.

Principal Subsidiaries

Venbo Comercio de Alimentos Ltda.

Principal Competitors

McDonald's Corporation.

Further Reading

Bruce, James, ''Frenzy of Fast-Food Franchises Spurs 'Go West' Movement in Brazil,'' *Journal of Commerce,* August 12, 1994, p. 5A.
Fontoura, Marília, ''Curve-se á lei de Greenberg,'' *Exame,* January 15, 1997, pp. 96–97.
Grangeia, Mario, ''Posso dar uma mordida?,'' *Exame,* April 9, 2003, pp. 66–68.
Hoge, Warren, ''The Fast-Food Rush in Brazil,'' *New York Times,* January 31, 1981, p. 29.
Murphy, Steven, ''Bob's Sells Downstream,'' *Business Latin America,* September 4, 2000, p. 7.
Ogier, Thierry, ''Life As a Burger King,'' *Latin Trade,* December 2000, pp. 44–47.
Wheatley, Jonathan, ''Slow Times for a Fast-Food Pioneer,'' *Business Week International Editions,* July 2, 2001, p. 31 (on ProQuest database).
Whitaker Penteado, J.R., ''Fast-Food Franchises Fight for Brazilian Aficionados,'' *Brandweek,* June 7, 1993, pp. 20–22, 24.

—Robert Halasz

Brookshire's

Brookshire Grocery Company

1600 West South West Loop 323
P.O. Box 1411
Tyler, Texas 75710
U.S.A.
Telephone: (903) 534-3000
Fax: (903) 534-2206
Web site: http://www.brookshires.com

Private Company
Incorporated: 1928
Employees: 12,000
Sales: $1.9 billion (2003 est.)
NAIC: 445110 Supermarkets and Other Grocery (Except Convenience) Stores

The Brookshire Grocery Company operates more than 150 supermarkets in Texas, Arkansas, Louisiana, and Mississippi. In addition to the standard fare of grocery items, company stores feature specialty departments including bakeries, delicatessens, floral shops, fresh fish and seafood counters, salad bars, and pharmacies. Many of the stores also sell gasoline. Long known for its concentration on customer service, the Texas-based company has three main operations: Brookshire Grocery, full-service supermarkets, which average around 40,000 square feet; Super 1 Stores, a no-frills, self-service warehouse format, which range from 80,000 to 100,000 square feet; and Ole Foods, supermarkets that cater to the Hispanic market. The nearly $2 billion company also boasts two distribution centers, two bakery plants, a dairy plant, a fleet of some 350 trucks, and its own manufacturing complex. Founded during the late 1920s, the company is widely respected for its long tradition of friendly service, clean stores, and technological innovation.

Early History

The humble origins of the Brookshire Grocery Company date back to 1928 and a 25-foot x 100-foot store in Tyler, Texas. The store was one of several stores in east Texas operated by the company's founder, Wood T. Brookshire, and his five brothers under the name Brookshire Brothers. The Brookshire brothers set out to build a local chain of grocery stores at a time when the chain store concept, which originated in the latter half of the 19th century with grocery giants such as the Atlantic & Pacific Tea Company (A & P) and the Kroger Company, had captured the imagination of many aspiring entrepreneurs. With mammoth chains such as A & P adding 10,000 stores during the decade, the Brookshire brothers attempted to build their own grocery empire by carving out a profitable niche in the east Texas market.

In keeping with the most progressive grocers of the era, the Brookshires adopted the self-service concept in their first stores. Customers, instead of first placing an order for a sales clerk to fill, made their own selections while following a more or less prescribed path designed to expose them to the appeal of the goods on the shelves. This innovative strategy, the forerunner to the modern supermarket, enabled grocers like the Brookshires to reduce operating expenses and, in turn, cut prices and build a strong customer base.

During the early 1930s, the supermarket gradually replaced the small grocery store. Like other grocers of the period, Brookshire operated its stores on a self-service basis and furnished its customers with larger displays of a wide variety of groceries as well as fresh meats, fruits, and vegetables. By dealing in a larger volume, the company was able to market its goods at aggressively low prices, while increasing profits and expanding its business.

In 1939, the Brookshire brothers dissolved their partnership, and Wood became the sole owner of three stores in Tyler, known by the trade name Brookshire's Food Stores, which later became the foundation for the 100-store company of the 1990s. Despite the economic hardships of the Great Depression, the company managed to expand its operations through the late 1930s: By the end of the decade, the fledgling grocery chain had opened its fourth store in the Tyler and Longview area, including the first air-conditioned store in east Texas.

The Postwar Period

Growth continued through the World War II years and the rest of the 1940s as five more stores were added to the east Texas area, in Winnsboro, Longview, Gladewater, and Kilgore.

Like many businesses across the country, Brookshire prospered during the favorable economic conditions of the postwar era; expansion continued at a steady rate.

The years following the war, however, also brought a new challenge to Brookshire Grocery and the rest of the industry. For more than a century, grocery stores were located on the Main Streets of the country and the downtown areas of large cities. As the population shifted from the cities to the suburbs following the war, though, serious parking problems arose in traditional shopping areas, creating the need for a new retail facility and a new grocery store location: the suburban shopping center. Not to be left behind by this change in the industry, Brookshire constructed its first shopping center store before the close of the 1940s.

With the favorable economic conditions of the 1950s and the Eisenhower years, came further expansion for the company. To keep up with the growing demand from new stores in Corsicana, Marshall, Paris, Greenville, and Mt. Pleasant, Brookshire constructed its first grocery warehouse in 1953. With the onset of a new decade, the 17-store chain extended its operations beyond the Texas state line for the first time, venturing into the Louisiana market and opening stores in Bossier City and Natchitoches. New stores in Wills Point, Terrell, Palestine, and Mineola, Texas, brought the total number of Brookshire stores to 31 by the end of the decade. In 1968, to better supply these existing stores and prepare for continued growth, the company erected a 175,000-square-foot distribution center in Tyler.

Expansion in the 1970s and 1980s

The 1970s proved to be a decade of record growth for Brookshire Grocery. By 1975, despite the obstacles of a national energy crisis and a recessionary economy, the company had opened 13 new stores and made its way onto the *Chain Store Age* list of the fastest growing grocers. Two years later Brookshire made its first appearance on the publication's list of the 100 largest food chains, recording an estimated $175 million in total revenue. During the remainder of the decade, revenue jumped more than 30 percent as the company inched its way up to number 76 on the list in a market dominated by multibillion dollar giants such as Safeway, Kroger, and A & P—despite operating in a comparatively small geographical area. While doubling its size to 62 supermarkets, Brookshire's did set up for business in a third state, opening three new stores in Arkansas as well as its first bakery plant.

This pattern of expansion continued into the early 1980s despite the recessionary conditions of the U.S. economy. In 1982, the company generated $350 million in revenue, having doubled its output in just seven years. By 1984, Brookshire operated more than 70 stores and employed more than 4,000 people in its three-state region. In its home base of Tyler, with a population of 75,000, the company's eight stores enjoyed a 40 percent market share, despite the presence of at least 15 grocery stores in the area.

The strategy that enabled the company to experience such steady growth to this point was simple: Beat the competition on strong and friendly service. As then president C.B. Hardin explained to Doug Harris of *Supermarket Business,* the company's strategy of "aggressive hospitality" demanded a strong commitment to service from its employees: "Our philosophy is when you come into one of our stores we want you to be greeted just as nice as if you were coming into our living room—because you're our guest, and the customer is our boss." With increasing competition from mainstays such as Kroger and newcomers such as Tom Thumb-Page, Brookshire fashioned its Southern hospitality into a well-orchestrated effort to please customers and stand out from the competition. With many of its stores located in oil-rich areas, the company attempted to outdo the competition on service rather than price, making sure that customers were not only greeted at the door when they entered and at the checkout when they left but given heartfelt greetings from stockers and service counter employees as well. "We'd rather overdo it than underdo it," Hardin told *Supermarket Business.*

It would take more than friendly service, though, for Brookshire to continue growing during the 1980s. As more and more competitors entered the scene, the company attempted to broaden its customer base by diversifying its operations and continuing its strategy of growth through geographical expansion. Chief among these developments was the company's opening of its first Super 1 Foods store in Alexandria, Louisiana, in 1984. In contrast to the traditional Brookshire store, with its elegant decor and state-of-the-art technology, the new line of stores cut back on the frills so that it could offer the lowest prices possible.

Between 1984 and 1990, the company opened 11 Super 1 Foods stores in Louisiana and Texas. Unlike competitors in the wholesale foods market such as Sam's Wholesale Club, the Super 1 stores required no membership fees and were generally smaller in size. The new warehouse-type environment enabled customers to save money—usually around $15 a week—by purchasing in larger quantities and bagging their own groceries. Although the Super 1 Foods stores were designed to keep labor costs low, they retained the colorful decor and many of the specialty departments that had become a fixture at the full-service stores and, in this way, distinguished themselves from many other competitors in the wholesale market.

One of the money-saving innovations at the company's warehouse-style stores could be found at the checkout stand. Whereas the full-service Brookshire's stores emphasized ambiance and an aesthetically pleasing checkout environment, the Super 1 units concentrated on getting customers through the checkout faster. To meet this goal, the company began installing triple-belt checkstands in its 65,000-square-foot Super 1 units. The "Tri-Belt" system features an initial belt at the head of the checkstand that carries items to the scanner position and a second belt that moves each customer's scanned and paid-for order to a bagging station where the consumer bags his or her own order.

While diversifying its operations in the mid-1980s, the company also attempted to reduce costs by taking advantage of the latest computer technology. In 1984 the company replaced its mechanical time-clocks with microcomputer-based time accounting systems. With more than 4,000 employees in its 70 stores, the manual processing of weekly payroll had become a monstrous task for the 18 payroll clerks who had to recalculate and verify all time-cards in less than 24 hours. The short turn-around time prevented clerks from correcting overpunches and illegal punches—errors that were costing the company thousands of dollars weekly. Once the new computerized accounting system was installed, though, store managers were able not only to reduce such discrepancies but better monitor employee overtime as well. With payroll processing time cut in half, the front office was able to spend more time collecting on bad checks and handling other administrative duties. The bottom line, as then personnel administration supervisor Dan Adcock stated in *Chain Store Age Executive,* was a savings of about $500 per week per store.

The 1990s and Beyond

One of the keys to Brookshire's continued success during the early 1990s was its traditional emphasis on serving the customer. Attracting shoppers to its Tyler stores in the face of an increasingly competitive market, however, required more than smiling cashiers and friendly stockers; it also meant responding to the cultural diversity and unique needs of its clientele. The transformation process for one Brookshire's store converted to a Super 1 Foods warehouse store, for instance, meant substantially increasing the Hispanic foods section to appeal to the area's small but rapidly expanding Hispanic population. By doubling the size of the Hispanic section through the addition of existing items and new foods such as corn tortilla mixes and sliced cactus and advertising in a local Hispanic paper, the store was able to attract customers from what had been, for the most part, an untapped market. By 1991, Hispanic shoppers represented nearly one-third of the store's total clientele.

Brookshire's transition into the discount foods market coincided with its move into the Dallas/Fort Worth area. New stores were opened in Allen, McKinney, and The Colony during the late 1980s. To keep pace with this steady expansion, the company added more than 250,000 square feet to its distribution center before the end of the decade, and in 1991, the company brought its first warehouse-type store to the area, opening a mammoth 100,000-square-foot Super 1 Foods in Plano. Two

years later, Brookshire increased its presence in the area's discount market, purchasing land for a new 70,000-square-foot Super 1 Foods in Garland. By 1995, the company had established a strong presence in the Dallas suburbs, with seven stores in operation.

The early and mid-1990s saw Brookshire solidify its presence in existing markets and venture into new territory. The company's expansion to the east resulted in the construction of a second distribution center in 1992, located in Monroe, Louisiana. The state also became the site of Brookshire's 100th store, which opened in Marksville, in 1994. That same year the company, while boosting its total revenue to an estimated $700 million, acquired a 491,000-square-foot manufacturing facility near Tyler.

In addition to opening its own stores, Brookshire sought to boost its share in various Texas markets by acquiring 16 stores from Thrift Mart, a $90 million, independent, family-run chain based in Granbury that got its start in the 1950s. Terms of the agreement were not released. The acquisition, which included stores in Fort Worth, Hurst, Aledo, and Granbury, represented the company's debut in the Fort Worth area and was heralded by company officials as a way to further increase the growing chain's buying power and offer its customers lower prices.

Brookshire also sought to better serve its customers by adding new services. In 1993 it launched the Brookshire Pharmacy Division, and by the end of the decade 73 stores would include pharmacies. The company opened its first Fuel Center in 1995, and over the years another 20 Brookshire's and Super 1 Foods stores would add gas stations to their operations.

In an attempt to maintain its reputation for customer service excellence, Brookshire entered into a multimillion dollar contract with the NCR Corporation for the latest in state-of-the art store automation technology. The installation plan, instituted in early 1996, called for an advanced checkout system that included an innovative, user-friendly, ATM-style interface designed to make checkouts faster and reduce employee training costs—by as much as 60 percent according to some estimates.

By improving the efficiency of its operations and by meeting the diverse needs of its customers through its upscale and warehouse stores, Brookshire entered the late 1990s hoping to ward off the threat from a new competitor into the grocery market: the supercenter, a combination general merchandise and grocery market under one big roof. Having opened its first supercenter in Texas in 1992, Wal-Mart, which controlled 42 percent of the discount retail market in 1995 and employed one out of every 200 employed people in the United States, attempted to carve its own niche in the $390 billion grocery business, opening its 54th supercenter in Texas and its 230th nationwide in 1995. Although the discount giant's increasing presence did not significantly affect Brookshire's larger markets, it did promise to threaten the company's market share in smaller communities where customers have to drive a greater distance to do their shopping and thus realize more benefits from the convenience of supercenters.

Despite the supercenter threat, Brookshire continued to expand by following the plan that had made it a success in the first place: finding ways to serve the needs of customers and embracing technology to maintain an edge in a highly competitive industry. In 1999 Brookshire was in the vanguard of retailers testing self-checkout technology, which it soon introduced to all of its stores. In 2000 the Tyler distribution center received a major upgrade, one of the most ambitious projects Brookshire ever took on. In addition to adding 50,000 square feet to its freezer facility, a new massive perishable warehouse was built as well. To serve the rapidly growing Hispanic population, Brookshire launched a third supermarket format: Ole Foods. The first store opened in Plano, Texas, in 2001. Another example of the company listening to its customers was the 2001 introduction of Le Carb Frozen Dessert, catering to customers practicing popular low-carb diets as well as to diabetics. Maintaining a strong relationship with employees was also a priority. In April 2002 Brookshire established an Employee Stock Ownership Plan, providing further incentive for the company's more than 12,000 employees to embrace Brookshire's culture.

With the new century, Brookshire continued to grow by acquisition, proving that it was able to succeed where others struggled. In April 2002 the company shed seven Dallas-area Super 1 Foods stores, a move that set up a pair of significant acquisitions a month later: Brookshire entered the Mississippi market in May 2002 by acquiring four Albertson's stores in the Jackson market, and bought 17 Winn-Dixie stores in North Texas, again in new markets for the company. The stores were located in the Fort Worth area, Denton, East Texas, and Wichita Falls. The 21 new stores were closed for a month to make the transition to the Brookshire's banner. It was a daunting task—training staff, stocking warehouses and supermarket shelves, and hiring drivers—but the company managed to open all the stores on schedule.

Competition from Wal-Mart and other retailers remained formidable, making innovation an even greater priority. On the technology side of the equation, Brookshire was once again an early user when it came to adopting new price optimization software that helped retailers set current prices by analyzing past sales performance. As a result, Brookshire was able to improve its price image with consumers, highly important in light of competition coming from so many quarters. A more customer-friendly innovation was the launch of a Kids Club, aimed at children ages 3 to 10. The program was tied into the parent's frequent shopper card, so that when parents bought certain items, the child received a toy or cookies from the bakery. In addition, children received birthday cards from the store and a newsletter that included stories and activities, as well as coupons. Members were also eligible for monthly prizes. The goal was more ambitious than simply having children influence the shopping decisions of parents. It was to establish an early relationship between Brookshire and its future customers. In this way, the success the company had enjoyed for three-quarters of a century could be extended to a new generation.

Principal Operating Units

Brookshire Grocery Stores; Super 1 Food Stores; Ole Foods.

Principal Competitors

Albertson's, Inc.; The Kroger Company; Wal-Mart Stores, Inc.

Further Reading

Amato-McCoy, Deena, "Self-Checkout Test Planned at Brookshire Grocery Units," *Supermarket News,* April 26, 1999, p. 21.

"Brookshire Finds a Better Way of Accounting for Its Time," *Chain Store Age Executive,* April 1985, pp. 67–68.

"Brookshire Grocery Covers All Bases," *Chain Store Age Executive,* December 1991, p. 28.

Doherty, Katherine, "Going It Alone: With a Dedicated Hard-Working Staff Brookshire Grocery Co. Masters the Art of Self Sufficiency," *Food Logistics,* March 15, 2003, p. 17.

Garry, Michael, "Spicing Up Sales," *Progressive Grocer,* April 1991, p. 34.

Halkias, Maria, "Wal-Mart, Kmart Set Sights on Small-Town Grocers' Turf," *Dallas Morning News,* July 7, 1995, p. 1D.

Harris, Doug, " 'Aggressive Hospitality' in Tyler, Texas," *Supermarket Business,* January 1984, pp. 39–40.

Lehbar, Godfrey M., *Chain Stores in America 1859–1962,* New York: Chain Store Publishing Corp., 1963.

Moses, Lucia, "Brookshire Grocery Creates Kids Club," *Supermarket News,* February 14, 2005, p. 29.

——, "Brookshire to Expand Pricing Strategy," *Supermarket News,* January 31, 2005, p. 47.

Narayan, Chandrika, "Brookshire's Plans Plano Super Store," *Dallas Times Herald,* July 20, 1991, p. 1B.

Piller, Can, "Tyler, Texas-Based Grocery Chain to Buy 17 Winn-Dixie Stores in North Texas," *Fort Worth Star-Telegram,* May 31, 2002.

Scott, Dave, "Brookshire's, Venture Grab Garland Site for New Stores," *Dallas Business Journal,* January 7, 1994, p. 1.

Wren, Worth, "Tyler Grocery Firm Buys 16 Thrift Mart Stores," *Fort Worth Star-Telegram,* October 4, 1995, p. 1.

—Jason Gallman
—update: Ed Dinger

Brown Jordan International Inc.

1801 North Andrews Avenue
Pompano Beach, Florida 33069
U.S.A.
Telephone: (954) 960-1117
Fax: (954) 960-1849
Web site: http://www.brownjordan.com

Private Company
Incorporated: 1994
Employees: 1,460
Sales: $346.3 million (2003)
NAIC: 337121 Upholstered Household Furniture
Manufacturing; 337124 Metal Household Furniture
Manufacturing; 337129 Wood Television, Radio, and
Sewing Machine Cabinet Manufacturing

Brown Jordan International Inc. (BJI), formerly known as WinsLoew Furniture Inc., operates as a designer, manufacturer, and marketer of furnishings and accessories to residential and commercial customers in the United States and abroad. The company's furnishings are sold under the brand names of Brown Jordan, Tommy Bahama, Pompeii, Winston, Molla, Vineyard, Atlantis, Stuart Clark, Casual Living, Tradewinds, Loewenstein, Charter, Lodging by Charter, Woodsmiths, Wabash Valley, Texacraft, and Tropic Craft. The company was born out of a 1994 merger of Winston Furniture Co. and Loewenstein Furniture Group. It operated as WinsLoew Furniture after the deal, acquired BJI in 2001, and adopted the BJI moniker in 2002.

Casual Furniture Since 1975

In December 1994 Winston Furniture Company, Inc. and Loewenstein Furniture Group, Inc. merged into WinsLoew Furniture, Inc. The merger pooled the interests and financial statements of the companies. Winston Furniture Company originated as a division of Marathon Corporation in 1975. By 1976, Winston management along with other investors acquired the aluminum furniture business of that division through a lever-

aged buyout (LBO). Over the next decade Winston grew, acquiring the wrought iron and tubular steel furniture business of Lyon-Shaw, Inc., a division of B.B. Walker Company, in 1986. Operating independently for more than a decade, Winston completed an initial public offering (IPO) of shares in August 1987. By 1988, however, Winston was purchased in a LBO by WF Acquisition Corporation, a company formed by affiliates of Trivest, Inc. specifically for the buyout. The two companies merged after the buyout, and Winston was able to reduce its indebtedness and expand its operations. In 1992, Winston was incorporated under the laws of the State of Delaware, and Winston Furniture Company of Alabama, Inc. became its sole operating subsidiary.

By 1994, Winston had become a leader in the casual furniture market. The company had pioneered the use of all-weather cushions on aluminum furniture in the 1970s and was awarded the 1993 Casual Furniture Manufacturer Leadership Award at the National Casual Furniture Market in Chicago, Illinois. Winston, which also had won the award in 1990 and had been a finalist for the award in each of its previous four years, was the only company to win the award twice. The award is based on the manufacturer's leadership in the areas of quality of goods, design, merchandising, customer service, ethics, communications, and trade relations. Winston continued to expand its casual furniture operations by purchasing all the assets of Texacraft, a privately held manufacturer of contract aluminum furniture, in 1994.

Loewenstein, Inc.: Contract Seating Since 1967

Loewenstein, Inc. was founded in 1967 as a manufacturer of contract seating for the hospitality market. Atlantis, an affiliate of Trivest, acquired the company in 1985 and Loewenstein operated as part of the "Atlantis Furniture Group" until 1990. The Atlantis Furniture Group consisted of Southern Wood Products, Inc., a manufacturer of promotionally priced RTA furniture; Gregson Furniture Industries, Inc., a manufacturer of traditional and transitional-styled seating for the office and institutional markets; and Excel Office and Contract, Inc., a manufacturer of contemporary and traditional-styled seating for the office furniture market. In 1990, Loewenstein was incorporated and purchased the Atlantis Furniture Group. In 1993, the company completed an IPO of common stock. The $17.2 million raised effectively retired all of Loewenstein's outstanding indebtedness and allowed for additional working capital.

As Loewenstein retired its debt, it expanded its futon offerings through acquisition. In 1993, Loewenstein purchased Shaffield Industries, Inc., a manufacturer of RTA furniture, including futons, chairs, tables, and related accessories under the brand name "From the Source." In 1994, Loewenstein acquired another futon manufacturer, New West Industries.

While Winston and Loewenstein operated separately and in different niche markets, their destinies were mingled because they shared certain officers. Earl W. Powell had founded Atlantis Plastics, Inc. in 1984, served as chairman of the board of Loewenstein since 1985, and was chairman of the board of Winston since 1988. In addition, Powell had cofounded Trivest, a Miami-based private investment firm that provided services to both Winston and Loewenstein, with Dr. Phillip T. George. Dr. George served as director of Loewenstein since 1985 and as director of Winston since 1989. Peter W. Klein served as director of Winston since 1988 and as director of Loewenstein since 1993; he also acted as secretary and general counsel of Trivest since 1986. Peter C. Brockway served as director of Winston since 1988 and executive officer, managing director, and executive vice-president of Trivest since 1986, 1991, and 1993, respectively. He also served as vice-president of Atlantis since 1986.

Although certain officers had informally discussed the possibility of merging Winston and Loewenstein, an official proposal came in 1994 from Earl W. Powell. He suggested a stock-for-stock, tax-free business combination. To investigate the potential of such a merger, the board of directors for each company appointed a committee of directors who were neither employees of Winston, Loewenstein, nor Trivest to study the proposal's feasibility.

At the time of the study, both companies were financially stable. Winston had sales of $33.7 million, and Loewenstein had sales of $66.6 million for the nine months ended September 30, 1994. The combined financial strength of the companies was hoped to allow the created company to expand product lines from a larger operating base, have better access to public and private financing due to the strength of a combined financial base, and enhance the attractiveness of company stock to investors because of a larger market capitalization. Independent analysts believed that the merger was fair from a financial standpoint. The merger was effected on December 16, 1994. Each outstanding share of common stock of Winston was converted into the right to receive one share of common stock of WinsLoew and each outstanding share of the common stock of Loewenstein was converted into the right to receive 1.05 share of common stock of WinsLoew.

Trivest played an important role in the history of both companies. Before the merger those officers controlling Winston and Loewenstein were affiliates of Trivest and controlled approximately 31.5 percent of Winston's outstanding common stock and approximately 34.3 percent of Loewenstein's. With the merger Trivest and affiliated parties would own 33.3 percent of the outstanding WinsLoew common stock. Until the merger, Trivest offered its specialized management services to both Winston and Loewenstein, receiving aggregate fees of $850,000 per year. In October 1994, WinsLoew entered a ten-year agreement with Trivest, Inc.; under the agreement, Trivest would provide corporate finance, financial relations, strategic and capital planning, and other management advice to WinsLoew for a base fee of $500,000, with increases for cost of living and additional businesses acquired.

Operating As One: Results of the 1994 Merger

Initially the pooled interests of the companies looked good. Operating results for the first year as WinsLoew Furniture, Inc. marked a 34 percent increase in sales to $137.8 million. An additional bonus came when WinsLoew won the 1994 Design Excellence Award from the Summer Casual Furniture Manufacturers Association for its tubular aluminum dining chair called Magnolia Sling.

The increase in sales and honor from the award did not cloud management's vision for the future, however. WinsLoew management introduced a strategic plan in mid-1995 to cut costs and improve efficiency in the coming years due to the manufacturing and marketing problems it saw in its low-end futons and Southern Wood division. The effects of the plan did not save the company from posting disappointing operating results after its second year. The management cited "higher raw material costs, competitive pricing pressures, and production inefficiencies," as well as the discontinuance of low-end futon production, for the decrease in income in 1995. WinsLoew had a net loss of $4.0 million in 1995, compared with a net income of $6.4 million in 1994. To further implement its strategic plan, WinsLoew sold its subsidiary Excel Office and Contract because its products were deemed "inconsistent with WinsLoew's," according to president and chief executive Bobby Tesney in *HFN*. Tesney added that the sale of Excel would "enhance profitability by reducing embedded costs and maximizing marketing opportunities in each of our product groups." He anticipated that the results of the sale along with increased sales and cost-cutting measures would be reflected in improved operating results for 1996.

The benefits of WinsLoew management's vision came in the fourth quarter of 1995, and the company continued to post increases in every quarter into 1997. Net income for 1996 was $8.3 million, compared with a net loss of $4.0 million the year before. Management noted that 1996 was a "very successful" year. In addition, the company reported improvement in the gross margins of each of its business segments. The company credited its "price increases, overhead reductions, production improvements, refocused or expanded marketing strategies, and new product designs" along with the consolidation of some warehousing and manufacturing facilities for its turnaround.

WinsLoew's numbers for 1996 far exceeded analysts' expectations. *Individual Investor* reported that analysts were "expecting just $0.77'' earnings per share, but WinsLoew had reached $0.95 earnings per share. Given WinsLoew management's stellar performance, analysts expected double-digit growth for the company in 1997 as well. Wallace W. Epperson, Jr., of Interstate/Johnson Lane noted in *Buyside* the difficulty of finding ''value'' or, even more rarely, companies ''exceptionally well-positioned in growth markets'' with a ''management team that has proven itself in difficult conditions.'' He concluded that WinsLoew offered all these attributes. Nancy Zambell of UnDiscovered Stocks, Inc. declared in *Buyside* that WinsLoew's earnings per share for 1996 was the '' 'proof-of-the-pudding' that WinsLoew has the management team to direct its future growth.'' In addition, WinsLoew's focus on national chain retailers was seen as good fuel to drive the company's growth, according to *Individual Investor*. The predictions seemed accurate by the end of the second quarter of 1997, when the company again reported earnings higher than analysts' estimates.

Product Improvement in the 1990s

The financial benefits reaped from WinsLoew management's strategic plan could not have been realized without the company's strong product offerings. More than 70 percent of WinsLoew's revenues came from the casual and contract seating groups. WinsLoew's casual residential furniture was marketed under the Winston label for aluminum furniture and under the Lyon-Shaw label for wrought iron. The September 1994 acquisition of Texacraft, a privately held manufacturer of aluminum, iron, wood, and fiberglass casual furniture, allowed WinsLoew to enter the contract casual furniture arena. WinsLoew augmented its quality of design by using stronger components than its medium-priced competitors and applying its exclusive Diamond bond paint finishing system, which gave the furniture a durable, chip- and fade-resistant protective finish.

At this time, contract seating was sold under the Loewenstein and Gregson labels. Loewenstein's Breeze chair won the International Interior Design Association and *Contract Design* magazine's APEX Award in the seating category in

1996. Entries in the design competition were judged on innovation, durability, performance, and value. The Breeze chair was designed by the Italian designer Carlo Bartoli, a man who ''uses technical solutions in an intelligent way, discreetly offered within the object almost as a bonus to the buyer,'' according to Jacques Toussaint in *Contemporary Designers*. ''He never cuts short his design component, such as aesthetics or function—these qualities are what place Bartoli among the most highly rated designers.'' To enhance its designs, Loewenstein improved its finishing process to produce the hardest and most vibrant finish in the industry. The electrostatic spray guns and three-dimensional ultraviolet drying system have increased efficiency in manufacturing and reduced the emission of volatile organic compounds 50 percent below permitted levels, a feat recognized appreciatively by the state of Florida.

WinsLoew marketed ready-to-assemble furniture under three labels: New West for futons and frames, MicroCentre for ergonomically designed computer furniture, and Southern Wood for promotionally priced spindle (including coffee tables, wall units, children's furniture, and TV carts) and flatline products (including bookshelves, computer desks, printer stands, and bath-related storage units). New West was ranked second among manufacturers in the futon industry. Part of the company's plans included eliminating the noncompetitive and low-margin futon products and broadening the market for futons by participating in non-futon trade shows. MicroCentre's computer workstations featured among other things the patented view-down monitor configuration. The design came from the research of ergonomist Stewart B. Leavitt. In light of the increasing numbers of health problems related to stress at work, Micro-Centre sponsored research by Leavitt in 1996. Leavitt studied how the height and placement of video display terminals affected vision comfort and related to healthcare issues. He discovered that the eyes could more easily focus when the monitor was placed 15 to 45 degrees below eye level. He also found that this positioning of the monitor could reduce eye strain, redness, and headaches over long periods.

As part of WinsLoew's strategy to curtail production of low-end products, WinsLoew drastically reduced the offerings in the Southern Wood line. WinsLoew did improve the designs of the remaining pieces, however, and invested nearly $1 million in new production equipment. The company anticipated that the more ''sophisticated'' designs would improve sales and profit margins. With WinsLoew's improved financial position and its efforts toward improving the quality of its product, many of the benefits of merging Winston and Loewenstein were only just becoming apparent in the late 1990s.

Changes in the Late 1990s and Beyond

During the late 1990s, WinsLoew remained focused on acquiring companies that manufactured furnishings at varying price points. Pompeii Furniture Industries, a manufacturer of high-end casual furniture for commercial markets, was acquired in 1998. During the following year, WinsLoew added Tropic Craft Aluminum Furniture Manufacturers, a maker of casual furniture for the contract and hospitality markets, to its arsenal. In addition to growth strategy, WinsLoew began to sell off unprofitable businesses that did not fit into the company's core line of casual furniture and contract seating. Included in its divestiture program was the Lyon-Shaw wrought iron casual furniture unit, which it sold to Woodard Inc. in 1997.

Changes were on the horizon for WinsLoew as it prepared to enter the new millennium. The first came in 1999, when a buyout group led by Chairman Earl Powell set plans in motion to acquire the company for $220 million and take it private. Trivest Furniture Corporation was created by the buyout partners and became WinsLoew's parent company after the deal. Over the next 18 months, the company grew through acquisition. It made its sixth and largest purchase in 2001 when it agreed to buy Brown Jordan International Inc. for $100 million. WinsLoew President and CEO Bobby Tesney commented on the purchase in a May 2001 *HFN* article claiming, ''The Brown Jordan name is number one in casual furniture today, and has been for many years. We think the name adds a lot to our presence in the market.'' Indeed, after the deal WinsLoew controlled 22 percent of the casual furniture market.

In early 2002, WinsLoew announced a major corporate restructuring in which all of its operational lines were consolidated under the WinsLoew Furniture Inc. corporate name. It shifted gears in May of that year and decided instead to adopt the Brown Jordan International Inc. (BJI) corporate moniker. Management hoped to capitalize on Brown Jordan's powerful brand name and reputation. In addition, the company shuttered its mass market headquarters in Ripon, Wisconsin, and moved key personnel to Pompano Beach, Florida. BJI also closed DesignResource, its creative division in Long Beach, California, and relocated it to Pompano Beach.

As an affiliate of Trivest Partners L.P., BJI's corporate mission was to position itself as the market leader in the retail, mass, and contract distribution channels. At this time, the company elected Bruce Albertson as president and CEO, while Tesney acted as vice-chairman. The executive group also included Jerry Camp, president of the retail market division; Dale Boles, president of the mass market division; and Darryl Rosser, president of the contract market division. With a solid executive team in place, a group of strong brands in its holdings, and a definitive business strategy, BJI appeared well positioned for success in the years to come.

Principal Competitors

Falcon Products Inc.; Meadowcraft Inc.; Virco Mfg. Corporation.

Further Reading

Allegrezza, Ray, ''Dealing in Metal,'' *HFN,* August 25, 1997, p. 15.
——, ''Execs Buy Excel Back from WinsLoew,'' *HFN,* December 4, 1995, p. 15.
''Analyst Roundtable,'' *Buyside,* April 1997.
Greenwald, Nathan, ''Hot Stocks: Momentum Investing,'' *Individual Investor,* April 1997, p. 94.
Meyer, Nancy, ''WinsLoew Assumes Brown Jordan Name, Consolidates Offices,'' *HFN,* May 13, 2002.
——, ''WinsLoew Furniture's Parent Company Buys Brown Jordan,'' *HFN,* May 14, 2001.
Ryan, Ken, ''Trivest Adds On to WinsLoew,'' *Buyouts,* May 21, 2001.
Toussaint, Jacques, ''Carlo Bartoli,'' *Contemporary Designers,* Detroit: St. James Press, 1996.
''WinsLoew—Acquires Tropic Craft,'' *CFO News,* July 1, 1998.
''WinsLoew Undergoes Corporate Makeover,'' *HFN,* February 25, 2002.

—Sara Pendergast
—update: Christina M. Stansell

C.R. Meyer and Sons Company

895 West 20th Avenue
Oshkosh, Wisconsin 54903-2157
U.S.A.
Telephone: (920) 235-3350
Fax: (920) 235-3419
Web site: http://www.crmeyer.com

Private Company
Incorporated: 1912
Employees: 500
Sales: $97.6 million (2005)
NAIC: 233000 Building, Developing, and General
    Contracting

Based in Oshkosh, Wisconsin, privately owned C.R. Meyer and Sons Company is one of the leading construction companies in the Midwest. Not only does the company offer a full range of general contracting services, it is also capable of designing buildings. Further capabilities include construction management and planning and consulting services. In addition, C.R. Meyer offers specialized services. Pre-engineered solutions include construction planning, value analysis, budgeting, bidding and estimating, material and equipment procurement, cost tracking and reporting, and project close out. The company also offers equipment moving and erection services. Included among the clients of C.R. Meyer are companies in such sectors as pulp and paper, mining, power generation, food and beverage, office facilities, healthcare, assisted living facilities, and financial services. In addition to the main office in Oshkosh, C.R. Meyer has an office in Rhinelander, Wisconsin, and maintains an equipment yard in both cities. The company has also opened an office in Grand Rapids, Minnesota, and owns Griese and Ross, a crane and heavy equipment rental company with locations in Oshkosh, Green Bay, Marshfield, and Tomahawk, Wisconsin.

Company Roots in the Late 19th Century

The man behind the C.R. Meyer name was Charles R. Meyer, a young German immigrant who came to Oshkosh in 1888 with little more than his mason's canvas bag. Inside were a trowel and wooden level, his only possessions of value. He was able to put the masonry skills he learned in Germany to good use in his new country. For the first dozen years, he concentrated on the stone fronts of homes, stores, and factories, many of which were related to Oshkosh's thriving lumber trade. Then, in 1900, a stroke of luck provided Meyer with an opportunity to branch out beyond stone masonry. He was a masonry subcontractor working on a paper plant when the carpenter on the project backed out, leaving the carpentry bid to Meyer. With this start, Meyer was able to become a general contractor in construction. His building projects were mostly small houses and stores in the Fox Valley area.

Meyer quickly established a reputation for superior workmanship, leading to increasingly larger projects, including mansions for the wealthy industrialists, as his area of operation gradually expanded throughout northeast Wisconsin, eventually reaching to Michigan's Upper Peninsula. In 1908, he built a mansion for the lumber baron and banker Edgar P. Sawyer, which later became the Oshkosh Public Museum. During the two decades of the 20th century, Meyer also built the Al Leach residence in Oshkosh, the Conway residence in Appleton, the Al Gilbert residence in Neenah, and the residence of Robert Lutz in Oshkosh. Throughout this period, Meyer also constructed a number of commercial and institutional projects, including the St. Elizabeth Hospital in Appleton, the massive Oshkosh Trunk Company plant, the Fox River Paper plant, the New German American Bank in Oshkosh, the Theda Clark Hospital in Neenah, the Sentry Insurance building in Stevens Point, the Jersild Knitting Company factory in Neenah, the Oshkosh Elk's Club, and the Webster Building in Oshkosh.

By now, Meyer was being helped by his sons Harry and Edward. In 1912, he incorporated the business as C.R. Meyer and Sons Company. The family construction business continued to thrive until the stock market crash of 1929. During the preceding decade, C.R. Meyer completed a number of significant building projects in Wisconsin, including the Athearn Hotel, the First Baptist Temple, the First Presbyterian Church, and the First National Bank, all located in Oshkosh. In addition, the company built the Riverside Paper Company plant in Appleton and facilities for the Neenah Paper Company and the Green Bay and Mississippi Canal Company. It was during this period that C.R. Meyer also became involved in other kinds of building projects, such as the Fox River Paper Dam in 1918 and the Lawe Street Bridge in Appleton in 1922, as well as other area dams and hydro facilities. The company also built a mansion for another lumber baron, Nathan Paine, whose residence one day would become Oshkosh's Paine Art Center and Gardens, considered an ''American Castle.''

Like most businesses in America, C.R. Meyer struggled as the country tumbled into the Great Depression. In 1932, Charles Meyer turned over the presidency of the company to Edward and the vice-presidency to Harry, on whose shoulders fell the responsibility of shepherding the business through these difficult times. At one juncture, the brothers were forced to mortgage all their possessions in order to keep C.R. Meyer in business. A stellar reputation earned over a period of decades, strong relationships with customers, and family friendships were also important in the company's ability to survive the 1930s. What few contracts there were during this time tended to go to C.R. Meyer. Important projects included Sunnyview Sanitarium, Merrill Junior High School, Mercy Hospital School of Nursing, and the Paine Lumber Company plant, all in Oshkosh; the Bergstrom Paper Company facility in Neenah; and the De Pere Bridge, the Paint River Dam, Little Chute Dam, Grandfather Falls Hydro Plant, and the Eastern Wisconsin Light, Heat and Power Company plant.

Postwar Building Boom

In 1939, Harry Meyer succeeded his brother as president of the family business, a position he held for the next 25 years. It was not until the United States entered World War II in late 1941 that the U.S. economy fully recovered. Following a brief recession after the war ended in 1945, the economy roared during the postwar years and C.R. Meyer benefited greatly from a sustained building boom. Business was so strong that in the late 1940s the company used some of its own resources to build itself a new 9,000-square-foot headquarters in downtown Oshkosh. For the most part, C.R. Meyer now focused on large public works projects and the construction of factories. Projects during the 1940s included the Peavy Falls Dam, the Tomahawk Dam, the Way Dam, the Rhinelander Paper Company plant, the Kimberly-Clark Globe Mill building, the Whiting-Plover Paper Company plant, and the Neenah Paper Company plant. Projects of the 1950s included the Butte des Morts Bridge, the State Street Bridge, Oregon Street Bridge, the Michigamme Falls dam, the hydroelectric plant at Big Quinnesec Falls, the Escanaba Steam Plant, the Cleveland Clifts Company Shaft Mine, the Marathon Paper plant in Menominee, Michigan, the Bayside Plant in Green Bay, the Bayside Pulliam Plant, the Nicolet Paper Company plant, and Oshkosh's Mercy Hospital.

A third generation took over C.R. Meyer in 1963 when Harry Meyer's son-in-law, Fred W. Pinkerton, became the company's president. A year later, a fourth generation became involved when Pinkerton's son, Fred M. Pinkerton, went to work for C.R. Meyer and began his grooming to one day take over the company. In reality, he began preparing to run the company from childhood. ''Everything I did in the high school years, working as a laborer or mason trader, my schooling years in Madison, my college years working with the company—I knew I was going to be involved in this company from the start,'' he told *Marketplace Magazine* in a 1995 interview. ''I wanted it, and I prepared for it. With my grandfather and my dad heavily involved in the business, many of our outings and fun times as a family revolved around business clients and business friendships. Those business friendships became personal friendships. It was all interrelated.'' Although he always expected to work in the family business, the younger Pinkerton, a fan of Frank Lloyd Wright, came close to dropping his college business classes to study architecture. Despite staying the course, his interest in design provided a key influence on the way he ran C.R. Meyer when he took over.

First, Fred M. Pinkerton would have to wait his turn. During the 22 years that his father led C.R. Meyer, the company constructed a number of significant projects, including the Bergstrom Paper Company plant, the Hewitt Machine Company facility, major additions to the Nicolet Paper Company facilities, several plants for the Oshkosh Truck Corporation, and the Wisconsin Tissue Mills plant. Additionally, in the early 1980s Fred W. Pinkerton oversaw the acquisition of Griese and Ross, which provided cranes and operators since its founding in 1973.

Fred M. Pinkerton Takes Over in the Mid-1980s

When Fred M. Pinkerton became president of C.R. Meyer following the death of his father in the mid-1980s, he continued the company's tradition of doing business by creating partnerships with clients. ''The key to the partnership approach is that everyone is together from day one,'' he explained to the *Northeastern Wisconsin Business Review* in a 1992 profile of the company. ''This allows for all partners to see the design stage in the works and give their input when certain needs arise.'' By forging a strong alliance between owner, architect-engineer, and construction firm (and in some cases an equipment supplier) and by having the parties meet on a regular basis throughout the construction process, C.R. Meyer was able to expedite work. ''For example,'' accord to the *Review*, ''SNE Enterprises Inc. selected C.R. Meyer to design and build a 660,000-square-foot manufacturing and office complex in Mosinee, Wisconsin. Using its partnership approach, Meyer was able to complete the $16 million project under budget and 1 month ahead of schedule.''

The addition of design capabilities was the most significant improvement the younger Pinkerton brought to C.R. Meyer after becoming company president, an outgrowth of his early interest in architecture. In 1995, he told *Marketplace Magazine,* ''When I graduated from school and came back to the business, I very early on saw the future of design-build, to become a support to an otherwise good, solid construction business. We have always had engineers and several draftsmen as far as I can remember employed in our office. I saw that opportunity involved, that I wanted to promote the design-build concept for

Key Dates:

1888: German immigrant and stone mason Charles R. Meyer immigrates to Wisconsin.
1890: Meyer expands beyond masonry.
1912: C.R. Meyer and Sons Company is incorporated.
1932: Meyer's son Edward Meyer assumes presidency.
1939: Edward's brother, Harry Meyer, become president.
1963: Harry Meyer's son-in-law Fred W. Pinkerton is named president.
1985: Following Pinkerton death, his son, Fred M. Pinkerton, heads the company.
1997: Pinkerton become chief executive officer; Phillip J. Martini is named president.
2002: The company opens an office in Grand Rapids, Minnesota.

C.R. Meyer. . . . I believe that clients—manufacturing industries, mills, and industrial firms—sensed the need for single-source responsibility.''

Although Pinkerton generally honored his father's advice, there was one area in which he followed his own judgment. He told the *Review* that his father once told him, ''Don't you ever put computers in here. That'll never work son.'' Realizing that it was just the cost that scared off his father, who had grown up parsimonious as a child of the Depression, Pinkerton embraced new technologies. The addition of computers and computer-assisted design systems were a key to the growth C.R. Meyer enjoyed as design-build company from the late 1980s onward. Turnaround time on a project could be greatly reduced while also providing cost effectiveness and the ability to make changes on the fly. Such flexibility was evident in a project the company completed for its own uses. Having outgrown their downtown offices, in 1989 C.R. Meyer converted a former airplane manufacturing building and hangar to suit the needs of a construction company. For several years, C.R. Meyer was the only construction firm in all of Wisconsin to offer computer-assisted design services.

Continued Success in the 1990s and Beyond

When C.R. Meyer entered the 1990s, it ranked number 173 on *Engineering News-Record's* list of the top 400 contractors in the United States. Within one year, the company jumped to number 158, boasting contracts worth $48.5 million. It now shied away from bridge construction and road projects, while adding specialties such as construction management services. In this way, C.R. Meyer became what Pinkerton called ''a mid-sized company with large-project capabilities.'' Not saddled with the overhead costs of a large company, C.R. Meyer enjoyed a great deal of flexibility. As Pinkerton told *Marketplace Maga-*

zine, ''We are able to gravitate towards industries that are successful and we are not dependent on an industry that might be in a down cycle. . . . In any economic cycle, there are always industry sectors that are thriving when the overall market isn't— and we have to be flexible to move toward those markets that are prospering.'' Major projects in the 1990s included the Sludge Burning Complex for Cross Pointe Paper in Park Falls, the Yankee dryer replacement at Wisconsin Tissue Mills In Menasha, the wastewater treatment plant at Packaging Corporation of America in Tomahawk, Berlin Memorial Hospital, the Riverside Medical Center in Waupaca, and the Cur*Med building in Oshkosh. C.R. Meyer also handled a pair of smaller jobs that were as much a labor of love as commerce: restoring the Oshkosh Public Museum that was housed in the Edgar P. Sawyer mansion it had built in the early 1900s and repairing the Nathan Paine mansion, home of the Paine Art Center, which it built in 1927, after the roof of the building burned off in a 1994 fire.

C.R. Meyer adjusted its management structure somewhat in the late 1990s. Pinkerton became chief executive officer in 1997 and turned over the presidency to Phillip J. Martini, who had served as vice-president for more than ten years. The company continue to pursue the same approach that made it successful for more than 100 years as it entered the 21st century. A yard was added in Rhinelander, Wisconsin, and in 2002 an office was opened in Grand Rapids, Minnesota. At the same time, C.R. Meyer was preparing for the future. Years earlier, Pinkerton told *Marketplace Magazine,* ''I want to be here through a successful transition from a family-owned business into the next generation that will manage C.R. Meyer and Sons. I will be here to ensure that our people who have given us their working lifetime are ensured that this will be in good hands for the next young people to carry on this business. It is important for me to prove that a fourth-generation business can successfully proceed into the fifth generation.''

Principal Divisions

Griese and Ross.

Principal Competitors

The Clark Construction Group; M.A. Mortsenson Company; The Walsh Group.

Further Reading

Howard, Thad, ''C. R. Meyer Excels at Building Area Landmarks,'' *Northeastern Wisconsin Business Review,* May 1, 1992, p. 23.
Prestegard, Steve, ''The Solution-Builder: C.R. Meyer and Son's Name Is on Some of the Area's Largest Construction Projects,'' *Marketplace Magazine,* August 15, 1995, p. 12.
''Scrapbook: C.R. Meyer and Sons Company,'' *C.R. Meyer and Sons Company,* 2003.

—Ed Dinger

California Pizza Kitchen Inc.

6053 W. Century Boulevard, 11th Floor
Los Angeles, California 90045
U.S.A.
Telephone: (310) 342-5000
Fax: (310) 342-4640
Web site: http://www.cpk.com

Public Company
Incorporated: 1985
Employees: 3,000
Sales: $422.5 million (2004)
Stock Exchanges: NASDAQ
Ticker Symbol: CPKI
NAIC: 72211 Full-Service Restaurants

California Pizza Kitchen Inc. was created in 1985 by attorneys Rick Rosenfield and Larry Flax. The company operates more than 150 full-service restaurants and 24 ASAP quick-service locations in 27 states and five countries. California Pizza Kitchen's menu was innovative from inception, offering unique pizzas topped with everything from barbecued chicken and duck, to grilled shrimp and Jamaican jerk chicken. It also serves a variety of salads, soups, pastas, sandwiches, appetizers, and desserts. California Pizza Kitchen's pizzas can be found in grocery store freezers as well, thanks to a partnership with Kraft Foods Inc.

Opening Its Doors in 1985

The founders of California Pizza Kitchen are Larry Flax and Rick Rosenfield. Flax, a native of Los Angeles, California, was educated at the University of Southern California Law School and served as an Assistant United States Attorney during the early 1970s. In that capacity, Flax worked as Chief of Civil Rights and as Assistant Chief of the Criminal Division for the United States Department of Justice. Rosenfield, a native of Chicago, worked as an attorney for the U.S. Department of Justice in Washington, D.C., and as Assistant U.S. Attorney for the Central District of California. Having met while pursuing their respective careers as assistant federal prosecutors, the two men struck up a friendship during the early 1970s and decided to form their own law firm. Concentrating on criminal defense

cases, in 1984 the two partners found themselves arguing a case before a Superior Court Judge in San Francisco. Flax and Rosenfield strongly believed that the facts of the case were in their favor, but the jury was unable to reach a verdict. Disillusioned by the hung jury, the two young men decided to leave the legal profession to seek a more rewarding career.

During their partnership, Flax and Rosenfield had offered legal services on a national basis, and in the course of their business travels they had sampled restaurants across the country and developed an enthusiasm for good food. Resolving to turn their enthusiasm into a business opportunity, they decided to open a restaurant. The two entrepreneurs took their lead from Wolfgang Puck, the master chef and owner of Spago restaurant in West Hollywood, who was known for creating pizzas with unusual toppings; the pair saw an opportunity to bring innovative pizza like Puck's to the mass market. The first California Pizza Kitchen was opened in Beverly Hills in 1985 and was an immediate success.

The strategy behind California Pizza Kitchen was simple. The owners wanted to provide a casual, upscale, family restaurant, with good food as the cornerstone of the enterprise. Most of the chain's kitchens are out in the open, so customers can watch the cooks preparing their pizzas. The restaurants are decorated with white tile to provide a clean, crisp atmosphere. The pizzas are baked in wood-burning ovens imported from Italy, whose designs had been perfected over a period of a few hundred years. The oven is fired to approximately 800 degrees Fahrenheit, and the pizza is cooked in three minutes in order to sear the ingredients. This results in a tastier—and, according to some cooks, a healthier—pizza. The partners were committed to creating designer pizzas with unusual toppings, such as duck sausage, Tandoori chicken, and goat cheese, an approach that not only attracted customers not normally inclined to eat pizza, but also enabled the company to take advantage of food trends within the industry. When the owners added pasta, salads, soft drinks, liquor, and desserts to the menu, California Pizza Kitchen was on the road to success.

1989 Expansion into Las Vegas

Although the company struggled during its first few years of operation and incurred some debt, sales of its pizza were always

Company Perspectives:

We believe our most defining success is our adherence to the philosophy that forms the foundation of our corporate culture, "R.O.C.K.," which stands for Respect, Opportunity, Communication and Kindness. It defines our relationships with our employees, vendors, partners, guests and stockholders and we know it provides the basis for our belief that CPK is an employer of choice. The R.O.C.K. philosophy also delivers a measurable return on investment for stockholders because employees who are motivated in a team environment can accomplish almost anything.

increasing. The company's big break came in 1989 when the flamboyant chairman of Golden Nugget casinos, Steve Wynn, struck a deal with Flax and Rosenfield to put a California Pizza Kitchen in the Mirage Hotel and Casino. Located in Las Vegas, the heart of the U.S. gambling industry, the new restaurant garnered $5.5 million in sales during its first year of operation. On weekends, according to the restaurant's manager, tables were turning over between 16 to 25 times within a 13-hour period. Unfortunately for Flax and Rosenfield, they did not own the restaurant in the Mirage Hotel and Casino. Wynn had arranged an unusual California Pizza Kitchen franchise. Yet the publicity that came from the success of the restaurant in Las Vegas opened doors to new opportunities in other parts of the country. Real estate developers were soon lobbying to place a California Pizza Kitchen in strategic locations for new malls and commercial developments.

In 1992 PepsiCo, Inc., located in Purchase, New York, bought a 50 percent interest in California Pizza Kitchen, which it later increased to 67 percent. In addition to its line of soft drink products, PepsiCo owned Pizza Hut, KFC (formerly known as Kentucky Fried Chicken), and Taco Bell. Management at PepsiCo wanted to gain more experience in operating full-service, moderately priced, casual-dining restaurants. The deal was finalized for $97 million, with Flax and Rosenfield receiving $20 million apiece, and PepsiCo assumed two seats out of the four on California Pizza Kitchen's board of directors. Not surprisingly, two of Taco Bell's officers were chosen for the two seats on the board. Flax and Rosenfield remained as co-chairs of the board of directors, with 50 percent voting control, and continued to direct the day-to-day operations of the company. The only change PepsiCo required in the agreement was for California Pizza to replace the sale of Coca-Cola products with PepsiCo's line of soft drinks.

The arrangement between PepsiCo and California Pizza Kitchen seemed to be a gift to Flax and Rosenfield. At the time of the deal, California Pizza Kitchen was generating approximately $60 million in annual sales from all its restaurants, with each one averaging a little more than $3 million. The number of employees had reached 1,700, the number of operating restaurants had risen to 25, and the ambitious entrepreneurs were pursuing a strategy to open a new unit each month. Although the owners were contemplating a public stock offering in order to continue their expansion program, they decided to accept PepsiCo's offer due to the generous terms of the agreement. Flax and Rosenfield realized that PepsiCo management wanted to

learn how to run an operation like theirs, and they were more than willing to teach people at PepsiCo what they knew in exchange for limitless expansion capital. Each new restaurant was costing nearly $1 million to open over an eight-month period, and Flax and Rosenfield did not want to interrupt their aggressive expansion plans.

California Pizza Kitchen was opening restaurants in upscale office buildings and pricey malls and as freestanding units in affluent areas. The company's restaurants were primarily located throughout the greater Los Angeles metropolitan area, but new units were opened on a monthly basis in major cities across the country, including Chicago and Atlanta. Except for two franchises in Las Vegas, and a limited partnership in Chicago, all of the restaurant units were owned by Flax and Rosenfield. Delighted by the chain's success, PepsiCo management was especially intrigued by the part played by the waitstaff in California Pizza Kitchen's achievement. When PepsiCo officials visited a number of California Pizza Kitchen units located in various areas of the country, they discovered an inordinately friendly and helpful staff of waiters and waitresses at each restaurant. Impressed by the process of selection, training, and retainment of employees, PepsiCo was determined to learn how to apply these techniques to its own restaurant operations.

Continuing Growth in the 1990s

The partnership between PepsiCo and California Pizza Kitchen flourished from the beginning. By the end of 1993, Flax and Rosenfield were operating 35 restaurants across the country and were planning an ambitious expansion drive of 50 new units per year in both 1994 and 1995. In 1993 the restaurant industry honored Flax and Rosenfield with the Golden Chain award, one of the plaudits that the partners found most satisfying out of all the accolades they received.

As their successes multiplied, Flax and Rosenfield began to devote even more attention than before to the development of personnel, which included more than 3,000 workers, 160 of whom were kitchen managers and general managers. Not only were the two men driving forces behind better service, but through their constant concern with internal coaching and promotion, they enhanced their employees' career opportunities. A former waiter and cook who had joined the company when it was only one month old was promoted to vice-president of back-of-the-house operations; a unit-level assistant manager became front-of-the-house operations vice-president; and the company's first waitress in the Beverly Hills restaurant became vice-president of training. The former lawyers also worked to improve the pay scale and benefits of their workers, securing, for example, a $2.3 million deal in special compensation and bonuses for company executives through negotiations with parent PepsiCo.

Throughout all of these developments, the focus of California Pizza Kitchen remained the food. The company offered 29 different pizza flavors, including duck sausage pizza, Thai chicken pizza, two-sausage pizza, tuna-melt pizza, mixed grill vegetarian pizza, goat cheese pizza, and eggplant Parmesan pizza, with prices ranging from $6.95 to $11.95.

The year 1994 was one of the best to date for the company. California Pizza Kitchen added 28 restaurants to reach a total of 70 units operating in 15 states and the District of Columbia. Sales also shot up to the $120 million milepost, a dramatic increase of 60 percent over the previous year. Surprisingly, only 40 percent of revenues were coming from the company's pizza menu: other items such as corn soup and barbecue chopped chicken salad were selling just as well. Per unit annual sales were still hovering around the $3 million mark.

By the beginning of 1995, California Pizza Kitchen was operating 78 restaurants in 18 states and in the District of Columbia. New food toppings and combinations were continually being added to the pizza menu, as were a host of new items such as Chicken Tequila Fettucine and Tuscan Bean Soup. Although Larry Flax and Richard Rosenfield remained firmly in control of the day-to-day operations of the restaurant chain, new management personnel from PepsiCo were becoming more and more an integral part of the company's decision-making process.

Changes in the Late 1990s and Beyond

Changes were on the horizon for California Pizza Kitchen as it entered the late 1990s. After spending nearly $100 million to expand the restaurant chain, PepsiCo shifted its business strategy and decided to jettison its restaurant holdings. As such, the company agreed to sell its interest in California Pizza Kitchen to venture capital firm Bruckmann, Rosser, Sherrill & Co. in 1997. Flax and Rosenfield retained a 25 percent interest in the company and Frederick Hipp was brought in to oversee daily operations as CEO.

California Pizza Kitchen returned to profitability in 1998 and also partnered with Kraft Foods Inc. to sell a line of frozen pizzas in grocery stores. During 2000 the company went public, raising $72.5 million in its initial public offering (IPO). The money was used to pay off debt and buy back preferred stock.

After the IPO, California Pizza Kitchen embarked on an aggressive growth strategy with Hipp at the helm. During 2003, 22 restaurants were opened. Some of the company's new locations, however, failed to meet profit expectations. As a result, the firm took cost-cutting measures that included shuttering its quality assurance department, stopping new menu rollouts, and raising the criteria for performance bonuses for managers. The company's founders, Flax and Rosenfield, were disenchanted with California Pizza Kitchen's direction and immediately set plans in motion to regain control of the company. Sure enough,

Hipp left his post in 2003, leaving Flax and Rosenfield positioned to restructure California Pizza Kitchen.

A cornerstone in the co-CEOs' strategy was to slow growth by making sure new restaurants were opened in desirable and profitable locations. During 2004, five new California Pizza Kitchens were opened. With granite counters, marble floors, flagstone walls, and wood tables, the company's new restaurant in the Irvine Spectrum Center in California showcased its look for the future. The new design was tailored to appeal to an older crowd—diners who would order cocktails with dinner. Flax and Rosenfield hoped that increased alcohol sales would bolster profits. They also returned the company's focus to its R.O.C.K. philosophy, which stood for respect, opportunity, communication, and kindness. This philosophy—a mantra the founders felt was ignored during previous management—guided its relationship with California Pizza Kitchen employees, customers, suppliers, and shareholders.

During 2004, comparable store sales increased by 8 percent, while revenues grew by 17.4 percent over the previous year. Earnings per share increased threefold over 2003 figures, a sure sign that California Pizza Kitchen was headed in the right direction. The company celebrated its 20th anniversary in 2005 and Flax and Rosenfield were confident that California Pizza Kitchen would continue to prosper in the years to come.

Principal Competitors

Brinker International Inc.; The Cheesecake Factory Incorporated; P.F. Chang's China Bistro Inc.

Further Reading

Albright, William, ''Everybody's Hot to Get in This Kitchen,'' *Houston Post,* December 9, 1994, p. 17.
Barret, Amy, ''Detergents, Aisle 2, Pizza Hut, Aisle 5,'' *Business Week,* June 7, 1993, pp. 88–89.
——, ''Pepsi Is Going After the Upper Crust,'' *Business Week,* June 7, 1993, p. 90.
''The Best of 1991,'' *Business Week,* January 13, 1992, p. 123.
Britt, Russ, ''California Pizza Kitchen Sells Slice,'' *Daily News,* May 21, 1992, p. 12.
''California Dreamin','' *Restaurants & Institutions,* April 1985, p. 27.
''CPK Gets Hipp Replacements,'' *Restaurant Business,* August 15, 2003.
Faust, Fred, ''Chain's Winning Strategy: Top Pizza with Americans' Favorites,'' *St. Louis Dispatch,* August 26, 1991, pp. 1–4.
Howard, Theresa, ''PepsiCo Acquires 50% of California Pizza Kitchen,'' *Nation's Restaurant News,* June 1, 1992, pp. 1–2.
Littlefield, Kinney, ''Pretty Is Part of Pizza Picture at New Takeout Eatery in Irvine,'' *Orange County Register,* May 28, 1993, p. 6.
Manley, Victoria, ''California Pizza Kitchen Opens in Monterey,'' *Monterey Country Herald,* January 25, 2005.
Martin, Richard, ''Larry Flax and Rick Rosenfield: Courting a New Success,'' *Nation's Restaurant News,* September 20, 1993, p. 18.
McCarthy, Michael J., ''PepsiCo Buys Its First Slice of Fancy Pizza,'' *Wall Street Journal,* May 21, 1992, p. B1(E).
Montgomery, Tiffany, ''Pizza Gets Redesigned,'' *Orange County Register,* August 1, 2004.
Morris, Kathleen, ''How to Have Your Pie and Eat It Too,'' *Business Week,* November 16, 1998.

—Thomas Derdak
—update: Christina M. Stansell

Carmike Cinemas, Inc.

1301 First Avenue
Columbus, Georgia 31901-2109
U.S.A.
Telephone: (706) 576-3400
Fax: (706) 576-2812
Web site: http://www.carmike.com

Public Company
Incorporated: 1982
Employees: 7,821
Sales: $494.5 million (2004)
Stock Exchanges: NASDAQ
Ticker Symbol: CKEC
NAIC: 512131 Motion Picture Theaters (except Drive-Ins)

Carmike Cinemas, Inc., is one of the largest movie theater chains by number of screens and theaters operated in the United States. The company operates 2,450 motion picture screens in 310 theaters in 37 states. During 2004, more than 63 million customers watched a movie on a Carmike screen. The company's theaters are located mainly in smaller cities, where they are frequently the only movie venues in town. In fact, more than 80 percent of its theaters are found in cities with populations fewer than 100,000. Aggressive expansion in the movie industry during the 1990s eventually led to problems for Carmike and its competitors. In August 2000, the company filed for Chapter 11 bankruptcy. It completed its reorganization in 2002 and has begun expanding slowly. In 2005, Carmike purchased George Kerasotes Corporation (GKC Theatres) in a $66 million deal.

Getting Started in 1982

Carmike's swift rise to prominence among movie exhibitors was the work of the Patrick family, a clan with a history in the theater business. Company Chairman Carl Patrick, Sr., was an executive with Martin Theaters, a Columbus, Georgia-based chain owned by another family. In 1969 Martin was purchased by Atlanta tycoon J.B. Fuqua, and it became part of Fuqua Industries. Although Patrick initially wanted his two sons, Mi-

chael and Carl, Jr., to stay away from the movie theater industry, Michael had other ideas.

While still a student at Georgia State University, Michael Patrick worked at the Rialto Theater in Atlanta, taking tickets and making popcorn. Shortly after that he accepted a job with Martin. Eventually, Carl, Sr., became president of Fuqua Industries, while Michael worked his way up to head of the company's movie theater division. When Fuqua decided to shed the division in 1982, the father and son team took hold of the theater chain in a leveraged management buyout. They then named the new company Carmike, a combination of the first names of brothers Carl, Jr. (who became a director, but remained uninvolved in company operations) and Michael.

With Carl, Sr., as chairman and chief executive, and Michael running the company's operations as president, Carmike embarked on a program of expansion at a time when many theater chains were holding back, fearful that movie-going was giving way to home video and cable television. In 1983 Carmike acquired Video Independent Theatres, Inc., adding 85 screens to the 265-screen base with which it had emerged from the Martin buyout. The company grew by building new theaters as well, adding 27 screens in 1982 and 18 in 1983 through its own construction projects. Carmike's strategy was clear from the outset. Patrick sought out smaller cities that he believed were underserved by movie theaters. Upon finding a good candidate, he then either purchased and expanded the existing theater or built a new multi-screen facility, often adjacent to the local mall. Using this method, Carmike expanded quickly throughout the South.

Carmike's management has credited a great deal of the company's success to I.Q. Zero, its unique computer system. Early on, Patrick realized that the small markets in which he was operating would not allow him much slack in controlling operating costs. To address this problem, he commissioned some Columbus, Georgia, friends to create a hardware and software package that would allow Carmike management to monitor the expenses and revenue of each Carmike theater to the most minute detail. The result was I.Q. Zero, a system unlike any other that existed in the industry. At the end of each business day, I.Q. Zero sent box office, concessions, and other types of information to company headquarters in Columbus. Using I.Q.

Zero, the company could access sales figures for a particular size of a particular brand of candy at one theater in Tennessee with the touch of a button. I.Q. Zero was also capable of alerting theater managers when their sales per person ratio has fallen below acceptable levels as determined by top management. By providing this kind of information, I.Q. Zero helped Carmike keep a tight rein on costs by substituting technology for management personnel wherever possible.

Growth Continuing in the Mid-1980s

The company's growth spurt continued unchecked through the middle of the 1980s. Although no existing theater chains were acquired in 1984 or 1985, Carmike built 55 new screens of its own during those two years. The year 1986 was especially eventful for Carmike. That year, the company acquired Essantee Theatres, Inc., adding 209 screens to its growing empire. In addition, 54 new screens were constructed. The Patricks took Carmike public in October 1986, with an initial over-the-counter stock offering, although the Patrick family retained about three-fourths of the company's voting stock. In the mid-1990s, the family held roughly 59 percent of the company's stock.

The company also met with some challenges, however, in 1986. Like many of its competitors, Carmike split markets in order to keep the upper hand in negotiations with movie studios for the rights to show new pictures. When this practice was ultimately deemed illegal, Carmike ended up paying a $325,000 fine for an antitrust violation. In spite of the scrutiny of regulators, Carmike carried on with its strategy of finding smaller-sized cities in which it could have a virtual monopoly on first run movies; the company was able to attain that status in some 60 percent of the markets in which it operated. The other key element in Carmike's approach was to show movies with the broadest possible appeal, carefully avoiding anything that could be construed as an art film.

By 1987 Carmike was earning $3 million on revenue of $84 million. The company continued to add screens by the dozen, and by 1988 the chain consisted of 670 screens in 216 movie theaters in 135 cities, still mostly located in the South, where it had become the biggest movie exhibitor in the region. Nationally, Carmike was fifth largest in terms of number of screens by this time. While the four theater chains that remained larger—General Cinema, United Artists Theatre Circuit, Cineplex Odeon, and AMC Entertainment—continued to butt heads with each other over the movie-going dollars generated by America's major population centers, Carmike sailed along by itself, opening multiscreen complexes in smaller markets, of which there seemed to be an endless supply.

Carmike brought another existing chain, the 116-screen Consolidated Theaters, Inc., into the fold in 1989, while adding another 35 screens of its own construction. Patrick also took his first vacation since launching the company. The company contin-

ued to prosper, with revenues approaching the $100 million mark, by bringing Hollywood's biggest, most mainstream movies into the sleepy towns of middle America. Because it maintained monopoly or near-monopoly positions in most of its markets, Carmike was able to negotiate better rates from movie distributors than could many of its competitors. Patrick was in a position, according to the *Wall Street Journal*'s Anita Sharpe, to tell Hollywood, ''Either you play Carmike Cinemas or Blockbuster Video.'' The company found savings in other areas as well. Its small town costs for constructing new theaters ran less than half of what such projects cost in prime suburban locations. Although ticket prices were lower at Carmike Cinemas than in big market theaters, Carmike's high-tech systems allowed it to expand the chain without adding large numbers of home office employees.

Gaining Market Share in the 1990s

As the 1990s began, Carmike's approach still ran contrary to that of its major competitors: While they were trying to become ''leaner and meaner,'' Carmike was still looking for new turf. Consequently, the 154 existing screens the company acquired in 1990 came from two of its biggest rivals, Cineplex Odeon and United Artists. On top of that, 24 new screens were constructed. With nearly 1,000 total screens in about 175 different markets, Carmike was established as a major force in the movie theater industry. Meanwhile, Hollywood studios were emphasizing the kinds of films that Carmike's customers favored—action movies featuring big-name stars. The Rambo-type movies went over especially well at the many Carmike theaters located near military facilities.

Over the next couple of years, Carmike picked up additional screens cast off by the likes of American Multi Cinema (AMC). Its biggest single leap in size came in 1991 with the addition of 353 screens in the form of a joint venture with Excellence Theaters. Carmike bought out its partners in that project two years later. By 1992 the company was operating 1,400 movie screens—twice the number it had in its possession only three years earlier—and posting revenues of $172 million. After buying out its joint venture partners in the Westwynn Theatres chain (formerly called Excellence) in 1993, Carmike was probably the third largest movie chain in the country, trailing only United Artists and AMC. The company also absorbed Manos Enterprises, a chain with 80 movie screens. That year, the company's revenue jumped to $242 million. As the chain continued to expand, Patrick and his team found ways to wring even more savings out of the I.Q. Zero system. The system took over yet more tasks formerly performed by humans, allowing management to reduce corporate overhead costs to a mere 2.5 percent of operating revenues, down from the 4 percent level the company had maintained for several years.

By the middle of 1993, Carmike had established a presence in 23 states in the South, Southwest, and Midwest. The company's 388 theaters contained a total of 1,560 screens. Again in 1994, Carmike picked up screens from other chains, built theaters of its own, and had a record year in just about every category. During 1994 the company acquired 178 screens from Cinema World, bought another 48 screens from General Cinema, and built five new complexes holding 43 screens. Carmike also added 15 new screens to complexes already in operation. Part of the financing for all of this growth came from a public

Key Dates:

1982: Carl Patrick, Sr., and his son, Michael Patrick, acquire Martin Theaters in a leveraged buyout; the company is renamed Carmike.
1983: Carmike acquires Video Independent Theatres Inc.
1986: Essantee Theatres Inc. is acquired; Carmike goes public.
1989: The company acquires Consolidated Theaters Inc.
1991: A joint venture with Excellence Theaters leads to the addition of 353 screens.
1995: By now, the company has 2,223 screens in its empire, less than 100 screens fewer than the number operated by United Artists.
2000: Carmike files for Chapter 11 bankruptcy.
2002: The company emerges from Chapter 11.
2005: GKC Theatres is acquired.

offering of $58 million worth of newly issued common stock, after which the Patricks still held the majority of voting interest in the company.

Buoyed by its five new acquisitions between the beginning of 1994 and the middle of 1995, Carmike narrowed the size gap between itself and industry leader United Artists considerably. By July 1995, the company had 2,223 screens in its empire, less than 100 screens fewer than the number operated by United Artists.

Meanwhile, Carmike's success in getting middle America to come to the movies made Patrick something of a guru among Hollywood executives. Top managers at entertainment companies such as Disney, Twentieth Century Fox, and Time Warner frequently turned to Patrick for projections about how certain films would do at the box office. Mogul Ted Turner consulted Patrick before his Turner Broadcasting System bought production companies New Line Cinema and Castle Rock Entertainment. By knowing the tastes of his small-town audience, Patrick was occasionally even able to make hits out of movies that were poorly received in big cities.

Many movie industry analysts considered Carmike the best-managed theater chain in the country for several years. The company's ability to churn out profits year after year while its competitors struggled to streamline and stem their losses seemed to support this opinion. Like all theater chains, however, Carmike was at the mercy of Hollywood. If the studios do not make movies that people want to see, the exhibitors suffered along with the producers. Carmike had clearly shown, though, that it was among the best at bringing in customers, regardless of the competition posed by VCRs, cable television, and high school football, and in spite of Hollywood's occasional inability to supply quality products. As long as people in small towns continue going to the movies, Carmike planned to build and buy theaters to serve that market.

Overcoming Challenges in the Late 1990s and Beyond

Expansion continued for Carmike during the latter half of the 1990s. In 1996, a vintage movie house opened its doors in

Lexington, Kentucky. Carmike partnered with Wal-Mart Stores, Inc. the following year to launch Hollywood Connection movie centers. The centers featured multiplex movie theaters, skating rinks, miniature golf, and arcades. During 1998, the company focused on upgrading and building nearly 300 screens with stadium seating.

During this time period, Carmike and its competitors aggressively pursued growth. This eventually caught up with the industry and by 2000, many companies found themselves with too many screens and not enough customers. An August 2000 *Wall Street Journal* article explained the situation, claiming, ''The rise of the so-called megaplex theaters, state-of-the-art facilities that sometimes have more than 20 screens at one location, quickly made the industry's older multiplexes obsolete. But even as theater chains scramble to close those older facilities, in many areas they have built too many of the new complexes.'' To make matters worse for Carmike, many of its large competitors were moving into the smaller markets it once dominated. During 1998 and 1999, the company posted losses of $31 million and $22 million, respectively, due in part to costs related to expansion.

As its financial position worsened, Carmike was forced to file for Chapter 11 bankruptcy protection in August 2000. During its reorganization, the company shuttered its unprofitable locations, restructured $650 million in debt, and got its financial situation back on track. Its reorganization plan was approved in January 2002.

With the bankruptcy behind it, Carmike cautiously moved forward with its growth plans. During 2004, the company opened three new theaters. It made a $66 million play for the George Kerasotes Corporation (GKC Theatres) in 2005. The deal added 30 theaters and 263 screens to its arsenal.

During 2005, weak box office sales continued to plague the industry. As a result, Carmike saw its competitors grow larger through merger activity. In June, AMC Entertainment and Loews Cineplex Entertainment announced a merger that would create a movie theater powerhouse with 450 theaters in 30 states and 13 countries. Regal Entertainment Group, a combination of Regal Cinemas, United Artists, and Edwards Theatres, remained the largest chain with 580 theaters and more than 6,600 screens in 40 states.

Carmike's strategy for the future was to develop its Carmike-plex, which featured stadium seating and digital sound. It planned to develop these theaters in markets with populations of 50,000 to 100,000—a market deemed too small for a megaplex. It also continued to rely on its I.Q. 2000 information technology system. Similar to its I.Q. Zero system, the I.Q. 2000 was used to control costs and streamline administrative functions. Although Carmike had experienced some troubles in the past, management was confident the company was positioned for success in the years to come.

Principal Subsidiaries

Wooden Nickel Pub, Inc.; Eastwynn Theatres Inc.; Military Services Inc.; Conway Theatres LLC.

Principal Competitors

AMC Entertainment Inc.; Cinemark Inc.; Regal Entertainment Group.

Further Reading

Barrett, William P., ''A Wal-Mart for the Movies,'' *Forbes,* August 22, 1988, pp. 60–61.

Blickstein, Jay, ''Small-Town Dixie Chain on Exhib Fast Track,'' *Variety,* March 30, 1992, p. 51.

''Box Office Bonanza,'' *Forbes,* March 27, 1993, p. 19.

Brach, Abby, ''Carmike Cinemas Experiences Success in Smaller Markets,'' *Columbus Ledger-Enquirer,* December 14, 1998.

Burke, Brad, ''Carmike Cinemas to Buy GKC,'' *Peoria Journal Star,* May 3, 2005.

Byrne, Harlan, ''Carmike Cinemas: Jurassic Park Could Help It Have a Dino-Mite Year,'' *Barron's,* June 28, 1993, pp. 39–40.

Clarke, Sara K., ''Movie Chain Merger Is Sign of Times,'' *Star-Ledger,* June 26, 2005.

Hawkins, Chuck, ''The Movie Mogul Who Thinks Small,'' *Business Week,* July 2, 1990, p. 37.

Levy, Harlan J., ''Tons of Screens, Not Enough Viewers,'' *New York Times,* March 11, 2001.

Marr, Merissa, ''Movie-Theater Chains Are Wary Amid Recovery,'' *Wall Street Journal,* May 17, 2004, p. C3.

''Now Playing, Carmike,'' *Forbes,* March 27, 1995, pp. 160–61.

Orwall, Bruce, ''Carmike Cinemas Files for Chapter 11 in Wake of Growth of 'Megaplex' Theaters,'' *Wall Street Journal,* August 9, 2000, p. B7.

Pendleton, Jennifer, ''Chain Sees Possibilities in Midst of Recession,'' *Variety,* March 30, 1992, p. 51.

Reingold, Jennifer, ''Carmike Cinemas: It Always Plays in Peoria,'' *Financial World,* March 14, 1995, pp. 20–22.

Sharpe, Anita, ''Last Picture Show,'' *Wall Street Journal,* July 12, 1995.

—Robert R. Jacobson
—update: Christina M. Stansell

CCC Information Services Group Inc.

World Trade Center Chicago
444 Merchandise Mart
Chicago, Illinois 60654-1005
U.S.A.
Telephone: (312) 222-4636
Toll Free: (800) 621-8070
Fax: (312) 527-2298
Web site: http://www.cccis.com

Public Company
Incorporated: 1980 as Certified Collateral Corporation
Employees: 1,120
Sales: $198.7 million (2004)
Stock Exchanges: NASDAQ
Ticker Symbol: CCCG
NAIC: 518111 Internet Service Providers

CCC Information Services Group Inc. is the publicly traded holding company for CCC Information Services Inc., a Chicago-based provider of software and services to help insurance companies, collision repair shops, and independent appraisers evaluate and settle automobile claims. The company's EZNet claims network of 350 insurance companies and 15,000 collision repair shops processes more than one million transactions each business day. CCC's signature product is 20-year-old CCC Valuescope, a system that determines the local market value of a vehicle. Additional products include CCC Pathways, a collision estimating tool used by insurers and repair shops; ClaimScope Navigator, a Web-based system that builds reports to help insurers compare their performance against competitors; and CCC Autoverse, providing insurers with data from appraisers to help them better manage the claim lifecycle.

Lawyer Founds Company in the 1970s

CCC was founded by Howard Allen Tullman, who was born in St. Louis in 1946. After earning his undergraduate degree from Northwestern University in 1967, he enrolled at Northwestern's School of Law, graduating in 1970. Following his admittance to the Illinois Bar, Tullman joined the Chicago law firm of Levy And Erens, where for the next ten years he specialized in Federal litigation. He became involved in some large class-action law cases which required him to maintain communications with thousands of people and led to the use of computerized databases. Out of this experience grew the idea to apply computer technology to the automobile claims process. In 1980, Tullman founded Certified Collateral Corporation, a partnership launched with a $300,000 investment, to provide car-valuation information to auto insurers, which used the data to set the value of losses on stolen vehicles or those involved in accidents. For decades, auto values were determined by the "blue book" and "red book" published guides. They were maintained manually, requiring adjustors to fill out spec sheets and mail them in, and the material then had to be assembled and printed. As a result, the information was far from timely. To keep its valuation system current, CCC created a massive database of car dealers' new and used inventories. Because the system, which was introduced in 1983, could be updated every few days and reflected the actual prices car dealers asked for used cars, insurance companies began to adopt the service. Moreover, many states did not allow insurance companies to share information, providing an opening for an independent database company like CCC.

In late 1983, Tullman took CCC public, raising $5 million to expand the business. Within two years, the company signed eight of the top U.S. auto insurers as customers and spread its operations to 20 states. CCC was used in 50,000 insurance claims in its first year, 100,000 in 1984, and well over 200,000 in 1985. In short order, all of the top 50 insurers in the United States became subscribers, and CCC's service was used to settle more than 80 percent of total loss claims. The *Chicago Sun-Times* in a 1985 company profile described the nature of the system: "Certified gets its blue book price information directly from dealers. In return, people who had had their cars stolen or destroyed and are looking for a certain type of used car, are referred to the dealers by Certified. Insurance companies tap into regional car price information through an automated telecommunications system. 'We constructed a circle that said we will help those insured [people] shop for a new car and we'll steer them back to the dealers. In the meantime, the dealers will

Company Perspectives:

CCC has one overriding goal: to put people back into their cars faster.

give us the price information that helps the insurance companies,' Tullman said.''

CCC also added the ability to check vehicles' 17-digit identification number (VIN), which insurance companies could use in the effort to eliminate fraud. At the time, it was estimated that about 10 percent of car insurance premiums were the result of claims filed on ''paper cars,'' vehicles reported as wrecked or stolen but which in reality did not exist. As described by the *Chicago Sun-Times,* ''In a typical fraud scheme, a person obtains a VIN number, perhaps from a junked car, and takes out policies with several companies. He later reports the car stolen and collects thousands of dollars from each insurer. 'Think about it,' Tullman said. 'How do most people buy car insurance? They pick up the phone and call their agent and he asks them for the VIN number. The agent never sees the car.' ''

Rapid Growth in the Mid-1980s

CCC grew at a rapid clip during its first few years, in 1986 reaching $13.8 million in sales, an 89.6 percent increase over 1985, and posting $2.2 million in net income, 26 percent better than the previous year. Tullman, who had other entrepreneurial interests, attempted to sell the company in 1986. Comp-U-Card International, a telephone marketer of legal services and merchandise, negotiated a $93.3 million stock transaction to acquire CCC, but the deal was eventually abandoned, reportedly due to differences in corporate cultures. The company now attempted to broaden its business and become a national clearinghouse of automobile information that not only served insurance companies but also banks, auto dealers, and possibly consumers. In keeping with this plan, the company changed its name to CCC Information Services Inc. It then completed a secondary offering of stock, underwritten by Morgan Stanley & Co., raising $15 million, the proceeds of which were earmarked to upgrade the company's infrastructure and to fund possible acquisitions.

Despite his ambitious plans for CCC, in the summer of 1987 Tullman again attempted to sell the company, this time to Fort Lauderdale-based SafeCard Services Inc., provider of credit card protection services, in a stock exchange valued at $99 million. However, this sale also fell through after American Express Co. announced that it would allow its contract with SafeCard to expire at year's end. As a result, SafeCard's stock plunged, and in a five-day span the company lost 40 percent of its market value. Because of the pending stock swap, CCC was pulled down as well, dropping approximately 30 percent in value. The acquisition was called off in October 1987 and CCC's stock began to rebound. By that time, the landscape for the company had changed in another way: for the first time in its history, CCC had to contend with serious competition in the form of AutoInfo Inc., a New York-based company that maintained a database of junkyard auto parts for insurance compa-

nies. AutoInfo aligned itself with Kelley Blue Book Co., an auto valuation publisher since 1929, to create a toll-free telephone service that provided an instant fair market valuation of a car to insurance appraisers and adjusters. Moreover, it charged about half of CCC's $29 transaction fee. In its favor, CCC was a well entrenched market leader, and AutoInfo proved in the long run to be a minor nuisance.

Tullman finally found a buyer in 1989, when David M. Phillips put together a group of investors to acquire CCC in a $60-million leveraged buyout. Phillips then took over as chairman and CEO of the company. Prior to CCC, Phillips had spent ten years at Citibank, where he ultimately served as a senior vice-president responsible for Latin American consumers businesses, including banks, life insurance companies, finance companies, and credit card firms. For his part, Tullman became involved in other startups and eventually became president of Chicago's Kendall College.

Under Phillips, CCC developed several new products during the 1990s. The company introduced EZEst in 1990, the first estimating tool in the auto industry that worked on a personal computer rather than a mainframe. Two years later, the company offered EZNet, the first system that connected insurers with repair shops. In this way, consumers would now find their claim data available to the repair shop as soon as they arrived. To continue to develop new products that would keep CCC in the forefront, Phillips needed more funding and in 1994 sold a 52-percent controlling interest to a White Plains, New York investment firm, White River Ventures Inc.

Phillips stayed on to run the now privately owned CCC, which in 1996 introduced Pathways, a suite of workflow-management products that dealt with the entire auto claims process. To raise funds for further product development, CCC was taken public once again in August 1996, raising $72 million. White River retained a significant stake, which Harvard University would inherit two years later when the school acquired the fund. For the year 1996, the company generated sales of $131 million, resulting in a net profit of $14.8 million. The next major product launch came in 1998 with the Pathways Image Library. It relied on the Internet to store and retrieve digital photos of cars used in the claims process. In this way, a mechanic in a repair shop could photograph a car and quickly send the image online to an insurer's claims office.

While CCC was building a solid reputation in the 1990s, especially with insurers, the company was not without its share of critics. Its Total Loss Valuation product was cited in a number of lawsuits filed against insurance companies by unhappy policyholders, who contended that insurers undervalued ''totaled'' vehicles. Plaintiff attorneys argued that the reason CCC was so popular with insurers was its proclivity for giving the lowest price possible for a total loss evaluation. CCC primarily based its valuation on the ''take price'' for a vehicle comparable to the one that was lost. Take Prices, according to the attorneys, excluded sales commissions and represented the lowest amount a dealer would sell a vehicle to a cash customer that day. Because CCC did not determine the settlement amount, it was not a party in the litigation. Furthermore, since insurance companies were its major customers, CCC suffered no adverse impact from the controversy.

Key Dates:

1980: Howard Tullman founds Certified Collateral Corporation.
1983: The company is taken public.
1986: The company's name is changed to CCC Information Services Inc.
1989: Tullman sells the company to a group led by David M. Philips.
1994: White Plains Ventures takes the company private.
1996: The company is taken public again.
1999: Phillips retires.
2003: Comp-Est Estimating Solutions Inc. is acquired.

New Leadership and Continued Growth: Late 1990s to Mid-2000s

After Phillips retired in April 1999, he was replaced by Githesh Ramamurthy, who had joined CCC as chief technology officer in 1992. Several years later, Ramamurthy won a patent for the company's claims processing software design. Having been a part of CCC major investment in new product development, he was eager to launch a new research and development push, this time to leverage the power of the Internet to increase the number of daily transactions from one million to ten million. He poured an estimate $100 million into new economy initiatives, as well as an expansion into Europe and a handful of business-to-business joint ventures, including one with partners Automatic Data Processing Inc. and Reynolds & Reynolds Co. to create a Web-based system for repair shops to help them find parts, arrange delivery, and then get their claims paid by insurers. In 2000, CCC launched DriveLogic, its integrated information system for Internet and wireless technology.

CCC's adoption of a new economy strategy was ill fated, however, as the Internet bubble burst and the stock market began to plummet in 2000. Previously debt free, CCC was now burdened with $60 million in debt and much of its cash flow was being consumed by its new ventures. Although sales increased to $184.6 million in 2000, the company lost $9.2 million. The following year, it lost another $30.6 million on sales of $187.9 million.

With the company on the verge of ruin, Ramamurthy was forced to take decisive steps. He withdrew from all of the new ventures, with the exception of DriveLogic, and slashed the company's 1,500 workforce almost in half. Ramamurthy also arranged for new financing of $35 million from New York-based Capricorn Holdings Inc. and Harvard. As a result of these steps, CCC was able to rebound in 2002, trimming its debt and returning to profitability, netting $22.7 million on sales of $191.9 million.

In 2003, CCC increased its repair shop customer base by acquiring Columbus, Ohio-based Comp-Est Estimating Solu-

tions Inc. from Hearst Corp. In addition to adding another 4,500 customers, CCC added additional electronic estimating and other tools used by collision repair shops. CCC also improved its position in the marketplace in 2003 by rolling out upgraded versions of CCC Pathways, CCC Autoverse, and CCC Pathways Professional Advantage. Although sales grew modestly in 2003, totaling $193.4 million, net income increased solidly to $26 million. Moreover, the company was well positioned to take advantage of an anticipated increase in information technology spending by its customers. In 2004, revenues reached $198.7 million, although net income slipped to $18.6 million. Nevertheless, CCC continued to position itself for ongoing growth. During the year, it introduced the first integrated estimating system, CCC Pathways Estimating Solution, version 4.2, which combined auditing, digital imaging, shop management, and frame-dimension applications in a single package, eliminating the need to refer to a separate CD-ROM for additional information or to buy a separate auditing tool. CCC looked to expand its reach beyond automobiles to the recreational vehicle and motorcycle industries, forging alliances with Duncan Systems, a leading player in the RV estimating data field, and Urban Publications, the leading provider of estimating services for motorcycles, ATVs, and scooters. For a start, CCC would resell its partners' products, but it was also launching an effort to incorporate them into other CCC systems. The company, as a result, looked to solidify its leading position in the claims marketplace.

Principal Subsidiaries

CCC Information Services Inc.

Principal Competitors

Applied Systems, Inc.; Automatic Data Processing, Inc.; Mitchell International, Inc.

Further Reading

Bonasia, J., ''CCC Software Hits Accelerator on Auto Insurance Process,'' *Investor's Business Daily*, November 5, 2002, p. A9.
Bremner, Brian, ''Cert. Collateral Expands Linkups,'' *Crain's Chicago Business*, May 18, 1987, p. 17.
——, ''Potent Rival Looms as Latest Threat to CCC,'' *Crain's Chicago Business*, October 12, 1987, p. 71.
''Company Fights Used-car Crime with Computers,'' *Chicago Sun-Times*, July 25, 1985, p. 94.
Gerrie, Sharon, ''Lawyers Go After Insurance Companies on Car Pricing,'' *Las Vegas Business Press*, September 13, 1999, p. 7.
Johnsson, Julie, ''Surviving the Net Wreck,'' *Crain's Chicago Business*, September 2, 2002, p. 4.
Lee, Murphy H., ''Big Contracts Fuel Car-repair Data Firm,'' *Crain's Chicago Business*, May 5, 1997, p. 20.
''Powering the Auto Claims Evolution,'' *Claims*, December 2001, p. A-4.

—Ed Dinger

Celera Genomics

45 Guide Drive
Rockville, Maryland 20850
United States
Telephone: (240) 453-3000
Toll Free: (877) 235-3721
Fax: (240) 453-4000
Web site: http://www.celera.com

Business Segment of Applera Corporation
Founded: 1998
Employees: 484
Sales: $60.1 million (2004)
NAIC: 325410 Pharmaceutical and Medicine Manufacturing; 325412 Pharmaceutical Preparation Manufacturing; 325413 In-Vitro Diagnostic Substance Manufacturing

Under the auspices of Applera Corporation, Celera Genomics is engaged primarily in the discovery and development of targeted therapeutics for cancer as well as for autoimmune and inflammatory diseases. The company also seeks to advance therapeutic antibody and selected small molecule drug programs together with other global technology leaders in the field. Celera's sister firm, Applied Biosystems, serves to market Celera's various databases, which provide data about the genomes of mice, fruit flies, bacteria, and other life forms to life sciences companies. Celera also derives revenue from subsidiary Paracel, a maker of computer hardware and software for genomic data analysis. Celera Diagnostics, its 50/50 joint venture with Applied Biosystems, focuses on the discovery, development, and commercialization of diagnostic equipment and technology.

Background of a Maverick Geneticist

One of the founders of Celera was J. Craig Venter, the maverick geneticist who sparked the famed race with the publicly-funded Human Genome Project (HGP), an international consortium of government and academic scientists in the United States and Europe, to produce the first map of the human genome. Venter grew up in Millbrae, California, a middle-class town outside of San Francisco. During the Vietnam War he was drafted into the Navy and served in the medical corps in Vietnam. After his tour of duty, Venter enrolled at San Mateo Community College and then at the University of California-San Diego with the aim of becoming a doctor. In just six years he had received a Ph.D. in physiology and pharmacology, and he then accepted a position as a junior faculty member at the State University of New York at Buffalo. Venter's academic research focused on analyzing the nature of proteins on the surface of brain cells that pick up chemical signals—neurotransmitters. He sought to understand how messages in the brain were sent and received. Opinionated and not always tactful, Venter was denied tenure in the pharmacology department but was picked up by the department of biochemistry.

Venter next relocated to Bethesda, Maryland, having accepted an appointment at the National Institutes of Health (NIH), which in the late 1980s and early 1990s was making slow progress in mapping the human genome under the leadership of James Watson, the co-founder of the double helix. As a member of the NIH's Human Genome Project, Venter's interest was piqued by the introduction of the first gene sequencing machine, which he saw as a way to speed up the identification of gene fragments dubbed "expressed sequence tags (EST)." Venter grew increasingly embittered, however, when Watson and others in NIH expressed little interest in his automated gene sequencing work.

After publishing his findings on EST in *Science* in June 1991, Venter caught the attention and funding of venture capitalist Wallace Steinberg, head of the New Jersey firm Health Care Investment Corporation. In 1992, Steinberg offered Venter an extraordinary deal; HealthCare would provide $70 million over seven years to a nonprofit institute run by Venter. In return, the new institute would turn over all proprietary commercial rights for any marketable discoveries it made to a profit-making firm formed by Steinberg. Venter also would receive 10 percent of the profitable company's stock. Venter called his new venture The Institute for Genomic Research (TIGR), recruited many of his NIH lab staff, and set up headquarters in Rockville, Maryland, a few miles north of Bethesda. Steinberg recruited William Haseltine, a leading AIDS researcher at Harvard, to lead the for-profit enterprise, which was named Human Genome Sciences (HGS). Under the terms of the arrangement, TIGR would search human tissue for expressed genes, sequence nucleotide fragments on automated machines, and compile the data onto massive databases. HGS would be given six months between the discovery of the gene fragments and their publication to analyze their functions. Venter could then publish the information, and the academic community and nonprofits could use the data for any purpose on the condition that HGS had first rights to commercialize any discoveries resulting from the data. HGS also could exercise a clause giving it another year to explore a gene's commercial promise and patent it if the gene proved medically promising before Venter could make the data public. The profits stemming from commercializing TIGR's discoveries would be funneled back to Venter's Institute. In 1995, TIGR achieved its first major success when Venter and Nobel Prize-winner Dr. Hamilton Smith mapped the genome of Haemophilus Influenzae, the bacterium that causes ear infections. The institute also mapped the H. Pylori bacterium and was working on mapping the genomes for the syphilis, cholera, and malaria bugs.

The 1998 Creation of Celera Genomics

In 1997, Steinberg died, and an increasing clash between Venter and Haseltine over research findings and competing agendas led to a split. Notorious for his aggressive approach to science and business, Haseltine aimed to form a multibillion global pharmaceutical company. He had also had been exercising the extension clause on numerous sequences, permitting little data out of TIGR to enter the public realm. Venter felt caught between being vilified by academics for withholding data and Haseltine's demands to withhold even more. Believing he was betrayed into serving HGS's sole commercial interests, Venter looked for a way out. In July 1997, HGS and TIGR issued simultaneous press releases that the two agreed to dissolve their partnership. To buy its freedom, TIGR gave up $38 million in funding from HGS but Venter retained the right to publish his genomics research whenever and however he wished.

In 1998, Michael Hunkapiller, developer of a new sequencing machine at Applied Biosystems (ABI), and Tony White, head of ABI's parent company, the Perkin-Elmer Corporation of Norwalk, Connecticut (later Applera Corporation), approached Venter to lead a new company. The idea was to use ABI's innovative sequencing technology that was ten times faster than existing equipment to map the complete human genome in three years, ahead of the government's 15-year $3 billion effort, at a fraction of the cost. Not wanting to repeat his experience with Haseltine, Venter demanded that the genome produced by the company be made publicly available.

Hunkapiller and White agreed on condition that the company would seek patents only on a few medically important genes. The agreement gave Venter a 5 percent stake in the new company, with TIGR receiving another 5 percent. Venter also was named president and chief scientific officer of the new company called Celera Genomics. The name of the firm was derived from the word "celerity," meaning swiftness of motion or rapidity— a definition intended to convey the speed with which Celera intended to accomplish its mission. Venter recruited most of his scientific talent from TIGR. Celera would utilize his rapid fire method known as the "random shotgun" approach, which served to sequence bits of genes that were pieced together in the end to create a map. Venter now planned to apply this method to decode the estimated 3.5 billion chemical letters of DNA that comprise human heredity by 2001. To accomplish this mission, Venter set up the world's greatest DNA sequencing factory with 300 machines developed in secret over the previous two years by Perkin-Elmer's West Coast subsidiary, Applied Biosystems.

With the cost of developing the human genome estimated at $300 million, Perkin Elmer expected a return on its investment. The question was how Celera would make a profit if it gave the genome away. Venter conceived of Celera not as a biotechnology firm but as an information company whose principal product would be a massive database of DNA centered on the human genome. Scientists, pharmaceutical companies, and others could access the fundamental sequence for free, but to probe the complete database, including data on genetic variability in humans and the genomes of other animals critical to biomedical research, would require a sliding fee. By developing and licensing genomic databases, Celera would become the definitive source of genomic information in the world, allowing for the development of new therapies, targeted diagnostics, and individualized medicine.

Challenging the Publicly-Funded Human Genome Project

From the start, Celera's ambitious plans raised suspicions among officials and scientists of the Human Genome Project (HGP) that Venter and Perkin-Elmer would try to monopolize the human code for profit, if not seize the scientific glory. Directors of the government sponsored project also worried about a cutoff of public funding if Congress believed the private sector was mapping the human genome more efficiently and at far less cost. Responding to the unexpected competition, lead scientists of the publicly-funded HGP announced they would complete the mapping of the human genome by 2003, two years ahead of schedule, and would produce a working draft by 2001 to match Celera's data.

In September 1998, Celera entered into its first significant collaboration since forming in May, agreeing to work with Paracel Inc., of Pasadena, California, to develop high resolution bioinformatics tools to analyze genomic information. Paracel's primary contribution was its GeneMatcher data analysis technology, which would assist Celera in its large-scale shotgun sequence assembly of the human genome. In the same month, Perkin-Elmer announced plans to distribute a new class of common stock to track the separate performance of its newly created Celera Genomics business unit. Perkin-Elmer believed the new stock structure would give Celera more autonomy and

---

Key Dates:

1998: Celera Genomics is founded by Dr. J. Craig Venter and the Perkin-Elmer Corporation.

2000: The *dropsophila* (fruit fly) sequence is published by Celera and Berkeley Dropsophila Genome Project; Celera announces the completion of its first draft of the human genome.

2001: Celera completes the first assembly of the mouse genome and acquires Axys Pharmaceuticals, a small molecule drug discovery company.

2002: Celera Genomics initiates new strategy for building its drug discovery and development business.

2004: Celera forges partnerships with leading drug discovery firms.

---

synergy with its Applied Biosystems venture to reach its commercial goals of developing and licensing genomic databases.

In May 1999, Perkin-Elmer shareholders approved a corporate reorganization, resulting in a name change to PE Corporation and the creation of separate securities for PE Biosystems Group and Celera Genomics Group that tracked the performance of the two business units. Celera also passed several milestones, including employing more than 300 employees, nearing the completion of laboratories and related facilities, working with Compaq Computer to establish one of the largest supercomputer centers in the world, and entering into database subscription deals with Amgen, Inc., Pharmacia & Upjohn, Inc., and Novartis Pharma, in addition to gene discovery agreements with Rhone-Poulec Rorer and Gemini Research Ltd. In September 1999, Celera also completed the sequencing phase in deciphering the genome of *dropsophila melanogaster*, the fruit fly—a model organism in biological research for more than 80 years. Because its DNA sequence and other characteristics made it the closest invertebrate research organism to humans, the sequencing of the *dropsophila* genome was anticipated to provide a valuable key to understanding the sequence of the human genome and human biology.

By November 1999, Celera was about one-third of the way toward mapping the human genome—well ahead in the race with the HGP consortium. While the publicly funded scientists questioned the accuracy of Celera's data, Venter insisted his map would be more precise than that of the consortium. Amid the acrimony, the two groups nevertheless felt pressure to collaborate to speed up the completion of the genome. Discussions between Celera and the HGP began as early as December 1998, but the international consortium—which insisted that gene discoveries should remain in the public realm—clashed with Celera's plans to acquire patents on its gene discoveries. The imbroglio between the public and private ventures first erupted publicly in March 2000 when discussions were still underway to jointly pool their data and publish results. An agreement and memorandum of understanding had been reached but eventually fell through due to pressure from American scientists and those in the United Kingdom's Wellstone Trust and Sanger Center, who charged Celera with trying to control the jointly produced genomic data. With the termination of discussions, the two sides only agreed to collaborate on a single publication date for their respective reports on the human genome.

In a surprise announcement before a U.S. House of Representatives hearing on the future of the HGP in April 2000, Venter said Celera had nearly completed the sequencing of the human code, laying claim to one of history's greatest milestones. With these words, Venter tried to declare Celera the winner in the long, closely watched race with the publicly funded consortium. The announcement caused Celera's stock to jump 19 percent in one day to $137 per share. Venter said Celera would complete an annotated map of the human genome by the end of the year, and that the company would make the genome available to researchers who wanted to use it, despite ongoing charges that the company intended to restrict access to the data. Venter, however, also defended Celera's plan to patent up to 500 genes. Soon after Venter's pronouncement, however, the HGP also claimed to be close to finishing its decoding rough draft. The private and public enterprises said they would now focus on finding where certain genes resided in the DNA sequence and what functions those genes controlled in order to produce medical treatments.

In June 2000, with the two sides putting aside their differences and racing to a draw, Celera and the public consortium held a much publicized ceremony at the White House in which they announced the simultaneous completion of a rough draft of the human genetic code. While scientists worldwide were jubilant by the news, Wall Street was less enthusiastic as the historic achievement seemed more scientific than commercial. Investors sold off shares in Celera, pushing its stock down to $109 per share. Celera's shares had been enormously volatile, ranging from a 52-week high of $256 to an abysmal low of around $7. For fiscal year 2000, Celera reported revenues of $42.7 million compared to $12.5 million for 1999. Revenue growth was attributed mainly to subscription agreements reached with major pharmaceutical companies. PE Corporation's chief executive officer Tony White—well aware of Wall Street's growing skepticism of Celera's business model as a seller of genetics data—said that Celera's primary focus would now turn to developing drugs and products around the raw information from the genome project. Once placed in sequence, scientists predicted the code would provide the key to new profitable blockbuster drugs that may cure cancer, heart disease, and other deadly diseases.

In November 2000, PE Corporation changed its name to Applera Corporation and announced the appointment of Kathy Ordonez, formerly with healthcare giant F. Hoffmann La Roche & Co., to create the molecular diagnostics business that would later become known as Celera Diagnostics. The initiative, started as part of Applied Biosystems with Celera actively participating, would seek to pursue opportunities in the rapidly evolving field of personalized medicine products and services based on the revolution in genomics research. At the same time, Celera expanded its operations by adding a protein research lab and hiring high-profile biologists to discover new proteins that could help researchers develop new drugs.

In 2001, Celera achieved more milestones in publishing its human genome paper in the premiere journal *Science*, receiving a $21 million NIH grant to sequence the rat genome, and completing the mapping of the genetic code of the mouse, the single important test organism in medical research. The company planned to make the data available only to companies and universities that subscribed to its database, rather than to all researchers. But one year later in 2002, the publicly funded international consortium led by the National Human Genome Research Institute publicized their own mouse genome map, which was made available worldwide without any restrictions. Celera also acquired Axys Pharmaceuticals of San Francisco, a biopharmaceutical company with expertise in the development of small molecule therapeutics, for $175 million as part of its strategy to transform itself into a profitable drug discovery and development business. By the end of fiscal 2001, Celera had increased revenues to $89.4 million stemming from subscription agreements with commercial and academic customers and from collaborations and service, but reported a net loss of $186.2 million due primarily to higher research and development costs.

Major Changes in the Early 2000s

In January 2002, Venter left the company, reportedly forced out by Applera Chief Executive Officer Tony White over differences about Celera's direction. Venter also had grown restless after the excitement of the genomics race faded and Celera and its corporate parent had turned their attention to drug discovery and development. In April, the company appointed Ordonez as Celera's new president. She faced the formidable task of transforming Celera from a genetic data provider into a drug company at a time when many investors had lost confidence in the firm. Its stock that once soared as high as $256 two years earlier had tumbled to little more than $14. Following her appointment, the company's stock had slipped 24 percent in one month, a vote of no confidence in Ordonez's qualifications to lead Celera's transformation after Venter's hasty departure.

Ordonez wasted little time in seeking to accelerate Celera's shift from marketing genetic data to developing drugs. In June 2002, she shed 132 employees or 16 percent of Celera's workforce from its DNA sequencing and information technology operations to realign the company. Celera also shifted its genetic information business, the Celera Discovery System, to its sister company, Applied Biosystems. The foray into drugmaking proved considerably more difficult than selling information as the company had no drugs in clinical trials and faced intense competition from existing drug companies. By January 2003, Celera's stock had plunged 58 percent in the previous 12 months. Nevertheless, the company had its advantages, including its database of the human genetic variations that scientists believed underlie disease. The company had been decoding these differences or chemical letters of the human genetic code called single-nucleotide polymorphisms (SNPs). Celera, moreover, had intellectual capital and $864 million in cash, one of the largest reserves in the biotechnology sector. This seemed to assure its survival over the long haul as it sought to develop new drugs. Analysts waged the company's immediate future on its diagnostics unit, which could earn a faster revenue stream by developing diagnostic tools for doctors and researchers. Celera also began to emphasize developing oral drugs for asthma, blood clotting, and osteoporosis, which it hoped to push through the early stages of human testing and into advance trials without relying on a major pharmaceutical company. Nevertheless, it would be years before Celera's drug candidates became eligible for Food and Drug Administration approval, a situation that explained why a company with so much cash and a trove of genetic data was finding it difficult to attract investors.

By the end of 2004, Celera's transformation into a drug development firm seemed to be maturing as it signed new deals with a number of pharmaceutical and biotechnology companies—including Abbott Laboratories, Seattle Genetics, Genentech, and General Electric—to provide potential targets for cancer drugs and new products for targeted medicine. The collaborative agreements were anticipated to help Celera's development while conserving its cash reserves of $700 million. Celera seemed to have withstood the worst of times in reinventing itself and could now look forward to making continued advancements in the drug discovery and diagnostic business.

Principal Operating Units

Celera Diagnostics (50%).

Principal Competitors

Human Genome Sciences; Incyte; ZymoGenetics.

Further Reading

Barbarao, Michael, and Terence Chea, ''Celera to Cut 132 Jobs, Refocus,'' *Washington Post*, June 12, 2002.

Bruno, Michael P., ''Human Genome Finally Translated,'' *Newsbytes*, June 26, 2000.

''Celera Genomics, Human Genome Project One Happy Family?,'' *Newsbytes*, June 20, 2000.

Chea, Terence, ''Guiding Celera's Change,'' *Washington Post*, May 9, 2002.

''Drug Target Alliance Formed,'' *Industries in Transition*, August 1999.

Gillis, Justin, ''Scientists Compile Map of Mouse Genome,'' *Washington Post*, May 7, 2002.

Jegalian, Karin, ''The Gene Factory,'' *Technology Review*, March-April 1999.

''Nice Job on the Genome. Now, Let's See Some Profits,'' *Business Week*, February 26, 2000.

''Perkin-Elmer Announces Proposed Distribution of Celera Genomics Targeted Stock,'' *Business Wire*, September 23, 1998.

Philipkoski, Kristen, ''Foes May Swim in Genome Pool,'' *Wired News*, November 16, 1999.

''Revenues, Loses Rise at Celera Genomics,'' *Newbytes*, July 29, 2000.

Roberts, Leslie, ''The Lord of the Flies,'' *U.S. News & World Report*, September 20, 1999.

''Rockville, Md.—Based Biotechnology Company Expands Operation,'' *Washington Times*, November 15, 2000.

Rosenwald, Michael S., ''Celera, Genetech Sign Cancer Drug Research Deal,'' *Washington Post*, September 29, 2004.

Seachrist, Lisa, ''Celera Completes Dropsophila Sequence; Starts Human Effort,'' *Bioworld Today*, September 10, 1999.

Shreeve, James, *The Genome War: How Craig Venter Tried to Capture the Code of Life and Save the World*, New York: Alfred A. Knopf, 2004.

Shrine, Jim, ''Race to Sequence Human Genome Continues: Celera, Paracel Team Up to Develop Bioinformatics,'' *Bioworld Today*, September 21, 1998.

Terry, Rob, ''Life after Venter,'' *Washington Post*, May 9, 2002.

Welsh, James, ''Investments—The Promise of Healthy Returns: Investors Can Score Big Profits in Biotechnology,'' *Financial Planning*, August 1, 2000.

—Bruce Montgomery

Charisma Brands LLC

25800 Commercentre Drive
Lake Forest, California 92630
U.S.A.
Telephone: (949) 595-7900
Fax: (949) 595-7913
Web site: http://www.charismabrands.com

Private Company
Incorporated: 1985 as International Beauty Supply
Employees: 300 (est.)
Sales: $20 million (2004 est.)
NAIC: 339930 Doll, Toy, and Game Manufacturing;
339931 Doll and Stuffed Toy Manufacturing; 339999
All Other Miscellaneous Manufacturing

Charisma Brands LLC sells dolls, jewelry, gifts, and collectibles under a variety of names. The firm is best known for its line of Marie Osmond collectible dolls. It also produces Magic Attic, Kewpie, and Saddy Gladdy dolls, accessories, and storybooks. The company's TCJC subsidiary markets jewelry and fashion accessories designed by Kenneth Jay Lane, Nolan Miller, Dennis Basso, and Bob Mackie. Many of Charisma's products are sold via the QVC television shopping network, while others are offered through catalogs, the Internet, and in retail stores. The firm is owned by members of management.

Origins

The roots of Charisma Brands date to 1985, when husband-and-wife entrepreneurs Louis and Tammy Knickerbocker founded a California-based firm called International Beauty Supply. The couple, who had earlier found success with Mexican restaurant chain Casa Lupita, soon began to market a home nail salon kit via cable televisions's Home Shopping Network.

After Louis Knickerbocker met plastic surgeon Michael Elam at a party, the company formed an offshoot called LaVie Cosmetics to make a face cream that the two men developed. Recruiting comedian and Elam patient Phyllis Diller as on-air spokesperson, the firm soon began to sell Creme de LaVie on the Home Shopping Network, taking orders for $997,000 worth in a single August 1988 weekend.

In 1989, another offshoot company, MLF Enterprises, was created. It would offer replicas of jewelry pieces owned by Charlie's Angels star Farrah Fawcett, who would also hawk the line on the Home Shopping Network. Not long afterward an additional division, Knickerbocker Creations, was launched as well. By 1990, the company was reportedly handling orders worth $18 million from the Home Shopping Network, which was nearly its exclusive source of revenue.

In 1990, he later alleged, Louis Knickerbocker was approached by Home Shopping Network chairman Roy Speer with a proposal that he secretly receive a 50 percent stake in Knickerbocker's businesses in exchange for arranging a $10 million line of credit. After checking with his lawyer about the propriety of such an offer, Knickerbocker declined it, which resulted in Speer banning the company's products from his network and then trying to woo away its celebrity spokespersons.

The firm soon reached a deal with rival shopping channel QVC, but Speer allegedly continued to keep track of its inner workings by paying Knickerbocker's executive vice-president to spy for him. The allegations surfaced several years later when government agencies began a probe of the Home Shopping Network's finances, which precipitated Speer's resignation as that firm's chairman and the sale of his controlling interest. Meanwhile, 1990 had also seen Knickerbocker drop Crème de LaVie face cream after co-inventor Michael Elam's medical license was revoked for malpractice and insurance fraud.

Marie Osmond Dolls Debut in 1991

In 1991, the company moved into a new product area with the introduction of Marie Osmond Fine Porcelain Collector Dolls. Doll aficionado Osmond helped design the new line, which would be sold via QVC and in stores like Toys "R" Us and JC Penney. Prices started at $25 and went as high as $6,000 for a limited-production special edition, with most selling for around $200. The first dolls debuted on QVC in November of 1991, with the company reporting sales of $1.4 million in four hours of air time. Osmond donated a portion of her proceeds

---

Key Dates:

1985: Louis and Tammy Knickerbocker found International Beauty Supply.
1991: The company begins to sell Marie Osmond Fine Porcelain Dolls via the QVC television shopping network.
1995: The firm, now known as L.L. Knickerbocker, goes public on NASDAQ.
1996: Jewelry companies are acquired.
1999: The firm is forced into bankruptcy by creditors.
2001: Brian Blosil acquires the assets of Knickerbocker; the firm becomes Marian LLC.
2004: Blosil sells the company to management; Marian's name is changed to Charisma Brands LLC.

---

to the Children's Miracle Network, a charity she helped establish in 1983.

The success of the Osmond dolls led to a similar deal the following year with former Mouseketeer and 1960s beach movie star Annette Funicello, who would sell a line of collectible bears under her name. Funicello suffered from multiple sclerosis, and part of the proceeds would fund a charity she had formed to help fight neurological diseases. Despite initial success with dolls and bears, by 1994 the company's annual sales had fallen to $7.8 million, with net earnings of $725,000.

In January 1995, Louis Knickerbocker's various businesses were merged into a single entity, the Rancho Santa Margarita, California-based L.L. Knickerbocker Company. That same month, the firm raised $4.9 million in an initial public offering (IPO) of stock on the NASDAQ Small Cap exchange. Of the 2.4 million shares extant, Louis Knickerbocker held 64 percent. The company used the funds to develop new products and to create television infomercials and a direct marketing sales campaign. At this time, the Marie Osmond doll line was the firm's biggest seller, accounting for approximately 40 percent of sales, with most of the remainder coming from Annette Funicello Collectible Bears and the ECT Ionizer, a product which purportedly removed harmful particles from indoor environments.

Following the IPO, L.L. Knickerbocker began signing a number of new licensing deals. Plans were soon announced to offer memorabilia and figurines based on the 1950s television program The Honeymooners, hair removal and skin care products, a recovery service for lost or stolen articles called Tracker, and a line of collectible angel dolls promoted by flamboyant fitness guru Richard Simmons. The firm also took a dip in the waters of the Internet, creating a joint venture with MultiMedia Magic Productions to develop "Electronic Storefronts" for on-line sales of a variety of products.

All of this activity, as well as new business from mail-order sales via advertisements in *Doll Reader* magazine, helped boost the company's stock value tenfold by mid-summer 1995, and in July the NASDAQ exchange moved it to the higher-profile National Market System. Over the summer, more new products were announced, including a series of videos called "Secrets of Modeling A-Z," which would be sold via infomercials.

With more attention directed toward the firm's once thinly traded stock, allegations began to surface that stockbroker Rafi Khan was somehow manipulating its price, and with reports of a possible Securities and Exchange Commission (SEC) investigation, it began falling. By late August, it had dropped to less than half of its recent peak, and then continued to slide.

In the fall of 1995, L.L. Knickerbocker began marketing its modeling videos via infomercials and selling the Tracker recovery service on QVC with help from actress Angie Dickinson, formerly the star of television's *Police Woman* series. The company also announced it would market a digital telephone with which users could make free long distance calls via the World Wide Web as well as a series of posters of company board member Farrah Fawcett, who had recently posed nude for Playboy magazine at the age of 48. Late in the year, L.L. Knickerbocker sold $3 million worth of new Christmas-themed Marie Osmond dolls in a single weekend on QVC, as the company announced plans to begin selling them through retail outlets like FAO Schwarz. QVC sales accounted for some 98 percent of revenues for the firm at this time.

In December 1995, a $10 million joint venture was formed with Paxson Communications to market products via informercials and through Paxson's new Shop at Home cable TV network. The first efforts included selling exercise devices endorsed by Olympian Florence Griffith Joyner and marketing Mr. Khalsa Numerology to compete with the successful Psychic Friends Network. For 1995, the firm reported sales of $13.1 million and earnings of $1.3 million.

Acquisitions and New Ventures in 1996

In March 1996, L.L. Knickerbocker entered a completely new business area by purchasing a 40 percent stake in Pure Energy Corp., a California firm that sought to produce an alternative motor fuel from industrial waste products. Pure Energy, which would be headed by Louis Knickerbocker, soon committed to invest $5.3 million in a wood-sludge conversion plant in Watertown, New York, which would also be funded by state and federal agencies and a chemical firm.

In the spring, the company expanded its offerings to jewelry through the acquisition of three companies: The Krasner Group, Inc. of Rhode Island, which sold jewelry designed by the likes of Kenneth Jay Lane and Nolan Miller on QVC, and Grant King International Co. Ltd. and S.L.S. Trading Co. Ltd., both of Thailand. The three new additions had total annual revenues of approximately $20 million.

In the summer of 1996, the firm bought a 25 percent stake in Insta-Heat Inc. and sister firm Self-Heating Container Corp. (later known as Ontro, Inc.), which had developed cans that could be heated by pressing a button on the bottom. Fall saw the addition of another Thai jewelry company, Harlyn International Co., and the signing of an agreement with country music superstar Barbara Mandrell to tout a line of jewelry on QVC. L.L. Knickerbocker also bought controlling interest in New England-based doll maker Georgetown Collection, Inc. and subsidiary Magic Attic Press for $1.68 million. The respective firms produced collectible porcelain dolls and 18-inch vinyl dolls for children that were modeled after the successful

American Girls line and sold with related storybooks and accessories.

In the summer of 1997, the company formed a joint venture with Arkenol Holdings to market alternative fuels in Asia, securing a new $20 million line of credit. Several of the company's recent ventures were now beginning to run into problems, with the Tracker service's telemarketers accused by the Federal Trade Commission of using scare tactics to sell unnecessary credit card insurance and Classy Lady hair removal devices abandoned when they did not receive Food and Drug Administration approval. The firm reported a loss of $4.4 million on sales of $68.3 million for the year.

The year 1998 saw L.L. Knickerbocker working to cut costs by consolidating its Far East offices into a single site in ShenZhen, China, and farming out Magic Attic Press book production and marketing to Millbrook Press. The company also secured $7 million in new financing from private investors, built a new silver manufacturing facility in Thailand, and took a 6.7 percent stake in Phoenix Environmental Ltd. in exchange for 2 percent of its Pure Energy holdings. The company continued to sign new licensing agreements as well, with recent additions including Disney, Universal Studios, and Kodak.

In July 1998, the SEC officially charged Rafi Khan and a partner of manipulating L.L. Knickerbocker stock five years earlier, though the company itself was not implicated. Khan agreed to cooperate with prosecutors and received a sentence of three years' probation and a five-year ban from the securities industry.

With losses continuing to mount, the company's stock price began falling steadily, ameliorated only slightly by announcements of new Internet sales efforts through Yahoo! and America Online. To help boost share value, the firm split off its holdings in the energy and self-heating container businesses by forming a new company called Knickerbocker Investments, Inc., which would be run by an independent advisory board. A short time later, another new unit, Knickerbocker WorldWide Co. was created to sell jewelry online. The company also relocated its Georgetown Collection business from Maine to California, consolidated related operations in Portland, Maine, and closed manufacturing facilities in Maine, New York, and Pennsylvania. One-quarter of the firm's 290 U.S. employees were laid off as a result of the downsizing, leaving a total of 450 worldwide. For 1998, L.L. Knickerbocker's revenues declined to $60 million and a whopping $28 million loss was reported.

Bankruptcy in 1999

With its Asian joint venture with Arkenol also recently declared a total loss, and having spent over $1 million on legal fees related to two separate lawsuits, by the summer of 1999 the company found itself in serious trouble. On August 23, as the firm's stock was coincidentally being delisted from the NASDAQ due to its low trading price, three of L.L. Knickerbocker's creditors filed a Chapter 7 petition in U.S. Bankruptcy Court seeking immediate payment of their debts. The firm began seeking a way out of liquidation, and in November it was allowed to convert from a Chapter 7 forced bankruptcy to a Chapter 11 reorganization and began negotiations with creditors. For the year, the company recorded revenues of $42.2 million and a loss of $11.2 million.

During the fall of 1999 and into early 2000, operations were streamlined by selling the unprofitable Georgetown Collection brand and discontinuing the Annette Funicello and Richard Simmons product lines. The firm also began to move away from the money-losing mail order area and toward retail sales, though QVC continued to account for nearly half of its earnings. For 2000, sales declined to $30.3 million, with a net loss of $3.4 million. The company's employee ranks had by now been whittled down to 357.

In July 2001, L.L. Knickerbocker accepted an offer of $6 million from Brian Blosil, the husband of Marie Osmond, to buy substantially all of its assets, which would form the basis of a newly formed company called Marian, LLC. Louis Knickerbocker subsequently filed a plan of liquidation with the bankruptcy court for the minimal remaining assets he held. The firm's founder later reappeared with a company called RG Global Lifestyles, Inc., that marketed dietary supplements and health and beauty aid products in Asia, as well as a device that created drinking water from air.

Now led by Marie Osmond's husband, in 2002 Marian LLC introduced new dolls like ''Butterfly Belle'' from the Adora Belle collection. The $100 doll was sold in a limited edition of 1,000. Osmond's product line also included other lines of dolls, figurines, storybooks, and accessories. Sales continued to be conducted via QVC as well as through catalogs, the Web, and retail outlets. The company was also marketing jewelry under the Kenneth Jay Lane and Nolan Miller brands via a subsidiary called TCJC.

In 2003, the Magic Attic brand was updated and relaunched for the Christmas shopping season. Five dolls, designed by Robert Tonner, were offered. The dolls came with costumes, accessories, and books. Though the 18-inch vinyl dolls had been inspired by the success of the American Girl brand, their accompanying stories focused on contemporary storylines, as opposed to the historical ones offered by the other firm. A complementary Web site was also created in which girls could enjoy games and other activities online. The dolls would be distributed via specialty retailers and priced at $74 each, slightly less than those of American Girl.

In February 2004, Brian Blosil sold a majority interest in Marian to its management, including CEO Anthony Shutts, and gave up his post as chairman. At this time, the company's name was changed to Charisma Brands LLC, after its 30-year old Rhode Island jewelry factory, Charisma Manufacturing. Marie Osmond would continue to license her doll line to the firm, which had also recently acquired licenses to make Kewpie dolls (based on Rose O'Neill's 1909 illustrations), and Saddy & Gladdy dolls (developed in 2003 by former teacher Lynn Huberman to help young children deal with emotional issues). The firm was actively developing its jewelry offerings at this time as well, with a new line of Bob Mackie-licensed items and the expansion of its existing products via the Kenneth Jay Lane Home Gift Collection and the Nolan Miller Apparel line.

After two decades pursuing diverse business interests, often under difficult circumstances, the company now known as

Charisma Brands LLC was now focused on dolls and jewelry items that were primarily marketed via the television shopping network QVC. With several established product lines and a group of experienced manager-owners at the helm, the firm had new hopes for future stability and profits.

Principal Subsidiaries

TCJC.

Principal Competitors

Roll International Corporation; Enesco Group, Inc.; The Boyds Collection, Ltd.; The Middleton Doll Company; IWI Holding Limited; Michael Anthony Jewelers, Inc.; LJ International, Inc.; American Girl LLC.

Further Reading

Barboza, David, ''Broker Runs Afoul of S.E.C. in Share Manipulation Case,'' *New York Times*, July 31, 1998, p. 2D.

Barron, Kelly, ''Celebrity-Product Maker Goes Public,'' *Orange County Register*, February 15, 1995, p. C2.

Byrnes, Nanette, ''Are Those Marie Osmond Dolls Really Worth $12 Million?,'' *Business Week*, September 4, 1995, p. 44.

''Endorser for Knickerbocker Had His Medical License Revoked,'' *Orange County Register*, August 16, 1995, p. C2.

Farnsworth, Chris, ''Knickerbocker Creditors File to Liquidate the Firm,'' *Orange County Register*, August 25, 1999, p. C2.

——, ''NASDAQ Dumps Knickerbocker,'' *Orange County Register*, August 26, 1999, p. C2.

Goldstein, Alan, ''Home Shopping Captures Jewel of an Angel,'' *St. Petersburg Times*, September 21, 1989, p. 1E.

——, ''Vendor Says Speer Wanted Secret Deal,'' *St. Petersburg Times*, June 22, 1993, p. 1E.

Greene, Jay, ''Knickerbocker Stock's 24% Dip May Mean Party's Over,'' *Orange County Register*, August 26, 1995, p. C1.

Haddock, Sharon M., ''Designing Dolls,'' *Deseret News*, September 11, 1997, p. C2.

Karkabi, Barbara, ''Made By Marie/Osmond's Porcelain Dolls Have a Fan Club All Their Own,'' *Houston Chronicle*, October 8, 1994, p. 1.

''L.L. Knickerbocker Shutting Down Porcelain-Doll Plant in Maine,'' *Dow Jones Online News*, September 28, 1998.

Lansner, Jonathan, ''Stars Alone Can't Save This Retailer,'' *Orange County Register*, April 27, 1999, p. C1.

Magnuson, Carolyn, ''Judge Asks L.L. Knickerbocker to Amend Reorg Plan,'' *Dow Jones News Service*, May 18, 2000.

O'Neal, Denise I., ''Kids' Hospitals Benefit from Osmond's 'Miracles' Doll,'' *Chicago Sun-Times*, June 3, 2005.

Orser, Dean, ''LL Knickerbocker: No Probe behind SEC, NASDAQ Queries,'' *Dow Jones News Service*, August 11, 1995.

Taylor, Cathy, ''Nudity Enters the Corporate Boardroom,'' *Orange County Register*, September 7, 1995, p. C1.

''Toy Maker Says It Will Reorganize,'' *Orange County Register*, November 16, 1999, p. C2.

—Frank Uhle

Checkers Drive-In Restaurants, Inc.

4300 West Cypress Street, Suite 600
Tampa, Florida 33607-4159
U.S.A.
Telephone: (813) 283-7000
Fax: (813) 283-7001
Web site: http://www.checkers.com

Public Company
Incorporated: 1986
Employees: 4,400
Sales: $194.25 million (2004)
Stock Exchanges: NASDAQ
Ticker Symbol: CHKR
NAIC: 722211 Limited-Service Restaurants

Checkers Drive-In Restaurants, Inc., is a major U.S. hamburger chain. Checkers, and sister brand Rally's Hamburgers, feature retro-styled, double drive-thru restaurants in the South and Midwest. In 2005, Checkers had 509 company owned or franchised restaurants under its own brand and about 364 under the name of Rally's Hamburgers. Both operated "double drive-thru" restaurants; Checkers was centered in the Southeast, while Rally's stronghold was the Midwest. With its distinctive black and white checkerboard squares surrounded by bright red and chrome, Checkers and Rally's took the fast food hamburger market by storm in the early 1990s. Quickly building hundreds of unique, vibrantly colored modular restaurants throughout the southeastern United States, their high volume double drive-through windows and low overhead allowed them to dominate the burger market, shocking the complacent Big Four (McDonald's, Burger King, Wendy's and Hardee's) and smaller regional hamburger chains. Checkers offered a simple menu with low-priced burgers and combination meals, and by 1993 the entire fast food industry was engaged in a ferocious price war with many fatalities. The consumer was the clear winner as burger chains and other fast food franchises opted to offer their own versions of "value"-priced items. The mid-1990s brought a slowdown and losses for Checkers and Rally's, and the two fumbled for new products and concepts as same-store sales slipped. Excessive growth led to a debt crisis, which was not resolved until both came under the influence of CKE Restaurants, which infused money and ideas into them and merged the two in 1999. Though the company came close to bankruptcy, it still had believers among franchisees, observers, and customers. New management restored an emphasis on the basics, initiated a popular new "You Gotta Eat" advertising campaign, and returned the company to a growth track.

Mid-1980s Birth of "The Champ"

Alabama native James E. Mattei, a successful real estate developer credited with renovating parts of downtown Mobile in the early 1980s to the tune of over $60 million, dabbled in the restaurant industry by building a few Wendy's franchises. When the restaurants didn't perform, Mattei ended up owning them and found that not only was half of the franchise's business from the drive-through window but the menu's most popular items were burger combination meals. To Mattei, the dining room, large parking lot, and extensive menu were an unnecessary drain on the restaurant. So why couldn't a pared down burger joint with an emphasis on faster service and a simple menu thrive where more cumbersome chains didn't? "That's how I ended up in this Checkers business," Mattei later told *Florida Trend* magazine in 1992.

Mattei, along with another real estate developer named Mark B. Reed, researched the hamburger market and culled ideas from several local and national chains. Six months before their first restaurant opened, a competitor named Rollo's debuted with drive-through windows on each side of a small, portable modular building in Mobile. The first Checkers (purportedly named after the ever-present Checker cabs) opened in April 1986 as a back-to-the-basics hamburger hut housed in a prefabricated modular building with no dining room or parking lot, but with two drive-throughs. Within months, Mattei and Reed opened three more Checkers, but their enthusiasm couldn't put the new chain into the black. When losses approached $20,000 per month, Mattei started looking for an additional partner. In 1987, he found Herbert G. Brown, a Florida businessman who had developed shopping centers, mobile home parks, and a drug store chain he sold to Jack Eckerd back in 1970. Brown had also been chairman of his own furniture business for nearly 40 years.

Company Perspectives:

Our mission is to operate with unstoppable passion and endless energy; to serve our guests with honesty; delivering the highest quality products for profit; with a smile on our face; while creating new opportunities for all employees and shareholders.

When Brown came on board, Reed faded into the background. Mattei sold half of Checkers to Brown, and the two expanded into Tampa, Florida. Next came nearby Clearwater, a sort of last ditch effort, since Checkers was still losing money. Remarkably, the Clearwater restaurant raked in $70,000 in its first month and $100,000 in its second. The new Checkers location and a heavily touted grand opening helped put the company on the map. Mattei and Brown also improved their product, eschewing the segment leaders' premade sandwiches for made-to-order burgers. Checkers offered a sparse menu, good food, and fast service, advertised at 30 seconds or less. The chain's signature sandwich became the ''Champ'' burger, a fully dressed quarter-pound of 100 percent ground beef for only 99 cents every day—this at a time when similar sandwiches at McDonald's and Burger King went for double Checkers' price or more. The average ticket was $3.40, and with two drive-throughs, twice the number of customers were served in half the time.

The Checkers Way: 1989–91

Checkers was different from its competitors in several key aspects in addition to its shiny 1950s art deco-styled buildings and uniquely seasoned french fries. First, every restaurant began with a prefabricated 700-square-foot, 70,000-lb. modular unit produced by Champion Modular Restaurant Company, Inc. (a wholly owned subsidiary of the company bought in bankruptcy court for $650,000), which was then transported by truck directly to the new location. The slender modular units were cheaper to produce (selling for $230,000 to franchisees), could be relocated or recycled if necessary, were up and running in under three weeks rather than months, cut down on real estate costs, and Checkers was assured of quality and consistency as each unit was identical and came complete with all equipment (appliances, fixtures, grills, and computerized sales systems) and supplies. Start-up costs for a new Checkers restaurant, less land and franchise fees (which ran around $25,000), averaged less than $440,000.

Second, Checkers installed two drive-throughs as well as a walk-up window and small patio with tables to seat about 40 at each restaurant. Customers received their food more quickly, and the added expense of a large dining room and parking lot were eliminated. Third, Checkers concentrated on a limited menu of sandwiches (burgers as well as fish and chicken sandwiches), seasoned fries, soft drinks, and milk shakes which employees quickly learned to prepare. Prices were low, preparation was easy, and Checkers maintained its brief delivery time of 30 seconds or less to consumers.

By 1989 Checkers had doubled its size from 1988 and the partners (with Mattei as CEO and Brown as chairman) ruled over an ever-growing enterprise, finishing the year with total revenues of over $8.7 million and net earnings of $71,000. The next year Checkers was still going strong but the competition was heating up with its closest competitor, the Louisville, Kentucky-based Rally's franchise. Rally's was the double drive-through segment leader yet fell on hard times in 1990, giving Checkers an opportunity to surge in the market. In December, however, Taco Bell purchased a 77-unit burger chain called Hot 'n Now to join the double drive-through fray. Hot 'n Now's calling card was a burger combo meal (burger, fries and medium drink) for only $1.17, and though the bottom-of-the-barrel pricing attracted notice, neither Checkers nor Rally's paid much attention to the upstart despite the formidable clout of Taco Bell's parent company, PepsiCo. Checkers ended 1990 with overall revenues of $25.3 million and net earnings over $1.5 million just as Rally's, under new management, readied for a comeback.

As Checkers gained prominence and drew customers away from other burger chains, analysts declared its formula a winner. Not only did Checkers save money with the Clearwater-based Champion producing its restaurant units, but cleared 10 percent or more for every modular restaurant sold to franchisees as well. Capable of producing over two dozen 14-by-28 foot buildings per month or 300-plus per year, Champion's sales brought in over $10 million or 24 percent of Checkers' overall revenue in 1991, and $1.4 million in earnings. On November 15, 1991, Checkers went public (under the ticker symbol CHKR) with shares priced at $16 each on a day when the Dow Jones fell 124 points. Nevertheless, Checkers' stock rose by 50 percent to $24.25 per share by the time the market closed, and the company realized proceeds of some $26 million. By the end of the year, Checkers had 119 restaurants (Rally's had 300), and total revenue climbed to $50.5 million with net earnings of $4 million. Despite the hoopla, a red flag was waving, as same-store sales had declined from $914,000 in 1990 to $894,000 in 1991, a little-noticed sign of trouble.

The Big Four Fight Back, 1992–93

In February 1992, Checkers promoted its first combo meal (Champ burger, small fries, and medium drink) for $2.29, followed by a chicken sandwich combo for $2.99—both a healthy 15 percent lower than most competitors' combinations. Margins improved in the first quarter, with even same-store sales rising 9.5 percent (helped by a four-point fall in food costs and the new combos), and Checkers moved full-steam ahead with expansion. Eight new restaurants opened by the end of March alone, and 32 more were slated for the rest of the year. In May, Checkers returned to Wall Street for a second stock offering, raising $36 million for additional growth. Amid a flurry of expansion, Checkers (which now had over 161 units) announced in July that it expected to bring its South Florida units from 15 to 50 by year-end. By concentrating in an already established market, Checkers hoped to keep marketing and operational costs to a minimum. Yet the downside of clustering was saturation, and when coupled with stiff competition from the Big Four and Rally's produced a considerable risk. Next came plans to build a second Champion manufacturing facility in Kentucky, Indiana, or Ohio to slash transportation costs and increase modular unit production.

Key Dates:

1985: Rally's is formed in Louisville, Kentucky.
1986: Two real estate developers launch Checkers Drive-In Restaurants in Mobile, Alabama.
1990: Revenues reach $25 million.
1991: Checkers goes public and has 85 stores in the Southeast.
1992: Revenues exceed $105 million.
1999: Checkers merges with Rally's.
2005: Checkers replaces McDonald's as official burger of NASCAR.

The company opened 106 new units in 1992 bringing the total number of Checkers to 225, or exactly half those of Rally's. In another competitive move, Rally's followed Checkers' lead and bought a modular restaurant producer, Beaman Inc., in North Carolina. Though Rally's was still the segment leader, in areas where Checkers penetrated the market first like Tampa and Orlando, Florida, and Mobile, Alabama, Checkers drove Rally's under in a relatively short time. Unfortunately, the reverse was true in areas heavily populated by Rally's, like New Orleans, where Checkers' units floundered. On average each Checkers restaurant systemwide brought in roughly $919,000 in 1992, which helped raise total revenues to just over $105.1 million and net earnings to $12.3 million for the year.

By 1993 the fast food hamburger market reached $25 billion or just over 31 percent of the total U.S. fast food market of $80 billion. The Big Four's restaurants numbered 25,000 across the country, compared to a mere 1,200 double drive-throughs units nationwide. While the Big Four had already lowered prices to compete with Checkers and Rally's, McDonald's and Burger King were also testing back-to-basics hamburger shops with double drive-throughs—the former with McDonald's Express and the latter with B.K. ExpressWay. Checkers' expansion continued with 181 new units, predominantly in the southeastern portion of the United States (as far west as Texas and easterly up to Pennsylvania), along with several developing markets in the Midwest. "Our first plan was to become a regional presence, then a national chain and in time, an international force," Brown told the *Tampa Bay Business Journal* in May. The company had certainly accomplished the regional presence and was well on its way to becoming a nationally known outfit.

By the third quarter of 1993, Checkers' revenues increased by 81 percent to $49 million and net earnings were strong at $4.1 million, a leap of 32 percent from the same period in 1992. Yet same-store sales dropped 5.3 percent systemwide from slower traffic and competition from both its own stores and others. Undeterred, Checkers continued to expand in Florida and elsewhere, including the InnerCity Foods Joint Venture Company (75 percent Checkers) with former Chicagoan La-Van Hawkins. Hawkins, who had previously owned 13 Checkers in Philadelphia and Atlanta, had recently sold them back to the company for $13 million in stock. The new joint venture began again in Philadelphia and Atlanta, with 11 Checkers restaurants in economically-depressed communities. The new stores provided 700 jobs while taking advantage of a largely untapped market. InnerCity and Checkers had plans to open as many as 35 additional units before the end of 1994.

Checkers also worked on an extensive advertising campaign to offset the gains of Burger King, McDonald's, and Wendy's, who reported strong sales from value-priced sandwiches and combo meals. Since Checkers had doubled its size annually for four straight years, all proceeds from the first and second stock offerings were depleted. Management considered a third offering, but decided instead to seek financing and utilize an existing credit line. At year-end, Checkers had opened 181 new stores for a total of 404 (227 company-operated and 177 franchised) in 20 states, including 163 restaurants located in Florida. While overall revenue for 1993 topped $189.5 million with net earnings of $15 million, the warning flags were again unfurled as the fourth quarter figures brought another decrease in same-store sales, this time to 10 percent systemwide.

Mid-1990s Debt Crisis

The dawn of 1994 found Checkers and its two chief competitors (Rally's and Hot 'n Now) faced with sagging sales, the triumph of the Big Four's value-pricing, and the successful emergence of several smaller regional burger chains. Faced with a declining and saturated marketplace, Rally's and Checkers struck a $2 million deal to eliminate direct competition by granting one another exclusive dominions in some Southern cities. Checkers bought nine Rally's in Atlanta and another nine in Miami; Rally's took over 18 Checkers units in Memphis, Raleigh, North Carolina, and Columbia, South Carolina, and three other areas. Hot 'n Now, however, no longer seemed a threat since Taco Bell "temporarily" closed some 40 restaurants in March. Also in March came the retirement of president and CEO Mattei, who was replaced by James F. White, Jr. as vice chairman and CEO. In August, Richard C. Postle, formerly of Kentucky Fried Chicken and Wendy's, joined Checkers as president and COO along with several second tier managers to help guide the company through its increasing difficulties. Brown, White, and Postle hoped to get through the transition by reducing operational costs, introducing new products, and concentrating on existing core markets.

At the end of the year, despite plans to open as many as 200 additional restaurants, the cost of too-rapid expansion and over-clustering caught up with Checkers. Faced with lawsuits by disgruntled shareholders over accounting practices, and another from franchisees who said the company blocked their plans to offer their own stock, Checkers reported revenues of $221 million and a net loss of $6.7 million, with same-store sales falling 14 percent systemwide. Segment leader Rally's suffered further losses in both 1993 ($10.1 million) and 1994 ($19.3 million). Yet a slight turnaround for Checkers had already begun with the continued success of the InnerCity Joint Venture with La-Van Hawkins and the introduction of the Monster Value Menu (featuring a myriad of food items for 99 cents), kids' meals, and a honey-grilled chicken sandwich. Rally's also tried something new, a third-pound burger called the Big Buford, and hoped the large sandwich's debut would help pull the company out of the red.

By January 1995 there were 496 Checkers restaurants (261 company-owned and operated and 235 franchises) in 23 states and the District of Columbia. Rumors swirled that the company might merge with former foe Rally's (whose stores numbered 526), seen as a natural progression by some considering both double drive-through chains still suffered same-store slumps and heightened competition from the Big Four. Instead, both chains turned to Mexican food: Rally's unveiled a cobranding marketing ploy with Green Burrito while Checkers experimented with L.A. Mex, its own in-house variety of Mexican fare. Priced from 99 cents to $2.99, L.A. Mex sold burritos, fajitas, nachos, tacos, and grilled chicken salads alongside its standard sandwiches and fries. The first Checkers/L.A. Mex prototype opened in July 1995 and immediately produced a double-digit sales increase at the location. Another 50 combination restaurants in the Tampa, St. Petersburg, and Sarasota (Florida) markets were planned by the end of January 1996. Additionally, Checkers started negotiating with another fast food chain (with a strong breakfast presence) about sharing space and menu items.

Mid-year Checkers again shuffled its top executives when Rick Postle departed and was replaced as CEO by Albert J. DiMarco, former head of the Nutri/System weight-control chain. The last four of the founders also left the board of directors, including chairman Herbert Brown. As its stock price languished, it attempted to restructure a $36 million debt (of an original $50 million borrowed) from its recent expansion. The company suspended its advertising on its way to posting a $46 million loss for 1996.

Checkers still had its believers. Even as it teetered precariously close to bankruptcy, the chain made *Success* magazine's list of best franchises to own in America. The publication appreciated its good relationship with franchisees.

New Backing and Merger in the Late 1990s

CKE Restaurants Inc. of Anaheim, California acquired most of Checkers' debt in November 1996. CKE was parent of the Carl's Jr. burger chain and Dallas-based Taco Bueno, and had recently obtained some equity in Rally's.

Albert DiMarco stepped down as CEO in December 1996 and was replaced by CKE COO Thomas Thompson. There was hope CKE could work the same magic it had used to turn around Carl's Jr. and Rally's. Part of the formula was a shift towards larger, more expensive burgers. Both Checkers and Rally's were experimenting with adding dine-in seating. Both restaurants could save on supplies by combining purchases with other CKE-affiliated companies, and by airing essentially the same television ads under their respective logos.

Former Applebee's head Jay Gillespie became Checkers CEO in November 1997 (former CEO Tom Thompson stayed as vice-chairman for a couple of years and later succeeded William P. Foley II as CEO of CKE). Previously instituted cost-control measures were beginning to take effect, he told *Nation's Restaurant News,* and same store sales were increasing. A merger of Checkers with Rally's Inc. was announced in 1997 and finally completed in August 1999. The combined independent double drive-through specialist had 900 corporate and franchises stores.

Franchise Focus for 2000 and Beyond

Daniel Dorsch succeeded Jay Gillespie as Checkers CEO in December 1999. Dorsch had a long track record as a successful franchisee with Taco Bell, KFC, and Papa John's. He vowed in the *Tampa Tribune* to bring excitement back to Checkers and Rally's, which were still losing money. He also trimmed administrative staff and sold more than 200 company-owned stores to experienced franchisees (which raised $50 million). "Franchisees are much better operators," Dorsch told *Florida.* "They have the people, passion, money and the community tie." Checkers closed the Champion Modular Restaurant unit in 2000.

The advertising was updated with the "You Gotta Eat" campaign beginning in January 2001. More successful and less controversial than some of the companies earlier efforts, it lasted for years and was cited as a significant factor in a turnaround. Checkers successfully defended the tagline against a lawsuit by New York restaurant coupon business YouGottaEat.com. Checkers also started sponsoring a number of professional and college sports teams. It eventually became the official hamburger of NASCAR in 2005, usurping McDonald's.

Dorsch recruited new managers and sweetened the incentive structure with vacations and car giveaways as the company began opening dozens of new restaurants a year at reduced franchise rates. (Many underperforming ones were shuttered.) Checkers expanded into Mexico through an alliance with Tribecca S.A. de C.V. Another franchisee opened a couple of stores in the West Bank.

Keith E. Sirois, formerly vice-president of franchise operations, succeeded Daniel Dorsch as president and CEO of Checkers in May 2003. Checkers had gotten a new chairman, Ronald Maggard, two years earlier, as William P. Foley II left that position (while retaining his role as chairman of CKE). By this time, Checkers' condition had vastly improved, even when measured by the vital same-store sales metric. Revenues were $194 million in 2004.

By 2005, Checkers had 509 company owned or franchised restaurants under its own brand, and about 364 under the Rally's name. Though a recovery seemed to be underway, the company was looking for strategies to boost its share price.

Principal Subsidiaries

CheckerCo, Inc.; Checkers of Puerto Rico, Inc.; Rally's of Ohio, Inc.

Principal Competitors

Back Yard Burgers, Inc.; Burger King Corporation; McDonald's Corporation; Sonic Corporation; Wendy's International Inc.

Further Reading

Albright, Mark, "4 Checkers Founders Leave Board," *St. Petersburg Times,* April 26, 1996, p. 1E.
——, "CEO at Checkers Resigns," *St. Petersburg Times,* December 18, 1996, p. 1E.
Barancik, Scott, "Checkers Changes Promote Efficiency," *St. Petersburg Times,* October 18, 2002.
——, "Food Fight: Web Site Says It Owns 'You Gotta Eat' Slogan," *St. Petersburg Times,* February 21, 2003, p. 1E.
Cebrzynski, Gregg, "Sales, Franchisee Approval Prompt Checkers' 'Gotta Eat' Ads," *Nation's Restaurant News,* May 31, 2004, p. 14.

''Checkers Drive-in Restaurants,'' *Barron's,* November 9, 1992, pp. 35–36.

De Lisser, Eleena, ''Fast-Food Drive-Throughs Lose Speed,'' *Wall Street Journal,* October 27, 1994, pp. 1B, 7B.

Green-Bishop, Joseph, ''Minority Business: Special Report,'' *Baltimore Business Journal,* September 16–22, 1994, pp. 29–30, 35.

Hagy, James R., ''After Fast Growth, What's the Next Move?,'' *Florida Trend,* November 1992, pp. 40–45.

Hamstra, Mark, ''CKE Crafts Merger of Checkers, Rally's: Chains Fused to Enhance Investor's $$,'' *Nation's Restaurant News,* April 7, 1997, p. 1.

Hayes, Jack, ''Drive-Thru Concepts Fight Back in Burger Price War,'' *Nation's Restaurant News,* April 3, 1995, pp. 1, 94.

——, ''Drive-Thru Players Rev Up for Test of Indoor Seating,'' *Nation's Restaurant News,* September 1, 1997, p. 3.

Howard, Theresa, ''Big 3 Shift Gears to Stay on Course,'' *Nation's Restaurant News,* April 11, 1994, pp. 1, 37, 40, 42.

——, ''Checkers 3rd-Q Net Jumps While Same-Store Sales Drop,'' *Nation's Restaurant News,* November 8, 1993, pp. 14, 101.

Hundley, Kris, ''Head of Florida-Based Fast Food Chain Makes Needed Improvements,'' *Florida,* August 3, 2000.

——, ''One Fast Fix, Coming Right Up,'' *St. Petersburg Times,* December 9, 1996, p. 10.

''In the Shop,'' *Restaurant Business,* October 10, 1995, pp. 70–76.

Keefe, Robert, ''Checkers Makes the CutFranchise-Wise, at Least,'' *St. Petersburg Times,* November 11, 1996, p. 3.

Liddle, Alan, ''Checkers Sees 1st Q Jump in Operating Income,'' *Nation's Restaurant News,* April 27, 1992, p. 14.

Martin, Richard, ''CKE Adds Checkers to Rally's Effort Fix,'' *Nation's Restaurant News,* November 25, 1996, p. 1.

Meadows, Andrew, ''Checkers Not Going Anywhere, CEO Says,'' *Tampa Tribune,* June 30, 2000, p. 1.

Mullins, Betsy, ''Fast-Moving Checkers Builds South Florida Base,'' *South Florida Business Journal,* July 6, 1992, pp. 1, 20.

Ossorio, Sonia, ''Prefabs Help Grease Burger Bottom Line,'' *Orlando Business Journal,* June 12, 1992, pp. 1, 38.

——, ''Checkers vs. Rally's for No. 1,'' *Tampa Bay Business Journal,* April 30, 1993, pp. 1, 12–13.

Peters, James, ''Hot Concepts! Checkers,'' *Nation's Restaurant News,* May 16, 2005.

——, ''Rebounding from Checkered Past, Drive-In Chain Cuts Debt,'' *Nation's Restaurant News,* September 17, 2001, p. 4.

Reinan, John, ''Checkers Names New CEO,'' *Tampa Tribune,* December 21, 1999, p. 1.

Rigsby, G.G., ''Checkers Confronts Deadline,'' *St. Petersburg Times,* August 30, 1996, p. 1E.

Sasso, Michael, ''Checkers Drive-In Restaurants Board Holds Million Stock Options,'' *Tampa Tribune,* May 19, 2005.

Smith, Katherine Snow, ''Checkers' Newest Market: The Nation's Inner Cities,'' *Tampa Bay Business,* January 21, 1994, pp. 1, 12.

——, ''Welcome to 99-Cent Land'' and ''Checkers' Midwest Modular Site to Save Money, Fuel Growth,'' *Tampa Bay Business,* September 3, 1993, pp. 1, 36, 37.

Zuber, Amy, ''Checkers Licensees Form Indy Group in Plan to Beef Up Chain,'' *Nation's Restaurant News,* April 8, 1996, p. 3.

——, ''Checkers-Rally's Merger Results in New Tactics to Boost Sagging Sales,'' *Nation's Restaurant News,* September 20, 1999, p. 1.

—Taryn Benbow-Pfalzgraf
—update: Frederick C. Ingram

Cheshire Building Society

**Cheshire House
Castle Street
Macclesfield SK11 6AF
United Kingdom
Telephone: (+44) 1625 434115
Fax: (+44) 1625 511198
Web site: http://www.cheshire.co.uk**

Private Company
Incorporated: 1870
Employees: 900
Total Assets: £4.4 billion ($7.8 billion) (2004)
NAIC: 522120 Savings Institutions

The Cheshire Building Society is one of the leading building societies in the United Kingdom and the largest building society in its core northwest England region. Based in Macclesfield, in Cheshire, the lender operates 52 branches, including its latest flagship branch opened in Manchester in 2004, as well as 13 property service branches. The Cheshire's branches typically serve the smaller towns and villages in the region and many were acquired through a string of mergers with smaller building societies during the 1970s and early 1980s. The Cheshire boasts more than 400,000 members, and total assets of £4.4 billion ($7.8 billion). That places the Cheshire in the 10th place among the United Kingdom's 63 remaining building societies. Nonetheless, the bank trails far behind the largest building society, Nationwide, with nearly 112 billion ($201 billion). In 2005, the Cheshire was said to have discussed the possibility of a merger with Derbyshire Building Society. In addition to its local branch network, the Cheshire has operated an Internet banking service, which has enabled the building society to penetrate the United Kingdom outside of its core region without the expense of establishing an expanded physical branch network. The Cheshire also operates two subsidiaries, the deposit-taking offshore vehicle Cheshire Guernsey Limited, and E-Mex Home Funding Ltd., which acquires and resells third-party mortgages. After several years of falling profits, in May 2005 the Cheshire replaced CEO Colin Whittle with Karen McCormick, who be-

came the only woman to head a U.K. building society. Under McCormick, the Cheshire has continued to affirm its intention to retain its building society status into the near future.

Origins of Building Societies in the 19th Century

Britain's industrialization stimulated a massive influx of population into the country's urban sector. The need for new housing quickly became a pressing concern, especially given the relatively low purchasing power of the average worker, to whom banks were unwilling to provide housing loans. In addition, the British financial community focus was on the London and the southeast regions. The need for home financing elsewhere in the country, particularly in the Midlands and the North, led to the development of a new type of financial tool, the mutual aid society.

The early mutual aid societies were formed by small groups of individuals from the same profession who pooled their resources in order to build houses. As each house was completed, members of the society would draw ballots to determine who would receive the house. Once all of the members had received housing, the society was disbanded. The mutual aid societies soon became known as building societies. The earliest societies were called "terminating" societies because of their temporary nature.

The earliest recorded building society in England was founded in Birmingham in 1775 and was known as Richard Ketley's. By the turn of the 19th century, a growing number of terminating societies had been established, although the movement was largely confined to the North and Midlands region. By the 1810s, the building society movement, previously operating under laws governing associations, began to attract specific legal recognition. In 1812, for example the British court ruled in favor of a building society for the first time in a claim against one of its members. The new legal basis for the building societies helped the movement grow. By 1825, the country counted more than 250 active building societies across the country.

A major milestone in the development of building societies came in 1832 with the passage of the so-called Great Reform Act. As the first piece of legislation governing voting rights in more than 150 years, the new legislation provided suffrage to

Company Perspectives:

The Cheshire sees world class quality customer service as the principal cornerstone of its success. By putting customers first, it has endeavoured to continue to provide a standard of service considered outstanding in its sector. The Board and Executive are firmly committed to maintaining growth, profitability and independence through a firmly held belief that mutuality works for the greater benefit of all its members.

property owners paying rents of at least forty shillings per year. The opportunity to gain voting rights, which shifted the balance of power in Great Britain toward the more populated urban centers, stimulated an upsurge in the number of building societies in the country.

The increase in building societies led to the passage of the first legislation specifically governing the new industry in 1836. This marked the first official recognition of building societies by the British government. As part of the legislation, building societies were required to receive certification from an overseer, later known as the Chief Registrar. Two years later, the Chief Registrar's office drafted a new series of ''Model Rules,'' applying the first standard to the industry.

By the 1840s, a number of building societies had begun to expand their conception to add savings deposit services as well. At the same time, societies began accepting deposits from members who were not seeking to build homes. Members were nevertheless able to benefit from leaving their savings with the society by receiving interest. This led to the proposal by James Henry James in 1845 for the creation of a new, ''permanent'' type of building society that remained in existence even after members had completed their homes. The first permanent building society, Metropolitan Equitable, appeared that same year. By the end of the decade, the industry began to make its first efforts at developing standards for calculating interest rates and repayment schedules. After permanent building societies had established themselves as alternative financial institutions, terminating societies still remained in business and endured into the 20th century, with the last terminating society shutting its doors in 1980.

The creation of the permanent building society took on still greater significance with the quickening industrialization, and concurrent urbanization, of England in the mid-19th century. The large population of urban workers, while low paid, was able to make up in collective wealth for the lesser financial worth of its individual members. The development of building societies with a permanent status enabled the groups to shift their model from providing direct funding for the construction of its members housing to providing loans, which were then repaid, with interest, into the common pool. The practice of balloting for loans was abandoned by many, but not all, of the new societies, since this method of attributing loans was open to abuse by gamblers.

By 1855, building societies themselves had begun to gather together into ''protection associations'' that developed lobbying strength to thwart government attempts to impose restrictive

legislation and increase taxes on the industry. In 1869, the building society movement set up a single, nationally operating protection association in London. The need for legislation was evident, however. In 1870, the British government launched an examination of the sector and passed the first Building Societies Act in 1874. By that time, the number of building societies had grown significantly. At the industry's height, more than 2,750 societies were in operation across the country. Among these was a small building society founded in Macclesfield, in Cheshire in the north of England, which, as the Cheshire Building Society, became one of the nation's oldest and largest building societies.

Merging for Scale in the 1970s

The Cheshire, like most institutions of its kind, focused on serving its local community, extending its services to outlying towns and villages in the area around Macclesfield. The 1874 legislation had placed limits on the range of services building societies were allowed to offer to its customers. For this reason, the Cheshire focused on providing mortgage and savings services.

The number of building societies began to drop off in the early years of the 20th century, in part because of mergers among the societies themselves. By 1910, there were fewer than 1,750 societies still in operation. This trend was to continue throughout the century, in large part because of pressure from further legislation and increased competition from the banking sector. The passage of the Building Societies Act of 1939 placed limits on mortgage securities available to building societies, while at the same time imposing the first in a series of mortgage rates increases. The development of new savings products by the country's banks further stiffened competition for building societies. In an effort to remain competitive, the industry entered an extended period of consolidation as the largely small-scale building societies merged together.

Building societies had also begun to raise their mortgage rates, a trend that started in 1939. This practice, along rising competition from the nation's banking sector for members' savings accounts, forced the beginnings of a shakeup in the U.K. building society market, which entered a long period of consolidation. The consolidation of the sector gathered momentum in the 1960s, after the passage of a new Building Societies Act in 1960 that placed limits on the size of loans, particularly corporate loans, made by building societies. The British government encouraged the further consolidation of the sector with the passage of an additional Building Society Act in 1962, which incorporated all previous legislation governing the sector. The result was a stream of mergers and acquisitions that continued into the 1990s.

The Cheshire Permanent Benefit Building Society, as it was then known, joined the drive toward consolidation in the late 1960s. In 1969, the society joined with a neighboring building society in Northwich to form the Cheshire and Northwich Building Society. The new group began a steady period of growth, reaching total assets of more than £28 million by 1972.

The Cheshire began seeking additional mergers throughout the 1970s. By the middle of the decade, the society added a number of other societies in the region, including the Winsford Permanent Building Society. The group's increasing strength

Key Dates:

1870: The Cheshire Permanent Benefit Building Society is founded in Macclesfield, Cheshire, England.
1969: The Cheshire merges with Northwich Building Society, becoming the Cheshire and Northwich Building Society.
1973: The Cheshire merges with the Winsford Building Society.
1980: The Cheshire merges with John Summers Building Society.
1981: Mergers with the Ashton Stamford and the Sandbach building societies are completed.
1982: The Cheshire merges with Leigh, Wigan and Accrington building societies.
1997: The Cheshire Guernsey Ltd is created.
2000: The society establishes E-Mex Home Funding Ltd.
2005: The Cheshire is rumored to have held merger talks with Derbyshire Building Society.

enabled it to boost its level of assets, which topped £60 million by 1976. By the end of the decade, the society's assets had grown to nearly £120 million. With 100,000 investing members, the society had become one of the Northwest region's three largest building societies. In recognition of its focus on the Cheshire region, the society had simplified its name to the Cheshire Building Society.

Into the early 1980s, the Cheshire continued negotiating mergers with its smaller neighbors. In 1980, for example, the Cheshire agreed to merge with the John Summers Building Society, which had been founded in 1901 to serve workers at the Summers Steel Works, later known as the Shotton Works and part of British Steel Corporation. As a result of that merger, the Cheshire not only added a branch office in Flint but also a new branch in Mold as well. In 1981, the Cheshire found two new merger partners: the Ashton Stamford and the Sandbach building societies. The latter merger gave the Cheshire its most southerly branch office, in Alsager, near Stoke on Trent.

The Cheshire largely completed its Cheshire region consolidation by 1982. In that year, the group made three significant mergers. The first was the addition of the Accrington and District Permanent Benefit Building Society. This merger also added the former operations of another Accrington building society, Accrington Victoria Permanent Benefit Building Society. The second merger of 1982 moved the Cheshire into Leigh, the result of the society's merging with Leigh Permanent. The third and final merger of the year, with Wigan Permanent Building Society, not only added a branch in Wigan but also a new branch office in Leyland as well.

Merger Candidate in the 2000s

In all, the Cheshire had completed 13 mergers through the 1980s and become the region's leading building society. During the 1990s, the society continued to build up its assets and by the early 2000s had become the United Kingdom's tenth-largest building society.

Concurrent with the Cheshire's growth, the building society sector underwent dramatic changes. The passage of a new Building Societies Act in 1986, amid sweeping changes in the legislation governing the British financial sector as a whole, had removed many of the restrictions on building societies and the financial products and services they were allowed to offer. Building societies were now also allowed to convert their status to shareholding corporations under the new legislation. The result was a further drop in the number of building societies in the United Kingdom. By the late 1990s, only 100 building societies remained, a figure that would drop to just 62 by 2005.

The Cheshire, however, remained committed to its mutual status. Nonetheless, the society responded to the changing market by developing new products and services in the late 1990s. In 1997, the company created Cheshire Guernsey Limited, a deposit-taking vehicle designed to take advantage of the liberal tax laws governing the Guernsey banking sector. In 2000, the Cheshire added a new mortgage products subsidiary, E-Mex Home Funding Ltd. That subsidiary was established in order to acquire and market mortgage products from third parties. In 2001, for example, E-Mex acquired its first £13 million package from Prudential Assurance Company. The company began making larger acquisitions toward mid-decade, such as a £90 million package from GMAC RFC in 2002 and a £144 million mortgage package in 2003.

The Cheshire remained committed to its northern regional operations. Nonetheless, it developed its own e-banking capacity, enabling it to begin offering mortgage and loan products to the rest of England for the first time. Meanwhile, the Cheshire took steps to fill a gaping hole in its branch office network when it opened a flagship office in Manchester, thus marking the society's entry into the region's largest urban market.

By 2005, the Cheshire had boosted its assets past £4.4 billion ($7.9 billion), placing it in the tenth position among the nation's top 20 building societies. Nevertheless, the Cheshire remained far behind the sector's leader, Nationwide, which had built up assets of nearly £112 billion. By mid-2005, under pressure of maintaining its competitiveness in a sector becoming increasingly international, the Cheshire was said to have begun discussions with similar-sized rival Derbyshire Building Society for a possible merger.

Principal Subsidiaries

E-Mex Home Funding Ltd.; Cheshire Guernsey Ltd.

Principal Competitors

Nationwide Building Society; Britannia Building Society; Yorkshire Building Society; Portman Building Society; Coventry Building Society; Chelsea Building Society; Skipton Building Society; Leeds & Holbeck Building Society; West Bromwich Building Society; Derbyshire Building Society.

Further Reading

''Change Is as Good as a Rest for Karen,'' *Manchester Evening News*, August 31, 2005.
''Cheshire Answers Surprise Demand for Long-term Products,'' *Financial Advisor*, July 7, 2005.

''Cheshire Becomes 20th building society in Euro-MTN market,'' *MTNWeek*, June 14, 2002, p.1.

''Cheshire Building Society,'' *What Investment*, October 2004, p. 12.

''Cheshire Chief Executive Quits,'' *Mortgage Strategy*, May 16, 2005, p. 12.

''Cheshire Fixes at 5.78% for Decade,'' *Money Marketing*, March 7, 2002, p. 24.

Clark, Lindsay, ''Net Helps Cheshire Move into South East,'' *Computer Weekly*, May 10, 2001, p. 13.

Dyson, Richard, ''Cheshire Chief Pays the Price for Tumbling Profit,'' *Daily Mail*, May 15, 2005.

——, ''Woman Takes the Helm at Ailing Lender,'' *Daily Mail*, May 22, 2005.

Prestridge, Jeff, ''Cheshire's Takeover War Alert,'' *Daily Mail*, June 26, 2005.

—M.L. Cohen

Coldwater Creek

Coldwater Creek Inc.

One Coldwater Creek Drive
Sandpoint, Idaho 83864
U.S.A.
Telephone: (208) 263-2266
Toll Free: (800) 262-0040
Fax: (208) 265-7108
Web site: http://www.coldwatercreek.com

Public Company
Incorporated: 1988
Employees: 5,402
Sales: $590.31 million (2004)
Stock Exchanges: NASDAQ
Ticker Symbol: CWTR
NAIC: 448120 Women's Clothing Stores; 454110
　　Electronic Shopping and Mail-Order Houses

Coldwater Creek Inc. is a U.S. marketer of apparel, gifts, jewelry, and accessories aimed at affluent women over 35. Originally a direct-mail business, the company has augmented its catalog sales with an online presence and brick-and-mortar stores. The retail shops have grown rapidly to account for half of total sales; by the end of 2004 Coldwater Creek had 114 full-line stores with plans for dozens more. The company is head-quartered in Sandpoint, Idaho and has facilities in Coeur d'Alene, Idaho and Parkersburg, West Virginia; its customer service representatives field up to 40,000 calls per day during the holidays. According to company founder Dennis Pence, great customer service for its busy, professional clientele has always been the foundation of the Coldwater Creek brand.

Yuppies Find an Outlet in the 1980s

Coldwater Creek had its source in the Hudson River. Dennis Pence had earned a philosophy degree at Antioch College in Ohio and was working in 1983 for Sony Corporation, as national marketing manager for consumer video products. Pence and his wife, Ann, who had been a copy director for Macy's California, decided to flee New York City in 1983 and start a business they could run from a pristine rural location. The site they chose was Sandpoint, in northern Idaho, population 5,000; the business was catalog sales, a competitive, crowded field that would offer 7,000 different titles by the mid-1990s.

Savings of $40,000, credit cards, and pawn shops launched the business. While Ann served as creative director, later to become chairman of the board upon the company's incorporation, Dennis headed the management side of the operation, eventually filling the roles of president and CEO. They communicated with their first clientele using a typewriter. They designed their own materials from the beginning. Early one-color catalogs were printed by the local newspaper; the first was only a brochure proffering 18 items. Print advertising rounded out their marketing media. The other necessary part of the formula was the mailing list. Initially, the couple maintained a roster of clients on hand-written 3-inch by 5-inch index cards. They concentrated their initial efforts on distinctive crafts supplied from small makers and other nature-related items, such as bird feeders and binoculars. In spite of their modest means, the Pences dedicated themselves to providing the highest levels of customer satisfaction. They put an extension cord on their telephone so they could bring it to their bedroom to fulfill the 24-hour service they advertised, Dennis Pence later told *Chain Store Age.*

The romantic appeal of their pristine location next to Lake Pend Oreille factored into the company's plan from the beginning. Another advantage of the site, once the Pences moved their operations out of their small apartment, was a motivated, loyal workforce. The isolated location proved a tough sale when recruiting skilled management talent, however. Later, when Pence considered relocating to West Virginia, the state of Utah subsidized job training and helped obtain money to develop the area's infrastructure.

Getting Colorful in the Mid-1980s

Northcountry, the company's first four-color catalog, debuted in 1985. This catalog of clothing, jewelry, and gifts would land most of the company's sales because of its broad appeal. In the mid-1990s, most items in *Northcountry* were priced between $15 and $90.

Writing and design were conducted in-house. The company maintained its own photographic studio and used outside photographers as well. Quality—in paper, printing, photography—was the watchword. Coldwater Creek commissioned original photography and artwork for the covers of its catalogs. Inside, pictures of rivers and mountains complemented photographs of the merchandise. Models were not used; the customer was not to be distracted by how the clothes would look on ideal bodies, but to relate to them directly, as if they were viewing them in a store. Color printing was done to the highest practical standard. Equally luxuriant were the purple prose captions describing the goods. The entire package was coordinated into a lushly illustrated narrative designed to take the targeted reader to a favorite place. Coldwater Creek's customers tended to be affluent, cultured female city dwellers who pined for outdoor spaces. The company made its first profit in 1986; at the time, the company had less than ten employees.

New Tools, New Lines in the 1990s

In 1991 and 1992, the company spent more than $1 million upgrading its computer system with a Hewlett-Packard minicomputer and software carefully customized to the company's requirements. The computing power was needed to process data on the millions of households that received the company's catalogs. Purchase records and demographic information were tracked; appropriate customers would be sent additional catalogs such as *Milepost Four* upon its introduction. To supplement its own data, the company rented mailing lists to identify prospects, who were started on *Northcountry,* which had the broadest variety and appeal of the Coldwater Creek catalogs. In addition to the equipment upgrades, new executive personnel were hired in 1992 to provide adequate administrative structure to the fast-growing company. In 1991, profits were $1.6 million on revenues of approximately $11 million.

High performance in customer satisfaction remained the company's focus. In 1992, the company reported a 3.5 percent merchandise return rate and minuscule abandoned call rates, as well as fulfillment accuracy and speed and call answering times that well exceeded industry standards. To provide the most knowledgeable assistance, merchandise samples were kept handy for the sales associates to answer detailed inquiries. Sales were $18.8 million in 1992.

New product lines stimulated sales in the mid-1990s. First introduced in the fall of 1993, *Spirit of the West* thrived in its niche of premium women's clothing and jewelry. As prices came down for the catalog's offerings, it proved even more successful. Beginning in 1996, a new spring edition boosted the line's sales further. From then on, the company's emphasis would be on

clothing rather than jewelry and accessories. Eventually the company would develop its own line of private-label apparel, allowing it to tailor its offerings and differentiate itself further. To win a younger audience, *Ecosong,* first mailed in fall 1994, offered lower priced gifts than *Northcountry,* most between $10 and $50. The Coldwater Creek Credit Card, also introduced in 1994, helped maintain the company's customer relationships.

Coldwater Creek continued to develop its infrastructure in the mid-1990s. From 1994 to 1996, nearly $20 million was spent to upgrade telecommunications systems (based on Northern Telecom telephone switches), data processing systems (based on the Hewlett Packard 3000 series), and distribution facilities. A new call center was built in more densely populated Coeur d'Alene, Idaho, 50 miles south of the company's original call center. The new facility provided redundancy and additional capacity for the company's considerable toll-free telephone traffic: 1.1 million phone calls in 1995 and 2.1 million in 1996. The center's 195 stations brought the company's total to 315. During the height of the 1995 holiday season, the company received about 9,000 calls per day. If one of the centers ran out of available operators, an alarm would sound and personnel at all levels would be obliged to answer calls. In addition, if either center should be rendered unavailable through natural disaster or equipment failure, calls would be forwarded to the other call center. Should both centers become inaccessible, calls could be routed to sales agents' homes. A redundant data processing system, in which orders entered at either location were automatically recorded instantaneously at both sites, also was installed at Coeur d'Alene. A total of 80 percent of orders was received through the telephone; the remaining orders were mailed or faxed.

Building on Mid-1990s Success

Coldwater Creek built a retail store in Sandpoint in 1995, converted from an entire two-story downtown shopping mall, perched atop a covered bridge. The 14,000-square-foot complex was eventually demarcated into stores for each of the catalogs as well as an ''outlet'' store. Other stores were opened a couple of years later in Seaside, Oregon and Jackson, Wyoming. Although the Pences chose Sandpoint because of its isolated location, tourist destinations were chosen at first to help raise brand awareness. Total sales were $75.9 million in 1995, producing earnings of $5.6 million.

To expand sales beyond the mostly female buyers into other members of the household, in spring 1996 Coldwater Creek introduced a men's clothing catalog, *Milepost Four,* which spurred sales. The average sale grew to $133 from $91 the previous year. *Milepost Four* would be sold off, however, in a couple of years.

In the fall of 1996, *Smithsonian Magazine* and the *New Yorker* ran advertisements supporting a national campaign to build the Coldwater Creek name, particularly to support its private-label apparel and store sales. Conversely, retail stores also helped establish the brand in the consumer's mind.

During the mid-1990s, the company's active customers increased in number from 30 to 50 percent per year. Half the sales were of apparel, the rest divided between jewelry and accessories. In 1994, sales were $43 million; in 1996 they reached

---

Key Dates:

1984: Coldwater Creek Inc. is formed; the first catalog offers 18 items.
1985: *Northcountry,* the company's core catalog, is introduced; the customer list has 2,000 names.
1992: The customer list has 700,000 names.
1993: The *Spirit* catalog is introduced.
1997: Coldwater Creek goes public on the NASDAQ.
1999: The first full-line retail store opens; online sales are launched.
2004: The company offers 3,000 items and has more than 15 million names on its customer list.

$143 million and profits amounted to $12 million. The company's vendor list had grown from only a handful of suppliers to more than 400 manufacturers. Coldwater Creek offered more than 4,200 different products through its catalogs, which reached four million mailboxes. Catalog distribution grew more than 50 percent per year from 1994 to 1996.

Going Public in 1997

Another way the company attempted to establish its name as a national brand on par with L.L. Bean was through its initial public offering (IPO) in January 1997, which raised $37.5 million. The Pences retained 75 percent ownership. Other benefits desired from the IPO were to make the company more attractive to management talent because of higher visibility and incentives such as stock options.

The company planned to heighten international efforts in 1997. Significant inroads had been established in Japan and Canada, which accounted for 10 percent of total net sales. In addition to increasing its mailings in those countries, Coldwater Creek also planned to enter the European market. Most of the company's products were made in either the United States or Canada.

Coldwater Creek's marketing efforts also began to flow into a new frontier, the Internet. Initially, the company's web site informed prospective customers about Coldwater Creek products and lore. They also could request a catalog online.

Coldwater Creek employees numbered more than 1,000 in 1997, most of which (745) were temporary. It had had fewer than 175 employees in 1993. Employment rolls swelled by as much as 300 during Christmas.

Coldwater Creek's operating figures continued to increase. From fiscal years 1995 to 1997 net sales rose from $45 million to $143 million, despite considerable increases in expenses such as paper and postage. Its unique setting, sophisticated approaches, and single-minded focus on the customer provided lessons that its well-heeled customers would be happy to see other businesses emulate.

Chain Store Age ranked Coldwater Creek the top High Performance Retailer for 1997 and 1998. "Our success has everything to do with intense customer focus," CEO Dennis Pence told the magazine. "We have never allowed ourselves to believe that we are smarter than the customer is or can anticipate what she wants. We take all our cues from her." In the late 1990s, the company had three years of 60 percent annual growth, a pace difficult to sustain.

New Channels in 1999

Coldwater Creek began a three-channel approach in 1999, just as its traditional catalog sales were losing steam in a slowdown that effected the industry as a whole. During the slowdown, the company made layoffs at its Idaho call centers while opening a new call center in Parkersburg, West Virginia. It also opened a nearby distribution center around the same time.

While maintaining the cachet of its upscale brand, Coldwater Creek would experience incredible growth online and through its new retail stores. In July 1999, the company began selling its full line—15,000 stockkeeping units—through its web site, www.coldwatercreek.com. The site proved more profitable than the catalog business after just two years. The web also proved a good way to move discontinued merchandise, and three of a dozen outlets were soon closed. Within a few years the online operation was accounting for one quarter of total sales. To enhance the online experience for the busy professional women it served, Coldwater Creek provided support via telephone, e-mail, and live chat. All of the company's agents were trained in phone and online service.

The greatest growth would come from brick-and-mortar locations, however. The company's first full-line retail store opened in November 1999. This would become Coldwater Creek's fastest growing channel.

There were some setbacks as the e-tail and retail businesses became established. An unexpected profit warning hammered Coldwater Creek's share price in early 2001, slashing its market cap from $374 million to $212 million on one cold February day. The company was well poised to outperform the rest of the economy as it slogged through the recession. During this time, founder Dennis Pence was replaced as CEO by company president Georgia Shonk-Simmons. After about a year and a half, in September 2002, Pence returned to the chief executive spot.

To help cut costs in a lean environment, the *Home* catalog and its associated web site were shut down in 2002, with the merchandise reassigned to other catalogs, mostly *Spirit of the West. Home* had featured hard goods, apparel, and jewelry. As the economy slowly improved, Coldwater Creek invested in ways to better serve its customers, opening a design studio in New York in 2004.

The company ended 2004 with 114 full-line retail stores, up from 66 in 2003 and 41 the previous year. By this time, retail sales accounted for half of Coldwater Creek's total revenues. The company also had two resort stores and 19 outlets. The company's market capitalization had risen to more than $1.1 billion from $197 million in just two years.

According to company literature, Coldwater Creek had 15 million names on its customer list, including 2.7 million active (12-month) buyers. The company's customer service reps fielded up to 40,000 calls per day during the 2004 holiday season.

Principal Competitors

Chico's FAS, Inc.; Dillard's, Inc.; The J. Jill Group, Inc.; Nordstrom, Inc.; The Talbots, Inc.

Further Reading

Case, John, "How to Launch an *Inc.* 500 Company," *Inc.,* October 1992.

——, "Looking for Jobs in All the Wrong Places," *Inc.,* March 1994.

Clark, Evan, "Coldwater Takes a Pounding," *WWD,* February 15, 2001, p. 5.

——, "Web Beats Catalog at Coldwater," *WWD,* September 22, 2000, p. 31.

Fenn, Donna, "Sooner or Later Almost Every *Inc.* 500 Company Hires an Ace Management Team. But How Soon—Or How Late?," *Inc. 500 Special Issue,* 1995.

Geranios, Nicholas K., "Catalog Company Tucked Away," *The State* (Columbia, S.C.), May 4, 1997, p. H5.

Gurchiek, Kathy, "Coldwater Creek Started in a Closet in Sandpoint, Idaho; Company Now Has 13 Million Customers," *Salt Lake Tribune,* September 14, 2003.

Miller, Paul, "Pence Retakes Coldwater Top Spot," *Catalog Age,* November 1, 2002.

Murphy, Anne, "Where the Growth Is: Hot Spots," *Inc. 500 Special Issue,* 1994.

Oberndorf, Shannon, "Coldwater Cools Off," *Catalog Age,* May 1999, p. 1.

Odell, Patricia, "Coldwater Kills Home Catalog," *Direct,* March 1, 2002, p. 11.

"Taking a Closer Look at Multimedia in Action," *Call Center,* October 1, 2001, p. 22.

Wilson, Marianne, "Coldwater Creek Is Still at the Top," *Chain Store Age,* November 1998, p. 74.

——, "Coldwater Creek Rises to the Top," *Chain Store Age,* November 1997, pp. 41 + .

—Frederick C. Ingram

Custom Chrome, Inc.

16100 Jacqueline Court
Morgan Hill, California 95037
U.S.A.
Telephone: (408) 778-0500
Fax: (408) 778-7001
Web site: http://www.customchrome.com

Wholly Owned Subsidiary of Global Motorsport Group,
Inc.
Incorporated: 1970
Employees: 180
Sales: $70 million (2004 est.)
NAIC: 336991 Motorcycle, Bicycle, and Parts
Manufacturing

Custom Chrome, Inc, is the world's largest independent supplier of aftermarket parts and accessories for Harley-Davidson motorcycles. Controlling approximately 20 percent of the aftermarket, the company is second only to Harley-Davidson itself. The more than 21,000 products offered by the company include replacement parts, custom parts, and accessories and apparel, which are distributed to dealers nationwide from warehouses in Louisville, Kentucky; Harrisburg, Pennsylvania; Visalia, California; Jacksonville, Florida; and Dallas, Texas. The company generates the majority of its revenue through the sale of its own products, ranging from transmissions to leather chaps, which are marketed under brand names such as RevTech, Premium, Dyno Power, Santee, Regency, Chrome Gear, and C.C. Raider. It also serves as a distributor of products offered by other manufacturers, such as Dunlop, Champion, Hastings, and Accel. Custom Chrome is a subsidiary of Global Motorsport Group, Inc., a holding company it created to facilitate expansion. Global Motorsport Group is owned by investment firm Stonington Partners.

Beginnings

Custom Chrome was founded in 1970 by Ignatius "Nace" Panzica, a 27-year-old mechanic who worked at a new car dealership and enjoyed racing and fixing up motorcycles. As an extension of his hobby, Panzica, along with three of his friends, opened a motorcycle accessory store in downtown San Jose, California. The new store, which they named Coast Motorcycle Accessories, was designed to meet the growing demand of the many riders they knew who customized their motorcycles with homemade parts not available on the market. The fledgling shop at that time had not yet limited itself to Harley-Davidson products but carried parts and accessories for all brands of motorcycles. The company's first order, in fact, was for Honda motorcycle bars. The most popular requests in the early days of the small shop, though, were for 16-inch rear wheels and spoke kits.

Panzica's original plans were to operate the business as a one-person shop, with the other three working only part-time, around the schedule of their full-time jobs. As vice-chairman and cofounder Ty Cruze explained to *Business Journal*, "I just started at the shop as a part-time job and then bought in as an investor. It was just through us being enthusiasts that we found we could purchase things at prices better than most dealers could . . . and it just grew." The success of the business prompted Panzica to alter his plans. Two years later, he diversified his retail store operation into wholesale parts as well, becoming a distributor as the dealer industry grew. In an attempt to reach Harley riders outside of the California region, Panzica and his friends came up with the idea that would define the company's marketing strategy for the next 25 years. Working on a kitchen table in one of their homes, they created a Custom Chrome catalog, publishing the first edition in 1973 and providing the advertising tool that made future growth possible.

Expansion in the 1970s

By 1975, Panzica's modest expectations for his one-person motorcycle parts shop had been surpassed. That year the company generated one million dollars in sales. The original store could no longer hold the inventory his growing customer base demanded, and the company leased a 5,000-square-foot warehouse down the street to make room for a wholesale operation. As the population of Harley riders (who as a group are noted for their obsession with making their bikes distinctive) continued to grow, the need for further expansion arose. In 1978, the company again moved its operations, leasing a 10,000-square-foot building nearby, its first industrial-type warehouse. Before the end of the decade, the company again doubled its size by relocating its business to a new 20,000-square-foot building in east San Jose.

As Custom Chrome entered the 1980s, it benefited from the increasing popularity of Harley-Davidson motorcycles and worked to obtain a dominant position in the market by the middle of the decade, supplying 60 to 70 percent of all aftermarket Harley parts, excluding the motorcycle company's own aftermarket production. In 1982, Custom Chrome completed its fourth move in six years, opening in a 40,000-square-foot building in Morgan Hill, California. A combination of several factors contributed to such rapid growth. First, the company skillfully cultivated its relationship with Harley-Davidson, both the primary source of its business and its chief competitor, by promoting the image of individualism, which was so much a part of the Harley mystique that appealed to the 250,000 members of the Harley Owners Group (HOG). Taking advantage of the almost fanatical desire Harley riders have to personalize their bikes as a statement of their individuality, Custom Chrome became an easily accessible source for customizing parts, supplying aftermarket shops to which the manufacturer, with a network of only about 600 dealers, could not sell. At the same time, Custom Chrome was able to offer its customers prices 10 to 15 percent lower than the competition, passing along the savings gained by manufacturing many of its parts in Taiwan. What is more, the company, which stocked parts for Harleys produced as early as 1936, was able to meet the unique needs of Harley enthusiasts who needed parts for their older bikes, ones that the manufacturer no longer carried.

Aggressive advertising also played a key role in the company's average annual sales growth during the early 1980s. Custom Chrome's marketing strategy at this time was carried out largely through its distinctive catalog, which not only provided attractive pictures of its product line but in addition supplied detailed information about the parts and offered suggestions for customizing and restoring as well. In 1982, the company's marketing department received its first Dealer's Choice "Best Catalog" award for its then 300-page publication, an award the company would receive again in 1983 and 1984.

Having emerged from the culture of Harley enthusiasts it now served, Custom Chrome knew firsthand the importance of customer service and the necessity of shipping orders as quickly and as inexpensively as possible. Accordingly, in 1985 the company introduced its "Eagle Express" freight program, enabling customers throughout the United States to receive their orders in three days by United Parcel Service (UPS) air ship-

ment while paying only UPS ground shipment prices. As the company continued to develop its extensive warehousing system through technological upgrades and new buildings, rapid delivery time continued to set the company apart from the competition and contribute to sales growth.

Harley Values Lead to Corporate Success: The Late 1980s

By 1986, Custom Chrome had developed into a 170-person company with sales in excess of $20 million. In addition, it now produced enough Harley parts to introduce a complete motorcycle kit. Although it had obviously come a long way from its origins as a small "biker hangout," it worked hard to project the unconventional image commonly associated with Harley-Davidson. Although Panzica and Cruze skillfully assembled a work force that included alumni from such companies as Hewlett-Packard Co. and Varian Associates Inc. and invested heavily in the latest computer technology to track inventory, they still ran the company with a laid-back attitude, preferring blue jeans and cowboy boots to pinstriped business suits, a strategy that managed to keep employee turnover relatively low. They decorated the walls of the corporate offices with Harley memorabilia rather than Ivy League degrees, underscoring the company's blue-collar roots and its commitment to its customers, many of whom were touring Harley-Davidson riders and Vietnam War veterans with a strong distaste for mainstream corporate values.

Maintaining this biker-friendly image and marketing strategy, however, did not prevent the company from building a state-of-the-art administration and 110,000-square-foot warehouse facility as its corporate headquarters in 1987. That same year, the company launched another first in the industry by organizing a Harley-Only Warehouse Dealer Show. Dubbed "The Greatest Show on Earth," the show was highly successful among Harley enthusiasts and vendors alike, setting the stage for what would become a mainstay in the Custom Chrome marketing strategy. Not only did the company make the show an annual event, it also began taking an active role in other consumer events for Harley-Davidson enthusiasts, such as the Black Hills Motorcycle Rally, a popular annual event held in Sturgis, South Dakota, and the annual Bike Week in Daytona, Florida. Participation in such events enabled the company to stay carefully attuned to the needs of its best customers and advertise its products at the same time.

As the decade drew to a close, business continued to prosper, especially in the eastern part of the United States. In contrast to other domestic vehicle manufacturers such as Chrysler, Ford, and General Motors, Harley-Davidson managed to boost sales and market share in the face of increasingly strong foreign competition. To keep up with the increasing demand and improve on its delivery time, the company again expanded its facilities, opening a new 85,000-square-foot building in Louisville, Kentucky, in 1988. A year later, Custom Chrome was awarded the Dealer's Choice Award for "Best Consumer Advertising" for the third time in a decade.

Although Custom Chrome benefited greatly from the success of Harley-Davidson during the 1980s, the relationship between the two companies has not been free of conflict. In 1989, the motorcycle manufacturer accused Custom Chrome of patent and trademark infringement, taking issue with its use of a brand name "Hawg," which closely resembled Harley's familiar trademark "Hog." At the same time, Custom Chrome brought a complaint against Harley-Davidson for packaging its products in a way that closely resembled the former's so-called "trade dress." A year later, the two parties settled their differences. Custom Chrome agreed to stop using the "Hawg" name by 1992, and Harley-Davidson agreed to stop using the distinctive packaging style.

Going Public and Continued Expansion in the 1990s

Although operating income continued to rise into the new decade, the company lacked the cash needed for further expansion and product research. A management-led leveraged buyout in 1989 by the Jordan Co. had resulted in the accumulation of enough debt to threaten the company's future growth. In 1991, after enduring two years of interest payments on the heavy debt load, Panzica took his 20-year-old company public to alleviate the debt burden. Having generated $39.6 million in revenues the previous year while consistently enjoying annual profit margins surpassing 40 percent for several years, the company hoped to raise enough capital to pay off the principal and accrued interest on loans and strengthen its credit line.

With its balance sheets stabilized, Custom Chrome was again ready to expand, creating the infrastructure for continued growth in the 1990s. A year after its initial public offering, the company opened a new 65,000-square-foot warehouse facility in Harrisburg, Pennsylvania. The new distribution facility made it possible for the company to provide one- to two-day delivery service for its customers in the entire New England area and on most of the East Coast.

The early 1990s proved to be years of strong growth for the company. Between 1991 and 1994, revenue jumped from $43.6

million to $74.9 million, while net income over the same period rose from a loss of $2.6 million to a profit of $6.4 million. Twice the size of its nearest independent competitor, the company enjoyed both the economies of scale and the financial strength to offer competitive prices and lead the industry in new product development at the same time. Despite such advantages, the company saw its market share decrease slightly in 1992 and 1993, primarily as a result of moves by small regional and national aftermarket competitors to undercut Custom Chrome's pricing on nonproprietary parts. In 1994, the company took several aggressive and highly publicized measures to ensure that its prices were indeed competitive. Such strategies included stamping the phrase "We Will Meet or Beat Any Printed Price" on its sales invoices and repositioning certain items within product lines in an attempt to make it easier for dealers to make comparisons with competitors' products. The intensive marketing program also stressed the company's record of superior performance and quick delivery time, qualities illustrated by three consecutive Dealer's Choice "Aftermarket Manufacturer of the Year" awards.

In October 1994, Custom Chrome was able to build upon its already strong reputation for customer service by constructing a 100,800-square-foot distribution facility in Visalia, California. The new site replaced Morgan Hill as the central distribution point for the company's markets throughout the western United States and was selected after talks with UPS confirmed that the Visalia location would improve the efficiency of Southern California deliveries, an important factor considering that the state accounted for 17 percent of the company's business. Once the company completed the monumental task of moving 13,000 part numbers to the new facility, it was able to guarantee one-day delivery to all of California and most of the western states.

As Custom Chrome entered the late 1990s, it sought to expand sales by cultivating relationships with existing customers, realizing that repeat business generated most of its revenue. In addition to bolstering its telemarketing program, the company increased its presence at motorcycle events throughout the country, transporting its newly assembled "mobile showroom," a custom-built truck and 48-foot trailer housing six Harley-Davidson motorcycles outfitted with the latest in Custom Chrome parts, to several events each year. Attendance at trade shows and events enables the company to monitor customer satisfaction and introduce the more than 300 new products it usually develops each year.

Restructuring for the 21st Century

The earnestness of Custom Chrome's desire to expand its business scope was expressed in several meaningful ways during the late 1990s. Panzica realized the company's growth was limited by its focus on serving Harley-Davidson customers, which prompted him to form a holding company to house his expansion efforts. "We know this market has walls," Panzica explained in an October 20, 1997 interview with the *Business Journal*, "so our future goals and vision is to expand into other areas of the motorcycle business." When Panzica made his remarks, he served as chief executive officer of Global Motorsport Group, Inc., a holding company formed several months earlier, in August 1997. Global became the parent company of Custom Chrome and its ancillary businesses Bad Kreuznach,

Germany-based Tom's Motorcycle Parts and Accessories; Tainan Hsien, Taiwan-based Custom Chrome Far East Ltd.; and a third company, acquired days after the formation of Global, Fort Worth, Texas-based Chrome Specialties, Inc.

Custom Chrome's closest rival after Harley-Davidson, Chrome Specialties was founded in 1984 by brothers Greg and John Kuelbs, who built the company into a $35 million-in-sales wholesale distributor by the time its was acquired by Global. Its addition to the Global family of companies added a network of 4,100 retailers worldwide that carried Chrome Specialties parts, giving the company the ability to offer aftermarket parts for Japanese-made Hondas, Yamahas, and Suzukis, Italian-made Ducatis, and British-made Triumphs.

In the wake of the Chrome Specialties acquisition, Global prepared for further expansion, but before the company could assume a greater profile in the aftermarket parts industry it attracted the attention of a corporate suitor. Golden Cycle LLC, a company formed expressively for the purpose of acquiring Global, launched a hostile takeover in March 1998. Golden Cycle, owned by the operator of a chain of retail motorcycle parts stores called Biker's Depot (a Global customer), met with stiff resistance to its offer. A series of lawsuits and countersuits dragged on for much of the year. Golden Cycle's efforts eventually were thwarted when Stonington Partners, an investment group, intervened and acquired Global, a transaction that returned Global to the private sector.

No longer a public company, but free to pursue its expansion plans, Global completed a giant step toward becoming a bigger, broader company as it entered the 21st century. In January 2000, the company acquired Motorcycle Stuff, a distributor based in Cape Girardeau, Missouri. Motorcycle Stuff boasted a diverse product line, offering parts for European and Japanese motorcycles, ATVs (All Terrain Vehicles), personal watercraft, and snowmobiles. "Motorcycle Stuff brings us national distribution and a new range of customers to involve everybody in the powersports business," Global's senior vice-president of sales and marketing said in a March 2000 interview with *Dealernews*. "We'll be adding another 5,000 dealer customers," the executive added.

As part of Global, the company it created, Custom Chrome was a distinct entity, as were the holding company's two other principal businesses, Chrome Specialties and Motorcycle Stuff. Custom Chrome's headquarter facilities were the same as Global's main offices; Chrome Specialties and Motorcycle Stuff each occupied the same quarters they had before being acquired by Global. During the first years of the 21st century, Global felt the weight of its acquisitions, strained by the debt taken on to add Chrome Specialties and Motorcycle Stuff to its operations. In October 2004, the financial pressure experienced by the company was eased somewhat when it secured a new $90 million credit facility, which was used to pay down some of its debt and strengthen its clash flow. The month also marked the first time Global combined trade shows for Custom Chrome and Motorcycle Stuff, an event held in Morgan Hill that attracted more than 2,000 people and roughly 1,200 dealerships.

As Custom Chrome and the rest of the Global businesses prepared for the future, they represented a powerful and diverse aftermarket parts organization. Custom Chrome, the catalyst of the Global empire, held sway in its niche, occupying a favorable position for the years ahead. In 2005, the company's catalog, a 1,400-page tome featuring more than 21,000 products, offered the most extensive parts selection in Custom Chrome's 35-year history. "Custom Chrome is the leader in their field," an advertising executive said in an April 4, 2005 interview with *Powersports Business*. "But there's still potential to do more and they recognize that. Overall, people now expect to be able to customize everything from music to a cup of coffee. And within the motorcycle industry, which has always valued individual expression, customization is more popular than ever, as is seen with the success of television shows and personalities entirely based on it."

Principal Subsidiaries

Custom Chrome Manufacturing, Inc.

Principal Competitors

Harley-Davidson, Inc.; Edelbrock Corporation; Hawk Corporation.

Further Reading

"Custom Chrome Names Mono Agency of Record," *Powersports Business*, April 4, 2005, p. 13.
Hayes, Mary, "Big 'Hog' Parts Seller Goes to Market," *Business Journal-San Jose*, October 14, 1991, p. 10.
Hildula, Scott, "Morgan Hill Firm Rings $20 Million in Hog Outfit Sales," *Business Journal*, October 27, 1986, pp. 1–2.
Jones, Danna M., " 'Nace' Panzica: Steers Motorcycle Parts Distributor to Public Success," *Business Journal*, August 30, 1993, p. 12.
Kontzer, Tony, "Custom Chrome Confirms Moving Local Distribution to Visalia," *Business Journal*, April 18, 1994, p. 7.
Labate, John, "Custom Chrome," *Fortune*, May 31, 1993, p. 99.
Taylor, Dennis, "Global Buyout Delayed by Bond Market," *Business Journal*, August 31, 1998, p. 1.
——, "Global May Be Rescued from Hostile Takeover," *Business Journal*, June 8, 1998, p. 1.
——, "Real Hostility Marks Takeover Attempt," *Business Journal*, April 20, 1998, p. 1.
Watanabe, Laurie, "Global Motorsport Adds Motorcycle Stuff to Its Powersports Line-Up," *Dealernews*, March 2000, p. 32.

—Jason Gallman
—update: Jeffrey L. Covell

Daniel Measurement and Control, Inc.

9720 Old Katy Road
Houston, Texas 77055
U.S.A.
Telephone: (713) 467-6000
Fax: (713) 827-3880
Web site: http://www.daniel.com

Wholly Owned Subsidiary of Emerson Electric Co.
Incorporated: 1946 as the Daniel Orifice Fitting Company
Employees: 1,600
Sales: $252 million (est.) (2004)
NAIC: 334513 Instruments and Related Product
   Manufacturing for Measuring, Displaying, and
   Controlling Industrial Process Variables; 332722 Bolt,
   Nut, Screw, Rivet, and Washer Manufacturing;
   332911 Industrial Valve Manufacturing; 332919 Other
   Metal Valve and Pipe Fitting Manufacturing; 332996
   Fabricated Pipe and Pipe Fitting Manufacturing;
   334514 Totalizing Fluid Meter and Counting Device
   Manufacturing

Daniel Measurement and Control, Inc. is a leading manufacturer of energy measurement technology, including systems to measure the flow of gases, liquids, and steam. In addition, the company is a major international producer of high-technology equipment to transmit, distribute, and market oil, gas, and various other energy commodities. The company is owned by Emerson Electric Co., operating as part of its parent company's Emerson Process Management division.

Company Founder Getting His Start in the Early 20th Century

Paul Daniel was born in Houston, Texas, on May 17, 1894. Educated in a one-room schoolhouse on the edge of the city, as a teenager Paul Daniel worked various odd jobs on the range in the burgeoning Texas metropolis. Yet as cattle raising became more and more modernized, and Houston began to lose its western ''shoot 'em up'' aura, the young man discovered that

work was getting scarcer and scarcer. Finally, after much deliberation, and with guarded encouragement from his parents, the young man traveled to southern California to seek his fortune.

Arriving in California without money or prospects in 1915, Daniel found a job at the El Segundo Refinery operated by Standard Oil Company, one of the largest and most successful enterprises in the history of American business. During his time at the refinery, Daniel learned all he could about the oil industry, and the new technology that was designed to speed and control the flow of oil through pipelines running across miles of almost uninhabitable terrain. In just two years, the ambitious and knowledgeable man from Texas had been promoted to the prestigious position of Tank Gauger at the refinery, one of the most sought-after and respected jobs within the Standard Oil Company.

Daniel volunteered to serve in the U.S. Army when America entered World War I in 1917. Although most of the recorded history about American involvement in World War I has focused on the European theatre, especially the fierce fighting around Belle Wood in the French countryside, American soldiers also fought against Germany in the Middle East and in Siberia. Daniel was assigned to the United States Army Siberian Expeditionary Force, which saw extensive action fighting alongside its Russian compatriots-in-arms. Daniel returned to the United States after two years of service, a wiser, stronger, and more determined man.

By 1920, Daniel was back in California working for the Pan-American Petroleum Company owned by an entrepreneur by the name of E.L. Dopheny. Under Dopheny's tutelage, Daniel learned more than ever about the oil industry and worked his way up the corporate ladder. Throughout the 1920s Daniel became acquainted with the intricacies of flow systems within the oil pipelines and, by 1928, he had risen to the position of assistant to the manager of the company's Natural Gas Division in Los Angeles, California.

The company was hard hit by the Great Depression in the early 1930s, and salaries were slashed dramatically. At first Daniel did not expect the economic hardships of the Depression to last very long, but when it became evident that no immediate relief was in sight, he grew worried about the security of his job.

Indeed, during the height of the Great Depression in the early and mid-1930s, Daniel was slowly phased out of work at the company. Forced to scrape by for a living, he worked any job he could get. At the same time, however, he never gave up his hope of working for the oil industry once again, and he started designing an orifice fitting that would allow for the changing of plates within the oil pipeline system without interrupting the flow of the oil or allowing significant leakage. After a few years of work on his design, he was rewarded with a patent for the "senior orifice fitting," as he called it, a creation whose fundamental design remains the standard in the pipeline industry at the present.

Starting a Business in the 1940s

With his patent in hand, and requests for the new device overwhelming him, Daniel decided to start his own business. The Daniel Orifice Fitting Company opened for business near the end of the Depression in Los Angeles, and began manufacturing orifice fittings, orifice plates, and meter tubes for the oil industry. Not long afterward, the company expanded its product line to include the manufacture of piston-controlled check-valves, orifice flanges, and Simplex plate holders. By the end of the decade, Daniel was head of a thriving business.

When America entered World War II in December 1941, the U.S. government contracted major oil companies to provide gas and oil to operate the tanks, jeeps, trucks, and various other motorized equipment used by soldiers in both the European and Pacific theatres. The major oil companies like Texaco and Standard Oil, in turn, contracted smaller firms to keep the flow of oil running smoothly. The Daniel Orifice Fitting Company benefited directly from these contracts. In fact, business expanded so rapidly that the company opened a small plant in Houston, hometown of the founder and owner.

By the war's end, the Daniel Orifice Fitting Company had grown dramatically and was poised to expand its manufacturing facilities and sales operations even further. Over the years, Paul Daniel had developed into a cautious but shrewd businessman, and he had grown to understand the value of expanding his company's operations in a slow but methodical manner. Gradually, throughout the 1950s, the company increased the number of its employees, built new manufacturing plants across the United States, and opened numerous sales and marketing offices, primarily in the western and southwestern regions of the country.

Expansion During the 1960s and 1970s

By the mid-1960s, after Paul Daniel had left the active management of the company, the Daniel Orifice Fitting Company counted more than 500 employees, five manufacturing plants located across the nation, ten sales offices, and 48 sales agency offices. In 1966, the board of directors decided to change the name of the company to Daniel Industries, Inc., to reflect the growing diversity of its product line and services.

The 1970s saw further expansion and growth for the company. Major acquisitions during this time included M&J Valve Company, an old and well-known firm that manufactured valves and gauges for the oil industry, and Oilfield Fabricating & Machine Company, one of the preeminent businesses in the supply of custom-made machine parts for oil and gas pipeline systems. In addition, management created a subsidiary named the Daniel Bolt Company, which was involved in the manufacture of products for oilfield machinery. Management also kept abreast of all the new developments in oilfield technology, and utilized innovations and new designs within the field to improve upon and expand the types of mechanical, electronic, and highly sophisticated computer-based products and systems the company was now producing. With the energy crisis at its peak during the mid- and late 1970s, and America determined to develop its own sources of energy in order to decrease dependence on foreign oil, Daniel Industries was at its high point.

Downturn During the 1980s and a Return to Basics

The most profitable period in the company's history lasted for about ten years. When the energy crisis faded, and the price of oil went down drastically, the entire American oil industry was hit hard. By the end of the decade, energy companies in the gas and oil industry had lost more than 370,000 jobs. Conservative estimates of job losses in the supporting industries were placed at more than one million. Daniel Industries faced its first real crisis, and management decided to return to the basics. This meant liquidating inventories, reducing capacity, and eliminating jobs. At the same time, management rededicated itself to manufacturing fewer but higher-quality products, streamlining manufacturing operations, encouraging innovative designs and product development, and improving customer service.

The most important development to come out of this difficult period was what became known as "partnership relationships" between Daniel Industries and both its customers and suppliers. A greater emphasis was placed on manufacturing quality products at competitive prices, with the common goal of minimizing total installation costs and operating expenses to the user. These partnership relationships were successful due to a number of strategic management innovations, including a material resource planning program, the use of computer numerical controlled machines and other highly specialized equipment, extensive employment of CAD/CAM systems, improved internal communications networks, and a new order-entry system.

The 1990s and Beyond

By the early 1990s, Daniel Industries had developed three main core businesses: metering, electronics, and pipeline valves. The core metering business included manufacture of

Key Dates:

Early 1940s: The Daniel Orifice Fitting Co. is established.
1950s: The company expands physically, building new manufacturing plants and opening sales and marketing offices across the country.
1966: The company changes its name to Daniel Industries, Inc.
1987: Daniel Industries completes its initial public offering of stock.
1995: Daniel Industries is sold to an investment group headed by entrepreneur Russell Ginn.
1996: Daniel acquires Bettis Corp. for $102 million, the largest acquisition in the company's history.
1999: Emerson Electric Co. acquires Daniel Industries.

the industry's standard Senior Orifice Fitting, as well as gas turbine meters, and ultrasonic flow meters. As the company's focus has shifted from liquid metering to value-added gas metering, management believed that the ultrasonic flow meter was the meter of the future for all gas pipeline systems. The electronics division, which became a part of the company's metering business, focused on manufacturing items such as Daniel flow computers for the worldwide market. The company's flow control valve business retained its traditional manufacturing role of producing gate valves for liquid pipeline systems. By the mid-1990s, the company had added a line of ball valves, as well as specialty control valves for use in gas pipelines and gas and liquid storage facilities.

During the early and mid-1990s, Daniel Industries made a commitment to expand its marketing worldwide as well as to increase its customer service locations internationally. A sales and service office was opened in Singapore to take advantage of one of the world's fastest growing gas producing markets. A sales office was opened in Moscow with the purpose of cultivating the emerging natural gas markets in Russia. An office in London was established to provide direct communication links with customers and engineering companies conducting operations in the North Sea. A subsidiary was formed in Germany—Daniel Messtechnik GmbH—to provide the company with access to developing markets in Eastern Europe. Other major offices included locations in Saudi Arabia, Scotland, and The Netherlands.

In 1995, management at the company decided to implement a comprehensive reorganization strategy to make all of the company's operations more effective, and to increase shareholder value. As the restructuring program successfully progressed, all of the assets of the company were sold to an investor group headed by Russell Ginn, a Houston-based entrepreneur. The change in ownership, however, did nothing to affect the expansion and growth of the company. In early 1996, the company purchased the Oilfield Fabricating & Machine Company and later in the year entered into an agreement with Framo Engineering A/S of Norway to market and sell the Norwegian firm's highly innovative multiphase flow metering system. At the same time, the company acquired Spectra-Tek International and concluded an agreement with Cooper Cameron Corporation to license worldwide that firm's geothermal gate valves and wellhead systems.

An End to Independence at the Dawn of the 21st Century

The second half of the 1990s proved to be an eventful period in Daniel Industries' history, a time of profound change that redefined the company's role in its industry. In 1996, Daniel Industries completed the largest acquisition in its history, the $102 million acquisition of Bettis Corporation. Waller, Texas-based Bettis manufactured actuators that were used to automate valves and control the flow of liquid for the same customers Daniel Industries served—natural gas and oil producers, transporters, and refineries. Bettis's six manufacturing plants became the new Bettis division of Daniel Industries, significantly increasing the company's stature. "You put these two companies together in 1997," Bettis's chairman, Nathan M. Avery, said in a September 18, 1996, interview with the *Houston Chronicle,* "and you're looking at a company with almost $300 million in revenues, good earnings, and a good balance sheet. We'll attract more shareholder interest."

Daniel Industries not only attracted more shareholder interest after the acquisition of Bettis, but also attracted the attention of a much larger rival in its industry. After sales reached $283 million in 1998, the company received an unsolicited takeover bid from an undisclosed company in March 1999. In a statement quoted in the March 16, 1999, issue of *PR Newswire,* Daniel Industries' chairman, Ronald Lassiter, hinted at what was expected to transpire. "Whether we choose to remain an independent company and continue to implement our strategic plan or become part of a larger concern," Lassiter said, "the people and products of Daniel industries will undoubtedly play a major role in shaping the future of the measurement and control industry." In May 1999, when Daniel Industries agreed to be acquired for $267 million, the corporate suitor was revealed to be St. Louis-based Emerson Electric Co., a conglomerate with $13.4 billion in sales active in process control, industrial automation, electronics, heating/ventilating/air-conditioning, appliance components, and electric motors markets.

When Daniel Industries joined Emerson, the company became part of the family of Fisher-Rosemount companies, a global leader in the process control industry, which was grouped within the Emerson Process Management division. Daniel Industries was renamed Daniel Measurement and Control, Inc., adopting the name of the company's manufacturing facility on Old Katy Road in Houston. Emerson acquired Daniel Industries because of the company's strengths in natural gas, which was expected to broaden the market penetration and increase the number of applications offered by Emerson. As a part of a division owned by its much larger parent company, Daniel Measurement and Control no longer reported its own financial figures and lost some of its individuality, but it continued to factor as an important player in its industry. By 2004, Emerson Process Management was a nearly $4 billion-in-sales business, with Daniel Measurement and Control responsible for only a fraction of the segment's revenue volume. The company's value was measured in other ways, predicated on the innovations of Paul Daniel and his successors. The introduction of the Daniel Series 1200 Turbine Flow Meter at the end of 2004 represented one of the ways the division was helping to contribute to the financial health of Emerson Process Management. The meter served the need for accurate flow measurement in low-volume fuel blending operations, a need created by environmental legislation requiring the use of ethanol as a gasoline oxygenate to achieve higher octane ratings. "Meeting the changing needs of the petroleum industry in this critical application is fundamental to the success of our customers," an Emerson Process Management executive said in a December 13, 2004, interview with *Product News Network.*

Principal Subsidiaries

Daniel Automation Company; Daniel Flow Products, Inc.; Daniel Valve Company; RBC Realty Inc.; Daniel Canada; Daniel Industries Ltd.; Daniel Messtechnik GmbH; Hytork International plc.

Principal Competitors

Tyco International Ltd.; Textron Inc.; SPX Corporation.

Further Reading

"Daniel Industries," *Oil and Gas Journal,* August 7, 1995, p. 68.

"Daniel Industries," *Wall Street Journal,* March 7, 1995, p. B2.

Durgin, Hillary, "Daniel Industries Will Acquire Bettis," *Houston Chronicle,* September 18, 1996, p. B1.

Fletcher, Sam, "Daniel Industries Sells Subsidiary," *Oil Daily,* June 26, 1995, p. 6.

——, "Management Buys Daniel En-Fab Systems from Parent Company for Undisclosed Price," *Oil Daily,* July 7, 1995, p. 2.

"Moorco Discloses Bid for Daniel Industries," *Wall Street Journal,* March 9, 1995, p. C15.

Perin, Monica, "Daniel Departure Ends Another Business Chapter," *Houston Business Journal,* June 4, 1999, p. 1.

"Turbine Flow Meters Aid in Low-Volume Fuel Blending," *Product News Network,* December 13, 2004, p. 32.

—Thomas Derdak
—update: Jeffrey L. Covell

DETROIT DIESEL
CORPORATION

Detroit Diesel Corporation

13400 West Outer Drive
Detroit, Michigan 48239-4001
U.S.A.
Telephone: (313) 592-5000
Fax: (313) 592-7323
Web site: http://www.detroitdiesel.com

Wholly Owned Subsidiary of DaimlerChrysler AG
Incorporated: 1987
Employees: 6,000
Sales: $2.3 billion (2002 est.)
NAIC: 336312 Gasoline Engine and Engine Parts
Manufacturing

A subsidiary of DaimlerChrysler AG since 2000, Detroit Diesel Corporation is the leading designer, manufacturer, and seller of medium and heavy-duty diesel engines serving the commercial truck, automotive, off-road, and marine markets. Detroit Diesel also services its engines through a global network of more than 2,700 authorized distributors and dealers. In addition, it manufactures two- and four-cycle engines for the international automotive market. Since the early 1990s, the company's Series 60 diesel engine, one of the first to take advantage of electronic engine controls, has been the best-selling heavy duty diesel engine on the market, but new engines are set to be introduced in 2007 to meet stricter Environmental Protection Agency (EPA) standards.

Origins

General Motors pioneered the development of practical, lightweight, powerful, and fast two- and four-cycle diesel engines. Initially the incentive to develop such engines came from the enormous profits available if diesel could replace steam in the locomotive industry. According to Alfred P. Sloan, president of GM during the 1920s and 1930s, Charles F. Kettering can be credited with the foresight and drive behind the practical application of diesel power. Kettering supervised experiments at GM as early as 1921 to develop a smaller, more efficient diesel. As Sloan tells the story in his memoirs *My Years With General Motors,* he

dropped by Kettering's office at the research laboratories one day and said, "Ket, why is it, recognizing the high efficiency of the diesel cycle, that it has never been more generally used?" Kettering explained that technical problems in diesel engine design up to that time had meant that the engines simply would not perform the way the engineers wanted them to. Sloan replied in his typically forthright manner, "Very well—we are now in the diesel engine business. You tell us how the engine should run and I will see that available manufacturing facilities are provided to capitalize the program."

The small, practical GM diesel engine might never have been developed, however, if Kettering had not also been a yachtsman. Kettering's fascination with diesel engines led him to purchase a diesel engine built by Winton Engines for use in his personal yacht. Kettering was so impressed with the Winton engine that he convinced Sloan to buy the Cleveland Ohio company. Alexander Winton, one of America's pioneer auto makers, was reportedly enthusiastic about the sale of his company to GM. He wanted to see the potential of diesel realized but knew that the cost of developing such an engine was beyond his scope. The apparently happy takeover was almost derailed by the market crash of 1929, but the sale went through in 1930. Simultaneously, GM purchased another Cleveland-based company, Electro-Motive Engineering Company, which had worked closely with Winton in the 1920s in their endeavor to develop a diesel-powered locomotive engine. The purchase of these companies was a great risk for GM in those economically turbulent times. The risk paid off but only after a number of years of intensive and often distressing research and development.

The break for the two-cycle GM diesel engine came when the company decided to use it as the power source for its dramatic reconstruction of an assembly line for the 1933 Chicago World's Fair. The diesels required continual repairs, prompting Kettering's son to comment that "the only part of the engine that worked well was the dip-stick." Nonetheless, locomotive companies were impressed with the power and efficiency of the engines compared to the steam locomotives they had been operating for years. Demonstration runs showed that a diesel-powered locomotive could cut the running time from Chicago to the West Coast by more than 20 hours. Once the industry decided to convert to diesel, GM had a corner on the market. No other major manufacturer built a diesel locomotive engine until after World War II. The success of the locomotive diesel foray prompted GM in 1937 to set up Detroit Diesel Engine Division to research, develop, and promote smaller diesel engines for marine and industrial use.

Aiming at a New Market in the Postwar Years

The importance of the railroad began a precipitous decline after World War II, but Detroit Diesel had already moved decisively into the truck and industrial sectors. Its main competitor in the postwar years, Cummins Engine Co., began to fight seriously for a share of the market in the 1960s. However, the trucking industry was booming, and it appeared to be an almost limitless market for the powerful diesel engines.

In 1970, Detroit Diesel Engine division was consolidated with GM's Allison division. Allison had been added to GM in 1929, during the same period of expansion and diversification that had seen the founding of Detroit Diesel. Allison played an important role in developing engines for aircraft used by American and Allied forces during World War II, producing an estimated 70,000 aircraft engines during the war. After World War II, GM decided that its future in the aircraft business rested with providing engines to other manufacturers, and it merged its Detroit Diesel and Allison divisions. In spite of the recession in the auto industry in the mid-1970s, Detroit Diesel Allison continued to perform well. By the beginning of the 1980s, Cummins had assumed the top spot in the diesel engine market, but Detroit Diesel still controlled a respectable 30 percent of the domestic market.

Over the next six years, however, Detroit Diesel underwent a precipitous decline, and by 1987 its market share had dwindled to less than 5 percent. The reasons for this calamitous fall are complex. In a 1985 article in *Automotive News,* L.F. Koci, then general manager of DDA and later president of the independent Detroit Diesel, cited an influx of diesel engines from Europe and Japan as a major cause of the drop in DDA sales. Although imports certainly contributed to falling sales, Detroit Diesel had lost much of its market share to the American Cummins Engine Co. A spokesman for Detroit Diesel after it had become an independent company acknowledged in a 1988 article in *Financial World* that ''in the late 1970s and early 1980s [DDA] was letting bad product out the door. The engines weren't performing well and we lost some good customers.'' Parent company General Motors had made some attempt to revitalize DDA; however, of the $50 billion spent on plant modernization by GM through the 1980s, only $100 million went towards the floundering DDA. It was a case of too little too late, and by 1987 GM began to look seriously for a buyer to take the beleaguered division off its hands.

New Ownership in the Late 1980s

The company did not look long. Roger Penske, the famous auto racer and wunderkind of the auto business world, was immediately intrigued at the prospect of reviving the lumbering old giant of the auto industry. By early 1988, Penske and GM had signed an agreement wherein Penske obtained ownership of 60 percent of Detroit Diesel's stock and GM secured the remaining 40 percent. Penske retained much of the old personnel at Detroit Diesel, continuing to employ engineers and management who had a long association with GM. Rather than overhauling the company by purging it of its old brass, he simply realigned the corporate goals. As reported in *Financial World* in 1988, he eliminated redundant computer costs and consolidated manufacturing operations in an effort to cut the operating budget by more than $70 million. However, he kept such longstanding Detroit Diesel employees as L.F. Koci, Detroit Diesel general manager at the time of the takeover.

In order to revive Detroit Diesel, Penske had to get results quickly. Within the first two years of independent operations, Detroit Diesel had more than doubled its market share. By 1993, this share had risen to 26 percent, mostly at the expense of its arch rival Cummins. Although under Penske's management revenues grew by more than 60 percent, heavy investments in research and development reduced profits to only 1 percent of sales. This low level of earnings, combined with a depressed American economy, led to two consecutive years of losses in 1990 and 1991. In the long run, however, Penske's persistence seemed to pay off: the company rebounded in 1992 and had a net income of over $20 million in 1993.

Aside from some cost-cutting measures and reorganization of the company, the early success of Penske's Detroit Diesel came on the strength of one item: the Series 60 engine. According to *Business Week* in 1991, the electronically controlled Series 60 engine was ''ground-breaking'' and, in addition to offering ''dramatically better fuel efficiency, it boasts nifty computerized features that diagnose mechanical problems and can monitor engine use—and thus track driver productivity.'' The Series 60, the first engine of its kind to be electronically controlled, was introduced during the first quarter of 1987. It was the product of a ''clean-sheet'' design that applied the latest technology to every stage of the manufacturing process, including production, assembly, and testing. Detroit Diesel originally claimed the engine needed an overhaul only once every 500,000 miles. The company later extended this boast to 750,000 miles. Over the next several years, the truck engines seemed to hold up well, and the $82 million that the Series 60 had brought the company by 1993 suggested that Detroit Diesel had overcome its reputation for unreliable products.

Joint Ventures Begin in the Early 1990s

Joint ventures with other major manufacturers further consolidated the revival of Detroit Diesel. German giant Mercedes-Benz entered into an agreement with Detroit Diesel in 1991 to develop electronic fuel delivery systems. As part of an engine development financing agreement, Diesel Project Development, a wholly owned subsidiary of Mercedes-Benz, bought $20 million of Detroit Diesel debentures in 1993, giving the German firm an 11 percent stake in the company. Volvo Penta also came to an

---

Key Dates:

1937: General Motors establishes Detroit Diesel Engine division.
1970: Detroit Diesel Engine division is consolidated with General Motor's Allison division.
1988: Roger Penske gains control of the company.
1993: Detroit Diesel is taken public.
2000: DaimlerChrysler AG acquires the company.

---

agreement in 1993 that promised Detroit Diesel exclusive rights to certain Volvo Penta marine diesel products within the NAFTA area. Perkins Engine, based in England, and Detroit Diesel made an agreement in 1988 that facilitated certain aspects of distribution. Perkins also agreed to manufacture some smaller engines for Detroit Diesel, providing them with a variety of engines ranging from 5 to 2,500 horsepower. In 1993, Detroit Diesel formed a joint venture company with RABA plc of Gyor, Hungary. The new company, named RABA-Detroit Diesel Hungary, Kft., reportedly will use RABA as its Eastern European manufacturing center, opening up an extensive potential market for products. Finally, in a return to its roots, Detroit Diesel entered into a "technology coalition" with Republic Locomotive to build new electronically controlled locomotive engines.

These joint ventures represent a strategy that each of the major U.S. engine makers, Detroit Diesel, Cummins Engine, and Caterpillar, had begun to employ by the early 1990s. Rather than continuing to fight each other for a dwindling share of the American market, each company attempted to increase foreign sales. The U.S. manufacturers hoped that forging ties with foreign companies would open European and Japanese markets, where potential sales were double what could be had in the U.S. market. The management of Detroit Diesel believed that the NAFTA and GATT agreements would "provide opportunities for growth even after considering the cyclical nature of the North American heavy-duty truck market."

Challenges and New Owners:
the Mid-1990s and Beyond

As Detroit Diesel faced the late 1990s, EPA standards for bus and truck engines posed the greatest challenge. The company had gotten the jump on the competition after the EPA set emission standards for the 1990s by being the first manufacturer to come out with an entirely new model. Due to the high-tech production system used on the Series 60, less than 1 percent of the engine's components needed modifications to meet the steep reductions in particulate emissions stipulated by the EPA in 1991 and 1994. The company's engines could be depended on to meet emission standards through 1997, but the future was not assured after that date.

Detroit Diesel hoped that the impressive amount of research and development the company had factored into its operating budget would ensure the company's edge in fuel efficiency and emission standards. A great deal of their research since the introduction of the Series 60 focused on developing engines that would run on cleaner fuels. Some of these experiments led to

test units that ran on natural gas as well as methanol, ethanol, and other alcohol-based fuels. If one of Detroit Diesel's competitors, however, developed a conventionally fueled model that could meet the emission standard before Detroit Diesel's experiments came to fruition, then the company would be set back considerably.

Despite the promising first few years of the Penske-owned Detroit Diesel, in the mid-1990s the company retained a large debt load from the lean and rebuilding periods. In an effort to offset this debt, the company completed an initial public offering (IPO) of 4.75 million shares of common stock in October of 1993. The result of the IPO was to offset the company's debt by $99 million. The ongoing series of joint ventures with companies both large and small, in the United States and overseas, positioned the company to broaden its market and product line.

All of these joint ventures were closely tied to the company's goal of using high-tech advancements to stay ahead of the competition as the industry faced ongoing pressure about environmental issues. The most significant advancement was the use of electronics to control fuel injection, allowing Detroit Diesel to easily meet all of the EPA standards. One of the much-touted advantages of the electronically controlled engines was that they were tamper-proof: timing was programmed at the factory and could not be adjusted. However, the electronic sophistication of the engines made by Detroit Diesel and other manufacturers also attracted scrutiny from the EPA and the Department of Justice. In 1998, Detroit Diesel and six other companies were fined $1 billion in a settlement with the EPA, Department of Justice, and the California Air Resources Board. Detroit Diesel's misconduct dated back ten years, when according to the EPA it first began incorporating "defeat devices" in their diesel engines. When being tested for emissions, the electronics recognized a test pattern and reduced the engine's emissions, but once the vehicle was determined to be on the open road the electronics allowed the engines to disregard pollution control levels. Of the seven companies fined, Detroit Diesel, which paid $83 million, sold the most engines.

In 1997, Penske attempted to expand Detroit Diesel's presence in the marine market with the acquisition of Outboard Marine Corp. Part of the plan was to use Outboard Marine to convert 50 of 800 auto centers Penske had acquired from Kmart Corporation in 1995 into marine and boat centers. The deal fell through, however, after two Outboard Marine shareholders topped Detroit Diesel's offer. Penske refused to budge on price and the acquisition was eventually aborted. After enthusiastically supporting the $500 million deal, Wall Street punished Detroit Diesel when the deal fell apart, bidding down the price of its stock. In addition, there was growing concern that the heavy-truck industry was poised for a decline. Detroit Diesel was heavily dependent on this sector, with heavy-truck engine sales accounting for 45 percent of revenues. To achieve some measure of diversification, Detroit Diesel entered the medium-duty truck market with the introduction of the Mercedes Benz 900 engine (MBE 900) in 1998, along with a new four-liter, six cylinder diesel engine targeting the pickup or sport utility vehicle market.

Detroit Diesel faced a number of challenges operating as a global company as the 1990s came to a close but management insisted in April 1999 that the company wished to remain independent. It soon became obvious, however, that given the pace of industry consolidation, Detroit Diesel would be hard pressed to remain competitive. With stricter diesel emission standards from the EPA on the horizon, the need for capital was going to be severe. Thus, in 2000 Detroit Diesel decided to join forces with DaimlerChrysler, which bought the rest of North America's fourth-largest engine maker in a $723 million deal that included the assumption of $300 million in debt. Daimler-Chrysler was now able to offer an integrated truck product around the world, as well as a chance to cut costs by purchasing engine production material in higher volumes. With Daimler-Chrysler's backing, Detroit Diesel looked to enter the light-duty diesel market and become more of a global player.

Detroit Diesel had to contend with a number of difficulties in the early 2000s. As part of the 1998 settlement with the EPA, Detroit Diesel had agreed to meet stringent nitrogen-oxide emissions standards by October 2002, rather than the original date of 2004. It proved to be a tougher task than anticipated, prompting the company to seek an extension. None was forthcoming, yet Detroit Diesel managed to meet the EPA standards and gain certification for its new Series 60 engine in the fall of 2002. Unfortunately, truck fleet customers held off buying the new engines, but eventually they would have to make the transition to EPA-compliant engines. In preparation for 2007's EPA heavy-duty on-highway engine standards, Detroit Diesel developed a new family of diesel engines. After the EPA standards were introduced in mid-2007, the company's Series 60, MBE 4000 and MBE 900 engines would be expected to coexist with the new engines until the existing lines were slated to be phased out by 2009.

Principal Competitors

Caterpillar Inc.; Cummins Power Generation; Navistar International Corporation.

Further Reading

Benoit, Ellen, "Jump Start," *Financial World*, November 1, 1988, pp. 42, 44.

Birkland, Carol, "High-Tech Diesels," *Fleet Equipment*, April 1996, p. 46.

Bohn, Joseph, "DDA Is Reorganizing Operations in Detroit," *Automotive News*, September 2, 1985, pp. 8, 42.

Brezonick, Mike, "Looking Beyond an Icon," *Diesel Progress North American Edition*, June 2005, p. 86.

Cochran, Thomas N., "On the Road Again: Why Mercedes-Benz Likes Roger Penske's Detroit Diesel," *Barron's*, September 27, 1993, pp. 13–14.

"Detroit Diesel and Raba Form a New Joint Venture Company to Assemble Engines in Hungary," Newswire Press Release, December 20, 1993.

"Detroit Diesel and Volvo Penta Announce Strategic U.S. Agreement," Newswire Press Release, February 16, 1994.

"Detroit Diesel to Produce Natural Gas, Alcohol Engines," *Automotive News*, July 2, 1990.

"Engines: Detroit Diesel Corp./Mercedes-Benz," *Fleet Owner*, August 2005, p. IV.

Kelly, Kevin, "Does Cummins Have the Oomph to Climb This Hill?" *Business Week*, November 4, 1991, pp. 66, 68.

Lowell, Jon, "Roger Roars Ahead: Penske Fires Up GM's Dying Diesels; Profits Replace Problems," *Ward's Auto World*, November 1988, pp. 30–34.

McCracken, Jeffrey, "Detroit Diesel Steadies," *Crain's Detroit Business*, February 16, 1998, p. 2.

——, "Feds Fine Diesel for Clean-Air Violations," *Crain's Detroit Business*, October 26, 1998, p. 3.

Mele, Jim, "The First Look at 1991 Engines," *Fleet Owner*, November 1989, pp. 76–85.

Miller, Scott, "DaimlerChrysler to Buy Detroit Diesel to Strengthen Its Dominance in Trucks," *Wall Street Journal*, July 21, 2000, p. A9.

"The Rising Rumble of American Diesels," *Business Week*, September 6, 1993, pp. 84, 86.

Rowan, Roger, "Those Dazzling Diesels," *Automotive News*, September 16, 1983, pp. 425–26.

Schwind, Gene, "A Clean-Sheet Approach to Engine Design and Manufacture," *Material Handling Engineering*, May 1987, pp. 61–63.

Sherefkin, Robert, "Detroit Diesel Picks Road with Fewest Financial Potholes," *Crain's Detroit Business*, September 11, 2000, p. 14.

Sloan, Alfred P., "Nonautomotive: Diesel Electric Locomotives, Appliances, Aviation," *My Years with General Motors*, New York: Doubleday, 1964, pp. 341–53.

Taylor, Alex III, "Rogert Penske Goes Boating," *Fortune*, August 4, 1997.

—Hilary Gopnik
—update: Donald Cameron McManus; Ed Dinger

Detroit Red Wings

600 Civic Center Drive
Detroit, Michigan 48226
U.S.A.
Telephone: (313) 396-7544
Fax: (313) 567-0296
Web site: http://www.detroitredwings.com

Wholly Owned Subsidiary of Ilitch Holdings Inc.
Founded: 1926
Employees: NA
Sales: $97 million (2004)
NAIC: 711211 Sports Teams and Clubs

Winner of ten Stanley Cup championships, the Detroit Red Wings are one of the most successful franchises in the National Hockey League (NHL). The team is backed by a passionate fan base and the deep pockets of its corporate parent, Ilitch Holdings Inc., the holding company for Michael Ilitch, who made his money with the Little Caesars pizza chain and also owns the Detroit Tigers major league baseball team, large portions of Detroit real estate, and other business interests. One of only a handful of NHL teams that had the financial resources to field a contending club every year, the Red Wings now face a different competitive environment after an impasse with players over a new collective bargaining agreement resulted in the cancellation of the 2004–05 season. Eventually a settlement was reached that called for a cap on the amount of money each club could spend on players.

NHL Taking Shape in the 1920s

Although the Red Wings are considered one of the NHL's "original six" clubs, the team actually joined the league a decade after it was established. The NHL's roots reach back to the 1910 merger of two so-called amateur Canadian hockey leagues who were weary of raiding one another's players at a bounty and decided to form the National Hockey Association (NHA). Soon, another professional league, the Pacific Coast Hockey Association (PCHA), was raiding NHA players, but the two circuits came to an accommodation and their regular season champions began playing for the Stanley Cup, which was first awarded in 1893 to the winner of a tournament of amateur hockey teams. The outbreak of World War I in 1914 disrupted play in the NHA and the teams' owners took the opportunity to reorganize and rid themselves of the nettlesome owner of the Toronto franchise. In a Montreal hotel on November 22, 1917 the National Hockey League was born, and it now played the PCHA for the Stanley Cup. The PCHA began to experience financial difficulties in the early 1920s and merged with another professional league, the Western Hockey League (WHL), whose franchises were generally located in small markets. Unable to pay the salaries offered by NHL teams, especially after the NHL began to expand to large American cities, WHL players were sold off. By 1926 only the NHL was left standing and the Stanley Cup became its exclusive property.

During the period of American expansion no fewer than five Detroit groups attempted to receive an NHL franchise. The winners were granted a franchise in May 1926 and in September of that year bought the entire roster of players of the WHL's Victoria Cougars at a cost of $100,000. The Cougars had won the Stanley Cup in 1925 and lost in the finals in 1926. In that first season as the Detroit Cougars, the team actually played its home games across the Detroit River in Windsor, Ontario, as it awaited the construction of its own building. Despite the purchase of talent, the Cougars got off to an inauspicious start, posting the worst record in the NHL for the 1926–27 season. Fans were not overly interested in paying to watch a losing club, and as a result the team finished its first year $80,000 in debt.

Prospects for the Detroit franchise began to pick up the next season. It moved into its new home, The Olympia, which at the time of its opening in 1927 housed the largest rink in the United States. That year also brought Jack Adams, who became the coach and general manager and would remain in charge for the next 35 years. Success did not come quickly, however, as the team failed to make the playoffs in three out of the next four years. Even changing the team's name from the Cougars to the Falcons in 1930 did nothing to turn around Detroit's fortunes. With the country mired in the Great Depression, the team was forced into receivership, and to make payroll Adams had to reach into his own pockets. But Adams and his hockey team would soon be rescued

104

Key Dates:

1926: A group of Detroit businessmen receive a National Hockey League franchise.
1932: James Norris acquires the team and changes its name to Red Wings.
1936: The Red Wings win their first Stanley Cup.
1952: Norris dies and leaves the team to his children.
1979: The team moves into the Joe Louis Arena.
1982: The Norris family sells the Red Wings to Michael Ilitch.
1997: The Red Wings win their first Stanley Cup in 42 years.
2002: The Red Wings win their tenth Stanley Cup.

from tight-fisted ownership in the form of a wealthy grain merchant, James Norris, who bought the team in the summer of 1932.

A Pair of Stanley Cups in the 1930s

Norris made his fortune trading in grain in Chicago but he grew up in Canada, where he was a star athlete, an accomplished tennis and squash player in addition to an amateur hockey player. He also had been a member of the Montreal Amateur Athletic Association (MAAA), a sporting club that because of its origins as a cycling club sported a logo of winged wheels. Norris had tried to establish a second NHL team in Chicago only to be blocked by the Chicago Blackhawks' owner. Instead Norris bought the struggling Detroit franchise and in October changed the team's name to the Red Wings. For a logo he modified the MAAA graphic, incorporating an automobile wheel and tire that was more appropriate to Detroit, the home of the U.S. auto industry. Free of money worries, Adams was now able to exhibit his talent as a coach and an executive and began assembling a winning team. The Red Wings lost in the Stanley Cup semifinals during their first year under Norris ownership and lost in the finals during the second. After failing to make the playoffs the team then won back-to-back Stanley Cups in 1936 and 1937.

Norris had a partner when he acquired the Detroit franchise and The Olympia, Arthur Michael Wirtz, a young Chicago real estate mogul. Together they also would acquire the Blackhawks' home, Chicago Stadium, and eventually the Blackhawks. The two men acquired interests in arenas and convention centers around the country, including Madison Square Garden in New York as well as facilities in St. Louis, Omaha, and Indianapolis. This circuit became the foundation for any number of ventures, including ice shows, the birth of the National Basketball Association, rodeo, college basketball doubleheaders, and professional boxing matches.

Other NHL franchises did not fare as well as the Red Wings during the Depression. Some transferred to other cities while others simply folded. By 1942 the league had just six teams—Boston, Chicago, Montreal, New York, Toronto, and Detroit—which would become known as the "Original Six." No new teams joined the NHL for another 25 years.

During the war years the Red Wings won a third Stanley Cup in 1943 and although a championship would escape the team for the rest of the decade it began to lay the foundation for one of the greatest teams ever to play in the NHL. Players included forward Ted Lindsay, defenseman Red Kelly, goalie Terry Sawchuk, and the legendary forward Gordie Howe, whose arrival in 1946 marked the beginning of a golden era in Red Wings' history. In 1950 Detroit regained the Stanley Cup, and in that year one of the team's most enduring traditions was born when a fan threw an octopus onto the Olympia ice. The eight tentacles represented the eight wins needed in the two best-of-seven series a team had to win in order to take the cup. Every Red Wings playoff run that followed would feature the appearance of numerous octopi hurled onto the ice to the delight of Red Wings' fans.

James Norris died in 1952, several months after the Red Wings won their fifth Stanley Cup, and ownership of the team passed to his children, Bruce Norris and Marguerite Norris. Marguerite was named president, becoming the NHL's first female executive. Growing up in Chicago, she had never seen the Red Wings play in Detroit. She held the position for four years before Bruce Norris took over. While she was president the team won two more Stanley Cup Championships. Although the team remained competitive for the next decade, these would be the last titles the team won for the next 40 years.

By the time the NHL expanded, doubling to 12 teams for the 1967–68 season, the Red Wings had descended into mediocrity. The team finished out of the playoffs 16 out of 18 years during this period, an especially poor showing given that only five of the league's 21 teams failed to qualify. The Red Wings moved to a new home, Joe Louis Arena, in December 1979, but even new accommodations were not enough of an attraction to lure fans to watch a talent-starved team. The season ticket base was reported to be 2,500 but had more likely slipped to just 1,500. It had been a slow, long decline for a proud organization, but by the early 1980s the Red Wings were a team saddled with debt and unable to fund the kind of organization required to field a contending club.

In June 1982 the Detroit Red Wings changed owners, when the club was purchased by Michael Ilitch for a paltry $11 million. A Detroit native, Ilitch, like James Norris, had been an athlete as a youth. He was a minor league baseball player in the Detroit Tigers' system whose career was prematurely ended by injury. Instead of sports, he turned his attention in the late 1950s to pizza, founding Little Caesars, which carved out a niche as a pick-up only operation. By controlling costs he was able to undercut the competition and open more shops. At the time Ilitch bought the Red Wings, Little Caesars was still a regional company, but within four years it would be a national player with about 1,000 units. Ilitch only bought the Red Wings after he failed in his attempt to acquire his beloved Tigers, who were wrested away by cross-town pizza rival, Domino's Tom Monaghan. Ten years later Ilitch would succeed in gaining control of the Tigers, but in the meantime he poured money into the Red Wings, building up every aspect of the team's malnourished organization as well as making improvements to Joe Louis Arena.

Although it took time for the Red Wings to assemble a winning team, Ilitch showed quicker results in restoring attendance through marketing efforts that included giving away free cars during games. The number of season ticket holders soon increased to 16,000 and once the team became contenders, losing in the Stanley Cup semifinals in 1987 and 1988, the Red Wings became one of the NHL's most valuable franchises. But the team took a step back during the 1989–90 season when it once again missed the playoffs.

Back on Top in the 1990s

The team promoted a bevy of young talent in the early 1990s that formed the nucleus of an excellent team, but it took the hiring of the NHL's most successful coach, Scott Bowman, in 1993 to mold that talent and bring in key veterans to forge a champion. A year later the Red Wings returned to the Stanley Cup finals for the first time since 1966. Although it lost four games to none to the New Jersey Devils, Detroit served notice that it was now a serious contender, and with Ilitch's dedication to winning it planned to maintain a place at the top of the league for years to come. After losing in the conference finals in 1996 to the eventual champions, the Colorado Avalanche, the Red Wings won their eighth Stanley Cup, the first since 1955, in the spring of 1997, sweeping the Philadelphia Flyers four games to none. Despite losing one of the league's best defensemen, Vladimir Konstantinov, whose career was ended by injuries suffered in an off-season automobile accident, Detroit defended their title the following year, this time sweeping the Washington Capitals.

Colorado continued to be an arch-nemesis of the Red Wings, defeating them in the second round of the playoffs two years in a row to close the 1990s. Detroit retooled its roster in the 2000s, bringing in a number of veteran players who meshed well with Bowman's system, the likes of older stars such as defenseman Chris Chelios; forwards Pat Verbeek, Luc Robitaille, and Brett Hull; and goalie Dominik Hasek. The additions to the roster resulted in the Red Wings accumulating a league-best 116 points in the regular season of 2001–02 and the team claiming its tenth Stanley Cup when it defeated the Buffalo Sabers. Bowman, who had now won nine Stanley Cups as a coach, stepped down as coach, although he would stay on as a consultant to the team.

Bowman was replaced behind the bench by Dave Lewis. The team remained very much a contender for the Stanley Cup, but failed to reach the finals the next two seasons. But by now the focus was no longer on the ice but in the board rooms where league officials and representatives for the players negotiated a new collective bargaining agreement. Although large market teams like Detroit, Philadelphia, Colorado, Montreal, Toronto, and New York Rangers were doing well, smaller market clubs were losing money and claimed they were unable to compete fairly against the bigger clubs. In truth, unbridled spending was no guarantee of success (witness the difficulty New York, Philadelphia, and Toronto had in winning a championship). But the small-market teams would not be satisfied with anything less than a cap on players' salaries, which they contended was way out of line with the kind of revenues the NHL was able to generate, in order to achieve some kind of fiscal certainty. From

the players' perspective, the owners had only themselves to blame for outbidding one another on players. Moreover, the cries of poverty were met with a degree of skepticism. Hockey was merely part of a greater whole, the arena business, as it had been from the days of Norris and Wirtz, who viewed hockey like concerts or conventions, as a way to fill dark nights on the arena calendar. The hockey business might have been struggling, but the arena business was thriving. In addition, the value of hockey franchises increased steadily. A case in point was the Red Wings, which according to *Forbes* was worth $248 million in 2004, a significant increase over the $11 million Ilitch paid for the club some 20 years earlier.

The players were adamantly opposed to the idea of a salary cap. After negotiations broke down between the players and league in 2004, the owners locked out the players, resulting in the cancellation of the 2004–05 season, the first time that a professional sports league had been forced to cancel an entire season because of a labor impasse. Both sides, realizing the tremendous harm being done to the sport, returned to the bargaining table and in the summer of 2005 finally hammered out an agreement that included a salary cap and an automatic cut in player salaries. The deal was in fact less favorable to the players than the final offer on the table before the season was canceled. Every club was now limited in the amount of money it could spend on players, who now changed teams at a dizzying clip. Many of the headlines in the summer of 2005 related to the player signings of small-market clubs. Whether the competitive balance in the NHL would be significantly altered remained to be seen. It was just as likely, however, that strong organizations like Detroit would continue to find a way to stand above the rest. Whether spectators would return to the arenas to watch hockey after a year's absence was also an open question. In Detroit, known for decades as Hockeytown, it was likely that the Red Wings would be welcomed back by its fans with open arms.

Principal Competitors

St. Louis Blues Hockey Club L.L.C.; Nashville Hockey Club LP; The Columbus Blue Jackets; Chicago Blackhawks (Wirtz Corporation).

Further Reading

Diamond, Dan, et al., *Total Hockey,* Kingston, N.Y.: Total Sports, 1998.

Greenland, Paul R., *Wings of Fire: The History of the Detroit Red Wings,* Rockford, Ill.: Turning Leaf Publications, 1997.

Henderson, Tom, "Profile: Mike Ilitch, Owner, Little Caesars, Detroit Red Wings," *Detroit Free Press,* August 9, 1982.

McGraw, Bill, "Ilitch's Local Success Is Legendary," *Detroit Free Press,* June 20, 2000.

Stein, Gil, *Power Plays: An Inside Look at the Big Business of the National Hockey League,* Secaucus, N.J.: Carol Publishing Group, 1997.

—Ed Dinger

A NAVARRE CORPORATION COMPANY

Encore Computer Corporation

6901 West Sunrise Boulevard
Fort Lauderdale, Florida 33313
U.S.A.
Telephone: (305) 587-2900
Fax: (305) 797-5793

Public Company
Founded: 1983
Employees: 1,330 (1988)
Sales: $4.7 million (1998)
Stock Exchanges: NASDAQ
NAIC: 334111 Electronic Computer Manufacturing

Encore Computer Corporation was one of the leading American manufacturers of open, scalable computer and storage systems for data centers and mission-critical applications. The company's highly innovative Memory Channel technology, coupled with its sophisticated Infinity 90 Series commercial parallel processing systems for mainframe computers, placed it at the forefront of the ever-changing computer systems industry. Yet from the very beginning of its existence, Encore struggled with financial problems. It ceased operations in 1999.

Origins

Encore Computer Corporation began its life under the most auspicious of circumstances. Kenneth G. Fisher, who had built the Prime Computer Company from a fledgling $7 million operation into a $350 million giant in just six short years, joined C. Gordon Bell and Henry Burkhardt III to form Encore in 1983. Bell had previously worked as an engineering vice-president at Digital Equipment Corporation, and Burkhardt had co-founded Data General Corporation. These three luminaries from the computer industry joined together to raise nearly $50 million to fund the startup of the new company. The trio intended to develop and market an extremely broad range of products, including desktop computers and large mainframes. With the market for computers worth over $31 billion at the time, Fisher and his colleagues felt certain they could secure a healthy portion of it for Encore.

At first, everything went according to plan. A technical staff was hired from the research laboratories at Carnegie-Mellon University in Pittsburgh, and a headquarters was established in Wellesley Hills, Massachusetts. Bell undertook the supervision of the engineering and design department, while Fisher and Burkhardt concentrated on finance, sales, and marketing. Encore acquired Hydra Computer Systems, Inc. to develop processors, Foundation Computer Systems, Inc. to write software, and Resolution Systems, Inc. to produce the terminals. The number of employees shot up to 110, and management projected early 1985 as the date for the initial models to roll out of the company's plant.

By January 1984, however, the company had lost $1.2 million. Undeterred by the costs incurred during the initial setup of Encore, Fisher, Bell, and Burkhardt forged ahead. During 1984 and 1985, the company concentrated on designing and marketing UNIX-based computers and terminal servers. During the same time, Encore developed a reputation as a leader in early symmetric and parallel multiprocessing designs for computers. Both the Defense Advanced Research Projects Agency, an office of the United States government, and the academic community became interested in the company's innovative software and architectural hardware. Members of these communities agreed to fund additional multiprocessing research conducted by Encore engineers. Armed with this ready financial backing, by 1988 Encore was able to build and deploy its own revolutionary design for a 32-way UNIX symmetrical multiprocessor with unprecedented computational abilities.

In order to build upon this technology, in 1989 Encore purchased the assets of the Computer Systems Division (CDS) of Gould Electronics. The Computer Systems Division of Gould dated back to 1961, a period when the competition between the United States and the Soviet Union for space technology encouraged numerous American firms to pursue contracts with the National Aeronautics and Space Administration (NASA). One of those companies, Systems Engineering Labs (SEL), targeted the field of data acquisition. SEL manufactured the industry's first 32-bit minicomputer, a development that spurred the explosion of the telemetry, energy, and vehicle simulation markets. SEL grew accordingly as it designed high

Key Dates:

1983: Kenneth G. Fisher, C. Gordon Bell, and Henry Burkhardt III found Encore Computer Corporation.

1985: Encore designs and markets a UNIX-based systems and leads the industry in development of early symmetric and parallel multiprocessors.

1988: The company releases a revolutionary 32-way UNIX symmetrical multiprocessor of unprecedented power.

1989: The company purchases a real-time computing business from Gould Electronics, a subsidiary of Japan Energy Corp.

1990: Encore introduces its Infinity 90 series open systems mainframes, which offer massive storage capacity and the ability to solve single system failures without disrupting an entire system.

1991: The company recapitalizes with the help of Japan Energy Corp. and its subsidiaries.

1992: Encore secures $150 million in financing from Japan Energy subsidiary Nippon Mining Co.

1994: Encore secures $100 million recapitalization from Gould.

1995: Encore receives an undisclosed amount of financing from Japan Energy Corporation.

1997: Gould again refinances Encore, for $40 million; Encore sells its memory business to Sun Microsystems Inc. for $185 million.

1998: Encore signs an agreement to sell its real-time business to Gores Technology Group for $3 million.

1999: The company liquidates and ceases operations in early January.

technology products for its customers in power utilities and aerospace.

In 1981, Gould recognized the leadership role Systems Engineering was playing in the superminicomputer industry. It purchased SEL and reorganized it under the name Computer Systems Division (CDS). As part of Gould, the new Computer Systems Division continued to design and manufacture computer systems for the simulation, energy, and telemetry markets. In 1985, CDS created a distributed shared memory system that became known as the Reflective Memory System. This system not only provided a simple memory model but also solved failure obstacles. The reflective memory system passively "reflected" memory updates to the memory boards on every one of the computers on the participating system. Each individual computer in a system possessed a reflective memory adapter and functioned as a repository for shared data. Armed with its own adapter, each computer was therefore protected from the failure of any other computer.

The strategy behind Encore's acquisition of Gould's Computer Systems Division was simple. Encore combined its own high technology symmetrical multiprocessing research and design advances with CSD's microprocessor-based systems and high-speed reflective memory system. The combination of high technology laid the groundwork for the development of Encore's Infinity 90 Series.

Infinity 90 was an open systems mainframe that provided I/O bandwidth and massive storage capacity. The topology of the system was designed to solve any single failure within a network without disrupting the entire system. Encore felt that the mainframe was a significant advance over traditional mainframe solutions to systems failures and storage capacity. Encore management believed the development of the Infinity 90 Series was the answer to their financial difficulties.

During the late 1980s and early 1990s, there was a detectable trend within the computer industry away from traditional proprietary computer technologies toward a "open systems" technology, that is, software and hardware manufactured to nonproprietary international standards and capable of running on machines regardless of their manufacturer. Nonetheless, the market for such technology remained very small. Encore committed over $76 million to develop a new generation of computer systems (the Infinity 90 Series and the Encore 90 Families) based on the open systems architecture, but demand for its products remained weak. Encore's new open systems technology did not generate the level of demand and income that management initially anticipated. At the same time, the company's older technology reached the final stages of its marketability and began to experience declining sales. The increasingly precarious financial position of the company began to affect the working relations of the founders, and Bell and Burkhardt decided to resign. Fisher remained chief executive officer and chairman of the board but was confronted with what seemed to be intractable financial problems. Sales of $215 million in 1990 dropped to $153 million by 1991.

Faced with declining revenues and a smaller customer base than originally projected, Fisher responded aggressively by implementing a complete restructuring of the company. He reduced Encore's number of employees, consolidated manufacturing and warehousing facilities, and devoted even more money to research and development. Pinched to generate a sufficient cash flow to pay for operating expenses, Fisher looked for help from the outside.

In 1991, Encore entered into an agreement with Japan Energy Corporation and a number of its subsidiaries to provide working capital for the financially strapped high-tech firm. The agreement included a revolving loan program amounting to $50 million and a refinanced loan amounting to $80 million. Fisher also agreed to a large exchange of stock for help in paying off Encore's growing debts.

With the assistance of Japan Energy, Fisher was able to obtain Encore additional time to prepare the Infinity 90 Series for market. When the Infinity 90 product line was introduced, however, the overall market conditions and the demand for open systems products did not increase significantly. Sales for 1992 dropped to $130 million. That year, the company was delisted by NASDAQ because it was unable to meet NASDAQ's $2 million minimum equity requirements for trading.

Anticipating future developments in the marketplace, Fisher reduced the level of sales to U.S. government agencies. With the end of the cold war in Europe, Fisher correctly perceived that the U.S. government, and especially the Department of Defense, would reduce its expenditures for computers and computer-related services. In 1992 and 1993, sales to various departments of the U.S. government amounted to 29 percent and 37 percent of the company's total net sales, respectively. To offset the potential damage that could be inflicted on Encore if the source of these revenues was reduced, he concentrated on expanding the Infinity 90 Series product line, still convinced of the application and high growth potentiality of non-traditional computer markets.

Encore, however, endured another disappointing year in 1993. The declining demand for open systems technology exceeded the projections of company management and, as a result, revenues continued to spiral downward. Estimates for international sales and growth of non-traditional computer markets were also significantly higher than actual sales and growth rates. At the end of fiscal 1993, the company reported sales of $93 million, a $35 million decrease from the previous year, and an operating loss of over $69 million. In light of these problems, Fisher was forced to reduce Encore's work force by 10 percent in June and an additional 8 percent in December of the same year. The company's European work force was reduced by approximately 20 percent. It marked the third straight year that the company had cut the number of workers it employed. Other cost-cutting measures included the elimination of excess sales and service offices.

With Fisher in firm control of Encore and a comprehensive restructuring program completed, the company's fortunes suddenly turned around. In late 1993 and early 1994, Encore management negotiated a major contract with Digital Equipment Corporation to license the company's connectivity technology for use in DEC's product line. This move, expected to produce a large amount of revenue through royalties, started to show results in early 1995. Encore also won a contract with the U.S. Department of Defense to replace and upgrade already employed IBM mainframes with its Infinity 90 Series at certain centers operated around the world. The first system was installed in January 1994. The Department of Defense was so pleased with the performance of this equipment that it concluded an agreement to install $20 million worth of Encore systems during the remainder of 1994.

Throughout 1994, Encore succeeded in winning additional contracts. The company reached an agreement with Amdahl Corporation to distribute an IBM-compatible storage system using a modified Infinity 90 mainframe computer. This was the first product designed and manufactured by Encore to be compatible with IBM's product environment, and the introduction of this system marked Encore's first foray into a $13 billion market. Encore noted that the product was the first in the industry with the ability to connect to an IBM system and provide storage functions, while at the same time perform as an open systems mainframe computer. The result was a five-year distribution partnership that amounted to over $1 billion. Finally, in early 1994, the company was recapitalized and began to sell its stock once again on the NASDAQ. By the end of fiscal 1994, Encore sales had rebounded to $130 million on the strength of Fisher's reconfiguration of Encore into an alternative mainframe and storage systems company.

Plotting a Downward Curve

The flicker of success proved to be a brief pause in Encore's decline. Nearly ten years after the deal, Encore still had not

recovered from its 1988 purchase of Gould's real-time computing business. The real-time enterprise developed and marketed data systems for such applications as military and civil aircraft simulators, utility power stations, and rapid transit systems that required computer processors capable of analyzing and responding to input at high speeds. A "business in decline," according to David Poppe of the *Miami Herald* (March 24, 1998), the real-time operation struggled despite having contracts with most major air carriers, including Boeing, Northrup Grumman, Electrabel, Lockheed, Raytheon, and Consolidated Edison.

Encore drew heavily on Gould and its then parent company Nippon Mining Co's resources, completing a $150 million recapitalization with Nippon Mining in 1992 and a $100 million debt-to-equity refinancing deal with Gould in 1994. In 1995, a recapitalization of undisclosed amount with Japan Energy Corp. allowed Encore to resume trading on NASDAQ, but the company continued to suffer steep losses. Between 1989 and 1998, the company lost over $228 million. In 1993, after its recapitalization with Nippon Mining, Encore's losses averaged nearly $6 million per month on revenues of about $7.79 million per month. In 1994, after the recapitalization through Gould, Encore's losses averaged about $3.4 million per month on revenues of about $6.48 million per month. David Poppe wrote, "Encore's continual need for financial aid caused Japan Energy Corp., the parent of Gould, to publicly describe Encore as a bone in its throat." Gould refinanced Encore again in 1997, converting $40 million of debt into preferred stock convertible to non-voting common stock at $3.25 per share, but the cash infusion was not enough to keep Encore from being removed to NASDAQ's Small Cap Market in early February of that year because the company failed to meet trading regulations for net tangible assets.

Into the Sunset

July 1997 marked the sale of Encore's storage products business to Sun Microsystems Inc., a Santa Clara, California-based technology firm known for such innovations as the universal software platform Java and other technologies important to the Internet and networking systems. The $185 million cash deal provided Sun with Encore's Datashare software and associated intellectual properties and technologies, which Sun intended to use to bolster its enterprise-level computing business. Led by Robert Collings and Paul Rosenblum, six Encore shareholders, who controlled over 5 percent of the company's stock, objected to the deal, which called for Encore to pay $154 million of the purchase price to Gould to retire debt and $17 million to management and employees in the form of severance payments and incentives. Shareholders would receive the remaining $7 million, or about 2.5 cents per share, only $4.3 million of which would come in the form of cash. Gould owned 49 percent of Encore's shares, however, so the opposition came to naught.

It was a deal that Sun came to regret. Sun hoped that the Encore software would aid in the development of a high-end intelligent storage system, but delays in packaging and delivery so diminished revenues from the software that Sun declared in its September 20, 2001, SEC filing that "future cash flow from the use of Encore's technology was determined to be negligible in fiscal 2000." Sun scrapped Encore's technology at a cost of $9 million and signed a deal to sell Hitachi Data Systems instead.

Encore Liquidated

Its primary business gone, Encore posted a loss of more than $20 million on revenues of over $8.33 million in 1997. By the end of the first quarter of 1998 in March, the company recorded a net loss of $766,000 on revenues of more than $4.7 million. That month, Encore announced the sale of its real-time computing business to Gores Technology Group, a technology acquisition company that purchased and managed high-tech organizations, for $3 million in cash. Under the terms of the sale, Gores operated Encore's real-time business between June 1, 1998 and January 8, 1999 for a fee of $100,000 per month, refundable to Encore on closure of the deal. During that time, Gores contracted with Compro to provide hardware service and refurbished products, reorganized Encore's European branches, and signed a new agreement with Encore's Japanese distributor. The management company also met with major customers and tailored the business, accelerating software releases and planning software and hardware upgrades to suit. Under Gores' management, sales increased 20 percent over the six months ending June 1998, and the real-time business began generating a net profit. The sale closed on January 8, 1999, and Encore ceased operations.

Principal Competitors

Dell Inc.; EMC Corporation; Hitachi Data Systems Corporation; International Business Machines Corporation.

Further Reading

"Acquisition: Encore and Sun Microsystems Sign Definitive Agreement for Encore's Storage Product Business," *EDGE: Work-Group Computing Report*, July 21, 1997, p. 1.

Baatz, E.B., "How to Win the Hearts (and Cash) Of Fickle Venture Capitalists," *Electronic Business*, June 1992, p. 96.

"Can Three Hotshots Make Encore Take Off?" *Business Week*, August 27, 1984, p. 93.

"Encore Computer Completes $40 Million Recapitalization," *Business Wire*, March 20, 1997, item 3201200.

"Encore Computer Shares Now Trade on NASDAQ SmallCap Market," *Business Wire*, February 6, 1997, item 2060179.

"Encore Sells Off Last of Its Business to Gores for $3M," *Computergram International*, January 7, 1999.

"Financial: Encore Reports First Quarter Financial Results," *EDGE: Work-Group Computing Report*, June 8, 1998, p. 42.

Freeman, Tyson, "Sun Takes $51M Charge on Bad Deals," *Daily Deal*, October 2, 2001.

"Gores Says Encore Real-Time Business Is Growing," *Computergram International*, January 11, 1999.

"GTG Concludes Encore Acquisition," *Business Wire*, January 8, 1999, item 0131.

"Joint Venture Expected to Boost Encore Sales," *South Florida Business Journal*, March 5, 1993, p. 23A.

LaPolla, Stephanie, "Vendors Promote Sharing in Heterogeneous Clusters," *PC Week*, December 16, 1996, p. 145.

"Monday Roundup," *Austin American-Statesman* (Texas), July 21, 1997, p. D2.

Ouellette, Tim, "Sun Rises in High-End Storage," *Computerworld*, July 28, 1997, p. 28.

Poppe, David, "Encore Computer Corp. Will Sell Last Unit, Liquidate," *Miami Herald*, March 24, 1998.

"Taking on Big Blue: Encore Stakes Future on New System," *South Florida Business Journal*, October 19, 1992, p. 15.

Turner, Alison, "Encore Computer Restructuring to Bolster Equity," *South Florida Business Journal*, February 11, 1994, p. 19A.

——, "Encore Shares Up as Firm Again Retools Financing," *South Florida Business Journal*, March 24, 1995, p. 5A.

—Thomas Derdak
—update: Jennifer Gariepy

Fiji Water LLC

361 South Side Drive
Basalt, Colorado 81621
U.S.A.
Telephone: (970) 927-7631
Toll Free: (877) 426-3454
Fax: (970) 920-1852
Web site: http://www.fijiwater.com

Wholly Owned Subsidiary of Roll International
    Corporation
Incorporated: 1993 as Nature's Best
Employees: 50 (est.)
Sales: $25 million (2004 est.)
NAIC: 312112 Bottled Water Manufacturing

A subsidiary of Roll International Corporation, Fiji Water LLC sells water in a distinctive square bottle under the Fiji Water label. The product has become the favorite bottled water of movie stars, rock musicians, and supermodels. Because of its chic appeal, Fiji Water also has benefited from some free product placement, appearing on the screen in such movies as *The Thomas Crown Affair* and *DodgeBall,* and television series *Ally McBeal, The West Wing, Friends, Felicity,* and *Just Shoot Me.* Fiji Water is even found in trendy restaurants, albeit corseted in a silver slipper. Moreover, some master chefs insist on cooking with Fiji Water. The company maintains that its water stands out because of its purity, drawn from a 17-mile-wide, 400-feet-deep aquifer on the Fiji island of Vitu Levu. The rainwater that filled the aquifer is 450 years old, according to carbon dating tests touted by the company, the result of rainwater that trickled through layers of rock and earth on a journey that took hundreds of years to complete. Hence Fiji Water predates the Industrial Revolution by a wide margin and has supposedly escaped the effects of centuries of pollution. The limited supply of Fiji Water, as well as the distance it must travel to reach a market, is a major factor in the company's business model, allowing it to sell the product at a premium price and placing subtle pressure on consumers to buy the water while it lasts. Of course, the Fiji Water company is

carefully controlling the flow of the water, periodically drilling holes to test the level to be certain the reservoir is not being depleted too quickly.

Founder's Launch of Business Career in the 1950s

The man behind the birth of Fiji Water was Canadian David Gilmour, son of an army officer-turned-businessman and an opera singer. As a child he traveled the world and, according to his recollections, developed a taste for exotic water. "From age 6, I had this feel for spring water," he told Danielle Herubin in a 1998 interview with the *Palm Beach Post.* "It was always a fascination, but I never found the perfect spring. It was always, in my opinion, flawed." Gilmour experienced a complete business career before resuming his fascination with water. He studied institutional management at the University of Toronto, and then following a one-year stint in the military started his business career in the 1950s, using $2,300 in savings to launch a company called Scan-Trade to import products from Scandinavia. Then in 1958 he teamed up with an old college friend, Peter Munk, to become involved in the hi-fi business. Their company, Clairtone, did well until they decided to try manufacturing televisions. The company failed amid some controversy, with accusations made that the two men had failed to keep shareholders adequately informed about how well the business was faring. Although Clairtone was liquidated by the government, Gilmour and Munk came away with some profits, which in the late 1960s they put to use building luxury hotels in the South Pacific, forming the Southern Pacific Hotel Corporation (SPHC), an enterprise that introduced Gilmour to Fiji and its more than 300 islands.

In 1971 Gilmour flew over the small uninhabited, 2,200-acre Fiji island of Wakaya and fell in love with its 32 pristine beaches. A year later he bought it for $1 million, and for the next 20 years used it as a family retreat. In the meantime, SPHC grew into the largest hotel chain in the region and was sold in 1981. Gilmour and Munk then used their hotel profits to form an oil exploration company that became Barrick Gold Corporation, involved in U.S. gold mining and acquiring Nevada's Goldstrike field, which turned out to be North America's largest gold field, producing 40,000 ounces a year. All the while, Gil-

Company Perspectives:

The company's mission is to establish Fiji Water as the most desired premium bottled water in the world.

mour began to develop the idea of building a luxury resort on Wakaya. In 1991 he opened the Wakaya Club, an exclusive ecologically sensitive resort. Gilmour dedicated the profits from the venture to the improvement of Fiji schools in honor of his daughter Erin. Her dream had been to teach art and history on Fiji. Gilmour sent her to Toronto to complete her education, but in 1983 she was found murdered in her apartment, a devastating, life-changing event for Gilmour.

Gilmour began developing a celebrity clientele for the Wayaka Club, the resort marketed solely by word of mouth. In 1999, *People* magazine offered a glimpse of life on Gilmour's pleasure isle: "Guests—including Tim Allen, Pierce Brosnan, Fran Drescher and Patrick Stewart—touch down on Wakaya's 2,500-foot airstrip in Gilmour's six-seater private plane and are greeted with a split of Taittinger champagne, tropical fruit and freshly baked ginger cookies. They then spend a luxurious week in one of nine thatched-roof guest villas, each complete with a four-poster rattan bed, a deluxe private bathroom and at least five employees to cater to their needs (cost: $1,200 to $1,400 per night). To enhance a sense of isolation from the outside world, Gilmour keeps the villas TV- and telephone-free. Recreation includes scuba diving amid dramatic coral reefs and hiking on scenic trails. For the less energetic, plenty of hammocks, masseuses and icy drinks await. Said Seattle racehorse breeder Karen Taylor shortly after arriving in April: 'I feel like I have landed on Fantasy Island.' "

The Wayaka resort served its guests native venison and vegetables and herbs grown on the island, but imported bottled French water. One day while playing golf on the island, Gilmour watched a guest drinking the imported water and it struck him as odd that he should have to send for water halfway around the globe when in all likelihood some of the purest water in the world was likely to be found close by—given Wayaka's virgin ecosystem, protected by a 1,500-mile buffer in all directions. Gilmour now enlisted the services of Barrick geologists to launch a search for the perfect water that had eluded him since childhood. They were eventually drawn to the island of Vitu Levu and a 50-acre parcel of land in the Yaqara Valley. Drilling and testing revealed a source of pure, delicious water, amply supplied with colloidal silica, which many believed helped to boost immune systems and counteract the effects of aging.

Building a Premium Brand in the 1990s

In 1993 Gilmour founded the production company of Fiji Water under the Nature's Best name, and then changed it to Natural Waters of Viti Limited in 1995, the same year the Fiji Water brand was created. The Fiji government granted the company a 99-year-lease in exchange for a royalty to tap the aquifer, and Gilmour invested $48 million to build a bottling plant on the site. In mid-1996 Gilmour recruited Aspen, Colorado businessman Doug Carlson to become cofounder and chief

executive officer of Natural Waters of Viti. Like Gilmour, Carlson had enjoyed a highly successful career in the hospitality industry. In the latter half of the 1980s he served as the CEO of The Aspen Club Companies, Aspen's largest hospitality company. Then prior to joining Gilmour he served as chief financial officer of The Aspen Skiing Company, a $100 million hospitality and ski resort company. It was not an easy task convincing him to join Fiji Water, however. Carlson told the *Denver Post* in December 2000 that it took "six phone calls to convince me to go from frozen water to melted water." Although he agreed to run Natural Waters of Viti, he did not relocate to Fiji, instead setting up headquarters in Basalt, Colorado, since it was in the United States where ultimately the company would either succeed or fail.

Initially Fiji Water was served to guests at The Wayaka Club and to SPHC resorts where Gilmour was connected. In June 1997 Fiji Water was introduced in the United States, first in the core markets of Los Angeles and Palm Beach, Florida, and then branching out to statewide distribution. It was sold in half-liter and 1½ liter squarish plastic bottles. The label was partially clear on the front so that in combination with a double-sided label on the back, it produced an eye-catching three-dimensional effect. Early in 1998 the product came to New York City and achieved national distribution over the course of the year. Fiji Water's timing proved to be fortuitous, as Evian and Perrier, the longtime best-selling French water brands began to falter, losing market share as well as their premium status to a multitude of new water brands, some of which were backed by deep-pocketed corporations like PepsiCo, Inc., the marketer of Aquafina and Dasani. Fiji Water's pitch as the purest water in the world allowed it to find a premium niche in a crowded marketplace. Gilmour continued to cultivate the brand's upscale image, convincing tony restaurants to carry Fiji Water. Jean George, one of Manhattan's top restaurants, balked at placing a plastic water bottle on its tables, although chef Jean-Gorges Vongerichten liked the water. After being shown a silver coaster that the restaurant used to make other bottles "table-worthy," Gilmour had a silver sleeve fashioned to fit the Fiji Water bottle. All eight of Vongerichten's Manhattan restaurants now began serving Fiji Water, priced at $10 for a liter bottle. In Hollywood it also made the menu at the Los Angeles Athletic Club, Le Dome, and the Chalet Gourmet.

Fiji Water enjoyed exceptional growth for a new product, increasing sales 250 percent from 1998 to 1999, and 242 percent to 2000. The product grew almost entirely by word of mouth, with some of the most famous people in the world acting as evangelists, including Jacqueline Bisset, Nicholas Cage, Elton John, Bruce Springsteen, Wesley Snipes, David Bowie, Elle MacPherson, Cindy Crawford, Rod Stewart, and Leonardo DiCaprio. Fiji Water also benefited from free product placement on films and television shows, although it soon had to pay for the exposure. Gilmour also was not above taking advantage of less common ways to promote his water. In 2000 Fiji underwent the third coup d'etat in its history, and a group of self-proclaimed nationalists seized the bottling plant and shut down production. The plant was almost entirely staffed by locals, who convinced the revolutionaries to leave. When international journalists descended upon Fiji to cover the coup, Gilmour tried to drum up interest in the plant takeover story as a way to promote the Fiji Water brand, but enjoyed little success.

Key Dates:

1993: The company is founded.
1996: Fiji Water is first produced and sold.
1997: Fiji Water is introduced in the United States in Los Angeles and Palm Beach.
1998: Fiji Water is introduced in New York City.
2000: A new bottling facility opens.
2004: The company is sold to Roll International.

Increasing Demand on an International Scale in the Early 2000s

Rising demand for Fiji Water led to the construction of a 110,000-square-foot, state-of-the-art bottling plant, completed in 2000 on the aquifer. Demand continued to build in the 2000s, leading to the airlifting of a new bottle line in 2004 to help increase capacity to more than 50 million cases a year. By now it was being sold in eight countries, marketed as Fiji Natural Mineral Water in Europe and Fiji Natural Spring Water in Australia.

In December 2004 Gilmour elected to sell Fiji Water to Roll International, controlled by one of Hollywood's richest couples, Stewart and Lynda Resnick, who made their fortune with Teleflora and gained notoriety through their ownership of the Franklin Mint, which became embroiled in a messy lawsuit with the Princess Diana Trusts over memorabilia sales. According to press reports, the Resnicks bought Fiji Water for approximately $50 million. They expressed their commitment to growing the business, while Gilmour planned to continue to play a role in the company's further development.

Principal Competitors

The Coca-Cola Company; Hawaiian Natural Water Company, Inc.; PepsiCo, Inc.

Further Reading

Austin, Marsha, ''Firm's Bottled Water from Fiji Grows in Popularity,'' *Denver Post,* December 26, 2000.

Helliger, Jeremy, and Vicki Sheff Cahan, ''Enchanted Isle: By Creating the Ultimate Retreat, David Gilmour Turned Tragedy into a Memorial,'' *People,* June 7, 1999, p. 73.

Herubin, Danielle, ''David Gilmour's Search for the Perfect Water,'' *Palm Beach Post,* April 6, 1998, p. 18.

''Island Water Floats on Luxury and Prestige,'' *Beverage Industry,* September 2000, p. 70.

McKay, Betsy, and Cynthia Cho, ''Water Works; How Fiji Brand Got Hip to Sip,'' *Wall Street Journal,* August 16, 2004, p. B1.

Milstead, David, ''L.A. Firm to Acquire Fiji Water,'' *Rocky Mountain News,* November 27, 2004, p. 2C.

Mortished, Carl, ''The Miner Who Struck Gold When He Found Water in Fiji,'' *The Times,* June 9, 2003, p. 27.

Ragogo, Matelita, ''Fiji Water Making Waves,'' *Pacific,* July 2003.

Todd, Heather, ''On an Island Paradise, Fiji Water Sets a Standard of Social Responsibility,'' *Beverage World,* January 15, 2005, p. 10.

—Ed Dinger

GELITA AG

Gelita AG

Uferstrasse 7
69412 Eberbach
Germany
Telephone: +49 (0) 62 71/84-21 90
Fax: +49 (0) 62 71/84-27 18
Web site: http://www.gelita.com

Private Company
Incorporated: 1878 as F. Drescher & Co.
Employees: 2,500
Sales: $549.3 million (2004)
NAIC: 325414 Biological Product (Except Diagnostic)
Manufacturing; 325998 All Other Miscellaneous
Chemical Product Manufacturing

Gelita AG is the world leader in the production of gelatin products. In 2004 Gelita, known until 2005 as DGF Stoess & Co. GmbH, produced some 78,000 tons of gelatin, for a broad variety of products, including foodstuffs, photography, pharmaceutical uses, and human nutrition. Gelita has factories on five continents, in the United Kingdom, France, Sweden, The Netherlands, the United States, Brazil, Mexico, Australia, New Zealand, South Africa, and China, as well as in its native Germany. In addition to its wide-reaching business interests, Gelita is involved in a number of social and community-based projects.

Producing Gelatin in the 19th Century

Gelita AG has its roots in the mid-19th century when gelatin underwent a transformation from a byproduct, produced by individual tanners, furriers, and butchers in small quantities from leftover animal bones and skins, to a product produced in vast quantities using rationalized industrial methods. The Gelita concern began to emerge between 1875 up to 1888 from a number of pioneer firms in southwestern Germany. The first was founded in 1875 by Amalius Schmidt, the first gelatin-maker to introduce automation to the production of gelatin in his factory near Schweinfurt, Germany. The cost of expansion, however, brought Schmidt into financial straits. Three years later creditors took over the works and teamed up with another

gelatin producer, F. Drescher, to form the firm, F. Drescher & Co. By the end of 1878, the Drescher factory was producing some 50 tons of gelatin annually. Over the coming years, Drescher continued to make improvements to his plant.

Drescher, however, was confronted with a knotty problem, one that had contributed to Schmidt's downfall—he had few distribution channels for his gelatin. Into the breach stepped Ch. W. Heinrichs, a gelatin distributor with such a broad base of customers that he could not find enough product to meet demand. Heinrichs first agreed to purchase Drescher's entire annual output, and then proposed becoming a partner in the company. Drescher rejected the offer at first but accepted when Heinrichs stopped purchasing Drescher's gelatin. Now a silent partner, Heinrichs brought his in-law, Heinrich Stoess, into Drescher & Co. Once inside Drescher with an effective sales force established, Stoess schemed to force Heinrichs out of the company. In the end, Stoess lost the power struggle and was himself forced to leave. Using the severance money he received from Drescher, however, Stoess set up his own gelatin company in Ziegelhausen, the Heidelberger Gelatine-Fabrik Stoess & Co., a company that by World War I would be one of the leading gelatin producers in Germany.

In May 1889, Drescher & Co. formally merged with Heinrichs's own gelatin factory in Hoechst, Germany to form Deutsche Gelatine-Fabriken (DGF) (German Gelatin Factories). DGF was established as a stock company. If a stockholder wanted to sell, however, other shareholders had to be given the right of first refusal, an arrangement that guaranteed control would remain in the hands of the owners and their families.

Both DGF and the Stoess firm produced edible gelatin for human consumption as well as photographic gelatin for the new medium that was just beginning to reach a broad public. In 1889–90 DGF produced 200 tons of gelatin, of which photographic gelatin constituted about 30 tons. By 1900 the company had established branches in London and Paris, and a sales office in New York, and was producing almost 350 tons of gelatin annually.

Meanwhile, in 1880, the brothers Paul and Werner Koepff had established a gelatin factory, Göppinger Gelatine and Leimfabrik,

Company Perspectives:

As gelatine experts and professionals, our primary focus is our core business gelatine with all its numerous fields of application (edible, photographic, pharmaceutical and special gelatine), including alternative raw materials. We are at the leading edge of the gelatine market and are fully customer-oriented. Our management is lean; we are flexible, fast and present throughout the world. We have a clear vision of the future and we are successful. We fully support the Mission & Values GELITA stands for and regard the GELITA brand as a very important company asset.

in Göppingen. The Koepff firm split its production almost evenly between edible and photographic gelatin. It was one of the first to rationalize the delivery of raw materials by laying rail lines directly up to the factory doors. By the dawn of the 20th century, DGF, one of the top two gelatin producers in the world, was buying some 15 percent of the Koepff firm's total output and in 1904 proposed a "financial cooperation" with its supplier. Although struggling with financial difficulties at the time, Koepff declined the offer, and a few months later declined another DGF offer to buy it outright. A brief upswing followed at the Koepff firm. After it expanded its factory, it found itself once again heavily indebted. When Paul Koepff (who by then was running the firm on his own) became seriously ill in 1911, he finally agreed to sell to DGF. The companies merged in 1911. Paul Koepff became the largest shareholder in DGF.

Overcoming Adversity in the Early 1900s

The German gelatin industry was hit hard by the start of World War I. It was abruptly cut off from foreign markets in Europe in 1914 and from the lucrative American market beginning in 1917. Raw materials were difficult to obtain. The workforce declined drastically because of conscription. Demand for gelatin in Germany plummeted. To bolster demand, DGF launched an aggressive campaign positioning gelatin as a nutritional supplement. Advertising was aimed directly at consumers; gelatin cookbooks were published and distributed. The strategy had little effect, however. After producing 720 tons in 1916–17, DGF production plunged to only 281 tons in 1919.

Both DGF and Stoess survived the war, and by 1920 DGF had resumed export relations, despite continuing shortages. A factor that contributed greatly to the upturn for both companies was an increased demand for high-quality, uniformly produced photographic gelatin. In the early 1920s both DGF and Stoess established exclusive supply deals with major film manufacturers, DGF with the German firm AGFA and Stoess with Eastman Kodak of Rochester, New York.

Heinrich Stoess had begun dealing with Eastman Kodak in 1893 and after the war ended they resumed their relationship, forging the first post-World War I German-American joint venture with the construction of the so-called Odin-Werke. A state-of-the-art factory for photographic gelatin in Eberbach, Germany completed in 1922, the Odin-Werke was a classic company town that included houses for workers, stores,

company-organized social clubs, and such. Business with Eastman Kodak was a boon to Stoess at the peak of the German postwar hyperinflation, when German currency was so rapidly devalued that within a year and a half the price of gelatin rocketed from 20 Marks per kilogram to 85,000 Marks per kilogram. The American dollars Eastman Kodak paid were stable currency that did not lose value overnight. With the same stroke of the pen, however, Stoess competitor DGF was forced to give up its Eastman Kodak business, and its valuable foreign income. By 1927 the market had changed again. Both AGFA and Eastman Kodak cut their photographic gelatin purchases from DGF and Stoess. To concentrate its resources, DGF relocated its headquarters to Schweinfurt and turned to Eastman Kodak subsidiaries elsewhere in the world for business.

Economic, Political, and Personal Challenges in the 1930s

Disaster struck in 1929. The Great Depression was a blow to the entire German gelatin industry. Stoess was hit with another tragedy as well. After completing the construction of a new factory in Eberbach, Heinrich Stoess made a trip to India. Shortly after his return, he suffered a major stroke that left him mute, paralyzed, and unable to lead the company. His son Walter took over the company reins. For the next ten years, the elder Stoess's condition was a closely held company secret, and in public statements it continued to attribute important company decisions to him. When he finally died in 1938, his obituary made no mention at all of his long illness and only then did his son officially take over the firm leadership.

With the Great Depression came a precipitous drop in demand for gelatin and DGF's undisputed German market leadership with 51 percent share of gelatin production meant little. Stoess was hit hard by the economic downturn. Its major plant, the Odin-Werke, was operating at greatly reduced capacity, and the firm had to cut its staff by more than 50 percent from that of the 1920s. The firm also shut its factory in Ziegelhausen down completely.

Later in the 1930s, however, both firms bounced back, and before long made Germany the world's leading producer of photographic and leaf gelatin. In 1934 DGF introduced the Gelita name as the umbrella brand for all of its gelatin products. The later 1930s were not without problems. The Nazis, who had come to power in 1933, had introduced strict laws governing the economic sphere. In 1937 DGF was charged with violations of foreign trade regulations. As a result, a number of company officials were arrested and spent time—sometimes weeks—in jail. Stoess was immune from such harassment for two reasons. It had resumed its relationship with Eastman Kodak in the United States and was bringing large amounts of badly needed foreign currency into Nazi Germany. Furthermore, Wilhelm Keppler, a member of the Stoess family, a leading executive at the firm, and a dedicated Nazi, was Hitler's leading economic advisor. Unfortunately for Stoess, Eastman Kodak and Keppler did not mix well. The American company objected to the close ties its partner firm apparently had with Hitler and demanded that Keppler leave if the partnership were to continue. Shortly afterward Keppler resigned and divested himself of all Stoess shares. By 1939, when World War II began, Stoess had doubled its 1932 production levels from 20 to 40 tons monthly.

Key Dates:

1875: Amalius Schmitt starts producing gelatin on an industrial basis in Schweinfurt.

1878: F. Drescher takes over Schmitt's gelatin factory.

1880: Göppinger Gelatine and Leimfabrik is founded by Paul and Heinrich Koepff, in Göppingen.

1888: Heinrich Stoess founds the Heidelberg Gelatine-Fabrik Stoess & Co. Ziegelhausen.

1908: The Koepff brothers link their Göppingen firm directly to the railway system.

1921: Stoess and Eastman Kodak jointly build Odin-Werke in Eberbach.

1934: Gelita is introduced as a brand name by DGF.

1945: American occupation authorities block the attempted merger of Stoess and DGF; Stoess is placed under "property control" by the occupation authorities.

1948: Heinrich Koepff of DGF is named co-manager of Stoess & Co. by Walter Stoess.

1950: R.P. Scherer GmbH is founded jointly by DGF, Stoess, and the American firm R.P. Scherer.

1972: DGF and Chemische Werke Stoess merge to form DGF Stoess & Co. GmbH.

1977: DGF Stoess Inc. is founded in Morris Plains, New York.

1977: Rohage GmbH is founded.

1992: Kind & Knox Gelatin Inc. of Sioux City, Iowa, is acquired.

2000: DGF Stoess celebrates its 125th anniversary.

2002: DGF Stoess moves into new headquarters in Eberbach.

2005: DGF Stoess changes its name to Gelita AG.

Destruction, Reconstruction, and New Products in the 1940s–50s

World War II brought further hard times to the German gelatin industry. By 1942 its export business had ceased entirely. DGF revenues dropped by 65 percent. Stoess was forced to close the Odin-Werke. With their workforces ravaged by conscription, both firms turned to slave labor—POWs, Jews from occupied countries, and others—to work their factories. By 1944 almost 20 percent of DGF's workforce consisted of forced labor. In the course of the war DGF suffered near total destruction of its most important factories from air raids. Stoess, on the other hand, came through virtually unhurt in spite of heavy bombing in the area of its Eberbach headquarters.

In 1942, for unknown reasons, Walter Stoess made overtures to DGF to buy his firm. Three years later the two companies merged. When the war ended just months later, however, American authorities declared the merger to be in violation of antitrust regulations and invalidated it. They also interred Walter Stoess as a Nazi war criminal and seized his company. It was not returned to him until 1948.

The reversal of the merger was difficult for both companies. In 1946 DGF had no production facilities to speak of, while Stoess had been seized and shut down by the American occupiers. Of the two, DGF was in far worse shape. Aside from

having no factories, its raw material and sales channels were nonexistent. In its first year of business after the war, it sold only one ton of leaf gelatin, less than one five-hundredth its 1932 sales. To bolster its position, the firm investigated new "special" gelatin applications, such as gelatin sponges for surgery, zinc glue, lime feed for livestock, food additives, aspic powder, and baking powder. These carried DGF through the first difficult postwar years when it manufactured 284.6 tons of special products—three times as much as gelatin products. The German currency reform in 1948 solved one serious problem. The new currency, the Deutsche Mark, was fixed at a more equitable exchange rate, and with it German firms could once again buy their raw materials on the world market. Gelatin production increased substantially. In the first half of 1948, before the reform, DGF produced 64 tons of gelatin; in the six months after the June reform it produced 242 tons. As production grew, gelatin products once again provided a larger and larger proportion of DGF sales.

In 1948 Walter Stoess was cleared of war crimes and his company was returned to him. Once back at his desk he made a decision that contributed greatly to the later merger of DGF and Stoess—he hired Paul Koepff's grandson Heinrich Koepff, who was a leading shareholder and ranking executive of DGF, as the co-manager of Stoess & Co. While serving at Stoess, Koepff retained his position at DGF—including full power of attorney at the firm. There was apparently minimal conflict of interest—at the time DGF produced primarily edible gelatin, while Stoess specialized in photographic and pharmaceutical gelatin.

In the early 1950s world demand for edible and photographic gelatins dropped again. The recent development of important new gelatin capsule technologies for medicine, however, seemed to point a way out of the downturn. Heinrich Koepff visited R.P. Scherer Co., a firm in Detroit, Michigan that was at the forefront of the field. Koepff persuaded the at first skeptical company to work with him, a project that became the first postwar German-American joint venture. The two firms built a new plant in Eberbach that incorporated the gelatin capsule advances pioneered by Scherer. The American company held a 51 percent share in the company called R.P. Scherer GmbH; Stoess and DGF shared a 49 percent interest. It was DGF and Stoess's first foothold in an area that would become the third great gelatin application—pharmaceutical gelatin. Pharmaceutical products enabled DGF to increase its annual revenues from DEM 30,000 in 1950 to DEM 2.34 million in 1954.

Expansion and Merger in the 1960s

In the remainder of the 1950s both Stoess and DGF concentrated on expanding and modernizing their production facilities. By 1960 Stoess was a considerably healthier company than DGF. The Eberbach firm was more effective, more profitable, and was situated in a better location than DGF. Heinrich Koepff, with a hand in both companies, launched efforts early in the 1960s toward a merger that would enable the two firms to solve various manufacturing and organizational problems, to rationalize production, and to phase out obsolete facilities. Certain members of the DGF board had long been hostile to Koepff's proposals, but by 1964 they had retired. Koepff in the meantime had consolidated his control of DGF, quietly buying up shares from the heirs of its original founders. In 1965 he made his move. Stoess purchased DGF outright. Immediately afterward, the most ineffective factories were shut down; production of the former competitors was consolidated and divided among the remaining plants. The merger was further consecrated one year later when Heinrich Koepff, the son of one of DGF's cofounders, married Gerda Stoess, the granddaughter of Stoess's founder. DGF remained a subsidiary of Stoess & Co. until 1972 when the two formally merged into DGF Stoess & Co. GmbH.

Expansion and Acquisitions in the 1970s

The 1970s saw the new firm grow. In 1968–69 it spun off its mineral feed division into a new firm, the Gesellschaft für Tierernährung (GfT) (the Society for Animal Nutrition). GfT produced feed for domestic livestock and premixes for industrial livestock production. After the spin-off GfT built a second feed factory, and by 2002 it had grown to one of the leading animal feed companies in Germany. In 1973 DGF Stoess acquired an interest in Scheidemandel AG, a glue maker much larger than DGF Stoess but that was going through a financial crisis. After the acquisition DGF Stoess provided capital for modernization of Scheidemandel plants. In 1979 DGF Stoess acquired an 80 percent share in the firm and by 2000 Scheidemandel existed only as an administrative unit (its factories had all been integrated into DGF Stoess). In 1978 Rohage GmbH was established. Using expertise acquired from Scheidemandel, Rohage was a raw materials trading company established to make DGF Stoess independent of individual suppliers by supplying the raw materials needed for gelatin manufacture. By 2000 Rohage had eight subsidiaries of its own together with an affiliate.

The firm expanded its activities in the United States in the late 1970s. In 1977 DGF Stoess Inc., a sales and marketing firm, was established in Morris Plains, New York. Around the same time the German company entered a joint venture with Davis Gelatine Ltd. of Australia to buy and modernize a gelatin factory in Calumet City, Illinois, which then operated as DynaGel Inc. When work on the 6,500-square-meter plant was completed in May 1981, it was the most modern gelatin factory in the United States.

Focusing on the Future in the 1980s

At the start of the 1980s DGF Stoess set out to define explicit goals and to establish effective strategies for achieving them. The principle goal was to increase the company's share in the German market by 34 percentage points and in the European market by ten percentage points by 1985. The following three areas were cited as critical to success: Special stress was placed on providing the best customer service; a secure self-financing capability was to be established to ensure uninterrupted growth potential; and new product development had to be accelerated, toward which a new R&D department was formed. Gelatin hydrolysate was seen as the most promising area for new product research. During the 1980s numerous applications for the material were found in food processing, pharmaceuticals, nutritional supplements, cosmetics, and perhaps most important, as a treatment for bone and joint problems.

In 1986 firm head Heinrich Koepff passed away. For the next couple of years the firm was run by a board of managers.

In 1988 Jörg Siebert was appointed the chairman of the DGF Stoess board. Siebert would lead the company into the new millennium.

One of Siebert's first moves was an attempt to acquire erstwhile partner capsule manufacturer R.P. Scherer. After the Tylenol scandal in 1985, which led to the loss of hundreds of thousands of dollars of orders for capsules, and a series of internal leadership intrigues had plunged the Detroit company into financial difficulties, it was put up for sale. To raise the funds necessary for a purchase, DGF Stoess converted its corporate form from a GmbH, a corporation with limited liability, to an Aktiengesellschaft (AG), or stock corporation, in 1989. Scherer's board rejected DGF Stoess's first offer, valued at about $341 million, but it invited DGF Stoess to submit a revised bid. Scherer responded to the new $377 million offer with a request for one dollar more per share. The additional expense, DGF Stoess felt, was too high. It broke off negotiations. The failed acquisition nonetheless had three positive results for DGF Stoess: It was transformed into a stock company, it secured financing sources for future expansion, and it laid the foundation for the company's future internationalization of its core gelatin business.

Further Expansion in the 1990s

Expansion into foreign markets was not long in coming. In 1992 DGF Stoess acquired Kind & Knox Gelatin Inc., a Sioux City, Iowa firm that had been producing gelatin products since 1890. The Kind & Knox main factory was completely renovated. In 1998 it was the most modern gelatin facility in North America. By the end of the 1990s, Kind & Knox was directly controlled and fully owned by DGF Stoess. Later the firm bought out Davis Gelatine's share in DynaGel and strengthened even further its presence in the world market; the move made DGF Stoess the world's largest producer of gelatin. During the 1990s subsidiaries for edible gelatin also were established in Great Britain and a firm was acquired in Sweden. In Germany in 1990 a new subsidiary, ATRO Protein Diät GmbH, was founded to produce dietary supplements capitalizing on the nutritional benefits of gelatin. In January 1998 UNIMELT GmbH was formed from the merger of two firms that processed animal fats. The subsidiary would the next year evolve into Gelita's animal fat group.

The decade was not characterized entirely by forward momentum, however. A drop in adhesives sales led the firm to shut down a factory in Wiesbaden in the early 1990s. The decline in the market led DGF Stoess to sell the Scheidemandel adhesives division altogether. In 1992 serious internal disagreements over the company's structure split the firm's upper ranks. One faction thought the company should be a privately run family business as it had always been, the other thought it should remain an AG. The conflict was so bitter that rumors circulated that the company would be sold. By the latter half of the decade, most opponents had left the company.

A New Identity in the 2000s

Going into the new century, the company restructured its operations once again to make them as efficient as possible. An important goal was to establish uniform, recognizable, and respected brand names by 2005. To that end in 1999 it concentrated all of its gelatin activities under a single corporate umbrella, the Gelita Group. The Gelita name, which was seen as representing quality and world leadership, was henceforth to be used on all gelatin products produced by the group. In addition, the Gelita Group, the UNIMELT Group for animal fats, and another group for all remaining business were placed under the administration of the operating unit, DGF Stoess. Meanwhile DGF Stoess AG was restructured into a holding company. Separate, easily distinguishable logos were developed for both DGF Stoess incarnations. On the occasion of its 125th anniversary in 2000, the company announced the construction of a new headquarters building in Eberbach. The building on the Neckar River was completed in 2002.

In 2005 stockholders voted to change Deutsche Gelatine-Fabriken Stoess AG to Gelita AG. That year also saw a 3.3 percent increase in sales over the previous year. In all revenues declined to DEM 454 million, a drop of DEM 18 million. Profits dropped in 2005 as well, from DEM 43 million to DEM 35 million.

Principal Subsidiaries

Gelita France SARL; Gelita Sweden AB; Gelita UK Ltd.; Gelita Deutschland GmbH; Gelita Nederland B.V.; Gelita USA Inc.; Gelita Mexico S. de R.L. de C.V.; Gelita DO BRAZIL Ltda.; Gelita Australia Pty. Ltd.; Gelita NZ. Ltd.; Gelita South Africa Pty. Ltd.; Gelita Tianjin International Trading Co. Ltd.

Principal Competitors

Atlantic Gelatin/Kraft Foods Global Inc.; Nitta Gelatin Canada, Inc.; PB Leiner; Geltech Co. Ltd.; Nitta Gelatin Inc.; Rousselot (Guangdong) Gelatin Co. Ltd.; Ewald Gelatine GmbH; Lapi Gelatine S.p.A.; Gelatines Weishardt S.A.

Further Reading

''DGF Stoess AG: The Gelatine Experts,'' *Nutraceuticals World,* June 2002, p. 89.

Donnan, Shawn, ''Goodman Moves on Buyback,'' *Financial Times,* March 9, 2002, p. 8.

''Gelita Establishes New Names,'' *Nutraceuticals World,* June 2003, p. 22.

Tode, Sven, *The Gelita Story—125 Years of DGF Stoess AG,* Hamburg, 2003.

''World Leader Gelita Arrives,'' *Gazeta Mercantil Online,* August 22, 2003, p. 1.

—Gerald E. Brennan

Gibbs and Dandy plc

P.O. Box 17, 226 Dallow Road
Luton LU1 1JG
United Kingdom
Telephone: (+44) 1582 798798
Fax: (+44) 1582 798799
Web site: http://www.gibbsanddandy.com

Public Company
Incorporated: 1920 as Gibbs and Dandy Ltd.
Employees: 322
Sales: £57.7 million ($107.10 million) (2004)
Stock Exchanges: London
Ticker Symbol: GDYO
NAIC: 423710 Hardware Merchant Wholesalers; 423390
    Other Construction Material Merchant Wholesalers;
    423610 Electrical Apparatus and Equipment, Wiring
    Supplies, and Related Equipment Merchant
    Wholesalers; 423720 Plumbing and Heating
    Equipment and Supplies (Hydronics) Merchant
    Wholesalers; 423830 Industrial Machinery and
    Equipment Merchant Wholesalers; 423840 Industrial
    Supplies Merchant Wholesalers; 444120 Paint and
    Wallpaper Stores; 444130 Hardware Stores; 444190
    Other Building Material Dealers

Gibbs and Dandy plc operates a network of builders' merchants in the United Kingdom, with a focus on the Northern Home Counties, South Midlands, and Thames Valley regions. The company operates nine branches featuring a complete range of building and plumbing materials, timber and joinery, as well as paint, glass, and electrical fittings and equipment. Customers range from major property developers and housing authorities to smaller builders and the home improvement and do-it-yourself markets. In addition to its Luton headquarters, the company operates branches in Bedford, Northampton, St. Ives, St. Neots, Slough, Maidenhead, Henley, and, Brackley. The acquisition of the Brackley branch was part of Gibbs & Dandy's plan to expand deeper into the South Midlands region in the second half of the 2000s. Gibbs & Dandy has been in operation since 1840 and has been listed on the London Stock Exchange since 1953. The company is led by chairman Christopher Roshier and managing directory R. Michael Dandy. In 2004, the company posted revenues of £57.7 million ($107.10 million).

Origins in the 19th Century

Luton was just a small town in the English countryside in the first half of the 19th century when Frederick Brown and Joseph Green established a shop on George Street. Opened in 1840, Brown and Green described their business as that of "Ironmongers, Iron and Steel Merchants and Hardwarement."

The Gibbs name became associated with the Luton builders' merchant market in 1867. In that year, GF Gibbs bought Brown and Green's company. Gibbs remained active in the business until nearly the end of the 19th century. During this time, the railroad came to Luton, sparking the town's growth into a major regional center. The ironmongers business evolved to meet the needs of the growing market, emerging as a major general builders' merchant for the fast-developing Luton area.

Gibbs retired in 1894, selling the business to brothers William and Percy Dandy. The Dandys decided to keep the Gibbs name, and the business became known as Gibbs and Dandy. The company grew strongly into the 20th century and continued to adapt to the changing building environment, adding new materials and departments, including electrical supplies. In 1920, Gibbs and Dandy formally incorporated as a limited liability company. At this time, the company described itself as "Builders' Merchants, Wholesale and Retail Ironmongers, Iron and Steel Stockholders, Paint and Colour Merchants and Electrical Wholesalers." By then, Gibbs and Dandy counted more than 8,000 customers.

Going Public in the 1950s

Over the next decades, Gibbs and Dandy maintained its prominence as a supplier to the local building market. During

119

Company Perspectives:

Our aims are to be the first choice supplier of building materials for professional tradesmen in our region; generate increasing real shareholder value; provide our customers with the right goods at the right time at the right price; encourage our employees to exceed our customers expectations and to act with integrity, and to provide them with good career opportunities.

Key Dates:

1840: Frederick Brown and Joseph Green launch Ironmongers, Iron and Steel Merchants and Hardwarement in Luton, England.
1867: GF Gibbs buys Brown and Green's business.
1894: Gibbs retires and sells the business to brothers William and Percy Dandy, who rename business Gibbs and Dandy.
1920: The company incorporates as Gibbs and Dandy Ltd.
1953: Gibbs and Dandy goes public, listing on the Birmingham Stock Exchange.
1968: Gibbs and Dandy and Frederic Gale Ltd. based in Bedford, merge under Gibbs and Dandy name.
1984: The company opens a branch in Northampton
1987: Three Luton branches are merged into a single site, which also becomes the company's headquarters, inaugurates a ''one-stop'' concept.
1990: Branches in St. Ives and St. Neots are acquired from David Smith Ltd; the Bedford branch converts to one-stop concept.
1996: The Northampton branch is moved to a larger location, which becomes a one-stop branch.
1997: Miller Morris and Brooker Ltd., with two branches in Slough and Maidenhead, is acquired.
2002: Elliott & Co is acquired, adding a new branch in Henley-on-Thames.
2004: Brackley Timber & Joinery Ltd. is acquired, adding new branch in Brackley.

this period, the company opened its first branch, in Dunstable. The company also boosted its presence in Luton with a new site.

The post-World War II period represented a return to growth for the U.K. building sector, and Gibbs and Dandy stood in a good position to profit from the expanding market. By then, the company had emerged as one of the leading suppliers of building materials not only in Luton but throughout the South Bedfordshire region. The company prepared for its continued growth, and in 1953 decided to go public, listing on the Birmingham Stock Exchange. The Dandy family remained active in the company and remained among its shareholders into the beginning of the 21st century.

The economic boom in the 1960s and the accelerated growth of the U.K. building market in general led Gibbs and Dandy to seek still greater expansion. In 1968, the company launched an offer to merge with another Bedfordshire builders' merchant, Frederic Gale, based in Bedford. Gale accepted the bid, worth some £340,000, and the two companies merged under the Gibbs and Dandy name. The combination of the two businesses created a regional leader with sales of £1.6 million at the beginning of the 1970s.

Over the next decade, Gibbs and Dandy grew again, adding a third site in Luton, in part to enable the company to expand its product offering to including heating, sanitaryware, and ''heavyside'' materials and equipment. In 1984, the company moved into Northampton, opening a branch office there. Three years later, Gibbs and Dandy consolidated its three Luton branches into a single location. The new Luton branch, built on a seven-acre site, also became the company's headquarters. At this time, the company began developing its 'one-stop' concept, offering a complete range of building materials and supplies for the professional and do-it-yourself markets.

Acquisitions into the 21st Century

Gibbs and Dandy eyed new expansion into the 1990s. At the beginning of the decade, the company acquired two new branches, in St. Neots and St. Ives, from David Smith Ltd. It also developed its Bedford branch into a second ''one-stop'' site.

The success of that concept led the company to expand its Northampton branch as well in the mid-1990s. Gibbs and Dandy purchased a larger site in that city's Heathfield Way and inaugurated its latest one-stop site in 1996. The boost in revenues and profitability enabled Gibbs and Dandy to prepare for further acquisitions into the second half of the decade. In 1997,

the company bought up Miller Morris and Brooker Ltd., adding two new branches, in Slough and Maidenhead. That purchase cost the company more than £3.6 million.

The consolidation of the U.K. builders' merchants market slowed somewhat into the beginning of the 2000s. By that time, Gibbs and Dandy had grown into a regional leader and one of the United Kingdom's top fifteen overall. By the end of 2000, the company's sales neared £45 million.

The company continued to seek out new acquisition opportunities. In 2002, Gibbs and Dandy expanded into Henly-on-Thames when it bought up Elliott & Co. Ltd. The company paid £2.1 million for the family-owned business.

The addition of Elliott & Co. helped boost the company's revenues past £51 million by the end of 2002. Gibbs and Dandy then took a break from its acquisitions as the building market softened, a result of the U.S. invasions of Afghanistan and Iraq.

By 2004, however, Gibbs and Dandy had located a fresh acquisition opportunity, buying up Brackley Timber & Joinery Ltd for £850,000. The purchase gave the company its ninth branch and established Gibbs and Dandy in Brackley, in Northamptonshire. The acquisition also fit in with the company's strategy of further expansion into the South Midlands region. The purchase also helped push total turnover past £57 million for the year. After 165 years in business, Gibbs and Dandy remained a prominent player in the U.K. builders' merchants market.

Principal Subsidiaries

Dandy Ltd.; Elliott & Co. (Henley) Limited; Gibbs and Dandy (Gales) Ltd.; Miller, Morris & Brooker (Holdings) Ltd.; Miller, Morris & Brooker (Holdings) Ltd.; One Stop Trade Building Centre Ltd..

Principal Competitors

Wolseley plc; Saint-Gobain plc; SIG plc; Jewson Ltd; FCX International plc; WM Owlett and Sons Ltd; C Brewer and Sons Ltd.; Solus Garden and Leisure Ltd.; Dormole Ltd.; Stax Trade Centres plc; Parker Merchanting; Eliza Tinsley Group plc; Hilti GB Ltd.

Further Reading

"Acquisition," *Daily Post*, December 3, 2004, p. 19.
"Builders Merchants Just Dandy," *Birmingham Post*, August 24, 2001, p. 26.
"Gibbs & Dandy," *Investors Chronicle*, March 12, 2004.
"Gibbs & Dandy," *Investors Chronicle*, September 3, 2004.

—M.L. Cohen

GiFi S.A.

Zone Industrielle La Boulbene, BP 40
Villeneuve-sur-Lot F-47301 Cedex
France
Telephone: +33 5 53 40 54 54
Fax: +33 5 53 40 54 6433
Web site: http://www.gifi.fr

Public Company
Incorporated: 1981
Employees: 2,487
Sales: EUR 440 million ($500 million) (2004)
Stock Exchanges: Euronext Paris
Ticker Symbol: 7509
NAIC: 424990 Other Miscellaneous Nondurable Goods
Merchant Wholesalers; 423990 Other Miscellaneous
Durable Goods Merchant Wholesalers

GiFi S.A. is France's leading retailer specialized in the low-priced, nongrocery category. The company, based in Villeneuve-sur-Lot, in the French southwest, operates a network of nearly 275 discount stores featuring a wide range of items, from home furnishings to toys to hardware, as well as textiles, auto parts, electronic goods, and compact discs and DVDs. Nearly three-quarters of the goods on sale at the group's stores are priced at EUR 4 or less. In a departure from the traditional discount goods channel, GiFi has launched its own branded lines in certain categories, including pet products (Doggy Dog), kitchen utensils (Cuisilux), and toys (Joubi). The company claims that more than 45 percent of the goods sold in its retail network originate from suppliers in France; most of the remainder come from Asian, especially Chinese, producers. GiFi has expanded rapidly in the first half of the 2000s; since 2000 the company has doubled its retail network. The company also has launched a refurbishment effort, converting a number of stores to a new large-scale Maxi GiFi concept, featuring more than 2,500 square meters of selling space. At mid-decade, the company has begun a move into international markets, acquiring 27 Idé stores in Belgium, and opening its first stores in Italy. The company also is preparing a launch into Spain. At the same time, GiFi has begun to diversify, acquiring discount clothing supplier Griff Plus in France. That acquisition brought the company a chain of 25 stores specialized in the sale of discounted brand name clothing. GiFi is listed on the Euronext Paris Stock Exchange. Founder Philippe Ginestet and family control more than 56 percent of the company's shares. In 2004 the company posted revenues of EUR 440 million ($500 million).

Discount Retailer in the 1980s

Philippe Ginestet's father sold animals in France's markets, exposing the younger Ginestet to the retail market at an early age. Yet Philippe Ginestet quickly displayed a talent especially for buying goods, seeking out the best prices, which he later resold at a profit. Later, in the 1970s, Ginestet went to work for Electrolux as a door-to-door salesman. There, Ginestet won an award for being the appliance giant's best salesman.

Ginestet's wife, however, was at the origin of Ginestet's conversion into one of France's leading retail entrepreneurs. In 1981, Ginestet's wife was seeking her own career direction. As Ginestet told *Le Passant Ordinaire,* "She was looking for something to do, so I bought her a store."

The Ginestets put together their savings, all of FRF 100,000 (approximately $10,000), and began seeking a location for their store near their home in Villeneuve-sur-Lot. The high rents of the city center, however, led the couple to the outskirts of town and the newly developing shopping district there. The Ginestets decided to launch a business as a "soldeur"—that is, selling end-of-range and de-stocked items—which at the time was a relatively new retail category. The Ginestets used Philippe Ginestet's name to form the name of their store: GiFi. The company then adopted the slogan: "Gifi Le Vrai Soldeur."

"At the time," Ginestet told *L'Entreprise,* "all one spoke about was the crisis and saving money. We therefore chose to surprise (our customers) with our prices and our choice of items." The Ginestets' choice proved a good one—by the end of its first year, the store had generated more than FRF 4 million in revenues. Ginestet quickly invested the steady stream of revenues into expansion, opening the second GiFi store just six months after the first. The strong sales at the GiFi stores also enabled the company to obtain credit from its suppliers, which in turn allowed it to turn a significant share of its revenues toward the opening of new stores. The growing network of GiFi stores provided the company with increased purchasing muscle; as its volumes increased, the company was able to negotiate still lower prices.

The company soon opened its fourth store, which marked a new milestone in the company's development. As Ginestet explained: ''Until then, we'd operated within the family. But with the fourth store, I needed to create a team.'' Seconded by a team of managers, Ginestet stepped up the company's store openings. By 1986, the company operated nine GiFi stores.

By then, however, Ginestet had recognized the limits of the ''soldeur'' concept, which left the company dependent on locating and negotiating for unsold stock. This meant that the choice of what appeared on its store shelves was often beyond the company's control. In 1986, therefore, Ginestet decided to convert GiFi's retail model to a low-priced formula. The company now turned directly to manufacturers and other wholesalers in order to build a more complete range of home furnishing goods and other nonfood items. As Ginestet explained to *Dynamique Commercial:* ''Between 1984 and 1988, a new concept appeared, that of factory outlet stores. I modified my format and Gifi Le Vrai Soldeur became Gifi Center. We made our purchases from wholesalers, remaining with the areas of gifts, decoration, toys, household textiles.''

Ginestet's intuition proved correct, and GiFi now entered a new phase of growth. Just two years later, the company had nearly tripled its store network. With 25 stores in operation, GiFi established a dedicated purchasing and distribution center in 1988. The new facility also provided the group with a more solid infrastructure as it pursued continued growth. Also that year, the company began purchasing operations in the Asian markets, often sourcing its goods directly from manufacturers.

National Network in the 1990s

These new supply channels enabled GiFi to move closer toward a department store concept (referred to by the company as product ''families''), expanding its range of goods into a more and more complete assortment. The wide range of products, coupled with the difficult economic climate at the begin-

ning of the 1990s, positioned GiFi and its low-priced concept as a fast-growing consumer favorite.

GiFi's retail network had reached 50 stores by 1993. In that year, the company added a number of new categories, notably textiles and cleaning and household products. The company continued adding new stores, topping 70 at mid-decade. By 1996, the company's sales had reached the equivalent of EUR 88 million. Yet GiFi remained more or less confined to the southwest region.

The company now put into place a strategy to launch it onto a national level. A key component of that strategy was Ginestet's willingness to bring in outside capital. In 1996, Ginestet organized a leveraged buyout of the company, selling 55 percent of the company to an investment partnership between Apax Partners & Cie and Fonds Partenaires du Groupe Lazard. The Ginestet family retained 45 percent of the company.

The company's new financial partners permitted GiFi to accelerate its growth. In just three years, the company nearly doubled its retail network again, becoming a nationally operating chain with nearly 130 stores by the end of 1999. The company's sales also had grown strongly, nearing the equivalent of EUR 150 million.

An important feature of the group's growth, and one that set it apart from most of its discount goods competitors, was the decision to launch a number of its own brands in the mid-1990s. As such the company added a line of pet products under the Doggy Dog brand. The company began selling a line of kitchen utensils, creating the Cuisilux brand. Last, GiFi added its own line of toys, called Joubi.

Going International in the 2000s

The 2000s marked GiFi's maturation into one of France's major retailing groups. Fueling the company's growth was its public offering, with a listing on the Euronext Paris Secondary Market in 2000. The listing reduced the stake held by Apax and Lazard by half. The public offering also gave Ginestet the opportunity to regain majority control of the company. After boosting his holding initially to 51 percent, Ginestet continued buying up blocks of shares in the company. By 2005, the Ginestet family's shareholding in the company had topped 56 percent.

Ginestet's confidence in the company's business model appeared well-founded. By 2002 the company had expanded its store network to 175 stores. GiFi also adopted a new strategy of extending its retail format to an international market. The company first targeted the French overseas departments, opening stores in Guyana and Guadeloupe. At the same time, GiFi maintained its store opening pace in France proper, extending its network to more than 200 stores by 2004.

Yet by then the company's international strategy had taken on still greater substance. In mid-2003, the company acquired a 50 percent stake in Idé, which operated a 27-store retail chain in Belgium. By 2004, GiFi had acquired full control of Idé and gained a significant presence in the Belgian discount retail market.

GiFi also had begun testing a new store format, that of the large-scale Maxi GiFi store format, featuring 2,500 square

Key Dates:

1981: Philippe Ginestet opens the first GiFi retail store in Villeneuve-sur-Lot, specialized in factory closeouts and unsold stock; a second store opens within the first year.
1986: With nine stores, GiFi converts to a low-priced retail concept.
1988: A central purchasing facility is opened and direct purchasing from Asian suppliers begins.
1993: The 50th store opens.
1996: Ginestet sells 55 percent of the company in a leveraged buyout in order to step up growth; the company launches its own brands of toys, pet products, and household utensils.
1999: The company tops 130 stores.
2000: GiFi goes public, listing on the Euronext Paris exchange; Ginestet boosts his shareholding to 51 percent (later 56 percent).
2002: The first international store openings occur in Guadeloupe and Guyana.
2003: The company acquires 50 percent of the 27-store Idé retail network in Belgium.
2004: The company acquires full control of Idé; the company opens its first stores in Italy and Spain; the Griff Plus brand name clothing store chain is acquired.

meters of selling space. Encouraged by the success of the format, the company launched a wider rollout, opening a total of ten stores by 2004. As part of that effort, the company began refurbishing and expanding a number of the stores throughout its network, and expected to open up to ten new Maxi GiFi stores by the end of 2005.

Having integrated its Belgian operations, the company turned its attention to new international markets. The company teamed up with a local partner to open a test store in Sassari, in the Sardinia region of Italy in 2004, and then opened a second store in Caligari. Neither store was an outright success, however, forcing the company to adapt its retail model to the Italian market.

Undeterred, GiFi moved into Spain at the end of 2004, opening two stores in Figueres and Terrassa. Soon after the company opened a third Spanish store, in Tarragona. The com-

pany also added to its operations in the French overseas departments, opening a store on the island of Réunion in 2004 as well.

GiFi reserved part of its energy for its domestic growth as well, opening a number of new stores through 2004. Significantly, the company made its first move to diversify its business, acquiring a 70 percent stake in the French discount brand name clothing retailer Griff Plus. That purchase, which was boosted to 100 percent by 2005, gave the company control of Griff Plus's 27-store retail network. GiFi quickly began adapting the chain, rolling out its own branded line of clothing, Able, in addition to Griff Plus's standard fare of discounted brand name labels.

By mid-2005, GiFi's total retail network had topped 270 stores and the company's revenues had reached EUR 440 million. Under the leadership of Philippe Ginestet, GiFi had grown into France's top retailer in the low-priced, nonfood segment. With the beginning of its international growth strategy, the company hoped to replicate that success on a European scale in the near future.

Principal Divisions

Distri Augny; Distri Beauvais; Distri Digne; Distri Essey Les Nancy; Distri Olivet; Distri Outreau; Distri Proville; Distri Romilly; Distri Sarreguemines; GiFi Diffusion; Gifi Mag; Gifies; Idé Belgium; Ingif.

Principal Competitors

Hyparlo S.A.; Logidis; Union des Cooperateurs d'Alsace S.A.; Carcoop France S.A.S.; GML France; EMC 2; Euro Textiles S.A.; Les Galeries; Nobladis.

Further Reading

De Parcevaux, Aude-Claire, "La réussite de 5 entrepreneurs: Philippe Ginestet, président de GiFi," *L'Entreprise,* November 21, 2002.
Desrayaud, Jean, "GiFi innove sur le marché discount," *Dynamique Commercial,* May-June 2002.
"GiFi, acquisition de l'enseigne 'Griff Plus,' " *Faire Savoir Faire,* January 16, 2004.
"GiFi poursuit son expansion," *Faire Savoir Faire,* November 26, 2004.
"GiFi, vingt ans d'expansion continue," *Faire Savoir Faire,* February 5, 2002.
Herreria, Michel, "L'aventure Gifi ou Bécassine au Palais Brongniart," *Le Passant Ordinaire,* June/July 2000.

—M.L. Cohen

something unexpected®

Gordmans, Inc.

12100 West Center Road Suite 1
Omaha, Nebraska 68144
U.S.A.
Telephone: (402) 691-4000
Fax: (402) 691-4001
Web site: http://www.gordmans.com

Private Company
Incorporated: 1915 as Richmans, Outfitters to the Family
Employees: 3,000
Sales: $350 million
NAIC: 448140 Family Clothing Stores; 452111
    Department Stores

Gordmans, Inc., is a discount retailer with 55 stores in 12 midwestern states. The company's stores sell name-brand clothing, shoes, accessories, and home fashion merchandise for up to 50 percent below department store prices.

Origins

As an enterprise started by the Richmans and developed into a regional chain of stores by the Gordmans, Gordmans, Inc. represents the work of two families. Gordmans was founded by Sam Richman, who left his native Russia and settled in Omaha, Nebraska, opening his own retail store in 1915 behind a small storefront that was part of a block-long building at the corner of 16th and Chicago. Richman's store, operating under the banner ''Richman's, Outfitters to the Family,'' housed his own family, who lived in the back of the store. Modest in size and purpose, Richman's retail store occupied the same quarters for the next 20 years, never aiming to be more than a small shop until a 1932 Chevy convertible pulled into town driven by an energetic, 22-year-old New Yorker. Dan Gordman was full of purpose, and he used the downtown Omaha shop to fulfill aspirations far more ambitious than those demonstrated by Richman.

In 1936, Gordman quit his job at Bloomingdales department store, packed all his belongings in his car, and set out for California. He was in pursuit of a dream 3,000 miles away, but he only got as far as Omaha, forced to stop because his car needed repairs and he was strapped for cash. Gordman's interest in becoming a successful retailer, meant to be realized in California, was instead fulfilled in Omaha. Within a year of his arrival in that city, Gordman had met Richman, become a full partner in his business, and married his daughter, Esther Richman, thoroughly committing his future to the small storefront on 16th and Chicago. The store quickly expanded as Gordman applied his experience at Bloomingdales to Richman's store, distinguishing himself as a skillful negotiator with buyers and attuned to the needs of customers. Within several years, Richman's store occupied the entire block at 16th and Chicago. A decade after Gordman's arrival, during the years immediately following World War II, a second store was purchased to the south of the original store. In the midst of the expansion, Gordman acquired Richman's interest in the company and changed the name of the company's two stores to ''Richman Gordman.''

Gordman managed the two Omaha stores for than a decade. During the 1960s, he was joined by his two sons, Jerry and Nelson, and his nephew Bob, the arrival of whom touched off a period of aggressive expansion. The company ventured out of its home market for the first time 1960s, opening a Richman Gordman in Lincoln, Nebraska, as well as three more stores in Omaha. The expansion efforts, which tripled the size of the retail outfit, offered no stumbling blocks, encouraging the family-run company to take its growth plans one step further. During the early 1970s, the company opened its first stores beyond Nebraska's borders, establishing two stores in Des Moines, Iowa, a third in Council Bluffs, Iowa, and a fourth in Topeka, Kansas. In 1974, the company opened a store in Grand Island, Nebraska. Richman Gordman, after nearly 30 years under the influence of Dan Gordman, had become a regional retail chain of note.

A New Retail Concept Is Created in 1975

Gordman's recognition as retailer stemmed not only from the increasing size of his company but also from the manner in which he presented his stores to the public. In Omaha, according to the company, Gordman was the first to introduce central checkouts, shopping carts, and self-service shoe departments to

Company Perspectives:

What is Gordmans all about? It's an exciting, fun-to-shop store that offers you a way to save up to 50 percent off prices you would find at a mall. Save on large assortments of name brand clothes for all ages, accessories, footwear, gifts, designer fragrances, fashion jewelry, accent furniture, home fashions and more-at big savings every day! Gordmans family of brand names includes most of those found in leading department and specialty stores. Check our price tags and discover savings up to 50% off department and specialty store regular prices! How do we do it? Unlike other retailers, we don't ask for any of the special considerations that are typically built into the selling price by manufacturers. As a result, we're able to pass those savings on to you. In addition, after having been in business for almost 100 years we've built thousands of strong, long term relationships with manufacturers throughout the country that allow us to negotiate incredibly low prices.

the retail realm. Richman Gordman stores also were credited with introducing the racetrack concept to a retail store's layout, a design that enabled customers to find a particular department by following a path describing the perimeter of a store. Gordman's innovations reached further, touching on a retail concept that recorded tremendous success at the end of the century and changed the dynamics of the retail sector. In 1975, one year after opening the Grand Island store, Gordman was beset by excess inventory. He also owned an empty building. By putting one into another, Gordman created a new business for his family-run enterprise, one that became the central strategic focus of the company in the 21st century.

Discount retail chains flourished during the 1990s, but Gordman enjoyed success with the concept decades earlier. In 1975, he opened a small store in Omaha on an experimental basis, hoping to use the store as way of getting rid of end-of-season merchandise that had been removed from the shelves of his department store chain. The store carried Richman Gordman merchandise, with each item selling for 50 percent less than it had at the company's department stores. Customers flocked to the store, turning the retail experiment into a new retail arm of the Gordman family called The ½ Price Store. Soon, the discount concept became more than an outlet for out-of-season Richman Gordman merchandise as growing demand prompted Gordman to dispatch buyers to negotiate for factory overstocks and in-season buyouts from apparel and accessories companies, which, in turn, spawned a separate corporate infrastructure to support the discount chain. By the end of the 1970s, six additional ½ Price Stores had opened.

The Gordman family retail business grew in two directions during the 1980s, expanding through both Richman Gordman Department Stores, Inc. and The ½ Price Stores, Inc. The two subsidiaries were controlled by the family's umbrella entity, Richman Gordman Stores, Inc. On the department store side of the business, six new Richman Gordman stores made their debut during the decade, additions that strengthened the retailer's presence in Omaha and Des Moines, where it already operated, and

provided entry into new markets such as Kansas City, Sioux Falls, South Dakota, and Wichita, Kansas. The Gordman's discount chain expanded at a greater pace during the 1980s, when nine new stores were opened in a five-state territory. By 1990, 75 years after Sam Richman opened his small shop in downtown Omaha, Richman Gordman Stores employed 4,000 workers and operated two retail chains, each comprising 16 stores.

Overcoming Challenges in the 1990s

The company's 75th anniversary marked the return of Dan Gordman's grandson to the family enterprise, a significant event at the beginning of what would prove to be an arduous decade for the Gordman businesses. Jeff Gordman grew up working in the family business, leaving Omaha after high school to attend The Wharton School at the University of Pennsylvania. After earning an undergraduate degree in economics, Gordman moved to New York City, where he joined Lehman Brothers as an investment banker. Following a stint on Wall Street, Gordman earned his master's degree in management from the Sloan School at the Massachusetts Institute of Technology, intending to pursue a career in strategy consulting. However, his plans changed after his grandfather issued an ultimatum. Dan Gordman threatened to sell the company unless his grandson returned to the family business. Jeff Gordman moved back to Omaha in 1990, rejoining Richman Gordman Stores at a critical period in its development.

When Gordman returned, he starting working at the company's stores in Kansas City and Lincoln before moving to the company's central offices, where he became part of Richman Gordman Stores' information technology group. Next, Gordman became a buyer for the company, but the duties associated with his job as well as the tasks assigned to virtually everyone else in the company soon were overshadowed by far more pressing demands. Richman Gordman Stores stood on the brink of insolvency, unable to pay its vendors and creditors. ''We lost sight of who we were as a company,'' Jeff Gordman reflected in a May 13, 2004, interview with the *Waterloo Courier,* referring to the darkest chapter in the company's existence. After closing four stores, the 26-store company filed for bankruptcy in 1992, awash in debt and lacking the strategic focus that had underpinned its development for decades. The company's two operating subsidiaries, Richman Gordman Department Stores and The ½ Price Stores, filed separate petitions for bankruptcy.

Gordman joined in the efforts to develop a plan for reorganization, applying his investment banking skills to help make Richman Gordman stores a going enterprise. The plan involved exiting the company's original department store business and focusing on one business instead, the ½ Price discount chain. The company emerged from bankruptcy protection in 1993 with its roster of stores winnowed further. Renamed Richman Gordman ½ Price Stores, Inc., the company staged its comeback in the business world with 21 stores operating under the ½ Price banner, but it continued to suffer financially during the ensuing years, reaching a tipping point midway through the decade. Gordman, seeing his family's company spiraling out of control again, decided to spearhead efforts for its salvation, launching his bid to take command of the company in 1996. ''The company was in a precarious financial position at the time, which gave me my chance,'' he explained in an April 12,

Key Dates:

1915: Sam Richman opens Richman's, Outfitters to the Family in Omaha, Nebraska.
1936: Dan Gordman arrives in Omaha and becomes Richman's partner.
1948: A second store, located in south Omaha, is acquired.
1960s: Expansion takes the company outside of Omaha for the first time.
1970s: The company ventures outside Nebraska for the first time, developing into a more than ten-store chain.
1975: Dan Gordman opens a discount shop, marking the birth of The ½ Price Stores concept.
1990: Dan Gordman's grandson, Jeff Gordman, joins the company on a full-time basis.
1992: The company files for bankruptcy, emerging as a discount chain one year later.
1996: Jeff Gordman is appointed chief executive officer.
2000: The company changes its name to Gordmans, Inc.
2004: Gordmans announces plans to double annual sales by the end of the decade.

2004 interview with the *Post-Crescent*. "I petitioned the chairman who was part of the creditor's committee. I said, 'Give me a shot at running this thing, otherwise it's going to go away.'" The chairman agreed to let Gordman take responsibility for the company, leading to the appointment of Gordman as chief executive officer in 1996.

When Gordman took the helm, the $220 million-in-sales company was pointed in the right direction but in dire need of major repairs. A number of changes were made over the course of the next several years, including additions to the company's management team, the implementation of policies designed to improve customer service, and the refinement of pricing strategies. Gordman remained committed to the decision to operate solely as a discounter, perceiving this to be the right direction for the company to pursue, but he believed wholesale changes needed to be implemented to support the pricing strategy. Essentially, an entirely new identity needed to be created for the company, prompting Gordman to remodel the stores, add themed sections for children and sports enthusiasts, and, as the final touch to the turnaround program, changing the name of the company. "The ½ Price moniker only represented one dimension of our business, that being price," Gordman explained in a May 13, 2004 interview with the *Waterloo Courier*. "I did not want to change the name to Gordmans," he continued. "I thought it carried negative equity, but our outside partners and internal associates took great pride in the family name. They were very connected to Gordmans." The company changed its name in 2000 from Richman Gordman ½ Price Stores, Inc. to Gordmans, Inc., omitting the apostrophe in its new corporate title "because apostrophes aren't cool," Gordman remarked in his interview with the *Waterloo Courier*.

The company's pace of expansion began to accelerate under its new identity as financial stability returned. Gordmans entered the decade with 32 stores, adding eight more stores by 2002, each featuring name-brand clothing, shoes, accessories, and home fashions at up to 50 percent below department store prices. During the next two years, the company opened four more stores and entered three new states, making Gordmans a 44-store chain with a presence in 12 Midwest states. "The future looks promising," Gordman remarked in a May 13, 2004 interview with the *Waterloo Courier*. "We hope to double sales in the next five years by expanding in new and existing markets, moving east." Gordman's more immediate plans called for expanding to 56 stores by the end of 2005, a goal the company had nearly met midway through the year. The opening of the company's first store in Indiana, a unit slated to debut in Evansville in September, and two stores in Illinois, both scheduled to open the following month, would lift its store count to 55. The future of the company, in terms of leadership, rested in the hands of Gordman, the only member of the Gordman family involved in the business. When asked in an April 12, 2004 interview with the *Post-Crescent* if another generation of his family might succeed him, Gordman responded, "My daughter might. She has some of the same characteristics that her daddy does. She's aggressive, she knows what she wants, she's very outgoing, and she's somewhat demanding, but it's hard to say," he said, before adding, "She's just 20-months old."

Principal Competitors

JC Penney Company, Inc.; Sears, Roebuck and Co.; Kohl's Corporation.

Further Reading

Alexander, Deborah, "Omaha, Neb.-Based Apparel, Home-Décor Retailer to Relocate, Open 4 New Stores," *Omaha World-Herald*, July 1, 2005, p. B1.
Palmer, Joel, "CEO of Retail Chain Gives Inspiring Speech to Waterloo, Iowa," *Waterloo Courier*, May 13, 2004, p. B2.
"Richman Gordman Files Chapter 11," *Daily News Record*, June 19, 1992, p. 10.
Wallenfang, Maureen, "Young CEO of Gordmans Opens Two New Stores in Fox Cities," *Post-Crescent*, April 12, 2004, p. B3.

—Jeffrey L. Covell

Greenpeace International

Ottho Heldringstraat 5
1066 AZ Amsterdam
Netherlands
Telephone: (+31) 20-514-81-50
Fax: (+31) 20-514-81-51
Web site: http://www.greenpeace.org

Nonprofit Organization
Incorporated: 1972 as Greenpeace Foundation
Sales: EUR 163.44 million ($205.1 million) (2003)
NAIC: 813310 Social Advocacy Organizations; 813311
    Human Rights Organizations; 813312 Environment,
    Conservation and Wildlife Organizations; 813319
    Other Social Advocacy Organizations

Greenpeace International is one of the world's best-known environmental action organizations. Backed by an international membership of nearly three million, the group operates 27 national and regional offices throughout the world. The group's overall operations are guided by its central office in Amsterdam, alternatively known as Stichting Greenpeace Council, while national and regional branches act according to local agendas. Greenpeace has achieved notoriety for its use of highly creative, non-violent means of calling attention to global environmental concerns. The organization's Rainbow Warrior is arguably one of the world's most widely recognized ocean-going vessels. Among the most memorable events in the group's existence was the bombing of the Rainbow Warrior by the French government. In 2005, it was revealed that orders for the attack came from then president François Mitterand himself. In addition to its media-grabbing confrontational events, Greenpeace also operates a strong lobbying wing, as well as its own research unit, providing the group with a second, more diplomatic approach. Greenpeace is an independent organization and refuses donations and grants from governments and corporations. Instead, the pressure group relies on financial funding from its international membership, as well as from grants and other private funds. In 2003, Greenpeace's income topped EUR 163 million ($205 million). Greenpeace International is led by chairman Anne Summers and international executive director Gerd Leipold.

Battling the Bomb in the 1970s

The U.S. military's testing of a 1.2 megaton nuclear bomb beneath Amchitka, part of the Aleutian Islands chain in Alaska, in 1969, inspired a series of protests by early environmental activists. After the United States announced in 1970 its intention to conduct a new test, this time of a 5-megaton bomb, under Amchitka, a group of Vancouver-based activists, including Canadians and expatriate Americans, came together to launch the ad hoc Don't Make A Wave Committee, initially as an offshoot of the Sierra Club. The name came from a slogan used during the protests the year earlier that had its source in warnings that underground nuclear testing might potentially unleash a tidal wave on the Canadian coast.

Among the protest group's founders were Dorothy and Irving Stowe, who were soon joined by Bill Darnell, Robert Hunter, Patrick Moore, Paul Cote, Jim and Marie Bohlen, Paul Watson, Ben and Dorothy Metcalfe, among others. Don't Make a Wave soon received endorsements from such organizations as the Sierra Club, the United Church of Canada, the B.C. Federation of Labour, and the Canadian Voice of Women.

During meetings for planning its protests, Marie Bohlen offhandedly suggested that the group simply sail a boat into the testing zone. The idea was later repeated to a reporter from the Vancouver Sun, thus forming the nucleus of a new form of social protest involving the use of emotionally laden, media-friendly images. At a subsequent meeting, the committee agreed to go ahead with the plan. Leaving that meeting, Bill Darnell coined the phrase "green peace." As Hunter later told the *Utne Reader:* "The term had a nice ring to it. It worked better in a headline than The Don't Make a Wave Committee. We decided to find a boat and call it Greenpeace."

Over the next year, the group raised funding (in part through the sale of buttons using the Greenpeace slogan as well as through benefit concerts featuring Joni Mitchell, Phil Ochs, James Taylor and others) and went in search of a boat to sail them into the testing zone. It was not until September 1971 that

Company Perspectives:

Our mission: Greenpeace is an independent, campaigning organisation that uses non-violent, creative confrontation to expose global environmental problems, and force solutions for a green and peaceful future. Greenpeace's goal is to ensure the ability of the Earth to nurture life in all its diversity. Greenpeace organises public campaigns for: The protection of oceans and ancient forests. The phase out of fossil fuels and the promotion of renewable energy to stop climate change. The elimination of toxic chemicals. The prevention of genetically modified organisms being released into nature. An end to the nuclear threat and nuclear contamination. Safe and sustainable trade. Greenpeace does not solicit or accept funding from governments, corporations or political parties. Greenpeace neither seeks nor accepts donations that could compromise its independence, aims, objectives or integrity. Greenpeace relies on the voluntary donations of individual supporters, and on grant support from foundations. Greenpeace is committed to the principles of non-violence, political independence and internationalism. In exposing threats to the environment and in working to find solutions, Greenpeace has no permanent allies or enemies.

they finally found a skipper willing to take them on. The boat, a halibut seiner piloted by Captain John Cormack, set sail at the end of September and reached Akutan Island before the crew was arrested and the ship turned back to Sand Point.

In the meantime, however, the group's action had receiving international media attention. The ship headed back to Vancouver where it was met by a new, larger vessel chartered by the Don't Make A Wave Committee. This vessel was renamed the Greenpeace and set sail again. During this second voyage, the crew members hatched plans to found a more permanent environmental protest organization, to be named Greenpeace Foundation. While the second attempt to reach Amchitka failed as well, the media attention nonetheless forced the U.S. government to postpone the second bomb test and ultimately drop the Aleutian testing program altogether.

Founding and Evolution of Greenpeace

Greenpeace Foundation was officially established in 1972. The group, which remained only loosely organized, inspired a number of similar movements around the world which also adopted the name Greenpeace. Among these was a group of protesters seeking to stop atmospheric nuclear testing by the French government at Moruroa, an atoll in the Pacific. The Greenpeace Foundation launched an appeal for skippers willing to sail into to the restricted testing area. David McTaggert, a Canadian and entrepreneur who had retired to his yacht in the South Pacific, agreed to sail the group into the exclusion zone. McTaggert's yacht was rammed. In a return trip to Moruroa the following year, McTaggert and crew were beaten by the French military. Images of the beating inspired an international outcry that successfully forced the French to abandon atmospheric testing.

By the end of the 1970s, McTaggert had emerged as the de facto leader of the Greenpeace movement and was to remain as the head of the organization into the 1990s. McTaggert was credited with reshaping the loose confederation of nine Greenpeace groups. The different groups, which often pursued their own agenda of issues, expanded Greenpeace's operations to include efforts to block whale-hunting and the slaughter of seal pups. Yet many of these groups had fallen into debt. In 1997, McTaggert stepped in to bail out the Greenpeace groups with his own funds. He then took effective control of Greenpeace, centralizing its operations into a new body, Greenpeace International, in 1979. Greenpeace then moved its headquarters from Vancouver to Washington, D.C. The organization also bought its first vessel, a trawler which was given the name Rainbow Warrior, taken from a Cree legend. The Rainbow Warrior, soon to become as well-known as Greenpeace itself, set sail in 1978.

Under McTaggert's leadership, Greenpeace narrowed its focus to a more limited range of environmental issues. Nuclear testing, however, remained a central concern for the group. In 1985, Greenpeace decided to take on the French government, which had not ended its nuclear testing program in the South Pacific, but simply moved it underground. After assisting in the evacuation of Rongelap Island, site of U.S. nuclear testing in the 1950s and 1960s, the Rainbow Warrior set sail for Moruroa in order to stop a new series of planned French nuclear tests. In response, the French government sent two Navy frogmen to attach bombs to the Greenpeace vessel. After initially denying its involvement in the attack, the French Navy finally admitted to the bombing, and, in 1987, agreed to pay damages to Greenpeace. It was not until 2005, however, that *Le Monde*, revealed that then President François Mitterand himself had ordered the bombing.

The resulting uproar over the bombing not only forced France to suspend its nuclear testing program, it also established Greenpeace International as a major force in the fast-growing global environmental activist movement. Donations began to pour into Greenpeace's offices. The group also recruited a growing number of activists eager to work for the cause and began expanding its network of national and regional offices. By the mid-2000s, the group operated offices in 27 countries, as well as three regional offices, reaching a total of more than 40 countries.

Environmental Force in the 21st Century

McTaggert retired from the organization in the early 1990s. By then, the momentum for Greenpeace's operations had shifted to Europe, which remained its primary source for donations into the next decade. In response, the group created a new central operating body, Stichting Greenpeace Council, which was established in Amsterdam to oversee the group's future growth. Greenpeace also shifted toward a more professional organizational structure, and began issuing annual reports in the 1990s.

Greenpeace growing stature as one of the world's most well-known and effective environmental activist groups helped it achieve a number of important victories in the 1990s. In 1991, the group's efforts to protect Antarctica led to the signing of the Antarctica Treaty, which placed a 50-year moratorium on

Key Dates:

1971: A group of environmental activists come together to protest the testing by the U.S. military of a 5-megaton bomb under Amchitka, part of the Aleutian Islands chain in Alaska.

1972: Greenpeace Foundation is founded and begins raising funds.

1979: David McTaggart, the central figure among various groups operating under the Greenpeace name, consolidates these diverse factions as Greenpeace International and assumes leadership of the organization into the mid-1990s.

1987: The French Navy admits to bombing a Greenpeace oceangoing vessel carrying protesters of France's nuclear testing in the Pacific Ocean and agrees to pay damages to the activist organization.

1991: The group's efforts to protect Antarctica result in the signing of the Antarctica Treaty, which placed a 50-year moratorium on mining in the region.

1992: Continuing pressure from Greenpeace leads the French government to agree to end its nuclear testing program.

1995: Due to the activities of Greenpeace, a summit is convened in which the United States, France, the United Kingdom, Russia, and China draft the Comprehensive Test Ban Treaty.

1998: Greenpeace successfully lobbies the European Union to set up controls on the use of genetically engineered (GE) crops by EU member nationals.

2003: The group's continued campaigning against GE crops and foods lead to the development of the Cartagena Protocol on Biosafety.

2005: *Le Monde* reveals that then President François Mitterand himself had ordered the bombing on the Greenpeace vessel involved in the protesting of France's nuclear testing in the Pacific Ocean.

mining in the region. The following year, continuing pressure from Greenpeace encouraged the French government to agree to end its nuclear testing program altogether, with the caveat that other nuclear powers agree to end their programs as well. This led to a summit in 1995 including the United States, France, the United Kingdom, Russia, and China and the drafting of the Comprehensive Test Ban Treaty.

One of the most visible campaigns taken on by Greenpeace in the late 1990s was its efforts to counter the growing use of genetically modified organisms in the agricultural and food industries. By 1998, Greenpeace had successfully lobbied the European Union to set up controls on the use of genetically engineered (GE) crops by EU member nationals. At the same time, the group's local efforts led to bans on GE crops in Austrian supermarkets, the enactment of sanctions that forbid the growing of GE crops with wild equivalents in France, and injunctions against imports of GE rapeseed by France and Greece, among other anti-GE policies enacted by EU member nations.

Other Greenpeace actions in late 1990s included attempts to limit the use of PVC, especially the initiation of a ban on the use of phthalates in PVC toys, put into place by the European Union in 1999. Into the 2000s, the organization took on the international logging industry, raising awareness of the alarmingly rapid destruction of the world's old-growth and tropical forests. The group's continued campaigning against GE crops and foods led to the development of the Cartagena Protocol on Biosafety in 2003. While often criticized, especially by its opponents, Greenpeace had established itself as a force to be reckoned with in the environmental arena.

Further Reading

Burnie, Shaun, ''Detonating the Mind Bomb,'' *Bulletin of the Atomic Scientists*, May-June 2005, p. 62.

Geiselman, Bruce, ''Off the Rails; Former Environmental Leader Blasts Movement,'' *Waste News*, April 25, 2005, p. 1.

Moore, Patrick, ''Failed Agenda Returns as HBN,'' *Plastic News*, June 27, 2005, p. 6.

''Profile: Blake Lee Harwood, Greenpeace,'' *PR Week*, April 26, 2002, p. 24.

Seccombe, Will, ''Apocalypse Bob,'' *Ryerson Review of Journalism*, spring 2003, p. 12.

Selle, Robert R., ''A Founder of Greenpeace,'' *World and I*, March 2003, p. 52.

Tickell, Oliver, ''Greenpeace Suffers in the Silly Season,'' *Guardian*, August 13, 1997.

Weyler, Rex, *Greenpeace: How a Group of Ecologists, Journalists, and Visionaries Changed the World*, Emmaus, Penn.: Rodale Books, 2004.

——, ''Waves of compassion,'' Utne Reader Web Specials Archive Issue. Available from http://www.utnereader.com.

—M.L. Cohen

Grill Concepts, Inc.

11661 San Vincente Boulevard, Suite 404
Los Angeles, California 90049
U.S.A.
Telephone: (310) 820-5559
Fax: (310) 820-6530
Web site: http://www.dailygrill.com

Public Company
Incorporated: 1985
Employees: 1,569
Sales: $47.57 million (2003)
Stock Exchanges: NASDAQ
Ticker Symbol: GRILE
NAIC: 722110 Full-Service Restaurants

Grill Concepts, Inc., operates two restaurant concepts, or formats, each with "Grill" in its name. Grill on the Alley is the more expensive of the two restaurant brands, offering more than 50 entrées of prime steak and fresh seafood. Daily Grill offers many of the same selections as its more expensive counterpart but in smaller portions and with less-expensive ingredients. The average dinner check at Grill on the Alley restaurants is $45 compared to an average of $22 at Daily Grill units. Grill on the Alley restaurants operate in Beverly Hills, Hollywood, San Jose, and Chicago. The San Jose and Chicago restaurants operate inside hotels, the Fairmont Hotel and the Westin Hotel, respectively. A number of the company's 20 Daily Grill restaurants operate inside hotels as well. One Daily Grill is located in the Tom Bradley International Terminal at Los Angeles International Airport. Daily Grill restaurants operate in California, Oregon, Texas, Illinois, and the greater Washington, D.C., area. Grill Concepts has an agreement with Starwood Hotels & Resorts Worldwide, Inc., one of the largest hotel and leisure companies in the world, to jointly develop restaurant properties within Starwood hotels. Starwood owns approximately 22 percent of Grill Concepts.

Origins

The dining format that spawned a chain of restaurants was created by three partners, Robert Spivak, Michael Weinstock, and Richard Shapiro. During the early 1980s, the founders, led by Spivak, began working on plans for a restaurant modeled after the traditional grill rooms found in San Francisco, Chicago, and New York during the 1930s and 1940s. The trio formed a limited partnership and opened their creation, Grill on the Alley, a fine-dining restaurant with black-and-white marbled floors, polished wooden booths, and dark-green upholstery that opened in Beverly Hills in 1984.

Offering entrées of prime steak and fresh seafood, Grill on the Alley was an upscale restaurant located between Wilshire Boulevard and Rodeo Drive, a perfect match for the community it served. For its chef, the Spivak-led team turned to John Sola, who played a prominent role in Grill Concepts' development for decades after being hired as opening chef. Originally, Sola wanted to be a blackjack dealer in Lake Tahoe, Southern California's haven of gambling and skiing, but Harrah's Hotel & Casino hired him to be a cook instead of a dealer. Sola distinguished himself quickly, becoming head saucier at Harrah's French restaurant. Next, he was hired as executive chef at a ski resort in the area, where he demonstrated sufficient skill and flair to attract the attention of Chef Rolph Nonnast at the Chronicle Restaurant in Santa Monica, California. Sola worked under Chef Nonnast for three years beginning in 1979, learning "many valuable lessons," according to his interview with *Chain Leader* in August 2002. "Most importantly," Sola remembered, "he taught me to keep it simple, to let the main part of the dish speak for itself." Spivak's dining concept, which was later described on the company's Web site as "a bastion of straightforward, classic American cuisine," was suited ideally to Sola's culinary skills. The restaurant proved to be a highly popular dining choice, known "for its power-dining clientele of entertainment industry movers and shakers," according to the May 22, 2000 issue of *Nation's Restaurant News,* which inducted the Grill on the Alley into its Fine Dining Hall of Fame in 1995.

After several successful years, Spivak and his partners began to think of expanding. The idea behind expanding was to create a scaled-down version of Grill on the Alley, one that would be more suitable for building into a chain of restaurants. The partners formed a company separate from the limited partnership that oversaw Grill on the Alley and developed a format that offered many of the same menu items as Grill on the Alley but at lower prices. The format debuted in September 1988, when

Company Perspectives:

Daily Grills continue their founders' commitment to serve big portions of traditional grill recipes, at affordable prices.

the first Daily Grill opened in Brentwood, California. Sola, who was named executive chef of Grill Concepts in 1988, created a menu that borrowed heavily from the offerings at Grill on the Alley, but he reduced the size of portions and substituted some ingredients to keep food prices down, resulting in an average Daily Grill check that was roughly half the price of a Grill on the Alley check. The shrimp cocktail recipe was identical at both restaurants, but Grill on the Alley used larger shrimp than Daily Grill, 16- to 20-count compared with 13- to 15-count. A New York steak at Grill on the Alley was a prime 16-ounce cut, while Daily Grill offered a 12-ounce Angus strip. In his August 2002 interview with *Chain Leader*, Sola explained some of the differences between the two formats, saying, "We've got to be a lot more basic with Daily Grill but have more leeway at Grill on the Alley. At Grill on the Alley, servers are careerists and very professional, and clientele is a bit more adventuresome. At Daily Grill, we have a much younger, more transient staff, and customers stick with what's familiar. If it's too exotic, they won't buy it."

Spivak and his partners, through two separate companies, controlled two dining concepts by the late 1980s, but the partners relied almost exclusively on the Daily Grill concept as their expansion vehicle. A second Daily Grill opened in Los Angeles 18 months after the Brentwood restaurant opened, beginning an expansion period that would see Grill Concepts open at least one new Daily Grill in Southern California every year during the first half of the 1990s. Restaurants were opened in Encino, Newport Beach, Studio City, and in Palm Desert at the El Paseo shopping center, dubbed the "Rodeo Drive of the Desert." The El Paseo restaurant, the company's sixth unit, opened in January 1994, concluding expansion for a brief period while Spivak and his team pondered their boldest move to date.

Daily Grill represented Spivak's vehicle for expansion. Nevertheless, his desire to accelerate expansion and greatly broaden the geographic scope of his operations required an additional element, which Spivak found in a publicly traded, New Jersey-based company named Magellan Restaurants Systems. Magellan operated three Pizzeria Uno restaurants that Spivak believed would enable his company to expand on the East Coast. In 1995, Magellan was purchased by Spivak and merged into Grill Concepts. The acquisition, which put Grill Concepts on the NASDAQ Exchange, was coupled with an announcement for accelerated expansion, ushering in an era of aggressive growth for the company.

Expansion in the Late 1990s

As Grill Concepts prepared for a period of more rapid growth, Spivak brought his two restaurant brands under the control of a single entity. In April 1996, Grill Concepts officially acquired the limited partnership that owned Grill on the Alley. Word of another acquisition soon followed, one that

promised to enlarge the company's stature considerably. In July 1996, Grill Concepts announced it had agreed to buy a bankrupt chain of 19 restaurants operating under the Hamburger Hamlet name. Based in Sherman Oaks, California, Hamburger Hamlet was founded in 1950 by Harry and Marilyn Lewis. After several successful decades, the company struggled when it fell into the hands of an investment group in the late 1980s, embarking on an ill-fated expansion campaign that eventually caused its financial collapse. Spivak, who was about to triple the size of his company with the $10 million acquisition, was excited by the prospects of the deal, declaring in a July 10, 1996 interview with the *Daily News*, "Our plan is to bring Hamburger Hamlet back to the glory days that Harry and Marilyn enjoyed with it." By October 1996, however, the mood at Grill Concepts' headquarters had changed. The company was forced to terminate the acquisition, unable to secure the financing to complete the deal.

By the time the Hamburger Hamlet deal was scuttled, Spivak had turned his attention to expanding the Daily Grill chain, fulfilling his promise in 1995 to accelerate the company's growth. In September 1996, the seventh Daily Grill opened, debuting in Irvine, California. The eighth Daily Grill put Grill Concepts in the record books. In January 1997, the company opened a unit in the Tom Bradley International Terminal at Los Angeles International Airport, an 8,300-square-foot Daily Grill that ranked as the largest full-service airport restaurant in the United States. Next, the company made the greatest geographic leap in its history, opening a Daily Grill in Washington, D.C., in March 1997, the first of four restaurants to open in the Washington area.

In 1998, the tenth anniversary of the Daily Grill chain, the company acted on several important decisions. During the year, Spivak and fellow executives decided the three franchised Pizzeria Uno restaurants did not fit the company's strategic plans. Accordingly, an exit strategy was devised, leading to the closure of the first Pizzeria Uno unit, a restaurant located in Media, Pennsylvania, in July 2000. One year later, the company sold a restaurant in South Plainfield, New Jersey, for $700,000, followed by the sale of the third unit in Cherry Hill, New Jersey, for $325,000 in April 2002, ending its involvement in the Pizzeria Uno business. In August 1998, the company forged a partnership that opened a new avenue of growth for both its restaurant properties, signing an agreement with Hotel Restaurant Properties, Inc. for assistance in locating suitable hotel locations for Daily Grill and Grill on the Alley restaurants. The agreement followed Grill Concepts' first experience with operating a restaurant inside a hotel. In May 1998, 14 years after the first Grill on the Alley opened, the company opened a second restaurant in the Fairmont Hotel in San Jose, California.

In the wake of the agreement with Hotel Restaurant Properties, the preferred mode of the expansion was to open Daily Grill and Grill on the Alley restaurants in hotels. The first Daily Grill to appear in a hotel opened in January 1999, when a restaurant was opened in the Hilton Hotel in Burbank, California. A restaurant at the Georgetown Inn in Washington, D.C., followed, debuting in April 1999. The following month, the 12th Daily Grill opened at Universal Citywalk, located in the Universal Studios Hollywood complex.

As Grill Concepts entered the 21st century, the company strengthened its commitment to operating in hotel properties and turned to both its restaurant formats for growth. After waiting 14 years before it added a second Grill on the Alley, the company opened its third restaurant two years later, selecting the Westin Hotel in Chicago as the location to showcase its upscale format. The Chicago restaurant opened in June 2000 and featured a wrap-around mahogany bar, a 100-seat lounge with a pianist who performed nightly, and a windowed wall that offered a panoramic view of Michigan Avenue. The Chicago opening was followed by the debut of another equally opulent Grill on the Alley in Hollywood. The Hollywood restaurant, which opened in November 2001, was located in the Hollywood & Highland complex, a facility that housed cinemas, retail shops, and a Renaissance Hotel.

Agreement with Starwood in 2001

Grill Concepts' affiliation with hotels was taken a step further in mid-2001. In July, Starwood Hotels & Resorts Worldwide, Inc. acquired a 12 percent stake in Grill Concepts, forming an equity-and-expansion pact with the restaurant company. White Plains, New York-based Starwood ranked as one of the largest hotel and leisure companies in the world, controlling 725 hotels, including the Sheraton, St. Regis, Westin, and W brands. According to the terms of the agreement either party could propose the development of a restaurant in a Starwood property. These restaurants would be jointly developed and operated by Starwood and Grill Concepts. The two companies had worked together on the Chicago Grill on the Alley, cultivating a relationship that culminated in the 2001 agreement. Starwood later increased its ownership interest in Grill Concepts to approximately 22 percent, as the giant, $5 billion-in-sales hotel company helped Spivak and his team expand the chain and enter new markets.

The first half the 2000s saw Grill Concepts add to its chain of Daily Grill units. Through its agreement with Starwood, the company entered Texas for the first time with a Daily Grill in Houston that opened in July 2002. The Houston restaurant was located in the Westin Galleria Hotel. The following year, the company entered Oregon for the first time, its third Starwood venture. The restaurant opened in Portland's Westin Hotel, a Starwood property. For the first time in its collaboration with hotels, the company was selected to manage a hotel's banquet facilities, a responsibility given to the Daily Grill in the Portland Westin.

In the years ahead, Grill Concepts was expected to continue to expand through its agreement with Starwood and on its own with non-hotel-based restaurants. After opening a Daily Grill in the Hyatt Hotel in Bethesda, Maryland, in 2004, the company opened its 20th Daily Grill close to home. In April 2005, a restaurant opened in Santa Monica in a 15-acre complex known as the Colorado Center. Although the company offered no specific goal for future expansion, the continued growth of both chains seemed a certainty, with hotel-based expansion to occupy most of the company's attention.

Principal Subsidiaries

GCI Inc.; Grill Concepts Management, Inc.

Principal Competitors

The Cheesecake Factory Inc.; Hillstone Restaurant Group; Morton's Restaurant Group, Inc.

Further Reading

Belgum, Deborah, ''Daily Meal,'' *Los Angeles Business Journal*, September 16, 2002, p. 14.

Flass, Rebecca, ''Daily Grill Is Latest Restaurant Brand Lured to Downtown,'' *Los Angeles Business Journal*, August 9, 2004, p. 9.

Glover, Kara, ''Well Done,'' *Los Angeles Business Journal*, August 5, 1996, p. 8.

''Grill Concepts Finishes '96 with Loss of $2.8M,'' *Nation's Restaurant News*, March 24, 1997, p. 12.

''Grill Concepts Inks Deal to Operate at Westin Portland Hotel,'' *Nation's Restaurant News*, June 9, 2003, p. 106.

''Grill Concepts Inks Three-Year Deal with Savista,'' *Nation's Restaurant News*, December 20, 2004, p. 86.

''Grill Concepts Opens Daily Grill Restaurant in Santa Monica's Colorado Center,'' *PR Newswire*, April 18, 2005, p. 21.

''Grill Concepts Slates June Debut for Chicago Branch of Grill on the Alley,'' *Nation's Restaurant News*, May 22, 2000, p. 48.

''Grill Nixes Hamlet Deal,'' *Nation's Restaurant News*, October 14, 1996, p. 4.

Martin, Richard, ''Daily Grill Offers Diners Free Meal, Kids' Carte,'' *Nation's Restaurant News*, August 24, 1992, p. 18.

Rogers, Monica, ''Daily Bread,'' *Chain Leader*, August 2002, p. 39.

Spector, Amy, ''Starwood Cooks Up Joint Venture, Buys 12% Stake in Grill Concepts,'' *Nation's Restaurant News*, June 4, 2001, p. 4.

Wilcox, Gregory J., ''Firm Seeks to Put Bite Back into Hamlets,'' *Daily News*, July 10, 1996, p. B1.

—Jeffrey L. Covell

Le Groupe **crit**

Groupe Crit S.A.

---

152 bis Ave. Gabriel Peri
Saint Ouen
F-93403 Cedex
France
Telephone: +33 1 49 18 55 55
Fax: +33 1 40 12 02 84
Web site: http://www.groupe-crit.com

Public Company
Incorporated: 1962 as Centre de Recherches Industrielles
    et Techniques
Employees: 3,500
Sales: EUR 1.12 billion ($1.6 billion) (2004)
Stock Exchanges: Euronext Paris
Ticker Symbol: CEN
NAIC: 488119 Other Airport Operations; 423860
    Transportation Equipment and Supplies (Except Motor
    Vehicles) Merchant Wholesalers; 492110 Couriers;
    541710 Research and Development in the Physical
    Sciences and Engineering Sciences; 541910 Marketing
    Research and Public Opinion Polling; 551112 Offices
    of Other Holding Companies; 561310 Employment
    Placement Agencies; 561612 Security Guards and
    Patrol Services; 561621 Security Systems Services
    (Except Locksmiths); 561720 Janitorial Services

Groupe Crit S.A. is one of the top five temporary employment providers in France. The company, based in Saint Ouen, operates more than 350 agencies throughout France. Since the early 2000s, Crit also has added a small number of agencies outside of France, namely in Switzerland, Germany, Spain, Italy, and Morocco. Crit's temporary employment services operate under a number of brand names, including Crit Intérim, Les Compagnons, Les Volants, Effika, and Mayday Travail Temporaire in France; Crit Intérim in Switzerland, Morocco, and Spain; and Propartner in Germany. Although Crit's temporary placement services covers the full range of employment areas, the company has a long-established position serving more specialized markets, such as engineering, research, graphic de-

sign or the restaurant sector. Temporary employment services represent nearly 90 percent of Crit's revenues, which topped EUR 1.1 billion in 2004. Crit is also active in two other sectors: airport services, through subsidiary Group Handling, which provides airport and cargo handling services at the Charles de Gaulle Roissy and Dublin International airports; and corporate services, including industrial engineering and maintenance services, consulting, and security services, among others. These operations represent 5 percent and 6 percent of Crit's sales, respectively. Listed on the Euronext Paris Stock Exchange's Secondary Market since 1999, Crit remains controlled by founder, chairman, and CEO Claude Guedj and family, who hold more than 69 percent of the company's shares.

Recognizing a Market in the 1960s

Claude Guedj founded the Centre de Recherches Industrielles et Techniques (Crit) in 1962 to provide consulting, engineering, and design services to the mechanical, electrical, and electronics industries. Very quickly, however, the company found itself sending out employees to work directly with its clients, providing onsite technical assistance and other services.

The temporary employment sector was still in its infancy in France at the time, and remained associated with unskilled labor. Yet Guedj recognized the potential market for placing temporary employees in highly skilled, technical positions. Through the 1960s, Guedj oriented Crit more and more toward the provision of temporary and short-term technical assistance services. Crit also expanded to include an increasingly wider range of industries and types of employment.

The French government passed new legislation regulating the temporary employment market in 1972, encouraging the development of the sector. Crit launched its own dedicated employment agency that same year, Crit Intérim. Through the end of the decade, Crit continued to expand and diversify its range of services, adding two new specialized subsidiaries, Les Compagnons and Les Volants, and targeting more specifically industries such as the automotive and construction industries.

During the 1970s, as well, Crit built up a secondary business providing support services to industries. The company began offering engineering, maintenance, subcontracting, and other services. By the end of the decade, Crit's range of services had grown to include industrial cleaning, security, and industrial equipment supply services. The development of France's nuclear power industry, in a government-led effort to reduce the country's dependence on fossil fuel imports, created a demand for specially trained and highly skilled temporary staff. Crit became an important player in this market as well, earning its nuclear power industry certification in 1979.

Crit began building a network of agencies through the 1980s and into the early 1990s. By 1995, the company had established offices covering nearly all of France. The company also had continued to add specialized divisions and subsidiaries, such as the creation of RHF, which focused on training and other human resources functions.

Acquisitions formed part of the group's growth, such as its purchase in 1995 of Delta Capital. That acquisition helped boost Crit's operations in the security services sector. The following year, Crit established a new subsidiary, AB Intérim. The company then bought up Interwork in 1997, adding that company's 29 agencies to Crit's network. By 1998, the company also had bought up two other temporary agencies, SOI Intérim and Free Work. By the end of that year, Crit's national network topped 90 agencies, with total group sales of EUR 176 million ($160 million).

International Growth in the New Century

Crit went public in 1999, listing its shares on the Euronext Paris Stock Exchange's Secondary Market. The listing enabled the company to begin planning new growth moves for the start of the 21st century. As part of that effort, the company redefined its strategy, turning its focus more specifically on its temporary employment operations and its multi-services arm. The change in strategy led Crit to sell off its industrial cleaning operations in 1999.

Crit then launched an aggressive expansion effort that saw its revenues triple by 1998, and then more than double again by 2005. The company began buying up a number of small-scale temporary employment specialists, including the acquisitions of ARS, Performances, and GTI in 1999. These purchases boosted the group's national network to nearly 120 by the end of the year.

The company also began building and diversifying its multiservices division. In 1999, the company acquired Europe Handling, which specialized in providing airport support services. Europe Handling was one of the most important in its sector in France, holding a prized contract for the country's main airport,

Charles de Gaulle, in Roissy, near Paris. In another move to expand its range of services, Crit acquired Otessa, a company focused on the special events market. Meanwhile, Crit had become interested in the international employment market, establishing Crit Intérim subsidiaries in Switzerland and Italy that year.

In 2000, Crit stepped up the expansion of its network of employment agencies, opening 12 new agencies in that year alone. These agencies were complemented by the establishment of five new offices focused on providing engineering and maintenance services. Also in 2000, Crit acquired ISS, which provided temporary employment services in the event, catering and restaurant, and reception sectors. Later that year, Crit added another temp group, Effika, focused on industrial services, and Mayday Travail Temporaire, with a specialty in the graphics, graphic design, and web design markets.

Crit completed the year 2000 with the purchase of Dublin-based CityJet Handling, renamed as Sky Handling Partner. The purchase significantly boosted Crit's new airport services wing, giving it the contract to service the Dublin International Airport. The following year, Crit's airport services arm scored another major success, when it won the contract to provide the airport support services at Paris Charles de Gaulle II. The company's sales also had grown accordingly, topping EUR 450 million that year.

In April 2001, Crit boosted its position in Switzerland with the acquisition of Equipe Emploi Services, a network of seven agencies in the country's French-speaking region. These were then placed under the company's Crit Intérim Suisse subsidiary.

In December 2001, Crit made a still more significant acquisition—that of larger rival Eurstt, then France's number four temporary employment group. The acquisition of Eurstt, which cost Crit EUR 125 million, boosted its national network to more than 350 agencies. The purchase also enabled Crit to expand into Germany, with three new agencies, and Spain, with six new agencies. By then, Crit had completed a five-to-one stock split, and received recognition from *Forbes* magazine as one of the 400 best small-company stocks in the world. The Eurstt acquisition, meanwhile, helped Crit top EUR 1 billion in sales, and also gave it the position as France's leading independent temporary employment agency, and number four overall.

Crit's expansion pace slowed a bit over the next two years as it worked on integrating its Eurstt acquisition. Nonetheless, the company continued to expand. In 2002, the company acquired Awac Technics and K Intérim. The following year, Crit entered Morocco, establishing a Crit Intérim subsidiary there. The company's airport services division meanwhile targeted Congo, establishing a new subsidiary there, Congo Handling. Back at home, Crit established a new specialized subsidiary, Crit Médical, which specialized in providing medical and paramedical personnel.

By the end of 2004, Congo Handling had imposed itself as a major player in its market, securing contracts with a number of airlines, including Air France, DHL, and others at the Brazzaville and Pointe Noire airports. In early 2005, the subsidiary added a new client, Toumai Air Tchad, for ground services at the Brazzaville airport. Crit's European airport services opera-

Key Dates:

1962: Claude Guedj forms the Centre de Recherches Industrielles et Techniques (Crit) to provide consulting, engineering, and design services.
1972: The company creates a temporary employment subsidiary, Crit Intérim, and expands its range of operations.
1979: The company receives certification for the nuclear power industry.
1995: Security services company Delta Capital is acquired.
1997: The company acquires Interwork, adding 29 agencies.
1999: Crit goes public on the Euronext Paris Stock Exchange; subsidiaries are established in Switzerland and Italy; the company enters the airport services sector with the purchase of Europe Handling.
2000: The company acquires Effika and Mayday Travail Temporaire; CityJet Handling (renamed as Sky Handling Partner) in Dublin is acquired.
2001: The company acquires Eurstt and becomes the leading independent French temporary employment group.
2002: Awac Technics and K Intérim are acquired.
2003: New subsidiaries Crit Intérim Maroc in Morocco and Congo Handling in Congo are established.

tions also were growing strongly, notably through Irish subsidiary Sky Handling Partner's contract in April 2005 to provide services for Iberworld, of Spain, and Air Transat, from Canada, at the Dublin International Airport.

By the end of 2004, Crit's operations included some 48 subsidiaries. The company launched the beginnings of a restructuring effort to simplify its operations, merging its GTI, CP, and K Intérim subsidiaries into its primary Crit Intérim subsidiary. With its dual focus, Crit expected to continue its success into the new century.

Principal Divisions

Congo Handling (Congo); Atiac; Awac Technics; Computer Assistance; Crit Center; Crit Intérim; Crit Intérim (Switzerland); Crit Maroc (Morocco); Crit Ressources Humaines (Canada); Crit Securite S.A.R.L.; Eurstt France; Eurstt S.A.; Euro Surete; Hillary; K Intérim; Laboralia; Les Compagnons; Les Volants; Otessa; Rush; Sci Cambraie; Sci Rigaud Premilhat; Sci Sarres De Colombe.

Principal Competitors

Manpower France S.A.S.; ADECCO Travail Temporaire S.A.; Inter Alsace; VediorBis S.A.S.; Intérim 25; Adia S.A.; Synergie Travail Temporaire.

Further Reading

"Crit Intérim: une politique de spécialisation et de proximité," *Esprit Club,* December 2003.
"Crit Takes Over Europe Handling," *Les Echos,* June 4, 1999, p. 25.
Felsted, Andrea, "Corporate Services in French Disposal," *Financial Times,* November 19, 2001, p. 26.
"Groupe Crit: contrats en Irlande et au Congo," *Boursarama,* April 18, 2005.

—M.L. Cohen

Groupe Limagrain

BP 1
Rue Limagrain
Chappes
F-63720
France
Telephone: (+33) 4 73 63 40 00
Fax: (+33) 4 73 63 40 44
Web site: http://www.limagrain.com

Private Cooperative Company
Incorporated: 1942 as Coopérative de Production et de
    Vente de Semences Sélectionnées du Massif Central
Employees: 5,400
Sales: EUR 1.1 billion ($1.31 billion) (2004)
NAIC: 111421 Nursery and Tree Production; 424210
    Drugs and Druggists' Sundries Merchant Wholesalers;
    424490 Other Grocery and Related Product Merchant
    Wholesalers; 424910 Farm Supplies Merchant
    Wholesalers; 541710 Research and Development in
    the Physical Sciences and Engineering Sciences

Groupe Limagrain is one of the world's leading producers of seeds, especially in Europe, where the group has long held the position as the top producer of corn, wheat, and other seeds for the professional market through its Anjou, Nickerson, and LG brands. Limagrain is also the world's leading supplier of seeds to the home gardening market and one of the top suppliers of vegetable seeds to the professional segment through its holding of Vilmorin Clause & Cie. The company is also active in the North American market through its 50 percent share of the AgReliant joint-venture in the United States and Canada, as well as its ownership of the Harris Moran Seed Company, among others. The company has also extended it reach into food products, supplying flour and other bakery ingredients through subsidiary Limagrain Céréales Ingrédients. In addition, the company owns Jacquet SA, France's second-largest industrial baking group. Acquisitions have formed an important part of Limagrain's growth and continue to play a role in its development. In 2004, for example, Limagrain acquired Westhove, in Blendeques in the north of France. In March 2005, the company purchased Advanta Seeds Inc., including its European businesses in corn, cereals, rapeseed, sunflower, and other vegetable seeds in Europe, and grass seed and sunflower seed production in Oregon and North Dakota in the United States. Limagrain remains unusual among the world's leading agro-industrial groups in that it has retained its status as a privately held cooperative, with 600 farmer-members based in the Auvergne region in France. In 2004, Limagrain posted sales of EUR 1.1 billion ($1.35 billion).

Wartime Beginnings

The Nazi occupation of France during World War II made it difficult for the country's farmers to ensure their seed supply. In 1942, a group of farmers in the Limagne plains area, near Clermont-Ferrand in the Auvergne region, joined together to create a cooperative to produce and distribute seeds. The new organization was called Coopérative de Production et de Vente de Semences Sélectionnées du Massif Central.

The cooperative at first specialized in the production of wheat seed. In the postwar period, however, the cooperative began investigating other seed markets. In the mid-1960s, it teamed up with the state-run research institute INRA in order to develop and produce new corn varieties. The cooperative adopted a new name, Limagrain in 1965, and in that year also decided to specialize in the research, development, and production of seeds for new corn varieties. By 1970, this effort led to the launch of the highly successful LG 11 corn variety.

During the 1970s, Limagrain, with its LG brand, emerged as a leading seed producer in France and increasingly throughout Europe as well. The cooperative also began seeking opportunities for expansion into other seed markets. In 1975, the group made its first significant acquisition when it purchased the venerable Vilmorin-Andrieux.

Vilmorin-Andrieux itself had its roots in the mid-18th century, when Madame Claude Geoffrey, who had already established a reputation as "maitresse grainetière" in Paris, married Pierre d'Andrieux, who served as seed supplier and botanist for King Louis XV. The couple opened a boutique in 1743 and in

1775 brought in son-in-law Philippe Victoire de Vilmorin. Vilmorin's grandson, Louis de Vilmorin, took over the company in the early 19th century and by the middle of the century had become recognized as one of the leading botanists of the day.

The acquisition of Vilmorin-Andrieux not only added the prominent brand name, it also added an entire new business in seeds for vegetables, fruits, and flowers and other ornamental plants. The purchase also paved the way for Limagrain's development into one of the world's major agro-industrial groups.

European Focus in the 1980s

Limagrain's expansion continued at the end of the 1970s and into the early 1980s. Acquisitions played an important role in the cooperative's growth, enabling it to extend itself into new areas of business and to consolidate its existing operations. Limagrain's next major acquisition came in 1979, when it acquired Tézier, in France. Founded in 1785 by Pierre Tézier, that company had long been a prominent supplier of vegetable seeds to the French market and had also developed a strong international presence as well. The combination of Vilmorin and Tézier under Limagrain boosted the cooperative to the leading ranks of European seed producers.

Limagrain made its first efforts to expand into the North American market at the beginning of the 1980s. After establishing a corn research facility in the United States in 1979, Limagrain added a production subsidiary with the purchase of Ferry Morse in 1981.

Ferry Morse had been formed in 1930 from the merger of two seed companies founded in the 19th century, DM Ferry Co, established in 1856, and CC Mores and Co., founded in 1874. The merged company grew strongly over the following decades and by the time of its acquisition by Vilmorin already held a leading position as a supplier of home garden seeds in the United States.

Nonetheless, Limagrain's primary focus into the early 1990s remained its expansion in Europe. The company also sought to extend its range of operations. In 1983, Limagrain set up its own corn mill, establishing itself as a supplier of grain to the food production industry. The cooperative also boosted its research and development component with the creation of a new plant biotech laboratory at the University of Clermont Ferrand in 1986.

Gardening had long been a prominent consumer market in France, and a significant proportion of the population cultivated their own vegetable gardens. The development of specialist retailers catering to the home gardening market encouraged Limagrain to create a dedicated umbrella structure for its various consumer-oriented operations. In 1989, the cooperative created Oxadis, which became the marketing and distribution operation for the Vilmorin and Tézier seed brands, as well as a line of pet foods and supplies, which were closely associated with the home gardening retail market.

Limagrain continued to expand its consumer operations and in 1990 acquired 80 percent of Flora-Frey, the leading seed brand in Germany. Following that acquisition, Limagrain created Ceres, a new holding company for its vegetable and flower seeds businesses, including Vilmorin, Tézier, Flora-Frey, Ferry Morris, and Oxadis. Then, in 1992, Limagrain renamed its gardening seeds operation Vilmorin & Cie., which then took over Ceres and its companies. This move preceded Vilmorin's public offering in that same year, when its shares were listed on the Paris Bourse. Limagrain remained the majority shareholder of Vilmorin, while Vilmorin became a vehicle for further growth for the cooperative through the 1990s.

Targeting North America in the 1990s

Limagrain had also taken significant steps toward becoming the leading seed supplier for the European market. In 1990, the company had acquired Anglo-Dutch company Nickerson-Zwaan. That purchase, which gave Limagrain prominent positions in the Netherlands and in the United Kingdom, represented the group's return to wheat seeds. Nickerson-Zwaan also added a variety of other crop seeds, including sugar beets, cabbage, gherkins, and lettuce.

The cooperative also deepened its interest in the consumer end market in the mid-1990s. In 1995, Limagrain became a major force in the French industrial breads market when it purchased Jacquet SA. That company had its origins in a small, family-owned bakery opened by Philibert Jacquet in Paris in 1880. Jacquet invented a new type of toast, Pain Grillé, which he patented and marketed under the Jacquet brand. In 1946, the Jacquet company was bought up by Lucien Joulin. Under Joulin, Jacquet became the first in France to produce pre-sliced, packaged bread. Sold at first in bakeries and shops in Paris, the new type of packaged proved popular, and in 1959 Jacquet opened a large-scale production facility to produce its Grand Blanc white bread. The rise of the supermarket in France presented a new opportunity for Jacquet, which quickly became a leading producer of packaged breads in that country.

In addition to its extension into this new consumer market, Limagrain had become interested in expanding into other markets. In the early 1990s, the cooperative redoubled its efforts to

Key Dates:

1942: A group of farmers create the Coopérative de Production et de Vente de Semences Sélectionnées du Massif Central in order to provide a dependable source of wheat seeds during World War II.

1965: The organization changes its name to Limagrain and specializes in the development of corn seeds.

1970: The highly successful LG 11 corn variety is launched.

1975: Expansion begins with the acquisition of garden seeds group Vilmorin.

1979: Seeds specialist Tézier is acquired.

1981: Limagrain purchases Ferry Morse Seeds in the United States.

1983: Production of cereals-based food ingredients is launched.

1989: Oxadis is created as a marketing wing for home garden seeds and pet supplies.

1990: Nickerson-Zwaan, a producer of wheat and vegetable seeds, is acquired.

1992: Vilmorin is listed on the Paris Stock Exchange.

1995: The cooperative expands into consumer and industrial bakery products with the purchase of Jacquet.

1997: Harris Moran Seed Company in the United States is acquired.

2000: Limagrain merges its North American corn seeds operation into AgReliant joint-venture with KWS.

2002: Limagrain Céréales Ingredients subsidiary is created to consolidate the group's food ingredients operations.

2003: A majority stake in Israel's Hazera, a world-leading producer of tomato seeds, is acquired.

2004: Limagrain purchases WestHove in France.

2005: The European vegetable seeds businesses of Advanta Seeds Inc. are acquired.

establish itself in North America. Once again, acquisitions formed a major part of the company's expansion strategy. In 1993, for example, the company acquired Biotechnica, based in Kansas City. This purchase was followed by the purchase of Ontario's KingAgro, a seed company with particular focus on the canola market. The company also began producing corn seed in the United States, launching this operation in 1994.

These and other acquisitions helped transform Limagrain into a truly global operation. Where previously Europe had accounted for some 95 percent of Limagrain's revenues, by the middle of the 1990s the North American market already represented more than 35 percent of the group's total income. In 1997, the cooperative boosted its North American presence again, this time acquiring one of the market's leading seeds suppliers, Harris Moran. That company had been formed in the early 1980s under parent company Celanese, a chemical company that had entered the seeds business in the early 1970s. Harris Moran was later taken over by Lafarge Coppee. In 1990, Lafarge Coppee joined with Rhone Poulenc to acquire a French seeds business as well, Clause.

This company too came under Limagrain's control following its acquisition of Harris Moran. Clause was then merged into Vilmorin, which became known as Vilmorin Clause & Cie.

GMOs and Global Growth in the 2000s

In 1997, Limagrain became the majority partner in the creation of Biogemma, which focused on the development of genetically modified organisms (GMOs). Despite the European restrictions on the use of GMOs, the creation of Biogemma was seen as a necessity in order to guarantee Limagrain's competitiveness in the future. The company also entered the development of plants for pharmaceutical uses, creating Meristem in 1997. One of that subsidiary's first patents, however, was revealed to be a means of creating a so-called "terminator" gene sequence that prevented seeds from germinating after harvest.

Limagrain reinforced its position in North American in 2000 when it formed a 50–50 joint venture with the U.S. company KWS. Called AgReliant, the new company combined Limagrain's North American corn seed operations with KWS's soybean business.

Two years later, in Europe, Limagrain moved to consolidate its various food ingredients operations under a single umbrella company, Limagrain Céréales Ingrédients (LCI). This company took over Limagrain's various ingredients brands, including DAFA enzymes, milling compensators, and improvers; MCT maize-based semolina ingredients; FCI texturing agents; and Sofalia food fibers.

As it moved toward mid-decade, Limagrain remained dedicated to its growth through acquisition strategy. In 2003, the company, through Vilmorin Clause & Cie, acquired a majority stake in Israel's Hazera, a leading producer of tomato seeds. The following year, the company added Germany's Carl Sperling & Co., a specialist in vegetable seeds, which was combined with Vilmorin Clause's Flora Frey operations. At the end of 2004, Limagrain boosted its grains business with the acquisition of France's Westhove, founded in Blendecques in 1854. This purchase was followed by the acquisition of Advanta Seeds Inc.'s vegetable seeds operations in Europe, as well as that company's sunflower and grass seeds operations in North Dakota and Oregon, respectively. Limagrain was by then counted among the world's top-ranking seeds producers, a feat the group achieved without abandoning its roots as an Auvergne region cooperative.

Principal Subsidiaries

AgReliant Genetics Inc. (Canada; 50%); AgReliant Genetics LLC (United States; 50%); Biogemma (55%); Clause/Tézier; Eurodur (44%); Ferry Morse (United States); Flora Frey/Sperling (Germany); Force Limagrain SA; Génoplante Valor SAS (48%); Harris Moran Seed Company; Hazera Genetics; Jacquet Céréales Technologies; Jacquet SA; Kyowa (Japan; 40%); Limagrain Central Europe; Limagrain Céréales Ingrédients; Limagrain Genetics; Limagrain Genetics Inc (United States); Limagrain Italia SpA (Italy); Limagrain Nederland BV (Netherlands); Limagrain Verneuil Holding; Limagrain-Nickerson GmbH (Germany); Maïs Angevin-Nickerson SA; Marco Polo Seeds (Thailand-Indonesia); Mikado (Japan; 20%); Nickerson International Research GEIE; Nickerson UK Ltd.; Oxadis; Société Meunière du Centre (36%); Soygenetics LLC (United States; 37%); Suttons Group Ltd. (United Kingdom); Ulice; Van den Berg BV (Netherlands); Vilmorin/Nickerson Zwaan.

Principal Competitors

Monsanto Company; Pioneer Hi-Bred International, Inc.; Syngenta.

Further Reading

"KWS, Limagrain Merge Interests in North America," *Feedstuffs*, February 14, 2000, p. 27.

"Limagrain Acquires Advanta Seeds Inc," *Chemical Market Reporter*, March 21, 2005, p. 11.

"Limagrain, la coopérative auvergnate rivale de Monsanto," *Monde*, August 25, 2001.

"Limagrain: le semencier génétique," *Expansion*, October 2003.

"Westhove Joins Limagrain," *International Food Ingredients*, December 2004, p. 12.

—M.L. Cohen

Groupe Open

202 Quai de Clichy
Clichy F-92110
France
Telephone: (+33) 1 40 87 97 97
Fax: (+33) 1 40 87 97 52
Web site: http://www.groupe-open.com

Public Company
Incorporated: 1989
Employees: 800
Sales: EUR 327.8 million ($400 million) (2004)
Stock Exchanges: Euronext Paris
Ticker Symbol: OPN
NAIC: 541512 Computer Systems Design Services

Groupe Open is one of France's leading and fastest-growing specialists in information technology (IT) and Web integration infrastructure and services, with a focus on the developing e-business and related interactive information systems. The company operates through two primary subsidiaries, Logix, targeting the IT professional market, and Innetis, which provides systems and services directly to corporations. In late 2004, the company boosted this latter business through the acquisition of a controlling stake in fellow French IT company Teamlog. Through its subsidiaries, Groupe Open provides design, development, implementation and support services that enable its customers to reposition their businesses toward a Web-integrated, e-business model. The company's clients include a number of major companies such as EDF, Air Liquide, Bouygues Telecom, Noos, Bred, Atos-Origin. At the same time, a strong share of Open's sales comes from the small-to-mid-sized market segment. Open has grown strongly since the late 1990s, in large part due to its transition from its original status as an IBM-based infrastructure reseller to a full-fledged IT services provider. Open's strategy calls for the company to double its sales by 2007 from 2004's EUR 328 million ($400 million). As part of this growth strategy, the company has launched an effort to expand internationally, using Logix as its spearhead. The company has also launched a series of acquisi-

tions, notably of Four Leaf Technologies and Commentor in the Scandinavian market in 2004, and CCG in the Netherlands in 2005. Logix is also present in Belgium, Spain, Hungary, Poland, and Morocco. Groupe Open is listed on the Euronext Paris Stock Exchange. Founder Frédéric Sébag is company chairman, and Guy Mamou-Mani is chief executive.

IBM Server Reseller in the 1980s

After earning a master's degree in mathematics, Frédéric Sébag began his career in 1985 as a sales engineer for the French IT services group Cosi. By 1987, Sébag had risen to the position of director for Cosi's sales department. The development of a new generation of server technology by IBM, along with the creation of the UNIX operating system, presented new opportunities in the French IT market. In 1989, at the age of 27, Sébag decided to form his own company, called Open Technologies. Open Technologies acted as a distributor for the sale and implementation of UNIX-based IBM servers in France. Open's relationship with and dependence on IBM remained strong throughout the 1990s. IBM's shareholding in Open reinforced the company's position as a de facto subsidiary of the U.S. computer giant.

Open began expanding its range of UNIX services in the early 1990s. In 1991, for example, the company created a new subsidiary, Open Ingénierie, dedicated toward the development of software for the UNIX system. The following year, the company created another subsidiary for its ASAP publishing and distribution operations, called Open Solutions. The addition of Laurent Sadoun, formerly sales director at Informix France, the previous year also led the way to the creation of Logix, a subsidiary dedicated to the sales and distribution for the group's UNIX software and systems. By the end of 1992, the company had restructured its operations, grouping its various businesses under a new holding company, Groupe Open, which retained direction of Open Technologies.

By then, however, Open found itself surrounded by a growing number of competitors. The company not only faced new rivals in the UNIX market but also new and competing servers and operating systems, especially NT from Microsoft. The economic pressures of this situation, combined with an interna-

---

Company Perspectives:

Groupe Open's Engineers/Consultants master the new technologies related to the e-business concept and have numerous certifications covering UNIX and Windows NT environments, Systems and Networks architectures, data storage and consolidation products as well as e-commerce tools. In addition, this team is made up of operational and organisational ERP experts whose aim is to integrate market solutions in order to deliver a full e-business information system, an on and/or off-line integrated management medium.

---

tional recession exacerbated by the first United States-led war against Iraq, led to a collapse of the French IT market.

Open was forced to restructure its operations in the mid-1990s. As part of the restructuring effort, the group refocused its subsidiaries to target specific market segments. Subsidiaries were then given greater autonomy, in order to respond more effectively to their markets. The company reorganized Groupe Open itself as a pure holding company, transferring the operations of Open Technologies to Open Ingénierie, which then changed its name to Open Technologies.

Groupe Open completed its restructuring with the creation of a new subsidiary in 1996, called Open Multimedia. That subsidiary was meant to enable Open's entry into the booming market for multimedia applications, which had become the fastest-growing segment of the computer industry in the late 1990s. Multimedia not only propelled the adoption of personal computers in the consumer retail sector, it also paved the way for significant development of Internet-based operations. Although the emerging importance of the Internet later led Open to reinvent itself to its advantage, the company's entry into the multimedia market proved to be a less fortuitous move. In 1997, Open shut down Open Multimedia, transferring its operations to Open Technologies.

In the meantime, Open had found a new vehicle for growth. In 1997, the company, through both Logix and Open Technologies, signed a new series of contracts with IBM for its new Risc System 6000. The contracts gave Open the top spot in France as a distributor of IBM's server technology, and the number three spot in the IBM server integration segment. The new IBM contracts launched a period of extraordinary growth for the company, helping it expand by some 370 percent between 1997 and 2000.

Meanwhile, Open had also initiated a new strategy to reduce its reliance on IBM. In 1997, Logix created a new subsidiary, Openway, launching the distribution of Sybase/Powersoft software products for both the UNIX and NT operating systems. Open also acquired a 17.5 percent stake in SIP, a company specializing in Microsoft Front Office applications for the financial market.

Services Focus in the Late 1990s

Toward the end of the 1990s, Open moved to shed its image as effectively an IBM subsidiary. In 1998, the company went public,

listing its shares on the Paris Bourse's Secondary Market. The public offering enabled the company to launch a new strategy, that of expanding into the services market. This direction offered a number of advantages for Open. An extension into the services sector helped reduce the group's reliance on its distribution and integration component, while also reducing its dependence on IBM for the major share of its revenues. Services also represented one of the fastest-growing segments of the IT market, and at the same time offered the prospective of far higher margins than the group's integration and distribution businesses.

The implementation of Open's services strategy crystallized with the arrival of Guy Mamou-Mani in 1998. Mamou-Mani had founded and led Manugistics, a French subsidiary of CSC-Go International, in 1995, while also becoming a top executive at CSC France.

Mamou-Mani took charge of creating a new Integration and Services division at Groupe Open. In 1999, the company acquired SQL Tech, a leading developer of Internet and intranet software. The company then reorganized its operations, bundling Open Technologies, Open Solutions, and SQL Tech into its Integration and Services division. The following year, that division was restructured into a new subsidiary, called Innetis, with Mamou-Mani as its CEO.

Innetis quickly began beefing up its range of services. Toward this end, the subsidiary made two strategic acquisitions in 2000. The first was that of Actinfo, which permitted the company to expand its services to the small-and-mid-sized market as well as giving it control of Actinfo.net, boosting its online services offering. The second acquisition, Value Add Consulting, allowed Innetis to begin providing consulting services as well.

Groupe Open's restructuring produced a new growth spurt for the company into the 2000s. Between 2000 and the end of 2004, the company had doubled its annual sales. While the Innetis services component provided part of this growth, the company's Logix unit remained a solid performer.

In particular, Logix provided Groupe Open with its spearhead into the international market. By the late 1990s, the company had recognized that in order to remain a force in the IT market, it would have to respond to the trend toward the increasing internationalization of the market. The company first entered Belgium in 1998, followed by Spain and Poland in 1999. At the same time, Logix moved to expand its Internet presence, launching its successful Logix.fr business-to-business portal. This fit in with Groupe Open's decision to focus on the e-business market for the new decade.

A new collapse in the international IT market in the early 2000s led Open to place further international expansion on hold. Nonetheless, the company's strong list of recurrent customers, which represented some 75 percent of the group's revenues, shielded Open from the worst effects of the IT market slowdown.

In 2002, the company reached a cooperation agreement with a new major player in the international IT market, Business Objects. Also in that year, the company's Innetis subsidiary boosted its range of services through the acquisition of fellow French group Owendo. Soon after Innetis unveiled the final

---
Key Dates:

1989: Frederic Sébag founds Open Technologies, a specialist in UNIX server implementation.
1991: Open Ingénierie is formed and begins developing software.
1992: Open Solutions and Logix distribution subsidiary are created; Open Ingénierie restructures under the holding company Groupe Open.
1998: Groupe Open goes public on Paris Stock Exchange's Secondary Market.
2004: Groupe Open agrees to acquire a controlling share of Teamlog.
---

version of its new software tools, WCM and XRP, providing Web site content management and back office applications. Innetis began building up its client list, with more than 50 packages sold by the end of 2004.

International Presence for the 2000s

In that year, Open renewed its international expansion effort, establishing a new Logix subsidiary in Amsterdam in April. Open also began looking for acquisition candidates to boost its European presence. This led the company to the Scandinavian market, where it acquired 80 percent of Denmark's Four Leaf Technologies. That company, which specialized in data storage solutions for the IT professionals sector, had established itself as a leader in the Nordic region, with operations in Denmark, Finland, Norway, and Sweden. Four Leaf became part of Logix. By the end of 2004, Logix had reinforced its Scandinavian operations with the purchase of Commentor, also based in Denmark, which was then placed under Four Leaf.

Setting itself a goal of doubling in size by 2007, Open continued its acquisition drive into 2005. The company acquired a stake in France's Teamlog in early 2004. This move led to an agreement giving Open a controlling interest in the company before the end of the year. In December 2004, Innetis acquired Obbisoft, a company that specialized in the development and distribution of logistics and transport support applications. By the beginning of 2005, Open had found its next target,

buying up CCG Europe, a Netherlands-based developer of storage software. While France remained Open's primary market, at 62 percent of its sales of nearly EUR 328 million in 2004, the company had successfully asserted itself as a rising star in the European IT services and integration markets.

Principal Subsidiaries

Commentor (Denmark; 67.93%); FINOVIA; Four Leaf Technologies (Norway; 79.92%); Four Leaf Technologies AB (Sweden; 79.92%); Four Leaf Technologies AS (Denmark; 79.92%); Four Leaf Technologies OY (Finland; 79.92%); GROUPE OPEN S.A.; IP Vista; LOG.X Maroc; LOGIX Benelux; LOGIX Iberia; LOGIX Nederland; LX Polska; OPENWAY SAS.

Principal Competitors

Volvo Information Technology AB; T-Systems GEI GmbH; gedas AG; Transiciel S.A.; Terra Networks S.A.; Sopra Conseil et Assistance en Informatique; GFI Informatique; Oberthur Card Systems; Computacenter France.

Further Reading

"Les ASP, cible du Groupe Open," *01 Informatique*, March 31, 2000.
Drothier, Yves, "La distribution d'infrastructure exige d'avoir une taille européenne," *JDN Solutions*, January 17, 2005.
"Frédéric Sebag vous a répondu," *Boursorama*, March 5, 2002.
"Groupe Open convoite Teamlog," *Vie Financiere*, January 7, 2005, p. 22.
Marquelty, Fabio, "Trois questions à Guy Mamou-Mani," *Le Journal des Finances*, January 22, 2005, p. 15.
"M. Sebag détient désormais 33,2% du capital de GROUPE OPEN," *Boursorama*, August 5, 2005.
Ruello, Alain, "Groupe Open va prendre le controle de Teamlog," *Echos*, January 25, 2005, p. 29.
Siccat, Armelle, "Groupe Open se porte bien," *Décision Distribution*, April 7, 2003.
Sounack, Laurent, "Le groupe Open accélère sa diversification dans les services," *Décision Micro*, February 7, 2000.
"Teamlog-Groupe Open," *Figaro Economique*, January 25, 2005, p. 6.
Thorel, Jérôme, "La deuxième chance d'Open Technologie," *Expansion*, May 14, 1998, p. 119.

—M.L. Cohen

High Falls Brewing Company LLC

445 St. Paul Street
Rochester, New York 14605
U.S.A.
Telephone: (585) 263-9403
Fax: (585) 546-5011
Web site: http://www.highfalls.com

Private Company
Incorporated: 1932 as Genesee Brewing Co.
Employees: 500 (est.)
Sales: $90 million (est.)
NAIC: 312120 Breweries

High Falls Brewing Company LLC is the seventh largest brewer of beer in the United States. The Rochester, New York-based firm distributes its products to most of the United States as well as parts of Canada and a handful of overseas markets. Its brands include JW Dundee's Honey Brown Lager, Genesee Cream Ale, Genny Light, Michael Shea's Irish Amber, and Koch's Golden Anniversary Beer. High Falls also serves as a contract brewer for firms like the Boston Beer Co., with as much as half of its output bearing other labels. The company is owned by members of management.

Roots

High Falls traces its origins to 1878, when Mathius Knodolf founded the Genesee Brewing Company in Rochester, New York, using a brewery that had been built in 1860. It took its name from the Seneca Indian word for the valley in which Rochester was located. In 1889 Knodolf's company and two others in the area were purchased by an English brewing syndicate, and the three companies' operations were consolidated into the Bartholomay Brewing Company, Ltd.

In January of 1919 the U.S. Congress passed the 18th Amendment to the Constitution, which banned the manufacture, transportation, or sale of alcoholic beverages. Like many others around the country, the brewery ceased operations, and its employees found new jobs.

One such worker was Louis Wehle, the company's superintendent. The son and grandson of brewers, Wehle had studied at the Rochester Institute of Technology before graduating from the National Brewers Academy in New York in 1911 and taking a job with Genesee. After Prohibition took effect in 1920 he became a grocer, and then in 1925 formed the Wehle Baking Company. He soon established a chain of bakeries, and sold the business for $1 million just before the stock market crash of 1929. In 1932, as repeal of the 18th amendment became imminent, Wehle decided to reactivate the Genesee brewery with several partners, and they invested $500,000 to renovate the dormant facility.

In September 1933 the new firm sold 50,000 shares of nonvoting stock in a public offering, and by the next year the Genesee Brewing Company was once again producing beers like the new 12 Horse Ale. The country was thirsty after more than a decade of Prohibition, and with Franklin Roosevelt's New Deal starting to bring the economy out of the Great Depression, sales took off. The firm's products were distributed regionally, primarily in New York State.

The 1940s saw Louis Wehle's longtime passion for outdoor sports lead his company to sponsor an annual statewide fishing contest that promoted conservation and sportsmanship, as well as the firm's beer. Louis Wehle also was involved in a number of humanitarian causes, and he served for more than a decade as head of the New York state March of Dimes campaign, which raised money to combat polio. The firm's success enabled him to live on a 1,700-acre estate near Rochester, which had its own harness racing track, duck-breeding grounds, and shooting range.

By the early 1950s Wehle had begun serving as board chairman, leaving day-to-day operation of the company to his son, John L. Wehle, who had attended Yale and the National Brewers Academy. Sales were strong during the decade, and after a record year of $22.5 million in revenues in 1957, the company spent $500,000 expanding its bottling operation.

Introduction of Cream Ale in 1960

In 1960 the company introduced Genesee Cream Ale, which would go on to become one of its most popular offerings. A lighter beer, Fyfe & Drum, was produced during this era as well.

Company Perspectives:

High Falls Brewing Company is perfectly positioned for future growth and opportunities. Although we continue to utilize the latest technologies available in brewing today, we hold true to the same time-honored traditions established decades ago by our very own brew master. And as such, we will continue to grow our family of High Falls brands to meet the demands of a growing segment of discerning and incredibly loyal customers and consumers.

In November of 1964 Louis Wehle died at the age of 75, and his controlling stake in the firm passed to his family.

The mid-1960s saw Genesee install the largest lauter tun brewing vessel in the world as it continued to upgrade its plant. In 1969 the company nearly finalized a merger with manufacturer Houdaille Industries, but the $31 million deal fell through. The firm recorded sales of $29.6 million for the fiscal year, and a profit of $2 million. In addition to marketing its own brews, the company also had begun distributing the Danish beer Carlsberg in the Northeast.

During the 1970s John Wehle oversaw an expansion of Genesee distribution to nearly half of the United States, and sales grew significantly. In 1978 the firm introduced a new light beer, Genny Light, which took the place of the similar Fyfe & Drum.

John Wehle had continued to lead the firm as chairman and CEO, and after several turnovers in the president's job, in March of 1982 his 35-year-old son John Wehle, Jr., was appointed to the post. During that year the company completed construction of a $3.4 million steam plant, which saved an estimated $100,000 per month in energy costs. The generator burned cardboard from boxes used to return deposit bottles, which New York and several other states had recently begun requiring.

The 1980s saw Genesee struggling to remain profitable, as mergers around the industry created larger and more powerful national competitors. Other factors impacting the firm's bottom line at this time included a heightened awareness of alcoholism in the United States and the resultant higher drinking ages, price cutting by competitors, and new competition from products like wine coolers.

Acquisition of Fred Koch Brewery in 1985

In February 1985 the company reached an agreement to acquire the struggling Fred Koch Brewery of Dunkirk, New York from its owner, Vaux Breweries PLC of England. After the sale, Genesee would continue to produce Koch's Golden Anniversary Beer and Black Horse Ale. For the fiscal year ending in mid-1985, Genesee recorded revenues of $141.5 million and earnings of $8.8 million.

In the fall of 1986 John Wehle, Jr., succeeded his father as CEO, though the senior Wehle would continue to serve as board chairman. The company's offerings now included Genesee Beer, Cream Ale, Light, Light Cream Ale, and 12 Horse Ale.

As earnings continued to fall in the face of industry consolidation, the company began looking for new ways to cut costs, and offered its employees bonuses for money-saving ideas. Genesee also formed a planning and development division to seek out other business opportunities, and subsequently partnered with Taylor-Bolane Associates, Inc. to create equipment rental company Cheyenne Leasing, and joined with Home Leasing Corp. to buy a 600-unit apartment complex in Columbus, Ohio.

In late 1987 Genesee created a new holding company called Genesee Corp. that would oversee all of its operations, and also bought Ontario Foods of Albion, New York, a processor and packer of dry food products like drink mixes. For 1988 the company, now the seventh largest brewer in the United States, reported sales of just less than $130 million, and a profit of $6.5 million.

In 1990 Genesee switched ad agencies as it sought to rebuild its sagging brands. The firm's advertising budget now stood at just $3.5 million, down from the $12 million of several years earlier. The following year saw introduction of a nonalcoholic beer, Genesee NA, which competed in a category that generated just 1 percent of total beer sales, but was growing rapidly.

In March 1992 the firm launched a new brand name, Michael Shea's Irish Amber. Sales of imported beers and smaller "microbrews" were growing rapidly at the time, and a number of larger breweries were trying to capture a part of that market with more specialized products. The firm was now on the rebound, with production increasing for the first time in five years to 2.22 million barrels, and sales hitting $145 million.

In November of 1993 John Wehle, Sr., died at age 76. He had served as board chairman until his death. The chairmanship was subsequently taken over by John, Jr., whose brother Charles S. "Chipp" Wehle would serve as senior vice-president.

Introduction of JW Dundee in 1994

In 1994 the company introduced several new varieties including Genny Ice, Michael Shea's Black & Tan, and JW Dundee's Honey Brown Lager. Like the Michael Shea brand, Dundee's was aimed at drinkers aged 21–35. The typical Genesee customer was a working class man, age 35 or older, and the firm was trying to reach a younger generation that appeared to place a higher value on flavor and perceived authenticity. The Shea's and Dundee's brands had some success in the firm's primary markets of New York, Pennsylvania, and Ohio, but made their greatest impact further afield in places like Chicago. Genesee beer was a lower-priced product, and the new brands enabled the company to charge the premium price of specialty beers.

Product introductions continued in 1995 with Genny Red and Michael Shea's Blonde Lager, and in 1996 the company created a new division called High Falls Brewing Co. to oversee its specialty beers, including new India Pale Ale. The company was following in the path of other old-line brewers that had created subsidiaries to put out microbrew-like drinks with no mention of the parent company. For the fiscal year ended in early 1996, Genesee reported that its Dundee's and O'Shea's beers accounted for 18 percent of total sales, double the amount of a year earlier. Dundee's had sold 2.6 million cases, up from 930,000 in its first year.

Key Dates:

1878: Genesee Brewing Company is founded in Rochester, New York.

1920: Production halts with the start of Prohibition.

1932: Louis Wehle reactivates Genesee brewery in anticipation of Repeal.

1960: Genesee Cream Ale debuts.

1964: Louis Wehle dies; control of the firm passes to his son, John Wehle.

1978: Genny Light is introduced.

1985: Fred Koch Brewery is acquired.

1986: The company starts investing in real estate, equipment leasing, and food businesses.

1992: Michael Shea's Irish Amber is introduced.

1993: John Wehle, Sr., dies; control of the firm passes to his son John Wehle, Jr.

1994: JW Dundee's Honey Brown, Genny Ice debut.

1996: The company begins brewing Sam Adams beer for Boston Beer Co.

2000: Contract brewing agreements are signed with Smirnoff Ice, Mike's Hard Lemonade; Genesee is sold to a group led by CEO Samuel Hubbard; the company is renamed High Falls.

2004: Two "craft" beers, JW Dundee's American Amber Lager and American Pale Ale, are added to the firm's offerings.

2005: High Falls takes on the distribution of three New Zealand beers made by Lion Nathan, and signs an agreement to have its beers distributed in Canada by Brick Brewing Co.

During 1996 the firm completed a $4 million upgrade of its bottling and packaging equipment and reached an agreement to market a Canadian company's beers in the United States. Genesee also scored a major coup by winning a contract to produce Sam Adams beer for the Boston Beer Co., which had no brewery of its own.

In the spring of 1997 the firm introduced a light version of the successful JW Dundee's Honey Brown Lager along with Genny Summer Brew, which was only available in the warmer months. The firm added two new companies to its food division during 1997 and 1998, Freedom Foods of Florida and TKI Foods of Illinois, at a total cost of $30 million.

For the fiscal year ended in May 1999, the company's brewing unit posted a loss of $4.7 million, as beer sales fell by 12.5 percent. The firm's nonbeer operations now made up more than a third of Genesee Corporation's income, which totaled $178.4 million. In August the company began considering an offer from Pabst to buy its beer brands. It was rejected, however, in large part because of the Wehle family's loyalty to Rochester and the jobs that would likely be lost there if Pabst relocated the brewing operations.

After the Pabst deal fell through, Genesee Brewing let 10 percent of its staff of 550 go as part of a new plan to cut costs and keep the struggling brewery in business. In December the company reintroduced 12 Horse Ale, which had originally been brewed in 1934. That same month a new suitor, Platinum Holdings of New York, struck a deal to buy the firm. Platinum already owned City Brewing Co. of LaCrosse, Wisconsin, which sold beer under a number of different brand names.

In March 2000 Genesee's 53-year-old chairman and primary shareholder, John L. Wehle, Jr., died of cancer. Control of the firm and its chairmanship passed to his brother Chipp, with Samuel Hubbard, the company's president since the preceding June, taking over as CEO of Genesee Corporation.

Sale to Management in 2000

In May the sale to Platinum Holdings fell apart amid recriminations on both sides. Shortly afterward a management-led buyout plan was put together, and in August the company reached an agreement for an investment group led by eight of the firm's executives, including CEO Hubbard, to acquire the brewing business for $25.8 million. The company's Ontario Foods unit and its other investments in real estate and equipment leasing would be divested separately. The purchase was funded in part by a $6.5 million federal grant and loan incentive package the firm had been awarded.

After the sale was completed in December of 2000, the company's name was changed to High Falls Brewing Co., reflecting management's desire to emphasize its specialty brews. The company would continue to produce its full line of beers and brew Sam Adams under contract to Boston Beer. High Falls also had recently signed agreements to make Mike's Hard Lemonade and Smirnoff Ice, a malt-based vodka drink. The company's plant was in good working order, and expanding contract production was a primary objective of the new owners. By now, one-half of the firm's brewing was contract work.

During 2001 High Falls spent some $11.5 million to add a new high-speed bottling line and other production equipment. Sixty-five new workers were hired, as the firm's contract work began to tap more of its 3.3 million barrel capacity.

The company was now actively seeking to rebuild its brands, which had suffered from a decline in marketing support. Even its most recent success, JW Dundee's, had slipped after peaking at 400,000 barrels in 1998. High Falls soon redesigned its packaging, and also boosted advertising spending, adding new point-of-purchase materials and, in 2002, the first Genesee television ads since the 1980s.

The firm ran into trouble in December 2002, when its Smirnoff bottling contract ended and it was unable to pay a $1 million note to former owner Genesee Corp. Efforts during 2003 to recapitalize in conjunction with a third party failed, and the company found itself unable to pay another $3 million payment at year's end. The year 2003 also had seen the launch of another new brand, Kipling Light, but the dark-colored, low-calorie beer made little impact.

In the late summer of 2004 the firm added two "craft" brews, JW Dundee's American Amber Lager and American Pale Ale. Samples of each were packaged with six-packs of Honey Brown to introduce them to the public.

In August 2004 Boston Beer told the company it would terminate its contract brewing work, and in November production ceased, leading to the layoffs of 30 employees. In late December High Falls was able to win the work back, however, narrowly averting a major financial crisis.

In early 2005 the firm took on distribution of three New Zealand beers made by Lion Nathan, and also signed a new agreement to have its beers distributed in Canada by Brick Brewing Co. By now High Falls brands were available in most of the continental United States, and parts of Canada, England, Ireland, and China.

With roots stretching back more than 125 years, High Falls Brewing Co. was one of the oldest beer makers in the United States. The firm was struggling to fend off competition from both industry giants and new upstarts, while working to redefine itself as a regional concern that made some nationally known products. Its new manager-owners were committed to keeping it afloat, but the road ahead looked rocky.

Principal Divisions

Fred Koch Brewery.

Principal Competitors

Anheuser-Busch Companies, Inc.; SABMiller plc; Molson Coors Brewing Company; Pabst Brewing Company; InBev USA; The Boston Beer Company, Inc.

Further Reading

"Boston Beer Renews High Falls Contract," *Modern Brewery Age,* January 10, 2005, p. 2.

"Bought by the Brewery Syndicate," *New York Times,* March 24, 1889, p. 2.

Cazentre, Don, "High Falls Brewing Co. Taps Craft Beer Drinkers," *Post Standard/Herald-Journal,* November 24, 2004, p. E1.

Daykin, Tom, "Pabst Looking at No. 5 Brewer," *Milwaukee Journal Sentinel,* August 27, 1999, p. 1.

——, "Plans to Buy Genesee Brewing Fall Through," *Milwaukee Journal Sentinel,* May 3, 2000, p. 35D.

"Genesee Brewery Chief John Wehle Jr. Dead at 53 After Long Bout with Cancer," *Modern Brewery Age,* March 20, 2000, p. 1.

"Genesee Says Mgmt. Buyout Is Complete," *Modern Brewery Age,* December 25, 2000, p. 1.

"Genesee to Be Sold to Platinum Holdings," *Modern Brewery Age,* December 27, 1999, p. 1.

"Houdaille and Genesee Drop Planned Merger," *Wall Street Journal,* April 22, 1969, p. 15.

"John Wehle Dies; Brewer Led Genesee," *Buffalo News,* November 8, 1993, p. C8.

Johnston, Phil, "Genesee Plays It Safe in Effort to Diversify," *Rochester Business Journal,* December 28, 1987, p. 1.

Le Beau, Christina, "Genesee Barrelage on a Roll, Bucking U.S. Trend," *Rochester Business Journal,* June 26, 1992, p. 5.

——, "Genesee Unveils Non-Alcoholic Brew," *Rochester Business Journal,* May 27, 1991, p. 1.

"Louis Wehle, 75, Ex-State Official," *New York Times,* November 22, 1964, p. 86.

Norris, Scott, "Genesee Offers Incentives in Bid to Reduce Costs," *Rochester Business Journal,* March 26, 1990, p. 8.

——, "Sales at Genesee Mirror Flat Growth in Industry," *Rochester Business Journal,* December 25, 1989, p. 11.

"Pheasants in His Brew," *New York Times,* June 7, 1956, p. 37.

"Plans to Reopen Brewery," *New York Times,* July 6, 1932, p. 12.

Pruzan, Todd, "Genesee Introduces High Falls Division for Upscale Brews," *Advertising Age,* June 10, 1996, p. 16.

Reid, Peter V.K., "Waking the Slumbering Giant," *Modern Brewery Age,* May 19, 2003, p. 6.

Roberts, Catherine, "Growth Slowing in Key Specialty-Beer Market," *Rochester Business Journal,* November 1, 1996, p. 1.

Schouest, Kim, "Up in Smoke," *Beverage World,* July 1, 1991, p. 60.

—Frank Uhle

HNI Corporation

414 East Third Street
Muscatine, Iowa 52761-0071
U.S.A.
Telephone: (563) 264-7400
Fax: (563) 264-7217
Web site: http://www.honi.com

Public Company
Incorporated: 1944 as Home-O-Nize Co.
Employees: 10,600
Sales: $2.09 billion (2004)
Stock Exchanges: New York
Ticker Symbol: HNI
NAIC: 337211 Wood Office Furniture Manufacturing;
    337214 Office Furniture (Except Wood) Manufacturing

HNI Corporation, formerly known as HON Industries Inc., is one of America's leading manufacturers and marketers of business furniture, workspace accessories, and hearth products. From small beginnings, the company developed into a thriving business with offices, manufacturing plants, distribution centers, and sales showrooms across the United States, Canada, and Mexico. The company's products, which range from office desks and chairs to fireplaces, are sold to dealers, wholesalers, warehouse clubs, retail superstores, and federal and state governments. Sales in 2004 exceeded $2 billion.

Early History

HON was conceived in a backyard in Iowa on a Sunday afternoon in 1943 by C. Maxwell Stanley and Clement T. Hanson. The two longtime friends were discussing the war, politics, and business, when Stanley proposed that he and Hanson start a manufacturing business after the war, one in which they could put into practice their common beliefs. Specifically, Stanley and Hanson agreed that good personal relations between management and workers were crucial to a company's success, but that American business, focusing only on making a profit, had ceased to treat employees with fairness and respect. Moreover, they believed that when the war was over, the United States

would see large unemployment figures. Their idea, therefore, was to build a successful company that would not only provide work for returning veterans, but would distinguish itself for its enlightened employee-management relations. Hanson thought it was a good idea and suggested inviting a mutual friend, H. Wood Miller, to join the business venture. Combined, the three had a variety of different attributes and experience to bring to their new business.

Stanley had earned a bachelor's degree in general engineering and a master's degree in hydraulic engineering, both from the University of Iowa, and had worked several years for engineering firms in Chicago and in Dubuque before arriving in Muscatine, Iowa, in 1932 at the depth of the Great Depression. There, he became a partner in a small engineering firm and built the business, which eventually became Stanley Consultants, Inc. A leader in the profession, Stanley authored *The Consulting Engineer,* a definitive text on private consulting.

Clement T. Hanson was a graduate of the College of Commerce at the University of Iowa. He had worked as an advertising executive for a firm in Iowa and as head of sales at a company in Illinois, developing along the way a keen interest and expertise in the areas of communications, public relations, and marketing. H. Wood Miller had spent several years studying design at the Art Institute of Chicago, eventually establishing his own design firm, the H. Wood Miller Company, which served several industrial clients.

Welcoming the challenge of creating and managing a new business, the three men began making plans. They were very confident in their abilities and eager to use them in a new venture. As Max Stanley stated, however, in *The HON Story,* "Our confident enthusiasm was matched only by our considerable naivete. Little did we understand the difficult problems and obstacles that new enterprises usually encounter. But this was as it should be. Had we foreseen the hurdles, we might never have ventured."

Predicting the huge postwar construction boom, Stanley, Hanson, and Miller decided to target the home market and, from there, narrowed down their ideas to focus on products for the kitchen. They eventually decided to enter the home appliance field with the manufacture of home freezers, followed by steel kitchen cabinets.

While considering what their company should be called, Hanson proposed Home-O-Nize. His colleagues liked the sound of it; the first syllable suggested the ultimate destination of their products, while the third syllable would be useful in creating future advertising slogans, such as "Economize with Home-O-Nize" or "Modernize with Home-O-Nize." Since Hanson, Miller, and Stanley had no actual production experience, they brought in Albert F. Uchtorff, president and owner of a sheet metal products manufacturing company, who offered his facilities for manufacture of the company's first product. On January 6, 1944, the four signed the Articles of Incorporation for the Home-O-Nize Company; offices were set up in Davenport, Iowa, and each of the four directors contributed $1,000 for ten shares of stock to the start-up project.

Product Development Beginning in 1944

That year, product development began. Miller made sketches for a deep freeze unit, as well as for some unique kitchen cabinets that could be quickly erected in a variety of configurations to custom fit a kitchen. Hanson and Miller began setting up a prototype shop, while Stanley began working with compressors. The company hired its first employee, who worked with the sheet metal on a part-time basis. Soon, the men opted to focus solely on realizing Miller's kitchen cabinet idea, rather than on freezer production.

Before actually introducing a product, however, the company met with adversity. Several disagreements between Uchtorff and the three company founders, over the direction and scope of Home-O-Nize, eventually prompted Uchtorff to sell his stock and resign from the fledgling board of directors. Uchtorff left what would become a successful project, and the company was left without a manufacturing plan and facilities.

Nevertheless, the three persevered, deciding that they would eventually establish their own manufacturing plant. First, however, they went ahead with their official presentation of the kitchen cabinet prototype, and distributors reacted with enthusiasm. Financing during this time was obtained through a

$100,000 loan from a federal agency as well as a successful stock sale; by the spring of 1947, 988 shares of Home-O-Nize had been sold to investors, and the three founders increased their shares as well.

After finding a suitable plant location in Muscatine, Iowa, hiring workers, investing in the necessary machinery, and securing a contract from Stampings Inc., the Home-O-Nize company manufactured its first product in April 1947; ironically, it was neither a freezer nor a kitchen cabinet that first left the plant, but instead an aluminum hood used in installing commercial gas at farms, residences, and businesses. A steel shortage in 1947 and 1948 prevented the company from ever realizing its original plans; as the founders waited out the shortage, they took on contract work that eventually would lead them into the office supply business.

The cutting of aluminum hoods for Stampings left a considerable amount of metal scraps, and the company soon found a use for them: The company began making anodized aluminum coasters for beverage glasses. Stamping the coasters with a company logo or a sailboat motif, Home-O-Nize marketed the coasters to businesses, which used them as gifts. They also began manufacturing aluminum ground markers to identify garden plants and recipe file boxes.

The development and sale of such three- by five-inch and four- by six-inch file boxes changed the direction of the company. Disappointed with its continuing inability to purchase steel for kitchen cabinets, and pleased with the market reception of the card file boxes, the company decided to direct its focus on office products. Green card files were produced for office use, red-and-white recipe files were made for the home, and red-and-black versions were sold to the Sunbeam Company in large quantities for use as premiums. Sales from the products made from scrap in 1947 amounted to almost $20,000.

During this time the group also developed programs and policies to support their continued belief that a company's success was based on good employee relations. While developing an employee manual, Hanson suggested that they refer to all employees as "members," a word that suggested, according to Stanley, "a greater sense of belonging and participation." In addition, at the onset, the company established an automatic cost-of-living adjustment keyed to the cost-of-living index. The company was among the first to establish such a program; most large corporations adopted this practice only under union pressure.

Overcoming Financial Problems in the Late 1940s and Early 1950s

With the help of a contract for farm equipment from John Deere's Harvester Works, 1948 became Home-O-Nize's first profitable year. The company was still under-financed, however, and sought additional contracts to keep its manufacturing plant busy. In 1949, Home-O-Nize signed a contract worth $450,000 with Associated Manufacturers, Inc. to produce a newly designed corn picker that attached directly to the front of a tractor. What seemed like a promising job, however, turned into "the greatest fiasco in the history of Home-O-Nize," according to Stanley. Home-O-Nize produced the corn picker, with designs provided by Associated that proved full of bugs; at its first field test, the corn picker failed after just one pass. Months of costly redesign ensued, for which, as it turned out, Associated was unable to pay. Litigation ensued, and Associated eventually defaulted on the contract, entering into bankruptcy.

As a result, Home-O-Nize was forced to reduce costs and that meant making some considerable staff reductions. The company salvaged what they could from inventory and wrote off a loss of $52,541 on the corn pickers. Moreover, with additional write-offs from their unrealized kitchen cabinet project, Home-O-Nize's cash position diminished by more than $100,000 during 1949. The company's financial position was at the worst level ever experienced.

The company survived, though, through loans, stock purchases, and a contract with the Bell Aircraft Company. On March 2, 1950, Home-O-Nize bought Bell's manufacturing rights to the Prime-Mover, an engine-powered wheelbarrow with a capacity of 1,000 pounds, and incorporated its subsidiary as The Prime-Mover Co. This purchase meant steady income and ultimately saved the company. The combined sales of Home-O-Nize and Prime-Mover totaled more than $600,000 at year-end 1950.

The period from 1951 to 1955 was known as Operation Independence Home-O-Nize, with a goal of expanding the Prime-Mover and office product businesses, and to decrease dependence on contract work. During the four-year period of Operation Independence, the company saw their basic objectives realized. By 1953, total consolidated sales passed the $1 million milestone and two years later exceeded $2 million. Profitability resumed in 1952, to start more than four decades of uninterrupted profits.

Office Products and Wholesaling Leading to Growth in the 1950s and 1960s

Office products were becoming the chief product line for Home-O-Nize during this time. In addition to its nonsuspension card files, the company began developing combination cabinets in 1953. One such product was the Unifile, which featured a unique one-key handle that operated plungers to lock all doors and drawers, and incorporated an optional interior security compartment. The Unifile was a steady seller from its introduction and would remain in the HON product line into the 1990s. Other products during this period were full-suspension filing cabinets, coat racks, and single pedestal desks with hairpin legs and matching tables. The company also began its name transition. Although the corporate name remained Home-O-Nize, the office products were branded H-O-N and given their own division within the company.

In the mid-1950s, the company strove for a greater market penetration through expanding sales of its office products and Prime-Movers, while raising productivity, improving the quality of products, and strengthening its financial position. The result was a decade of explosive growth. Annual sales passed $5 million in 1961 and surpassed $10 million in 1965. The number of members working at the company more than tripled, from less than 200 in 1956 to more than 500 by the end of 1965. During this period, H. Wood Miller left Home-O-Nize to focus more closely on his industrial design work. He remained a shareholder, however, and, on occasion, assisted the company's engineers with design projects.

The HON line of office equipment during this time grew to include products such as steel drawer card cabinets, steel cash boxes, the HONOR line of products for the schoolroom, and the VS (standing for Very Special) line of higher-end office products. The company also acquired Luxco Company of La Crosse, Wisconsin, a manufacturer of chairs, stools, and machine stands, introducing HON to the seating industry.

The major marketing breakthrough of the time, however, was HON's entry into the wholesale marketplace. By 1965, the company was serving about 75 wholesalers located throughout the United States, with about 35 percent of its furniture reaching dealers through this channel. Home-O-Nize also began selling HON products to Sears, Roebuck & Co., for retail to small businesses or consumers who maintained offices in their home. Continuing efficiency and expansion into new plant locations helped with growth during this period.

The 1960s also brought changes in management and in the company name. Stanley M. Howe was appointed executive vice-president of the company in 1961, and became president in 1964. Howe had joined Home-O-Nize in 1948, as the assistant to the head of the planning division. Proving himself a manufacturing genius and a shrewd administrative leader, Howe shared the founders' vision of growth and had become vice-president of production by 1954. He would later become chairman of HON after the death of Max Stanley in 1984. Having long ago shifted its focus away from manufacturing products for the kitchen and home, the company changed its name in 1968 to HON Industries, Inc.

Expansion in the Late 1960s–80s

Geographic expansion and acquisitions characterized the late 1960s and 1970s at HON. In 1967, the company purchased a plant site in Cedartown, Georgia, marking its first move out of Iowa on the way to becoming a national manufacturer. The introduction of computers in 1968 helped in the management and control of operations of the growing company. By 1969, net sales were $25 million. During this time, cofounder Clement Hanson retired from HON.

Under the leadership of CEO Stanley, the company continued to add to its holdings. Holga Metal Products of Van Nuys, California, was acquired in 1971, giving the company a manufacturing facility in the rapidly growing southern California region. Corry Jamestown of Corry, Pennsylvania, was acquired in 1972, HON's first venture into the higher-priced segment of the office furniture market. HON then bought Norman Bates Inc. of Anaheim, California, their first venture into wood manufacturing. To serve the East Coast markets, HON opened a plant in Virginia. The acquisition of Murphy-Miller of Owensboro, Kentucky, put HON into the wood seating business in 1977. By 1979, net sales surpassed $198 million, an eightfold increase since 1969.

HON Industries expansion continued in the 1980s. Heibert Inc. of Carson, California, brought HON into high-quality wood furniture and wood office systems furniture. Heatilator, the leading name in prefabricated fireplaces, became part of HON Industries in 1981. J.K. Rischel Company, manufacturers of traditional wood office furniture, was purchased in 1982, and the next year, HON acquired 35 percent of Ring King Visibles, a rapidly growing office products company. In 1986, the company acquired Budget Panels, Inc. of Kent, Washington.

In the spring of 1986, two years after the death of Maxwell Stanley, and after nearly a tenfold increase in sales from 1972 to 1985, HON was notified that it had become a *Fortune* 500 company. The company had a record of making 124 consecutive quarterly common stock dividends by 1985. In fact, cash dividends from a single share of stock issued by Home-O-Nize in its first public offering in 1946 totaled more than $10,600 by 1985.

By 1987, under the leadership of Chairman and President Stanley Howe, HON had become known as the most efficient producer in the industry worldwide, capable of producing a desk every minute, a file every 40 seconds, and a chair every 20 seconds. Company sales reached $555 million that year, which also marked HON's 40th year in operation.

The XLM Company was established during this time to manufacture a unique new design of budget file cabinets to be sold through mass merchandisers, and the company consolidated its Corry Jamestown and Hiebert divisions into a new operation known as the CorryHiebert Corporation. After a difficult decision, HON sold Prime-Mover to BT Industries, a worldwide materials handling equipment company; the sale benefited shareholders, as the company received a $8.3 million after-tax gain. In 1989, HON acquired The Gunlocke Company, of Wayland, New York, an established architectural and design firm for office furniture. Moreover, the remaining shares of Ring King Visibles were purchased and the company became a wholly owned subsidiary of HON.

Success Continuing in the 1990s

The 1990s saw the rise to prominence of the home office, as estimates suggested that 26 million Americans did some part-time work at home and another 25 percent worked full-time at home. This trend gave way to the emergence of two new major outlets of office furniture: warehouse clubs and office product superstores, such as Office Depot. HON moved quickly to become a major supplier to these retailers.

In March 1990, Jack D. Michaels, formerly the president and CEO of Hussmann Corp., was named president of HON Industries. Michaels was eventually given the position of CEO as well, while Howe remained on as chairman of the board. Under Michaels, HON made a long-term commitment to explore and develop international opportunities with the formation of HON Export Limited. In 1991, the company had its first decline in sales in four decades, caused by a flat growth in the office furniture industry and the lowest level of housing starts since World War II.

In following years, however, sales increased again. In 1993, the company made record investments in new product development, new capital equipment, new business ventures, and member development. Although HON was forced to close its Corry-Hiebert Corporation office, it entered a new market through the acquisition of the DOVRE brand of cast iron fireplaces and wood stoves, which were manufactured and marketed through Heatilator. According to a 1995 *Fortune* article, HON was one of America's most admired companies in the furniture industry in the mid-1990s. Moreover, the company had positioned itself for continued growth and success into the 21st century. With a corporate goal of doubling its profit by the year 2000, HON was maintaining its leadership position nationally and was expanding its presence internationally.

Late 1990s and Beyond

With a solid strategy in place, HON's good fortunes continued in the late 1990s and beyond. Its hearth division grew significantly during this time period through a series of acquisitions. During 1996, the company purchased Heat-N-Glow Fireplace Products Inc. Subsidiary Hearth & Home Technologies Inc. was created shortly after the deal was completed. Aladdin Steel Products Inc. was acquired in 1998. Two years later, American Fireplace Company and the Allied Group were bought and merged into HON's Fireside Hearth & Home division.

During 1997, HON's sales exceeded $1 billion for the first time, proving that it was on strong financial footing. With the exception of 1995—when the company lost two major customers—earnings had climbed steadily. Whereas the company entered the new millennium poised for additional growth, it faced challenges related to changes in consumer spending, heightened competition, and an overall economic slowdown. During 2001, HON announced that it would shutter three plants as part of a restructuring effort. The firm expected to save $12 million per year as a result of the closures.

HON's business efforts were successful and it garnered a noticeable share of industry accolades during this time period. The company was honored as one of the World's Top Best-Managed Companies by *IndustryWeek* in 2000. It also was named one of the 400 Best Big Companies in America by *Forbes* magazine in 2000 and 2001. In 2003, the company was named the most admired company in the furniture industry by *Fortune* magazine.

During 2004, the company made several key acquisitions to bolster its office furniture line. It purchased Paoli Inc., a provider of wood case goods and seating; Omni Remanufacturing Inc., a paneling and office furniture services firm; and Architectural Installations Atlanta Inc., another office furniture service company. HON also expanded its hearth business by adding Hearth and Home Distributors of Delaware Inc. and Edward George Company to its arsenal.

HON Industries changed its name to HNI Corporation in 2004. The adoption of a new corporate moniker was part of a strategy that focused on managing independent brands. By adhering to the corporate vision set in place by the company's founders—to be profitable, to be economically sound, to pursue profitable growth, to provide quality products, to be a great place to work, and to be a responsible corporate citizen—HNI had set itself apart from its competitors. Its longstanding history of success left management confident that HNI would prosper in the years to come.

Principal Subsidiaries

Allied Fireside, Inc.; Allsteel Inc.; Maxon Furniture Inc.; The Gunlocke Company LLC; Hearth & Home Technologies Inc.; HNI Asia LLC; HFM Partners; HNI Services LLC; HTI Hungary LLC; Holga Inc.; The HON Company; HNI International Inc.

Principal Competitors

Haworth Inc.; Herman Miller Inc.; Steelcase Inc.

Further Reading

DeWitte, Dave, ''Officer Furniture Maker HON Industries Plans Name Change to HNI Corp.,'' *Knight Ridder/Tribune Business News,* March 23, 2004.

Driscoll, Lisa, ''Compensating for Workers' Comp Costs,'' *Business Week,* February 3, 1992, p. 72.

Francett, Barbara, ''Using Price to Change Buying Patterns,'' *Computerworld,* October 29, 1990, p. 116.

''HON Industries Inc.—HNI to Acquire Paoli Inc. from Klaussner Furniture,'' *Knight Ridder/Tribune Business News,* March 23, 2004.

''HON Industries to Close 3 Plants in Restructuring,'' *Reuters News,* July 24, 2001.

Jacob, Rahul, ''Corporate Reputation,'' *Fortune,* March 6, 1995, pp. 54–90.

LaBar, Gregg, ''Getting Work Off Employees' Backs,'' *Occupational Hazards,* April 1991, pp. 27–31.

Palmer, Joel, ''The Legacy Continues,'' *Business Record,* October 12, 1998, p. 13.

Stanley, C. Maxwell, and James H. Soltow, *The HON Story,* Ames: Iowa State University Press, 1991.

Welsh, Tricia, ''Best and Worst Corporate Reputations,'' *Fortune,* February 7, 1994, pp. 58–69.

—Beth Watson Highman
—update: Christina M. Stansell

In-N-Out Burgers Inc.

4199 Campus Drive, 9th Floor
Irvine, California 92612
U.S.A.
Telephone: (949) 509-6200
Fax: (949) 509-6389
Web site: http://www.in-n-out.com

Private Company
Incorporated: 1948
Employees: 3,500
Sales: $285 million (2002 est.)
NAIC: 722211 Limited-Service Restaurants

In-N-Out Burgers Inc. is a leading fast-food retail chain with more than 200 locations in California, Arizona, and Nevada. Known for its made-to-order hamburgers, fresh ingredients, and efficient service, it has maintained the same basic menu and a simple, customer-friendly philosophy since its founding in 1948. The company serves up hamburgers, cheeseburgers, the Double-Double, French fries, malts, shakes, and sodas. The restaurants do not use microwaves, heat lamps, or freezers, guaranteeing that each guest's order is fresh and made-to-order. In-N-Out Burger is a private, family-run, non-franchised company.

Dawn of the Drive-Thru

In-N-Out Burger started in the Los Angeles suburb of Baldwin Park, California, in 1948. Harry Snyder developed the idea of a drive-thru hamburger restaurant where customers would be able to order their food via a two-way speaker unit. This was a rather novel idea, as most hamburger stands of the post-World War II era employed carhops to serve food to customers seated in their cars. Thus, Harry Snyder and his wife, Esther, opened what is said to be California's first drive-thru restaurant. The menu was limited to burgers, french fries, soft drinks, and milk shakes. The Snyders' priorities were simple: serve customers high-quality, fresh food with efficient, friendly service in a clean and tidy environment. This business philosophy and the original menu have remained largely unchanged throughout the years.

It was very important to the Snyders to maintain control of each location in order to continue achieving the high standards they had set as In-N-Out Burger's norm. Consequently, Harry and Esther Snyder did not rush to open further outlets. In fact, three years passed before they added a second In-N-Out Burger location. This new outlet was in the San Gabriel Valley east of Los Angeles in the town of Covina. As Californians became progressively car dependent and fast-food drive-thru restaurants grew in popularity, the Snyders gradually added more outlets, some with double-lane drive-thru service to accommodate more customers. The Snyders' two sons, Rich and Guy, began working at In-N-Out Burger at an early age. They were expected to work in the restaurants and learn the business from the ground up.

Harry Snyder oversaw In-N-Out Burger until 1976, when he passed away from cancer. By then, In-N-Out Burger had grown to 18 units, all in Los Angeles County. At the age of 24, Rich Snyder assumed the role of president. His older brother, Guy, became vice-president, and Esther continued to work in the accounting department.

Corporate Strategy

Though Rich Snyder had plans for In-N-Out Burger's expansion and growth, one thing he would not change after taking over as president was the menu, which included the following items: Double-Doubles (a double cheeseburger), cheeseburgers, hamburgers, French fries, milk, coffee, pink lemonade, iced tea and various sodas, and milk shakes in vanilla, chocolate, or strawberry. The only addition to the original menu was a lemon-lime soda. A non-menu item that eventually gained word-of-mouth popularity in Southern California was the Animal, a Double-Double with grilled onions and extra sauce (all In-N-Out burgers came with a special sauce somewhat similar to Thousand Island dressing), which was voted "Best Off-the-Menu Special" in the 1996 *Buzz Magazine* restaurant awards.

Refusing to change the menu was unusual for a fast-food chain, but adding other items, the Snyders feared, would affect the quality of the food and the service. By keeping the menu short, In-N-Out Burger could maintain control and guarantee high-caliber food. In the July 24, 1989, issue of *Forbes,* Rich

153

Snyder stated, "It's hard enough to sell burgers, fries and drinks right. And when you start adding things, it gets worse."

Rich Snyder remained true to his parents' goal of serving only the freshest foods available. None of the ingredients were frozen, and no microwaves were used. All items were made to order, contributing to what some in the food industry considered a long wait for a fast-food hamburger. The milk shakes were made with real ice cream, and the burgers were 100 percent beef. The beef was ground and formed into patties by In-N-Out workers at the Baldwin Park facility. The lettuce was broken into leaves by hand, and the buns were baked fresh using an old-fashioned sponge dough that took six to eight hours to rise. The potatoes for the french fries were shipped in burlap sacks to the outlets, where associates cut them by hand. In-N-Out has used Southern California-grown Kennebec potatoes, which are said to be ideal for frying. The French fries have always been fried in cholesterol-free vegetable oil.

Rich Snyder also maintained his family's opposition to franchising. While McDonald's, which began the same year as In-N-Out, decided to franchise in 1954, the Snyders, though inundated with franchise inquiries, remained firm. They thought franchising would cause them to lose control of In-N-Out Burger and the business philosophy they had worked so hard to achieve and maintain. As Rich Snyder commented about franchising in *Forbes:* "My feeling is I would be prostituting my parents by doing that. There is money to be made by doing those things, but you lose something, and I don't want to lose what I was raised with all my life." Fast growth was not one of the Snyders' goals, but they did have plans for In-N-Out Burger's expansion.

The Snyders were also committed to viewing employees as if they were family members. Employees, called associates, were treated with respect. Pay was a step above that at other fast-food restaurants. In 1989, part-time associates earned $6 per hour, well above the minimum wage of $4.25. Managers made an average of $63,000 annually. The combination of intensive training and good wages parlayed the associates into capable and friendly workers. At In-N-Out, the customer did not receive a pile of change but had the change counted back out loud. Because the Snyders demonstrated their appreciation of the associates, employee loyalty has been high at In-N-Out Burger. Some associates have been with the company for more than 20 years, and many have worked their way up from entry-level to managerial positions.

Growth in the 1980s

Soon after taking the reins at In-N-Out Burger, Rich Snyder founded a commissary at the In-N-Out Burger headquarters in

Baldwin Park. The establishment of this commissary, where In-N-Out Burger could receive, store, and ship equipment and food supplies to its outlets, gave In-N-Out Burger quality control over all In-N-Out ingredients. The commissary was a busy location: hamburger patties were formed, potatoes were checked for blemishes and quality, equipment was maintained, and supplies were received and distributed to In-N-Out locations. Rich Snyder also established the In-N-Out University in 1983. The university, a training school for new managers, reinforced In-N-Out Burger's business tenets and standards and ensured uniformity of management techniques and methods.

The number of outlets continued to grow steadily under Rich Snyder's guidance. Expansion, however, was still a slow process, which can be partly attributed to the difficulties involved in securing building permits. Because In-N-Out Burger's food was cooked to order, the average wait at a drive-thru was approximately 12 minutes, significantly longer than at other fast-food drive-thru restaurants. This long wait occasionally resulted in traffic jams along busy urban streets, which caused city officials to delay building permits for In-N-Out Burger.

In-N-Out Burger changed tactics in the late 1980s and chose to open fewer double-lane drive-thru units and more restaurants with one drive-thru lane plus indoor and outdoor seating for patrons. The Snyders felt this change would accommodate larger crowds and better serve the customer, which was still one of their top priorities. Another change was their decision to lease property rather than to purchase it. Until 1989, In-N-Out Burger purchased most of their property. This meant seeking lower-priced locations, which were usually in outlying, suburban areas. Leasing property allowed In-N-Out to venture into more metropolitan areas with high property values, such as Santa Monica and West Los Angeles.

During Harry Snyder's leadership, expansion was limited to the Los Angeles County area. Rich Snyder decided to take In-N-Out Burger south of Los Angeles County to the growing counties of Orange, Riverside, and San Bernardino. Most of the outlets were strategically located near freeway or highway off-ramps in highly visible locations to cater to the car-reliant customer.

Rich Snyder also expanded the company's non-food items. At In-N-Out, customers could purchase not only a juicy burger but also T-shirts, bumper stickers, and caps. Because of the success of the T-shirts, Rich Snyder in 1989 began a mail-order catalog, which eventually also included pins, key chains, mugs, and golf balls. Most of the T-shirts were emblazoned with artists' renderings of vintage cars parked outside In-N-Out Burger restaurants, reinforcing the nostalgic spirit that pervaded In-N-Out.

In-N-Out Burger became active in donating funds to the prevention of child abuse in 1986. The In-N-Out Burger Foundation was established, and every April In-N-Out sponsored a company-wide fund-raising campaign. Canisters were placed in all In-N-Out outlets. In-N-Out matched three dollars for every dollar given up to $100,000. In-N-Out Burger also hosted a Children's Benefit Golf Tournament every spring. The money raised from this event was added to funds collected from the stores. All funds were then donated to various organizations

Key Dates:

1948: Harry and Esther Snyder open the first In-N-Out Burger.
1976: Harry Snyder dies; there are 18 In-N-Outs in operation.
1983: In-N-Out University is formed to train restaurant associates.
1989: An In-N-Out mail order catalog is launched.
1990: A store opens in San Diego county.
1993: Rich Snyder is killed in a plane crash; Esther Snyder takes over as president and Guy Snyder is named chairman.
1999: Guy Snyder dies at age 49.

throughout California with the intent to help abused and neglected children.

Corporate Changes in the Early 1990s

By the time Rich Snyder readied In-N-Out Burger to venture out of the Los Angeles area and into San Diego County in 1990, he had brought the number of locations up to 55. The first San Diego location was in Lemon Grove, south of the city of San Diego. The second unit, planned for northern San Diego County, was in Vista.

As In-N-Out Burger outlets were spreading outside Los Angeles County, Rich Snyder decided to relocate the corporate headquarters and the In-N-Out University from Baldwin Park to Irvine, California, a city 45 miles south in Orange County. The move, which took place in 1994, affected most of In-N-Out Burger's 200 corporate employees. The commissary, including the maintenance, meat plant, and warehouse employees, would remain in Baldwin Park. Irvine was home to the corporate offices of many other food-service giants, including Taco Bell, Red Robin, and El Torito. Another factor that might have been involved in selecting Irvine was that Rich Snyder resided in Newport Beach, located less than ten miles from Irvine.

On December 14, 1993, just months away from moving the corporate headquarters to Irvine, Rich Snyder was killed in a commuter plane crash. Snyder was on board an executive jet when it crash-landed at Irvine's John Wayne Airport. Snyder, Philip R. West (a childhood friend of Snyder's who was In-N-Out Burger's chief operating officer and executive vice-president), Jack Sims (another friend), and two pilots were killed. They were returning from a one-day trip to scout possible In-N-Out locations in Southern California and also to attend the opening of a Fresno store. Snyder and West had a personal agreement not to fly on the same plane together but apparently had broken the policy for this flight. It is believed that Rich's mother, Esther, had also been aboard the plane, but she chose to deplane at an earlier stop.

Rich Snyder was 41 years old at the time of his death. He had been married for the first time just a year before and had a daughter. During his tenure as president, he had increased the number of In-N-Out Burger units from 18 to 93. A born-again Christian, philanthropist, and conservative Republican supporter, he began each company meeting with the Pledge of Allegiance.

Rich Snyder led In-N-Out Burger to tremendous growth while maintaining the simple philosophy his parents adopted in 1948.

Continued Expansion in the Mid-1990s

As a result of Rich Snyder's untimely death, Esther Snyder assumed the role of president and continued to work in the corporate offices. Rich's brother, Guy Snyder, who had been an executive vice-president but had not been actively participating in daily management duties at the time of Rich's death, was named chairman of the board. Rich Snyder's widow was appointed to the board of directors.

In April 1994, the corporate headquarters relocated to Irvine, California, as planned. Expansion continued under Guy Snyder's direction, with new In-N-Out Burger outlets opening in northern California and Las Vegas, Nevada, as well as in towns with existing In-N-Out outlets. In-N-Out offered rentable cookout trailers for special occasions or corporate functions. Despite this growth, Guy Snyder did not stray from his family's business outlook and continued to promote simplicity, efficiency, and fresh, cooked-to-order food.

By the late 1990s, with more than 120 outlets in California and Nevada, In-N-Out Burger showed no signs of slowing down, and as the number of their restaurants grew, so did their popularity. In-N-Out Burger was the winner, for example, in the quick-service burger division in the 1997 *Restaurants & Institutions* annual poll. In-N-Out beat Wendy's, which had won the category for the previous eight years. According to the February 1, 1997, issue of *Restaurants & Institutions,* the criteria upon which the restaurants were judged included quality of food, menu variety, service, atmosphere, value, cleanliness, and convenience. In-N-Out Burger ranked first in four (quality of food, service, value, and cleanliness) of the seven categories. It was quite a coup for the family-owned chain, as this was the first year In-N-Out Burger was eligible to compete in the survey. In-N-Out Burger scored highly in the customer-loyalty category as well, with many respondents ranking it highest in overall satisfaction.

Within its base of Southern California, In-N-Out was also maintaining a popular, almost cult-like following. In Pasadena Weekly's ''Best of 1996'' readers' poll, In-N-Out Burger won the categories ''Best Fast Food'' and ''Best Burger.'' According to the July 24, 1989, issue of *Forbes,* In-N-Out Burger's following included movie stars and corporate executives. Bob Hope, David Letterman, Farrah Fawcett, and Ryan O'Neal were among some of In-N-Out's more famous patrons.

Late 1990s and Beyond

Success continued for In-N-Out in the late 1990s. Steady and calculated growth continued, and by 1999 there were 140 restaurants scattered throughout California and Nevada. In-N-Out was dealt a tragic blow that year when Guy Snyder died suddenly in his home in December at age 49. Esther, outliving her husband and two sons, reassumed the role of president and pledged to maintain the founding philosophy that she and her husband had created so many years ago.

In-N-Out continued opening new locations in the early 2000s at a pace of approximately ten per year. The chain's following was stronger than ever, and its sales often outpaced its competitors. Restaurant sales tracker Technomic estimated the company's 2002 revenue at $285 million, up 10 percent over the previous year's figure. Meanwhile, sales at McDonald's were stagnant and Burger King's sales had dropped by 3.4 percent. An In-N-Out fan summed up his perspective in an August 2005 *Oakland Tribune* article, claiming, ''I think In-N-Out is like Starbucks. Even if there is one on every corner, people will still come.''

The chain's popularity often led entrepreneurs to ''copycat'' In-N-Out's strategy. For example, the company filed suit against James Van Blaricum in 2001 for turning his Lightning Burgers restaurant in Texas into an In-N-Out look-a-like. Van Blaricum allegedly told former employees to steal ideas from In-N-Out and had them sneak into In-N-Out restaurants to take pictures. He even froze an In-N-Out hamburger and took it to a lab for testing. As part of an out-of-court settlement, Van Blaricum agreed to pay $250,000 to In-N-Out, transfer all restaurant assets to the company, and stay out of the hamburger business for at least ten years. In-N-Out found itself involved in a similar trademark infringement suit in 2003 with Gerald Hans Rizza and Marie Manriquez Rizza.

During this time period, the company expanded its presence in California and Nevada and began opening stores in Arizona. Esther Snyder, now in her 80s, remained at the helm of In-N-Out. The lack of third-generation family to run the business, however, left many industry observers wondering what would happen to the chain in the years to come. Nevertheless, company executives maintained that In-N-Out would continue to operate as a privately run entity and had no plans to go public or to franchise the chain.

Principal Competitors

Burger King Corp.; Jack in the Box Inc.; McDonald's Corp.

Further Reading

''Burgers: In-N-Out Burger,'' *Restaurants & Institutions*, September 1, 2004, p. 50.

''Familiarity Breeds Contempt from In-N-Out Burger,'' *Restaurants & Institutions*, June 1, 2002, p. 26.

Martin, Richard, ''In-N-Out Burger Pulls Away from Drive-thru-only Focus,'' *Nation's Restaurant News*, June 19, 1989, pp. 3–4.

——, ''Top In-N-Out Burger Execs Killed in Calif. Plane Crash,'' *Nation's Restaurant News*, January 3, 1994, pp. 1–2.

Paris, Ellen, ''Where Bob Hope Buys His Burgers,'' *Forbes*, July 24, 1989, pp. 46–48.

Puzo, Daniel P., ''America's Favorite Chains,'' *Restaurants & Institutions*, February 1, 1997, pp. 26–34.

Spector, Amy, ''In-N-Out CEO Snyder Dead at 49,'' *Nation's Restaurant News*, December 20, 1999, p. 3.

Steere, Mike, ''A Timeless Recipe for Success,'' *Business 2.0*, September 2003.

Tice, Carol, ''In-N-Out Burgers: With an Emphasis on Quality, This Fast Feed Shows Its Rare Appeal,'' *Nation's Restaurant News*, January 28, 2002.

Wong, Scott, ''Fremont Gets In-N-Out That May Prove Bigger Is Better,'' *Oakland Tribune*, August 14, 2005.

Wright, Nils J., ''In-N-Out Burger Wants into Sacramento Area,'' *Business Journal Serving Greater Sacramento*, July 18, 1994, p. 1.

—Mariko Fujinaka
—update: Christina M. Stansell

International Speedway Corporation

P.O. Box 2801
Daytona Beach, Florida 32120-2801
U.S.A.
Telephone: (386) 254-2700
Fax: (386) 947-6816
Web site: http://www.iscmotorsports.com

Public Company
Incorporated: 1953
Employees: 1,000
Sales: $647.8 million (2004)
Stock Exchanges: NASDAQ
Ticker Symbol: ISCA
NAIC: 711212 Racetracks

With 11 racetracks hosting more than 100 auto racing events each year, International Speedway Corporation (ISC) is the largest motorsports operator in the United States. Some of its tracks include California Speedway, Darlington Raceway, Daytona International Speedway, Martinsville Speedway, Talladega Superspeedway, and Watkins Glen International. The company also owns MRN Radio, the largest independent sports radio network in the United States; Daytona USA, the official NASCAR motorsports attraction in Daytona Beach; Americrown Service Corporation, a catering service and food and beverage concessions provider; and Motorsports International, a manufacturer of motorsports-related merchandise. The France family owns 35 percent of ISC and also controls NASCAR, the National Association for Stock Car Auto Racing.

Early History

The history of racing and the legendary names of automotive competition in the Daytona Beach area of the state of Florida can be traced back to 1903. Legend has it that racing on the beach started when two gentlemen entered into a friendly wager as to which one of them had the most reliable and fastest "horseless carriage." That one wager, and resulting race, gave rise to what soon became known as the "Birthplace of Speed." Within a very short time, the wagers between gentlemen stopped but the competition to settle who had the fastest automobile continued. As word of the competition grew, and more people began to visit Daytona Beach just to view the automotive races, even the nascent film industry took an interest. The 1905 silent movie, *Automobile Races at Ormond, Florida,* provided the first glimmerings of an allure that would attract people for years to come. Suddenly, throngs of people came to watch the speed trials for the ever-improving motorized road vehicles. One of the most famous of all the speed trials during these early years involved Ransom E. Olds, the creator of what was later known as the "Oldsmobile" and the first man to engage in a race on Daytona Beach in a timed run.

During the years leading up to World War I, Daytona Beach attracted competitors from around the world to test the speed of their automobiles. In fact, most of the land speed records set during the early part of the 20th century were accomplished by drivers at Daytona Beach. Although the advent of World War I and America's involvement in the European conflict slowed the development of Daytona Beach as the gathering place for land speed trials, nonetheless, the attraction to the Florida location experienced an immediate resurgence following the end of the war in November of 1918.

Through the 1920s, and even during the height of the Great Depression, Daytona Beach attracted drivers who competed in speed time trials. As the Daytona Beach races grew in reputation and prominence, drivers from as far away as Britain, France, Italy, Hungary, Germany, and Spain became regular competitors. Major H.O.D. Segrave of Great Britain was the first man to exceed 200 mph on the beach. Frank Lockhart from the United States died on the same stretch of beach while attempting to establish a new speed record. As the motor car developed in both power and speed, however, the organizers of the Daytona Beach speed trials soon recognized that racing cars were outgrowing the facilities available at the beach. As a result of these developments, it was decided that the speed trials should be relocated to the Bonneville Salt Flats in the state of Utah. The last (and one of the legendary) land speed trials on Daytona Beach was held in March 1935, when Sir Malcolm Campbell in his famous Bluebird V set the best speed ever recorded on the beach at 276 mph.

Having already firmly established an international reputation as the ''Birthplace of Speed'' in the automotive racing industry, the organizers of the original Daytona Beach speed trials began looking for something new to continue the area's famous legacy. They found it in stock car racing. Although not a brand new sport, the organizing committee initiated a decidedly innovative approach. Regularly scheduled stock car races would be held on a course that combined a portion of Daytona Beach with a portion of a public road. The original course of 3.2 miles incorporated a north turn immediately south of the center of the city of Daytona. Running approximately 1.5 miles on the beach and then turning 1.5 miles onto a paved public highway, the two sections of the course were connected by banked sand turns. The inaugural race on March 8, 1936 signaled the start of a new era in the history of racing at Daytona Beach. Most of the initial competitors were from the United States, but as the reputation of the race grew, drivers from around the world began to flock to the beach once again. Not satisfied with sitting on their laurels, the organizers decided to take the next step and on January 24, 1937, inaugurated the Daytona 200 motorcycle race, the first of its kind in racing history.

World War II and the Postwar Years

Because of the reconfiguration of most American industrial factories in the name of national defense, racing at Daytona Beach was suspended for the duration of World War II. Most of the organizers closely associated with the racing at Daytona Beach were either serving in the Armed Forces or working in various industrial capacities for the American war effort. When the war ended in the summer of 1945, the organizers banded together once again to restart the racing tradition at Daytona Beach.

One of the most important influences on the postwar era of racing at Daytona was a man named Bill France. France, a mechanic from a local shop in Daytona, had entered the first stock car race in March 1935. Although he had finished fifth in the race, he developed a lifelong enthusiasm for the sport of racing. During the war, France worked as a welder and mechanic building submarine chasers at the Daytona Beach Boat Works. But when the war ended, he once again took his place among the competitors at Daytona Beach.

After the 1946 racing season had come to an end, France decided to retire from competitive racing and devote his energies to promoting stock car and motorcycle racing on the beach. A tireless and enthusiastic man, in 1947 France initiated the organizational meetings for what was to become NASCAR, the National Association for Stock Car Auto Racing. NASCAR was established in 1948, and France and NASCAR became the driving force behind Daytona Beach racing.

One of the most important actions taken by France and NASCAR during the years after World War II was the promotion of a new design for the beach/road course in Daytona. The racing circuit was moved down to the south end of the beach, near Ponce Inlet, primarily because of the growth in Daytona. The newly designed course measured 2.2 miles for stock cars and 4.1 miles for motorcycles. Yet France soon realized that the continued and rapid growth in both Daytona's population and the racing crowds signaled the end of racing on the beach. Consequently, in April of 1953, France decided to form his own corporation, Bill France Racing, and begin planning the construction of a permanent speedway facility in Daytona.

By 1955, France's dream of a modern speedway facility in Daytona began to take shape when he entered into negotiations with the Daytona Beach Racing and Recreational Facilities Authority to construct and operate a $2.5 million motorsports arena. After private funding had been arranged for building the facility, the most up-to-date engineering and construction methods were used to follow the blueprint for a 2.5-mile tri-oval circuit that incorporated 31-degree banking in both its east and west turns. France changed the company's name to Daytona International Speedway Corporation in 1955.

In November 1957, the Daytona Beach Racing and Recreational Facilities Authority signed an agreement with France and his Daytona International Speedway to lease the property indefinitely. One year later, the beach/road course was used the final time for auto racing.

With much fanfare and publicity, the Daytona International Speedway hosted its inaugural race on February 22, 1959. The first Daytona 500 fielded an array of 59 cars and posted a sweepstakes award totaling $67,760. More than 41,000 people were in attendance to watch the first race of the Daytona 500. As history would have it, they were not disappointed. The finish of the race was too close to call, yet Johnny Beauchamp was declared the ''unofficial winner'' and basked in the adulation of Victory Lane. Unfortunately for Beauchamp, the final results were determined three days later by a clip of newsreel that provided conclusive evidence that Lee Petty had won the close race in his Oldsmobile. The first of many close stock car races that enhanced the reputation of Daytona International Speedway, it was followed by another dramatic finish on July 4th when Fireball Roberts won the first Firecracker 250 stock car race in a modified Pontiac.

The Growth of Racing from the 1960s through the 1990s

During the next three decades, many new races were added to the schedule of Daytona International Speedway. The last motorcycle race on Daytona Beach was held in 1960; one year later it was moved to the Speedway, with Roger Reiman winning the first Daytona 200 on a Harley-Davidson. In 1962, Dan Gurney won the first Daytona Continental Sports Car Race in a Lotus Ford. Other races established during these years included the Pepsi 400; the Daytona Speedweeks, a 16-day preliminary set of races that initiated the major league racing season; the

Key Dates:

1947: Bill France initiates the organizational meetings for what is to become NASCAR, the National Association for Stock Car Auto Racing.

1948: NASCAR is established; France and NASCAR become the driving force behind Daytona Beach racing.

1953: France creates Bill France Racing.

1959: Daytona International Speedway hosts its inaugural race.

1968: The company changes its name to International Speedway Corp.

1982: Darlington Raceway in South Carolina is purchased.

1999: ISC completes its merger with Penske Motorsports Inc.

2004: North Carolina Speedway is sold; funds from the sale are used to purchase Martinsville Speedway in Virginia.

Rolex 24 at Daytona; the Exxon World SportsCar Championship and Supreme GT Series; the Busch Clash and Daytona ARCA 200; the ARCA Bondo/Mar-Hyde Supercar Series; the Gatorade 125-Mile Qualifying Races for the NASCAR Winston Cup, which determined the entrants for the Daytona 500; the Discount Auto Parts 200; the Firebird International Race of Champions; and the Daytona 300 NASCAR Busch Race. The company officially adopted the International Speedway Corporation (ISC) moniker in 1968.

By the early 1980s, ISC had become so famous that the running of the 25th anniversary of the Daytona 500 was a major international sports event. Drivers from more than 20 countries competed for the honor of driving in Victory Lane, which was won by Cale Yarborough in his Super-Pontiac. In 1984, President Ronald Reagan was the Grand Marshal for the NASCAR Winston Cup Race, won by Richard Petty. During these years, corporate sponsorship of racing at Daytona increased dramatically. Racing became known as one of the few sports where commercialism was not only accepted but expected. As a result, major corporations such as Ford, Chevrolet, Gatorade, DuPont, Goodyear, Anheuser-Busch, STP, and Western Auto signed on to sponsor major races at Daytona Speedway, which had the effect of significantly offsetting costs associated with those races.

ISC, which was first headed by Bill French and then by his son, began to expand its holdings during the 1980s and 1990s. Darlington Raceway in South Carolina was purchased in 1982, and Tucson Raceway in Arizona also was acquired. In addition, management decided to acquire a 50 percent interest in Watkins Glen International Road Course in New York in 1983.

The company purchased a 12 percent interest in Penske Motorsports Inc., the owner and operator of Michigan International Speedway and Nazareth Speedway in Pennsylvania in 1996. It also initiated construction of a new, state-of-the-art California Speedway, located near Los Angeles. At the same time, ISC expanded into areas other than speedway operation and management and racing promotion. Americrown Service Corporation was formed by International Speedway Corporation to operate the food, beverage, and souvenir concession stands at the Daytona, Talladega, and Darlington speedways. Also responsible for providing catering services to corporate customers in suites at these facilities, in 1995 Americrown expanded its services to other unaffiliated sporting events, such as the LPGA championships. International Speedway Corporation added a radio station to its holdings, MRN Radio Network, to produce and syndicate races promoted by the company. Finally, in July 1996, the company opened Daytona USA, a motorsports museum and theme park complex that includes attractions such as interactive media, racing exhibits, theaters, and a racing museum.

At this time, one of the fastest growing spectator sports in the United States was stock car racing, and ISC was at the forefront of its development and promotion. More than 70 stock car, sports car, truck, and motorcycle races were held annually at the company's properties, and nearly 80 percent of its income was derived from NASCAR sanctioned races at Daytona, Talladega, and Darlington. With revenues consistently on the rise, International Speedway Corporation had a clear road ahead for ever-larger profits.

Racing into the Late 1990s and Beyond

Success led to additional growth and expansion for ISC as it prepared to enter the new millennium. In 1997, it acquired the remaining shares of Watkins Glen International and Phoenix International Raceway. During 1999, ISC purchased all remaining shares of Penske Motorsports Inc. The deal added four tracks to ISC's burgeoning holdings, including California Speedway, Michigan Speedway, N.C. Speedway, and Nazareth Speedway. ISC also acquired Richmond International Speedway in a $215 million deal.

During the late 1990s, the company set plans in motion to build a new motorsports facility in Kansas City, Kansas and Chicago, Illinois. Ground was broken in 2000 and the new speedways hosted their inaugural NASCAR Winston Cup Races in 2001. The company also partnered with Donald Trump to develop a motorsports facility in the New York area. In 2003, Nextel Communications Inc. usurped Winston's 32-year position as the sponsor of NASCAR's premier racing series. As such, the Nextel Cup Series was born out of a ten-year, $750 million sponsorship deal. Brian France, son of France, Jr., was named chairman and CEO of NASCAR that year while daughter Lesa France Kennedy became ISC's first female president.

ISC's close ties with NASCAR left it in an enviable position in the industry, but often left smaller competitors crying foul at its monopoly-like control. NASCAR made changes to its 2004 Nextel Cup championship schedule, favoring larger ISC markets versus smaller markets in the South. A Speedway Motorsports shareholder filed suit against NASCAR, claiming the schedule change gave an unfair advantage to ISC. The suit was settled eventually and as part of the agreement, ISC sold its North Carolina Speedway to Speedway Motorsports. ISC acquired Martinsville Speedway in Virginia in 2004—it used the money gained from the sale of its North Carolina track to fund the purchase.

By now, ISC's growth seemed unstoppable. The company's revenues had grown steadily since the 1990s, climbing from

$418 million in 2000 to $648 million in 2004. More than 85 percent of 2004 revenues stemmed from NASCAR events. According to the company, NASCAR was the second highest-rated sport on television. It had 75 million fans across the United States. In fact, one in three American adults claimed to be a fan and during 2004, 17 of the top 20 highest-attended sporting events in the United States were NASCAR events. With a growing fan base, an expanding presence across the United States, and the top position in the motorsports industry, ISC was on the right track for success in the years to come.

Principal Subsidiaries

Americrown Service Corporation; ASC Holdings, Inc.; ASC Promotions, Inc.; The California Speedway Corporation; Chicago Holdings, Inc.; Darlington Raceway of South Carolina, LLC; Daytona International Speedway, LLC; Event Equipment Leasing, Inc.; Event Support Corporation; Great Western Sports, Inc.; HBP, INC.; Homestead-Miami Speedway, LLC; International Speedway, Inc.; ISC.Com, LLC; ISC Properties, Inc.; ISC Publications, Inc.; Kansas Speedway Corporation; Kansas Speedway Development Corporation; Leisure Racing, Inc.; Martinsville International, Inc.; Miami Speedway Corporation; Michigan International Speedway, Inc.; Motor Racing Network, Inc.; Motorsports Acceptance Corporation; The Motorsports Alliance, LLC; Motorsports International Corporation; New York International Speedway Corporation; North American Testing Company; Pennsylvania International Raceway, Inc.; Phoenix Speedway Corporation; Raceway Associates, LLC; Richmond International Raceway, Inc.; Rocky Mountain Speedway Corporation; Southeastern Hay & Nursery, Inc.; Talladega Superspeedway LLC; Watkins Glen International, Inc.; 88 Corporation; 380 Development LLC.

Principal Competitors

Dover Motorsports Inc.; National Association for Stock Car Auto Racing, Inc.; Speedway Motorsports Inc.

Further Reading

Bernstein, Viv, "Next Generation of NASCAR's Ruling Family Puts New Face on Sport," *New York Times,* February 20, 2005.

Cohen, Adam, "Blowing the Wheels Off Bubba," *Time,* February 26, 1996, pp. 56–57.

"From the Green to the Pits," *Forbes,* July 4, 1994, p. 20.

"International Speedway Expands," *Wall Street Journal,* December 2, 1999.

Lowry, Tom, "The Prince of NASCAR," *Business Week,* February 23, 2004, p. 90.

Mitchell, Mary A., "Racing Museum Revs Up," *Travel Weekly,* July 11, 1996, p. F3.

——, "Winter Business Picks Up Speed," *Travel Weekly,* March 21, 1994, p. F26.

"NASCAR: Unsafe at This Speed?," *Business Week,* November 1, 1999, p. 90.

Powell, Tom, "NASCAR Touring Show To Make Debut in August," *Amusement Business,* May 23, 1994, p. 15.

Rouch, Chris, "Red Necks, White Socks, and Blue Chip Sponsors," *Business Week,* August 15, 1994, p. 74.

Sullivan, Lee, "Brickyard Brickbats," *Forbes,* April 11, 1994, p. 20.

Waddell, Ray, "Interactive Motorsports Attraction Daytona USA To Open Summer '96," *Amusement Business,* September 4, 1995, p. 34.

——, "New Daytona USA Tops Projections," *Amusement Business,* August 5, 1996, p. 43.

—Thomas Derdak
—update: Christina M. Stansell

JSP Corporation

4-2-3 Marunouchi, Chiyoda-ku
Tokyo
100-0005
Japan
Telephone: (+81) 3 6212 6300
Fax: (+81) 3 6212 6302
Web site: http://www.co-jsp.co.jp

Public Company
Incorporated: 1962 as Nihon (Japan) Styrene Paper
Employees: 747
Sales: ¥77,724 million ($735.3 million) (2004)
Stock Exchanges: Tokyo
Ticker Symbol: JSP
NAIC: 326150 Urethane and Other Foam Product
    (Except Polystyrene) Manufacturing

JSP Corporation is the world's largest producer of expanded polypropylene plastics (EPP), backed by its proprietary beads foaming and extrusion foaming processes. The company, which developed the first EPPs in the 1970s, markets these materials under the P-Block, ARPOR (in North America), and EPPOR brand names, as well as its Super Blow line of hybrid foam technology products. The company has also been a pioneer in the development of biodegradable plastics, such as its Green Block packaging products. These products are said to break down completely into carbon dioxide and water when in contact with soil. JSP subgroups its product lines into four primary categories: Sheets, Beads, Boards, and others. Applications using JSP's products include styrene paper; P-Pearl polypropylene foam sheeting used as a food packaging material; Acryace sheeting used in the construction of rear-projection television screens; Miramat polyethylene foam sheets, used as a cushioning material; packaging materials under the Caplon, P-Board, P-Mat, Miranet, and other brands; P-EPP (porous expanded polypropylene), used for acoustical paneling, among other applications; P-Block and ARPOR, which are used in the production of automobile bumper systems; expanded polyethylene, providing molded protective packaging; and cross-linked expanded polyethylene, used for a variety of cushioning applications, from sports equipment to flooring under-liners. JSP Corporation is an internationally operating business, with production plants in the United States, Mexico, France, Germany, Italy, Korea, Taiwan, Singapore, and China, in addition to 11 production facilities in Japan. The company also operates a number of research and development facilities and in the mid-2000s has been focusing its research and development efforts on creating new product applications for its core technologies. Japan remains the group's largest market, with nearly 74 percent of sales of ¥77,724 million ($735.3 million) in 2004. Mitsubishi Chemical is JSP's largest shareholder, following the merger of Mitsubishi Chemical Foam Plastic into JSP in 2003. JSP is listed on the Tokyo Stock Exchange and led by chairman Masaaki Harada and president Rokurou Inoue.

Polystyrene Specialist in the 1960s

JSP Corporation's roots trace back to the 1950s with the founding of Japan Gas Chemical in 1951 and Nihon Plastic and Chemical Co in 1957. Those two companies merged together to form Nihon (or Japan) Gas Chemical Co in 1961. One result of the merger was the creation of a dedicated unit for the production of foamed polystyrene, and especially polystyrene "paper," that is polystyrene formed into sheets. The new subsidiary was named Nihon Styrene Paper (JSP) and launched its operations at a production plant attached to Nihon Gas Chemical's newly built Hiratsuka Research Laboratory, which opened in 1962.

The creation of plastics-based packaging materials, especially polystyrene paper, played an important role in the development of the packaging industry. The new materials were lightweight (since they were composed 95 percent of air), capable of being produced as food-grade materials, were waterproof, provided superior cushioning, and were easily molded to a variety of shapes. Yet the production of styrene paper and foamed polystyrene in general required the mastery of sophisticated technology.

This technology advantage helped Nihon Styrene Paper quickly to assert itself as a leading producer of styrene paper in Japan, particularly in the second half of the 1960s. The com-

---

Company Perspectives:

Reinforcing Our Foundation Through the Merger with MFP. To prosper in international competition and maintain our edge amid ongoing globalization of markets, we must accelerate the pace of technological development, R&D, and product application development. We also need to re-cover our investments more quickly. We have combined our research programs with MFP's research programs in the July 2003 merger, a move that is expected to deliver syner-gistic benefits. Moreover, the integration of MFP's upstream technologies with JSP's downstream strengths will further expedite the commercialization process.

---

pany's emphasis on research and development paid off in 1967, when the company launched a new generation of styrene-based packaging material. The new proprietary sheeting was marketed under the name Miramat, becoming JSP's first branded product.

JSP's growth coincided with the rise of Japan as a leading global industrial center, a top exporter of electronic and other goods to world markets. Indeed, JSP's foamed polystyrene-based packaging materials played an important role in enabling Japan to develop its export market, providing a cheaper, lighter, and more efficient packing material. The company's foamed packaging materials were also adopted by a variety of industries, including Japan's large fishing industry. The company's polystyrene containers quickly replaced cardboard as a means of transporting fish to shore and across the country.

In 1971, Japan Gas Chemical merged with another fast-growing chemicals company, Mitsubishi Edogawa Chemcial Co., forming Mitsubishi Gas Chemical Company. The new entity then became the parent of Nihon Styrene Paper, which later was renamed as JSP Corporation. The Edogawa company was one of the country's oldest chemicals producers, estab-lished as a Mitsubishi partnership in 1918.

Expanding Production in the 1970s

As part of one of Japan's leading chemical groups, JSP now had the resources to expand its production in the 1970s. The company opened a new plant in Kanuma in 1971. This was followed by the opening of the company's Kansai Plant in 1975 and by the construction of the Kyushu Plant in 1978.

JSP continued developing new products in the 1970s. In 1977, the company launched its Miraboard line of styrene paper created specifically for the food industry. The new type of packaging material could be formed into a variety of shapes and had the important quality of being heat resistant. In this way, the company backed the growth of a new segment of processed and ready-to-eat foods. The company's products were also in de-mand by the fast food and restaurant industries.

Yet JSP had also begun to imagine other uses for its polysty-rene beyond the packaging industry. In 1978, the company launched a new product, called Mirafoam, providing paneling and insulation products for the construction industry. By then, environmental concerns about the use of polystyrene foam had

led JSP to form a new company in 1974 for the production of foam recycling machinery.

JSP also sought to exploit its technological advance in the international market at the end of the 1970s. This led the company to acquire a stake in France's Douff SA in 1978. The company then transferred the technology and equipment needed to produce Miramat packaging materials for the French and European markets. JSP later acquired control of the French company, which was renamed Sealed Air Packaging SA.

Japan remained JSP's primary market, however, and in 1980 the company opened a new plant in Hokkaido in order to accom-modate rising demand for its polystyrene products. The com-pany's research and development efforts paid off again in 1982 when JSP launched a new type of foamed polystyrene, dubbed P-Block. The new material was developed specifically for Ja-pan's fast-growing automotive industry, providing the core for a new generation of lightweight, plastic bumper systems. The rapid adoption of the new materials by Japanese automakers helped them gain a competitive edge as they made a massive entry into the United States and other auto markets.

International Growth in the 1980s and 1990s

The new material provided the company with an entry into the U.S. market in the 1980s, as American automakers re-sponded to the rising sales of Japanese cars in the United States with smaller, more fuel-efficient automobile models. In 1985, JSP launched a U.S. subsidiary, JSP America Inc., in order to make investments in that market. This effort led the company to form a manufacturing joint venture with Arco in order to pro-duce P-Block for the North American market. The joint-venture was named Arco/JSP Co. By 1986, JSP had launched a wholly owned U.S. manufacturing subsidiary, J&V Foam Products.

JSP also prepared a range of new products for the end of the decade. In 1988, the company achieved a first breakthrough with the launch of its Mirawoody Green packaging technology. The new product provided a more environmentally friendly packaging material than its standard polystyrene products.

JSP's research and development efforts continued to facili-tate the company's growth through the end of the decade. In 1989, JSP launched production of two new material brands: L-Block and Caplon. Also in that year, the company formally changed its name to JSP Corporation. This move came ahead of the company's public listing on the Tokyo Stock Exchange's Second Section, in 1990.

The name change came ahead of a new and more aggressive drive to expand the company's operations internationally. In 1991, the company expanded its Arco/JSP joint-venture to Eu-rope, opening a new subsidiary in Belgium. That year, the also company set up a joint venture in Korea, called KOSPA, in order to produce polystyrene foam products for the Korean automotive industry. The KOSPA joint venture was established as a vertically integrated operation, producing the raw materials needed to make polypropylene foam as well as the final foam products themselves.

JSP entered Taiwan in 1992, setting up the joint-venture Taiwan JSP Chemical Co Ltd. The following year, the company

Key Dates:

1962: Nihon (or Japan) Styrene Paper Company is established as a result of a merger between Japan Gas Chemical Co and Nihon Plastic and Chemical Co. to produce polystyrene paper products for the packaging industry.

1967: Miramat packaging material for food and other industries is launched.

1978: The company expands internationally for the first time with an investment in Douff SA, in France, which begins producing JSP's Miramat packaging material.

1982: P-Block foam, used as the core for automotive bumper systems, is launched.

1985: The company forms a joint venture with Arco to produce P-Block for the North American market.

1989: The company's name is changed to JSP Corporation.

1990: The company lists on the Tokyo Stock Exchange's Second Section.

1993: The company acquires control of Arco/JSP and changes its name to JSP International, which becomes spearhead for the group's international expansion.

1998: Green Block biodegradable packaging material is introduced.

2003: JSP absorbs Mitsubishi Chemical Foam Plastic Corporation, consolidating its position as a world leader in its market.

bought out Arco and renamed the Arco/JSP operation as JSP International. Now directly controlled by JSP Corporation, JSP International launched an aggressive drive to establish itself as a global supplier of foamed bumper systems to the worldwide automotive industry. The company began expanding its production capacity, adding two new plants in the United States and a third, under subsidiary JSP Foam Products, in Singapore in 1995. The following year, the company's JSP America Inc. subsidiary took over its J&V Foam Products subsidiary in the United States.

In the United States, the company's fortunes rose after the passage of legislation establishing stricter automotive safety standards, including the use of impact-absorbent padding on the interior side of vehicle doors starting in 1996. Automakers were also increasingly adopting foam-core bumper systems, and by the late 1990s more than half of all U.S. cars featured this type of system. JSP itself claimed a 60 percent share of that product category.

In addition to its success in the United States, JSP had become a major supplier to the European automotive industry, notably the safety-conscious Volvo Corporation. The company boosted its European manufacturing operations when it established JSP International Manufacturing in France. In 1997, JSP also set up a manufacturing subsidiary in Toluca, Mexico.

New Product Applications and Expansion into the 2000s

In the 1990s, JSP launched several new products and brands, while extending its technology at the same time. At the begin-

ning of the decade, for example, the company debuted its system for creating non-freon foamed plastic. The new system helped eliminate the highly polluting freon from the plastics production process.

The company also rolled out new packaging grade materials, such as the launch of Mirafit, a housing material, in 1993, and P-Pearl, developed for the food packaging industry and launched in 1994. The following year, the company released another new packaging material, P-Board. Then, in 1998, the company achieved a significant breakthrough with the launch of its Green Block packaging material. The environmentally friendly product claimed to be 100 percent biodegradable, breaking down into carbon dioxide and water in the soil. In 2000, the company debuted its next generation of packaging products, Mirafreeze.

JSP entered Germany in 2001, buying up a manufacturer of molding materials and equipment to establish JSP International Gmbh & Co. The following year, JSP moved to mainland China, setting up JSP Plastics (Zuxi) Co. That subsidiary was followed by a second Chinese operation, JSP International Trading (Shanghai) Co. in 2004. By then, the company had also added a new manufacturing facility in Tullahoma, Tennessee, in 2002.

The following year, JSP confirmed its position as the world's leading manufacturer of foamed plastic products when it agreed to merge with Mitsubishi Chemical Foam Plastic Corporation (MFP). The addition of MFP complemented JSP's own production with a specialty in the production of expanded polystyrene. With the addition of MFP's sales of ¥13 billion per year, JSP Corporation's total sales topped ¥77 billion ($750 million) by the end of 2004.

Difficult market conditions, including the soaring price of crude oil as a result of the invasion of Iraq by the United States, forced JSP to cut back its expandable polystyrene production by as much as 20 percent starting in mid-2004. Yet the company continued to seek to expand its other operations, especially on an international level. In January 2005, JSP announced its intention to build a new plant in the Czech Republic in order to produce expanded polypropylene foam in order to meet rising demand for EPP-based bumper cores and automotive interior shock absorption systems. The new plant, with an initial capacity of 7,000 tons per year, was expected to be operational in 2006 and to double its capacity by 2014. With this expansion, JSP Corporation demonstrated its intention to remain the world's leading producer of polypropylene and polystyrene foam products well into the 21st century.

Principal Subsidiaries

Japan Xanpak Corporation; KP Corporation; Japan Repromachine Industries Co., Ltd.; Seihoku Packaging Company; Japan Acryace Corporation; JSP Molding Corporation; MIRAX Corporation; Kansai Plast Corporation; Yukasansho Kenzai Co., Ltd.; Hokuryou Eps Co., Ltd.; Honsyu Yuka Co., Ltd.; JSP International Group Ltd. (Unitee States); JSP International LLC. (United States); JSP Mold, LLC. (United States); JSP Licenses, Inc. (United States); JSP International Specialty Foams LLC. (United States); JSP Automotive Interiors LLC

(United States); JSP International de Mexico, S.A. de C.V. (Mexico); JSP International SARL (France); JSP International GmbH & Co. KG (Germany); JSP International GmbH (Germany); JSP International SRL (Italy); Sealed Air Packaging S.A.S. (France); KOSPA Corporation (Korea); Korea Special Products Co., Ltd. (Korea); Taiwan JSP Chemical Co., Ltd. (Taiwan); JSP Foam Products, Pte. Ltd. (Singapore); JSP Foam Products Hong Kong Limited (China); JSP Plastics (Wuxi) Co. Ltd. (China); JSP International Trading (Shanghai) Co., Ltd. (China).

Principal Competitors

KGM Industries Ghana Ltd.; Abplast Products PLC; Dow Chemical Co; E A Juffali and Brothers; Tekni-Plex Inc; Continental AG; HeidelbergCement AG; Nuqul Group of Cos.; Phoenix Brushware; Stirol Joint Stock Co.; Kaneka Corporation; Nitto Denko Corporation.

Further Reading

"JSP Corp (New Factory)," *Japan-U.S. Business Report*, November 1999.

"JSP Corporation to Build Plastics Plant in Cheb," *Access Czech Republic Business Bulletin*, October 4, 2004.

"JSP-Mitsubishi Foams Merger," *Chemical Business NewsBase—Chemical Week*, October 30, 2002.

"JSP Set to Cut Back EPS (Expandable Polystyrene) Beads Production by 20%," *Asia Africa Intelligence Wire*, July 1, 2004.

"JSP Slates New Czech Expanded PP Beads Plant by 2006," *Chemical Business Newsbase—Japan Chemical Week*, January 13, 2005.

—M.L. Cohen

King Nut Company

31900 Solon Road
Solon, Ohio 44139
U.S.A.
Telephone: (440) 248-8484
Toll Free: (800) 860-5464
Fax: (440) 248-0153
Web site: http://www.kingnut.com

Private Company
Incorporated: 1937
Employees: 150
Sales: $35 million
NAIC: 311423 Dried and Dehydrated Food Manufacturing; 311911 Roasted Nuts and Peanut Butter Manufacturing; 311423 Cookie and Cracker Manufacturing; 311919 Other Snack Food Manufacturing; 206401 Candy and Confectionary Manufacturers; 206801 Salted and Roasted Nuts and Seeds; 544101 Candy and Confectionary; 594713 Gift Baskets and Parcels

King Nut Company processes, packages, and distributes nuts, dried fruits, pretzels, and snack mixes to supermarkets, drugstores, food service companies, convenience stores, gift companies, mass merchandisers, and airlines. Its products sell under the Kings, Peterson's Nut, and Summer Harvest brands. The company also produces private label nuts and snacks.

A Small Regional Company: 1937–89

Husband and wife, Earl and Edna Balliette, founded King Nut Company in Cleveland, Ohio, in 1937. They ran their small nut roasting and packaging business together, with Edna managing the office and Earl in charge of other business functions. During the late years of the Depression, King Nut sold nut products to local restaurants and taverns.

When Earl died in 1952, Edna Balliette took over the company, assisted by her brother, Michael Krempa. Balliette later became president of the Peanut Butter and Nut Processors Association, a position she held until she retired in 1989, when she was over 80 years of age.

King Nut grew slowly during its first five decades, and its sales remained regional. In the 1970s, it moved from Cleveland to Solon, Ohio. When Balliette sold the company to Kanan Enterprises in 1989, the company's account list consisted of mostly local retailers, a few national vending firms, and the Cleveland Municipal Stadium. King Nut's annual sales of nuts and dried fruits totaled about $5 million. Its annual growth was less than 10 percent a year, and its employees numbered fewer than 30. Local rival, Peterson Nut, which had been founded by Charles Peterson in Cleveland, Ohio, in 1927, was twice the size of the King Nut Company.

Michael Kanan, the company's new president and chief executive officer, set about to create a national profile for King Nut. Kanan had been an executive vice-president of the Michigan-based Everfresh Juice Company. Upon purchasing King Nut, he moved to Bainbridge, Ohio, with his wife and persuaded his son, Martin, to leave his job with a Detroit automotive-parts supplier to become King Nut's vice-president and director of sales and marketing. Another son, Matthew, joined the company in 1997.

King Nut under New Ownership

During the Kanans first seven years in charge of the company, King Nut's sales increased to $14 million, and its peanut volume increased more than six times to five million pounds. The number of employees more than doubled to 70. By 1996, King Nut's snacks were in vending machines throughout the country and sold at major retailers, including Revco, Finast, Drug Emporium, and Stop-N-Shop. Martin Kanan went after business with the major airlines aggressively, and, after five years, King Nut landed its first airline contract with US Airways in 1994. When Anheuser-Busch closed its Eagle Snacks subsidiary, the company got the break it had been seeking. Agreements with Trans World Airlines, Northwest Airlines, and Continental Airlines followed. By 1995, King Nut had contracts with five national airlines, which accounted for 150 million bags of peanuts and pretzels a year.

Company Perspectives:

To be the best tasting, value-priced, fastest-selling supplier to the supermarket, drug, mass merchandise, vending, airline, food service, convenience store, soft serve, ingredient, gift, and private label industries—ultimately serving the consumer with the value added snack products we produce and supply. We will achieve our mission by having imagination and vision; challenging ourselves everyday to be the best and to always offer the better value.

In the mid-1990s, King Nut modified its equipment to handle the snack mixes (nuts and pretzels or nuts and sesame sticks) that were becoming more popular with airlines as customers' tastes changed and concern arose about peanut allergies. In addition, King Nut began to produce private label items for companies, such as Amish Farms, and non-nut snacks for retail sale under its own Kings Delicious and Summer Harvest brand names.

By 1997, King Nut was processing one million pounds of nuts (cashews, peanuts, almonds, pistachios, and more) as well as other snack items such as pretzels each week at its plant in Solon, Ohio. However, the American public had begun to perceive nuts as an unhealthy snack, and supermarket sales of jarred, canned, and bagged nuts fell. In fact, only unshelled nuts saw an increase in sales in 1995, as consumers shied away from nuts as a high-fat, and therefore unhealthy, snack food. In 1997, the Snack Food Association, which had been founded in the early 1940s, reported that snack nuts and party mixes were two of only a few product types that had experienced significant sales growth that year. Nut manufacturers, in an attempt to combat the public's negative perception of nuts, sought to educate consumers about the differences between the fatty acids found in nuts and the saturated fats of junk foods. They also sought to win contracts with the airlines to supply in-flight snacks, some of which included items other than nuts, such as pretzels.

In 1998, King Nut Company, whose contracts now included American, Delta, and America West, in addition to other carriers, supplied 250 million bags of peanuts to the airlines. The company built a 10,000-square-foot addition, which it almost immediately outgrew, that included additional storage space and converted a loading dock into a retail store. In 1999, it experimented briefly with storefront retailing. However, according to Michael Kanan in a 2000 *Inside Business* article, the "location was not good. We didn't get a lot of foot traffic."

A Major Provider of Nuts and Snack Foods in the 2000s

By 2000, King Nut Company had grown to become a major player in the lucrative airline in-flight snack market, several times larger than its local competitor, Peterson Nut Company. The latter had been owned by Fairmont Snacks Group since 1988. Some 60 percent of King Nut Company's business came from its snack sales to airlines. It employed about 100 people in its 60,000-square-foot facility and produced about 300 million bags of nuts, pretzels, dried fruit, and snack mixes annually. Sales had tripled throughout the 1990s. Still, the more visible

Peterson Nut overshadowed King Nut in the minds of many northeast Ohioans.

In fact, Peterson Nut had been foundering since the early 1990s after being acquired by Fairmont Snacks Group. In the summer of 1998, employees complaining of low wages and poor working conditions at the company voted to be represented by the AFL-CIO. In addition to its union problems, Peterson was letting some of its accounts fall by the wayside, and King Nut readily took these over. Nevertheless, Peterson Nut continued to outstrip King Nut in catalog and fund-raising sales and at the local ballpark.

In the late 1990s, King Nut began to sell the front panel on its in-flight snack packages as advertising space. It reserved the back panel for its own branding information. The approach, which its creator, Los Angeles-based food broker Harvey Alpert & Co., called "brand in the hand," provided for a split in proceeds between King Nut and the airlines. Most often, the space was sold to Internet marketers that targeted the typically high-income, educated air traveler.

"Unlike watching a TV commercial, you can't walk away from this, when you're on an airplane, you sit there and eat the whole snack," Martin Kanan explained in a 2000 *BrandPackaging* article. Kanan estimated that his company's snack packages held air travelers' attention for at least 30 seconds, which was plenty of time for them to look at both front and back panels. In 2000, King Nut's front panels advertised the Weather Channel, the Winter Olympics, and Kenneth Cole. The company was now supplying in the vicinity of 300 million snack packages to the airlines each year.

In the summer of 2001, King Nut, with 98 employees, expanded its operations again, moving its edible nuts and snacks roasting and packaging operation to a building it purchased on Solon Road. In addition, the company also introduced resealable, stand-up pouches for its nuts, snack mixes, and dried fruits. It was also planning to increase its work force to 120 employees by the year 2009. However, after the terrorist attacks against the United States on September 11, 2001, the decrease in air travel led the airlines to default on their orders for in-flight snacks. King Nut, in turn, laid off close to 50 people that fall.

Once air travel started up again, the demand for snacks resumed and even increased. With the major airlines no longer offering in-flight meals, they instead turned to supplying passengers with additional snacks. King Nut, which in 2001 was the snack supplier for United Airlines, American Airlines, Delta Airlines, Continental Airlines, US Airways, Trans World Airlines, America West Airlines, and Southwest Airlines, began packaging not just nuts but nut mixes, pretzels, granola mixes, and breakfast snacks for the airlines.

In March 2003, Kanan Enterprises purchased Peterson Nut and Fairmont Snacks brands from the Peterson Nut Company of Cleveland, Ohio and added most of Peterson Nut's 30 employees. The acquisition meant expansion into the upscale gifts market and additional sales to grocery and convenience stores. It also brought with it the business of Jacobs Field, in downtown Cleveland, home to the Cleveland Indians, and a store directly across from the stadium.

<table>
<tr><td colspan="2" align="center">**Key Dates:**</td></tr>
<tr><td>**1927:**</td><td>Charles Peterson founds Peterson Nut.</td></tr>
<tr><td>**1934:**</td><td>Peterson sells Peterson Nut to Don Kelling.</td></tr>
<tr><td>**1937:**</td><td>Edna and Earl Balliette found King Nut Company.</td></tr>
<tr><td>**1988:**</td><td>Fairmont Snack Group buys Peterson Nut.</td></tr>
<tr><td>**1989:**</td><td>Edna Balliette retires and sells King Nut to Kanan Enterprises.</td></tr>
<tr><td>**2003:**</td><td>Kanan Enterprises buys Peterson Nut and Fairmont Snacks and merges it with King Nut.</td></tr>
</table>

King Nut's and Peterson Nut's combined markets promised a future of continued growth for the company. In 2004, King Nut supplied more than 500 million packages to most of the major airlines in the United States and several international carriers. Peterson Nut's retail business moved to a new store with four times more parking and signed a five-year lease on the space.

Principal Subsidiaries

Kanan Enterprises Inc.; Kanan Realty LLC.

Principal Competitors

Diamond Foods Inc.; Frito-Lay Company; Kraft Foods, Inc.

Further Reading

George, Jim, and Jim Peters, ''The 'Billboard' on Packages Yields Advertising Revenue,'' *BrandPackaging*, November 2000, p. 12.

Hitt, Jack, ''Are Brands Out of Hand?'' *Fast Company*, December 2000, p. 51.

Johnson, Terrence L., ''King Nut Out of Its Shell: Father and Son Use Contracts with Airlines to Turn Sleepy Distributor into Booming Company That Has Tripled Revenues in Just Seven Years,'' *Plain Dealer*, June 21, 1996, p. 1C.

Sweeney, Shari M., ''Working for Peanuts,'' *Inside Business*, June 2000.

—Carrie Rothburd

The Knot, Inc.

462 Broadway, 6th Floor
New York, New York 10013
U.S.A.
Telephone: (212) 219-8555
Toll Free: (877) 843-5668
Fax: (212) 219-1929
Web site: http://www.theknot.com

Public Company
Incorporated: 1996
Employees: 235
Sales: $41.40 million (2004)
Stock Exchanges: NASDAQ
Ticker Symbol: KNOT
NAIC: 516110 Internet Publishing and Broadcasting;
    511120 Periodical Publishers; 511130 Book Publishers

The Knot, Inc., is one of America's leading sources of information and products for couples planning a wedding. The firm operates a web site, theknot.com, which offers informative articles, chat rooms, and personal wedding web pages, plus an online gift registry with more than 15,000 items from the likes of Target, Michael C. Fina, Linens 'n Things, and Fortunoff. The company also owns related web sites, including thenest.com, which caters to newly married couples; promspot.com, for teens; and greatgirl friends.com and greatboyfriends.com, which are subscription-based online dating services. Other Knot offerings include the nationally distributed *The Knot Weddings* magazine, regional wedding planning magazines that appear in 23 markets, and book series published by Broadway Books and Chronicle Books. Co-founder and executive editor Carley Roney has become a well-known wedding expert, with frequent television appearances and a syndicated wedding advice column.

Beginnings

The Knot was founded in 1996 by Carley Roney, David Liu, Rob Fassino, and Michael Wolfson, who had met while attending New York University's school of Film and Television in the late 1980s. Roney and Liu married in 1993, and the problems they experienced organizing the event left them wishing for a more up-to-date and practical planning guide than they had been able to find.

At this time the World Wide Web was gaining popularity for its ability to house large amounts of data that could easily be manipulated and updated, and made available around the clock. Sensing an opportunity, the friends decided to form a company to develop online content to help couples through the wedding planning process, which typically involved months of planning, hundreds of details, (tens-of) thousands of dollars in expense, and many potential pitfalls. Naming their new venture The Knot (after "tying the knot," an informal expression for marriage), they set about developing a guide to the wedding planning process that would be modern, practical, and stylish, with a dash of urban flair. The potential market was sizable, with some 2.3 million couples married each year in the United States, and the total wedding industry generating an estimated $35 billion in revenues. The four partners had experience in a variety of media endeavors, with Roney and Liu having recently headed a firm called RunTime, Inc., which worked on projects for many well-known clients.

In June 1996 they successfully pitched their idea to America Online (AOL), which agreed to put up funding. In September wedding content developed by The Knot appeared on AOL exclusively for its members. The offerings included articles on wedding planning, cost-saving tips, information about necessities like gowns and photographers, and "chat rooms" where brides-to-be could compare notes. Though primarily intended for women (who traditionally did the bulk of wedding planning), there was also information for grooms-to-be about things such as buying a ring and how to tie a bow tie. After their new company was incorporated, Liu took the titles of chairman and CEO and Roney was designated editor-in-chief.

In July 1997 The Knot launched a standalone web site, theknot.com, and the following April Hummer Winblad Venture Partners invested several million dollars in the company to fund further growth. By now, less than a year after its launch, the firm's site was attracting 250,000 unique users per month, with 300 registering to join the online community each day. The site

Company Perspectives:

The Knot has quickly become America's leading wedding brand reaching out to millions of engaged couples each year through our award-winning website, books, magazines, and broadcast offerings. Our trademark fresh voice and real-world sensibility, down-to-earth editorials, easy-to-use tools, and convenient, comprehensive gift registry and wedding supplies store keep America's brides and grooms coming back time and again.

had grown to feature an extensive database of products and services, including photos of more than 8,000 gowns and a list of wedding photographers searchable by area code and price, as well as honeymoon travel package auctions, more than 3,000 articles on wedding topics, 32 different editorial features that were frequently updated, and chat rooms. The free site was supported by advertisers like Lenox China, Wamsutta, Kodak, and Godiva Chocolatiers, though it was still operating in the red.

In June 1998 theknot.com was rated the best wedding site online by Yahoo! Internet Life, and in November the firm launched an online gift registry, which partnered with numerous retailers to allow couples to pre-select gifts. Items they chose could then be purchased by wedding guests online, with The Knot taking a cut. Revenues for 1998 were $1 million, but the firm recorded a loss of $1.5 million.

In January 1999 the first in a series of three Knot books was published by Random House imprint Broadway Books. *The Knot Complete Guide to Weddings in the Real World* offered practical advice for brides-to-be on all aspects of the wedding day. The book helped boost the web site's traffic, and during the month the firm recorded visits by more than 900,000 unique users, with 1,000 new members joining per day.

In April 1999 cable shopping channel QVC invested $15 million in The Knot, which made it the company's single largest stakeholder. The deal would quadruple the size of the online gift registry to more than 10,000 products, and the two companies would begin to cross-promote each other's offerings. In the summer The Knot also acquired online wedding products supplier Bridalink.com and online travel planner Click Trips, and signed marketing alliances with the likes of jewelry retailer Mondera.com and NextCard Internet Visa.

Initial Public Offering in December 1999

Internet-based businesses were now gaining the rapt attention of Wall Street, and in December 1999 the firm went public on the NASDAQ with a 3.5-million-share offering that raised $35 million. Major stakeholders continued to be QVC, with 36.4 percent of the firm, Hummer Winblad, with 18.3 percent, and AOL, with 8.1 percent. Each of the four original founders owned 5 percent, with the company's 100 employees also given stakes. The Knot recorded revenues of $5.1 million and losses of $9.2 million for the year. Theknot.com now had 500,000 members.

In February 2000 the company bought Weddingpages, Inc. for $8.5 million. The latter firm published quarterly regional

wedding magazines in 50 markets, which would be re-branded to incorporate The Knot name. A new annual publication, *Wedding Gowns,* also was launched by the company. The 400-page magazine showed photographs of 1,400 dresses, with minimal editorial content or advertising.

The spring of 2000 saw The Knot form a joint venture with retailer H. Stern, called The Knot Brazil, which would operate a Portuguese-language Knot site. Stern, which owned a chain of 175 luxury goods and jewelry stores in 15 countries, would be half-owner of the operation, which was seen as a first step toward becoming the leading online wedding resource worldwide.

In April the firm launched a wedding planning web site for the New York metropolitan area, the first in a series for regional markets around the United States. The Knot also began sending new members a free information-packed three-ring binder to use as a wedding planning organizer, which included discreet advertisements like a ring size gauge from Mondera and a budget workbook from MBNA. Although the company's demographic was overwhelmingly female, in the spring of 2000 an alliance was formed with Playboy.com to offer that firm's bachelor party planning content on theknot.com.

In June 2000 NBC-TV's *Today Show* began running a ten-part series called ''Today Ties the Knot,'' in which a couple's wedding was planned with input from the show's viewers. Boosted by the heightened visibility, in August the company's web site recorded its one millionth registered user.

In the fall The Knot announced marketing partnerships with Linens 'n Things and Fortunoff, and relaunched honeymoon travel planning web site clicktrips.com, which had been purchased the previous year. In November the company was named the premier wedding content provider for MSN, and also signed a deal with Chronicle Books for two books that would focus on wedding gowns and flowers.

The year 2001 saw partnerships formed with a variety of additional firms, including Barnes & Noble, Lifetime Television, Sunbeam Corp., and Yahoo! Shopping, but the company also was beginning to experience problems on several fronts. One was a revolt by most of the regional franchisors of its Weddingpages magazines, who sought a legal injunction against a ban on their use of the Knot name, which was later resolved through mediation. Another was the company's stock price, which, like that of many dot.coms, had taken a tumble. In August it was de-listed from the NASDAQ and moved to the over-the-counter market. New web site members continued to be added, however, and late summer saw the two millionth registration on theknot.com. For fiscal 2001, the firm recorded sales of $24.1 million and a loss of $15.8 million.

May Department Stores Co. Buying a Stake in 2002

In February 2002 The May Department Stores Company invested $5 million in the firm, securing a 19.5 percent ownership stake. May operated 439 department stores under names like Hecht's, Strawbridge's, Famous-Barr, and Filene's, as well as 150 David's Bridal stores, and the two firms began to cross-promote each others' products and services.

Key Dates:

1996: The Knot, Inc. is founded and begins supplying wedding content to AOL.
1997: The company launches theknot.com web site.
1998: Hummer Winblad buys a stake in the firm; an online gift registry is introduced.
1999: QVC invests $15 million in the firm; Bridalink and Click Trips are acquired.
1999: An initial public offering raises $35 million.
2000: The firm acquires magazine publisher Weddingpages, Inc. for $8.5 million.
2002: May Department Stores invests $5 million in the company.
2004: Thenest.com web site is launched; a partnership with Michael C. Fina is formed.
2005: The GreatBoyfriends LLC online dating firm is bought; online videos are added; a partnership with Target's Club Wedd gift registry is formed.

August 2002 saw theknot.com reach three million registered users. The average member stayed active for 12 months, so this cumulative total included a number who were no longer using the site. In September the firm's national magazine, *The Knot Weddings,* was distributed to newsstands nationwide. For the year, revenues increased to $29.5 million, while losses fell to $5.1 million.

In January 2003 the Oxygen cable network aired *Real Weddings from The Knot,* a six-part reality television series hosted by Carley Roney that showed couples' actual weddings. In February the firm extended its content provider relationships with AOL and MSN, and in April The Knot partnered with ABC-TV's *The View* for a four-week series showcasing the "fantasy weddings" of the series' four hosts.

The spring of 2003 saw the launch of promspot.com, a Knot knockoff that was targeted at high schoolers preparing to attend a prom dance, and the formation of a strategic alliance with Evite.com, an online invitation service. In September, Carley Roney signed with Scripps Howard to write a weekly advice column that would be syndicated to 70 newspapers around the United States.

In November The Knot, which had recently begun operating in the black, sold 2.8 million new shares of stock to institutional investors for $3.75 each. Revenues for 2003 hit $36.7 million, and earnings amounted to $1.1 million. By year's end the stock price had returned to the $5 range, 20 times the figure of several years earlier, though still half of the offering price in December 1999.

In January 2004, another season of *Real Weddings from The Knot* aired on the Oxygen network. The firm was now also working on developing video content for Comcast.net's Relationships Channel, which would incorporate elements of theknot.com for Comcast cable Internet subscribers. In June, the firm's regional weddings magazines were relaunched. Now serving only about 25 U.S. markets, they featured advice from Carley Roney, photo-stories on weddings in each area, and a directory of hundreds of local wedding-related vendors and service providers. Revenues for 2004 continued to grow, at $41.4 million, with earnings inching upward to $1.3 million.

In January 2005 The Knot acquired GreatBoyfriends LLC, which operated two subscription-based dating web sites, greatboyfriends.com and greatgirlfriends.com, which the firm would later overhaul and relaunch. The Knot had also recently created a site called thenest.com, which targeted newly married couples.

In February, the syndicated game show *Who Wants To Be a Millionaire* did a Knot-themed week of programs in which engaged couples tried to win money to spend on their weddings. March saw the firm's stock re-listed on the NASDAQ and in April, a major new partnership was announced with retailer Target, whose gift registry was the largest in the world. The Club Wedd registry would be featured prominently on theknot.com, while Target's own registry site would incorporate Knot content. A similar deal had been signed several months earlier with china, crystal, and jewelry retailer Michael C. Fina.

The month of April also saw rival WeddingChannel.com file suit against The Knot, alleging patent infringement. The firm vowed a vigorous defense. In May a compact disc was released by Sony Classical called *The Knot Collection of Ceremony & Wedding Music,* which was designed to assist brides in choosing music for their weddings.

By the summer of 2005 theknot.com had firmly established itself as the most popular wedding web site on the Internet. It boasted more than one million active members, with a total of 2.1 million unique visitors each month. The average user viewed the site nine times monthly, and spent 20 minutes per visit. The firm claimed a "click-through" rate of 15 percent on the site's banner ads, compared with 0.1 percent for the Internet as a whole. Users of theknot.com were 85 percent female and had an annual household income of more than $60,000.

Approximately half of the company's revenues were now derived from advertising, with about a quarter each coming from merchandise sales and publishing. Most of the firm's content was created at its headquarters in New York, but it also operated a technical facility in Austin, Texas, and an order-fulfillment center in Redding, California.

In less than a decade The Knot, Inc. had become one of the best-known brands in the now $70 billion U.S. wedding industry, with its flagship web site boasting more than one million active members. The firm had built up a portfolio that extended to books, magazines, television programs, a newspaper advice column, and spin-off web sites, and it looked toward future growth as the wedding planning industry continued to migrate online.

Principal Subsidiaries

Weddingpages, Inc.; Click Trips, Inc.

Principal Competitors

WeddingChannel.com, Inc.; Conde Nast Publications, Inc.; Fairchild Publications, Inc.; iVillage Inc.; Martha Stewart Living Omnimedia, Inc.; Amazon.com, Inc.; Yahoo! Inc.

Further Reading

Adler, Carlye, ''48 Hours with Theknot.com,'' *Fortune,* February 7, 2000, p. 194C.

Braunstein, Peter, ''Theknot and Diamond Engage in Partnership,'' *Women's Wear Daily,* November 28, 2000, p. 16.

Dalin, Shera, ''Who's Hot, Who's Knot,'' *St. Louis Post-Dispatch,* April 8, 2005, p. B1.

Hass, Nancy, ''At the .com Wedding,'' *New York Times,* December 5, 1999, Sec. 9, p. 5.

Huhn, Mary, ''Another E-zine Gets Inky—theknot.com Spawns a Catalog,'' *New York Post,* February 23, 2000, p. 38.

Key, Angela, ''Tying The Knot on the Net,'' *Fortune,* July 25, 2000, p. 320.

''The Knot Gets Victory in NY Court,'' *Women's Wear Daily,* September 5, 2001, p. 6.

Kwok, Chern Yeh, ''May Co. Ties the Knot with Nuptial Site,'' *St. Louis Post-Dispatch,* February 26, 2002, p. C1.

Mack, Ann M., ''The Knot Releases Wedding Box,'' *ADWEEK Eastern Edition,* March 20, 2000, p. 68.

''The Marrying Kind—Pittsburgher Who Co-Founded Internet Wedding Company Gets Chance to Walk Down Aisle,'' *Pittsburgh Post-Gazette,* April 15, 2000, p. B14.

''Online Wedding Business Thriving—QVC Will Tie Theknot.com,'' *New Orleans Times-Picayune,* April 15, 1999, p. C1.

Oser, Kris, ''TheKnot.com Seeks to Extend Its Engagements,'' *Advertising Age,* May 23, 2005, p. 144.

Russo, Ed, ''Weddingpages Agrees to Sell to Online Rival,'' *Omaha World-Herald,* February 3, 2000, p. 18.

Schwartz, Evan I., ''With Billions in Spending By and For the Soon-To-Be-Married at Stake, the Race for Top Bridal Site Is Heating Up,'' *New York Times,* June 21, 1999, p. 4C.

Tedeschi, Bob, ''Some Web Sites Are Producing TV-Type Shows and Showing Them Around the Clock, A Contrast to Video-on-Demand,'' *New York Times,* March 14, 2005, p. 5.

Webb, Carla, ''Dot Karma,'' *HFN,* March 12, 2001, p. 36.

''Weddingpages Seeks to Untie Theknot.com,'' *Women's Wear Daily,* October 27, 2000, p. 20.

Young, Vicki M., ''The Knot Loses $3.2M in 4th Qtr,'' *Women's Wear Daily,* February 14, 2000, p. 16.

—Frank Uhle

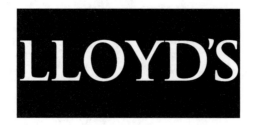

Lloyd's

1 Lime Street
London EC3M 7HA
United Kingdom
Telephone: + 44 7327-1000
Fax: + 44 7327-5599
Web site: http://www.lloyds.com

Private Company
Incorporated: 1871 as Society of Lloyd's
Employees: 582
Total Assets: $237.5 billion (2003)
NAIC: 524210 Insurance Agencies and Brokerages

Perhaps the world's most famous insurance group, Lloyd's is a uniquely organized insurance market. It does not sell insurance per se, but regulates a market through which insurance contracts are transacted. The organization is a society of individuals—and, since 1994, corporations—that accept liability for claims under insurances accepted on their behalf. In a nutshell, Lloyd's brokers act on behalf of their clients. Underwriters accept risk from the brokers for the syndicates, which, in turn, are the actual business units that sell insurance—they provide insurance after a premium is paid—in the Lloyd's market. In 2005, there were 62 underwriting syndicates that covered all classes of business from more than 200 countries across the globe. Lloyd's had the capacity to accept insurance premiums of more than £13.7 billion ($26 billion) in 2005. The United States is the largest geographical market for Lloyd's, accounting for 34 percent of business in 2004. Lloyd's is the world's sixth largest reinsurer.

Over the course of its more than three centuries in business, this unique group has brokered policies for the routine (it is Great Britain's leading automotive insurer) as well as the weird. Unusual contracts written at Lloyd's have included the following: a food critic who insured his taste buds for £250,000; a comedy troupe that took out a policy to cover the risk that an audience might die laughing; and rock star Bruce Springsteen, who insured his voice for £3.5 million. Although the group's most famous claim is probably the sinking of the Titanic in 1912, numerous and massive claims in the late 1980s and early 1990s threatened to "sink" the venerable Lloyd's.

Prompted by aggregate losses of more than £7.9 billion ($12.4 billion) from 1988 through 1992, Lloyd's was compelled to reform some long-held precepts. For more than 300 years, individual underwriting members, called Names, accepted unlimited personal liability for the policies they signed. Facing a lawsuit that eventually cost the group more than £3 billion, Lloyd's formally inaugurated limited individual liability in 1993. The creation of Equitas, a separate reinsurer to assume all of Lloyd's pre-1993 liabilities, was intended to set Lloyd's back on the trail to profitability.

Origins As 17th-Century Coffeehouse

In 1688, Edward Lloyd opened a coffeehouse in Tower Street, London, near the docks. He sought to attract a clientele of persons connected with shipping and, in particular, marine underwriters, those willing to transact marine insurance. By 1689 he was well established. In 1691 his coffeehouse moved to Lombard Street. Lloyd provided shipping intelligence. After his death in 1713 the business was carried on by a succession of masters. From 1734 the business published *Lloyd's List*, a newspaper featuring shipping news. The paper still appears daily.

In the early 18th century Lloyd's became the main, though not the only, place where marine underwriters congregated. The Bubble Act of 1720 gave two newly formed corporations, The London Assurance and The Royal Exchange Assurance, the exclusive right to transact marine insurance as corporations, but expressly allowed individual private underwriters to continue operating. The two corporations exercised the utmost caution and took only a fraction of the growing market, leaving scope for private underwriters. Some of these also were willing to effect gambling insurances, where the policyholder did not stand to lose financially if the event insured against occurred, that is, he had no insurable interest. Such insurances on ships and cargoes were forbidden by an Act of 1745 but persisted on lives and specific events.

In 1769 some underwriters who disapproved of gambling insurances broke away. They persuaded a Lloyd's waiter,

Thomas Fielding, to open a New Lloyd's Coffee House, which, in five years, drove the old one out of business. The new Lloyd's became cramped. In 1771 nine merchants, underwriters, and brokers formed a committee that took over the premises and appointed two masters to run them. Lloyd's moved into the Royal Exchange in 1773. By the Life Assurance Act, 1774, Parliament prohibited gambling insurance on lives, thus vindicating the stand of those who had reorganized Lloyd's.

In 1779 Lloyd's had only 179 subscribers. These enjoyed the sole right of entry to the underwriting room at Lloyd's. The wars with France from 1792 to 1815 brought great prosperity for marine insurers, among them John Julius Angerstein, an underwriter and broker who served as chairman in 1786, from 1790 to 1796, and again in 1806. At the height of the wars the number of subscribers rose to more than 2,000.

Declining Membership in the Early 19th Century

British entrepreneurs chafed at the law against new marine insurance companies. In 1824 the Bubble Act was at last repealed, but peace had signaled a decline in marine insurance. The number of subscribers fell from 2,150 in 1814 to 953 in 1843. In 1846, to raise money, a higher subscription was imposed on those subscribers who underwrote insurances; only 189 paid. In 1844, the committee of Lloyd's abolished the office of the masters and assumed full responsibility, through its secretary, for administering the market.

In 1848 Captain G.A. Halsted of the Royal Navy was appointed secretary, a post he held for 20 years. From 1850 Lloyd's began to appoint politically prestigious persons from outside its own community to the chairmanship. The most notable was G.J. Goschen, a young liberal member of Parliament who later became chancellor of the exchequer. He was chairman from 1869 to 1886 and again from 1893 to 1901. After 1901 Lloyd's reverted to having chairmen who worked in the market.

During the first half of the 19th century the committee was concerned, in large part, with intelligence-gathering for the benefit of Lloyd's members. Beginning in 1811 it appointed firms and persons in ports throughout the world to provide shipping information. By 1829 there were more than 350 Lloyd's Agents, as they were called. Lloyd's Agents receive no remuneration except for services rendered to underwriters such as surveying damaged property. They could, however, hope for some commercial advantage from their association with Lloyd's.

Marine underwriters have always felt the need for information about ship construction. As early as 1760 they formed a registration society that published a book of details of ships for the use of subscribers only. In 1798 shipowners began publishing a similar book. In 1834 the two publications were merged to form Lloyd's Register of Shipping, administered by a committee representing shipowners, merchants, and marine underwriters. The register operated as a corporation separate from Lloyd's.

The provision of intelligence loomed large in the work of Henry Hozier, who was secretary from 1874 to 1906. In addition to strengthening the central staff of Lloyd's, he saw the desirability of getting information promptly, and set up coastal telegraph stations for that purpose. By 1884 Lloyd's had 17 stations at home and six abroad. They worked in cooperation with the Admiralty. Hozier was knighted. He was a pioneer of wireless telegraphy, which Lloyd's used early in the 20th century.

Incorporation in 1871

For much of the 19th century the committee exercised little power over its underwriting members. Lloyd's remained a loosely run club. Not until 1851 did a general meeting resolve that any member becoming bankrupt should forfeit his membership. Legislation was sought to strengthen the committee's powers. The Lloyd's Act, 1871, made Lloyd's a corporation, the Society of Lloyd's. The objectives of the society were stated as the carrying on of marine insurance by members and the collection and publication of intelligence. At that time the participation of Lloyd's in nonmarine insurance was negligible and the Act made no reference to it or, indeed, to insurance brokers.

Between 1849 and 1870 the underwriting membership of Lloyd's had doubled. The committee became increasingly concerned to see that applicants for membership had the necessary means to support their underwriting. From 1856, in a few cases, guarantees or deposits were required, but it was not until 1882 that they became mandatory. Even then they related only to marine insurance.

After 1871 the volume of nonmarine insurance became significant. Its growth was due, in large part, to the efforts of C.E. Heath, an underwriter who began his own business in 1881. Aside from transacting fire insurance he pioneered new forms such as all risks insurance on property on land, and on household burglary. C.E. Heath underwrote on behalf of a syndicate that in 1887 consisted of 15 Names.

The years 1875 to 1900 saw the accelerating development of Lloyd's in two respects. Thanks to the activities of Lloyd's brokers, much business began to reach Lloyd's from the United States and other overseas sources. Reinsurance, that is, the acceptance of liabilities assumed by direct insurers under their own policies, came to be transacted at Lloyd's, which pioneered novel forms of reinsurance contracts.

Standards Set Under Heath in the Early 20th Century

In 1908, at Heath's prompting, Lloyd's took steps toward tightening security under Lloyd's policies. A general meeting agreed that all underwriters should provide certificates of solvency from approved auditors and that premiums be held in trust accounts for the payment of claims. This had beneficial effects in the following year. The Assurance Companies Act, passed in 1909, which for the first time imposed a measure of regulation on companies transacting the main classes of general insurance, left to the Corporation of Lloyd's the primary responsibility for regulating Lloyd's underwriters, as did subsequent regulatory Acts.

World War I affected Lloyd's favorably, creating a large demand for war-risk coverage at high premiums. The state took 80 percent of the war risk on ships, leaving 20 percent to private underwriters. The state also insured cargoes at sea at fixed rates, leaving underwriters free to offer lower rates for any business they wanted. They made large profits on the desirable cargo business while the state was losing money on the residue. Insurance of war risk on property on land was left to private enterprise for three years. Lloyd's took the lead in providing coverage where most insurance companies were unwilling to do so. The business proved profitable.

At Lloyd's, all policies were prepared by brokers who then had to take them to the underwriting room for signature on behalf of all the syndicates concerned, a tedious process. In 1916, to save clerical labor, the committee sanctioned an optional system whereby policies could be signed on behalf of all the underwriters concerned in a new bureau, Lloyd's Policy Signing Bureau. In 1924 use of the bureau, renamed Lloyd's Policy Signing Office, became mandatory.

The first quarter of the 20th century saw the development of three new classes of insurance—motor, aviation, and credit. Credit insurance involved a guarantee that monies due would be paid. In 1923, one syndicate transacting this business failed through reckless underwriting. The committee of Lloyd's banned future direct insurance by way of financial guarantees but allowed reinsurance of such business to continue.

The reputation of Lloyd's depended on claims being met by underwriters. Some underwriting syndicates had the potential to fail through dishonesty or poor underwriting. In 1927 Lloyd's set up a central fund, financed by a continuing small levy on premiums. This fund was held in trust for the benefit of policyholders whose claims were not met.

In World War II Lloyd's again prospered, although war risks were undertaken by the government. Special arrangements had to be made to protect the company's U.S. business. Lloyd's established a U.S. trust fund into which all premiums in U.S. dollars had to be paid and held for the benefit of policyholders.

The first half of the 20th century was a profitable time for Lloyd's. Its underwriters proved themselves more flexible than insurance companies. They identified risks overcharged by company cartel rates and, by selective underwriting, skimmed the cream of the business. Large insurances had to be shared among many individual underwriters. The increasing size of insurances led to a growth in the size of syndicates. In 1890 a syndicate with ten Names was exceptional. By 1952 there were 16 syndicates with 100 Names or more. The largest had more than 300 Names. Large syndicates developed for motor insurance, of which Lloyd's had no more than 5 percent of the £100 million market in 1950.

The growth of Lloyd's had three consequences. First, the need for further underwriting capacity started a hunt for new Names to provide the capital required. Brokers were well placed to find people. They also organized underwriting syndicates. A number, called underwriting agents, acted as both members' agents and managing agents. Second, the various interests at Lloyd's formed market associations to deal collectively with the problems they encountered. Marine underwriters formed their own association within Lloyd's in 1909. An association for fire and accident—nonmarine—underwriters was formed in 1910 and Lloyd's Insurance Brokers' Association was founded. Although underwriters at Lloyd's wrote the group's first auto policy in 1901—it was a marine policy that purported the vehicle to be ''a ship navigating on dry land''—Lloyd's Motor Underwriters' Association was not formed until 1931. Lloyd's Aviation Underwriters' Association dates from 1935. Third, pressure on space at the Royal Exchange became acute. In 1928 Lloyd's moved out to specially built premises in Leadenhall Street.

Rapid Growth in the Postwar Era

The years following 1950 saw the most spectacular growth at Lloyd's. In 1957 a further building had to be opened on an adjoining site across Lime Street. In 1983 the old Leadenhall Street building was demolished and Lloyd's commissioned a new structure, designed by Richard Rogers, for the site. This was opened in 1986, with the Lime Street building being retained. Meanwhile much work had been transferred to outstations at Chatham and Colchester.

Between 1952 and 1968 the membership of Lloyd's nearly doubled, from 3,157 to 6,052. In considering how to increase underwriting capacity, Lloyd's appointed a working party under the chairmanship of the Earl of Cromer. Meanwhile, in 1968, membership, hitherto confined to the commonwealth, was opened to nationals of all countries. Eligibility was extended to

British women in 1970. It was not until 1972 that women were admitted to the underwriting room.

The Cromer working party issued its report in 1970. It favored the admission of corporations as members, but this recommendation was not adopted. Thanks to the profitability of Lloyd's, however, membership again rose steeply, reaching 20,145 in 1982 and 33,532 in 1988, although by 1990 it had fallen to 28,770.

One growth area after 1950 was U.K. motor insurance. Lloyd's held one-sixth of the market, thanks in part to a modification of the company's normal procedure, which required all business to be transacted in the underwriting room. Since 1965, Lloyd's allowed motor syndicates to deal directly with non-Lloyd's intermediaries if they were sponsored by a Lloyd's broker. Motor syndicates, therefore, could operate as if they were insurance companies.

During this time period, about half of the company's business was derived from the United States. U.S. insurance brokers cast envious eyes on Lloyd's brokers, who alone had access to Lloyd's and, therefore, received commissions on all business placed there. The big Lloyd's brokers found themselves exposed to takeover overtures from their U.S. counterparts. In 1979 Marsh & McLennan, the largest U.S. broker, acquired C.T. Bowring. In 1982 Alexander & Alexander acquired Alexander Howden. Since 1982 two Lloyd's brokers have acquired two large U.S. brokers: Sedgwick took over Fred S. James and Willis Faber merged with Corroon & Black.

In a market such as that of Lloyd's, where hundreds of enterprises competed from time to time, unsatisfactory situations arise. One such event was the affair of the Sasse syndicate in 1976. Its active underwriter authorized an underwriting firm in New York to write business on his syndicate's behalf. The firm transacted a large volume of bad business, which led to heavy losses. The Sasse syndicate exceeded the premium income it was authorized to write. Some members of the syndicate, faced with heavy calls, sued Lloyd's, alleging that losses arose from a failure to supervise. It became apparent that the machinery of Lloyd's was not working properly. In 1979 the committee appointed a working party under the chairmanship of Sir Henry Fisher to examine self-regulation at Lloyd's. The working party reported in 1980. It made 79 recommendations for improvements. Apart from a general tightening up, the working party recommended a new governing body with wider powers. It drew attention to the growing influence of the big brokers. In 1978 the six largest brokerage groups had placed more than half of Lloyd's business and the proportion was growing.

Record Profits in the 1980s Giving Way to Unprecedented Losses in the 1990s

Lloyd's accepted the main recommendations and sought legislative powers to bring them into effect. The result was the Lloyd's Act of 1982. This act put a new body, the Council of Lloyd's, over the committee, which had consisted of 16 persons, mainly underwriters, active in the Lloyd's market. The council was to include, in addition to the 16 committee members, eight representatives of the Names not working in the market—external members—and three nominated persons not

members of Lloyd's. At the prompting of the governor of the Bank of England, prominent accountant Ian Hay Davison was appointed chief executive and became a nominated person and one of three deputy chairmen of Lloyd's. The Act also provided for the separation of brokers and managing agents. They were to divest themselves of financial interests in each other. The separation was achieved by 1987.

At about the time of the Act, scandals erupted involving two leading broker groups. Large amounts of premiums had been siphoned off from some profitable syndicates by means of reinsurance with companies in which the chairmen and other directors of the groups had a financial interest. The reverberations of these events continued for some years with expulsions and suspensions, but none involved any loss to policyholders as distinct from Names. Lloyd's premium income did not suffer. The council made determined efforts to stamp out internal abuses.

In 1986 the government appointed the Neill Committee to consider whether those who participated at Lloyd's as Names had protection comparable with that provided for investors under the Financial Services Act of 1986. The following year the committee reported a number of shortcomings and made 70 recommendations for remedy. They included an amendment to the constitution of the council by which it would consist of 12 working members of Lloyd's, eight representatives of external members, and eight nominated members from outside Lloyd's, including the chief executive, so that the working members would be in the minority. The council accepted the recommendations beginning with the change to its membership. In three years most of the other changes were implemented.

Lloyd's appeared to be on a roll in the 1980s, chalking up record net income in 1986 and attracting thousands of nouveau riche to swell the ranks of Names to a high of 32,433 in 1988. But that veneer of success was shattered in the late 1980s, when a string of large claims brought massive losses to bear on the 300-year-old institution. Claims stemming from marine disasters such as the 1988 explosion of the Piper Alpha oil rig and the 1989 Exxon Valdez oil spill combined with natural disasters including the San Francisco earthquake and Hurricane Hugo, both in 1989. Final accounting for 1988 (which was not reported until 1991 due to a three-year lag in the Lloyd's financial reporting cycle) revealed a net loss of £509 million, Lloyd's first shortfall in more than two decades. At the same time, the Lloyd's U.S. operations were hit with retrospective liability for disability caused by asbestosis and for pollution damage. Faced with personal financial ruin, thousands of Names refused to honor their debts, instead launching preemptive lawsuits against Lloyd's for recourse. Thousands more Names resigned, shrinking Lloyd's membership to less than 10,000 by 1997; three even committed suicide. With individual and syndicate failures mounting, Lloyd's racked up five consecutive losses totaling £7.9 billion ($12.4 billion) from 1988 through 1992.

The crisis compelled extraordinary, heretofore unthinkable, changes at Lloyd's. Guided by former broker Chairman David Rowland, several reforms were set in motion in 1993. For the first time in its history, Lloyd's permitted corporate and institutional investors to underwrite policies. The first corporate members joined the organization in 1994. In a revolutionary departure from the long-held principle of unlimited liability, Lloyd's restricted individual Names' financial obligations to 80 percent of premium income, with excess losses reverting to a reserve funded by annual membership dues. It created a reinsurer, dubbed Equitas in 1994, to assume all liabilities incurred by Lloyd's prior to 1993. The new entity was funded by £859 million levied on Lloyd's' remaining members. In 1996, Lloyd's adopted annual accounting and achieved a £3.1 billion settlement with litigants after a long and bitter standoff.

In spite of the obstacles it encountered in the late 1980s and early 1990s, Lloyd's remained the largest and most innovative insurance market in the world during the mid-1990s. In fact, its overall assets increased from £17.9 billion in 1990 to £27.3 billion in 1995. Lloyd's returned to profitability in 1993, recording net income of £1.1 billion that year and a preliminary profit of £1 billion in 1994 as well.

The Late 1990s and Beyond

Changes continued for Lloyd's into the late 1990s and beyond. It completed its Reconstruction and Renewal plan in early 1997, which structured Lloyd's into five main operating segments, including Members' Services, Insurance Services, Facilities Management, Business Development, and a North American unit. It also dropped the "of London" portion of its moniker, opting to be known simply as Lloyd's. Problems related to its pre-1993 liabilities left it pursuing payment from many of its former members for underwriting losses well into the late 1990s. Lloyd's was seeking $231.1 million from former Names that failed to comply with the earlier settlement.

The new millennium brought with it a new era of catastrophic events. The terrorist attacks of September 11, 2001, in New York and Washington wreaked havoc on the insurance industry. The market experienced its worst year in 2001, when claims skyrocketed to £2.66 billion. Three years later, the market was once again hit hard by natural disasters including hurricanes, earthquakes, and tidal waves. Total claims reached £1.33 billion.

The insurance industry as a whole was on the cusp of major change during this time period as businesses faced a new realm of risk. Many companies were forced to protect against international fraud, corrupt practices, technology risks, terrorism, and compensation claims. In response to the changing business environment, Lloyd's syndicates began to offer a host of new products, including terrorism and political violence insurance, Home Value Protection insurance, Nannycare, which offered nannies protection against liability claims, and Club Esurance, a product offering businesses protection against system crashes and hacking activity.

In 2003, Lloyd's adopted a new franchise model, a cornerstone in its business strategy that signaled yet another significant shift in focus away from Names to corporate customers. According to Lloyd's, the model altered its status from regulating the market to commercially managing the market. This new structure had a threefold purpose: to develop and sustain a commercial business environment; to position Lloyd's as the top market in the insurance industry; and to develop a group of well-managed and efficient businesses.

Despite the unprecedented natural disasters in 2004—the worst year for natural catastrophes in history—Lloyd's secured a profit of £1.35 billion. Nevertheless, the events over the past several years had forced the industry to rethink risk management and contract certainty, a term for agreeing on final contract terms before inception. Whereas Lloyd's appeared poised for success in the future, its management team was on its toes keeping pace with ever-changing industry demands.

Principal Competitors

Allianz AG; AXA; Marsh & McLennan Companies Inc.

Further Reading

Ashworth, Jon, "Shake-up at Lloyd's Threatens to Put Hundreds of Jobs at Risk," *Times,* November 15, 1995, p. 26.

Brown, Antony, *Hazard Unlimited,* Colchester: Lloyd's of London Press, 1987.

Cockerell, Hugh, *Lloyd's of London: A Portrait,* Cambridge: Woodhead-Faulkner, 1984.

Davison, Ian Hay, *A View of the Room: Lloyd's Change and Disclosure,* London: Weidenfeld and Nicolson, 1987.

England, Robert Stowe, "At the Brink: Facing Unpaid Debts Close to $1.7 Billion, Lloyd's of London Fights for Its Life," *Financial World,* November 21, 1995, pp. 70–72.

Fleming, Charles, "Moving the Market: Lloyd's Pretax Profit Drops 28%," *Wall Street Journal,* April 7, 2005, p. C3.

Flower, Raymond, and Michael Wynn Jones, *Lloyd's of London: An Illustrated History,* Colchester: Lloyd's of London Press, 1981.

The Future of Lloyd's and the London Insurance Market, New York: Practicing Law Institute, 1992.

Gibb, D.E.W., *Lloyd's of London: A Study in Individualism,* London: Macmillan, 1957.

Goddard, Sarah, "Lloyd's Puts on a New Face," *Business Insurance,* April 28, 1997.

——, "Lloyd's Resolving Nagging Problems," *Business Insurance,* August 31, 1998.

Gunn, Cathy, *Nightmare on Lime Street: Whatever Happened to Lloyd's of London?,* London: Smith Gryphon Publishers, 1993.

Hodgson, Godfrey, *Lloyd's of London: A Reputation at Risk,* London: Penguin Books, 1986.

"Leaking at the Seams," *Economist,* January 26, 1991, pp. 69–70.

Lloyd's of London: A New World of Capital—Is the Genie Out of the Bottle?, Hartford, Conn.: Conning & Co., 1996.

Pitt, William, "An Outsider's Insider Tackles the Mess at Lloyd's," *Institutional Investor,* February 1993, pp. 143–45.

Proctor, Patrick, *For Whom the Bell Tolls,* Harlow: Matching Press, 1996.

Raphael, Adam, *Ultimate Risk,* London: Corgi Books, 1995.

"Regulatory Arrangements at Lloyd's: Report of the Committee of Enquiry," *Neill Report,* London: HMSO, 1987.

"Sir David Rowland: Master Communicator Spearheads Reconstruction of Lloyd's," *Business Insurance,* October 30, 1997.

White, Patrick, *Lloyd's: Post Reconstruction and Renewal,* London: FT Financial Publishing, 1997.

Wright, Charles, and C.E. Fayle, *A History of Lloyd's from the Founding of Lloyd's Coffee House to the Present Day,* London: Macmillan, 1928.

—Hugh Cockerell
—updates: April Dougal Gasbarre;
Christina M. Stansell

ZICAM.

Matrixx Initiatives, Inc.

742 North 24th Street, Suite 455
Phoenix, Arizona 85016
U.S.A.
Telephone: (602) 385-8888
Fax: (602) 387-4112
Web site: http://www.zicam.com

Public Company
Incorporated: 1996 as Gum Tech International, Inc.
Employees: 15
Sales: $60.2 million (2003)
Stock Exchanges: NASDAQ
Ticker Symbol: MTXX
NAIC: 325410 Pharmaceutical and Medicine Manufacturing; 325411 Medicinal and Botanical Manufacturing; 325412 Pharmaceutical Preparation Manufacturing

Matrixx Initiatives, Inc., develops, produces, markets, and sells over-the-counter pharmaceuticals, most notably the product Zicam, a patented homeopathic remedy for the common cold with a unique delivery system. Through the Zicam LLC subsidiary, Matrixx offers a total of ten different products for the cough and cold market.

1994–99: Producing and Marketing Gums With Health Benefits

Matrixx traces its roots to Gum Tech International, which in 1994 introduced ''hope in a box of gum,'' according to a 1994 *Atlanta Journal & Constitution* article. Its cherry-flavored Love Gum with ginseng was reputed to increase ''romantic power'' and to make those who chewed it feel good and energized. In its first three months of sales at two California quick stops and a gift shop, Love Gum made $250,000 in sales, leading Gum Tech to expand its products to make gums designed to provide health benefits to consumers: Buzz Gum to boost energy, Smoker's Gum to whiten teeth, Orient Express Gum to improve memory, and PMS and Hangover Gum with pain relievers and vitamins.

Two years later, Gum Tech held its initial public offering on Nasdaq. By 1997, it had relocated to Phoenix, Arizona, and its line of functional chewing gums had grown to include Calcium Supplement Gum, High Gear Energy Gum, non-nicotine Cig-Arrest Gum, and gums for oral hygiene, weight loss, and antioxidant properties. Deciding to forsake the health food market in favor of mass-merchandising, the company aimed to create a worldwide distribution network for its products. It also began producing gums for other companies in addition to its own line of branded gums, including two gums for General Nutrition Companies in 1997. In 1998, it added a memory and concentration enhancing gum, a nicotine chewing gum, a dental gum, and a gum with Acutrim for other companies.

The increase in business created the need for additional space, and in 1998, Gum Tech, with the only stainless steel gum-manufacturing facility registered with the Food and Drug Administration to manufacture gum with over-the-counter drug products, leased an additional 32,000-square-foot facility in which to expand its warehouse and packaging capabilities. The company's sales of $5.2 million that year were 40 percent more than they had been in 1997; still Gum Tech registered a loss of roughly $6.2 million.

1999: Zicam Debuts

In 1999, Gum Tech added another distribution agreement with Herbalife International Inc. for energy gum, then embarked upon a new direction with BioDelivery Technologies, Inc. Biodelivery Technologies specialized in the development of unique systems for the delivery of bioactive compounds. The two companies' joint venture, Gel Tech LLC of Woodland Hills, California, introduced Zicam Cold Remedy, a new homeopathic cold remedy that used a nasal gel to deliver an ionic zinc emulsification formula. Initial research showed that Zicam reduced the duration of the common cold from ten to 14 days to one to three days. Zicam sold at supermarkets, such as Fry's and Albertsons, and drug stores, such as Rite Aid, Genovese, Eckerd Drug, King Kullen, American Drug Stores, Basha's, Kroger, as well as Wal-Mart.

Gel Tech moved forward on clinical research to prove conclusively Zicam's ability to reduce the duration of cold symptoms, and to explore its ability to prevent their onset and to relieve symptoms caused by allergic reactions to airborne allergens. Zicam was thought to work because zinc gluconate, the weak organic salt in Zicam nasal gel, interfered with viral attachment to the intercellular adhesion molecule-1 receptor (ICAM-1) on airway cells. Zinc gluconate dissolves to form positively charged zinc ions and negatively charged gluconate, a compound found in all human tissues. Late in 1999, in an article that was to have been published by the *American Journal of Infection Control*—but was pulled because its contents were leaked to the press before publication—the first controlled study of intranasal zinc formulation suggested the product's effectiveness.

In 2000, the first phase of Gel Tech's own research revealed that Zicam reduced the duration of the common cold by 78 percent when taken at the onset of symptoms. The second phase of research recorded a reduction of 71 percent. Also in 2000, the online peer-reviewed journal, the *Internet Journal of Family Practice*, conducted a double-blind study that proved Zicam Allergy Relief, introduced that year, was "very effective in relieving primary allergy symptoms such as hay fever, nasal and ocular symptoms . . . ," reducing severity of allergic symptoms by 52 percent. A study published in *Ear, Nose & Throat Journal* reported that Zicam reduced the duration of the common cold by an average of 75 percent when taken at the onset of symptoms.

Other research focused on the efficacy of nasal sprays in quickly relieving congestion, part of a nationwide movement toward prevention in the treatment of colds and allergies. In 2000, after research proved that saline sprays, in particular, played a preventive role against allergy symptoms, the market for nasal products reached $382 million in 2000, with Zicam the No. 9 brand in its category with sales of $9.9 million. Zicam products were now available at more than 50,000 drug stores, grocery stores, pharmacies, mass merchants, and convenience stores in United States. The company received a patent for its "method of delivering zinc ions in a nasal gel to the nasal membrane to relieve the symptoms of the common cold."

The Rise of Zicam in the Early 2000s

Product sales increased 49 percent in 2001, generating $61 million in revenues, revealing growing consumer acceptance of the Zicam brand in the midst of a weak cold season during which overall sales of over-the-counter cold remedies decreased. Thanks in part to Gel Tech's 2001 agreement to distribute its cold remedy to General Nutrition Centers and Vitamin

World stores nation wide, Zicam had become one of the top five best-selling cold products in the United States. Gum Tech sold the manufacturing operations, contracts, and assets associated with its gum business and 200,000 shares of Gum Tech to the Wm. Wrigley Jr. Co. for $25 million and used the proceeds of the sale to enhance its marketing of Zicam products. It then purchased the remaining shares of Gel Tech LLC.

A favorable judgment in 2002 on a patent infringement case that the company filed in behalf of its Zicam products in January 2000 helped reinforce Zicam's position as the No. 4 nasal product after Afrin, Primatene Mist, and Nasal-Crom. In fact, the mild winter of 2001 to 2002 had weakened sales for most cough and cold products as had the scare over anthrax-tainted letters. Since the anthrax virus when inhaled causes flu-like symptoms, more people with upper respiratory symptoms opted to see their doctor rather than buy an over-the-counter remedy. Afrin, Primatene Mist, and Nasal-Crom all posted a decline in sales for the year ending February 2002. Zicam, however, posted double-digit gains.

Gum Tech changed its name mid-year in 2002 to Matrixx Initiatives, Inc., to reflect its exit from the functional chewing gum market, and by August, Zicam had moved to the No. 3 slot in the cold remedy product line-up. In September 2002, it introduced five new Zicam brand products: Zicam Cold Remedy Swabs, Zicam Kids-Size Cold Remedy Swabs, Zicam Extreme Congestion Relief, Zicam Sinus Relief, and Zicam Nasal Moisturizer.

The company's growth in sales continued strong. During 2002, revenues increased 47 percent to $23.5 million from $16.1 million in 2001. The company's net income for the year was $1.4 million as compared to a loss of $4.8 million the year before. By 2003, that figure was $3.3 million on sales of $43.5 million, an 85 percent increase above 2002 sales. Zicam Cold Remedy nasal spray had also moved into the No. 2 spot for nasal sprays purchased in the United States, behind only Afrin.

In 2003, Matrixx Initiatives again brought new products to market: Zicam Cold Remedy Chewables, RapidMelts, and Oral Mist products were designed to appeal to consumers uncomfortable with nasal applications. A problem with the company's swab manufacturer led to the launch of new type of swab in 2004. And, in 2005, Matrixx Initiatives introduced the first over-the-counter spray treatment for coughs.

Matrixx Initiatives responded promptly to an early 2004 Dow Jones "In the Money Report" that focused on the possibility that Zicam nasal products could cause lost or diminished olfactory function, or anosmia. A press release announced that "[a]ll Zicam products are marketed according to FDA guidelines for homeopathic medicine . . ." and went on to say that Matrixx believed statements alleging that intranasal Zicam products cause anosmia (loss of smell) were completely unfounded and misleading . . . "In no clinical trial of intranasal zinc gluconate gel products has there been a single report of lost or diminished olfactory function . . ."

Fortunately for Matrixx, consumer acceptance of Zicam was largely unaffected by the report. The line continued to grow about 50 percent a year, contributing to a 30 percent annual compound sales increase from 1999 to 2004, the year in which

Key Dates:

1994: Gum Tech begins business in North Hollywood, California.
1996: Gum Tech holds its first public offering.
1997: Gum Tech relocates to Phoenix, Arizona.
1998: The company leases an additional 32,000-square-foot facility.
1999: Gum Tech forms Gel Tech LLC with Biodelivery Technologies and introduces Zicam Cold Remedy.
2000: Gum Tech adds Zicam Allergy Relief.
2001: Gum Tech sells its gum business to the Wm. Wrigley Jr. Company and purchases the remaining shares of Gel Tech LLC.
2002: The company changes its name to Matrixx Initiatives, Inc. and introduces five new Zicam brand products.
2003: Matrixx brings three new Zicam products to market.

the company's revenues reached $60.2 million. The company also continued to branch out into the nasal health market, increasing its line of offerings in 2005 to include a new product called Nasal Comfort. This hyper-tonic aqueous solution con-

tained essential salts oils to cleanse and moisturize the nose and thereby increase nasal cavity function during respiration.

Principal Subsidiaries

Zicam LLC.

Principal Competitors

K-V Pharmaceutical Company, NutraMax Products Inc., Perrigo Company, QLT USA, The Quigley Corporation.

Further Reading

''Common Cold: New Research Supports Efficacy of Zincum Gluconicum Nasal Gel,'' *TB & Outbreaks Week*, January 21, 2003, p.10.
''Journal Won't Publish 'Leaked' Zicam Results,'' *Nutraceuticals International*, December 1999, p. 12.
''Rhinovirus: Homeopathic Remedy Reduces Duration of Common Cold,'' *Health & Medicine Week*, May 1–8, 2000, p. 23.
''Rhinovirus: New Patent Awarded for Zicam Secures, Expands Exclusive Cold Remedy Formula,'' *Virus Weekly*, May 7, 2002, p. 10.
''Zicam Allergy Relief Pilot Study Published in Peer-reviewed Online Medical Journal,'' *Chemical Business Newsbase*, September 13, 2000.

—Carrie Rothburd

Mayfield Dairy Farms, Inc.

4 Mayfield Lane
Athens, Tennessee 37371
U.S.A.
Telephone: (423) 745-2151
Toll Free: (800) 629-3435
Fax: (423) 746-1782
Web site: http://www.mayfielddairy.com

Wholly Owned Subsidiary of Dean Foods Company
Incorporated: 1957
Sales: $200 million (2004 est.)
Employees: 1,800
NAIC: 31151 Dairy Product (Except Frozen) Manufacturing; 311511 Fluid Milk Manufacturing; 311520 Ice Cream and Frozen Dessert Manufacturing

Mayfield Dairy Farms, Inc., produces and distributes milk and ice cream products in nine southeastern states. The company has been run by the Mayfield family since its start in 1923. In 1990, it became a subsidiary of Dean Foods.

1923–80s: A Family-Owned Creamery Expands Beyond Tennessee

Thomas B. Mayfield, Jr., and his wife, Goldie, started Mayfield Creamery in 1923. Mayfield, Jr., came from a family with a long tradition in farming. In the 1820s, his great grandfather, Jesse Mayfield, started a farm in McMinn County, Tennessee, and began peddling his surplus milk to neighbors in the surrounding Athens community. In the 1870s, Mayfield's father, Thomas B. Mayfield, Sr., began raising and selling horses, Jersey cows, and Berkshire hogs. Mayfield, Sr., his wife, and their son, Thomas B. Mayfield, Jr., purchased 45 Jersey cows in 1912 and established Live Oak Farms, selling milk to the residents of McMinn County from a horse-drawn buggy. In 1922, the Mayfield family completed a new milk plant and began marketing the first pasteurized milk between Chattanooga and Knoxville.

Throughout the Great Depression, the Mayfields supported Mayfield Creamery's operations by borrowing capital to expand and maintain full employment. When Mayfield, Jr., died in 1937, Thomas B. Mayfield III took over the company with the help of a family friend, Tom Harrison. Mayfield III, and his brother, Scott, mortgaged the family farm to build the most modern milk plant in the southeastern United States when they returned from World War II. In 1950, the company opened its first full-scale production facility in Athens, Tennessee. Continuing its steady expansion, Mayfield Creamery opened its first distribution center in Chattanooga, Tennessee in 1954. Another company first occurred in 1955 when Mayfield converted its milk fleet from ice-cooled to refrigerated trucks. This innovation enabled the company to ship its products throughout the southeastern United States.

In 1958, Mayfield became the first dairy in the United States to install an Aerovac vacreator. This imported device from New Zealand superheated the milk in a vacuum to remove unwanted odors and flavors. "You get a slight cooked flavor consumers perceive as richness," Rob Mayfield explained in a 2004 *Dairy Field* article. "It tastes the same year round." However, although Mayfield favored this technology and continued to use it for its ability to produce milk with a consistently fresh flavor, the dairy industry as a whole did not adopt it. The following year, the company continued its expansion by opening a Knoxville distribution facility.

In the 1960s, Mayfield began focusing on ice cream production and innovation. To this end, in 1962, the company purchased equipment that enabled it to freeze its packaged ice cream faster, yielding a smoother-textured product. Around the same time, Thomas B. Mayfield, III also developed the first zipper-opening ice cream carton, which the company called the Zip-II carton. The carton, which resealed tightly, offered the advantage of preserving the ice cream's freshness for future servings.

As Mayfield's products grew in popularity throughout the southeastern United States, the company began expanding its production capacity outside of Tennessee. In 1977, the company entered the Atlanta market by purchasing the Aristocrat Ice Cream Company. This business strategy proved to be a big success; Mayfield's ice cream sales exploded throughout north Georgia and Atlanta. Mayfield was the best-selling ice cream in

Atlanta in 1980, and the following year *Time* magazine selected Mayfield's ice cream as "the best ice cream in the world."

1980s–90s: New Directions, Steady Growth, and a Change of Ownership

Throughout the 1980s, Mayfield continued to introduce new products and to streamline its operations. In the early 1980s, it was the first company to make and fill its own milk jugs in a continuous operation. Then, in 1983, the company introduced its trademark yellow gallon milk jug to block out light and thus protect the flavor and nutrients in milk. As American's concern for health and nutrition grew, Mayfield began to capitalize on the trend, marketing Nu-Trish A/B in east Tennessee in 1987. This new milk product contained a combined culture of acidophilus and bifidum—two bacteria beneficial to digestion. In 1989, Mayfield began distributing many of its products via vending machines and introduced its low-fat frozen yogurt, which soon became a best-seller in the United States.

By 1990, Mayfield's annual sales exceeded $110 million and the company's customers spanned from eastern Tennessee to northern Georgia. In that same year, Dean Foods Company purchased Mayfield and the company began investing in plant renovations, installing modern processing and packaging equipment. It also set up ice cream distribution centers throughout the southeast, beginning with centers in Tennessee, Virginia, and South Carolina in 1993.

The sale of the dairy was a time of soul-searching for the great-grandsons of the first Thomas B. Mayfield. "When we sold in 1990, I had to decide what my role [in the business] was going to be," revealed Scott, Jr. (Scottie) in a 1997 *Chattanooga Free Press* article. He and his brother opted to stay at the helm of the family business. At the time, milk consumption nationwide was down and milk price supports were being phased out. However, sales of ice cream were still steady in the mid-1990s. Mayfield was selling ice cream in seven southeastern states. Although vanilla still reigned as the company's most popular type of ice cream, Mayfield introduced a whole new line of flavors.

Milk sales continued to slump, and, in early 1995, faced with the necessity of replacing two extremely old paperboard carton machines in its plant, the company decided to look to its past for inspiration for its future. According to president Scottie Mayfield, "[W]e knew the company was going to make in investment in equipment, the question was if there was a better way for us to package our milk. . . . It was a big decision, going in a completely different direction than any dairy had ever tried . . . [b]ut we thought it was the best way to appeal to on-the-go consumers and get them to drink more milk," he was quoted in a 2004 *Dairy Field* article. So, in September 1995, Mayfield introduced an entirely new package: a plastic bottle shaped like an old-fashioned glass milk bottle. The bottle—called a

Chug—featured a twist-on, resealable, tamper-evident cap and fit in a car cup holder, both of which features helped it compete with single-serve juices and sodas.

Unfortunately, the new bottle did not initially attract many of Mayfield Dairy's regular vending customers whose vending machines were equipped only to handle paperboard cartons. As a result of the switch, the company immediately lost about 40 percent of its vending customers. Other vendors accommodated Mayfield; however they remained tentative about customer response because of the accompanying need to increase pricing. In the end, though, customers voted heartily in favor of the Chug packaging, and, by 1996, the company's vending business was slowly returning back to its paperboard levels. Soon, Mayfield was adding products to its line of Chug products, including lemonade and Jungle Juice. "On one hand, the customers who stuck with us have all seen increases in sales . . . on the other hand, now that the word has gotten out about how well the old-style bottle is doing in the vending machines, we are getting new inquiries from customers," Scottie Mayfield could recall proudly in a 1996 *Beverage World* article.

At the same time, poor weather in 1996 led to high costs for soybeans, corn, hay, and other feed grains for cows and put a damper on milk production. Dairy farmers had to cut back on herd size and feed their cows less. The cost of milk cost increased to between $2.50 and $3.00 per gallon. The situation continued through 1997 leading to only modest annual increases in dairy consumption overall and no growth in fluid milk. Regardless of the poor market, Mayfield, as a subsidiary of a large conglomerate, Dean Foods, continued to grow. By 1996, the company was building a new milk processing plant on a 20-acre site in Braselton, Tennessee. The plant had the capacity to receive milk seven days a week. Raw milk was stored in 50,000-gallon silos, and cream was stored in 8,000-gallon cream silos. Mix-proof valves in the receiving area, eliminated the need to disconnect hoses when switching from pumping milk out of a truck to cleaning the truck. The 70,000-square foot project cost upwards of $15 million to build and included a visitors center with ice cream parlor, gift shop, and a theater. It processed 150,000 gallons of skim, 2-percent, whole, and chocolate milk per day. The plant serviced the Georgia, South Carolina, and North Carolina school markets with gallon and half-gallon plastic bottles and half-pint cartons of milk.

Growth continued for the company through the rest of the 1990s. In 1997, Mayfield purchased Tri-State Dairy's facilities in Georgia and used the buildings acquired as distribution centers for milk and ice cream. By 1997, Mayfield was processing 50 million gallons of milk and 12 million gallons of ice cream in 30 flavors annually. In 1999, it became the official milk of Zoo Atlanta through the year 2001. In commemoration of its 75th anniversary that year, it introduced its milk in old-fashioned glass milk bottles.

2000 and Beyond: Focusing on Ice Cream

Mayfield entered into an alliance with Barber Dairy in 2000 to distribute Mayfield's ice cream throughout Alabama, creating a line of products called Select. Consumers reacted positively to the new line and sales rose, making Mayfield the number one brand of vanilla in Atlanta and East Tennessee.

Key Dates:

1900: Thomas B. Mayfield, Jr., begins a dairy operation with 45 Jersey cows.
1923: Mayfield Creamery begins operations in Athens, Tennessee.
1937: Thomas B. Mayfield, Jr., dies and Thomas B. Mayfield III takes over the company.
1950: Mayfield Dairy completes construction of a new milk facility.
1977: The company purchases the Aristocrat Ice Cream Company.
1990: Dean Foods Company purchases Mayfield Dairy.
1995: The company adds four additional distribution facilities in Georgia.
1997: Mayfield began production at its new milk plant in Braselton, Georgia; company purchases the facilities of Tri-State Dairy on Georgia.
2000: Mayfield forms an alliance with Barber Dairy.

In 2002, Mayfield expanded its ice cream products and services. At this point, it replaced Barber's ice cream with its full Classic line, adding novelties such as its Brown Cows, Fudge Bars, ice cream sandwiches, and Banana Pops. Also in 2002, it introduced packaging for its ice cream with the new "click-top" ice cream lid.

Between 2000 and 2002, Mayfield invested $17 million in plant modernization and expansion and established seven addi-tional distribution centers, six in Alabama and one in Florida. Also in 2002, the company introduced a new ice cream package made of millennium board, a paper product that improved insulation, better preserving freshness, while reducing crushing and damage.

In 2004, the dairy industry experienced the biggest price hike ever, an increase of 50 to 60 cents per gallon of milk. Mayfield, however, remained strong, adding low-carb ice cream to its line and continuing to develop new flavors. "We're trying our best to sometimes get ahead of and sometimes catch up and try to stay with consumers and their needs," Scottie Mayfield announced in an Associated Press wire.

Further Reading

Behrendt, Cathy, "Dean Foods Reinvents Milk," *Business and Industry*, September 1997, p. 26.
Dudlicek, James, "Chugging Along," *Dairy Field*, October 2004, p. 1.
Mans, Jack, "Georgia on Their Minds," *Dairy Foods*, March 1999, p. 53.
"Packaging That 'Works Right Now' Helps Sell the Good at Mayfield Dairy," *BrandPackaging*, January 2003, p. 30.
Schackleford, Chris, "A Family Scoop: For Four Generations the Mayfield Family Has Been a Step Ahead of Consumer's Tastes in New Trends and Flavors in Ice Cream," *Chattanooga Free Press*, December 1997, p. 11.
Sfiligoj, Eric, "Bring Your Milk Money and Spare Some Change for Water," *Beverage World*, May 31, 1996, p. 18.

—Carrie Rothburd

Mecalux S.A.

Avda Gran Via 72-78
L'Hospitalet de Llobregat
E-08902
Spain
Telephone: (+34) 93 261 69 00
Fax: (+34) 93 336 02 60
Web site: http://www.mecalux.com

Public Company
Incorporated: 1966; 1969 as Mecalux
Employees: 2,100
Sales: EUR 241.5 million ($312 million) (2004)
Stock Exchanges: Madrid
Ticker Symbol: MLX
NAIC: 337215 Showcase, Partition, Shelving, and Locker
    Manufacturing; 423440 Other Commercial Equipment
    Merchant Wholesalers

Mecalux S.A. specializes in the design and manufacturing of warehousing systems, specifically the production of shelving systems. The Spanish company is that country's market leader, claiming a share of some 50 percent of the domestic market. Spain is also Mecalux's largest market, accounting for roughly half of its sales, which topped EUR 241 million ($312 million) in 2004. In addition, Mecalux is a major player in the heavily fragmented European shelving market, claiming market leadership in France, Italy, Greece, and Portugal. Together, the European market represents 74 percent of the group's revenues. Overall, Mecalux's share of the European market is estimated at 7 percent. Farther abroad, the company also holds a leading share of the Argentinian market. The South American market as a whole accounts for 4 percent of sales, while the U.S. market generated 17 percent of the group's revenues in 2004. Mecalux supports its international presence with manufacturing facilities in a number of markets, including Mexico (Tijuana), Poland (Gliwice), the United States (Chicago), France (Toulouse), and Argentina (Buenos Aires), as well as sales and marketing subsidiaries in a number of countries. Altogether, Mecalux is present in some 50 countries. In 2004, the company acquired fellow Spanish warehousing systems group Esmena. Mecalux also operates subsidiary Logismarket, which produces an industrial directory featuring more than 20,000 logistics, storage, packaging, and industry equipment products. Mecalux has also begun a diversification into automated warehouse systems, developing robotics-based systems for the automatic handling of boxes and pallets. The company's fourth division is its publishing division, Mecalux News, which publishes a monthly Spanish-language magazine for the logistics and warehousing markets and a corresponding French-language quarterly. In 2005, the company boosted its robotics division with the acquisition of the automated storage systems division of the ThyssenKrupp group. Mecalux is listed on the Madrid Stock Exchange but remains dominated by the founding Carillo family, which holds more than 56 percent of the company's shares. Founder José Luis Carillo remains the company's president.

Origins as a Shelving Firm in the 1960s

José Luis Carrillo opened a small workshop in Barcelona in 1966, where he began producing lightweight metal shelves for the area's stores and warehouses. Demand for Carrillo's shelves grew quickly, and by 1969 Carrillo decided to industrialize production. Carrillo incorporated his company as Mecalux that year, and at the same time launched Mecalux beyond the local market. In support of this, Mecalux opened sales offices in Seville, Valencia, and Madrid. By 1972, Mecalux had expanded its sales network to include all of Spain. Backing the company's expansion was the opening of its first large-scale facility. The 3,000-square-meter building opened in 1970.

The increased capacity enabled Mecalux to extend its operations from its base in shelving production to include a wider range of warehousing functions. As part of this effort, the company began developing its own pallet racket systems and products in 1974. The success of this line helped Mecalux achieve strong growth through the 1970s. In order to meet demand, the company expanded its production and warehousing facilities, doubling the size of its main facility.

Spain's economic boom in the late 1970s and early 1980s, following the death of Francisco Franco and the development of a democratic government, provided a strong market for Mecalux's growth. The company quickly established itself as one of the country's leading shelving and warehousing systems producers. By the end of the 20th century, Mecalux had claimed the outright lead in the market, with some 50 percent of the total Spanish shelving market.

Mecalux also successfully turned toward the international market. In 1982, the company entered neighboring France, setting up a sales office in Paris. The company soon imposed itself on the French market, later becoming the market leader in that country. At the same time, Mecalux made its first expansion overseas, launching a production subsidiary in Argentina in 1984. Supported by a 6,000-square-meter facility there, Mecalux became the dominant shelving producer in that market as well.

Back at home, Mecalux moved into a new headquarters building in Barcelona in 1984. At the same time, the company expanded its product line again, now extending its operations to include turnkey warehousing systems. The company also boosted its production capacity at mid-decade, opening a new 35,000-square-meter plant in Cornella, in Barcelona, in 1986.

With this increased capacity, Mecalux was able to turn its attention toward conquering new markets. The company moved into the United Kingdom and Germany, establishing sales offices in these markets. By the beginning of the 1990s, the company had boosted its operations in France and Portugal as well. In both of these countries, Mecalux became the leading player in the shelving and warehousing systems markets.

Public Offering in the 1990s

Mecalux's continued advance into the international shelving and warehousing market encouraged it to invest nearly EUR 8 million in order to reequip and expand its main Cornella plant by 1994. The company continued opening sales offices in Portugal, then turned to Italy in 1995, opening its first sales office there.

In order to step up its expansion, Mecalux sought new capital in the mid-1990s. The company first turned to the institutional market, generating more than EUR 19 million from an investment group led by Mercapital. With this funding, the company launched construction of a new 15,0000-square-meter logistics facility in Barcelona. Mecalux also extended its operations into the publishing realm, with the debut of Mecalux News. Devoted to the logistics market, the magazine grew into a monthly with a Spanish circulation of 30,000. The company later added a French-language version, which it published as a quarterly.

Mecalux targeted the Americas for growth in the late 1990s, adding a sales branch in Chile in 1996. In 1997, the company supported its entry into the North American market with the opening of a manufacturing plant in Tijuana, Mexico. Production at the facility, which boasted some 30,000 square meters of production space, was launched in 1998.

Following completion of the Tijuana plant, Mecalux added sales offices in Tijuana and Monterrey, in Mexico, as well as in Los Angeles. The U.S. market became one of the company's fastest growing markets and by the mid-2000s represented some 17 percent of group sales.

Closer to home, the company added production capacity in France, buying a facility in Toulouse. That plant enabled the company to extend its range with light shelving products, such as for use in filing cabinets. Mecalux also extended its range to include office partitioning systems.

Mecalux continued to add sales branches, opening offices in Bologna and Padua, in Italy, and in Bordeaux, France, in 1998. The company turned to the Eastern European market the following year, with the opening of its first branches in Poland and the Czech Republic. Also in 1999, Mecalux went public, listing its shares on the Madrid and Barcelona Stock Exchanges. José Luis Carrillo, who still served as president of the company, continued to maintain a direct controlling stake of more than 56 percent, with his shareholding extended to some 70 percent through indirect holdings.

International Leader for the 21st Century

Mecalux's international network grew again in 2000 with an entry into Belgium and Austria, as well as new offices opened in Poland and the Czech Republic. The company's interest in the Eastern European market received a new boost the following year, when Mecalux launched construction of a new plant in Gliwice, Poland. The initial phase of the facility featured 25,000 square meters of production space, costing the company some EUR 28 million.

The year 2001 also marked two important milestones for the company. The first was the creation of subsidiary Logismarket, in partnership with Accenture. Logismarket served as a business-to-business catalog and portal for the international logistics community, backed by a print catalog with a European circulation of 225,000, as well as a CD-ROM edition with a circulation of 270,000, and a Web site, Logismarket.com, with a directory listing more than 2,500 companies and more than 22,000 products.

The second milestone of 2001 was Mecalux's decision to diversify into a fast-emerging warehousing category: robotics and automated systems. In support of this effort, the company created a new division, Mecalux Robotica, which began developing a line of automated warehouse systems. The division grew quickly, and by the middle of the 2000s represented more than 10 percent of company sales.

The company continued adding new branches, extending its reach in Spain and France in 2001, and boosting its Italian presence with the opening of a larger office and warehouse facility in Milan in 2002. In the meantime, the company pre-

Key Dates:

1966: José Luis Carrillo begins producing light metal shelves in a workshop in Barcelona.

1969: The company incorporates as Mecalux and launches industrial production.

1970: A new 3,000-square-meter production plant opens.

1974: The business expands into pallet racking systems.

1982: The company expands internationally, opening a sales office in Paris, France.

1984: Mecalux enters Argentina with a 6,000-square-meter production plant.

1986: The company launches construction of new 35,000-square-meter plant in Cornellá, Barcelona.

1991: Mecalux expands into the United Kingdom and Portugal.

1995: The company enters Italy.

1997: Mecalux builds a 30,000-square-meter plant in Tijuana, Mexico, and expands into the North American market.

1999: The company goes public, listing on the Madrid and Barcelona Stock Exchanges, and enters Poland and the Czech Republic.

2001: Mecalux debuts its b2b directory and Web site Logismarket, creates an automated warehouse systems division (Mecalux Robotica), builds a production plant in Gliwice, Poland, and completes the first phase of a 280,000-square-foot plant outside of Chicago.

2004: Esmena, in Spain, is acquired.

2005: Mecalux acquires the automated storage systems division of the ThyssenKrupp group.

pared to accelerate its penetration of the U.S. market. In 2001, the company began construction of a massive 280,000-square-feet production facility in Melrose Park, Illinois, near Chicago. The first phase of the plant launched production in early 2002.

By then, Mecalux had already established itself as the market leader in much of southern Europe. The company then targeted the northern European market for future growth. In 2002, Mecalux launched a new drive to expand into the region, especially into the German market, supported by the opening of new sales branches in Hamburg, Stuttgart, Munich, Frankfurt, and Dusseldorf. In that year, the company also added new branches to its French subsidiary, which now boasted 12 sales centers throughout France.

The downturn of the international economy at the beginning of the 2000s put a crimp into Mecalux's growth. By 2004, however, the company was ready to launch a new growth effort. Mecalux now turned toward acquisitions for its expansion, reaching an agreement to acquire fellow Spanish company Esmena in 2004. Esmena was founded in 1956 and launched its own shelving operations in the late 1990s before being acquired by steel group Corporación Gestamp in 2000.

As Mecalux finalized the Esmena acquisition in the first half of 2005, it continued to seek acquisition opportunities. The next purchase came in July 2005, when the company reached an agreement to purchase the automated storage systems division of Germany's ThyssenKrupp group for EUR 5.25 million ($6.1 million). The acquisition complemented two aspects of Mecalux's growth strategy, boosting its northern European presence while at the same time enhancing its robotics operations. By then, Mecalux claimed a 7 percent share of Europe's fragmented warehouse systems market and ranked among the market's world leaders.

Principal Subsidiaries

Mecalux Argentina, S.A.; Mecalux Belgium, S.A.; Mecalux Brasil, Ltda.; Mecalux Chile, Ltda.; Mecalux Estantes, Lda. (Portugal); Mecalux France; Mecalux Gmbh A(Germany); Mecalux Levante, S.A.; Mecalux Mexico, S.A. De C.V.; Mecalux Milano, S.R.L. (Italy); Mecalux Servis, S.A.; Mecalux Servis, S.A.; Mecalux Sp. Z O.O. (Poland); Mecalux U.K. Ltd; Mecalux USA, Inc.; S.Gallardo, SL

Principal Competitors

Siemens Dematic; FKI plc; Daifuku Co., Ltd; Schaefer Holding International, GmbH; Murata Machinery Ltd; Swisslog Holding, Ab; Kardex AG; Columbus McKinnon Corporation; Vanderlande Industries BV.

Further Reading

"Mecalux," *Material Handling Management*, December 2002, p. 53.
"Mecalux to Open New Manufacturing Plant," *Modern Materials Handling*, January 2001, p. 27.

—M.L. Cohen

The Melting Pot Restaurants, Inc.

8810 Twin Lakes Boulevard
Tampa, Florida 33614
U.S.A.
Telephone: (813) 881-0055
Toll Free: (800) 783-0867
Fax: (813) 889-9361
Web site: http://www.meltingpot.com

Private Company
Incorporated: 1985
Employees: 2,300
Sales: $115 million (2004 est.)
NAIC: 722110 Full-Service Restaurants

The Melting Pot Restaurants, Inc., is a Tampa, Florida-based private company that operates the largest fondue restaurant chain in the United States, comprising more than 85 units, most of which are franchised operations. While the chain is a player in the romantic dining niche, Melting Pot's upscale dining experience is also a popular choice for social gatherings and corporate dinner parties. Customers do their own cooking at the table using inset burners while the wait staff provides the ingredients, regulates the heat, and observes for customer safety. Because a full-course fondue meal is a time-consuming experience, lasting at least two hours, table turnover is limited. However, Melting Pot makes up for this disadvantage by saving on kitchen staff due to simple prep needs and by commanding an average check of around $40, aided in large part by the sale of a broad line of wines, cognacs, cordials, and specialty drinks. At some units, the chain is also adding late-night business for customers looking for dessert fondue and wine after a night out. Unlike the simple fondue offerings from an earlier era, Melting Pot offers a four-course meal: choice of a cheese fondue as an appetizer, choice of salad, an entree, and a chocolate fondue dessert with such dipping ingredients as strawberries, bananas, pineapple, cheesecake, marshmallows, and pound cake. Entrees include steak, chicken, duck, lobster, shrimp, and a vegetarian offering. They are paired with such dipping sauces as gorgonzola port, lemon pepper, Louisiana hot sauce, teriyaki glaze, curry, horseradish, and garlic

Dijon butter. The chain has also upgraded the cooking medium, which was once limited to peanut oil. Entree cooking can now be done Coq au Vin, which relies on Burgundy wine, mushrooms, garlic, and fresh herbs; Court Bouillon, a seasoned vegetable broth low in salt and cholesterol free; Bourguignonne, which employs canola oil and fondue batters; Majo, a Caribbean broth flavored with citrus and garlic. Melting Pot is run by chief executive officer Mark Johnston and his brother Robert Johnston, president and chief operating officer.

Fondue's Popularity Peaks in the 1970s

A Swiss tradition, fondue began to gain exposure in the United States following World War II. In the mid-1950s, New York's Chalet Swiss restaurant began cooking meat cubes in hot oil in a communal pot creating Fondue Bourguignonne, making fondue dining a common pastime. It became even more popular during the 1960s when the restaurant introduced chocolate fondue. As a result, the fondue pot became a standard wedding gift, one which, after being used on one or two occasions, was generally relegated to the closet, primarily because using it involved laborious procedures, including the preparation of sauces to achieve a variety of flavors. Fondue restaurants cropped up to relieve diners of the tedious chores of fondue cooking, and they prospered into the 1970s before customers grew tired of the limited fare and the novelty of sharing a community pot wore off. Coming in at the tail end of the trend, businessmen Bruce Knoechel and Roy Nelson opened the first Melting Pot restaurant in Maitland, Florida, close to Orlando. It was a modest operation consisting of four tables and a two-course menu: Swiss cheese fondue and beef fondue done in the Bourguignonne style. The restaurant was successful enough to lead Knoechel and Nelson to open a second location in Orlando in 1976.

Mark Johnston, while working his way through college, was an employee at the Maitland restaurant. He became enamored with the fondue concept and convinced the owners to grant him a franchise. Using his savings, he tried to open restaurants in Orlando and Tampa, but he was unable to obtain a liquor license in Tampa and entering the Orlando market proved too expensive. It was not until 1979 that he was able to bring in his brothers, Mike and Bob, the latter still in high school, and, with

Company Perspectives:

The Melting Pot provides a unique, upscale and intimate dining experience with its assortment of fondue, cooked at the table by the guests. It is the perfect location of a romantic evening, corporate dinner party or friendly gathering.

$14,000 they scraped together, open the first Melting Pot franchise restaurant, located in the basement of a Tallahassee oyster bar. The fondue restaurant did well enough to enable the Johnston brothers to open their second Melting Pot two years later, in 1981, in a Tampa location.

Johnston Brothers Take Over Melting Pot in the Mid-1980s

Aside from the Johnston brothers franchise, Knoechel and Nelson franchised only one other unit, which opened in Gainesville, Florida, in 1984. The Johnston brothers wanted to add more restaurants, but they also wanted to be part of a franchise system set up and committed to growth, something that Knoechel and Nelson were not prepared to do. Thus, in 1985, the brothers bought out the Melting Pot founders, who then served as mentors to the young men, encouraging them to pursue their goals and buoying their belief in the Melting Pot concept. The Johnstons formed a franchise development company and quickly added two new company-owned stores, in Clearwater and St. Petersburg, Florida. Trying to run their restaurants while also acting as a franchiser proved difficult, resulting in slower growth than the brothers anticipated.

The next decade turned into a trial-and-error phase, as the brothers added franchised units (generally one or two a year, often awarded to regular Melting Pot customers) and refined the elements of the Melting Pot concept. In some respects, they reinvented the fondue niche, their goal being to create an upscale restaurant with a high check average. To support greater franchising, they beefed up their business structure, in particular the training program for franchisees. They also honed their marketing approach, which in the beginning was based almost solely on simplistic considerations of demographics and location and led to the establishment of Melting Pots in some areas that were either too seasonal or transient. In addition, the chain often settled for B sites in shopping centers that had limited visibility. These units were ultimately closed. The marketing message was also in need of fine tuning, originally positioning the restaurant as the kind of place to bring out-of-town friends who did not have a Melting Pot at home. The Johnstons conducted focus groups of loyal customers, first-time customers, and customers who had not dined at a Melting Pot recently. Out of the accumulated information, the company was able to determine the nature of Melting Pot's core customers, then employed more sophisticated demographic tools to locate markets with the highest concentrations of that customer profile. Melting Pot now gravitated to A sites that had more drive-by traffic and were located in high density bedroom communities with larger amounts of disposable income. As a result, sites fitting this new profile experienced much higher sales. The new marketing message portrayed Melting Pot as the kind of special restaurant that out-of-town friends would want to visit *because* their commu-

nity had one and they liked the social experience. The Johnstons also wanted to portray Melting Pot as a place to go any night of the week, while at the same time maintaining the focus on the event-dining experience Melting Pot had to offer.

Another key element in refining the restaurant's business model involved the menu. In the early years, the chain added variety but made the mistake of offering combinations that allowed customers to sample every item on the menu, thus offering them little incentive to make a return visit in the near future. Melting Pot therefore reworked its offerings, which helped create repeat business. In the 1990s, when diners had become more health conscious, Melting Pot supplemented the menu with such items as pork, duck, lobster, and shrimp in the Bourguignonne style. The chain also added the other fondue styles of cooking meat cubes in broth.

By 1995, when the chain totaled 26 units, Melting Pot was ready to ramp up its franchising efforts. In that year, the company introduced a new training program for franchisees, and throughout the rest of the 1990s Melting Pot opened three to five new restaurants each year. After initially focusing on Florida, Melting Pot branched out to Georgia and the Carolinas before targeting the Midwest and Mid-Atlantic states as well as Arizona. Of the new restaurants that opened in 1996, for example, one was in Buffalo Grove, Illinois, and another in Columbus, Ohio. The chain enjoyed particular success attracting franchisees who did not have experience in restaurant ownership and management because their lack of expertise could be remedied by the company's strong training program. Furthermore, the Melting Pot concept was relatively simple and low in cost for an upscale dining operation. As one franchisee explained to *Chain Leader* in a 2003 company profile, ''What was appealing is that overhead is low. There are no ovens, fryers or hood systems. And you don't have to hire a chef and give him 50 percent of the profits to develop great menu items.''

This mid-1990s expansion phase was supported by across-the-board upgrades. In 1997, a new logo was introduced as well as a new ad campaign that emphasized the refined message that Melting Pot was an out-of-the-ordinary dining experience not limited to a special occasion but perfect for any night of the week. The chain rolled out a revamped menu in the same year that added eight new entrees. In addition, the wine list was expanded. Consumer research also resulted in other changes: larger portions, better presentation, and front of the house staff was increased. A server assistant was introduced to cater to guests, making sure water glasses were refilled, serving coffee, and helping out as necessary. Moreover, the chain updated its look, which was intended to make the decor more attractive to male customers. All too often, women had come to a Melting Pot for a festive night with their friends, but they failed to return with boyfriends and husbands. The chain's earth tones were now replaced with bolder colors: purple, mustard, and gaucho green. Beige floor tiles gave way to carpeting, tables and booths were enlarged, and lighting made brighter. To keep the conversion costs to a minimum for franchisees, Melting Pot hired a Tampa company to build the tables, booths, and lights, which were then trucked to the restaurants and installed by representatives of the designer and builder. New restaurants also took advantage of the arrangement to reduce the time it took to open from 120 days to 90 days.

Accelerated Growth in the 2000s

In 2001, Melting Pot picked up the pace by adding new restaurants, opening ten to reach 46 units in size, only four of which were company owned. The chain opened another ten in both 2002 and 2003. To keep the concept fresh, in 2002 Melting Pot hired a new director of design, Amy Gil, who brought a new interior look to the restaurants, which now included artwork from local artists. "As for interior colors," in the words of *Chain Leader,* "the older deep purple, mustard yellow, dark olive and rust are being replaced with softer purples, light olive and burgundy. Ceilings are painted a mossy gold. . . . 'We want to have a feeling that makes a guest say, "It's all about me"',' says Gil. 'They have to be comfortable enough to sit for several hours.' " One challenge she faced was creating intimate spaces for couples while accommodating large parties, since, unlike other restaurants, the electrical wiring at Melting Pot precluded moving tables together. The new interior design allowed Melting Pot to accommodate groups from eight to more than 40, while glass panels between booths provided the privacy couples desired.

Another part of the ongoing refinement of the Melting Pot concept involved the beverage program, with alcohol accounting for about 20 percent of sales. Wine rooms were added so that some of the restaurants were able to offer as many as 250 different wines. In addition to achieving greater variety, the chain helped to boost alcohol sales, and check averages, by pairing appropriate wines with entrees in the menu. Servers were also trained to make wine suggestions.

Melting Pot reached the $100 million mark in systemwide sales in 2002. The expansion pace again picked up in 2004 as the chain added 16 new locations, and in 2005 it planned to celebrate its 30th anniversary by opening its 100th restaurant. By 2010, the Johnstons hoped to reach 175 units, primarily taking advantage of opportunities in the Midwest and West, as well as some growth possibilities in the Northeast, in particular Long Island. The company was also exploring the possibility of taking the Melting Pot concept international.

Principal Competitors

The Cheesecake Factory Inc.; Main Street Restaurant Group Inc.; Wolfgang Puck Worldwide, Inc.

Further Reading

Bruno, Karen, "Melting Pot Revitalizes Fondue as 12th Unit Opens," *Nation's Restaurant News,* January 12, 1987, p. 2.

Clancy, Carole, "Melting Pot Stirs Up Plans to Expand, Updates Its look, Menu," *Tampa Bay Business Journal,* September 26, 1997.

Frumpkin, Paul, "Melting Pot Dips into Past to Resurrect Fondue-Inspired Eatery," *Nation's Restaurant News,* July 22, 2002, p. 24.

Meadows, Andrew, "Melting Pot Restaurant Chain Experiences Unprecedented Growth," *Tampa Tribune,* July 26, 2003.

Smith, Devlin, "And Now For Something Different," *Entrepreneur.com,* February 11, 2002.

Walkup, Carolyn, "Melting Pot Takes Fondue Concept into the Future," *Nation's Restaurant News,* March 10, 1997, p. 130.

Whitaker, Aja, "Brothers Find Fondue Secret to Success," *Business Journal* (Tampa), January 10, 2003, p. 4.

Zimmerman, Christine, "Slam Dunk," *Chain Leader,* April 2003, p. 49.

—Ed Dinger

Meredith Corporation

1716 Locust Street
Des Moines, Iowa 50309-3023
U.S.A.
Telephone: (515) 284-3000
Toll Free: (800) 284-4236
Fax: (515) 284-2700
Web site: http://www.meredith.com

Public Company
Incorporated: 1905
Employees: 2696
Sales: $1.22 billion (2005)
Stock Exchanges: New York
Ticker Symbol: MDP
NAIC: 511120 Periodical Publishers; 511130 Book
    Publishers; 513112 Radio Stations; 513120 Television
    Broadcasting

Meredith Corporation is a leading U.S. media company that is focused primarily on magazines and broadcasting. It is best known for publishing two of America's most popular magazines: *Better Homes and Gardens* and *Ladies' Home Journal*. About 75 percent of the diversified media company's revenue comes from its magazine business, which publishes 17 major brands plus about 160 special interest titles. The company also has more than 300 books in print, including the best-selling, red-and-white checkerboard-covered *Better Homes and Gardens Cookbook*. In addition, the company owns and operates 14 television stations, primarily in smaller markets such as Flint, Michigan, and Ocala, Florida, as well as one radio station. Meredith's diverse media projects focus for the most part on home and family. It maintains a large consumer database and has two-dozen Web sites, as well as extensive licensing agreements.

Early History

The seeds that started the Meredith Corporation were given to Edwin Thomas (E. T.) Meredith as a wedding present. On E.T. Meredith's wedding day, his grandfather gave him several gold pieces, the controlling interest in his newspaper, and a note that said, "Sink or swim." After returning his grandfather's newspaper to financial health, Meredith sold it for a profit and began publishing a service-oriented farm magazine called *Successful Farming* in 1902. The magazine grew quickly, from a starting circulation of 500 to more than half a million subscribers by 1914. The staff had grown proportionately, from five employees in 1902 to almost 200 in 1912. In 1999, the company had more than 2,500 employees and still occupied the same building that was established as company headquarters in 1912. The building went through some expansion, including an $18 million renovation completed in 1980.

After serving a year as Woodrow Wilson's Secretary of Agriculture, E.T. Meredith returned to his company in 1920 and decided to publish more magazines. In 1922, the company purchased one magazine, *Dairy Farmer,* and launched another, *Fruit, Garden and Home.* Meredith tried to make *Dairy Farmer* a national success for five years before merging it with *Successful Farming.* Unable to make a profit until 1927, *Fruit, Garden and Home,* a magazine similar to *Successful Farming* for the home and family, had start-up difficulties as well. At first, advertisers paid $450 per black-and-white page in *Fruit, Garden and Home,* as opposed to *Successful Farming*'s rate of $1,800 per black-and-white page. After a name change in 1924 to *Better Homes and Gardens,* the magazine's fortunes turned around, allowing it to command $1,800 per black-and-white page of advertising by 1925.

By the time of E.T. Meredith's death in 1928, the year he was considered a candidate for the U.S. presidency, *Better Homes and Gardens* and *Successful Farming* had reached a combined circulation of 2.5 million. After World War II, *Better Homes and Gardens* had surpassed *McCall's, Good Housekeeping,* and *Ladies' Home Journal* to become the leading monthly magazine. Holding a circulation of about eight million for more than two decades, *Better Homes and Gardens* remained a powerful magazine into the 1990s, when it ranked third largest in the United States, behind only *Reader's Digest* and *National Geographic.*

Meredith capitalized on the success of *Better Homes and Gardens* magazine and began publishing the *Better Homes and*

Gardens Cook Book in 1930. Magazine subscribers received complimentary copies of the first edition, and book sales grew rapidly. The cookbook became one of the best-selling hardback books in America, with more than 29 million copies sold by its eleventh edition in 1995. The company has since used the *Better Homes and Gardens* name to further its profits, using it to sell special interest publications starting in 1937, to open a real estate service in 1978, and to offer garden tools at 2,000 Wal-Mart stores starting in 1994.

Diversification in the Postwar Years

To raise the capital necessary to diversify its interests, the company began offering stock to the public in 1946. Over the next ten years, Meredith bought three television stations and opened a commercial printing business. By 1965, the company was listed on the New York Stock Exchange. By 1969, the company had formed a printing partnership with the Burda family of West Germany, which would grow into one of the largest printing businesses in the United States.

In 1978, Meredith began a franchise-operated real estate business under the "Better Homes and Gardens" name. "It's a natural extension of the product franchise," Meredith chairperson Robert Burnett told *Advertising Age*. By 1985, the business challenged established realtors like Century 21 and Coldwell Banker, according to *Advertising Age*. The real estate business had grown to include about 700 firms, which owned and operated about 1,300 offices and had 24,000 sales associates by 1994. Company headquarters supplied the franchisees with marketing, management, and sales training information.

Although Meredith was publicly owned, it had a long history of only cautiously seeking investors. In 1985, however, it turned into "a very different kind of company," Paine Webber analyst J. Kendrick Noble told *Advertising Age*. At that time, Meredith began welcoming interest in its operations. Meredith also started sponsoring art exhibits in New York and giving presentations to security analysts. The change occurred to fuel a growth strategy that helped make it a Fortune 500 company.

At the beginning of the 1980s, Meredith's interests included a printing business, a fulfillment system, a real estate franchise, four television stations, and three magazines: *Better Homes and Gardens, Metropolitan Home,* and *Successful Farming.* The company expanded quickly during the 1980s, entering the video market with Meredith Video Publishing, purchasing

three television stations, launching seven new magazines, publishing a Korean edition of *Better Homes and Gardens* magazine (an Australian edition had been published since 1978), and purchasing *Ladies' Home Journal,* the sixth largest women's service magazine when ranked by circulation at the time of the purchase in 1986.

Focusing in the 1990s

Despite its acquisitions and expansion, however, the company soon floundered. In 1992, Meredith had a net loss of $6.3 million. In response, management decided to streamline Meredith, ridding the company of ancillary businesses. To soften the blow of a nationwide advertising slump it felt in its magazines and television stations, Meredith sold its 50 percent interest in the Meredith/Burda printing partnership to R.R. Donnelley & Sons Company of Chicago in 1990. Given the high costs of remaining competitive in the printing business, Meredith president Jack Rehm felt the sale was smart, telling *Business Record,* "We had to make a choice to either get bigger or else to get out. We felt we could better use our resources in our other businesses and depart the printing business." To further streamline, Meredith sold its fulfillment business to Neodata of Boulder, Colorado, in 1991, and two television stations were sold off in 1993. Moreover, the company's work force was cut by 7 percent, to 2,000, between 1992 and 1994.

Meredith's cuts and investments allowed it to focus on what it did best. E.T. Meredith III told *Business Week* in 1994, "We're going back to what we were: a successful magazine and broadcasting company." Meredith planned to add three or four magazines per year. Realizing that advertising profits might never be as high as they were during the lucrative 1980s, the company earmarked $400 million for additional television and magazine acquisitions, according to *Business Week.* In addition, the company developed customized marketing programs that could create tailored packages of Meredith's magazine and book publishing, real estate service, and television stations for advertisers' specific needs. By 1994, company profits had started to climb again, jumping 23 percent over 1993 to $22.9 million on revenues of $799 million.

Meredith's streamlining helped the company take advantage of its unique niche, the home and family. Meredith sold its chic magazine, *Metropolitan Home,* to Hachette Filipacchi Magazines, the publishers of *Elle,* and introduced several new titles that targeted different domestic topics, such as *Country Home, Country America, WOOD, Midwest Living,* and *American Patchwork & Quilting.* Meredith's new magazines met with significant success, with growing circulations of 200,000 to one million. Shari Wall, senior vice-president at J. Walter Thompson in Chicago, noted Meredith's fortuitous position in the market, telling *Business Week* that "their thrust of family and home is the hot thing for the 1990s." Meredith, too, eagerly publicized its area of focus. In 1993, the company launched an advertising campaign for its magazine group that asserted "If it has to do with home and family, it has to be in Meredith." The campaign featured black-and-white pictures of real families having fun together.

Although Meredith promoted itself aggressively to advertisers, it relied most heavily on its subscribers, who fueled the company's rebound. Circulation for most of the company's

Key Dates:

1902: E.T. Meredith begins publishing *Successful Farming.*
1922: *Dairy Farmer* and *Fruit, Garden and Home* magazines are acquired.
1924: *Fruit, Garden and Home* is renamed *Better Homes and Gardens.*
1930: A *Better Homes and Gardens* cookbook is launched.
1936: The company offers shares to the public.
1948: Meredith enters the television broadcasting business.
1965: Meredith lists on the New York Stock Exchange.
1986: *Ladies' Home Journal* is acquired.
1993: Meredith's Des Moines headquarters is flooded.
1998: Revenues top $1 billion; *More* magazine launched.
2002: Meredith buys *American Baby* for $115 million.
2005: The company posts a year of record revenue; Meredith buys titles from Gruner + Jahr for $350 million.

magazines was up in 1993, but company president Jack Rehm told the *New York Times* that "the reason we have succeeded with so many magazine titles in the last several years is that we are able to get readers to really pay for the magazines. We must count much more on the reader to generate the revenue stream than the advertiser. Historically, that has not been true, and magazines who were overly dependent on advertising were the ones who really suffered." In 1993, Meredith's magazine subscription and newsstand revenues accounted for 32.2 percent of the company revenues, or $257.45 million, and magazine advertising revenues made up 29.6 percent, with $236.81 million.

Meredith's *Better Homes and Gardens* magazine proved a good example of the company's success in managing large publications. *Better Homes and Gardens* led the shelter magazine industry in ad revenues and pages in 1988, offering its advertisers an audience four times the size of its next competitor, according to *Marketing and Media Decisions.* A four-color page cost $103,480 in *Better Homes and Gardens;* in *Architectural Digest, Better Homes and Gardens'* closest competitor in shelter magazines, a similar advertisement cost $28,490. According to some analysts, *Better Homes and Gardens'* fortunes can be traced to the trend toward home and hearth that started in the late 1980s and early 1990s; the magazine benefited because it bridged the home and women's service categories.

Meredith took a conservative approach to changing its flagship magazine, refusing to bow to the shifting winds of publishing fashion. For example, when faced with "single, disenfranchised dropouts" at advertising agencies in the 1960s who were "insulted that we would continue to publish [*Better Homes and Gardens*] when [they] didn't think it should exist," Burnett told *Advertising Age,* "It was tempting to say, 'We've got to change *Better Homes and Gardens* and get with it.' " Meredith remained committed, however, to the magazine's focus on home and family.

To keep the magazine contemporary, Meredith continually made subtle changes rather than doing major redesigns every

five years like other magazines. According to Burnett, in an article in *Advertising Age,* rapid change was likely to alienate readers. Burnett commented that "the worst thing that could happen is for your best friend to show up with a changed personality; it's a shock and a negative." The magazine's enhancements for 1994 included the addition of puzzles and games for parents and their children. The company's strategy paid off, as *Better Homes and Gardens* continued to be a leader in its category.

In 1994, Meredith's several large circulation magazines and book clubs generated a subscriber database of 63 million, the largest in the United States. Meredith began exploiting this database for profit in 1992, as the company's marketing department began using it to give editors valuable feedback on their magazine's readership, as well as to cross-promote books and magazine spin-offs, target direct mail programs for advertisers, research new markets, and test new products. The company also used the database to aid in the launch of a new magazine called *Crayola Kids,* to insert specialized ads in targeted magazines for an auto advertiser, and to put in targeted editorials in *Better Homes and Gardens* issues. The database also helped to turn around the fortunes of Meredith's book division. Despite its more than 30 years of experience in database marketing, during which it had also used rented lists, Meredith did not consider itself a very sophisticated user of its own resource. Clem Svede, vice-president and director of consumer marketing, noted in *Direct* that "when someone asks how our database is doing, we say 'We think we're at the top of our class—but we're only in the first grade.' "

In 1993, the company faced a challenge in the form of a natural disaster. Massive flooding in the Midwest that year, particularly in Iowa, reached the company's Des Moines headquarters, ruining the company's mainframe computer system. As a result, the company was forced to install a new desktop publishing network about eight months earlier than planned. Under the guidance of Robert Furstenau, director of production and technology for Meredith's magazines, the company converted to the new system in about two days. Meredith immediately purchased $400,000 worth of Macintosh computers and peripheral equipment, installed them in a rented space, and flew in software specialists from around the country to give 103 editorial employees two weeks of training information in a few hours. Despite the chaotic atmosphere, no deadlines were missed, and in the long run the desktop system has reduced the company's pre-press production costs. Furstenau told the *Des Moines Register* that the flood "has got to be one of the better things that has happened to magazine production at Meredith in a long time."

Changes in the Late 1990s

The company had floundered in the early 1990s, with erratic earnings, a rather staid image, and thin operating margins well below the publishing industry average. Yet it had great assets, particularly in its under-exploited customer database and in its *Better Homes and Gardens* brand name recognition. In 1994, the company announced ambitious plans to launch new magazine titles, buy more television stations, swing lucrative licensing deals, and expand its book publishing division. The book division ultimately did not pay off, and in 1995 the company sold its book club to Book of the Month Club and reduced its commitment to book publishing. In other areas, however, Meredith was right on track. It managed to launch new magazine titles with great skill, primarily because it learned to target audiences using its existing customer database. Although other media companies such as Hearst and Time Warner also had massive databases, Meredith's was singular in that its customers were very similar, described in a December 4, 1994 *Forbes* article as "nesters—people who are interested in their homes and in spending money to make them better." Thus it was not too difficult for Meredith to cull the list and find, for example, people with older homes: a good market for its *Traditional Home* magazine and the related *Renovation Style*. Other new titles in the mid-1990s were *American Patchwork & Quilting* and *Home Garden*. The company managed to hold costs for new magazines down to $2 million to $3 million, considered impressively low in the publishing industry, and most turned a profit within two to three years. The company also embarked on a successful licensing deal in 1994, letting mass-marketer Wal-Mart open Better Homes and Gardens Garden Centers in more than 2,000 stores. These sold gardening equipment marked with the "Better Homes and Gardens" name, as well as the magazine itself and other Meredith gardening titles. The deal with Wal-Mart led to minimum royalties of $3 million for each of the first three years and $5 million for the next two years. Meredith also brokered the *Better Homes and Gardens* name by publishing small booklets for sale at checkout counters with titles like *Garden, Deck & Landscape Planner*. The company had 40 such books by 1995 and printed a total of 35 million copies. By the mid-1990s, such brand extensions were leading to impressive earnings: the company told *Forbes* in 1995 that it derived $1.05 in income from brand extensions for every dollar of revenue the magazine *Better Homes and Gardens* earned.

In its broadcasting segment, Meredith also performed as planned. By 1996, the company had seven stations, and these contributed more than 40 percent of the firm's profit. In 1997, the company purchased three more television stations, picking them up for $435 million from First Media Television. This acquisition gave Meredith stations in Orlando, Florida; Greenville, South Carolina; and Bend, Oregon. They were small markets but increased Meredith's share of the nation's television market from 5 percent to 8 percent. By 1998, Meredith owned 11 stations, and these accounted for about 18 percent of the company's total revenue. Its stations were all in small markets, yet most of them were predicted to be strong growth areas. In late 1998, Meredith negotiated to buy its first station in a top-ten market, Atlanta's WGNX. Not only was Atlanta a major market, but it was one of the country's fastest growing television markets.

By 1999, Meredith seemed to be in very good shape. Its big advantage was that its core product—home-related publications and products—was more and more the "in" thing. The number of people aged 45 to 54 was increasing as the baby boomers aged, and this demographic tended to spend the most on home-related goods. The old-fashioned appeal of *Better Homes and Gardens* and the other Meredith publications seemed likely to be back in style with a vengeance in the coming decade. The company had managed to shed unprofitable businesses such as its real estate venture and much of its book publishing and

concentrate on what it knew best. In addition, Meredith was able to make useful cross-connections between its publishing and broadcasting sectors in order to launch, for example, a syndicated *Better Homes and Gardens* television show. Financially, the company was in record shape, with sales topping $1 billion for the first time in fiscal 1998.

Meredith's share price and earnings reached unprecedented heights in the late 1990s. *Folio: The Magazine for Magazine Management* lauded Meredith's creativity while noting fiscal prowess. *Folio* called Meredith "the gatekeeper to the American family." With its database of more than 60 million names, the company was able to tailor its marketing for the benefit of advertisers. It was also early to spot new trends. Meredith launched a new magazine in 2000 to capitalize upon the emerging popularity of scrapbooking.

In Tune in the 2000s

In the general recession following the September 11, 2001, terrorist attacks on the United States, the company worked to maintain its momentum on a number of fronts, Meredith officials told *Advertising Age*. It was developing book titles with The Learning Channel's "Trading Spaces" show in addition to its wildly successful Home Depot series, launched in 1995. *Ladies' Home Journal* was reworked to make it more enticing to advertisers. Meredith's focus on family life seemed in step with the feeling of the country after the attacks, observed *Business Week*. The baby boomers had already been aging into a time of life said to be more concerned with home furnishing and decoration.

Meredith acquired *American Baby* magazine from Primedia in December 2002 for $115 million. The new parent invested in an extensive revamping of the title, which had a circulation of two million as well as Spanish language offerings and an Internet presence.

Meredith achieved a notable milestone with its *More* magazine, launched in 1998, which had nearly tripled in circulation to one million copies. According to *Crain's New York Business,* it was the first successful lifestyle magazine aimed at women over 40.

Branding exercises at Meredith were going through some adjustment. A new line of "Better Homes and Gardens" home furnishings was being marketed through home sales reps, while the name was being dropped from the real estate brokerage.

Still Growing in 2005

Meredith reported the highest income in its history, $128.1 million, for the fiscal year ended June 30, 2005. The company continued to get bigger. On July 1, 2005, Meredith closed a $350 million deal to buy *Family Circle, Fitness, Parents, Child,* and *Ser Padres* from Gruner + Jahr Publishing USA. Gruner + Jahr's *Rosie* and *YM* magazines had folded in a circulation misstatement scandal, but observers were optimistic the titles Meredith bought would thrive under Meredith's solid circulation methods.

In addition to taking over one of *Better Homes and Gardens'* top rivals, *Family Circle,* the purchase expanded Meredith's reach with younger women and Hispanics. This enhanced its competition with giant Time Inc. and allowed Meredith to connect advertisers with females at every stage of life.

Following the purchases from Gruner + Jahr, Meredith organized its publishing operations into the Parenting Group, Women's Lifestyle Group, and Mass Reach Group. The Parenting Group was launching *Siempre Mujer* for Spanish speakers in September 2005.

With a circulation of 7.6 million, *Better Homes and Gardens,* the jewel of the Mass Reach Group, was the third largest magazine in the United States. According to *MEDIAWEEK,* Meredith was second only to Time Inc. in terms of readers. The Gruner + Jahr acquisitions lifted its combined circulation from 20 million to 30 million. Its consumer database contained 75 million names.

Former CEO and grandson of the company founder, Edwin T. "Ted" Meredith III, passed away in February 2003. He was considered responsible for keeping the company centered in Des Moines. Meredith's recent acquisitions had shifted had left it with more publishing employees in New York City than Iowa for the first time in its history, noted *Advertising Age.* A priority for then-chairman and CEO Bill Kerr was to keep the company's culture focused on the heartland, according to *Business Week.*

Kerr, who had joined Meredith in 1991 after heading the magazine group of the New York Times Co., was planning to retire in June 2006 after nine years at the top job. His likely successor was president and chief operating officer Steve Lacy, who had started with the company in 1998 as vice-president and chief financial officer.

Principal Subsidiaries

Meredith Holding Company.

Principal Divisions

Broadcasting; Publishing.

Principal Operating Units

Mass Reach Group; Parenting Group; Women's Lifestyle Group.

Principal Competitors

Hachette Filipacchi Media U.S., Inc.; Hearst Corporation; Time Inc.

Further Reading

Brown, Kathi Ann, *Meredith: The First 100 Years*, Des Moines, Iowa: Meredith Corporation, 2002.

Carmody, Deirdre, "A Focus on Home, Hearth and Profit," *New York Times*, October 4, 1993, p. C7.

Chase, Brett, "Meredith Leaves Printing Behind, Looks to Future," *Business Record*, January 13, 1992, p. 2.

Creamer, Matthew, "Meredith's First Step Is to Remove Tarnish from Titles; Good Track Record for Boosting Circulation, But G&J Scandal Lingers," *Advertising Age*, May 30, 2005, p. 4.

Cyr, Diane, "Database Magic at Meredith," *Direct*, February 1994.

Ebert, Larry Kai, "Meredith at 75: Multi-Media Expansion," *Advertising Age*, October 31, 1977, pp. 3, 78, 80.

Flamm, Matthew, "Getting Better with Age; 'More' Magazine Finds the Formula to Succeed with Women Over 40," *Crain's New York Business*, December 20, 2004, p. 3.

Granatstein, Lisa, "Baby Steps: Meredith Nurtures AB Group," *MEDIAWEEK*, January 19, 2004, pp. 3233.

——, "Media Elite: William Kerr, Chairman/CEO, Meredith Corp.," *MEDIAWEEK*, January 26, 2004, p. 29.

Ives, Nat, "Meet the Sexiest Men in Magazines, or, How Des Moines-Based Meredith Became a Hot House," *Advertising Age*, August 1, 2005, p. 1.

Kasler, Dale, "Meredith Veteran Named New Better Homes Editor," *Des Moines Register*, April 6, 1993.

——, "Meredith Will Launch "Big' Gardening Magazine," *Des Moines Register*, July 4, 1994, p. 3.

——, "The Talk of the Industry: Flood a Boon for Meredith," *Des Moines Register*, September 13, 1993.

Levin, Gary, "Meredith: Growing Up with an '800-lb. Gorilla,'" *Advertising Age*, March 11, 1985.

Lovell, Michael, "A CEO Who Loved the Outdoors, Flying and His Employees: Ted Meredith, Grandson of the Media Company's Founder, Dies at 69," *Business Record* (Des Moines), February 10, 2003.

——, "From Farming to TV, Meredith Has Grown with America," *Business Record* (Des Moines), December 9, 2002, pp. 1+.

——, "Meredith's Reach Extends Beyond Its Titles," *Business Record* (Des Moines), December 16, 2002, pp. 1, 89.

McDougall, Paul, "Meredith: Gatekeeper to the American Family," *Folio*, April 1, 1999, p. 30.

Melcher, Richard A., "Homes, Gardens—And a Tidy Turnaround," *Business Week*, August 22, 1994, pp. 55–56.

Podems, Ruth, "Serving Families for 77 Years," *Target Marketing*, September 1989, pp. 18–24.

Pollock, Jim, "Focused Style Has Lacy on Track for Meredith's Top Job," *Des Moines Business Record*, January 17, 2005, p. 8.

Schnuer, Jenna, "Publishing Executive of the Year: Stephen M. Lacy," *Advertising Age*, October 20, 2003, p. S12.

Smith, Stephanie, "The Mother of All Deals," *MEDIAWEEK*, May 30, 2005.

Weber, Joseph, "Bull's-Eye in the Heartland; Iowa's Meredith Rides the Home-and-Hearth Wave," *Business Week*, June 23, 2003, p. 54.

Weller, Sam, "Meredith Publishing and Home Depot's Effort Produces Bestsellers," *Publishers Weekly*, August 10, 1998, p. 242.

Williams, Scott, "Realtor Links Up with Chain," *Seattle Times*, July 15, 1992, p. B4.

—Sara Pendergast
—updates: A. Woodward; Frederick C. Ingram

monster

Monster Worldwide Inc.

622 3rd Avenue, 39th Floor
New York, New York 10017
U.S.A.
Telephone: (212) 351-7000
Fax: (212) 658-0541
Web site: http://www.monsterworldwide.com

Public Company
Founded: 1967 as Telephone Marketing Programs
Employees: 5,000
Gross Billings: $845.5 million (2004)
Stock Exchanges: NASDAQ
Ticker Symbol: MNST
NAIC: 541810 Advertising Agencies

Monster Worldwide Inc., formerly known as TMP Worldwide Inc., oversees the operations of Monster, the largest online career search Web site, and TMP Worldwide, one of the largest recruitment advertising agency networks in the world. With over 58 million job seeker members, Monster is the 14th most-visited Web site on the Internet. Its database is home to over 49 million resumes, which are perused by over 200,000 member companies looking for prospective employees.

Yellow Pages Specialist in the 1980s

The company was founded in 1967 by Andrew J. McKelvey as Telephone Marketing Programs, a specialist in placing advertisements in Yellow Pages telephone books. By 1980, the New York City-based company also had offices in Chicago, Los Angeles, Miami, Toronto, London, and Milan. Its gross annual billings had reached about $35 million, which, at 15 percent commission, came to more than $5 million in revenue. Telephone Marketing Systems was placing ads for clients such as Ryder Systems and Econo-Car in the nation's 5,700 directories. The company also held a three-year consulting contract with the French government.

Telephone Marketing Programs had $67.5 million in gross billings and $10 million in gross income in 1983, all stemming from Yellow Pages advertising. "We saw a tremendous opportunity to consolidate in the early 1980s," McKelvey later told Hugh Pope of the *Wall Street Journal*. "We learned how to buy agencies, how to merge them, and our market share grew steadily. The average agency doesn't want to go into Yellow Page advertising. They want to make award-winning commercials. But what we do is just as creative."

In 1985, when Telephone Marketing Programs ranked 67th among U.S. advertising agencies, its gross billings were $103.3 million and its revenues $15.3 million. TMP now had seven major offices and six sales units nationwide. In 1986, it opened TMP Japan Inc. in Tokyo as a joint venture. In France, it was in the initial phase of making advertisement placements by electronic delivery.

Telephone Marketing Programs was benefiting from a proliferation of new Yellow Pages directories as a result of the government-mandated breakup of the American Telephone & Telegraph Co. (AT&T). This was forcing advertisers to expand their budgets for directory advertising, and, largely as a result, Yellow Pages revenues rose 19 percent to nearly $7 billion in 1985. To accommodate national advertisers unwilling to spend more money, however, TMP, in an effort to target the best buys for its clients, was beginning to survey customers in a variety of markets to determine which directories they used and how often they used them.

By the end of the 1980s, Telephone Marketing Programs was the largest advertising agency in the Yellow Pages field. In 1989, its gross billings reached $270 million and its gross income climbed to $40.5 million, of which all but $3 million was in the United States. The company now had 17 offices. It gained 22 clients in that year, including giant firms such as Avis, Coca-Cola, CVS, Hitachi, and SmithKline-Beecham, while losing only seven. The company's billings and earnings reached $501 million and $59.7 million, respectively, in 1992. By 1994, it commanded a 40 percent share of the Yellow Pages market, including such major clients as General Motors and Ryder Trucks.

Recruitment Advertising Player: 1993–95

TMP Worldwide entered the field of recruitment advertising in 1993 when it purchased Chicago-based Bentley, Barnes &

Company Perspectives:

At Monster Worldwide, we help individuals get ahead. We help them search, explore and discover opportunity. To stretch. To reach, strive and accomplish. To achieve. To arrive at the special place where talent and potential meet. Where a dream is fulfilled. A fire is ignited. Magic happens. To make a difference. At Monster Worldwide, we understand the unique potential we have. Not only to grow a company but to develop an entire industry. An opportunity to be seized. And fulfilled.

Lynn, an agency with about $50 million in annual capitalized billing, of which recruitment advertising accounted for roughly 75 percent. TMP sold the agency's consumer division to Ayer Inc. in 1994.

Paul Austermuehle, a Bentley, Barnes vice-president who was made president, said the following year that TMP's advanced Yellow Pages technology had helped his agency discover new revenue streams. TMP's heavy investments in computerization and technology, for example, enabled a longtime Bentley, Barnes client to meet a Clear Air Act mandate by reducing the number of commuters who were driving to and from work without passengers. "We're only just now discovering how to make the best use of all the things our TMP marriage provides," Austermuehle told Ylonda Gault of *Crain's New York Business.*

Like Yellow Pages advertisements, recruitment, or classified advertising was an unglamorous, labor-intensive part of the advertising business neglected by many name agencies because of relatively low profit margins. TMP Worldwide followed the Bentley, Barnes purchase with seven other acquisitions of agencies specializing in recruitment in the following year. These included Deutsch Shea & Evans, Merling Marx, and Chavin & Lambert of New York City and Rogers and Associates of Santa Clara, California. The additions raised TMP's recruitment billings to about $125 million a year and made it the third-largest recruitment agency in the United States and the nation's nineteenth largest advertising agency overall. In 1994, the company lost $2.5 million on commissions and fees of $86.2 million.

Founded in 1981, Rogers & Associates was the second-largest advertising agency in Silicon Valley, with California offices in Los Angeles, San Diego, and San Francisco as well as Santa Clara, plus offices in Chicago, Dallas, Miami, and Tampa. Curtis Rogers became president of TMP Worldwide's new recruitment division, while his partner, Steve Schmidt, was appointed president of the parent company's interactive/new media division, with responsibility for "Career Taxi," a Web site enabling clients to create an online brochure for attractive prospective job applicants.

By early 1995, TMP Worldwide's roster of acquired recruitment agencies had reached 12. Of TMP's 70 offices, 25 were focusing on recruitment advertising. TMP's billings in 1995 included $200 million from classified recruitment advertisements in newspapers and other publications. Its acquisitions that year included two competitors in the Boston-area recruit-

ment ad business: Adion and the Haughey Group. TMP's 2,500 recruitment advertising clients at the end of 1995 included Cigna, Nike, Dean Witter Reynolds, and Gateway 2000.

Adion founder Jeff Taylor became head of TMP Interactive, which was put in charge of the "Monster Board" recruitment Web site Taylor created in 1994. He later told Rex Crum of *Boston Business Journal,* "I knew the business [of Monster Board] was bigger than New England, but almost all the ads and job seekers were from New England. By selling, I was able to utilize the infrastructure of TMP and grow the business." At the end of 1995, Monster Board was listing more than 7,000 positions from U.S. and Canadian employers, receiving resumes from 48 countries, and registering 15,000 hits a day.

TMP Worldwide was not ignoring its core Yellow Pages business, which among its 2,100 clients in 1995 included Ford Motor Co., MCI Communications, Hallmark Cards, Pizza Hut, and United Van Lines. Its gross Yellow Pages billings of $425 million in 1995 accounted for 30 percent of the total billings in this field by U.S. agencies, three times the share of its nearest competitor. An important 1995 acquisition was the purchase of Dallas-based GTE Directories Corp.'s Yellow Pages business and assets from U.S. West. By contrast, TMP held only a 7 percent share of the recruitment advertising market. TMP had net income of $3.2 million on commissions and fees of $123.9 million in 1995, marking an end to at least four years of deficits.

Publicly Owned Powerhouse: 1996–99

TMP Worldwide spent more than $25 million to acquire 12 companies in 1996 and, at the end of the year, had acquired 36 companies since the beginning of 1994 with estimated total gross annual billings of about $350 million. The company made its initial public offering in December 1996, raising $80.5 million by offering a majority of its outstanding Class A shares of common stock at $14 a share. This sum almost exactly matched the company's long-term debt at the end of the year and enabled it to borrow more money for more acquisitions. McKelvey remained president and chairman of TMP and continued to hold 60 percent of the company, including all the Class B shares, which had ten times the voting power of the Class A shares.

TMP Worldwide registered commissions and fees of $162.6 million in 1996. It lost $52.4 million after taking a charge of $52 million for issuing stock to existing shareholders of TMP's predecessor companies in exchange for their shares in these companies. By July 1997, when TMP sold 2.4 million more shares to the public, its stock was trading at $22.25 a share.

TMP Worldwide's overseas acquisitions included the 1996 purchase of the recruiting firm Neville Jeffrees Australia Pty Limited for $25 million. TMP had purchased eight companies in 1997, including Belgian and Dutch recruitment agencies, at a total expense of $18 million by July, when it landed Austin Knight, the largest such agency in Great Britain, with 1996 gross billings of £134.4 million (about $210 million), commissions and fees of £29.3 million (about $45 million), and 24 offices worldwide. Collateral lines of business brought its annual revenues to more than £70 million (about $110 million). Its clients included Sony Electronics, British Gas, Schweppes, Nestlé, and Yahoo! TMP now had a presence in 11 countries

---

Key Dates:

1967: Andrew J. McKelvey establishes Telephone Marketing Programs.
1993: TMP enters the field of recruitment advertising when it purchases Chicago-based Bentley, Barnes & Lynn.
1994: Adion founder Jeff Taylor creates the "Monster Board" recruitment Web site.
1995: The company acquires Adion; Taylor becomes head of TMP Interactive.
1996: TMP goes public.
1998: By now, Monster Board is the Internet's top job-search site.
1999: Monster Board, Online Career Center, and MedSearch combine to form Monster.com.
2000: Monstermoving.com is launched.
2003: TMP changes its name to Monster Worldwide Inc.
2005: Monster Worldwide sells its North American and Japanese Yellow Pages division.

---

and 80 offices worldwide. Other 1997 acquisitions included the British companies MSL Group and Lonsdale Advertising and a U.S. agency, Johnson Recruitment Advertising. TMP's 1997 revenues came to $329.5 million and its net income to $10.7 million.

By this time, TMP Worldwide was placing the advertisements of all its print clients online at Web sites that included not only Monster Board but Online Career Center, the Internet's earliest career site; MedSearch, the main online classified-ad service for the healthcare industry, and Be the Boss, a site promoting opportunities in franchising. Founded in 1992 by Bill and Susan Warren, Indianapolis-based Online Career Center continued to be run by Bill Warren.

By late 1998, Monster Board was listing 50,000 job postings and receiving more than two million visitors a month, making it the Internet's top job-search site. Prospective employees paid nothing, while the cost to employers began at $175 for 60 days. The service was available in five countries. In January 1999, Monster Board, Online Career Center, and MedSearch combined to form Monster.com. During the second quarter of 1998, Monster.com had an operating profit of $455,000 on revenues of $10.7 million. Monster.com's revenues for the first quarter of 1999 reached $20.1 million. In May 1999, it was serving 42,000 clients, listing 204,000 jobs, holding more than 1.3 million active resumes, and recording 7.6 million hits per month. It was planning to introduce, in July 1999, Monster Talent Market 1.0, a service to connect job searchers with contractors, consultants, freelancers, and small business owners.

TMP Worldwide had made 14 acquisitions in 1998 by mid-October of that year. Among these was Stocking Advertising and Public Relations, one of the oldest agencies in the Washington, D.C., area, with annual revenue of $11 million. TMP paid for the purchase with stock valued at $14.5 million. The company had gross billings of $1.4 billion in 1998, including about $794.2 million for recruitment advertising and about $485.2

million for Yellow Pages advertising. Commissions and fees came to $406.8 million, including $48.5 million in Internet revenue. Net income was $4.2 million.

TMP Worldwide's list of 17,000 clients in 1998 included more than 80 of the Fortune 100 companies and about 400 of the Fortune 500. The company maintained 71 offices in the United States and 46 abroad. Its long-term debt was $118 million at the end of the year. McKelvey held 37.2 percent of TMP's shares in March 1999. The company's growing Internet business was not lost on investors, who bid its stock to a peak of $93 a share in the spring of 1999.

TMP Worldwide's ravenous appetite for acquisitions showed no sign of slowing in 1999. In January, it announced the acquisition of three European recruitment agencies: the German firms Bonde & Schmah and PMM Management Consultants and the French company Sources, SA. The latter purchase, combined with TMP's other operations in France, put the company into a leadership position in the recruitment advertising industry in that country, according to McKelvey. Also in January 1999, TMP Worldwide acquired Morgan & Banks Ltd., its biggest acquisition to date, for more than 5.1 million shares of TMP stock. This Australian company was providing permanent recruitment of personnel ranging from mid-level executives through clerks and was also engaged in temporary contracting and human resources consulting.

TMP Worldwide entered the executive search field in March 1999 when it agreed to buy LAI Worldwide Inc., a firm based in New York City, for more than $80 million in stock. According to Joann S. Lublin of the *Wall Street Journal,* McKelvey told an interviewer, "We are [now] going to be a big player at the upper end . . . starting with [college] internships running through the whole gamut ending with CEOs." LAI was merged with TASA Worldwide, TMP's executive search division, with Robert L. Pearson, LAI's chief executive officer, to run the operation jointly with Michael Squires, TASA's president.

During the first quarter of 1999, temporary contracts accounted for 30 percent of TMP Worldwide's sales; recruitment advertising for 24 percent; search and selection, 22 percent; Yellow Pages, 13 percent; and Monster.com, 11 percent. McKelvey indicated that the company name would probably be changed to TMP.com when the bulk of its revenue was coming from the Internet. He said that he believed recruitment advertisements, Yellow Pages ads, and executive searches eventually would converge on the Internet and that TMP wanted to acquire businesses promoting online advertisements to Yellow Pages advertisers.

Changes in the New Century: 2000–05

TMP's growth continued well into the year 2000. The company remained hot on the acquisition trail adding HW Group, based in the United Kingdom, and Illsley Bourbonnais, a Toronto-based executive head-hunting firm, to its arsenal. It also purchased System One Services and VirtualRelocation.com. TMP expanded its presence on the Web that year by launching Monstermoving.com, a relocation and moving Web site, and ChiefMonster.com, an executive job-search site. Late in the year, it acquired Jobtrak.com.

TMP made a play for HotJobs.com, the second-largest job-search site, in 2001. The company's plans were thwarted, however, when Yahoo! Inc. trumped its offer late in the year. By now, several challenges had forced TMP and its Monster.com subsidiary to make some changes in its strategy. A weakening economy and growing unemployment rates lead to job cuts and falling profits. In fact, during 2002 TMP reported a loss of nearly $535 million, due mainly to weak business operations at its offline staffing and executive search division as well as a charge related to its costly acquisition spree. As such, TMP retooled its operations in 2003 and decided to spin off its unprofitable executive search business. TMP changed its name to Monster Worldwide Inc. that year, signaling the company's focus on its Web-based business.

During 2004, Monster acquired Military Advantage Inc., a company offering military men and women career services via the military.com Web site. It also purchased Tickle Inc., a firm offering personality testing and career assessment services. In an attempt to bolster its international business, Monster acquired jobpilot GmbH, a leading European online career firm, and Emailjob.com, a French job-search site; it also secured a 40 percent interest in China HR, a Chinese job-search company.

In June 2005, Monster sold its North American and Japanese Yellow Pages division to Audax Group in an $80 million deal. According to the company, the sale enabled Monster Worldwide to focus on its core online recruitment business. That same month, Jeff Taylor announced he planned to leave the company in August to start a new online venture that would be partially funded by Monster Worldwide.

During the early 2000s, the company experienced many ups and downs but overall survived the dot-com crash that had wiped out many Internet-based firms. By 2004, its financials appeared to be back on track with gains in both revenues and profits. Monster had a presence in 27 countries across the globe, giving it access to over three billion people. The company had indeed come a long way from its Yellow Pages roots in 1967. Management was confident that Monster would continue its successful run as the leading online recruitment firm in the years to come.

Principal Operating Units

Monster; Advertising and Communications; Directional Marketing.

Principal Competitors

CareerBuilder Inc.; HotJobs.com Ltd.; Kforce Inc.

Further Reading

Barker, Robert, "Monster's Monstrous Appetite for Cash," *Business Week*, May 17, 2004.

Crum, Rex, "Monster of His Dreams," *Boston Business Journal*, November 6, 1998, p. 3.

Dougherty, Philip H., "A Yellow Pages Specialist," *New York Times*, May 29, 1980, p. D15.

Edwards, Paul L., "Exec Looks Forward to Yellow Pages Growth," *Advertising Age*, May 19, 1986, p. 74.

Gabriel, Frederick, "Stock Soars As Ad Firm Employs New Lines to Provide Growth," *Crain's New York Business*, June 2, 1997, p. 4.

Gault, Ylonda, "No Glamour, Just Gains," *Crain's New York Business*, September 5, 1994, pp. 3, 31.

Hodges, Jane, "IPO Provides TMP Chief with More Fuel for Growth," *Advertising Age*, January 6, 1997, p. 29.

Hyten, Todd, "Recruitment Ad Firms Sold to TMP Worldwide," *Boston Business Journal*, January 5, 1996, p. 3.

Kontzer, Tony, "Valley's 2nd-Largest Ad Shop Sold," *Business Journal-San Jose*, February 27, 1995, p. 1.

Kramli, Beth, "TMP Worldwide Announces Agreement to Acquire Austin," *Business Wire*, July 21, 1997.

La Monica, Paul R., "Some Kind of Monster," *Business 2.0*, March 3, 2005.

Lublin, Joann S., "TMP Worldwide Agrees to Acquire Exec-Search Firm," *Wall Street Journal*, March 12, 1999, p. B2.

McLean, Bethany, "A Scary Monster," *Fortune*, December 22, 2003.

"Monster Founder Leaving," *New York Times*, June 14, 2005.

Pope, Hugh, "Yellow Pages Agency TMP Steps into Spotlight with Global Moves," *Wall Street Journal*, January 16, 1997, p. B11.

Schaff, William, "The Value of TMP's Monster," *Informationweek*, May 17, 1999, p. 154.

Schoettle, Anthony, "On-Line Employment Sites Search for Niche," *Indianapolis Business Journal*, October 26, 1998, p. 9A.

"U.S. Agency to Create Recruitment Ad Giant," *People Management*, August 7, 1997, p. 10.

—Robert Halasz
—update: Christina M. Stansell

National Aquarium in Baltimore, Inc.

Pier 3
East Pratt Street
Baltimore, Maryland
U.S.A.
Telephone: (410) 576-3800
Web site: http://www.aqua.org

Nonprofit Corporation
Incorporated: 1981
Employees: 300 (1995)
Sales: $43.00 million (2003)
NAIC: 541710 Research and Development in the
Physical, Engineering, and Life Sciences 712120
Historical Sites; 712130 Zoos and Botanical Gardens;
712190 Nature Parks and Other Similar Institutions

National Aquarium in Baltimore, Inc., runs one of the country's leading aquariums: the National Aquarium in Baltimore (NAB). Owned by city government, NAB is Baltimore's largest paid tourist attraction, with 1.6 million visitors a year, 75 percent from out-of-state. The aquarium is involved in a number of education, conservation, and research programs.

The centerpiece of Baltimore's Inner Harbor urban revitalization, NAB has a national reputation for family appeal. Its success helped spawn aquariums in other cities such as St. Louis and Atlanta. The National Aquarium in Baltimore hosts more than 10,500 specimens of more than 560 species. Its management also runs the much smaller National Aquarium in Washington, D.C.

Origins

The National Aquarium in Baltimore (NAB) was created during a period of urban renewal. Its August 8, 1981 opening followed closely upon a new convention center and retail development in the Inner Harbor. Three years in the making, the aquarium cost $21.3 million, which was mostly provided by the City of Baltimore. Congress gave the aquarium its name (if not any funds), although there was already an existing National

Aquarium in the Interior Department's basement. (NAB would take over management of the smaller aquarium in 2003.)

The largest of several tanks contained the Atlantic coral reef exhibit, which held one-third of the aquarium's one million gallons. The coral reef tank and one below it dedicated to the open ocean were both shaped like doughnuts, allowing visitors to be surrounded by sharks behind the glass of the two aquariums.

NAB originally hosted 6,000 specimens of 600 different species, including birds, amphibians, reptiles, and mammals, in a facility seven stories high. About 100 people were employed in their care. A 65-foot tall simulated rain forest capped the building's five levels.

In its first year, the National Aquarium in Baltimore attracted more than twice as many visitors as expected. By 1985, it was estimated to have an economic impact exceeding $80 million a year. In 1990, NAB had 5,000 specimens of aquatic animals and an economic impact of $130 million.

A New Home for Marine Mammals in 1990

The National Aquarium promoted environmental conservation through its award-winning educational programs. It emphasized the importance of pure water to various ecosystems. From the beginning, the institution was involved in studies of Chesapeake Bay's water quality. In spite of such efforts, NAB and other aquariums weathered a wave of criticism from activists opposed to keeping dolphins in captivity.

The Marine Mammal Pavilion opened at the end of 1990. This 94,000-square-foot addition showcased the aquarium's three beluga whales and five Atlantic bottlenose dolphins in a tank of 1.2 million gallons surrounded by a 1,300-seat amphitheater. There was also a life-size sculpture of a humpback whale. The addition cost $35 million to build.

The Atlantic Coral Reef and Open Ocean tanks underwent a $13 million renovation in 1993 and 1994 to repair corrosion damage to steel-reinforced concrete and make improvements. An elaborate laser show entertained visitors during their closure. The aquarium was then staffed by about 300 paid employees. There were also more than 500 volunteers, including 100 scuba divers.

In the late 1990s, NAB had an annual budget of more than $20 million; admissions and concessions provided about 60 percent of funds. The aquarium had about 1.7 million visitors a year, including 650,000 children under the age of 11. 75,000 Maryland school children attended for free.

Keeping It Fresh for 2000 and Beyond

An existing rain forest exhibit was expanded in 1999 with an aquatic riverbank. To refresh its offerings, the aquarium began bringing in traveling exhibits. One of these, an exhibit on jellyfish, remained for two years. Television advertising at the time was promoting the aquarium as a fun and inspirational educational experience. ''Our vision is that connecting people with aquatic wildlife makes a better world for both,'' the acquarium's marketing director told the Baltimore *Sun.*

Dozens of six-foot-long fiberglass fish sculptures placed throughout downtown Baltimore helped celebrate the aquarium's 20th anniversary in 2001. During that year, the aquarium uncorked a wildly popular exhibit on seahorses that filled nine tanks with specimens from the Pacific Ocean and Chesapeake Bay. It later became a traveling exhibit, touring as far away as Italy.

Visitor demand prompted NAB allow more public access to its operations. In 2002, it began taking small groups of visitors to view the exhibits behind the scenes through its new Immersion Tours. Other appropriately named programs were Breakfast with the Dolphins and Sleeping with the Sharks. An aquarium representative told Baltimore's *Daily Record,* ''Studies show in the museum industry if you don't freshen your product you're at risk of losing three percent of your business annually.''

In 2003, NAB opened its sleepovers, ever popular with special groups and friends of the aquarium, to nonmembers. However, it experienced lower revenues as a result of a significant drop in donations and grants in a weak national economy.

NAB began managing the National Aquarium in Washington in September 2003. According to the *Baltimore Sun,* the goal was to become the leader in training aquarium professionals.

The National Aquarium in Washington, D.C., claimed to be the oldest in the country. Originally formed in 1873 as part of the Anderson School of Natural History in Woods Cross, Massachusetts, it was moved to Washington, D.C., in 1888. Located in the headquarters of what was then called the Fish Commission, in 1934 it was moved to the new Department of Commerce building on 14th Street and Constitution Avenue. The Commerce Department oversaw the Bureau of Fisheries, which later helped form the U.S. Fish and Wildlife Service.

In the 1960s, the National Aquarium in Washington, D.C., had about 100 species, mostly freshwater varieties, displayed in 47 wall tanks each holding between 50 and 2,000 gallons. (A 6,000-gallon tank was later obtained.) It operated as a private nonprofit when its federal funding was discontinued following the opening of the aquarium in Baltimore, which received only its name, not money, from Congress. In spite of its smaller size, the D.C. aquarium housed some rare species that NAB did not have, such as a chambered nautilus.

NAB hired Event Network Inc. to manage its concessions in late 2004. The San Diego company also handled retail operations for other major aquariums. NAB had gift shop sales of about $4 million a year; the new arrangement was expected to boost net income from them to more than $1 million, reported the *Baltimore Business Journal.*

An exhibit based on an Australian river gorge habitat opened in the spring of 2005. It cost $66 million to create and was sponsored by Discovery Communications, which acquired the right to name it after its cable channel. "Animal Planet Australia: Wild Extremes" was NAB's most expensive expansion to date. It included more than 3,000 specimens and featured a 35-foot waterfall. The 65,000-square-foot glass pavilion built to contain the exhibit expanded the aquarium by one-third. A spokesperson told the local *Daily Record* that Australia's Northern Territory environment was chosen because it was unlike anything depicted in the United States.

A Zagat survey had rated NAB the second-best aquarium in the country, after Monterey Bay Aquarium, for family travelers. The aquarium continued efforts to grow bigger and better. A $112 million expansion was scheduled to open in the spring of 2007.

Principal Competitors

Maryland Science Center; Monterey Bay Aquarium; Mystic Aquarium; National Zoological Park; Shedd Aquarium Society.

Further Reading

Allen, Karen Tanner, "Finding Finned Friends," *Washington Post*, Weekend Sec., March 27, 1998.

Arney, June, "Baltimore Aquarium to Take Over Management of Washington, D.C. Aquarium," *Baltimore Sun*, September 4, 2003.

"Baltimore Aquarium and Zoo Revenues Down; Search Continues for New Funding Resources," *Daily Record* (Baltimore), July 3, 2003.

"Baltimore's Natl. Aquarium Marks 13th Anniversary," *Amusement Business,* January 23, 1995, p. 24.

"Bathtub Snorkeling an Image to Woo Them; New TV Ads with a Touch of Fantasy Aim to Persuade Viewers That Visiting the National Aquarium Is Fun as Well as Educational," *Baltimore Sun*, March 16, 1999, p. 1C.

Calos, Katherine, "The Reef Is Ready . . . at Aquarium," *Richmond Times-Dispatch*, April 6, 1995, p. D4.

Culbertson, D.C., "Deep Sleep in a Shark Lair; Slumber Party at Baltimore National Aquarium," *Washington Times*, July 17, 2003, p. M14.

Dash, Julekha, "National Aquarium to Outsource Retail," *Baltimore Business Journal*, October 29, 2004.

DeFord, Susan, "Baltimore Art Exhibit Advances Swimmingly; Columbia Resident Hatched Fish Idea," *Washington Post*, July 5, 2001, p. T5.

"The Day of the Dolphins; Behind the Scenes at the National Aquarium in Baltimore," *Washington Post*, October 24, 2000, p. C15.

El-Khoury, Tamara, and Bill Atkinson, "Animal Planet Gets Naming Rights to New Pavilion at National Aquarium," *Baltimore Sun*, June 18, 2004.

Goldberg, Karen, "Hooked on Dolphins; Public Has Whale of a Good Time at Aquarium in Baltimore," *Washington Times*, April 2002, p. D4.

Kercheval, Nancy, "Baltimore Aquarium Helps Preserve Endangered Seahorse," *Daily Record* (Baltimore), April 5, 2001.

Kridler, Kara, "Baltimore's National Aquarium Exhibit to Showcase Australia's Northern Territory," *Daily Record* (Baltimore), February 27, 2004.

Lipscomb, Hetty, "A Feeding Frenzy at Commerce," *Washington Post*, Weekend Sec., June 10, 2005.

McManus, Kevin, "In the Jaws of an Aquarium," *Washington Post*, August 10, 1990.

Miller, Bruce, "Nat'l Aquarium in Baltimore Now Offers Behind-the-Scenes Tours," *Daily Record* (Baltimore), October 19, 2002.

The National Aquarium, Washington, D.C.: U.S. Department of the Interior, Fish and Wildlife Service, Bureau of Sport Fisheries and Wildlife, Circular 93, 1960.

"Nat'l Aquarium in Baltimore to Host Adults-Only Sleepover," *Daily Record* (Baltimore), January 9, 2003.

Pendered, David, "Aquarium Provides Tourists Reason to Spend Time, Money in Baltimore," *Atlanta Journal and Constitution*, June 2, 2003.

Piccoli, Sean, "Baltimore Takes a Dive (for Dolphins)," *Washington Times*, December 27, 1990, p. M4.

"Q&A: WBR Talks with James A. Flick Jr. and David M. Pittenger," *Warfield's Business Record*, Sec. 1, January 6, 1995, p. 27.

Samuel, Paul D., "Aquarium Turns on the Lights to Mask $12.7M Renovation," *Warfield's Business Record*, Sec. 1, October 8, 1993, p. 4.

Schaffer, Athena, "Aquariums Find Success with Life on the Road," *Amusement Business*, April 20, 1998, p. 18.

"Survey: National Aquarium in Baltimore No. 2 in U.S.," *Daily Record* (Baltimore), May 27, 2004.

Uhlenbrock, Tom, "Tank Tale: Aquarium Anchors Baltimore Renewal," *St. Louis Post-Dispatch*, November 5, 1989, p. A1.

Valentine, Paul W., "Md. Aquarium Readies New Mammal Pavilion," *Washington Post*, September 14, 1989, p. A30.

Webster, Bayard, "Baltimore Aquarium: Birds, Fish, Reptiles Adapt to New Life," *New York Times*, August 18, 1981, p. C3.

Wilgoren, Debbi, "Couple Makes Fish a Family Affair," *Washington Post*, March 22, 1990.

Worden, Amy, "Aquarium Divers Plumb Depths of Dedication," *Plain Dealer* (Cleveland), March 24, 1996, p. 7F.

—Frederick C. Ingram

Newly Weds Foods, Inc.

4140 West Fullerton Avenue
Chicago, Illinois 60639
U.S.A.
Telephone: (773) 489-7000
Toll Free: (800) 621-7521
Fax: (773) 489-2799
Web site: http://www.newlywedsfoods.com

Private Company
Incorporated: 1932 as Newly Weds Baking Co.
Employees: 1,700
Sales: $400 million (2002 est.)
NAIC: 311940 Seasoning and Dressing Manufacturing

Newly Weds Foods, Inc., is a Chicago-based family-owned company with a global reach, making breadings, batters, seasonings, rubs, and marinades for the food processing and service industries, primarily servicing restaurant chains. Although generally taken for granted, food coatings play an important role in the food industry. Not only do glazes and rubs enhance flavors, they provide an appealing look to consumers. Moreover, they seal in moisture and help prevent dehydration, thus retarding freezer burn and the cost of wasted products. Batters help to offset the varying moisture levels and fat and protein content in meats, poultry, vegetables, and other organic products, as well as offset differences in processing machinery, water quality, line speed, and set-up time. Food manufacturers also gain a way to distinguish their products on the basis of taste, texture, and look. In addition, spice blends and seasoning are engineered to provide visual appeal, longer flavor retention, and cleaner flavor release. Newly Weds' formulated seasonings accommodate 46 world cuisines. In addition, Newly Weds product lines include cures, deli and sausage seasonings, function mustards, sauces, binders, browning agents, stuffing crumbs, dry soups, English muffins, and capsicums, including red peppers, chili powders, and paprika. Newly Weds Foods also offers customers a number of value-added services such as sensory evaluation, packaging development services, and consulting services on how to integrate new products, or changes to existing products, into a customer's processing operation. Furthermore, the company offers the services of a proprietary marketing tool, FlavorTrak, a database that profiles and tracks menu items from more than 500 restaurant chains. FlavorTrak helps customers keep track of market trends and is a useful tool for research and development purposes as well as sales and marketing. Newly Weds' 12 state-of-the-art plants are located in the United States, Australia, Canada, China, Israel, New Zealand, Thailand, and the United Kingdom. The company also maintains eight regional laboratories in the United States and 18 sales offices and distribution centers throughout the world.

Origins Date to 1930s

Newly Weds Foods was founded in Chicago in 1932 as Newly Weds Baking Co. by Paul Angell, who was originally interested in developing new dessert ideas and created the first ice cream roll cake. Because it married sheet cake and ice cream, he called the specialty "Newly Weds," a name which he would apply to the company as well. For the first 20 years, Newly Weds' focus was on the cake roll business, but in the early 1950s Angell recognized the emerging importance of the frozen foods industry and the need for appropriate breadings and batters. Using bakery-based technology to produce breading and batter mixes, primarily used on seafood, Newly Weds began to serve this niche and by getting an early start became the leading producer of customized food coatings in the United States, a distinction the company would never relinquish. While the company continued to produce the sheet cake used in making Newly Weds ice cream roll well into the 1990s, the breadings and batter business rapidly eclipsed the dessert business. In 1958, Newly Weds began producing English muffins, an item it continues to sell.

The popularity of fried and breaded foods grew rapidly in the 1960s and 1970s. A major turning point in the history of the company took place in 1977 when it introduced the Japanese-style bread crumb to the United States. The "J-crumb" became Newly Weds' signature product. A 1984 *Quick Frozen Foods'* article described it as "an elongated sliver with a light porous texture which produces a crispy yet tender bite." It was formulated for use in conventional, convection, or microwave ovens, and its color and texture could be altered "from pink to white to toasted, double-toasted or golden, in fine, medium or coarse granulations.'' J-crumbs offered other low-cost benefits as well. It was suitable for a wide range of products in a variety of applications, had a longer frying tolerance, and possessed excellent holding qualities under heat lamps. The J-crumb played a key role in Newly Weds expanding from seafood items to providing coatings suitable for veal, cheese, mushrooms, and cauliflower in addition to other vegetables and fruits.

Becoming a ''Little Big Company'' in the 1980s

By now headed by a second generation in Charles T. Angell, son of the founder, Newly Weds began expanding its geographic reach in 1979 when it established a United Kingdom operation by way of a joint venture with a British company to establish a European presence. An even more important change occurred a year later when Newly Weds opened a second production site in Watertown, Massachusetts, ushering in a decade of significant growth, much of it achieved through strategic acquisitions. ''In Mr. Angell's words,'' wrote Laurie Gorton in a 1993 company profile for *Baking & Snack,* ''during the 1980s, Newly Weds moved from being a big little company to being a little big company.'' The goal after that was to become ''a big company, 'plain and simple.' '' In 1983, the company moved into the markets of the Pacific Rim by establishing a presence in Australia through a joint venture with a local company. Newly Weds became involved in the formulated seasonings business through the 1988 acquisition of St. Louis-based Spicecraft Company, which manufactured and blended spices for food processors. A year later Newly Weds opened a batters and breadings processing plant in Springdale, Arkansas, encompassing 100,000 square feet. The $9 million plant was strategically located within the southeastern poultry processing industry. All the while, the original Chicago facility was expanded and upgraded to keep up with the rising demand for Newly Weds' products. The decade closed with the harvesting of the company's first capsicum crop.

Newly Weds continued to expand in the early 1990s. In 1991, it forged a partnership with RHM Ingredients, a British supplier of food ingredients. Together they established a joint venture, New Food Ingredients France, to supply food coatings and flavor systems to French food processors. A year later, Newly Weds looked north of the U.S. border, establishing an alliance with Toronto-based UFL Foods Inc., a food ingredients supplier that would become responsible for the sale of Newly Weds batter and breading sales in all of Canada, the company's largest export market, followed by Mexico and Central and South American countries. During this period, the company bought a building adjacent to its Chicago campus to house a new research and development unit, offices, and production lines for J-crumbs as well as a new ''American bread crumb,'' or ABC-crumb. As a result of this and other additions, the Chicago site now covered 14 acres and housed 380,000-square-

feet of operations. Newly Weds opened a fourth U.S. manufacturing facility in 1992, a $17 million, 135,000-square-foot plant located in Cleveland, Tennessee, built to accommodate the increasing demand for Newly Weds' products in the Southeast and able to produce more than 100 million pounds of crumbs each year. At this time, the Springdale facility was expanded by 50,000 square feet. In early 1993, Newly Weds once again grew externally, acquiring Gardner, Kansas-based Kate Industries from Con Agra, Inc. Generating about $10 million in annual sales, Kate manufactured multi-grain blends, a new product for Newly Weds, as well as batters and other mixes sold to food processors, snack food companies, and industrial bakers.

In addition to American-style bread crumbs, which gave coated foods a homemade look, new products developed by Newly Weds in the early 1990s included Barrier Dip 2000, a pre-frying dip system that significantly cut the amount of fat absorbed by a breaded product while improving freezer storage life, and Newly Crisp crumbs, which gave baked items the taste and texture of fried foods while cutting fat and eliminating the need for messy and demanding deep fryers. Most schools, for example, did not use fryers and were a prime market for the baking product. Consumer demand for less fat was also a key factor in Newly Weds' move into marinades and glazes, products intended to compensate for a projected reduction in the demand for battered and breaded products. However, the products quickly developed into a category of their own, appealing especially to consumers with nutritional concerns.

The company's expansion program continued in the mid-1990s. In 1995, Newly Weds moved into the markets of the Middle East by establishing a joint venture in Israel. A year later, Newly Weds was once again on the acquisition path, completing three significant purchases. It added Tacoma, Washington-based Specialty Foods Inc., a blender of ingredients primarily used in the seafood industry; Decatur, Alabama-based BMB Specialty Co., a manufacturer of batters, breadings, and food coatings; and F.W. Witt & Co., a Yorkville, Illinois, maker of dry and liquid seasoning blends for the sausage industry. Also during this period, Newly Weds developed its FlavorTrak menu trend tracking system, which debuted in 1996 and would be upgraded on an ongoing basis.

Newly Weds grew on a number of fronts in the final years of the 1990s. In 1998, it opened a new plant and research and development operation in Beijing, China. In that same year, it opened a Technical Services Center in Idaho Falls, Idaho, and acquired its Canadian partner, UFL Foods, the addition of which supplemented Newly Weds' capabilities in seasonings as well as packaging. In 1999, Newly Weds bolstered its Canadian business by acquiring Edmonton-based Norac Technologies, while adding rosemary-based antioxidants to Newly Weds' product mix. Also in 1999, the company completed an expansion and remodeling of the Yorkville plant it picked up in the F.W. Witt acquisition and bought Tri-State Specialties Inc., yet another seasonings firm. When the century came to a close, Newly Weds was generating annual sales in the $340 million range, according to published reports.

More Acquisitions and Expansion in the 2000s

A series of acquisitions were completed in the early 2000s. The Chicago Spice Co., an Illinois-based full service maker of blended seasonings, rubs, glazes, sauces, and marinades and provider of portion control packaging services was picked up in June 2000. In early 2001, Newly Weds acquired Flavorite Laboratories, a Memphis, Tennessee-based developer and supplier of customized seasonings for meat, poultry, side dishes, and snacks, as well as gravies, marinades, sauces, glazes, and soups. The addition of Flavorite's capabilities prompted Charles Angell to comment in a press statement that Newly Weds was "now a full service ingredient powerhouse for the product development community."

Far from complacent, Newly Weds continued to make strategic acquisitions. In 2002, it acquired long-time British partner RHM Ingredients, fortifying Newly Weds' position in the United Kingdom and Europe. Later in the year, Boston-based Dirigo Spice Corp. was purchased, supplementing the Watertown, Massachusetts, operation and the company's business in the Northeast. Dirigo produced seasonings and ingredients for meats, seafoods, baker and snack items, cheese and dip mixes, salad dressings, sauces, and soup mixes, as well as other specialty items.

Newly Weds further strengthened it business in continental Europe with the 2003 acquisition of Helmond, Holland-based HPI. Also in 2003, Newly Weds bought Chicago-based Heller Seasonings & Ingredients and its three production facilities located in Bethlehem, Pennsylvania; Modesto, California; and Bedford Park, Illinois, where a full research and development unit was also housed. Heller provided seasonings and custom

spices for use in meat processing, snack foods, prepared foods, side dishes, dressings, dip, soups, and sauces. Newly Weds also grew internally during the early 2000s. The Horn Lake, Tennessee, facility was expanded in 2001, then in 2004 a $10 million expansion was launched, resulting in a 260,000-square-foot plant, the largest the company owned, capable of manufacturing Newly Weds' complete line of spices, marinades, seasonings, and other food coatings. The commitment to the Memphis-area plant was indicative of its strategic location, an overnight point to Chicago, Kansas City, Atlanta, Dallas, and New Orleans.

Newly Weds had to contend with changing consumer tastes over the years. For example, the battered-and-breaded meat segment, essentially anything labeled "fried," experienced difficulty as consumers became more health conscious, especially due to the popularity of low-carbohydrate diets such as the Atkins Diet. All food developers faced a major challenge on the horizon: the nutritional guidelines regarding trans fats scheduled to go into effect in January 2006. Regardless, Newly Weds' researchers continually looked for ways to address these and other concerns, developing new technologies to produce healthier, yet flavorful coating combinations. Advances in coatings also helped in the development of more appealing microwavable products that remained crispy after they came out of the oven. The three-prong goal of Newly Wed researchers was to create batters and breadings that allowed for quicker preparation, provided better quality, and, perhaps most important of all, tasted good.

Principal Competitors

International Flavors & Fragrances, Inc.; Kerry Group plc; McCormick & Company, Inc.

Further Reading

Gorton, Laurie, "Baking Crumb ABCs," *Baking & Snack*, August 1, 1993.
"Japanese-Style Bread Crumbs Offer Help to Processor of Ethnic Specialties," *Quick Frozen Foods*, January 1984, p. 30.
Lofton, Dewanna, "Chicago-Based Food Company Eyes Horn Lake, Miss.,-Based Seasoning-Product Firm," *Commercial Appeal*, September 7, 2000.
"Newly Weds Foods Has Seen the Future," *Quick Frozen Foods International*, October 1992, p. 141.
"No, We Don't Make Wedding Cakes . . . Yet!," *Frozen & Chilled Foods*, March-April 2005, p. S27.
Sheffield, Michael, "Newly Weds Foods Expanding Horn Lake Plant," *Memphis Business Journal*, May 28, 2004, p. 1.
White, Lisa, "The Cover Up," *National Provisioner*, April 2005.

—Ed Dinger

Northwest Airlines Corporation

2700 Lone Oak Parkway
Eagan, Minnesota 55121
U.S.A.
Telephone: (612) 726-2111
Fax: (612) 726-7123
Web site: http://www.nwa.com

Public Company
Incorporated: 1926 as Northwest Airways
Employees: 39,342
Sales: $11.279 billion (2004)
Stock Exchanges: NASDAQ
Ticker Symbol: NWAC
NAIC: 481111 Scheduled Passenger Air Transportation;
481112 Scheduled Freight Air Transportation

Northwest Airlines Corporation is a holding company whose primary interest is Northwest Airlines Inc., America's oldest carrier with continuous name identification and the world's fourth oldest and largest airline. Based in Minneapolis, the airline offers both domestic and international flight service to some 750 cities in 120 countries. In September 2005, in an industry plagued by debt and rising oil prices, Northwest filed for Chapter 11 bankruptcy protection, reporting debts of some $17 billion. The company vowed to continue operations while it restructured.

Roaring to Life in the 1920s

The history of Northwest can be traced to the 1920s. After passage of the Kelly Airmail bill in 1926 the Ford Transport Company, a subsidiary of the auto manufacturer, was awarded the Chicago to St. Paul airmail route. They commenced business on June 7 of that year, but a series of airplane crashes over the summer forced Ford to sell the company to Northwest Airways by October. Northwest ran Ford's open-cockpit, single-engine biplanes until the winter weather compelled them to cease operations. In the spring of 1927 Northwest resumed business. By July the company was hauling passengers on their short trunk routes. Once again, however, the harsh northern winter forced them to close for the season.

During the flying seasons of 1928 to 1933 Northwest secured an expansion of routes through the Dakotas and Montana, and eventually to Seattle, Washington. The man largely responsible for the company's westward growth was Croil Hunter. While Hunter only occupied a position in middle management, it was his initiative to enter new markets and win new airmail routes that gave Northwest its early preeminence. By 1933 Hunter was vice-president and general manager of the airline.

In the years before World War II Northwest directed its expansion eastward to New York. The company survived the government's temporary suspension of airmail contracts in 1934 with virtually no loss in business, and began operating mail services and passenger routes along the northern corridor. Moreover, new and modified airplanes enabled Northwest to continue operations through the winter. The planes were modified further when it became obvious that finding light-colored, downed planes in the snow was a difficult task. The tail fins of all the company's planes have since been painted a bright, contrasting red. In 1937 Croil Hunter, who had been credited with the airline's success, was named president of the company.

In the attempt to establish northern routes to Asia, Northwest pilots made expeditions to Alaska and across the Aleutian Islands. The northern route had been passed up by Pan Am, which was unable to win landing rights in the Soviet maritime provinces and Japan. Instead, Pan Am decided to open a route to the Philippines and China, via Hawaii and Guam. Pan Am crossed the ocean first, but Northwest held the promise of a faster route.

When the Americans became involved in World War II in 1941, Northwest was chosen to operate the military support routes to the strategically important Aleutian Islands. The airline's experience with cold weather aviation and its predominance in the region made it a logical choice. The Army Air Corps flew its C-46s, C-47s, B-25, and B-26 bombers directly from the production line to Northwest facilities in Minneapolis, Minnesota, and Vandalia, Ohio, in order for them to be modified for cold weather and long distance routes. Northwest's expertise in this area contributed significantly to the effectiveness of the Allied war effort.

During the war passenger flights were strictly limited to people with priority status. Regardless of the suspension of commercial business, however, Northwest benefited from the war. With a healthy military allowance from the War Department, Northwest improved its facilities and upgraded its technology.

Postwar Competition

When the war ended Northwest lobbied the Civil Aeronautics Board to award the airline rights to fly to the Orient from Alaska. This so-called "great circle" route was actually about two thousand miles shorter than Pan Am's transpacific route. When Congress rejected airline magnate Juan Trippe's proposal to make Pan Am America's international flag carrier, the Civil Aeronautics Board was free to certify Northwest for "great circle" routes to the Orient.

With the government's reaffirmation of competition within the industry, all the companies hurried to modernize their airline fleets. It was both a matter of cost-efficiency and prestige. Northwest looked to the Martin Company's new 202 airliner to replace the aging DC-3 model, and complement the company's fleet of Boeing 377 Stratocruisers. The Stratocruiser, with its lower level bar and intimate "honeymoon suites," was extremely popular with newlyweds and business travelers. The Martin 202, however, did not remain in service for very long; its reputation for malfunctioning became widespread. Fortunately, the 202 was quickly replaced by the DC-4.

When the Korean War started in 1950, Northwest employed many of its DC-4s to assist the United Nations forces. They ferried men and transported equipment, including bomber engines and surgical supplies, to various points in Japan and Korea. The military utilization of the airline, which lasted for several years, was carried out without any interruption of its regular commercial services.

In 1952 Hunter relinquished the presidency to Harold R. Harris, but retained his position as chairman of the board. After two uneventful years Harris was replaced by Donald Nyrop. After he received his law degree, Nyrop served in the military transport group during World War II. Later, he headed the Civil Aeronautics Board. For many years after joining Northwest he set an austere tone for the organization. For example, the Minneapolis headquarters was located in a large windowless building that he planned would become a maintenance hangar at some point in the future. Nyrop also had a chart showing the inverse relationship between the number of vice-presidents and profits. Needless to say, Northwest had a minimal number of vice-presidents.

On the other hand, Nyrop brought Northwest into the jet age quickly, purchasing the Lockheed L-188 prop-jet Electra, the DC-8, and the Boeing 707 and 727. Through the early 1960s Northwest consolidated its service across the northern United States and along the "great circle" to its Asian destinations. Profits were consistent and growth remained slow and cautious.

Perhaps the one outstanding event of the period occurred on Thanksgiving Eve of 1971. A man who identified himself as Dan Cooper boarded a Northwest 727 in Portland, Oregon, bound for Seattle, Washington. He claimed to have a bomb and demanded $200,000 and two parachutes. His demands were met and the airplane departed. Somewhere over southwestern Washington, at about 25,000 feet, Cooper ordered the airplane's rear bottom door opened. He walked down the stairs and jumped into the densely clouded, cold and black night. Cooper and most of the money were never found. He was, however, rumored to have died in a New York hospital in 1982.

In 1978, after 24 years in charge, Donald Nyrop retired. He was replaced by Joseph M. Lapensky, an accountant who was promoted from within the company. Many industry analysts expected Lapensky to continue Nyrop's management policy. In fact, Lapensky must be regarded as an interim figure, one who represented a definite but subtle change in direction for the company.

Soaring Under Deregulation in the 1980s

Lapensky inherited the leadership on the eve of deregulation. For many of the large airlines the new era of competition resulted in the loss of large amounts of revenue. Northwest, however, was quite firmly established in its various markets, and remained largely unchallenged. Lapensky's most important problem, however, was the ruptured state of labor relations which resulted from his predecessor's attempts to weaken the unions. In one instance, when Northwest employees threatened to strike, Nyrop decided to confront the unions. He enlisted the help of a 15-airline mutual aid fund established to enable the companies to withstand the effects of a long-term strike. When Nyrop realized the effort was stalemated, he gave in to union demands. Nyrop's union problem became Lapensky's union problem, and before long Lapensky retired.

In October 1983 Steven G. Rothmeier became Northwest's new president. Rothmeier gained Lapensky's favor after writing a paper on a deregulated airline market as a student at the University of Chicago. Rothmeier's case study of Northwest had so impressed people at the airline that they offered him a job in 1983. Like Lapensky, he rose through the company, albeit quickly, to the top executive position. Under new management the airline formed a holding company, Northwest Airlines, Inc., which assumed responsibility for the airline and its subsidiaries. On January 1, 1985, Rothmeier was named chief executive officer, confirming his position as the leader of Northwest.

In 1985 United Airlines proposed to buy the Asian and Pacific routes of Northwest's competitor Pan Am. Rothmeier led the opposition to the sale, arguing that it would leave only two airlines competing in Asia. Northwest invested many years of negotiation and costly waiting to achieve and maintain its Pacific markets. According to Rothmeier, it was hardly fair that United could simply purchase a competitive share. Regardless of the opposition, the sale of Pan Am's Asian routes to United was approved in 1986.

Northwest, which had suffered from not having a computerized reservations system, purchased a large share of TWA's PARS system, which the two companies jointly operate. The company has also made arrangements with four smaller independent airlines to generate more "feeder" traffic to Northwest.

In 1986 Northwest purchased its regional competitor Republic Airlines. The $884 million sale barely won federal approval since the two airlines operated many of the same routes. At first the Civil Aeronautics Board was concerned that Northwest would operate monopolies in too many markets. Republic had established hubs in Detroit and Memphis, in addition to Minneapolis. However, Republic's north-south route structure provided the ideal "feeder" for Northwest's longer-haul east-west structure, despite a certain amount of overlap. As a result of this merger, John F. Horn was named president of Northwest and NWA, Inc. Rothmeier, still chief executive officer, assumed the position of chairman, vacant since Lapensky's retirement in May 1985.

Prior to the merger, Republic flew to over 100 cities in 34 states, Canada, and the Caribbean. Northwest's network covered 74 cities in 27 states and 16 countries in Western Europe, the Far East, and the Caribbean. Until the purchase of Republic Airlines, Northwest had always been "underleveraged," or virtually free of debt. Northwest's management used to be proud of this fact, but came to recognize that, for tax and other purposes, it was good to carry "some debt."

In 1989 financiers Alfred Checchi and Gary Wilson bought control of Northwest in a $3.65 billion leveraged buyout deal, after which the airline became a private company. One year later, former Beatrice CEO Frederick Rentschler was named Northwest's new CEO. One of the first tasks facing the new management was rectifying the service record of the airline, whose poor service and on-time performance record in recent years led dissatisfied business travelers to give it the unfortunate nickname "Northworst." Flush with optimism over the company's future, Checchi and Wilson embarked on a program of acquiring the assets of other airlines and committed $450 million through the year 1995 to improving service. They purchased Eastern Airlines' Washington, D.C., hub, bought Asian routes from Hawaiian Airlines, and made their desire to deal further well-known—at various times, they began negotiations to buy all or major portions of Continental, Midway, and Qantas.

However, Northwest was soon struck by business and image setbacks. Two 1990 incidents—the conviction of several Northwest pilots for flying under the influence of alcohol and a runway collision of two Northwest jets, killing eight, which was later blamed on crew error—tarnished the airline's public reputation further. The airline's hopes to expand through acquisitions proved hampered by its $4.2 billion debt, the product of the leveraged buyout coupled with extant debt from the purchase of Republic, which left the airline with a negative net worth. Moreover, Northwest was hit by the general financial troubles that affected the industry in the late 1980s, including rising fuel costs, declining traffic caused by a weakening economy, and pricing wars. In 1990 and 1991, when these problems were exacerbated by recession and war in the Middle East, Northwest lost $618 million. As leading airline United began aggressive expansion into the Pacific market, Northwest's inability to match United's purchases left it vulnerable in its traditionally strongest area.

Management attempted a number of plans to raise operating funds, including pursuing incentive funds from the state of Minnesota, in which the airline is based. In 1991, the company received $835 million in aid from the state for opening two maintenance bases there. In order to stave off bankruptcy, the company also embarked on an aggressive cost-cutting campaign, cutting service by a third at its Washington, D.C., hub and seeking concessions from its six unions, although many of its workers already received wages below the industry average.

Northwest appeared to have escaped the catastrophic effects of recession and deregulation that felled such competitors as Eastern and Pan Am, but its massive debt left it at a disadvantage at a time when other airlines were employing a strategy of buying routes and expanding globally. However, Checchi and Wilson's creative debt-cutting measures and their expenditures to improve the airline's service record bore some fruit: in 1991 the airline finished first in on-time performance, a category in which it had been dubbed the worst.

A Merger in the 1990s

In 1992 Northwest and KLM Royal Dutch Airlines applied to the United States Transportation Department to merge the operations of the two companies and function as one. Since the United States had recently signed a treaty with the Netherlands allowing companies a good deal of leeway, the Transportation Department approved the combination, allowing Northwest and KLM to coordinate prices, available seats, sales forces, and data, while sharing revenues. An added bonus was the injection of KLM's equity stake in the company. The alliance nearly doubled the pair's share of transatlantic traffic, to 12 percent.

Fortunately for Northwest, the industry pulled out of its slump by 1994. A public stock offering early in the year reflected investors' optimism. Northwest posted revenues of $8.33 billion for the year and income of $830 million. These figures rose to $9.09 billion and $902 million in 1995.

Although the Northwest/KLM alliance proved fruitful for investors on both sides of the Atlantic—Wilson and Checchi's 20 percent stake grew from $40 million to nearly $1 billion and KLM's $400 million investment reached a value of $1.6 billion—a bitter power struggle unfolded behind the scenes. KLM's overtures for more control of Northwest prompted Wilson and Checchi to insert "poison pill" provisions into Northwest's charter preventing KLM from acquiring more than its 19 percent share of the company. This in turn prompted a lawsuit from KLM, which also lobbied to loosen the regulations preventing foreign companies from owning controlling interests in U.S. airlines. In addition, KLM President Pieter Bouw's separate discussions with the pilots' union—the two parties together controlled half of Northwest—infuriated Wilson, according to Fortune.

Even this relationship could be mended, however. Bouw resigned as KLM president in May 1997. By August, KLM had dropped its poison pill lawsuit and agreed to sell back its Northwest shares gradually through the year 2000. The working bonds seemed as strong as ever: the pair announced their considerable cargo operations would cooperate more closely, and the expanded KLM alliance gave Northwest a passage to India (via Amsterdam) beginning in June 1997.

At the same time, Northwest's Pacific operations were threatened by political forces abroad. Northwest had already suffered from an excess of capacity in Japan, and the Japanese government sought to curtail the carrier's rights to fly passengers beyond Japan to other Asian destinations. Nevertheless, Northwest's $10.23 billion in revenues brought in a net income of $596.5 million. At approximately $2 billion, its debt had been reduced to half the 1993 level.

A strike by Northwest pilots, eager to claim their share of the company's bounty and opposed to various management strategies, finally grounded the airline in late August 1998. Northwest laid off 31,000 employees during the crisis and did not resume full operations until September 21. The shutdown resulted in a $224 million loss for the third quarter of 1998 on revenues of $1.93 billion (the carrier had earned $290 million in the third quarter of the previous year).

Although its confrontations with KLM and its labor problems seemed to have been resolved, Northwest would have to successfully navigate the U.S. government's interests as well as those of the Japanese. Northwest's announced intentions to purchase control of Continental Airlines, the fifth largest U.S. carrier, prompted scrutiny from the Justice Department, as did its ''predatory'' price competition against budget carriers such as Pro Air and Reno Air.

Northwest's losses deepened to $285 million by the end of 1998, its stock reaching a year-end low of $18.63 per share, a 71 percent drop from the first-quarter high of $65.31. Two more profitable years followed, with net income of $300 million in 1999 and $256 million in 2000. The airline's lingering troubles were exacerbated, however, by such factors as a general economic downturn beginning in 2000; the September 11, 2001, attacks on the World Trade Center and Pentagon; subsequent wars in Afghanistan and Iraq; and the Severe Acute Respiratory Syndrome (SARS) epidemic of November 2002 to July 2003, all of which kept non-business and even some business travelers at home. Coupled with ever-increasing jet fuel costs, the global drop in travel sent Northwest scurrying to cut costs wherever possible as 2001's $423 million loss was followed by steep drops in stock prices and losses of over $1.7 billion between 2002 and 2005. Federal aid relating to the September 11 attacks in the amount of $249 million and an additional $61 million in writedowns helped lessen Northwest's losses by $100 million in

2001, but prospects continued to look gloomy. By year end 2004, Northwest's stock had dropped to $7.09, down almost 90 percent from its 1998 high. Only a one-time writedown taken in 2003 prevented Northwest from showing a loss of $265 million that year; the airline finished 2003 in the black with a net income of $248 million, compared to losses of $798 million one year earlier. The relief was only temporary, however; in 2004, the company posted net losses of $862 million.

Rate Hikes, New Fees, No Pretzels

To counter the losses, Northwest began laying off workers and scaling back amenities for its coach services, even eliminating the small bag of pretzels given to passengers in flight, a move that company sources estimated would cut $2 million in costs per year. Transpacific and Asian routes and a Detroit-to-Rome nonstop service were cut in 2001. Four of the airline's facilities—reservations centers in New York State and Hawaii, a flight attendant base in Chicago, and a pilot base in Honolulu—were shut down in 2001. The company stated in a press release: ''We will continue our aggressive plans to acquire new aircraft, modernize our hub airport facilities, especially the new $1.2 billion Detroit Midfield complex, and enhance premium World Business Class and first class products.''

In August 2004, Northwest courted the wrath of the travel industry by attempting to offset $180 million in booking fees incurred through discount travel Internet sites and travel agents by levying a $7.50 fee per round-trip ticket and a $3.25 fee per one-way ticket. Calling the fees the equivalent of a fare increase, agents and Internet discounters immediately lashed back, threatening to stop booking Northwest flights or to feature Northwest's fares less prominently on web sites. SABRE Group, a large booking agency, filed suit with the airline for breach of contract and moved Northwest listings to a less prominent spot on their Internet site, prompting Northwest to file a countersuit for breach of contract. A few days after the initial announcement, Northwest rescinded the fees because other airlines failed to match them.

In June 2005, another attempt at raising fares failed for similar reasons. A $50 each-way hike in costs for business travelers, $5 to $10 increases in fares that competed with discount carriers' fares, and a two-night stay provision added on to certain fares were overturned when competing airlines refused to match Northwest's prices and stay requirements. Chairman Gary Wilson responded to Northwest's troubles by dumping 59 percent of his shares in the company, valued at $15.1 million, causing stock price to dive 12 percent amid rumors of impending bankruptcy. Desperate for cost savings and effectively unable to increase rates, the airline instituted a $50 per person fee (capped at $200 per family) for employees and eligible family members who wished to participate in the airline's longstanding employee benefit, ''pass travel,'' free travel in empty seats available at flight time.

The fee imposed on pass travel was only one of the concessions Northwest attempted to wring from its employees, most of whom were represented by four unions: the Air Line Pilots Association International (ALPA), the International Association of Machinists & Aerospace Workers (IAM, which represents agents, clerks, equipment service employees, and stock clerks), the Professional Flight Attendants Association (PFAA), and the

Aircraft Mechanics Fraternal Association (AMFA). From its early days Northwest was known for its acrimonious relationship with its workers, and its labor relations in the harsh business environment at the beginning of the 21st century proved no exception to history. Seeking to cut $1 billion in labor costs, the airline demanded $35 million in pay, benefit, and job cuts from its nonunion workers, then turned to the labor unions for more.

In 2005, Northwest's problems came to a head. As the economic recession deepened and oil prices rose precipitously, Northwest's mechanics went on strike, and a few weeks later Northwest announced that it would seek bankruptcy protection under Chapter 11, coincidentally on the same day as competitor Delta. Recovery in the industry, which suffered losses of some $30 billion in the early 2000s, was a much-discussed topic. Airline bankruptcy attorney William Rochelle, quoted in a September 2005 *Associated Press* article, postulated ''We are reading the first page in a thriller that will end either in resurrection or the death and burial of an entire industry as we know it today.''

Principal Subsidiaries

Northwest Airlines, Inc.; MLT Vacations Inc.; Northwest PARS, Inc.

Principal Competitors

AMR Corporation; Delta Air Lines, Inc.; UAL Corporation.

Further Reading

Arndt, Michael, ''Northwest's CEO Deplanes,'' *Business Week Online*, October 4, 2004.

''Bad News Hurts Airline's Stock,'' *Seattle Times*, June 14, 2005, p. C2.

''Bill Could Ward Off Chapter 11 for Delta, Northwest, CEOs Say,'' *Airline Business Report*, June 20, 2005.

Broderick, Richard, ''Aircraft Mechanics Negotiate Contract with Airline,'' *St. Paul Ledger*, April 19, 2001.

Burr, Barry B., ''Penalty Possible,'' *Pensions & Investments*, February 3, 2003, p. 23.

Carey, Susan, ''Northwest May Be Heading for Chapter 11,'' *Wall Street Journal*, June 13, 2005, p. C1.

Compart, Andrew, ''NWA Fees Target Consumers, Trade,'' *Travel Weekly*, August 30, 2004, p. 1.

Daniel, Caroline, ''U.S. Airlines Hit by Ratings Downgrades,'' *Financial Times*, July 1, 2002, p. 27.

Davies, R.E.G., *Airlines of the U.S. Since 1914*, New York: Putnam, 1972.

De Young, Dirk, and Tim Huber, ''Northwest Deal Will Boost Cargo,'' *Minneapolis-St. Paul CityBusiness*, August 1, 1997.

Doyle, Andrew, ''Operations: Crisis-Hit Airlines Shed Routes, Jobs,'' *Flight International*, April 1, 2003, p. 8.

Elliott, Stuart, ''American Companies Are Adjusting Almost Everything that Represents Them Overseas,'' *The New York Times*, April 4, 2003, p. C5.

Fedor, Liz, ''Is NWA Following a Strike Path?,'' *Star Tribune* (Minneapolis), June 2, 2005, p. 1D.

——, ''Chairman's Sales Fuel NWA Bankruptcy Fears,'' *Star Tribune* (Minneapolis), June 14, 2005, p. 1D.

——, ''Managers Training to Be Northwest Flight Attendants,'' *Star Tribune* (Minneapolis), June 15, 2005, p. 2D.

''Fitch Downgrades Northwest Airlines to 'CCC+'; Outlook Negative,'' *Business Wire*, June 1, 2005.

Flesher, John, ''Large Airlines Must Cut Costs to Survive,'' *Grand Rapids Press* (Michigan), June 3, 2005, p. C2.

Freed, Joshua, ''Delta, Northwest Seek Bankruptcy Protection,'' *Associated Press*, September 15, 2005.

Greenhouse, Steven, ''Toll Mounts as Northwest Plans to Cut 10,000 Jobs,'' *New York Times*, September 22, 2001, p. C5.

Gwynne, S.C., ''Flying into Trouble,'' *Time*, February 24, 1997.

Jackson, Robert, *The Sky Their Frontier: The Story of the World's Pioneer Airplanes and Routes, 1920–1940*, Airlife, Ltd., 1983.

Johnson, Tim J., ''Northwest Strike Sparks PR Battle,'' *Minneapolis-St. Paul CityBusiness*, September 7, 1998.

Kaydo, Chad, ''Northwest Airlines Strikes Out,'' *Sales & Marketing Management*, November 1998, p. 22.

Keane, Angela Grelling, ''Northwest Is Ready,'' *Traffic World*, October 27, 2003, p. 24.

Kelly, Kevin, ''A Midcourse Correction for Northwest,'' *Business Week*, July 13, 1992.

Kontzer, Tony, ''Northwest Airlines Imposes Charge for Independent Web Sites,'' *InternetWeek*, August 27, 2004.

Laibich, Kenneth, ''Winners in the Air Wars,'' *Fortune*, May 11, 1987.

Martinez, Michelle, ''Airport Unit Lures New Airlines, but Northwest Is Sensitive to Competition,'' *Crain's Detroit Business*, April 4, 2005, p. 3.

Maynard, Micheline, ''For Air Travelers, the Frill Is Gone,'' *International Herald Tribune*, June 10, 2005, p. 12.

McKenna, Ed, ''Freight Flies Higher,'' *Traffic World*, November 1, 2004, p. 29.

——, '' 'Robust' Year for Air Cargo,'' *Traffic World*, January 31, 2005, p. 29.

Moylan, Martin J., ''Northwest Airlines Mechanics Ready for Strike,'' *Saint Paul Pioneer Press* (Minnesota), June 2, 2005.

——, ''Mechanics Talk Tough,'' *Saint Paul Pioneer Press* (Minnesota), June 9, 2005.

——, ''Northwest Airlines Employees Will Have to Pay Fee for 'Pass Travel' Program,'' *Saint Paul Pioneer Press* (Minnesota), June 11, 2005.

——, ''Northwest Mechanics, Cleaners Union to Accept Concessions,'' *Saint Paul Pioneer Press* (Minnesota), June 25, 2005.

''Negotiations Leave Northwest Airlines Circling,'' *Corporate Report-Minnesota*, August 1997.

''Northwest Adds,'' *Air Cargo World*, February 2005, p. 5.

''Northwest Airlines,'' *Air Transport World*, July 2004, p. 89

''Northwest Asks Pilots for 20% Pay Cuts,'' *The New York Times*, February 27, 2003, p. C3.

''Northwest Has Loss and Sees No Upturn Soon,'' *The New York Times*, April 17, 2003, p. C4.

''Northwest Pilots Agree Labour Deal,'' *Airline Business*, November 1, 2004, p. 16.

''Northwest Shares Tumble 12%,'' *Cincinnati Post*, June 14, 2005, p. C9.

Reinan, John, ''Up in the Air: Seven Days on Northwest Airlines,'' *Star Tribune* (Minneapolis), August 29, 2005,

Torbenson, Eric, ''Northwest's Fare Hike Fails,'' *Dallas Morning News*, June 14, 2005.

Tully, Shawn, ''The Big Daddy of CFO's,'' *Fortune*, November 13, 1995.

Tully, Shawn, and Therese Eiben, ''Northwest and KLM: The Alliance from Hell,'' *Fortune*, June 24, 1996.

''U.S. Airlines Flying Low,'' *Corporate Finance*, November 2004, p. 4.

''U.S. Bailout Helps Northwest Post a Profit,'' *The New York Times*, June 27, 2005, p. C12.

Zagorin, Adam, ''Hunting the Predators,'' *Time*, April 20, 1998.

Zellner, Wendy, ''How Northwest Gives Competition a Bad Name,'' *Business Week*, March 16, 1998, p. 34.

—John Simley

—updates: James Poniewozik; Frederick C. Ingram; Jennifer Gariepy

Ocean Beauty Seafoods, Inc.

1100 West Ewing Street
Seattle, Washington 98199-1321
U.S.A.
Telephone: (206) 285-6800
Fax: (206) 285-9190
Web site: http://www.oceanbeauty.com

Private Company
Founded: 1910 as Washington Fish & Oyster
Employees: 250
Sales: $500 million (2003 est.)
NAIC: 311711 Seafood Canning; 311712 Fresh and
   Frozen Seafood Processing.

Based in Seattle, Washington, privately owned Ocean Beauty Seafoods, Inc. is one of the largest vertically integrated seafood companies in the Pacific Northwest. Although the company buys fish from all over the world, it specializes in seafood products originating in the waters of Alaska, Canada, and the Pacific Northwest. It then processes and distributes the seafood in facilities located in Alaska and the lower 48 states. In addition to the Ocean Beauty label, the company also sell its products under another 20 brand names, such as Ocean Bonita, Sea Choice, LASCCO, Three Star, Icy Point, Tribe, Pink Beauty, Searchlight, Commander, and Neptune. Customers include commodity buyers, retail buyers, food service buyers, private labels, and export buyers. Production facilities are located in Copper River/Cordova in Prince William Sound, home to a major salmon run; Naknek in southwestern Alaska, the world's largest sockeye fishery; Petersburg, Alaska, the largest chum fishery in the state; Kodiak, Alaska's second largest fishing port, where fresh, frozen and canned salmon, as well as halibut, perch, cod, pollock, flatfish, and herring are produced year round; Nikiski, one of Alaska's premiere fresh water salmon fisheries; Alitak, a remote processing plant at the south end of Kodiak Island in Alaska; and Excursion Inlet, located 40 miles west of Juneau. Ocean Beauty maintains distribution operations in Astoria, Washington; Boise, Idaho; Dallas, Texas;

Phoenix, Arizona; Portland, Oregon; Salt Lake City, Utah; and Seattle and Spokane, Washington.

Company Heritage Dates to the Early 1900s

Originally known as Washington Fish & Oyster, Ocean Beauty was founded in Seattle, Washington, in 1910. During the 1930s, the company first became involved in Alaska, decades before the territory achieved statehood, by opening a processing operation there. Over the years, Ocean Beauty expanded on its Alaskan business, becoming in 1954 the first seafood company to portion and vacuum pack Alaska seafood steaks and fillets. Then, in the 1960s, the company bought the oldest and largest seafood production plant in Kodiak, Alaska, established in 1911, to process the catch from Alaska's central gulf, a thriving area where some of the most fertile fishing grounds converged. Species included salmon, cod, halibut, herring, and pollock.

During the early decades of its history, Ocean Beauty also expanded its distribution capabilities. In 1948, the company opened a Spokane, Washington, branch to sell seafood to customers in the Inland Empire, an area between the Cascade Range and the Rocky Mountains, comprising eastern Washington, eastern Oregon, northern Idaho, and western Montana. The Pocatello, Idaho, distribution operation was launched in 1956 as Idaho Fish & Poultry and served customers in southeast Idaho. A year later, a Boise, Idaho, branch was added. Ocean Beauty moved into the Montana market in 1964, when it opened an office in Helena to distribute the company's seafood products that were either flown in or trucked in.

In 1978, Ocean Beauty opened a production plant in Cordova, Alaska, a remote town situated on Prince William Sound and close to the world-famous Copper River, where some of the more prized salmon in the world thrived. Salmon are born in fresh water, migrate to the ocean to feed, then return to their natal river as adults, swimming against the current, to lay their eggs and die. Because the flow of the Copper River is so strong and the distance, some 300 miles, to the headwaters so long, only the hardiest salmon are able to make the journey. Hence, they possess a high oil content to provide protection from the freezing waters that originate in the surrounding glacier-etched

Company Perspectives:
Setting the standard for quality since 1910.

mountains, making Copper River King and Sockeye salmon some of the world's best-tasting fish. Moreover, they are high in Omega 3 oil, which many people believe lowers cholesterol, allowing this product to command a premium price.

Ownership Change in Late 1970s

In 1979, Ocean Beauty was acquired by Sealaska Corporation, an Alaskan regional Native-owned corporation established several years earlier by the United States government. The creation of Sealaska and a dozen other for-profit regional corporations was the culmination of a century-long dispute over the ownership of aboriginal homelands. Soon after the United States purchased Alaska from Russia in 1867, the Tlingit Indians objected to the transaction, rightly pointing out that they and other Native tribes had inhabited the land for centuries before the Russians established their first settlement in 1784. Hence, the Russians should not be able to sell something that they never owned. The Tlingits were, in fact, shrewd businessmen, legendary for their trading skills. As an increasing number of Americans encroached on their lands over the ensuing decades, the Tlingits eventually turned to the U.S. courts, filing a lawsuit in the U.S. Court of Claims in 1947.

As the issue lingered in the court system, the problem of land claims only worsened after Alaska was granted statehood in 1959, because the terms of the act allowed Alaska the right to take possession of 100 million acres of land for development. Natives became concerned that such development might threaten their traditional lifestyle, and given the nature of some of the proposed projects, they had cause for concern. For example, the U.S. Army Corps of Engineers wanted to build a massive dam on the Yukon River to generate electricity, in the process submerging a number of Athabascan villages and forcing the relocation of more than 1,000 natives. Then there was Project Chariot, an idea floated by the U.S. Atomic Energy Commission, which wanted to set off a nuclear device to blast out a harbor at Cape Thompson to allow the shipping of minerals and other goods from northwest Alaska. While the economic advantages were obvious, no one considered the effects radioactive contamination might have on the Native population. Project Chariot caused such outrage that the first statewide Native newspaper, the *Tundra Times*, was established, providing a forum for Native land claims and other grievances. Next, the Alaska Federation of Natives was created and the land claim issue became its primary focus. In 1965, the Natives scored a major victory when U.S. Interior Secretary Stewart Udall granted a freeze on all land transfers pending a resolution to the Native claims. Perhaps the most important factor that led to a settlement was the 1968 discovery of oil on Alaska's North Slope. The major oil companies wanted access to the oil and to build a pipeline, but could not proceed as long as Native land claims were still outstanding. They eventually put their support behind the Alaska Natives. A settlement was reached in 1971 with the passage of the Alaska Native Claims Act (ANCSA),

which awarded the Alaska Natives $962.5 million and 44 million acres of land. To manage the assets, the government formed a dozen regional corporations; a 13th was later created for Alaska Natives living outside the state. Each Alaska Native born on or before December 18, 1971 received 100 shares of stock in their regional corporation. In exchange, the Natives gave up their aboriginal land claims and surrendered their aboriginal hunting and fishing right.

Representing Tlingit, Haidi, and Tsimshian Natives, Sealaska was the largest of the regional corporations with $93 million and 220,000 acres of timber land. Its directors decided not to pursue passive investments, such as oil leases, opting instead to invest in businesses that were important to the community. In addition to timber, Sealaska became involved in the seafood industry, which had played an important role in the area economy for many years, as well as the lives of many Sealaska shareholders. The purchase of Ocean Beauty was advantageous because the processor could purchase the catch of some shareholders while employing others in the plants, thereby circulating money throughout the region and building up local communities.

Unfortunately, Sealaska and Ocean Beauty suffered immediate setbacks. When a Belgian man died from botulism poisoning after eating salmon, the Food and Drug Administration recalled all canned salmon packed in 1980 and 1981 from eight Ocean Beauty processing plants in Alaska. The parent company also had to endure a stumbling timber industry and extremely high interest rates in the early 1980s. The situation became so dire that Sealaska was on the verge of declaring bankruptcy by the end of 1982. The company managed to recover, due in large part to the performance of Ocean Beauty, which in addition to the botulism scare was able to overcome a collapse in crab stock and low salmon returns.

During the 1980s, Ocean Beauty significantly expanded its processing and distribution operations. In 1982, it opened a distribution branch in Astoria, Washington, to serve customers in Oregon and Washington; this was supplemented by a nearby production facility. Also in 1982, Ocean Beauty established a distributorship in Salt Lake City that became the largest in the state of Utah. It not only served customers in Utah but those in Wyoming and Nevada as well. Ocean Beauty built up its processing capacity in 1984, acquiring a facility in Petersburg, Alaska, that offered both canning and freezing capabilities. Like many Ocean Beauty plants, it was seasonally operated, from late June to mid-September. Another development in 1984 was the opening of the Seattle distribution branch, which shared space with the company's headquarters and acted as a hub for seafood coming in from Alaska, Canada, Oregon, and Washington. In 1988, Ocean Beauty acquired another seasonal processing plant, this one in Naknek, Alaska. Operating seven days a week, 24 hours a day from late April to mid-August, the Naknek plant, located on Bristol Bay, processed salmon as well as herring. Another significant development was the 1989 launch of a processing vessel. Spanning 225 feet in length, the Ocean Pride was capable of accommodating more than 140 crew members and workers. The ship followed the fishing fleet into the Bering Sea, where king crab and bairdi and oplilo tanner crab were caught. By having a floating processing operation nearby, the fisherman did not have to leave the grounds to make the difficult, time-consuming trek through rough winter seas to

<table>
<tr><td colspan="2">Key Dates:</td></tr>
<tr><td>1910:</td><td>Washington Fish & Oyster is founded.</td></tr>
<tr><td>1954:</td><td>The company becomes the first to vacuum pack Alaskan seafood.</td></tr>
<tr><td>1979:</td><td>The company is acquired by Sealaska Corporation.</td></tr>
<tr><td>1984:</td><td>A Petersburg, Alaska, facility is acquired.</td></tr>
<tr><td>1990:</td><td>Ika Muda International acquires the company.</td></tr>
<tr><td>1995:</td><td>All distribution operations adopt the Ocean Beauty name.</td></tr>
<tr><td>2001:</td><td>Landlock Seafood acquisition opens the Texas market.</td></tr>
<tr><td>2004:</td><td>A Phoenix distribution branch opens.</td></tr>
</table>

southern delivery points. Moreover, they cut down on the ''dead loss'' of crab on board.

Ocean Beauty Put Up for Sales in the Late 1980s

In the latter half of the 1980s, the market for Alaskan seafood prospered. Most of it was exported to Pacific Rim countries, in particular Japan. By the end of the decade, Ocean Beauty, operating twelve processing facilities and eight regional distribution centers in five western states, processed and marketed more than 100 million pounds of seafood, generating annual sales of nearly $200 million and accounting for about three-quarters of Sealaska's total revenues. As a result, the parent company rebounded in the 1980s after posting just three profitable years during its first decade of existence. In 1989, Sealaska was named the Governor's Alaskan Exporter of the Year due to its strong timber and seafood sales. Because the company wanted to pursue other business opportunities, it elected to put Ocean Beauty on the block in late 1989, the result of a formal strategic review initiated several months earlier. By the end of August 1990, the terms of a sale were completed and Ocean Beauty was acquired by Ika Muda International, a company based in Pekalongan, Indonesia. Ika Muda was Indonesia's largest prawn producer and also maintained seafood processing and trading operations in the Far East and the United States. Sealaska realized a $14.6 million profit on the deal.

A group of local investors bought back the company in the 1990s, but as it had done during Sealaska's tenure, Ocean Beauty continued to expand over the course of the decade regardless of who owned it. A three-million pound capacity cold-storage facility was added to the Kodiak plant in 1992, allowing the company to lay away seafood during production peaks. This surplus could then be used for value-added production when the plant was less busy. In 1995, Ocean Beauty acquired a pair of specialty companies: Los Angeles Smoking & Curing Company (Lascco) and Three Star Smoked Fish Company. Lascco had been in business since 1921 processing smoked fish and pickled fish products, while Three Star had been producing similar products on the West Coast since 1938. Another smoked fish operation, Boston-based Rite Foods, would be acquired in 1999 to flesh out this specialty division. In 1995, Ocean Beauty also took steps to build up some brand recognition, as its distribution operations in Astoria, Boise, Helena, Pocatello, Portland, Salt Lake City, Seattle, and Spokane all adopted the Ocean Beauty name. By the end of the decade, Ocean Beauty sales topped the $300 million mark.

In the early years of the 21st century, expansion continued for Ocean Beauty. In 2000, it acquired Monroe, Washington-based Circle Sea, a company with 20 years of experience producing and marketing smoked and pickled products for foodservice and retail customers. Ocean Beauty moved into the Texas market in 2001 with the purchase of Landlock Seafood Co. of Carrollton, Texas, a seafood processing company founded in 1978 and the leading seafood distributor to the Dallas, Fort Worth, and Houston markets. With Ocean Beauty's backing, Landlock was able to move into other untapped markets in the Southwest. In the fall of 2002, Ocean Beauty agreed to merge its operation with that of Los Angeles-based Prospect Enterprises to create a new seafood-distribution company with combined sales of $325. However, the deal was scuttled by early 2003. Also in 2002, Ocean Beauty acquired three Alaskan production plants: Cook Inlet Processing, located on the Nikiski Peninsula, and processing plants located in Alitak and Excursion Inlet purchased from Wards Cove Packing Co. Ocean Beauty opened a new distribution operation in Phoenix in July 2004. In that same year, it also acquired several noteworthy brands, including Commander Sardines, Port Clyde Sardines and Fish Steaks, and Neptune Minced Clams. With annual revenues in the neighborhood of $500 million, Ocean Beauty now ranked among the top ten of North American seafood suppliers.

Principal Competitors

Bumble Bee Seafoods, L.L.C.; Heritage Salmon; Peter Pan Seafoods, Inc.

Further Reading

Brown, Cathy, ''Sealaska Corp. Has Benefited from Tlingit and Haida Traditions in Trading,'' *Juneau Empire*, January 17, 1999.

Brown, Cathy, Lori Thomson, and Svend Holst, ''A Struggle For Land,'' *Juneau Empire*, January 17, 1999.

Mallott, Byron, ''Sealaska Has Best Profit Year in 1987,'' *Alaska Journal of Commerce*, June 6, 1988, p. 7.

Manna, Victor, ''Sealaksa Changes Course,'' *Alaska Business Monthly*, March 1990, p. 12.

''Sealaska Charts a New but Liquid Course,'' *Alaska Journal of Commerce*, December 25, 1989, p. 13.

Tremaine, Richard, ''Catching Seafood Dollars in Alaska,'' *Alaska Business Monthly*, October 1989, p. 91.

—Ed Dinger

OENEO S.A.

7 rue Louis Murat
Paris F-75008
France
Telephone: +33 1 58 36 10 90
Fax: +33 1 42 25 03 41
Web site: http://www.OENEO.com

Public Company
Incorporated: 1838 as Tonnellerie Moreau
Employees: 1,576
Sales: EUR 162.7 million ($205 million) (2004)
Stock Exchanges: Euronext Paris
Ticker Symbol: SABT
NAIC: 321920 Wood Container and Pallet Manufacturing

Formerly known as Sabaté Diosos S.A., OENEO S.A. is a major player in the international wine industry. The company is the world's second largest producer of cork-based and other closure systems, and is also the world's leading producer of oak casks. Slightly more than half of the group's revenues, which amounted to nearly EUR 163 million ($205 million) in 2004, come from its oak cast operations. France represents the company's single largest market, at 35 percent of sales, while the rest of Europe adds another 36 percent to sales. North America accounts for 17 percent of group sales. In the mid-2000s, OENEO has shifted the focus of its wine closure production to emphasize its "technological" closures, and especially its patented Altec synthetic corks and the new DIAM wine closure system, introduced in 2005. As such, the company has sold off its natural cork production unit, as well as other noncore operations, such as its cork flooring subsidiary. The company also has re-centered its oak cask manufacturing business around its French production unit, shutting down its oak staves mill in Iowa. The company hopes that these measures will help it restore its profitability after several years of losses. OENEO is listed on the Euronext Paris Stock Exchange.

Cork Maker in the 1930s

Modeste Sabaté was a journalist in his native Catalan, Spain, who fled his country when Ferdinand Franco came to power after the Spanish Civil War. Sabaté settled in Roussillon, near the Spanish border and the French Mediterranean basin. In 1939, Sabaté founded a company and began producing corks. He was joined by sons Augustin, Alex, Bernard, and Georges in 1960.

Cork had been used as a bottle stopper since the 1600s, when Dom Perignon fashioned the first cork for his famous champagne. Cork was quickly adopted for the so-called tranquil wines as well and, before long, cork had become synonymous with bottled wine. At first centered in the south of France, the cork industry gradually moved south, following the richest areas of the cork-producing oak, Quercus Suber in the Catalan region of Spain and Portugal. One of the earliest of the industrial cork makers appeared in Spain in the 1750s.

Cork remained a fairly rare commodity, growing only in certain areas along the Mediterranean basin. The growth cycle of the cork oak was rather long—more than 30 years for the maturation of a tree. Harvesting cork was a delicate process as well. A first harvest, culling the so-called male bark from the 30-year-old tree, exposed the underlying female or mother bark, which then required a further 9 to 11 years of growth before the cork could be harvested. The production of finished cork itself required another year to two years of effort.

Yet cork's success among French and international winemakers came from the natural material's qualities, allowing just enough air to pass through to aid in the oxidation process of aging fine wines, while being flexible enough to provide a tight seal for the bottle. Nonetheless, cork was not without its shortcomings. Being rare, it was rather expensive for bottlers of cheaper wines. In addition, cork was long plagued by its vulnerability to 2,4,6-trichloroanisole, or TCA, a chemical compound capable of tainting wine—producing the musty, off-flavors of so-called corked wines. The wine industry began a search for a means of eliminating TCA.

Modeste and sons, especially Augustin Sabaté, began building the company into one of France's leading cork producers. The company also took a leading role in the search for means of reducing, if not eliminating entirely, TCA from their corks. In 1985, the company patented a new method for cleaning cork, using hydrogen peroxide and dubbed SBM by Sabaté. The inven-

Company Perspectives:

Present in all major wine producing regions, OENEO is the only international group to propose a global offer of value added products and services to the wine industry. OENEO is the largest manufacturer of barrels for fine wines and the second largest provider of cork based closures in the world.

tion represented somewhat of a breakthrough for the wine industry and helped Sabaté capture a leading position among the world's cork makers. Modeste Sabaté died in 1986, and Augustin Sabaté took over as head of the family-owned company.

Integrated Wine Products Provider at the Turn of the 21st Century

The French wine industry stimulated the creation of other industries aside from cork making. One of the most important of these, at least as far as the fame of French wines was concerned, was that of the production of the casks used for aging wines. Crafted (typically by hand until rather late in the 20th century) from a specific species of French oak, the casks became essential to the quality of French wines.

An early cooperage was that of Tonnellerie Moreau, based in Charente, a region of western France near the Bordeaux wine industry. Founded in 1838, that company enjoyed a degree of prominence up until World War I. Moreau was joined by other cooperages, including Sequin, founded in 1870. The two companies were later brought together under Remy Martin, which took a majority share in Moreau in 1958 and reoriented the company toward the production of casks for Remy Martin's core cognac and related spirits products. Remy Martin acquired full control of the company in 1972. By the late 1970s, more than 70 percent of the company's sales came from its parent company. By then, however, Sequin Moreau had decided to refocus itself as a producer of casks for the Bordeaux wine producers, then for other wine producer regions of France. After successfully imposing itself as a leading cooperage for the French market, Sequin Moreau began attacking the international market, opening an office in Australia in 1988 and an office in Napa, California, in 1992. The company also diversified into producing casks from other species of oak, notably from Russia and North America.

Another fast-growing cooperage was that of Tonnellerie Radoux, founded in 1947 by Robert Radoux. That company crafted its cask after the traditional fashion until the arrival of Radoux's son, Christian, as the company's head. The younger Radoux converted the company to limited liability status in 1982 and began industrializing much of its production processes, while maintaining nonetheless traditional methods, materials, and designs. In the late 1980s and early 1990s, Radoux began to seek greater vertical integration, buying up Sciage de Berry in 1987 and France Merrain in 1991 to ensure its supply of cask components. The company also launched its own wine-making ingredients distribution subsidiary in 1991.

Radoux sold out to investor Michel de Tapol in 1997. Two years later, Tapol merged Radoux with Sequin Moreau, one of its primary competitors. The new company, dubbed Diosos,

became the world's leading producer of oak casks for the wine market. Remy Martin, meanwhile, remained a major shareholder in the company.

During this time, Sabaté also had been growing strongly. The SBM patent had helped establish the quality of Sabaté's cork, and the company soon grew to become the main rival for industry leader Corticeira Amorim, of Portugal. A major step in Sabaté's development came with its acquisition of Spain's Corchos de Mérida, a company specialized in raw product purchasing and storage. This acquisition enabled the company to begin the process toward creating a vertically integrated production chain. The Mérida acquisition notably helped the company ensure the supply and quality of its raw cork requirements.

The company's requirements were growing steadily in the late 1980s. Under Augustin Sabaté, the company now turned toward industrializing its production process. In 1991, the company completed construction of a new 65,000-square-meter headquarters and production facility in the town of Ceret. The company then was able to begin converting its production processes to comply with ISO 9002 regulations, a certificate the company obtained in 1995. In 1994, Sabaté confirmed its intention to build its position, placing its stock on the Paris Stock Exchange's unlisted market. One year later, however, the company transferred its listing to the Parisian Exchange's Secondary Market.

Sabaté's public offering and new production facility also enabled it to pursue development of a new product—a new cork material that the company dubbed Altec. The introduction of Altec allowed Sabaté to straddle an ongoing argument among wine producers of the virtues of natural cork versus newer artificial corks then appearing on the market. Altec was in fact a hybrid of natural and artificial materials, using cork powder produced from a purified cork and combining that with a material developed for Sabaté by Akso Nobel. The new Altec presented a number of interesting properties, notably a greater elasticity than natural cork, as well as a greater resistance to TCA tainting, while retaining some of natural cork's porosity.

Launched in 1995, Altec made steady inroads among wine producers, particularly on the international scene. By 1997, the company was selling more than 200 million units per year, some 80 percent of which were sold to the United States. By then, Sabaté had opened an office in the United States, under subsidiary Sabaté USA, located near the heart of the California wine-producing region, which began operations in 1995. Sabaté continued to seek means to ensure its vertical integration, and in 1996, the company created a new subsidiary, Sabaté Maroc, a company specialized in the purchasing and treatment of raw cork. A year later, the company expanded horizontally, acquiring cork flooring and materials specialist Aplicork, based in Spain.

Augustin Sabaté died in 1998 and son Marc Sabaté took over as the company's president. By then, Sabaté had sold more than one billion Altec corks, confirming the product's success. That number was to double again just two years later. The company faced a slight setback, however. Sabaté initially had claimed that Altec was entirely TCA-free. A series of TCA taints among its customers, however, forced the company to admit that it was impossible to eliminate the possibility of TCA tainting entirely. Despite a range of bad publicity, the extent of the TCA tainting

Key Dates:

1838: Tonnellerie Moreau, later a founding member of Diosos, is founded.

1870: Seguin, another member of the later Diosos company, begins producing casks.

1939: Modeste Sabaté starts up a cork production company in Rousillon, France.

1947: Robert Radoux begins crafting casks.

1958: Moreau and Sequin merge and Remy Martin becomes a majority shareholder.

1960: Modeste Sabaté is joined by sons Augustin, Alex, Bernard, and Georges.

1972: Remy Martin acquires full control of Moreau Seguin, which produces casks for cognac and eau-de-vie.

1977: Christian Radoux takes over his father's business and introduces industrial production methods.

1979: Moreau Seguin begins producing casks for the French wine industry.

1985: Sabaté patents the SBM cork cleansing process.

1986: Sabaté acquires Corchos de Mérida of Spain.

1990: Seguin Moreau begins international expansion and begins producing casks using Russian and American oaks.

1991: Sabaté opens a new 65,000-square-meter headquarters and production facility in Ceret, France.

1994: Sabaté launches its first public offering on the Parisian unlisted securities market.

1995: Sabaté joins the Paris Stock Exchange's Secondary Market.

1999: Moreau Seguin and Radoux merge to form Diosos S.A.

2000: Sabaté and Diosos merge to form Sabaté Diosos S.A.

2003: Company name is changed to OENEO.

remained limited to a very small percentage of all bottles using Altec corks. The setback barely slowed down the rise of Altec sales in Sabaté's revenues; by 2001, Altec represented some 45 percent of Sabaté's cork sales.

Sabaté moved to expand its bottle-stopping range as it turned toward the new century. In 1999, the company acquired two other companies, including Switzerland's Suber, a producer of cork for high-quality wines, as well as screwtop caps. Sabaté's entry into this latter category represented its growing determination to follow the trend toward internationalization of the wine industry, which saw consumers turning away from France to embrace new wines from other parts of the world. Screwtop caps were widely considered the best means of closing a bottle of wine. Although French winemakers—and their customers—refused to consider abandoning natural corks, especially for high-quality wines meant to age for long periods of time, other markets, such as Australia, were proving more and more receptive to the idea of adopting screwtop caps. Among the notable advantages of this system was the virtual absence of TCA tainting. Later in 1999, Sabaté took a stake in Sibel, a maker of corks for champagne and sparkling wines. By 2000, the company had completed its takeover of Sibel, taking 100 percent control.

Sabaté's determination to place itself in line with developments in the worldwide wine industry led it to make a more dramatic move in 2000. In that year the company announced that it had reached an agreement to merge with Diosos S.A., creating Sabaté Diosos S.A. The merger doubled Sabaté in size, as both the cork division and the cooperage division produced more than EUR 100 million in revenues. Under terms of the agreement, Marc Sabaté and Michel de Tapol agreed to function as co-CEOs of the enlarged group, which sought to position itself as a provider of services and products to the wine industry. Although greeted with some skepticism by stock market observers—who criticized in particular the lack of production synergies between the two companies—Sabaté Diosos remained confident that the merger would enable both sides of the larger group to take advantage of its widened distribution network as it wooed the world's winemakers.

The company, which continued to enlarge its production facilities in Ceret, moved to boost its customer service capacity as well. In 2002, the company opened new finishing facilities in South Africa and in California, increasing the range and depth of its services for its customers in those markets. The following year, Sabaté Diosos opened a new stave mill in Bloomfield, Iowa, in an effort to produce lower-cost casks based on American woods for the U.S. market. Also in 2003, the company, through local partnerships, added new finishing operations in Australia, Italy, and Chile. In that year, as well, the company expanded its cask-making capacity through the acquisition of Australia-based Schahinger.

New Name and New Focus in the Mid-2000s

Yet the hoped-for synergies from the merger Sabaté Diosos never appeared, just as the company struggled amid the difficult economic climate of the early 2000s. The company's sales appeared to enter a freefall, with revenues dropping from below EUR 202 million at the end of 2002 to less than EUR 163 million at the end of 2004. Already by 2002, the company was forced to take steps to counter its downward spiral. Among its first moves was to eliminate its dual-leadership—a move made as much to restore investor confidence in the group's direction. Michel de Tapol left the company; Marc Sabaté stepped down as well, turning over the CEO spot to Gérard Epin, formerly CEO at Sonepar Distribution, a distributor of electrical products.

Epin led a restructuring of Sabaté Diosos, refocusing the company around a core of wine closures and casks. As part of that effort, the company shut down its parquet floor production division, then sold off its transportation operations and its nonwine-related cork products activities in 2003. Following its restructuring, Sabaté Diosos decided to change its name in order to reinforce its new focus on the wine industry. In June 2003, the company became known as OENEO S.A.

Yet OENEO's difficulties continued into mid-decade. Notably, its new Iowa mill failed to live up to the company's expectations, as U.S. winemakers continued to use wood chips for their lower-priced wines; yet the Iowa mill's American wood casks were seen as unsuitable for higher-priced wines. After the mill lost nearly $1.2 million in 2004, OENEO sold off the plant in January 2005.

Meanwhile, the continued shift away from traditional cork wine closures, especially in the international market, led OENEO to restructure its cork-making operation in 2004. As part of that restructuring, the company abandoned its natural cork operations and re-centered its closures division on its technical corks, synthetique closures, and especially its "technological" cork production.

Backing up its refocusing effort, OENEO launched two new closure products at the beginning of 2005. The first was a new type of twist-on cap, called the S-cap. More important to the group's future, however, was the unveiling of its newest technological cork in January 2005. Called the DIAM (or Diamond) and developed in conjunction with the French Atomic Energy Commission, the new closures were produced using a process similar to that used to produce decaffeinated coffee. The resulting taint-proof cork was greeted enthusiastically by the international wine industry. With a new name and backed by the success of its DIAM and Altec technological corks, OENEO expected to remain a leading player in the global wine closures market into the 21st century.

Principal Subsidiaries

Corchos de Mérida S.A.; Sabaté Maroc SARL; Altec S.A.; Suber Suisse S.A.; SC Finance; Diosos S.A.

Principal Competitors

Corticeira Amorim; Sociedade Gestora de Participaoes Sociais, S.A.; Supreme Corq Inc.; Tonnellerie Francois Freres S.A.; Tonnellerie Vicard S.A.; Nadalie-Tonnellerie Ludonnaise S.A.; Tonnellerie Taransaud S.A.; Tonnellerie Saury S.A.; Tonnellerie Bouts S.A.

Further Reading

"Les bouchons d'OENEO," *L'Expansion,* October 29, 2003.

Brockhoff, Anne, "OENEO Sells Iowa Oak Stave Mill," *just-drinks.com,* January 14, 2005.

Cuny, Delphine, "Scepticisme sur le regroupement Sabaté-Diosos," *La Tribune,* October 24, 2000.

Hiaring, Philip, "Sabaté," *Wines & Vines,* August 1999.

Hunter Gordon, Kim, "OENEO and the Diamond Route to Recovery," *Beverage Daily.com,* January 20, 2005.

Kinetz, Erika, "Cork and Barrel Makers Face Risks Too," *International Herald Tribune,* June 23, 2001.

Matterson, Helen, "OENEO Uncorked Down Under," *Australasian Business Intelligence,* February 14, 2005.

Mowbray, Simon, "Cork Producer Claims Its Research Has Come with a Solution to Wine Taint," *Grocer,* July 27, 2004, p. 54.

"New Closures Force OENEO to Change Tack," *Australasian Business Intelligence,* March 7, 2005.

"OENEO's Process Is Veritas Validated," *Wines & Vines,* July 2005, p. 10.

"Plastic Wine Stoppers: A Corking Row," *Economist,* June 5, 1999.

"Sabaté Diosos abaisse ses perspectives de croissance," *La Tribune,* July 25, 2001.

"Sabate Diosos to Restructure Its Cork Activity," *Les Echos,* October 2, 2002.

—M.L. Cohen

The Oilgear Company

2300 South 51st Street
Milwaukee, Wisconsin 53219-2340
U.S.A.
Telephone: (414) 327-1700
Fax: (414) 327-0532
Web site: http://www.oilgear.com

Public Company
Incorporated: 1921
Employees: 750
Sales: $94.4 million (2004)
Stock Exchanges: NASDAQ
Ticker Symbol: OLGR
NAIC: 333996 Fluid Power Pump and Motor
Manufacturing

Sometimes confused as an energy company, The Oilgear Company, based in Milwaukee, Wisconsin, is a global manufacturer of products that rely on fluid power—the use of pressurized fluids in the case of hydraulics and pressurized gas in pneumatics—to perform mechanical tasks. Oilgear products include hydraulic pumps, motors, valves, fluid meters, and the electronic systems needed to control fluid power. A wide variety of industries are customers, including automotive, chemical, petroleum, food, lumber, machine tool, metals, mining, plastics, and rubber. In addition to the United States, the company maintains facilities—combining manufacturing, service, and training—around the world, in Australia, France, Germany, India, Italy, Japan, Korea, Mexico, Singapore, and the United Kingdom. Sales engineering support is offered in more than 50 countries. Although a public company listed on the NASDAQ, Oilgear is 46 percent-owned by an employee stock plan.

Heritage Dating to the 1880s

Oilgear grew out of Bucyrus International, Inc., a Milwaukee-based manufacturer of mining equipment founded in 1880 in Bucyrus, Ohio. Its founder, Daniel P. Eells, originally bought the idle Bucyrus Machine Company to produce equipment for the railroads, such as locomotive drive wheels, car wheels and axles, and hand cars. But the company changed in focus in 1882 when two railroads contracted Bucyrus to make steam shovels for use in railroad construction. Eells sensed a business opportunity and began concentrating on the manufacture of excavating equipment, used not only for laying railroads but mining and public works projects as well. Business was so strong that Bucyrus outgrew its facilities and relocated to South Milwaukee County, which offered the company financial incentives to move to Wisconsin. Bucyrus excavating equipment was used in many of the major construction projects of the day, including the building of the Panama Canal. In 1911 it ceased to be a family-owned business when it merged with two competitors to become a public company, named Bucyrus Company. Along the way Bucyrus introduced a number of innovations as it achieved a reputation as a top-notch manufacturer of heavy-duty excavating equipment. It was no wonder that the company would be involved in the use of hydraulics, in particular fluid power, to provide power to the massive components of its equipment.

The Oilgear Company was founded in 1921, growing out of efforts at Bucyrus. According to the Founding Industries of Wisconsin project, it was founded by three men: E.K. Swigart, Walter Ferris, and W.E. Magie. Although never flashy, the company was a success from the outset, never suffering a loss, able to weather periodic downturns in the economy, including the Great Depression of the 1930s. Oilgear started out producing a single hydraulic press line, but gradually expanded its offerings to cater to a growing range of industries. During the 1950s it became a global player, opening offices in Mexico, Great Britain, France, Germany, and Italy, as well as Australia to serve the Pacific Rim. The company was best known for big systems offering high pressures. It was not until the 1970s that the company tried to grow by external means. It acquired Petrodyne Co., in 1972, followed by the purchase of Ball Manufacturing Inc. in 1978. A major market for the company was petroleum exploration, but when the offshore oil drilling market collapsed in the late 1970s, Oilgear once again proved its flexibility in finding new growth opportunities, in particular through the marriage of computer technology with hydraulics, setting the stage for the modern era of the company.

Oilgear was one of the first companies to use microprocessors with hydraulics, and in the early 1980s began to beef up its research and development budgets to build complete computer-control systems, buying only the memory chips, to find more industry applications for its products. One significant success story during this period was the introduction of large, high-pressure forging presses that sold for as much as $4 million, used to make aluminum windows, pots and pans, plywood, plastic automotive panels, car wheels, and construction machinery. On the other end of the scale, Oilgear made small hydraulic units and component pumps used in machine tools and riding mowers. Annual sales totaled about $40 million in the mid-1980s, but by the end of the decade increased by 50 percent to $61.8 million. Net income held steady around the $1.7 million mark, due primarily to the company's ongoing need to invest in R&D and make large capital equipment purchases in order to remain competitive.

Entering the 1990s with Little Recognition

As Oilgear entered the 1990s, it was described by the *Milwaukee Sentinel* as the Rodney Dangerfield of Milwaukee industry: "Despite a solid record of earnings and equipment that is used in everything from theme park rides to riding mowers and the production of aluminum windows, Oilgear may not get the respect it deserves. . . . its products are hardly well-known to the average consumer even in the company's home town." Oilgear's longtime president, Carl L. Gosewehr, explained, "We don't build an end product. You don't drive an Oilgear pump around your yard to cut your lawn." Nevertheless, the company was well respected in the hydraulics field, finding a way to prosper as a niche operator. "We go to the marketplace with specific features, unique features, things that offer the customer more. We fit only in those markets where people are looking for additional features," Gosewehr explained to the *Sentinel*.

With a recession hurting domestic sales, Oilgear's international business became a focal point in the early 1990s. At the start of the decade, overseas sales accounted for about 45 percent of all revenues. In addition to its three manufacturing plants—located in Milwaukee; Freemont, Nebraska; and Longview, Texas—the company at this stage also operated plants in England and Spain as well as a licensed operation in Japan. To take advantage of projected growth in Latin America and the Pacific Rim, the Mexican and Australian offices were expanded. In addition, new one-person offices were established in Singapore and Brazil in 1992. (Several years earlier, in 1987, Oilgear had attempted to enter the Brazilian power fluid market by way of a joint venture, an effort that failed to take root.)

In 1991 Gosewehr retired, replaced by Otto F. Klieve, followed by 27-year Oilgear veteran David Zuege, the company's current chief executive, who took charge in December 1995. The former chief financial officer inherited the reins of a company that generated sales of $82.1 million and net income of $2.2 million in 1994, Oilgear's most profitable year since 1990. Despite changes in leadership, the company continued to follow its strategy of pursuing niche opportunities. While the main product at the time was piston pumps, new products were in development for the mobile market, for a new lawn mower product and sweepers, skidders, and drive fans for use in buses. The company also launched an effort to boost Asian sales and offset declines in the European market. Asian countries were still using old hydraulic technologies relying on water as a medium and were ripe to make the transition to Oilgear's more advanced products, which relied on oil as a medium. In early 1997 Oilgear established a manufacturing presence in the region. Rather than look to China like its competitors, Oilgear elected to enter the market through India. It forged a joint venture with Harman Engineers, an Indian automation and process controls manufacturer. Oilgear retained a 51 percent interest in the business, named Harman Oilgear Ltd. In addition to geographic expansion, the venture was intended to serve the consumer food processing sector, growing rapidly in Asia and expected to enjoy continued growth for the next decade. Oilgear also looked to expand in Central and South America by opening a sales and service facility in Brazil. Another area of opportunity for Oilgear was the return to oil drilling applications after 20 years. With oil exploration on the upswing, Oilgear began developing systems to moor and stabilize offshore drilling platforms. For the year 1997 Oilgear recorded sales of $90.9 million and net income of $2.7 million.

Despite softness in the U.S. fluid power industry in 1998, Oilgear enjoyed record sales, totaling $96.8 million. Nevertheless, profit margins were hurt by the drop in demand as well as problems in launching new products and a depression that visited Asia. Management responded with some cost-cutting initiatives, resulting in a drop in net income to $575,000 for the year. Most of the problems occurred at the tail end of 1998. Zuege told those gathered at the annual shareholders meeting that the fourth quarter was disappointing, adding, "That is one of my great understatements. We weren't disappointed. We were crushed with the results of the fourth quarter." The company suffered a fourth quarter loss of $682,000. To shore up the company, salaries were cut and some jobs eliminated, but it was clear that Oilgear still faced a period of uncertainty. Although Zuege felt the company may have experienced the worst of the bad times, he told shareholders, "We don't see a dramatic turnaround in the immediate future."

While sales dipped to $90.7 million in 1999, cost containment steps taken in 1998 helped Oilgear to restore profitability, as net income increased 131 percent to $1.3 million. At the same time the company was able to increase the engineering and development budget to introduce enhancements and launch new products to help the company remain competitive during difficult times in the fluid power industry. The company also looked to improve its marketing by forming an alliance with East Aurora, New York-based Moog Inc., a global manufacturer of precision control components and systems. Products from the two companies were often integrated. The new arrangement called for Oilgear and Moog to do joint marketing and sales, making it easier for customers to do business with

---

Key Dates:

1921: The company is founded.
1972: Petrodyne Co. is acquired.
1978: Ball Manufacturing is acquired.
1995: David Zuege is named chief executive.
1997: A joint venture is formed with Harman Engineers, a manufacturer in India.
2000: The power fluid market crashes.
2004: Oilgear returns to profitability.

---

both of them while receiving a better system at a more competitive price.

New Century, New Challenges

Strong growth at the end of 1999 appeared to bode well for Oilgear as it entered a new century, but 2000 proved to be another difficult year. Sales improved modestly to $92.3 million, but earnings declined again, totaling just $800,000, due primarily to a softening in the U.S. fluid power market in the second half of the year and the depressed Euro and other undervalued currencies. Nevertheless, Oilgear continued to invest in R&D, well aware that a major reason the company was able to do as well as it did during tough times was its technological edge. Given that the United States now slipped into recession, as did the world economy, and the world fluid power market as a result was crippled, the company needed every advantage it could find. Sales fell to $82.6 million and the company posted a net loss of $1.7 million for the year. Cost cutting was once again the order of the day, the implementing of which actually resulted in a slight profit in the fourth quarter, preventing 2001 from becoming even a worse experience for Oilgear. While fat was trimmed, the company refuse to cut muscle, continuing to invest in product development. It also looked to serve customers wherever they could be found. In 2001 Oilgear formed a subsidiary in Japan to do business in that market, replacing a joint venture licensing arrangement that had struggled during Japan's own recession.

There were glimmers of hopes of increased sales in early 2002, but they proved to be a mirage. Simply put, the company made components that were part of end products, but if the end products were not being sold there were no customers for the components. Now even the cost-cutting measures affected

R&D: In 2002 the company spent $1.7 million on product development compared with $2.1 million in 2001. Oilgear also closed one of its three U.S. plants, the facility in Longview, Texas. A company that had prided itself on an ability to turn a profit even under the most difficult of conditions now found itself awash in red ink. In 2002 sales dipped to $75.3 million and the net loss increased to nearly $5.5 million. When the economy began to recover in 2003, the fluid power industry lagged behind. Sales for Oilgear improved somewhat to $81 million, but the company lost another $1.8 million.

As the worldwide economy continued to rebound in 2004, Oilgear finally began to see a recovery in its business as well. The company was profitable in all four quarters, and the company returned to the black for the year, when it recorded sales of $94.4 million and net income of $423,000. Moreover, Oilgear enjoyed sales increases in the United States, Europe, and Asia. The company began 2005 with the highest backlog of orders in its history, boding well for Oilgear's continued comeback.

Principal Subsidiaries

Oilgear Towler GmbH; Oilgear Towler Ltd; Oilgear Towler S.A.; Oilgear Towler Australia Pty. Ltd.; Oilgear Mexicana S.A. de C.V.; Oilgear do Brazil Hydraulica Ltda.; Oilgear Towler Japan Co.; Oilgear Towler Polyhydron Pvt. Ltd. (51%).

Principal Competitors

Haskel International, Inc.; Koyo Seiko Co., Ltd.; SC Hydraulic Engineering, Inc.

Further Reading

Barnes, Brooks, "Milwaukee-Based Oilgear Forms Joint Venture in India," *Milwaukee Journal Sentinel*, March 21, 1997, p. 32.
——, "Oilgear Tries to Add a Little Sizzle," *Milwaukee Journal Sentinel*, April 6, 1997, p. 1.
Bennett, Keith W., "Fluid Power Keeps Pumping," *Iron Age*, February 7, 1983, p. 28.
Doherty, Chuck, "Like Dangerfield, Oilgear May Not Be Getting the Respect It Deserves," *Milwaukee Sentinel*, July 12, 1990, p. 4.
Gallun, Alby, "As Fluid Power Market Slips, Oilgear Loses Traction," *Business Journal-Milwaukee*, April 23, 1999, p. 6.
Hawkins, Lee, Jr., "Oilgear Forms Alliance with N.Y. Company," *Milwaukee, Journal Sentinel*, June 9, 1999, p. 2.
Holley, Paul, "Hyping Hydraulics—Taking a "Solid Company" into the Future," *Business Journal—Milwaukee*, March 9, 1996, p. 19.

—Ed Dinger

Okuma Holdings Inc.

5-25-1 Shima-Oguchi, Ohguchi-cho
Niwa-gun 480-0193
Japan
Telephone: (+81) 587 95 7820
Fax: (+81) 587 95 4807
Web site: http://www.okuma.co.jp

Public Company
Incorporated: 1898 as Okuma Noodle Machine Co.
Employees: 1,895
Sales: $822 million (2004)
Stock Exchanges: Tokyo
NAIC: 332721 Precision Turned Product Manufacturing;
    333319 Other Commercial and Service Industry
    Machinery Manufacturing; 333515 Cutting Tool and
    Machine Tool Accessory Manufacturing; 333518
    Other Metalworking Machinery Manufacturing

Okuma Holdings Inc. is the name adopted in 2005 for the merged operations of Okuma Corporation and two affiliated companies, Okuma & Howa Machinery Ltd. and Okuma Engineering Co. The new company is one of Japan's and the world's largest manufacturers of computer-numerical-control (CNC) machinery and systems. The company, which stemmed from a maker of noodle machinery at the turn of the 20th century, produces a wide range of machinery for every industry. The company's largest production is in machining centers, which combine a range of production processes into a single, comprehensive system. Machining centers represent 50 percent of the group's sales, which are expected to top ¥136 billion ($1.3 billion) by the end of the enlarged company's 2006 fiscal year. Lathes represent Okuma's second-largest product category at over 30 percent. The company also produces multitasking machines, enabling a variety of production processes from a single centralized system. This category represents 14 percent of sales. Japan remains Okuma's core market, accounting for more than 46 percent of revenues. Elsewhere in the Asia Pacific region, the company generates more than 14 percent of sales, a number which was expected to grow with the company's launch of a lathe-making joint-venture, Hangzhou Feeler Takamatsu Machinery Co., in January 2005. Okuma has also maintained a sales and manufacturing presence in North and South America, especially in the United States, since the early 1980s. That market accounted for 26 percent of group sales in its 2005 fiscal year. In addition, Okuma exports to Europe, which represents approximately 14 percent of sales. Junro Kashiwa, who serves as president and CEO of Okuma Corp. will become chairman of Okuma Holdings. Upon completion of the merger, the listing for Okuma Holdings will replace those of Okuma Corp., Okuma & Howa, and Okuma Engineering.

Beginnings at the Turn of the 20th Century

Okuma was founded in 1898 by 28-year-old Eiichi Okuma in Nagoya, Japan. The company was initially founded to produce machinery for the manufacture of noodles. Okuma then adapted his operations to the make cigarette machines, as well as machinery for woodworking and printing. The extension of his business led Okuma to become interested in building the machines needed to produce the machines, and in 1904 his company began producing its first machine tools.

Machine tools became the company's specialty by the end of World War I. In 1918, Okuma changed its name to reflect its new focus, becoming Okuma Machinery Works Ltd. At this time, the company began manufacturing lathes, a line that remained one of the company's largest product groups into the 21st century. Okuma grew strongly in the run-up to World War I, and by the end of the 1930s the company had captured the leading position in the Japanese machine tools market.

Okuma remained a market leading in the postwar years as well. In particular, the company played an important role in developing technologies that enabled Japan to achieve its impressive industrial growth in the second half of the century. This process began in 1953, when the company expanded its line to include radial drilling machines. By the end of the decade, the company had introduced its first high-speed lathes. This latter category represented an important development in the production of machinery and in the manufacture of machine tools themselves.

The introduction of the first numerical-controlled (NC) machinery represented an opportunity for Okuma in the 1960s. In

---

Company Perspectives:

Development, manufacture and sales of NC machine tools and systems based on an overall integrated approach. One of the world's foremost companies in the field of machine tools, Okuma is the only Japanese machine tool manufacturer with sophisticated mechatronics know-how to build machines and controls precisely for each other. The corporate logo symbolizes this approach as—Your Single Source For Machine & Control.

1963, the company introduced its own NC-controller featuring absolute position encoding capability. Okuma's early extension into the NC technology enabled it to capture a major share of the market, and the company remained one of the only Japanese companies to include capacity in both machine tools and the NC systems to drive them. By 1966, the company had combined the two, producing its first NC lathe.

By then, the company had launched production of double machining centers, debuting its first in 1964. This product category enabled Okuma to play a major role in the support of the Japan's hosting of the Olympic Games, as well as in the construction of the country's high-speed train system and the development of Japan's industry in general. By 2004, the company had sold more than 6,000 double machining centers.

Okuma's growth led it to begin development of a new manufacturing facility and headquarters, in Oguchi, which saw its first phase of construction completed in 1970. By 1979, the company had completed the second phase of the Oguchi plant, at which time it began relocating its headquarters to the new facility. The process was largely completed in 1980, marking the company's departure from Nagoya after more than 80 years.

In the meantime, Okuma had adopted the newly emerging computer technology that revolutionized the world of manufacturing in the 1970s and 1980s. The company released its first computer-numerical-control (CNC) system in 1973. The success of that venture led Okuma to convert all of its NC machinery to use CNC technology.

International Expansion in the 1980s

Okuma added a number of new products in the early 1980s. In 1981, for example, the company produced its first vertical machining centers. The following year, it created a new generation of lathes, the LC15 NC. At the same time, Okuma began to expand externally for the first time. In 1980, for example, the company acquired a stake in another major Japanese machine tool company, Howa Industry, which became known as Okuma & Howa Machinery. Howa stemmed from the spin off of Howa Corporation's machine tools division in 1943. Under the name Howa Industry, the company launched its first six-foot lathe in 1945 and later went public, listing first on the Nagoya Stock Exchange in 1949, before joining the Tokyo Stock Exchange in 1961. Three years later, Howa Industry built a new production facility in Konan, Aichi, which became its headquarters. Okuma & Howa, which remained a separate, independently listed com-

pany, developed a particular expertise in producing machine tools for Japan's, and later the world's, car makers.

Okuma turned toward the international market in the 1980s. It first entered the United States with a sales subsidiary in New York in 1984. The creation of a new trade agreement between the United States and Japan during the 1980s, which placed restrictions on Japanese imports, led Okuma to launch a manufacturing subsidiary in the United States as well. The company invested some $30 million to establish a plant in North Carolina in 1987. In the same year, affiliate Okuma & Howa also set up a plant in the United States.

Back at home, Okuma set up its second production plant in 1988, in Kani, completing the first phase of its construction in that year. The second phase of the Kani plant's construction was completed just three years later. The expansion of the company's production capacity played an important part in the company's international expansion strategy, supporting the extension of its sales operations into new markets. In 1988, Okuma added a sales and service subsidiary in Germany, giving the company its first foothold in the European market. As with its U.S. extension, the company's Okuma & Howa affiliate also set up a sales and marketing subsidiary in Germany that year. In addition, Okuma began expanding into the Asian market as well, establishing a branch in Singapore in 1990.

Merging for Leadership in the 2000s

Okuma continued developing new machine tools and systems through the 1990s. In 1994, the company debuted a new generation of lathes. This advance was followed by the launch of its MX-V and MX-H horizontal machine centers the following year, and the Space Turn series of NC lathes in 1997.

On the international front, the company consolidated its U.S. operations, transferring its sales and marketing business to its North Carolina manufacturing plant in 1995. In 1997, Okuma moved into Taiwan, establishing the Tatung Okuma Co. joint venture for that market. The two companies by then had built up a relationship over more than 20 years, beginning with the transfer of Okuma high-speed precision lather technology in 1976.

Okuma next turned to the Australia and New Zealand markets, acquiring Atlas CNC Machines Ltd. in 2000. That company stemmed from Gilbert Lodge and Company, founded in 1908, which became a leader in the Australian and New Zealand machine tools market over the next decades. Gilbert Lodge was acquired by Atlas Steels in 1985, changed its name to Atlas CNC in 1992, then was acquired by Email Ltd. in 1995. Atlas CNC's purchase by Okuma came after the joint takeover of Email by Smorgon and Onesteel in 2000. In 2002, Atlas CNC was renamed as Okuma Australia Pty Ltd.

While Japan remained Okuma's primary market, continuing to account for more than 46 percent of the group's sales in 2005, the company had successfully balanced its domestic sales with a strong international presence. The Asian market remained a target of the company's expansion efforts, and in 2003 Okuma entered the fastest-growing country in the region. In that year, the company established a presence in mainland China with the launch of the joint-venture BYJC-Okuma (Beijing) Machine Tool Co.

Key Dates:

1898: Eiichi Okuma founds a company in Nagoya, Japan, to produce machinery for noodle making, later adding the production of cigarette machines and other equipment.
1904: The company launches production of machine tools.
1918: The company becomes Okuma Machinery Works Ltd.
1943: Howa Machinery (later Howa Industries) is created as a spinoff of the machine tools division of Howa Heavy Industries.
1958: Okuma launches the production of high-speed lathes.
1963: Okuma launches its first self-developed NC controller.
1976: The company begins a technology transfer relationship with Tatung of Taiwan.
1980: A stake in Howa Industries, which becomes Okuma & Howa, is acquired; construction of the new Oguchi plant and headquarters is completed.
1984: Okuma enters the United States with a sales and marketing subsidiary in New York.
1987: A U.S. manufacturing subsidiary is established in North Carolina.
1988: A sales and marketing subsidiary is established in Germany.
1990: The company opens a branch in Singapore.
1991: The company changes its name to Okuma Corporation.
1997: Tatung-Okuma joint venture in Taiwan is created.
2000: Atlas CNC, which becomes basis of Okuma Australia Pty Ltd, is acquired.
2003: Okuma enters China through its BYJC-Okuma joint venture in Beijing.
2005: The company launches a new mainland China joint venture with Taiwan's Fair Friend and creates Okuma Holdings Inc. through a merger of Okuma Corporation, Okuma & Howa, and Okuma Engineering.

In 2004, Okuma stepped up its mainland presence, teaming up with Taiwan's Fair Friend in order to create Hangzhou Feeler Takamatsu Machinery Company in Hangzhou City. That company launched operations at the beginning of 2005.

By then, Okuma ranked among the world leaders in the machine tools market. In 2005, the company moved to consolidate its position, reaching an agreement with Okuma & Howa and another publicly listed associate, Okuma Engineering Co., to form a three-way merger. The result of the merger was the creation of a new holding company, Okuma Holdings Inc., which took over the stock market listings of all three companies. In this way, Okuma boosted its total revenues to more than ¥136 billion ($1.33 billion). Junro Kashiwa, who had served as president and CEO, was then named as chairman of the new, larger company. Okuma Holdings expected to uphold the long tradition of the Okuma name as a machine tool leader into the 21st century.

Principal Subsidiaries

Okuma America Corporation; Okuma Australia Pty Ltd; Okuma Europe GmbH; Okuma Latino Americana Comercio Ltda; Okuma Machinery (Shanghai) Co., Ltd; Okuma Singapore; Okuma Techno (Thailand) Ltd; Tatung-Okuma Co., Ltd.

Principal Competitors

Sulinskiy Metallurgical Works Joint Stock Co.; Gurevsk Metallurgical Plant Joint Stock Co.; Halma plc; Koninklijke Nedschroef Holding N.V.; MacLean-Fogg Co.; Société Legris S.A.; Alumasc Group PLC; San Shing Fastech Corporation; Ideal Standard France S.A.; B Elliott Ltd.; Helvar Merca Oy Ab.

Further Reading

"How the Okuma/Okuma & Howa Merger Will Shake Out," *Metalworking Insiders' Report*, May 15, 2005, p. 2.
"How Two Japanese Builders Are Betting on the Market in China," *Metalworking Insiders' Report*, November 15, 2004, p. 4.
Kelley, Katherine A., "Ten Thousand Machines Made," *Modern Machine Shop*, March 2000, p. 114.
"Okuma Companies Merging Management," *American Machinist*, March 2005, p. 22.
"Okuma Copes by Shifting Production, Moving Upmarket," *Metalworking Insiders' Report*, November 28, 2001, p. 1.
"Okuma in Cooperative Research in China," *Metalworking Insiders' Report*, June 15, 2005, p. 5.
"Okuma Plans Merger with Two Affiliates," *Metalworking Insiders' Report*, January 15, 2005, p. 1.
Ushio, Shota, "Okuma Milestone," *Metalworking Insiders' Report*, July 31, 2004, p. 6.

—M.L. Cohen

Old Town

Old Town Canoe Company

35 Middle Street
Old Town, Maine 04468
U.S.A.
Telephone: (207) 827-5513
Fax: (207) 827-2779
Web site: http://www.oldtowncanoe.com

Wholly-Owned Subsidiary of Johnson Outdoors, Inc.
Incorporated: 1902 as Robertson and Old Town Canoe
    Company
Employees: 250
Sales: $30 million (2004 est.)
NAIC: 326199 All Other Plastics Product Manufacturing;
    336612 Boat Building; 81149 Other Personal and
    Household Goods Repair and Maintenance

The Old Town Canoe Company is one of the world's leading manufacturers of canoes and kayaks. It is a key part of Johnson Outdoors Inc.'s Paddlesports division, which also includes the Ocean Kayak and Necky Kayak brands. Old Town's canoes are sold at about 900 dealers throughout the world, most of them specialty stores. While the company has pioneered modern materials use in personal watercraft, a few canoes are still made using wood-and-canvas construction techniques that date back to the 19th century.

Old Town Origins

Old Town, Maine, was known for its watercraft even before loggers plied the Penobscot River with their wooden bateaux in the 1800s. The Old Town Canoe Company traces its origins to 1900, when it was formed to make a different type of boat, the wood-and-canvas canoe. This was evolved from the birch bark canoes of the local Penobscot Indians, a connection Old Town Canoe would feature in its advertising. According to one report, there were 15 other canoe factories nearby at the time.

Then called the Indian Old Town Canoe Company, the new enterprise was backed by members of the entrepreneurial Gray family, who had ventures in logging, hardware, and owned a wildly successful salve for horses called Bickmore's Gall Cure

(the latter would also endure for more than 100 years). George and Herbert Gray hired Alfred E. Wickett to run the canoe operation (he left in 1914).

The first few canoes were made behind the Grays' hardware store, but within a few months fabrication moved into two floors of an industrial building. Strong demand prompted several other moves to increasingly larger facilities.

Old Town built about 250 canoes in its first year. The company aimed for a wide market from the beginning, advertising in recreation publications as well as producing an annual catalog. According to Susan Audette's thorough history of the company, the distribution network for the horse salve was easily tapped for canoe sales. Audette notes that ready access to rail service was another factor in the firm's success.

Early models often featured sails. Sponsons, or floats, were also popular additions. Buyers had the choice of different designs and three grades of materials and finish. Soon the company was offering rowboats of canvas-covered construction as a lightweight alternative to traditional all-wood models.

The company was incorporated as Robertson & Old Town Canoe Company in 1902, establishing a partnership with Auburndale, Massachusetts, canoe maker John Ralph Robertson. George and Herbert Gray held most of the shares, while the latter served as president. Robertson, who already had his own popular business based on the Charles River, left Old Town in 1903 and it was reincorporated without his name. (He later lent his expertise to building racing canoes and even the wood-and-canvas shell for record-setting Stanley Steamer automobile.)

Sales were about $25,000 in 1905. The company was soon making between 200 and 400 canoes per month. The product line was expanded to include shorter (15-foot) and longer (34-foot) models. The latter were called "War Canoes" and were designed for several people. By 1908 Old Town was also selling motorized models.

It was the largest canoe manufacturer of more than a dozen in the area, employing 50 people. The crafts were already being sold as far away as Europe and South America. Carleton Canoe

Company, a supplier of cedar planks to Old Town, was acquired in 1910 (and would be consolidated with Old Town in 1934).

While the logging industry dwindled, New Englanders were taking to the woods, and the water, by the thousands. Old Town was expected to sell 6,000 canoes in 1914 before World War I intervened. As men went to war, noted Audette, the company tailored advertising to the women who started working, and earning money. The company also supplied the military with paddles.

A Square Stern model was introduced in 1917 specifically to accommodate new outboard motors. In 1923, Old Town became the first distributor for the Johnson Motor Company.

Sales exceeded $500,000 in 1927. Sam Gray became company president following his father's death in 1928. Sam Gray is described by Audette as a tireless and creative marketer. He began the enduring practice of giving away four-foot canoe replicas as promotional gifts to dealers who ordered complete railcars of 40 canoes. Those who ordered two railcars had the option of an eight-foot version. These models were highly prized and credited with boosting sales considerably.

In 1931, Old Town was able to produce about 1,600 canoes, about half the state of Maine's total, in spite of the Great Depression. Its products were available in more than 50 different colorful designs in the 1930s.

The company found itself scrambling for workers and materials with the arrival of World War II. This led Old Town to conduct its own logging operations until 1956. The plant was unionized during the war.

New Materials After World War II

The postwar years saw several different models introduced to encourage a newly affluent society to get out on the water. There was an emphasis on speed, noted Audette, with more powerful outboard motors available. Old Town's all-wood motorboats were among its strongest sellers in the 1950s and 1960s. Sam Gray died in 1961. By then his sons Braley and Deane were at the helm.

Technological advances extended to the industry. Grumman Corporation, a maker of aluminum-hulled warplanes, began making metal canoes by the thousands. Old Town saw production crash to a mere 200 canoes a year in the early 1960s, noted Audette, when Grumman was making almost ten times as many.

Old Town eschewed the use of plywood, unlike some of its competitors, but began working with fiberglass in the mid-

1960s after acquiring the talents of pioneering designer Walter King, who helped develop the company's first large motorboat, the 24-foot Atlantis. Fiberglass and other new materials helped Old Town regain its lead against aluminum craft.

The company's vessels have made man extraordinary voyages. One enterprising sailor crossed the Atlantic in a 13.5-foot Old Town sailboat in 1965.

Another new material, Royalex (a brand of ABS plastic) was added in the 1970s when Old Town designer Lew Gilman developed new methods for producing molds with it. Though expensive (upwards of $350 at the time), the Royalex kayaks became popular for their durability. Old Town had introduced its first kayak in 1940, but interest in whitewater sports did not explode until the 1970s.

Large motorboats, which cost up to $11,000, were dropped from the product line in the mid-1970s due to increasing competition and dwindling demand in the face of oil shortages. Old Town was then selling 5,000 canoes a year—a healthy number, but one-quarter of the production of Coleman, which dominated the low-end market.

1970s–80s: New Ownership and Profitability

Old Town Canoe was acquired by Johnson Diversified in December 1974. Sam Johnson of S.C. Johnson Wax fame had been building a portfolio of outdoor-related companies.

The substantial corporate backing allowed the company to modernize its back office functions, marketing, and production methods. At the same time, there remained a place for traditional wood-and-canvas canoe construction.

Old Town began distributing Lettmann and Prijon kayaks in 1979, and for a few years stopped selling kayaks under its own brand. Old Town's Discovery line of canoes was introduced in 1984. These employed a three-layer polyethylene hull developed by Lew Gilman. The strong, affordable, lightweight canoes were popular enough to return Old Town to profitability for the first time in ten years, noted Audette. Old Town became the world's largest producer of canoes as aluminum canoes fell out of favor. According to Rhode Island's *Providence Journal*, Old Town had more production space (181,000 square feet) than all other canoe makers in the United States combined. At this time, Old Town was also selling kits, complete with wood, for buyers to construct at home.

Old Town acquired the White Canoe Company in October 1984. Formed in 1888, White predated Old Town by ten years and had been a training ground for some of its top talent.

In 1989, the *Wall Street Journal* reported Old Town was peddling more than 22,000 canoes a year, accounting for one-quarter of industry sales. Grayling, Michigan's Carlisle Paddles Inc. was acquired in 1990.

Kayaking Grows in the 1990s

In 1990 Old Town began distributing the Dimension brand of sit-upon kayaks for Quebec's Plastiques LPA, Ltd. Old Town bought the company in 1997. With the canoe market flat, in

Key Dates:

1898: The company's first canoe is built behind Gray hardware store in Old Town, Maine.
1910: Carleton Canoe Company is acquired.
1928: Sam Gray becomes company president following the death of his father, George Gray.
1961: Sam Gray dies, leaving the business to sons Braley and Deane.
1974: Johnson Diversified acquires Old Town.
1984: Affordable Discovery canoes revitalize sales; White Canoe Company is acquired.
1990: Carlisle Paddles Inc. is acquired; Old Town begins selling Dimension sit-upon kayaks.
1997: Ferndale, Washington's Ocean Kayak is acquired.
1999: The Old Town factory is expanded.
2000: Parent company Johnson Outdoors Inc. is organized.
2004: Old Town builds its one millionth boat.

1995, Old Town again began selling its own brand of kayaks. By 1998 they accounted for 40 percent of sales. Old Town was distributed through 800 outlets worldwide, most of them specialty stores. The L.L. Bean catalog was among its largest retailers. Canada, Japan, and Germany were top markets. Other acquisitions in the late 1990s extended Old Town's product line further. These included Leisure Life, Ltd., maker of pedal boats, and West Coast manufacturer Ocean Kayak.

Old Town Canoe celebrated its 100th anniversary in 1998. Some of its earliest wood canoes were still in service. The company had become one of Old Town's leading tourist attractions. Its 200,000 square foot factory was a focal point of the city's riverfront redevelopment. Old Town's canoe business had outlasted several other once-prominent local industries: logging, shoes, textiles, and pie plates.

The company bought New Zealand's Pacific Kayaks around 2000. Old Town continued to work to meet the booming demand for kayaks at its home plant. It soon began making them out of fiberglass for weight savings.

Old Town Canoe was a key part of the Johnson Outdoors Paddlesports division, which also included Ocean Kayak and Necky Kayaks. Together, they offered an array of choices for different types of paddlers: recreational for the majority of users as well as sit-on-top, enthusiast, touring, and whitewater models. Old Town began its one-millionth boat in 2003 and 2004, an 18-foot, wood-and-canvas OTCA (Old Town Canoe Model A) destined for display at company headquarters. For 2005, it introduced a new production model of its 1903 Charles River canoe using modern materials.

By this time, the market for kayaks had peaked, reported the *Portland Press Herald.* One analyst told the paper that Old Town typically accounted for more than one-third of Johnson's watercraft revenues, which were about $80 million a year. Growing European sales, though a small portion of the total, prompted Johnson Outdoors to open a distribution center in France. There were plans to eventually move production into a modern manufacturing plant in the United States.

Principal Competitors

Confluence Holdings Corporation.

Further Reading

Audette, Susan T., and David E. Baker, *The Old Town Canoe Company: Our First Hundred Years,* Gardiner, Maine: Tilbury House, 1998.

Bloch, Jessica, "Old Town Turns 100; World-Renowned Builder to Mark Anniversary with Special Line," *Bangor Daily News,* January 2, 1998.

Bongartz, Roy, "Wood Canoe Holds Fast in Changing Times," *Providence Journal,* May 12, 1985, p. T10.

Brownstein, Andrew, "Old Town Reviving Riverfront; Canoe Maker Anchor of Project Catering to Outdoors Enthusiasts," *Bangor Daily News,* July 31, 1998.

——, "Old Town Ups Canoe Incentives; City Approves TIF to Make Way for Firm's Speedy Expansion," *Bangor Daily News,* September 1, 1998.

Gray, S.B., "How We Built New Markets for an Old Product," *System: The Magazine of Business,* January 1927, pp. 56–58.

Hauger, Nok-Noi, "Old Town Floats Milestone; Canoe Maker Marks Centennial; Millionth Boat the Crowning Event," *Bangor Daily News,* July 31, 2003, p. A1.

Ingrassia, Paul, "Today It's Possible to Sail a 'Freighter' and Call It a Canoe—In the Paddle-Pushing Market There Are Models Galore; Some for Canoodling, Too," *Wall Street Journal,* July 24, 1989, p. 1.

Levy, Michael, "Canoemakers Change Course to Stay in Mainstream," *Buffalo News,* June 26, 1994, p. B9.

"More Enjoy Lighter Side of Paddling; Technology Trims Ounces But It Comes with a Higher Price," *Portland Press Herald,* April 15, 2001, p. 6D.

"Old Town Canoe Company—One of the Most Phenomenally Successful Industrial Enterprises in Eastern Maine," *Old Town Enterprise,* March 3, 1905, p. 1.

Shaw, Dick, "Old Town Canoe Co.'s First Century Chronicled," *Bangor Daily News,* March 4, 1999.

Stettner, Morey, "Turn Employees into Innovators," *Investor's Business Daily,* June 13, 2005, p. A13.

Taylor, Rod, "Peddling Premium Paddling," *Promo,* June 1, 2004, p. 7.

Turcotte, Deborah, "Old Town's Kayaks Outsell Canoes," *Bangor Daily News,* August 8, 2000.

Turkel, Tux, "Course Correction; Manufacturing Methods That Have Sustained Old Town Canoe for a Century Are in Dire Need of Modernizing," *Portland Press Herald,* September 7, 2003, p. 1F.

—Frederick C. Ingram

1-800-GOT-JUNK? LLC

300-1523 West 3rd Avenue
Vancouver, British Columbia V6J 1J8
Canada
Telephone: (800) 710-5865
Toll Free: (800) 468-5865
Web site: http://www.1800gotjunk.com

Private Company
Incorporated: 1989 as The Rubbish Boys
Employees: 1,000 (est.)
Sales: $75 million (2005 est.)
NAIC: 562119 Other Waste Collection

1-800-GOT-JUNK? LLC bills itself as "North America's largest junk removal service" with more than 150 franchised locations in the United States and Canada. The firm's blue, green, and white trucks pick up items that are too big for curbside garbage collection, but not large enough to merit a heavy-duty waste hauling service. Fees are based on the volume of truck space filled, with a typical job running about $290. The firm's clientele includes homeowners, property management companies, construction firms, and corporations. The company is owned by founder and CEO Brian Scudamore.

Beginnings

The company known as 1-800-GOT-JUNK? was founded as The Rubbish Boys in 1989 by Brian Scudamore in Vancouver, British Columbia, Canada. Born in San Francisco, Scudamore had moved with his parents to Vancouver at eight and had shown an entrepreneurial spirit from a young age, delivering papers at nine, washing cars for money at 11, and selling candy and snacks to his classmates at 14.

Scudamore's studies sometimes took a back seat to his side activities, and he dropped out of high school one class shy of graduation, though he managed to secure admission to a community college for the fall of 1989. He began to look for summer work to pay for his tuition, but the job market was tight, and he could not find employment. One day, while sitting in the drive-through lane of a local McDonald's, the 19-year-old found himself staring idly at a truck full of junk in front of him.

For Scudamore, it was a "Eureka" moment—he decided then and there to begin hauling trash.

The next day he withdrew $700 from the bank to buy an old Ford pickup truck, and made preparations to get business cards and flyers printed. Seeking to give his one-man junk-hauling operation the illusion of size, he dubbed it The Rubbish Boys, adding the slogan, "We'll Stash Your Trash in a Flash!" He painted his new business phone number, 738-JUNK, on the plywood sides he had attached to the back of the truck, and waited for the phone to ring.

Work soon began trickling in, and by summer's end Scudamore had made a profit of $1,700. After his first year in college he revived the trash hauling business for another summer, but in the fall he began taking business management classes at the distant University of Montreal. He decided to transfer to the University of British Columbia in Vancouver after a year, however, so he could run his trash hauling business year-round.

In 1993, with the successful business demanding more and more of his attention, Scudamore decided to quit school to pick up junk full time. Although his surgeon father was appalled, in the newly incorporated firm's first year of full-time operation, revenues hit $100,000.

In 1994 Scudamore opened a small office in Vancouver to serve as a dispatch center for the three trucks he now owned, and the following year he began developing custom computer software to use for scheduling, marketing, and accounting. In 1995 a branch operation was launched in Victoria, British Columbia, with a partner, and in 1996 The Rubbish Boys recorded $1 million in revenues for the first time.

The year 1997 saw the company hire Paul Guy, who had been the general manager of College Pro Painters in British Columbia, to help develop a franchise plan. That same year, the firm's first American location was set up in Seattle, Washington.

Name Change to 1-800-GOT-JUNK? in 1998

In 1998 Scudamore made the decision to change both the company's name and its phone number to 1-800-GOT-JUNK to provide more marketing punch. The number already belonged to a state agency in Idaho, and it took him several weeks to convince the official in charge to give it up. The company subsequently painted the number in large type on the sides of its trucks, enabling them to double as mobile billboards. 1-800-GOT-JUNK? staff also had begun using several "guerrilla marketing" tactics to promote the firm, including putting signs on telephone poles, placing company flyers on homeowners' doorknobs between deliveries, and parking trucks near stores like Home Depot where potential clients might lurk. Later, the firm's employees would don blue wigs and stand at intersections to wave signs advertising the company.

Scudamore's years of experience as a junk hauler had given him ample time to hone his own approach to the business. Declaring his goal to be "the Federal Express of junk removal," he focused on earning a reputation for service, reliability, and professionalism, projecting expansion to a total of 30 locations by 2003. He was the sole owner of the firm, having shed an early partner, and its growth had been financed entirely through internally generated funds or loans that had been quickly repaid.

In 1999 consultant Paul Guy quit to open a location of his own in Toronto, Ontario, kicking off the firm's new franchise program. The franchise fee was $20,000 plus a royalty of 8 percent of revenues, as well as 7 percent to fund the call center and 1 percent for national advertising. With truck and office rental and other initial expenses, the total start-up cost was in the neighborhood of $50,000. Many new franchises were started by people who had grown tired of their careers in the corporate world. The entry costs were relatively low, and after several years of hauling junk themselves while the business grew, they could hire college students or other young workers to do the bulk of the manual labor.

The company's Vancouver headquarters handled all incoming orders and scheduling of pickups, which helped standardize customer service systemwide, and also allowed individual operators to focus on doing field work, rather than dwelling on administrative tasks. Orders could be placed via the call center or the company's web site, and a completed order would be routed to the local franchise via the Internet and scheduled in a two-hour window. The franchisee called customers to confirm arrival time about a half hour ahead, and then made a follow-up call afterward to verify that they were satisfied.

The firm's typical pickup fee was $300 for a 15-cubic-yard load, which included two hours of labor. Additional labor was $22 per hour. Jobs were typically scheduled a day or two in advance, but same-day service was also available. A franchisee might expect to do as many as eight or more pickups in a day.

The company's staff wore uniforms and presented clients with a printed price list—a stark contrast to the stereotypically shabby appearance of the small-time trash hauler, whose fee might vary depending on the perceived size of a customer's wallet. The firm required that each truck be washed daily, and if they were not maintained well, the company could cancel the franchise.

1-800-GOT-JUNK? did not accept hazardous materials such as paint or chemicals, and attempted to recycle most of what was picked up. Drivers got first dibs on usable items, though most were taken to charitable organizations like Goodwill Industries. The firm's fees included the cost of dropoff at a local dump, which gave its employees an incentive to recycle, as it was usually free or even sometimes generated a small amount of revenue. As much as 60 percent of what was picked up was recycled. Approximately three-fourths of the firm's business took place between April and October, when moving or home renovation projects brought much work.

All of 1-800-GOT-JUNK?'s operations utilized the firm's own JunkNet software, an Internet-based application that each franchisee used to get daily scheduling information as well as to perform management, payroll, and accounting tasks. The software also could send text messages to drivers' cellular telephones.

Rapid Expansion Beginning in 2000

Franchising inquiries were beginning to pour in; during 2000 all available locations in Canada were snapped up, and franchises began to open around the United States in cities like Portland, San Francisco, Minneapolis, Chicago, and Buffalo, New York. The pace of growth increased even more rapidly in 2001, and by the end of that year the firm had 31 locations.

In 2002 1-800-GOT-JUNK? moved its headquarters into a 9,000-square-foot location in Vancouver that had been vacated by a bankrupt dot.com. Dubbed "The Junktion," the space was outfitted with office furniture that had been purchased for 10 cents on the dollar, along with items that had been salvaged from refuse pickups.

The firm's call center now employed 32 customer service representatives, who handled between 800 and 1,000 calls per day. Most were answered live, rather than by a computerized system, and virtually all calls were taken within 60 seconds. To serve all of North America, the center was open from 4:30 a.m. to 8:30 p.m. Pacific time. As with 1-800-GOT-JUNK?'s other employees, call center staff members were given incentives, which included commissions and preferred call routing for those who closed the highest percentage of sales. For 2002, the company, which now had 400 employees, took in revenues estimated at $7 million.

1-800-GOT-JUNK? was receiving media attention from the likes of CNN and *Fortune* magazine, and interested parties were flooding the firm with requests for new franchises. The company offered a money-back guarantee to the select few it chose if a franchise did not have revenues of more than $100,000 in its first year.

In October 2003 the firm unveiled a new online booking option that enabled clients to set up service without any human interaction. It was promoted with motorcades of 1-800-GOT-JUNK? trucks through the company's franchise markets. For 2003 systemwide revenues topped $12 million, with the Vancou-

Key Dates:

1989: Brian Scudamore founds The Rubbish Boys in Vancouver, British Columbia.
1994: The firm, now with three trucks, opens an office in Vancouver.
1995: A branch location opens in Victoria, British Columbia; development of JunkNet software begins.
1996: Revenues top $1 million.
1997: The first U.S. location opens in Seattle, Washington.
1998: The company phone number and name is changed to 1-800-GOT-JUNK
1999: A franchising program begins with a new location in Toronto.
2002: The headquarters and call center are moved to a 9,000-square-foot space.
2005: Locations top 150; the first overseas unit is added in Australia.

ver, Toronto, and San Francisco territories accounting for more than $1 million each. The company was now averaging $238 per pickup, which corresponded to half a truckload of trash.

100th Franchise in 2004

In July 2004 the firm celebrated the awarding of its 100th franchise. 1-800-GOT-JUNK? now served 46 metropolitan areas in the United States and Canada, with 90 percent of franchises located south of the border. Sales had increased more than 100 percent for the fourth consecutive year, with systemwide revenues hitting $38.6 million.

A franchise now cost $18,000 for an exclusive territory with a population of 125,000, plus another $6,000 for a marketing package. Additional territories were priced at $8,000 each. The firm continued to collect approximately 15 percent of gross revenues in royalties and to fund call center operations.

In May 2005 1-800-GOT-JUNK? announced that it would begin using MapPoint Location Server software on its Vancouver trucks as part of a Microsoft pilot project. Drivers would carry Web-enabled smart phones that could display work orders and maps, and the cell-phone locating capabilities of Sprint would pinpoint the closest truck to a pickup, which would reduce fuel costs and driving time.

The spring also saw the firm forge an alliance with Oakleaf Waste Management, which represented a network of 3,500 independent haulers. Oakleaf would refer business to 1-800-GOT-JUNK? in exchange for a 5 percent referral fee.

By the summer of 2005 the firm had awarded more than 150 franchises, including one that was set to open in Sydney, Australia. Systemwide revenues of $75 million were projected for the year.

A little more than 15 years after Brian Scudamore had started a summertime trash hauling service, 1-800-GOT-JUNK? LLC had grown into a 150-franchise chain with a presence in 48 of the top 50 markets in North America. The firm's high-tech approach to what had once been the province of small-time operators with rusty pickup trucks was one key to its success, as was a healthy dose of marketing flair. Under its young owner's continued guidance, the company's future appeared bright.

Principal Competitors

Allied Waste Industries, Inc.; Waste Management, Inc.; Republic Services, Inc.; Goodwill Industries International, Inc.; The Salvation Army National Corporation; Trashbusters Rubbish Company Ltd.

Further Reading

Armitage, Alix, ''A Dirty, Rotten Success Story,'' *Seattle Times,* August 1, 2001, p. E3.

Couvillion, Ellyn, ''Turning Clutter into Cash,'' *Baton Rouge Advocate,* September 21, 2003, p. 1I.

Green, Frank, ''Trash-Hauling Chain's Business Is Picking Up,'' *San Diego Union-Tribune,* May 8, 2003, p. C1.

Higgins, Marguerite, ''One Man's Junk Is Another's Business Success,'' *Washington Post,* August 18, 2003.

Hurley, Becky, ''In the Spotlight—1-800-GOT-JUNK Franchisee Finds an Alternative to the 'Cubicle Life,' '' *Colorado Springs Business Journal,* August 9, 2002, p. 2.

Ingram, Mathew, ''Trash Removal Firm Dumps Paper Schedule for Smart Phone,'' *Globe and Mail,* June 16, 2005, p. B13.

Johnson, Jim, ''Canadian Hauler Finds His Calling,'' *Waste News,* July 8, 2002, p. 15.

Martin, Justin, ''Cash from Trash,'' *Fortune Small Business,* November 1, 2003, p. 53.

O'Herron, Jennifer, ''Talking Trash: In an Industry Not Known for Customer Service, 1-800-GOT-JUNK's Call Center Is Out to Set the Standard,'' *Call Center,* September 1, 2002, p. 56.

Quinn, Shirley, ''High-Tech Solutions for a Low-Tech Industry,'' *Franchising World,* May 1, 2000, p. 39.

Schultz, Beth, ''Talkin' Trash: One Outfit's Story of E-Commerce,'' *Network World,* April 11, 2005, p. 1.

Stoller, Gary, ''Rubbish Boy Turned Junk into His Career: Entrepreneurial Spirit Struck at Young Age,'' *USA Today,* June 13, 2005, p. B7.

Stueck, Wendy, ''Firms Aim to Clean Up in Trash Business,'' *Globe and Mail,* June 16, 1999, p. B10.

Waisberg, Deena, ''Humble King of the Junkyard,'' *National Post,* June 11, 2005, p. FW4.

—Frank Uhle

Oregon Freeze Dry, Inc.

525 25th Avenue S.W.
P.O. Box 1048
Albany, Oregon 97321
U.S.A.
Telephone: (541) 926-6001
Toll Free: (877) 366-3877
Fax: (541) 967-6527
Web site: http://www.ofd.com

Private Company
Incorporated: 1963
Employees: 300
Sales: $63.20 million (2004 est.)
NAIC: 325411 Medicinal and Botanical Manufacturing;
325412 Pharmaceutical Preparation Manufacturing;
325414 Biological Product (Except Diagnostic)
Manufacturing; 311423 Dried and Dehydrated Food
Manufacturing

Oregon Freeze Dry, Inc., is one of the world's leading processors of freeze-dried products. A leader in technology, the company designs and builds its own equipment and has processed more than 400 different products, including full meals. Oregon Freeze Dry has expanded beyond food markets into chemicals, pharmaceuticals, and biologicals. The company has two plants in Oregon, representing 70 percent of North American freeze-drying capacity. Oregon Freeze Dry also has a subsidiary in the United Kingdom and a joint venture in Denmark.

Origins

According to a 1996 *Scientific American* article by company president Herbert Aschkenasy, the concept of freeze drying dates back at least to the ancient Incas of Peru, who would preserve potatoes in the low temperature and low pressure environment of the Andean heights. The process was used during World War II to preserve blood plasma and drugs.

Applications for freeze drying in the 1950s and 1960s largely involved food products. The process consists of fast freezing a food or biological product and then removing its moisture in a vacuum chamber at temperatures well below freezing. The product is then sealed in packaging that will keep out oxygen and moisture, and it becomes edible again when opened and reconstituted with water. Freeze dried food items proved less prone to collapse, retained more flavor, and rehydrated more quickly than those dried by heat. With about 98 percent of water removed, freeze-dried foods typically weighed 80 to 90 percent less than fresh. Freeze dried foods could be kept at room temperature for two or more years. Drawbacks to the process were that it used a lot of electricity and was relatively expensive.

Oregon Freeze Dry was formed in 1963 in Oregon's Willamette Valley to produce dried sliced strawberries for a General Foods breakfast cereal called Post Toasties corn flakes. General Foods executive Ellis Byer was the enterprise's first general manager and later its president and chairman as well.

Oregon Freeze Dry was soon working to produce an alternative to canned rations for the military. It also supplied food for NASA's Apollo space program and developed meals for nuclear submarine crews and ''Long Range Patrol Subsistence'' in Vietnam. By the late 1960s, Oregon Freeze Dry was a publicly traded company with annual sales of about $5 million.

Going Outdoors in the 1970s

The work in military rations led to the introduction of Mountain House brand freeze dried food for backpackers in 1970. Mountain House representatives claimed its products tasted better than those of competitors since the ingredients were cooked together before freeze drying. Within a few years Mountain House was marketing more than 100 different products. Oregon Freeze Dry also owned the Tea Kettle brand of backpacker food.

Oregon Freeze Dry had sales of $10.2 million in the 1975 fiscal year and net income reached $511,000. According to *The New York Times*, Oregon Freeze Dry had successfully reduced its dependence on government contracts (once its sole business) to just one-seventh of its sales.

Oregon Freeze Dry developed a line of freeze dried meals for senior citizens in the late 1970s under the Easy Meal brand.

NASA supplied research and testing for the concept under a congressional mandate to improve nutrition for the elderly. Oregon Freeze Dry also realized success during this time as American consumers became increasingly interested in food security and survivalism.

By the late 1970s Oregon Freeze Dry was attracting the attention of larger food companies in a burgeoning era of corporate shopping sprees. In 1978, Oregon Freeze Dry was acquired by the Seven-Up Company, which itself would become a subsidiary of Phillip Morris Cos. Inc.

Private Label in the 1980s

In 1982, Oregon Freeze Dry began supplying private label customers. One early client was Nutri-System Inc., a weight loss company for which Oregon Freeze Dry developed a line of products. The company also supplied the Lipton Company with freeze-dried chicken and vegetables for its soups, and tested its own line of freeze dried fruit chips under the Goodbody Snacks brand.

Although less than 1 percent of packaged foods were freeze dried, according to *Smithsonian,* Oregon Freeze Dry was nevertheless the world's largest freeze dried food producer. (The company did not process instant coffee, which was a considerable industry in itself.) Oregon Freeze Dry controlled approximately half of the market for outdoor recreation foods in the United States in the mid-1980s. Although that industry was beginning to lag, as Baby Boomers aged and backpacking as recreation experienced a decline, it was a small part of Oregon Freeze Dry's total business. Industry analysts estimated that Oregon Freeze Dry had reached sales of $50 million a year.

In September 1986, Herbert Aschkenasy, who had become company president in 1981, led an employee buyout of the company after Pepsico acquired its corporate parent Seven-Up from Philip Morris.

In the late 1980s, freeze drying was capturing attention for new industrial uses. Oregon Freeze Dry was attempting to make the freeze drying of ceramics, such as superconductors, commercially viable. Interest in biotechnology was prompting new applications in that area. For example, probiotics such as lactic acid bacteria could be freeze-dried for storage. On at least one occasion, Oregon Freeze Dry helped an archive recover from a flood by freeze-drying books and documents.

New Demands in the 1990s

Operation Desert Storm in the early 1990s resulted in unprecedented demand for Oregon Freeze Dry's military provisions. Employment at Oregon Freeze Dry reached a temporary peak of

600 workers as the company filled a $62 million order for three million cans of chicken, beef, and pork chops to go into the B rations supplied to military kitchens in Iraq. Oregon Freeze Dry was also packaging a $6 million hamburger bun order.

Oregon Freeze Dry further expanded into the chemical, pharmaceutical, and biological markets in the 1990s. These efforts included a deal to freeze dry wound dressings for Carrington Laboratories of Irving, Texas.

In 1995 Oregon Freeze Dry formed a joint venture in Preston, England, called Commercial Freeze Dry Ltd. to produce a range of freeze-dried items. Zeneca Group was an equal partner in the venture until June 1999, when it was bought by Oregon Freeze Dry.

Oregon Freeze Dry overhauled production processes at its three Oregon plants in 1997 using the theory of constraints (TOC) and enterprise resources planning (ERP) software. According to a case study in the *Production & Inventory Management Journal,* smaller batch sizes (tied to dryer capacity) allowed Oregon Freeze Dry to reduce inventory levels and lead times while increasing on-time deliveries.

These improvements helped Oregon Freeze Dry's Mountain House label meet a big increase in demand caused by the stockpiling that accompanied fears of massive computer crashes at the turn of the century. In addition to its pouches popular with backpackers, Oregon Freeze Dry also packaged food in cans for long-term emergency preparedness storage. (The company was not involved in the emerging market for self-heating meals.)

More Fruit and Cereal After 2000

Another European producer was acquired by Oregon Freeze Dry through a joint venture in March 2000. DLG/Agrova Food joined Oregon Freeze Dry in the purchase of Danish Freeze Dry A/S, which was formed in 1964 and had sales of about DKK 80 million a year. Oregon Freeze Dry's U.K. business, Commercial Freeze Dry Ltd., became a subsidiary of Danish Freeze Dry.

In 2002 the company won a contract reminiscent of its earliest business. Kellogg ordered sliced strawberries to add to its Special K cereal (a European version had been a big hit in 1999). General Mills also began adding Oregon Freeze Dry's berries to two new varieties of Cheerios cereal, including the popular Berry Burst version. Other cereal brands soon clamored for freeze dried fruit.

Oregon Freeze Dry continued to find new and interesting applications for its technology. It assisted an Oregon company in packaging blue-green algae as a dietary supplement. The company was also processing an artificial diet for lacewings, a beneficial predatory insect, for a California insect supplier that was raising them for the agricultural market. With production capacity in North America, at its Danish joint venture, and at the U.K. subsidiary, Oregon Freeze Dry was well equipped to meet traditional food needs as well as to explore new applications for the freeze dry process.

Principal Subsidiaries

Danish Freeze Dry A/S (Denmark; 50%).

Principal Divisions

Food; Advanced & Specialty Products.

Principal Competitors

American Outdoor Products, Inc.; Freeze-Dry Foods Ltd.; Richmoor Corporation; TyRy, Inc.

Further Reading

Ainsworth, Susan Jones, "Freeze Drying Stirs New Interest," *Chemical Week,* February 17, 1988, p. 42.

"Albany Company Provides Fruit for Cheerios," *Associated Press State & Local Wire,* April 14, 2003.

"Albany Company Seeks New Way to Raise Lacewings," *Associated Press State & Local Wire,* August 6, 2003.

Aschkenasy, Herbert, "Working Knowledge," *Scientific American,* September 1996.

Brenneman, Kristina, "Corporate Strategies: Love That Slimy Green Scum," *Portland Business Journal,* September 22, 2000.

Colby, Richard, "Gulf Military Needs Stretch Oregon Firms; Defense Contracts for Tank Parts and Dried Foods Get Priority Attention and Boost Local Payrolls," *Oregonian* (Portland), December 19, 1990, p. E1.

"Delicious Hot Meal Without Cooking: Simply Adding Hot Water to Freeze Dried Foods Produces Complete Meals in 5–10 Minutes; Products Are Specially Designed for Senior Citizens," *Food Engineering,* March 1978, p. EF22.

Dunne, Mike, "Thriving on Survival—Nervousness Helps Industry," *Daily News of Los Angeles,* March 19, 1988, p. B1.

"Gourmet C-Rations," *Newsweek,* November 13, 1967, p. 95.

Green, Warren, "Field-Testing the New Freeze-Dried Foods for Outdoorsmen," *The New York Times,* April 7, 1974.

Groves, Martha, "Shrinking Market—Freeze-Dried Food Fight Is Taking Its Toll," *Los Angeles Times,* August 19, 1986, Bus. Sec., p. 4.

Harris, David L., "Freeze-Dried Fruit Is a Fresh Trend in the World of Breakfast Cereal," *Boston Globe,* July 9, 2003, p. E4.

Hopson, Janet, "The Freeze-Drying Technique Makes for Movable Feasts," *Smithsonian,* July 1983, pp. 91 +.

Johnson, Kelly, "End of the World Sale; Y2K Worriers Store Up Freeze-Dried Food," *Sacramento Business Journal,* February 26, 1999.

La Ganga, Maria L., "Food Processors Kept Busy Feeding Troops in Mideast," *Los Angeles Times,* January 22, 1991, p. D1.

Mans, Jack, "Computers in Cool Control at Country's Largest Freeze-Drying Company," *Prepared Foods,* November 1985, pp. 89 +.

Metz, Robert, "Market Place: Difficulties for 3 Small Growth Concerns," *The New York Times,* January 7, 1977, p. D2.

Muir, Frederick M., "11 Firms Hope to Right the Books at L.A. Library," *Los Angeles Times,* August 13, 1987.

Neiman, Janet, "Seven-Up Foods Unit Plans Fruit Snacks Test," *Advertising Age,* December 13, 1982, p. 20.

Nicholls, Walter, "Whether It's Summer Camping or a Y2K Emergency, Dinner Is in the Bag," *Washington Post,* July 21, 1999, p. F1.

Norman, Steve, "Oregon Freeze Dry Gains New Berry Business," *Associated Press State & Local Wire,* March 10, 2002.

Umble, Michael, Elisabeth Umble, and Larry Von Deylen, "Integrating Enterprise Resources Planning and Theory of Constraints: A Case Study," *Production & Inventory Management Journal,* April 1, 2001, pp. 43–48.

—Frederick C. Ingram

Petco Animal Supplies, Inc.

9125 Rehco Road
San Diego, California 92121
U.S.A.
Telephone: (858) 453-7845
Toll Free: (877) 738-6742
Fax: (858) 677-3095
Web site: http://www.petco.com

Public Company
Incorporated: 1965
Employees: 16,900
Sales: $1.81 million (2005)
Stock Exchanges: NASDAQ
Ticker Symbol: PETC
NAIC: 453910 Pet & Pet Supplies Stores

Petco Animal Supplies, Inc., is the second-largest pet food and supplies retailer in the United States, operating a chain of 740 stores in 47 states and the District of Columbia. The company's stores sell more than 10,000 pet-related products, including pet food, supplies, grooming products, toys, small pets such as fish, birds, and other small animals (no cats or dogs), and veterinary supplies. Petco's principal format is a 12,000- to 15,000-square-foot store located near neighborhood shopping destinations.

Birth of the Petco Superstore

Petco had been operating as a retailer of pet food and supplies for nearly 30 years before the company launched its bid to become the dominant national player in its industry. Founded in 1965, the company competed during its first decades as one of the hundreds of regional pet merchandisers scattered across the country who found it difficult to operate under the shadow of the all-powerful supermarkets. In the battle to lure pet owners into their stores, the supermarkets prevailed comfortably, accounting for 95 percent of all the pet food sold in the country. Their dominance came at the expense of specialized retailers like Petco, but beginning in the mid-1980s the stifling grip

maintained by the supermarkets started to weaken. The cause for the change was part of a pervasive transformation of the retail industry as whole in which massive ''warehouse'' discount stores and ''superstores'' secured a substantial foothold in the retail sector. Along with the growing prominence of these new retail formats, the diversity of pet products—particularly food—increased, providing a lucrative niche for the specialized retailers to exploit. Supermarkets had held sway by stocking their shelves with popular brands such as Alpo, Kal Kan, and Purina, but beginning in the mid-1980s new premium brands of pet food were introduced into the market. Premium brands such as IAMS, Science Diet, and Nutro that offered higher levels of nutrition than the supermarket brands became increasingly popular among pet owners, and specialized pet products stores were the only retailers to carry such brands. The changing dynamics of the pet products industry led to the decreasing strength of the supermarkets and the growing prominence of retailers such as Petco. Between the mid-1980s and the mid-1990s, the percentage of pet food sold in supermarkets slipped from 95 percent to 50 percent, with specialized pet products retailers, warehouse clubs, and mass merchandisers accounting for the change. The conditions were prime for Petco's growth and expansion into a national chain. In the reshaping of the pet products industry, the nearly 30-year-old regional retailer played a leading role.

Petco did not begin to transform into a national force until after its 1994 initial public offering (IPO) of stock, but the individual who spearheaded the mid-1990s expansion arrived as the decade began. Brian K. Devine joined Petco in August 1990, bringing with him 20 years of retail experience. Prior to his arrival at Petco, Devine had served as president for Krause's Sofa Factory, a furniture retailer and manufacturer, but the bulk of his professional experience came from his association with Toys ''R'' Us, a retailer of children's toys. From 1970 to 1988, Devine served in various capacities for the specialty retailer, including as senior vice-president in charge of growth, development, and operations and as the chain's director of stores. His background in specialty retailing contributed to the personality of Petco as a national retailer, distinguishing it from its main rival. Yet the company did not take on this personality until it fully embraced the superstore concept. The transition from operating traditional stores to superstores had begun by the early 1990s, when there were nearly 200 Petco stores of various sizes in operation. The majority of the stores consisted of Petco's traditional units, which measured roughly 3,500 square feet. The company had discovered, however, that it could achieve greater customer traffic, sales volume, and profitability with a larger format: Petco's prototype superstore. Petco's superstores were five times larger than the company's traditional units, stocking a full range of pet food and supplies, as well as fish aquarium systems, reptiles, and other small animals, selections generally not available at the traditional stores. By the end of 1991, the company had established 37 superstores, recording sufficient success with the new format to persuade executives to direct expansion efforts toward the establishment of additional superstores. Although Petco officials had not abandoned the traditional concept and would continue to operate smaller units that were profitable, the first half of the 1990s would see an increasing number of Petco superstores and a decline in the number of traditional stores.

By the end of 1992, there were 208 Petco stores in operation, 76 of which were superstores. The following year, the number of superstores exceeded the number of traditional stores for the first time, with the 239-unit chain comprising 132 superstores and 107 traditional stores. By this point, the success of the superstore concept encouraged the company to expand more rapidly and give the superstore concept a national reach. To expand at a greater rate and to take advantage of market conditions primed for a company with Petco's characteristics, Devine, who was named chairman of the corporation in January 1994, decided to take the company public. Petco's initial public offering (IPO) was completed in March 1994, giving the company the financial resources to step up its expansion, something Devine intended to do through acquisitions of smaller pet merchandise chains.

Mid-1990s Expansion

Over the course of the ensuing year-and-a-half, Petco completed 12 acquisitions representing 100 stores located in 16 states, converting the purchased units to its superstore format. Petco's superstores carried a merchandise assortment of more than 10,000 items, which was far more than the 400 items generally stocked by supermarkets. Inside the stores, the shelves were stocked with premium cat and dog food, grooming products, toys, and a broad assortment of pet-related items whose diversity was intended to stimulate impulse purchases. Confronted with crab-and-tuna-flavored cat treats, peanut butter-flavored dog biscuits, orthopedic dog beds, bird beak conditioners, pet greeting cards, and numerous other pet-related items, customers responded by generally buying more than they originally intended. It was a

marketing strategy one Petco employee summarized by saying, "They'll come in to just buy dog food and end up buying toys and treats." Petco customers admitted as much, their buying habits typified by one customer who explained, "I usually pick up something that I didn't intend to buy. I even look at the dog stuff and I don't have a dog."

Aside from tantalizing its customers with a vast array of pet products, Petco devoted considerable effort to ways in which products were presented to customers. One of the signature traits of the chain was its practice of incorporating the merchandising ideas of other retailers, including competitors big and small and retailers outside the pet products industry. The company's senior vice-president of merchandising and distribution traveled worldwide searching for innovative ideas from his visits to other stores. For example, the idea for a brochure stand that began appearing in Petco superstores was first seen by a Petco executive in a hardware store in Europe. The inspiration for a pet bar stocked with pet treats similar to a salad bar for humans was taken from a chain of pet stores in Boston. The result was the adoption of market-proven merchandising techniques and the elimination through assimilation of merchandising advantages held by competitors.

The rewards for capturing the spending dollars of pet owners were vast, estimated at $20 billion by the mid-1990s. Vying for a share of the annual, pet owner expenditures were legions of small, independent pet shops, supermarkets, mass merchandisers, and convenience stores. Petco perceived itself to be competition with all such pet products retailers, but the most obvious rival was the only other publicly held, national pet merchandise chain, Phoenix-based PETsMART Inc. Industry pundits preferred to view the two sprawling chains as waging a battle against one another for national supremacy, but Petco officials emphasized the distinctions separating the two companies and downplayed the drama of two industry heavyweights competing head to head. "There's a giant difference," Devine explained. "They're catering more toward the grocery store user and the mass-market customer. We're catering more to the specialty retail customer. We both sort of picked our niches." The niches occupied by the two companies were reflective of the different professional backgrounds of the leaders who controlled each company. Devine's years at Toys "R" Us influenced his decision to position Petco as a specialty retailer, whereas PETsMART's president and chief executive officer, Mark Hansen, used his experience as a grocery store veteran to pattern PETsMART after the supermarket model of high turnover and lower profitability. Accordingly, PETsMART focused on stocking less expensive merchandise in larger, 26,000-square-foot stores. Petco, on the other hand, based its strategy on retailing more expensive merchandise in smaller, 15,000-square-foot stores.

The contrasting philosophies of PETsMART and Petco also affected each company's real estate strategy, which was part of the reason Devine did not perceive the success of Petco as being dependent on the demise of PETsMART. Generally, the two chains were not side-by-side competitors; instead, each moved into distinct areas, pursuing different demographics. Typically, PETsMART located its superstores in what were referred to as "power centers" alongside other superstores and warehouse stores like Home Depot, Costco, and Staples, hoping to draw

Key Dates:

1965: Petco is founded.
1990: Brian K. Devine joins Petco and spearheads the development of superstores.
1993: The 239-store chain includes 132 superstores.
1994: Devine is named chairman and Petco completes its initial public offering (IPO) of stock.
1997: The 81-store PetCare chain is acquired.
2000: In a $600 million buyout, Petco returns to the private sector.
2002: Petco returns to the public sector, raising more than $275 million in a second IPO.
2003: Petco signs a naming rights package for the San Diego Padres' new stadium, which opens in 2004 as Petco Park.
2004: Expansion centers on the company's new ''Pisces'' format.

customers from outside their immediate neighborhoods. Petco, in contrast, established its stores within neighborhoods, positioning its premium outlets in local shopping centers anchored by supermarkets, venues frequented by the company's target customers who accounted for 70 percent of its consumer base. ''The educated woman is our best customer,'' explained Devine. ''She's the best premium food customer. We try to place our stores where they shop on a regular basis. We try to go with the upscale grocer if possible.''

Difficulties in the Late 1990s

With Petco and PETsMART occupying separate turfs and together controlling only 5 percent of a $20 billion market, there was substantial room for expansion as the two companies faced the late 1990s. Devine foresaw the expansion of Petco to 1,250 stores, roughly four times the size of the chain by the end of 1996. However, as the company pursued its ambitious goal it faltered, sparking criticism that it had been over-zealous in its growth plans. Problems surfaced after the company registered an aggressive year of expansion in 1997, when 104 stores were added to the chain, with the majority of the new units coming from the acquisition of the 81-store PetCare chain, which operated in nine states in the Midwest and the South. The process of efficiently incorporating the new stores into the company's fold and continuing to transform from a 3,000-square-foot format to a superstore format proved to be difficult. As a result of the acquisitions that increased the company's store count to more than 430 units and extended its presence into 31 states, crippling financial losses were incurred. During the first half of 1998, Petco racked up more than $8 million in net losses. The company's stock, which had swelled to more than $30 per share in 1997, plunged to nearly $5 per share. One stock analyst offered his opinion, explaining, ''The company has had problems because, frankly, they expanded their business too much, too fast. The company's costs got a little out of line of what they should have been.'' To make matters worse, the company also faced three class action shareholder lawsuits charging management with securities violations and fraud. The acquisition of nearly 20 retail chains since the 1994 IPO caused considerable strain

on the once vibrant chain, but the late 1990s witnessed the recovery of the company that touted itself as the ''premier specialty retailer of pet food and supplies in the United States.''

By the early months of 1999, Petco began to display signs of vitality. The company had eased back on its acquisition campaign and focused on invigorating the profitability of its existing stores. The stores acquired in 1997 that had precipitated the company's downfall were expected to begin producing as well as the other units by the end of 1999. Analysts, who previously had warily distanced themselves from the company, began to view Petco's prospects more positively. The cause for their more sanguine outlook derived from the company's emphasis on producing returns to shareholders and its new growth strategy. Petco operated 476 stores in 37 states and planned to add to its store count, but expansion in the years ahead was expected to come from the construction of new stores rather than through acquisitions, thereby avoiding the pitfalls of converting stores to the Petco format. In 1999, the company planned to build 40 new stores. As Petco pushed ahead with its plans, its future success depended on producing consistent earnings growth, something that eluded the company during the 1990s. A perennially growing market and a tighter control on profitability, however, engendered optimism for the 21st century.

Optimism began to fade at the turn of the 21st century as Petco found itself in a defensive position again. Just as the company was beginning to recover from the financial difficulties of the late 1990s, its resurgence was cut short by its investment in an Internet start-up, Petopia.com, ensnaring Petco in the spectacular collapse of the dot-com industry. Further, after The Procter & Gamble Company acquired IAMS in 1999, Petco no longer enjoyed its exclusive distribution deal with the popular pet food brand, which exacerbated the losses stemming from the investment in Petopia.com. In response to the difficulties, the company chose to return to the private sector, perceiving its stock to be undervalued. In 2000, with the help of the Los Angeles-based equity firm Leonard Green and Partners, a $600 million buyout was completed. Out of the public eye, Petco focused on curing its ills, building 53 new superstores, closing 19 underperforming units, and developing a new format to inject vitality in the chain. By 2002, the Devine-led enterprise was ready to sell itself on Wall Street again.

New Formats for the Future

For the second time in its history, Petco completed an IPO. In February 2002, the 561-store chain raised more than $275 million from its stock offering, touting its new ''Millennium'' format to investors. Millennium stores, which were more focused on the supplies side of the business, featured merchandise grouped by pet category rather than by product category, beginning as a test format that quickly was embraced by Devine and his senior executives. By the end of 2002, there were 79 Millennium stores operating, with plans to add 60 new Millennium units annually for the next several years. Ultimately, management revealed during the year, the goal was to make Petco a 1,250-store chain.

Back in a positive, growth-oriented mind set, Petco's management pressed ahead, seeking to double the size of the chain. In 2003, a deal was announced that did nothing to advance the chain towards its goal of 1,250 stores, but one that did much to heighten awareness of the Petco name. In January, the company announced a 22-year naming rights package for the new stadium of Major League Baseball's San Diego Padres that resulted in Petco's home city baseball stadium, which was unveiled in April 2004, being named Petco Park. As the San Diego Padres prepared to play in the new stadium, Devine passed his title as chief executive officer to Petco's chief financial officer, James Myers, who joined Petco in 1990, the same year Devine joined the company. Devine remained the company's chairman, taking responsibility for shaping overall corporate strategy, which was expressed in a significant fashion several months after Meyers' promotion. In June 2004, Petco experimented with a new store format at its store in Escondido, California, where the first prototype of the "Pisces" format was tested. The Pisces format featured a larger line of fish and aquatic supplies than traditional stores along with a wide-open, "racetrack" store layout. This format proved to be as popular as that of Millennium units. By March 2005, the Pisces format had been incorporated in nearly 70 stores, with plans calling for more than 100 Petco stores to use the concept by the end of 2005. As Petco plotted its expansion plans for the years ahead, the Pisces format gripped management's attention. "This store concept," the company's president proclaimed in a March 14, 2005 interview with *DSN Retailing Today*, "is the future of pet retailing."

Principal Subsidiaries

International Pet Supplies and Distribution, Inc.; Petco Southwest, Inc.; Pet Concepts International; PM Management Incorporated; Petco Southwest, L.P.; Petco Animal Supplies Stores, Inc.; E-Pet Services; E-Pet services, LLC; 17187 Yukon Inc. (Canada).

Principal Competitors

PETsMART, Inc.; Costco Wholesale Corporation; Wal-Mart Stores, Inc.

Further Reading

Allen, Mike, "Dog Days Hound Petco in Wake of Stock Drop," *San Diego Business Journal*, October 12, 1998, p. 4.

——, "Petco Park the Name of Padres' New Home in 2004," *San Diego Business Journal*, January 27, 2003, p. 3.

Basas, Susan M., "Petco Animal Supplies Inc.," *Investor's Business Daily*, December 5, 2002, p. A7.

Buttita, Bob, "Petco Set to Acquire 81 Pet Care Superstore Outlets," *Pet Product News*, November 1997, p. 4.

Chadwell, John, "Power Brokers," *Pet Product News*, July 1996, p. 62.

Creno, Glen, "Pet Superstore Chains Gear Up for All Out War," *Knight-Ridder/Tribune Business News*, March 22, 1997.

Desjardins, Doug, "Petco Roars Back into the Public Sector," *DSN Retailing Today*, March 11, 2002, p. 5.

——, "Petco's Pisces Is Bigger Fish Tale," *DSN Retailing Today*, March 14, 2005, p. 26.

Fugazy, Danielle, "Petco Tries Out Public Market a Second Time," *IPO Reporter*, February 25, 2002, p. ITEM02056001.

"New CEO for Petco," *San Diego Business Journal*, February 23, 2004, p. 4.

Rooney, Brian, "Pet Food Retailer Booms into National Chain," *Business Journal*, May 30, 1988, p. 5.

Sahm, Phil, "Petco Plans to Open 4 Utah Stores," *Knight-Ridder/Tribune Business News*, April 7, 1999.

Scally, Robert, "The Clever Copy Cat," *Discount Store News*, December 8, 1997, p. 71.

—Jeffrey L. Covell

Petróleos de Venezuela S.A.

Edif. Petróleos de Venezuela
Avenida Libertador, La Campiña
Apartado Postal 169
Caracas, 1010-A
Venezuela
Telephone: (212) 708-4111
Fax: (212) 708 4661
Web site: http://www.pdvsa.com.ve

State-Owned Company
Incorporated: 1976
Employees: 46,920
Sales: $46.25 billion (2001)
NAIC: 211111 Crude Petroleum and Natural Gas
    Extraction; 211112 Natural Gas Liquid Extraction;
    213111 Drilling Oil and Gas Wells

Petróleos de Venezuela S.A. (PDVSA) is wholly owned by the Venezuelan state and is the holding company for the national petroleum industry. PDVSA has proved reserves of 77.2 billion barrels of oil—the largest proved reserves outside of the Middle East. Along with its domestic exploration and production business, the company has refining and marketing operations in the Caribbean, Europe, and the United States. Its CITGO Petroleum subsidiary supplies gasoline to retail locations across the United States. The company has experienced turmoil in recent years due to the leadership of Venezuelan President Hugo Chavez. A labor strike in 2002 led to serious losses in oil production and more than 18,000 employees were fired as a result. Rafael Ramirez was named president of PDVSA in 2004.

Early History

Oil has been known and used in Venezuela since seepages were found on the shores of Lake Maracaibo during the colonial period, which ended in 1910. The first formal concession for its exploitation, however, was not awarded until August 24, 1865, when Camilo Ferrand procured the rights from the president of Zulia state. In 1876, a report submitted to the president of Zulia on the petroleum and asphalt deposits in the Maracaibo basin indicated the existence of an oil seep near Tarra, producing 5,760 gallons a day. The first oil company incorporated in the country was the Compañia Nacional Minera Petrólia del Táchira, formed on October 12, 1878. A succession of grants followed during the 19th century, and the systematic exploitation of the country's large hydrocarbon reserves started during the 27-year dictatorship of General Juan Vicente Gómez, which lasted from 1908 to 1935.

The major foreign oil companies were attracted to the country because of the expectation of large oil deposits, the country's relative political stability compared with the rest of Latin America at the time, and the favorable terms offered for the exploration of the country's oil resources. Venezuela, unlike the Middle East or Iran, devised a concessionary system whereby most oil companies could operate, regardless of nationality, and production costs were much lower than in the United States, which accounted for 70 percent of total world oil production at the time.

Venezuela's move toward controlling its oil industry took a significant step in 1943, when the new hydrocarbon law integrated all oil legislation. Five years later, in 1948, the Venezuelan congress passed a new income tax law, establishing the so-called 50–50 system that would become a landmark in relations between the international oil companies and the governments of the various oil-producing countries. This system refers to an agreement whereby concurrent owners bear all expenses equally. In 1959 the national government decided to grant no further concessions, thus ending a system that dated back to the previous century. A further fundamental step toward achieving full control of the country's oil wealth was taken in April 1960 when the Corporación Venezolana de Petroleo (CVP), a national oil company, was established to enable the country to acquire greater experience in all areas of the oil industry. CVP was to operate in competition with foreign concessionaires in the country and was to be the official instrument of the country's petroleum policy. The Service Contracts system was introduced in 1967 through a partial reform of the Hydrocarbons Law, allowing the nation to negotiate with foreign companies under more advantageous conditions.

Company Perspectives:

Petróleos de Venezuela, S.A. (PDVSA) contributes to the national development based on a high sense of joined responsibility which flows in parallel directions heading both towards a common end while supporting part of the PDVSA's socio-economic structure and that of the country as well. This joined-responsibility principle governs all the operations within the oil business dynamic. PDVSA bears a great responsibility as a driven force for the national development, and in consequence, for keeping national security and its implications through the profits obtained from the commercialization of its products and its tax payments. Due to the new PDVSA's approach based on the relation with the environment and the importance given to people as owners of oil and as final destiny of the benefits resulting from hydrocarbons and their by-products activities, a wide sense of joined responsibility has prevailed. Communities, cooperatives and the main national industry have joined their efforts to become fully part of programs and projects surrounded by an atmosphere of cooperation and proactivity.

During the administration of Rafael Caldera the initiative in oil matters shifted from the executive to congress, which increased corporation taxes on oil business and allowed the government unilaterally to determine reference prices for crude oil. The government also began to feel that the previous policy of awarding service contracts would not be successful because it would not provide a more viable alternative to the outright nationalization of the industry. At the same time it was felt that the companies—which would lose their concessions at a given date—were not investing enough to maintain their equipment and fields in working order, and without any guarantees of future profits the companies would disinvest and hand over the concessions in 1983, when the concessions expired, in a poor state. It was debatable whether the government would be entitled to the companies' capital equipment, and production appeared to be on the decline.

As a result, in 1971 the Hydrocarbons Reversion Law was enacted, aimed at ensuring the continuity and efficiency of the country's oil activities after the concessions expired in 1983. The law provided for all industry assets to revert to the nation on the expiration of the concessions, and for the government to appropriate all concessions not being exploited. In addition, the law established that companies would have to deposit 10 percent of their assets with the government to ensure that all such assets would be properly maintained by the companies until complete reversion took place.

Further steps toward nationalization were taken through a series of laws covering the natural gas industry, the domestic petroleum products market, and the merchant marine. By the autumn of 1973 the possibility of an early reversion before 1983 was introduced and started to gain acceptance, replacing the original plan to start nationalizing the industry from 1983. In his last presidential address, Caldera urged the new incumbent, Carlos Andrés Pérez of Acción Democrática, to nationalize the industry. The new government also believed that the oil indus-

try was disinvesting; for instance, the number of exploration wells drilled had declined from 589 in 1958 to 148 in 1973, causing the reserves-to-production ratio to decline. On March 22, 1974, a committee was set up to prepare a draft bill whereby the state itself would maintain the industry and trade of hydrocarbons.

On August 29, 1975, the Organic Law Reserving to the State the Industry and Commerce of Hydrocarbons was enacted, allowing the government to take full control of the oil industry on January 1, 1976. The assets of the industry were acquired from the ex-concessionaires based on a net book value of $1.17 billion.

PDVSA Taking Control in 1978

The nationalization of the industry required the creation of a functional structure that would allow normal operation to continue within the new legal scheme. A holding company, PDVSA, was established to coordinate, supervise, control, and plan the activities of its subsidiaries made up of the 14 former operating companies. PDVSA's oil would be marketed through the major international oil companies Exxon, Shell, and Gulf, thus guaranteeing the company a stable market share. PDVSA reserved the right to reduce the volume of oil placed in this manner by 10 percent after the first year, and by 20 percent in the second year. The new company also would receive technical assistance in exploring and refining from the former operating companies, which would be paid at a rate that varied between 16¢ and 30¢ per barrel. The original 14 operating subsidiaries were integrated in 1977 into four major companies, Lagoven, Maraven, Meneven and Corpoven. On March 1, 1978, PDVSA assumed full responsibility for the country's petrochemical industry when the government transferred the ownership of Petroquímica de Venezuela S.A. (Pequiven) to PDVSA. Pequiven had two petrochemical complexes: Morón in Carabobo state and El Tablazo in Zulia state. Morón manufactured fertilizers as well as several chemicals for the domestic market. The El Tablazo plant produced olefins, caustic soda, and chlorine, which are sold to other nearby industries.

Although PDVSA was a state enterprise, it was expected to finance its normal investment program from its own resources, under a 10 percent cash flow mechanism whereby 10 percent of pre-tax export sales profits could be retained for the purpose of reinvestment by the company. The board of directors reported to an assembly constituted by the minister of energy and mines, who presided over it, and to those members of the Executive Cabinet designated by the president of the republic. PDVSA operated under broad policy guidelines issued by the government.

PDVSA in the Late 1980s

During 1989, PDVSA produced around 1.6 million barrels of oil and condensate per day. It owned 12 refineries with an overall processing capacity of 1.75 million barrels per day, of which 945,000 million barrels per day were processed in Venezuela and the rest in the United States, Europe, and the Dutch Antilles. The most important domestic refineries in terms of capacity were Amuay with 630,000 barrels per day and Cardón with 350,000 barrels per day. Prior to nationalization, Venezuela's refineries had been geared to use low gravity oil to produce heavy fuel oil for export to its traditional market, the northeast United States. At the time of nationalization, heavy fuel oil accounted for 61 percent of total products exported. After nationalization, PDVSA began to diversify its exports, seeking to increase its supply of white products—gasoline and jet fuel—which were traditionally more in demand and afforded a higher profit margin. With this goal in mind, between 1978 and 1987, the company decided to upgrade its refineries in Amuay, Cardón, and El Palito to reduce the proportion of residual fuels obtained in the refining process and increase the proportion of naphtha, gasoline, and distillates. With further upgrading and conversion facilities, the refineries were able to use a higher proportion of heavier crudes, which represented the major volume of reserves in the country. The upgrading of PDVSA's refineries was two-thirds completed when it was halted in 1986 because of low oil prices. Although heavy fuel yield dropped from 61 percent in 1976 to 27 percent in 1986, it was still too high in 1991 for PDVSA's key U.S. market, where heavy fuel oil amounted to only 8 percent of total demand.

During the late 1980s, PDVSA supplied the domestic market with approximately 335,000 barrels per day of petroleum products, which represented approximately 20 percent of total production. PDVSA supplied local markets through its four main operating subsidiaries, Lagoven, Maraven, Meneven, and Corpoven, which operated supply depots and about 1,600 petrol stations. The products sold were petrol, aviation fuel, diesel fuel, lubricants, kerosene, and asphalt, with petrol accounting for almost half of total consumption.

One of PDVSA's most important international marketing strategies at this time was its joint venture participation in foreign manufacturing and marketing companies, which had accelerated significantly since 1986, when oil prices fell below $10 per barrel and it was difficult to place oil. PDVSA decided to secure long-term outlets for its crude oil by increasing its presence in foreign downstream markets, mainly in the United States and Europe. It had slightly less than 800,000 barrels per day of refining capacity and leased a 300,000-barrels-per-day refinery in Curacao in the Dutch Antilles. PDVSA's first downstream venture outside Venezuela took place in West Germany

in 1983 when it entered into a joint venture partnership with Veba Oel to supply 155,000 barrels of oil per day.

Through its ownership of CITGO Petroleum Corporation, PDVSA also owned refineries at Lake Charles, Louisiana, and refineries at Corpus Christi, Texas. Subsidiary Propernyn PDVSA bought 50 percent of CITGO from the Southland Corporation. In 1990 Propernyn became the sole owner of CITGO. On October 31, 1989, PDVSA acquired 50 percent of Unocal's downstream assets in the midwestern United States. With this acquisition, PDVSA gained access to a deep conversion refinery near Chicago with an installed capacity of 153,000 barrels per day, as well as distribution and marketing facilities in Illinois, Michigan, Iowa, Ohio, and Wisconsin. PDVSA also owned minority stakes in two refineries in Sweden and one in Belgium.

The proportion of light and medium crude oil in Venezuela's export package declined between 1976 and 1984, with a complementary increase in the volume of heavy crude exports. As a result of PDVSA's exploration record, this trend was reversed in 1985, so that by 1988 exports of light and medium crudes accounted for 50 percent of PDVSA's crude export package. The United States was PDVSA's main market, accounting for 54 percent or 891,000 barrels per day of total exports in 1988, with Europe in second place with 205,000 barrels per day or 12.4 percent.

PDVSA's proved reserves rose from 18.2 billion barrels in 1976 to 58.35 billion barrels in 1989. This was the result of increased exploration activity and the addition of 26 billion barrels from the Orinoco oil belt. Prior to nationalization, only 33 exploratory wells had been drilled between 1971 and 1976, compared with 58 wells in 1976 and 225 in 1982.

PDVSA's success in exploration resulted mainly from discoveries made around 1987 at El Furrial in the eastern state of Monagas, with estimated reserves of 538 million barrels and with an upside potential of 1.1 billion barrels, in the Ceuta South-Southeast field in Lake Maracaibo with estimated recoverable reserves of one billion barrels, and in the Guafita field in Apure, next to the Caño Limón field in Colombia, with estimated recoverable reserves of 500 million barrels. Additional reserves from the Orinoco oil belt also contributed to the company's reserves. These discoveries added between 10 and 12 billion barrels of light and medium grade crude oil to a reserve base that was disproportionately biased toward heavier oils.

These discoveries were expected to have a profound impact on the country's crude export mix, as the Monagas prospects, which currently produced 80,000 barrels per day of light oil, were expected to reach plateau production—the stable production period before the field declines—of 500,000 barrels per day in 1994. The Ceuta field produced 100,000 barrels per day and was expected to reach 200,000 barrels per day in 1993.

Since the trend toward heavy oil was reversed with the discoveries of light oil in Monagas and Apure, PDVSA continued to concentrate its exploration efforts on finding light and medium oil, and between 1988 and 1993 planned to drill 112 exploration wells to add a possible 9.4 billion barrels of reserves to the existing 58 billion barrels. The exploration effort was concentrated on the Furrial-Musipán geological trend in Monagas, where 51 wells were to be drilled, and on the

North-Central section of Lake Maracaibo, where 43 wells were to be drilled.

PDVSA also was developing its large Orinoco oil belt using a new patented production method. This field covered an area of approximately 42,000 square kilometers and was considered one of the most important untapped reserves of heavy oil in the world. The estimated oil in situ was around two trillion barrels. The treated heavy oil was known as orimulsion, with recoverable reserves estimated at 267 billion barrels, equivalent on a calorific basis to all of South Africa's coal reserves and to all of the United States' crude reserves. Orimulsion was a rival product to coal and according to PDVSA was not intended to compete with heavy fuel oil. Commercial marketing of the fuel started at a modest level of 20,000 barrels per day, but was expected to reach 600,000 barrels per day by the middle of the decade.

Gas reserves in the country in the 1980s were estimated at 93 trillion cubic feet of gas. At this time, gas production was between 3.6 million and 3.8 million cubic feet of gas per day, of which one-third was sold locally, about one-third reinjected into the reservoirs, 21 percent used by the oil industry, and 5 percent flared. Major switching from oil to gas was not envisaged until 1992, after completion of the Nurgas pipeline from Anozategui to the West.

In 1987 PDVSA started exporting coal from western Venezuela through its subsidiary, Carbozulia. Initial exports started at 500,000 tons but were expected to reach 6.5 million tons by 1995.

In its first year of operation, PDVSA received net income of $825.6 million, increasing to $1.88 billion in 1977, but with the decline in oil prices the company's net income also suffered, falling to $731 million in 1988. For tax purposes, PDVSA was treated by the Venezuelan government like any other business entity. The company paid royalties, and income taxes were based on the export values of the oil and products sold. PDVSA did not enjoy any tax privilege except for the tax-free receipt of 10 percent of the net income from its subsidiaries' export sales, which, for accounting and tax purposes, was viewed as a cost incurred by the subsidiaries. The government's fiscal share, composed of royalties, income tax, and other taxes, amounted to $5.64 billion in 1988, representing almost 60 percent of total revenues of $9.51 billion. During the early 1990s, PDVSA continued to invest in its production facilities with the intention of increasing production. It also intended to increase its presence in the European downstream sector through acquisitions. In 1992, the country allowed foreign investment in its oil fields for the first time since PDVSA was nationalized.

Upheaval in the 1990s and Beyond

Under the direction of Luis Guisti, PDVSA spent much of the 1990s determined to double production capacity. As part of this strategy, PDVSA focused its efforts on securing lucrative partnerships. The company worked with Shell, Exxon, and Mitsubishi on the Mariscal Sucre project, which was created to explore and develop liquefied natural gas (LNG) resources in the Paria Peninsula and the East Coast of Margarita. In 1996, the company opened up ten of its oil fields to foreign oil firms.

As part of the specialized exploration and development contracts, foreign companies had to evenly share their profits with the Venezuelan government. In 1998, PDVSA restructured its organization and created three main divisions: PDVSA Exploration and Production, PDVSA Manufacture and Marketing, and PDVSA Services.

PDVSA's future changed dramatically in December 1998 when former paratrooper Hugo Chavez was elected president. Chavez shuttered many of Guisti's plans and focused on bringing the company back under tight government control. His poor treatment of company officials, the firing of many top executives, and his overall management of the oil company led to growing discontent. By 2002, PDVSA employees and opponents of Chavez planned to halt oil production, which had serious implications for the Venezuelan economy. Humberto Calderon Berti, the former Minister of Energy and Mines, offered his thoughts on the strike in an April 2002 *New York Times* article. ''This can only end with the president resigning,'' he claimed. ''All Venezuelans from all walks of life, from all social strata, from all the political and ideological sectors, must take part in the stoppage. This is about him or us. It is a choice between democracy or dictatorship.''

By now, Venezuela's economy was faltering and there was major political unrest in the country. During this time, Chavez was briefly overthrown by a military coup. In an attempt to appease PDVSA employees and protesters, Chavez removed his appointees from the PDVSA board and tapped the former head of OPEC, Ali Rodriguez, to lead the oil company. Political turmoil continued, however, and a second major strike followed in December 2002. Overall, the work stoppage cost the Venezuelan government billions of dollars. Approximately 18,000 employees were fired for their part in the strike.

During this time, relations between the United States and Venezuela were strained. The United States did not support Chavez, and the populist leader accused the United States of endorsing the 2002 coup d'etat and even plotting an assassination attempt. Both countries, however, were in a unique situation. The United States depended on Venezuela for 15 percent of its oil imports and Venezuela exported 60 percent of its oil to the United States.

Although Chavez certainly had his opponents, he gathered support from the poor working class. Using revenues from PDVSA, he funded many social programs that provided education and food to poverty-stricken Venezuelans. Chavez idolized independence hero Simon Bolivar and his movement became known as the Bolivarian Revolution. Chavez's social programs were successful and in August 2004 he beat a recall referendum set forth by his opposition. Many expected him to win another six-year term in the 2006 elections.

As a result of the unrest over the past several years, PDVSA oil output was suffering. Production levels were falling by as much as 25 percent per year and, according to OPEC, the company's daily output was 2.6 million barrels a day—down from 3.3 million in 1997. Venezuela became increasingly dependent on foreign investment to increase its production. Nevertheless, Chavez increased royalties on refining projects in the Orinoco region from 1 percent to 16.66 percent in October

2004. New ventures would have to pay 30 percent in royalties and allow PDVSA to take a 51 percent stake.

PDVSA had faced a challenging chapter in its history during the late 1990s and early years of the new millennium. Although much of the upheaval appeared to be in its past, only time would tell if the company would bounce back from the devastating oil strikes of 2002. Venezuela's economy was dependent on the health of the oil industry. Indeed, continued foreign investment in the country's oil fields was necessary for success in the years to come.

Principal Subsidiaries

Lyondell-CITGO Refining Company LP (United States; 41%); Needle Coker (United States; 25%); Chalmette Refining LLC (United States; 50%); Merey Sweeny (United States; 50%); Hovensa LLC (United States; 50%); Ruhr Oel GmbH (Germany; 50%); AB Nynas Petroleum (Sweden; 50%); Monomeros Colombo-Venezolanos (Columbia; 47%); Petrozuata (49%); Fertinitro (35%); Metor, C.A. (38%); Carbones del Guasare S.A. (49%); Super Octanos, C.A. (49%); Ceraven (49%); Profalca (35%); Intesa (40%); PDVSA Petroleo, S.A.; Petroquimica de Venezuela, S.A. (Pequiven); Bitumenes Orinoco, S.A. (BITOR); Deltaven, S.A.; Carbones del Zulia, S.A. (Carbozulia); PDV Holding, Inc.; PDVSA Finance Ltd.

Principal Competitors

Exxon Mobil Corporation; Petróleos Mexicanos; Saudi Arabian Oil Company.

Further Reading

Coronel, Gustavo, *The Nationalization of the Venezuelan Oil Industry,* Lexington, Mass.: Lexington Books, 1983.

Forero, Juan, ''Venezuela Woes Worsen As State Oil Company Calls Strike,'' *New York Times,* April 9, 2002.

Lifsher, Marc, ''Strike in Venezuela Shows Signs of Winding Down,'' *Wall Street Journal,* January 8, 2003, p. A10.

Marquis, Christopher, ''A Bitter Chavez Castigates U.S.,'' *The New York Times,* March 18, 2004.

Martínez, Aníbal R., *Venezuelan Oil: Development and Chronology,* London: Elsevier Applied Science, 1989.

Millard, Peter, ''Venezuela Assails Past Oil Contracts,'' *Wall Street Journal,* June 8, 2005, p. B5D.

O'Grady, Mary Anastasia, ''Oil Wells Refuse to Obey Chavez Commands,'' *Wall Street Journal,* May 20, 2005, p. A15.

Petras, James, E., Morris Morley, and Steven Smith, *The Nationalization of Venezuelan Oil,* New York: Praeger Publishers, 1977.

''Petroven—Petróleos de Venezuela S.A.,'' *OPEC Bulletin Supplement,* April 24, 1978.

''OPEC Member Country Profile—Venezuela,'' *OPEC Bulletin Supplement,* December 11, 1978.

''PDVSA—Petróleos de Venezuela S.A.,'' *OPEC Bulletin Supplement,* February 18, 1980.

''PDVSA Shifts Course Under Chavez Presidency,'' *Oil Daily,* June 1, 1999.

Philip, George, *Oil and Politics in Latin America,* Cambridge: Cambridge University Press, 1982.

Smith, Geri, ''Killing the Golden Goose?,'' *Business Week,* March 14, 2005.

Sullivan, William M., and Brian S. McBeth, *Petroleum in Venezuela: A Bibliography,* Boston: G.K. Hall & Co., 1985.

—Brian S. McBeth
—update: Christina M. Stansell

Pope Resources LP

19245 10th Avenue N.E.
Poulsbo, Washington 98370
U.S.A.
Telephone: (360) 697-6626
Fax: (360) 697-1156
Web site: http://www.poperesources.com

Private Company
Incorporated: 1985
Employees: 72
Sales: $39.64 million (2004)
Stock Exchanges: NASDAQ
Ticker Symbol: POPZ
NAIC: 113110 Timber Tract Operations; 236115 New
    Single-Family Housing Construction (Except
    Operative Builders)

Pope Resources LP owns and manages timberland and real estate in Washington state. The company operates through two primary subsidiaries, Olympic Resource Management and Olympic Property Group. Olympic Resource Management owns approximately 115,000 acres of timberland in western Washington and manages timberland for other owners, serving as a forestry consultant. Olympic Property Group owns a 2,600-acre portfolio of residential and commercial development lands, including the town site of Port Gamble, Washington.

Origins of a Spinoff

Pope Resources sprang from one of the oldest timber companies in the Pacific Northwest, making its debut as a separate company nearly 150 years after its progenitor was established. The company was formed from certain assets controlled by Pope & Talbot, Inc., a lumber company that started in the barging business in 1849 in San Francisco. Founders Andrew Jackson Pope and Frederic Talbot diversified into the lumber business several months after starting their company, and arrived in the Pacific Northwest three years later, establishing a company named Puget Mill Company on the Puget Sound in what later became the town of Port Gamble. Puget Mill quickly became the largest business on the Puget Sound, establishing a presence in nearby Port Ludlow shortly after the Civil War. Both Port Gamble and Port Ludlow figured as prominent components of Pope Resources' business more than a century later.

The assets inherited by Pope Resources drew their origins from Pope & Talbot's timber holdings, which by the beginning of the 1880s totaled 150,000 acres. The other aspect of Pope Resources' business—real estate development—had its roots in Pope & Talbot's holdings in Port Gamble and Port Ludlow. The company first began to build a real estate development business, which initially produced lackluster results, in the years preceding World War I. Pope & Talbot, the name adopted by Puget Mill in 1940, later renewed its involvement in real estate development, but its timber assets experienced growth decade after decade, representing the mainstay of the company's business. By the 1950s, Pope & Talbot owned more than one billion board feet of timber, possessing more than an ample supply of wood to warrant its diversification into an integrated wood products company. The company began to shape itself into a manufacturer as well as a harvester during the 1950s, either acquiring or building facilities to manufacture timber-derivative products. Pope & Talbot added a particleboard plant, a veneer mill, a wood treatment facility, and a plywood plant. During the 1970s, the company entered the pulp and paper business, followed by further diversification during the 1980s, when it entered the consumer products market by adding tissue and diaper plants.

As Pope & Talbot flowered into a vertically integrated wood products company, it also delved into other, nontimber-related businesses. It began dabbling in real estate ventures again during the 1960s, undertaking its most ambitious development project in Port Ludlow, on land purchased by the company in 1878. Pope & Talbot began development at Port Ludlow in 1968, constructing a new marina, restaurant, beach club, condominiums, sports facilities, and a championship golf course. The company wanted to make the development a vacation-home resort, initially anticipating a community with 1,200 homes. Although the company sold the lots for all the home sites, the project fell short of becoming the vacation-home paradise envisioned by its creators. Construction costs soared as the rate

Company Perspectives:

At Pope Resources we have worked hard over many years to cultivate a reputation for honesty, fairness, and integrity. We are known for our stewardship of the land, respect for the communities in which we do business, and the straight-forward transparency with which we communicate to the investment marketplace. Collectively, such actions and be-haviors as these generate a public trust that we view as critical for us to maintain in support of our value-building enterprise. As one means of upholding that cultivated trust, we have set for ourselves high standards of ethical conduct.

of inflation escalated during the late 1960s and early 1970s, exacerbating the underlying problem with the project: the market did not contain a sufficient number of recreational home buyers. In the end, only 450 homes were built.

Pope Resources was born from a strategic decision by executives at Pope & Talbot. By the 1980s, growing concern over the environmental impact of logging was reducing logging activity and increasing the cost of timber, prompting officials to take action. They decided to reduce the company's exposure to the timber market in the Pacific Northwest, a decision that led Pope & Talbot to spin off its real estate and timber holdings in Washington to the company's shareholders. A master limited partnership was created in 1985 named Pope Resources, a company given more than 70,000 acres of timberland on the Olympic Peninsula, the resort in Port Ludlow, ownership of the historic section of Port Gamble, and other assets. The company's annual sales upon its release from Pope & Talbot were less than $20 million, the starting-off point for a collection of assets that were more than a century old.

One of the first projects undertaken by Pope Resources involved a return to the vacation-home resort project in Port Ludlow. The growing population in the Puget Sound area had created a potentially larger market for recreational homebuyers, but the company wanted to be sure, wishing to avoid the miscalculation of the late 1960s. A marketing study was commissioned from a national research firm in 1984, while Pope & Talbot still oversaw the real estate development operations, the first of three studies commissioned to determine the viability of further developing the site located near the head of Hood Canal. The last study was completed in 1988, revealing that the company should target those in or close to retirement rather than vacation-home buyers. With a potential customer base identified, the company pressed ahead with the project, a development that would become known as New Port Ludlow. To gain approval for the project and appease the Protect Ludlow Bay Committee, Pope Resources spent $2 million to improve waste treatment facilities at Port Ludlow built under the aegis of Pope & Talbot, which residents complained were inadequate. Next, the company built the amenities for the New Port Ludlow project before constructing the homes. "They're not buying future promises," Pope Resources vice-president of development remarked in a June 18, 1990 interview with *Puget Sound Business Journal.* Pope Resources constructed a $2 million, 16,000-square-foot recreation center with an auditorium and workshop areas, a pool and spa, and other

fitness facilities before beginning work on the $100 million, 800-home adult community.

The New Port Ludlow development was the most conspicuous demonstration of Pope Resources' existence during its first decade in business. The company achieved nominal growth, but it kept a low profile, characterized as a "caretaker" company by a major shareholder in the April 30, 1999, issue of the *Puget Sound Business Journal.* The company remained in the shadows until its president and chief executive officer, George Folquet, retired in December 1995. When Folquet retired, two of the company's board members decided to recruit a new leader to invigorate the Pope Resources organization. Peter T. Pope, the president and chief executive officer of Pope & Talbot, and his cousin's husband, Adolphus Andrews, Jr., whose families owned one-fifth of Pope Resources, began looking for a new leader and found a veteran timber executive named Gary F. Tucker.

Tucker Tenure Beginning in 1996

Tucker spearheaded a dramatic makeover of Pope Resources, ushering in a period of accelerated growth that marked the company's first expression of independence from Pope & Talbot. Pope Resources was no longer a "caretaker" company, but it took roughly a decade for the company to assert its own personality. The credit, for better or worse, went to Tucker, who arrived in January 1996 after twice retiring from a lengthy career in the timber industry. Tucker spent years working for Seattle-based Plum Creek Timber Co., the former timber arm of Burlington Northern. He retired as the company's vice-president of resources in 1989, but emerged from retirement in a matter of months to found his own company, Trees Inc., a consulting firm that managed 2.1 million acres of private forest for the Hancock Timber Resource Group, an investment component of John Hancock Financial Services. Tucker, who was 60 years old when he joined Pope Resources, approached his new job with the zeal of a rising executive, promising wholesale changes that would change the company's corporate culture and trigger unprecedented growth in new directions. "Gary has taken a totally different tack," a colleague explained in an April 30, 1999 interview with *Puget Sound Business Journal.* "Almost from day one, Gary seemed to be an exceedingly ambitious fellow."

Tucker stamped the beginning of a new Pope Resources era with pervasive changes. He hired new executives from high-profile companies such as Boise Cascade Corp., Weyerhaeuser Co., and MacCaw Cellular Communications Inc. He instilled a new workplace environment that was more tolerant of risk, more creative, and more collaborative. After examining the company's operations, Tucker sought to expand on the company's two traditional lines of business. The company made most of its money by logging and selling trees from its 76,000 acres of forest on the Olympic Peninsula. A smaller portion of its revenue was derived from the real estate division, which owned 4,000 acres in the Puget Sound area, as well as the Port Ludlow development and the town site of historic Port Gamble. Tucker, a year after his arrival, began adding to the operations he inherited, executing what he considered to be his masterstroke in 1997, when Olympic Resource Management LLC (ORM) was formed as a new subsidiary. ORM was formed to manage forests owned by other companies, marking a new line of business for Pope Resources that Tucker believed could carry the company toward much greater

---

Key Dates:

1985: Pope & Talbot spins off its timber and real estate assets in Washington as a master limited partnership named Pope Resources.

1996: Gary F. Tucker is named president and chief executive officer, beginning a period of expansion for Pope Resources.

1997: Olympic Resource Management is formed, marking Pope Resources' entry in the forestry consulting business.

1998: Pope Resources acquires Simons Reid Collins, a Canadian timber consulting business.

2000: Allen Symington replaces Tucker, touching off a divestiture program aimed at narrowing Pope Resources' strategic focus.

2001: The acquisition of 44,500 acres of timberland in Washington increases Pope Resources' timber assets by 60 percent.

2002: David L. Nunes replaces Symington and sells the company's Canadian consulting business.

2004: Pope Resources acquires 1,339 acres of timberland in Jefferson County, Washington.

---

heights. "Our goals for Olympic Resource Management are ambitious," he explained in a March 17, 1997 interview with *Business Wire.* "We expect significant growth within two years. If we meet our targets, ORM could be managing in excess of $1 billion in investments within five years."

ORM was the centerpiece of Tucker's makeover, but not the only significant change to the company's organizational structure during his tenure. The new subsidiary gained a considerable foothold in its new business in 1998, winning a contract to manage more than 500,000 acres of forest in Washington, Oregon, California, and British Columbia owned by Tucker's former employer, Hancock Timber Resource Group. At roughly the same time, Tucker made further organizational changes, reorganizing Pope Resources' real estate, real estate development, and utilities assets into separate companies. Olympic Property Group L.L.C. was formed as a holding company for subsidiaries Olympic Resorts L.L.C., Olympic Real Estate and Development, Inc., and Olympic Water and Sewer, Inc. Olympic Resorts was given ownership of the 27-hole golf course at Port Ludlow, a commercial development called Village Center, and a recreational vehicle park, which were to be managed, along with a 300-slip marina, by Olympic Real Estate and Development. The water and sewer utilities serving Port Ludlow were bundled under the control of Olympic Water and Sewer. Before the end of what had been a busy year for Pope Resources, Tucker made a final addition to the company's operations. In December, he acquired Simons Reid Collins, a timber consultant that managed approximately 60,000 acres of forest on Vancouver Island.

A Change in Leadership for the 21st Century

Tucker's sweeping changes helped reverse a two-year decline in sales and earnings, sparking a 43 percent increase in

sales in 1998 to a record $43 million, but his era ended abruptly. The "exceedingly ambitious" Tucker had proved to be just that, at least in the minds of some Pope Resources officials. Tucker resigned in May 2000 after increasing the company's workforce from 56 in 1996 to 257 in 1999. His replacement, Allen Symington, was hired in September 2000 as Pope Resources' chairman and chief executive officer, and immediately announced measures to reverse some of Tucker's actions. "There needs to be efforts undertaken to get this thing back on track," said Bruce Sherman, the chairman of Private Capital Management Inc., which owned 38 percent of Pope Resources, in a December 15, 2000 interview with *Puget Sound Business Journal.* Symington, a former executive at U.S. Timberlands Co. LP, which owned 670,000 acres of timberland in Oregon and Washington, announced a strategic makeover of his own, designed to narrow the company's focus on growing and managing timberlands.

Symington's overhaul focused on divesting some of the Tucker-inspired additions to Pope Resources, but ORM, the centerpiece of Tucker's makeover, was retained. Before Symington began to whittle down the company's interests, however, he completed the first timberland acquisition in Pope Resources' history. In February 2001, the company agreed to buy 44,500 acres of forest in Washington's Skamania and Lewis counties from Plum Creek Timber Co. for $54 million. The acquisition increased Pope Resources' timberland by 60 percent, giving the company 118,500 acres, but the deal offered more than just an increase in assets. Most of Pope Resources' trees at the time were either young or ready to be logged, whereas the Plum Creek timberland contained many trees in the mid-range age classes, thereby by balancing Pope Resources' timber assets.

The divestitures began not long after the Plum Creek deal was announced. In August 2001, the company sold the Port Ludlow development for $16.7 million. Next, a planned transition in leadership took place. Symington was replaced as chief executive officer in January 2002 by David L. Nunes, who had been promoted to president concurrent with Symington's appointment as chief executive officer in September 2000. Nunes, who spent nine years working for Weyerhaeuser Co. before joining Pope Resources in 1997, continued pursuing Symington's objective of creating a slimmed-down Pope Resources. In November 2002, he announced plans to exit the forestry consulting business in Canada, which had developed from the 1998 acquisition of Simons Reid Collins. "We have come to recognize that this business provides only limited synergy with our core timberland management business and has additionally suffered due to the protracted softwood lumber dispute between the United States and Canada," Nunes explained in a November 5, 2002 interview with *Canadian Corporate News.*

The contrasting philosophies of the Tucker and the Symington/Nunes leadership tenures created equally contrasting financial results. Pope Resources collected $50.6 million in revenue in 2000, the year Tucker resigned. By 2004, the company's revenue volume had shrunk to $39.6 million. Growth was achieved in profitability between the two periods, however, encouraging Nunes to press forward with the company's more focused strategic approach. In 2000, Pope Resources registered a net loss of $6.2 million. In 2004, the company posted a net profit of $10.1 million. As Nunes prepared for the future, he was expected to pursue growth but only within the narrowed scope of the company's focus. An acquisition announced in late 2004 conformed to the strategic vision of the company, offering a blueprint for the future. In October 2004, the company announced it was acquiring 1,339 acres of timberland interspersed among acreage it already owned in Jefferson County. "This property includes a significant volume of high-quality merchantable timber, which we expect to harvest over the next few years," said Nunes, in a statement quoted by *UPI NewsTrack* on October 25, 2004. The acquisition was the company's last major deal before celebrations of its 20th anniversary began, a milestone that had its roots in a more than century-old business.

Principal Subsidiaries

ORM, Inc.; OPG Properties LLC; OPG Port Gamble LLC; Olympic Resource Management LLC; Olympic International LLC; Olympic Resource Management CP LLC; Olympic Property Group I LLC; Olympic Real Estate Development LLC; Harbor Hill LLC.

Principal Competitors

Hampton Affiliates; Pacific Fiber Company LP; Simpson Investment Company.

Further Reading

Erb, George, "A New Creed: Pope Resources Gets a Makeover," *Puget Sound Business Journal,* April 30, 1999, p. 1.

——, "New Forests for Pope to Manage," *Puget Sound Business Journal,* March 31, 2000, p. 3.

Hayes, John R., "The Tree Option," *Forbes,* June 26, 1989, p. 268.

Milburn, Karen, "Pope Res. Tries Again at Port Ludlow," *Puget Sound Business Journal,* June 18, 1990, p. 16A.

"Pope Resources Announces Appointment of New Chief Executive Officer," *Business Wire,* January 9, 2002, p. 375.

"Pope Resources Announces Exit of Canadian Consulting Business," *Canadian Corporate News,* November 5, 2002, p. 1008308u2674.

"Pope Resources Buys 1,339 Acres," *UPI NewsTrack,* October 25, 2004, p. 12.

"Pope Resources CEO Steps Down," *Puget Sound Business Journal,* May 12, 2000, p. 20.

"Pope Resources Creates New Companies," *Business Wire,* May 1, 1998, p. 05010239.

"Pope Resources Makes Timberland Purchase," *Puget Sound Business Journal,* February 23, 2001, p. 21.

"Pope Resources Remake Has a Big Shareholder's Blessing," *Puget Sound Business Journal,* December 15, 2000, p. 9.

"Pope Sells Resort for $16.7 Million," *Puget Sound Business Journal,* August 10, 2001, p. 3.

Virgin, Bill, "Company Sees the Forest," *Seattle Post-Intelligencer,* February 28, 1998, p. B3.

—Jeffrey L. Covell

PPR S.A.

10, Avenue Hoche
75381 Paris
Cedex 08
France
Telephone: (33) 1 45 64 61 00
Fax: (33) 1 44 90 62 25
Web site: http://www.pprgroup.com

Public Company
Incorporated: 1972 as Au Printemps S.A.
Employees: 93,397
Sales: EUR 24.2 billion ($33 billion) (2004)
Stock Exchanges: Paris
Ticker Symbol: PP
NAIC: 452110 Department Stores; 454110 Electronic
    Shopping and Mail-Order Houses

PPR S.A., formerly known as Pinault-Printemps-Redoute S.A., is the third-largest luxury retail group in the world. The group went through a major reorganization in the early years of the new millennium, selling off its holdings in timber, electrical equipment, and consumer credit services. During this time, PPR increased its stake in the Gucci Group, eventually securing a 99.4 percent interest in the luxury concern whose brands include Gucci, Yves Saint Laurent, Bottega Veneta, YSL Beaute, Boucheron, Sergio Rossi, Bedat & Co., Alexander McQueen, Stella McCartney, and Balenciaga. PPR's retail establishments include Printemps, Conforama, Redcats, Fnac, and CFAO. Francois Henri Pinault, the founder's son, took over as CEO in 2005.

Mid-19th Century Origins

In 1865, 31-year-old Jules Jaluzot, who had been a department head at Bon Marche, France's oldest department store, opened Au Printemps, a small store on the corner of boulevard Haussmann and rue du Havre in Paris. The store consisted of a basement for stock, a ground floor, and the mezzanine of a residential building, some 200 square meters in all. Au Printemps was a rapid success and Jaluzot purchased the upper floors of the building. By 1870 the staff had grown from 30 to 250. The acquisition of adjacent buildings followed, and the store soon occupied a whole block on boulevard Haussmann, between rue du Havre and rue Caumartin. As its reputation grew, Jaluzot began mail-order operations in France and other European countries, with catalogs in different languages.

In 1881 a fire destroyed two-thirds of the somewhat ramshackle store, which by then employed more than 700 people. Jaluzot decided to rebuild immediately, turning the business into a societe en commandite par actions—limited partnership—called Jaluzot & Cie. This form of company was common in France at the time, consisting of a managing partner (or partners) and shareholders who played no part in the management of the business. The managing partner, appointed for life, named his co-partners and successors and was guaranteed a fixed percentage of the profits—in this case, 18 percent. He was also entirely responsible for any debts incurred by the company. Jules Jaluzot provided about 35 percent of the capital of the new company, and the shareholders provided the rest. In 1882 the new department store was opened. It occupied a ground area of 2,900 square meters and had six floors, occupying the entire area between rue de Provence and rue Caumartin. Further commercial success followed, but Jaluzot, a Member of Parliament for his native Nievre and a prominent figure in Paris society, became involved in financial speculation of various sorts. In 1905 he speculated in sugar, using his own money and also in the name of and with capital from Au Printemps (Printemps), but this venture failed and he had to resign. His initials, JJ, can still be seen in the ceramic tiles on the facade of his 1882 store. His place as managing partner was taken by Gustave Laguionie, who had worked alongside Jaluzot at Au Printemps from 1867 to 1882, before leaving to become director of a wholesale business in piece goods. In 1907 Laguionie, then age 64, named his 23-year-old son Pierre as joint managing partner, and in the same year the foundation stone was laid for an adjacent store between rue Caumartin and rue Charras. The new building was opened in 1910. It was larger than the first store, occupying six floors, with a ground floor of 5,000 square meters.

Adopting Modern Management Strategies in the Early 20th Century

Gustave Laguionie died in 1920, leaving the business under the control of his son Pierre, alongside Alcide Poulet, named

Company Perspectives:

PPR's goal is to be one of the world's most admired companies for its capacity to seduce and surprise its customers, its outstanding products and services, its constant drive to improve performance and its corporate ethics.

partner in 1920. In 1921 there was another disaster when the 1910 store partially burned down; rebuilding began immediately and the store was reopened in 1924. Adjacent buildings were acquired in rue du Havre and used for mail-order operations (then about 20 percent of total sales) and small stores were purchased in Le Havre, Rouen, and Lille in 1928 and 1929. Furthermore, some independent retailers became affiliated with Printemps for the purchase of merchandise. More important were the changes in management methods. Between 1926 and 1930 a number of innovations were introduced. Advertising and sales promotion formed an integral part of the selling activities of the firm, which adopted a strict budget. A house magazine was started in addition to training and research departments. In 1929 the functions of buying and selling were separated instead of being the responsibility of a single department head, and a separate buying company, the Societe Parisienne d'Achats en Commun (SAPAC), was founded. In 1930 a system of budgetary control was introduced, by which each major activity had a planned budget of expenditure and results. In 1928 Pierre Laguionie became a founding member of the International Association of Department Stores, a society for management research.

The year 1931 saw Printemps involved in an entirely new form of retailing, the limited-price variety store. In that year the first Prisunic store opened in Paris, operated by Prisunic S.A., a wholly controlled subsidiary. A central buying company, SAPAC-Prisunic, was created in 1932, and by 1935 there were eight Prisunic stores in operation, four in Paris and four in the provinces, with another 30 stores operated by retailers affiliated with SAPAC. In 1932 one of the first groups to become a Prisunic affiliate was Maus Freres of Geneva, which opened Prisunic stores in eastern France with French associates, including Pierre Levy, the textile manufacturer. In 1936, however, a law was passed forbidding companies to open more one-price stores. This virtually brought to an end the expansion of Prisunic through new stores, but progress was made with affiliated stores, as in most cases these were establishments that did not necessarily carry the Prisunic name.

Wartime Difficulties Yielding to Postwar Growth

At the outbreak of World War II the Printemps group consisted of the Paris store and seven stores elsewhere in France, plus 20 stores affiliated with the SAPAC buying organization. The Prisunic division had ten stores of its own and 60 affiliated stores, which employed about 5,500 workers. The group was still a limited partnership, and after the death of Alcide Poulet in 1928, Pierre Laguionie appointed his two brothers-in-law, Georges Marindaz (who died in 1931) and Charles Vigneras, as co-partners. Both were married to daughters of Gustave Laguionie.

The war, the German occupation, and the postwar shortages of merchandise meant a period of survival rather than of growth.

But with the economic recovery starting in the early 1950s expansion again gathered pace, in two overlapping phases. The first was vigorous growth of the Prisunic variety store chain from 1950 to 1965. The number of Prisunic stores owned by the group rose from 13 in 1950 to more than 80 in 1965, and in the same period the number of affiliated stores rose from 80 to more than 230. Affiliated stores were a very effective way of earning commission on sales and increasing the purchasing power of the central buying organization with virtually no investment in land, buildings, or stock. Furthermore, it was no secret that, for the Printemps group, the Prisunic operation was extremely profitable and provided capital for the subsequent growth of the department store division.

Starting in 1954, the buildings of the Paris department store were completely transformed. Although the facades were untouched, the interiors were changed beyond recognition. All nonselling activities were transferred to the outskirts of the city, the enormous lightwells were filled in to provide selling space, the buildings on the north side of rue du Havre became the large Brummell menswear and sporting goods store, new banks of escalators were installed, and in 1963 two additional sales floors were built on top of the 1882 building. Selling space in these units was increased from 32,000 square meters in 1950 to 45,000 in 1970. Apart from the main store, heavy investments were made in rebuilding, enlarging, and modernizing seven provincial stores between 1956 and 1964. In the latter years a completely new store was built in Paris at the Nation, and in 1969 the Printemps opened its first store in the Parly-2 regional shopping center near Paris.

Corporate Reorganization in the 1970s

The various activities of the group during these years were handled mostly by separate limited partnerships, which by the early 1970s numbered more than 120, including 50 separate Prisunic companies. This structure was adopted in part because the managing partners did not want to risk their personal wealth in other activities but also because of the effects of the La Patente tax, which, until it was reformed, increased in proportion to the number of people employed by each company. The slowing of Prisunic's profitable expansion from 1965 onward and the heavy capital expenditure by the department store division, which did not lead to immediate returns, led shareholders and the managing partners to realize that the limited partnership system was no longer an effective way of running a diversified business employing more than 13,000 people. Furthermore, Pierre Laguionie was by this time 87 years old and wanted to retire from active management. In 1971 the managing partners, Pierre Laguionie and his nephew Jean Vigneras, son of Charles Vigneras, who had died in 1970, agreed with the shareholders to consolidate the partnerships into a limited company, or societe anonyme.

The process was not a simple one. Capital had to be found for the managing partners, and some interested parties were more concerned with the group's real estate value than its commercial activities. Eventually an agreement was reached with the Swiss retail group, Maus-Nordmann of Geneva. Maus-Nordmann, a private family company, operated a chain of more than 60 department stores in Switzerland and owned a store chain, P.A. Bergner, in the United States. They were also familiar with the French retail industry since they had important shareholdings in the department store groups Nouvelles

Key Dates:

1865: Jules Jaluzot opens Au Printemps.
1881: A fire destroys two-thirds of the store; Jaluzot turns the business into a limited partnership called Jaluzot & Cie.
1931: The first Prisunic store opens in Paris.
1972: Au Printemps S.A. is established.
1987: The company launches its bid for La Redoute S.A.
1992: Francois Pinault's Groupe Pinault acquires a controlling (two-thirds) stake in Printemps.
1994: The companies merge as Pinault-Printemps-Redoute S.A. after Printemps acquires the remaining 46 percent of Redoute.
1995: Serge Weinberg takes over as CEO.
2000: A 42 percent stake in Gucci Group N.V. is acquired.
2004: The company's stake in Gucci increases to 99.4 percent.
2005: Francois Henri Pinault is named Weinberg's successor; the company changes its name to PPR S.A.

Galeries Reunies (SFNGR) and Bazar de l'Hotel de Ville (BHV). Perhaps most important, the Maus-Nordman group had become an affiliate of Prisunic as early as 1932. By 1970 its company, Societe Alsacienne de Magasins S.A. (SAMAG), had 45 affiliated Prisunic stores in eastern France. In a series of complicated transactions that involved the transfer of the assets of SAMAG to Printemps, the withdrawal of Maus-Nordmann from its holdings in SFNGR and BHV, and the compensation of the managing partners, a new company—Au Printemps S.A.—came into being in 1972. The Maus-Nordmann group owned 34 percent of the share capital, a figure that increased to 42.7 percent 20 years later, while the next largest shareholder held 6 percent. Pierre Laguionie was made honorary president, and Jean Vigneras continued for a while as president director general. But Laguionie died in 1978 and Vigneras withdrew in the same year, thus ending some 70 years of control and management by the Laguionie family.

The first five years of the new company were not easy. The French economy was in recession following the oil crisis, the profits of the company fell, and the new management was faced with commitments that had been entered into by the previous management, such as opening new stores in shopping centers in the Paris area. These included stores in Velizy, opened in 1972; Creteil, opened in 1974; and Galaxie in Paris, opened in 1976. These new stores were not very profitable. Eventually the Creteil store was closed, and a contract to open a store in the Defense shopping center was canceled.

The Prisunic variety store division, though profitable, was no longer expanding. Competition from hypermarkets (combined grocery and general merchandise stores) and specialty shops had reduced the general appeal of variety stores, and emphasis was placed on the development of supermarkets and increasing food sales in the downtown locations of most of the stores. As a result of the stagnation of the variety stores, an attempt was made to develop the Escale chain of hypermarkets. The first of these opened in 1969, and by 1972 there were five in operation. Printemps realized that it did not have the expertise to start up a new hypermarket chain, and by 1976 its Escale stores had been transferred to the established Euromarche group of hypermarkets, with Printemps acquiring a 26 percent share in Euromarche S.A.

New Management, New Direction Beginning in the Late 1970s

The years from 1977, however, were to see the beginning of a transformation in the activities of the Printemps group that was possibly more important than the opening of the Prisunic variety stores in the 1930s. Responsible for this change were Jean-Jacques Delort, who was appointed managing director in 1978 and had joined the group 18 months earlier, and his president, Bertrand Maus. Commercial strategy consisted of four main policies. First was the recognition that well-managed department stores and variety stores could, provided with the necessary investments, continue to be profitable. These methods of retailing, however, did not constitute important areas of expansion and growth. Second, commercial activities in the food sector offered growth prospects, particularly in more modern forms such as supermarkets, hypermarkets, and affiliated food stores. Third, specialty stores and home shopping, including mail order and shopping by telephone, were growing retail sectors. Fourth, when opportunities occurred or could be created, the export of know-how and merchandise was to be pursued vigorously. These policies dominated the activities of Printemps beginning in 1978.

No great change took place in the number of owned department and variety stores. Some smaller stores were closed, a few new stores were acquired or built, and investments continued to be made in existing stores. In the case of Prisunic, emphasis continued to be placed on increasing food sales and by 1980 food accounted for 58 percent of Prisunic's total sales. At the same time the concept of exporting department and variety store expertise and merchandise gathered strength. In 1979 an important agreement was made with Japan's Daiei retailing group to open Printemps department stores in Japan. Printemps provided the expertise and Daiei the building, so Printemps's capital investment was negligible. Daiei opened several such stores in Japan and similar agreements were made in other countries, including Portugal. By the early 1980s there were 11 stores outside France carrying the Printemps name, and a larger number affiliated with Printemps for supplies of merchandise. Prisunic followed a similar policy, and soon there were Prisunic or Escale (large supermarket) stores in French territories overseas and in Greece and Portugal. Specialty nonfood retailing was developed in the menswear market. In 1974 the Printemps group had opened a specialty menswear store called Brummell in Toulouse. But perhaps the most important step forward took place in 1980 when Printemps bought a 40 percent share in Magasins Armand Thiery et Sigrand (ATS), an existing menswear chain. This shareholding was increased to 80 percent in 1981 and 87.4 percent by the early 1980s.

In 1984 an entirely different type of move was made with the purchase of 51 percent of Disco S.A., a food wholesaling group, and 99 percent of a related company called Discol S.A. In association with seven other wholesalers, Disco, the second largest food wholesaler in France, supplied more than 1,500 affiliated food retailers. Discol acted as a food wholesaler to restaurants, schools, and hospitals, and was France's second largest firm in this sector. Together Disco and Discol owned and operated 18 food distribution centers and their associated firms had a further 38. These acquisitions, along with the significant food sales of Prisunic stores, afforded Printemps a strong presence in France's food industry.

Acquisition of La Redoute in the Late 1980s

Printemps's most dramatic acquisition took place in 1987–88, when first 15 percent, then 20 percent, then 32 percent, and finally, on an agreed bid, 54.7 percent of the shares of La Redoute S.A., the largest mail-order company in France, passed to its control. Founded in 1831, La Redoute owned not only two smaller mail-order firms in France, Vert Baudet and Maison de Valerie, but also controlled Vestro, the second largest mail-order company in Italy, and the Prenatal chain of stores, which boasted more than 325 branches in Italy, Spain, Austria, Germany, and Portugal. Since Printemps took control, mail-order selling was developed in the Benelux countries and Portugal and an agreement was made with Sears Canada. La Redoute's 25 percent share of Empire Stores, the fifth largest mail-order firm in the United Kingdom, was increased in 1991 to virtually complete control at 98.9 percent.

In the hypermarket retail sector, the Printemps group had acquired a 25 percent interest in the Euromarche hypermarket company in 1975. Through crossholdings in Viniprix S.A., this share rose to 43.5 percent by 1986. The profits of Euromarche fell, however, in 1987 and 1988, and in 1989 the firm incurred a heavy loss, with only a marginal improvement in 1990. Unable to control the management of Euromarche, Printemps disposed of its share in 1991, selling it at a profit to the hypermarket group Carrefour.

Another, but less important, change occurred in 1991 when the Printemps group sold the Disco food wholesale company. In effect, however, this made little difference to the commitment of the Printemps group to food wholesaling. While giving up the day-to-day operation of wholesale depots, Printemps, through its Prisunic buying organization, remained the chief source of supply for the 1,775 franchised retailers of Disco.

In December 1992, Francois Pinault's Groupe Pinault, which had itself only just gone public in 1988, acquired a controlling (two-thirds) stake in Printemps. Since the 1960s, Pinault had expanded his business from a small timber company into a FRF 40 billion conglomerate with interests in distribution and retailing. The companies merged as Pinault-Printemps-Redoute S.A. (PPR) in 1994 after Printemps acquired the 46 percent of Redoute it did not already own. Over the first half of the 1990s, the conglomerate's sales increased from FRF 31.3 billion ($5.6 billion) in 1991 to FRF 77.8 billion ($15.4 billion) in 1995.

Having guided a successful reorganization of France's Le Bon Marche, Philippe Vendry returned to Printemps in 1995 to guide a revitalization of the chain. Vendry had advanced to the post of managing director of Printemps during his 22-year career at the chain before leaving in 1987 to serve as president of Le Bon Marche. According to Katherine Weisman of *WWD*

magazine, he earned a reputation as "France's Dr. Retail" in the intervening years. His multifaceted prescription for Printemps included limiting its merchandise to five key categories: women's apparel, men's apparel, home furnishings, cosmetics, and leisure goods. Store remodelings reorganized goods into product "universes," as contrasted with traditional "bazaar-style" displays. Vendry also hoped to improve customer service, which he himself admitted was "lousy." Strategies to improve back-office operations included development of computer automation, centralization of purchasing, and market research. Whether these changes would improve Printemps's sagging operations [the chain suffered a FRF 34 million ($6.7 million) loss in 1995] remained to be seen.

Despite Printemps's poor showing, the group as a whole achieved a FRF 1.5 billion net income, nearly triple the pro forma profit of FRF .5 billion of 1993. At this time, management felt that the company's broad diversification protected it from negative economic forces and positioned it well to take advantage of upturns.

Changes in the Late 1990s and Beyond

During the remainder of the 1990s, PPR significantly expanded its holdings. Through its subsidiaries, PPR added French-based music and book retailer Fnac and SCOA, a West African pharmaceuticals supplier, to its arsenal. Its electrical equipment supplier, Rexel, also grew by making a variety of strategic purchases. Meanwhile, PPR launched a new women's lingerie chain, Orcanta, in 1996. During 1998, the company purchased Guilbert, Europe's largest office supply and equipment concern, as well as a 49.9 percent interest in Brylane, a large mail-order company based in the United States. It acquired the remaining shares of Brylane in 1999. In 2000, France's largest computer retailer, Surcouf, was added to PPR's holdings.

PPR made its move into the luxury goods sector of the retail market that year when it set its sights on Gucci Group N.V. It secured a 42 percent interest in the firm, which set off a bitter battle with competitor LVMH Moët Hennessy Louis Vuitton S.A. At the time of PPR's purchase, LVMH was making a hostile play to acquire Gucci. PPR stepped in as a white knight, made its purchase, and destroyed any chance that LVMH had to acquire the Italian company. PPR and LVHM battled it out in courts for over two years and finally came to an agreement in September 2001. As part of the deal, PPR agreed to acquire 8.6 million Gucci shares from LVMH for $812 million. The purchase raised its stake in Gucci to 53.2 percent. During that year, Gucci acquired Bottega Veneta and Balenciaga and also inked signed partnership agreements with Stella McCartney and Alexander McQueen.

Under the direction of Serge Weinberg, PPR transformed itself from an unwieldy conglomerate into a luxury retail group in the early years of the new millennium. Starting in 2002, PPR began the process of restructuring. It increased its stake in Gucci to 54.4 percent, sold the Guilbert mail-order business to Staples Inc., and began selling off its credit and financial services business. During 2003, its stake in Gucci increased to 67.6 percent. It also sold its timber arm, Pinault Bois & Materiaux, to U.K.-based Wolseley PLC and sold Guilbert's contract business to Office Depot. Rexel, its electrical equipment subsidiary, was sold in 2004.

The *pièce de résistance* in PPR's strategy was gaining a majority control of the Gucci empire, and in 2004, its stake was raised to 99.4 percent. With the restructuring complete, Weinberg stepped down to start his own investment business in 2005. Francois Henri Pinault, son of PPR's founder, took over in March. The company officially adopted the PPR S.A. corporate moniker that year. Pinault commented on his strategy for the future in an April 2005 *WWD* article, claiming, ''The approach we have is to be in the right business at the right time. It's the approach of an investor. I don't want to put all my eggs in one basket. I'm really here to build something and to keep on building a group.'' Indeed, as the third largest luxury group in the world, PPR appeared to be well positioned for future growth. Only time would tell, however, if its venture into luxury retail would pay off.

Principal Operating Units

Gucci Group N.V.; Printemps; Redcat; Fnac; Conforama; CFAO.

Principal Competitors

Carrefour S.A.; LVMH Moët Hennessy Louis Vuitton S.A.

Further Reading

Aktar, Alev, ''Printemps To Expand Self-Service Concept, *WWD*, August 4, 1995, p. 5.

''Au Printemps Profits in '91 Boosted by Sale of Hypermarket Stake,'' *WWD*, March 30, 1992, p. 15.

Carracalla, Jean-Paul, *Le Roman du Printemps, Histoire d'un Grand Magasin*, Paris: Denoél, 1989.

Carreyrou, John, ''At Last, Gucci Settlement Suits Men Behind PPR, LVMH,'' *Wall Street Journal*, September 11, 2001.

D'Aulnay, Sophie, ''French Facelifts: Department Stores Say It's Time To Compete on a New, Focused Level,'' *Daily News Record*, October 30, 1995, p. 7.

Dumas, Solange, *Cent ans de Jeunesse*, Paris: Printania, 1965.

''Founder's Son to Take Over at PPR,'' *International Herald Tribune*, February 4, 2005.

Mac Orlan, Pierre, *Le Printemps*, Paris: Ed. Gallimard, 1930.

''PPR's Net Jumped 46% in 2004,'' *Wall Street Journal Europe*, March 18, 2005.

''Printemps, in Denver, Shuts Doors,'' *Daily News Record*, April 6, 1989, p. 3.

Raper, Sarah, ''Pinault Buys 40.56 Percent of Au Printemps Group,'' *WWD*, November 26, 1991, p. 10.

Rives, Marcel, *Traite d'Economie Commercial*, Paris: Presses Universitaires de France, 1958.

''Share and Share Unlike,'' *Economist*, December 21, 1991, pp. 94–95.

Socha, Miles, ''Rising Son,'' *WWD*, April 11, 2005.

Tahmincioglu, Eve, ''Printemps' U.S. Future Rocky,'' *Footwear News*, April 3, 1989, p. 12.

Weisman, Katherine, ''Bourse Probing Redoute, Pinault-Printemps Merger,'' *WWD*, March 28, 1994, p. 15.

——, ''Printemps' Stock Price Still on Rise After Buying Conforama,'' *WWD*, April 27, 1992, p. 2.

——, ''Putting Printemps into Gear,'' *WWD*, May 18, 1995, p. 14.

—James B. Jefferys
—updates: April Dougal Gasbarre;
Christina M. Stansell

 **Progress Energy**

Progress Energy, Inc.

410 West Wilmington Street
Raleigh, North Carolina 27601-1748
U.S.A.
Telephone: (919) 546-6111
Fax: (919) 546-2920
Web site: http://www.progress-energy.com

Public Company
Incorporated: 1908 as Carolina Power & Light Company
Employees: 15,700
Sales: $9.8 billion (2004)
Stock Exchanges: New York
Ticker Symbol: PGN
NAIC: 221121 Electric Bulk Power Transmission and
    Control

Progress Energy, Inc., is a regional utility holding company formed in 1999 to combine the assets of Carolina Power & Light and Florida Power. The Raleigh, North Carolina-based company uses both nuclear and fossil-fueled power plants, capable of generating more than 24,000 megawatts of electricity, to serve nearly three million customers in North Carolina, South Carolina, and Florida. In addition, the company is involved in such nonregulated businesses as energy marketing, broadband capacity, and natural gas production. Progress Energy is a public company listed on the New York Stock Exchange.

Electricity Comes to the Carolinas in the 1880s

In the 15 years following the destruction visited upon the South during the Civil War, North and South Carolina rapidly rebuilt their economies, proving especially successful in the textile, tobacco, and furniture industries. An increasing amount of capital from the North flowed into the area. Although tobacco processing would become king of the local economy, textile production was also a major industry in the region, one in need of new power sources. Hence, textile factories played a key role in bringing electricity to the Carolinas. In 1879, Thomas Edison patented his first incandescent lamp, and three years later opened the United States's first electric lighting plant, the Pearl

Street Station, in New York City. Although more remotely located, the Carolinas were receptive to the new technology. The first electric lights in the region were installed in a Salem, North Carolina, factory in 1881. The first North Carolina city to receive electric service was Raleigh in 1885. Although electricity spread to most of the area's larger cities by the turn of the 20th century, it was a far from a prosperous enterprise.

In the early 1890s, electric service was provided to the Carolinas by a number of small, independently operated systems with poor voltage regulation, leading to frequent outages. Three of these companies merged in 1908 to form Carolina Power & Light Company. The largest was Raleigh Electric Company, organized in 1881 as the Raleigh Street Railway Company to operate electric streetcars in the city. It was reorganized in 1894 as the Raleigh Electric Company, but it was unable to find customers beyond street lights, streetcars, and nearby textile mills. Ownership of the struggling business passed to General Electric (GE) when Raleigh Electric could not pay for its equipment. In 1905, controlling interest was acquired by Electric Bond and Share Company of New York, a GE-controlled holding company formed that year to provide financing to small utilities, which in many cases, like Raleigh Electric, had used securities as part payments for electrical equipment. In 1906, the holding company picked up Cape Fear Power Company and Consumers Lights and Power of Sanford-Jonesboro. The three small utilities served just 1,100 customers in Raleigh, Sanford, and Jonesboro, plus a few Fayetteville textile mills. It required little insight to conclude that the companies should be consolidated, which they were on February 19, 1908.

Under new management, led by Col. Charles E. Johnson and backed by the deep pockets of Electric Bond and Share, Carolina Power & Light began to pursue the growth that had eluded its founding companies. At the time, the company mostly powered streetcars and provided street lighting, and even then the streets were turned off in the middle of the night, when people were presumed asleep, then turned back on shortly before dawn. Household electrical use was virtually nonexistent, and attracting residential customers was made more difficult by consistent breakdowns in the system. However, as Carolina Power & Light improved service and expanded its operations, small municipal electric companies took notice and asked the company

---

Company Perspectives:

Progress Energy, headquartered in Raleigh, N.C., is a Fortune 250 diversified energy company with more than 24,000 megawatts of generation capacity and $9 billion in annual revenues.

---

to take over the job of supplying power to their communities. In this way, Carolina Power & Light added towns like Henderson, Oxford, and Goldboro to its service area. For the time being, the company's principal business remained lighting, illuminating streets and the interiors of businesses and a few well-to-do homes. Electric power's chief competitors for the lighting market were the local gas companies, the two sides waging war through advertisements in the local press. In Raleigh, Carolina Power & Light won out and acquired Standard Gas & Electric Company in 1911, consolidating the city's gas and electric service. A year later, the company grew further through acquisitions by acquiring Asheville Power & Light Company and a competing power system operating in Goldsboro.

Industrial Sales Grow in 1910s

Early on, Carolina Power & Light set its sights on the textile mills that were opening in the Piedmont and Coast Plains area, and it funded the completion of a hydroelectric power plant located in Blewett Falls that had been forced into receivership in 1909. The plant became operational in June 1912, and the company extended lines to the mills as well as nearby towns, such as Rockingham, Hamlet, and Wadesboro. Within the year, lines were strung across the South Carolina border to serve the town of Cheraw. Unfortunately, the business from area textile mills that Carolina Power & Light so coveted was not forthcoming. Two separate sales efforts in the two years leading up to the plant coming on line failed to land any mills or other large industries as customers. A Macon, Georgia, General Electric sales manager named Clinton N. Rackliffe was hired to tackle the problem of selling industrial power. Using the railroads and horse-drawn transportation, he scoured the countryside, visiting with owners of cotton mills and other large factories, struggling to convince them that a small electric motor could furnish the same amount of power to their equipment as the complicated network of steam engines, water turbines, belts, and drive shafts that they had long relied upon. Rackliffe's first customer was Wadesboro Cotton Mill; after that success, sales began to grow.

With the advent of World War I in August 1914, Carolina Power & Light was forced to cut back on its expansion because certain materials were not available. As a result, the company added no generating capacity and few additional transmission lines. Nevertheless, it did benefit because business picked up in the textile industry, leading to the construction of new mills, which now preferred to buy electric power and invest the money they would have spent on steam plants into textile machinery that could make more products. Moreover, coal was rationed and rose in price, prompting mills to turn to the power companies to supply their needs.

After a recession that immediately followed World War I ended in November 1918, the U.S. economy experienced a major boom. Carolina Power & Light steadily added generating capacity and customers, while its corporate parent, Electric Bond and Share, continued to accumulate utility assets. In 1926, Carolina Power & Light was reincorporated to add three operating companies and a construction firm owned by Electric Bond and Share: Yadkin River Power Company, Asheville Power & Light Company, Pigeon River Power Company, and Carolina Power Company. The consolidated company provided retail service to 100 communities and wholesale power to another 29. Over the next ten years, Carolina Power & Light added another 142 communities to its service area, but during that time the company would have to weather the worst of the Great Depression that was ushered in by the stock crash of 1929 and lingered throughout the 1930s. The challenges of this period were not fully overcome until the jolt the economy received from World War II military spending. During the tough times, textile mills cut back on production and their use of electricity while residential customers decided against purchasing the new household electrical appliances that were just beginning to become popular before the crash. In addition, many people let their electric wiring go dead and reverted to kerosene lamps. Anticipating industrial expansion in the Carolinas during the 1930s, the company had invested in a major expansion of its production capacity only to see much of it unused. As a result of all these factors, revenues fell, the company paid no dividends from 1933 to 1936, and salaries were cut across the board.

Carolina Power & Light's excess capacity would soon be needed, however. By 1940, it was becoming clear, at least to the government, that the United States would eventually be drawn into the war raging in Europe. The country took steps to put itself on a war footing, and Carolina Power & Light took steps to add even more generating capacity to meet the increasing need for electricity in the Carolinas. Wartime spending revived the U.S. economy and reawakened consumer confidence, leading to a postwar boom. To meet increasing demand for power, and to catch up on building the system curtailed by wartime shortages of materials, the company grew on all fronts, expanding capacity, laying new transmission lines, and adding radio communications to improve repair and maintenance services. During the postwar years, the company was especially successful in signing up rural customers, which for the past 20 years had resisted the change but now embraced electricity. In 1948 alone, Carolina Power & Light added 3,000 miles of rural lines and 19,253 new rural customers. The company also underwent an ownership change during this period. For a number of years, all of the company's stock had been held by a Electric Bond and Share subsidiary, National Power & Light Company. In 1940, acting in accord with the Public Utility Holding Company Act, the Securities and Exchange Commission initiated dissolution proceedings on National Power & Light. There was a possibility that Carolina Power & Light might be divided up into smaller parts, but in the end the company was broken off as a whole. In August 1946, the company's shares were distributed to National Power & Light shareholders, half of which went to Electric Bond and Share. In December of that year, the newly independent company gained a listing on the New York Stock Exchange. Within two years, Electric Bond and Share sold off all of its shares.

In the early 1950s, Carolina Power & Light looked to expand eastward and took steps to build a new power plant in the eastern fringe of its service area. Then, in 1952, it solidified its position in the region by acquiring Tide Water Power Company. It would be the last acquisition for nearly 50 years. The company was satisfied with building its business within the area it had already staked out. It launched an atomic energy program and opened a nuclear power plant, but because it was a state-regulated utility with guaranteed rates of return, management tended to be conservative, and Carolina Power & Light turned into a sleepy little utility barely noticed by Wall Street, content to grow in line with its territory's increasing population and economic development.

Late 1980s Bring Changing Business Landscape

Conditions for utilities began to change in the late 1980s, when the U.S. Congress passed laws to make possible wholesale power sales and energy trading as utilities began to share grids and buy and sell electricity from one another. In 1992, Carolina Power & Light brought in a new president and chief operating officer, William Cavanaugh, a 23-year veteran of New Orleans-based Entergy, to help chief executive officer and chairman Sherwood Smith, but the company remained cautious about embracing the new opportunities presented to utilities. Carolina Power & Light was financially sound and located in one of the fastest growing parts of the country. As Cavanaugh told *Business North Carolina* in 2003, ''Why would we want to go off overseas or anywhere else where we didn't know the landscape.'' Meanwhile, Charlotte-based Duke Energy, founded around the same time as Carolina Power & Light, took a different approach, spending millions on trading floors and power plants in California, where deregulation was in full bloom. Even after Cavanaugh succeeded Smith as CEO and chairman, Carolina Power & Light opposed deregulation in North Carolina, crossing swords with Duke's more aggressive board of directors, which viewed Enron as a role model. Cavanaugh was suspicious of Enron, however, and its attempts to lure away customers, telling *Business North Carolina,* ''They were saying things like, 'We'll sell you a 10-year contract, but I want all the profits recorded in the first year because that's how I make my bonus.' I sat in this boardroom with the directors and tried to figure out how they were doing all this marketing and trading. You could see their volume, but you couldn't see where they were making anything.''

Anticipating that deregulation would occur in North Carolina, Carolina Power & Light began to look for ways to diversify. It acquired North Carolina Natural Gas for $354 million, thereby moving into an area in which management believed the company needed to become involved if deregulation took place. It also entered the hot telecommunications field. However, North Carolina ultimately held off on deregulation, in large part because of California's experience and the demise of Enron, leading the company to divest North Carolina Natural Gas and to write down more than $200 million in its telecommunications subsidiaries. One deal completed during this time did pan out—the $5.3 billion acquisition in 1999 of Florida Progress, the holding company for Florida Power, the second largest utility in Florida.

A New Name for a New Century

Florida Progress was founded in the 1890s as St. Petersburg Electric Light & Power Company and took the name Florida Power in 1927. During the 1980s, it veered away from its traditional business, becoming involved in such areas as equipment leasing, life insurance, railroads, barge lines, and coal mines. The strategy did not pay off, and in the late 1990s Florida Progress put itself on the block. It engaged in talks with a British utility company, Scottish Power, but they fell apart in April 1999, leading to the sale to Carolina Power & Light later in the year. Carolina Power & Light, which had 1.2 million customers in North Carolina and South Carolina, added Florida Progress's 1.3 million customers in the west and central sections of Florida, transforming Carolina Power & Light into a regional utility, one of the ten largest generators of electricity in the United States. The acquisition provided entry into a coveted market and supplied the kind of increased revenues the company was looking for without leaving the Southeast.

In December 2000, Carolina Power & Light changed its name to Progress Energy, Inc., although it continued to do business in the Carolinas under its old name and as Florida Power in Florida. That would change a year later when the company began operating in both the Carolinas and Florida under the Progress Energy brand. While customers may have been comfortable with the old names, it was easier to sell the company to investors by telling them Progress Energy had operations in the South, rather than explaining that it did business under one name in one market and a second name in another. Aside from name changes, the company also began selling off some of the non-core assets inherited from Florida Progress, many of which proved difficult to unload as the economy soured in the early 2000s. The company also had to contend with a drop in business caused by the recession, as well as low wholesale prices and a heavy debt load.

In 2004, Cavanaugh retired, a move he had planned to make two years earlier. However, in light of the Enron scandal taking place at the time, which led to industry turmoil, he was persuaded to remain at his post until conditions improved. He was replaced by Robert McGehee, who joined the company as general counsel in 1997 and was promoted to president and chief operating officer in 2002. McGehee took over a company that faced a number of challenges but also one that possessed the potential to enjoy strong growth in the future.

Principal Subsidiaries

Progress Fuel Corporation; Progress Energy Corporation; Progress Energy Service Company LLC; Progress Ventures Inc.; Progress Telecom.

Principal Competitors

Duke Energy Corporation; FPL Group, Inc.; Southern Company.

Further Reading

Brooks, Ricks, ''Carolina Power-Florida Progress Deal Forms Giant, Putting Pressure on Rivals,'' *Wall Street Journal*, August 24, 1999, p. B11.

Deogun, Nikhil, ''Carolina Power & Light to Buy Florida Progress for $5.3 Billion,'' *Wall Street Journal*, August 23, 199, p. A3.

Holson, Laura M., ''Carolina Power May Be Buying Florida Utility,'' *New York Times*, August 21, 1999, p. C1.

Martin, Edward, ''Watts Up, Doc?,'' *Business North Carolina*, November 2003.

Price, Dudley, ''Corporate Parent to Eliminate Carolina Power & Light,'' *News & Observer*, October 3, 2002.

Riley, Jack, *Carolina Power & Light Company, 1908–1958*, Raleigh, North Carolina: Carolina Power & Light Company, 1958, 338 p.

Sutton, Louis V., *Carolina Power & Light Company, 1908–1958*, New York: Newcomen Society in North America, 1958, 32 p.

—Ed Dinger

Purolator Products Company

100 Westwood Place, Suite 200
Brentwood, Tennessee 37027
U.S.A.
Telephone: (615) 221-7433
Toll Free: (800) 526-4250
Fax: (615) 221-7182
Web site: http://www.pureoil.com

Wholly Owned Subsidiary of ArvinMeritor, Inc.
Incorporated: 1976 as Facet Enterprises, Inc.
Employees: 400
Sales: $30 million (2004 est.)
NAIC: 336399 All Other Motor Vehicle Parts
   Manufacturing

A leading manufacturer of automotive filters in the United States, Purolator Products Company is a subsidiary of global automotive supplier ArvinMeritor, Inc., forming part of the company's light vehicle aftermarket division. The original Purolator filter, invented in 1923, was the first replaceable oil filter for automotive motors. Since that time, Purolator brand filters have been marketed by a string of companies, and today the Purolator name is found on more than 2,000 part numbers used for automotive, light truck, and other applications. In addition to oil filters, Purolator products include engine air filters, cabin air filters, fuel filters, transmission filters, PCV valves, and breathers. Purolator maintains its headquarters in Brentwood, Tennessee.

Facet Enterprises is Created in the Mid-1970s

The Bendix Corporation spun off Facet Enterprises, Inc. as an independent company in 1976. The formation of Facet (an acronym for Filters, Automotive Components, and Environmental Technology) was the result of a settlement of a nine-year dispute between Bendix Corp. and the Federal Trade Commission (FTC). Bendix's 1967 purchase of Fram, a producer of automotive and industrial filters, had been challenged by the FTC on the grounds that, with this merger, too much of the filtration industry would be controlled by one firm. After drawn out negotiations, Bendix agreed to spin off several of its filter operations as Facet Enterprises.

Although Facet was created primarily in order to satisfy the FTC ruling, Bendix also planned to have the new company absorb the enormous pension costs of employees at three recently discontinued Bendix divisions. The Facet spin off was regarded by some analysts as a calculated move by Bendix to dump the pension funds by linking them to a new company whose assets were less than half of the liability of the cost of the pension fund. One year after the divestiture, Facet chairman, James B. Treacey, estimated that $34 million of the $51 million liability inherited by the new company was the result of employees who had retired or been terminated prior to the divestiture. It seemed impossible at the time that the company could ever succeed and Wall Street observers dubbed the new Facet "the company launched to fail." After eight years of dispute and threatened litigation, some funds were recovered from Bendix retroactively to offset the pension load.

Despite its inauspicious beginning, Facet Enterprises survived to become the leading filter manufacturer in the United States. By the early 1980s, under President James Malone, Facet's primary markets were in the automotive and ventilation segments of the filter industry, although the company also manufactured a variety of specialized filters for industrial use. Facet's automotive filters, which generated about one-third of the company's sales, were sold primarily as "private label" products to retailers like Sears and Kmart, who then placed their own brand name on the products. Facet was the third largest manufacturer in the private label segment of the automotive filter market, which itself accounted for a large proportion of total industry sales. By 1985, Facet was recording net income of $2.5 million on sales of $171 million.

Facet Purchases Purolator in 1987

The genesis of a new company named Purolator Products occurred in 1987 when Facet Enterprises purchased the filter manufacturing end of Purolator, Inc. for $67 million. The Purolator name had been associated with automotive filters ever since 1923, when Ernest Sweetland invented the first replace-

253

Company Perspectives:

At Purolator, quality is a way of life and it is synonymous with customer satisfaction.

---

able automotive oil filter using treated cotton waste. The new filter required fewer oil changes and provided cleaner oil to the engine, reducing engine wear. Sweetland named his invention ''Pure Oil Later,'' which became the basis for the Purolator line of auto parts. Purolator remained a major force in the auto parts industry through much of the 20th century. During the 1960s, Purolator entered the courier business, and by the late 1980s this segment of the company's operations had become so successful that Purolator was looking to shed its automotive divisions.

The acquisition of Purolator's filter operations gave Facet a broader geographical base from which to service customers. Facet's automotive filter plants were located in Dexter, Missouri, and Salt Lake City, Utah, creating distribution problems for customers in the eastern United States. Management reasoned that they could deliver the filter that the customer wanted more efficiently if they had plants on both the East and West Coasts. Purolator's manufacturing plants in Fayetteville, North Carolina, and Ontario, Canada, provided the perfect solution to Facet's distribution problems. With the addition of Purolator's facilities, Facet would have access to 1.3 million square feet of manufacturing capabilities.

Market research indicated that Facet did not enjoy high brand recognition among consumers, ranking well behind the top three branded filters: Fram, AC-Delco, and Purolator. The four next most recognized brands, however, were all Facet manufactured filters under private labels. In fact, Facet's private label filters accounted for a greater market share than the number one branded filter, Fram. By acquiring Purolator, Facet hoped to capitalize on that company's high profile brand name. With the acquisition, Facet became the country's largest automotive filter manufacturer, controlling an impressive 30 percent of the market. Net income doubled to $4.9 million on sales of $280 million. Automotive filters were generating over 75 percent of sales for the company with heating and ventilation filters providing the bulk of the remainder.

Pennzoil Purchases Facet in 1988

Lured by Facet's market share Houston-based Pennzoil Corporation purchased Facet in 1988 for $233 million. Pennzoil was drawn to the acquisition by Facet's potential as an attractive combination with Pennzoil's growing ''quick lube'' business, the industry's term for the single service quick oil change outlets that had been springing up across the country since the early 1980s. Pennzoil was one of the leading suppliers of motor oil to the quick lube segment, and Facet provided private label filters to the three largest quick lube operators: Jiffy-Lube, Minit-Lube, and Valvoline Rapid Oil Change.

The same strategy that had encouraged the purchase of Purolator led to another major merger when two years later, in 1989, Facet acquired Servodyne Corporation. Servodyne, originally a West Coast filter and cartridge manufacturer, had ac-

quired a large number of filter distribution companies during the 1980s making them an attractive partner for Facet. In 1990, the new company, Facet-Servodyne, Inc., officially changed its name to Purolator Products, Inc. in an effort to capitalize on the superior brand recognition of the Purolator name. President and CEO, James R. Malone explained the strategy to *Tulsa World*, ''This is the first step in a corporate strategy which will eventually replace the Facet name with the highly respected and much better known Purolator name.''

Most of Facet's business, had been in private label sales of filters to other automotive aftermarket suppliers before the purchase of Purolator and the subsequent name change. After the name change, Purolator began a two-tiered sales strategy, continuing to supply filters for private label use and promoting its own high profile Purolator brand and distinctive logo. Nevertheless private label sales continued to account for the lion's share of Purolator Product's activity in the automotive sector.

Pennzoil Sours on Purolator

When Pennzoil bought Facet in 1988, the company controlled about 32 percent of the automotive filter market. By 1990, this figure had climbed to almost 40 percent with sales reaching over $420 million. In spite of the sales growth, Pennzoil almost immediately began to regret the purchase of Facet and did not foresee realizing a return on their investment. The hoped-for savings in transportation costs in delivering filters to customers was not realized on the balance sheet, as the cost of purchasing and managing the company outstripped Purolator Product's income and the advantage that it offered to Pennzoil's quick lube venture. In addition, Pennzoil's purchase of Jiffy Lube in 1989 set the company up as a direct competitor to other quick lube operators who quickly dropped Facet as a supplier. By 1989, the newly named Purolator Products Company was recording a net loss of $7 million.

Despite having sunk approximately $61 million into their new acquisition within two years, Pennzoil became anxious to unload the money losing Purolator. Pennzoil was prepared to bite the bullet and take a loss on the Facet-Purolator transaction, announcing to shareholders that they expected to lose up to $125 million on the divestiture. Even this estimate, however, turned out to be wishful thinking, as all offers fell well short of Pennzoil's asking price. Pennzoil was not willing to give the company away for nothing, despite its being a serious cash drain, because Purolator was still the dominant manufacturer in the automotive filter market. Compounding the lack of a reasonable offer on Purolator was a disagreement between Pennzoil and the Internal Revenue Service. During the late 1980s, tax laws had been revised to limit the deductions large corporations could claim on the sale of unproductive subsidiaries. Pennzoil had been counting on claiming $102.5 million in losses on Purolator as a discontinued operation for the fourth quarter of 1990, but the new ruling reduced this figure to only $60 million.

Purolator Rebounds in the 1990s

Frustrated in its attempt to sell Purolator Products, Pennzoil developed a new tactic in dealing with its unfortunate purchase. In April 1990, Pennzoil fired 25 Purolator executives. President and CEO James Malone was replaced by turnaround specialist

Key Dates:

1923: Ernest Sweetland invents the Purolator filter and forms Purolator, Inc.
1967: Bendix Corporation acquires Fram filter business.
1974: Bendix spins off its filter business as Facet Enterprises, Inc.
1987: Facet acquires Purolator.
1990: Facet changes its name to Purolator Products, Inc.
1994: Mark IV Industries, Inc. acquires Purolator.
1999: Purolator is sold to Arvin Industries Inc.; Mark IV sells non-automotive Purolator assets to CLARCOR Inc.
2000: Arvin merges with Meritor Automotive Inc.; Purolator moves its headquarters to Brentwood, Tennessee.
2005: North Carolina Purolator plant is slated for sale.

Roman Boruta. Boruta and his team liked what they saw in most aspects of the company and were confident that Purolator Products still had great potential. At the same time Boruta discovered that the company had essentially been buying business by accepting any contract, even at a loss, in order to maintain or boost market share. Boruta explained the situation to *Automotive Marketing:* ''They were taking every contract, no matter what the price, no matter what the cost implications. We had one customer where the cost of sales was much higher than the cost of producing it. I'm sure they had good reasons for doing this but I don't know what they were. . . . Some people think volume cures a lot of sins, that's what was happening. The property and equipment was all right. But accounts receivable was terrible. There were 50% past due accounts.''

Boruta's first order of business was to collect the outstanding accounts even if contracts were put in jeopardy. New customers were researched before contracts were finalized and tighter payment schedules were written into new contracts. At the same time, Boruta renegotiated prices with major clients. Even at the risk of losing the company's contract, which represented 14 percent of overall sales, Boruta sought and obtained a 6 percent price increase from automotive giant Ford. Although the focus of the reorganization was on improving accounts, manufacturing costs were also streamlined most notably by closing the outdated Canadian plant, putting 200 employees out of work. Overall, the Purolator work force was reduced by approximately 900. After recording a net loss of about $50 million in 1991, Purolator Products had a net income of approximately $13 million the following year.

As Purolator's bottom line improved, new bids came in from aftermarket companies wanting to purchase the refurbished company, but as Pennzoil Chief Executive Officer James L. Pate told the *Wall Street Journal,* ''I wouldn't even entertain an offer, we've decided to keep it.'' The following year, Pennzoil spun off Purolator Products, offering ten million shares to the public in October 1992 and severing all ties with its troubled subsidiary. Rationalizing the apparent about-face, CEO Pate told *Tulsa World* that Pennzoil would focus on ''areas it considers strategic to future business.'' With Pennzoil divesting itself

of Purolator to focus on its strong suit, oil and gas refining, Purolator was once again an independent company.

When Purolator was spun off by Pennzoil in 1992, the company was organized into four business segments. The company's automotive products segment, providing about 75 percent of sales, produced automotive oil, air, and fuel filters for virtually all automobiles and light duty trucks then operated in North America. Approximately 90 percent of these sales were to the aftermarket sector for vehicle repair and maintenance. The remainder went to original equipment manufacturers like Ford and Chrysler for placement in new vehicles. The company's plant in Fayetteville, North Carolina, was the world's largest automotive filter manufacturing plants. Analysts estimated that the company's share of the U.S. automotive filter market was once again at about 30 percent. In addition to domestic operations, Purolator established a European sales, marketing, and distribution subsidiary, Purolator Filter GmbH, and continued to control a 39.3 percent equity interest in Purolator India Limited, a company that had been started by Purolator back in the 1960s.

Purolator's second largest segment was made up of air filtration products manufactured and distributed through the company's wholly owned subsidiary Purolator Products Air Filtration Company. Although this subsidiary made up only 13 percent of Purolator sales, it was one of the largest U.S. manufacturers of air filtration products for heating, ventilation, and air conditioning systems. These products were marketed under both the Purolator and Facet brand names. The remainder of Purolator's sales were provided by the separations systems segment, conducted through the company's wholly owned subsidiary, Facet International, and the industrial filter products segment, managed by the company's Facet Filter Products Division.

Mark IV Acquires Purolator

By 1993, after one year as an independent company, Purolator sales had climbed back up to $435 million, and the company was back in the black with net income of $17.8 million. The company's new-found independence was short lived, however, as in 1994 Mark IV Industries, Inc. acquired Purolator Products Company for $260 million. Mark IV was a diversified manufacturer of engineered systems and components for power transmission, fluid power and transfer, and filtration applications for industrial and automotive customers.

In 1997, Mark IV undertook a major reorganization which saw the original Purolator Products broken up into a variety of operating units. The company's main automotive filter product line became the basis for Mark IV's automotive aftermarket unit along with Mark IV's automotive belt and hose manufacturer, Dayco Products. Purolator Products Air Filtration Company, Facet International, and Purolator Filter Products were transferred to Mark IV's industrial operating unit.

As part of Mark IV's integration of Purolator Products, the company's manufacturing plant in Dexter, Missouri, was closed, while facilities in Fayetteville, North Carolina, were expanded and a 506,000-square-foot distribution center was built to supply all of the needs of the company's customers in the eastern United States. Mark IV management was confident that this reorganization would increase profit margins and allow Purolator Products to take full advantage of their dominant market share in automotive filters.

Poor conditions in the automobile aftermarket business soon led to difficulties for Mark IV, however. Profits dipped in 1998, as did the company's stock price, forcing management to engineer a restructuring program. In early 1999, Mark IV elected to sell Purolator's automotive filter business to Arvin Industries, Inc. for $276 million and the assumption of $69 million in debt. Later in the year, Mark IV sold Purolator's specialty filters business to CLARCOR Inc., creating Purolator Facet, Inc., which would share the Purolator heritage. Although a break-even transaction, the sale of Purolator at least allowed Mark IV to reduce its debt load and provide the funds needed to invest in the company's auto transmission and air intake businesses.

Founded in 1921, Arvin started out making mufflers, car heaters, and catalytic converters and in the 1980s emerged as the world largest producer of tire valves and tubes as well as a major manufacturer of automotive exhaust systems and gas-charged lift supports. Because Arvin and Purolator served many of the same customers and relied on similar distribution channels, they were deemed a good fit, their combination creating cost-reduction opportunities as well synergies that could bring in new retail and wholesale customers. One of the cost-reduction steps that followed included the closing of Purolator's Tulsa headquarters at the end of 1999. The company set up shop in Arvin's offices in Brentwood, Tennessee.

Purolator soon became part of an even larger organization, when in 2000 Arvin merged with Meritor Automotive Inc. to create ArvinMeritor Inc., a global enterprise with 120 facilities located in 25 countries, employing 36,000 people. With combined revenues of $7.5 billion the company offered a wide range of systems and components for light vehicles, commercial trucks, and trailers, serving both original equipment manufacturers and the aftermarket, Purolator's niche.

Not only did ArvinMeritor face the difficult task of integrating two massive organizations, it also had to contend with the effects of a poor economy. Over the next few years, the company looked to sell off non-essential operations in order to focus on core businesses. In 2004, management put the light vehicle services division up for sale, a decision that had an impact on Purolator, despite being part of the light vehicle aftermarket division. Purolator's Fayetteville, North Carolina, plant was included in the light vehicle services division and slated to be part of the sale. Although it remained a productive facility, Fayetteville was expendable in light of declining sales combined with high steel prices and high gas prices. In 2005, the plant cut employment but a buyer had not been found.

Principal Competitors

AC Delco; Robert Bosch GmbH; Jiffy Lube International, Inc.

Further Reading

"Anatomy of a Turnaround at Purolator: Volume Does Not Cure Financial Sins," *Automotive Marketing*, October 1991, pp. 18–22.

"Arvin Inc. Plans to Acquire Purolator Auto Filter Business," *Aftermarket Business*, March 1999, p. 14.

Byrne, Harlan S., "Purolator Products," *Barron's*, July 19, 1993, pp. 25–26.

Casesa, J., "Purolator Products—Company Report," Wertheim Schroder & Co., Inc., August 17, 1993.

Curtis, Bruce, "Facet Deal to Enhance Standing," *Business Chronicle*, December 15, 1986, p. 1.

"Facet and Fram Continue to Dominate the Oil Filter Market," *Automotive Marketing*, September 1989, pp. 18–22.

"Facet—Company Profile," *Automotive Marketing*, December 1987, p. 70.

"Facet 'Launched to Fail' Buying Two Purolator Units," *American Metal Market*, December 15, 1986, pp. 4–5.

Hartley, Tom, "Purolator Products is Mark IV's 2nd Largest Acquisition," *Business First of Buffalo*, October 10, 1994, p. 5.

"IRS Cracks Down on Sale of Subsidiaries," *The Wall Street Journal*, March 27, 1990, p. 2A.

"Mark IV Industries to Acquire Purolator in $264 Million Pact," *The Wall Street Journal*, October 4, 1994, p. 5B.

"Marriage of Supplier Giants Off to Smooth Start," *Automotive News*, July 31, 2000, p. 22F.

Maurer, Mitch, "Facet Combines Divisions," *Tulsa World*, August 30, 1989, p. 1B.

——, "New Purolator Head Boruta Making Turnaround Attempt," *Tulsa World*, September 9, 1990, pp. 1–5G.

——, "Pennzoil Offering Purolator for Sale," *Tulsa World*, October 28, 1992, p. 1B.

Parker, Claire, "Purolator Cuts Staff at Fayetteville, N.C. Plant," *Fayetteville Observer* (Fayetteville, North Carolina), August 16, 2005.

Pritchard, Catherine, "Purolator to Expand Plant Capacity," *Observer Times*, August 19, 1995, p. 7.

Robinson, David, "Vice-President of Mark IV Unit, Son-in-Law to Pay $221,789 in Fines for Insider Trading," *Buffalo News*, April 30, 1997, p. 13B.

Solomon, Caleb, "Pennzoil Plans to Begin Restructuring, Decides to Retain Purolator Products," *The Wall Street Journal*, August 16, 1991, p. 3A.

——, "Pennzoil to Offer Shares to Public in Purolator Unit," *The Wall Street Journal*, October 28, 1992, p. 7A.

Strong, Michael, "Sluggish Industry Makes Life After Merger Difficult for ArvinMeritor," *Crain's Detroit Business*, June 11, 2001, p. 4.

Williams, Fred O., "Mark IV to Sell Purolator Automotive Filter Business," *Buffalo News*, February 9, 1999, p. E4.

—Hilary Gopnik
—update: Ed Dinger

RedPrairie Corporation

20700 Swenson Drive
Waukesha, Wisconsin 53186
U.S.A.
Telephone: (262) 317-2000
Toll Free: (877) 733-7724
Fax: (262) 317-2001
Web site: http://www.redprairie.com

Wholly Owned Subsidiary of Francisco Partners
Incorporated: 1975 as McHugh Freeman & Associates
Employees: 600
Sales: $72.7 billion (2004)
NAIC: 511210 Software Publishers

Based in Waukesha, Wisconsin, RedPrairie Corporation is a leading global supplier of software that companies use to manage virtually every aspect of their supply chains. According to RedPrairie, its DigitaLogistix software suite includes modules for transportation management, warehouse management, and labor productivity management, as well as logistics command and control, supply chain analytics, global visibility, and role-based collaboration via the World Wide Web. In addition, the company offers solutions for inventory optimization, supply chain security, mobile resource management, and international trade logistics, as well as applications for radio frequency identification (RFID). In addition to developing and marketing its own software, RedPrairie resells equipment from other vendors, including Intermec, Hewlett-Packard, Symbol Technologies, Psion Teklogix, and LXE. The company also provides a number of services, ranging from logistics operations analysis and implementation to training and support. RedPrairie's customer base spans a number of industry segments, from healthcare, pharmaceuticals, consumer goods, food-beverage. retail, industrial-wholesale, automotive and service parts, electronics, and third party logistics. In addition to its Wisconsin headquarters, RedPrairie has U.S. sales and service offices in Eden Prairie, Minnesota; Raleigh, North Carolina; and Charlotte, North Carolina. Internationally, the company has offices in the United Kingdom (York and Stokenchurch); Paris; Ninove, Belgium; and Oosterhout, Netherlands.

Formative Years: 1975–89

RedPrairie was founded in 1975 when Jim McHugh and Doug Freeman, who were both working in the information systems department of Miller Brewing Co., decided to form their own computer consulting and software development business. Operating under the name McHugh Freeman & Associates, the partners initially focused on providing traditional information technology (IT) consulting services. Freeman parted ways with the company in 1983, eventually moving to San Jose, California, to operate a software catalog distribution company.

By the mid-1980s, McHugh Freeman was working with companies like Compaq Computer and Quaker Oats to computerize their distribution centers. Specifically, the company's involvement in the automation of storage and retrieval systems (AS/RS) for distribution centers and warehouses gave it pioneer status in this particular niche.

According to the company, by this time "McHugh Freeman had used its accumulated expertise to create one of the first comprehensive packaged warehouse management systems (WMS). It combined over a decade of warehouse management consulting and software development into a packaged solution for rapid deployment in Tier One warehouses and distribution centers."

By the end of the 1980s, McHugh Freeman had developed enough of a reputation that three companies were interested in acquiring it. From its offices in Brookfield, Wisconsin, McHugh employed 34 people and generated sales of $3 million to $5 million in 1989. That year, McHugh Freeman was acquired by St. Louis-based Alvey Holdings Inc., a materials handling systems manufacturer, for an undisclosed amount.

Consolidation and Expansion: 1990–2001

McHugh Freeman's acquisition by Alvey, which eventually changed its name to Pinnacle Automation, provided much-needed capital for expansion during the early 1990s. In addition, it gave McHugh the resources to branch out into other areas of the supply chain industry.

Company Perspectives:

The history of RedPrairie is a monument to the expertise, dedication, hard work, and experience needed to guarantee our clients' success in achieving total logistics excellence. Our sole focus has always been on providing the best functionality, technology and services for Supply Chain Execution. As a result, our clients have experienced 100% successful implementations and we count many of the best known names in business among our clients.

By 1994, McHugh Freeman had relocated to nearby Waukesha, Wisconsin. That year, the company's sales were projected to reach $25 million to $30 million. Senior vice-president Ritch J. Durheim, who had joined McHugh Freeman in 1977, was named president and chief operating officer. Cofounder Jim McHugh remained chairman and CEO. McHugh Freeman employed 150 workers in 1994, up from roughly 85 the previous year. The majority of the company's workforce was comprised of computer programmers and software engineers.

Limited only by the availability of skilled workers, McHugh Freeman was growing at a rapid clip during the mid-1990s. In fact, the company was expanding so quickly that it needed more spacious facilities for its headquarters. Subsequently, by 1994 McHugh had hired Told Development to erect a four-story, 86,000-square-foot office building. By leasing more than half of the new structure, which it planned to occupy by the end of 1995, McHugh Freeman would expand its space by about 50 percent.

In addition to its software products, by the mid-1990s McHugh sold related gear, including radio frequency equipment, bar code applicators and readers, and special computer terminals that its customers mounted directly onto forklifts. Packaged together, the company's solutions typically cost clients, which included Miller Brewing Co., Procter & Gamble, Pepsi-Cola, BASF Corp., Nabisco, Digital Equipment Corp., Gallo Wine, and Spiegel, between $1 million and $3 million.

By August 1995, McHugh was marketing its DM Plus software suite for distribution centers and warehouses. Incorporating ORACLE database technology, the UNIX-based software ran on the HP/9000 platform and provided capabilities in a number of areas, including cycle counting and productivity reporting, value-added order processing, shipping, inventory management, cross docking, wave planning and release, yard management, scheduling, put-away, picking, receiving, replenishment, and location management.

McHugh's DM Plus product was RFID compatible, and also supported a graphical user interface. The latter feature was in keeping with a larger industry trend, as companies sought to offer more user-friendly, "point-and-click" applications, as well as more "off-the-shelf" software that companies could use and upgrade from without the costs associated with custom solutions.

In October 1995, McHugh Freeman opened a regional office in Atlanta, Georgia. The following January, the company acquired Weseley Software Development Corporation, which had

created an advanced transportation management and optimization solution called TRACS.

By early 1997, DM Plus v.4.10 had been introduced. The new version ran on both the IBM RS/6000 and HP/9000 platforms and included new features, including parcel manifest interface management and small parcel, less-than-truckload shipment processing.

Heading into the late 1990s, a number of important developments happened at McHugh Freeman. The company's first name change came in August of 1997, following a restructuring that combined McHugh Freeman and Weseley Software into one firm named McHugh Software International Inc.

Following its name change, McHugh Software acquired Brookfield, Wisconsin-based Software Architects Inc. (SAI) in April of the following year. While McHugh historically had focused on larger clients with sales exceeding $1 billion, SAI had developed a WMS intended for companies with sales of $500 million to $1 billion, namely in the third-party logistics and technology sectors.

McHugh eventually blended aspects of SAI's software, which had a unique architecture, throughout its own product mix. According to the company, this allowed McHugh to provide logistics firms with "unmatched configurability and flexibility." This was an important move, because the industry was demanding software that was highly flexible and capable of managing multiple variables, such as different languages, specific SKU attributes such as color and size, and labels that met the standards of different countries.

According to the July 1998 issue of *Export Today,* the late 1990s were a volatile time for software firms, and customers were urged to think carefully before committing to a particular WMS. Nevertheless, the rewards of implementing the right system were significant. In addition to reducing inventory levels and improving tracking, one industry analyst cited productivity gains in the range of 15 to 30 percent.

Major developments continued as the decade's end approached. First came McHugh Software's acquisition of the Minneapolis-based industrial consultancy Gagnon & Associates. The May 1998 deal gave McHugh new capabilities in the productivity solutions arena. With the addition of Gagnon's labor management systems and services, McHugh claimed it was able to offer a comprehensive array of supply chain solutions.

In the August 1998 issue of *Logistics,* Pinnacle Automation president and CEO Stephen J. O'Neill remarked: "The addition of Gagnon's labor-management functionality to McHugh's product suite gives McHugh the unique ability to provide leading-edge logistics software combined with the industry's recognized leader in productivity solutions."

Several months later, O'Neill announced that Pinnacle was spinning off McHugh Software. In conjunction with GE Capital, the private equity firm Advent International purchased a minority equity stake in McHugh Software valued at an estimated $50 million. In the December 1998 issue of *Transportation & Distribution,* O'Neill said the spin-off would "provide the management and capital structure necessary for McHugh to

Key Dates:

1975: Jim McHugh and Doug Freeman form McHugh Freeman & Associates.

1983: Freeman leaves the company; midway through the 1980s, McHugh Freeman develops one of the first warehouse management systems.

1989: McHugh Freeman is acquired by St. Louis-based Alvey Holdings Inc., which later becomes Pinnacle Automation.

1996: McHugh Freeman acquires Weseley Software.

1997: McHugh Freeman and Weseley Software are combined into one firm named McHugh Software International Inc.

2001: McHugh reports a net loss on revenues of approximately $70 million.

2002: McHugh Software adopts the name RedPrairie Corporation.

2003: RedPrairie opens an Asia/Pacific headquarters in Shanghai, China.

2005: Francisco Partners acquires RedPrairie.

realize its full potential, and allow Pinnacle to focus its resources and efforts on its systems business.''

In early 1999, Cypress Associates' John Hill indicated that the market for automated material handling systems was worth $4.5 billion in 1998, with WMS systems accounting for approximately 60 percent of that total. Although McHugh's revenues dropped 21 percent between 1998 and 1999, the company remained focused on competition, devoting 24 percent of its 1999 revenues to research and development.

As McHugh prepared to compete within this promising market during the 2000s, it named Joseph Broderick as its president and CEO. With 20 years of industry experience, including the installation of some 550 supply chain systems, Broderick came to McHugh Software from Manugistics. He was tapped to provide leadership in the areas of professional services, engineering, marketing, and sales.

McHugh Software kicked off the 21st century with several product-related developments. In May 2000, the company entered into an agreement with Boulder, Colorado-based SyVox, a developer of speech recognition technology, which added interactive voice capabilities to McHugh's systems.

The Logistics Suite was introduced three months later, providing new customers with logistics software modules that were between 80 and 90 percent pre-built for a wide span of business sectors, ranging from consumer products and e-commerce to those dealing in packaged chemicals, electronics, and spare parts.

By this time, McHugh had developed the nickname ''McHuge'' by some industry players, according to *Frontline Solutions Europe.* The nickname stemmed from what McHugh executive vice-president of sales and marketing Steve Tonissen called the company's ''anything for a buck'' policy, whereby it would commit to just about any firm that wanted to buy its software, even if the customer's business was not the best fit for the product.

Under the watch of new CEO Joseph Broderick, Tonissen replaced 80 percent of McHugh's sales force, and the company began to do a better job of focusing. The two men decided the company would concentrate on consumer packaged goods companies in the food and beverage sector, high-tech and electronics firms, dot-com companies, third-party logistics firms, and those dealing in parts. The company backed away from other industry sectors, including clothing retail, to the point of cutting ties with a few large customers and effectively foregoing millions of dollars in business. McHugh reported a net loss in 2001, on revenues of approximately $70 million.

In January 2002, John G. Jazwiec was named as McHugh Software's CEO. About three months later, McHugh established an RFID Center of Excellence in conjunction with other companies (Marconi InfoChain, Georgia-Pacific, Chep International, Intermec Technologies Corp., and Unilever) that supported the use of radio frequency identification. RFID involves the use of small radio tags that are able to communicate with a networked device known as a reader. These tags, which may contain a variety of data, can be affixed to or embedded within pallets, cartons, merchandise, or parts that companies and retailers need to track.

In the April 15, 2002 issue of *Food Logistics,* Unilever supply chain futurist Simon Ellis said: ''Potentially, RFID chips and readers can smooth Collaborative Planning, Forecasting and Replenishment, as well as execution level functionality within the DC [distribution center], possibly even to the point of eliminating mundane tasks such as issuing purchase orders or advance ship notices. For retailers, this pilot is the first step toward addressing their biggest problem—the last 50 feet, getting product to the shelf.''

New Business Model in 2002

After only a few months at the helm, Jazwiec led McHugh through the most significant change process in its history. On May 22, 2002, McHugh Software radically altered its business model by implementing a shared risk-reward program that guaranteed results for its customers. As the company explained, this involved ''totally aligning its corporate culture, processes and products to deliver superior, measurable logistics results.'' One of the main reasons for this shift was to convince companies that had made logistics systems investments during the previous decade that doing so again would be cost-effective.

Along with a new business model that focused on gain sharing, the company also adopted the name RedPrairie Corporation to differentiate itself from other industry players and redefine its image. As *Traffic World* explained in its May 27, 2002 issue, many within the industry still thought of McHugh as a WMS vendor, when in fact less than 25 percent of the company's revenues were generated by WMS systems.

On the creative side, Ken Hanson, executive creative director of McHugh's ad agency, Milwaukee-based Hanson Dodge, elaborated on the words that made up the new name. In the June 3, 2002 issue of *Adweek Midwest Edition,* he explained that the color red was ''a striking image'' that was ''almost nonexistent in technology.'' Hanson further explained that the prairie concept denoted a peaceful place in an industry that was anything but peaceful.

Moving forward, Jazwiec explained that while McHugh was known as a software company, RedPrairie's identity would be very different. In the quest to save customers money, he noted the possible acquisition of other firms involved with logistics functions such as automation and material handling.

The company's name was not the only thing to be changed. The title of chief executive officer was changed to that of "results leader," executive vice-presidents became "results leaders" in their respective areas, and employees became "customer advocates." Services and software products were referred to as the "RedPrairie Approach." Beyond new titles, employee performance was linked with customer performance.

Because customers were not required to make sizable up-front investments under the new model, RedPrairie was able to concentrate on more mid-sized and small firms. In the past, it had focused mainly on larger corporations. According to the aforementioned *Traffic World* article, RedPrairie's gain-sharing approach typically required companies to share 25 percent of their first-year savings. However, firms that chose to invest more up front could gain-share less.

In addition to its corporate transformation, it also was in May 2002 that McHugh released a new version of its LENS information portal, a product that allowed logistics providers to process transactions via the World Wide Web. LENS 3.0 gave McHugh customers roles-based collaborative processing capabilities, as well as the ability to track shipments in real time from order through delivery. It also gave logistics firms greater agility and allowed them to minimize inventory levels.

In December 2003, RedPrairie opened Asia/Pacific headquarters in Shanghai, China. This was quickly followed by a major deal that expanded the company's size and international reach: the February 2004 acquisition of High Wycombe, United Kingdom-based LIS, a top SCE provider. LIS was integrated into RedPrairie's Europe, Middle East, and Africa (EMEA) division, which was placed under former LIS CEO Martin Hiscox. According to the company, the deal bolstered its status as player in local European markets, with offices that could offer multi-lingual sales and support.

According to the *Milwaukee Journal Sentinel,* in addition to extending RedPrairie's international reach, the LIS deal also increased the company's size by about 250 employees, bringing the total workforce to approximately 600 employees. Although RedPrairie already was the industry's second-place WMS vendor, the acquisition brought the company closer to industry leader Manhattan Associates in this area. Combined revenues of both firms were expected to total $130 million in 2004.

In 2005, Francisco Partners, a Menlo Park, California-based private equity firm focused on the technology sector, acquired RedPrairie from private investors that included Vestar Equity Partners and Advent International. In the April 19, 2005 issue of *Traffic World,* Jazwiec commented: "This acquisition will expand our opportunities to better leverage RedPrairie's leadership position for accelerated growth, both organically and through further acquisitions."

Principal Competitors

HighJump Software, Inc.; Manhattan Associates Incorporated; Provia International Inc.

Further Reading

Fauber, John, "The Warehouse Goes High-Tech," *Milwaukee Journal,* June 29, 1994.

"Firm Names Durheim President," *Milwaukee Sentinel,* May 9, 1994.

"Francisco Partners Acquires RedPrairie," *Traffic World,* April 19, 2005.

Gertzen, Jason, "Waukesha, Wis.-Based RedPrairie to Acquire Foothold in Europe," *Milwaukee Journal Sentinel,* February 12, 2004.

Hickey, Kathleen, "McHugh Now RedPrairie," *Traffic World,* May 27, 2002.

"In Brief . . . ," *Automatic I.D. News,* September 1999.

Jensen, Trevor, "Simply Red," *Adweek Midwest Edition,* June 3, 2002.

"McHugh Buys Consulting Firm," *Logistics,* August 1998.

"McHugh Buys Software Architects," *Logistics,* March 1998.

"McHugh Changes Name, Market Approach; Rider Joins Team," *Warehousing Management,* June 2002.

"McHugh Freeman Accepts Offer," *Milwaukee Journal,* May 1, 1989.

"McHugh Software Adds Event Management," *Industrial Distribution,* May 2002.

"McHugh Software on the Move," *Transportation & Distribution,* December 1998.

"Name Change," *Material Handling Engineering,* October 1997.

"RFID Center of Excellence Formed," *Food Logistics,* April 15, 2002.

Slee, Kendall, "SKUing Relationships," *Export Today,* July 1998.

"Suite Success," *Works Management,* August 2000.

"The Top Five," *Frontline Solutions Europe,* October 2000.

"Two More Industry Deals Announced," *Logistics Management & Distribution Report,* May 2000.

"UNIX-Based, Integrated System Does It All for Distribution Centers," *Automatic I.D. News,* August 1995.

"WMS CEOs: 'Turn Data Flow into Cash Flow,' " *Supply Chain Flow,* April 1999.

—Paul R. Greenland

The Regence Group

200 S.W. Market Street
Portland, Oregon 97201
U.S.A.
Telephone: (503) 225-5221
Toll Free: 800 452-7278
Fax: (503) 225-5274
Web site: http://www.regence.com

Private Company
Incorporated: 1996 as The Benchmark Group
Employees: 6,000
Total Assets: $6.7 billion (2003)
NAIC: 524113 Direct Life Insurance Carriers; 524114 Direct Health and Medical Insurance Carriers

The Regence Group is the largest operating group of BlueCross BlueShield companies in the Northwestern United States. Through its subsidiary companies—Regence BlueCross BlueShield of Oregon, Regence BlueCross BlueShield of Utah, Regence BlueShield in Washington, and Regence BlueShield of Idaho—the non-profit company provides health insurance products and related services to nearly three million members and has close to 39,000 providers in its networks. The company also provides life, disability, and short-term medical insurance through its Regence Life & Health Insurance subsidiary. The BlueCross BlueShield Association, of which Regence is a member, consists of more than 50 independent Blue Cross and Blue Shield companies nationwide. Most are huge nonprofit corporations, the descendants of hospital and doctor associations founded in the 1930s and earlier.

Mid-1990s Formation of The Regence Group

In 1995, as an increasing number of BlueCross BlueShield companies were merging to take advantage of economies of scale and to become more attractive to employers with workers in more than one state, four BlueCross BlueShield providers in the Northwestern United States formed a ground-breaking affiliation in Portland, Oregon. King County Medical, Pierce County Medical, and BlueCross BlueShield of Oregon, with one other Blue Shield participating under contract, formed a non-profit regional health plan called The Benchmark Group. Benchmark's purpose was to share best practices, databases, and strategic planning among its affiliates; to save money through group purchasing of supplies and technology; to consolidate background functions such as information technology, human resources, legal and finance; to develop uniform products and a regional network of providers; and to market a single package to multi-state employers.

The initiative was designed to become a new business model for Blue Cross and Blue Shield groups nationwide that wanted to preserve their locally focused no-for-profit heritage, according to Richard Woolworth, who later became chief executive officer in a 2001 *Lewiston Morning Tribune* article. "We can do this without actually merging and without losing what we've always been—not-for-profit organizations with a commitment to local communities, our customers and community service."

Benchmark had no separate officers or employees. Its officers were the chief executives of each of the operating companies with the head of BlueCross BlueShield of Oregon acting as the affiliation's chief executive. Each plan continued to operate from its separate facility under its own board of directors; and each appointed directors to the Benchmark board in proportion to its size: nine from Oregon, seven from King County, and three each from Pierce County and Idaho. Together the non-profit companies had 2.3 million customers and $2.8 billion in annual revenues.

In 1996, the four companies launched the Pacific Northwest's first regional health plan, a preferred provider organization that targeted large companies with employees and encompassed more than 20,000 providers and 120 hospitals. The advantage to a multi-state single plan for employers was two-fold: it allowed companies to get rates based on their entire pool of workers and allowed them to deal with one insurer instead of several. Benchmark also offered life insurance, Medicare HMO programs, and workers compensation coverage.

Additions and realignments took place among The Benchmark Group's members. BlueCross BlueShield of Utah joined the group in 1996. In 1997, King County Medical BlueShield,

---

Company Perspectives:

It is our mission to provide customers with the best value in health, dental, vision and life insurance benefits, and administrative services. We will accomplish this by being customer focused and market driven, using the strengths, synergy and opportunities created by The Regence Group of health plans. It is our responsibility to ensure the availability of affordable, quality health insurance products in our service area. We have an obligation to effectively manage costs and to provide customers with a choice of competitively priced, quality health products in return for their investment. We are committed to keep health-care costs as low as possible for our customers. This is being achieved through the negotiation of fair rates for health-care services. We are dedicated to these principles and are working diligently to fulfill the common vision of The Regence Group: to set the industry standard in health-care access, financing and service.

---

which was dominant in Tacoma, and Pierce County Medical Bureau, which was strong in Seattle, merged into a new company named Regence Washington Health. The merger resulted in the largest medical insurer in Washington. Benchmark, too, changed its name to The Regence Group, Regence being a combination of "region" and "alliance." The Regence Group's affiliates changed their names accordingly to Regence BlueCross BlueShield of Oregon and Regence BlueShield of Idaho. All together The Regence Group's members served 2.4 million medical subscribers.

Structural Changes Through the Year 2000

The late 1990s continued to be a hard time financially for health insurance companies. Regence Blue Shield of Washington responded to the need for cost-cutting in 1999 by discontinuing new individual health insurance plans in Washington. The 50,000 individuals already enrolled kept their coverage. A year later, once the state insurance board in Washington approved a new law that allowed insurance companies to impose longer (up to nine-month) waiting periods for individual plans, Regence Blue Shield resumed offering the individual plans. The new Washington law also allowed insurers to direct the sickest 8 percent of applicants: those with congenital and congestive heart failure, coronary artery disease, kidney failure, an HIV or AIDS diagnosis, or needing an organ transplant—to the state's high-risk plan, while at the same time requiring insurers to offer maternity and prescription benefits that had been cut by carriers in recent years. Regence BlueShield of Washington began offering three plans, two of which include prescription drug, preventive care, and maternity benefits. The third plan offered basic coverage only.

As another aspect of change, The Regence Group formed its own not-for-profit pharmacy benefits management service in 1999, and in 2000 it joined with Myhealthbank to jointly develop defined-contribution health care "solutions" for employers. The first arrangement of its kind in the country, Myhealthbank allowed employers to tailor their workers' group benefits by making financial contributions into employees' per-

sonal health bank accounts. Each employee then selected his or her individual insurance coverage from a range of contribution levels to medical, dental, pharmacy, disability and life insurance plans. Any remainder in an individual's account could be put toward such things as co-payments on medications, alternative care services, or medical devices.

The Regence Group underwent internal structural changes as well in the early years of the new century. In 2000, John Ruch, president of Regence BlueCross BlueShield of Idaho became president of BlueCross BlueShield of Utah as well. He replaced Jed Pitcher, who became president and chief operating officer of The Regence Group in Portland, Oregon. Pitcher had worked in a variety of positions at BlueCross BlueShield of Utah for 30 years and had been its president and chief executive officer for 20 years.

Meanwhile in Idaho, Regence BlueShield was moving a majority of its executive team out of its Lewiston offices to Boise. Another 40 percent of its Lewiston executives were reassigned as part of a consolidation plan that called for moving most of the executive team out of the Lewiston office in the coming two to five years in order to improve the company's productivity. In a separate move, this one to offices in Lewiston's new business and technology park, created about 100 new jobs for claims analysts. The newly formed claims processing unit covered new customers joining The Regence Group in Idaho, Washington, Oregon, and Utah.

Challenges in the Early 2000s

By 2001, The Regence Group had three million members. As part of the ongoing trend among the nation's Blue Cross and Blue Shield plans to work together to compete against national health plans such as Aetna and United Healthcare, the company embarked on plans to join with Chicago-based Health Care Service Corp., the nonprofit owner of BlueCross BlueShield of Illinois, New Mexico, and Texas. The new alliance stood to make The Regence Group the largest non-profit health insurance organization in the nation with nearly 10 million customers and 16,000 employees.

Consumer advocates were concerned about the deal, suspecting that it would reduce customer choice, raise premiums, drive down payments to physicians, force small medical groups out of practice, and put aspects of The Regence Group's business beyond the reach of state regulators. At the time, several Blues nationwide were becoming for-profit stock companies for the opportunity to sell stock to raise money for expansion and new technology. Regence insisted that it remained committed to the organization's not-for-profit mission, and, after a year spent developing the plan, the two companies dropped it. However, one of the leading factors in the decision to withdraw was not consumer protection, but the discovery that neither entity would save money in moving to a single, shared claims processing system.

The company continued struggled with profit losses in the early years of the new century, despite revenues of $6.2 billion in 2002. Faced with health care benefit expenses that rose more than eight times the rate of inflation in Oregon and Washington, many employers in those states chose to have their higher wage earners pay proportionately more of the cost of their health

Key Dates:

1995: The Benchmark Group forms out of four BlueCross BlueShield providers in Oregon, Washington, and Idaho.
1996: The Benchmark Group launches the Pacific Northwest's first regional health plan; BlueCross BlueShield of Utah joins the group.
1997: King County Medical BlueShield and Pierce County Medical Bureau merge to become Regence Washington Health; Benchmark changes its name to The Regence Group; the other members adopt the Regence name.
1999: The Regence Group establishes a nonprofit pharmacy benefits management service.
2000: The company joins with Myhealthbank.

insurance premiums. ''You'll see more employers cutting back on [health insurance] programs dramatically . . . and some employers even getting out of providing health insurance altogether,'' predicted Pitcher of the future state of affairs, in a 2003 *Salt Lake Tribune* article. The Regence Group itself launched a four-tiered system for its own 2,000 employees. Despite such changes, the company still faced higher medical claims and falling membership.

There were also several changes of guard in 2003. Mark B. Ganz became the company's president and chief operating officer, succeeding Pitcher, under whose tenure the company had grown from 300,000 customers in 1980 to 615,000 in 2003. Ganz had been part of the formation of The Benchmark Group, and since 2001, he was president of Regence BlueCross BlueShield of Oregon. He was replaced by J. Bart McMullan, Jr.

Regence BlueShield of Idaho also got a new president in the person of John Stellmon, replacing Ruch, who had been president of Idaho and Utah since 1997. Ruch was replaced in Utah by Scott Ideson, who had been with the company since 1999. Mary McWilliams, who had been president of Regence BlueShield in Washington since 2000 remained in her position.

In addition, the company began another round of restructuring in late 2003 that continued into 2004. It created a single, coordinated claims and membership system that included all four states. It reduced its operating budget by 13 percent across the board, initiated a 10 to 15 percent cut in its executive ranks across the four states, instituted layoffs of 170 workers, and

increased the rate of lower-cost generic prescription drugs that members took. It also began encouraging its members that used some of the more prescribed drugs (Celexa, Zoloft, Lipitor, Zocor, and Vioxx) to buy higher-dosage pills and split them in half. The controversial program, called the Half Tablet Program, issued pill splitters to members, who doubled their supply of medication, while halving their co-payments and trips to the pharmacy. Concern among health care practitioners primarily cited the possibility that patients might take incorrect dosages.

The Regence Group also launched a new product platform for employers in 2003 that it extended to members in 2004. Based on a collection of preferred provider plans, enrollees chose from multiple benefit tiers and provider panels that allowed them to tailor their benefits to meet desired price points. The company looked to this platform as a means of ensuring its affordability and, thus, profitability, as it anticipated a future of ongoing increases in health care costs to both consumer and insurer.

Principal Subsidiaries

Regence BlueCross BlueShield of Oregon; Regence BlueCross BlueShield of Utah; Regence BlueShield; Regence BlueShield of Idaho; Regence Life & Health Insurance Company.

Principal Competitors

Pacificare Health Systems Inc.

Further Reading

Beason, Tyrone, ''Activists Suspect Insurers' Motives; Regence Won't Stay Nonprofit Once Deal Is Done, States Warned,'' *Seattle Times*, September 7, 2000, p. C2.
Gollhofer, John G., ''Insurance Consolidation Puts Health Care at Risk,'' *Seattle Post-Intelligencer*, January 8, 2000, p. A7.
Herzog, Boaz, ''Regence is Singing the Blues for Now,'' *Oregonian*, April 10, 2004, p. B 8.
——, ''Splitting for Savings,'' *Oregonian*, September 9, 2004, p. D1.
——, Strategies Seek to Cool Health Care Costs,'' *Oregonian*, May 11, 2004, p. D1.
''Regence Wants to Join Up With Other Midwest Blues,'' *Lewiston Morning Tribune*, March 18, 2001, p. 3E.
Mitchell, Lesley, ''Businesses Rethink Health Care Benefits,'' *Salt Lake Tribune*, December 7, 2003, p. E1.
Rojas-Burke, Joe, ''Regence Drops Plans to Form No. 1 Insurer,'' *Oregonian*, August 16, 2001, p. D1.
Rothschild, Mary, ''Individual Insurance Back on Sale; New Law Drew Insurers to Market Again,'' *Seattle Times*, December 3, 2000, p. B1.

—Carrie Rothburd

RENAULT

Renault S.A.

13-15 quai Le Gallo
92513 Boulogne-Billancourt
Cedex
France
Telephone: (+33) 1-76-84-50-50
Fax: (+33) 1-41-04-51-49
Web site: http://www.renault.com

Public Company
Incorporated: 1945 as Regie Nationale des Usines
   Renault
Employees: 130,573
Sales: $55 billion(2004)
Stock Exchanges: Euronext Paris
Ticker Symbol: RNO
NAIC: 336111 Automobile Manufacturing; 336211 Motor
   Vehicle Body Manufacturing; 336312 Gasoline
   Engine and Engine Parts Manufacturing; 336322
   Other Motor Vehicle Electrical and Electronic
   Equipment Manufacturing; 336399 All Other Motor
   Vehicle Parts Manufacturing; 522220 Sales Financing

One of the world's pioneering auto makers, Renault S.A. is also one of Europe's largest. Renault's annual revenue of more than $55 billion, along with its payroll of more than 130,000 employees in 2004, also makes it one of France's flagship corporations. Renault manufactures automobiles in partnership with Renault-Nissan Motor in Japan, Dacia in Romania, Renault-Samsung Motors in Korea, and Dong Feng Motor Corp. in China. In addition to the company's automobile division, Renault's finance division is one of France's largest credit providers, principally underwriting the purchase of the company's automobiles. After a rocky period in the mid-1990s, marked by the former government-run company's privatization and capped by stagnating sales and the failed attempt to fuse the company with Sweden's Volvo, Renault has recaptured both its market position and its spirit. Upon setting a new company production record of 2.2 million vehicles in 1998, Renault announced intentions to double that number by the year 2010, while increasing the share of its foreign sales to 50 percent of total sales, compared with just 20 percent in 1997. Under CEO and Chairman Louis Schweitzer, Renault has taken strong steps to meet its goal, including the opening of a FRF 4 billion production facility in Brazil in December 1998 and the cementing of crucial business alliances in Asia and Eastern Europe.

Automobile Pioneer

The closest parallel in the French automobile industry to Henry Ford was Louis Renault. His youthful interest in mechanical contrivances, especially steam engines and electrical devices, was accepted by his well-to-do family, and he was allowed to have his own workshop on the family's property.

Soon after he finished his military service and his father passed away, Louis convinced his older brothers Fernand and Marcel each to invest FRF 30,000 to build an automobile firm, which would be called Renault Freres. In 1899, Renault Freres received its first down payments for motor cars at FRF 1,000 per vehicle. Primarily an assembly operation in the early years, Renault Freres expanded operations as fast as it could acquire components and erect buildings. Engines, tires, radiators, gears, steel, and electrical equipment all came from other companies. By 1899, the industry had already generated a considerable range of specialist component firms. Marcel Renault soon joined the active management of the company to lessen the workload of his brother Louis, who preferred to work in the shop rather than attend to commercial details. By 1901, the company had become the eighth-largest firm in the automobile industry based on its small, inexpensive, and reliable car. The company's success should not be measured only by sales and profits, however, but also by its imitators. Louis Renault's transmission system, for example, was eagerly copied by other small car manufacturers.

Perhaps the most important ingredient in the firm's early success was the publicity Renault's cars received as a consequence of their racing prowess. Both Marcel and Louis Renault were expert racing drivers, and they were victorious in numerous international events. Unfortunately, in 1903, while competing in the Paris-Madrid race, Marcel Renault was killed. Louis immediately withdrew his cars from the racing circuit, and his company did not compete again for several years.

After 1905, Renault's taxicab became its largest selling product. Work began on this line late in that year when the company won an order for 250 chassis. The large orders for cabs soon made Renault the most important French automobile producer.

The firm did considerable export business during this period. In 1912, for example, nearly 100 Renault cabs were in service in Mexico City, and Renaults outnumbered all of the other types of taxicabs in Melbourne. By 1914, the company had 31 dealers in foreign countries, from Yalta to Shanghai. Louis Renault himself did not take as much interest in these marketing matters as he did in the technical aspects of his business. He considered himself more of an inventor than anything else and took out in his own name about 700 patents for devices that he had made personally or that had been developed in his factory.

Like several other automobile firms, Renault participated in the development of aviation in France. In 1907, the company began to experiment with aircraft engines, attempting to extract the most power possible from lightweight, air-cooled motors. While somewhat successful technically, this activity brought no profits at the time. Nevertheless, the discoveries and the experience that resulted found their justification in the war that soon followed. During World War I, the company became an important manufacturer of all sorts of military equipment, including aviation engines and the light tanks that proved so effective in 1918.

Postwar Technocracy

After the war, the Renault factory expanded. Nonetheless, though the firm remained among the top producers in France during the interwar period, Louis Renault was slow to adopt new technical and organizational ideas. This reluctance significantly hindered the company's growth. In addition, when Paris was liberated near the end of World War II, Louis Renault was jailed on a charge of Nazi collaboration. He died in prison before his case could be examined, and the provisional government of Charles de Gaulle nationalized the company. The government installed some inspired technocrats to operate the company along commercial lines, and they made it into a showpiece of French industry. The firm built up its own production of machine tools, and its factory was the first in Europe to use automation. In 1948, the company began to manufacture a miniature car called the Quatre Chevaux (4 CV or hp), which had been planned secretly during the war by Renault technicians.

The Quatre Chevaux proved to be a symbol of the social philosophy that has guided Renault ever since, first under Pierre Lefaucheux and then under his successor Pierre Dreyfus. An idealistic kind of technocrat, Dreyfus regarded the car as a social instrument that every family had a right to possess. Therefore, the firm concentrated on a large production of relatively small and inexpensive cars, the models gradually growing in size as French incomes and living standards rose. The other feature of this social philosophy was the idea that a firm owes its workers not only a wage but also as full and happy a life as possible. With state support, Renault led the field in welfare and labor relations.

It is possible to view the introduction of the Quatre Chevaux either as an example of effective business management or as the use of a state firm to provide a lower-cost product. During the 1950s and 1960s, the company maintained its record for effective product innovation. The Dauphine was manufactured to fit into the market opening between the inexpensive economy models and the higher-priced models. The new model soon became quite popular and outsold all others for the next five years. A second distinctive aspect of Renault's success has been its emphasis on exports. It was one of the first companies in the automobile industry to make a serious effort to develop a sales organization in the United States.

Because of the interest in Renault cars in the United States, the company was aiming initially to penetrate the market by supplying 1,000 cars per month. However, the United States ordered no fewer than 3,000 cars in only one month. Consequently, Renault increased their daily production rate from 300 to approximately 500 units, with company production facilities working near capacity for months in advance. Continued expansion into the international automobile market remained one of the company's main concerns for years, and plans were therefore made for the construction of plants abroad. Sales agreements using existing local networks were made in Brazil, Argentina, Algeria, and India.

By the end of 1959, Renault was estimated to be the sixth-largest automobile manufacturer in the world. At the beginning of 1960, when the U.S. automobile market began to shrink, sales of the Dauphine dropped by 33 percent in comparison with the previous year. It was a period of stagnation on the U.S. domestic market and, as a result, Renault was faced with the problem of adjusting to the specific requirements of the American motorist.

In France, meanwhile, preparations were underway for new car models, which would be known as the R-4 and the R-8. These were vehicles that had a third side window on a four-door body. Subsequently, an error was made on a project that was to have been a large six-cylinder vehicle. Once the accounts had been completed, it was discovered that the price of the car ought to have been 25 percent higher than originally planned. The swift and decisive intervention of Renault's chairman, Pierre Dreyfus, established the parameters of the new car, which was to have four cylinders, a functional styling, and a competitive price. The result was the R-16, which remained in production until the mid-1970s and had features that have been retained into the 21st century. As a parallel development to car production, Renault also had begun to manufacture the Estafette, a

Key Dates:

1899: Louis, Marcel, and Ferdinand Renault sell the first of Louis' cars for 30,000 francs each.
1903: Marcel Renault dies in a racing accident.
1905: Renault becomes a leading French auto manufacturer on the strength of its taxicabs.
1907: The company begins building aircraft engines.
1914: The company has 31 dealers in foreign countries.
1918: Renault is an important manufacturer of war materiel, including light tanks and aircraft engines.
1945: Louis Renault dies in jail awaiting trial for collaboration with the Nazis; the company is nationalized.
1948: The Quatre Chevaux is released.
1957: The Dauphine is successfully introduced in the U.S. market.
1959: Renault is the world's sixth-largest automaker.
1960: U.S. auto market shrinks; Dauphine sales drop 33 percent.
1966: Highly successful R-16 is introduced; it remains in production until the mid-1970s.
1977: Renault purchases 46.4 percent of American Motors (AMC) and begins producing the Alliance and the Encore, both American versions of Renault models.

1979: American Motors becomes the exclusive importer and distributor of Renault vehicles in the United States; Renault markets AMC vehicles abroad.
1982: Renault takes full control of AMC.
1987: Renault withdraws from the U.S. market after sustaining heavy losses and sells AMC to Chrysler.
1990: Renault begins privatization.
1993: A partnership deal with Volvo fails.
1996: Renault loses $680 million due to a European recession, shrinking sales, and increasing global competition.
1997: Cost-cutting restores Renault to profitability.
1998: Renault produces a record 2.2 million vehicles.
1999: Renault purchases a controlling share of Nissan, begins selling off non-core companies, and purchases Romanian automaker Dacia.
2000: Nissan becomes profitable again; Renault purchases Korean firm Samsung Motors.
2003: The last of Renault's non-core businesses is divested.
2004: Renault-Nissan enters a joint agreement with Chinese automaker Dong Feng Motor Corp.
2005: Renault-Nissan is the fourth-largest automaker in the world.

commercial vehicle for door-to-door deliveries, which was replaced by another model in the beginning of the 1980s.

During the 1970s, Renault went through a period of significant expansion. The success of the R-5, a particularly well-designed and highly reliable vehicle, allowed Renault to stay at the top of the European league of manufacturers. At the same time, a widely based program initiated in 1977 enabled the firm to purchase 46.4 percent of the shares in American Motors in 1980. The U.S. company then began production of the Alliance and the Encore, corresponding to European versions of the Renault.

The relationship began in 1979 when the two corporations signed an agreement. American Motors became the exclusive North American importer and distributor of Renault cars, and the French corporation would market American Motors products in France and several other countries. This was followed by the direct purchase of approximately $500 million in American Motors securities. American Motors chairman Gerald Meyers resigned in 1982 and was replaced by Paul Tippett, Jr., who then named Renault's Jose Dedeurwaerder as president and chief operating officer. Other Renault personnel took their places in the corporation and on the board of directors as the first modern trans-Atlantic company was established.

Regrouping in the 1980s and 1990s

By the mid-1980s, however, Renault's small deficit had turned into a $1.5 billion loss. Georges Besse arrived in 1985 with a mandate to prevent any further losses. Besse, a pragmatic engineer who had rescued the state-owned Pechiney Metals Group, was unable to go much beyond symbolic measures in helping the company. The Socialist government in France had backed away from tough industrial decisions that it feared

would hurt the party in national elections. In addition, Besse's timing was unfortunate since powerful French communists had been arguing that Renault should worry more about upgrading French operations and protecting French jobs than spending money abroad on American Motors. The communists claimed that there was an imbalance between investments needed at home and expansion abroad. AMC's losses in 1986 made those arguments even more compelling. Nonetheless, Besse was able to cut some 20,000 jobs from the payroll, while instilling a new profit-driven culture in the government-owned company.

In November 1986, Besse was assassinated by the French terrorist organization Direct Action. This event, however, was not the only one that had an adverse effect on Renault. The company also was suffering from a series of poor marketing judgments that had reduced its share of the domestic auto market. Once the largest car manufacturer in Europe, Renault had slipped to sixth place. Besse's successor, Raymond Levy, pushed through Besse's restructuring of the company, eliminating an additional 30,000 jobs and leading the company toward its privatization in the 1990s.

In March 1987, Renault announced that it would withdraw from the U.S. market by selling its share in American Motors to the Chrysler Corporation. Under this agreement, which American Motors voted to accept, Renault was to receive over $200 million for its AMC shares and bonds over a period of five years. The company was also paid royalties from Chrysler's marketing of AMC's newly launched Premier. In exchange, Renault agreed to export between $2 billion and $3 billion worth of automatic components to Chrysler.

In 1990, the former Regie Nationale des Usines Renault converted its status to that of Renault S.A., a first step toward privatization. At the same time, the company entered into agreement with Volvo to merge the two companies' operations, including an exchange of shares that would give the Swedish automotive maker as much as 20 percent of Renault. This ambitious cross-ownership plan fell through in 1993 when Volvo's shareholders rejected the plan.

The Volvo failure would prove only the beginning of a somber period in Renault's history. Hit by an extended European recession, facing dwindling market share and increasing global competition, Renault would slip into losses by 1996. Nevertheless, under a new CEO and chairman, Renault had already begun to strike back against misfortune. In the early 1990s, despite the poor economic climate, Renault began expanding its international presence, building new operations and cooperation agreements in such countries as Turkey, China, and the Czech Republic, as well as strengthening the company's Latin American operations and entering the Russian market. Whereas Renault had previously done little to enter the growing Asian countries, the company now began to move toward building a presence in these developing markets.

More importantly, Renault—driven more and more by the need to provide profits, as the French government's position was reduced from 80 percent to just 45 percent by 1995—went back to the drawing board for its new car designs. Indeed, during the 1990s the company would appear to recapture the spirit of innovation that had produced the indomitable R-4 and R-5 with the introduction of the Clio in 1992, which would take the lead as France's best-selling car. In 1993, the company debuted the Twingo, another success. In the larger-sized realm, Renault continued to dazzle auto buyers with the popular Megane (the number two selling car in France), the minivan Espace, and 1997's hit Kangoo.

The company's net loss in 1996 of FRF 5 billion, chiefly due to rising production costs, proved only a temporary setback. A streamlining of the organization and the reduction of production costs by nearly FRF 4,000 per automobile would return the company to profitability the following year. In 1998, the company forecast an all-time production record of 2.2 million vehicles. According to CEO Schweitzer, however, by the year 2010 this record would seem ancient history. Continued cost-cutting measures were expected to produce some FRF 20 billion in savings, while the company's strategy called for production to reach more than four million vehicles per year, with foreign sales to account for some 50 percent of the company's total, compared with just 20 percent in the late 1990s. As a primary step toward this goal, Renault prepared to open a new FRF 4 billion production facility in Brazil in December 1998.

Refocusing on Core Strengths

Cost-cutting lifted Renault out of its 1996 losses of $680 million to earnings of $1.5 billion in 1998 and a combined profit in 1998 and 1999 of $1.65 billion. A series of divestitures followed that refocused the company on its core automobile business. In 1999, the carmaker sold its subsidiary Renault Automation to Italy's Comau. In 2000, Renault Véhicules Industriels, the automaker's heavy truck division, was sold to Volvo AB for $1.6 billion. Renault received a 15 percent stake in Volvo and paid the Swedish automaker $460 million for an-

other 5 percent of Volvo's shares. The deal, which included U.S.-based Mack Trucks as well as Renault's European truck operations, made Volvo the world's second-largest truck manufacturer after Mercedes-Benz and the third-largest maker of heavy diesel engines. Though the Volvo, Renault, and Mack brand names were kept separate, the companies' powertrain, purchasing, and product development divisions merged. Renault's logistics unit CATFrance was sold to the European consortium Global Automotive Logistics in 2001, and Fiat-owned truck manufacturer Iveco purchased Renault's bus unit, Irisbus, the same year. In 2003, the French automaker divested itself of the last of its non-core businesses, selling 51 percent of Renault Agriculture to Germany's Claas, the largest European manufacturer of farm equipment.

With the divestitures and returned profits came new acquisitions intended to strengthen Renault's global presence, especially in Asia. In September 1999, the company purchased a 73 percent stake in the Romanian firm Automobile Dacia Pitesti S.A. in order to gain a foothold in the expanding Eastern European auto market. In 2000, Renault bought 70 percent of the South Korean Samsung Group's faltering automotive unit for $512 million, renaming it Renault Samsung Motors Corp. Renault made the venture break even two years ahead of schedule in 2002 and positioned the Korean automaker to serve as the center of its Asian operations. In November 2004, Renault pledged $571 million over three years to develop new gasoline engines and begin production of sport-utility vehicles at Renault Samsung's Busan, South Korea, factory by 2007.

Risky Alliance Pays Off

By far the most important acquisition Renault made at the turn of the 21st century was its 1999 purchase of 36.8 percent of the Japanese company Nissan Motor. The deal was considered a mistake by many industry watchers. Nissan was in difficult financial straits due to a weak Asian economy and ineffective marketing in the United States. Critics cited poor brand identity, unexciting car design, and a lack of features that would distinguish Nissan's products from those of competitors. The Japanese company had entered into merger talks with Daimler-Chrysler, which withdrew its offer after examining Nissan's finances. Differences in Japanese accounting practices made it nearly impossible for Daimler-Chrysler accountants to calculate precisely the extent of Nissan's debts. According to Japanese accounting rules, assets were reported at historical purchase prices rather than current market prices, and the financial obligations of a company's subsidiaries were not reported in the main company's financials. As a result, considerable liabilities could be hidden in subsidiaries' books. Nissan claimed $16.7 billion in debt, but analysts estimated the company's actual debt at almost twice that amount. Industry watchers looked askance at Renault, only in its second profitable year after near-bankruptcy, entering into such a complicated financial tangle. In addition, other commentators cited Renault's failure in the U.S. market as evidence that it lacked the wherewithal to aid Nissan in overcoming its marketing problems and strengthening its U.S. market presence.

The $5 billion deal, the largest foreign investment ever made in a Japanese company, created the world's fifth-largest automaker, measured by unit sales. The Renault and Nissan brands maintained their individual identities and focused on their strongest markets: Renault in Europe and Latin America and Nissan in Asia and North America. The French company appointed cost-cutting whiz Carlos Ghosn president of Renault-Nissan and charged him with generating $3.3 billion in savings between 2000 and 2002. During 1999, the new management closed five plants and idled 16, 500 workers, an action unprecedented in Japanese business. In 2000, Ghosn cut Nissan's workforce by 6 percent and reduced component costs by 10 percent. He also made plans to reduce Nissan's underutilized production capacity by more than half, cut suppliers from 1,145 to 600 over three years, close sales outlets in Japan, and streamline dealer networks in Europe and the United States. By the end of 2000, commentators hailed the Renault-Nissan deal as a brilliant union of automakers with high-volume production in three key global auto markets—Europe, Asia, and the United States. Nissan's strengths in engineering and manufacturing and Renault's expertise in cost-cutting and new product development were perceived as an extremely strong match. Analysts expected Nissan to contribute nearly half of Renault's $1.32 billion earnings in 2000, the Japanese automaker's second full-year profit in nine years. The two companies formed a new joint firm in the Netherlands to combine planning for parts and materials purchasing, manufacturing, and sales. The alliance was intended to cut costs further by sharing vehicle technology while maintaining separate looks and feels for their different product lines. In 2002, Renault paid $1.6 billion to raise its share of Nissan to 44 percent, and Nissan purchased a 15 percent stake in Renault.

The streamlining of dealer networks begun at Nissan was extended to Renault's enterprise as well. The companies consolidated dealerships and distribution networks around the globe. The French company cut its number of European dealers from 2,500 in 1995 down to 2,000 in 2000, eventually reducing the number to 800. The cuts were intended to save $777 million in sales and service operations by 2003. In 2002, Renault began marketing new and used Renaults through a Web site in the United Kingdom. The site's success was such that the company expanded the program with Web sites in Spain, France, Brazil, and Germany in 2004.

In February 2005, the alliance widely predicted to fail reported that it sold 5,785,231 vehicles in 2004, an 8 percent increase over 2003. With 9.6 percent of the global market, Renault-Nissan was the fourth-largest automaker in the world. The company also announced that its chief executive officer of 13 years, Louis Schweitzer, was handing over the CEO job to Nissan President Carlos Ghosn. Schweitzer's departure came on the heels of a record year. Operating profits in 2004 totaled $1.74 billion more than those of 2003, which was also a record year. In 2004, the company entered into a joint venture with China's Dong Feng Motor Corp. to operate a production facility, building on a 50–50 2003 venture between Nissan and Dong Feng to assemble low-cost parts for the subcompact

Sunny at a plant in Guangdong Province, China. In 2005, Renault and Nissan were singularly positioned to serve the fast-growing Asian market, and the company did so well worldwide that it was able to raise shareholder dividends 29 percent.

Principal Divisions

Automotive; Financing.

Principal Competitors

General Motors Corporation; Peugeot S.A.; Volkswagen AG.

Further Reading

Barnard, Bruce, "Renault's Renaissance," *Europe*, July 2000, p. R.
——, "Renault," *Europe*, April 2002, p. S4.
Choy, Jon, "Renault's Bid for Nissan Spotlights Japanese Accounting Practices," *JEI Report 1999*, March 26, 1999.
Debontride, Xavier, "Bresil, Turquie, Russe: Renault reve son avenir a long terme," *Echoes*, September 30, 1998, p. 54.
Farhi, Stephane, "Volvo, Renault Create Truck Giant," *Automotive News*, May 1, 2004, p. 4.
"Golding's Analysis: Renault," *just-auto.com*, February 8, 2005.
Ihlwan, Moon, and Chester Dawson, "A French Recipe to Savor," *Business Week*, October 7, 2002, p. 28.
Laux, James M., *In First Gear: The French Automobile Industry to 1914*, Liverpool, U.K.: Liverpool University Press, 1976.
Mader, Ian, "Renault Reveals New Investment for South Korean Affiliate," *America's Intelligence Wire*, November 30, 2004.
McLintock, J. Dewar, *Renault: The Cars and the Charisma*, Cambridge: Stevens, 1983.
"Nissan, Renault to Set Up Joint Firm," *Yomiuri Shimbun/Daily Yomiuri*, October 17, 2001, item YOSH19343887.
"Nissan-Renault Ranks 4th in Terms of Global Sales," *Knight-Ridder/Tribune Business News*, February 2, 2005, item 05033032.
"Nissan to Aid Renault's Profits More than Expected," *The New York Times*, November 22, 2000, p. C4.
Reeve, Steve, "Renault to Drive European Sales via Online Expansion," *Precision Marketing*, September 6, 2002, p. 9.
"Renault, China's Dongfeng to Set Up Joint Auto Production Firm," *Japan Transportation Scan*, July 6, 2004.
"Renault to Back Dealers Online," *Marketing*, August 4, 2004, p. 9.
"Renault to Invest $5B in Nissan Merger," *United Press International*, March 29, 1999, item 1008086u0713.
Routier, Airy, "Le dieteticien de Renault," *Challenges*, April 1998, p. 78.
Saint-Seine, Sylviane, "Renault Hopes to Save through Dealer Network Restructuring," *Automotive News Europe*, October 8, 2001, p. 23.
——, "Agriculture Deal Marks End of Renault Sell-Offs," *Automotive News Europe*, March 24, 2003, p. 17.
Souffrant, Rebecca, "Mack Trucks Included in Volvo Plan to Buy Renault," *Commercial Carrier Journal*, February 2001, p. 12.
Truett, Richard, "Renault Designers Think 'Frenchness,' Not Retro," *Automotive News*, January 21, 2002, p. 56.
"Two Blind Mice," *Delaney Report*, March 22, 1999, p. 2.

—updates: M.L. Cohen; Jennifer Gariepy

Repco Corporation Ltd.

362 Wellington Road
Mulgrave
VIC 3170
Australia
Telephone: +61 3 9566 5444
Fax: +61 3 9561 9538
Web site: http://www.repco.com.au

Public Company
Incorporated: 1922 as Automotive Grinding Company
Employees: 3,600
Sales: AUD 862.3 million ($659.8 million) (2005)
Stock Exchanges: Australian
Ticker Symbol: RCL
NAIC: 441310 Automotive Parts and Accessories Stores

One of the flagships of the Australian manufacturing sector in the mid-20th century, Repco Corporation Ltd. has entered the 21st century as the leading retail reseller of automotive after-market parts and accessories in the Australian and New Zealand markets. The company operates a network of more than 430 branches throughout Australia and New Zealand and expects to boost its chain to more than 500 stores by 2008. The majority of the group's operations come from its Repco auto parts network, with more than 400 stores in Australia and New Zealand. Since 2003, the company, which traditionally targeted the trade market, has begun converting its store network to a dual format targeting both trade and retail customers. As part of that effort, the company also has been relocating many of its branches to more consumer-oriented retail locations. In addition to the Repco store network, Repco includes the Ingram automotive components import and distribution business, and the Mc-Leod's motorcycle accessories business, both acquired from Alesco in December 2004. Another Repco division is Ashdown, which specializes in automotive electrical components, air conditioning, and fuel injection products. Ashdown operates its own network of 19 branches in Australia. In 2000, Repco began targeting the performance market with the creation of Motospecs, which specializes in the import and distribution of high-performance transmission, fuel, four-wheel drive, and other products. Founded in the early 1920s, Repco was part of the PacDun conglomerate (now known as Ansell) through the 1990s, before being spun off in a management buyout in 2001. The company has been listed on the Australian Stock Exchange since 2003. Michael R. Brown serves as company chairman, and Peter Mummery is the group's managing director.

Anticipating the Australian Automotive Market in the 1920s

The origins of Repco lay in the early 1920s, when Geoff Russell returned from service in World War I. Russell had recognized an opportunity for entering the automotive market. At the time, Australia had not yet developed its automobile market, and relied on imports. Yet the limited availability of spare and replacement parts made it difficult to repair the imported cars. Russell entered this market, founding a business reconditioning automobile engines. In 1922, Russell set up shop in a shed in Collinwood, a suburb of Melbourne, calling the business the Automotive Grinding Company.

By 1924, Russell's business had grown enough to enable him to move the company to larger quarters in Carlton. A number of other entrepreneurs had entered the spare parts manufacturing market. At the same time, other companies developed with a specialty in importing spare parts. Yet obtaining parts and components remained difficult through the 1920s. In 1926, therefore, Russell decided to team up with a friend, Bill Ryan, who had been working for a business importing spare parts. The partners founded Replacement Parts Pty. Ltd. (Repco), setting the stage for what was to become one of Australia's manufacturing giants.

The year 1927 marked a new opportunity for the young Repco. In that year, Ford and General Motors came to Australia to set up the country's automotive manufacturing sector. The arrival of the two automotive giants, and the resulting increased availability of automobiles in Australia, provided a strong foundation for Repco's own growth.

In addition to developing their own import operation, Russell and Ryan began establishing a network of shops, eventually expanding to serve the entire Victoria region. The stores not only sold spare parts, but also produced parts in their own workshops. The company grew strongly, especially during the Depression years when many consumers sought to extend the lives of their vehicles rather than purchase new cars. During the 1930s, as well, Repco launched its first advertising campaigns, helping to boost its position in the market.

By the mid-1930s, the company had developed a central position in the Australian automobile market. Boasting more than 500 employees, the company's strong sales network had enabled it to build up its manufacturing wing as well. In the second half of the decade, the company's own production accounted for more than two-thirds of its retail sales. In the late 1930s, Russell bought out partner Ryan's stake in the business. Then, in 1937, Russell combined the group's operations into a single business, Repco Limited, which was then listed on the Melbourne Stock Exchange. Russell himself died in 1946.

Postwar Manufacturing Giant

World War II provided a boost to Repco's manufacturing operations. As the company turned its production to support of the war effort, the company also expanded its production capacity. In 1942, the company constructed new production facilities dedicated to its defense manufacturing business. This increased capacity in turn led the company to seek further expansion of its manufacturing operations, particularly during the postwar period.

Following the end of the war, the company began acquiring a number of other Australian automotive parts companies, such as PBR Corporation, founded by the Paton brothers in the 1920s and specialized in the production of automotive braking systems. The expansion of its manufacturing range placed Repco in position to become a key player in a new development: the creation of the first ''Australian'' automobile.

Encouraged by the Australian government, which had been seeking to stimulate a homegrown automotive industry since the 1930s, General Motors Holden announced plans in 1944 to develop an automobile designed in Australia. More than 90 percent of the components for the mid-sized, affordable car were also to be manufactured in Australia. Repco and its subsidiaries quickly joined the Holden project as a major provider of components and systems for the automobile design. The Holden project also meant that for the first time Repco was not merely producing replacement parts. Instead, the company became responsible for the design and development of a number of Holden components,

such as its pistons and cables, as well as a number of engine and brake components. Through its own growth and its acquisitions, the company's manufacturing base grew strongly. By the beginning of the 1960s, Repco controlled some 14 factories.

Repco's entry into original design manufacturing led the company into a new and exciting area in the 1950s. In 1954, one of the company's engineers, Charlie Dean, led a team in designing and building the Maybach race car. The Maybach was purchased and driven by a noted racing driver of the time, Stan Jones, who won the New Zealand Grand Prix with the car that year.

Recognizing the advertising potential in developing a racing car division, Repco became one of the sponsors for the Phillip Island Racing Club in 1955. The next major step in Repco's racing career came in 1958, when the company was approached by an up-and-coming Australian driver, Jack Brabham. Repco initially provided technical assistance to Brabham, who founded his own company, Motor Racing Developments, in England, to build cars for the Formula One circuit. The partnership helped Brabham win the Formula One World Championship twice, in 1959 and 1960.

The company's partnership with Brabham strengthened in the early 1960s, when Repco and Brabham collaborated on the design of a new vehicle, called the Repco Brabham. By the mid-1960s, the Repco Brabham had begun winning races, and in 1966 Brabham became the first driver to win the Formula One World Championship in a car bearing his own name. The Repco-designed engine was also the first Australian engine to win a world championship.

Repco's involvement in international racing was short-lived. By the end of the 1960s, the increasing professionalism of international racing circuits, as well as rapidly developing technological improvements in racing car design, had driven up the cost of participation. The arrival of a new engine design, the Cosgrove, in 1968 meant that Repco too would have to design and build a completely new engine to remain competitive. Repco decided that the cost of building a new engine was too high, and decided to exit Formula One racing. By the early 1970s, the company had abandoned racing altogether.

Nonetheless, racing had enabled Repco to build an international reputation. The success of the Repco Brabham—and the steadily growing popularity of racing in general—enabled the company and its subsidiaries to being targeting the export market, a rarity for Australian manufacturers of the time. The company continued acquiring other car parts manufacturers during the 1960s, and opened a number of new production facilities as well. The period saw Repco develop expertise in a number of related areas, such as compressed air systems, hydraulic hoses and systems, and control valves. By the end of the decade, Repco operated nearly 40 factories across Australia and had become one of the country's top manufacturing icons.

Retail Focus in the 1980s

The boom in the automotive market came to an abrupt halt in the early 1970s. The sudden increase of oil prices in 1973 caught the industry—and most of the industrialized world's economy—off guard. In addition, Repco was hit by a string of management changes during the period. At the same time,

Key Dates:

1922: Geoff Russell founds the Automotive Grinding Company in Collingwood, near Melbourne.
1926: Russell joins with Bill Ryan and sets up Replacement Parts Pty., opening their first parts shop.
1937: The company goes public as Repco Limited.
1947: The company joins in the design and production of the Holden, the first Australian-designed automobile.
1954: A Repco engineering team builds its first racing car.
1960: Repco controls 14 factories.
1968: The company begins its exit from the racing circuit.
1981: After a diversification drive during the 1970s, the company restructures under the new Repco Corporation Ltd.; the company opens its first store in New Zealand.
1985: Corporate raider Ariadne acquires Repco.
1986: Repco exits manufacturing to focus exclusively on distribution.
1988: Pacific Dunlop acquires Repco and changes its name to Pacific Automotive; the first dual-format store is launched in New Zealand.
1991: The company acquires Ashdown, an electrical parts specialist.
1996: The company launches its first dual-format store in Australia.
1998: The Appco network in New Zealand is acquired.
2000: The company launches high-performance parts specialist Motospecs.
2001: Pacific Dunlop sells off Pacific Automotive to a management buyout.
2003: The company is renamed Repco and launches a new public offering.

Repco launched a new diversification strategy, which led the company into disparate sectors such as hardware, finance, manufacturing batteries, air-conditioning systems, and even management of gymnasiums.

Yet the company failed in its efforts to recapture its former growth rate. Investor confidence also was falling, amid continued management changes and structural reorganizations, including the creation of a new holding company, Repco Corporation Ltd., to oversee the now highly diversified group. The company's lagging share price left it vulnerable in the early 1980s to a newly developing trend in the international investment community—that of the appearance of a number of flamboyant and highly aggressive corporate raiders. In 1981, Repco entered New Zealand, establishing its first store there.

Repco sought to protect itself, and boost its share price, by launching a sell-off of a number of its underperforming and noncore holdings. The company's efforts were not enough, however, and in 1985 the company fell prey to investment group Ariadne. Under Ariadne, Repco's breakup was accelerated. By 1986, Repco had shed its manufacturing operations altogether and was regrouped around its automotive parts distribution network. Those operations had by then expand to cover all of Australia.

Ariadne itself fell victim to the collapse of the corporate raider market in the late 1980s. As a result, Repco itself was sold to Pacific Dunlop, more familiarly known as PacDun, in 1988. Under PacDun, Repco's name was changed to Pacific Automotive, with Repco becoming the company's core brand. Under PacDun, Pacific Automotive grew to include a number of prominent auto parts distribution businesses, including Ashdown, acquired in 1991. That company focused on the distribution of electrical components, later building up a network of nearly 20 trade-oriented stores by the beginning of the 2000s. PacDun also built up a second business, specialized in automotive tires, called South Pacific Tyres.

Under PacDun, the company continued to build up its auto parts distribution activities, focusing especially on its chain of Repco stores. Traditionally, the company had targeted the market for trade professionals. As such, the group's stores generally were located away from consumer retail areas. In 1988, however, the company developed a new dual-format store, designed to appeal to both professionals and the consumer retail market. The first dual-format store opened in New Zealand.

By 1996, the company had decided to expand the dual-format store concept to its Australian operations, in part to counter the increasing strength of a number of its competitors. The company also sought to expand its operations through acquisition, notably with the purchase of the Appco network of trade-oriented auto parts shops in New Zealand in 1998. The company formed an auto parts wholesaling joint venture with Atkins Carlyle, called CarParts. In 2000, Pacific Automotive launched Motospecs, specialized in the distribution of high-performance aftermarket parts and accessories.

In the late 1990s and into the 2000s, however, PacDun had begun to struggle to maintain profitability. With its share price slipping—dropping as low as AUD 1.25 per share by 2001—PacDun found a new major shareholder in U.S.-based investment fund Shamrock Holdings. By 2001, Shamrock forced PacDun to undergo its own restructuring, and in May of that year PacDun announced its intention to sell off both Pacific Automotive and South Pacific Tyres. By the end of that year, the company had completed the sell-off, in a management buyout backed by several private equity groups, worth AUD 270 million.

Following the buyout, the company changed its name, becoming Automotive Parts Group. In 2002, the company decided to focus on its trade and retail distribution operations, selling off its 50 percent of CarParts. The company, which had been restructuring its core Repco business, then launched a new expansion strategy, calling for an increase in its number of stores to 500 by 2008, and the conversion of all of its Repco stores to the dual format. That operation required an extensive investment, in large part in order to relocate its centers to more retail-oriented locations.

To back its new strategy, the company regrouped its businesses under a new name, Repco, and then returned to the stock market, launching its public offering in October 2003. The new Repco counted on remaining Australia's automotive parts distribution leader, and began preparing an acquisition drive. This led the company to seek out purchases of smaller and independent businesses. Yet the company also targeted larger operations, such as its December 2004 purchase of Ingram, a leading distributor of electrical car parts, and McLeod's, a specialist in motorcycle accessories, from Alesco for AUD 90.5 million. These purchases helped boost Repco's share of the Australian electrical car parts segment to 50 percent, and the company's sales grew to more than AUD 860 million ($660 million) by 2005. After more than 80 years, Repco remained a fixture in the Australian automotive industry.

Principal Divisions

Repco; Ashdown; Motospecs; Ingram; McLeod Accessories.

Principal Competitors

Coles Myer Ltd.; Super Cheap Auto Proprietary Ltd.; Strathfield Group Ltd.; Auto One Proprietary Ltd.; Burson Automotive Proprietary Ltd.; Tyrepower Ltd.

Further Reading

Galacho, Olga, "More Parts for Repco," *Herald Sun,* December 15, 2004.

Hughes, Anthony, "Repco Poised for Further Acquisitions," *Australasian Business Intelligence,* December 15, 2004.

Jones, Chris, "Good Gain Has Repco Buzzing," *Herald Sun,* August 9, 2005.

Pickard, Derek, "Sale of the Century," *Automotive Aftermarket,* May 2001.

"Repco in Growth Rev-up," *Mercury,* September 8, 2004.

Rochfort, Scott, "Repco Gets Alesco Automotive," *Sydney Morning Herald,* December 15, 2004.

Simon, Evans, "Good Buys Pay Dividends for Repco," *Australian Financial Review,* August 9, 2005.

—M.L. Cohen

Ripley Entertainment, Inc.

7576 Kingspointe Parkway #188
Orlando, Florida 32819
U.S.A.
Telephone: (407) 345-8010
Fax: (407) 345-0801
Web site: http://www.ripleys.com

Wholly-Owned Subsidiary of the Jim Pattison Group
Incorporated: 1949 as Ripley's Believe It or Not
Employees: 225
Sales: $150 million (2005 est.)
NAIC: 713110 Amusement and Theme Parks; 712130
     Zoos and Botanical Gardens; 713990 All Other
     Amusement and Recreation Industries

Ripley Entertainment, Inc., manages a chain of more than 40 entertainment attractions located at tourist destinations in North America, Asia, and Europe. They include about 25 Ripley's "Believe It or Not" museums, which display unusual items like shrunken heads and elaborate models made from matchsticks; three Ripley's Haunted Adventures, which use live actors and props to scare visitors; three Ripley's aquariums; four Louis Tussaud's Wax Museums; five Guinness World of Records museums; three miniature golf courses; and a sightseeing tour bus firm. The company owns about one-third of the attractions, with the rest held by franchisees. Ripley Entertainment also produces a daily comic strip that appears in 200 newspapers around the world, books, television programs, computer games, and other entertainment products based on the Ripley's "Believe It or Not" comic strip that was created by Robert Ripley in 1918. The firm has been owned since 1985 by Canadian billionaire Jim Pattison.

Origins

The founder and namesake of Ripley Entertainment, Leroy Ripley, was born in Santa Rosa, California, in December of 1890 (though many sources cite 1893). Ripley began working from a young age, first for a tombstone engraver, then as a semi-professional baseball player and advertising artist. In 1908, he sold a cartoon to a national magazine. The following year he began to draw sports cartoons for the *San Francisco Bulletin* and later the *Chronicle*. In 1912, Ripley moved to New York, where he began drawing sports cartoons for the *Globe* the following January. At his editor's urging, he signed them with the more "athletic" first name of Robert, which he soon adopted as his own.

On December 19, 1918, Ripley published a cartoon he called "Champs and Chumps," which featured interesting and obscure sports facts about such things as a backwards race and a broad jump on ice. Though he had composed it merely to fill up space on a slow news day, it got a favorable response, and the paper began running it weekly. Its scope soon broadened to include unusual non-sports items, and on October 16, 1919, the cartoon's name was changed to "Believe It or Not."

In 1923, the *Globe* folded and Ripley began working for the *New York Evening News*, where he hired Norbert Pearlroth to help perform research for the "Believe It or Not" strip, which was now running daily. Pearlroth, who was fluent in 14 languages, began using the vast resources of the New York Public Library to uncover a steady stream of material for the comic.

During the 1920s, Ripley published books on handball, travel, and boxing with minimal success, but in 1929 his first compilation of "Believe It Or Not" cartoons reached the best-seller lists. Its sales were helped by the recent controversy over an item he had run which stated that Charles Lindbergh was not the first person to cross the Atlantic non-stop by air, but the 67th. Ripley received more than 150,000 angry letters and telegrams protesting his "lie," but the scrupulously accurate cartoonist had his facts correct: a team of two Britons had accomplished the feat by plane in 1919, followed by two dirigibles that had each carried more than 30. Lindbergh, in 1927, had merely been the first to do so alone.

The success of Ripley's book led to an offer of $100,000 per year from William Randolph Hearst's King Features Syndicate, which soon gave his cartoon a world-wide audience. At its peak, it would reach as many as 80 million readers a day via publication in 300 newspapers in 33 countries.

The 1930s were a heady time for Ripley, who began a long-running weekly radio show for NBC and other networks, shot a series of nearly two dozen short subject films for Vitaphone, and traveled the world in search of ever more exotic discoveries. He became a household name, and the first cartoonist to earn a million dollars from his work.

Odditorium Debuts in 1933

In 1933, Ripley opened what he called an ''Odditorium'' at the Chicago World's Fair that featured unusual items he had collected along with performances by sideshow acts like contortionists, sword swallowers, and a girl who had been born without arms or legs. It was one of the best-attended attractions at the fair, and after it closed the Odditorium made stops around the country at events like the California-Pacific Exhibition in San Diego and the 1939 New York World's Fair. The year 1939 also saw an Odditorium opened in Times Square by Ripley's firm International Oddities, Inc., but it closed a year later.

Though his foreign travels were halted by the onset of World War II, during the 1940s Ripley continued his daily comic strip and radio work and also began to focus on licensing his name for a host of products that ranged from trading cards to women's clothing. In 1949, he made the switch from radio to the new medium of television, but shortly after completing the 13th episode of his new program, Robert Ripley had a heart attack and died.

After his death, Ripley's business affairs were taken over by his younger brother Douglas. His manager, Doug Storer, oversaw publication of the newspaper cartoon, which continued to be compiled by Norbert Pearlroth, with the drawing done by Paul Frehm. A public auction of Ripley's estate was held, and many of the oddities he had collected were purchased by John Arthur, who opened a new, permanent ''Believe It or Not'' museum in St. Augustine, Florida, in 1950.

Douglas Ripley soon proved incapable of managing the business, and Storer and Arthur took control. During the 1950s, many books, magazines, and comic books bearing the Ripley imprint were published, and museums opened in Las Vegas (1952), Atlantic City (1954, closed 1957), and New York City (1957). In 1959, Storer retired, leaving the firm in the hands of John Arthur.

In 1963, Arthur joined with a Canadian, T. Alec Rigby, to open a museum in Niagara Falls, Canada, and Rigby soon opened additional ones in San Francisco and Chicago, as well as acquiring the Louis Tussaud Wax Museum nameplate. In 1969, Rigby became the sole owner of Ripley's ''Believe It or Not''

enterprise and moved the firm's headquarters from New York to Toronto, where it became known as Ripley's International, Ltd.

Expansion continued in the 1970s, with museums opened in Gatlinburg, Tennessee (1970), Ripley's home town of Santa Rosa, California (1971), Blackpool, England (1972), and Myrtle Beach, South Carolina (1976). The firm's New York museum was shuttered in 1972, while the Blackpool one closed in 1976.

Ripley's ''Believe It or Not'' returned to television in 1982 with a series hosted by actor Jack Palance that ran for four seasons. The television exposure helped boost interest in the firm's museums, which saw revenues increase by 40 percent. By the mid-1980s, new locations had opened in Ocean City, Maryland, and on the French Riviera.

Acquisition by Jim Pattison Group in 1985

In early 1985, Ripley's International was sold to the Jim Pattison Group of Vancouver, British Columbia, for a reported $6 million. Pattison had become one of Canada's wealthiest men by assembling a group of companies that included car dealerships, radio stations, and a sign and outdoor advertising company.

With an infusion of $5 million from Pattison, a new expansion plan was developed, and the firm began franchising its museum concept. The first franchised site opened in 1986 in Newport, Oregon, and others soon followed in Las Vegas and New Orleans. In 1987, the firm's Chicago museum closed, but the next year new museums opened at Surfer's Paradise, Australia, and San Antonio, Texas. By this time, there were a total of 11 ''Believe It or Not'' museums and three Louis Tussaud Wax Museums in operation.

In 1989, the firm's publishing unit signed with United Media, ending a 60-year relationship with King Features Syndicate. A new museum was also opened in the Dallas suburb of Grand Prairie, Texas, and in December company veteran Bob Masterson was appointed president. The start of the 1990s saw a spate of new museum openings in various cities, including Orlando, Florida; Seoul, South Korea; Blackpool, England; and Buena Park, California. The firm's New Orleans museum was shuttered, however, as its family entertainment offerings had proven incompatible with the adult-oriented French Quarter where it was located.

In 1991, the firm unveiled a new type of attraction in Gatlinburg, Tennessee. Ripley's Moving Theater had seats that moved in synchronization with a high-resolution 70mm film image, creating a heightened sense of reality as viewers experienced a variety of thrills. The following July, the Gatlinburg, Tennessee, Ripley's museum burned to the ground, destroying nearly all of its contents.

The year 1992 saw new franchised museums opened in Mexico City; Great Yarmouth, England; Hollywood, California; and Orlando, Florida. The latter locale was a typical entry in the firm's chain. The $2 million museum, whose eye-catching exterior was designed to appear as if it was falling into a sinkhole, boasted 9,000 square feet of exhibit space. Nearly a dozen themed galleries used music, sound effects, and videos to enhance the display of several hundred items, which ranged

Key Dates:

1918: Robert Ripley publishes his first comic strip of odd facts in the *New York Globe.*

1929: King Features Syndicate signs Ripley, bringing his comic strip to a worldwide audience.

1933: The first ''Odditorium'' opens at the Chicago World's Fair with exhibits and live acts.

1949: Ripley dies after filming the thirteenth episode of his TV show, and the firm is taken over by his brother.

1950: A new Ripley museum opens in St. Augustine, Florida.

1950s: Doug Storer and John Arthur take over the firm; Las Vegas, New York, and Atlantic City museums open.

1960s: Niagara Falls, Chicago, and San Francisco museums open; L. Tussaud is acquired.

1969: T. Alec Rigby becomes the sole owner of the firm.

1970s: New museums open in Tennessee, Southern Carolina, and England.

1982: A *Believe It or Not* television series hosted by Jack Palance debuts.

1985: Jim Pattison Group of Vancouver, British Columbia, Canada buys the Ripley firm.

1986: The first franchised museum opens in Oregon; others follow in the United States and abroad.

1991: The first Ripley's Moving Theater opens in Gatlinburg, Tennessee.

1997: Ripley's Aquarium opens in Myrtle Beach, South Carolina.

1999: The first Ripley's Haunted Adventure opens in Gatlinburg.

2000: A new Ripley's television series debuts on the cable station TBS; a Gatlinburg aquarium opens.

2004: Work begins on $200 million hotel, waterpark, and aquarium in Niagara Falls.

from a shrunken head and medieval torture devices to a ten-foot section of the Berlin Wall and a two-thirds scale model of a 1907 Rolls Royce made from one million matchsticks.

To keep the displays fresh, each year 15 to 20 percent of the museum would be changed, as repeat customers accounted for an estimated 30 percent of the firm's business. Parent company Ripley Entertainment owned the objects on display and maintained a warehouse full of items which were constantly being added to. While some were purchased at auction or from dealers, many were brought in by the public.

Headquarters Moved to Florida in 1993

In 1993, the firm, now known as Ripley Entertainment, Inc., moved its headquarters to Orlando, Florida, and celebrated the 75th anniversary of the ''Believe It or Not'' strip with special exhibits at the firm's museums, a two-hour television special on the TBS cable network, an animated children's TV series, and a book titled *Dear Mr. Ripley* that compiled some of the millions of letters Ripley's fans had sent him. The company, which had

published over 70 books by this time, continued to create a daily ''Believe It or Not'' cartoon that appeared in some 200 papers in more than 40 countries. In 1993, a new franchised museum opened in Key West, Florida, and the following year another in Branson, Missouri.

At this time, the company's leadership began looking at new ways for the firm to grow. Ripley Entertainment had always located its attractions at tourist destination spots like Niagara Falls or the Alamo, where a family might go on a days-long vacation trip but exhaust the possibilities of the main attraction in an afternoon. The firm's museums offered one intriguing way to spend the remainder of their time, and Bob Masterson and the company's other executives sought out other unusual and memorable ways to entertain families.

In January 1995, Ripley Entertainment announced that it would build a new high-tech aquarium in Myrtle Beach, South Carolina. The $36 million facility would feature displays of exotic fish, some interactive elements, a restaurant, and a gift shop. In February, a new Ripley's museum and Moving Theater opened in Pattaya, Thailand, and in March the firm reached an agreement to purchase two Guinness World of Records museums and take over the administration of seven others. Ripley would also have the option of franchising additional ones. In April, the rebuilt Gatlinburg Ripley's museum was opened. A handful of items that had survived its predecessor's fire were displayed, but most exhibits were new. At 17,500 square feet, it had double the space of the earlier museum and was the largest in the firm's chain, which now numbered 24. Other Odditoriums were opened during the year in Jakarta, Indonesia, and Manila, Philippines, though the former was later closed due to political turmoil in that country. To open a museum, the firm reportedly charged a $5 million franchise fee and 15 percent of revenues.

Aquarium Opens in 1997

In 1997, the Myrtle Beach aquarium began operations. Its exhibits included a 600,000-gallon shipwreck-themed shark tank which visitors walked through via a 310-foot acrylic tunnel, a ray pool where the flat fish could be touched, an Amazon rain forest habitat, and the Sea-for-Yourself Discovery Center, which was shaped like a submarine. The facility was rounded out with a gift shop and two restaurants. Admission was $12.95 for adults and $6.95 for children, slightly more than what the firm's museums charged.

Expansion to Asia continued with franchised museums in Taegu, South Korea, and Hong Kong in 1997 and in Kuala Lumpur, Malaysia, and Ghuangzhou, China, in 1998. Also in 1998, a Guinness franchise also opened in Talchung, Taiwan, and the company began working with merchandising firm Sony Signatures to reposition the Ripley brand worldwide by developing new books, computer games, and other entertainment products.

In October 1999, Ripley paid a total of $1.3 million for more than 50 items that had belonged to the late Marilyn Monroe, including shoes, clothing, photographs, her driver's license, and her makeup case. They would be displayed at the firm's Hollywood museum before traveling to others in the chain.

Gatlinburg, Tennessee, located near the Great Smoky Mountains National Park (the most popular U.S. national park) had long been one of the firm's prime markets, and in 1999 another new concept, Ripley's Haunted Adventure, was unveiled there. It featured several themed rooms in which live actors delivered chills to visitors. In late 2000, the Ripley's Aquarium of the Smokies, built at a cost of $50 million, also opened in Gatlinburg.

New Television Series in 2000

In January 2000, a new hour-long Ripley's *Believe It Or Not* television series, hosted by actor Dean Cain, debuted on TBS with the largest audience for an original series premiere, excluding sports, in basic cable history. New Haunted Adventures attractions also opened in 2001 in Myrtle Beach and in 2002 in San Antonio. Yet another new concept was Davy Crockett Mini-Golf, which opened in Gatlinburg in July 2002.

By now, the firm had more than 40 attractions in nine countries, which brought in 11 million visitors per year. Of the 25 "Believe It or Not" museums, the company owned seven, as well as all three Ripley's Moving Theaters (which had recently been converted to show 3D movies), two Haunted Adventures, and both aquariums. Only one of the six Guinness World of Records facilities, in Orlando, was owned by the firm, and that unit, which had opened in 2000, closed the same year.

In the fall of 2002, Ripley Entertainment signed an agreement with Paramount Pictures to develop a film series about Robert Ripley's adventures, which was expected to resemble "a goofy version" of Steven Spielberg's Indiana Jones films. Revenues for the year were estimated at $85 million, with profits put at $30 million.

In 2003, new franchised Ripley's museums were opened in Key West, Florida, and New Orleans, the latter replacing a closed Planet Hollywood restaurant there. After making offers on failing aquarium operations in Denver, Colorado, and Duluth, Minnesota, the firm took control of the latter in early 2003.

In January 2004, Ripley bought the Grand Prairie and San Antonio, Texas, Ripley's museums and adjoining wax museums from their owner. The firm would refurbish the former and rebrand the latter as Louis Tussaud Wax Museums. Early 2004 also saw acquisition of the Big Red Train tour bus company in St. Augustine, Florida. Revenues had doubled within the previous three years and were expected to double again in the next three, according to CEO Masterson.

In early 2004, the firm announced plans to build a $200 million complex near Niagara Falls, Canada, called The Great Wolf Lodge Waterpark Resort. Expected to open in late 2005 or 2006, it would include a 404-room hotel and an indoor waterpark, with a separate Ripley's Aquarium to be completed nearby a year later. The hotel-waterpark concept had been licensed from The Great Lakes Co. of Madison, Wisconsin, which would manage it for the first five years. A new Ripley's museum in Spain and two new mini-golf courses were also slated to open in 2005, and the firm was considering a $350 million project for Singapore and acquisitions of other attractions, including planetariums and science and history museums.

Ripley Entertainment, Inc. had taken cartoonist Robert Ripley's fascination for strange and entertaining facts into a new high-concept dimension with its chain of Ripley's "Believe It or Not" museums and had also branched out into wax museums, movie theaters, aquariums, haunted houses, and more. With nine decades of experience satisfying the public's seemingly endless appetite for the bizarre and unexplained, the firm looked forward to many more years of entertainment to come.

Principal Competitors

Landry's Restaurant, Inc.; Busch Entertainment Corp.; The Tussauds Group; Universal Parks & Resorts; The Walt Disney Company; Six Flags, Inc.; Cedar Fair, L.P.

Further Reading

Clark, James C., "Believe It or Not, Ripley's Is an Empire," *Austin-American Statesman*, August 29, 1992, p. D4.

Fingersh, Julie, "Ripley's Considers International Sites," *Amusement Business*, October 19, 1992, p. 18.

Groeller, Greg, "Orlando, Fla.-Based Ripley's Explores New Tourist Ideas," *Orlando Sentinel*, July 26, 2004.

Hall, Cheryl, "On the Trail of the Bizarre, Ripley's Curator Circles the Globe for Curiosities," *Dallas Morning News*, October 12, 1993, p. 1D.

Jackson, Jerry W., "TV Show, Oddities Lure Visitors to Ripley's Attraction in Orlando, Fla.," *Orlando Sentinel*, March 18, 2002.

Kit, Zorianna, "Par Eyes Films of Ripley's Oddities," *Hollywood Reporter*, September 18, 2002, p. 1.

Mitchell, Mary A., "Ripley's Museum Reports Steady Traffic, Especially at Night," *Travel Weekly*, December 7, 1992, p. 93.

Morgan, Philip, "Believe It! Born Poor, Wizard of Odd Became Wealthy and Famous!," *Tampa Tribune*, June 15, 1999, p. 1.

——, "Believe It! Ripley Museums Around the World Get Weird Stuff from a Warehouse—in Orlando," *Tampa Tribune*, June 15, 1999, p. 1.

Muret, Don, "Believe It or Not—Ripley Continues Expansion in Far East," *Amusement Business*, August 18, 1997, p. 34.

O'Brien, Tim, "Believe It or Not, Ripley's to Build Sea Aquariums," *Amusement Business*, January 23, 1995, p. 1.

——, "Bob Masterson a Believer in Ripley's Brand," *Amusement Business*, July 30, 2001, p. 1.

Patterson, Kelly D., "A Marketing Plan With Teeth—Ripley's Plan New Products, Ventures," *Dallas Morning News*, July 30, 1998, p. 1C.

Reuter, Lisa, "Ripley's Aquarium Angles for Tourists along Grand Strand," *Columbus Dispatch*, March 16, 1997, p. 5I.

"Ripley, 'Believe It or Not' Creator, Dies of Heart Attack," *Washington Post*, May 28, 1949, p. B2.

"Ripley's Believe It or Not History." Available at http://www.ripleys.com/broadband/history.html, July 4, 2005.

"Ripley's to Be Acquired By Canadian Businessman," *Wall Street Journal*, December 13, 1984.

Tugores, Mathias, "Ripley Believe Him or Not," *Business Review Weekly*, August 31, 1998, p. 92.

—Frank Uhle

Royal Caribbean Cruises Ltd.

1050 Caribbean Way
Miami, Florida 33132
U.S.A.
Telephone: (305) 539-6000
Fax: (305) 374-7354
Web site: http://www.royalcaribbean.com

Public Company
Founded: 1969
Employees: 38,870
Sales: $4.56 billion (2004)
Stock Exchanges: New York
Ticker Symbol: RCL
NAIC: 483112 Deep Sea Passenger Transportation

Royal Caribbean Cruises Ltd. is the world's second largest cruise company (behind top-ranking Carnival Corporation), with 29 cruise ships and a total of 60,590 passenger berths as of August 2005. Founded in 1969, the company has been instrumental in changing the cruise industry from a trans-ocean carrier service into a vacation option in and of itself. Royal Caribbean offers a variety of different itineraries and its ships call at more than 160 destinations in the Caribbean, Bahamas, Mexico, Alaska, Europe, Bermuda, Panama Canal, Hawaii, New England, and Canada. The company, a Liberian corporation, operates under two separate brands, Royal Caribbean International and Celebrity Cruises. Although the company operates globally in terms of its itineraries and destinations, nearly 85 percent of its passengers are from North America. After pleading guilty to charges of illegal dumping and obstruction of justice in the late 1990s, Royal Caribbean has pledged to clean up its act. In 2004, the company began installing Advanced Wastewater Purification systems on its fleet.

Early History

Royal Caribbean Cruises Ltd. can trace its history to the beginning of today's passenger cruise industry. When three major Norwegian shipping companies founded the Royal Caribbean Cruise Line in 1969, a cruise was an around-the-world or trans-ocean voyage on a large passenger liner, and was something only the wealthy could afford. According to Cruise Lines International Association, an industry trade group, an estimated half a million passengers took cruises of three nights or more in 1970, the year Royal Caribbean began offering cruises.

The company built and operated three ships during the 1970s, offering cruises throughout the Caribbean. In fact, Royal Caribbean was the first line to design ships specifically for warm water year-round cruising. Prior to this, a cruise line company would use its passenger liners for cruises in the Caribbean in the months they were not transporting people across the Atlantic or Pacific.

Royal Caribbean's first vessel, the 700-passenger *Song of Norway,* began service in November 1970, and introduced glass-walled dining rooms, expansive sun decks located in the middle of the ship, and the company's signature Viking Crown Lounge projecting out from the ship's funnel, high above the sea. Edwin Stephan, one of the company's founders and Royal Caribbean's president at the time, got the idea for the lounge from the revolving restaurant atop the Space Needle at the 1962 World's Fair in Seattle. He anticipated that not only would passengers have a terrific view from this cocktail and observation lounge, but its design would set the vessel apart from other ships and make Royal Caribbean vessels instantly recognizable.

In 1971, the *Nordic Prince* entered service in the Caribbean and the company began offering passengers air/sea vacations, with the airfare to Miami included in the price of the cruise. The following year, with the introduction of the *Sun Viking,* Royal Caribbean became the biggest cruise line in the Caribbean with weekly departures from Miami on seven- and 14-day vacations.

For the remainder of the decade, Royal Caribbean focused on establishing its name brand. To do this, it concentrated on ensuring a consistent high quality for all its cruises and on generating and meeting demand. In 1973 it opened a marketing office in London and, in 1978, took the unprecedented step of cutting the *Song of Norway* in two and adding an 85-foot midsection, increasing the passenger capacity to 1,000. This was the first cruise ship to be lengthened in this way. In 1980, the same thing was done to the *Nordic Prince.* As Royal Caribbean entered the

---

Company Perspectives:

We always provide service with a friendly greeting and a smile. We anticipate the needs of our customers. We make all effort to exceed our customers' expectations. We take ownership of any problem that is brought to our attention. We engage in conduct that enhances our corporate reputation and employee morale. We are committed to act in the highest ethical manner and respect the rights and dignity of others. We are loyal to Royal Caribbean and Celebrity Cruises, and strive for continuous improvement in everything we do.

1980s, the three ships in its fleet ranged in size from 18,445 to 23,149 tons, with berths for 714 to 1,012 passengers.

The 1980s: Resort-Style Cruising on Megaships

The *Song of America* debuted in 1982. Weighing 37,584 tons and with 1,402 berths, it was the largest cruise ship built in 20 years. The new ship enabled Royal Caribbean to expand its itineraries, and in 1985 it moved outside the Caribbean for the first time, offering summer cruises to Bermuda from New York City.

The cruise industry grew as the target population—middle- and upper-income people—grew older and richer, quadrupling in the 15 years Royal Caribbean had been on the seas. In 1985, more than two million passengers took cruises marketed in North America, according to a *Forbes* article, with nearly two-thirds of them heading for the Caribbean. Projections were that the demand would only increase.

Cruise companies began a building spree in anticipation of the demand, taking advantage of low interest rates and shipyards eager for the business. Royal Caribbean initiated its first major capital expansion program, expanding *Viking Serenade* by 536 berths and building four new ships in four years. The new ships developed the "megaship" concept and introduced resort-style cruising. The first of the new vessels, the 874-foot *Sovereign of the Seas,* entered service in 1988. It weighed more than 73,000 tons, had berths for 2,276 passengers, and featured two indoor/outdoor cafes, two glass elevators, a five-story atrium, and nearly three football fields of open deck on which passengers could stroll.

In April 1988, Richard Fain was named chairman and CEO of the company. Two months later, Royal Caribbean and Admiral Cruises, a passenger cruise service that had operated for almost 100 years, combined their operations, although each kept their separate brand identity. Later that year the company underwent a fundamental ownership change. First, one of the original founding companies, Anders Wilhelmsen & Co., became the sole owner by buying out the other two partner companies. Then Wilhelmsen entered into a joint agreement with the Pritzker family (owners of Hyatt Hotels Corp. and other holdings) and the Ofer family, owners of a large shipping company. The result, once the process was completed in 1992, was that A. Wilhelmsen A/S, a Norwegian corporation, and Cruise Associates, a Bahamian general partnership, became the principal owners of Royal Caribbean. Members of the Wilhelmsen family of Norway controlled A. Wilhelmsen A/S and members of the Pritzker family of Chicago and of the Ofer family controlled Cruise Associates.

1990–94: Passengers Growing Younger

In 1990, while the ownership restructuring was going on, Royal Caribbean opened its new headquarters at the port of Miami and consolidated all functions in one location. The *Nordic Empress* entered service, the first ship built specifically for short cruises such as the company's three- and four-night cruises in the Bahamas. With the addition of *Viking Serenade,* the company also added seasonal cruises to Alaska as well as to Europe.

Travel agents played a critical part in the company's operations, with some 30,000 independent agencies making essentially all the bookings for the cruises. To simplify that process, Royal Caribbean introduced CruiseMatch 2000, the world's first automated cruise booking system for travel agents. The new computer system allowed travel agents direct access to the company's computer reservation system, making it easy to book cruises. The year ended unhappily, however, when a shipyard fire damaged *Monarch of the Seas,* delaying its launch.

Monarch did enter service in 1991. Royal Caribbean's largest vessel at the time, weighing nearly 74,000 tons, with berths for more than 2,300 passengers, the new ship was based in San Juan. *Viking Serenade* was rebuilt for short cruises, adding berth capacity, a new dining room and cafe, and a Viking Crown Lounge. This enabled the company to enter the year-round Mexico market with three- and four-night cruises from Los Angeles. The company also established an international sales and marketing department to increase the number and percentage of its passengers from outside North America. That department oversaw operations of the company's sales offices in London, Oslo, and Frankfurt.

Royal Caribbean's strategy in the very competitive cruise/vacation market was to target the upper portion of the "mass" market, promising a quality product for slightly more money than other volume competitors such as Carnival Cruise Lines. But to fill its ships during a recession (and a war in the Persian Gulf, which affected cruises in the Mediterranean), the company had to offer discount prices. That factor, combined with the costs of servicing the debt from its shipbuilding activities, led to a sharp drop in profits in 1991.

With the entry of the final megaship in its expansion program, the *Majesty of the Seas,* in 1992, Royal Caribbean became the first cruise line to offer year-round megaship cruises in the major Caribbean markets. The building program begun in 1987 had more than tripled the company's number of berths, to 14,228, and brought the fleet's number to nine ships. That year also saw the end of Admiral Cruises, when Royal Caribbean sold its two-ship fleet and discontinued service.

During 1992 the company introduced Enterprise 2000, the company's new computer information system, which was used for reservations, passenger ticketing, sales tools used by the company's sales force, and tools for travel agents.

Royal Caribbean also initiated its "Save the Waves" program to preserve the environment by not dumping things overboard. In addition, each ship recycled about 20,000 alumi-

Key Dates:

1969: Three major Norwegian shipping companies establish the Royal Caribbean Cruise Line.

1970: Royal Caribbean's first vessel, the 700-passenger *Song of Norway,* begins service.

1978: The *Song of Norway* is cut in two to add an 85-foot midsection, which increases the passenger capacity to 1,000.

1982: The *Song of America* debuts; weighing 37,584 tons and with 1,402 berths it is the largest cruise ship built in 20 years.

1992: A. Wilhelmsen A.S., a Norwegian corporation, and Cruise Associates, a Bahamian general partnership, become the principal owners of Royal Caribbean.

1993: Royal Caribbean goes public.

1996: Celebrity Cruise Line Inc. is acquired.

1999: Royal Caribbean pleads guilty to 21 counts of polluting and agrees to pay an $18 million fine.

2004: The company begins installing new advanced wastewater treatment plants on its ships.

num cans each week, and the company purchased more than one million pounds of recycled products each year.

With its fleet in order, the company took action to reduce its debt, beginning with its first public debt offering of $126 million subordinated notes in 1992. The following year Royal Caribbean went public, offering 11.5 million shares of common stock on the New York Stock Exchange. During 1994, the company was able to lower its borrowing rates by refinancing its banking arrangements with a $750 million revolving credit facility. It then issued $125 million in senior notes. By the end of the year, the company had reduced its debt-to-capital ratio to 47 percent from a high of 75 percent in 1992. The company also built a second office facility in Miami to accommodate the Passenger Services Department.

Royal Caribbean celebrated 1994 with a 5 percent increase in revenues and a 28 percent rise in net income, without adding to its fleet capacity. Part of that success may have come from the company's advertisements on cable television. Over the years, the cruise industry's audience had expanded to include younger adults, not just those nearing or in retirement. Royal Caribbean targeted people 25 to 54 who made $40,000 or more. Rather than focusing on opportunities to socialize or nonstop activities, it positioned itself as ''a vacation during which people can relax completely in their own way: with a trip to the spa, a jog around the deck, or a day on the white sands of an island beach,'' as described in a 1995 article in *MediaWeek.* In addition, recognizing the reality of that younger market, the company offered activities to entertain children.

''Two Great Brands . . . One Great Vacation Company'': 1995 and Beyond

The battle for consumers' leisure dollars continued to intensify, with cruise lines, resorts, and timeshare developers concentrating on offering all-inclusive vacations. Between 1995

and 1998, Royal Caribbean undertook its second major capital expansion program, building six Vision-class ships at a cost of approximately $1.5 billion. Each new ship used more than two acres of glass in the design and featured a seven-deck atrium with glass elevators, skylights and glass walls, a pool and entertainment complex covered by a moveable glass roof, a two-deck main dining room, a state-of-the-art show theater, a glass-encased indoor/outdoor cafe, and a shopping mall.

The largest of these new ships carried 2,000 passengers and weighed 75,000 tons. The smallest had 1,804 berths and weighed 70,000 tons, twice the number of people and three times the weight of the original *Song of Norway.* The expansion anticipated increasing the company's berth capacity by approximately 74 percent, from 14,228 to more than 24,700 berths.

The first of the new vessels, the *Legend of the Seas,* entered service in 1995, bringing the Viking Lounge silhouette to Hawaii and expanding Royal Caribbean's cruises in Alaska. The ship's amenities included an 18-hole miniature golf course with all the features, water hazards, and proportions of an average golf course; not surprising, perhaps, with Royal Caribbean the official cruise line of the Professional Golfers' Association.

Designed to be faster than most cruise ships, the new vessels permitted more flexibility in itinerary planning. The company entered the Far East market and was the first to offer year-round cruises there and in Southeast Asia. Two more new ships began cruises in 1996, the 1,800-berth *Splendor of the Seas* and the 1,950-berth *Grandeur of the Seas.* Also in 1995, the company sold the *Nordic Prince,* one of its original three ships, for approximately $55 million, realizing a gain of some $19.2 million.

Royal Caribbean's offerings in the Caribbean also included stops at two private company-operated destinations: CocoCay, an island in the Bahamas owned by the company, and Labadee, a peninsula on the north coast of Haiti leased by the company. Passengers could shop at artisan markets, eat picnics along the beach, and windsurf, snorkel, and sail. In 1995 the company added to these the industry's first on-shore club, the Crown & Anchor, at St. Thomas in the U.S. Virgin Islands.

In December 1995, a series of class-action suits were filed alleging that the company misrepresented to its passengers the amount of its port charge expenses. These were followed in 1996 with class-action suits alleging that seven cruise lines, including Royal Caribbean, should have paid commissions to travel agents on port charges included in the price of cruise fares. In February 1997, Royal Caribbean and other companies agreed that all components of the cruise ticket price, other than governmental taxes and fees, would be included in the advertised price.

During 1996, some 973,000 passengers went on Royal Caribbean cruises, over 100,000 more than sailed in 1995. That year saw the sale of another of the company's original ships, the *Song of Norway,* for $40 million (a gain of $10.3 million), and the establishment of the $1 million Royal Caribbean Ocean Fund.

In July, Royal Caribbean bought Celebrity Cruise Line Inc. for $515 million. Celebrity became a wholly owned subsidiary and continued to operate under its own brand name. Celebrity served the premium cruise vacation market, owned five ships with approximately 8,200 berths, and offered 40 different itineraries ranging from 6 to 18 nights, and stopping in more than 50 ports in Alaska, Bermuda, the Caribbean, and through the Panama Canal. The addition of Celebrity Cruises greatly enhanced the company's presence in the premium destination market of one- and two-week cruises, and its acquisition increased Royal Caribbean's total market share in 1996 to approximately 27 percent of the 4.7 million North Americans who went on cruises that year.

Royal Caribbean continued its capital expansion program by contracting for two Eagle-class ships to be delivered in the fall of 1999 and 2000. These were to be the largest passenger cruise ships built at the time, each weighing 130,000 tons and accommodating 3,100 passengers, and were being designed to attract families and those seeking active sports and entertainment activities. Among the planned amenities: rock climbing facilities, conference centers, and a wedding chapel.

During January 1997 a new television advertising campaign debuted, introducing a new brand identity—Royal Caribbean International—and presenting Royal Caribbean as a global vacation brand with a focus on worldwide cruise vacations. That same month, the company and two of Hyatt Hotels' Puerto Rican properties began jointly marketing what was a first in the Caribbean, a week-long vacation package that included both a cruise and a stay at a hotel. To attract new passengers, Royal Caribbean also marketed its vessels as conference sites for groups ranging from romance writers to dental anesthesiologists, and combined cruising and golf with Golf Ahoy!, a shore excursion program for people who would rather play golf than shop, sunbathe, or sightsee. To help passengers finance their cruise, the company announced "CruiseLoans," allowing people to charge all the expenses, including upgrades, excursions, and onboard spending. The program was administered by Citicorp's Citibank NA.

In the fall of 1997, the company sold $9 million of stock to repay some of its debt and announced that it would sell the *Sun Viking,* its smallest ship and the last of its original three vessels, to Star Cruises for $30 million. At the same time, Celebrity Cruises took delivery of the 1,850-berth *Mercury,* the last of a five-ship expansion program begun in 1990, bringing its total fleet capacity to some 8,200 berths.

With its two brands, Royal Caribbean Cruises, Ltd. had strong name recognition in both the popular, warm-weather vacation market and the seasonal cruise market. Its new ships received press attention because of their size and facilities. Between 1996 and 2000, the company expected to increase its berth capacity by 102 percent, to 38,000. Other cruise lines were doing the same, as industry capacity was expected to grow 12.4 percent in 1998 and 11.7 percent in 1999, according to the Cruise Line Industry Association. With the number of passengers growing only at an average 7.6 percent a year since 1981, Royal Caribbean Cruises would need to use all of its creativity and traditional service quality to attract new passengers to cruising in order to fill their ships.

Overcoming Rough Seas in the Late 1990s and Beyond

During the late 1990s, Royal Caribbean was forced to fend off negative publicity when it became embroiled in several lawsuits related to dumping oil and hazardous chemicals in coastal waters around the United States. In 1998, the company pled guilty to obstruction of justice for attempting to cover up its illegal dumping practices. Royal Caribbean faced five years probation and agreed to pay a $9 million fine. Trouble continued the following year, however, when the company was indicted on additional charges of dumping toxic solvents in New York Harbor, and oil and toxic chemicals from its photo and dry cleaning shops in waters near Miami, the Virgin Islands, Los Angeles, and the Inside Passage in Alaska. Royal Caribbean pled guilty to 21 counts of polluting and faced an $18 million fine. The state of Alaska also sued the company and in 2000 the firm paid out $3.3 million to the state to settle the charges.

During this time period, the cruise industry as a whole felt pressure from environmental groups to clean up their act. According to these groups, sewage from cruise ships contributed to a host of problems including contamination of the world's oceans. Oceana, an organization created to protect the ocean, launched a campaign against Royal Caribbean in the early years of the new millennium. Before ships set out to sea, the group would fly a banner behind an airplane that read, "Got Sewage? Royal Caribbean Dumps Daily." In May 2004, Royal Caribbean agreed to install new advanced wastewater treatment plants on its ships.

Despite the troubles brought on by the litigation, Royal Caribbean continued expansion efforts in the late 1990s and beyond. In 1999, the company launched *Voyager of the Seas,* a 142,000-ton, 3,114-passenger ship. *Explorer of the Seas* entered service the following year and was the first ship to include an atmospheric and marine laboratory on board. *Radiance of the Seas,* a 90,090-ton, 2,100-guest ship set sail the following year and was the first Royal Caribbean vessel to use gas turbines. *Brilliance of the Seas, Serenade of the Seas,* and *Jewel of the Seas*—all Radiance-class ships—were launched in 2002, 2003, and 2004, respectively.

During 2004, Royal Caribbean began offering cruises to the Galapagos Islands via its Celebrity Xpeditions line. It also announced the launch of its new *Freedom of the Seas* ship in 2006. With a 3,600-guest capacity, the *Freedom* would be the largest cruise ship in the world. Even as rising fuel costs threatened company revenue in 2004 and 2005, Royal Caribbean experienced marked success. Net income grew to $474.7 million in 2004 while earning per share increased by 59 percent over the previous year. Revenues also increased by more than 20 percent in 2004 and occupancy was at an all-time high. With its dumping problems behind it, Royal Caribbean appeared to have set sail into a prosperous future.

Principal Subsidiaries

Adventure of the Seas Inc.; Blue Sapphire Marine Inc.; Cape Liberty Cruise Port LLC: Celebrity Cruise Lines Inc.; Cruise Mar Investment Inc.; Enchantment of the Seas Inc.; Esker Marine Shipping Inc.; Explorer of the Seas Inc.; Fantasia Cruising Inc.; Galapagos Cruises Inc.; Grandeur of the Seas Inc.; Infinity Inc.; Islas Galapagos Turismo y Vapores CA; Jewel of the Seas Inc.; Majesty of the Seas Inc.; Mariner of the Seas Inc.; Millennium Inc.; Monarch of the Seas Inc.; Navigator of the Seas Inc.; Nordic Empress Shipping Inc.; Radiance of the

Seas Inc.; RCL UK Ltd.; Rhapsody of the Seas Inc.; Royal Caribbean Cruise Lines A.S.; Royal Celebrity Tours Inc.; Seabrook Maritime Inc.; Serenade of the Seas Inc.; Sovereign of the Seas Shipping Inc.; Summit Inc.; Universal Cruise Holdings Ltd.; Vision of the Seas Inc.; Voyager of the Seas Inc.; Zenith Shipping Corporation.

Principal Competitors

Carnival Corporation; NCL Corporation; Star Cruises Ltd.

Further Reading

Behar, Richard, ''Floating Resorts,'' *Forbes,* January 26, 1987, p. 62.

DeGeorge, Gail, ''Royal Caribbean May Be Taking on Water,'' *Business Week,* May 25, 1992, p. 34.

Hannafin, Matt, ''Celebrity Eschews Megaships for Little Adventures,'' *Boston Herald,* February 19, 2004.

Keates, Nancy, ''Danielle and Joey Urban Can't Believe Mickey Mouse Let Them Down,'' *Wall Street Journal,* October 24, 1997.

McDowell, Edwin, ''In Alaska, Cruise Line Chief Offers Apology for Dumping,'' *The New York Times,* August 26, 1999.

''RCCL Reaffirms Its Commitment to the Ocean Environment,'' *Travel Weekly,* November 4, 1996, p. C19.

''RCCL to Debut 'Legend of the Links,' '' *Travel Weekly,* November 7, 1994, p. C22.

Rice, Faye, ''What to Do on Your Summer Vacation,'' *Fortune,* June 12, 1995, p. 20.

''Sea Change,'' *Travel Weekly,* January 9, 1997, p. 20.

''Trolling for Cruisers Among Upscale Viewers,'' *MediaWeek,* May 27, 1995, p. S22.

Wald, Matthew L., ''Cruise Line Pleads Guilty to Dumping of Chemicals,'' *The New York Times,* July 22, 1999.

——, ''A Cruise Line Starts to Clean Up After Itself,'' *New York Times,* November 28, 2004.

—Ellen D. Wernick
—update: Christina M. Stansell

Rural Press Ltd.

159 Bells Line of Road
North Richmond
NSW 2754
Australia
Telephone: +61 2 4570 4444
Fax: +61 2 4570 4663
Web site: http://www.ruralpress.com

Public Company
Incorporated: 1988
Employees: 2,899
Sales: AUD 515.11 million ($400.20 million) (2004)
Stock Exchanges: Australian
Ticker Symbol: RPL
NAIC: 511110 Newspaper Publishers; 511120 Periodical
   Publishers; 515112 Radio Stations

Rural Press Ltd. is Australia's leading publisher of newspapers and magazines targeting the rural and agricultural markets. The company publishes more than 140 titles, including the daily newspapers *Canberra Times* and *Burnie Advocate,* and weekly newspapers including *North Queensland Register, Queensland Country Life, The Land* (the group's oldest agricultural holding), *Stock & Land, Stock Journal,* and *Farm Weekly*. Monthly titles include *Agriculture Today* and *Australian Cotton Outlook* in New South Wales, *Farmer & Grazier* in Queensland, and *Queensland Farmer*. In addition, Rural Press publishes nearly 100 local newspapers. Rural Press's nearly 20 magazine titles include *Alternate Farmer, Australian Farm Journal, Australasian Flowers, Australian Horticulture, Farmer & Stockowner, Friday Mag, Good Fruit & Vegetables, Hoofs & Horns, Landcare,* and *The Grower,* among others. The company also publishes several titles in New Zealand, including *Straight Furrow, The Dairyman,* and *AgTrader*. Since the late 1990s, Rural Press also has built up an impressive portfolio of rural- and agricultural-related magazines and newspapers in the United States, including the Farm Progress Group, acquired in 1997 and featuring 35 state-focused editions. The company also operates a number of web sites targeting the Australian rural and farmer

market. Rural Press has built up a network of ten rural radio stations in Australia, including River94.9 FM Ipswich, 5RM Berri, 5RIV FM Berri, 1557 Wild Country, and 5CS Port Pirie (SA). Rural Press emerged from the breakup of the Fairfax publishing group in the late 1980s, and remains controlled by the John B. Fairfax wing of the Fairfax family. In the 2000s, however, the company has been rumored to have entered merger talks with John B. Fairfax Holdings, which controls the other half of the former Fairfax group. Rural Press is listed on the Australian Stock Exchange. In 2004, the company's revenues topped AUD ($400 million). John B. Fairfax remains company chairman. Brian K. McCarthy serves as managing director.

Founding an Australian Publishing Empire in the 19th Century

Rural Press's roots lay in the development of the Fairfax family publishing empire. John Fairfax, a native of Warwickshire, England, had published two newspapers in Leamington before emigrating to Australia in the late 1830s. In 1841, Fairfax acquired his first Australian paper, the *Sydney Herald,* which grew into the country's largest newspaper, with a circulation of 4,000 by 1851. The following year Fairfax was joined by son Charles, and the company became known as John Fairfax & Sons. After Fairfax died in 1877, the company was taken over by two other sons (Charles died in 1863), who expanded the business with the launch of a second newspaper that same year. James Reading Fairfax became sole owner of the company in 1886, backed by sons James Oswald and Geoffrey.

The Fairfax company converted to the status of limited corporation in 1916. James Reading had remained as head of the company until his death in 1919, at which time James Oswald took over the company's lead until his own death in 1926. In that year, his son, Warwick Fairfax, became head of the company, a position he would maintain until 1987.

Throughout this time, the Fairfax company expanded to become one of Australia's leading publishing and media groups. In addition to its own newspaper launches, the company grew through a number of acquisitions, such as the purchase in 1934 of *Home and Art* in Australia, as well as the *Illawarra*

Mercury, through the purchase of *South Coast Times* in 1969, among many others. In 1971, the company launched its own national weekend paper, the *National Times.* Yet the *Sydney Morning Herald* remained the group's flagship.

The company also acquired stakes in a number of Australian media groups, such as the purchase of 45 percent of the *Newcastle Morning Herald* and the *Newcastle Sun* in 1961, and a minority stake in David Syme & Co., publisher of the *Melbourne Herald,* among other titles. The company later acquired majority control of the Syme company, passing the 50 percent mark in 1972. The company also acquired full control of the Newcastle titles in 1978. In that year, as well, Fairfax acquired control of the radio group Macquarie Broadcasting Holdings.

In the meantime, Fairfax had begun to explore interests beyond newspaper publishing. In 1955, the company acquired the license to operate the television channel ATN7 in the Sydney market. To help pay for its extension into broadcasting, the company went public in 1956. The Fairfax family maintained control of the company for the time being. By the early 1980s, however, the family's shareholding had slipped below majority control. This left the company vulnerable to a takeover—which came in 1981 from Holme a Court.

The company successfully fought off that bid, and launched a new expansion policy in the 1980s. An important part of the group's growth came from a rapid expansion into Australia's regional newspaper market, and especially the market for rural and agricultural publications.

The Fairfax company's involvement in Australia's rural and agricultural newspaper market stemmed from its 1970 purchase of a 25 percent stake in the Land Group, publisher of Australia's oldest newspaper dedicated to Australia's farm community, *The Land.* Launched in 1911, *The Land* took on the mission of promoting the interests of the country's agricultural community, more specifically, in its New South Wales market. Fairfax continued to increase its shareholding in the Land Group, eventually acquiring control of the company.

Rural Specialist in the 1980s

The takeover attempt from Holme a Court at the beginning of the 1980s had far-reaching consequences for the Fairfax company. When Warwick Fairfax died in 1987, his son, also named Warwick, took over as head of the family's shareholders group. In 1988, Warwick Fairfax, fearful of the possibility of another hostile takeover attempt, launched his own takeover offer in order to de-list the company from the stock exchange. Another faction of the Fairfax family, led by half-brother John B. Fairfax, opposed the takeover, however.

Warwick Fairfax formed Tryart Pty. Ltd. as a takeover vehicle, which acquired the Fairfax group for AUD 2.25 billion—including a cash payment to the John B. Fairfax faction. Yet Tryart quickly stumbled over its heavy debt taken on in order to complete the takeover and was forced to sell off a number of assets, such as its rural publications, including *The Land,* and the Courier group of suburban newspaper titles. These were picked up by John B. Fairfax and brother Timothy as the cornerstones for their new publishing empire, Rural Press. The Fairfax brothers subsequently merged the Courier titles with the holdings of another family-controlled media group, Hannan, creating Independent Print Media Group (IPMG). In the meantime, Tryart continued to flounder; when the stock market crashed at the end of the decade, the company was forced to declare bankruptcy. A new group of investors bought up the company, which continued to be known as John B. Fairfax Holdings, in 1990, marking the end of the Fairfax family's involvement in what remained as one of Australia's top media groups.

Rural Press started off the 1990s as a specialist publisher of rural and regional newspaper and magazines dedicated to Australia's farming and agricultural community. This position was boosted with the purchase of a 60 percent stake in *The Examiner,* serving Launceston, in 1991. The company soon began to spread its wings into other media, however, and in 1993, the company entered radio broadcasting, acquiring its first radio licenses. The company continued acquiring stations, including Queensland Maranoa stations in 1994 and the Cairns-Townsville-Mackay radio network in 1995. By the middle of the 1990s, Rural Press's radio holdings included 27 radio licenses in Queensland, South Australia, and Western Australia.

The year 1995 marked a significant milestone for the development of Rural Press, when the company acquired Macquarie Publications. That purchase included some 56 newspapers and magazines focused on the New South Wales market, including daily, weekly, and monthly titles. Formed in 1949, after husband-and-wife team Leo and Pat Armati purchased the *Dubbo Liberal,* the Macquarie Group had grown into Australia's leading regional publishing company by the early 1990s. Among Rural Press's newly acquired titles were Macquarie flagships such as *Western Magazine, Town & Country Magazine,* and *Southern Weekly Magazine.*

Rural Press boosted its penetration of the rural market with the creation of the Farming Online web site in 1996. The following year, the company breached another new frontier when it purchased the Farm Progress Group. Based in the United States, Farm Progress was that market's leading farming and rural publishing group, with 26 regional editions covering 43 states. Farm Progress also held the United States' oldest farming title, *Prairie Farmer,* which was launched in 1841, as well as *Feedstuffs,* introduced in 1873, and the leading title targeting the U.S. livestock feed industry.

The acquisition of Farm Progress led Rural Press to sell off most of its broadcasting assets, at least temporarily, that same year. The company sold off its Broadcast Division to DMG Regional Radio, for AUD 88 million. By 1998, however, the company staged a return to radio, buying up Coast & Country Broadcasting Services Pty. Limited, which operated two radio stations in Port Lincoln and Port Pirie. The purchase boosted the group's portfolio of radio stations to five.

Major Australian Media Group in the New Century

Acquisitions played a major role in Rural Press's development into the mid-2000s. In 1998, the company purchased Federal Capital Press of Australia Pty. Ltd., paying AUD 164 million to acquire its holdings. Federal titles included *Canberra Times, Sunday Times, The Chronicle,* a free weekly, and *Valley View,* a free tabloid. In that year, the company relaunched its revitalized Broadcast Division, which operated primarily through a joint venture established with Unitel Corporation. Rural Press's share of the joint venture, called Star Broadcasting Network Pty. Ltd., stood at 50.1 percent. In 1999, the company launched its seventh station, Magic FM, in Port Lincoln.

Other acquisitions followed into the 2000s, including the purchase of the *Bellingen Shire Courier Sun,* based in the New South Wales North Coast, and a 50 percent stake in *Golden Mail,* a free weekly serving Kalgoorlie, in Western Australia, both acquired in 2001. The following year, the company bought up *The Bendigo Advertiser* and the *Wimmera Mail-Times,* both serving Horsham, Victoria.

Rural Press sought new acquisition opportunities in order to boost its portfolio of titles. Its next purchase came in 2003, when it bid AUD 47.6 million to acquire 85 percent of Harris & Co., a publishing group based in Tasmania, which held the remaining 40 percent of the *Launceston Examiner.* Another prominent Harris title was the *Burnie Advocate.*

In the meantime, the Fairfax family sold off its half of IPMG, raising AUD 200 million ($134 million), in 2003. That sale came amid rumors that Rural Press had been involved in merger talks with John B. Fairfax, a move that would create Australia's leading media group. The two sides denied their interest in merging, however.

Instead, Rural Press maintained its acquisition drive. In 2003, the company acquired full control of the Star Broadcasting Network, which by then had grown to ten stations. Then, at the end of 2004, the company struck again, buying several titles, including the *Hepburn Shire Advocate* in Victoria and the *Senior Post* in Western Australia. In December of that year, the company added the *Moree Champion* in New South Wales and the *Goondiwindi Argus* in Queensland. With more than 140 titles, Rural Press remained true to the Fairfax family tradition of Australian media dominance in the new century.

Principal Subsidiaries

Agricultural Publishers Pty. Ltd.; Bridge Printing Office Pty. Ltd. S.A.; Canweb Printing Pty. Ltd.; Country Publishers Pty. Ltd. S.A.; Cudgegong Newspapers Pty. Ltd.; Esperance Holdings Pty. Ltd.; Examiner Properties Pty. Ltd.; Farming Online Pty. Ltd.; Farm Progress Holding Co, Inc.; Golden Mail Pty. Ltd.; Harris and Company Pty. Ltd. (85%); Hibiscus Happynings Pty. Ltd.; Hunter Distribution Network Pty. Ltd. VIC; J & R Graphics Pty. Ltd.; Macleay Valley Happynings Pty. Ltd.; Media Investments Pty. Ltd. S.A.; Merredin Advertiser Pty Ltd.; Mountain Press Pty Ltd. (88%); Northern Newspapers Pty. Ltd. S.A.; NZ Rural Press Ltd.; Port Lincoln Times Pty. Ltd. S.A.; ProAg Pty. Ltd.; Queensland Community Newspapers Pty. Ltd.; Regional Printers Pty. Ltd.; Regional Publishers (VIC) Pty. Ltd.; Regional Publishers (Western Victoria) Pty. Ltd.; Regional Publishers Pty. Ltd.; RP Interive Pty. Ltd.; RPL Technology Pty. Ltd.; Rural Press (North Queensland) Pty. Ltd.; Rural Press (USA) Ltd.; Rural Press Printing (Victoria) Pty. Ltd.; Rural Press Printing Pty. Ltd.; Rural Press Regional Media (WA) Pty. Ltd.; Rural Press USA Inc.; Rural Press Pty. Ltd.; Rural Publishers Pty. Ltd. S.A.; Regional Media Pty. Ltd. S.A.; Snowy Mountains Publications Pty. Ltd.; Star Broadcasting Network Pty. Ltd.; Stock Journal Publishers Pty. Ltd. S.A.; The Advocate Newspaper Pty. Ltd.; The Barossa News Pty. Ltd. S.A.; The Examiner Newspaper Pty. Ltd.; The Federal Capital Press of Australia Pty. Ltd.; The Miller Publishing Co., Inc; The Printing Press Pty. Ltd.; The Queanbeyan Age Pty. Ltd.; Tofua Holdings Pty. Ltd.; West Australian Rural Media Pty. Ltd. WA; Western Australian Primary Industry Press Pty. Ltd. WA; Western Magazine Pty. Ltd. (75%); Whyalla News Properties Pty. Ltd. S.A.

Principal Divisions

Regional Publishing; Architectural Publishing; Printing; Broadcasting; Interactive.

Principal Competitors

News Corporation Ltd.; AAPT Ltd.; John B. Fairfax Holdings Ltd.; Independent Print Media Group; Publishing and Broadcasting Ltd.; APN News and Media Ltd.; Independent Newspapers Ltd.

Further Reading

''Australia's Fairfax Family Sells Stake in IPMG for US$ 134.4 mln,'' *AsiaPulse News,* July 2, 2003.

''Australia's Rural Press Fall Short of Harris & Co. Acquisition,'' *Asia Pulse,* December 30, 2003.

Buffini, Fiona, ''Rural Press in the Thick of the Action,'' *Australasian Business Intelligence,* February 14, 2005.

''Fairfax, Rural Press Merger Talks Denied,'' *B&T,* September 16, 2002.

Kappelle, Liza, ''Publisher Tunes in to Radio,'' *Courier-Mail,* September 7, 2004.

''Rural Press Chief Can't See Any Black Holes Looming,'' *SMH,* February 11, 2005.

Ryan, Rosemary, ''Newspapers Target Rich Seniors,'' *Australasian Business Intelligence,* March 24, 2005.

Shoebridge, Neil, ''Rural Press Keen to Stay in the Hunt,'' *Australasian Business Intelligence,* February 10, 2005.

—M.L. Cohen

Sabre Holdings Corporation

3150 Sabre Drive
Southlake, Texas 7609
U.S.A.
Telephone: (682) 605-1000
Fax: (682) 605-8267
Web site: http://www.Sabre-holdings.com

Public Company
Incorporated: 1996
Employees: 9,000
Sales: $2.13 billion (2004)
Stock Exchanges: New York
Ticker Symbol: TSG
SIC: 561510 Travel Agencies; 518210 Data Processing,
     Hosting and Related Services

Sabre Holdings Corporation is a leading distributor of electronic travel-related products and services in the world. The company provides information technology (IT) solutions to the travel and transportation industry which allow travel agents worldwide to electronically access booking information for airlines, railways, cruises, tours, hotels, and rental cars. In doing so, Sabre operates one of the largest privately owned real-time computer systems. The company also offers individual customers the option to set up travel reservations on the Internet through its easySabre and Travelocity services.

The Early Years

Although Sabre has been a freestanding entity for only a few years, its beginnings date back to 1946, when American Airlines brought computer technology to the travel industry with the Magnetronic Reservisor. One of the first computerized reservations systems, Magnetronic Reservisor was advanced to include basic computer file technology, so that a reservation agent could automatically check availability and sell or cancel seats. Later in the decade, American Airlines and IBM joined together to announce the Semi-Automated Business Research Environment—Sabre. The system cost an unprecedented $40

million, including expenses for initial research and development as well as the actual installation of the system.

After being introduced, Sabre evolved into an electronic gateway to provide access to reservation information about all types of travel-related items, including airlines, cars, and hotel reservations. The technology used to make reservations was also adapted to act as a means for customers to secure items such as flowers, theater tickets, and bon voyage gifts. Additionally, other services were provided to varied markets such as insurance providers, retailers, broadcasters, financial institutions, and manufacturers.

Growth in the 1980s and 1990s

In 1985, consumers with their own personal computers were introduced to the easySabre system, which offered individuals the access and ability to make travel-related arrangements in the comfort of their own homes. For the most part, however, the company provided its services to corporate clientele. In fact, until 1988, Sabre provided services only to AMR Corporation (AMR), its parent company, and one of AMR's other subsidiaries, American Airlines. Sabre's software and systems management services helped distinguish American as one of the most technologically advanced airlines.

At the end of the 1980s, Sabre's services began to be offered to other companies, including more than 130,000 travel agency terminals worldwide. The business gained by the addition of these travel agent customers came to represent over 50 percent of Sabre's IT revenue. By the mid-1990s, in fact, the company estimated that more than 40 percent of all travel agency airline bookings were made through Sabre, representing 65.8 percent of the company's revenues.

In the 1990s, Sabre provided its IT services to over 450 clients in 73 countries. Through this non-reservation-based area, Sabre worked with its parent, AMR, and with other transportation and financial services companies which had data problems. The company maintained three regional offices across the globe: one in Dallas/Ft. Worth, Texas; one in Sydney, Australia; and one in London, England. Each of these units was responsible for all aspects of Sabre's business and also provided support to local offices in their respective regions.

Independence from AMR in 1996

April 1996 brought the beginnings of Sabre's repositioning as a separate legal entity from AMR. The decision to do so was made based on Sabre's position as one of the nation's largest computerized reservation services, as well as on its strong growth in the IT field. A prospectus was filed with the U.S. Securities and Exchange Commission which covered an initial public offering of as much as $550 million of Class A common stock. Approximately 20 percent of this stock was offered by late summer in 1996, causing parent company AMR's stock to jump 5.5 percent.

Sabre's executives noted that the company's performance during its first year as a public company was the best in its history. Booking volumes outside the United States grew at a compound annual rate of 28 percent, and during 1996 the company introduced new products for both of their primary areas of business: information technology solutions and electronic travel distribution.

In the midst of continued positive change and growth for Sabre, one of its travel agent reservation software products was identified in an investigation of its fellow AMR subsidiary, American Airlines. Allegations were made that the company had programmed bias into the computer reservation system used by travel agencies, meaning that add-on software used when booking with Sabre's product was biased toward American's flights. The allegations were made against American by Northwest Airlines and The Department of Transportation in October 1996. Developed by Sabre, "Preference MAAnager" was said to have violated rules against building bias into computer reservation system displays. This particular software could reorder flights on the agents' screens either to highlight or show only American flights, even though the Department of Transportation had made it illegal to bias a reservation system in 1984. In 1992, however, the department had decided that travel agents could install add-on software, such as "Preference MAAnager," from third-party vendors. A Department of Transportation administrative law judge later ruled that American was not technically violating federal rules by offering "Preference MAAnager" free to travel agents.

Innovations in Technology: 1996–98

In March 1996, the company joined together with Worldview Systems Corporation to create and introduce "Travelo-

city" for use by those individuals looking to make their own travel arrangements online. This Web site communicated directly with the Sabre reservation system and was soon the largest travel site on the World Wide Web that was not an airline-run site. The Web site's system was developed for those individuals who wished to peruse and purchase travel industry offerings via their personal computers. Attempting to lure customers onto the Web by offering extras that were not available from a traditional agent, Travelocity had a traveler-paging option to provide the customer with booking information up to a maximum of five flights. Other features available online through Travelocity included an instant travel reservation system, a lowest-fare finding device, electronic ticketing, consolidator fares for pre-purchased bulk sales to travel agencies, international booking capability, and a travel agency directory.

After its introduction, Travelocity soon registered in excess of 1.6 million members and began logging about 15 million hits monthly. This helped the site earn a ranking among the Top 25 Web sites used at work, according to two separate research firms, RelevantKnowledge and Media Metrix. For every online booking transaction, Sabre received approximately 5 percent from the airline, car rental company, or hotel (arrangements made through a travel agent earned $3 per purchase). Travelocity made more than $100 million in travel-related bookings on the Web in 1997, its first full year of operation. Industry analysts noted the sudden increase in travel industry revenues that originated online from sites like Travelocity and predicted that the percentage of industry revenues garnered online would only continue to increase in coming years. According to the Travel Industry Association of America, the $827 million worth of bookings which were made in 1997 represented a mere 1 percent of earnings in the travel industry. The Travel Industry Association predicted this figure could reach 5 percent by the year 2000, however.

Also launched in 1996 was Sabre Business Travel Solutions (Sabre BTS), the company's online corporate travel management service. This gave both business travelers and their travel counselors, either separately or together, an easy and convenient way to make or change their own travel plans according to corporate policies through their computers, with 24-hour access and travel agency support. In addition to automating travel planning and reporting, Sabre BTS was also designed to cut up to 30 percent of the costs associated with business travel management. The products offered consisted of integrated modules for travel booking, policy compliance, and expense reporting. Able to track all travel-related spending ranging from pre-planning to reimbursement, businesses could save as much as 30 percent in total travel management costs by using Sabre BTS. An additional feature of Sabre BTS was an overhead map of the airplane with all available seats mapped out, noting such details as exit rows, first-class accommodations, and the location of the galley. Any specific seat could be reserved, changed, or canceled by the user at any time before travel. By March 1998, Sabre BTS was used by 120 customers, more than any other system for corporate travel management.

Sabre was awarded six patents in July 1997 by the U.S. Patent and Trademark Office for new information management systems technology. Covered by the patents were the Availability Processor for reservation inventory control applications, CRSSim tech-

---

Key Dates:

1946: American Airlines purchases the Magnetronic Reservoir, an early computer reservations system; a later partnership with IBM produces the Semi-Automated Business Research Environment (Sabre).

1985: The easySabre system for personal computers is launched.

1988: Sabre begins expanding its clientele beyond American Airlines and other subsidiaries of holding company AMR Corporation.

1990s: Sabre provides its information technology services to over 450 clients in 73 countries.

1996: Sabre separates from AMR Corporation and goes public; Travelocity and Business Travel Solutions are introduced.

1997: Internet-based Planet Sabre is introduced; the company purchases US Airways Group's information technology assets.

1998: Sabre enters a joint venture with travel services company ABACUS International Holdings.

1999: Sabre renames itself Sabre Holdings Corporation.

2000s: Waning airline revenues spark crisis over the cost of using such global distribution systems (GDSs) as Sabre.

---

nology for business-generating computer reservations systems, the Shell Communication Interface Program, the SQL Mapper, and Interactive Analysis System—or Datawise—technologies.

In 1998, Sabre BTS was redesigned to offer new features such as the ability to access departure and arrival gates and times, restrictions, cancellation terms, and ticketing guidelines. The user could receive an automated pre-travel authorization of booked reservation via e-mail. Also included was an updated car rental and hotel booking process, which allowed travelers at separate company sites the ability to add personal preferences such as frequent flyer numbers.

Announcement of an alliance with MobileStar Network Corp. was made in August 1998. This arrangement would supply travelers greater mobile access to their travel plans through wireless high-speed access to the Sabre BTS online booking tool. Connecting through their laptop via a PC card device with a small radio and ethernet local area network adapter, the new Sabre system allowed users to connect with its network without the bother of having to find an analog phone line. That same month, Sabre BTS was upgraded once again to include information such as online hotel maps, weather information, and group travel-related information. Sabre also announced plans to team up with IBM to develop a "next generation" corporate travel management solution. The combination of Sabre BTS's policy compliance tools and online booking and IBM's Web-based Electronic Expense Reporting Solution would provide the consumer with easy installation, ongoing customer support, and the convenience of Web access to all of their booking and expense reporting tools.

Planet Sabre, the industry's first Internet-enabled application for travel agencies, was introduced in early February 1997.

Using the same technology that had been developed for Travelocity, Planet Sabre integrated every tool a travel agent could need into one customizable desktop display. This easy-to-use Microsoft Windows 95-based software suite greatly simplified the booking of travel arrangements. Through Planet Sabre or Turbo Sabre, the company offered a private Web site for travel agents called Sabre AgentExplorer. The site featured a customized city pair chart showing the lowest published airfare available for those pairs of cities most frequented by their customers. The bulletin board also showed details regarding the fares, which included the previous lowest fare and the airline offering the fare, among others.

Development Strategies in the Late 1990s

A $4.3 billion, 25-year contract between US Airways Group Inc. and Sabre Group Holdings, Inc. was signed December 12, 1997, selling off US Airways' information technology assets. The deal was arranged so that Sabre could run US Airways' data center operations, communications and help desks, and software applications, while also providing hardware and personnel. Additionally, the contract called for significant support by Sabre for the airline's ground and flight operations, maintenance and engineering activities, internal reservations system, sales, and cargo operations. All US Airways' software was scheduled to be converted to a Sabre application by 1999.

February 1998 brought another multimillion-dollar agreement for the company. ABACUS International Holdings Ltd. and Sabre signed a joint venture agreement called ABACUS International, a new Singapore-based travel services company. In this agreement, Sabre was to invest $139 million in cash, plus about $100 million in assets, while becoming the provider of computer reservations for the company. In a second agreement, over 7,000 ABACUS travel agencies across the world adopted a customized version of the Sabre reservations service, which was called "ABACUS powered by Sabre." This venture added almost 150,000 terminals in more than 40,000 travel agencies in 108 countries and positioned Sabre to become a key player in Asian travel technology.

In a 1998 effort to bolster customer confidence in the safety of Sabre's online reservation and purchase systems, the company introduced its Shop Safe Guarantee. By using the site's secure server, this service would be provided in the event of credit fraud and reimburse the individual's liability fee up to $50. Travelocity joined the Better Business Bureau (BBB) online initiative, which was dedicated to ethical online marketing practices. The site's BBB online profile could be viewed through the Travelocity Web site.

Throughout many different industries, Sabre has been recognized as a leader in information technology solutions and operations. Among the awards the company has earned are the ORSA Award for "The Best Operations Research Group in the Country (U.S.A.)" (first recipient) by the Operations Research Society of America, the Franz Edelman Award for "Best Operations Research Project in the World" by the Institute of Management Sciences, the Network World User Excellence Award, the UNIX-Expo Award—International Excellence in Open Systems, the Datamation Client Server Award, the Partners in Leadership Award, the Strategic Mission Award, the ESPRIT

Award, the Object Management Group Object Application Award, the Business Traveler International Magazine Award, and the People's Voice Award.

Just a few short years after Sabre incorporated as a publicly held company, its personnel and expertise had led it to become one of the largest travel service providers in the world. Through its combination of strengths, Sabre was able to provide its customers with cutting-edge technology and over 150 products and services that could be used by groups ranging from airlines to foodservice providers. Its unequaled customer service offered support 365 days per year to those clients with Sabre intelligent workstations, communications networks, and printers. As the 20th century came to a close, Sabre seemed to be poised for further growth and innovation in the future.

Record Years Round Out the 20th Century

Sabre ended 1998 with a record net profit of $231.9 million, an increase of 16 percent over 1997, on revenues of $2.3 billion, 29 percent higher than 1997. Much of the year was spent preparing for two large rollouts of modifications to computer systems: Y2K system compliance repairs and the conversion of US Airways' computer system to a Sabre application. Technicians spent over one million hours on the latter project, which involved over 30,000 computers and printers at 400 locations around the globe. The rollout itself was completed literally overnight, in less than six hours during the night of December 5, 1998.

In March 1999, the company rolled out another change, renaming itself from Sabre Group Holdings to Sabre Holdings Corporation and streamlining its business units into two major branches. The company's legacy travel distribution business comprised one branch. The other branch, which reflected Sabre's ongoing drive toward diversifying its client base, provided information technology outsourcing. Clients of this, the fastest-growing of Sabre's business segments, included American Airlines, US Airways, and Canadian Airlines, as well as hotels, car rental companies, cruise lines, and electronic ticket distributors worldwide. The London Underground and the French railway system contracted for software to handle complex scheduling and routing information. Other technology clients included oil and gas companies, manufacturers, and financial companies.

By July 1999, Sabre's operating income rose 11 percent over 1998, reaching $77 million, or 59 cents per share, beating Wall Street estimates of 56 cents per share. Analysts noted that the company achieved its gains despite a general decline in profits among air carriers because of its stable $4 per ticket booking fee, which ensured steady income in the face of market fluctuations that cut into airlines' bottom lines. In order to strengthen the business's position, AMR, the parent company of American Airlines, Sabre, and the regional carrier American Eagle, spun off its 83 percent stake in the travel technology company. The move was expected to increase Sabre's business opportunities with non-AMR companies, which grew from 58 percent of Sabre's clientele in 1994 to nearly 70 percent in 1997. This fell below the 15 to 25 percent per year increases the company desired to offset leveling-off of revenues in the increasingly crowded travel industry.

Changing the Way the Travel Business Is Done

By 2001, Sabre was not alone in the online travel marketplace. Competitors including European-based Amadeus, Microsoft spinoff Expedia, Worldspan, Galileo, and Orbitz, many with origins in airline-owned computer reservation systems similar to Sabre, offered online travel booking. It was a market that could only grow so much, however, and saturation coupled with a decline in leisure travel after the terrorist attacks on the United States of September 11, 2001 slowed airline business. Rising fuel costs struck another blow to the air travel industry and sent carriers scrambling for ways to cut costs and remain solvent. One of the carriers' targets was the fees charged by Sabre and other booking services.

In 2002, fees charged to airlines by global distribution systems (GDSs) were expected to top $2.2 billion. Such fees averaged around $4.36 per ticket, according to a study commissioned by Orbitz and conducted by Global Aviation Associates. Sabre responded to increasing complaints from airlines by devising a corporate travel booking application, Get-There. The application was used to book fares through Corporate Connect, a program that offered airlines 50 percent off fees on tickets. Sabre passed the cost of the fee cuts on to travel agents by ceasing to pay them incentives in the form of per-ticket commissions. Once a travel agency signed on with Sabre, thus getting access to somewhat cheaper fares, it would no longer receive commissions on corporate travel bookings. The solution proved unpopular with agents, who pointed out that the less-expensive fares could already be accessed through airlines' Web sites, thus negating any value the program might have for agencies. Sabre's competing GDSs, however, concurred that eliminating commissions to agents and changing the way ticket bookings were made and paid for were essential to the continued health of the industry. Northwest Airlines made an attempt in August 2004 to steer travelers away from GDSs, agents, and ticket counters by slapping a set of fees on such purchases. The $7.50 fee attached to GDS bookings by the airline inspired Sabre to move Northwest fare information to a less prominent spot on its GDS displays on the grounds that Northwest violated fare contracts negotiated with Sabre. Northwest responded by filing a breach of contract suit in a federal court in the airline's home state of Minnesota. Sabre replied in kind with a breach of contract suit in a federal court in its home state of Texas. Although Northwest backed down and repealed the new fees, the message to the travel booking industry was clear: agency commissions must be cut. In 2005, Sabre reported it had paid GDS users $36 million more in fees in 2004 than it paid in 2003, down from an increase of $63 million between 2003 and 2002.

Principal Subsidiaries

Sabre Airline Solutions; Sabre Travel Network; Travelocity.

Principal Competitors

Expedia Inc.; Galileo Inc.; Orbitz Inc.; Worldspan Technologies Inc.; Amadeus Global Travel Distribution S.A.

Further Reading

Allen, Margaret, "Magistrate's Ruling Has Travel Agents on Defensive," *Dallas Business Journal*, December 5, 1997, p. 14.

Berry, Kate, "Travel Stock Jumps on Sales, Internet News," *Wall Street Journal*, April 20, 1998, p. B11L.

Browning, E.S., and Scott McCartney, "Heard on the Street: AMR's Offering of Sabre Shares Seeks to Tap Hidden Value in Reservations, Consulting Unit," *Wall Street Journal*, October 7, 1996, p. C2.

Caldwell, Bruce, "Separation Anxiety for IT?," *Information Week*, April 22, 1998, p. 18.

Campbell, Jay, "Sabre Biz Sites Besiege Market," *Travel News*, April 28, 2003, p. 1.

Compart, Andrew, Jerry Limone, Michael Milligan, and Dennis Schaal, "Agents Applaud U.S. Airways-Sabre Fare Plan," *Travel Weekly*, October 28, 2002, p. 155.

Donoghue, J.A., "The Big Switch," *Air Transport World*, October 2003, p. 42.

Flint, Perry, "Sabre Unleashed," *Air Transport World*, November 1996, pp. 95–96.

Foley, John, "Sabre's Challenge," *Information Week*, August 18, 1997, p. 83.

Forster, Julie, "Northwest Sues Ticket Distributor Sabre," *Knight-Ridder/Tribune News Service*, August 26, 2004, item K2699.

Jonas, David, "GDS Incentive Growth Slows," *Business Travel News*, March 21, 2005, p. 4.

Madden, John, "Sabre Rattles Its Own Cage in Restructuring," *PC Week*, April 5, 1999, p. 64.

Mauer, Jennifer Fron, "AMR Strike Could Be a Boon for Online Travel Industry," *Dow Jones News Service*, February 14, 1997.

McCartney, Scott, "AMR Moves Closer to Spinoff of Sabre Group," *Wall Street Journal*, August 9, 1996, p. C2.

——, "U.S. Charges American Airlines Puts Bias Toward Carrier in Reservation Service," *Wall Street Journal*, October 29, 1996, p. A8.

Michels, Jennifer, "Sabre Takes a Stab at GDS Costs with Corporate Connect Plan," *Travel Agent*, July 29, 2002, p. 10.

Reed, Dan, "Demand for Air Travel Boosts Earnings at Fort Worth, Texas-Based Sabre," *Knight-Ridder/Tribune Business News*, July 21, 1999.

——, "Fort Worth, Texas-Based American Airlines Begins Stock Spinoff," *Knight-Ridder/Tribune Business News*, March 1, 2000.

——, "Profits Hit Record Levels for Fort Worth, Texas-Based Travel Firm," *Knight-Ridder/Tribune Business News*, May 17, 1999.

"Sabre to Slash Agent Payouts," *Travel Trade Gazette UK & Ireland*, December 1, 2003, p. 4.

Shippy, D'Ann Mabray, "Layoffs Announced at Fort Worth, Texas-Based Travel Reservations Firm," *Knight-Ridder/Tribune Business News*, September 1, 1999.

Vijayan, Jaikumar, "Sabre Lands U.S. Airways Outsourcing," *Computerworld*, September 22, 1997, p. 43.

Wagner, Mitch, "Travel Service Providers Broaden Online Offerings," *Computerworld*, July 21, 1997, p.49.

—Melissa West
—update: Jennifer Gariepy

Saul Ewing LLP

1500 Market Street, 38th Floor
Philadelphia, Pennsylvania 19102-2186
U.S.A.
Telephone: (215) 972-7777
Fax: (215) 972-7725
Web site: http://www.saul.com

Private Company
Founded: 1921 as Saul, Ewing, Remick & Saul
Employees: 530
Sales: $118.5 million (2004)
NAIC: 541110 Offices of Lawyers

Saul Ewing LLP is a major mid-Atlantic multidisciplinary law firm, employing more than 250 attorneys and another 325 supporting professional staff. In addition to its headquarters in Philadelphia, Pennsylvania, the firm maintains offices in Chesterbrook and Harrisburg, Pennsylvania; Newark and Princeton, New Jersey; Wilmington, Delaware; Baltimore, Maryland; and Washington, D.C. Saul Ewing does work in more than 20 major areas of law, including healthcare; bankruptcy and restructuring; litigation; business; labor; real estate; public finance; personal wealth, estates, and trusts; utilities; and environmental. Clients range from individuals to corporations, their needs met by a cross-practice approach that employs teams of attorneys with varied expertise. Saul Ewing is organized as a partnership, led by an executive committee and a managing partner elected for a four-year term. Providing further structure are department chairs and office managing partners.

Heritage Dating to the 1800s

Saul Ewing traces its lineage to one of the greatest attorneys in U.S. history, John Graver Johnson, a man who ''in the opinion of some well-qualified judges [was] the greatest lawyer in the English-speaking world,'' *The New York Times* wrote at the time of his death. His illustrious legal career notwithstanding, Johnson today is best remembered for donating more than 1,200 paintings to the Philadelphia Museum of Art. The son of a blacksmith, he was born in 1841. At a time when law schools were not the

custom, Johnson learned his trade after high school by serving as a document clerk in a law office. At 21, he was admitted to the bar and launched his distinguished career. He was only 28 when he became general counsel for the Pennsylvania Company, a major bank and trust company that today is part of the Wachovia family. At that time, Johnson played an instrumental role in the creation of the new Philadelphia Naval Yard at League Island. Johnson combined a photographic memory with an incisive intellect to become one of the most sought-after attorneys in the country, serving the interests of industry barons such as Andrew Carnegie, J.P. Morgan, Henry Clay Frick, and John D. Rockefeller. He also marched to his own drummer, refusing to travel to New York City, forcing prominent men to visit his Philadelphia offices where they would often be seated next to everyday people, whose much smaller cases he took on at reduced rates. Everyone was made to wait their turn. Johnson was also known to charge modestly for the work he did for corporate clients, a practice that caused occasional embarrassment for co-counsels who presented much higher bills for performing far less work. Nevertheless, Johnson became a wealthy man, due in large part to his enormous capacity for work, allowing him to indulge in his passion for collecting art, a field in which he was self-taught. After a legal career that lasted more than half a century, Johnson handled more than 10,000 court cases, including a staggering 168 cases before the U.S. Supreme Court. Today, only a handful of attorneys argue as many as ten cases before the Supreme Court.

When Johnson, who operated as a sole practitioner, died in April 1917, his law practice was taken over by his salaried associates, who formed the firm of Pritchard, Saul, Bayard & Evans, which maintained offices at 1835–43 Land Title Building in Philadelphia. In March 1921 the firm was dissolved and a split of attorneys occurred, leading to the foundation of today's Saul Ewing. Saul Ewing was originally formed as a general law practice called Saul, Ewing, Remick & Saul. Unlike Johnson, all of the partners, graduates of the University of Pennsylvania, had law school educations. The managing partner was a Johnson protégé, Maurice Bower Saul, who was also an important real estate developer. In 1925 the firm moved into new offices in the Packard Building at 15th and Chestnut Streets, a Saul project. His brother, Walter Biddle Saul, was the litigator, specializing in construction law and associated areas. Walter

Company Perspectives:

At Saul Ewing, we are dedicated to the key values of excellence, energy and enthusiasm: excellence in our legal services, the energy to succeed, and an enthusiasm for understanding and being responsive to our clients' needs. These core values are the hallmarks of our 85 years of service to clients.

Saul also was president of the Philadelphia School Board in the early 1950s and is the only living person after whom a Philadelphia public school (the Saul Agricultural High School) was named. Joseph Neff Ewing and Raymond M. Remick, who had become partners in Pritchard, Saul, Bayard & Evans in 1920, were well-respected real estate and estate lawyers, respectively. Remick wrote the treatise still used in Pennsylvania regarding trust and estate law.

Naming Earl G. Harrison As Partner in the Early 1940s

Shortly before the United States entered World War II in December 1941, the firm added Earl G. Harrison as a partner and changed its name to Saul, Ewing, Remick & Harrison. Eleven Saul Ewing attorneys and two clerks volunteered to serve in the military. By the end of the war all of the attorneys had attained officer rank, three won Bronze Stars, and Robert Sayre received the Legion of Merit. In the early 1950s Sayre achieved acclaim by defending Philadelphia teachers on a pro bono basis during the McCarthy anti-Communist witch hunts. During the war, Harrison, himself a World War I veteran, served as the United States Immigration Commissioner. Shortly after the fighting in Europe ended he was directed by President Truman to inspect the displaced persons camps in Europe housing Jewish concentration camp survivors. In his report to the president he wrote, ''We appear to be treating the Jews as the Nazis treated them, except we do not exterminate them.'' His recommendations became American policy and were instrumental in the United States prodding the British into permitting Jewish emigration to Palestine, eventually leading to the birth of Israel.

Early on, the historic contributions of its attorneys notwithstanding, Saul Ewing was very much a Philadelphia-focused law firm, representing some of the city's most important companies as well as developing a thriving regional municipal finance practice, heavily involved in the issuance of bonds for significant public works projects. The size of the firm increased modestly, from 20 attorneys in 1925 to 65 in 1975, when it moved to new accommodations at Centre Square West where Broad and Market Streets intersect in the heart of Philadelphia's Center City. During most of this time the firm was headed by Maurice Saul, ''the Boss,'' as he was called by associates. He retired in 1960, and died in 1974. He was succeeded as managing partner by Fred VanDenbergh, who served in that capacity until 1978. At this point the firm began to elect managing partners for three-year terms, which eventually evolved into four-year terms. Robert Sayre served as the firm's first elected managing partner.

Saul Ewing embarked on a period of significant growth during the 1980s, adding practices as well as expanding geo-graphically. In the early 1980s the firm added a healthcare practice and moved into Philadelphia's western suburbs, opening an office in Malvern to serve companies located along the Route 202 corridor in neighboring Chester County. Also during this time, litigation partner John J. Barrett, Jr., won a $6 million verdict against Mobil Oil, at the time a tremendous jury victory. The firm expanded by adding an office in Wilmington, Delaware, and added environmental and bankruptcy and reorganization practices. The firm further expanded by opening an office in Pennsylvania's capital city of Harrisburg. In the late 1980s, Saul Ewing opened an office in Princeton, New Jersey, to serve clients in the Princeton-Trenton, New Jersey corridor. To support its rapid expansion, Saul Ewing launched a major recruitment drive in the middle of the decade, hiring 15 attorneys in one stroke to add more litigators and bolster the firm's capabilities in business law.

In May 1986, then Philadelphia Police Commissioner Kevin M. Tucker appointed a 14-member Task Force to review the ''status and potential of the Philadelphia Police Department.'' The panel, composed of distinguished Philadelphians, included not one, but two Saul Ewing attorneys, Henry S. ''Hank'' Ruth, Jr., and J. Clayton Undercofler, III. Hank Ruth had started his legal career in the 1970s at Saul Ewing and left for Washington, D.C., where he was the last of four prosecutors in the Watergate scandal. Ruth returned to Saul Ewing after his career in Washington and served on the police commissioner's task force. The task force published a report and Hank Ruth was appointed the Vice Chair of the Philadelphia Advisory Group of ten other prominent Philadelphians to oversee the implementation of the recommendations. Two years later, Pennsylvania Governor Robert P. Casey tapped Undercofler to assume chairmanship of the Southeastern Pennsylvania Transportation Authority (SEPTA) board. The *Philadelphia Inquirer* called Mr. Undercofler a ''diplomat and a tenacious leader'' who ''effectively ended the squabbling on the SEPTA board.'' Several years later, Undercofler and partner David Moffitt served as special counsel to the Pennsylvania House of Representatives Judiciary Committee in connection with the impeachment of a Pennsylvania Supreme Court Justice. In 1990, Saul Ewing partners John Stoviak and Paul Hummer, as well as several associates, represented the Commonwealth of Pennsylvania in court cases brought by insurers challenging the constitutionality of what was a new auto insurance reform act. And, in a tie to the firm's founder, John G. Johnson, Saul Ewing's real estate lawyers in the late 1990s participated in the revitalization of the Philadelphia Naval Yard, successfully transforming the site into a thriving commercial hub.

In the early 1990s many law firms were adversely impacted by a recession that led to corporations reducing outside legal services, prompting a wave of mergers between law firms looking to fortify their balance sheets. At the time, Saul Ewing was Philadelphia's 13th largest law firm with 142 attorneys, most based in Philadelphia. As the economy rebounded, business picked up and Saul Ewing once again added attorneys, seeking to bolster its regional presence.

Late 1990s: A Major Merger

In September 1998 Saul Ewing merged with a smaller Baltimore law firm, Weinberg & Green, founded in 1920 by Leonard

Key Dates:

1917: Upon the death of Philadelphia attorney John Graver Johnson, the practice is taken over by Pritchard, Saul, Bayard & Evans.
1920: Weinberg & Sweeten is established in Baltimore.
1921: Pritchard, Saul is dissolved, resulting in the birth of Saul Ewing, led by Maurice Saul.
1930: Weinberg & Sweeten becomes Weinberg & Green.
1974: Maurice Saul dies.
1998: Saul, Ewing, Remick & Saul is merged with Weinberg & Green.
2000: The firm is renamed Saul Ewing LLP.
2003: A Washington, D.C., office is opened.
2005: A Newark, New Jersey, office is opened.

Weinberg and Howard Sweeten as Weinberg & Sweeten. It became Weinberg & Green in 1930 after the arrival of wunderkind attorney Howard Green, who despite being just 21 years of age held a Ph.D. and a law degree. When it merged with Saul Ewing, Weinberg & Green had 63 lawyers and a reputation for meeting the needs of closely held and emerging companies across a number of disciplines. The cultures of the two firms complemented one another, as did their specialties. According to the *Philadelphia Inquirer,* "The firms said they hope that by combining their legal staffs, they will significantly increase business in such specialized services as employee rights and pensions to health care and the environment. The deal broadens the geographic reach of both firms—their combined territory will stretch from New York to Maryland." Writing for the *Baltimore Business Journal,* Heather Reese maintained that the merger was "indicative of the direction in which the legal industry has begun to move. With businesses growing and expanding, law firms are looking for ways to meet their clients' legal and geographical needs, which often means joining forces. 'The law firms are looking to their clients and what their clients are looking for and need as they become more national in scope,' said Joseph Altonji of law firm consultant Hildebrandt Inc." Reese also wrote that the merger allowed both firms "to expand the depth of their practices—Weinberg & Green by adding stronger securities, public finances and health care practices, and Saul Ewing by growing its tax and labor and employee benefits groups."

After Saul Ewing and Weinberg & Green consolidated their operations, the combined firm truncated its name in 2000, becoming Saul Ewing LLP. A year later the firm expanded its specialties by launching a Baltimore-based human resources consulting group called Workplace Initiatives, or WISE. Unlike other large law firms in the area that housed labor and employment practices providing employment consulting and legal services, WISE offered packaged services to help businesses prevent problems by making sure they were in compliance with an increasing number of complex federal, state, and local workplace laws. WISE started out by focusing on mid-Atlantic region employers.

Leading the firm during this transitional period was Stephen S. Aichele, who took over as managing partner in 2001 after Litigation Partner John Stoviak stepped down after serving as managing partner for eight years. Aichele joined Saul Ewing in 1976 as a summer student and distinguished himself in the early 1990s when at 42 he assumed leadership of the real estate department at a time when the recession had devastated the sector. Under his guidance, the unit thrived, growing from 17 lawyers to 40. Taking the reins of the entire firm, he was now determined to raise the profile of Saul Ewing, which over the years had done little to court publicity. In addition, Aichele wanted to deepen the firm's bench. "The (firm's) Baby Boomers didn't have a strong generation above us," he told *Philadelphia Business Journal,* lamenting a weakness in the firm over the previous 15 years. "The danger is that we'll stay in those positions until we're 60 and lose a whole generation behind us. We need to make sure we get out of the way soon enough and bring along another generation." Aichele was not adverse to shaking things up. In 2002 the firm hired former lawyer-turned-marketing guru David H. Freeman to teach Saul Ewing attorneys sales and marketing techniques to attract new business and develop rainmakers. "Whenever you say sales, marketing or business development, people immediately leap to the Golden Arches," Aichele told Baltimore's *Daily Record.* Rather, the emphasis was on attorneys building personal relationships with clients to develop influence and trust that would lead to further business. The program also helped attorneys cope with rejection. "Lawyers like immediate success," Aichele said. "They were successful in high school, successful in college, successful in law school. Sales is 90 percent failure, and in marketing there is no expectation of work each time you make a call." Other concepts the program taught was how to better listen to clients and to start thinking like a potential client's lawyer before being retained.

Given the Baltimore office's proximity to Washington, D.C., in October 2003, Saul Ewing established an office in the nation's capital, not only to serve clients' needs in the District of Columbia but in northern Virginia as well. To advance the firm's strategic plan of becoming a mid-Atlantic powerhouse, in 2005 Saul Ewing opened an office in the New York City metropolitan area, established in Newark, New Jersey, by a group of public utilities lawyers. It was a natural expansion as Saul Ewing already did utility work in Princeton, Harrisburg, and Washington, D.C. In addition, the Newark office provided Saul Ewing with a toehold in a key market where the firm hoped to pick up clients in areas such as litigation and real estate law.

Saul Ewing had become one of the predominant law firms serving the mid-Atlantic region, a true generalist with successes across the legal spectrum. Its Bankruptcy and Restructuring Department won a high-profile case in front of the Fourth Circuit Court of Appeals establishing the rights of a licensor of software to preclude a debtor from returning the licensor's license rights without the licensor's sanction. The Business Department represented an IT consulting firm on a $60 million merger, and the Litigation Department scored a summary judgment for one of the largest petrochemical corporations. Moreover, the firm in 2005 became one of the first mid-Atlantic firms to hire a diversity program manager and pro bono counsel.

In early 2005, the firm launched "We're All In," a firm-wide initiative to provide legal assistance to low-income elderly and veterans living in the communities where Saul Ewing has offices. Through the program, the firm pledged to give a minimum of 25 hours per attorney each year to help meet the overwhelming needs of the elderly and veterans.

Principal Competitors

Adelberg, Rudow, Dorf & Hendler LLC; Venable LLP; Wiley, Rein & Fielding LLP; Wolf, Block, Schorr and Solis-Cohen.

Further Reading

Feiler, Jeremy, "Saul Ewing's New Head Sets His Course of Action," *Philadelphia Business Journal,* February 15, 2002.

Fernandez, Bob, "Philadelphia Legal Firm to Merge with Baltimore Law Practice," *Philadelphia Inquirer,* September 11, 1998.

Geier, Peter, "Philadelphia-Based Saul Ewing Law Firm Trains Attorneys in Sales and Marketing Concepts," *Daily Record* (Baltimore), July 18, 2003.

Reese, Heather, "Weinberg Merger No Surprise to Other Firms," *Baltimore Business Journal,* September 18, 1998, p. 9.

Rulison, Larry, "Saul Ewing Forms HR Business," *Baltimore Business Journal,* May 11, 2001, p. 5.

St. John, Gerard J., "This Is Our Bar," *Philadelphia Lawyer,* Winter 2002.

—Ed Dinger

ScanSource, Inc.

6 Logue Court
Greenville, South Carolina 29615
U.S.A.
Telephone: (864) 288-2432
Toll Free: (800) 944-2432
Fax: (864) 288-1165
Web site: http://www.scansource.com

Public Company
Incorporated: 1992 as ScanSource, Inc.
Employees: 887
Sales: $1.47 billion (2005)
Stock Exchanges: NASDAQ
Ticker Symbol: SCSC
NAIC: 423430 Computer and Computer Peripheral
    Equipment and Software Merchant Wholesalers

ScanSource, Inc., is a leading specialty technology distributor. It supplies value-added resellers with bar code scanners and printers, magnetic stripe readers, and other tools for electronic inventory management. ScanSource has distribution centers in Memphis, Toronto, Mexico, and Belgium. Its offerings include more than 34,000 products from more than 60 manufacturers. Most of its more than 16,000 customers supply solutions to SMBs (small to medium businesses).

Origins

ScanSource was formed at the end of 1992 to service resellers of point-of-sale (POS) and auto identification (AutoID) equipment. This labor-saving technology allowed the transfer of data without manual input of each character and included such devices as bar code and label printers, laser scanners, and magnetic stripe readers. AutoID technology was spreading pervasively into many other uses aside from inventory control, materials handling, distribution, shipping, and warehouse management. Scientific researchers were discovering its uses as well. POS products included terminals, receipt printers, pole displays, cash drawers, and peripheral equipment. ScanSource was known as the only AutoID and POS distributor that did not sell to end users.

Gates/FA Distributing Inc. provided logistical support for the joint venture with one of its former CEOs, Steve Owings, who also had led the PC maker Argent Technologies, Inc. (Both companies were located in Greenville, South Carolina.)

By 1991, large retail chains were devotees of bar code scanners and printers. Although smaller businesses were beginning to use them in PC-based applications, these types of devices typically were not carried by microcomputer resellers. Cash register companies had been supplying this market. ScanSource's backers felt that therein lay an excellent opportunity to capture a large share of the $2.5 billion bar coding market.

The company started with 19 employees. Demand increased steadily from the beginning. Within a few months, ScanSource was representing about 20 vendors, including AutoID market leader Symbol Technologies Inc., Fargo Electronics Inc., and Star Micronics America. Business continued to pour in as retail inventory management grew more complex. At the same time, AutoID and POS equipment were becoming more standardized, less dependent upon proprietary technology. This was expected to spur growth in the AutoID segment at an annual rate of 14 percent through the end of the century. The AutoID market was valued at $2.2 billion; the POS equipment market was valued at $2.6 billion.

In May 1993, ScanSource bought Marietta, Georgia-based Alpha Data Systems Inc., a ten-year-old company. The transaction introduced a national client list to ScanSource. The purchase of the equipment distribution portion of MicroBiz Corporation of Spring Valley, New York soon followed. The transaction was valued at approximately $650,000. MicroBiz, a $4-million-a-year company, developed PC-based POS software for small retail stores.

ScanSource ended its first fiscal year in June 1993, having lost $243,242 on sales of $2.4 million in its first seven months. The next six months, however, saw a profit of $64,597 on sales of $6.5 million, and fiscal year 1993–94 ended with sales of $16.1 million and a $352,000 profit.

An initial public offering in March 1994 raised $4.6 million in capital. The stock was a lively seller and within a couple of

---

Company Perspectives:

We believe in honesty and integrity in everything that we do. There is no alternative. We highly value our customers and vendors and are committed to meeting their needs quickly and fairly. We believe each employee's opinion counts and deserves respect. We encourage innovation and creativity from every employee, in every department. Mistakes that arise from good intentions and hard work are distinguished from those arising from lack of effort or carelessness. We are committed to an environment that respects and values the diverse backgrounds, interests and talents of our employees. We protect our company resources to benefit those who depend on us, such as our employees and shareholders. We are committed to helping those less fortunate in our communities by giving our time, talents and resources.

---

months the share price had nearly tripled from $5 to $14. Gates/FA owned a 12.5 percent stake, while Stephen Owings owned 15 percent. Fast growth was part of the plan. Company founders expected to reach $100 million in sales within five years.

Dropping Gates/FA in July 1994

With Arrow Electronics Inc.'s impending acquisition of Gates/FA, ScanSource cut ties to its partner in July 1994. Arrow also had begun to compete in the POS market. ScanSource was compensated $1.4 million to make up for losing its warehouse partner.

ScanSource found an operational replacement for Gates/FA in MicroAge Inc. The firm's warehouse and MIS agreement began in the fall of 1994. MicroAge, however, did not provide financing support. MicroAge's warehouse facilities were located in Cincinnati.

Several new product lines enhanced ScanSource revenues in 1995: Epson America receipt printers, Zebra Technologies bar code label printers, and Micro-Touch POS touch screen monitors. PC-based POS units continued to rise in popularity in small retail applications. At the same time, the Windows operating system reached new levels of acceptance, prompting upgrading throughout the market. ScanSource competed against 50 other distributors in the POS market, including a dozen specializing in products for small business. Besides peripherals such as pole displays, cash drawers, and scanners, ScanSource also offered specialized software suited to various retail applications.

ScanSource revenues reached $90 million in 1996, when the company had 101 employees. ScanSource, which had an exclusive relationship with IBM, was well positioned when the computer maker unveiled its new PC-based SureOne POS system in February 1996. ScanSource expected to sell 10,000 units per year with an end price of about $3,000 each. IBM's new integrated system contrasted with the typical set-up patched together by resellers and was backed by more marketing savvy.

A leading data collection technology company, Intermec Corporation, tapped ScanSource to service its value-added resellers (VARs) in February 1997. Intermec cited ScanSource's experience with this particular market as a deciding factor in choosing the company. At this time, ScanSource already had a state-of-the-art shipping facility in Memphis, Tennessee, as well as regional sales offices in Canada and the United States.

ScanSource created its Professional Services Group to focus on hand-held, wireless data collection devices. Clients for these products required extra support through the installation process. ScanSource used special events to grow its market. The Solutions USA show, co-sponsored by Globelle, introduced hundreds of resellers to new products from dozens of vendors. Transition Marketing, Inc. was created in fiscal 1996 by ScanSource and Globelle Corporation to sponsor such trade shows. (Globelle later sold back its shares in the venture.) ScanSource also cooperated with vendors in advertising through trade periodicals, direct mail, and other promotional avenues.

In 1997 ScanSource acquired another PC-oriented distributor, POS ProVisions of Canada, for $4.3 million worth of stock. ProVisions had 15 employees and garnered $12 million in annual sales.

New Ventures in the Late 1990s

ScanSource created Catalyst Telecom in 1997 to distribute business telephone and computer telephony integration (CTI) products. Telephony products included business telephone systems and fax and data applications. ScanSource worked with Lucent Technologies to bring this to fruition, marketing Lucent's telephone handsets, cables, and voice mail equipment. ScanSource bought telephony company ProCom Supply the same year. In 1998 the company added The CTI Authority, Inc., a maker of computer-based voice messaging devices, which had sales of $8 million a year.

ScanSource boasted a compound annual growth rate of 80 percent between 1994 and 1997. Operating income increased at a 92 percent compound annual rate during the same time period. In its 1996–97 fiscal year, ScanSource had $2.5 million in profits on revenues of $93.9 million. It aimed to double sales in 1999 as the POS, AutoID, and telephony markets moved further away from direct sales. Employees numbered 131 in August 1997.

As PC-based applications began to become important in commercial security systems, ScanSource planned to enter that market as well, most likely through acquisition. An additional stock offering raised $26 million in capital that could be used toward this purpose. (The offering, delayed because of low share prices, had originally aimed for $32.5 million.) ScanSource also was considering expanding into the Canadian CTI market.

Lucent began to require ScanSource subsidiary Catalyst and other distributors to stock more parts for its switches to facilitate their timely delivery, rather than waiting for orders to be placed to begin building them. Having the distributors complete the assembly allowed the switches to be shipped in a matter of days versus up to six weeks.

ScanSource continued using road shows to recruit PC-oriented VARs to its line of POS, AutoID, and CTI products. TechTeach '99 featured educational seminars from some of the top vendors, such as IBM, Lucent, and Symbol, designed to help resellers enter new markets. PC VARs accounted for ap-

Key Dates:

1992: ScanSource formed as joint venture of Gates/FA Distributing Inc.
1993: Alpha Data Systems and MicroBiz acquired.
1994: Company goes public, enters alliance with Micro-Age Inc.
1996: Transition Marketing trade show venture formed with Canada's Globelle Corporation.
1997: POS ProVisions of Canada and ProCom Supply acquired; Catalyst Telecom unit formed.
1998: The CTI Authority, Inc. acquired.
2001: Company opens European unit, expands in Latin America.
2004: Revenues exceed $1 billion.

proximately half of ScanSource's 9,300 clients. The rest were specialty technology VARs.

In 1998 ScanSource launched Catalyst Commerce and the Internet Fulfillment Group to allow customers to place orders over the Internet. They also could check inventories and get delivery tracking information on-line.

Both ScanSource and Catalyst Telecom achieved ISO 9002 certification in 1999. The process was completed in just eight months. The ISO 9000-series documents internationally accepted standards of quality management and assurance.

ScanSource's new ventures-business telephones, Catalyst Commerce, CTI, and Canada-performed as well as its core bar code and POS business, according to Mike Baur, company president.

Still Growing After 2000

The rapidly growing company retooled its management team in January 2000. Company president Michael Baur took the CEO role as Steven Owings stepped down to lead the Catalyst Commerce unit while remaining chairman of ScanSource. Three new management positions were created around the same time.

Sales were $494.7 million in fiscal 2000 with income of $13.8 million. The figures continued to rise, reaching sales of $630.7 million in 2001 and income of $16.5 million. With such results, its shares fared better than many tech stocks. After plunging to $27 when the Internet bubble burst, within a year it was about $50 (though off a pre-bubble high of $73).

ScanSource acquired e-commerce solution provider Black Arrow Capital Inc. in March 2000. Black Arrow had developed a new web store aimed at bar code resellers. A leading POS supplier, NCR, was added to ScanSource's partners in November 2000. ScanSource was aiming to convince more resellers to carry POS equipment. Selling points were higher margins and compatibility with the PC and networking market.

Azerty, Inc.'s PositiveID unit, a distributor of bar code equipment, was acquired in 2001. Another significant acquisi-

tion was the purchase of Pinacor's computer telephony integration (CTI) sales unit.

In 2002 ScanSource opened a new unit, Reseller Services. It offered solution providers a web portal allowing their clients to access the entire ScanSource inventory online, while the resellers could set their own prices.

The federal government and healthcare providers were expected to be large markets for new wireless and Voice over IP (VoIP) solutions as well as the data collection tools that had been proven in manufacturing and distribution, CEO Mike Baur said in *Computer Reseller News*. The Catalyst Telecom unit was enlisting resellers for a new voice-and-data IP system from Avaya. NEC was another VoIP supplier for ScanSource.

In 2003 large retailers were making orders again, company CEO Mike Baur told *VARbusiness*. However, leading broadline resellers Ingram Micro Inc. and Tech Data Corporation were muscling into the POS arena. HP became a supplier to ScanSource around January 2004, offering an affordable, Web-enabled POS platform aimed at the SMB (small to medium business) market. ScanSource soon unveil Solution City, an online resource to help resellers provide solutions for ten specific markets.

Established a security unit in the fall of 2004. Around the same time, ScanSource joined Microsoft Corporation in developing specialized POS bundles for small to midsized businesses (SMBs) in the beer and wine, apparel, sporting goods, and gift markets.

Another new technology embraced by ScanSource was RFID. According to Computer Reseller News, Wal-Mart and the Department of Defense were mandating their suppliers collectively spend possibly billions of dollars to become RFID compliant. ScanSource's top RFID suppliers included Intermac, Zebra, and Symbol Technologies.

The company was expanding its business abroad. A sales office opened in Mexico in 2001. ScanSource acquired a U.K. AIDC and POS distributor and opened a European unit in Belgium in 2002 while entering the Latin American market through the acquisition of POS distributor NetPoint International. In 2005 ScanSource added a sales office in Toronto, a few years after an earlier office there had been closed. The company also maintained a branch in Vancouver. Europdata Connect UK Ltd. (EDC), which had offices in Britain, Sweden and the Netherlands, was acquired in April 2005.

Sales were up 23 percent in fiscal 2005 to $1.5 billion. Income rose 19 percent to $36 million. *Forbes* magazine ranked it 83rd on its list of the Best Big Companies in America. *Business Week*, *Fortune*, and others noted its remarkable growth year after year.

Principal Subsidiaries

4100 Quest, LLC; ScanSource Properties, LLC; Partner Services, Inc. f/k/a ChannelMax, Inc.; ScanSource Security Distribution, Inc.; ScanSource Canada, Inc.; ScanSource de Mexico S de RL de CV (76%); Outsourcing Unlimited, Inc. (88%); Netpoint International, Inc. (76%); ScanSource France SARL;

ScanSource Europe Ltd. (United Kingdom); ScanSource UK Ltd.; ScanSource EDC Ltd. (United Kingdom); ScanSource Europe SPRL (Belgium) ScanSource Germany GmbH; ScanSource Europe (Italia) Sede Secondaria.

Principal Divisions

Catalyst Telecom; Paracon; ScanSource.

Principal Competitors

Ingram Micro Inc.; Peak Technologies, Inc.; Tech Data Corporation; Westcon Group.

Further Reading

Bennett, Jeff, ''ScanSource May Go on Acquisition Hunt,'' *Greenville News,* December 4, 1997, p. 6D.

Campbell, Scott, ''Distributors Look Past the Pond,'' *Computer Reseller News,* March 11, 2002, p. 66.

——, ''Lucent's Distributors Promise Faster Delivery of Switches,'' *Computer Reseller News,* January 4, 1999.

Del Nibletto, Paolo, ''ScanSource Expands in Canada,'' *Computer Dealer News,* March 4, 2005, p. 8.

Dennis, Donnette, ''Bar-Code Buy: ScanSource to Acquire Black Arrow,'' *Computer Reseller News,* March 13, 2000, p. 63.

DuPlessis, Jim, ''Two South Carolina Companies Barely Touched by Recession,'' *Knight Ridder/Tribune Business News,* June 1, 2003.

Gresock, Sam, ''Fortune Lists Two South Carolina Firms Among Fastest-Growing Businesses,'' *State* (Columbia, S.C.), August 16, 2001.

——, ''Greenville, S.C.-Based Technology Firm Fills Three Management Positions,'' *State* (Columbia, S.C.), January 20, 2000.

——, ''Stock in Greenville, S.C.-Based ScanSource Holds Steady,'' *State* (Columbia, S.C.), August 19, 2001.

Gros, Michael, and Edward F. Moltzen, ''ScanSource Urges VARs to Focus on Verticals,'' *Computer Reseller News,* June 21, 2004, p. 43.

Hausman, Eric, ''Mobile Solutions on Upswing,'' *Computer Reseller News,* May 19, 1997, pp. 47–48.

Lang, Steven, and Rob Wright, ''ScanSource Continues Convergence PushSeeks 300 VARs to Cater to the SMB Market Via Its Catalyst Telecom Division,'' *VARbusiness,* February 7, 2005, p. 52.

Lingblom, Marie, ''New Reseller Services Division, ScanSource Partners Laud Distributor's Support Services,'' *Computer Reseller News,* October 7, 2002, p. 156.

——, ''ScanSource to Take Solution Providers Into New Verticals,'' *Computer Reseller News,* February 3, 2003, p. 56.

Linsenbach, Sharon, ''ScanSource in Tune with RFID Wave,'' *Computer Reseller News,* October 25, 2004, p. 43.

——, ''Specialty Retail SMB BundlesMarket Heats Up As ScanSource, Microsoft Add Fuel To POS Fire,'' *Computer Reseller News,* November 15, 2004, p. 14.

Longwell, John, ''Gates F/A To Distribute Bar-Coding Hardware-Enters into Joint Venture with Ex-CEO,'' *Computer Reseller News,* January 11, 1993, p. 131.

——, ''IBM Aims PC POS System at Channel,'' *Computer Reseller News,* January 22, 1996.

——, ''Specialty Distributors Add Markets,'' *Computer Reseller News,* May 10, 1993, p. 115.

Maloney, David, ''Partners in Success,'' *Industrial Distribution,* February 2000, p. M8.

Moltzen, Edward F., ''ScanSource Launches VAR Seminars,'' *Computer Reseller News,* March 8, 1999, p. 32.

Pepe, Michele, ''Auto ID Spotlight TechTeach: Come One, Come All to POS Arena,'' *Computer Reseller News,* December 13, 1999, p. 127.

Pereira, Pedro, ''Scanning the Field: Distributor Eyes New Markets,'' *Computer Reseller News,* March 2, 1998, pp. 57–58.

Rushing, R.W., ''ScanSource Targets Point-of-Sale Niche,'' *Computer Reseller News,* May 23, 1994, p. 44.

''Scanning a New Venture,'' *Computer Reseller News,* August 16, 1993, p. 63.

Terdoslavich, William, ''POS Specialists Mine Growth Niche,'' *Computer Reseller News,* October 20, 1997, pp. 34–35.

Thompson, Samantha, ''ScanSource Goes Public, Stock Climbs,'' *Greenville News,* March 24, 1994, p. 7D.

——, ''ScanSource Pulls Plug on Offering,'' *Greenville News,* March 25, 1997, p. 8D.

Werner, Ben, ''Cash Registers Keep Ringing for ScanSource,'' *State* (Columbia, S.C.), January 30, 2005.

——, ''CEO Pitches South Carolina-Based Scan-Technology Firm's Hot Sales in New York,'' *State* (Columbia, S.C.), June 21, 2004.

Wright, Rob, ''ScanSource's POS Business Shines Brightly As It Signs on Its Newest Vendor Partner: HP,'' *VARbusiness,* January 12, 2004, p. 60.

——, ''ScanSource Surges Beyond Point-Of-Sales Under CEO Mike Baur, ScanSource Has Also Expanded, Regionally and Technologically,'' *VARBusiness,* September 13, 2004, p. 72.

—Frederick C. Ingram

Seibu Railway Company Ltd.

1-11-1 Kusunokidai
Tokorozawa City
Saitama Prefecture
Japan
Telephone: (42) 926-2035
Fax: (42) 926-2237
Web site: http://www.seibu-group.co.jp

Public Company
Incorporated: 1912 as Musashino Railway Company
Employees: 15,751
Sales: $3.92 billion (2004)
Stock Exchanges: Tokyo
Ticker Symbol: SBUR F
NAIC: 482111 Line-Haul Railroads; 71399 All Other
Amusement and Recreation Industries

Seibu Railway Company Ltd. (Seibu Railway) is one of Japan's leading railway operators and the nucleus of the Seibu Railway Group of companies, whose interests range from railways to real estate development and hotel operation to the ownership of one of Japan's leading baseball teams. Overall, the company owns 81 hotels, 52 golf courses, and 36 ski resorts. Chairman Yoshiaki Tsutsumi—once dubbed the richest businessman in the world by *Forbes* magazine—was arrested on charges of insider trading and falsifying financial documents in early 2005. The scandal surrounding his arrest and an enormous debt load related to real estate development ventures forced the company to begin to restructure its holdings in 2005.

Early History

The origins of Seibu Railway lie in a railway company called Musashino Railway Company, founded in 1912 by one of Japan's most famous entrepreneurs, Yasujido Tsutsumi. He was a Tokyo-based businessman who was seeking to profit from Japan's fast-growing economy. In 1872 Japan's first railway was opened, providing transport between the cities of Yokohama and Tokyo. The ensuing 40 years saw Japan industrialize at a fast pace. The government's policy was to encourage private investors to develop the infrastructure, and it became apparent that the electric railway would be the dominant form of public transport in the Tokyo area. The government began awarding licenses to investors who wished to develop and build track along major routes. Tsutsumi obtained a license for the construction and operation of an electric railway between Ikebukuro in central Tokyo and the outlying town of Tokorozawa. The government, as it had done with all the private railways, issued guidelines on the fares that could be charged. Tsutsumi succeeded in raising ¥1 million in capital for the company, Musashino Railway Company (Musashino). Construction began in 1912 and was completed three years later, when passenger services between Ikebukuro and Hanno, on route to Tokorozawa, commenced. The initial trains were steam-driven, as the 44-kilometer route was not electrified. Electrification took place in 1922, and the track was extended to Tokorozawa. In the following year, however, the Tokyo area experienced a catastrophic earthquake, with devastating consequences for the infrastructure. Large portions of the Musashino track were ruined, and reconstruction took more than a year. Musashino, and the city of Tokyo in general, recovered quickly, however, and by 1927 the company was able to open a new service between the city of Nerima, near Tokorozawa, and Ikebukuro. The service was double-track, permitting trains to run more frequently.

By 1930 Tokyo was one of the largest metropolitan areas in the world, with a population of more than three million. The agricultural areas surrounding the city gradually became residential as the city grew. To a large extent the growth was most pronounced in the vicinity of major rail routes, and Musashino saw steady housing development along its two routes. This meant a growth in passenger volume and revenue. The company continued to invest in track, converting all to double by 1930. Branch lines were built from the main lines to cater to local residential areas. Musashino's main rival at this time was the Tokyo Express Railway Company (Tokyu), under the leadership of Keita Gotoh. Gotoh and Tsutsumi became fierce rivals, as Gotoh's strategy was to take over smaller railway companies and thus expand his empire. Indeed, by the late 1930s Gotoh's company had swallowed up almost all the private railways in the Tokyo area, one of the exceptions being Musashino. The two

Key Dates:

1912:   Yasujido Tsutsumi establishes Musashino Railway Company.
1940:   The company acquires Tamako Railway Company.
1946:   Musashino becomes known as Seibu Railway Co. Ltd.
1968:   Seibu Railway's train tracking system is computerized and television monitors are placed along the lines.
1976:   Seibu Railway completes the building of the Seibu Shinjuku Building.
1989:   Yoshiaki Tsutsumi is named chairman.
2004:   Auditors discover that Kukodu Corp. has misrepresented its equity stake in Seibu Railway; Tsutsumi resigns.
2005:   Tsutsumi pleads guilty on charges of insider trading and falsifying financial documents.

companies also were faced with competition from the nationally owned railway network covering the whole of Tokyo. Musashino flourished, however, and in 1940 acquired Tamako Railway Company, which also had escaped takeover by Gotoh, and with it an additional service in the vicinity of its network.

In the early 1940s Japan was preparing for full-scale war with the Allies. All major companies were ordered by the military government to play their part in this effort, and Musashino contributed by supplying railway freight cars. In 1944 Musashino's tracks were severely damaged by the bombing raids carried out by the U.S. Air Force and at the time of Japan's surrender in August 1945 its infrastructure was in need of rebuilding. Following the occupation, the U.S. command began the process of dismantling the huge Japanese industrial conglomerates that had emerged before the war. Tokyu was split up but Musashino, being smaller, was left with its routes intact. With Tsutsumi still in charge, the company became known as Seibu Railway Co. Ltd. (Seibu Railway) in 1946.

Rebuilding and Expanding in the Postwar Era

Seibu Railway began the rebuilding of its track, aided by grants from the government, which was in turn subsidized by the U.S. government. As well as rebuilding the old lines, Seibu Railway began the development of routes from Shinjuku, another major central Tokyo station, to suburban regions. The company also bought a baseball team, the Seibu Lions, in 1949. A stadium was built in the vicinity of Tokorozawa and the team soon came to dominate its league. Seibu Railway also began to develop the real estate it owned in the vicinity of its track. This became a lucrative source of income for the company, in addition to its core railway business. The company continued to invest in its infrastructure, with the 1950s being a time of extensive track expansion. The station platforms were expanded to accommodate longer trains, and the frequency of services along the major Shinjuku and Ikebukuro routes increased. In 1963 a ten-car express train service between Ikebukuro and Tokorozawa was inaugurated. In the following year the company built a large railway car depot at Koteshi, along the route,

to service its rapidly growing fleet of railway cars. At that time the emphasis for Seibu Railway was on speed of service. Tokyo's population was growing rapidly, with the residential regions around Seibu's lines forming a continuous metropolitan region. The majority of the residents commuted to work in the center of Tokyo, and the morning rush-hour on Seibu Railway's lines was becoming increasingly congested. While expanding its services, Seibu Railway was aware of the safety risks of transporting hundreds of thousands of passengers daily. In 1968 Seibu Railway's train tracking system was computerized and television monitors were placed along the lines. Tokyo's many level-crossings had long been a source of accidents, so Seibu Railway installed automatic safety systems at its crossings in 1969; as a result, fatalities fell dramatically.

Seibu continued to develop its real estate and in 1973 completed a huge underground complex in Ikebukuro Station. This complex included shops and restaurants as well as Seibu Railway's terminals. The development of Shinjuku Station followed in 1974. In 1976 Seibu Railway completed the building of the Seibu Shinjuku Building, its first major piece of real estate near Shinjuku Station. Toward the end of the 1970s Seibu Railway installed a computerized switching system. The company also invested heavily in station improvement, building new stations, including Tamako Station in 1961, and renovating others.

With a large stake in the ownership of the company, Yasujido Tsutsumi's family was one of the wealthiest in Japan. Although the ailing Yasujido died in 1989, he had passed control of the company over to his son Yoshiaki in the 1970s. Seibu Railway's traditional rivalry with Tokyu had diminished as both companies grew into diversified conglomerates. The 1980s saw Seibu Railway diversify into resort development, beginning with a project on the Hawaiian island of Maui in 1987. The company continued to develop family homes along its railway lines. In the late 1980s, with the boom in Japanese real estate prices, the leasing of Seibu Railway property in central Tokyo became lucrative.

1990s and Beyond

In the early 1990s Seibu Railway ranked fourth behind the Tobu, Tokyu, and Odakyu Railway Companies in terms of passenger volume among private railway firms in the Tokyo area. Seibu Railway's railway business continued to be the core of the business, although in percentage revenue terms it was on a par with the company's resort and tourism businesses. The latter accounted for around 40 percent of revenue each, with the remaining 20 percent coming from real estate. The company's baseball team was extremely successful, winning the Japan Series three years in succession in the late 1980s. Yoshiaki Tsutsumi, who became chairman in 1989, planned on future diversification, having opened two large hotels in Hawaii and Yokohama in 1990. That same year, *Forbes* magazine gave Tsutsumi the title of the richest businessman in the world.

The company opened the first Burger King fast-food outlet in Japan in 1993 as part of a joint venture. It also teamed up with the Saison Group to provide satellite broadcasting in Japan. In 1996, its Hawaiian subsidiary finished the $35 million restoration of the Mauna Kea Beach Hotel. The hotel was considered one of the finest on the island. The company continued to work closely with local governments to develop leisure properties. Seibu Railway designed the resorts, while the government constructed roads and the needed infrastructure. By the end of the 1990s, Seibu Railway had more than 80 hotels, 52 golf courses, and 36 ski resorts in its portfolio.

During this time, the company's railway operations remained on track, but profits began to dwindle at its real estate and leisure businesses. In the early 1990s, Japan's housing market had collapsed and in just a few years its economy had bottomed out. Faltering sales at Seibu Railway's real estate subsidiary forced the company to post a loss in 1996. Continued problems in the leisure sector led to a $33.86 million loss in 1999.

Seibu Railway forged ahead, determined to restore the profitability of its leisure business. It began to shutter money-losing operations at its real estate and golf subsidiaries. In 2003, it partnered with competitor Odakyu Electric Railway Co. to develop a tourist spot in Hakone, a hot spring resort area.

Seibu Railway's future was changed dramatically during the early years of the new millennium when the company was hit by a major scandal. In March 2004, six top executives were arrested on charges that they bribed corporate racketeers. A few months later, an auditor discovered discrepancies in Seibu Railway's ownership structure. Kokudo Corporation—a privately held company controlled by Tsutsumi—had misrepresented the size of its equity stake. In October 2004, Tsutsumi was forced to resign. In early 2005, he was arrested on claims of insider trading and falsifying financial statements. A March 2005 *Asian Wall Street Journal* article explained the situation. "Prosecutors allege that Mr. Tsutsumi conspired with several executives to falsify Seibu Railway's 2003 financial statement, which said Kokudo's stake in Seibu Railway was 43.16% instead of the actual 64.83%. The falsification was allegedly an attempt to hide the fact that a handful of top executives owned too much of the railway—a violation of Tokyo Stock Exchange rules." As such, the company was delisted from the exchange in December 2004. The scandal took its toll on company operations as well as those involved in it. Former Seibu president, Terumasa Koyanagi, committed suicide shortly after being questioned for his involvement.

Takashi Goto became Seibu Railway's new president in 2005 and Naoki Hirano was elected chairman. The two men were charged with restructuring the struggling company, which was carrying a $13.3 billion debt load and posted an $81 million loss in 2004. Although there was speculation that foreign investors would purchase Seibu Railway, the company's future remained up in the air.

Principal Subsidiaries

Seibu Construction Co., Ltd. (50%); Seibu Zoen Co., Ltd. (24.2%); Izu Hakone Railway Co., Ltd. (48.6%); Shinmachi Jari Co., Ltd. (46.1%); Ikebukuro Shooing Park Co., Ltd. (20.3%); Ohmi Railway Corporation (75.7%); Seibu Golf Corporation; Seibu Estate Corporation; Ohmi Kanko Co., Ltd. (69.4%); Seibu Travel Co., Ltd. (50%); Yodosei Corporation (89.7%); Musashino Jisho Co., Ltd.; Seibu Real Estate Sales Co., Ltd.; Lokerani Resort Corporation (U.S.A.; 72.7%); Moanam Corporation (U.S.A.); Nuiaina Corporation (U.S.A.); Seibu Unyu Co., Ltd. (94.1%); Seibu Bus Co., Ltd. (99.5%); Seibu Hire Co., Ltd.; Kyushu Seibu Unyu Co., Ltd.; Toshimaen Co., Ltd.; Seibu Real Estate Co., Ltd.; Makena Golf Corporation (U.S.A.); Hawaii Prince Hotel Waikiki Corporation (U.S.A.); Mauna Kea Beach Hotel Corporation (U.S.A.); Hapuna Neach Prince Hotel Corporation (U.S.A.).

Principal Competitors

Keio Electric Railway Co., Ltd.; Kintetsu Corporation; Tobu Railway Co., Ltd.

Further Reading

"Japanese Railway Tycoon Held in Insider-Trading Allegations," *Asian Wall Street Journal,* March 4, 2005.

"Land Fall: Seibu's Era of Development Projects Is History," *Asahi Evening News,* March 3, 2005.

"Parent Company Biggest Obstacle to Seibu Revival," *Nikkei Report,* May 25, 2005.

Rowley, Ian, and Hiroko Tahiro, "Seibu: Vultures Are Circling," *Business Week,* May 23, 2005.

"Scandal-Tainted Kokudo Eyes Full-Scale Restructuring," *Japan Weekly Monitor,* November 15, 2004.

"Seibu Still Cleaning Up Bubble Residue," *Nikkei Report,* December 11, 2003.

Zaun, Todd, "Guilty Plea in Big Financial Scandal in Japan," *The New York Times,* June 17, 2005.

—Dylan Tanner
—update: Christina M. Stansell

Shochiku Company Ltd.

4-1-1 Tsukiji, Chuo-ku
Tokyo 104-8422
Japan
Telephone: (+81) 3 5550 1533
Fax: (+81) 3 5550 1639
Web site: http://www.shochiku.co.jp

Public Company
Incorporated: 1895
Employees: 1,485
Sales: ¥9.61 billion ($836.20 million) (2005)
Stock Exchanges: Tokyo
Ticker Symbol: 9601
NAIC: 512131 Motion Picture Theaters, Except Drive-In;
   512120 Motion Picture and Video Distribution;
   711320 Promoters of Performing Arts, Sports, and
   Similar Events without Facilities

Shochiku Company Ltd. is one of Japan's oldest and largest vertically integrated film and theatrical production companies. With origins in traditional Kabuki theater, the company continues to operate the famed Kabuki-za Theater in Tokyo, Shochiku has long played a central role in the Japanese film industry, releasing the works of such cinema greats as Yasujiro Ozu, Hiroshi Shimizu, Nagisa Oshima, Takeshi Kitano, and Akira Kurosawa. The company is also behind the immensely popular Tora-san series, the world's longest running film series, with nearly 50 movies produced over nearly three decades. Film production remains a vital part of the group's revenues, representing some 20 percent or more of sales. The company's Kabuki theater operations, which include productions throughout Japan, account for an additional 10 percent of the company's sales, which topped ¥9.61 billion ($836.20 million) in 2005. Shochiku has adopted a vertical integration strategy in order to compete in the 2000s. The company not only produces films, it distributes them through its network of movie theaters. Through Shochiku Multiplex Theatres and other subsidiaries, the company operates some 300 screens in 50 theaters, including the Movix mulitplex theater chain. Shochiku, which owns

one of Japan's most extensive film collections, produces television programming, including animated series such as the Gundam robots and Ultraman franchises. In 2005, the company created a dedicated animation division in order to increase its production of animated programming. Shochiku has also deepened its vertical integration through development of video and DVD production and distribution.

Kabuki Beginnings in the 19th Century

Brothers Matsujiro Shirai and Takejiro Ohtani founded a Kabuki theater company in Kyoto in 1895, combining the Chinese pronunciation of the first characters of their own names to form the company name Shochiku. The brothers quickly developed into prominent players in the Kabuki theater circuit, and by 1914 the company had taken over the Kabuki-za Theater in Tokyo. That theater was widely recognized as being Japan's most important Kabuki showcase. Into the beginning of the 2000s, the Kabuki-za continued to produce 50 shows per week.

Yet the 400-year-old Kabuki and Japan's other traditional theater forms had already begun to face a serious challenge from a new entertainment form: cinema. The first Japanese film production company had appeared shortly before World War I. At the same time, Japanese audiences were deserting the country's Kabuki theaters for the many films arriving from the United States. Shochiku recognized that its own future lay in adopting the new art form, and the company launched its own film production in 1920. The company built its own production studio in Kamata, in southern Tokyo. By the end of the year, Shochiku had already released its first film, *Island Woman.*

The company's entry into film production became all the more important after a fire destroyed the Kabuki-za theater in 1921. Shochiku began work on rebuilding the complex, which was completed in 1924. In the meantime, Shochiku's film production moved closer to its central role in the company's operations.

The success of the company's early film production led it to seek expansion, and in 1924 Shochiku listed on the Tokyo and Osaka Stock Exchanges. Shochiku also began attracting a number of talented directors who helped establish Japan as one of the world's film centers. Among the most famous of Japan's directors was Yasujiro Ozu, who joined Shochiku as an assistant soon after the company launched its own film production. By 1927, Ozu had been allowed to direct as well, completing his first film, *Sword of Penitence*. Ozu remained with Shochiku throughout his prestigious film career. Other noted contemporaries included Mikio Naruse, Heinosuke Gosho, and Hiroshi Shimizu.

Shochiku also played a key role in the modernization of Japanese cinema. In 1931, the company released Japan's first "talkie." Called *Madam to Nyobo,* roughly translated as "Proprietress and Wife," the film was seen as an allegory for the film industry's, and the country's, own acceptance of the trend toward modernization. *Madam to Nyobo* was a critical and popular success for Shochiku, firmly establishing the company as one of Japan's top two film producers in the prewar period.

While Shochiku continued to produce silent films for several more years, sound clearly represented the future of Japanese cinema. In order to develop its sound technology, Shochiku built a new production studio, at Ofuna. That facility was completed in 1936, at which time the Kamata studio was closed down. The Ofuna studio remained Shochiku's primary production facility until the turn of the 21st century.

Postwar Development

Shochiku continued to produce films during World War II, but soon fell foul of the country's military authorities, which judged that the company's film lacked appropriate nationalistic fervor. Shochiku fortunes fell during the war years; the success of the film *47 Ronin,* a costume drama directed by Kenji Mizoguchi, helped saved the company from financial ruin.

In the aftermath of World War II, the Japanese film industry was more or less dismantled, with many of the country's film production companies put out of business. Shochiku remained one of the few survivors of this period and joined in with two other feature film producers, Toho and Dai Nippon, as well as several makers of short films, to create a voluntary industry oversight body, the Union of Motion Picture Producers.

Shochiku was able to return to film production by the end of the decade. In 1949, the company relisted its stock, now on the Tokyo, Osaka, Nagoya, Fukuoka, and Sapporo Stock Exchanges. In the meantime, the company was also forced to rebuild the Kabuki-za theater again, which had been bombed during the war. The theater reopened in 1951. That year also saw a new advancement for Shochiku and the Japanese film industry in general, when Shochiku released the country's first

color film, a comedy called *Carmen Comes Home.* The film was not only the first color film in the country, it also used the very first stock of color film produced by Fuji, setting the stage for Fuji Film's emergence as a world leader in that market.

Shochiku faced difficulties in the late 1950s and early 1960s. The Japanese cinema market focused primarily on the country's major urban centers. Theaters, however, were often owned directly by the film producers who showed only their own films or films by partners. In this way, Toho had managed to secure the exclusive rights to much of the output of the Hollywood studios. Shochiku searched for its own partners in order to maintain its competitiveness. In 1960, the company created a partnership with Tokyu Recreation, which was a prominent real estate holder and cinema operator. The agreement gave Shochiku access to Tokyu's cinema network, which meant access to its audience as well.

The partnership played a role in Shochiku's survival during a severe industry downturn in the late 1960s, as film attendance began to decline with the growth of other forms of entertainment, especially television. Shochiku managed to weather this period, bolstered by the huge success of its first Tora-san film in 1969. Directed by Yoji Yamada and starring Kiyoshi Atsumi, the Tora-san film series was to become the world's longest-running film franchise, with 48 films produced between 1969 and 1995, the year of Atsumi's death. The Tora-san series represented a steady and important revenue source for Shochiku.

In 1975, Shochiku completed its Togeki headquarters building in Tokyo. The new headquarters featured a view of the company's Kabuki-za Theater. From there, the company oversaw its development through a new boom period for Japanese cinema, which peaked between the mid-1980s and early 1990s. In 1987, the company distribution business received a lift with the construction of the Mullion shopping center and entertainment complex in Tokyo. That building was one of the first to feature several cinemas in the same complex. Of the three theaters in the Mullion center, three were owned by Shochiku.

Vertical Integration for the 2000s

The Mullion complex paved the way to a revolution in the Japanese film industry. In 1993, the legendary Hollywood studio of Warner Bros. teamed up with local partner Mycal to open Japan's first multiplex theater. The new type of theater, which featured 12 screens or more, represented a dramatic transformation of the Japanese film distribution market. One significant change was that the new theaters tended to open in the country's suburban market, a radical departure from the traditional focus on the country's main urban centers. In addition, the availability of multiple screens encouraged distributors to seek films from a variety of film producers. This trend was further encouraged by the creation of partnerships among film companies, often a necessity due to high real estate prices, to build and operate the new multiplex theaters.

Shochiku created a dedicated theater subsidiary in 1996. Called Shochiku Multiplex Theaters, the new subsidiary began building and managing theaters for the company. Shochiku opened its first multiplex in 1997, making it the pioneer Japanese company in this enterprise. The company created its own once again falling, Shochiku underwent a restructuring at the beginning of the 2000s, adopting a new vertical integration strategy.

The company now sought to expand its operations not only in film production and distribution but also in related areas such as video and DVD production and distribution, as well as venturing into the sales of ancillary products such as toys and T-shirts. Shochiku also boosted its range of television programming, particularly its production of lucrative animated series. This latter category represented a vast new market, given the huge global demand for Japanese anime movies and the corresponding market for licensed toys and other products. In order to capitalize on its own successful animated production, such as the Gundam robot series and the Ultraman series, Shochiku established a dedicated animation division in 2004.

Shochiku's fortunes were once again on an upswing. Buoyed by its renewed box office success, the company sales neared ¥10 billion ($950 million) for the first time in 2005. Celebrating its 110th anniversary that year, Shochiku remained the leading steward of Japan's Kabuki tradition as well as one of its most important film groups.

Principal Subsidiaries

Shochiku Aruze Communications (50%); Shochiku International; Shochiku Multiplex Theaters.

Principal Competitors

Toho Company Ltd; Toei Company Ltd; Kadokawa Company Ltd.; Digital Adventure Inc; Cameo Interactive Ltd; DynEd Japan KK; 4D; Acclaim Japan.

Further Reading

Bull, Brett, "Toon Unit Zap-up: Studio Aims for Global Animation Market," *Variety,* April 25, 2005, p. A6.
Elley, Derek, " 'Gentle Giant' Carves Its Niche," *Variety,* April 25, 2005, p. A14.
Lally, Kevin, "Japanese Titan: 110-year-old Shochiku Wins Exhibition Honor," *Film Journal International,* April 2005, p. 82.
Leong, Anthony, "The Sword and the Dollar: Samurai Pix Lead Studio's Foreign Push," *Variety,* April 25, 2005, p. A2.
Murdoch, Blake, "Shochiku Beefing Up Slate to Boost Its Market Share," *Hollywood Reporter,* May 18, 2004, p. 16.
Rosenberg, Scott, "A Shochiku Landmark," *Film Journal International,* February 2005, p. 25.
Saki, Tad, "Shochiku Shares Its H'w'd Game Plan," *Variety,* July 9, 2001, p. 39.
Schwarzacher, Lukas, "Conglom Clock," *Variety,* April 25, 2005, p. A4.
——, "Film Arm Hopes to Match Record '04 Perf," *Variety,* April 25, 2005, p. A2.
——, "Studio's Sun Rises Anew from Kabuki to Film," *Variety,* April 25, 2005, p. A1.

—M.L. Cohen

theater brand, Movix, which became its flagship distribution vehicle. By 2005, the Movix chain included 13 multiplexes with a total of 124 screens. Shochiku itself directly controlled its 13 traditional theaters, with a total of 33 screens, while three other subsidiaries operated an additonal 27 screens.

Led by Toru Okuyama during the 1990s, Shochiku made an attempt to diversify its film production business, which had long favored so-called "middle class dramas." In an effort led by Okuyama's son Kazuyoshi, the company began producing a new range of films, including action films such as Sonatine, released in 1993. The new range of films was also designed to increase Shochiku's penetration of the foreign market, as Japan's action films, especially its "ninja" films, began building a worldwide audience.

Yet the Okuyamas' aggressive strategy clashed with the company's more conservative board of directors, which ousted the pair in 1998. The Okuyama's were in part victims of a new downturn in the Japanese film industry. The rise of the video game market, coupled with the explosion of the Internet, the arrival of satellite, and other new entertainment forms, began draining off Japanese moviegoers. With its financial position

Sleeman Breweries Ltd.

551 Clair Road West
Guelph, Ontario N1L 1E9
Canada
Telephone: (519) 822-1834
Fax: (519) 822-0430
Web site: http://www.sleeman.com

Public Company
Incorporated: 1984 as Antebi Enterprises Inc.
Employees: 900
Sales: $177.1 million (2004)
Stock Exchanges: Toronto
Ticker Symbol: ALE
NAIC: 312120 Breweries

Based in the small town of Guelph, Ontario, Sleeman Breweries, Ltd. is Canada's leading brewer and distributor of premium beer and the third largest brewing company overall—albeit a distant third behind Labatt Brewing Company Ltd. and Molson Companies Ltd. Drawing on vintage family recipes Sleeman makes a variety of special brews, such as its bestselling Sleeman's Cream Ale and Honey Brown Lager. Sleeman brews are available in the United States and the United Kingdom on a limited basis. The company produces a number of regional Canadian brands, including Okanagan Spring and Shaftebury in British Columbia and Alberta, Unibroue in Quebec and Ontario, and Maclays in Atlantic Canada. Sleeman Breweries also distributes a variety of international premium beers throughout Canada, including Samuel Adams, Grolsch, and Pilsner Urquell; Guinness in British Columbia and Quebec; and provides contract production for Japan's Sapporo beer. In addition to its position on the high end of the market, Sleeman Breweries is involved in the value-price category through the acquisition of the Stroh portfolio of brands in Canada, which include Stroh, Old Milwaukee, Colt 45, Pabst, and Schlitz. The company operates five breweries in Canada as well as one in LaCrosse, Wisconsin. Sleeman Breweries is a public company listed on the Toronto Stock Exchange.

Founder: 1960s High School Dropout

Sleeman Breweries founder, chief executive officer, and chairman, John W. Sleeman, was born in Toronto in 1953, the son of a Bell Canada executive who did not drink. At the age of 16 he dropped out of school, determined to become a millionaire by the age of 30. His business education was limited to management training at McDonald's and the practical experience of being a McDonald's manager at such a young age. When he was 19 Sleeman moved to England and fell in love with the pub culture, so much so that when he returned to Canada a few years later, in 1977, he started his own pub called Monahan's in the Toronto suburb of Oakville. To supply his pub with the kind of beer he had enjoyed in England he began importing British beers and was soon supplying other establishments. This sideline proved so successful that in 1977 he sold the pub and cofounded Imported Beer Co. to distribute imported beers such as Guinness, Double Diamond, and Heineken to bars throughout Canada. Well before his 30th birthday Sleeman met his goal of becoming a millionaire.

Sleeman might have spent the rest of his business career as an import distributor had it not been for a visit paid to his home one day in 1984 by his father's sister, Florian. She brought with her a small leather-bound notebook and an antique clear bottle that had been kept in a trunk for the past half-century. Sleeman told *Profit* in a 1996 interview that his aunt told him, " 'It's time you found out about your heritage.' She showed me a recipe book for a brewery, and said, 'Did you know your family was in the beer business?' I said, 'No, that's a strange coincidence.' She says, 'Well, here's a recipe book. Would you think about restarting it?' " Sleeman was reluctant at first to give up his successful distribution business to become a brewer, but he was fascinated with the family history about which his father had never spoken.

The Sleeman family's connection to Canadian beer brewing dated back to 1834 when a young brewmaster named John H. Sleeman emigrated from Cornwall, England, and settled near Guelph, a small Canadian town that apparently loved its beer. According to a history of Guelph, by 1843 the community had a population of 700 and nine breweries. One of the earliest operations was established in 1827 by James Hodgert. Sleeman

Company Perspectives:

Today, Sleeman is one of the fastest growing premium brewers in North America. Throughout our lineage, brewing the highest quality beer has been an unwavering passion for the Sleeman family.

became the manager but soon moved to St. David's to open his own brewery, the Stamford Spring Brewery. He sold the business in 1845 and moved back to Guelph and worked at Hodgerts Brewery until opening the Silver Creek Brewery in 1851. His son, George, became his partner in 1862 and the sole owner five years later when the elder Sleeman retired. George's son, George A. Sleeman, became involved in the business in 1886. It was in 1898 that George Sleeman created the recipe for Sleeman Cream Ale, which he wrote down in the personal notebook Aunt Florian gave John W. Sleeman nearly 90 years later.

Sleeman Brothers Caught Smuggling in the 1930s

With the start of the new century the family business was incorporated as The Sleeman Brewing and Malting Co. Ltd. By this time the brewery was using the clear bottles that became a family trademark, one of which was stored in a trunk along with the recipe book. But the enterprise fell on hard times in 1916 when the Canada Temperance Act went into effect and the company was limited to selling malt and ginger ale. George Sleeman died in 1926, leaving the brewery business in the hands of his sons, George A. and Henry O. Sleeman. In the meantime, across the Detroit River in the United States, Prohibition also had gone into effect in 1919, although Americans' thirst for alcohol did not slacken. Rather, it increased, providing the Sleeman brothers with an opportunity to meet that demand. They smuggled beer across the border in farm wagons, buried under fresh vegetables bound for the U.S. market. The Ontario police grew wise to the trick, however, and caught the brothers red-handed in 1933, just a few months before Prohibition was repealed. The Canadian authorities were less concerned about selling alcohol into the United States than they were about being cut out of the action, telling the Sleeman brothers that even though they were making beer illegally they could have an export permit, sell wherever they wanted to, but they would have to pay taxes. Still, the Sleemans refused to cooperate. In the end, they were forced to sell the brewery to pay the tax bill. The family's involvement with smuggling became a matter of shame, explaining why John W. Sleeman was 31 years old before he learned about the colorful past of his forebears.

Sleeman was in no hurry to revive the family brewery despite his aunt's encouragement. "I was already financially successful, and I didn't really want to gamble all that on a new venture," he told *Profit*. "So I thought about it for a couple of years. She kept asking how things were going and I kept stalling. Finally she used guilt—that always works—and she said, 'I'm getting old and I could die soon. I'd like you to start the brewery. It would mean a lot to me.'" Nevertheless, Sleeman remained hesitant. "I contacted Standard Brands . . . and I said, 'You're the last registered owners of my granfather's

company. Would you be interested in letting me have the company back?' I expected a 'yes, for a million dollars' type of answer, and they, to my surprise, came back and said, 'It's a wonderful idea. Pay us $1 and you can use the company.'" Next, Sleeman decided to check out the trademark rights to the logo on the bottle his aunt gave him. Using a beaver and a maple leaf, they closely resembled the Canadian Pacific logo. He wrote to Canadian Pacific to learn if they had any objection to his using the design, and again to his surprise (or perhaps disappointment) he was told he was free to do as he pleased. "So I was running out of reasons why I shouldn't start the brewery," Sleeman said.

In October 1985 Sleeman reincorporated The Sleeman Brewing and Malting Co. Ltd. To finance the building of a small brewery Sleeman turned to banks, as he had done with his previous ventures, receiving a $3 million loan. He also sold a stake in the business to Detroit-based Stroh Brewing Co. It was on the advice of Stroh that Sleeman held back on opening the facility because the quality of the beer was not yet good enough and the brewery risked losing credibility with beer drinkers that it might never regain. Sleeman's Canadian bank, however, grew concerned about the delay and the project going over budget, lost faith in the business, and called in the loan, giving Sleeman just 30 days to pay them back. Other Canadian banks refused to loan the money, and it was only the intervention of Stroh that kept the project alive, introducing Sleeman to the National Bank of Detroit. Sleeman lost his house paying back the Canadian bank, but the package the Detroit bank put together was enough to pay off the rest of the earlier loan and still leave the brewery with some working capital.

The first pints of Sleeman Cream Ale were first poured in August 1988, and the first bottles filled in October. A few months later, in February 1989, Silver Creek Lager, another family recipe, was reintroduced to the Ontario market, followed in May by the introduction of Toronto Light Lager. Also in 1989 Sleeman began to brew and distribute Stroh's and Stroh's Light brands in the Ontario market. Within two years the company had attained a 1 percent market share in Ontario, Canada's most populous province and largest beer market, and the brewery had doubled its capacity to 200,000 hectolitres. In conjunction with Stroh, the company began marketing Sleeman Cream Ale in Detroit, but it proved a tough sale even with Stroh's marketing efforts behind it. As a result, Sleeman decided to concentrate on the Canadian market, with its goal to become the dominant premium beer brewer in the country before looking elsewhere. Neither did Sleeman have any interest in going toe-to-toe with Labatt or Molson or even badmouthing the giants as did the other microbrewers. In fact, Sleeman relied on Labatt and Molson to sell them their used equipment.

Successful Mid-1990s Entry into the Quebec Market

During the early 1990s Sleeman concentrated on adding new products and entering new Canadian markets. In 1992 the company introduced Sleeman Premium Light, a low-calorie lager. A year later the brewery returned to the family recipe book, unveiling Sleeman Original Dark, an all-natural, all-malt ale. Also in 1993 Sleeman began selling Sleeman Cream Ale and Sleeman Silver Creek Lager in British Columbia. A number of territories followed in 1994: Alberta, Manitoba, and Quebec.

Key Dates:

1834: Brewmaster John H. Sleeman emigrates to Canada.
1851: Sleeman opens Silver Creek Brewery.
1933: Sleeman's grandsons, George A. and Henry Sleeman, are forced out of the business after getting caught smuggling beer into the United States.
1988: John W. Sleeman reopens the family brewery.
1996: Sleeman Breweries is taken public in a reverse merger.
1998: Upper Canada Brewing Company and Brasserie Seigneuriale Inc. are acquired.
1999: A licensing agreement to distribute Stroh brands in Canada is signed.
2000: The Maritime Beer Company is acquired.
2004: Unibroue Inc. is acquired.

French-speaking Quebec offered a particular challenge, however. The province marched to its own drummer, preferring ales over lagers, unlike the rest of the country. It also was not especially open to an Anglophone brand like Sleeman, but John Sleeman won over many of the residents by his willingness to serve as the brewery's spokesperson, despite his halting French. Sleeman claimed that when he first visited the recording studio it was with the understanding that someone else was going to do the commercials, but it was just a trick. The company could not afford an announcer anyway, so Sleeman stepped in. What he lacked in delivery and fluency he made up for in sincerity and a willingness to try. The result was tremendous growth in the sale of Sleeman products in Quebec over the next few years.

Sleeman bought back Stroh's interest in the company in 1994, and the production of Stroh brands returned to the United States. In that same year, Sleeman agreed to a reverse merger with Allied Strategies Inc., owner of Okanagan Spring Brewery of Vernon, British Columbia, one of the best known microbreweries in Western Canada, in a deal that would not be finalized in more than a year, resulting in a company with a new name: Sleeman Breweries Ltd. The merger was attractive to Sleeman on a number of levels. It gave the company national scope, elevating it above the crowd in the consolidating microbrewery segment. Sleeman Breweries could then use economy of scale to save money by centralizing administrative functions and use its increased purchasing power to save money on such basic commodities as bottles, cartons, and caps. It also could command better terms on financing. In 1996, Sleeman Breweries changed banks after several fruitful years with National Bank of Detroit, which realized the company had outgrown it and actually advised Sleeman on how to approach national banks. This time, John Sleeman did not go cap in hand to lenders. Rather, they bid on his business, with The Bank of Nova Scotia winning out, and which was later joined by the Bank of Montreal. Moreover, the reverse merger with Allied Strategies, listed on the Vancouver Stock Exchange, provided Sleeman Breweries with access to the equity markets.

In 1996 the company made a public offering of stock, the proceeds of which were used to fund further acquisitions in the second half of the 1990s as Sleeman Breweries became a consolidation vehicle. The company's stock would now trade on the more prestigious Toronto Stock Exchange. In 1998 Sleeman Breweries completed a pair of significant acquisitions: Upper Canada Brewing Company and Brasserie Seigneuriale Inc. of Boucherville, Quebec. Also of note in 1998, Sleeman Breweries introduced Maple Brown Ale and its products became available in the United Kingdom. The company closed the decade by acquiring Shaftebury Brewing Company Ltd. of Vancouver, the third largest craft-brewer in British Columbia, and by signing a new deal with Stroh, this time a 15-year licensing agreement to the Stroh family of brands in Canada. In this way, Sleeman Breweries staked out a position in the popular price category to complement its premium craft business, both areas enjoying growth, unlike the middle sector dominated by Molson and Labatt. Once again, the company was looking to avoid competing against Canada's top two brewers, content to do business on either side of them, in both the top end and lower end of the price spectrum. In addition, by adding the Stroh brands to the mix, Sleeman Breweries was able to beef up its national distribution network, which in turn led to distribution agreements with foreign brewers such as Scotland's Scottish & Newcastle PLC and Boston Beer, maker of the popular Samuel Adams beer. These alliances then provided Sleeman Breweries with an opportunity to export its products through its new partners.

Sleeman Breweries began the new century where it left off in the old, acquiring another microbrewery, Maritime Beer Company, based in Nova Scotia. A year later Quebec's Northern Goose Beer Company was added. Then, in June 2004, Sleeman Breweries bought Quebec's largest microbrewery, Unibroue Inc. The company also forged new alliances in the early 2000s. It agreed to distribute South African Breweries' Pilsner Urquell and the Strongbow brand of premium packaged and draught cider for England's H.P. Bulmer Ltd. In 2002 it also signed an agreement with Japan's Sapporo Breweries Ltd. to provide contract production for Sapporo products in the United States. Moreover, Sleeman Breweries continued to launch new products into the market. The first Sleeman can in family history, a barrel-shaped design, was offered in 2002 and a low-carb beer, Sleeman Clear, was introduced in 2003. The company dipped into the family recipe book yet again in 2004, unveiling Fine Porter, a limited-edition brew, the first in what was known as the John Sleeman Presents series. In 2005 the company introduced Sleeman Original Draught, an unpasteurized lager.

Principal Subsidiaries

The Sleeman Brewing & Malting Co. Ltd.; Sleeman Unibroue Inc.

Principal Competitors

Big Rock Brewery Income Trust; Brick Brewing Co. Ltd.; Gambrinus Company Inc.; InBev.

Further Reading

Aubun, Benoit, ''Beer and Bad French,'' *Maclean's,* September 17, 2001, p. 32.

Brent, Paul, ''Labelling John Sleeman,'' *Financial Post,* July 20, 1996, p. 10.

Cherney, Elena, ''Canadian Brewery Seeks to Export Success to U.S. Market,'' *Wall Street Journal,* July 24, 2001, p. B2.

Febbell, Tom, ''No Small Beer,'' *Maclean's,* June 17, 1996, p. 26.

Oliver, Marlane, ''The Top 10 Things I Wish I'd Known,'' *Profit,* December 1, 1996, p. 24.

Wilson-Smith, Anthony, ''Ale in the Family,'' *Maclean's,* May 3, 1999, p. 41.

Yasmin, Glanville, ''The Challenges of Growth,'' *CA Magazine,* May 2000, p. 20.

—Ed Dinger

Sorbee International Ltd.

9990 Global Road
Philadelphia, Pennsylvania 19115
U.S.A.
Telephone: (215) 677-5200
Toll Free: (800) 654-3997
Fax: (215) 677-7736
Web site: http://www.sorbee.com

Private Company
Founded: 1978
Employees: 25
Sales: $35 million (2003 est.)
NAIC: 311340 Nonchocolate Confectionery
   Manufacturing

Philadelphia, Pennsylvania-based Sorbee International Ltd. is a manufacturer, distributor, and importer of sugar-free hard candy, soft candy, chocolates, chocolate bars, cookies, cereals, fruit spreads, and syrups. The company's other brands include DreamCandy, which in addition to offering low-fat, low-calorie chocolate bars is being positioned to move into other non-sugar niche markets; and Global Brands, a private label importer of chocolate bars, cereals, and other products. A private company, Sorbee is headed by its founder, Eliot Stone.

Company Founded in the Late 1970s

Eliot Stone grew up in Philadelphia, Pennsylvania, the son of Dr. Harold G. Stone, who ran a company, Medical Products Laboratories, Inc., that specialized in fluoride pharmaceuticals, selling what it called Ethical Dental Pharmaceuticals and Public Health products to dentists, doctors, pediatricians, hospitals, and clinics. The younger Stone went to work for MPL in the 1970s but soon turned his attention to the sugar-free candy business. According to Edward Prewitt writing for *Fortune* in a 1988 article, "In 1977, when a dentist gave his kids lollipops after cleaning their teeth, Stone began Sorbee International, now the world's leading manufacturer of sugar-free candy." *Philadelphia Business Journal,* however, offered a slightly different version of the story in a 1986 profile of Stone: "In 1978

. . . he noticed the lollipops that dentists gave out were high in sugar content. 'It seemed a little silly to me for a dentist to be giving sugary candy to a kid who had just had a cavity or two filled,' he said." His interest aroused, Stone did some research, which led him to the dyrogenated dextrose sweetener called sorbitol, a sweet-tasting non-sugar substance. In 1978, he invested $100,000 to launch a company named after the sweetener, Sorbee and developed a sugar-free lollipop. Samples were sent out to drum up interest, then the company began to market the products to dentists, taking advantage of MPL's nationwide distribution channels to professionals in this field.

Sugar-free candy was an extremely small part of the confection industry, with sales at the time mostly limited to diabetics. Sorbee succeeded in carving out a niche selling to dentists and in the 1980s began to expand its distribution in response to telephone calls and letters it received from parents whose children had received the Sorbee lollipops at their dentist, wanting to know where they could buy the candy. The company began selling the product direct to customers, but the demand was such that it began seeking out other ways to distributed the lollipops. Sorbee first established itself in the retail channel through health food stores, but as sales increased, the company was able to move into drug stores, supermarkets, and other stores. Around 1984, Sorbee began expanding its line, adding two or more new products each year. By the mid-1980s, the company employed some 100 people and was generating sales "in eight figures," as Stone told *Philadelphia Business Journal.*

Stone Sidetracked by Video Business in 1980s

While Stone was working 12-hour days launching Sorbee, he became involved in another venture, again growing out of a personal experience. In 1983, he and his wife grew frustrated while visiting a video rental store because they could not find the tape they wanted and the clerk was rude. At the time, rental stores kept the tapes behind the counter and customers waited in line had to ask the clerk if a particular title was available or not. "I looked around," he told *Philadelphia Business Journal,* "and I saw all these people in the same situation we were in, and walking out because they couldn't find the movie they wanted. I thought 'I could run a video store better than this.' "

309

In September 1983, he invested $300,000 to open a Philadelphia video store with 6,000 movies, employing a different system, one now taken for granted: empty boxes of available movies were displayed in the open for browsing, and when customers brought the box to the counter, they knew it was available. The venture was only four months old when Stone opened two more stores, launching the West Coast Video chain, the name intended to conjure associations with Hollywood.

Stone turned over the running of Sorbee to his father while he and his partner, Richard J. Abt, began franchising the West Coast concept in 1985. In 1988, the company acquired National Video, a network of 455 stores, so that with more than 650 stores in the fold, West Coast Video was briefly the largest video chain in the country. Although West Coast added another 200 units at its peak, other players emerged, most notably Blockbuster Entertainment, whose superstore format proved so popular that it surpassed West Coast Video. In 1991, West Coast Video tried to transform itself into a pure franchising company by selling its 59 company-owned and limited partnership stores to franchisees, part of a move that was to culminate in an initial public offering of stock. Less than a year later, however, the company's general partner, Stone-owned Red Lion Entertainment, the entity that owned the company-owned stores, filed for Chapter 11 bankruptcy protection, and West Coast Video Enterprises soon filed as well. Later in 1992, a reorganization plan was accepted that in part called for Stone to pay $375,000 out of his own pocket and pledge $1 million in Sorbee stock, a deal that would pay creditors 25 cents on every dollar owed. In exchange, creditors gave up their right to pursue legal action against Stone. He remained in charge of the company after it emerged from bankruptcy and changed the name to West Coast Entertainment, but it never recaptured the momentum of earlier years. In 1995, it was acquired by Marion, Ohio-based Giant Video Inc., at which point Stone severed his ties to the company he started.

Although it is uncertain how involved Stone was in the running of Sorbee during the time he headed West Coast Video, it seems likely, given his reputation as a workaholic, that he kept close tabs on operations. The sugarless candy niche had undergone a number of significant changes since Stone sold his first lollipop to a dentist office. New and improved bulking agents and sweeteners had come onto the market, allowing candymakers to produce sugarless hard candy that was almost identical to sugar hard candy in terms of feel, look, taste, and even the way it crunched. As a result of improving products, the sugarless candy category experienced steady growth in the 1980s. Moreover, an increasing number of consumers were turning to all manner of sugarless and low-fat products during the 1980s, including sugarless chewing gum, sugar-free sodas, and low-fat ice cream. Sorbee was one of the main beneficiaries of the trend that continued into the 1990s. In 1991, the company enjoyed a 12 percent increase in sales. It was only a matter of

time before the big candy manufacturers took note of the money being made on the fast-growing sugarless candy niche, even though at the time it accounted for just 1 percent of the market. A key moment in the industry came in 1992 when M&M/Mars introduced the Milky Way II Bar, which contained less fat and about 25 percent fewer calories than the original Milky Way. It was one of the early attempts in the pursuit of a tasty, low-calorie chocolate, perhaps the ultimate challenge in the candy industry, which was divided between chocolate and non-chocolate products.

Regarding low-fat chocolate, Kitty Kevin wrote in a 1995 *Food Processing* article: "If the question of low-fat chocolate were merely one of finding an appropriate fat substitute—even though matching the characteristics of cocoa butter is quite daunting—it surely would have been accomplished by now. But the question is much more complex because of the legal definition of chocolate. Current legal standards don't allow for the replacement of milk fats or cocoa butter in chocolate. That leaves confectioners with few options other than to use less chocolate or change its particle distribution." Technically speaking, chocolate is the suspension of cocoa and sucrose particles in cocoa butter. To make a low-fat chocolate, therefore, required researchers to reduce the amount of fat needed to suspend the particles without sacrificing taste or texture.

Dream Bar Launched in the Mid-1990s

In the early 1990s, Sorbee launched the Dream Foods Co. division to make its play in the low-fat chocolate bar arena. In July 1994 it introduced the one-ounce DreamCandy Bar, imported from Wales, containing three grams of fat and 88 calories. It took the minimalist approach to producing a low-fat product, using real milk chocolate but making it chewy with the addition of caramel, honey, and nougat, and the use of polydextrose as a bulking agent also added to the bar's taste. It was sold in supermarket, convenience, and drug stores, and response was so strong that a second product in the Dream Bar line made its debut in 1996, the Peanut Butter Crisp DreamCandy bar. It combined peanut butter and crisps with a wrapping of real milk chocolate. It had 3.5 grams of fat and 100 calories. A year later, the WOW bar, a crunchy chocolate-covered peanut butter bar was introduced. With 3.5 grams of fat and 120 calories, it was slightly more fattening than the previous entries in the line. In 1995, Sorbee also introduced sugar-free bagged chocolates under its own label, including chocolate-covered peanut butter, cocoa creams, and peppermint patties.

During the 1990s, sugarless candies made increasing inroads in the coveted supermarket channel. To drive sales the company offered samples to consumers, conducted promotional price reductions, and also invested in television advertising. In 1997, the company signed Richard Simmons, the popular fitness personality, to act as the spokesman for the Dream line of candy bars. His name and face also appeared on the packaging, which exclaimed, "You're not dreaming, these are delicious!" Another significant marketing endeavor, launched in 1998, involved licensing. Sorbee brought out a line of sugar-free hard candy, using isomalt and aspartame, under the Kraft Foods' Crystal Light brand name, available in the four Crystal Light powdered diet drink mix flavors: lemonade, tropical fruit, assorted fruit, and iced tea. Sorbee signed another licensing

Key Dates:

1978: Sorbee International Ltd. is founded.
1994: The first Dream Bar is introduced.
1997: Richard Simmons is signed as a spokesperson.
1998: Sorbee signs a licensing deal with Krafts' Crystal Light and Country Time Lemonade labels.
2004: Sorbee petitions for Chapter 11 bankruptcy protection.

deal with Kraft to sell sugarless hard candy under the Country Time Lemonade name. As the 1990s came to an end, the diet candy category was experiencing faster growth than candy overall, with low-fat chocolate the fastest growing part of it. Sorbee took advantage of the trend by introducing chocolate-covered cream wafers and also brought out a new upscale line of foil-wrapped hard candy. At the same time, Sorbee looked to become involved in regular chocolate as well, closing out the decade by introducing a line of affordably priced, boxed Belgian chocolates called Sweet Obsession. The two editions—the Classic Assorted Collection of 18 varieties of milk, white, and dark chocolates with flavored centers, and the Classic Coffee Collections of 16 chocolates with coffee-flavored centers—were priced between Godiva and Russell Stover.

With the start of the 2000s, Sorbee continued to add to its sugar-free products. After a great deal of research and consumer taste testing, the company debuted a line of five sugar-free cookies using the no-calorie sweetener Splenda. They included animal cookies, peanut butter, soft baked oatmeal, crunchy chocolate, and soft baked chocolate. Sorbee also added sugar-free, individually foil-wrapped jelly candies available in cherry, lemon, raspberry, peach, strawberry, and lemon flavors. In addition, the company introduced sugar-free milk and dark chocolate-flavored truffles, creams, and caramels. In early 2001, Sorbee brought out a new line of sugar-free hard candies, which came in chocolate, butterscotch, and coffee flavors.

Despite a downturn in the economy, sales of all candies continued to grow in the early 2000s. The sugarless candy segment then benefited greatly from the dramatic popularity of the Atkins diet and other low-carb diets. As explained by *Candy Industry* in a September 2003 article, "Many low-carb products are sugarfree. When sugar is removed from a product, the carbohydrate count in the product is often lower. That explains how manufacturers like Sorbee . . . can easily make the move to also offering low-carb products. Sorbee recently changed its sugar-free chocolate bags and bars to include labeling for low-carb dieters. The new labeling provides the net-carb count on each bag."

Presumably, Sorbee prospered during the low-carb craze while it lasted, although the financial state of the private company has always been closely guarded. Nevertheless, on April 13, 2004, Sorbee petitioned the court in the Eastern District of Pennsylvania for Chapter 11 bankruptcy protection. According to the filing the company had $2,655,522 in total assets, compared to $3,057,720 in debts. When the company would emerge from Chapter 11 and in what form remained to be determined.

Principal Competitors

Hillside Candy LLC; The Hershey Company; Kraft Foods Inc.

Further Reading

Fuhrman, Elizabeth, "The Low-Carb Bonanza," *Candy Industry*, September 2003, p. 38.

Kaplan, Andrew, "Small Niche, Big Potential," *U.S. Distribution Journal*, February 15, 1995, p. 16.

Kevin, Kitty, "Low-Fat Chocolate: The Impossible Dream?," *Food Processing*, May 1995, p. 85.

Kulpa, Jennifer, "Diet Sales Bulge in Candy Aisles," *Drug Store News*, November 15, 1999, p. 79.

Prewitt, Edward, "On the Rise," *Fortune*, November 21, 1988, p. 204.

Rogen, Ed, "Lights, Cameras . . . Success," *Philadelphia Business Journal*, June 2, 1986, p. 1.

Rutherford, Andrea C., "Candy Firms Roll out 'Healthy' Sweets, but Snackers May Sour on the Products," *Wall Street Journal*, August 10, 1992, p. B1.

Sectzer, Jessie Ray, "Hard Candies Remain Up Even As Economy Struggles," *Candy Industry*, February 2002, p. 36.

—Ed Dinger

Southern Poverty Law Center, Inc.

400 Washington Avenue
Montgomery, Alabama 36104
U.S.A.
Telephone: (334) 956-8200
Fax: (334) 956-8483
Web site: http://www.splcenter.org

Nonprofit Organization
Incorporated: 1971
Employees: 105
Total Assets: $36.65 million (2003)
NAIC: 541190 Other Legal Services; 813311 Human
    Rights Organizations

The Southern Poverty Law Center, Inc. (SPLC) is an organization that seeks to improve civil rights for poor Americans and immigrants through legal action, the gathering of intelligence on hate groups, and education. It is best known for a series of lawsuits that helped shut down white supremacist groups by winning large monetary judgments for their victims, while others have improved conditions for prisoners and other institutionalized persons and protected the rights of children and immigrants. The organization's Intelligence Project (formerly Klanwatch) monitors the activities of hate groups around the United States and publishes the quarterly *Intelligence Report* for law enforcement officials, while the Immigrant Justice Project takes on cases involving abuse of immigrants in the southern United States. The SPLC's education wing, tolerance.org, creates and distributes educational materials for use in K-12 classrooms, including a Web site and a semi-annual magazine that is sent to 500,000 educators. The organization also publishes trial strategy manuals and offers grants to attorneys through its Strategic Litigation Grant Project. The SPLC does not charge clients for its services but is funded by donations and interest drawn from its $136 million endowment fund.

Beginnings

The Southern Poverty Law Center was founded in 1971 by two white lawyers in Montgomery, Alabama, Morris Dees and Joseph J. Levin, Jr., who banded together to form an organization that would take up the plight of poor Southern blacks in the legal arena. They would perform their work pro bono, with no charge to their clients.

Born in 1936 to a family of Alabama farmers, Dees had founded a direct marketing company as an undergraduate at the University of Alabama to sell birthday cakes by mail, and after graduating from law school in 1960 went on to sell such items as cookbooks, hair cream, and tractor cushions. He began to practice law in Montgomery, and although in 1961 he represented a white man accused of beating a freedom rider, he felt strong sympathy for the plight of blacks in the still largely segregated South. In February 1968, after a night spent reading a biography of crusading lawyer Clarence Darrow at a snowed-in airport, he made a decision to take up the cause of civil rights. One of his first successes was a case which led to the integration of the all-white Montgomery YMCA. In 1969, Dees sold his highly successful publishing company, Fuller & Dees Marketing Group, to Times Mirror for $6 million, and turned to civil rights law full-time.

Joseph Levin, born in 1943, had also gotten his law degree from the University of Alabama, and, after two years in the U.S. Army, returned to work in his father's law practice in Montgomery. He had seen racism firsthand while at college when the Ku Klux Klan had burned a cross in the yard of his Jewish fraternity house. Watching Dees's efforts to challenge the racist status quo in Montgomery, Levin decided to help. The pair went into practice together, and Levin & Dees soon evolved into the SPLC. Its primary purpose, according to Dees's 1991 book *A Season For Justice,* was "to fight the effects of poverty with innovative lawsuits and education programs." It would attempt to end "customs, practices, and laws that were used to keep low-income blacks and whites powerless."

Seeking a prominent Civil Rights activist to head the new organization, the pair recruited Julian Bond for the title of honorary president. Born in 1940, Bond had helped found the influential Student Nonviolent Coordinating Committee (SNCC) and been nominated for vice-president at the 1968 Democratic National Convention, where he had given a memorable speech, though he was not able to accept the nomination because of his age.

Company Perspectives:

Throughout its history, the Center has worked to make the nation's Constitutional ideals a reality. The Center's legal department fights all forms of discrimination and works to protect society's most vulnerable members, handling innovative cases that few lawyers are willing to take. Over three decades, it has achieved significant legal victories, including landmark Supreme Court decisions and crushing jury verdicts against hate groups.

Soon after incorporating the SPLC, seasoned marketer Dees started a direct mail fundraising campaign, sending out 25,000 letters to members of groups like the American Civil Liberties Union. The organization received enough donations to hire a small staff and take on more cases, and after Dees raised $24 million for the unsuccessful 1972 presidential bid of Democratic Senator George McGovern, he received a copy of the campaign's mailing list of 700,000 names, which was used to raise further contributions for the SPLC.

One of the organization's first notable cases was *Nixon v. Brewer,* which focused on giving poor blacks and whites better representation in the Alabama state legislature. The case was a success and led to the state changing its rules to require a single representative per voting district rather than the former ''at large'' method which tended to favor whites.

Another of the SPLC's early cases was *Paradise v. Allen,* a 1972 lawsuit that sought to integrate the all-white ranks of the Alabama State Police. After the state was ordered to hire one black trooper for every white one hired until the force was 25 percent black, the state tried a variety of means to avoid compliance. The case was settled by the U.S. Supreme Court in 1987 in favor of the SPLC's client.

Other cases of the early 1970s forced the federal government to change Department of Defense regulations that denied some benefits to dependents of servicewomen and led to prison reforms in Alabama, with the judge calling the prisons ''wholly unfit for human habitation'' in his ruling.

Though it typically stuck with class action lawsuits, the SPLC was also taking on more cases for individuals, primarily those involving the death penalty. One of the first of these was that of the ''Tarboro Three,'' a trio of young black men sentenced to death for allegedly raping a white woman in 1973. The SPLC found a witness who contradicted the testimony of the victim and other exculpatory evidence, and the men were ultimately given a much-reduced sentence and released. Other well-known cases included that of Joan Little, a black woman who killed a white prison guard she claimed was trying to rape her, and Johnny Ross, convicted of raping a white woman in Louisiana in 1975 and sentenced to death at age 16. Both had their death sentences reversed.

The year 1976 saw Julian Bond give up the title of SPLC president, while Dees took time off to help raise funds for presidential candidate Jimmy Carter. Levin, who had served as the SPLC's legal director for its first five years and worked on

more than 50 major cases, supervised Carter's Justice Department transition team and then remained in Washington to serve in the administration. In 1979, he went into private law practice in Washington, though he remained involved with the SPLC as its president and board chairman.

In 1976, the SPLC also started a new operation called Team Defense, for which its attorneys developed strategies to fight death penalty cases that were shared with other lawyers via seminars and a series of manuals. In 1977, a dispute over fundraising methods between Dees and the head of the Team Defense Project, Millard Farmer, resulted in lawsuits between the two and Farmer leaving the organization.

Successes of this era included a lawsuit that helped end job requirements that discriminated against women seeking to work in Alabama as prison guards and a suit against a cotton mill by a worker who had contracted a respiratory disease from the dust he inhaled while working there, which cost him his job when he became too ill to work. He received a financial settlement, and the case led to federal regulations limiting the amount of dust to which workers could be exposed. By 1979, the SPLC had a staff of five lawyers and two investigators, and an endowment of more than $5 million.

In 1979, at a peaceful protest march in Decatur, Alabama, more than 100 Klansmen attacked marchers with bats and guns. Many were beaten, and two were shot in the head. The FBI investigated but did not charge the Klansmen, though a black marcher was charged with assault. The SPLC soon got involved, filing a civil suit against the Invisible Empire of the Knights of the Ku Klux Klan and several of its members. The lawsuit was later resolved in a ruling that several Klansmen pay damages, perform civil service, and refrain from supremacist activities. The organization also uncovered new evidence in the case, which led to the convictions of nine of the Klansmen.

Klanwatch Founded in 1981

Largely as a result of that case, in 1981 the SPLC founded a new unit called Klanwatch to monitor and report on the activities of hate organizations around the United States. Shortly after its formation, the SPLC filed suit against another group of Klansmen in Texas who had been training in paramilitary camps. When an association of white shrimp fishermen recruited them to help frighten off a rival group of Vietnamese immigrant fishermen, the Klan threatened the latter and allegedly burned some of their boats. The judge issued an injunction against the Klan intimidating the fishermen and later forced them to disband their training camp.

In 1983, an arsonist set fire to the firm's offices in Montgomery. Though it had evidently been set in an attempt to destroy the organization's Klan files, many documents critical to the case were undamaged. Two Klan members and a Klan sympathizer later pled guilty and were sentenced to prison. Dees and other staffers received frequent threats of violence, and they were often escorted by armed guards, while the firm's offices and Dees's home were kept under guard around the clock.

The 1984 case of *Beulah Mae Donald v. United Klans of America* brought a new weapon to the SPLC's arsenal, one that it would use many times in the future. In 1981, Donald's son

Michael had been killed at random by Klan members who sought to intimidate blacks in Mobile, Alabama, after an interracial jury had acquitted a black man accused of killing a policeman. Though the two Klansmen who killed Donald were later convicted, the SPLC decided to seek a further level of relief by suing the Klan group they belonged to for monetary damages. In 1987, the case was settled with an award of $7 million to Ms. Donald. As a result, the Klan's headquarters building was turned over to her, and the organization was effectively shut down.

In 1989, the SPLC won a similar judgment for $12.5 million against White Aryan Resistance founder Tom Metzger for the family of an Egyptian college student murdered by white supremacists in Portland, Oregon, who had been encouraged by Metzger to commit the act. The 1980s also saw an important victory in the area of tax equity, with owners of coal mines in Kentucky forced to pay a greater share of taxes on their coal reserves, resulting in improved funding for local schools and the creation of new jobs.

In 1989, the SPLC unveiled the Civil Rights Memorial, designed by Vietnam War Memorial architect Mia Lin, across the street from its Montgomery headquarters. Featuring the names of more than 30 individuals killed in the struggle for civil rights, it became a major tourist attraction for the city.

Teaching Tolerance Introduced in 1991

In 1991, the organization founded a new program called Teaching Tolerance to give educators help in promoting respect for diversity. It published a semi-annual magazine and also offered teaching materials and multimedia kits to K-12 educators in 55,000 schools, as well as grants for those creating programs in their communities. A decade later it would extend its offerings with a Web site, www.tolerance.org.

Continuing to take up controversial subjects, in 1992 the SPLC sued the governor of Alabama over the state's use of the Confederate battle flag over the capitol dome. The suit was successful, and it was taken down. During the 1990s the firm also took on a number of cases involving prisoners' rights, winning changes in the way inmates were hospitalized, expanding the reading materials they were allowed, and ending use of a humiliating device called the "hitching post" and the revived chain gang. Other cases of this period won improved rights for immigrants, resulting in the state giving driver's license tests in eight different languages, and free provision of medically necessary transportation for Medicaid patients.

In 1994, a new Klanwatch offshoot, the Militia Task Force, was formed, and the organization's intelligence-gathering operations were later merged to create the Intelligence Project. It would monitor a fluctuating number of about 800 hate groups, with the quarterly *Intelligence Report* mailed out to 60,000 law enforcement agencies.

In 1996, cofounder Joseph Levin moved back to Montgomery to take the post of chief executive officer of the organization. By now, the SPLJ's endowment totaled $68 million, and it had a budget of more than $7 million a year. It was receiving contributions from some 300,000 supporters.

SPLC Wins $21.5 Million from Klan Group in 1998

A 1996 SPLC lawsuit against the Christian Knights of the Ku Klux Klan and several related organizations and individuals resulted in the highest judgment ever against a hate group. After a 100-year old black church was burned to the ground as part of a string of similar arson fires, the SPLC sued the groups thought to be responsible, and in 1998 won a $37.8 million judgment, which was later reduced to $21.5 million by a judge. The defendants were forced to give up their land and headquarters, which effectively killed off the Christian Knights organization. Like other such judgments, the victims received only a small portion of the total awarded, as most Klan groups had little in the way of assets.

In 1998, the SPLC sued on behalf of a black homeless teenager who had been denied admission to two Alabama high schools. Shortly after the suit was filed, she was admitted, and the state Board of Education later agreed to abide by the federal McKinney Act requiring educational access for homeless children.

In 2000, the SPLC won a $6.3 million judgment against Richard Butler and the Aryan Nations that resulted in the loss of their 20-acre compound in Idaho. It was later turned into a park by the plaintiffs, whose car had been shot at from the compound in 1998.

The year 2000 also saw the SPLC move into a new highly secure six-story headquarters beside the Civil Rights Memorial. This facility would house its staff of 70 and provide room for growth. The SPLC's endowment now stood at $120 million, and during the year it took in $44 million in fundraising and investment income and spent $13 million on operations.

In November 2000, the organization and Dees were profiled in a highly critical article in *Harper's* magazine. The writer of the article echoed comments made over the years by other critics: the firm's emphasis on fundraising well beyond its current needs, its relatively small percentage of black employees, and the reputed unhappiness of many who worked there were all touched on, with some calling Dees the "televangelist" of the civil rights movement. He responded that many of the complaints had been made by disgruntled former employees and that the endowment was necessary to keep the organization positioned for long term survival.

SPLC lawsuits of the early 2000s helped secure immigrant children the right to counsel in deportation hearings and further improved healthcare and living conditions for prisoners. Another resulted in the removal of a two-and-a-half ton monument displaying the Ten Commandments in the rotunda of the state's judicial building.

In 2003, Levin stepped down from the SPLC's top post and became president emeritus. J. Richard Cohen would serve as president and CEO, with San Diego attorney James McElroy taking the role of board chair. The same year saw a new suit filed against an anti-immigrant paramilitary group called Ranch Rescue, which had allegedly captured a group of illegal Salvadorean immigrants, held them hostage, and terrorized them. The following year, a new unit, the Immigrant Justice Project, was founded to help protect the rights of immigrants in nine southern states.

In August 2005, the Ranch Rescue case was decided in favor of the immigrants, who were awarded financial settlements from several of their attackers, as well as the 70-acre Camp Thunderbird, the group's headquarters. The year also saw a new Civil Rights Memorial visitor center added that featured in-depth information about those honored there.

After more than 30 years of fighting for the rights of the oppressed, the Southern Poverty Law Center continued to seek justice for Americans who otherwise would have no voice. The organization had helped secure improvements in rights for minorities, prisoners, children, and immigrants, as well as bringing some of the country's most violent hate groups to their knees. The battle was far from over, however, and the organization continued to take on new cases in its quest for justice.

Principal Operating Units

www.tolerance.org; Intelligence Project; Immigrant Justice Project.

Further Reading

Brinkley, Douglas, "Fighting the Good Fight," *New Orleans Times-Picayune*, June 9, 1996, p. E7.

Dees, Morris, and Steve Fiffer, *A Season For Justice: The Life and Times of Civil Rights Lawyer Morris Dees*, New York: Charles Scribner's Sons, 1991.

Elliott, Stuart, "A Marketer of Civil Rights Who Has Made a Difference," *The New York Times*, May 15, 1991, p. D20.

"Fire Damages Alabama Center That Battles Klan," *The New York Times*, July 31, 1993, p. 1A.

Gannon, Julie, "We Can't Affort Not to Fight," *Trial*, January 1, 1997, p. 18.

Hudson, Mike, "Nurturing Justice or Cashing In?," *Roanoke Times & World News*, August 27, 2003, p. 1.

"Klan Must Pay $37 Million for Inciting Church Fire," *The New York Times*, July 25, 1998, p. A7.

London, Robb, "Sending a $12.5 Million Message to a Hate Group," *The New York Times*, October 26, 1990, p. B20.

Morlin, Bill, "Dees' Center Has Compiled Extensive Resume," *Spokesman Review*, January 26, 1999, p. A4.

Morse, Dan, "Does Center Practice What It Preaches?," *St. Petersburg Times*, April 3, 1994, p. 5D.

"New Legal Center in Alabama Seeks to Aid the Poor Politically and Economically," *The New York Times*, February 20, 1972, p. 40.

Sack, Kevin, "A Son of Alabama Takes on Americans Who Live to Hate," *The New York Times*, May 12, 1996, p. 7D.

Schmidt, William E., "Black Is Handed Deed to Offices of Klan Group," *The New York Times*, May 20, 1987, p. A18.

Silverstein, Ken, "The Church of Morris Dees," *Harper's Magazine*, November 1, 2000, pp. 54–57.

Smothers, Ronald, "Memorial Honors the Victims of Racial Violence," *The New York Times*, November 4, 1989, p. 7.

Stevens, William K., "Judge Issues Ban on Klan Threat to Vietnamese," *The New York Times*, May 15, 1981, p. A14.

Stone, Andrea, "Morris Dees: At Center of the Racial Storm," *USA Today*, August 3, 1996, p. 7A.

"'Team Defense' Uses New Methods to Avoid Death Penalty for Clients," *The New York Times*, December 5, 1976, p. 60.

Thomas, Jo, "Courthouse Klan-Fighter Takes on Aryan Nations," *The New York Times*, August 29, 2000, p. A14.

Toner, Robin, "A Mother's Struggle with the Klan," *The New York Times*, March 8, 1987, p. 25.

Wilkie, Curtis, "Lawsuits Prove to Be a Big Gun in Anti-Klan Arsenal," *Boston Globe*, June 17, 1993, p. 1.

—Frank Uhle

Stericycle, Inc.

28161 North Keith Drive
Lake Forest, Illinois 60045
U.S.A.
Telephone: (847) 367-5910
Toll Free: (800) 643-0240
Fax: (847) 367-9493
Web site: http://www.stericycle.com

Public Company
Incorporated: 1989
Employees: 3,545
Sales: $516.2 million
Stock Exchanges: NASDAQ
Ticker Symbol: SRCL
NAIC: 562211 Hazardous Waste Treatment and Disposal

Stericycle, Inc., is the largest medical waste management company in the United States, with additional operations in Puerto Rico, Canada, Mexico, and the United Kingdom. Approximately 310,000 of the company's customers are small medical waste producers, such as doctors and dentists offices, outpatient clinics, and long-term and sub-acute care facilities, while another 7,500 customers, such as hospitals and blood banks, are major medical waste generators. General medical waste is either incinerated, or rendered into a recyclable material or usable fuel by means of autoclaving, which relies on high pressure and temperature to destroy pathogens, or Stericycle's proprietary electro-thermal, deactivation technology (EDT), which disinfects waste by means of low-frequency radio waves. Specific services include the Bio Systems Sharps Management Program, involved in the entire life cycle of the sharp medical tool, from procurement to disposal and verification to meet regulatory compliance; Stericycle Direct Return, helping customers manage expired medications; and Stericycle Infection Control Management Software, an infection tracking system intended to prevent the outbreak of costly hospital-acquired infections. The Company also markets Steri Safe Disinfectant Cleaner, a hospital-grade multipurpose disinfectant and cleaner. Stericycle is a public company based in Lake Forest, Illinois, its stock traded on the NASDAQ.

Company Emerges From 1980s Classroom Exercise

Stericycle was conceived by Dr. James Sharp, a physician who returned to school to earn a Masters of Business Administration. While studying startups and writing business plans, he developed the idea of a waste medical disposal company to complete a class exercise in 1986. The problem of medical waste became major news during the summer of 1987 when on several occasions used syringes, blood bags, gauze dressings, and other items washed up on a 50-mile stretch of New Jersey beaches, which had to be closed for reasons of public safety, resulting in the loss of $1 billion in tourism for the state. The problem was likely caused by illegal dumpers, and no incidents of this magnitude occurred again. Nevertheless, medical wastes in smaller quantities washed ashore in virtually all coastal states, and hospitals were known to toss bloody surgical gowns and others wastes into dumpsters. To quell the public outcry, Congress enacted the Medical Waste Tracking Act of 1988, a tepid response that called for a two-year pilot program to track materials that came in contact with blood or other body fluids in ten states. The publicity surrounding the issue also led to a number of entrepreneurs launching medical waste disposal companies, although many of them were fly-by-night affairs that did nothing more than burn or bury the waste. Sharp's business model for a medical waste disposal company also gained currency and became the subject of a newspaper article that caught the attention of businessman David Lane, who had experience in the healthcare and environmental management industries. He contacted Sharp and decided to turn Sharp's classroom business plan into a reality.

Sharp and Lane secured $7.1 million in seed money from John Patience, a partner in the Deerfield, Illinois-based venture capital firm of Marquette Venture Partners. Stericycle was incorporated in Delaware in March 1989 and opened its first plant, located in Arkansas, in February 1990. Just a month later, the founders began to step aside, bringing in a professional manager in the form of Jack W. Schuler, who became chief executive officer and chairman of the board. Schuler had 17 years of experience at Abbott Laboratories, where he rose to the rank of president and chief operating officer. Not only did Schuler provide invaluable contacts from his days at Abbott, he also brought with him a patent for the EDT technology, making

Stericycle the first company in the $1 billion medical waste industry to possess a disposal process that produced recyclable material as an end product.

By the end of 1991, Stericycle had a roster of a dozen customers and revenues of $1.6 million. It was a small player with great ambitions, despite facing stiff competition from well-heeled solid-waste companies like Waste Management Inc. and Browning-Ferris Industries Inc. (BFI), which saw medical waste as a bundling opportunity. They could negotiate a single price with a hospital, for instance, that would include taking care of all of its wastes. As a result, the big players charged less to collect medical waste than the specialized companies could, and BFI and Waste Management began to gobble up the small companies. With its technological savvy, Stericycle was able to hold on during this period until tighter Environmental Protection Agency (EPA) regulations and increased fines began to change the industry dynamic and specialists were able to gain an edge. In the meantime, Stericycle filed an antitrust lawsuit against BFI in 1993. The matter was settled a couple years later.

New CEO Takes Over in Early 1990s

In May 1992, Schuler brought in a new CEO, Mark C. Miller, a 15-year veteran at Abbott, where he had served as vice-president in charge of operations in Africa, the Pacific, and Asia. According to Kathleen Murray writing in the November-December 1993 issue of *Chief Executive,* Miller "was in line to become CEO. But somehow, he found the idea of running an established company stifling, and he bolted for Stericycle. 'I realized that part of what I enjoyed was a team of people who are charged up to create something,' says Miller, an affable and easygoing former high school football star. 'It was that new buzz of creating.' "

All told, Stericycle raised $50.1 million from venture partners, which in addition to Marquette included State Farm Mutual Automobile Insurance Co. and Baxter Healthcare Corp. Baxter also forged an alliance to develop technologies to convert plastic syringes into recyclable fibrous materials, which would then be used to make the plastic containers to hold used medical sharps. A major selling point for Stericycle was its ability to recycle medical waste, rather than rely on landfills and incinerations. Not until January 1992 did the company open its first full-scale EDT treatment facility, located in More, Washington. Three more facilities opened in 1993, in Loma Linda, California; Woonsocket, Rhode Island; and Yorkville, Wisconsin. Starting in 1993, Stericycle also began spending some of its cash to grow the business through acquisitions. The first deal, completed in August 1993, was the purchase of Portland, Oregon-based Therm-Tec Destruction Service of Oregon, Inc. Next, in March 1994, Stericycle bought the assets of Recovery Corporation of Illinois, including containers, transportation equipment, and customer list. Later in the year, Stericycle added Safe Way Disposal Systems,

Inc., a Middletown, Connecticut-based company doing business in Connecticut, New York, Rhode Island, and Massachusetts. Another acquisition followed in 1995: the assets of Safetech Health Care of Valencia, California. Largely due to these acquisitions, Stericycle saw its revenues increase from $5 million in 1992 to more than $21.3 million in 1995, a total that ranked the company second, albeit a distant second, in the medical waste disposal field to BFI. The company was still racking up losses, having burned through $38 million since its launch, but was well on its way to achieving profitability.

Stericycle completed four more acquisitions in the first half of 1996, including Bio-Med of Oregon, Inc. and WMU Medical Services of New England, Inc. in the month of January, and Santa Ana, California-based Doctors Environmental Control, Inc. and Sharps Incinerator of Fort, Inc. of Fort Atkinson, Wisconsin in May. To fund further growth, the company prepared to make an initial public offering (IPO) of stock in the second half of 1996. Underwritten by New York firms Dillon Read & Co. and Salomon Brothers and Chicago-based William Blair & Co., the IPO was completed in late August, netting the company $27.6 million.

In 1997, Stericycle acquired seven more companies with locations in New York, New Jersey, Washington, D.C., Baltimore, Ohio, Wisconsin, and Arizona. The additional business helped Stericycle to increase revenues to $46.2 million in 1997 and net income of $1.4 million, representing the company's first profitable year in its short history. Prospects for continued growth were also bolstered in 1997 by the issuance of new clean air standards by the EPA that targeted medical waste incinerators, calling for reduced levels of mercury, dioxins, carbon monoxide, and lead emissions. Stericycle further benefited because of its EDT technology as many competitors became willing acquisition candidates, opting to sell out rather than make the investment to upgrade their incinerators.

With 7 percent of the market, Stericycle still trailed BFI by a wide margin, but it became the industry's most aggressive consolidator and was not shy about stating its goal of becoming number one. In 1998, Stericycle completed 13 acquisitions, including BFI's Arizona business. The company also entered into a joint venture with a Mexican company to form MEDAM S.A. de C.V. and acquire Repesa S.A. de C.V., one of the largest medical waste service providers in Mexico. In addition, Stericycle licensed its ETD technology for use in Brazil. For the year, Stericycle increased sales to $66.7 million, resulting in net income of $5.7 million. Ironically, Stericycle also became the subject of anti-trust litigation in 1998, accused of colluding with BFI to divide territories in Utah, Arizona, Colorado. The matter was settled five years later, with Stericycle agreeing to pay a civil penalty and assume costs, while neither admitting nor denying guilt.

In some respects, possible collusion with BFI had become a moot point. After long expressing a desire to acquire its larger rival, changing circumstance made the dream a reality in 1999. Allied Waste Industries Inc. agreed to acquire BFI in a $7.3 billion deal and simultaneously announced that it would unload assets with at least $900 million in an effort to pare its debt. Allied was more than willing to part with the medical waste business, and Stericycle was a ready buyer, especially well situated because the third largest competitor in the industry, Florida-based Med/

```
┌─────────────────────────────────────────────┐
│               Key Dates:                     │
│                                              │
│ 1989:   Stericycle is incorporated.          │
│ 1992:   Mark Miller is named CEO.            │
│ 1996:   The company makes an initial public  │
│         offering of stock.                   │
│ 1999:   Browning-Ferris Industries is        │
│         acquired.                            │
│ 2004:   Stericycle enters the United Kingdom.│
└─────────────────────────────────────────────┘
```

Waste Inc., was struggling and had recently hired an investment banking firm to help it sort through its strategic options. There was a likelihood, nevertheless, that buyout funds or another company might be interested in BFI, prompting Stericycle to agree to pay $410.5 million for the company, which many analysts estimated was worth $240 to $300 million. However, with its strong balance sheet, Stericycle was able to secure the necessary funding to acquire a rival nearly three times its size. Another important factor in the BFI acquisition was that Stericycle eliminated a competitor that had been charging a low price for its service because of its bundling approach. Stericycle was now able to raise prices more in line with market realities, thus adding to the cash flow necessary to service the debt it took on to acquire BFI. As the unrivaled leader in its field, of course, Stericycle was not above cutting rating rates in select markets to thwart the aspirations of smaller competitors. In addition to BFI, Stericycle completed 14 other acquisitions in 1999. As a result, it placed tenth on *Fortune* magazine's annual list of the 100 fastest growing companies in America.

Selective Acquisitions in the 2000s

Stericycle entered the 2000s with a more selective approach to acquisitions, now focusing on tuck-ins in areas it already served. By gaining geographical density, management hoped to use its infrastructure as a competitive edge to win new accounts. Nevertheless, Stericycle remained open to acquiring a company in a new service area if the economics made sense. It also continued to pursue international opportunities to license its patented technologies. In 2000, Stericycle acquired seven companies, followed by seven more in 2001, including the purchase of Enviro-Med Canada, Inc. to move into the Canadian market. Sales jumped to $323.7 million in 2000 and improved to $359 million in 2001, while net income totaled $14.5 million in 2000 and $14.7 million in 2001 (held down due to high energy costs). At this stage, Stericycle controlled about 20 percent of the market, the only national player in the medical waste disposal field, 12 times larger than its nearest competitor, Med/Waste. Prospects were also buoyed by new clean-air rules set to go into effect in 2002, which would prompt many hospitals to shut down their incinerators and turn to companies like Stericycle to dispose of their medical wastes. The company had successfully integrated the BFI operations, and Wall Street rewarded the company's performance by aggressively bidding up the price of its stock.

External growth continued in 2002, when Stericycle added nine more companies in the United States. It also added to its Canadian business by acquiring Pyroval, Inc., based in Quebec. A key acquisition in 2002, although not completed until 2003, was

the $41.5 million purchase of Scherer Healthcare Inc., the addition of which moved Stericycle into a new line of business, the disposal of sharp medical waste items. In January 2004, the company launched its Bio Systems Sharps Management Program to offer customers a complete turnkey solution for the handling of sharps. Sales grew to $401.5 million in 2002, while net income ballooned to $45.7 million. A dozen more acquisitions were completed in 2003 and 2004, including three Mexican companies: Proterm de Mexico S.A. de C.V., Sterimed S.A.de C.V., and Bio-Infex Servicios y Technologia S.A. de C.V. In 2004, Stericycle entered the United Kingdom through the acquisition of White Rose Environmental Limited. Sales totaled $453.2 million in 2003 and reached $516.2 million in 2004, while net income grew to $65.8 million in 2003 and $78.2 million in 2004.

There was new competition on the horizon in 2005 in the form of giant Waste Management Inc., which had sold most of its medical waste disposal business to Stericycle in 1996 and now decided to reenter the field. Regardless, Stericycle was well positioned to answer the challenged. In addition, demographics favored the company's long-term prospects: with an aging U.S. population requiring more medical attention in the years to come, an increasing amount of medical waste would have to be disposed of, and Stericycle was poised to pick up a major slice of the additional business.

Principal Subsidiaries

American Medical Disposal, Inc.; BFI Medical Waste Inc.; Enviromed, Inc.; Scherer Laboratories, Inc.

Principal Competitors

Med/Waste Inc.; Waste Management Inc.

Further Reading

Alpert, Bill, "Tech Trader: Does Stericycle Have Too Much Market Clout?," *Barron's*, July 29, 2002, p. T1.

Chase, Brett, "War For Medical Waste Brews," *Crain's Chicago Business*, April 25, 2005, p. 4.

Comerford, Mike, "Targeting Bigger Game, Ex-Abbott Labs President Takes Chance as Stericycle Aims for Bigger Rival," *Daily Herald*, April 28, 1999, p. 1.

Keefe, Lisa M., "Stericycle Beats Start-up Odds," *Crain's Chicago Business*, July 9, 1990, p. 17.

Miller, James. P., "Lake, Forest, Ill., Medical-Waste Disposal Firm Is Positive About Acquisition," *Chicago Tribune*, June 1, 2001.

Murray, Kathleen, "Mark C. Miller," *Chief Executive*, November-December 1993, p. 29.

Oloroso, Arsenio, Jr., "Flush with IPO Cash, Stericycle Maps Expansion, Buyout Plans," *Crain's Chicago Business*, September 16, 1996, p. 32.

——, "Stericycle Aiming for Top of the Heap," *Crain's Chicago Business*, May 4, 1998, p. 4.

Redfearn, Suz, "Stericycle Inc./Lake Forst, Illinois Waste Manager Acquires Real Taste for Deals," *Investor's Business Daily*, March 28, 2001, p. A10.

Sostron, Carolyn Pye, "Stericycle Crowned King of Medical Waste Management," *Healthcare Purchasing News*, July 1999, p. 1.

—Ed Dinger

Sun Hydraulics Corporation

1500 West University Parkway
Sarasota, Florida 34243
U.S.A.
Telephone: (941) 362-1200
Fax: (941) 355-4497
Web site: http://www.sunhydraulics.com

Public Company
Incorporated: 1970
Employees: 678
Sales: $94.5 million (2004)
Stock Exchanges: NASDAQ
Ticker Symbol: SNHY
NAIC: 332999 All Other Miscellaneous Fabricated Metal
   Product Manufacturing

Sun Hydraulics Corporation is a Sarasota, Florida-based designer and manufacturer of high-performance, screw-in hydraulic cartridge valves and manifolds, crucial components in fluid power systems used to control force, speed, and motion. The products are used in a wide variety of construction, agricultural, and utility equipment; machine tools; and material handling equipment. Although more expensive than conventional hydraulic valves, Sun's screw-in cartridge valves use a two-piece floating style construction that offers equipment designers greater flexibility, better performance, and a longer life span. In addition to a pair of manufacturing facilities in Sarasota, Sun also operates plants in the United Kingdom, Germany, Korea, and China (through a joint venture). Aside from its innovative products, what sets Sun apart is its unusual organization, the subject of three Harvard Business School case studies. The company has no private offices, job descriptions, or organizational charts. The only job titles are state mandated due to Sun's public status. Employees are granted a great deal of discretion to implement changes as they see fit. The corporate culture has been a primary reason why Sun has enjoyed steady growth since 1970 in spite of dips in the economy along the way.

Founder's Frustration with 1960s Corporate Bureaucracy

Sun's founder, Robert E. Koski, was instrumental in the growth of Mentor, Ohio-based Dynamic Controls, Inc., maker of fluid power control products. After starting out as a product engineer in 1959, over the course of the next decade the Dartmouth College graduate worked his way up through the ranks, including stints in industrial sales, marketing, and product development. Ultimately he became vice-president and director of corporate development, the number 2 position in the organization behind the founder. During that stretch of time Dynamic Controls grew from $600,000 in annual sales to $5 million, but Koski became frustrated with the way the company grew in terms of organization and culture. Not only with his employer but elsewhere he encountered companies that he believed were organized to stifle human contributions. He developed his own management theories, as well as a new hydraulic valve he wanted to pursue, but found no backing from management at Dynamic Controls. Instead, in early 1970, at the age of 40, he quit, determined to launch a company to implement his ideas.

Taking an engineering approach to starting a business, Koski spent most of the first year planning and designing. He elected to stay in the fluid control business with which he was familiar, believing there was room for entry, and selected the name Sun Hydraulics Corporation. He also decided to locate his business in Sarasota, where his former employer had a satellite operation producing hydraulic systems for pleasure boats. Another hydraulic manufacturer also was operating in the area, and he believed he would be able to attract talented people, especially those unhappy with life at a hierarchical company—precisely the kind of employees he wanted. Moreover, Sarasota was growing and offered excellent transportation options. Koski conceived of a horizontal organization to the business, hoping to avoid the "ossification" that resulted from the reliance on a typical vertical organizational chart. At Dynamic Controls, he told Harvard Business School for one of its case studies, people had been given titles, but "as the company outgrew their capabilities and needed to hire or promote more talented people who would appear on the organization chart as their superiors, there was no place the old-timers could go that would satisfy

Company Perspectives:

Sun Hydraulics offers the most comprehensive line of screw-in hydraulic cartridge valves and manifolds in the world. These products provide machine designers the opportunity to develop unique, reliable solutions for hydraulic control applications.

their egos. They had to leave. They could not stay and save face with all the other employees. They had to leave.'' As a model, Koski looked to the way the DuPont Chemical Company ran its laboratories during the 1920s and 1930s when there was a shortage of trained scientists. Out of necessity senior and junior scientists were teamed together and given a great deal of latitude to move from project to project. It was a system that resulted in a period of great innovation at DuPont. For Sun, Koski envisioned a company with no hierarchy, titles, firm job descriptions, reporting relationships, or even close supervision. In the words of a Harvard Business School case study, ''People would be expected to decide for themselves, based on widely shared information on operations, how best to contribute to the company's objectives. Both manufacturing and office personnel would be expected to work with others in the organization whenever they deemed it necessary to accomplish their tasks. 'Horizontal management' would encourage the formation of 'natural clusters' or groups to achieve whatever work had to be done.'' As a further reflection of employee freedom and self-imposed reliability, Sun also would forego the use of quality inspectors. All employees were to take responsibility for the quality of their own work.

Koski wrote out his ideas in a 34-page business plan that he sent to four Sarasota-area banks and other potential investors. In it he described his management philosophy as well as an overview of the fluid power components industry and the Sun product and a detailed ten-year projection of financial and other criteria. He offered three levels of growth projections—pessimistic, realistic, and optimistic—in terms of sales, the number of employees, and the amount of floor space needed. Koski secured the financial backing and launched Sun in 1970 with his wife and one employee. After ten years, Koski looked back and found that with inflation taken into account Sun had come within a percentage point of his optimistic projection.

New Plant Needed by the 1980s

Overall, Sun grew in an orderly way despite the loose structure. The original plant built in 1970 was expanded in 1975, and then in 1980 the company opened a new plant five times as large as the original one. The company turned a profit after its second year and over the course of the first 15 years sales improved at an annual clip of 30 percent to 35 percent, at a time when the industry average was 25 percent. Sun also was better able to weather an industrywide slump in 1982 and 1983 and avoided laying off any employees. In addition, Sun was able to price many of its products 10 percent lower than the competition yet recorded profits that were about twice as much as the industry average. It had a stellar reputation, recognized for its innovative design, quality workmanship, and ethical business dealings.

Although the shape the company culture would assume with so few rules in place had been far from predictable, there was no doubt that Koski's management principles—or lack of them—played a major role in the company's success.

In the office area only the controller and his assistant had enclosed offices, while everyone else, including Koski, relied on workplaces separated only by waist-high walls. Meetings were impromptu, generally growing out of a conversation that required input from other employees. In the shop there were a dozen family groups, each with one informal lead person, who generally emerged naturally. As much as possible the company avoided the use of such titles as supervisor, foreman, and manager, only relying on them as a way to help newcomers to know where to go for help. Employees also were cross-trained in a natural way. They helped out as needed and switched departments as their interests changed. Within a family group, many of the members were able to do all or most of the jobs within it. The shop employees worked four ten-hour days, then used their own discretion about coming in on Fridays and Saturdays to work overtime, and they did not necessarily have to be working in their own departments.

New employees were hired to fill a ''vacuum'' when one became apparent, but the main qualifications were personal and it was not a given that the new employee would even fill the vacuum. As a Harvard Business School case study revealed, ''One engineer, who had been hired with a product development function in mind, had 'become intrigued with the computer' in his first days on the job, and since he concentrated entirely on creating new programming applications.'' In another instance, a market-oriented engineer spent quite a few months '' 'wandering around' learning more about the market. [Colleagues] were certain that one way or another his wandering would be of benefit to the company.''

By 1985 Sun employed 170 people and despite its growing size had been able to maintain its cherished corporate culture. One concern was that the company was overly dependent on Koski and his vision for the company, that unless a way could be found to make him less important on a personal level the company would lapse into conventionality with his departure.

Over the next several years Koski made a conscious effort to remove himself, and Sun began to function with only a modicum of input from him. Not only was the Sarasota operation proving that his personality was not the key to the success of his business model, but the company also was able to create similar structure in new operations, launched in the United Kingdom in 1985 and Germany in 1990. In Sarasota, in the meantime, Sun added 100 employees between 1985 and 1991. During this period Koski also groomed his successor, Clyde Nixon.

A Cornell University-educated engineer and former Naval officer with a Harvard MBA, Nixon had first met Koski in 1979 when as president of a hydraulics manufacturer, Double A Products Co., he attempted to buy Sun. Koski was not interested in selling, but the two men established a business relationship: Koski was eager to find another company to serve as competition in Sun's high-performance niche because many end users were reluctant to switch to the type of valves and manifolds Sun had to offer if there was only one supplier. The

Key Dates:

1970: The company is founded by Robert Koski.
1980: A new plant opens in Sarasota, Florida.
1985: A U.K. plant opens.
1990: A German plant opens.
1997: The company is taken public.
2003: A jointly owned plant is established in China.

two companies forged an alliance in 1982 but three years later Double A was acquired and the relationship was severed. In 1988, looking for a new challenge, Nixon contacted Sun and Koski invited him to join the company and take a year to "wander around and see what he thought he could do." Despite being offered three other more conventional job offers, Nixon opted to work for Sun. At the end of his year-long "wandering" in Koski's view, or "apprenticeship" in his own mind, Nixon took over as president.

Controlling Growth in the 1990s

As Sun entered the 1990s it had to find a way to harness its growth in a number of ways. Employee initiatives resulted in new shop floor scheduling software and robotics that was far ahead of the work being done at many university and national laboratory centers. But the technology was complex and had to be maintained. Still, when the company experienced an electrical problem that shut down the scheduling system for a month, Sun was able to maintain production around 80 percent; other companies likely would have been forced to shut down production entirely. Employees also were lax about buying equipment and services on their own, often neglecting to tell the accounting department. Improved purchasing procedures were instituted, but Koski and Nixon were hesitant to tamper too much with the latitude afforded employees that was such a vital part of the company's culture and success. Sun continued to develop innovative products. Rather than try simply to satisfy customer needs, the company developed products that the customers did not know they needed—yet. As Koski told the Harvard Business School case writers in a 1991 follow-up study, "I think some of our new patented products will still be recognizably in use a hundred years from now. It's difficult for me to picture how these products could have been developed in a large hierarchical company." Many of these cutting-edge products were not even listed in the company catalogue. Rather, customers simply learned about them by word of mouth and the company lost a great deal of sales simply because other potential users were unaware of the products. As a result, Sun took steps in the early 1990s to publish a comprehensive catalog on a more timely basis.

Sales grew from $32.4 million in 1993 to more than $55 million in 1995 when the company launched an international expansion into Europe and Asia. Sun experienced a frustrating 1996, due in large measure to limitations in capacity. Nevertheless, the company was not deterred from taking the next step in its development: going public in January 1997. In a televised interview on CNNfn's *Street Sweep,* Koski explained the decision to file for a public offering of stock: "It's the rite of

passage as far as I'm concerned because we need to be a multinational company. Our multi-national customer-partners need to know more about us and it was time to get it done and we were free at the moment." The offering also allowed some insiders to cash in equity and the stock was now available to use as an incentive to retain key people—but was not to be used to recruit people. All told, the offering netted $18.3 million, with $10 million going to existing stockholders and the balance used to pay down debt and for general corporate purposes. To conform with the requirements of being a public company, Sun had to assign titles to people—chairman, president, vice-president, secretary, and treasurer—but it continued to march to its own drummer. Business cards did not use the titles, and even the typical "Letter to Shareholders" in the annual report became "Observations from Bob Koski and Clyde Nixon," in which Koski penned a few thoughts followed by Nixon's response.

Sun opened new plants in Sarasota and Germany and hired 100 new employees in 1997, when sales grew to $64.2 million and net income amounted to $4.7 million. In 1998 Sun acquired its Korean operation, the first acquisition in company history. The price of the company stock was stagnant but did not affect the way management ran the company, although they were somewhat mystified over the workings of the market, an experience that would only heighten with the years. To alleviate the capacity problems of the mid-1990s, Sun began making significant investments in capital equipment to take advantage of spikes in demand during business cycle upturns. The company also established an important alliance with a German company, Rexroth, which would become a customer and developer of Sun's unique screw-in valve system. Again, the goal was to create a competitor in order to create a greater share of the $650 million cartridge valve market.

Sun's sales approached $80 million in 2000, but then demand began to dip and the economy slumped. Rather than retrench, Sun invested for the future and waited for conditions to improve. In a joint venture with a distributor it also established a plant in China to take advantage of the explosive growth in that country's manufacturing sector. In addition Sun opened sales offices in France and Kansas City, where it also planned to eventually establish a manufacturing capability to produce certain products made by the U.K. operation. By having a domestic plant producing the items, delivery times could be significantly shortened. Although sales declined over the next few years, the company remained profitable.

Business turned around significantly in 2004, when sales jumped from $70.8 million the prior year to $94.5 million, and net income increased from $2.17 million to $7.83 million. The price of the company's stock also began to climb. As Sun entered 2005 the price soared, increasing 96 percent in a matter of 28 trading days to significantly more than $30 before ebbing somewhat. The year was clearly shaping up to be even better than 2004, and the investments made in the late 1990s positioned Sun to enjoy ongoing success.

Principal Subsidiaries

Sun Hydraulik Holdings Ltd.; Sun Hydraulics Ltd.; Sun Hydraulic GmbH; Sun Hydraulics Korea Corporation.

Principal Competitors

Koch Enterprises Inc.; Mark IV Industries Inc.; Sauer-Danfoss Inc.

Further Reading

Henderson, Andre, "Corporate Freedom," *Florida Trend,* August 1, 1997, p. 54.

Hielscher, John, "Sun Hydraulics Stock Surges," *Sarasota Herald Tribune,* April 9, 2005, p. D1.

Mitseas, Catherine, "Valve Maker Develops Unique Path to Growth," *Business Journal (Serving Greater Tampa Bay),* May 21, 1999, p. 1.

Sauer, Matthew, "Sun Looks to Wall Street To Keep It Hot," *Sarasota Herald Tribune,* November 18, 1996, p. 8.

—Ed Dinger

Sunglass Hut
INTERNATIONAL

Sunglass Hut International, Inc.

4000 Luxottica Place
Madison, Ohio 45040
U.S.A.
Telephone: (513) 583-6000
Toll Free: (800) 786-4527
Fax: (800) 786-4327
Web site: http://www.sunglasshut.com

Wholly Owned Subsidiary of Luxottica Group S.p.A.
Incorporated: 1971
Employees: 9,174
Sales: $679.7 million (2004)
NAIC: 453998 All Other Miscellaneous Store Retailers
   (Except Tobacco Stores)

Sunglass Hut International, Inc. is the world's largest specialty retailer of nonprescription sunglasses. The company operates 1,858 stores, 1,584 of which are located in North America. Overseas, the company operates 110 stores in Europe and 164 stores in Australia, New Zealand, and Singapore. Sunglass Hut is focused on fashion eyewear, operating as part of Luxottica Group S.p.A., the world's largest eyewear company, but it also operates more than 300 stores that sell watches under the names Watch Station and Watch World. Other North American retail subsidiaries owned by Luxottica include LensCrafters, Inc., Pearle Vision, Inc., and licensed brand stores located in stores operated by Sears, Roebuck and Co., Target Corporation, and BJ's Wholesale Club, Inc.

The Early Years

Sunglass Hut was founded in 1971 by Sanford Ziff in Miami, Florida. Ziff, an optometrist at the time, had decided that the people in Miami could benefit from protective eyewear in the Florida sun, while he himself could capitalize on the popularity of sunglasses as a wardrobe accessory. He opened a freestanding kiosk in an aisle of Miami's Dadeland Mall, called it the "Sunglass Hut," and sold his fashionable frames at price points of $20 and more. His idea was an almost immediate success, and he found that, for the most part, customers were willing to give in to impulse shopping when it came to accessories.

The success of his first kiosk prompted Ziff to open other Sunglass Hut locations in the Miami area. His family climbed aboard and began to help him expand his small enterprise. As he opened more kiosks, and later, actual stores, Ziff's wife Helene took on a role as the director of personnel. He continued to handle the purchasing and daily operations of the new company, while she dealt with the employees who were hired to staff the stores. As the business continued to expand, the Ziffs' son, Dean, began to handle business aspects related to the company's growth and expansion into new areas.

The Sunglass Hut business continued in that fashion for the next decade, slowly and steadily adding store locations and entering new market areas in a calculated and yet ambitious manner. By the time Sunglass Hut celebrated its 15-year anniversary in 1986, it was composed of more than 100 store units and was achieving sales of more than $24 million a year. At that point, Ziff began formulating an aggressive, five-year expansion plan that would make his business more visible on a national level. His only uncertainty was whether he had the capital actually to finance his idea.

After a great deal of thought regarding his financial situation, both on a personal and a business level, Ziff began to search for an investor to purchase a portion of Sunglass Hut. He decided that he would sell off the majority of his equity in the company, use the proceeds to fund his expansion plan, and give his remaining share of Sunglass Hut to his son. After exploring many different suitors and their offers, Ziff decided to team up with an investment firm from Connecticut called Kidd, Kamm & Co., which had offered more than $35 million for a 75 percent stake in Sunglass Hut. The new investors agreed to Ziff's terms, which dictated that he would retain the company's management team while also shifting part ownership of the company to his son.

1988–92: The Rapid Worldwide Expansion of Sunglass Hut

Following the partial acquisition of Sunglass Hut by Kidd, Kamm & Co., the business was incorporated under the name Sunglass Hut International, Inc. Ziff and his new partners then began to execute his plans for growth. For two years, they worked together to increase the number of Sunglass Hut stores

---

Company Perspectives:

The Sunglass Hut strategy is to offer customers a dominant assortment of the most wanted sunglasses in a convenient fun shopping environment, staffed by friendly, knowledgeable sales associates who are trained to provide a high level of service.

---

in the marketplace, as well as upgrade existing units and add new products to the company's line. Ziff and his management team were actually responsible for taking care of these tasks, while the investors simply offered the financial backing.

Then in 1989, at the age of 64, Ziff left his company in the control of his partners and retired from the business. The Ziff family still held an almost 25 percent stake in Sunglass Hut in Dean's name but was no longer involved in the day-to-day operation of the business. Meanwhile, the company's management continued to push forward with the aggressive expansion and acquisition phase. By 1991, the company's annual sales had quadrupled and soon surpassed the $100 million mark. At that time, the Ziffs sold the portion of Sunglass Hut that remained in their control. It was later estimated that the family received more than $25 million when it sold the company, a figure that included the proceeds from the first sale transaction, all related fees, and the sale of the final 25 percent.

The following year, the Sunglass Hut chain included almost 450 store units, and sales figures were continuing to rise. But, unfortunately, sales for sunglasses retailing at $30 or more declined for the first time in almost a decade, which actually caused a decrease in same-store sales for the year. The company essentially was selling more sunglasses only because it had more stores open; overall, the decline in same-store sales ate away at the company's profits for the year. One highlight that year, however, was the acquisition of competitors Sun Mark, Inc. and Sunglass Marketing, Inc., which included the addition of 134 stores, bringing the Sunglass Hut total to almost 600.

The 1990s: Success As a Publicly Held Company

The year 1993 marked the entrance of Sunglass Hut International, Inc. into the public domain, as the company's stock was offered for sale in an initial public offering that spring. The sale earned Sunglass Hut $70 million, which was immediately used to rid the company of $41 million in long-term debt and to repurchase $11 million in its preferred stock. The remainder of the proceeds then were used to fund further expansion that was in the works, including the addition of another 200 stores in the United States and Europe. In addition, Wallis Arnold Enterprises, Inc. was purchased at the end of the year.

In 1994, during its first full year as a publicly held company, Sunglass Hut either opened or acquired from competitors more than 225 new store locations. The company also entered a joint venture agreement with Sunglass World, the largest specialty retailer of sunglasses in Australia, to open and operate almost 80 Sunglass Huts there. Meanwhile, the company had been working to strengthen its relatively new direct-mail sunglass sales operation. Some wondered why Sunglass Hut would

bother selling its items by mail order, when the practice was often expensive because of the costs related to shipping items and to an increase in returns. But Sunglass Hut's mail-order division averaged $110 per transaction, versus an average of $80 per transaction inside its store units. In that way, the mail-order operation not only paid for itself (and then some), but also enabled the company to reach a wider base of consumers.

Sunglass Hut continued to open new store units rapidly in 1995, everywhere from airport terminals to outlet centers and leased spaces in department stores, in addition to its traditional stores in malls and on city streets. The company also began planning to expand into the sale of prescription sunglasses in selected markets. Testing of the idea began early in the year. Another notable occurrence in 1995 was the acquisition of NFL League MVP Steve Young as the spokesman for the company's new "SunGear" brand private-label items. In addition to the rollout of SunGear, another new member of the Sunglass Hut family included Sunsations Sunglass Company, which was an Indiana-based sunglass retailer, the national chain of which was made up of 350 stores in 44 different states. Sunsations was acquired in June, and in October and November Sunglass Hut also completed the acquisitions of Sunglass World Holdings Pty. Ltd. and of Sun Shades 501 Ltd.

In 1996 the company achieved record sales that broke the half-billion mark, topping off at $527.1 million. At that point, Sunglass Hut International possessed a 30 percent share of the sunglass market in the United States. The company was operating more than 1,700 stores throughout the world, with approximately 1,425 of those being in the United States and the remainder spread throughout Canada, Australia, Europe, Puerto Rico, the U.S. Virgin Islands, and Mexico.

That year, Sunglass Hut committed itself to two major projects for the future. First, the company entered a joint venture agreement with Royal Sporting House Pte. Ltd. of Singapore to open Sunglass Hut stores in Southeast Asia. Under the terms of the agreement, each company would own 50 percent of the venture initially, with Sunglass Hut International possessing the right to purchase Royal Sporting's portion after five years. Another major plan that was set in motion in 1996 was the company's entrance into the business of selling watches through a new enterprise called "Watch Station." With the introduction of Watch Station, Sunglass Hut was looking to revitalize a somewhat inactive watch market that had been dominated by department stores for years. The first Watch Station was opened as a freestanding kiosk in Miami's Dadeland Mall, the same place where Sunglass Hut had begun 25 years earlier.

Sunglass Hut at the Turn of the 21st Century

The foray into selling watches proved to be a boon to Sunglass Hut's business, giving the company a new avenue of growth at a time when its mainstay business was beginning to suffer financially. As the company entered the late 1990s, profits began to deteriorate, prompting management to implement a program aimed at creating a leaner, more profitable organization. In 1998, the company closed 250 stores, reduced the number of vendors it dealt with by more than 50 percent, and reduced the selection of brands and styles it stocked by 90

Key Dates:

1971: Sanford Ziff opens the first Sunglass Hut, a kiosk in Miami, Florida.
1986: After opening his 100th store, Ziff sells 75 percent of the company to finance its expansion.
1992: Sunglass Hut acquires Sun Mark, Inc. and Sunglass Marketing, Inc.
1993: Sunglass Hut completes its initial public offering of stock.
1995: Sunglass Hut begins to sell prescription sunglasses.
1996: The 1,700-store chain collects more than $500 million in sales; the first Watch Station is opened.
1998: Sunglass Hut exits the prescription sunglass business and begins stocking watches at select Sunglass Hut units.
2000: Watch World International, Inc. is acquired.
2001: Luxottica Group S.p.A. acquires Sunglass Hut.
2004: Sunglass Huts completes a program aimed at refining its brand identity.

percent. The year also marked the end of the company's involvement in the prescription eyewear business. Eye-X, which had developed into a 26-store chain during the previous three years, was shut down, but the loss of one business line was compensated for by the success of Watch Station. In 1998, after registering encouraging results from operating Watch Station units, the company began experimenting with combination stores, stocking some Sunglass Huts with watches. The experiment was successful, fueling expansion in three directions: the addition of Sunglass Hut units, Watch Station units, and stores that stocked merchandise from both concepts. In 2000, management delved deeper into the watch business, acquiring the 118-store Watch World International chain in a $30 million deal. At the time of the purchase, the company's Watch Station chain consisted of 110 stores and the number of its combination stores reached nearly 200. "The watches appeal to roughly the same demographic as the sunglasses, essentially an affluent young person, but the company is getting higher sales volume and improved return on the converted stores," an analyst noted in a March 3, 2000 interview with *Daily News Record*.

At roughly the same time the Watch World acquisition was completed, interest from an Italian suitor set the stage for a new chapter in Sunglass Hut's history. Luxottica Group S.p.A., the world's largest eyewear company, was determined to increase its retail presence in North America. In 1995, Luxottica acquired the LensCrafters Optical retail chain, following up with the purchase of the eyewear division of Bausch & Lomb, which included brands such as Ray-Ban, Revo, Arnette, and Killer Loop, in 1999. The company's founder and chairman, Leonardo Del Vecchio, perceived Sunglass Hut as an ideal addition to his sprawling retail empire and he began acquiring the company's shares. In the spring of 2000, a firm Del Vecchio controlled acquired a 5.6 percent stake in Sunglass Hut before informing the company of his buyout intentions at the end of April 2000. Sunglass Hut management flew to Luxottica's headquarters in Milan, but the two sides were unable to agree on a price. Several counterproposals were made until the parties agreed in early

2001 to complete the deal. In February, Luxottica paid $653 million for Sunglass Hut, gaining more than 1,300 Sunglass Hut stores, 430 combination stores, and 228 stores that operated under either the Watch Station or Watch World banner. Added to the 864 LensCrafters stores in the United States and Canada, the acquisition gave Luxottica more than 2,500 retail locations in North America.

Under Luxottica's control, Sunglass Hut became part of the eyewear armada assembled by Del Vecchio. The company maintained its lead as the largest retailer of nonprescription sunglasses in North America during the first years of the 21st century, but expansion took a back seat to other issues as the company celebrated its 30th anniversary and prepared for the years ahead. In 2003, Sunglass Hut, at Luxottica's behest, began to reposition its brand identity, emphasizing the fashion element of its market, which was expressed in the 2004 advertising campaign, "Spontaneous Expression." The campaign, which also included the remodeling of stores, coincided with a promotional partnership with *Rolling Stone* magazine. The collaboration focused on celebrations for the magazine's "50 Years of Rock and Roll," for which Sunglass Hut sponsored a section featuring musicians wearing Luxottica sunglass frames such as Revo and Ray-Ban. The year also marked the arrival of a new member to the Luxottica optical family. In October 2004, Del Vecchio acquired Cole National, the second largest operator of optical retail stores in North America. The acquisition included more than 2,100 stores operating under the names Pearle Vision, Sears Optical, Target Optical, and BJ's Optical, further consolidating Luxottica's stalwart position in North America.

Principal Subsidiaries

Sunglass Hut International, Inc.; Sunglass Hut Corporation; Sunmark, Inc.; Sunglass Marketing, Inc.; Sunglass Hut of California; Sunglass Hut Trading Corporation; Sunglass Hut Realty Corporation; Sunglass Hut of Canada, Ltd.; Sunglass Hut of Puerto Rico, Inc.; Sunglass Hut of Virgin Islands, Inc.; Sunglass Hut Capitola, Inc.; Sunglass Hut of Florida, Inc.; Sunglass Hut (U.K.) Ltd.; Sunglass Hut Acquisition Corporation; Sunglass Hut of Mexico, Inc.; Sunglass Hut Holding of Mexico, Inc.; IHS Distribution Corporation; IHS Procurement Corporation; Sunglass Hut de Mexico, S.A. de C.V.; Distribuidora Mexicana de Articulos para Sol, S.A. de C.V. (Mexico); Sunglass Hut France; SHI Sales Corporation; Wallis Arnold Enterprises, Inc.; Wallis Arnold Enterprises, Inc.; Sunshade Optique (U.K.) Ltd.; Solstar (U.K.) Ltd.; Sunglass Hut Holding of France, Inc.; Sunglass Hut of Northern France, Inc.; Sunglass Hut of Southern France, Inc.; Watch World International, Inc.

Principal Competitors

Marchon Eyewear, Inc.; Swiss Army Brands, Inc.; Oakley, Inc.; Gargoyles, Inc.

Further Reading

Hanover, Dan, "Sunglass Hut's Eyes Are Focused on the Internet," *Chain Store Age,* September 1998, p. 188.
Hill, Andrew, "Sunglass Hut Finds Italian Buyer," *Financial Times,* February 23, 2001, p. 32.

Kar, Arnold J., "Sunglass Hut Finds a Winning Combination," *Daily News Record,* March 3, 2000, p. 11.

Kletter, Melanie, "Strutting Their Stuff; Swimwear Firms Take to the Runways at the Newest 7th on Sixth Show," *WWD,* July 7, 2005, p. 14s.

Lyons, David, "Persistence Paid Off for Suitor of Sunglass Hut," *Miami Daily Business Review,* March 7, 2001, p. A1.

Miracle, Barbara, "Sunglass Hut: Rose-Colored Glasses," *Florida Trend,* August 1993, p. 8.

Salomon, R.S., Jr., "Three Bombed-Out Stocks to Buy Now," *Forbes,* December 16, 1996, p. 393.

Spragins, Ellyn E., "Seize the Time," *Inc.,* January 1989, p. 116.

Underwood, Elaine, "Time Flies: Sunglass Hut Plots To Shake Up Watch Biz," *Brandweek,* April 1, 1996, p. 1.

Weitzman, Jennifer, "Sunglass Hut to Buy Rival," *WWD,* May 8, 2000, p. 32.

—Laura E. Whiteley
—update: Jeffrey L. Covell

Syms Corporation

SYMS | AN EDUCATED CONSUMER IS OUR BEST CUSTOMER°

Syms Way
Secaucus, New Jersey 07094
U.S.A.
Telephone: (201) 902-9600
Fax: (201) 902-9874
Web site: http://www.syms.com

Public Company
Incorporated: 1983
Employees: 1,749
Sales: $283.6 million (2005)
Stock Exchanges: New York
Ticker Symbol: SYM
NAIC: 448140 Family Clothing Stores

Syms Corporation operates a chain of off-price apparel stores under the Syms name, selling men's clothing and haberdashery, women's clothing, children's wear, shoes, luggage, and fragrances. The company operates 37 stores in 15 states, gearing its stores to the quality-minded but price-conscious middle-income buyer. Syms is unusual among discounters because it discloses future price changes, enabling customers to return at a later date for a larger discount. The company collects more than half of its revenues from selling men's tailored clothes and haberdashery. Syms maintains a 277,000-square-foot distribution center at its headquarters in Secaucus, New Jersey.

Business Launched in 1959

Sy Merns was a radio sportscaster in the early 1950s when he left this field to join his older brother George's discount clothing store, inherited from their father, on Greenwich Street in lower Manhattan. As Sy's daughter Marcy described the situation in her 1992 book *Mind Your Own Business and Keep It in the Family,* Sy Merns labored for six years to come up with $6,000, the agreed-on amount for 20 percent of the business. At the end of this period, however, George said 20 percent of the store was now worth much more, so Sy left, about 1959, to open, with a partner, a rival clothing store around the corner in 2,000 square feet of space, an enterprise that he named "Sy Merns." Since "Merns Mart" was the name of George's store, he went to court and forced his brother to change the name. Sy then abbreviated the name of his store to "Syms" and, eventually, took it as his legal surname, apparently in 1986.

Syms bought brand-name menswear irregulars at less than wholesale prices and, after removing the labels at the manufacturer's insistence, sold the merchandise at about 40 percent below retail, offering the widest selection possible. By 1967, there were five Syms stores, all in the rapidly developing low-rent area on the western fringe of Manhattan's financial district. Three of them were scheduled for demolition, two to make way for the giant World Trade Center. With a lease running through May 1968, Merns was refusing to vacate another of the five so that U.S. Steel Corp. could construct a 50-story office building unless he received a payment in six figures. According to his daughter, he "prevailed and became a real estate legend." Merns bought out his partner in 1968.

Syms opened a small Miami store in 1969, which moved to a larger location in Hallendale, Florida, in 1975. A small Buffalo store opened in 1970. By 1974, the single remaining Manhattan location was on Park Place, still on the western fringe of the financial district but now occupying 36,000 square feet. The company had opened its first suburban store in Bergen County, New Jersey, and in 1974 it opened another one, in Roslyn, Long Island. In 1978, it opened its first store in the Washington, D.C., metropolitan area, in Falls Church, Virginia.

Syms did not advertise its wares until 1971, when accountants told the boss that the money saved by not doing so would be lost to taxes anyway. As a former broadcaster, Merns announced his own commercials. The company broadcast its first television commercial, with Merns again as its representative, in 1974, the same year it adopted "An Educated Consumer Is Our Best Consumer" slogan that would become increasingly familiar to New Yorkers. It began selling women's clothing in 1971.

Syms had net income of $4 million on net sales of $72.1 million in 1979. The following year, when it had eight units, the enterprise purchased A. Sulka & Co., a prestigious retailer of men's haberdashery, established in 1895, with a store on Fifth Avenue in midtown Manhattan and another in London. There was also a second New York City store and a San Francisco one. In 1983, Sulka acquired a Paris operation. Leased Sulka departments were placed in Philadelphia, Houston, and Chicago department stores in 1983, 1984, and 1985, respectively. A Sulka store on Manhattan's Park Avenue became the chain's flagship in 1985, and a Troy, Michigan, outlet was added in 1988. The Sulka chain was sold in 1989.

More Stores, Bigger Profits in the 1980s

There were ten Syms stores in the fall of 1982. By now, manufacturer's labels appeared in all the clothing, women's as well as men's, accompanied by a tag listing both the nationally advertised price and the sharply discounted Syms price. Sy Syms, appearing in his own television spots and writing his own copy, would deliver messages such as, "If a garment doesn't have a recognizable name on it, it's not advisable to buy it." He was receiving goods from hundreds of manufacturers, one of whom told Walter McQuade of *Fortune* magazine, "You have to bite the bullet and get rid of mistakes. I called Sy and dickered. . . . A soft touch he's not, but he doesn't gouge. He keeps his commitments." Free of debt, Syms paid promptly out of cash flow, sometimes within ten days. In 1981, the chain sold more than 150,000 men's suits with more than 200 well-known brand names.

In a 1985 *Forbes* article, however, Richard Behar wrote that Syms was "sometimes hoodwinking its 'educated consumers' and sometimes selling them inferior-grade garments that can be mistaken for top-of-the-line goods." Behar reported that, for example, although Syms was the largest customer in the United States for "leftover" Givenchy suits, these were "visibly of lower overall quality than the Givenchys that are sold in department stores." He added that Syms had agreed to remove the Givenchy label before the customer was allowed to take the suit out of the store. "On balance," Behar concluded, "it seems clear that a good deal of Syms' merchandise is, in fact, manufactured specifically for it and is not 'leftover' in the accepted sense of the word."

This challenge to Syms's credibility did not go unanswered. Interviewed by Jay Palmer of *Barron's* in 1988, the founder's feisty eldest child, by now second in command to her father, insisted, "Despite what you have read elsewhere, the suit that you buy from Syms is made by the same people from the same fabric and the same patterns at the same factory and with the same workmanship as the suit with the same label sold at much higher prices in other stores. We are talking fabrics, not finished suits, when Syms buys from the suit maker. . . . We always ask them to make the suits up into the more conservative, lower-

priced lines because that is what does best at Syms. Critics who look at our suits and compare them elsewhere don't compare like with like."

Syms, like other off-price retailers, saved its customers money by not putting up a front. There were no mannequins to display the merchandise; the dressing rooms had no separate stalls and were dimly lit; alterations, gift wrapping, and deliveries were extra; only Syms's own credit card was accepted; and the stretched-thin sales staff received no commissions. Syms maintained it held no sales, but its stores frequently announced "dividends," especially on rainy and snowy days, and certain women's garments were marked down every ten days until sold. Some 64 percent of Syms's $179.2 million in 1983 sales was generated by men's tailored clothes and haberdashery and 32 percent by women's dresses, suits, separates, and accessories. A small portion of the merchandise, mostly sweaters, jackets, and shirts, was being sold under the company's own "S" private label, but by 1987 brand or designer names were on all garments in Syms stores.

Syms made its initial public offering in 1983, clearing nearly $30 million in selling shares of its stock. Sy Syms, according to Behar, pocketed about $25 million and also retained control of 80 percent of the stock. To the 11 existing Syms stores, the company added, in 1984, new ones in two Chicago suburbs, Niles and Addison, and a Philadelphia suburb, Cherry Hill, New Jersey. By this time the Hallendale, Florida, store had moved to Fort Lauderdale, the Buffalo store had moved to nearby Williamsville, two outlets were in Boston suburbs, a second New Jersey store had opened in Woodbridge, and Westchester County, New York, also had a Syms store.

Expansion continued at a rapid pace in subsequent years. A second Philadelphia-area store opened in 1985 in King of Prussia, Pennsylvania. New Syms stores were established in 1986 in Monroeville, Pennsylvania, and Secaucus, New Jersey. In 1987, the chain opened stores in Norcross, Georgia; Southfield, Michigan; Brentwood, Missouri; and North Randall, Ohio. The following year, new stores opened in Hurst, Texas (outside Dallas), and in Charlotte and Henrietta, New York. The company moved its headquarters and warehouse from Lyndhurst, New Jersey, to Secaucus in 1987. That year was Syms's tenth consecutive year of record sales and net income. Its operating margin before taxes (once, at 14 percent, the highest of any U.S. retailer) remained at a comfortable 12.5 percent. The chain, in 1988, was no longer cutting out famous-name labels before buyers left the stores, but it continued its policy of not mentioning manufacturers' names in its advertising.

Sticking to a Successful Formula in the 1990s

Syms moved its Roslyn store to Westbury in 1989 and opened new stores in Baltimore, Houston, and Tampa in 1990. In the recessionary fiscal year ended February 28, 1991, profits slipped for the first time since 1977. The chain, which in 1992 owned, rather than leased, 18 of its stores, compared with only one in 1983, found itself overstocked with merchandise and was forced to slash its prices. Almost a dozen new Syms stores opened during the next few years, but revenues remained stagnant and net income dropped in 1994 to the lowest level since 1982. Industry observers noted that retailers like Syms were facing increased competition from other off-price stores, discounters, and department stores.

With company stock selling in late 1995 for only $8 a share, compared to $15 a share in its initial public offering a dozen years earlier, Sy Syms explored the possibility of taking his company private, although he ultimately rejected the idea because of the need to take on a major debt load. In the fiscal year ended March 1, 1997, Syms recorded its highest profit level in seven years. The company opened a second Manhattan outlet in midtown, on high-rent Park Avenue, in late 1996. Despite the location, a retail consultant, Alan Millstein, told Beth Fitzgerald of the *Newark Star-Ledger* that Syms ''runs the homeliest looking stores in retailing,'' adding that even the new Park Avenue store ''looks like a used airplane hangar—but it's jammed full of people.''

Its momentum restored, Syms announced in April 1997 plans to open 19 new stores over the next four years, including four in Los Angeles and two each in San Francisco, Seattle, and Toronto, thereby establishing a presence on the West Coast and in Canada for the first time. The Atlanta, Baltimore, Detroit, Houston, and Miami metropolitan areas, plus the Princeton, New Jersey, area, were slated to receive second units. For Atlanta, Detroit, and Miami, this was accomplished in 1998. A Syms opened in Boston in the same year, and similar downtown outlets were scheduled for Chicago and Washington, D.C. In April 1999, Syms opened its twelfth store in the metropolitan New York City area, in Lawrenceville, New Jersey. The chain's stores were averaging 40,000 square feet in size and holding some 8,000 suits on average.

Marcy Syms, president since 1983 and chief operating officer since 1984, succeeded her father as chief executive officer in January 1998. She vowed not to make any major changes, retaining the chain's large selection of merchandise and its no-frills ambience, telling Jean Palmieri of *DNR/Daily News Record,* ''We see no need to fool around with a successful formula.'' Two younger brothers were serving as vice-presidents. At 71, Sy Syms retained the position of chairman and continued to come into the office every day. He owned about 41 percent of the company's shares of stock at this time, and members of his family held another 11 percent.

In the fiscal year ended February 28, 1998, the company registered record net income of $23 million, sending its stock price to the $15-a-share level. The fiscal year ended February 27, 1999 was not as rosy for Syms as the previous one, however. Net sales fell $9 million, to $343.9 million, and net income dropped $5.5 million, to $17.5 million. Men's tailored clothes and haberdashery accounted for 53 percent of sales; women's dresses, suits, separates, and accessories, for 31 percent; shoes, 8 percent; children's wear, 6 percent; and luggage, domestics, and fragrances, 2 percent. The company blamed the downturn on an undersupply of the lower-priced brands that its customers were seeking. Syms's stock dropped back to the $8-a-share level. The chain continued its record, however, of never losing money in a quarter, much less a year. Always conservatively financed, it had a long-term debt of only $400,000 in early 1998.

A Lackluster Start in the 21st Century

Syms's disciplined attitude toward debt and the fact that it owned most of its stores, rather than leased them, ranked as arguably the chain's strongest qualities at the turn of the 21st century. Instead of expanding its chain, Syms retreated during the first years of the decade, closing stores as a way to restore the financial vitality once exuded by the company. In 2000, when there were 48 Syms stores in operation, the company's net income plunged from $17.4 million to $2.2 million, an 87 percent decline, on a slight decline in revenues. The financial difficulties continued as the company faced stiff competition from other discount retailers such as Men's Wearhouse, leading some critics to wonder whether the company's strategy needed to be altered. Marcy Syms, despite the lackluster results reported by the company, remained steadfast to the concept developed by her father. ''Our message has remained consistent, and we've stayed true to our original concept,'' she remarked in a May 10, 2002 interview with the *Dallas Morning News.* ''We sell a name you know at a price that will knock your socks off.''

When Marcy Syms made her remarks, the number of Syms stores had been reduced to 42, but the closure of unprofitable stores did little to change the company's overall financial state. The end of 2002 marked the company's second consecutive year of posting an annual loss. Sales for the year dropped substantially, falling from $342 million to $287 million. The financial slide continued until 2005, when the pattern of four consecutive years of losses and three consecutive years of declining revenues came to an end. For the year, sales were up 3 percent to $283 million, still well below the $342 million collected in 2001, and earnings reached $2 million, up markedly from the nearly $5 million loss posted the previous year. The company's store count by this point had been whittled down to 37 after three closures during the year in North Carolina, Maryland, and New Jersey. Looking ahead, Marcy Syms and her management team hoped the year's financial totals augured the beginning of better times at the company, as they guided Sy Syms's business toward a half-century of existence as a discount apparel retailer.

Principal Subsidiaries

Generic Products Inc.; The Rothschild's Haberdashery Ltd.; SYL Inc.; Syms Advertising, Inc.

Principal Competitors

Federated Department Stores, Inc.; Filene's Basement Corporation; The May Department Stores Company.

Further Reading

Behar, Richard, "Hi, This Is Sy Syms," *Forbes*, September 9, 1985, pp. 30–32.

"Company Spotlight #194: Syms Corp.," *Crain's New York Business*, May 23, 2005, p. 22.

Fitzgerald, Beth, "Syms Stays Ahead of the Retail Pack by Meeting Customer Expectations," *Newark Star-Ledger*, April 9, 1997, pp. 37–38.

Furman, Phyllis, "Sy, Marcy Outrun Apparel Downturn," *Crain's New York Business*, January 27, 1992, pp. 1, 41.

Gellers, Stan, "Syms Schools Consumers on Better Suits," *DNR/Daily News Record*, April 23, 1997, pp. 2, 14.

——, "Syms Set to Embark on Major Expansion," *DNR/Daily News Record*, April 25, 1997, cover, p. 1.

Kaplan, Don, "Syms Steps Out on Park Avenue," *DNR/Daily News Record*, November 22, 1996, p. 3.

——, "Syms Sticking to Its 'Values,'" *DNR/Daily News Record*, December 12, 1994, pp. 10–11.

Lasseter, Diana G., "Sy Syms Wants to Take Syms Private," *BUSINESS News New Jersey*, October 4, 1995, p. 8.

Lipowicz, Alice, "Retail's Slow Summer Tests Syms' Fiber," *Crain's New York Business*, October 5, 1998, p. 40.

"Marcy Syms Discusses How Retail and Her Family Business Are Entering a New Era," *BUSINESS News New Jersey*, November 29, 1995, p. 25.

McQuade, Walter, "The Man Who Makes Millions on Mistakes," *Fortune*, September 6, 1982, pp. 106–08, 110, 112, 116.

Palmer, Jay, "Fancy Labels, Plain Prices," *Barron's*, September 26, 1988, pp. 18, 20, 47.

Palmieri, Jean E., "It's Marcy's Turn to Educate the Consumers," *DNR/Daily News Record*, April 29, 1998, pp. 4–5.

Prial, Frank J., "Small Haberdashery Upsets U.S. Steel's Skyscraper Project," *Wall Street Journal*, September 18, 1967, pp. 1, 21.

Quinn, Steve, "Clothing Store Has Tentative Deal to Take Old Plano, Texas, Homeplace Site.," *Dallas Morning News*, May 10, 2002, p. B2.

Syms, Marcy, Mind Your Own Business and Keep It in the Family, New York: Mastermedia Ltd., 1992.

"Syms Profits Freefal 87 Percent in Year," *Daily News Record*, May 5, 2000, p. 24.

Wipperfurth, Heike, "Stock Watch: Syms Racks Up Hefty Gain," *Crain's New York Business*, August 12, 2002, p. 35.

—Robert Halasz
—update: Jeffrey L. Covell

Taco Bell Corporation

17901 Von Karman
Irvine, California 92614
U.S.A.
Telephone: (949) 863-4500
Fax: (949) 863-2252
Web site: http://www.tacobell.com

Wholly Owned Subsidiary of YUM! Brands Inc.
Incorporated: 1962
Employees: 166,000
Sales: $1.7 billion (2004)
NAIC: 722211 Limited-Service Restaurants

Taco Bell Corporation is a California-based fast service restaurant chain that specializes in Mexican-style fast food. Taco Bell, with 2004 combined company and franchisee sales reaching $5.7 billion dollars, holds the largest share of the Mexican-style restaurant market in the United States. More than 35 million consumers visit a Taco Bell each week and over 80 percent of its 6,500 locations are franchised. The company, with restaurants in Canada, Guam, Aruba, Dominican Republic, Chile, Costa Rica, Guatemala, Puerto Rico, Ecuador, Hawaii, Asia, and Europe, operates as a subsidiary of YUM! Brands Inc., the largest restaurant company in the world.

Taco Bell Precursor Opens in 1946

In 1946, Glen Bell, a World War II veteran, opened a hot dog stand in San Bernardino, California. The 23-year-old Bell decided to start his own business after working for a local gas company and a railroad system. Having bought a gas refrigerator at a discount from the gas company, Bell sold it for $400 and used the money to secure a lease for the food stand site and to buy building materials. Confident that the postwar economy would support his endeavor, Bell opened the shutters of ''Bell's Drive In'' for business later that year.

Bell began unassumingly, remaining a one-person operation and serving only take-out food. His first day of business brought in $20 over a 16-hour day. Working long hours (the stand's hours of operation extended from nine a.m. to midnight), he eventually averaged $150 a day in business during his first year.

In 1952, Bell sold his first stand and set about building an improved version. His new menu was comprised of hamburgers and hot dogs, then staples of the emerging fast food industry. Coincidentally, just as Bell built his second stand, the McDonald brothers were building their first fast food restaurant, also in San Bernardino. By 1955, Ray Kroc, a traveling salesman touting milk shake machines, would link up with the McDonald brothers and form the giant McDonald's hamburger chain.

Bell Experiments with Tacos in 1950s

The phenomenal worldwide success of the McDonald's restaurant chain would come later. However, its successful beginnings in San Bernardino were enough to prompt Bell to find a niche in the fledgling Mexican-style food business. He settled on selling tacos by volume, rather than making and stuffing them individually, as was the case in full-service restaurants. As Bell later noted in a 1978 speech to a Taco Bell franchise convention, ''My plan for experimenting with tacos was to obtain a location in a Mexican neighborhood. That way, if tacos were successful, potential competitors would write it off to the location and assume that the idea wouldn't sell anywhere else.''

After choosing a location in a Hispanic neighborhood of San Bernardino, Bell began selling a chili dog from which he eventually developed his traditional taco sauce. He also developed taco shells that could be easily and quickly fried and later stuffed with ingredients. This stand was so small that Bell sold his first tacos at 19 cents each from a window on the side.

In 1953, Bell opened a second stand in Barstow, near San Bernardino. Tacos sold well in that locale as well, and Bell recruited Ed Hackbarth to run the stand. A year later, Bell began the construction of three Taco Tia stands in San Bernardino, Redlands, and Riverside. When the new stores were completed a year later, Bell achieved $18,000 in sales in his first month.

A small commissary was soon built to serve the three Taco Tia outlets and three other Bell's Drive In outlets. Here vegetables were prepared daily, as were taco shells and sauces. To maintain freshness, meat was cooked at the individual restaurants.

In 1956, Bell sold his three Taco Tia restaurants to fund his expansion into the Los Angeles restaurant market. A reces-

---

Company Perspectives:

Taco Bell works with its suppliers to deliver great tasting, high quality food. Our food is topped, layered, loaded, melted, and grilled fresh for you, right when you order it. This means two things. First, you get your food prepared exactly how you want it. And second, it always tastes fresh.

---

sionary economic atmosphere, however, drove up construction costs. Bell eventually went into partnership with four members of the Los Angeles Rams professional football team to reduce his start-up risk. In 1958, they formed the El Taco restaurant chain, which included a central commissary to serve up to 100 units. Three outlets were initially opened, producing profits of $3,000 after the first year of business.

First Taco Bell in 1962

Bell wanted to remain independent, however, so in 1962 he again sold his share in a successful restaurant chain and, a year later, opened the first Taco Bell outlet in Downey. Eight more outlets were built in the Long Beach, Paramount, and Los Angeles regions.

During this period, the concept of franchising was catching on, first with car dealerships and then throughout the restaurant industry. Bell quickly seized on the idea. In 1964, Kermit Becky, a former Los Angeles policeman, purchased the first Taco Bell franchise in the South Bay area of Los Angeles. Other franchise buyers followed.

In 1965, Bell hired Robert McKay as general manager of the company to help franchise Taco Bell. McKay would later recall the challenge before him in *Forbes:* "Franchising was really hot. Everyone wanted franchises in the mid-sixties. Then came the shakeout a few years later and franchising no longer was the easy game it once was."

Public Offering in 1966

The following year, the Taco Bell chain went public on the Pacific Stock Exchange, enabling Bell to receive bank financing for the first time. Previously, all financing had been secured on a private basis. (The first Taco Bell was opened with 40 shares, each worth $100 and held mostly by Bell's family.)

In 1967, McKay was named president of Taco Bell. At that time, the company owned 12 restaurants with an additional 325 franchises. By 1970, Taco Bell had become a $6 million operation, producing annual profits of approximately $150,000. The fast food chain's success soon drew the attention of PepsiCo Inc., the snack food and soft drinks giant, which was seeking to diversify into the restaurant business.

During this time, Pizza Hut, a PepsiCo subsidiary, launched Taco Kid, a Mexican food concept to challenge Taco Bell. The launch failed, and Pizza Hut soon had to write off its investment. PepsiCo then altered its strategy and began wooing Glen Bell in order to buy Taco Bell outright. In February 1978, a deal was struck in which the Mexican fast food chain was purchased for just under $125 million in stock.

PepsiCo Leadership in the Late 1970s

PepsiCo's strategy in acquiring Taco Bell was simple: the fast food chain dominated the Mexican food market, so PepsiCo was buying market share. For PepsiCo, the challenge was to make Taco Bell less a regional ethnic food phenomenon and more a national fast food chain. Glen Bell had originally sought to set Taco Bell apart from other fast food chains, McDonald's in particular, and its preeminent position among other Mexican food chains, almost all of them regional or local rivals, was already secure.

PepsiCo's decision to reposition Taco Bell was a challenge to the fast food giants on a national scale. The PepsiCo strategy emphasized that Taco Bell outlets would sport spartan simplicity in decor and menu, with a concentration on predictable quality, affordable prices, and clean and convenient surroundings. Taco Bell also moved swiftly to redesign the company logo. The old logo, an Hispanic man dozing under a giant sombrero, was replaced by a sparkling bell atop the company name. As Larry Higby, senior vice-president of marketing at Taco Bell, noted in *Advertising Age,* "Usually when you try to turn something around, you look to develop breakthrough advertising. But we came to exactly the opposite conclusion: we needed to look more mainstream."

The strategy worked. Taco Bell grew rapidly during the early 1980s. By 1983, when John E. Martin took over as president, the chain had 1,600 outlets in 47 U.S. states, producing a total of $918 million in sales. The average Taco Bell franchise claimed sales of $680,000 that year, a significant increase over the franchise average of $325,000 in sales only three years earlier. As a measure of market strength, Taco Bell's nearest rival in the Mexican fast food segment was Naugles, a California-based chain with only 160 outlets and 1983 sales of $84 million.

A 1985 advertising campaign typified the company's mainstream approach. The television spots stressed that Taco Bell offered the same ingredients as its burger rivals: beef, cheese, and tomatoes. It simply served the ingredients up in a different and, according to the company, more satisfying way. The campaign's tag-line, "Just Made for You," reminded consumers that more than 60 percent of Taco Bell products were custom-made and that no dish was prepared until it was ordered to ensure freshness. By 1986, Taco Bell had grown to 2,400 outlets with just over $1.4 billion in sales. Television advertising that year called Taco Bell "the cure for the common meal," a pointed allusion to the staple foods offered by its competitors.

New Taco Bell outlets were also different from earlier models. The traditional arched windows and red-tile roofs were retained but with the addition of exterior stucco. Interiors featured skylights, silk plants, and light-colored wood. New dishes, such as seafood salads and grilled chicken, were added to menus, and drive-through windows became a standard feature.

Successful Pricing and Production Changes in the Late 1980s

In 1986, Taco Bell expanded overseas by opening a restaurant in London, England. Two years later, Taco Bell made widespread pricing and production changes. The resulting lower price of

<table>
<tr><td colspan="2">Key Dates:</td></tr>
<tr><td>1946:</td><td>Glen Bell opens a hot dog stand in San Bernardino, California.</td></tr>
<tr><td>1962:</td><td>Taco Bell is established.</td></tr>
<tr><td>1964:</td><td>Taco Bell begins to franchise.</td></tr>
<tr><td>1966:</td><td>The company goes public.</td></tr>
<tr><td>1978:</td><td>PepsiCo Inc. buys Taco Bell.</td></tr>
<tr><td>1986:</td><td>The company opens its first international restaurant in London, England.</td></tr>
<tr><td>1993:</td><td>A line of taco shells, salsa, and refried beans hits supermarket shelves.</td></tr>
<tr><td>1997:</td><td>PepsiCo spins off its restaurant division as Tricon Global Restaurants Inc.</td></tr>
<tr><td>2002:</td><td>Tricon changes its name to YUM! Brands Inc.</td></tr>
</table>

many of the items on the Taco Bell menu forced rival hamburger chains to follow suit. On the production side, Taco Bell began contracting out much of its food preparation, including the dicing and slicing of vegetables and the frying of taco shells, in order to get the kitchen out of the restaurant. Just-in-time inventory controls were added to all outlets, resulting in reduced overhead costs. Electronic information systems installed in all Taco Bell outlets cut down significantly on management paperwork. Staff responsibilities changed as well, as Taco Bell reversed the 70 percent kitchen and 30 percent dining room ratio in all its outlets. As Zane Leshner, the company's senior vice-president for operations, commented in *Financial World* in 1991: "We no longer dedicate an awful lot of labor and space to doing things that have no customer value at all." The strategy paid dividends for Taco Bell. The streamlining steps enabled the Mexican fast food chain to raise its profits by 25 percent annually during the late 1980s, a time when it was sharply dropping its prices.

The company's success, coming when the late 1980s recession led to savage price-cutting and cutthroat competition in the fast food industry, impressed industry analysts. A 1991 article in the *Harvard Business Review* named Taco Bell as the best performer in the fast food industry at the time, surpassing traditional market leader McDonald's. The authors wrote, "If McDonald's is the epitome of the old industrialized service model, Taco Bell represents the new, redesigned model in many important respects."

To keep customers focused on Taco Bell's menu, the company in 1991 introduced a three-tiered value menu. Most products on the menu, from original tacos and bean burritos to cinnamon twists, would be sold at three main price levels: 59 cents, 79 cents, and 99 cents. In addition, new menu items introduced in 1991 included steak burritos to lure dinner customers and a test breakfast menu. These changes helped the company to achieve 60 percent more sales in 1991 than two years earlier.

Expansion in the 1990s

New Taco Bell outlets were also being added to the company's stable. The number had grown from 2,193 units in 1985 to 3,273 in 1990, marking an annual growth rate of 8.3 percent. That growth rate continued in the early 1990s as Taco Bell

opened some new franchises and many new company-owned restaurants. In 1992, Taco Bell opened outlets in Aruba, South Korea, and Saudi Arabia, bringing the number of international locations to 11. In the United States, Taco Bell pursued several unconventional approaches to expand opportunities for sales. In addition to opening new restaurants, the company introduced Taco Bell Express, small outlets with a limited menu and little or no seating, in airports, business cafeterias, and sports stadiums. Street carts took this idea a step further.

In addition, to take advantage of the growing take-home food market, Taco Bell forged agreements with supermarkets for counters within their stores. Although such counters created competition for the supermarket's own deli stands, the increased traffic through the store and the percentage the supermarkets got from the fast food sales was felt to offset any business stolen from delis. Taco Bell also entered the supermarket venue through a line of taco shells, salsa, and refried beans in 1993. In all, CEO John E. Martin hoped to have 250,000 distribution points by the next century.

However, this aggressive expansion raised the ire of many franchisees, who felt the new restaurants and outlets threatened their own sales. A comparison of Taco Bell Corp.'s profits and average sales growth per store seemed to validate the franchisees' fears: between 1989 and 1992, the company's operating profits had grown by approximately $100 million, whereas average sales growth per store had fallen from about 16 percent to 7 percent a year. Some franchisees also felt threatened by the company's move toward more company-owned stores. CEO Martin claimed that the problem stemmed from franchisees' unwillingness to change. "Sometimes you have to lead people kicking and screaming to the right answer," he explained to Amy Barrett of *Business Week*.

Parent company PepsiCo's attitude toward aggressive expansion reversed itself in the mid-1990s, however. Its hefty investment in new outlets and company-owned stores failed to provide an adequate return, especially when compared to its other core businesses. Its restaurants, including Taco Bell, had operating margins of 7 percent, whereas its beverage division was seeing margins of 13 percent, and its snack division, 17 percent. The initial solution tried by Roger Enrico, the new chairman and CEO, was to reduce the percentage of outlets owned by the company, which stood at 60 percent in 1995. Rather than have company money tied up in capital, Taco Bell could rely on franchisee investment, a strategy followed by McDonald's, which owned only 20 percent of its restaurants in 1995.

Spinoff in 1997

Still, this step did not satisfy PepsiCo's need for a greater return on its assets, and the company prepared to sell its restaurant division. In the late 1990s, PepsiCo drew together its restaurant businesses, including Pizza Hut, Taco Bell, and Kentucky Fried Chicken (KFC), placing them in a single division. All operations were now overseen by a single senior manager, and most back office operations, including payroll, data processing, and accounts payable, were combined. In January 1997, the company announced plans to spin off this restaurant division, creating an independent publicly traded company called Tricon Global Restaurants, Inc. The formal plan, approved by PepsiCo board of directors in August 1997, stipulated that each PepsiCo share-holder would receive one share of Tricon stock for every ten shares of PepsiCo stock owned. The plan also required Tricon to pay a one-time distribution of $4.5 billion at the time of the spinoff. The deal was approved by the Securities and Exchange Commission and completed on October 6, 1997.

Enrico explained the move: "Our goal in taking these steps is to dramatically sharpen PepsiCo's focus. Our restaurant business has tremendous financial strength and a very bright future. However, given the distinctly different dynamics of restaurants and packaged goods, we believe all our businesses can better flourish with two separate and distinct managements and corporate structures."

After the spinoff was complete, Tricon immediately began to implement new strategies intended to bolster revenues and profits. The company also looked to strengthen its relations with its franchise locations. In the case of Taco Bell, the company began selling off company-owned stores to its franchisees. It also launched a new advertising campaign featuring a talking Chihuahua at the end of 1997. Management hoped the new campaign as well as the addition of several new menu offerings including the Gordita, Chalupas, and Grande Meals would shore up sales in the late 1990s.

Despite its efforts, Taco Bell was pushed to shelve the popular advertising campaign featuring the Chihuahua in 1999 after its franchisees demanded that future commercials tout the company's fresh food. Prompted by faltering sales, the firm launched its "Think Outside the Bun" slogan in an attempt to lure customers to its new, fresher products. At the same time, two men filed suit against chain claiming the firm stole their advertising idea for the talking Chihuahua. In 2003, a federal jury awarded $30.1 million to the two men. Taco Bell planned to appeal the verdict.

Overcoming Problems in the 2000s

Weak sales, rising cheese prices, and growing franchisee debt followed the company into the 21st century. During 2000, Taco Bell took a $26 million charge for expenses related to franchisee debts. At the same time, the company was forced to recall the taco shells used in its restaurants after it was discovered that the taco shells sold in supermarkets contained genetically modified corn, which was not approved for human consumption. While the shells used in the restaurants were not linked to the shells sold in grocery stores, Taco Bell voluntarily set the recall in motion.

Emil Brolick, Taco Bell's president and chief concept officer, commented on the company's overall situation in a February 2001 *Wall Street Journal* article, claiming, "We are not doing a great job in terms of quality, in terms of friendliness, in terms of speed, in terms of cleanliness in the store." To remedy this situation, the company began to focus on offering menu items with improved quality and replaced its ground beef and refried beans with thicker, tastier products. It also added more upscale menu items including steak tacos, quesadillas, Grilled Stuft Burritos, and Border Bowls, which featured grilled chicken, salsa, red tortilla strips, seasoned rice and beans, and a three-cheese blend over a bed of iceberg lettuce.

Taco Bell's strategy appeared to pay off when sales began to rebound in 2002. In fact, the company began performing better than the other chains in YUM! Brands' arsenal. (In 2002, Taco Bell's parent company changed its name to YUM! Brands Inc. after it acquired A&W All American Food Restaurants and Long John Silver's.) Taco Bell launched its Big Bell Value Menu in 2004, which offered seven items priced under $1.29, including a half-pound bean burrito and a half-pound beef and potato burrito. It also launched Mountain Dew Baja Blast, a lime-flavored drink made exclusively for Taco Bell.

Under Brolick's leadership, Taco Bell had reformed its financial record and by 2004 was in the midst of its third consecutive year of sustained growth. That year, Taco Bell came to an agreement with the Coalition of Immokalee Workers (CIW), ending a long-running boycott by the group of tomato farm laborers in Florida. As part of the agreement, Taco Bell agreed to pay a penny-per-pound surcharge on tomatoes and also work to improve farm labor standards and pay policies. With recalls, lawsuits, and boycotts behind it, Taco Bell appeared to be well positioned for success in the years to come.

Principal Competitors

Del Taco Inc.; Doctor's Associates Inc.; McDonald's Corp.

Further Reading

Barrett, Amy, "Indigestion at Taco Bell," *Business Week*, December 14, 1992, pp. 66–67.
——, "Detergents, Aisle 2. Pizza Hut, Aisle 5," *Business Week*, June 7, 1993, pp. 82–83.
Bell, Glen, "Getting Here," Irvine, Calif: Taco Bell Inc., 1978 (speech to Taco Bell franchise convention).
Garber, Amy, "Taco Bell: 'No Quiero Jury's $30M Verdict,'" *Nation's Restaurant News*, June 16, 2003.
——, "Emil Brolick," *Nation's Restaurant News*, October 4, 2004.
Ordonez, Jennifer, "Taco Bell Chief Has New Tactic: Be Like Wendy's," *Wall Street Journal*, February 23, 2001, p. B1.
Papiernik, Richard L., "Despite Improvement, Tricon Continues Attempts to Remedy Ailing Taco Bell Chain," *Nation's Restaurant News*, May 14 2001.
"A Promising Manana," *Forbes*, August 1, 1977.
"Restaurants Without Kitchens," *Financial World*, November 26, 1991.
Rudnitsky, Howard, "Leaner Cuisine," *Forbes*, March 27, 1995, pp. 43–44.
Schlesinger, Leonard, and James Heskett, "The Service-Driven Service Company," *Harvard Business Review*, September-October, 1991.
Sellers, Patricia, "Pepsico's Shedding Ugly Pounds," *Fortune*, June 26, 1995, pp. 94–95.
——, "Why Pepsi Needs to Become More Like Coke," *Fortune*, March 3, 1997, pp. 26–27.
"Taco Bell, Farmworkers Settle Tomato Dispute," *Nation's Restaurant News*, March 21, 2005.
"Taco Bell Secures Fast-Food Presence," *Advertising Age*, July 16, 1984.
"Taco Bell Wants to Take a Bite Out of Burgers," *Business Week*, August 8, 1986.
Whalen, Jeanne, and Jeff Jensen, "Taco Bell Hearing Call of the Border," *Advertising Age*, July 10, 1995, p. 6.

—Etan Vlessing
—updates: Susan Windisch Brown;
Christina M. Stansell

Tech Data Corporation

5350 Tech Data Drive
Clearwater, Florida 33760-3122
U.S.A.
Telephone: (727) 539-7429
Toll Free: (800) 237-8931
Fax: (727) 538-7803
Web site: http://www.techdata.com

Public Company
Incorporated: 1974
Employees: 8,500
Sales: $19.79 billion (2004)
Stock Exchanges: NASDAQ
Ticker Symbol: TECD
NAIC: 421430 Computer and Computer Peripheral
    Equipment and Software Wholesalers

Tech Data Corporation is one of the world's largest distributors of computer products. The company's customer base is composed of over 90,000 value-added resellers and retail dealers located in more than 100 countries. Its product line contains more than 75,000 different items, including computers, printers, monitors, disk drives, networking equipment, and software. Tech Data distributes products from 1,000 manufacturers and publishers. Tech Data was Florida's largest publicly held firm, according to *Florida Trend.* Keys to the company's success in a low-margin, rapidly changing market include attention to detail and low debt levels.

Company Formed in 1974

When Tech Data was founded in 1974, it bore little resemblance to the industry giant it has grown to become. The company was started by Edward Raymund to market computer supplies to large institutions in central Florida. Its customers at that time were end-users rather than resellers, primarily hospitals and government agencies. From Tech Data, these end-users purchased disk packs, tape, and other data-processing paraphernalia for use with their mainframe and mini computers.

By the early 1980s, the company had annual sales of about $2 million. Around that time, several developments both inside

the company and in the computer industry as a whole led to profound changes in the way Tech Data was to do business. The emergence of personal computers (PCs) in 1980 created an exciting new market niche that was wide open for exploitation. When Raymund decided to pursue a share of the market for PC supplies, however, he met with resistance on the part of his field sales force. Raymund's plan involved the expansion of the company's telemarketing operation, and the field sales staff, which relied on large institutional customers, perceived this as a threat to their dominant position in the company.

Also during this time, Steven Raymund, Edward's 25-year-old son, came to work for the company. Put to work on the upcoming Tech Data catalog, Steve initially had no intention of making the situation permanent. Gradually, however, his interest in the company's operations increased. As the elder Raymund began spending less time at Tech Data to concentrate on his other company, Tech Rep Associates, Steven Raymund took on more responsibilities, eventually becoming operations manager at Tech Data. This development did not sit at all well with the sales force, which had hoped to buy the company out from Raymund in the near future; Steven Raymund's sudden rise to prominence meant that a buyout was unlikely.

Early 1980s Shift to Wholesale

About a month after Steven Raymund received his new title, a group consisting of Tech Data's key salespeople staged a coup of sorts. Five of them gathered at the office on a Saturday and proceeded to photocopy all of the company's customer records and vendor information. The following Monday, Raymund found letters of resignation on his desk from the five, who then went to work for a nearby competitor. The impact of this mass desertion at Tech Data was immediate and brutal. It quickly became apparent that the salespeople had taken many of the company's best customers with them. Monthly sales figures dropped by more than 50 percent, and the company began losing money. In fact, the situation became so bad that the elder Raymund considered shuttering Tech Data so that he could devote more resources to his other company, which was thriving.

Instead, the Raymunds undertook a radical shift in strategy. Rather than replace the departed field sales force, they beefed up their telemarketing staff, which was much less expensive to support. They then began to aggressively court computer dealers in addition to end-users. The company also began to pay more attention to direct mail, purchasing mailing lists and sending out catalogs in greater numbers. By the middle of 1983, Tech Data was once again making money. About that time, the company began dealing in PC products such as disk drives, printers, and keyboards. Selling to dealers rather than users proved so successful that by the end of fiscal 1984 the company had withdrawn from the end-user market entirely, and its transformation into a wholesale distributor was complete. That year, Steve Raymund was named chief operating officer, and the following year he became chief executive officer.

In 1986, Tech Data offered its stock to the public for the first time, entering the market at $9.75 a share. Annual sales had reached $37 million by this time. Marketing primarily to value-added resellers, which sold computer equipment and supplies to small and medium-sized businesses, Tech Data grew at a remarkable rate through the rest of the 1980s. Sales nearly doubled in 1987, reaching $72 million. The company doubled its sales again, to $149 million, the following year.

In 1989, Tech Data made its move northward with the acquisition of ParityPlus, a modest Canadian microcomputer distributor. The Canadian operation, purchased for just over $1 million in cash, was subsequently renamed Tech Data Canada. By the end of fiscal 1989, the company's coast-to-coast network of ten distribution centers was in place, and its work force had grown to 430. Sales for the year were $247 million.

Struggles and Successes in the Early 1990s

After reporting impressive earnings for several years in a row, Tech Data stumbled slightly in 1990. Although its sales grew to $348 million for the year, the company's net income

was cut in half. This off year was attributed in part on the bankruptcy of a major customer, Bulldog Computer Products of Atlanta, which cost Tech Data $1 million. Mismanagement and theft of inventory, including accounting errors and reported thievery at the company's Los Angeles warehouse, resulted in another $4 million in red ink. Raymund reacted to these problems with a combination of tightened inventory controls and cost-cutting measures. The company's executive rank was thinned out, and the frequency of inventory checks was switched from yearly to quarterly.

By 1991, Tech Data had turned things around. That year, Steve Raymund succeeded his father as chairman of the company's board of directors. Tech Data had settled in among the top five computer distributors in the United States and was an acknowledged leader in the distribution of local area network (LAN) and network products. For the year, Tech Data reported earnings of $6.7 million on sales of $442 million. The company began stocking the products of several well known manufacturers around this time. Among the companies whose wares Tech Data began selling in the early 1990s were Compaq, Conner Peripherals (a leading maker of disk drives), Toshiba, and Lexmark (a typewriter and printer spin-off of IBM).

By 1992, the company had about 25,000 customers, 70 percent of which were value-added resellers. The rest consisted of large national retailers. In March 1992, Tech Data added software to its line for the first time, helping to close the gap between Tech Data and its largest competitors, Ingram Micro and Merisel, Inc., where software was already generating about 40 percent of those companies' revenues. Forty software companies were quickly added to Tech Data's list of suppliers.

Tech Data also benefited increasingly from the desire on the part of PC manufacturers to cut distribution costs. Since selling to a distributor required less effort than selling directly to dealers, more and more producers of computer equipment were drawn to companies like Tech Data as the most efficient channel for selling their goods. Eventually, even the largest companies in the computer industry began to feel that selling through wholesale distributors was necessary if they were to remain competitive with such up-and-coming concerns as AST Research and Dell.

For fiscal 1992, revenues at Tech Data rose to $647 million. In January 1993, Tech Data made an important breakthrough when it received authorization to begin selling certain Microsoft system and application software products to value-added resellers. IBM and Apple were also added to the list of companies whose products were available through Tech Data. With these major producers in the fold, Tech Data's numbers jumped impressively once again. The company reported earnings of $19.8 million on sales of $979 million for 1993. During that year, Tech Data also sought to expand internationally, and, toward that end, an export division was established early in the year. Based in Miami, the division was designed to serve the Latin American market.

International Expansion in the Mid- to Late 1990s

For fiscal 1993, Tech Data's sales increased 57 percent to $1.53 billion. Record earnings of $30.2 million were reported as

Key Dates:

1974: Tech Data is launched to market mainframe and mini computer supplies to large institutions.

1981: Sales are $2 million; the company has ten employees.

1983: The company is profitable again after a shift to the PC reseller market.

1985: Steven Raymund, son of founder Edward Raymund, becomes CEO.

1986: The company goes public.

1989: Parity Plus (Tech Data Canada) is acquired.

1992: Software is added to the company's product lineup.

1993: Microsoft, Apple, and IBM products are added; an export division is established in Miami.

1994: Distributors are acquired in California; revenues exceed $2 billion.

1998: The company acquires control of leading European distributor Computer 2000.

1999: Canada's Globelle Corporation is acquired.

2003: Azlan Group, European distributor of networking products, is acquired.

well. In a flurry of activity, the company announced the addition of several major software companies to its line of offerings. In January 1994, Tech Data completed the acquisition of Software Resource Inc., a software distributor based in Novato, California. This acquisition enabled the company to begin offering several well known software lines, most importantly those of Borland International and WordPerfect Corporation. In March, Tech Data beefed up its international operations with the acquisition of Softmart International, S.A., a privately-held French distributor of PC products. The list of software companies represented in Tech Data warehouses grew in 1994 with the inclusion of Lotus, Aldus, and Computer Associates.

In the mid-1990s, Tech Data appeared to be narrowing the margin by which it trailed its larger competitors, Merisel and Ingram. By devoting a greater share of its work force to customer support and shoring up its software business and international operations, Tech Data stood to increase its overall market share, further solidifying its position as a leader among distributors of computer products.

Revenues exceeded $2 billion in 1994. Tech Data's inventory, worth $350 million, included 20,000 products from 600 manufacturers. As Tech Data's volume grew, the company was spending $29 million on a new computer system, nearly the equivalent of its $30 million net income. It also invested heavily in training for its 450 sales reps and 130 technical support people who handled thousands of calls every day on behalf of its 45,000 customers. The workforce was growing rapidly, exceeding 2,600 employees by 1996. *Computerworld* ranked it second among the best places to work due to compensation, the potential for advancement, and other factors.

Unfortunately, the new computer system crashed in 1995. A number of customers and investors took their business elsewhere. However, noted *Florida Trend,* Tech Data was able to turn yet

another crisis into a launching pad for the next stage in its growth. By 1997, it was reporting record profits and annual revenues of $4.6 billion, and its stock price was twice pre-crash levels.

An enduring side benefit of the computer upgrade was e-commerce capability; 40 percent of Tech Data's orders were handled online by 1997. Soon (before rival Ingram Micro), the company was building Web-based storefronts for its customers, reported *Computer Reseller News.* By this time, Tech Data was the world's second-largest PC distributor but had less than half the revenues of Ingram Micro, which had recently acquired the distribution operations of another large rival, Intelligent Electronics Inc., and was buying up overseas companies as well.

Traditionally known for organic growth, Tech Data expanded its international operations in the late 1990s through acquisitions. In 1997, it bought a 77 percent controlling interest in the $1 billion German PC products distributor Macrotron AG. This was sold to Ingram Micro the next year, however, in the aftermath of a larger acquisition.

In 1998, the company paid Klockner & Co. AG $395 million in stock for its 80 percent holding in Munich-based distributor Computer 2000 AG (the remaining shares were picked up in 2000). This purchase lifted Tech Data's total revenues to nearly $12 billion, noted *Computer Reseller News.* Computer 2000 had operations in more than 30 countries, some (in the Middle East and South America) new to Tech Data, but its own expansion quest had failed after heavy losses after it bought U.S. distributor AmeriQuest Technologies. After putting the company's U.S. operations in the hands of company president Tony Ibarguen, CEO Steve Raymund temporarily moved to Paris to be closer to the expanding business in Europe.

In the western hemisphere, Tech Data set up distribution centers in Sao Paulo, Brazil and Miami. Globelle Corporation was added in 1999, doubling the size of Tech Data's Canadian business north of the border.

Post-Bubble Survival

Sales were about $20 billion in 2000. The rise of the Internet had helped the information technology (IT) market grow. However, some distributors were failing even before the tech bubble burst, including CHS Electronics, one of Tech Data's nearer rivals, which collapsed in 1998. Demand slowed and more buyers bought directly from manufacturers such as Dell. As the market slowed, Tech Data cut its workforce by one-fifth in 2001.

Revenues slipped to $15.7 billion for the fiscal year ended January 31, 2003. In March 2003, Tech Data bought Europe's Azlan Group, a distributor of networking products, for $227 million. CEO Steve Raymund was steering the company towards new technologies in IP telephony, the digital home, and IT convergence, he told *Computer Reseller News.*

As noted by *Computer Database,* severe competition awaited distributors beginning to benefit from an improving economy. Nevertheless, Tech Data's sales again approached $20 billion in the fiscal year ended January 31, 2005. Tech Data was the world's second-largest distributor of computer products behind Ingram Micro Inc. With SYNNEX Corporation, they made up the industry's "Big Three."

Principal Subsidiaries

Azlan Group Limited (United Kingdom); TD Brasil, Ltda.; Tech Data Canada Corporation; Tech Data Education, Inc.; Tech Data Finance, SPV, Inc.; Tech Data Deutschland GmbH; Tech Data Europe GmbH; Tech Data Latin America, Inc.

Principal Competitors

Ingram Micro Inc.; SYNNEX Corporation.

Further Reading

Campbell, Scott, "Steve Raymund," *Computer Reseller News*, November 10, 1999.

Doyle, T.C., and John Longwell, "Tech Data to Expand Reach via Software-Signing Spree," *Computer Reseller News*, February 14, 1994.

Dubashi, Jagannath, "Tech Data: There's Gold in Them VAR Hills," *Financial World,* May 12, 1992, p. 14.

Finegan, Jay, "Turning Point," *Inc.*, April 1989, pp. 106–07.

"Inside Tech Data," *Tampa Tribune*, June 28, 1993.

Quickel, Stephen W., "Tech Data Muscles onto Others' Turf," *Electronic Business Buyer*, September 1993, p. 32.

Rooney, Paul A., "Tech Data Mastering Growth," *Tampa Bay Business Journal*, April 12, 1991, p. 1.

Scholl, Jaye, "Cool Cat with a Hot Hand," *Barron's*, Januray 6, 1992, p. 16.

—Robert R. Jacobson
—update: Frederick C. Ingram

Thomasville®

Thomasville Furniture Industries, Inc.

401 East Main Street
Thomasville, North Carolina 27360
U.S.A.
Telephone: (336) 472-4000
Toll Free: (800) 225-0265
Fax: (336) 472-4085
Web site: http://www.thomasville.com

*Wholly Owned Subsidiary of Furniture Brands
   International Inc.*
Incorporated: 1904 as Thomasville Chair Company
Employees: 4,300
Sales: $800 million (2004 est.)
NAIC: 337121 Upholstered Household Furniture
   Manufacturing

Thomasville Furniture Industries, Inc., is a leading manufacturer of upper medium to higher-priced dining room, bedroom, upholstered, and occasional furniture. The company is also the economic keystone of Thomasville, North Carolina, with half the company's work force living and working there. The landmark Big Chair—an 18-foot reproduction of a Duncan Phyfe design first erected in 1922 and rebuilt in 1951—remains in the town square as a symbol of the company's long-standing (and well-seated) success. The chair's size also remains a tribute to the company's growth. By 2005, Thomasville Furniture had become a subsidiary of a Fortune 500 parent, Furniture Brands International, Inc., and was displaying its wares in 144 Thomasville Galleries and 157 Thomasville Home Furnishings Stores nationwide. Through one of the furniture industry's most aggressive marketing campaigns, the company's brand name continued to work itself into the American mindset, in order to better position its products for the nation's living-room set of the future.

Origins

Founded in 1904 with $10,000 and a turnover of 180 chairs a day, Thomasville Chair Company was one of many small chair manufacturers in the region. By 1907, the fledgling enterprise owed $2,000 in lumber fees to T.J. Finch and his brother, D.F.

Finch. The brothers had already distinguished themselves as prominent entrepreneurs by farming timber, producing and selling lumber, and helping found a telephone company and two banks. In addition, T.J. Finch was the sheriff of Randolph County. Within a year of reluctantly accepting payment in stock in lieu of the young company's scarce cash, the brothers moved to "protect their investment" by buying out the remaining shares. By the end of that year, T.J. Finch occupied the company's presidential seat.

True to their nature, the Finch family didn't sit still for long. By 1908, the company reported profits on sales of $91,522. A year later, total assets were nearly doubled by the acquisition of Bard Lumber and Manufacturing Company. Moreover, T.J. Finch positioned the growing company for vertical integration, starting a machine shop, a three-story building for wrapping and upholstery operations and inventory, and one of the largest veneer plants in the South. The 1914 acquisition of Cramer Furniture Co. more than doubled the company's size once again, and by 1917 sales topped $1 million. Meanwhile, T.J. Finch had begun delegating key responsibilities to his son, T. Austin Finch, with an eye on the next generation of success.

Postwar Diversification

Following World War I, new emphasis was placed on diversification of product line to accommodate customer demand. The first in-house designers were hired in 1925. Alliances were formed with other furniture manufacturers so that Thomasville chairs could be marketed as integral parts of furniture sets. Chairs were crafted by Thomasville, tables by St. Johns Table Co. of Michigan, and buffets by B.F. Huntley Furniture Co. of Winston-Salem. These wares, peddled by the first national sales force in the furniture industry, proved so successful that T. Austin Finch positioned the company to produce them on its own. By 1927, Thomasville offered a complete line of dining room furniture, distinguishing itself as the most diversified producer in the industry.

After T. Austin Finch ascended to the Thomasville presidency in 1927, he positioned the company for higher quality products and trendsetting innovation. Rather than cut wages,

Company Perspectives:

Thomasville Furniture Industries is a full-line manufacturer founded in Thomasville, North Carolina, in 1904. Today, although business trends and home styles continue to change, the company remains committed to its rich heritage of quality, beauty and innovation. Thomasville believes the true value of its furniture lies in the sense of comfort, the touch of romance and the possibility of self-expression it provides. Thomasville is a living brand of aspirations and dreams.

prices, and quality during the strain of the Depression years, the company stepped up to a higher grade of furniture—a move that involved immediate risks, but that set Thomasville apart from its competitors when the economic storm clouds cleared later that decade. Initiative in automation helped the company produce its higher-end products more efficiently, as well. In 1937, the company installed one of the first conveyor systems in the industry and retrofitted its equipment for automated processes. Meanwhile, T. Austin's brother, Doak Finch, played a growing role in the company's operations. For example, he contracted a manufacturer of automatic nail machines for shoemaking to design the first such machines for the furniture industry. Following T. Austin's death in 1943, the younger brother continued the lineage of Finch company presidents.

During World War II, 65 percent of Thomasville's efforts were geared toward government orders. From army double deck bunk beds to wood plugs for bombs, tent stakes, and spatulas, the company's products had moved from domestic sitting rooms to overseas battle fields. Stores of consumer furniture were sold exclusively to customers who had bought from Thomasville before the war.

The postwar era was marked by strong economic recovery on all domestic fronts, with a prominent share of the furniture market moving to the South. Large, biannual exhibits—in April and October—served as forums for furniture makers to showcase their products. Thomasville launched marketing campaigns designed to get potential consumers right into the factory, and in 1958, the company opened a massive, four-story showroom that dwarfed those of virtually all its competitors.

1960s Public Offering

The 1960s ushered in a period of unprecedented growth, spurred by a series of mergers that changed not only the scope of the company's client base, but its name. In 1961, Thomasville Chair Company merged with B.F. Huntley Co., continuing a 35-year alliance in marketing and developing complete furniture packages. The new entity, renamed Thomasville Furniture Industries, went public in April 1962 and began selling shares on the New York Stock Exchange in 1964. With greater resources at hand, the company broadened both its product line and its client base, moving decisively into contemporary styles and forging strong ties with business clients, such as hotels, in the contract furniture market.

Starting in the late 1960s, the company took great strides in quality control by pioneering the industry's first Environmental

Simulation Package Testing Laboratory. Using climatized chambers and specialized machines to simulate variable conditions, these facilitates helped assure the durability of packaging and, ultimately, the condition of Thomasville's delivered goods.

In 1968, Thomasville Furniture became a subsidiary of Armstrong Cork Company, a leading industrial firm with a history dating back to 1860, when Thomas M. Armstrong and John D. Glass began producing cork bottle stoppers in a one-room shop. By the time Armstrong acquired Thomasville, it had become a major industrial manufacturer. Shortly thereafter, its name was changed to Armstrong World Industries to better reflect its diversified product line, which ultimately ranged from industrial floor coverings to carpets, wood products, furniture, adhesives and sealants, and gaskets by the 1990s.

Under Armstrong's parentage, Thomasville continued its pattern of growth through acquisitions that had started in the early 1960s. Indeed, the 1960s were fruitful years for mergers with a number of valuable companies: Phoenix Chair Company in 1964; Founders Furniture Company in 1965; Western Carolina Furniture Company in 1966; and Caldwell Furniture Company in 1968. During the 1970s, the company continued to expand its operations with the start up of the Armstrong furniture line, a lower priced line of bedroom furniture. Under the leadership of Frederick Starr, who became president and CEO in 1982 that growth continued. Key mergers and facility developments included Gilliam Furniture Inc. in May 1986; construction of a new plant at Carysbrook, Virginia, in June 1986; the Westchester Group of Companies in November 1987; Gordon's Inc. in August 1988; and construction of a 40,000 square-foot addition to one of its Thomasville dining room furniture plants in late 1988.

With recessionary trends in the early 1990s, Thomasville lost some of the growth momentum that it had enjoyed during the boom of the mid- to late 1980s. The furniture industry was particularly recession-prone for two key reasons: most consumers were quick to put off furniture purchases in bad times; and furniture sales were highly dependent on real estate, which was hit hard by recession. Moreover, as analyst Wallace Eppeson, Jr., noted in a January 1994 Business-North Carolina article, furniture sales historically remained stalled long after recessions were over—reflecting in large part the deferrable nature of the product. Still, Starr took few draconian measures to curtail the ambitious plans he had begun on the crest of the 1980s. Drawing on the expertise of financial officers running complex computer programs in late 1990, Thomasville calculated its likely profits if the company were to suffer 10, 15, or 20 percent reductions in sales. Concluding that medium-term growth might be flat, but not detrimental, Starr and his team positioned the company for continued growth in the not-to-distant future. ''We really do not want to close plants. ... We've got great plants, great people. You can't get them back if you close them,'' Starr told John Burgess in a November 25, 1990 article for *The Washington Post.*

Cost Cutting in the 1990s

Rather than close plants or severely cut back on operations, therefore, Thomasville moved to lighten its financial burden with a series of effective cost reduction measures in the early

1990s. The company stepped up programs to reduce production and distribution time, to improve quality, and to restructure its salaried and hourly organizations. The company also shifted production toward lower-cost items that would perform better in hard times, such as upholstered and non-assembled furniture. In addition, in 1991 Thomasville moved into a key, new market that promised exceptional growth: furniture equipped with electronic components. In an October 25, 1993 article for Investor's Business Daily, Kathleen M. Berry reported that sales of such furniture designs were expected to reach $3 billion by 1995. To tap that potential, Thomasville struck an alliance with Holland's Philips Electronic NV, collaborating on new entertainment centers or home theater systems with price tags between $10,000 and $12,000. The company also made cross-merchandising arrangements in 1993 with Eastman House to sell mattresses and quilted bedsets with its beds and also began to develop its international business.

In an effort to maximize its share of a stagnant market, Thomasville redoubled marketing and advertising efforts that it had started aggressively pursuing in the 1980s. Such a strategy provided an appreciable advantage in an industry that tended to neglect consumer advertising. Although furniture makers shipped $18 billion in products each year, manufacturers spent only $170 million annually on consumer advertising, the Home Furnishing Council estimated in *Advertising Age* on January 10, 1994. (Furniture manufacturers traditionally spent their marketing money on trade ads, leaving the task of consumer advertising to retailers.) Thomasville was among a small minority of exceptions. As early as 1989, the company initiated a $10 million-plus television ad campaign. Moreover, Thomasville forged ahead in its "galleries" program, consisting of free-standing stores that displayed only the company's products, as well as fully furnished displays in retailing stores. The push was a success: between 1982 and 1988, Thomasville saw its sales double to $360 million.

Along with their advantages, Thomasville's marketing efforts caused some troubles for the company. In April 1988, a group of North Carolina discount retailers filed two antitrust federal court challenges against Thomasville. In May, the retailers pressed for a bill in the General Assembly that would permit them to sell furniture by mail and toll-free telephone. They claimed that the furniture manufacturer was placing excessive restrictions on retailers by forbidding them from selling Thomasville goods over the phone to customers who had never set foot in the showroom or to solicit business outside the local area. Thomasville argued that it was merely protecting the rights of furniture manufacturers to draw customers into the showroom, where they could see a broad complement of furniture. he company also intended to stop "free riding" customers who shopped at their local galleries and then ordered goods from afar, often at lower prices. In June 1989, Thomasville amended its distribution policy by which retailers could sell to any client in the state and to any mail or telephone customers they had prior to June 8. By the end of November 1989, this compromise had prompted the retailers to drop the suit.

In mid-1994, Thomasville consolidated the lessons of all its past marketing efforts. The company combined direct mail, TV, and print advertising for a nationwide image campaign developed by Pascale & Associates, a Greensboro, North Carolina, agency. Promotion of a new product line, Country Inns & Back Roads, was directed at a target audience of upscale women interested in antiques, museum art, cooking, and gardening. Pascale started the campaign by issuing three separate direct mail postcards, taking out billboards, and placing three newspaper ads, all of which aroused consumer interest without showing the actual product line. Capitalizing on the anticipation from that first phase, the campaign depended on a second phase: a combination of mini-catalog mailers, retailer brochures, newspaper ads, and radio and TV spots that actually described the furniture products.

New Ownership in the 1990s

In 1995, Thomasville Furniture was acquired for $339 million by Furniture Brands International, Inc., a St. Louis-based corporation which owns Broyhill, Lane, Drexel Heritage, Maitland-Smith, and other furniture-making companies. Furniture Brands was ranked as the country's leading maker of residential furniture.

The late 1990s saw a rapid expansion in the number of Thomasville Home Furnishings stores. In 1997, 20 stores were opened. Another 25 were opened in 1998. At the same time, Thomasville approached dozens of independent furniture retailers about opening free-standing stores selling only Thomasville furniture. Nearly 100 such stores were opened by the turn of the century.

Despite the rapid growth in sales outlets, the late 1990s were a troubling time for Thomasville. Competition from foreign manufacturers resulted in many layoffs and plant closings. The disturbing trend continued into the new century: between 2001 and 2005 alone, Thomasville cut over 2,800 jobs. In mid-2005 it was announced that Thomasville would shut down seven furniture plants in North Carolina by November. It was the largest layoff in the company's history. Since the 1990s, the number of Thomasville employees dropped from about 8,000 to 4,300. Dave Masters, Thomasville Furniture general manager of personnel and safety, told Amber Veverka in the *Charlotte Observer*, "We've just got too much domestic capacity and we're trying to lower that to balance our domestic and import production." An increasing percentage of Thomasville furniture was manufactured overseas and brought in from China, the Phillipines, and Mexico. Paul Dascoli, executive vice-president of Thomasville, told Richard Craver of the *Winston-Salem Journal* that once the company's restructuring was complete, "only 25 percent of Thomasville's wooden furniture would be made domestically."

New Designs in a New Century

To help revive the company's competitiveness, Thomasville has introduced two distinctive lines of furniture based on famous figures of literature and film. In 2000, "Ernest Hemingway: The Collection of a Lifetime" was launched, named after the novelist well known for his love of big game hunting, bullfighting, and deep sea fishing. The collection consists of five categories, each inspired by a region or country with which the globe-trotting Hemingway is associated: Paris, Kenya, Havana, Key West, and Ketchum, Idaho. The furniture is meant to suggest Hemingway's robust, outdoorsy image and is aimed at what Matthew Grimm in *American Demographics* called "America's bookish, aging, Sunday Times-ritualizing baby boomers." Speaking to Sandra O'Loughlin in *Brandweek*, Thomasville vice-president of brand development Mitch Scott stated: "The Ernest Hemingway collection is an extremely successful collection and continues to perform extremely well."

In the spring of 2003, the "Bogart Collection" was introduced, named after the legendary film star Humphrey Bogart and inspired by the classic furniture designs of the 1930s and 1940s. The collection includes over 100 pieces of furniture. The Bogart Collection seeks to evoke, O'Loughlin noted, "the glamour and sophistication of Hollywood's heyday." An extensive advertising campaign launched the collection, featuring a Bogart lookalike posing amid the furniture.

Thomasville teamed with Progress Lighting in early 2004. Under the arrangement, Progress made and sold lighting fixtures "designed to coordinate with current Thomasville Furniture collections, down to the design details and finishes," as Nancy Meyer explained in *HFN: The Weekly Newspaper for the Home Furnishing Network*. Jim Decker, Progress Lighting vice-president of brand management, told Meyer that the arrangement with Thomasville had proven profitable: "From our standpoint, the value of the Thomasville brand, and the consumer recognition we hoped it would have, have more than surpassed our expectations. It's coming through in spades."

In 2005, Thomasville furniture was sold in 144 Thomasville Galleries, 157 Thomasville Home Furnishings Stores, as well as in over 400 independent retail stores. In addition, business furniture manufactured by its subsidiary Creative Interiors is sold in the Target and Wal-Mart retail chains. While stiff competition from foreign manufacturers still threatened the domestic furniture-making industry, Thomasville Furniture introduced new concepts and partnerships which promised to keep the company at the forefront of the field.

Principal Divisions

Thomasville Cabinetry; Thomasville Lighting; Founders Furniture; Pearson; Hickory Chair; Creative Interiors; Hickory Business Furniture; Thomasville Contract.

Principal Competitors

Bassett Furniture Industries Inc.; Ethan Allen Interiors Inc.; La-Z-Boy Inc.; Hooker Furniture Corporation.

Further Reading

Benscoter, Jana, "Thomasville to Shut 7 Furniture Plants in North Carolina by November," *High Point Enterprise*, June 8, 2005.

Berry, Kathleen M., "Furniture and Electronics Makers Form Alliances," *Investor's Business Daily,* October 25, 1993, p. 4.

Brown, Nicholas, "Furniture Discounters Drop Suit Against Thomasville," *Greensboro News & Record,* November 29, 1989, p. B5.

Brown, Nicholas, "Thomasville Gallery Program a Success," *Greensboro News & Record,* November 6, 1989, p. C3.

Burgess, John, "Fighting to Stay Fit: Economy's Failing Vital Signs Force Firms to Find Cures," *Washington Post,* November 25, 1990, p. H1.

Craver, Richard, "Thomasville Furniture Industries to Close Plants," *Winston-Salem Journal,* June 8, 2005.

Gattuso, Greg, "The Advertising Road Less Travelled; Marketing Technique of Thomasville Furniture Industries, Inc.," *Direct Marketing Magazine,* June 1994, p. 20.

Gault, Ylonda, "Traditional Furniture Seeks City Market," *Crain's New York Business,* July 8, 1991, p. 28.

Gaylor, Ginny, "Bogart among Top Names to Headline in High Point," *Home Accents Today,* October, 2002, p. 12.

Grimm, Matthew, "Live Large, at Home: The Myth That Was Hemingway Now Furnishes Boomers' Dreams," *American Demographics,* June, 2000.

"Have a Seat and Wait: That's What the Furniture Industry is Doing," *Business-North Carolina,* January 1994, p. 73.

Johnson, Bradley, "A Dispute in the Gallery," *Greensboro News & Record,* April 10, 1989, p. C10.

Johnson, Paul B., "Thomasville Furniture to Close Statesville, N.C., Plant with 118 Jobs at Stake," *High Point Enterprise,* July 2, 2004.

Kelt, Deborah, "Thomasville Lenox: Double Date," *HFD: The Weekly Home Furnishings Newspaper*, April 19, 1993, p. M2.

Kramp, Kelly, "Thomasville Braces for Reality of Loss," *High Point Enterprise,* June 12, 2005.

Kunkel, Karl, "Category Remains Hot," *HFN: The Weekly Newspaper for the Home Furnishing Network*, October 18, 1999, p. 36.

Meyer, Nancy, "Retailers: Chances Are There to Co-Market Thomasville Lighting, Furniture," *HFN: The Weekly Newspaper for the Home Furnishing Network,* October 11, 2004, p. 116.

O'Loughlin, Sandra, "Bogart Stars as Thomasville Plays It Again," *Brandweek,* January 20, 2003, p. 4.

Schancupp, Pam, "Matching Linen for Restonic, Thomasville Beds," *HFD: The Weekly Home Furnishings Newspaper*, May 3, 1993, p. 26.

Sloan, Pat, "Furniture Maker Builds on TV Ads," *Advertising Age,* December 5, 1988, p. 12.

Steenhuysen, Julie, "Finally, Furniture Makers Fashion Ads," *Advertising Age,* January 10, 1994, p. S2.

Switzer, Liz, "Thomasville on a Roll: Company Fine-Tunes with New Stores, Advertising," *HFN: The Weekly Newspaper for the Home Furnishing Network,* August 24, 1998, p. 21.

"Thomasville, Progress Partner in Lighting Venture," *Home Accents Today,* February, 2004, p. 10.

"Thomasville to Launch Bogart-Themed Furniture," *Brandweek,* May 21, 2001, p. 5.

Van Der, Pool Lisa, "Thomasville Goes Contemporary: 'Where Style Lives' Branding Puts Furniture Maker in a New Light," *ADWEEK Southwest,* March 11, 2002, p. 6.

Veverka, Amber, "Imports, Automation Take Toll on North Carolina Furniture Industry," *Charlotte Observer,* September 26, 2002.

—Kerstan Cohen
—update: Thomas Wiloch

The Tokyo Electric Power Company

1-3, Uchisaiwai-cho, 1-chome
Chiyoda-ku, Tokyo 100-8560
Japan
Telephone: (+03) 4216-1111
Fax: (+03) 4216-2539
Web site: http://www.tepco.co.jp

Public Company
Incorporated: 1951
Employees: 51,694
Sales: ¥5.05 trillion ($45.9 billion) (2004)
Stock Exchanges: Tokyo Osaka Nagoya Niigata
Ticker Symbol: TKECF
NAIC: 221111 Hydroelectric Power Generation; 221112 Fossil Fuel Electric Power Generation; 221113 Nuclear Electric Power Generation; 221119 Other Electric Power Generation; 221121 Electric Bulk Power Transmission and Control; 221122 Electric Power Distribution

The Tokyo Electric Power Company (TEPCO) is one of the world's largest electric utility companies. Japan has ten major regional power companies but TEPCO alone supplies approximately one-third of Japan's electricity. In fiscal year 2004, the company distributed 286.7 billion kilowatt-hours (kWh) of electricity to 28 million industrial, commercial, and individual customers in Tokyo and the surrounding area. TEPCO's total generating capacity is nearly 63,000 megawatts (MW). It has 190 thermal, nuclear, hydro, and wind power plants in its arsenal. Deregulation of Japan's electric market began in 1995 and since that time TEPCO has been diversifying its holdings. The company is also working to restore public faith in nuclear power after a scandal in 2002 forced the temporary shutdown of its 17 nuclear power plants.

Early History

TEPCO has its roots in Japan's first electric utility, Tokyo Electric Lighting Company, which emerged in the mid-1880s, although TEPCO dates its incorporation from 1951, the year in which the Japanese electric power industry returned to private ownership after government monopoly control during World War II.

Even as the world's first public power stations were being established in London and New York in 1882, the Meiji government, in its effort to modernize Japan, formed an Institute of Technology. English and other foreign experts were invited to Tokyo to train the Japanese in the technology. In November 1885, Tokyo Electric Lighting Company used a Japanese-made portable generator to light 40 incandescent lamps in the Bank of Tokyo. Regular service began the following year when the company, capitalized at ¥200,000, was granted a charter to generate and distribute electricity and sell lighting accessories. A coal-fired thermal station, generating 25 kilowatts (kW), began operating in November 1887. By 1892, 14,100 lamps had been installed in post offices, banks, ministries, and Japan's first modern factories.

Tokyo Electric Lighting Company used thermal plants because coal was plentiful; the only other domestic energy resource, major river systems, was beyond the range of its primitive transmission technology. Hydroelectric power generation, introduced by the city of Kyoto in 1891, would become Japan's leading prewar electricity source, but was available to Tokyo only over long-distance trunk lines.

The company began to consolidate neighborhood thermal plants and by 1897 had ten units in Asakusa Kuramae power station, aggregating a capacity of 2,390 kW. Distribution efficiency improved in 1907 with 55 kilovolts (kV) transmission. By 1911, the company was also making tungsten bulbs.

Industry Law Takes Effect in 1911

The government consolidated ad hoc legislation over the rapidly growing industry by enacting an Electric Utility Industry Law in 1911. From then on, power plants had to be licensed, and regulation began providing for common use of transmission lines. War, too, had become a spur to growth. The Sino-Japanese war of 1894 to 1895 boosted Japanese industry with its procurement demands. At the same time, tramcar systems proliferated in Tokyo and other Japanese cities.

Company Perspectives:

Our group management principle is to contribute to the realization of affluent living and a pleasant environment by offering optimal energy services. The TEPCO group promotes this management principle, and strives to become the top energy service provider in line with the following three group management guidelines: win the trust of society; survive the struggle in competition; and foster people and technologies.

Following the 1904 to 1905 Russo-Japanese War, the government promoted heavy industry, and the electric power industry also grew rapidly, becoming second only to banks in terms of capital. Tokyo Electric Lighting Company, now able to draw power from hydroelectric stations in the hinterland, remained the largest utility in the country even as the number of generating and distribution companies rose from 11 in 1892 to 1,752 by 1915. Its service region encompassed the political capital, a major university center, and a burgeoning of satellite heavy-and light-industrial complexes and their international trading ports.

Japan was allied with Britain and France in World War I. While British and French industries were occupied in war production, exports of Japanese light-industrial goods to Europe soared, notably raw silk but also tea, toys, household utensils, and machine parts. In 1925, the total number of companies in the electricity utility field peaked at around 3,000.

In September 1923, however, there came a huge setback, the Great Kanto Earthquake, accompanied by fires which destroyed much of Tokyo and Yokohama. International aid poured in and the restoring of utilities was given the highest priority. By 1924, the company was again moving forward in the development of a national grid among Japanese companies importing American equipment which produced current at 50 hertz (Hz). Companies in western Japan, including Osaka, had opted for German equipment, delivering 60Hz. New transmission technology could deliver and convert hydroelectric power from the hinterland mountain regions. This began the wide area electric power exchange system, which continues to overcome power shortages in the Tokyo region.

In the 1920s, Europe was again producing light-industrial goods, and the Japanese economy slid into severe depression. Japan's leading export, raw silk, slumped by more than half. There was fierce competition in the electric power industry. In some cases, three power companies supplied a single customer at different times of the day. Tokyo Electric Lighting Company began absorbing bankrupt competitors during an industry shake-out.

By 1928, it was the largest of the Big Five utilities operating the self-regulating Electric Power Control Council. In general, Japan's industries were adopting the cartel system in an effort to stabilize the marketplace. At the same time, militarist factions were turning the nation toward war in mainland China. By 1932, the government began enforcing a revised Electric Utility Industry Law. This gave the bureaucrats the final say on rates, company mergers, and even expropriation of utilities for military production.

State Control in the Late 1930s and Early 1940s

By 1937, governments increasingly dominated by personalities wanting to emulate the German and Italian imperialist regimes had led Japan into full-scale war against China. Tokyo Electric Lighting Company, along with the rest of the industry, came under state control in 1938. The core legislation established the Japan Electric Generation and Transmission Company (JEGTCO) or Nippon Hasso Den. The Electric Utility Bureau of the Ministry of Communications supervised the industry. The Japanese government wanted to ensure an abundant supply of cheap electricity for military production. Government permission was required for rate levels, building new power stations, or installing transmission lines. Tokyo Electric Lighting Company was at that time a component of what was, in effect, one of the largest electricity companies in the world.

By 1942, the framework for exerting state control over the electric power industry was firmly in place. In 1943, the task of supervision passed to the Electric Power Office of the Ministry of Munitions. The industry thus became part of the mobilization for global war. Hydroelectric power development took priority, and 17 new plants were built on river systems across the country. The Tokyo region could use only coal-fired thermal plants locally. The military planning brought a national grid closer to reality, and Tokyo and most of eastern Japan was standardized on 50Hz current while western Japan used 60Hz. At the same time, military intervention had, in fact, slowed down development in the utility industry. In the four years before World War II, electricity production capacity had been increasing at an annual rate of 600 MW. During the war years, annual growth in capacity declined to an average 170 MW.

Postwar Occupation

When Japan surrendered in 1945, Tokyo had been bombed and burned to rubble. Facilities of the former Tokyo Electric Lighting Company represented a large proportion of the 44 percent of thermal power plant capacity that had been destroyed nationwide. The JEGTCO monopoly was transferred to the Ministry of Commerce and Industry, forerunner of the Ministry of International Trade and Industry (MITI). The American-led military occupation authorities of Japan initially intended to return the nation to the level of an agricultural economy. By August 1946, surviving equipment in some 20 war-damaged thermal power plants had been included among factory machinery which was to be shipped to Asian countries invaded by Japan in part-payment of war reparations.

The national industrial base had been almost halved by air-raid destruction, and, with the munitions factories closed, Japan started out anew in 1945 with a surplus of electric power capacity to demand. With their legendary energy, however, the Japanese began to reconstruct factories from whatever machinery was available. As early as 1946, electric power demand increased by 25 percent and rose by an average of 10 percent for the next several years.

The Allied occupation at first refused to allow new capacity to be added, fearing that this might be a first step toward rearmament. By 1948, the JEGTCO monopoly was targeted for breakup, along with other industrial and financial concentrations such as the *zaibatsu*. Just how this was to be accomplished became a heated

Key Dates:

1886: Tokyo Electric Lighting Company is granted a charter to generate and distribute electricity and sell lighting accessories.
1911: The Electric Utility Industry Law is enacted.
1938: Tokyo Electric Lighting Company comes under state control.
1951: TEPCO incorporates as the Japanese electric power industry returns to private ownership.
1955: TEPCO research laboratories begin exploring nuclear power.
1966: Pilot nuclear power plants begin operating in Japan.
1970: The Minami-Yokohama Thermal Power Station becomes the first in the world to use liquefied natural gas (LNG) from Alaska.
1989: TEPCO cable television system is established.
1995: Changes in the Electricity Utilities Industry Law allow competition to enter into the electricity generation and supply market.
2000: The retail sector of Japan's electric power industry begins to deregulate.
2002: The company is forced to temporarily close its 17 nuclear reactors.
2005: The retail electric power market continues to deregulate.

issue between the Japanese leaders and the Allied occupation planners, who debated whether centralized state control should continue or utilities should return to private ownership. The situation was complicated by the rising power of unions encouraged by occupation policies. Paradoxically, unions in the electric power industry tended to favor state control for job security, and from 1946 often-violent strikes began with the aim of ensuring a future for domestic coal fuel, among other issues.

The Cold War began to change U.S. priorities for Japan: to support the strategy of containing Stalinist communism, it was becoming more desirable to have an industrially strong Japan with at least a military capability for self-defense. One of the most influential Japanese voices regarding electricity utility reform proved to be that of Yasuzaemon Matsunaga. This Meiji era entrepreneur was an important link between the prewar Tokyo Electric Lighting Company and the TEPCO that emerged in 1951. He had no direct business ties to the Tokyo utility but was a role model for Kazutaka Kikawada, who became TEPCO president during the high-growth economic breakthrough of the 1960s.

Matsunaga had prospered in western Japanese electric utilities and electric railways early in the century. By 1924, he was president of the Japan Electric Association. He opposed the military takeover, and when the JEGTCO monopoly was imposed in 1938 he retired to private life. In the postwar debate over future policy, he championed the private enterprise solution and his views prevailed.

TEPCO Begins Operation in 1951

While the debate continued, in May 1949 the MITI was established, and its Agency of Natural Resources assumed con-

trol of utilities. Finally, on November 24, 1950, the government invoked occupation powers to force reform legislation through parliament. From December 1950, a Public Utilities Commission comprising businessmen and academics, free of political control, divided the nation into nine regions, each with a privately owned electric power company, to begin operating in May 1951. TEPCO assumed the assets and liabilities of JEGTCO in the Tokyo region, including a subsidiary, the Kanto Power Distribution Company.

The Korean War had been underway since June 1950, and from its inception TEPCO played a leading role in supplying power to a still-occupied and capital-starved Japan. TEPCO relied on power transferred from distant hydroelectric stations for 80 percent of the supply for the Tokyo region.

The Korean War was the first of a succession of unforeseen circumstances fostering the Japanese economic miracle. It stimulated the first postwar boom because Japan was the main rear-base for American-led United Nations forces turning back the invasion of South Korea by communist North Korea. The extent to which U.S. policy toward Japan had been reversed is indicated by the fact that in April 1952 MITI was permitted to exclude thermal power station equipment from the list of machinery earmarked, in principle at least, for shipment abroad as war reparations.

TEPCO began increasing rates to profitable levels and cash flow was helped further by an easing of the tax structure, allowing more generous depreciation write-offs. What was emerging was the uniquely Japanese modification of classic free-enterprise capitalism based on competition but also due consideration for overriding national goals. At an early stage, TEPCO management gave priority to developing a new generation of managerial talent. In-house training courses reached the level of university education. State planning continued to have a role, especially for ensuring stability of supply for something as crucial as energy.

While TEPCO and the other regional companies were evolving as private enterprises, as early as 1951 Matsunaga succeeded in establishing a Central Research Institute for the Electric Power Industry. By 1952, the Prime Minister's Office had added an administrative Electric Power Development Coordination Council. A government-financed Electric Power Development Company, Ltd. (EPDC), capitalized at ¥100 billion, took on the job of developing major new hydroelectric power stations.

The Allied occupation ended in April 1952. By November, a Federation of Electric Power Companies had been organized and numerous symposiums and study groups debated whether the country should limit itself to the domestically available coal and hydroelectric energy resources. External events were to influence the outcome once more; in particular, technology became available from the United States and Europe, and oil became less expensive.

Studies began on the potential of nuclear power as early as 1954, although Japan was as barren of uranium ores as it was of oil. TEPCO research laboratories began exploring nuclear power in 1955, ahead of the promulgation in December of that year of an Atomic Energy Basic Law to guide the industry. In January 1956, the Prime Minister's Office added an Atomic Energy Commission to its roster of administrative bodies. The

Japan Atomic Energy Research Institute (JAERI), funded by both the government and the industry, opened in the same year. A separate entity, the Japan Atomic Power Company, followed in November 1957. TEPCO could coordinate its nuclear future through these and other supplementary organizations.

In 1958, the company became a founding member of the Japan Electric Power Information Center (JEPIC), whose major purpose was to promote technological exchanges with American and European utilities. High-voltage transmission and bridging the disparate frequencies in the eastern and western halves of the country became priorities. In 1959, a new Central Electric Power Council supervised the opening of the Tadami Line, linking the 50Hz system of TEPCO and the hydroelectric plants of the Tohoku Electric Power Company far to the northeast of Tokyo.

In 1961, Kazutaka Kikawada became president of TEPCO. Kikawada had joined the Tokyo Electric Lighting Company in 1926 during the depression Japan's economy experienced at this time. He had studied economics at Tokyo Imperial University and developed an interest in the problems of unemployment and social welfare. He took the TEPCO helm just as Prime Minister Hayato Ikeda was launching a program to double the national income within a decade, boosting public spending, reducing taxes, and lowering interest rates. Ikeda, who had become prime minister in 1960, was disabled by cancer in 1964. By then, however, Japan had joined the Organization for Economic Cooperation and Development (OECD) and had developed a domestic market whose prospering consumers would underpin manufacturing growth in the decades ahead.

Matsunaga, who had headed yet another commission planning the way forward for utilities in 1960, had been Kikawada's entrepreneurial model. As TEPCO president, in 1963 Kikawada also became chairman of the Keizai Doyukai, the Japan Association of Corporate Executives. This business association, formed in 1946, focused mainly on the appropriate role of private enterprise in improving the quality of Japanese life in general. It eventually became affiliated with six similar business organizations in Europe, the United States, and Australia involved in developing a private-sector role for easing global economic problems. Kikawada also became chairman of an advisory Economic Council of the Economic Planning Agency during 1966 and 1967.

Exploring New Sources of Power: 1960s–1980s

The prosperity of the 1960s brought a proliferation of electric home appliances and air-conditioning. TEPCO's peak demand season shifted from winter to summer, and the Tokyo region needed more and more supplementary power. In October 1965, the 50Hz system of eastern Japan was able for the first time to exchange power easily with the 60Hz system of western Japan through a sophisticated frequency converter station in central Japan. From 1963, thermal power generation had taken the lead over hydroelectric sources nationwide. By 1973, TEPCO's long-term development plan, applying large-scale thermal power generation technology, had quadrupled the company's capacity of eight years earlier.

Increasing American involvement in Vietnam throughout the 1960s accounted in part for orders flooding into Japan.

Heavy metal and chemical industries developed rapidly. As in the Korean War, Japan provided a major Asian support base, repairing air, land, and sea-battle equipment and supplying many materials and services. While U.S. industry met wartime priorities, new export markets opened for Japan, notably in consumer electronics. TEPCO, teamed with Japan's general trading houses (sogo shosha), began to diversify its overseas sources of fuel. Japan was following the rest of the industrial world into an era of oil-fired thermal power generation.

With the expansion of the coal-burning utility industry in Japan, air pollution began to reach critical levels, and in 1967 TEPCO turned to Indonesia for low-sulfur Minas crude oil. In 1970, its Minami-Yokohama Thermal Power Station became the first in the world to use liquefied natural gas (LNG), from Alaska. By 1973, coal-firing had been discontinued. Pilot nuclear power plants had begun operating in 1966. In 1971, TEPCO began operating Japan's third boiling-water reactor (BWR). The main supplier of the reactor and technology was General Electric of the United States.

TEPCO located its nuclear power plants far from the crowded capital region, on the coast of Fukushima prefecture to the north, the service region of its longtime partner, the Tohoku Electric Power Company. By 1979, five further BWR reactors had been added to the Fukushima No. 1 complex. The company now used its own technology and contracted construction to other Japanese corporations that were experts in the field. Despite potential earthquake hazards that could result in catastrophic events at nuclear power facilities, nuclear power began gaining ascendancy, mainly to reduce air pollution. In 1970, the government legislated severe controls on air, land, and water pollution. An Environmental Agency on the American model emerged in 1971. The oil crisis of 1973 to 1974 reinforced commitment to a nuclear future.

TEPCO declared a state of emergency and began shifting away from oil, a process accelerated by the second oil crisis at the end of the 1970s. Between 1973 and 1981, the share of nuclear fuel in the overall fuel mix increased from 3 percent to 21 percent. LNG consumption rose from 1.4 million tons annually to 6.9 million tons. The share of oil in thermal power generation declined from 90 percent to 56 percent. The company also researched new coal-burning technologies, from Coal-Oil-Mixture to the gassification of raw coal. By 1984, one major thermal power station had been converted back to improved coal fuel, and another was planned for 1993 in a joint-venture with Tohoku Electric Power Company.

The company entered the 1990s under the leadership of Gaishi Hiraiwa. Hiraiwa was elevated to chairman and chief executive officer in 1984. After graduating from Tokyo Imperial University Faculty of Law, and after briefly joining Tokyo Electric Lighting Company in 1939, he was drafted into the army and sent to war in China. After the war, he rose to become TEPCO's president in 1976. Hiraiwa was chairman of the Economic Council advising the government and in December 1990 was elevated from vice-president to chairman of the powerful Federation of Economic Organizations (Keidanren).

Under Hiraiwa's leadership in the 1980s, TEPCO moved into the realm of high technology applied far beyond the boundaries of the electric power industry. In 1980, Japan adopted a Law for Promoting Development and Introduction of Alternative Energies to Oil. By 1991, TEPCO was operating 13 of the 17 nuclear reactors installed in operating power stations; two more were under construction and another was in the advanced planning stage. The Three Mile Island and Chernobyl nuclear accidents revived popular opposition to nuclear technology in Japan. This delayed but did not halt the development of nuclear power. TEPCO and the government emphasized a net gain in combating conventional pollution, which was still severe in Japan. A need for more generating capacity became evident in the 1991 summer peak demand season when Tokyo was close to requiring rationing.

TEPCO in the Early to Mid-1990s

At this time, TEPCO imported uranium ores from the United States, Canada, Australia, and Niger. Specialized processing was carried out in the United States, Canada, the United Kingdom, and France, and spent nuclear fuel was sent to the United Kingdom and France for reprocessing. (By 2001, spent nuclear fuel was no longer shipped abroad.) Both uranium enrichment and spent-fuel reprocessing started to be carried out in Japan, however, and nuclear power stations added repositories for low-level wastes. In 1991, nuclear power accounted for 28 percent of TEPCO's total generation. This was projected to reach 39 percent by the year 2000.

TEPCO fully considered national policy needs in its business decisions. Since the 1970s, the main contractors for its nuclear power plants had been Toshiba and Hitachi. To ease trade friction, equipment orders for two new plants were switched to the General Electric Company (GEC) of the United States. TEPCO also turned to GEC for advanced gas turbines and generators to enhance the efficiency of thermal plants fired by LNG. In 1991, TEPCO was the world's largest user of LNG (along with liquified petroleum gas). The LNG share in TEPCO's thermal power fuel mix increased from 10 percent in 1973 to 56 percent in 1991. TEPCO bought from suppliers as far afield as Alaska, Brunei, Abu Dhabi (Das Island), Malaysia, Indonesia, and Australia. Through trading houses such as Mitsubishi Corporation and Mitsui & Company, it seemed likely that TEPCO would have access to Russian LNG resources on Sakhalin Island and possibly on the Siberian mainland if Russia followed through on invitations for shared development with Japan.

Oil had dwindled from 47 percent of TEPCO's total generating facilities in 1970 to 21 percent in 1990, and was projected to shrink to 15 percent by 2000 even before the Gulf War provoked new concern about supply stability. Hydroelectric power, representing 88 percent of supply in 1952, the company's first full year of operation, leveled off at around 9 percent; it survives for peak load demand fluctuations in a strategy of nuclear power for "base load" and LNG for "middle load." Coal was returned to the list of fuels in less-polluting guises, partly because the new technologies made it possible to begin buying American and other coals as well as Australian coal as a trade-balancing measure.

TEPCO was heavily involved, domestically and internationally, in research and development (R&D). In 1991 the central Engineering R&D Administration alone had 400 staff. Already

TEPCO was using new types of chemical fuel cells for local electricity supplies and electric power storage cells to help during peak demand, harbingers of future alternatives. Like many Japanese corporations, TEPCO maximized the application of its technology and expertise wherever opportunity beckoned.

In 1986, for example, when the Japanese government began to liberalize the telecommunications market, previously monopolized by Nippon Telegraph and Telephone Corp. (NTT), TEPCO used its expertise in computerized power grid communications in joining with two *sogo shosha* to form Tokyo Telecommunications Network Company, Inc. (TTNet) to develop an optical fiber digital network for facsimile, data, and public telephone services. This led to mobile communications and, in 1989, a TEPCO cable television system. The founding president of TTNet was Kazuo Fujimori, who had joined TEPCO in 1951 as an engineer and had become executive vice-president.

Research into nuclear power plant safety under earthquake conditions was also being applied to prototype high-rise buildings which could adjust to withstand earthquake vibrations. This was a contribution to Tokyo's major waterfront urban redevelopment projects. In seeking to reduce peak demand, TEPCO technologies gave Tokyo its first district air-conditioning system using waste heat on the heat-pump principle. In some cases, the heat was extracted from river waters warmed by factory discharge, while in others heat was recovered from sewage beneath high-rise "new towns." TEPCO recycled 60 percent of the copper used in power lines. TEPCO's laboratories were researching high-temperature industrial ceramics, superconductivity, and artificial intelligence for computers.

During the 1990s, TEPCO was involved with major international research projects in the United States and Europe while encouraging visits from overseas students and scientists. TEPCO technology enabled the company to achieve the world's lowest levels of sulfur dioxide and carbon dioxide emissions. In addition, research revealed the photosynthesis potential of seaweed for absorbing carbon dioxide. At the 1991 Tokyo Auto Show, TEPCO displayed an electric car prototype that could reach 170 kilometers per hour and could drive the 500 kilometers to Osaka without a battery recharge. Because of these wide-ranging activities, the company began to refer to itself as the TEPCO Group. It entered international capital markets with the issue of corporate bonds.

Challenges in the Late 1990s and Beyond

During the 1990s, the electricity industry in Japan began its deregulation process. In 1995, changes in the Electricity Utilities Industry Law allowed competition to enter into the electricity generation and supply market. Then, in 1996, a wholesale electric power bidding system enabled non-electric power companies to sell electricity to electric power companies. In March 2000, retail sales of electricity were partially deregulated, allowing large-lot customers—those demanding large amounts of electricity—to choose their power supplier. The retail sector continued the deregulation process in April 2005. This sector of the industry accounted for nearly 60 percent of TEPCO's electricity sales.

The intent of deregulation was to foster competition, which in turn would lower the electricity costs in the country. The deregulation was slow to change the Japanese industry, however, and during 2001 TEPCO and the other regional companies still controlled 99 percent of the market. In fact, only six Japanese-based companies, other than the original ten, supplied power to large customers, including retail businesses and office buildings. This accounted for a mere 0.2 percent share of the overall utility market.

During Japan's deregulation process, the nation as a whole was suffering due to an economic downturn. Demand for electric power fell, leaving TEPCO focused on developing new sources of income and revenue. In 1997, the company became Japan's first electric concern to sell LNG. In addition, it stepped into the Internet service provider arena when it partnered with several U.S. firms to create SpeedNet. Telecommunications firm POWEREDCOM was also launched at this time in partnership with other Japanese electric firms. In 2001, the company announced plans to construct Vietnam's first independent power plant.

TEPCO completed construction on the largest nuclear plant in the world in 1997. This was achieved despite public sentiment in Japan, which remained hostile towards the development of nuclear power due to several fatal accidents and scandals. According to a March 2000 *Business Week* article, nuclear power accounted for nearly 35 percent of Japan's electricity. In fact, for much of the 1990s, Japan's industry had aggressively focused on shifting from expensive and polluting coal-fired plants to nuclear power. Due to concerns over the safety of these nuclear facilities, Japan's government was forced to rethink its expansion efforts, cut back on its nuclear development plans, and find alternative sources of power. Nevertheless, it hoped nuclear power would be supplying over 40 percent of Japan's energy needs by 2011.

Despite public opposition to nuclear power, TEPCO continued to promote it as an environmentally friendly form of energy. Disaster struck in 2002, however, after the company admitted to falsifying safety documents related to its nuclear facilities. Engineers had failed to report 29 incidents of serious leaks and cracks in reactors at three of its nuclear plants during the late 1980s and 1990s. As a consequence of these revelations, the Japanese government ordered the temporary shutdown of TEPCO's 17 nuclear facilities. This left Tokyo in the midst of a power shortage during the hot summer months. Three of its plants were allowed to restart by 2003, and the remaining facilities were back online by the end of 2004.

The scandal proved costly to TEPCO, affecting its bottom line by ¥2 billion, as well as to its customers and the industry as a whole. During the shutdown, replacement power cost nearly 50 percent more than nuclear power, leaving its customers footing a much larger bill. At the same time, trust in Japan's nuclear energy facilities and the companies that supplied nu-clear power was shaky at best. The government hoped to regain consumer confidence, especially since nuclear power remained at the forefront of the country's energy strategy.

During 2004, TEPCO launched a new management plan entitled Management Vision 2010. A cornerstone in this new strategy was shoring up faith in the company's nuclear program. The company also focused on overcoming competition brought on by deregulation, developing new technologies, and expanding into new business areas. With the nuclear scandal behind it, TEPCO looked to the future and was determined to restore its image as low-cost, high-quality electric power supplier.

Principal Subsidiaries

The Tokyo Electric Generation Company Ltd.; POWEREDCOM Inc. (83.8%); AT TOKYO Corp. (52%); TEPCO Cable Television Inc. (85.4%); TEPCO Systems Corporation; Toden Real Estate Co Inc.; Toshin Building Co. Ltd.; Toden Kogyo Co. Ltd.; Tokyo TOSHI Service Company; Tokyo Electric Power Environmental Engineering Company Inc.; Tokyo Electric Power Home Service Company Ltd.; Tokyo Densetsu Service Co. Ltd.; Tokyo Living Service Co. Ltd.; Tokyo Electric Power Services Co. Ltd.; Toden Kokoku Co. Ltd. (80.2%); Tokyo Electric Power Company International B.V.; Pacific LNG Shipping Ltd. (70%).

Principal Competitors

Chubu Electric Power Company Inc.; The Chugoku Electric Power Company Inc.; The Kansai Electric Power Company Inc.

Further Reading

Battersby, Amanda, ''A Spot of Bother for Tepco,'' *Upstream*, February 20, 2004.

Bremner, Brian, ''Tokyo's Nuclear Dilemma,'' *Business Week*, March 15, 2000.

''Going Nuclear, Maybe,'' *Petroleum Economist*, June 1, 2004.

''Darkness Falls on Tokyo,'' *The Economist*, July 19, 2003.

Dawson, Chester, ''Japan: A Nuclear Powerhouse Dims,'' *Business Week*, November 15, 2004.

French, Howard W., ''Tokyo Is Told: Go Nuclear or Go Dark,'' *The New York Times*, April 13, 2003.

Hein, Laura E., *Fueling Growth: The Energy Revolution and Economic Policy in Postwar Japan*, London: Harvard University Press, 1990.

Japan Electric Power Information Center, *History of the Electric Power Industry in Japan*, Tokyo: JEPIC, 1988.

''Japan Prepares for Free-For-All,'' *Power Economist*, April 1, 2000.

Morse, Andrew, ''Nuclear Accident Kills 4 in Japan,'' *Wall Street Journal*, August 10, 2004.

Ozaki, Robert S., *Human Capitalism: the Japanese Enterprise System as World Model*, Tokyo: Kodansha International, 1991.

—Rowland G. Gould
—update: Christina M. Stansell

Tone Brothers, Inc.

2301 S.E. Tone's Drive
Ankeny, Iowa 50021-8888
U.S.A.
Telephone: (515) 965-2711
Fax: (515) 965-2803
Web site: http://www.tones.com

Wholly Owned Subsidary of Associated British
 Foods plc
Incorporated: 1873
Employees: 1,000
Sales: $232.3 million (2003)
NAIC: 311942 Spice and Extract Manufacturing; 311822
 Flour Mixes and Dough Manufacturing from
 Purchased Flour; 311999 All Other Miscellaneous
 Food Manufacturing

Tone Brothers, Inc., is the country's oldest spice company, as well as its second largest, behind industry leader McCormick & Company, Inc. Still based near Des Moines, Iowa, where it was established in 1873, Tone is noted for being the first company west of the Mississippi to sell roasted coffee (in the 1880s), and for introducing clear plastic, hermetically sealed packages with flip-top lids for spices (in the 1980s). By the late 1990s, Tone produced more than 250 varieties of seasonings and mixes. Under the ownership of Burns Philp & Company Ltd. in the mid-1990s, Tone also became the distributor of Durkee Spices, Fleischmann's Yeast, and Spice Islands products. Tone is also the leading supplier of spices to national warehouse club chains. Through the 1980s and 1990s Tone and its employees faced challenges as the company passed through several owners, each of whom changed the company's focus and then quickly sold it. In the mid-1990s, Tone became part of the American operations of parent Burns Philp; in 1997 Tone came under the auspices of the newly created Burns Philp Foodservice division, existing as a brand name only. In 2004, Burns Philp sold its spice and yeast businesses to Associated British Foods plc, which merged Tone with its North American division, ACH Food Companies, Inc.

A Pioneering Company in the 19th Century

In 1873 Jehiel Tone, who was born in New York and had worked for a coffee and spice company in Michigan, convinced his brother I.E. Tone to head west with him and start their own business. The brothers came to Des Moines, Iowa, which had just become the state capital, and chose it as the home of Tone Brothers, Inc. At first, the company sold only coffee and spices, and the original staff consisted of Jehiel Tone, I.E. Tone, Aunt Mary, and "Mother." For the next century Tone would continue as a family business, even as it greatly expanded in size.

Within its first 25 years, Tone had set up a sales force that marketed coffee, tea, and spices. It had become the first company west of the Mississippi to sell roasted coffee, which before that time had consisted of whole green beans that were roasted over wood stoves at home. (The notion of selling ground roasted coffee beans came years later.) And it had become the first company in the United States to sell pure ground pepper, as opposed to the widely used blend that contained ground olive stones and lamp black for added color. Tone's also introduced the concept of individual packages for spices, and began to sell them in orange-and-black boxes.

The New Century Brings New Ideas

In the late 1890s, I.E. Tone's son, Jay E. Tone, Sr., graduated from the Massachusetts Institute of Technology as a chemical engineer. He brought this knowledge to the family business, and soon the company was selling extracts as well as coffee, tea, and spices. Lemon extract was the most popular of Tone's extracts. The company, still based in Des Moines, began to sell its products in other Midwestern states.

By the 1930s Tone's was importing coffee, tea, and raw spices from several countries. Jay Tone, Sr., became company president in 1939, and soon afterward he and his brother Fred introduced a new product: "pressure packed" ground coffee in cans, which eliminated the common problem of coffee spoilage. Jay Tone, Sr., remained president of Tone for 30 years and continued to work in his office regularly until the age of 96. In 1969, soon after his son, Jay Tone, Jr., assumed the presidency, the company's family ownership came to an end, when it was

Company Perspectives:

We believe brands make a difference, whether it is one of our leading consumer brands or customer brands. We believe brands are fundamental to creating value and driving differentiation within the food industry. Brands, and their unique attributes and associations, help build consumer loyalty and trust which are essential to driving sustained business growth and profitability.

sold to Mid-Continent Bottlers, another Des Moines company. Jay Tone, Sr., died four years later, at the age of 100. He had been born the same year that Tone's was established, and lived to see its entire first century.

Tone Ground Up by New Owners

During the 1970s Tone's new owner, Mid-Continent Bottlers, initiated major changes in the business, while retaining a Tone family member as president (first Jay Tone, Jr., and then Jay Tone III). Coffee and tea sales were discontinued, and Tone concentrated completely on spices. While a new company headquarters was set up in Des Moines, annual sales remained stagnant at $4 million, and the new owners decided to change the company's old approach of dealing only with a few large customers. Instead, products would be sold in a wider market. In addition to selling to retail customers, a new division was established to market Tone's products to foodservice distributors and chefs.

However, as the 1970s closed, Mid-Continent Bottlers itself was caught up in the corporate acquisition frenzy of the times. In 1978 Universal Foods, of Milwaukee, bought Mid-Continent. Shortly thereafter, Tone found itself on the market again, and in 1979 it was acquired by a group of Des Moines investors. The first person outside of the Tone family to become president of the company was Hal Ashby.

Under this new ownership, sales at Tone jumped to $12 million within two years. The company began to make inroads in the area of technological innovation, such as its development of a process to cryogenically grind spices (freezing and grinding them at extremely low temperatures, up to 200 degrees below zero) and its use of clear plastic, hermetically sealed spice containers with flip-top lids. Sales rose sharply to $25 million in 1984. The following year, another new president, F. Christopher Kruger, was named.

In the 1980s Tone's became acknowledged as a leader in the foodservice industry, as well as the leading spice supplier to warehouse clubs. Consumers became interested in new spices, particularly blends with an ethnic twist. Tone developed a new line of products, including fajita and taco seasonings and a 13-spice Italian blend. Its annual sales neared $50 million as the 1980s drew to a close, and it moved to more modern facilities in Des Moines. Once again Tone became attractive to a new buyer.

Sale to Rykoff-Sexton in 1989

In early 1989 Tone once again found itself in the hands of new owners, this time Rykoff-Sexton, Inc., a manufacturer and distributor of products for the food service industry. Rykoff-Sexton itself had recently been formed by the merger of S.E. Rykoff & Co. (in Los Angeles) and Sexton (in Chicago). The new conglomerate became heavily involved in mergers and acquisitions.

Under Rykoff-Sexton's ownership, Tone's operations once again were redefined. All sidelines, such as candy and pasta, were eliminated. A joint venture was formed with Devon Plantations, in India, to assure that Tone's would have a reliable source for the five million pounds of pepper it purchased each year. A new line of salt-free and MSG-free spice blends for health-conscious consumers was created. Tone's emerged as the supplier of virtually all spices to the growing number of warehouse clubs throughout the country. By this time, the company produced more than 250 different seasonings and mixes, requiring it to build a new, technologically advanced plant in Ankeny, Iowa, which was completed in 1994. Annual sales that year reached $90 million.

Sale to Burns Philp in 1994

At this point, employees of the increasingly successful Tone found once again that their company was to be sold to a new owner. In mid-1994 Rykoff-Sexton announced its plans to sell Tone to Burns Philp & Company Limited, an Australian leader in the manufacture of food ingredients. According to Rykoff-Sexton's president, Mark Van Stekelenburg, his company sold Tone's in order to focus on its core foodservice and distribution operations. Burns Philp, on the other hand, wanted to expand its industrial spice business, and acquired Tone along with several other food product businesses in the United States. These acquisitions made Burns Philp the world's second largest producer of spices, behind McCormick & Co., Inc. It set up a new North American division, and managing director Ian Clack clearly envisioned a race to make Burns Philp the world's largest spice company.

The transition from Rykoff-Sexton to Burns Philp parentage was not smooth. Shortly after the sale was announced, Tone had to recall almost six tons of ground nutmeg that had been contaminated with aflatoxin. Then Burns Philp initiated arbitration proceedings against Rykoff-Sexton, claiming for reasons not fully disclosed that events occurred prior to the acquisition that had reduced Tone's value. This matter was not settled until late 1996.

Meanwhile, Burns Philp decided to merge all of its North American operations in Iowa, requiring immediate construction of yet another new plant at a cost of over $12 million, and resulting in the closing of facilities in Nevada and Pennsylvania that Burns Philp had just purchased. This new state-of-the-art facility, completed in 1996, was designed for production and distribution of Tone's products, as well as several for other newly acquired Burns Philp products, such as Durkee Spices and Fleischmann's Yeast. It also would serve as the research and development facility for all of Burns Philp's spices and food ingredients.

Burns Philp definitely underestimated the response of the spice industry leader, McCormick & Co., Inc., to its new competitor. Suddenly Burns Philp found itself in the midst of a nasty situation that several analysts described as a spice war. McCormick began to pour millions of dollars into an attempt to keep retailers from stocking its competitor's spices. In 1995 it spent $210 million on ''shelf space agreements,'' under which retailers would carry only McCormick products for a set time period (often several years). In return, the retailers would be paid ''slotting fees'' for carrying McCormick spices, which sharply reduced the actual price they paid for these spices.

The effect on Tone's sales and on Burns Philp was immediate and devastating. Tone's 1995 profits dropped 47 percent, from $58 million to $31 million. The year 1996 was a financial disaster for Burns Philp, with losses of almost $62 million largely attributed to the spice war. In that year's annual report, managing director Ian Clack acknowledged that the company had underestimated the competition in the international market, as well as the effort it would take to manage a worldwide food business.

By early 1997 it was obvious to Burns Philp that its acquisitions program had been a huge mistake. Only a little over two years after buying them, Burns Philp announced its intention to sell all of its North American spice operations, including Tone's, Durkee, Spice Islands, and other operations. In a May 1997 letter to Burns Philp shareholders, chairman Alan McGregor succinctly noted that, ''we do not have the time or resources required to generate the returns necessary from the herb and spice businesses.'' Instead, Burns Philp would regroup and refocus on its still-profitable yeast business, using proceeds from the sale to reduce its debt and to take advantage of unspecified ''current opportunities.''

Burns Philp also announced that managing director Ian Clack, who had initiated the company's purchase of Tone's and its entry into the global spice business, had decided to retire. Two days later, Burns Philp publicly disclosed that the U.S. Federal Trade Commission was investigating the spice industry for possible anti-competitive activity. Burns Philp executives claimed that the investigation centered on McCormick's use of ''slotting fees,'' which had set off the spice war. However, they acknowledged that the FTC had subpoenaed Burns Philp's records as well.

In July 1997 Burns Philp announced that Tom Degnan, former vice-president at Universal Foods Corporation (a global food company based in the United States), would become its new managing director. Degnan would bring with him extensive experience in global operations and in the yeast business, which Burns Philp hoped to make its core operation once it had sold its other holdings.

In July 1997 pepper prices rose to their highest level ever, rising 70 percent by May of that year. This increase was due to the combined forces of market speculation and (more seriously) drought conditions in Brazil and Indonesia, two of the major producers of pepper. This event was expected to cause a major long-term expense for a company that purchased several million pounds of pepper each year.

Sudden Collapse in the Late 1990s

In November 1997 Burns Philp collapsed suddenly, shortly after New Zealand billionaire Graeme Hunt seized a 19.9 percent controlling stake in the Australian company at a cost of A$262 million and less than a month after announcing that the spice business would be sold off. In the ensuing fire sale of its assets Burns Philp wrote down the book value of its spice business by $700 million and attempted to sell the concern to its U.S. management for $235 million. The sale failed to materialize, and Burns Philp executed a $300 million recapitalization as its share price plummeted from $2 to 25 cents per share and its debt swelled to $1.3 billion.

The company struggled to reform around its core yeast and vinegar businesses. Although the spice business remained unsold, a growing trend in the use of gourmet spices in home cooking offered a promising boost to Tone and Burns Philp's other seasoning brands, which had taken a whipping from McCormick in 1995 and 1996. Tone launched the brand Spice Islands World Flavors, a line of eight blends including Jamaican Jerk seasoning, the Indian mix Garam Masala, Louisiana Cajun seasoning, and the French blend Herbes de Provence. Despite a decline in home cookery that had eroded the spice market at the end of the 20th century, Tone held high hopes for the new line, since exotic ethnic spices were known to generate 75 percent more profit than such old standbys as salt and pepper, making the new blends attractive to retailers. Seth Pemsler, vice-president of marketing and sales for Tone's retail division, told George Lazarus of the *Chicago Tribune* that the company hoped to double its Spice Islands revenues from $50 million by 2003 or 2005.

A Long-Awaited Sale

In 2004, the long-awaited suitor for Burns Philp's herb and spice business appeared: Associated British Foods plc (ABF), an international giant encompassing food, ingredients, and retail operations worldwide, with annual sales of £5.26 billion and more than 35,000 employees. Tone and Burns Philp's yeast and bakery ingredients businesses fetched $1.35 billion in July 2004. Analysts estimated the value of Tone Brothers between

$200 million and $400 million; ABF did not report specific figures for the spice company purchase. Tone merged into ABF's North American grocery and food service division ACH Food Companies, Inc., joining numerous well-known brands, including Twinings Tea, Argo Corn Starch, Karo corn syrups, and Ovaltine. The company announced that its new parent would provide "a platform for expansion into the growing spices and seasonings categories."

ABF's chief executive, Peter Jackson remarked, "These businesses are a perfect fit for ABF," and noted that strong revenues and market positions along with their international scope provided excellent opportunities for growth. The company planned to focus on growing in the areas of gourmet spices and food club sales, while applying ACH's expertise in food service and private label sales to further enhance growth in those areas.

Principal Competitors

McCormick & Company, Inc.

Further Reading

"ACH Food Companies, Inc. Announces Acquisition of Tone Brothers, Inc.," *Business Wire,* July 22, 2004.

"Associated British Foods Buys Tone," *UPI NewsTrack,* July 22, 2004.

"Australia: Burns Philp Saw Better Half-Year Profit," *Australian Financial Review,* January 30, 2002.

"Australian Concern To Sell Its Spice Unit," *The New York Times,* October 4, 1997, p. B3.

"Australian Spice Maker to Sell Foreign Units," *The New York Times,* May 20, 1997, p. D21.

Blitzer, Carol, "Small Companies Work Wholesale, Distribution Field," *San Francisco Business Times,* December 13, 1991, p. S1.

"Burns Philp Celebrates the Completion of $12.3 Million Spice Facility Expansion in Ankeny, Iowa," *Business Wire,* November 10, 1995.

"Burns Philp Food Inc.," *Chemical Marketing Reporter,* May 1, 1995, p. 23.

"Burns Philp Fire Sale Follows Company Collapse," *Chemical Market Reporter,* May 4, 1998, p. 3.

"Burns Philp: Pepper Prices Nothing to Sneeze At," *PR Newswire,* August 13, 1997.

"Industry News: ABS Purchases Yeast and Spices Units," *Food Ingredient News* 12, no. 8, August 2004.

Lazarus, George, "Chicago Tribune Marketing Column," *Chicago Tribune,* May 9, 2000.

Leicester, John, "Associated British Foods Buying Tone Brothers," *America's Intelligence Wire,* July 23, 2004.

"Los Angeles Food Firm Buying Tone Brothers," *Des Moines Register,* March 10, 1989, p. S7.

Morton, Kate Miller, "Memphis, Tenn.-Based ACH Food Whets Appetite for Acquisitions," *Commercial Appeal* (Memphis), September 3, 2004.

"Non-Symmetrical Spice Containers Receive Added Strength," *Chilton's Food Engineering,* May 1990, p. 80.

"Price War is Drag on Tone's, Parent," *Des Moines Register,* February 15, 1996, p. S8.

"Recall Notice—Tone Brothers Ground Nutmeg," *FDA Enforcement Report,* August 30, 1995.

"Rykoff-Sexton Arbitration Resolved," *PR Newswire,* October 11, 1996.

"Rykoff-Sexton Completes Sale of Tone Brothers Subsidiary to Burns Philp," *PR Newswire,* October 28, 1994.

Sherman, Jean, and David Tuller, "Shaking Up the Spice Industry," *Working Woman,* October 1987, p. 78.

Somerville, Sean, "McCormick Reportedly Is Under Probe," *Baltimore Sun,* May 22, 1997, p. 1C.

"Spice Concern Sale Is Off," *The New York Times,* November 7, 1997, p. C11.

Stensholt, John, and Nicholas Way, "Spice Speculation," *Business Review Weekly* 26, no. 29, July 29, 2004, p. 25

"Tone in Pepper Venture," *Des Moines Register,* February 11, 1992, p. S8.

"Tone's Iowa Plant Wins Out," *Des Moines Register,* April 7, 1995, p. A1.

Tone's: 124 Years of Innovation and Progress, Ankeny, Iowa: Tone Brothers, Inc., 1997.

"Tone's Purchased by Aussies," *Des Moines Register,* August 24, 1994, p. S8.

"Tone's Savors Taste of Success," *Des Moines Register,* December 21, 1992, p. B1.

"U.S. Spice Business Changes Hands," *Food Institute Report* 30, July 26, 2004, p. 7.

—Gerry Azzata
—update: Jennifer Gariepy

True Value Company

8600 West Bryn Mawr Avenue
Chicago, Illinois 60631-3505
U.S.A.
Telephone: (773) 695-5000
Fax: (773) 695-6516
Web site: http://www.truevaluecompany.com

Cooperative Company
Founded: 1997
Employees: 2,800
Sales: $2.02 billion (2004)
NAIC: 444130 Hardware Stores; 444190 Other Building
Material Dealers; 444220 Nursery and Garden Centers

True Value Company, formerly known as TruServ Corporation, was formed on July 1, 1997, by the merger of Cotter & Company and ServiStar Coast to Coast Corporation. As a cooperative, True Value supports more than 6,200 independent retailers in the United States and 54 other countries. The retail names making up the True Value cooperative are: True Value, Grand Rental Station, Taylor Rental, Home & Garden Showplace, Induserve Supply, and Party Central. Problems related to the 1997 merger and accounting irregularities forced True Value to restructure its operations, cut jobs, and divest certain businesses in the early 2000s. The company adopted its current moniker in 2005.

Company Roots: 1855–1910

The companies that combined to form TruServ Corporation were deeply rooted in the wholesale hardware business. Hibbard Spencer Bartlett & Company, a hardware wholesaler that eventually developed the True Value name, was founded in 1855. American Hardware & Supply Company, the precursor of ServiStar Corporation and the first wholesale hardware cooperative in the United States, was established in 1910, and Coast to Coast Corporation grew from a wholesale hardware cooperative formed in 1928.

In 1910, harnesses were a big hardware seller and there were only 46 states in the Union when 20 hardware store owners

from western Pennsylvania, West Virginia, and Virginia came together. The hardware industry was made up of hundreds of small independent stores whose owners bought their merchandise from various wholesalers, such as Hibbard's.

The men who met in Pittsburgh that day were looking for a way to cut their costs and keep their prices competitive. They decided to form a nonprofit cooperative that would serve as their own wholesaler and distributor. As members of a co-op, they could pool their buying power to negotiate better prices for hardware from manufacturers and then sell the merchandise with a small markup to themselves and other hardware dealers who owned the shares of the co-op. The annual profits that were not invested in the company would be returned at the end of the year to the dealer-owners, who reduced costs by consolidating their distribution, operating, and promotional activities into one company.

The company's charter was approved and the first stockholders' meeting of American Hardware & Supply Company was held on October 25, 1910. The company began operating out of a warehouse in Pittsburgh.

Building a Company: 1911–48

Over the next 20 years, American Hardware demonstrated that a low-cost cooperative wholesaler made sense in the hardware business, and by 1929 sales were just over $1 million. Others liked the concept and followed American's lead. In 1928, the Melamed brothers of Minneapolis, Minnesota, established a franchise-store cooperative that would become the Coast to Coast Corporation.

Meanwhile, Hibbard Spencer Bartlett & Company, which was not a cooperative, was increasing its marketing activities throughout the Midwest. In 1928, the company published its first "Toy Parade" consumer catalog and invited dealers to its first Toy Show. In 1932, Hibbard's introduced a new private-brand line of hand tools under the True Value label. To help dealers increase sales, Hibbard's developed a kit of marketing aids, introduced a Dealers' Service Department and set up a model store at its headquarters where dealers could get marketing suggestions.

During World War II, Hibbard's tried a new approach by opening nine company-owned stores using the True Value

---

Company Perspectives:

True Value Company is a cooperative comprised of members who are entrepreneur-retailers. Ours is a Members-First focus. We are committed to empowering the independent retailer by setting industry and market standards with our niche businesses and unique brand of creative marketing, wide product assortment, award-winning merchandising and technology, quality training and business expertise.

---

name. The company's regular customers did not like the competition, and Hibbard's closed the test stores after the war.

The fourth company in the TruServ history, Cotter & Company, came on the scene in 1948. The company's founder, John M. Cotter, started in the hardware business a few years after American Hardware & Supply Company was incorporated when, at the age of 12, he went to work in a neighborhood hardware store in St. Paul, Minnesota. After high school, Cotter worked as a salesman for a regional hardware wholesaler, then in his own hardware store, in Eau Claire, Wisconsin. In his mid-20s, Cotter went back on the road, eventually working for a Chicago-based merchandising group.

In the late 1940s, competition from discount stores and other chain operations caused independent dealers to increasingly turn to low-cost distributors. In his review of Edward R. Kantowicz's biography of John Cotter in Chilton's *Hardware Age*, Jim Cory explained that Cotter ''stumbled on dealer-ownership by accident.'' He had noticed, as a young salesman, that ''the best, the busiest, the cleanest hardware store in every town . . . belonged to Our Own Hardware Company,'' a Minnesota-based dealer-owned cooperative.

At a convention of Our Own early in 1947, Cotter began chatting with Bill Stout, the general manager of American Hardware. As Kantowicz wrote, ''Cotter and Stout, talking long into the night, looked up the *Hardware Age* dealer listing for Illinois, Michigan, Iowa, and Indiana and determined that there was room for a dealer-owned wholesaler in Chicago.'' By that time, there were some dozen hardware cooperatives around the country serving small and widely separated regions, and their share of the market was tiny. Ace Hardware, the largest of the cooperatives, had sales in 1948 of $10 million. Hibbard's, in contrast, dominated the Midwest with sales of over $28 million.

A few months after his talk with Stout, John Cotter and 12 hardware dealers founded Cotter & Company in Sycamore, Illinois, and the new wholesale cooperative opened for business in January 1948. Operating out of a rented warehouse in Chicago, Cotter & Company offered ''hardware merchandise at attractive prices, a barebones warehouse operation, semi-annual dealer markets, consumer advertising, and merchandising help for the retailer,'' according to Kantowicz. Cotter went back out on the road, spending six months visiting Midwest dealers to convince them to put up the $1,500 it would cost to buy shares in his co-op.

The Hibbard's Takeover: 1950–62

From its experience with the True Value test stores during World War II, Hibbard's had learned the value of having stores buy everything from one wholesaler with a complete merchandising and operating plan. In the 1950s, Hibbard's acquired several smaller wholesalers around the Midwest and started a voluntary chain of franchise dealers who bought most of their merchandise from Hibbard's and used the company's True Value ads and promotions. In 1956, the company reached record sales volume of $33 million.

Deciding to concentrate on the True Value franchise, Hibbard's stopped selling to thousands of small accounts and laid off many of its salesmen. The company ended the decade with a chain of nearly 1,000 dealers and four distribution centers, with stores from the Appalachian Mountains to the Rockies, and sales of $19 million.

However, Hibbard's underwent another change as well during the 1950s. As it bought up rival wholesalers, the company went after their real estate, not their hardware business. Eventually it reached a point where all its net income was coming from real estate and other investments, with the hardware business some years actually operating at a loss. In 1962, the board of directors decided to liquidate the hardware business, which had been around for more than 100 years, and establish the company instead as a real estate investment firm.

John Cotter had been busy acquiring and raiding smaller rivals in the Midwest as well as outside the region, and Cotter & Company had surpassed Hibbard's in sales volume in 1960. Cotter had also been keeping a close eye on happenings at Hibbard's and had figured out what was happening with the company's hardware business. In 1961, he secretly indicated that he was interested in buying Hibbard's assets. Although nothing came of that approach, when the Hibbard board decided to sell, Cotter & Company was their first choice.

Cotter wanted access to the True Value dealers before other wholesalers recruited them. According to Kantowicz, the Hibbard's takeover was one of the best-kept secrets in business history. During the summer and fall of 1962, John Cotter and a small number of his top people met secretly with Hibbard's directors and a handful of senior-level employees to hammer out the deal, using code names throughout the process.

The final price for all of Hibbard's assets was $2.5 million, including $2,500 for the True Value trademark. Cotter and Hibbard's announced the sale the day after Thanksgiving, and most of the 400 Hibbard's dealers agreed to become shareholders in the Cotter & Company co-op. Not only were dealers allowed to continue to use the True Value name, Cotter & Company members decided to add that name to all their stores. Cotter's acquisition of Hibbard's increased the company's sales 56 percent and, for what was certainly one of the true values in business history, gave Cotter a brand name that would become its national identity.

Fine-tuning Store Programs: 1960s–80s

Cotter & Company honed its True Value advertising and store programs, setting a model for low-cost distributors and helping to keep independent hardware retailers competitive with discount and chain stores. In 1966, the company's sales topped $100 million, making it the largest hardware distributor

Key Dates:

1855: Hibbard Spencer Bartlett & Company is established.
1910: American Hardware & Supply Company, the precursor of ServiStar Corporation and the first wholesale hardware cooperative in the United States, is created.
1928: The Melamed brothers of Minneapolis, Minnesota, establish a franchise-store cooperative that eventually becomes the Coast to Coast Corporation.
1932: Hibbard's introduces a new private-brand line of hand tools under the True Value label.
1948: Cotter & Company is established.
1962: Cotter acquires Hibbard in a $2.5 million deal.
1990: ServiStar merges with Coast to Coast to form a $1.8 billion international co-op.
1997: TruServ Corporation is formed by the merger of Cotter & Co. and ServiStar Coast to Coast Corporation.
1999: Accounting irregularities force the company to post a $131 million loss.
2003: The company settles a Securities and Exchange Commission investigation into its accounting practices.
2005: TruServ changes its name to True Value Company.

in the country. Cotter's success and the company's methods were felt beyond the Midwest.

In Pennsylvania, American Hardware moved into a new facility in rural East Butler, a town north of Pittsburgh, in 1960, and expanded its inventory, hired new personnel, and implemented new procedures. In 1965, the company, with 450 members and sales of around $18 million, began to expand through a series of acquisitions. In 1977, the company instituted its ServiStar advertising program, planning to create a voluntary chain of owner-dealers. By the end of the 1970s, after 15 years of expansion, American had increased the number of members to 3,500 and had sales of slightly over $300 million. Sales volume at Cotter and Company topped $1 billion in 1979.

American's ServiStar program was completely voluntary. When American introduced the ServiStar concept, the approach was simply to get the ServiStar sign in the window. As American president Larry Zehfuss explained in an article in the October 1983 issues of *Chilton's Hardware Age,* "We'd go in, sign the store, show the dealer how the program worked, and tell him to call us if he had any problems."

However, following a share-of-market analysis that showed the company was getting only a small percentage of the ServiStar dealers' purchases, American increased its sales staff and went after those purchases, implementing an array of marketing and merchandising services and expanding the ServiStar private label program to include plumbing and electrical equipment, as well as such items as brooms and garbage cans, along with the more familiar paint and paint sundries. In the process, American became the first hardware cooperative to establish a customer service department.

Over the next several years, dealers' average purchases increased substantially, and by 1983 some 2,100 of American's owner-dealers displayed the ServiStar sign and accounted for 70 percent of the company's sales. That same year, consumer recognition of the ServiStar name topped 50 percent. Aiming to increase that recognition to 90 percent by the end of the 1980s, the company began making large advertising investments ($10 million in 1985), using magazines, newspapers, circulars, and television ads to actually sell the product. In 1987, the company had sales of $1.1 billion, and nearly 4,000 hardware, lumber, rental, and home and garden centers across the country. In 1988, in recognition of the growing diversity of its business, American changed its corporate name to ServiStar Corporation.

John M. Cotter died in 1989, at age 85, having built Cotter & Company into a $2.1 billion company with over 8,000 members. A wheeler-dealer, master politician and manager, and a champion of dealer-ownership, Cotter witnessed and contributed to a major transformation of the hardware industry during his 73 years in the business. However, another transformation was occurring in the industry as independent, neighborhood dealers began losing customers to giant home improvement chains such as Lowe's and Home Depot, and Sears began opening freestanding hardware and paint stores that were smaller than the superstores but larger than most independents and offered well-known brand names.

Competing with the "Big Box" Chains: 1990–95

The introduction of the giant chains combined with a recession in the housing market sent the independent dealers and their wholesalers scrambling. Trying to preserve membership as well as gain new members, the cooperatives focused on new services and leaner operations.

Cotter & Company, where John's son Daniel was president and CEO, stressed regionalization, adding thousands of items to their merchandise offerings to meet the needs of different geographic markets. The company, along with other hardware wholesalers, also targeted the home remodeling market.

ServiStar expanded westward, gaining members in the Northwest and Rocky Mountain states, and strengthened services for its different niche markets. Some 200 of the co-op's members who operated garden centers as well as the many hardware and lumber center dealers who sold lawn and garden merchandise had been complaining that the company was not meeting their needs in terms of products, especially plants, or advertising. After looking at their complaints, ServiStar developed a complete marketing campaign called Home & Garden Showplace geared to retailers who operated garden centers. In 1990, the company opened the prototype Home & Garden Showplace store, in Amherst, New York, near Buffalo.

In July 1990, ServiStar merged with Denver-based Coast to Coast to form a $1.8 billion international co-op. Coast to Coast, the company founded by the Melamed brothers in 1928, and its parent company, Amdura, had been in bankruptcy proceedings and had lost about 200 of its 1,000 stores when ServiStar bought it for $25 million. The company, with dealer owners primarily in the Midwest and West, operated two types of stores: Coast to Coast Total Hardware and Coast to Coast Home and Auto, selling automotive merchandise from mufflers to waxes to tires. The merger was a boost to both companies; after one year, sales rose 16 percent and profits rose 46 percent.

In 1993, ServiStar Coast to Coast added to its rental business with the purchase of the 288 franchise units of Taylor Rental Corp., a subsidiary of The Stanley Works. Each qualified franchisee was offered a licensing agreement from the co-op, with a reduction in pricing averaging 12 percent. The Taylor stores and the company's 260 Grand Rental Station locations made ServiStar the largest general rental chain in the United States.

As the superstore home center chains continued to grow, the presidents of the four largest hardware co-ops met "to help members fight the chain stores," Dan Cotter explained to *National Home Center News*. Presidents from ServiStar Coast to Coast, Ace Hardware, and Hardware Wholesalers, Inc. joined Cotter. To avoid antitrust accusations, the presidents did not discuss pricing or a "co-op of co-ops," but as a result of the sessions both Cotter & Company and ServiStar Coast to Coast individually began exploring merger opportunities. Each independently identified the other as the best match.

The merger was not the only route for expansion. Both companies were also moving into other countries. In 1994, Cotter established True Value International, an independently operated division based in Georgia, to serve stores outside the United States. ServiStar, which had opened its first store outside the United States in 1971, in Bermuda as an executive perk, also had numerous members in other countries.

A New Company: 1996–97

In July 1996, Dan Cotter and Paul Pentz met privately to discuss the possibility of merging the two co-ops. In December, the joint boards unanimously approved the merger and proposed it to their membership. In January 1997, the two presidents addressed the companies' conventions, and beginning in February more than 6,000 retailers attended a series of over 500 town hall meetings across the country to answer questions and address concerns.

In March, Cotter's Tru-Test facilities produced their first batch of ServiStar paint, and in April the merger received 95 percent approval from the memberships. The new corporation, headquartered in Chicago, was officially created on July 1, 1997. Dan Cotter was named chairman and CEO, and ServiStar's president Paul Pentz delayed his retirement to become president, COO, and a director.

The history of TruServ up to this point had been the history of the hardware industry over the past 150 years. It included distribution innovations, bitter rivalries, novel marketing and sales techniques, community involvement, and retailer raids. Primarily, however, it was the story of independent hardware retailers joining together to be more successful at selling while maintaining their service, product knowledge, and personal involvement in the community—the traditional strengths of the hardware retailer. The creation of TruServ was the next step in this long history, and whether it would withstand the competition of the "big box" stores remained unknown.

Overcoming Problems in the Late 1990s and Beyond

President Don Hoye was named CEO in 1999. His position at the helm of TruServ was short-lived, however, and marked by an accounting scandal, lawsuits, and falling sales. During a 1999 audit, accounting irregularities topping out at $100 million were discovered, leading to a $131 million loss that year. To make matters worse, integration problems relating to the 1997 merger were taking their toll. Overall, the merger had cost nearly $60 million and left the co-op with three different inventory tracking systems. Orders began to be left unfilled, causing members to become disgruntled and leading them to search for new suppliers. As a result, over 2,100 stores left the TruServ co-op by 2001.

Lackluster sales, increased competition, and lawsuits related to the accounting mishap continued to plague the company in the 2000s. During 2000, TruServ sold its lumber and building materials business. The company also shuttered its Canadian operations and initiated a series of job cuts. In the spring of 2001, the co-op defaulted on a $200 million loan and was struggling under a $540 million debt load. Hoye resigned later that year, and Pamela Forbes Lieberman, TruServ's CFO and COO, was named his replacement.

During 2003, TruServ settled a Securities and Exchange Commission (SEC) investigation without formally admitting or denying the charges. A March 2003 *SEC News Digest* explained the commission's findings: "From approximately July 1997 through the end of 1999, TruServ's accounting systems and internal controls related to inventory management were inadequate. The Order finds that these deficiencies caused TruServ to understate expenses, which resulted in overstatement of net income, during 1998 and 1999." TruServ agreed to comply with securities laws as a result of the findings.

With the accounting issues behind it, TruServ looked ahead to the future. It worked to cut expenses and decrease its debt load. The company's merchandising department was completely restructured, leaving four divisional vice-presidents reporting to the chief merchandising officer. Lieberman left her post in late 2004, and Lyle Heidemann, a former Sears executive, was named her replacement in June 2005. He was charged with increasing membership and bolstering product sales while fending off increasingly intense competition.

As part of its turnaround strategy, TruServ adopted the True Value corporate moniker in early 2005. By this time, the company appeared to be recovering slowly. Net income had doubled in 2004 over the previous year, reaching $43.2 million. Debt continued to drop, and while 355 members exited the co-op, 202 new members signed up. True Value's management was confident it was on the right track for success in the future. Only time would tell, however, if True Value's problems were truly a thing of the past.

Principal Competitors

The Home Depot Inc.; Lowe's Companies Inc.; Wal-Mart Stores Inc.

Further Reading

"American Hardware Supply: Style Is the Difference," *Chilton's Hardware Age*, October 1983, p. 64.

Bamford, Jan, "SERVISTAR Has Home Town Flavor," *Pittsburgh Business Times & Journal*, September 26, 1988, p. 9S.

Carlo, Andrew M., "True Value Charts a New Course," *Home Channel News*, March 7, 2005.

"Co-op Presidents Join Together to Fight Chains," *National Home Center News*, May 24, 1993, p. 5.

Cory, Jim, "Book Reviews—John Cotter: 70 Years of Hardware," *Chilton's Hardware Age*, March, 1987, p. 108.

Feder, Barnaby J., "Independents Have a Weapon Against the "Big Boxes,' " *The New York Times*, June 11, 1997.

Frieswick, Kris, "Of Mergers and Margins: How the True Value/ServiStar Merger Will Impact the Hardware Manufacturing World," *Manufacturing Marketplace*, December 1996.

Guy, Sandra, "Ex-Sears Exec Heidemann Takes Helm at True Value Co-op," *Chicago Sun-Times*, June 7, 2005, p. 55.

Hoover, Jon, "ServiStar Adds Garden Center to Its Program Line-up," *Chilton's Hardware Age*, February 1990, p. 59.

"Hoye Resigns as TruServ CEO," *Do-it-Yourself Retailing*, August 1, 2001, p. 19.

"Introducing a Retail Co-op as Unique as You Are," Chicago: TruServ Corporation, 1997.

Jackson, Susan, and Tim Smart, "Mom and Pop Fight Back," *Business Week*, April 14, 1997, p. 46.

Kantowicz, Edward R., "Hardware Hardball: The Building of True Value," *Crain's Chicago Business*, January 12, 1987, p. 41

——, *John Cotter: 70 Years of Hardware*, Chicago: Cotter & Company, 1987.

Murphy, H. Lee, "A Wrenching Time: Cotter Tries to Hammer Out Hardware Combo," *Crain's Chicago Business*, Mary 5, 1997, p. 4.

"No Longer Just Coasting Along," *Do-It-Yourself Retailing*, May 1991, p. 85.

Rouvalis, Christina, "Smitty's: Where Muscovites Come to Shop," *Pittsburgh Post-Gazette*, October 16, 1991, p. 23.

"SEC Charges Former Chief Financial Officer of TruServ Corporation with Causing the Company's Violations of Financial Reporting, Books and Records and Internal Controls Laws," *SEC Digest*, March 5, 2003.

"ServiStar and Coast to Coast Mark 1st Merger Anniversary," *Aftermarket Business*, October 1, 1991, p. 17.

"Servistar to Acquire Taylor Rental Franchise," *Chilton's Hardware Age*, July 1993, p. 28.

Sutton, Rodney K., and Carollyn Schierhorn, "Co-ops and Buying Clubs Plot New Strategies," *Building Supply Home Centers*, August 1990, p. 90.

Tatge, Mark, "Ill-Serv'd TruServ, the Largest Hardware Co-op in the U.S., Has Burned Its Members-And Set Fire to Itself," *Forbes*, May 28, 2001, p. 121.

—Ellen D. Wernick
—update: Christina M. Stansell

Union Carbide Corporation

Union Carbide Corporation
400 West Sam Houston Parkway South
Houston, Texas 77042
U.S.A.
Telephone: (713) 798-2016
Fax: (713) 978-2394
Web site: http://www.unioncarbide.com

Wholly Owned Subsidiary of The Dow Chemical Company
Incorporated: 1917 as Union Carbide & Carbon
   Corporation
Employees: 3,800
Sales: $5.86 billion (2004)
NAIC: 3251 Basic Chemical Manufacturing

Union Carbide Corporation is the world's largest producer of ethylene glycol, commonly used as antifreeze, and is a leading manufacturer of the world's most widely used plastic, polyethylene. In spite of a disaster at its Bhopal, India, pesticide plant in 1984 that resulted in numerous deaths and serious health problems for people living in the region, as well as a devastating takeover attempt that followed, the corporation remained one of top 20 exporters in the United States in the early 1990s. Union Carbide pioneered the petrochemicals industry and introduced the first two modern plastics. The company became known as "chemist to the chemical industry and metallurgist to the metals industry" because of its production of many of the building blocks of those two industries.

Origins

The Union Carbide & Carbon Corporation (UCC) was formed in 1917 from the combination of four companies: Union Carbide Co. (incorporated 1898), Linde Air Products Co. (incorporated 1907), National Carbon Co., Inc. (incorporated 1899), and Prest-O-Lite Co., Inc. (incorporated 1913). The new entity was organized as a holding company, with its four members acting relatively autonomously and cooperating where their businesses converged.

The merger combined what had often been competing interests to form an industrial chemicals powerhouse. The oldest member of the quartet, Union Carbide, had been formed to manufacture calcium carbide, which was used in the production of metal alloys. A by-product of alloying calcium carbide with aluminum was acetylene, a gas that company executives hoped would prove useful for street and household lighting. When Thomas Edison's electric incandescent light bulbs proved more practical for most lighting, however, it looked as if Union Carbide's acetylene lighting business was obsolete. Luckily, a French researcher discovered that acetylene could be burned in oxygen to produce a hot, metal-cutting flame. A whole new market for the gas emerged, and UCC was ready to take advantage of it.

The company continued to manufacture calcium carbide at plants in Sault Ste. Marie, Michigan, and Niagara Falls, New York, and by 1900 the Union Carbide's capital stock stood at $6 million. Union Carbide combined America's first commercial high-carbon ferrochrome process, which had been developed by company founder Major James T. Moorhead in the late 1890s, with a metal alloying business acquired in 1906. The subsidiary created a line of metals composed of iron and one or more other metals, known in the industry as ferroalloys. Ferroalloys made the production of alloy steels more efficient because they could be incorporated more easily with steel to create new metals with specific properties. Union Carbide's low-carbon ferrochrome, for example, was a precursor of modern stainless steel.

Union Carbide had been involved with the Linde Air Products Co. through joint acetylene experiments for about six years before the formation of the UCC holding company. As one of America's first oxygen-producing concerns and, after 1917, part of one of the country's largest chemical companies, Linde soon became the world's largest producer of industrial gases such as acetylene, hydrogen, and nitrogen. These gases formed the foundation of the petrochemical industry. The Prest-O-Lite Company had been one of Union Carbide's primary competitors for most of the two companies' histories, but three years of cooperative acetylene experiments among UCC, Prest-O-Lite, and Linde made the merger smoother. Before the turn of the 20th century, National Carbon Co. had produced the first commercial dry cell battery and offered it under the Eveready trademark. The well-known brand would be a UCC staple for the next seven decades.

With combined research efforts and a national push for new technologies to help win World War I, further developments came in rapid succession at Union Carbide. New products included batteries for portable radios and corrosion and heat-resistant ferroalloys that strengthened the steel used to build skyscrapers, bridges, and automobiles. The government's need for ethylene during the "Great War" also generated interest in hydrocarbon byproducts. These substances were made from calcium carbide and would later become the raw materials for the production of plastics, synthetic rubber, fibers, solvents, explosives, and industrial chemicals. In 1919, the first production of synthetic ethylene began. Ethylene would develop into the industry's most important industrial hydrocarbon, eventually used in polyethylene (plastics), polystyrene (Styrofoam), and antifreeze, among other products. Union Carbide's Prestone brand ethylene glycol soon became the top-selling antifreeze, a position it held throughout the 20th century.

The new corporate structure enabled UCC to leverage the combined assets of its four primary subsidiaries and embark on an acquisitions spree that was not halted even by the Great Depression. In 1919 alone, the company acquired an acetylene manufacturer, created Canadian subsidiaries of National Carbon Co. and Prest-O-Lite, and purchased a new headquarters at 42nd Street and Madison Avenue in New York City. This new home served the company until the late 1970s. During the 1920s, Union Carbide expanded its overseas interests with the acquisition of a Norwegian hydroelectric plant in 1925 and a calcium carbide/ferroalloy plant in that same country in 1929. The holding company added to its battery business with the purchase of Manhattan Electrical Supply Co. in 1926. UCC annexed two domestic industrial gas interests in 1928 and strengthened its industrial electric furnace business with the acquisition of the Acheson Graphite Corporation in 1928.

U.S. Vanadium Co. Acquired

One of the most vital acquisitions UCC made during the 1920s was that of U.S. Vanadium Co.'s Colorado mine, mill,

and reduction plant in 1926. Carbide's subsequent vanadium research was a truly corporate venture that coordinated several of the company's subsidiaries and eventually involved the company in the government's atomic energy program. Uranium-bearing materials were located and provided by U.S. Vanadium. UCC scientists demonstrated that gaseous diffusion could be used to separate quantities of uranium-235 and contracted with the federal government in 1943 to operate the Oak Ridge Gaseous Diffusion Plant. After intensive research, UCC's Linde Company perfected a refining process for treating uranium concentrates. A plant was built and operated by the Electro Metallurgical Company (acquired in 1922) to provide extensive metallurgical research and manufacture uranium. Finally, Union Carbide and Carbon Research Laboratories contributed to the development of the atomic weapon itself.

In 1939, UCC acquired the Bakelite Corporation, which developed the first modern plastic, phenol formaldehyde. In 1941, Carbide made permanent-press fabrics possible with its development of glyoxal.

Union Carbide earned a reputation for developing raw materials for the chemical and metals industries during World War II. Since natural rubber was in very short supply during the war, the company resumed its experiments with butene, a hydrocarbon that was developed into a synthetic rubber. Modern neoprene is a familiar example of butene's application.

Postwar prosperity camouflaged nagging problems at UCC: the company was chalking up a bad track record of discovering new substances and processes but not capitalizing on them. For example, UCC pioneered urethanes, but did not commit enough financial resources to the new field in time to profit. The company also made permanent-press fabrics possible with its development of glyoxal, but could not come up with a consumer product that maximized its profit potential. It often ended up riding the coattails of movements it had spawned. Union Carbide's program of internal promotion engendered company loyalty, but it also stifled creativity. The company started a slide into relative mediocrity that, with few exceptions, would consume the next three decades.

A succession of well-meaning chief executives kept UCC in "turnaround mode." Under the direction of CFO Morse G. Dial, Carbide absorbed its major operating subsidiaries and formally relinquished its holding company status in 1949. Dial hoped to reverse the excessive autonomy at UCC by creating a "President's Office" composed of the corporation's division heads. The company name was changed to Union Carbide Corporation in 1957 to reflect its reorganization from a holding company to a diversified corporation. By that time, Union Carbide and Carbon Corporation had established some 400 plants in the United States and Canada, in addition to overseas affiliates. The company went from having 18 autonomous divisions to just four primary domestic groups: Union Carbide Chemicals Co., Linde Co., Union Carbide Plastics Co., and Union Carbide Consumer Products Co. Even though these corporate segments were technically divisions, the retention of the word "company" in each section's name represented the perpetuation of the decentralized management structure of a holding company, and its detrimental effect on Union Carbide continued.

Key Dates:

1917: The company is incorporated as Union Carbide & Carbon Corporation and acquires Linde Air Products Company, National Carbon Company, Inc., Prest-O-Lite Company, Inc., and Union Carbide Company.

1920: Carbide and Carbon Chemicals Corporation is established.

1926: U.S. Vanadium Company is acquired.

1939: The company merges with Bakelite Corporation.

1957: The company's name is changed to Union Carbide Corporation.

1959: Union Carbide Consumer Products Company is formed.

1984: A gas leak at a plant in Bhopal, India, results in tragic loss of life.

1986: Amerchol Corporation is acquired.

1989: Union Carbide Corporation becomes a holding company owning the subsidiaries UCAR Carbon Company, Union Carbide Industrial Gases Inc., and Union Carbide Chemicals and Plastics Company, Inc.

1992: Union Carbide Industrial Gases is spun-off as an independent company named Praxair, Inc.

1994: Union Carbide launches a joint venture, Polimeri Europa, with EniChem.

1997: Union Carbide launches a joint venture, Univation Technologies, with Exxon Chemical Company.

1998: Union Carbide launches a joint venture in Malaysia with Petronas.

1999: Union Carbide launches a joint venture with Tosco Corporation.

2001: Union Carbide is acquired by the Dow Chemical Company.

UCC Develops Polyethylene

Polyethylene, a plastic used in squeeze bottles (high-density polyethylene), as well as in films and sheeting (low-density polyethylene), became Union Carbide's largest dollar-volume product after World War II. An olefins division was set up in the 1950s to supply low-cost raw materials for the chemicals and plastics industry in the 1950s. For several years, the company sold these plastics to other manufacturers. However, Carbide finally did capitalize on this discovery in 1964, when Glad branded plastic wraps, bags, and straws were introduced. Within just four years, Glad became the leading brand in its market.

By the 1960s, Union Carbide occupied the top spot in many of its primary fields, including industrial gases, carbon electrodes for industrial electric furnaces, batteries, atomic energy, polyethylene plastic, and ferroalloys. In 1965, the conglomerate's sales topped $2 billion for the first time. From 1956 to 1966, Union Carbide parlayed a few plants in a dozen countries into 60 major subsidiary and associated companies with plants in 30 countries serving over 100 markets. International operations of the conglomerate contributed 29 percent of its annual sales, and by mid-decade the company name was changed to Union Carbide International Co. to reflect its increased global presence.

In spite of consistently rising sales, which doubled from 1960 to 1970 to $3 million, Union Carbide's profits plummeted and stayed low from 1966 to 1971. Carbide could claim leading market shares, but top shares of low-margin commodities still equaled low profits. Industry-wide overcapacity in ferroalloys ran as high as 70 percent in the early 1960s, and prices for these products fell 25 percent. The company was compelled to cut its ferroalloys work force by 40 percent and close a major plant at Niagara Falls. To make matters worse, the market for low-density polyethylene stagnated for the first time in over 20 years.

Union Carbide was still the second-largest chemical producer in the United States, but it invariably lagged behind most of its competitors in terms of growth and profitability during this period. Misguided investments in petroleum, pharmaceuticals, semi-conductors, mattresses, and undersea equipment, combined with a $1 billion petrochemicals complex at Taft, Louisiana, which ran in the red for the last three years of the 1960s, further tarnished Union Carbide's standing. Not surprisingly, the conglomerate's stock dropped from $75 in 1965 to $45 in 1968 as the company "earned a reputation for aimless fumbling," according to *Business Week*.

Unfortunately for Union Carbide, environmental complaints about the company's Marietta, Ohio, ferroalloy plant came to a head in 1971, when consumer champion Ralph Nader brought a decade of local residents' complaints into the national spotlight. For four years, the conglomerate had largely ignored public and government efforts to make it clean up several plants that were polluting the air over West Virginia. Union Carbide's resistance to outside influence gave it the public image of a reactionary bully concerned only with profits and scornful of the environment, a stigma that the company would bear for years to come. In 1971, UCC capitulated to federal orders that it immediately use more expensive low-sulphur coal to reduce noxious sulfur dioxide emissions by 40 percent. The company was given a fall 1974 deadline to install $8 million in advanced emissions scrubbers.

The bad news continued, as the recession of 1970 and 1971 hammered commodities companies like UCC, with the chemicals and plastics markets entering another cycle of overcapacity. From 1968 to 1973, UCC's sales grew by only 4 percent annually, well below the industry average. CFO and president F. Perry Wilson, who had been promoted to those offices in 1971, made his bid to turn Union Carbide around. His restructuring plan included three primary changes. First, he tried to pare back peripheral activities and focus on plastics and chemicals. Among the businesses sold were a bedding company, most of UCC's oil and gas interests, a pollution-monitoring devices business, a plastic container line, a fibers business, a jewelry line, and an insect repellant business. Second, he worked to shift the corporate focus from market share to profitability. Finally, Wilson tried to plan capital and capacity investments so that UCC could avoid the inefficiencies and plummeting prices that had accompanied industry-wide overcapacity in the past.

A New Business Development department was formed in 1970 to coordinate the three areas outside of chemicals and plastics that Wilson did not sell: Biomedical Systems, Marine Foods, and Agricultural Systems. Another key organizational change was the disbanding of the Consumer & Related Products Division, which had contributed 22 percent of UCC's annual revenues. The Eveready business was split off into a Battery Products Division, while Glad and Prestone were coordinated in a division with the production of their raw materials. Despite the fragmentation of the Consumer Products Division, Wilson said that he hoped that consumer products would contribute 50 percent of UCC's revenues in the future. He recognized that these relatively stable, high-margin product lines sustained Union Carbide through economic downturns.

For a few years, it looked as if the new strategy was working. From 1973 to 1981, earnings per share rose 100 percent. UCC increased productivity dramatically during the late 1960s and early 1970s to keep its corporate head above water. From 1967 to 1973, physical output of chemicals and plastics rose 60 percent, while per-pound production costs were cut by one-third. William S. Sneath continued these trends when he became chairman and CEO in 1977. Still, the company found itself increasingly strapped for cash. Steadily rising expenses in Europe resulted in a $32 million loss in 1978, which forced Carbide to divest virtually all of its European petrochemicals and plastics operations. That same year, UCC was forced by its creditors to retire $292 million in long-term debt, which forced it to borrow another $300 million in 1979. That year, Carbide's Standard & Poor's credit rating fell from AA to A+, and its stock fell as low as 42 percent below its $61 book value.

Chairman Sneath embarked on another round of cost-cutting in 1980, pruning the executive staff by 1,000 and divesting a total of 39 businesses. Sneath retained five primary businesses: graphite electrodes, batteries, agricultural products, polyethylene, and industrial gases. By 1980, Carbide had 116,000 employees at over 500 plants, mines, and laboratories in 130 countries, bringing in over $9 billion in annual sales. Sneath embarked on a plan to invest profits into high-margin consumer goods and specialty chemicals.

Disaster Strikes in India

The disaster at Union Carbide's pesticide plant in Bhopal, India, in December 1984 struck the corporation just as it was beginning to make lasting strides toward profitability. UCC had established battery plants in India as early as the mid-1920s and had seven plants with 5,000 employees there by 1967. India's chronic food shortages precipitated a government-sponsored "Green Revolution" in the 1960s, with the country's socialist government eager to join Union Carbide in establishing pesticide and fertilizer plants. In 1975, the Indian government granted Union Carbide a license to manufacture pesticides, and a plant was built on the sparsely populated outskirts of the regional capital of Bhopal. The plant drew more than 900,000 people to Bhopal by 1984. This plant was built, owned, and operated by Union Carbide India, Limited (UCIL), in which Union Carbide Corporation held just over half the stock.

In December 1984, at least five tons of methyl isocyanate gas (MIC) seeped out of the plant over a 30 minute period. Union Carbide maintained that the accident, which killed 3,800 people and permanently injured another 10,000, was sabotage. *Newsweek* magazine called the incident "the worst industrial accident in history." According to a statement posted on the Union Carbide Web site, "An initial investigation by Union Carbide experts reported that a large volume of water had apparently been introduced into the MIC tank, causing a chemical reaction forcing the chemical release valve to open and allowed the gas to leak. A committee of experts working on behalf of the Indian government conducted its own investigation and reached the same conclusion. An independent investigation by the engineering consulting firm Arthur D. Little determined that the water could only have been introduced into the tank deliberately, since safety systems were in place and operational that would have prevented water from entering the tank by accident.''

Five senior Indian executives of Union Carbide were arrested. The Indian government charged Warren Anderson, chairman of Union Carbide's board, with "corporate and criminal liability" and accused the Union Carbide management of "cruel and wanton negligence." Many class action suits were filed against Union Carbide on behalf of the victims. In April 1988, a court in India ordered Carbide to pay $192 million in "interim" damages. Union Carbide and the Indian government reached a much-criticized settlement for $470 million in 1989. In 1994, Carbide sold its share of the Bhopal plant to MacLeod Russell (India) Limited. Proceeds of the sale were used to fund a hospital in Bhopal for victims of the tragedy.

In addition to the human toll, the incident set off a chain reaction at Carbide. By 1985, the company's market value dropped by two-thirds to less than $3 billion, and GAF Corporation's Samuel Heyman accumulated enough stock to mount a hostile takeover bid of $5.3 billion. After working for two decades to expand its consumer products lines, Carbide was forced to sell off its Consumer Products Division, a profitable group that included Glad trash bags, Eveready batteries, Prestone, and STP automotive products, for $840 million. The corporation borrowed $2.8 billion, raised a total of $3.6 billion in asset sales, and repurchased $4.4 billion in stock to repulse Heyman's attack.

Carbide scaled back to the three main business lines (chemicals and plastics, industrial gases, and carbon products) that were once its strength and benefited from sharply reduced interest rates and falling costs of petrochemical feedstocks. Nevertheless, the company had lost the safety net provided by its consumer products. Union Carbide's debt stood at 63 percent of capital, and its equity was cut to a quarter of its former value. Income rose 78 percent in 1987 to $232 million, but high debt service made it hard for the company to develop and introduce new products. In 1988, UCC reduced its debt by more than $400 million and increase equity by almost $600 million.

By 1988, Union Carbide's corporate identity had begun to take clearer shape. Sales hit $8.3 billion (one-third below the 1981 peak), profits were up to more than $300 million, and the company had a new CEO, Robert D. Kennedy. His goals for the company included growth, an ambitious prospect in the face of depleted finances. His solution was to trim operating expenses and generate profits. Between 1984 and 1988, payroll was reduced from 98,000 employees to 43,000, while Carbide set up joint ventures with British Petroleum Co. and Allied-Signal Corporation and made a few modest acquisitions.

In 1989, Carbide advanced slightly on its long journey toward financial recovery. Net income was $573 million. Profits in the chemicals and plastics divisions put Carbide in the number two spot on the list of the top ten publicly traded companies in America. The company succeeded in reducing its debt-to-capital ratio to below 50 percent and invested $181 million in research and development. That year, the company introduced its proprietary LIHDE Oxygen Combustion System, which used pure oxygen to burn organic wastes.

Carbide's fate was far from settled. A $3.3 billion debt stymied both diversification and overseas expansion. Carbide's sales were dependent on cyclical commodities such as polyethylene, and as the chemical industry stumbled, earnings declined. Net income decreased 46 percent from 1990. The brightest prospects were in the industrial gas unit: Carbide remained number one in North America in that industry, with $2.4 billion in sales.

The company launched a "work simplification program" in the early 1990s. The program had a cost reduction goal of $400 million a year by the end of 1994. Carbide progressed toward this goal by repurchasing 20 million shares, spinning off two small businesses, and selling 50 percent of its carbon business in 1990.

As a fitting mark to Union Carbide's 75th anniversary in 1992, the company had the year's best-performing stock on the Dow Jones list of 30 industrials. Carbide was half way to achieving its $400 million cost reduction goal and had endured a loss of $187 million. The dramatically smaller corporation had shifted its focus from diversification to becoming a low-cost leader in basic chemicals. This strategy included uncharacteristic environmentalism: Carbide anticipated "inevitable government mandates on waste reduction and recycling" when it started reprocessing plastic bottles in 1992. After Bhopal, UCC's efforts helped raise industry performance standards and levels worldwide, and the company was praised for its "responsible care" efforts.

Expansion through Joint Ventures

During the 1990s, Union Carbide expanded its business worldwide by engaging in joint ventures with both American and foreign companies. In 1994, Carbide announced a joint venture with EniChem, a European chemicals company, to develop, manufacture, and sell polyethylene under the name Polimeri Europa. Each company would own 50 percent of the new firm. The arrangement would make Carbide and EniChem the largest producers of polyethylene in western Europe. EniChem's existing polyethylene plants in Germany, France, and Italy were made part of the new company, while a new 400,000-tons-a-year plant in Brindisi, Italy, was planned.

The year 1996 saw further expansion internationally when Carbide announced a joint venture with China's Shanghai Petrochemical Co., Ltd. to manufacture and sell latex polymer emulsions under the name Shanghai Petrochemical Union Carbide Emulsion Systems Co., Ltd. The new company would construct a plant in Jinshanwei, China, near Shanghai. A second expansion into the Chinese market came later in 1996 with Carbide's subsidiary Amerchol Corp. announcing that it would be constructing a plant in Guangdong Province, China.

Carbide teamed with Exxon Chemical Company in 1997 to create the joint venture company Univation Technologies. Combining both Carbide's and Exxon's patented polyethylene manufacturing processes, Univation would manufacture polyethylene using these processes and license the technologies. Univation would also license the super condensed mode technology, which doubles polyethylene production.

Carbide expanded its presence in Asia with the 1999 announcement of a joint venture with Petronas, the national oil company of Malaysia. The two firms would build a petrochemical complex in Malaysia focusing on ethylene oxide and its derivatives and oxo alcohols and oxo derivatives. In 2001, the Kerteh Integrated Petrochemicals Complex opened, with Union Carbide owning 24 percent of the project.

Another joint venture was announced in 1999. Carbide and Tosco Corp. joined in a 50–50 venture to combine their polypropylene business. The deal was expected to take Carbide, ranked eighth in North America among makers of polypropylene, into the top five producers. Under the agreement, Tosco would build a 775 million-pound-per-year plant in Linden, New Jersey, while Carbide would contribute its two plants in Seadrift, Texas, and Norco, Louisiana.

Acquisition by Dow Chemical

On August 4, 1999, it was announced that Union Carbide would become a subsidiary of The Dow Chemical Company. The next two years saw negotiations between the two firms on the terms of the deal. Negotiations were also held with the European Commission and the Federal Trade Commission to get government approval of such a large merger. As part of the agreement, Dow was obliged to divest some of its holdings, including its gas-phase polyethylene metallocene technology, while Carbide had to divest its 50 percent ownership in Polimeri Europa, its joint venture with EniChem. Finally, all discussion was over and Dow acquired Carbide for $11.6 billion on February 6, 2001. The deal created the world's second-largest chemical company, just behind DuPont. According to Michael Parker, chairman and CEO of Dow, quoted by Robert Brown in *Chemical Market Reporter:* "While the negotiations took longer than first imagined, we are pleased with the outcome and consider it a win-win for everyone involved." Union Carbide chairman and CEO William H. Joyce called the deal, according to Joseph Chang in *Chemical Market Reporter,* "the right move at a good time. In a consolidating chemical industry where fewer, more powerful companies will exist, the combination of Dow and Union Carbide now sets the standard for the industry."

Since the acquisition, Carbide has seen generally positive financial growth. In 1999, the company posted net sales of $5.87 billion and a profit of $291 million. In 2000, net sales were $6.52 billion with a profit of $162 million. The next two years saw losses on lower net sales. 2001 sales were $5.4 billion with a loss of $699 million, while 2002 sales were $4.78 billion with a loss of $510 million. In 2003, however, Carbide moved into the black again with net sales of $5.16 billion and a profit of $313 million. This trend continued in 2004 with net sales of $5.86 billion and a profit of $687 million. For the first quarter of 2005, Carbide reported net sales of $1.68 billion and a profit of $280 million. As Union Carbide faced the 21st century with rising sales and profits, its chemical products continued to be essential to the manufacturing of countless other products throughout the world.

Principal Subsidiaries

Amerchol Corporation; Amko Service Company; Bayox, Inc.; Beaucar Minerals, Inc.; BEK III Inc.; Be-Kan, Inc.; Bentley Sales Co. Inc.; Blue Creek Coal Company, Inc.; Catalyst Technology, Inc.; Cellulosic Products, Inc.; Chemicals Marine Fleet, Inc.; Dexter Realty Corporation; Gas Technics Gases and Equipment Centers of Eastern Pennsylvania, Inc.; Gas Technics Gases and Equipment Centers of New Jersey, Inc.; Gas Technics Gases and Equipment Centers of Ohio, Inc.; Global Industrial Corporation; Hampton Roads Welders Supply Company, Inc.; Harvey Company; Innovative Membrane Systems, Inc.; International Cryogenic Equipment Corporation; Iweco, Inc.; Karba Minerals, Inc.; KSC Liquidation, Inc.; XTI Chemicals, Inc.; Linde Homecare Medical Systems, Inc.; Linox Welding Supply Co.; London Chemical Company, Inc.; Media Buyers Inc.; Merritt-Holland Company; Mon-Arc Welding Supply, Inc.; Nova Tran Corporation; Paulsboro Packaging Inc.; Phoenix Research Corporation; Polysak, Inc.; Prentiss Glycol Company; Presto Hartford, Inc.; Presto Welding Supplies, Inc.; Seadrift Pipeline Corporation; Soilsery, Inc.; South Charleston Sewage Treatment Company; UCAR Capital Corporation; UCAR Energy Services Corporation; UCAR Interam, Inc.; UCAR Louisiana Pipeline Company; UCAR Pipeline Incorporated; UCORE Ltd.; Umetco Minerals Exploration; Umetco Minerals Sales Corporation; Unigas, Inc.; Union Carbide Africa and Middle East, Inc.; Union Carbide Canada Ltd.; Union Carbide Caribe, Inc.; Union Carbide Communications Company, Inc.; Union Carbide Engineering and Hydrocarbons Service Company, Inc.; Union Carbide Engineering and Technology Services; Union Carbide Ethylene Oxide/Glycol Company; Union Carbide Europe, Inc.; Union Carbide Films-Packaging, Inc.; Union Carbide Grafito, Inc.; Union Carbide Imaging Systems, Inc.; Union Carbide Industrial Services Company; Union Carbide Inter-America, Inc.; Union Carbide International Capital Corporation; Union Carbide International Sales Corporation; Union Carbide Polyolefins Development Company, Inc.; UNISON Transformer Services, Inc.; UOP LLC; Vametco Minerals Corporation; V.B. Anderson Co.; Welders Service Center of Nebraska, Inc.; Wolfe Welding Supply Company, Inc.

Principal Competitors

BASF AG; Huntsman International LLC; Total Petrochemicals, Inc.

Further Reading

Berman, Phyllis, "Dow's Pocket Has a Hole," *Forbes Global*, March 31, 2003, p. 34.
Brown, Robert, "Dow, Carbide Ink $7.4 Billion Mega-Merger," *Chemical Market Reporter*, February 12, 2001, p. 1.
"Carbide, Enichem Form PE Powerhouse," *Chemical Marketing Reporter*, August 8, 1994, p. 3.
"Carbide Lays Out Its Strategy through 1983," *Chemical Week*, September 19, 1979, p. 49.
Chang, Joseph, "Dow Chemical, Union Carbide to Merge in $11.6 Billion Deal," *Chemical Market Reporter*, August 9, 1999, p. 1.
"A Corporate Polluter Learns the Hard Way," *Business Week*, February 6, 1971, pp. 52–56.
"The Cure for a Chemical Giant," *Business Week*, July 14, 1973, pp. 88–92.
Denton, Timothy, "Exxon, Union Carbide Launch Univation Metallocene Venture," *Chemical Market Reporter*, April 21, 1997, p. 1.
"Dow Completes Merger with Union Carbide," *Adhesives & Sealants Industry*, April 2001, p. 11.
"Dow Performance Chemicals: Stronger, Better, Global; Integration of Union Carbide Products and Services Repositions Key Dow Business," *Adhesives & Sealants Industry*, March 2002, p. 26.
"Dow Shuts Seadrift Olefins Plant," *Chemical Market Reporter*, July 14, 2003, p. 3.
Esposito, Frank, "Carbide Forms Joint Venture; New Partner to Build PP Plant," *Plastics News*, February 15, 1999, p. 3.
Everest, Larry, *Behold the Poison Cloud: Union Carbide's Bhopal Massacre*, Chicago: Banner Press, 1986.
"Giant with a (Giant) Headache," *Forbes*, December 1, 1968, pp. 24–26.
Hoffman, Charles B., "Union Carbide Formula Calls for Higher Net," *Barron's*, April 16, 1973, pp. 31, 39.
"How Union Carbide Has Cleaned up Its Image," *Business Week*, August 2, 1978, p. 46.
Jackson, Tony, "Bhopal's Awkward Truth: The 1984 Union Carbide Disaster Holds Lessons for Governments That Try to Control Companies' Activities, Says Tony Jackson," *Financial Times*, September 5, 2002, p. 17.
Lappen, Alyssa A., "Breaking Up Is Hard to Do," *Forbes*, December 10, 1990, p. 102.
"Last Original Union Carbide Plant to Close," *Industrial Maintenance & Plant Operation*, November 2001, p. 6.
Levy, Robert, "The Man from Uncarb," *Dun's Review & Modern Industry*, July 1966, pp. 46–48.
Menzies, Hugh D., "Union Carbide Raises Its Voice," *Fortune*, September 25, 1978, pp. 86–88.
"A New Union Carbide Is Slowly Starting to Gel," *Business Week*, April 18, 1986, p. 68.
Norman, James R., "Carbide Saves Itself—But Was It Worth It?," *Business Week*, January 20, 1986, p. 26.
Sissell, Kara, "20 Years after Bhopal: Charting Progress of Plant Safety," *Chemical Week*, December 15, 2004, p. 19.
"Turnaround Year for Union Carbide?," *Financial World*, January 5, 1972, pp. 5, 23.
"Union Carbide," *Rubber World*, July 1996, p. 8.
"Union Carbide," *Rubber World*, December 1996, p. 8.
"Union Carbide Reported Record Net Income of $915 Million in 1995 on Sales of $5.888 Billion," *Rubber World*, March 1996, p. 12.
"Union Carbide: Revolution without the 'R'," *Forbes*, November 1, 1963, pp. 22–26.

—April S. Dougal
—updates: Marinell Landa; Thomas Wiloch

United Dairy Farmers, Inc.

3955 Montgomery Road
Cincinnati, Ohio 45212
U.S.A.
Telephone: (513) 396-8700
Toll Free: (800) 833-9911
Fax: (513) 396-8736
Web site: http://www.udfinc.com

Private Company
Incorporated: 1940
Sales : $300 million (2004)
Employees: 3,000
NAIC: 31151 Dairy Product (Except Frozen)
Manufacturing; 311511 Fluid Milk Manufacturing;
311520 Ice Cream and Frozen Dessert Manufacturing;
424430 Dairy Product (Except Dried or Canned)
Merchant Wholesalers; 445120 Convenience Stores;
447110 Gasoline Stations with Convenience Stores

Founded by the Lindner family in 1940, United Dairy Farmers, Inc., remains a closely held family business managed by Robert Lindner, Sr., and his sons Brad, Robert, Jr., and David. The company manufactures and distributes branded milk, ice creams, and dairy products under the United Dairy Farmers trademark, as well as the following branded items: Homemade Brand Premium Ice Cream, Krazy Kreams, and Micro Shake. In addition, the company owns and operates almost 200 dairy/convenience stores in with ice cream parlors, which are famous for their made-to-order, hand-dipped malts, shakes, freezes, sundaes, and ice cream sodas.

Early Years: Revolutionizing the Dairy Industry

In 1940, Carl Lindner introduced an innovative dairy concept in Norwood, Ohio. At the time, almost all milk was delivered in quarts to customers' front doors and paid for on a weekly or monthly basis. Identifying a business opportunity, Lindner created a new model for milk distribution: milk and other dairy products sold cash-and-carry at his company's onsite store.

Lindner called his company United Dairy Farmers in acknowledgment of its milk suppliers. Lindner's entire family (his wife Clara and their four children, Dorothy, Carl, Jr., Robert, and Richard) dedicated themselves to making Lindner's company a success. They rebuilt used dairy production equipment and fashioned cabinets and signs for the company's new store.

On May 8, 1940, Lindner's dairy plant and adjacent 20- by 50-foot store opened. It was the first of its kind, as were its gallon and half-gallon bottles of milk. Store hours were from eight in the morning to ten at night seven days a week. The store sold its milk for 28 cents a gallon, half the cost of home-delivered milk. It also sold other dairy products, such as butter, cottage cheese, eggs, and buttermilk. Although Lindner's dairy did not extend credit to its customers, his business model enabled him to sell dairy products at a much lower cost than home-delivery dairies because he had done away with delivery expenses. For many customers, this reduced cost was a welcome break. On opening day, the store's sales topped eight dollars, a definite success.

In fact, the store was so successful that its competitive presence displeased local home-delivery dairymen. After business hours on opening day, two dairymen attacked Carl Lindner in the store's driveway. Fortunately, he was able to break free, and he later settled out of court with his attackers for $1,000.

1940–50: Company Growth and Diversification

UDF soon became a local favorite. The company's popularity and success helped it to expand throughout the 1940s. The Lindners subsequently opened a second store in Norwood, a third in nearby Silverton, and a fourth in St. Bernard. As the business grew, the family remained in active control of company operations: Dorothy managed the books from an office in the corner of the boiler room; Carl, Jr., directed market expansion efforts and real estate acquisitions; Robert oversaw ice cream and milk production; and Richard managed the physical facilities and maintenance.

UDF undertook plant expansions and renovations that increased production capacity throughout the 1940s. By 1950, there were nine UDF stores, and the company's office had relocated to

Company Perspectives:

Since our family opened the first United Dairy Farmers cash-and-carry dairy store in Norwood, Ohio over 60 years ago, we have been committed to making affordable, quality ice cream and selling it with fast friendly service in clean, bright stores. Three generations later, with almost 200 UDF stores and ice cream sold in numerous states, we still make our milk and ice cream on the site where the first store stood. At United Dairy Farmers, if we put our name on it, you can be sure we're proud of it!

the building next door to the original plant. After the untimely death of Carl Lindner, Sr., in 1952, his children took over the company, which continued to grow. By 1958, the company's most major plant expansion to date was complete. Its plant was equipped with two continuous ice cream freezers, half-gallon and pint ice cream fillers, a half-gallon bottle filler, a bottle washer, and 12 stainless steel milk-holding tanks adjacent to a new receiving dock. By this time, the company owned 22 stores.

In the late 1950s, the Lindner family's interest in the financial aspects of business ownership led to the formation of American Financial Corporation (AFC) and the purchase of the Thriftway grocery chain. While her brothers remained in charge of UDF, Dorothy Lindner took over management of AFC. By 1960, UDF owned and operated about 30 stores in and around Cincinnati, many of which sold lines of bread, cookies, lunch meat, and cheeses as well as the original UDF fresh dairy products.

A change in management roles took place among family members in the 1960s. Richard Lindner left UDF in 1965 to take over Thriftway. Carl, Jr., and Robert focused on expanding AFC holdings while also operating UDF. They used profits from their dairy business to help finance acquisitions of banks and insurance firms. Toward the end of the decade, they oversaw a major UDF store remodeling program that added merchandising space for approximately 1,200 convenience grocery products in the dairy and food sections. Throughout the 1970s, the business continued to grow, and in 1977, some UDF stores began to sell UDF brand gasoline.

1980s–90s: A New Generation Focuses on Specialization and Expansion

The second generation of Lindners entered the family business in the early 1980s. Robert Lindner's sons, Jeff and Brad, focused their attention on expanding ice cream sales by adding the Homemade Brand premium ice cream line in 1982. Homemade Brand was also introduced in local stores and soon began to garner awards: *People* magazine rated its Cookies 'n' Cream the Number One "Exotic" Flavor in 1984, while shortly thereafter, *Cincinnati Magazine* named Homemade Brand "Best" for its Cherry Cordial ice cream. By 1986, Homemade Brand ice cream sold in major grocery chains and independent stores in five states, firmly establishing the company's wholesale operations. In 1987, UDF introduced another first, the MicroShake frozen milkshake, which thawed and became ready to eat in the microwave.

The company's retail chain also grew under the direction of Robert Lindner, Jr., who succeeded his father as president in 1985. By the early 1990s, there were about 200 UDF stores, and the company's new superstores sold fast-food as well as ice cream in sit-down parlors and pumped UDF brand gasoline. The company was rated as one of the 100 top privately-owned companies in the Tristate area that included Cincinnati, northern Indianapolis, and northern Kentucky; its ice cream was considered among top 15 American brands. However, the Lindner family was still not content to rest and planned to offer new services and products in order to maintain the company's leadership role in the dairy and convenience store markets.

Thus, in 1994, UDF joined a national buying association, Convenience Equipment and Supplies Enterprises (CEASE), to gain access to greater buying power. By 1995, the company was distributing its full line of dairy products in Ohio, West Virginia, western Maryland, and Pennsylvania. That same year, UDF bought Borden's Valley Bell Dairy's four operations, which manufactured frozen desserts and other dairy products. Part of the purchase deal specified that UDF would continue to manufacture Borden's products under the brand names of Borden, Meadow Gold, and Valley Bell. Winn-Dixie also purchased Thriftway stores from the Lindner family in 1995.

UDF continued to grow during the late 1990s despite a steep increase in the cost of soybeans, corn, hay, and other feed grains that put a damper on milk production and led to a jump in the cost of milk. These market forces affected modest annual increases in dairy consumption overall, and no growth in fluid sales. In 1997, seeking to overcome these obstacles, UDF sought to tap into the adult and young adult on-the-go markets by introducing 16-ounce, resealable jugs of milk, tea, spring water, and sports drinks.

That same year, UDF became the focus of unwelcome publicity when civil rights groups called for a boycott of the company on the grounds that UDF stores discriminated against black workers. UDF countered that nearly 19 percent of its 3,000 employees were black. and pledged to improve its existing anti-discrimination policies. However, the company became embroiled in a series of lawsuits brought by two black workers in Columbus who said they were fired and called derogatory names at work because of their race. Although ultimately, UDF was found not guilty of racial discrimination in two separate jury trials, one juror was quoted in a 2000 *Columbus Dispatch* article as saying that hiring and firing within the company appeared to be arbitrary: "UDF has a lot of personnel problems. They have bad policies or no policies for dealing with rape, sex, and age discrimination. They need to get their house in order."

Another hardship occurred for UDF in 1998 when it began to face greater competition as a result of industry consolidation throughout the greater Cincinnati area. Prior to that year, the company's main milk competition came from other independent dairies, but Suiza Food Corporation and Dean Foods bought up the last of the independent dairies in the region and began muscling in on UDF territory. In June, Thriftway, owned by Winn-Dixie Inc. since 1995, switched to Dean Foods as its dairy supplier, and although UDF picked up a contract with IGA Supermarkets, this did not offset the Thriftway loss. "We're going to have to figure out how to generate more fluid

Key Dates:

1940: Carl Lindner, Sr., and his four children open the first United Dairy Farmers (UDF) store in Cincinnati, Ohio.

1952: Lindner dies and his children take over the company.

1958: UDF expands and modernizes its plant.

1961: The Lindner family buys Thriftway Inc.

1977: UDF stores begin to sell UDF brand gasoline.

1982: The company introduces its Homemade Brand Premium Ice Cream.

1984: *People* magazine rates Homemade Brand Cookies 'n' Cream ice cream its Number One "exotic" flavor.

1985: Robert Lindner, Jr., succeeds his father as president of the company.

1995: UDF buys Borden's Valley Bell Dairy operations; Winn-Dixie buys Thriftway from the Lindner family.

1998: Brad Lindner becomes UDF president and chief executive officer.

2001: The company begins to sell Mobil branded gasoline.

business without knocking on one door and getting a huge account," announced Brad Lindner, who became UDF president and chief executive officer in 2000 in a *Business Courier* article of that year. "So we have to look to go a bit further outside our geography, or look to another channel of business."

In 2001, UDF began to sell Mobil branded gasoline at 108 of its dairy/convenience store locations in Ohio and Kentucky, after upgrading pumps and underground storage tanks, adding canopies and Mobil signs, and switching the stores' credit card processing system. The partnership meant that UDF would be assured a supply of gas from Mobil in the event of a petroleum shortage and could bank on greater profits form gasoline sales since some customers had regarded UDF gas as suspect. In addition, national statistics showed that people who bought braded fuel were more likely to buy the more profitable premium and mid-grade gasolines. According to Brad Lindner, the partnership also meant a change for the company internally. "We've been independent and could so whatever we wanted," he said in a 2000 *Business Courier* article. "Now we're going to be joined at the hip with a huge organization . . . That's going to be an adaptation culturally."

In 2001, the company also expanded its business into the Dayton, Ohio market. The expansion included the construction of new stores and the conversion of existing stores into a larger format, some of which would include car wash facilities. In the years following, the company continued to grow with the addition of new stores and by introducing new ice cream flavors under both the Homemade Brand and United Dairy Farmer labels. In 2005, it placed first for its Homemade Brand Chocolate Ice Cream in a survey conducted by the Cincinnati Enquirer.

Principal Competitors

7-Eleven Inc., Kroger Co., Sheetz Inc.

Further Reading

"Banana Republican: Man in the News, Carl Lindner," *Financial Times*, November 14, 1998, p. 15.

Melcer, Rachel, "Mobil Could Fuel UDF Growth," *Business Courier*, November 17, 2000, p. 3.

Ruth, Robert, "Allegations of Racism at Center of Lawsuit in Third UDF Case," *Columbus Dispatch*, April 25, 2000, p. 6C.

——, "Jury Clears UDF in Racial Suit," *Columbus Dispatch*, February 18, 2000, p. 1 D.

——, "UDF Wins in Federal Court; Race Not a Motive in Firings, Jury Finds" *Columbus Dispatch*, October 6, 1998, p. 1A.

"UDF Joins CEASE Family," *National Petroleum News*, October 1994, p. 96.

Williams, Brian, "Milking a Package For All That It's Worth," *Columbus Dispatch*, September 25, 1998, p. 1F.

—Carrie Rothburd

urban outfitters inc.

Urban Outfitters, Inc.

1809 Walnut Street
Philadelphia, Pennsylvania 19103
U.S.A.
Telephone: (215) 564-2313
Fax: (215) 568-1549
Web site: http://www.urbanoutfitters.com

Public Company
Incorporated: 1976
Employees: 6,200
Sales: $827.8 million (2005)
Stock Exchanges: NASDAQ
Ticker Symbol: URBN
NAIC: 448140 Family Clothing Stores

Urban Outfitters, Inc., operates specialty retail stores under the Urban Outfitters, Anthropologie, and Free People banners. The company operates two business segments: the lifestyle merchandising retail segment, which oversees store operations, and a wholesale apparel business. Both Urban Outfitters and Anthropologie offer customers hip and trendy apparel and home furnishings through retail locations, catalogs, and Web sites. The first Free People store opened in 2002. The freepeople.com Web site soon followed. As of January 2005, Urban Outfitters Inc. operated 65 Anthropologie stores, two Free People retail locations, and 75 Urban Outfitter stores in the United States, Canada, and the United Kingdom.

Beginnings

Urban Outfitters was created in 1970 by two retail novices, anthropology graduate Richard Hayne and his former roommate at Lehigh University, Scott Belair. Hayne was just back from two years working with Eskimos in Alaska as a VISTA Volunteer; Belair was a second-year student at Wharton School of Business and needed a project for his entrepreneur workshop. Over beer one night, the two came up with the idea of a store for college and graduate students, selling inexpensive clothes and items for dorm rooms and apartments. Pooling $5,000, they opened the Free People Store in Philadelphia, near the campus of the University of

Pennsylvania. In a 400-square-feet store decorated with packing crates and beat-up furniture, they offered inexpensive second-hand clothing, Indian fabrics, scented candles, T-shirts, drug paraphernalia, and ethnic jewelry. "I was that market," Hayne told Dan Shaw of *The New York Times* in 1994, adding that "Everyone associated with the store was that market."

The store was a success. "Belair got an A on the project," according to Robert La Franco in a *Forbes* article, "and went on to Wall Street, where he started his own bankruptcy workout business." Hayne stayed with the business, adding such merchandise as coffee mugs and glassware to the product line. In 1976, he moved to larger quarters near the university, changed the store's name to Urban Outfitters, and incorporated the company. In 1980, with sales around $3 million, Hayne opened a second store, in Cambridge, Massachusetts, close to several colleges.

In 1987, Hayne hired Kenneth Cleeland as chief financial officer. Cleeland, a graduate of George Washington University, had held financial positions with several wholesale and retail companies. At Urban Outfitters, he instituted financial controls to deal with shoplifting problems and Hayne's rather casual bookkeeping practices. Profits increased, and Cleeland helped Hayne borrow $3 million to open six new stores within three years.

New stores in the chain followed the original concept and were located in metropolitan areas near college students. By 1995, Urban Outfitters stores would be established in Madison, Wisconsin; Ann Arbor, Michigan; Boston; Minneapolis; Seattle; New York; Washington, D.C.; Chicago; and Portland, Oregon. Moreover, the chain would also secure a presence in California, with five locations in college towns. Even when Hayne was tempted to drift from his original concept, store locations kept the company focused on its college-age market.

The new stores maintained Hayne's "counterculture" approach, and the company relied heavily on its buildings and interior displays to entice customers to enter, explore its stores, and buy its goods. "We always use renovated buildings," Hayne told the *Washington Post* in a 1993 feature. "Other stores will go into a mall and put their image into a space, where we use an existing space to enhance our image. None of our stores look alike. We go into these old buildings and adapt them

---

Company Perspectives:

Our established ability to understand our customers and connect with them on an emotional level is the reason for our success. The reason for this success is that our brands— Urban Outfitters, Anthropologie and Free People—are both compelling and distinct. Each brand chooses a particular customer segment, and once chosen, sets out to create sustainable points of distinction with that segment. In the retail brands we design innovative stores that resonate with the target audience; offer an eclectic mix of merchandise in which hard and soft goods are cross merchandised; and construct unique product displays that incorporate found objects into creative selling vignettes. The emphasis is on creativity. Our goal is to offer a product assortment and an environment so compelling and distinctive that the customer feels an empathetic connection to the brand and is persuaded to buy.

---

for ourselves,'' he noted. In Washington, D.C., for example, the company took over a Woolworth's store, complete with worn wooden floors, exposed brick walls, and a steel staircase to the basement. The Ann Arbor store was established in an old theater, and other locations included a former bank and stock exchange. In 1993, Urban Outfitters stores averaged approximately 9,000 selling square feet.

The decor within each stores was also unique, although the atmosphere remained similar throughout the chain—casual and fun. Much of this was due to the staff and the company's policy of listening to its customers. Hayne hired staff within the targeted age group and depended on their personal style to guide merchandising strategies. Staff decided on the music to be played, even bringing in their own compact disks, and department managers were made responsible for the look of their sections. ''We have to come up with creative inventions for fixtures and displays,'' housewares manager 27-year-old Susan Duckworth explained in the *Washington Post,* adding that ''It's the only place I've worked where you can bring an old crate to work, make something out of it and [the bosses] love it.''

''We try to appeal to the mainstream and those who want to cross the line every once in a while; we do stay abreast of fashion trends,'' Sala Patterson, an 18-year-old sales associate explained in the *Washington Post* article. According to a 1995 *Forbes* story, Hayne spent $4 million a year on salaries and expenses for over 75 young fashion buyers who checked out neighborhoods in the United States, London, and Paris to report on hot trends. The chain's unconventional atmosphere, merchandise, and music attracted students younger than 18 as well. As one 15-year-old explained to the *Washington Post,* ''It's such a down-to-earth place, it's not a chain like the Gap and J. Crew. Everything's really different.''

Urban Outfitters prepared its management, merchandising, and buying staff by recruiting recent college graduates and qualified store employees and sending them through a six- to nine-month ''Management Development Program.'' While in the program, participants had a series of rotations between stores and the home office. A ''Manager-in-Training'' program offered the on-the-job experience needed to become a departmental, assistant, or store manager.

As the company grew, it took steps to keep its organizational structure relatively stable. Employees were eligible for profit sharing and stock options and took turns producing *Urban World,* a quarterly in-house newsletter. Articles in the newsletter included reports from various branches and profiles of employees and customers, providing market research as well as internal communications. In 1993, the company initiated it ''Shared Fate'' program, designed to increase team management and give every employee the responsibility and authority to make decisions to increase productivity.

Recognizing that private label merchandise generally yielded higher gross profit margins than brand name merchandise, Hayne created a wholesale division in 1984 to design, produce, and sell its own line of junior sportswear. Michael Schultz joined the company in 1986 as president of Urban Wholesale, Inc. Schultz had previously served as president of Andrew Fezza International Division of Levi Strauss & Company and as a vice-president of merchandising at Pierre Cardin.

Success Continues in the Early 1990s

In 1990, Urban Wholesale replaced its signature Urban Outfitters collection brand with three separate labels: Ecote, Free People, and Anthropologie. The three apparel labels each targeted a different audience. Ecote produced solid and printed casual rayon dresses in styles ranging from baby dolls to A-lines and made up about 60 percent of the business in 1991. The Free People label produced sixties-era inspired designs and hip casualwear, while Anthropologie made young women's casual wear, primarily cotton, wool, and silk sweaters. Schultz expected Anthropologie to become the wholesale division's biggest label because it was the most adaptable. As reported in *Women's Wear Daily,* before the change, 70 percent of the division's sales were to department stores and 30 percent to specialty stores. In 1991, it was just the opposite, as wholesale volume had grown 50 percent, from $10 million in 1989 to $15 million in 1990.

In 1993 and 1994, the Urban Wholesale division had revenue gains in excess of 76 percent and 56 percent, respectively. The company attributed this growth primarily to more and larger orders for the Anthropologie line from small and medium-sized specialty apparel stores. It should be noted that while much of the inventory of the company's stores was from the three labels, buyers for Urban Outfitters and Anthropologie did not automatically buy from the wholesale division. Urban Outfitters and Anthropologie accounted for 28.8 percent and 0.3 percent of Urban Wholesale's total revenue in 1992, according to the company prospectus. By 1994, goods from Urban Wholesale shipped outside the United States, particularly to Japan, comprised 6 percent of total sales. Merchandise made in the United States represented about 20 percent of the division's production.

As the number of stores grew and the wholesale division was revamped, company sales increased. In 1990, net sales amounted to $37.4 million. In 1991, sales increased 17.3 percent to $43.9 million. Most of the increase, 75 percent, was due to new stores opened in 1990 and 1991. The largest selling product category in Urban Outfitters stores was women's apparel. In 1992, it accounted for one-third of total sales, followed by footwear and accessories at 27 percent, men's apparel at 22 percent, and apartment wares and gifts at 18 percent.

In October 1992, Hayne opened the first Anthropologie store in a renovated automobile dealership in Wayne, Pennsylvania, outside Philadelphia, and named Glen Senk president. After 16 years of selling T-shirts, jeans, and work boots, and with his original chain doing well, Hayne thus took the company's strategy to older, more established shoppers living in the suburbs of major metropolitan areas. Anthropologie targeted customers who were focused on family, home, and career, with interests in travel, the arts, gardening, and reading. The Wayne store featured an espresso bar and placed greater emphasis on "hard-goods" such as furniture and a variety of home, garden, and tabletop products, including books and ceramics.

The decor of Anthropologie tended to be rustic and ecologically conscious. Product lines were intermixed and arranged in a variety of displays. For example, an antique bed might serve as the anchor for a section containing linens, towels, nightgowns, lingerie, soap, bath oils, picture frames, and mirrors. Another small area might feature children's clothes, books, toys, and note cards, while birdhouses and diaries of handmade paper might be found alongside men's sweaters and pants.

During 1992, company sales grew to $59.1 million, a 34.7 percent increase. The wholesale division introduced the Co-operative product line of fashion basics, consisting mostly of lower-priced cotton knit tops and sweaters. Profits also increased with the successful expansion of the company's higher-margin private label program.

Urban Outfitters Goes Public in 1993

During 1993, Hayne opened two more Urban Outfitters stores, in San Francisco and Costa Mesa. Comparable store sales increased by 18 percent and total sales exceeded $500 per selling square foot for the first time. The wholesale division opened a large sales office in New York. Prices at Urban Outfitters stores during 1993 ranged from 75 cents for greeting cards to $450 for a World War I-style leather bomber jacket. At the Anthropologie store, prices ranged from $1.00 for a greeting card to $1,500 for an antique Mexican cabinet. The company implemented its "Shared Fate" program for employees and initiated a company-wide profit-sharing plan. Total sales for the year grew at 43 percent. In November, Urban Outfitters went public at $18 a share, raising over $13 million in capital through the initial public offering.

Hayne used the capital to continue his strategic plan of growth by adding new stores on the retail side of the business and attracting new customers to the wholesale division while increasing sales to existing ones. In 1994, he opened three new Urban Outfitters stores, two in Chicago and one in Pasadena, and indicated that he planned to open three or four new stores each year for next three years, some of which were planned to be located outside the United States, either in Canada, Europe, or both. Based on the success of the Wayne, Pennsylvania, store, two more Anthropologie stores were opened in 1994, in Westport, Connecticut, and Rockville, Maryland, just outside Washington, D.C. In the company's annual report that year, Hayne indicated he hoped to open three to four additional Anthropologie stores each year and that the company would invest heavily in expanding the Anthropologie division. Overall company sales grew by 30 percent from 1993. Recognizing that high rates of growth would be difficult to maintain, the company set a goal of 20 percent annual growth.

In 1995, an Urban Outfitters store opened in Portland, Oregon, and lease signings were announced in Austin, Texas, and Tempe, Arizona, moving the company into the Southwest. With steadily increasing sales during this time, the company gained a ranking as number 76 on the *Business Week* list of hot growth companies. As it neared the end of the 20th century, the Urban Outfitters and Anthropologie chains appeared to be going strong, and, after a quarter century, Hayne and his staff were still successfully anticipating and responding to shifts in fashion trends and the changing tastes of their customers.

Late 1990s and Beyond

Urban Outfitters entered the late 1990s on solid ground. Despite having to close its first location near the University of Pennsylvania due to poor sales, the company forged ahead with is growth plans, buoyed by strong sales at its remaining outlets. In 1998, Anthropologie launched its direct-to-consumer catalog. Later that year, Urban Outfitters made its debut in London, opening its first store on Kensington High Street. During this period, Urban Outfitters' expansion was comparatively slower than many retail chains, however, despite the fact that it putting considerable effort into market research before deciding to open a store. Company officials called each location a "complete lifestyle" store and were diligent in making sure it knew what its target customers wanted. Hayne explained the lifestyle label in a November 1998 *Retail Week* article. "We have this concept where we have a unique and singular group of people that we are trying to service and we have a concept that emphasizes the lifestyle approach to servicing these customers. The product category to us is not particularly important, as long as we can make money, but the lifestyle is incredibly important."

Urban Outfitters continued its lifestyle strategy in the 2000s and experienced marked success. It expanded its store count while sales and profits increased. Fifteen stores were opened in 2000, 12 in 2001, and 15 in 2002. During 2003, approximately 20 Anthropologie stores opened their doors while 20 Urban Outfitters locations were added to the company's growing arsenal. The Urban Outfitters catalog was launched that year.

The company opened its first Free People store in the Garden State Plaza Mall in Paramus, New Jersey, in November 2002. A second location followed in December 2004 in Arlington, Virginia. During that year, Urban Outfitters was one of the most successful retailers, securing a revenue increase of nearly 50 percent while net income rose by 87 percent over the previous year.

With a solid financial record in place, Urban Outfitters planned to continue its expansion efforts in the coming years. Management hoped to increase store count by 20 percent per year, emphasizing that each location would continue to have its lifestyle focus. By 2005, there were over 75 Urban Outfitters stores in the United States, Canada, and the United Kingdom. Over 65 Anthropologie stores accounted for nearly 39 percent of net sales in 2005. Its success in recent years left it in a enviable position among its competitors. Indeed, Urban Outfitters Inc. had a strong following, a solid strategy in place, and years of success under its belt. Hayne was confident that the company would remain a retail powerhouse well into the future.

Principal Subsidiaries

Urban Outfitters, Inc.; Anthropologie, Inc.; Urban Outfitters Wholesale, Inc.; Urban Outfitters UK Ltd.; Urban Outfitters (Delaware), Inc.; Anthropologie (Delaware), Inc.; Urban Outfitters West LLC; Urban Outfitters Direct LLC; Anthropologie Direct LLC; Inter-Urban, Inc.; U.O.D. Inc.; U.O.D. Secondary, Inc.; UO Fenwick, Inc.; Urban Outfitters Canada, Inc.; Urban Outfitters Ireland Ltd.; Free People LLC; UOGC, Inc.; Urban Outfitters Holdings LLC; Anthropologie Holdings LLC; urbanoutfitters.com LP; anthropologie.com LP; Freepeople.com LLC.

Principal Competitors

Gap Inc.; Buckle Inc.; Limited Brands Inc.; Pier 1 Imports Inc.

Further Reading

Barrett, Amy, "Hot Growth Companies," *Business Week*, May 22, 1995.
"Company Chops Its Roots," *Harrisburg Patriot*, May 29, 1997, p. B9.
Gilstrap, Peter, "Not-So-Radical Chic," *Washington Post Magazine*, September 12, 1993, p. 31.
Gordon, Maryellen, "Urban Outfitters' New Route," *Women's Wear Daily*, sportswear report supplement, January 2, 1991, p. 4.
Greenburg, Cara, "For School, Romance and Ripped Seams," *New York Times*, September 5, 1993, Sec. 9, p. 14.
Hamner, Susanna, "Lessons from a Retail Rebel," *Business 2.0*, June 1, 2005.
La Franco, Robert, "It's All About Visuals," *Forbes*, May 22, 1995.
Shaw, Dan, "For Yubbies (Young Urban Bourgeois Bohemians)," *The New York Times*, July 10, 1994, p. 31.
Sherwood, James, "Urban Warrior," *Independent*, October 18, 1998.
"Urban Lifestyle," *Retail Week*, November 20, 1998.
Zinn, Laura, et al, "Teens—Here Comes the Biggest Wave," *Business Week*, April 11, 1994.

—Ellen D. Wernick
—update: Christina M. Stansell

V Verbatim.

Verbatim Corporation

1200 W.T. Harris Boulevard
Charlotte, North Carolina 28262
U.S.A.
Telephone: (704) 547-6500
Fax: (704) 547-6813
Web site: http://www.verbatim.com

Wholly Owned Subsidiary of Mitsubishi Chemical
   Corporation
Incorporated: 1969 as Information Terminals Corporation
Employees: 60
Sales: $130 million (2005)
NAIC: 334613 Magnetic and Optical Recording Media
   Manufacturing

One of the world's most recognized data storage technology developers, Verbatim Corporation was one of the first manufacturers in the floppy disk industry, making its start several years after its founding in 1969. By virtue of a licensing agreement reached by the company's founder with International Business Machines (IBM), Verbatim began manufacturing floppy disks in the early 1970s, and has kept pace with the ever-changing marketplace since that time. Based in Charlotte, North Carolina, Verbatim operates as a subsidiary of Mitsubishi Chemical Corporation. Its product line includes CD recordable media, DVD recordable media, printable media, LightScribe media, USB drives, memory cards, and printer supplies.

Early History

By the mid-1960s Reid Anderson had devoted much of his life to his professional career. During the 1940s and 1950s, Anderson had spent 17 years working for Bell Laboratories developing electronic switching and storage devices, then moved on to NCR Corporation, spending two years there before arriving at the Stanford Research Institute, where he developed new products for an additional five years. Aged 46 when he ended his stay at Stanford Research Institute, Anderson was an unlikely candidate for entering into the frequently disappointing world of entrepreneurship, but in 1964 he did just that, leaving

his position at Stanford Research Institute to start his own company. Although it would be another five years before Anderson pointed himself in the right direction, his first fateful steps in 1964 would lead to the founding of one of the world's preeminent companies in the computer disk industry.

While employed at Stanford Research Institute, Anderson had been working on developing new products for an assortment of companies, "essentially starting new businesses for various companies," as he would later reflect to *Forbes.* His entrepreneurial spirit aroused, Anderson used a transistorized metronome-tuner he had designed to launch his own small business making metronomes for musicians like himself, an amateur clarinet player. The confluence of hobby and profession worked well, but after three years Anderson came to the realization that he had exhausted the market for metronomes in his area and, consequently, began looking for another business opportunity.

Following his three-year metronome venture, Anderson teamed up with a business consultant named Ray Jacobson and formed Anderson Jacobson, which produced acoustic data couplers, devices that permitted computer data to be transmitted over telephone lines. Before long, however, Anderson was drawn to the lucrative possibilities of another product. After recalling his years at Bell Laboratories when he worked on the development of magnetized tape in cassettes, Anderson was hopeful that the relatively new technology employed in the production of magnetized cassette tape would realize tremendous financial gains for a savvy entrepreneur. Anderson approached his business cohort about the idea of changing their product line, but Jacobson balked at the proposal, leaving it up to Anderson to launch the business himself.

The year was 1969 and Anderson was in his 50s, preparing to establish his own company after two less-than-spectacular efforts. He borrowed money from a bank and convinced several friends and relatives to loan him additional cash, giving him enough capital to found Information Terminals, which would be renamed Verbatim and develop into the largest manufacturer of magnetic computer floppy disks in the world. Before Anderson's fledgling company would begin its meteoric rise, however, one essential ingredient needed to be added: Information

371

Company Perspectives:

As a subsidiary of Mitsubishi Chemical Corporation, a recognized world leader in the chemical and computer industries, Verbatim is ideally positioned to take advantage of changes in the market while continuing to challenge the frontiers of data storage.

Terminals had been founded to manufacture data cassettes, not floppy disks. Anderson made the pivotal switch to that product four years after starting Information Terminals when he realized data cassettes would soon be outdated by faster 8-inch floppy disks. Floppy disks, which were used for recording, storing, and retrieving computerized data, were a revolutionary product first introduced by IBM in 1973. Anderson approached IBM, asking the behemoth company if he could license the new floppy disk technology, and IBM, more concerned with selling its expensive computers than selling $5 disks, agreed.

Explosive Growth in the 1970s Leads to Challenges

Annual sales at Anderson's Sunnyvale, California-based company before and after the licensing agreement with IBM provided ample and tangible proof of the boon floppy disk production represented. Sales in 1972 were a respectable $480,000, but two years later Anderson's signal licensing agreement with IBM had driven his company's annual revenue total to $4.3 million. Earnings had spiraled upward as well, enabling Verbatim to net more than half of what it had grossed two years earlier. Among the company's products were 8-inch floppy disks and 5.25-inch floppy disks, both of which would drive Verbatim's annual sales upward during the 1970s. By 1976, the company's annual sales had nearly tripled in two years' time, jumping to $12 million. Three years later, in 1979, the same year Verbatim became a publicly owned company, annual sales surged to $36 million, and the following year sales eclipsed the $50 million mark.

Verbatim's growth during the 1970s had been incredibly vigorous, transcending Anderson's hopeful expectations and outstripping all other floppy disk manufacturers, but as the 1980s began Verbatim became a victim of its own success. Rapid expansion had engendered a sprawling, loosely organized management structure. Uninhibited success, which had flourished for a decade, bred a debilitating complacency, and quickly the company found itself in trouble. Annual sales, which had swelled exponentially since Anderson approached IBM about obtaining a licensing agreement, recorded only a modest gain at the beginning of the 1980s, inching from $50 million in 1980 to $53 million in 1981, one year after earnings had plunged 43 percent.

At the heart of Verbatim's lackluster financial results were quality control problems wrought by lackadaisical production management and overconfidence that the future would be as bright as the past. The company had let its guard down and customers started to complain, beginning in 1980 when problems with Verbatim's floppy disks began to surface. Specifically, Verbatim had used an incorrect chemical formulation for the material used to coat their disks' media base, which was exacerbated by additional problems with the protective liner used in the disks' jackets. As the number of complaints mounted, Verbatim reeled and its once stalwart financial growth came to a stop.

The company announced a massive recall of its faulty disks, establishing a $1.5 million reserve against returns, but a recall solved only one of the many problems that had spread throughout Verbatim. To eradicate the complacency that had deleteriously affected the company, Verbatim's board of directors voted for wholesale changes, hiring Malcom Northrup, a technology manager at Rockwell International's semiconductor division, as chief executive in January 1981 and relegating Anderson to the chairman's office, which he would occupy temporarily before making his final exit from the company he had created. In the wake of this major change in leadership, Verbatim's manufacturing and testing procedures were improved and automated, giving birth to a new high-quality Datalife line of disks, which were sold with a five-year guarantee, the first in the industry.

Rebounding in the 1980s

With a new production management team installed and quality control procedures revamped, Verbatim surged back, recording a robust gain in annual sales from $53 million in 1981 to $85 million in 1983, particularly encouraging in light of the recessionary economic conditions characterizing the early 1980s. By 1983, Verbatim was touting itself as the world's largest supplier of floppy disks, supported by production facilities in the United States, Ireland, Australia, and Japan. The company's embarrassing episode with its customers had taught management a lesson, leading Verbatim to completely restructure its sales and distribution network to develop retail business, focusing on the end-user rather than distributors, software companies, and other manufacturers. As an essential part of this important strategic shift, the company launched a $4 million promotional effort in 1983, aiming its sales pitch directly at secretaries, small-business owners, educators, researchers, and computer aficionados, an audience Verbatim had previously ignored.

After the sweeping changes were completed, Verbatim once again stood on stable ground. The company trailed only IBM in the market for 8-inch disks, but held a commanding lead in the larger 5.25-inch market, making it the overall industry leader as the industry itself was set to expand substantially. In 1983 the floppy disk industry represented a $500 million market, a total that was expected to eclipse $1 billion by 1985 and reach $4 billion by the end of the decade. Considering Verbatim's number-one position in the industry and that floppy disk sales accounted for roughly 85 percent of its sales, growth prognostications such as those published in 1983 spurred expectations that the company would record commensurate growth. Ahead, however, were troubled years for Verbatim as floppy disk manufacturers became involved in a high-priced race to pioneer technological developments and as a global price war weeded out all but the strongest.

The Eastman Kodak Purchase: 1985

In 1985 Eastman Kodak Co., like numerous other large corporations, wanted to expedite its entry into the floppy disk business and share in the enormous profits that were expected to come. The company had introduced its own line of 8-, 5.25-, and 3.5-inch disks in late 1984, forming its Electronic Media Manufacturing division to superintend new business, but time was crucial and the company needed to quicken the pace. The acquisition of Verbatim presented Eastman Kodak with an opportunity to do so. In March 1985, Eastman Kodak announced its $174 million bid for Verbatim, promising to retain the company's management after its acquisition and to operate the floppy disk manufacturer as a wholly owned subsidiary.

Verbatim, meanwhile, had once again fallen on hard times, for painfully familiar reasons. Confusion about floppy disk media specifications for its largest customer, IBM, had led to the cancellation of future orders. This cancellation compounded the company's other ails, as laggard personal computer sales led to declining operating results for Verbatim. The company laid off 400 employees the week before Eastman Kodak announced its intention to acquire Verbatim, leading industry observers to speculate that Verbatim had sought Eastman Kodak out, hoping a parent company could alleviate some of its financial problems; however, it was never confirmed who approached whom first.

As the decade progressed, with Verbatim now operating as part of Eastman Kodak's Mass Memory unit, the floppy disk market became increasingly competitive, particularly because of the rapid rise of Japanese floppy disk manufacturers. By 1988, Verbatim had enough and filed a complaint with the U.S. Department of Commerce alleging that Japanese companies were violating U.S. trade laws by selling their 3.5-inch disks at prices well below fair market value. In response to the federal inquiry triggered by Verbatim, three major Japanese manufacturers, Sony Corporation, Maxell Corporation, and Kao Corporation, increased the competitive and pricing pressures they were exerting on U.S. manufacturers by opening production facilities in the United States and doubling production capacity. Adding further to Verbatim's difficulties were reported problems with the quality of its disks, which had been surfacing for a decade, preventing the company from securing large contracts with major software companies and computer manufacturers.

Sale to Mitsubishi Chemical in 1990

Against the backdrop of alleged dumping practices by Japanese manufacturers and Verbatim's increasingly precarious position, Mitsubishi Chemical Corporation, a Japanese chemical conglomerate that also manufactured optical disks and other information products, was assuming a more aggressive posture, hoping to establish a greater presence in both the U.S. and Japanese floppy disk markets as the 1990s began. Concurrently, Eastman Kodak was implementing a billion-dollar divestiture program aimed at shedding its noncore businesses. The common denominator in each company's divergent strategies was Verbatim, a nonessential component of the Eastman Kodak empire and an attractive asset for the acquisitive-minded Mitsubishi Chemical Corporation. In a transaction valued at an estimated $200 million, Mitsubishi Chemical acquired Verbatim in 1990, making Mitsubishi Chemical the largest competitor in the U.S. market for floppy disks and a considerably stronger global competitor with the absorption of Verbatim's worldwide sales network.

With a new parent company supporting its growth, Verbatim entered the 1990s invigorated, intent on becoming a more well-rounded company. The acquisition of Carlisle Memory Products in 1992 and its entry in the memory card and CD-ROM markets helped to engender a significant transformation at Verbatim, as the company diversified from its mainstay floppy disk business to become what it termed the world's largest media manufacturer. In the three years since its acquisition by Mitsubishi Chemical, the company had introduced more new image and data storage products than any other company, introducing five new product lines, featuring 16 entirely new products, in 1993 alone. On the heels of this pervasive diversification, Verbatim formed a joint venture with Sanyo Laser Products in October 1994, creating one of the largest independent CD-ROM and audio-CD producers in North America.

Despite Verbatim's focus on developing innovative products and earning the reputation as one of the industry's premier manufacturers, competitive and pricing pressures continued to hound the company as it entered the mid-1990s. In November 1994, one month after forming its joint venture with Sanyo Laser Products, Verbatim laid off 100 employees—primarily production workers—at its Charlotte, North Carolina, facility. Conversely, the company established sales offices in Argentina, Chile, Columbia, and Venezuela in July 1994, hoping to capture a lucrative portion of the burgeoning South American computer market. Both Verbatim's retreat in Charlotte and its expansion in South America were indicative of the tenuous ground occupied by even the industry's largest players in the global battle for dominance, the rigors of which were not expected to lessen as Verbatim's management plotted their course for the remainder of the decade.

The Late 1990s and Beyond

Verbatim went online in 1998, taking advantage of new opportunities afforded by the Internet. This move was particularly helpful to its Australian subsidiary, which used the Web to bolster sales and increase recognition. A Verbatim executive explained the initiative in a 1998 *Practical Accountant* article claiming, ''Our company's electronic business strategy was to help us provide our network of distributors and resellers with a 24-hour virtual store, improve our staff productivity, and get ahead of the competition.''

As part of Mitsubishi Chemical's Performance Products business segment, Verbatim entered the new millennium on solid ground. It continued to keep pace with ever-changing technology, offering new and innovative products under the Verbatim label. As CD and DVD burners gained popularity with personal computer users, the company put CD and DVD recordable media at the forefront of its product line. In 2003, the company launched its Digital Vinyl CD-R media. Each disc looked like a vinyl 45 record—the label side of the CD-R was even grooved like a 45 record.

By 2005, Verbatim was ranked the leading supplier of recordable CD and DVD media in the world by independent research firm Santa Clara Consulting Group (SCCG). According to the firm, Verbatim and its Japanese counterpart, Mitsubishi Kagaku Media, held 12.1 percent of the CD-R market and 14.6 percent of the recordable DVD market. As the leader, Verbatim stood in an enviable position. A May 2005 *Business Wire* explained, "The market for recordable CD and DVD media is being driven by the growing demand for DVD burners that write to both CD and DVD media. SCCG forecasts the worldwide installed base of DVD writers will grow from less than 100 million to over 180 million by the end of 2005. With CDs playing a vital role for recording personal music, photos and home videos, analysts expect the market for CD media to be fairly stable in the coming years." The market for DVD media was expected to increase at a more rapid rate—from 1.4 billion in 2004 to more than 3.1 billion in 2005.

During this time period, Verbatim was known throughout the industry for often being first to market new products, including higher-speed media; double-layer discs, which included more storage space; VideoGard hard coat technology; and unique products like DigitalMovie DVDs, which looked like movie reels. It also launched Blu-ray and High Definition DVD (HD-DVD) recordable and rewritable media in anticipation of the release of high definition drives and recorders in late 2005. As the leading supplier of media storage products, Verbatim

stood on familiar ground. The company had learned from the mistakes of the 1970s and 1980s, however, and had emerged as a solid, customer-friendly company. Indeed, Verbatim appeared poised for growth in the years to come.

Principal Competitors

Hitachi Maxell Ltd.; Sony Corporation; TDK Corporation.

Further Reading

"Case Study: Verbatim Picks Accpac," *Practical Accountant,* November 1998, p. S7.

Isaac, Daniel, "Verbatim Left Adrift as Disk Probe Brings Industry Sea Change," *PC Week,* February 20, 1989, p. 65.

"Kodak Offers $174M in Bid for Verbatim," *Electronic News,* March 18, 1985, p. 20.

"MKC Slims Down and Beefs Up," *Chemical Week,* April 4, 1990, p. 10.

Nathans, Stephen F., "The Editor's Spin," *Emedia,* January 2003, p. 8.

Shipley, Chris, "Verbatim Lays Off 400," *PC Week,* November 12, 1985, p. 184.

"Verbatim Increases Lead in Recordable and Rewritable CD and DVD Media Markets," *Business Wire,* May 31, 2005.

"Verbatim/MKM Announces Development Plans for Blu-ray and HD-DVD Media," *Business Wire,* January 4, 2005.

"Verbatim: Taking Charge of Change," *Managing Office Technology,* July 1993, p. 71.

Verna, Paul, "Sanyo Forms Venture with Verbatim," *Billboard,* October 15, 1994, p. 86.

Weigner, Kathleen K., "The One That Almost Got Away," *Forbes,* January 31, 1983, p. 46.

Wingis, Chuck, "Verbatim Widens Its View of Expanding 'Floppy Disc' Field," *Advertising Age,* March 21, 1983, p. 4.

—Jeffrey L. Covell
—update: Christina M. Stansell

VICTORINOX·

Victorinox AG

Schmiedgasse 57
CH-6438
Ibach-Schwyz
Switzerland
Telephone: 41 (0) 41 81 81 211
Fax: 41 (0) 41 81 81 511
Web site: http://www.victorinox.com

Private Company
Incorporated: 1891 as Swiss Cutlery Guild
Employees: 1,000
Sales: $337.1 million (2005 est.)
NAIC: 332211 Cutlery and Flatware (Except Precious)
Manufacturing; 332212 Hand and Edge Tool
Manufacturing

For more than 100 years, Victorinox AG has supplied knives to Swiss Army soldiers. Each day, the company produces 34,000 Swiss Army knives, 38,000 pocket tools, and 30,000 household, kitchen, and professional knives. Approximately 90 percent of its production is exported to more than 100 countries. From repairing the space shuttle to emergency tracheotomies, Victorinox's products have been used throughout the world. In fact, several U.S. presidents have commissioned personalized versions of the Swiss Army pocket knife and the Museum of Modern Art in New York features Victorinox's products in its design collection.

19th-Century Alpine Origins

Carl Elsener was born in 1860 to Balthasar Elsener-Ott, one of a long line of haberdashers in Zug, Switzerland. Instead of taking up hats, Elsener learned the craft of knife-making and apprenticed in Paris and Tuttlingen, Germany, where he specialized in surgical quality instruments and razors. Elsener began making knives for himself on January 1, 1884, in Ibach, south of Geneva in the pastoral canton of Schwyz, the birthplace of the Swiss Confederation. A former mill on the Tobelach River (Tobel Stream) housed Elsener's first workshop. The first Swiss Army knives were reproductions of pocket knives mass-produced in Soligen, Ger-

many. A blade, punch, can opener, and screwdriver folded into the knife's handle. Elsener began making them for the Swiss Army in 1891, after organizing the Swiss Cutlery Guild of 37 craftsmen in order to ease the district's severe employment deficit, which was forcing its agricultural labor base to seek greener pastures in foreign lands.

Elsener was not the only knife maker granted a contract. Although the Fabrique nationale d'armes in Bern had turned down the chance to supply pocket knives for the army, the Forges de Vallorbe was another early supplier. Around the dawn of the 20th century, Paul Boechat & Cie (based in the Francophone Jura canton), later to become Wenger S.A., also became a supplier, giving rise to decades of apparently contradictory claims of authenticity from the rival manufacturers. The Swiss government would continue to maintain the right of both of these two companies to manufacture official Swiss Army knives.

Many variations of the original Soldier's Knife ensued: farmers, students, and cadets alike could have their own namesake folding assortment of tools. Elsener's stroke of genius came when he whittled down the original knife's clunky design, adding two new features for the benefit of officers, who unlike enlistees typically had to buy their own knives. A small, sharp "erasing" blade was useful for scraping off mistakes in paperwork handwritten by pen. A corkscrew helped enhance the officers' dining and socializing. The six blades required only two springs. The "Offiziersmesser," the official knife of the Swiss Army, was registered for trademark protection on June 12, 1897. When later offered for sale to civilians, the knives sported bright red handles to aid their visibility in snow. The original Army models were housed simply in a metal case.

The company's tinkering did not end with the Officer's Knife. Its success spawned knives with various additional appendages, including a saw, scissors, tweezers, and magnifying glass. The Swiss Champ performed 30 different functions. The 24-tool "Champion" has been displayed in New York's Museum of Modern Art and the Staatliches Museum fur Angewandte Kunst in Munich as a pinnacle of product design. In the 1990s, it retailed for about $90; the six-blade Classic sold for $18.

The company began using a Swiss White Cross to identify its wares in 1909. Elsener dubbed the line with the trademark "Victoria" in honor of his mother, who died the same year. The -inox suffix was attached in 1921, a designation for the stainless steel newly introduced into the knives' production. In the 1920s, the field of craftsmen supplying pocket knives to the Swiss Army was thinned to only Victorinox and Wenger.

Mid 20th-Century Rise to Prominence

In 1937, the Forschner Butcher Scale Company of New Britain, Connecticut, began importing Victorinox butcher knives. American buyers were not introduced to Swiss Army Knives en masse, however, until they were sold at overseas army bases after World War II. Forschner was also a venerable family-owned business, founded in 1855. Swiss Army knives replaced butcher scales in its product lineup after it was sold in 1957.

So compact were the knives that appendages often served more than one function. For example, in 1951 Victorinox received a patent for its new can opener, which was said to work easily and not leave ragged edges. The end of the can opener had been fashioned into a small screwdriver blade. (One unstated function that had always been included with screwdriver blades was that they spared the knife blades from being ruined in prying open containers or twisting screws loose.) Victorinox also made the knife lighter by using aluminum alloy rather than nickel and silver in the separators.

In 1960, the KGB and Soviet press mulled over a Swiss Army knife, among the ingenious Western spy equipment found on Francis Gary Powers when his U2 was downed over Russia. Victorinox maintained an enduring relationship with pilots, who had a natural affinity for compact, lightweight devices. One aviator even reported using his Swiss Army knife to free himself from burning wreckage. The knives would later be carried aboard the space shuttle.

Forschner became the exclusive Victorinox distributor for the United States in 1972. This was documented formally in 1983. Forschner was sold again in 1974, to investor Louis Marx, Jr., who sold the knives through mass-market retailers instead of just outdoor supply stores. The company went public in 1981; one significant investor was Charles Elsener, president of Victorinox.

In 1976, Victorinox began supplying the Germany army with pocket knives—sporting a German eagle rather than the Swiss cross. After the United States, Germany was the firm's biggest market.

Spinning Off New Products into the 1980s and 1990s

Some earlier brand extensions were the survival kits Victorinox had assembled as a natural complement to its pocket-knives. A broader diversification began in earnest after Forschner registered the Swiss Army name as a trademark in the 1980s, clearing the way for product spinoffs such as sunglasses and wristwatches. The watches, which retailed between $75 and $500, performed beyond expectations. The granting of the trademark provoked some public questioning since the Swiss Military Department did not require royalty payments in return. It did stipulate, however, that such products be made in Switzerland and be of "exceptional quality." In 1996, Forschner, then known as Swiss Army Brands, did agree to pay royalties, however.

The deal prompted a lawsuit from Precise Imports Corp., U.S. and Canadian importer of Wenger knives, which was settled in 1992. Forschner retained the rights to use the Swiss Army trademark on its compasses, timepieces, and sunglasses, while Precise could use it in marketing other non-knife items. Watches under the Wenger brand did appear in stores opposite Victorinox brand watches (made by a separate Swiss supplier). In 1992 and 1993, Canada and the Caribbean were added to Forschner's exclusive sales territory.

The connotation of quality possessed by Swiss Army knives helped U.S. distributor Forschner build a considerable business selling the knives as promotional items imprinted with sponsor's logos. Lyndon Johnson reportedly gave away 4,000 of the knives embossed with his signature, starting an enduring White House tradition. Approximately 100 companies bundled Swiss Army knives with their wares to entice consumers in the 1990s. Massachusetts-based Cyrk, Inc. specialized in this type of marketing.

Pharmaceutical companies such as Eli Lilly bought hundreds of thousands of the knives to promote new drugs. In 1989, Forschner sold nearly $10 million worth of them this way. The knives made medical news more than once, being used by doctors in emergency in-flight tracheotomy operations to save choking airline passengers. Not surprisingly, a special blade was eventually created for this purpose, as well as a tool for pulling cotton out of medicine bottles.

The renewed vigor of Victorinox in the 1980s and 1990s inevitably began to arouse competitors. Schrade Cutlery introduced a German version of the knife. Wenger made an agreement with Buck in 1991 to market knives under the well-known American brand name.

In 1992, Forschner sued to prevent the Arrow Trading Co. from importing Chinese clones displaying a white cross and shield and the words "Swiss Army." Victorinox introduced the genuine article to the Chinese market in 1993, when worldwide sales totaled $148 million (only $83,000 of this garnered in China).

Various refinements helped broaden the knife's appeal. Victorinox attempted to make the knives more attractive to female buyers by offering them in various colors. The Executive model, a small knife featuring tools such as a nail file and orange peeler, sought to cut out a place for Swiss Army knives in the business world. The SwissCard embodied the concept in the form of a "credit card" a fraction of an inch thick, which sported a toothpick, tweezers, letter opener, pen, and scissors.

In the mid-1990s, Victorinox had an 80 percent market share for Swiss Army knives outside Switzerland. Sales to the Swiss

Key Dates:

1884: Carl Elsener begins making knives in Ibach.
1891: Elsener begins to make knives for the Swiss Army.
1897: The "Offiziersmesser," the official knife of the Swiss Army, is registered for trademark protection.
1909: The company begins using a Swiss White Cross to identify its wares; Elsener dubs the line with the trademark "Victoria" in honor of his deceased mother.
1921: The -inox suffix is attached, a designation for the stainless steel newly introduced into the knives' production.
1937: The Forschner Butcher Scale Company of New Britain, Connecticut, begins importing Victorinox butcher knives.
1972: Forschner becomes the exclusive Victorinox distributor for the United States.
1976: Victorinox begins to supply the German army with pocket knives.
1996: Forschner changes its name to Swiss Army Brands Inc. (SABI).
2002: The company acquires all remaining shares of SABI.
2005: Victorinox acquires competitor Wenger.

Army itself had dwindled to less than 1 percent of the company's output. Victorinox also made kitchen knives carrying the Forschner brand name, as well as daggers and kitchen knives for the Swiss Army. Victorinox made 400 different chefs' knives as well as at least as many variations on the Swiss Army knife. Only a fraction of these models (40), however, were marketed in the United States.

Forschner changed its name to Swiss Army Brands, Inc. (SABI) in the middle of the decade to reflect the company's principal focus. Its sales were $130.01 million in 1996. Swiss Army brand extensions earned nearly half of this; the knives themselves earned slightly more than one-third.

Cutting into New Turf and a New Century

As it approached the new millennium, Victorinox exported 90 percent of its production. As Carl Elsener reported, "We receive many letters from abroad which make us proud of our product, but also of Switzerland. To be able to advertise Switzerland and Swiss quality is a great honour for Victorinox."

Elsener summarily dismissed the concept of moving pocket knife production overseas in order to slash labor costs and customs duties. He cited the company's stated mission of providing employment in its rural environment (headquartered in a town with a population of 3,500) as well as the selling power of Swiss craftsmanship. The plant manufactured 34,000 pocket-knives per day.

Victorinox boasted of its new factory's efforts to minimize ecological impact. The plant was heated primarily through energy recovered from its own manufacturing operations. In addition, 100 adjacent apartments also shared this heat source. Other environmental conservation measures included recycling industrial waste.

Victorinox AG celebrated the 100th anniversary of its "Offiziersmesser" in 1997. Although the Swiss Army knife had remained a bestseller throughout the century, the firm continued to refine its mainstay as well as develop new products. The calls of new markets, such as Latin America, could be heard echoing through the Alps, and the village's workshops hummed with activity in response.

The company was well positioned to handle the challenges it faced in the new millennium. The terrorist attacks in 2001, which led to strict travel restrictions and a slowdown in consumer spending, cut into company sales of Swiss Army knives. In fact, sales of Victorinox's knives reportedly fell by as much as 50 percent when the knives were no longer allowed on planes. The opening of a new SABI store in New York's SoHo district was also set back by more than a month as a result of the attacks. The company experienced another blow in 2003 when Switzerland decided to cut its military forces by one half.

Despite facing uncertain times, Victorinox forged ahead. It teamed up with SABI in 2001 to create Victorinox Swiss Army Watch AG, an international watch company. It purchased the remaining shares of SABI the following year, taking the U.S.-based company private. Sue Rechner, SABI's new president, commented on the deal in an October 2002 *National Jeweler* article. "Now that we don't have to worry about shareholders," she claimed, "we will be far more flexible and agile. The purchase by Victorinox allows us to be more competitive, because we can redeploy resources at the drop of a hat. We can concentrate on our core business, instead of worrying about how to make money in the short-term."

Victorinox's next big move came in 2005 when it added competitor Wenger S.A. to its arsenal. Both companies maintained their individual identities and expected the union to be beneficial on several levels. For Wenger, it provided much needed financial relief and would allow production to continue. The merger also kept the manufacture of genuine Swiss Army knives in Switzerland and put both companies on solid footing to compete with cheap imitations that were surfacing abroad, especially in China. Together, Victorinox and Wenger produced more than 25.7 million knives each year.

Victorinox's strategy during this time period included the introduction of unique and inventive products while continuing the longstanding tradition of providing top quality knives, pocket tools, and watches. Many new versions of the Swiss Army knife were being launched in order to combat weak sales. New knives that had flash memory sticks, glow-in-the-dark handles, and other digital features were hitting store shelves. Wenger introduced Evolution, a new line of ergonomic knives, to the American market in 2005. Although Victorinox had battled unprecedented challenges over the past several years, it stood in an enviable position as the sole manufacturer of the genuine Swiss Army knife. Carl Elsener and his management team were confident the company was prepared to overcome any future challenges that may come its way.

Principal Competitors

Buck Knives Inc.; Swank Inc.; Timex Corporation.

Further Reading

Andreae, Christopher, ''Definitely Officer Material,'' *Christian Science Monitor,* June 25, 1997.

Bourjaily, Philip, ''The Swiss Army Knife,'' *Sports Afield,* July 1, 1994.

Bucher, Delf, ''Pfiffige Werkzeugkästen für sämtliche Hosentaschen,'' *Tages-Anzeiger,* February 2, 1997.

''But Will They Open Cans?,'' *Time,* September 10, 1990, p. 63.

George, Rose, ''The Swiss Army Knife: Survival of the Sharpest,'' *Irish Independent,* May 10 2005.

Harding, Luke, ''G2: Cut Down: A Blade, a Bottle Opener, and a File,'' *Guardian,* July 5, 2005.

Meeks, Fleming, ''Blade Runner,'' *Forbes,* October 15, 1990.

Merki, Kurt-Emil, ''Nicht jedermann hat's im Sack,'' *Tages-Anzeiger,* February 2, 1997.

Norman, Geoffrey, ''Making the Blade,'' *Forbes,* November 25, 1991.

Olson, Elizabeth, ''Still Swiss and Still Sharp,'' *New York Times,* May 1, 2005.

Pullin, Richard, ''Swiss Army Alleges Trademark Infringement,'' *Reuters Business Report,* December 18, 1996.

Rychetnik, Joseph, ''A Perplexity of Pocket Tools,'' *Knives '96,* Northbrook, Ill.: DBI Books, 1995, pp. 21–29.

Sains, Ariane, ''Swiss Army Swells Ranks,'' *Adweek's Marketing Week,* June 4, 1990, p. 24.

Strandberg, Keith W., ''Victorinox Buys Back Shares of Swiss Army Brands,'' *National Jeweler,* October 1, 2002.

Strauss, Gary, ''Swiss Army Forced to Get Resourceful,'' *USA Today,* November 1, 2001.

''Swiss Army Knife Cuts Wide Swath: Profits Rise As It Carves Bigger Niche,'' *Charlotte Observer,* September 6, 1992, p. 7B.

''Swiss Victorinox Buys Local Wenger,'' *German News Digest,* April 26, 2005.

Tagliabue, John, ''Red-Hot Battle Over Red-Handled Knives: Distributor of Famous Swiss Army Gadget Sues to Stop Sales of Chinese Knockoffs,'' *Charlotte Observer,* September 11, 1994.

Weiser, Benjamin, ''It Slices, It Dices, It Outrages the Swiss: A Ruling Favoring Chinese Imitations Cuts Army Knife's Original Makers to the Bone,'' *Washington Post,* July 30, 1994.

—Frederick C. Ingram
—update: Christina M. Stansell

Virbac Corporation

3200 Meacham Boulevard
Fort Worth, Texas 76137
U.S.A.
Telephone: (817) 831-5030
Fax: (817) 831-8327
Web site: http://www.virbaccorp.com

Public Company
Incorporated: 1987 as Virbac Inc.
Employees: 262
Sales: $67.1 million (2003)
Stock Exchanges: Pink Sheets
Ticker Symbol: VBAC
NAIC: 325412 Pharmaceutical Preparation Manufacturing

Virbac Corporation is a Fort Worth, Texas-based manufacturer of health and pet-care products, primarily for cats and dogs, such as shampoos and skin care products, dental products, vitamins and supplements, medicated feed additives, flea and tick products, wormers, ear cleaners, and hairball remedies. In addition, the company makes tropical fish products, including aquarium water conditioners and test strips. To a lesser degree, Virbac is involved in the specialty chemical business, producing rodenticides, pest control products, and home, lawn, and garden products. Virbac also offers private label and contract manufacturing services for animal health and specialty chemicals industries. The company maintains two major facilities. Its Fort Worth 127,000-square-foot operation houses manufacturing, warehousing, distribution, and office functions. Most of Virbac's products not regulated by the Environmental Protection Agency (EPA) are manufactured in Fort Worth. The second plant, 176,000 square feet in size, is located in Bridgeton, Missouri. Because it is an EPA and Food and Drug Administration (FDA) registered facility, it manufactures most of the company's EPA and FDA regulated products. Bridgeton also handles Virbac's contract manufacturing business. Virbac is a public company, majority owned by France-based Virbac SA. Its shares are traded on a Pink Sheets basis, due to a delisting by the NASDAQ following an accounting scandal that emerged in 2003 and resulted in the resignation of the chief executive officer and the chief financial officer, as well as a probe by the Securities and Exchange Commission (SEC).

Company Founded in Early 1980s

Virbac considers its founder to be Roger Brandt, a Texas businessman involved in the pharmaceutical industry. In 1981, he spotted an opening in the pet-care field to produce skin care products developed specifically for dogs. At the time, veterinarians had nothing to prescribe for dogs other than human dermatological products, but these were not suited to the task. Brandt formed a company called Allerderm in 1982 to address this need, initially producing anti-itch shampoos. Over the next five years, the business established itself in the pet-care field and attracted the attention of Virbac SA, a global veterinary pharmaceutical manufacturer. The French company acquired Allerderm in 1987 and changed its name to Virbac Inc., then sold off part of the company in a public offering of stock held in 1994. Virbac performed well in the 1990s, as did the entire pet industry, which was worth about $25 billion by the later years of that decade and enjoying annual growth in the 15 percent range. To form a larger and more competitive business, in 1999 Virbac, which was doing about $15 million a year in sales, was merged with a larger pet-care company, Agri-Nutrition Group, a St. Louis-area manufacturer of dental hygiene, nutritional, and grooming products for cats and dogs that was doing about $35 million in business each year.

Agri-Nutrition Gains Independence in Early 1990s

Agri-Nutrition grew out of the Health Industries Business of Purina Mills Inc. In 1993, an investor group acquired the unit through a subsidiary called PM Resources, Inc. (PM standing for Purina Mills), which then became part of a Delaware corporation, PM Agri-Nutrition Group, formed three months later. In July 1994, the company was taken public, netting $12.1 million that was used to fuel expansion. The company assumed the Agri-Nutrition Group Ltd. name in March 1995, and by the end of the month paid $3.3 million for Zema Corporation, a North Carolina maker of health care and pet grooming products. In August of that year, Agri-Nutrition spent another $5.5 million for St. JON Laboratories, a Los Angeles-based company that manufactured oral hygiene, dermatological, and gastrointestinal products for cats and dogs and also maintained a London, United Kingdom-based subsidiary, St. JON VRx Products. Next, in September 1997, Agri-Nutrition paid nearly $2.5 million in cash and stock to acquire Mardel Laboratories, a Glendale Heights, Illinois, company that manufactured and marketed pet care products for cats, dogs, birds, small animals, and fresh water and marine fish. It also offered pond accessories. Agri-Nutrition now split its business into two units: the Pet Health Care Division, focusing on pet owners, and PM Resources, which took care of the company's private label and contract manufacturing operations.

Although Agri-Nutrition was more than twice as large as Virbac Inc., the later was considered the acquirer because its parent company, Virbac SA received 60 percent of the voting stock of the combined business. The merger was completed in March 1999, with Pascal Boissy, president of Virbac SA, assuming the chairmanship, and Virbac's CEO Dr. Brian A. Crook staying on as chief executive. Agri-Nutrition's CEO, Bruce G. Baker, became an executive vice-president of the enlarged company, which settled on the large Fort Worth facility as its headquarters. Crook's tenure would be brief, however. Within a matter of weeks he resigned to "pursue other interests," according to a company statement, and was replaced by Thomas L. Bell. The son of a truck driver, the 40-year-old Bell had devoted his adult working life to the animal and livestock healthcare industry. After earning a chemistry degree, with a minor in business administration, from Mount Union College in Ohio, he took a job as a sales representative in the animal health division of Diamond Shamrock. Several years later he joined the Fort Dodge Animal Health subsidiary of American Cyanamid, where he spent 13 years, rising to the rank of vice-president for the International Animal Health and Nutrition Division.

Virbac devoted the rest of 1999 to consolidating and streamlining its business. Agri-Nutrition's Chicago and Los Angeles distribution facilities were shut down and their operations transferred to Fort Worth. All of the Chicago manufacturing was also moved to Texas, as were much of the Los Angeles manufacturing operations, leaving only a limited amount of production and marketing business to be conducted in California. In time, that would also be eliminated, leaving just the manufacturing units in Fort Worth and the St. Louis area.

With its house in order, Virbac anticipated that within a few years it would increase revenues, which totaled less than $44 million in fiscal 1999, to $100 million by the end of 2004, as well as $20 million in earnings. Management was banking on its relationship with Virbac SA to spur growth, as well as riding the wave of the pet industry, one of the strongest growing sectors of the U.S. economy. It signed agreements to have Virbac SA distribute its products internationally, as well as to distribute

Virbac SA's products in the United States and Canada. Virbac also had two drugs in development to treat horse parasites, and pharmaceutical Pfizer was set to market and distribute them under a 15-year agreement, pending approval from the FDA.

Virbac achieved a solid start in its first full year since the merger, recording sales of $53.7 million in 2000, a 10 percent improvement over the combined sales from the previous year. As a result of increased sales and cost savings from the consolidation of the two operations, the company realized net income of more than $3.6 million. Virbac benefited from the increase sale of oral hygiene and dermatological products and a bump in its contract manufacturing business. Virbac's consumer brands division also acquired the rights to Pet-Tabs, a cat and dog nutritional supplement, that management hoped would add another $5 million in sales in 2001. Business was also boosted in 2001 with the introduction of Iverhart Plus, a dog heartworm prevention product. In addition, the company gained FDA approval for the two Pfizer products and began manufacturing Worm-X, a dog wormer, and Virbamec, a wormer for cattle. To accommodate is expanded production, a 1,500-square-foot manufacturing suite was added to the Bridgeton plant. Bell touted the potential of the three new products, telling the press that they offered a $640 million market opportunity. If true, the company was well on its way to meeting Bell's announced goal of "reaching a $20 million bottom line on a $100 million top line by 2004."

At the end of 2001, management reported revenues of $60.6 million and net income of $1.3 million, a far cry from keeping pace with Bell's goal, and eventually these numbers would come under scrutiny. In the meantime, the task of reaching the $100 million level grew even more difficult as Virbac began experiencing increased competition in the pet store sales channel as well as from products sold by mass merchants, affecting sales in all product categories. To offset this deteriorating situation, the company began seeking ways to sell their products through mass-market outlets such as supermarkets, drug store chains, and discounters. Revenues were also hurt by the decision to cut back on low-margin contract manufacturing in order to devote resources to Virbac's branded products. For the year 2002, management reported sales of $63.8 million and net income of $3.4 million.

In 2003, Virbac sought to improve its product mix by increasing its presence in the animal pharmaceutical business through acquisition. In August, it added Delmarva Laboratories, a small Virginia-based veterinary pharmaceuticals company that manufactured two antibiotics and two euthanasia drugs. A month later, Virbac paid $15.1 million for the veterinary medicine business of King Pharmaceuticals, a Tennessee pharmaceutical company that primarily manufactured drugs for human consumption and was looking to divest non-core products. As a result, Virbac added several products in the small-animal endocrinology market as well as products to treat gland-related conditions, the most important of which was Soloxine, used in dogs as a thyroid hormone replacement. Other King products included Pancrezyme, Tumil-K, Uroeze, and Ammonil.

Scandal Emerges in Fall 2003

Wall Street was pleased with the acquisitions, as reflected by the rising price of company shares, which reached a high of

Key Dates:

1982: Allerderm is founded.
1987: Virbac SA acquires Allerderm, which is renamed Virbac Inc.
1993: Agri-Nutrition is founded.
1994: Agri-Nutrition is taken public.
1999: Virbac and Agri-Nutrition merge.
2004: Accounting errors lead to the resignation of Virbac's CEO and CFO.

$8.73 at the end of October. Just two weeks later, however, Virbac became mired in scandal. An outside auditor, PricewaterhouseCoopers, raised serious questions about the company's accounting practices and refused to sign off on its third quarter numbers. The price of Virbac shares plunged, slipping 22 percent before the NASDAQ halted the trading of the stock until the company was able to provide some clarification. In mid-December 2003, Virbac admitted that it had been improperly counting revenue since 2001. At the same time, it announced that Bell was taking a voluntary leave of absence with pay until an investigation was completed by the company's audit committee. David Eller, a Houston drug industry executive, was hired to step in as interim CEO.

According to the *Fort Worth Star-Telegram*, Virbac booked revenues for products that were either returned later or destroyed after the lapse of their expiration date. Moreover, the company "shipped products from its veterinary division to wholesalers during the final days of several quarters to boost revenues in those quarters but held off on final delivery until the subsequent quarters had begun." Virbac also "booked revenue from some products in its manufacturing and livestock division at the time of shipment. Those orders should have been treated as consignments, with no revenue counted until Virbac had been paid, the company said." As a result, Virbac's net income had been inflated by $900,000 in 2001 and $1.3 million in 2002. Reported sales fell from $60.6 million to $56.3 million in 2001, and $62 million from $63.8 million in 2002.

Law firms representing shareholders wasted little time in filing lawsuits against Virbac, alleging it had misrepresented its

financial condition. Then, in January 2004, the NASDAQ delisted the company, and Bell, along with CFO Joseph Rougraff, resigned. Soon the SEC launched a probe, the scope and nature of which was uncertain until January 2005, when the company received a "Wells notice," a formal warning the SEC issued to companies, indicating that the commission might pursue civil action. Not only did the company face the prospect of SEC penalties and have to contend with shareholder suits, it also had to deal with lenders. The company's mounting legal and accounting fees left insufficient cash to repay borrowing. As a result, Virbac announced in May 2005 that if lenders failed to renegotiate the terms of several loans it might seek bankruptcy protection. At least for the near term, Virbac's prospects were in question.

Principal Subsidiaries

PM Resources, Inc.; St. JON Laboratories, Inc.; Francodex Laboratories, Inc.; Virbac AH, Inc.

Principal Competitors

The Hartz Mountain Corporation; Heska Corporation; IDEXX Labs, Inc.

Further Reading

Banstetter, Trebor, "Fort Worth, Texas-Based Maker of Pet Health Products Touts New Offerings," *Fort Worth Star Telegram*, February 1, 2000.

Manning, Margie, "Bow WOW!," *St. Louis Business Journal*, March 15, 2002, p. 1.

Perotin, Maria M., "Animal Products Maker Virbac Issues Notice on Debt," *Fort Worth Star-Telegram*, May 10, 2005.

——, "Texas-Based Animal Health Products Maker Admits to Inflating Revenue," *Fort Worth Star-Telegram*, December 19, 2003.

Shlachter, Barry, "Trading of Stock Halted for Fort Worth, Texas Animal Health Products Maker," *Fort Worth Star-Telegram*, November 14, 2003.

Smith, Rod, "Agri-Nutrition, Virbac Complete Pet Care Merger," *Feedstuffs*, April 5, 1999, p. 6.

Yu, Roger, "Animal-Drug Maker Virbac's CEO, CFO Quit Amid Profit Scandal," *Dallas Morning News*, February 10, 2004.

—Ed Dinger

W Jordan (Cereals) Ltd.

Holme Mills, Langford Road
Biggleswade SG18 9JY
United Kingdom
Telephone: (+44) 1767 318222
Fax: (+44) 1767 600695
Web site: http://www.jordans.co.uk

Private Company
Incorporated: 1981
Employees: 420
Sales: £93.2 million ($165.75 million) (2003)
NAIC: 311230 Breakfast Cereal Manufacturing

W Jordan (Cereals) Ltd. is the United Kingdom's largest independently owned breakfast cereals and snacks producers. Owned and operated by the Jordan family, under brothers William J. and David Jordan, the company has established itself as a major among the global breakfast cereal by targeting the ''natural'' cereals niche. The company produces a variety of additive-free cereals, including its top-selling Country Crispy and its first cereal, Original Crunchy, among others. The company produces its own line of cereal bars, and since the 2000s has added a number of other snack foods, including chips. Initially a producer of organic cereals, Jordan was nevertheless a pioneering member of the Guild of Conservation Grade Producers, which allows farmers and food producers to operate under a less stringent set of requirements than those followed by organic food manufacturers. Jordan has also joined with fellow natural foods producer Yeo Valley to launch a venture in order to place vending machines featuring its foods in Britain's schools, thus offering to students an alternative to traditional snacks and soft drinks. Jordan remained based in Biggleswade, where the Jordan family has operated flour mills since the 1800s. In 2005, the company celebrated its 150th anniversary.

Origins as a 19th Century Miller

The Jordan family were originally farmers in the North Bedfordshire region of England, with roots dating back to the 18th century and perhaps earlier. Toward the end of that century, William Jordan began renting out his draught horses to the local miller. Jordan's son, also named William, took over the operation of the family farm around the turn of the 19th century and led the family into milling itself, buying up a mill at Eaton Socon. Jordan's sons Alfred and William III continued in the milling and flour trade. Alfred went to Biggleswade, renting the Holme Mill there, while William set up a flour depot in London. Later, William Jordan III returned to Bedfordshire, where he took over operation of the Holme Mill in 1855.

The Jordan family continued to lease the Holme Mill into the 1890s. In 1893, however, the family purchased the mill outright. They then remodeled the mill, replacing the original millstones with new rolling mill equipment in 1896. Just three years later, however, the mill burned down. The family rebuilt the mill, designed from the outset as a rolling mill. In this way, the Jordans' mill became one of the most modern and efficient in the region.

William Jordan III remained in control of the Holme Mill until his death at the age of 93. (His son William IV had meanwhile set up his own mill nearby). The mill was then bought by William III's grandson, William V, who had returned from a stint as a pilot for the British Air Force during World War II. William V maintained the mill's flour operation but also extended the business in the 1950s, using the mill's waste product to launch a business producing animal feed. Jordan also built a strong business providing flour packaged under third-party and private-label brand names.

The next generation of Jordans, David and older brother William VI, who preferred to be called Bill, came of age in the 1960s. Bill Jordan initially became a professional musician, touring the United Kingdom and the United States as a drummer in a band in the late 1960s and early 1970s. While in the United States, however, Bill Jordan was introduced to the newly emerging category of health foods, most importantly the first organic cereals. One of the earliest and most popular of the new cereals was called granola, which featured toasted oats and honey.

Breakfast Cereal Producer in the 1970s

Bill Jordan gave up touring as a musician in the early 1970s in order to return to Biggleswade and launch his own granola recipe for the U.K. market. Jordan, who later oversaw the company's commercial development, was joined by brother David, who became responsible for leading the group's production. Together with an engineering partner, the Jordans designed their first production line, built around a used bakery oven. By 1972, the brothers had developed their own granola recipe, which they called Original Crunchy, based on all-natural ingredients. Soon after, they set out touring Britain's county fairs and food exhibitions in order to drum up customers. In the meantime, William Jordan V maintained the company's animal feed and flour business.

The early years were difficult ones for the company as the Jordans met with reluctance from the U.K. retail sector to accept the new type of cereal. Slowly, however, the company managed to win over a growing number of customers. Jordan was aided by the increasing awareness among British consumers of nutrition, health, and environmental issues. By 1980, the company had managed to place its cereals on the shelves of a number of the United Kingdom's small but growing network of health food stores.

The company incorporated in 1981 as W Jordan (Cereals) Ltd. By then, Jordan had launched its breakthrough product, the Original Crunchy Bar, presenting the company's granola recipe in a cereal bar format. Introduced in 1980, this product paved the way for the company's acceptance by the United Kingdom's mainstream grocers. Supermarket group Waitrose Ltd., one of the country's largest, became the first in the mainstream retailers sector to place Jordan products on its shelves.

Strong sales of the Jordan brand in the Waitrose network provided the company with the calling card it needed to win shelf space among Britain's other retailers, especially market leaders such as Teisco and Sainsbury. Jordan capitalized on its popularity, rolling out a wider range of products. Among these, the company extended its breakfast cereals range with new cereals and recipes, including muesli, as well as its own line of Jordan brand flour. Toward the end of the 1980s, Jordan made its first effort to move into the snack food category, launching a bagged snack called Oatsters.

In the mid-1980s, Jordan backed the formation of a new control body, the Guild of Conservation Food Producers, which established less restrictive farming practices than those required for the organic foods label. Part of the company's motivation for this was to make production easier for its producer farmers. Under the Conservation Grade label, land was no longer required to lay fallow for a three-year period, and certain classes of biodegradable fertilizers and pesticides were permitted. The Guild of Conservation Food Producers eventually attracted some 250 farmers as well as about 25 food manufacturers.

International Success in the 1990s

Sales of the Original Crunchy bar continued strongly through the decade. However, Jordan lost its leadership spot in the category to the marketing might of Mars and Quaker Oats, which launched their own cereal bars. By the early 1990s, Jordan's share of the U.K. cereals market was on the decline. In response, the company launched a multi-million pound advertising campaign. The company also developed a number of new recipes to appeal to developing consumer tastes, adding the Frusli brand, as well as a new cereal featuring freeze-dried strawberries, Country Crisp, introduced in 1991. That cereal provided Jordan with a new bestselling product. Country Crisp remained the company's largest-selling cereal into the mid-2000s.

Having established itself as a leading national brand, Jordan began a drive to transform its name into an international cereals brand. The company moved onto the European continent, then launched its cereals in the United States. As part of its drive to become an international brand, Jordan displayed a certain flexibility in order to appeal to local preferences. An example of this was the company's entry in France, which it began by producing cereals featuring bittersweet dark chocolate, the chocolate variety preferred by French consumers. This flexibility paid off for the company. By the mid-2000s, France had become the company's largest export market, accounting for more than half of the company's foreign sales.

Jordan continued rolling out new recipes into the late 1990s and early 2000s. The company made a new attempt to crack the snack food market with the launch of a new line of Oven Crisped Chips in 2000. This line, which featured flavors such as Sun-dried Tomato and Sour Cream and Chives, offered a low-fat alternative to traditional potato chips.

New Products for the 21st Century

Concerns over British nutritional habits, along with the growing problem of obesity in the United Kingdom, offered Jordan a new opportunity in the early 2000s. The presence of vending machines stocked with snack foods and soft drinks in the country's school system came under intense criticism as efforts got underway to change the country's eating habits. In 2002, Jordan teamed up with another natural foods producer, Yeo Valley, to launch a new class of vending machine featuring healthier food choices, including Jordan's own snack foods. As part of that effort, the two companies formed the joint venture The Organic and Natural Food Company. Branded as the Green Machine, the joint venture began testing its first vending machines, which also featured organic fruit juices, in early 2002. By 2003, the company had placed more than 100 Green

Key Dates:

1855: William Jordan acquires a lease to Holmes Mill in Biggleswade, England.
1893: Jordan purchases Holmes Mill, replacing the original millstones with new rolling mill equipment.
1972: Bill and David Jordan develop a granola cereal recipe, called Original Crunchy, and launch its production using a secondhand bakers oven.
1980: Original Crunchy Bar is launched.
1981: Supermarket group Waitrose agrees to stock Jordans cereals; the company incorporates as W Jordan (Cereals) Ltd.
1985: Jordans becomes a founding member of the Guild for Conservation Food Producers, establishing the Conservation Grade label.
1991: The best-selling Country Crisp cereal is introduced; the company begins international sales operations and makes its first attempt to enter the snack food category with the launch of Oatsters.
2000: Oven-Crisped Chips are launched as part of a re-entry into the snack food market.
2002: The Organic and Natural Food Company is created as a joint venture with Yeo Valley in order to introduce Green Machine vending machines.
2004: Construction begins on a 63,000-square-foot warehouse and distribution facility in Biggleswade.
2005: Bill Jordan is made a Member of the Order of the British Empire (MBE).

Machines in the country's schools. The success of the concept led the company to decide to roll out the vending machine to the general market starting in 2003.

The Jordans backed their company's development into an international brand by hiring an increasing number of non-family members, building a professional management team. The company continued this process in 2002 when both Bill and David Jordan, who had been serving as joint managing directors, moved into the chairman and vice-chairman positions, respectively. In their place, the company named Edward Olphin, formerly the company's business development director, and Rob Hitchins, who had been finance director, as new joint managing directors.

Jordan grew quickly into the mid-2000s, encouraging the company to launch a £20 million ($35 million) expansion effort in 2004. A centerpiece of the investment program was the construction of a new 63,000-square-foot warehouse and a distribution center in Biggsleswade, slated for completion before the end of 2005.

The new facility was designed to provide a home for a number of successful new products, including a new line of Frusli Bar varieties launched in 2002. In 2004, the company debuted a new line of cereal bars, the Luxury Bars, as well as low-fat muesli, Special Fruit Muesli.

By 2005, Jordan had successfully exported its products to nearly 25 countries worldwide, including Europe and the United States, as well as a number of Asian and Middle East markets. International sales by then represented some 24 percent of the group's total sales, which neared £95 million at mid-decade. In recognition of the group's contribution to the United Kingdom's organic foods market, the company won a Queen's Award in 2003. This was followed by the award of an MBE (Member of the Order of the British Empire) to Bill Jordan himself in early 2005. One of the United Kingdom's most popular cereals companies, Jordan also remained among the most successful independent concerns in its market sector.

Principal Subsidiaries

The Organic and Natural Food Company (50%).

Principal Competitors

Altria Group Inc.; Kraft Foods North America Inc.; General Mills Inc.; Kellogg Co.; Associated British Foods PLC; Dr. August Oetker KG; Quaker Oats Co.; Orkla ASA; Royal Numico N.V.

Further Reading

"Crunchy Bars Go Far to Earn Firm a Queen's Award," *Biggleswade Chronicle*, January 8, 2003.
"Cereal Company Invests 20m in Expansion Plans," *Grocer*, March 20, 2004, p. 14.
Forrest, Tracy, "No Junk Please—We're Jordans!," *Super Marketing*, May 1, 1992, p. 50.
Mason, Tania, "Jordans Ties with Yeo Valley to Push Health in Schools," *Marketing*, January 31, 2002, p. 4.
"Organic Honours," *Natrual Products Online*, January 31, 2005.

—M.L. Cohen

W.R. Berkley Corporation

475 Steamboat Road
Greenwich, Connecticut 06830
U.S.A.
Telephone: (203) 629-3000
Fax: (203) 769-4098
Web site: http://www.wrbc.com

Public Company
Incorporated: 1967 as Fine-Vest Services, Inc.
Employees: 4,736
Total Assets: $11.45 billion (2004)
Stock Exchanges: New York
Ticker Symbol: BER
NAIC: 524126 Direct Property and Casualty Insurance
   Carriers

W.R. Berkley Corporation is an insurance holding company with five major business segments: regional property casualty; specialty lines; reinsurance; alternative markets; and international. Through its subsidiaries, W.R. Berkley operates as a leading commercial lines property casualty insurance provider. The company's numerous specialty and regional subsidiaries are located in 27 states while its international arm oversees operations in Argentina and Asia.

Early History

W.R. Berkley Corporation is the creation of entrepreneur and investor William R. Berkley. Berkley got his start as an investor at the age of 12, when he began using spare money from his lawn-mowing business to buy stocks. Among his top picks at the time was Decca Record Company, which signed many of the most promising British rock artists of the 1960s. Decca's stock jumped in price from $13 to $42, encouraging Berkley to become to pursue further ventures in the stock market. In the late 1960s, the brilliant Berkley attended Harvard's business school, where he and a classmate ran a $2 million mutual fund out of their four-bedroom apartment. The fund, which formed the foundation for W.R. Berkley's predecessor (Berkley Dean & Co.), was a smash-

ing success. Its assets ballooned to $10 million by the time Berkley was out of college, and it turned out to be one of the hottest mutual funds of the period.

Berkley earned a reputation at Harvard as brilliant, arrogant, and boastful. "This guy was very confident, there's no doubt," recalled Dennis Duggan, a reporter that profiled Berkley in the 1960s for *New York Newsday.* Duggan added, "He said he'd be rich. He wanted to be one of the richest people in America. He was arrogant; he exuded it." Berkley's swaggering style earned him a cream pie in the face from his contemptuous Harvard classmates, but it apparently also helped to make him very wealthy. By the time Berkley was 23 years old, in fact, Berkley Dean & Co. was managing $10 million in mutual fund assets, as well as $15 million in other investments, and generating nearly $1 billion in annual revenues. Berkley would later attribute his cockiness to youth and simplistic views of the world but not before building the multi-million-dollar insurance holding company that became W.R. Berkley Corporation.

Berkley succeeded in the stock market during the 1960s and early 1970s by purchasing the stocks of companies with earnings that were growing faster than the economy. He was widely publicized at the time as an investment genius for his ability to sniff out undervalued stocks. In reality, much of his success at the time was the result of a strong bull market that complemented his investment strategy. When the market stalled in the early 1970s, Berkley's investment performance waned. Berkley bailed out of the stock-picking business and decided to jump into the insurance business with the purchase of Houston General Insurance Co. He bought the company because the sale price was low. However, it represented the first of a large portfolio of companies, rather than stocks, that Berkley would accrue during the next 20 years.

Growth in the 1970s and Early 1980s

Berkley took his company public in 1973 as W.R. Berkley Corporation. He invested proceeds from the offering in Houston General. Like many of his stock picks, the Houston General investment soared. Berkley sold the company 14 months later for nearly twice the purchase price. He used profits from the sale to buy other insurers. Berkley's strategy in the insurance business during the 1970s was multi-faceted. Importantly, Berkley recognized an pivotal emerging industry trend: changing financial controls for property-casualty insurers were rapidly increasing the number of investment dollars available per each dollar of capital held by the companies. The additional investment pool meant that insurers could invest more conservatively in government bonds and other low-risk instruments and still rack up healthy profits. Markets were slow to realize the significance of the changing financial controls, so Berkley was able to buy insurance companies at very low prices in relation to their future worth.

Aside from the investment dynamics of the insurance industry during the 1970s and 1980s, Berkley planned to profit from a unique operating strategy. He believed that many insurance companies, in an effort to impress competitors and customers, had grown too large. They had succeeded in setting up giant, nationwide networks that allowed them to benefit from economies of scale related to marketing, investing, and data processing. In doing so, however, they had forfeited benefits associated with operating intimately with local and regional markets. Thus, Berkley's plan was to purchase a network of independent, regional insurance companies. He then reduced expenses; one example of this strategy was the centralization of data processing tasks. At the same time, he would allow each of his companies to operate autonomously in their respective regions. In this way, managers of the subsidiaries could respond to the intricacies of their local markets and provide more personalized service to customers.

Throughout the 1970s and early 1980s, Berkley purchased a string of insurance companies, most of which he whipped into high-profit performers. In addition to regional insurers, Berkley utilized his strategy to break into the specialty insurance business. Berkley subsidiaries were eventually offering several types of unique coverage. For example, W.R. Berkley was one of only a handful of American insurance organizations that offered collision insurance on Rolls-Royces. Another of its exotic policies protected sports tournament directors from having to pay big prizes to lucky winners who, for example, shot a hole-in-one to win a contest at a golf tournament or made a record-size catch at a fishing contest. "The laws of probability are in our favor," Berkley explained in the March 1987 *Money*, adding, "Because we insure 100 sports tournaments, for example, it is unlikely we will have to pay off on very many."

Berkley achieved above average returns from his insurance companies during the 1970s and early 1980s. Furthermore, he managed to do so without incurring excessive debt or jeopardizing the financial stability of his companies. The fiscal strength of W.R. Berkley became apparent during the property-casualty industry blowout of the early 1980s. Indeed, many property-casualty insurers suffered huge losses during the downturn because returns from investments soured and claim payments outstripped investment income. Berkley, by contrast, had sacked away large cash reserves in preparation for the downturn. Furthermore, he had wisely invested most of the assets from his companies in conservative, low-risk instruments that were less impacted by stagnant stock markets.

Success Continues in the 1980s and 1990s

Besides surviving the industry shakeout relatively unscathed, Berkley took advantage of market conditions during the early and mid-1980s. For example, in his typical nonconformist style, Berkley jumped into the commercial truck insurance business during the mid-1980s while most of his competitors were trying to get out. Most commercial truck insurers at the time were suffering heavy losses for a variety of economic and regulatory reasons. Berkley, sensing an upturn in that niche, purchased Carolina Casualty Insurance Co. The market rebounded and the company was able to increase its premium volume by more than 50 percent over a five-year period.

It eventually became clear to investors that, despite Berkley's investment background and skills, the key ingredient to his company's success during the 1970s and 1980s was sound management and operating strategies. While other companies enjoyed temporary bursts of success by making risky boom-and-bust investments, Berkley's prudent business tactics allowed his company to enjoy moderate returns when investment markets were down and big gains when markets were strong. Providing evidence of the company's value-added strategy were a number of innovations that W.R. Berkley had pioneered. For example, the company was one of the first insurers to market a captive risk-retention group to businesses; the "self-insurance" groups effectively enabled companies to handle insurance needs without traditional policies. Berkley was also a pioneer in the field of environmental insurance, which protects companies against liability from accidents such as oil and chemical spills.

By 1986, the sprawling W.R. Berkley Corporation was generating about $400 million in annual revenue, an increase of nearly 100 percent over 1985. Throughout the late 1980s and early 1990s, the company's annual revenue fluctuated between $415 million and $450 million. Profits, however, grew from $7 million in 1985 to $30 million in 1986 before leveling out around a healthy $50 million annually throughout the late 1980s and into the mid-1990s. Those sales and profit figures reflected Berkley's emphasis on steady profitability rather than growth. "Profit is sanity. Volume is vanity," Berkley was quoted as saying in the July 26, 1993 issue of *Business Insurance*.

Besides capturing fat profits from his portfolio of more than 20 insurance companies, Berkley became engaged in a number of other businesses that interested him. In 1981, for example, he started National Guardian Corporation, a company that installed and serviced alarm systems. Berkley got the idea to launch the

Key Dates:

1967: William R. Berkley establishes the predecessor to W.R. Berkley Corp.
1973: The company goes public.
1981: Berkley establishes the National Guardian Corporation.
1986: W.R. Berkley is generating about $400 million in annual revenue.
1998: Preferred Employers Insurance Co. is launched.
2002: The company purchases a 20.1 percent interest Kiln plc.
2004: W.R. Berkley reports its highest net income to date.

venture after he had an alarm installed in his own home. After trying to start the company from scratch, he decided instead to build it by acquiring his competitors. Between 1983 and 1987, he purchased nearly 100 companies at a cost of about $130 million. By 1987, the company was employing 6,000 workers, generating income of $5.5 million annually, and providing alarm and security guard services throughout the northeastern United States.

In addition to National Guardian, Berkley launched Finevest Services Inc. in 1987. The venture stemmed from Berkley's chance purchase of a dairy company, which got him interested in the food business. Finevest was established as an investment and consulting firm with interests in the food and food distribution industry. Finevest Foods was created in 1987 as a holding company for four food companies that Berkley had purchased since January 1986. By 1988, Finevest Foods was distributing more than 2,200 frozen food products to 18 states. Also during the late 1980s, Berkley fired up Strategic Information Inc. to get in on the booming computer/communications industry. The firm was created to specialize in market research, and Berkley hoped to use the company to support his insurance and food holdings.

Although Berkley tinkered with other business ventures, the W.R. Berkley insurance operations remained the core of his personal empire. In fact, some of his other investments soured during the recession of the late 1980s and early 1990s. Finevest, for example, finally went bankrupt in 1991 and ended up costing Berkley a whopping $20 million. "Financially, it was a great deal of money," Berkley acknowledged in *Business Week* for September 21, 1992, adding "but that's life." In contrast, W.R. Berkley continued to flourish despite an ugly industry shakeout in the property-casualty insurance business. Indeed, as they had in the late 1970s and early 1980s, many of Berkley's competitors loaded up on risky investments such as real estate and junk bonds in an effort to boost returns. When the bottom fell out of the market, those companies got burned. Berkley, with its conservative investment portfolio and profitable operating strategy, sustained steady revenues and even managed to boost investment income. The result was healthy, relatively constant profitability.

Going into the mid-1990s, W.R. Berkley Corporation was following a strategy of creating new insurance companies and divisions rather than purchasing existing companies. Among other benefits, the strategy was designed to reduce tax liabilities.

Berkley was also increasing its emphasis on managed care in the mid-1990s and expanding overseas with planned investments in Central and South America and Asia. Finally, Berkley was stepping up its investments in the reinsurance business. Although net income dipped in 1994, W.R. Berkley continued to outperform the industry average in terms of profitability (excluding investment income). Furthermore, the company boasted a capital surplus far above the government-required minimum and above the industry average, which reflected W.R. Berkley's excellent financial condition. With an estimated net worth approaching $500 million in 1995, Berkley had achieved his youthful goal of becoming one of the wealthiest men in the United States.

W.R. Berkley in the Late 1990s and Beyond

Merger activity and turbulent global economies began to change the landscape of the insurance industry in the late 1990s. Sure enough, rumors began to surface that W.R. Berkley was looking for a suitor. After considering its options, the company chose to remain on its own and instead focused on bolstering its holdings. At this time, W.R. Berkley strengthened its reach abroad through a joint venture with Northwestern Mutual Life Insurance Co. The venture launched its first business in Argentina and planned to expand into the Philippines, Brazil, and Uruguay. International expansion was slow and deliberate, however, especially after a major financial crisis hit Asian markets.

An industry downturn led to a fall in earnings in 1998 and a loss in 1999. The company remained steadfast in its strategy to focus on specialty insurance markets that many other insurance companies left alone or were exiting. For example, W.R. Berkley created Preferred Employers Insurance Co. in 1998 to operate in California's workers' compensation market. The new subsidiary targeted small companies that were traditionally ignored by the larger insurance and managed care concerns.

W.R. Berkley's successful business strategy left it on solid ground as it entered the 2000s. It restructured its reinsurance business to focus on excess-of-loss reinsurance and changed the subsidiary's name from Signet Star Reinsurance to Berkley Insurance. It also launched InsurBanc, which offered financial services to existing clients. Not all of W.R. Berkley's ventures during this time period were successful. In 2000, the company announced plans to sell auto insurance through Priceline.com. The deal failed to reach fruition when a slowdown in earnings forced Priceline.com to scrap the deal in early 2001. W.R. Berkley also shuttered its personal lines operations in order to focus on commercial lines.

Despite these minor setbacks, the company remained focus on expansion into specialty markets. Eyeing London as a key growth area, W.R. Berkley purchased a 20.1 percent stake in Kiln plc, a Lloyd's insurer that had experienced significant losses due to the September 11, 2001, terrorist attacks against the United States. In 2003, it launched W.R. Berkley Insurance Europe Ltd. in London to write professional indemnity insurance. It also created Berkley Medical Excess Underwriters LLC to provide medical malpractice excess insurance and reinsurance coverage to hospitals and hospital associations.

During this time, W.R. Berkley stood in an enviable position as market conditions in the property casualty insurance arena remained strong. Net premiums increased from $1.5 billion in 2000 to $3.7 billion in 2003, and in 2004 they climbed to $4.3 billion. Net income also increased by 28 percent that year, reaching an all time high of $4.97 per share. By now, the company was operating as one of the 15 largest commercial lines property casualty insurance writers in the United States.

Principal Divisions

Regional Property Casualty Insurance; Reinsurance; Specialty Insurance; Alternative Markets; International.

Principal Competitors

The Allstate Corporation; American International Group Inc.; State Farm Mutual Automobile Insurance Company.

Further Reading

''Berkley Moves into Calif. Workers' Comp Mart.,'' *Insurance Finance & Investment*, July 13, 1998.

''Berkley: Underwriting Profits Key,'' *Insurance Accounting*, September 30, 2002.

Berkley, William R., ''W.R. Berkley Corp. Names John J. Kinsella President and CEO of Admiral Insurance Co.,'' *PR Newswire*, May 26, 1994.

Bryant, Adam, ''Greenwich-based Firm Hopes Market's Not Cold to Public Stock Offering,'' *Southern Connecticut Business Journal*, March 7, 1988, p. 1.

Cone, Edward F., ''Boy Wonder Grows Up,'' *Forbes*, February 20, 1989, p. 49.

Goodman, Jordan E., and Walter L. Updegrave, ''Earnings from Insuring Against a Big Fish,'' *Money*, March 1987, p. 8.

Marcial, Gene G., ''A Champ in Casualty,'' *Business Week*, July 18, 2005, p. 90.

McDonald, Lee, ''Ready for a Change,'' *Best's Review*, August 1, 2001.

Montgomery, Shep, ''Great River Forms New Insurance Company,'' *Mississippi Business Journal*, March 7, 1994, p. 1.

Porter, John W., ''National Guardian Grows at Alarming Rate,'' *Intercorp*, November 13, 1987, p. 11.

Reeves, Amy, ''W.R. Berkley Corp.,'' *Investor's Business Daily*, January 8, 2003.

Schachner, Michael, ''Berkley's Strategy Proves a Winner for His Collection of P/C Insurers,'' *Business Insurance*, July 26, 1993, p. 1.

Smart, Tim, ''William Berkley Had a Hard Act to Follow: Himself,'' *Business Week*, September 21, 1992, p. 80.

''Think Globally, Move Carefully,'' *Best's Review*, Property-Casualty Insurance Edition, April 1, 1998.

—Dave Mote
—update: Christina M. Stansell

Winbond Electronics Corporation

4 Creation Road III, Science-Based Industrial Park
Hsinchu
Taiwan
Telephone: +886 3 577 0066
Fax: +886 2 2798 4382
Web site: http://www.winbond.com.tw

Public Company
Incorporated: 1987
Employees: 3,800
Sales: TWD 31.21 billion ($980.02 billion) (2004)
Stock Exchanges: Taiwan
Ticker Symbol: 2344
NAIC: 334413 Semiconductor and Related Device Manufacturing; 334412 Printed Circuit Board Manufacturing; 334111 Electronic Computer Manufacturing; 334210 Telephone Apparatus Manufacturing; 334220 Radio and Television Broadcasting and Wireless Communications Equipment Manufacturing; 334310 Audio and Video Equipment Manufacturing

Winbond Electronics Corporation is one of Taiwan's leading developers and manufacturers of integrated semiconductor devices (ICs). The company operates primarily through two divisions: the Logic IC Business Group and the Memory IC Business Group. The latter represents the largest part of Winbond's business, with products including DRAMs, Flash Memory, and Pseudo SRAMs. Memory products accounted for nearly 70 percent of the group's sales of more than TWD 31 billion ($980 million) in 2004. The company's Logic IC group develops and manufactures IC products for various markets, such as consumer electronics (mobile camera phone chips, gaming consoles, mobile and wireless multimedia components, etc.), as well as ICs for TFT-LCD screens, computer motherboards, and the like. Logic Products represented nearly 29 percent of Winbond's revenues in 2004. Asia, and especially the dominant Taiwanese electronics market, remains Winbond's primary market, accounting for more than 92 percent of the group's revenues. Winbond is also present in the United States and Europe, which accounted for just 4.75 percent and 3 percent of the group's 2004 sales, respectively. The company operates three fabs in Taiwan; the company expected to open a new fab by the end of 2005, which was expected to reach full production by 2006. Winbond is listed on the Taiwan Stock Exchange.

ERSO Offshoot in the 1980s

Taiwan targeted the electronics market as early as the mid-1960s, importing technology from the United States and Europe, with an early emphasis on the CMOS market. By the late 1970s, Taiwan had emerged as an important center for the world electronics market. Although the country had initially imported technology through a series of technology transfer agreements, it also established its own research and development expertise. This effort occurred in large part under the auspices of the Taiwanese government's Electronics Research Organization (ERSO), controlled by the Industrial Technology Research Institute (ITRI).

ERSO/ITRI served as a seedbed for much of Taiwan's electronics and semiconductor industry. In addition to providing financial and technical support for the industry, ERSO and ITRI also provided significant infrastructure support. Such was the case in 1980 with the construction of the Hsinchu Science-based Industrial Park. ERSO also created a number of important players in the market, such as Taiwan Semiconductor Manufacturing Corporation (TSMC) and United Microelectronics Corporation (UMC) both in the early 1980s.

Dr. Ding-yuan Yang was one of the founding members of ERSO, leading the group of engineers trained at RCA in the late 1970s. Back in Taiwan, Yang became responsible for setting up ERSO's demonstration laboratory, before becoming chief of the institution's computer development group. There, Yang led ERSO's entry into the specialized chipset market.

The growth of Taiwan's electronics market, and the success of TSMC, UMC, and other ERSO spinoffs, led Yang, and seven other engineers at ERSO, to decide to enter the private sphere as well. In 1987, Yang lined up an investor, Walsin Lihwa Corporation, and established Winbond Electronics Corporation. Unlike TSMC and UMC, the new company was not directly controlled

Company Perspectives:

The company's vision is to be the most successful "Mobile Electronics Solutions" provider in the world. To increase productivity and the fun in life for all people.

by ERSO. Nonetheless, Winbond enjoyed strong support from ERSO, including the use of ERSO's original Hsinchu laboratory and the transfer of an additional team of 40 engineers. ERSO also sent Yang to study Business Administration at Stanford University. Of importance, Yang's relationship with ERSO and ITRI (he was later to be named as head of planning and marketing for ITRI) also enabled Winbond to start up its operations based on a license for ERSO's CMOS chip technology.

By the end of 1987, Winbond had established its first fab and had launched production of its first IC products. The company quickly expanded into building chipsets based on Intel's 286, then 386, and later, 486 microprocessors, becoming a major player in that all-important IC segment. By 1988, the company also had launched production of wafers. This enabled Winbond to expand into various specialty chipset markets, such as for video display controllers, as well as voice and other early multimedia ICs in 1989, and then add its first integrated circuit for the newly established LCD market in 1990.

Winbond began building its international sales market at that time as well. In 1990, the company established subsidiaries in the United States and in Hong Kong. Winbond also continued to develop its technology, emerging as one of the Asian IC industry's top innovators into the mid-1990s. Among the company's achievements during this time was the development (with ERSO) of the ISDN U-transceiver and, in partnership with Symphony, the one-micron CMOS 386 and 486 chipset families, both in 1991. By then, the company had entered the memory market, developing its first high-speed SRAM chips.

Technology Acquisitions in the 1990s

Into the mid-1990s, Winbond continued to step up its technology, achieving 0.8 micron production in 1992, then 0.6 micron in 1993. In 1994 the company became the first in Asia to develop a single-chip design MPEG video decoder IC. In that year, as well, Winbond launched production of 0.5 micron SRAMs. This effort was supported by the completion of the company's new Fab 2 in 1995. Also in that year, Winbond went public, listing on the Taiwan Stock Exchange.

The public offering enabled Winbond to begin planning a new phase of growth. The company entered a licensing agreement with Toshiba Corporation to design and produce a series of DRAM and high-speed SRAM chips for the Japanese electronics giant. Winbond also began construction of its third fab. Completed in May 1996, Fab 3 was subsequently destroyed by fire later that same year. Forced to rebuild, the company's next fab, Fab 4, launched pilot production—of Toshiba technology-based 64M DRAMs—by the end of 1997.

In the meantime, Winbond had continued to step up its technology, launching 0.4 micron IC production in 1998. By

Key Dates:

1987: Dr. Ding-yuan Yang, a founding member of Taiwan's ERSO, leaves the company to found Winbond Electronics Corporation and begins construction of Fab 1.
1989: The company establishes its first foreign office in Hong Kong.
1990: The company establishes a subsidiary in the United States.
1992: Production is launched at Fab 2.
1994: The company releases the first Asian-built single-chip MPEG video decoder.
1995: The company's public offering is made on the Taiwan Stock Exchange.
1998: The company acquires Information Storage Systems of California as part of a drive to acquire new technologies.
2001: The company opens subsidiaries in Japan and Shanghai, China; 46 percent of NexFlash Technology Inc., based in California, is acquired.
2002: The company signs a technology partnership agreement with Infineon Technologies AG.
2004: The Infineon partnership is expanded and construction of a new 12-inch fab is launched.
2005: The company acquires full control of NexFlash Technology.

May of that year, the company had successfully completed a pilot run of 0.25 micron DRAMs as well. The company also launched a new part of its growth strategy in 1998, when it made its first acquisition, of California's Information Storage Devices. That company specialized in IC-based voice recording and playback devices. It also marked the début of Winbond's drive to add technology through acquisition.

Winbond's next acquisitions came in 1999, when it bought up Bright Micro Electronics, as well as Cirrus Logic's Thin Film Transistor operations, both located in the United States. Together with Information Storage Devices, the new acquisitions were merged into Winbond's U.S. subsidiary. Also that year, the company licensed new TFT-LCD driver and IC technology from Vivid Semiconductor.

The company then teamed up with Toshiba and Fujitsu to develop new 0.13 micron DRAM processing technology. The partnership also included an agreement for the joint development of a future 0.11 micron technology. In the meantime, Winbond continued to expand its facilities, opening a new Fab Automation & Facility Engineering Center in June 2000, followed by the completion of the group's Fab 5, and its first computer-integrated manufacturing system.

Winbond added to its international sales and marketing force with the creation of two new subsidiaries in 2001, in Japan and in Shanghai, China. The new subsidiaries also expanded the group's research and development operations. The company next formed a partnership with Japan's Sharp Corporation for the development of new ACT1 Flash memory technology.

Memory Focus in the 2000s

By the mid-2000s, Winbond had begun to refocus itself on the memory market. By the middle of the decade, memory products formed nearly 70 percent of the company's sales. Most of the company's memory sales came from the DRAM category, supported by the establishment of a new Technology R&D Group in 2003. The new division consisted of a Memory Technology Center, dedicated to developing new DRAM technologies, and an Emerging Technology Center and a Novel Device Structure Center.

After Toshiba announced its decision to exit the DRAM market in the early 2000s, Winbond was forced to seek a new technology partner. The company found its new partner soon after it signed a first technology transfer agreement with Germany's Infineon Technology AG. After the successful development of a 0.11 micron process, the two companies signed a new agreement in 2004 to develop a 0.09 micron technology.

In support of this, Winbond launched construction of a new 12-inch fab at the end of 2004. Construction of the new facility was expected to be completed by the end of 2005. After completion of initial pilot production, the company hoped to launch full-scale production at the fab by 2006.

In the meantime, Winbond continued its shift toward a focus on the memory market. In 2001, the company had invested in the United States' NexFlash Technologies, based in Silicon Valley and specialized in the development of high-density flash memory technology. In June 2005, Winbond acquired full control of NexFlash, providing a complement to the company's own focus on low-density flash memory products. Winbond expected to remain a central player in the global IC market into the new century.

Principal Subsidiaries

Baystar Holding Ltd.; Goldbond LLC; Marketplace Management Ltd.; Mobile Magic Design Corporation; Newfound Asian Corporation; NexFlash Technologies, Inc. (52.35%); Peaceful River Corporation; Pigeon Creek Holding Co., Ltd.; Winbond Electronics Corporation America; Winbond Electronics Corporation Japan; Winbond Electronics (H.K.) Ltd.; Winbond Electronics (Shanghai) Ltd.; Winbond Int'l Corporation; Win Investment Corporation.

Principal Competitors

Taiwan Semiconductor Manufacturing Corporation; United Microelectronics Corporation.

Further Reading

Carroll, Mark, and David Lammers, ''Winbond Rides MPEG Wave,'' *Electronic Engineering Times,* April 10, 1995, p. 29.

Clendenin, Mike, ''Life After Toshiba,'' *Electronic Engineering Times,* December 26, 2001, p. 4.

Fuller, Douglas B., et al., ''Leading, Following or Cooked Goose? Innovation Successes and Failures in Taiwan's Electronics Industry,'' *Industry and Innovation,* June 2003, p. 179.

Manners, David, ''Blossoming into a Market Leader,'' *Electronics Weekly,* October 28, 1992, p. 17.

Murphy, Tom, ''Full Stream Ahead for Taiwan Foundries: Only Winbond Derails Chipmaking Production,'' *Electronic Business Asia,* January 2002, p. 12.

''Winbond Electronics Corp. (Expansion),'' *Solid State Technology,* November 2004, p. S16.

''Winbond Electronics Corp. (to Build a New Wafer Plant in Taiwan),'' *Solid State Technology,* August 2003, p. 20.

''Winbond Stakes Out Europe,'' *Electronic Buyers' News,* November 27, 2000, p. 28.

—M.L. Cohen

WINMARK

C O R P O R A T I O N

Winmark Corporation

4200 Dahlberg Drive, Suite 100
Minneapolis, Minnesota 55422-4837
U.S.A.
Telephone: (763) 520-8500
Toll Free: (800) 567-6600
Fax: (763) 520-8410
Web site: http://www.winmarkcorporation.com

Public Company
Incorporated: 1988 as Play It Again Sports Franchise
   Corp.
Employees: 122
Sales: $26.6 million (2004)
Stock Exchanges: NASDAQ
Ticker Symbol: WINA
NAIC: 339992 Musical Instrument Manufacturing;
   423910 Sporting and Recreational Goods and Supplies
   Merchant Wholesalers; 448130 Children's and
   Infants' Clothing Stores

Winmark Corporation pioneered what the company calls the "ultra-high-value" retailing niche. High quality used products are sold alongside new goods in a traditional retail store format. The rapidly growing company began with Play It Again Sports, which is ranked among the largest sporting-goods chains in the United States, with 410 stores in 2005. Its other three franchised businesses are Once Upon A Child (with 208 stores), Plato's Closet (with 133 stores), and Music Go Round (with 40 stores). All of these operations buy, sell, trade, and consign used and new merchandise. In addition, Winmark also offers business services, including equipment leasing, under the name Winmark Business Solutions.

Origins

Martha Morris was inspired to develop the Play It Again Sports concept in 1983 when she had trouble reselling a nearly new $200 backpack. She borrowed $15,000 from a friend's parents, and the two women started a used sporting equipment store in a vacated tombstone shop near a Minneapolis cemetery. Morris bought out her friend within a few months. Boosted by local television coverage, she sold about $120,000 of used equipment during her first year of business. Initially she sold everything on consignment, but she later began buying used equipment outright and selling new goods, such as sales representative samples, last year's models, and retailers' out-of-season equipment.

Financial success and customer feedback told Morris the idea could work elsewhere, so in mid-1988 she went to a franchise development consulting firm for help. K. Jeffrey Dahlberg and Ronald G. Olson, the owners of Franchise Business Systems, Inc. (FBS), had their doubts at first about the potential for a used sporting goods chain. In a 1994 *Fortune* magazine article Olson said, "Her store looked like a garage sale with hours." Nevertheless, the numbers showed them she was also pulling in a lot of business, so FBS took her on as a client.

The Minneapolis *Star Tribune* for March 8, 1992, Dick Youngblood wrote, "Her instincts were bull's-eye accurate. Despite limited capital, the business grew in 18 months to 19 franchise operations in six states, taking 1989 revenues to more than $800,000, which included sales at the two stores Morris owned then plus the franchise and royalty fees. Sales of the franchised stores alone totaled $1.3 million." Dahlberg and Olson used their combined expertise to polish the entrepreneurial nugget into a gemstone.

Dahlberg acquired his franchising know-how in his family-run hearing-aid business. He began developing the Miracle Ear Centers network when he was named president of Dahlberg, Inc. in 1983. However, the combination of uneven earnings and franchise startup costs of $10 to $15 million caused friction with his father and a power struggle with a group of California investment firms that held 20 percent of the company stock. In 1986, only a few months after being named CEO of Dahlberg, Inc., he left the company.

A friend introduced Dahlberg to Olson, who had 20 years of retail experience with companies such as Dayton Hudson Corporation and on his own. The two men formed FBS in 1986 as a franchise development, marketing, and investment firm.

Among the franchise systems they helped build were a 250-store eye-care chain and a 100-store dry-cleaning chain. Olson was left to run the day-to-day business of the consulting firm, while Dahlberg reconciled with his father and returned to lead the hearing-aid business in 1988.

Play It Again Sports in 1990s

In 1990, Dahlberg and Olson bought the franchising operation of Play It Again Sports for more than $1 million plus five years of royalty payments. Dahlberg became chairman and Olson served as president and CEO of the company. The next year, Morris decided to sell them her three retail stores as well, but she signed on as a consultant. By the end of 1991, 134 Play It Again Sports franchise stores were open in 41 states and Canada.

In January 1992, Dahlberg and Olson purchased Sports Traders, Inc., an independent wholesaler owned by Jim Van Buskirk, an early owner of Play It Again Sports. Van Buskirk acquired a 50 percent interest in the first Morris store in 1986, but the next year he left to develop his own Play It Again Sports stores. The wholesale business he started supplied both his and Morris's stores with new goods to supplement the selection of used sporting equipment purchased from the public. As part of the purchase agreement, Van Buskirk's Play It Again Sports stores continued to operate separately from the growing franchise system.

Play It Again Sports franchises were being sold at a rapid pace. Dahlberg and Olson were able to draw from a pool of middle managers displaced by corporate downsizing. The men believed the Play It Again Sports concept could be translated into other retail areas and began acquiring successfully established businesses in the used goods market. In November 1992, Dahlberg and Olson purchased franchising and royalty rights from Once Upon A Child, Inc., a Columbus, Ohio-based, 22-store chain selling children's clothing, furniture, and toys. The chain had been started by local retailers Dennis and Lynn Blum in 1985.

Dahlberg resigned as president and CEO of Dahlberg, Inc. at the end of 1992 in order to devote himself full time to the expanding Play It Again Sports business. Dahlberg, Inc., its sales and earnings boosted by the franchise system Dahlberg had built, was sold to Bausch & Lomb in 1993 for $138 million.

A Name Change in 1993

In February 1993, Olson and Dahlberg opened the first corporate-owned Once Upon A Child store. All of their 16 Twin Cities franchises were sold before mid-year. Also in 1993, the company purchased assets of Hi Tech Consignments, a musical instrument and audio equipment retailer (renamed Music Go Round) and Computer Renaissance, Inc., a retailer of close-out and used computers. In recognition of the changes, Play It Again Sports Franchise Corp. was renamed Grow Biz International, Inc.

In August 1993, an initial public offering (IPO) was announced: 1.6 million common shares at $10 per share. The Grow Biz stock price jumped to $15 per share during the first trading day. The company raised about $16.7 million from the IPO. Revenues for 1993 increased 89 percent over the previous year to $51.8 million. By the end of the year, 490 stores were open in the United States and Canada; eight of those stores were owned by the corporation. An additional 282 franchises had been awarded for future opening.

In the *Twin Cities Business Monthly* for December 1993, Gillian Judge wrote, ''The company's recent rapid growth hasn't been without repercussions, and some of the newest franchisees of Once Upon A Child shops grumble that the system has some kinks to work out before it runs as well as Play It Again Sports.'' In order to bolster franchise support Grow Biz began to decentralize operations. During 1994, the company began individualizing concept support and leadership.

Grow Biz's 1994 revenues grew to $83.6 million; net income was $1.4 million, a 300 percent increase over the previous year. The first Canadian Once Upon A Child store was among the record 243 Grow Biz stores opened in 1994. The company added a fifth business concept that year, compact disc stores. Grow Biz purchased assets, franchising, and royalty rights of CDX Audio Development, Inc., of Green Bay, Wisconsin, which operated 43 CD Exchange stores.

In 1994, the company topped both *Fortune* and *Inc.* magazines' lists of the fastest-growing American public companies. According to *Fortune,* Grow Biz had experienced an annual growth rate of 285 percent in terms of total revenues over the past five years. In an *Investor's Business Daily* article by Claire Mencke, Olson pointed out that initially the company's rapid growth was unexpected. ''But it happened that we brought together a lot of trends: value pricing starting with the used product, the trend in recycling, and the availability of a lot of strip-shopping center real estate.''

Despite the acclaim, 1994 also had its bleaker moments. Grow Biz stock price fell by 15.7 percent in October when lower-than-expected third quarter earnings were announced. According to an October 22, 1994 *Star Tribune* article, the earnings' setback was caused by a reduction in the projected number of store openings for the year, due to a tight strip-mall real estate market and losses related to foreign investments.

The company had begun to franchise Play It Again Sports stores internationally in 1991. In 1993, Grow Biz entered into joint venture agreements to franchise stores in Europe and Mexico. However toward year-end 1994, Grow Biz withdrew from the Mexican market, closing both of its corporate-owned stores. The company also suffered losses in its corporate-owned German venture, but the franchised stores there continued to operate.

In *Corporate Report Minnesota* for April 1995, Lee Schafer noted that the Play It Again Sports franchises were moneymakers for their owners, a situation that was atypical of the franchise environment at the time. However, Schafer pointed out that analysts had some reservations about the other concepts. The computer stores faced uncertainty related to rapidly changing technology, the strength of franchisees among the kids clothes and toys concept was being questioned, and the disc businesses faced stiff competition from new disc sellers. Olson disputed this and said in the same article that Grow Biz was "concentrating on becoming operationally strong" in all five concept areas.

Grow Biz gave its franchisees support and assistance in the following areas: advertising and marketing, centralized buying and warehouse services, point-of-sale computerized information systems, management training, and store opening assistance. It also provided periodic field support visits. The franchisees were generally required to comply with guidelines regarding store design, the use of television advertising focusing on the buy-sell concept, and standardized merchandise purchasing processes. An initial franchise fee cost $20,000. Franchisees also paid an annual royalty of 3 to 5 percent of gross revenues.

Grow Biz more than doubled the size of its distribution facilities in 1995 and consolidated operations at its headquarters. Revenues for 1995 topped $100 million, while net income climbed 47 percent to $2 million. Royalty revenue jumped 51 percent to $11.6 million. By year-end 1995, a total of 1,311 franchises had been awarded: 965 stores were open, including 57 stores in Canada, eight in Europe, and one in Australia.

In early 1995, all the Grow Biz concepts except Music Go Round were ranked first in their categories in *Entrepreneur* magazine's Annual Franchise 500. Music Go Round, the smallest of the five Grow Biz concepts with 11 U.S. stores in operation, generated $4 million in revenues in 1995. Customers ranged from parents seeking a place to buy or sell musical instruments for their children to professional musicians upgrading their equipment.

Among Computer Renaissance's best customers were first-time computer buyers and sellers and small business owners. The company also purchased used computers from corporations upgrading their systems and from liquidators. Only about 20 percent of store inventory was new. Unlike the other Grow Biz concepts, which typically purchased used goods ready for resale, the corporation refurbished used computers and provided franchise operations with technical assistance. Revenues for the 64 U.S. and Canadian stores in operation in 1995 were $23 million.

Compact disc industry sales grew by 33.6 percent in 1994, according to company figures. With Disc Go Round, Grow Biz was positioning itself to capitalize on the strength of the relatively new industry plus the growing CD-ROM market. Disc Go Round's 1995 revenues were $17 million, and all of its 99 stores in operation were in the United States and Canada. The typical franchisee and customer were younger than those of the other Grow Biz concepts.

Once Upon A Child stores targeted parents with children under 12 years of age. "Gently-used" items, which were sold for one-third to one-half of the new retail price, made up about 80 percent of the Once Upon A Child product mix in 1995. The 164 stores open that year generated $37 million in sales. In contrast, Play It Again Sports had 674 stores in operation in 1995 and generated $255 million in revenues.

In 1998, a new franchise concept, ReTool, was launched. ReTool focused on buying and reselling used and reconditioned tools. In much the same manner as the other Grow Biz franchises, ReTool aimed at the typical consumer looking to sell tools he no longer needed and buy tools he did need at a discount.

Olson said a May 1996 article by Susan Reda in *Stores* that Grow Biz "raised the bar in terms of consumers' expectations" of used goods. He went on to say, "There's no longer a stigma attached to buying used items."

Changes in the 21st Century

Grow Biz had seen a growth in the number of stores in the 1990s, but that growth was apparently too fast. In 2000, the company showed a loss of $350,700. The 2000s saw big changes at the company. John Morgan acquired control of Grow Biz in 2000. A former partner in Winthrop Leasing, Morgan had sold his company and retired in 1999. However, retirement did not suit him and Morgan looked around for new business opportunities. As the chief executive officer, Morgan brought in a new management team to run the company. Jeffrey Dahlberg and Ron Olson, while not involved in operations, each continued to own 20 percent of the company's stock, while Morgan owned another 20 percent. In 2001, Grow Biz was renamed Winmark Corporation.

Among the changes instituted by Morgan to revive the company was to close down the ailing Disc Go Round and Computer Renaissance franchises in 2000. The ReTool franchise was shut down in late 2001. The concept had never worked out as well as expected. As Morgan told John Hoogesteger in *CityBusiness* for December 7, 2001, "People don't normally sell old tools. Even tools they rarely use they keep around in case they need them at some point." In the three years the franchise was in operation, only 17 stores had been opened. Weaker stores in the other franchises were also shut down during this period of reorganization. In 2002, Winmark began purchasing an interest in Archiver's, a photography service provider specializing in preserving old photographs. By early 2004, Winmark owned nearly 20 percent of the company's stock.

Winmark's new Plato's Closet franchise, retailing used clothing for the teenage market, was a success. Developed by the same couple who had come up with Once Upon A Child, Dennis and Lynn Blum, the franchise name was suggested by their son, who had been studying the Greek philosopher in school. Focusing on "gently-used" trendy clothing not yet out of style in the rapidly changing teen market, each Plato's Closet store was between 2,500 to 3,200 square feet in size and contained some 98 percent used clothing and 2 percent new clothing. Most prices were some 70 percent below the new merchandise price. By 2005, there were over 130 Plato's Closet stores in operation.

The financial picture for Winmark improved dramatically in the first five years of the 21st century. With the closing of stores that were not performing, the company saw a profit of $3.2 million in 2001. This trend continued in the following years: $3.8 million profit in 2002, $4 million in 2003, and almost $4.1 million in 2004. In the first quarter of 2005, Winmark posted a net income of nearly $700,000. According to Neal St. Anthony in the *Star Tribune* for April 13, 2004, since Morgan took over the company, Winmark's "performance has turned around and the return on equity has averaged more than 30 percent annually." By March 2005, Winmark operated a total of 791 stores in North America.

In 2003, Winmark expanded its activities to become a service supplier to franchise owners and small business in general with the launch of Winmark Business Solutions (WBS), a free service that offered small business owners negotiated discount pricing from such vendors as accountants, office supply retailers, printers, and Web designers. WBS also leased equipment to small businesses. Under this arrangement, a business owner could choose the type of equipment needed and a particular vendor, and WBS would purchase that item and lease it to him. The lease deal allowed the business owner to free his cash for other purposes. The business concept was similar to that followed by Morgan's old company, Winthrop Leasing. While the leasing business was still a small part of Winmark's financial picture, company officers were optimistic about its future as a complement to the firm's franchising operations in the used goods market. While Winmark's success could propel more franchisers to develop competing national used product chains, the company was banking on its growing name recognition to help it continue to draw consumers to buy and sell merchandise and on potential franchisees to choose their concepts over other options.

Principal Competitors

Goodwill Industries International, Inc.; The Sports Authority, Inc.; Wal-Mart Stores, Inc.

Further Reading

Apgar, Sally, "Play It Again Owner Buys CD Exchange Company," *Star Tribune* (Minneapolis), July 6, 1994, p. 3D.

Beran, George, "Retail Renegade," *St. Paul Pioneer Press,* January 16, 1994.

Daniel, Fran, "Greensboro, N.C., Couple Finds Success in Retail-Resale Chains," *Winston-Salem Journal* (Winston-Salem, North Carolina), August 21, 2002.

DePass, Dee, "Inc. Magazine Selects Grow Biz International as Fastest Growing Small Corporation In Nation," *Star Tribune* (Minneapolis), April 29, 1994, p. 1D.

Fiedelholtz, Sara, "Cashing In on Teen Fashion Fickleness," *Chicago Sun-Times,* August 26, 2004.

"Grow Biz Becomes Winmark," *CityBusiness* (Minneapolis), November 23, 2001, p. 33.

Hoogesteger, John, "Winmark Unscrewing ReTool Line," *CityBusiness* (Minneapolis), December 7, 2001, p. 1.

Iverson, Doug, "Dain Analyst Predicts Growth for Grow Biz," *St. Paul Pioneer Press*, October 11, 1993.

Jossi, Frank, "Inside Small Business," *CityBusiness*, August 19, 1994, p. 13.

Judge, Gillian, "Play It Again," *Twin Cities Business Monthly*, December 1993, pp. 54–58.

Kaeter, Margaret, "Trash for Cash," *Twin Cities Business Monthly*, March 1996, pp. 44–48.

Kaplan, David, "Houston Chronicle Moneymakers Column," *Houston Chronicle*, May 11, 2005.

Kinsey, Michelle, "Dress for Less," *Star Press* (Muncie, Indiana), August 31, 2004.

Marcotty, Josephine, "Jeffrey Dahlberg Resigns Positions at Dahlberg to Devote Full Attention to Play It Again Sports," *Star Tribune* (Minneapolis), December 18, 1992, p. 1D.

——, "Play It Again Sports Franchise Corp. Discussing Public Stock Offering in '93," *Star Tribune* (Minneapolis), May 6, 1993, p. 1D.

——, "Franchise by Franchise, He's Built His Career," *Star Tribune* (Minneapolis), January 17, 1994.

McCartney, Jim, "Play It Again Sports Franchiser Expands," *St. Paul Pioneer Press*, May 6, 1993.

——, "Media Replay Opens Store in Uptown, Minneapolis, Minnesota," *St. Paul Pioneer Press*, December 29, 1994.

Mencken, Claire, "Mining an Untapped Market for Used Goods," *Investor's Business Daily*, September 19, 1994.

Nevius, C.W., "Dublin: Plato's Closet Resells 'In' Clothes Before They Are 'Out,'" *San Francisco Chronicle*, June 10, 2005.

Pokela, Barbara, "A Used Ski Is Still a Ski That Can Be Sold at Play It Again Sports," *Star Tribune* (Minneapolis), September 15, 1986, p. 8M.

Ratliff, Duke, "Grow Biz: A Recycling Retailer," *Discount Merchandiser*, May 1996, pp. 92–96.

Reda, Susan, "Beyond Discounting," *Stores*, May 1996, pp. 24–26.

Reichard, Kevin, "Used Equipment Has New Life at Computer Renaissance," *CityBusiness*, January 21, 1994, p. 13.

St. Anthony, Neal, "Once Again, Morgan Delivers the Goods; Under His Control, Winmark Posts Record Earnings," *Star Tribune* (Minneapolis), April 13, 2004, p. 1D.

Schafer, Lee, "As the Cookie Crumbles . . . ," *Corporate Report Minnesota*, April 1995, pp. 39–40.

Serwer, Andrew E., "Lessons from America's Fastest-Growing Companies," *Fortune*, August 8, 1994, pp. 42–45.

"Shares of Grow Biz International Fall 15.7% After It Reports Lower-Than-Expected Earnings," *Star Tribune* (Minneapolis), October 22, 1994.

Singer, Leah, "A Great Vintage," *Success*, June 1994, p. 24.

Steinberg, Susan, "Franchisers of the Future," *Success*, November 1996, p. 92.

Warshaw, Michael, ed., "Renegades," *Success*, January-February 1996, p. 32.

Waters, Jennifer, "Grow Biz to Expand into New Campus," *CityBusiness*, June 2, 1995, p. 6.

"Winmark Business Solutions," *Franchising World*, November-December, 2004, p. 71.

Youngblood, Dick, "Making the Right Moves Pays Off," *Star Tribune* (Minneapolis), March 8, 1992, p. 2D.

——, "He Proved California Investors Wrong—And Then Some," *Star Tribune* (Minneapolis), June 29, 1992, p. 2D.

——, "The Play It Again Sports Franchisers Plan to Sell Idea Again and Again. . . . ," *Star Tribune* (Minneapolis), September 23, 1992, p. 2D.

——, "Jeff Dahlberg Finds That There's No Biz Like Grow Biz," *Star Tribune* (Minneapolis), May 2, 1994, p. 2D.

——, "Seven Twin Cities Firms on Fast-Grower List," *Star Tribune* (Minneapolis), May 3, 1996, p. 3D.

—Kathleen Peippo
—update: Thomas Wiloch

Zacky Farms LLC

2020 South East Avenue
Fresno, California 93721
U.S.A.
Telephone: (559) 486-2310
Toll Free: (800) 999-8202
Fax: (559) 443-2706
Web site: http://www.zacky.com

Private Company
Incorporated: 1955
Employees: 1,100
Sales: $100 million (2003)
NAIC: 112330 Turkey Production

Zacky Farms LLC is a family-owned, Fresno, California-based poultry company that, after starting out in the 1920s involved in eggs and chickens, is now focused on turkey. The operation is vertically integrated: Zacky hatches its own turkeys, feeds the flock from its own granaries, then processes the birds in its own plants and delivers the finished product on a company-owned fleet of trucks. Since the 1950s, Zacky has avoided using hormones, preservatives, and additives and now offers free-range turkeys, which are allowed to roam freely and feed on a special diet of corn and natural grains. Zacky's turkey products include whole turkeys, fresh ground turkey, turkey patties, vacuum-packed breasts, skinless and boneless turkey parts, sliced turkey breast, turkey sausage, and turkey-based lunch meats. In addition, the company's Stockton, California, plant is able to process beef, pork, and chicken along with turkey to produce hot dogs and luncheon meats, either in bulk or vacuum packed. Zacky markets its products under the Zacky Farms and Westerner brands and also does private label work. In addition, Zacky offers a foodservice line of products.

Origins

Zacky Farms was founded by Samuel Zacky, who was born in Kiev, Russia, in 1897 and 11 years later immigrated with his family to the United States. They eventually settled in the quiet farm town of Los Angeles, California, around the same time that the fledgling movie industry was beginning to take root. As a teenager, Zacky peddled nuts and fruits. By 1928, he had saved enough money to enter the poultry business, opening Sam's Poultry Market, located at the corner of Slauson and Western Avenues in Los Angeles. He sold chickens, turkeys, and ducks on both a retail and wholesale basis. The birds were ''dressed while U wait.'' Customers selected live birds bought from a local farm, and these were then killed, plucked, and gutted on the spot. To supply the store, Zacky eventually bought a ranch in Van Nuys, California, where in addition to hens and fryers he raised rabbits.

At that time, the poultry industry was undergoing dramatic changes. Previously the part-time occupation of women and children, the poultry industry came of age in the 20th century. Poultry science programs were launched at American colleges, leading to the development of mass production techniques that made small-farm chicken enterprises obsolete. Red meat rationing during World War II resulted in increased consumption of chicken, a demand met in large part by the introduction of battery cages arranged in rows and tiers. This arrangement became the standard way to raise chickens for both eggs and broilers. After the war, Americans continued to consume eggs and chicken at the same rate, although over the long term consumers began to cut back on eggs and ate more chicken, tipping the traditional balance in the poultry industry. Another phenomenon of the postwar 1940s was the rise of supermarkets and suburbs. When World War II ended, Samuel Zacky sold his ranch to buy a poultry market in Monterey Park, California, where his three sons (Albert, Robert, and Harry) began to help out. It was primarily a retail operation, but the younger Zackys correctly surmised that the emerging supermarket channel offered a tremendous growth opportunity. The family business now made the transition from a retail to a wholesale business and from being a local provider to becoming a state-wide provider.

Zacky Farms Incorporated in the Mid-1950s

In late 1953, the family launched a wholesale operations called Zacky and Sons, and soon afterward opened its first processing plant, located in South El Monte, California. In

1955, Zacky Farms was incorporated. Even then the family was beginning to think in "natural" terms and looking to develop a vertically integrated company. Bob Zacky's wife, Lillian, who went to work for the business in 1956, told *Los Angeles Magazine* in a 1993 profile, "We began raising our own chickens, building our own ranches, manufacturing our own feed." Much of this activity took place after the company's founder, Samuel Zacky, who had remained very much involved in the company until the end, died in 1964. Albert and Robert Zacky took charge and continued to build the poultry operation, with Albert responsible for raising the birds and Robert distributing the product. Zacky built a chicken hatchery in 1967.

One of the most significant steps taken by the company occurred in 1971, when Zacky acquired a larger poultry business, British-owned Balfour Guthrie, which brought with it the Fresno Feed Mill and extended Zacky's presence to central California. The mill was upgraded and expanded in order to provide Zacky and its multi-million-bird flock with the various types of feeds they needed. It was also during this period that the family business brought in experienced outsiders, Hank Frederick and Saul Brand, who played instrumental roles in Zacky's continued growth in the 1970s. A Southern California distribution center was established out of an El Monte rabbit operation the company acquired. Zacky ended the 1970s by opening a state-of-the-industry, 150,000-square-foot chicken processing facility in Fresno that was capable of processing more than one million chickens a week.

Zacky added turkey to the mix in 1984 with the purchase of Swift and Company's turkey assets, which included hatcheries, growout ranches, a processing plant, a packaging building, and a cold storage facility. A year later, Zacky added to its turkey business through another acquisition, this time buying Poppy Foods Company. As a result of these moves, Zacky was now a fully integrated chicken and turkey operation. The company raised its own flocks, fed from the products of its mills, and the birds were then processed in Zacky's plants and sold through its distribution network. The chicken products were mostly sold in state, but Zacky turkey products could be found throughout the West. Moreover, the South El Monte facility became a major California distributor of beef, pork, lamb, and fish products. Nevertheless, the focus remained very much on poultry, especially in light of shifting consumer tastes. In 1987, Americans, who were becoming increasingly more health conscious, ate more poultry than beef for the first time in history, a trend that would continue. Turkey in particular, which was once primarily reserved for holiday dinners, was now finding its way into the diets of Americans throughout the year because its low-fat, high-protein content.

It was during the late 1980s that Lillian Zacky became the voice of Zacky Farms and launched a successful, long-running series of radio spots. As she told *Los Angeles Magazine* in the 1993 profile the publication ran on her, after going to work for the family business in 1956 she did "a little bit of everything." "Somebody would call and ask for accounts receivable. I'd say, 'Just a moment, please,' wait 10 seconds and come back and say, 'Accounts receivable. May I help you?'" That was "probably why Bob suggested me for the radio spots. He knew I had a flair for the theatrical." Nevertheless, she had to audition for the job with a dozen other people. The spots featured her pretending to talk on the telephone, lending a folksy charm as she regaled listeners with stories about Zacky Farms. Listeners responded well to the spots, leading many people to send her letters asking for personal advice. "I think people respond to that fact that I don't sound trained or fussed over." Regardless, the advertising campaign played a key role in Zacky Farm's steady growth in sales. By the end of the 1980s, the company was expanding once again to meet rising demand, committing more than $16 million to build a new protein conversion plant in Fresno; a new hatchery in Kerman, California, adding 300,000 chickens each week to the production cycle; and a new feed mill near Traver, California, the largest animal feed mill west of Denver. Not only did these additions help Zacky to satisfy the growing demand for its products in Southern California, they helped the company in its efforts to gain market share in central and northern California.

Facilities Added and Expanded in the 1990s

Zacky entered the 1990s as California's second largest poultry grower, processor, and supplier, trailing only Livingston, California-based Foster Farms. The company continued to enjoy strong growth, leading to the upgrading of current facilities and the addition of others. A new feed mill that Zacky opened in Traver in 1991 was one of the poultry industry's first automated operations. Later in the decade, the company bought a Stockton processing facility from the Safeway supermarket chain. With the help of a government incentive package, Zacky initiated a major expansion in Fresno in 1996. A 75,000-square-foot addition to a cold storage plant increased storage capacity by 13 million pounds, allowing Zacky to handle all of its storage needs internally rather than contract some out to a public freezer. The Fresno turkey processing operation also received an additional 5,000 square feet of space, a move that consolidated functions that had previously been divided between two buildings. Moreover, the new equipment that was part of the expansion was more energy-efficient and used less water.

All told, the project cost $12 million, the first installment on $124 million worth of investment the company envisioned for the Fresno operation over the next 20 years. The next phase took place in late 1999, when Zacky launched a $10.4 million capital improvement project on two Fresno facilities. At a cost of $3.4 million, about 18,000 square feet of the turkey-processing plant was remodeled in order to permit the production of new turkey products: fresh turkey parts, sliced turkey breast, ground turkey, and turkey sausage. It was all part of an effort to tap into the growing market for fresh tray-packed turkey products. Zacky spent another $7 million to expand its Fresno chicken-processing plant, adding 40,000-square-feet of space to include a new weighing area, staging and shipping area, and boxing room, as well as an employee facility. Both projects were completed in the early weeks of 2000. Also during the course of the 1990s, Zacky added a new hatchery.

Focusing on Turkey

Zacky was not the only poultry company to ramp up production. Foster Farms followed suit, as did companies across the country. However, excessive expansion resulted in a market crunch in the chicken industry, which during the early years of the 21st century experienced the poorest conditions it had faced in 20 years. Zacky also had to contend with a misfortune that adversely impacted the company's ability to compete when, in April 2000, Albert Zacky, president of Zacky Farms, died of an apparent heart attack at the age of 71. Aside from the loss of his leadership, the family business faced a hefty inheritance tax bill, placing a financial burden on the company's operations.

In March 2001, Zacky Farms agreed to sell its chicken operations to Foster Farms, with Albert Zacky citing the federal inheritance tax as the compelling reason for the sale. Foster Farms took over Zacky's 35 live production ranches, feed mill, hatchery, the Fresno processing plant, and a Los Angeles distribution center. As a result, Foster Farms would move up the rankings in what was already a consolidated industry. Instead of being the tenth largest chicken producer in the United States, it was now number eight.

Zacky, its name long associated with chickens in the mind of California consumers, now focused exclusively on turkey products. The money received from the sale to Foster Farms was used to pay off the inheritance taxes and to invest in the company's turkey operations. As part of its commitment to the turkey business, Zacky moved its corporate offices from El Monte near Los Angeles to Fresno in 2003. The company's chief executive officer told the *Fresno Bee,* "Having our offices near our existing plant site will expedite daily operational issues as well as the flow of information to our employees. The offices were included in a new 12,000-square-foot structure that also housed a new kitchen where turkey recipes could be developed and tested.

In some ways, selling off the chicken operation gave Zacky a new lease on life. Lillian Zacky told the press that Zacky Farms took on the spirit of "a young company just starting to grow again." Controlling all aspects of the process, from the breeding of the turkeys to delivery, Zacky was well positioned to take advantage of turkey's ever-growing popularity with consumers, whether it be with a traditional whole turkey or a turkey frank. Moreover, most of the major turkey companies were located east of the Rocky Mountains, providing Zacky with an opportunity to enjoy strong growth in the western states, where the company's longtime, well-earned reputation for selling a quality product, combined with superior customer service, gave it a clear edge over the competition.

Principal Divisions

Consumer Products; Foodservice Products.

Principal Competitors

Foster Poultry Farms; Tyson Foods Inc.; Smithfield Foods Inc.

Further Reading

Andrade, Dereck, "Zacky Selling to Foster Poultry Deal May Involve 1,500 Jobs," *Daily News* (Los Angeles, California), March 29, 2001, p. B2.

Benjamin, Marc, "Zacky Farms chief Al Zacky Dies in Los Angeles at Age 71," *Fresno Bee*, April 27, 2000, p. C1.

Britton, Charles, "Zacky Farms . . . It IS No Turkey," *Southern California Business*, November 1, 1987, p. 6.

Gallagher, Erica, "Learning to Fly," *Food and Drink*, July-August 2004.

Haughton, Natalie, "Celebrate: Lillian Zacky Salutes the Fourth," *Daily News* (Los Angeles, California), June 27, 1996, p. H1.

Rodriguez, Robert, "Zacky Moves to Fresno," *Fresno Bee*, June 14, 2002, p. C1.

Russell, Jeremy, "Alive and Kicking," *National Provisioner*, December 2002, p. S29.

Smith, Rod, "Foster Farms Calls Acquisition 'Ideal' for Company, Consumers," *Feedstuffs*, April 2, 2001, p. 1.

Well, Jeffrey, "The Queen of Cluck," *Los Angeles Magazine*, August 1, 1993, p. 46.

—Ed Dinger

INDEX TO COMPANIES

Index to Companies

Listings in this index are arranged in alphabetical order under the company name. Company names beginning with a letter or proper name such as Eli Lilly & Co. will be found under the first letter of the company name. Definite articles (The, Le, La) are ignored for alphabetical purposes as are forms of incorporation that precede the company name (AB, NV). Company names printed in bold type have full, historical essays on the page numbers appearing in bold. Updates to entries that appeared in earlier volumes are signified by the notation **(upd.)**. Company names in light type are references within an essay to that company, not full historical essays. This index is cumulative with volume numbers printed in bold type.

Apple Bank for Savings, 59 51–53
Apple Computer, Inc., III 115–16; **6**
  218–20 (upd.); **36** 48–51 (upd.); **38** 69;
  71 19
Apple Orthodontix, Inc., **35** 325
Apple South, Inc. *See* Avado Brands, Inc.
Applebee's International Inc., 14 29–31;
  19 258; **20** 159; **21** 362; **31** 40; **35**
  38–41 (upd.)
Applera Corporation, **74** 71
Appleton Papers, **I** 426
Appleton Wire Works Corp., **8** 13
**Appliance Recycling Centers of America,
  Inc., 42** 13–16
Applica Incorporated, 43 32–36 (upd.)
Applied Beverage Systems Ltd., **21** 339
Applied Biomedical Corp., **47** 4
Applied Bioscience International, Inc., 10
  105–07
Applied Biosystems, **74** 72
Applied Color Systems, **III** 424
Applied Communications, Inc., **6** 280; **11**
  151; **25** 496; **29** 477–79
Applied Data Research, Inc., **18** 31–32
Applied Digital Data Systems Inc., **9** 514
Applied Engineering Services, Inc. *See* The
  AES Corporation.
Applied Films Corporation, 12 121; **35**
  148; **48** 28–31
Applied Industrial Materials Corporation,
  22 544, 547
Applied Komatsu Technology, Inc., **10** 109
Applied Laser Systems, **31** 124
Applied Learning International, **IV** 680
Applied Materials, Inc., 10 108–09; **18**
  382–84; **46** 31–34 (upd.)
Applied Micro Circuits Corporation, 38
  53–55
Applied Network Technology, Inc., **25** 162
Applied Power Inc., 9 26–28; **32** 47–51
  (upd.)
Applied Programming Technologies, Inc.,
  12 61
Applied Solar Energy, **8** 26
Applied Technology Corp., **11** 87
Applied Thermal Technologies, Inc., **29** 5
Approvisionnement Atlantique, **II** 652; **51**
  303
Apria Healthcare Inc., **43** 266
Aprilia SpA, 17 24–26
Aprolis, **72** 159
APS. *See* Arizona Public Service
  Company.
APS Healthcare, **17** 166, 168
APSA, **63** 214
AptarGroup, Inc., 69 38–41
Apura GmbH, **IV** 325
Aqua Alliance Inc., 32 52–54 (upd.)
Aqua Cool Pure Bottled Water, **52** 188
Aqua de Oro Venture, **58** 23
Aquafin N.V., **12** 443; **38** 427
Aquarium Supply Co., **12** 230
Aquarius Group. *See* Club Mediterranee
  SA.
Aquarius Platinum Ltd., 63 38–40
Aquatech, **53** 232
Aquila Energy Corp., **6** 593
Aquila, Inc., 50 37–40 (upd.)
Aquitaine. *See* Société Nationale des
  Petroles d'Aquitaine.
AR Accessories Group, Inc., 23 20–22
AR-TIK Systems, Inc., **10** 372
ARA Services, II 607–08; **21** 507; **25** 181.
  See also Aramark.

Arab-Israel Bank Ltd., **60** 50
Arab Japanese Insurance Co., **III** 296
Arab Leasing International Finance, **72** 85
Arab Radio & Television, **72** 85
Arabian American Oil Co. *See* Saudi
  Arabian Oil Co.
Arabian Gulf Oil Company. *See* Natinal
  Oil Corporation.
Arabian Investment Banking Corp., **15** 94;
  26 53; **47** 361
Aracruz Celulose S.A., 57 45–47
Aral AG, 62 12–15
ARAMARK Corporation, 13 48–50; **16**
  228; **21** 114–15; **35** 415; **41** 21–24
Aramco. *See* Arabian American Oil Co.;
  Saudi Arabian Oil Company.
Aramis Inc., **30** 191
Arandell Corporation, 37 16–18
Arapuã. *See* Lojas Arapuã S.A.
Aratex Inc., **13** 49
ARBED S.A., IV 24–27, 53; **22** 41–45
  (upd.); **26** 83; **42** 414
Arbeitsgemeinschaft der öffentlich-
  rechtlichen Rundfunkanstalten der
  Bundesrepublick. *See* ARD.
The Arbitron Company, 10 255, 359; **13**
  5; **38** 56–61
Arbor Acres, **13** 103
Arbor Drugs Inc., 12 21–23. *See also*
  CVS Corporation.
Arbor International, **18** 542
Arbor Living Centers Inc., **6** 478
Arby's Inc., II 614; **8** 536–37; **14** 32–34,
  351; **58** 323
ARC. *See* American Rug Craftsmen.
ARC International Corporation, **27** 57
ARC Materials Corp., **III** 688
ARC Propulsion, **13** 462
ARCA. *See* Appliance Recycling Centers
  of America, Inc.
Arcadia Company, **14** 138
Arcadia Group plc, 28 27–30 (upd.),
  95–96
Arcadia Partners, **17** 321
Arcadian Corporation, **18** 433; **27** 317–18
Arcadian Marine Service, Inc., **6** 530
Arcadis NV, 26 21–24
Arcata Corporation, **12** 413
Arcata National Corp., **9** 305
Arcelor S.A., **65** 311
ARCH Air Medical Service, Inc., **53** 29
Arch Mineral Corporation, 7 32–34
Arch Petroleum Inc., **39** 331
Arch Wireless, Inc., 39 23–26; **41** 265,
  267
Archbold Container Co., **35** 390
Archbold Ladder Co., **12** 433
Archer-Daniels-Midland Co., I 419–21; **7**
  432–33, 241 **8** 53; **11** 21–23 (upd.); **17**
  207; **22** 85, 426; **23** 384; **25** 241; **31**
  234; **32** 55–59 (upd.)
Archer Management Services Inc., **24** 360
Archibald Candy Corporation, **36** 309; **71**
  22
Archie Comics Publications, Inc., 63
  41–44
Archipelago RediBook, **48** 226, 228
Archon Corporation, 74 23–26 (upd.)
Archstone-Smith Trust, 49 27–30
Archway Cookies, Inc., 29 29–31
ArcLight, LLC, **50** 123
ARCO. *See* Atlantic Richfield Company.
ARCO Chemical Company, 10 110–11
ARCO Comfort Products Co., **26** 4

Arco Electronics, **9** 323
Arco Pharmaceuticals, Inc., **31** 346
Arcon Corporation, **26** 287
Arcor S.A.I.C., 66 7–9
Arcorp Properties, **70** 226
Arctco, Inc., 12 400–01; **16** 31–34; **35**
  349, 351
Arctic Alaska Fisheries Corporation, **14**
  515; **50** 493–94
Arctic Cat Inc., 40 46–50 (upd.)
Arctic Enterprises, **34** 44
Arctic Slope Regional Corporation, 38
  62–65
ARD, 41 25–29
Ardal og Sunndal Verk AS, **10** 439
Arden Group, Inc., 29 32–35
Ardent Risk Services, Inc. *See* General Re
  Corporation.
Ardent Software Inc., **59** 54–55
Argenbright Security Inc. *See* Securicor
  Plc.
Argentaria Caja Postal y Banco
  Hipotecario S.A. *See* Banco Bilbao
  Vizcaya Argentaria S.A.
Argentaurum A.G. *See* Pall Corporation.
Argentine National Bank, **14** 46
Argon Medical, **12** 327
Argonaut, **10** 520–22
Argos, **I** 426; **22** 72; **50** 117
Argos Retail Group, **47** 165, 169
Argos Soditic, **43** 147, 149
Argosy Gaming Company, 21 38–41
Argosy Group LP, **27** 197
Argus Corp., **IV** 611
Argus Energy, **7** 538
Argus Motor Company, **16** 7
Arguss Communications, Inc., **57** 120
Argyle Television Inc., **19** 204
Argyll Group PLC, I 241; **II** 609–10,
  656; **12** 152–53; **24** 418. *See also*
  Safeway PLC.
Aria Communications, Inc. *See* Ascend
  Communications, Inc.
Ariba, Inc., 38 432; **57** 48–51
Ariel Capital Management, **28** 421
Ariens Company, 48 32–34
Aries Technology, **25** 305
Ariete S.P.A. *See* De'Longhi S.p.A.
Aris Industries, Inc., 15 275; **16** 35–38
Arista Laboratories Inc., **51** 249, 251
Aristech Chemical Corp., **12** 342
Aristocrat Leisure Limited, 54 14–16
Aristokraft Inc. *See* MasterBrand Cabinets,
  Inc.
The Aristotle Corporation, 62 16–18
Arizona Airways, **22** 219
AriZona Beverages. *See* Ferolito, Vultaggio
  & Sons
Arizona Daily Star, **58** 282
Arizona Edison Co., **6** 545
Arizona Growth Capital, Inc., **18** 513
Arizona One, **24** 455
Arizona Public Service Company, **6**
  545–47; **19** 376, 412; **26** 359; **28**
  425–26; **54** 290
Arizona Refrigeration Supplies, **14** 297–98
Arjo Wiggins Appleton p.l.c., 13 458; **27**
  513; **34** 38–40
Ark Restaurants Corp., 20 25–27
Arkansas Best Corporation, 16 39–41;
  19 455; **42** 410
Arkansas Louisiana Gas Company. *See*
  Arkla, Inc.
Arkia, **23** 184, 186–87

Christensen Boyles Corporation, 19 247;
26 68–71
Christensen Company, 8 397
Christiaensen, 26 160
The Christian Broadcasting Network,
Inc., 13 279; 52 83–85; 57 392
Christian Dalloz SA, 40 96–98
Christian Dior S.A., 19 86–88; 23 237,
242; 49 90–93 (upd.)
Christian Salvesen Plc, 45 10, 100–03
The Christian Science Publishing
Society, 55 99–102
Christian Supply Centers, Inc., 45 352
Christiana Bank og Kredietklasse, 40 336
Christie, Mitchell & Mitchell, 7 344
Christie's International plc, 15 98–101;
39 81–85 (upd.); 49 325
Christofle Orfevrerie, 44 206
Christofle SA, 40 99–102
Christopher & Banks Corporation, 42
73–75
Christopher Charters, Inc. See Kitty Hawk,
Inc.
Chromalloy American Corp., 13 461; 54
330
Chromalloy Gas Turbine Corp., 13 462; 54
331
Chromatic Color, 13 227–28
Chromcraft Revington, Inc., 15 102–05;
26 100
Chromium Corporation, 52 103–05
Chrompack, Inc., 48 410
The Chronicle Publishing Company,
Inc., 23 119–22
Chronimed Inc., 26 72–75
Chronoservice, 27 475
Chrysalis Group plc, 22 194; 40 103–06
Chrysler Corporation, I 144–45; 11
53–55 (upd.). See also DaimlerChrysler
AG
Chrysler Financial Company, LLC, 45 262
CHS Inc., 60 86–89
CHT Steel Company Ltd., 51 352
CH2M Hill Ltd., 22 136–38
Chubb Corporation, III 220–22, 368; 11
481; 14 108–10 (upd.); 29 256; 37
83–87 (upd.); 45 109
Chubb, PLC, 50 133–36
Chubb Security plc, 44 258
Chubu Electric Power Company, Inc., V
571–73; 46 90–93 (upd.)
Chuck E. Cheese, 13 472–74; 31 94
Chugach Alaska Corporation, 60 90–93
Chugai Boyeki Co. Ltd., 44 441
Chugai Pharmaceutical Co., Ltd., 8
215–16; 10 79; 50 137–40
Chugai Shogyo Shimposha. See Nihon
Keizai Shimbun, Inc.
Chugoku Electric Power Company Inc.,
V 574–76; 53 101–04 (upd.)
Chugoku Funai Electric Company Ltd., 62
150
Chunghwa Picture Tubes, 23 469
Chuo Rika Kogyo Corp., 56 238
Chuo Trust & Banking Co. See Yasuda
Trust and Banking Company, Limited.
Chupa Chups S.A., 38 133–35
Church & Company, 45 342, 344
Church & Dwight Co., Inc., 29 112–15;
68 78–82 (upd.)
Church and Tower Group, 19 254
Church's Chicken, 7 26–28; 15 345; 23
468; 32 13–14; 66 56–59

Churchill Downs Incorporated, 29
116–19
Churchill Insurance Co. Ltd., III 404
CI Holdings, Limited, 53 120
Cia Hering, 72 66–68
Cianbro Corporation, 14 111–13
Cianchette Brothers, Inc. See Cianbro
Corporation.
Ciba-Geigy Ltd., I 632–34; 8 108–11
(upd.). See also Novartis AG.
CIBC. See Canadian Imperial Bank of
Commerce.
CIBC Wood Gundy Securities Corp., 24
482
Ciber, Inc., 18 110–12
Ciby 2000, 24 79
CIC. See Commercial Intertech
Corporation.
CIC Investors #13 LP, 60 130
CICI, 11 184
Cie Continental d'Importation, 10 249
Cie des Lampes, 9 9
Cie Générale d'Electro-Ceramique, 9 9
Cie.Generale des Eaux S.A., 24 327
CIENA Corporation, 54 68–71
Cifra, S.A. de C.V., 8 556; 12 63–65; 26
524; 34 197–98; 35 320; 63 430. See
also Wal-Mart de Mexico, S.A. de C.V.
Cifunsa. See Compania Fundidora del
Norte, S.A.
Ciga Group, 54 345, 347
Cigarrera La Moderna, 21 260; 22 73
Cigarros la Tabacelera Mexicana
(Cigatam), 21 259
CIGNA Corporation, III 223–27; 10 30;
11 243; 22 139–44 (upd.), 269; 38 18;
45 104–10 (upd.)
CIGWELD, 19 442
Cii-HB, III 678; 16 122
Cilbarco, II 25
CILCORP Energy Services Inc., 60 27
Cilva Holdings PLC, 6 358
Cima, 14 224–25
CIMA Precision Spring Europa, 55 305–06
Cimaron Communications Corp., 38 54
Cimarron Utilities Company, 6 580
CIMCO Ltd., 21 499–501
Cimeco S.A. See Grupo Clarín S.A.
Cimenteries CBR S.A., 23 325, 327
Ciments Français, 40 107–10
Ciments Lafarge France/Quebec. See
Lafarge Cement
Cimos, 7 37
Cinar Corporation, 40 111–14
Cincinnati Bell, Inc., 6 316–18; 29 250,
252
Cincinnati Electronics Corp., II 25
Cincinnati Financial Corporation, 16
102–04; 44 89–92 (upd.)
Cincinnati Gas & Electric Company, 6
465–68, 481–82
Cincinnati Lamb Inc., 72 69–71
Cincinnati Milacron Inc., 12 66–69. See
also Milacron, Inc.
Cincom Systems Inc., 15 106–08
Cine-Groupe, 35 279
Cinecentrum, IV 591
Cinemark, 21 362; 23 125
CinemaSource, 58 167
Cinemax, IV 675; 7 222–24, 528–29; 23
276
Cinemex, 71 256

Cineplex Odeon Corporation, II 145, 6
161–63; 14 87; 23 123–26 (upd.); 33
432
Cinerama Group, 67 291
Cinnabon Inc., 13 435–37; 23 127–29; 32
12, 15
Cinquième Saison, 38 200, 202
Cinram International, Inc., 43 107–10
Cinsa. See Compania Industrial del Norte,
S.A.
Cintas Corporation, 16 228; 21 114–16,
507; 30 455; 51 74–77 (upd.)
Cintra. See Concesiones de Infraestructuras
de Transportes, S.A.; Corporacion
Internacional de Aviacion, S.A. de C.V.
Cinven, 49 451; 63 49–50
Cipal-Parc Astérix, 27 10
Ciprial S.A., 27 260
CIPSCO Inc., 6 469–72, 505–06. See
also Ameren Corporation.
CIR. See Compagnie Industriali Riunite
S.p.A.
Circa Pharmaceuticals, 16 529; 56 375
Circle A Ginger Ale Company, 9 177
Circle International Group Inc., 17 216; 59
171
The Circle K Company, II 619–20; 7
113–14, 372, 374; 20 138–40 (upd.); 25
125; 26 447; 49 17
Circle Plastics, 9 323
Circon Corporation, 21 117–20
Circuit City Stores, Inc., 9 120–22; 29
120–24 (upd.); 65 109–14 (upd.)
Circus Circus Enterprises, Inc., 6
203–05; 19 377, 379
Circus Distribution, Inc. See DC Shoes,
Inc.
Circus Knie, 29 126
Circus World, 16 389–90
Cirque du Soleil Inc., 29 125–28
Cirrus Design Corporation, 44 93–95
Cirrus Logic, Inc., 9 334; 11 56–57; 25
117; 48 90–93 (upd.)
CIS Acquisition Corporation, 56 134
CIS Mortgage Maker Ltd., 51 89
Cisco Systems, Inc., 11 58–60; 34
111–15 (upd.); 36 300; 38 430; 43 251
Cise, 24 79
Cisneros Group of Companies, 47 312;
54 72–75
CIT Alcatel, 9 9–10
CIT Financial Corp., 8 117; 12 207
CIT Group, Inc., 13 446, 536; 63 404
Citadel Communications Corporation,
35 102–05
Citadel General, III 404
Citadel, Inc., 27 46
CitFed Bancorp, Inc., 16 105–07
CITGO Petroleum Corporation, II
660–61; IV 391–93, 508; 7 491; 31
113–17 (upd.); 32 414, 416–17; 45 252,
254
Citibanc Group, Inc., 11 456
Citibank, III 243, 340; 9 124; 10 150; 11
418; 13 146; 14 101; 23 3–4, 482; 25
180, 542; 50 6; 59 121, 124–25. See
also Citigroup Inc
Citibank of Mexico, 34 82
CITIC Pacific Ltd., 16 481; 18 113–15;
20 134
Citicasters Inc., 23 293–94
Citicorp, II 253–55; III 397; 7 212–13; 8
196; 9 123–26 (upd.), 441; 10 463, 469;
11 140; 12 30, 310, 334; 13 535; 14

German-American Car Company. *See* GATX.

The German Society. *See* The Legal Aid Society.

GERPI, **51** 16

Gerrard Group, **61** 270, 272

Gerresheimer Glas AG, 43 186–89

Gerrity Oil & Gas Corporation, **11** 28; **24** 379–80

Gerry Weber International AG, 63 169–72

GESA. *See* General Europea S.A.

Gesbancaya, **II** 196

Geschmay Group, **51** 14

Gesellschaft für musikalische Aufführungs- und mechanische Vervielfältigungsrechte. *See* GEMA.

Gesellschaft für Tierernährung, **74** 117

GET Manufacturing Inc., **36** 300

Getchell Gold Corporation, **61** 292

Getronics NV, 39 176–78

Getty Images, Inc., 31 216–18

Getty Oil Co., **6** 457; **8** 526; **11** 27; **17** 501; **18** 488; **27** 216; **47** 436. *See also* ChevronTexaco.

Getz Corp., **IV** 137

Gevaert. *See* Agfa Gevaert Group N.V.

Gevity HR, Inc., 63 173–77

Geyser Peak Winery, **58** 196

GFI Informatique SA, 49 165–68

GfK Aktiengesellschaft, 49 169–72

GFL Mining Services Ltd., **62** 164

GFS. *See* Gordon Food Service Inc.

GFS Realty Inc., **II** 633

GGT Group, **44** 198

GHI, **28** 155, 157

Ghirardelli Chocolate Company, 24 480; **27** 105; **30 218–20**

GI Communications, **10** 321

GI Export Corp. *See* Johnston Industries, Inc.

GIAG, **16** 122

Gianni Versace SpA, 22 238–40

Giant Bicycle Inc., **19** 384

Giant Cement Holding, Inc., 23 224–26

Giant Eagle, Inc., **12** 390–91; **13** 237

Giant Food Inc., II 633–35, 656; **13** 282, 284; **15** 532; **16** 313; **22 241–44 (upd.);** **24** 462; **60** 307

Giant Industries, Inc., 19 175–77; 61 114–18 (upd.)

Giant Resources, **III** 729

Giant Stores, Inc., **7** 113; **25** 124

Giant TC, Inc. *See* Campo Electronics, Appliances & Computers, Inc.

Giant Tire & Rubber Company, **8** 126

Giant-Vac Manufacturing Inc., **64** 355

Giant Video Corporation, **29** 503

Giant Wholesale, **II** 625

GIB Group, V 63–66; 26 158–62 (upd.)

Gibbons, Green, van Amerongen Ltd., **II** 605; **9** 94; **12** 28; **19** 360

Gibbs and Dandy plc, 74 119–21

Gibbs Construction, **25** 404

GIBCO Corp., **17** 287, 289

Gibraltar Casualty Co., **III** 340

Gibraltar Steel Corporation, 37 164–67

Gibson, Dunn & Crutcher LLP, 36 249–52; 37 292

Gibson Greetings, Inc., 7 24; **12 207–10;** **16** 256; **21** 426–28; **22** 34–35; **59** 35, 37

Gibson Guitar Corp., 16 237–40

Gibson McDonald Furniture Co., **14** 236

GIC. *See* The Goodyear Tire & Rubber Company.

Giddings & Lewis, Inc., 10 328–30

GiFi S.A., 74 122–24

Giftmaster Inc., **26** 439–40

Gil-Wel Manufacturing Company, **17** 440

Gilbane, Inc., 34 191–93

Gilbert & John Greenall Limited, **21** 246

Gilbert Lane Personnel, Inc., **9** 326

Gildon Metal Enterprises, **7** 96

Gilead Sciences, Inc., 54 129–31

Gilkey Bros. *See* Puget Sound Tug and Barge Company.

Gill Interprovincial Lines, **27** 473

Gillett Holdings, Inc., 7 199–201; 11 543, 545; **43** 437–38

The Gillette Company, III 27–30; 20 249–53 (upd.); 23 54–57; 68 171–76 (upd.)

Gilliam Furniture Inc., **12** 475

Gilliam Manufacturing Co., **8** 530

Gilliam S.A., **61** 104

Gilman & Ciocia, Inc., 72 148–50

Gilman Paper Co., **37** 178

Gilmore Steel Corporation. *See* Oregon Steel Mills, Inc.

Gilroy Foods, **27** 299

Gimbel Brothers, Inc. *See* Saks Holdings, Inc.

Gimbel's Department Store, **I** 426–27; **8** 59; **22** 72; **50** 117–18

Gimelli Productions AG, **73** 332

Gindick Productions, **6** 28

Gingiss Group, **60** 5

Ginn & Co., **IV** 672; **19** 405

Ginnie Mae. *See* Government National Mortgage Association.

Gino's East, **21** 362

Ginsber Beer Group, **15** 47; **38** 77

Giorgio Armani S.p.A., 45 180–83

Giorgio Beverly Hills, Inc., **26** 384

Giraud Restaurant System Co. Ltd. *See* Odakyu Electric Railway Co., Ltd.

Girbaud, **17** 513; **31** 261

Girl Scouts of the USA, 35 193–96

Giro Sport Designs International Inc., **16** 53; **44** 53–54

GiroCredit Bank, **69** 156

Girod, **19** 50

Girsa S.A., **23** 170

Girvin, Inc., **16** 297

Gist-Brocades Co., **III** 53; **26** 384

Git-n-Go Corporation, **60** 160

The Gitano Group, Inc., 8 219–21; 20 136 **25** 167; **37** 81

La Giulia Ind. S.P.A., **72** 272

GIV. *See* Granite Industries of Vermont, Inc.

Givaudan SA, 43 190–93

GIW Industries Inc., **62** 217

GJM International Ltd., **25** 121–22

GK Technologies Incorporated, **10** 547

GKH Partners, **29** 295

GKN plc, III 493–96; 38 208–13 (upd.); **42** 47; **47** 7, 9, 279–80

Glacier Bancorp, Inc., 35 197–200

Glacier Park, Inc. *See* Viad Corp.

Glacier Water Services, Inc., 47 155–58

Glamar Group plc, **14** 224

Glamis Gold, Ltd., 54 132–35

Glamor Shops, Inc., **14** 93

Glanbia plc, 38 196, 198; **59 204–07,** 364

Glass Glover Plc, **52** 419

Glasstite, Inc., **33** 360–61

GlasTec, **II** 420

Glastron. *See* Genmar Holdings, Inc.

Glatfelter Wood Pulp Company, **8** 413

Glaxo Holdings plc, I 639–41, 643, 668, 675, 693; **9 263–65 (upd.); 10** 551; **11** 173; **20** 39; **26** 31; **34** 284; **38** 365; **50** 56; **54** 130

GlaxoSmithKline plc, 46 201–08 (upd.)

Gleason Corporation, 24 184–87

Glemby Co. Inc., **70** 262

Glen & Co., **I** 453

Glen Alden Corp., **15** 247

Glen-Gery Corporation, **14** 249

Glencairn Ltd., **25** 418

Glencore International AG, 52 71, 73; **73** 391–92

The Glenlyte Group, **29** 469

Glenlyte Thomas Group LLC, **29** 466

Glenmoor Partners, **70** 34–35

Glenn Advertising Agency, **25** 90

Glenn Pleass Holdings Pty. Ltd., **21** 339

GLF-Eastern States Association, **7** 17

Glico. *See* Ezaki Glico Company Ltd.

The Glidden Company, I 353; **8 222–24;** **21** 545

Glimcher Co., **26** 262

Glitsch International, Inc. *See* Foster Wheeler Corp.

Global Access, **31** 469

Global Apparel Sourcing Ltd., **22** 223

Global Berry Farms LLC, 62 154–56

Global BMC (Mauritius) Holdings Ltd., **62** 55

Global Card Holdings Inc., **68** 45

Global Communications of New York, Inc., **45** 261

Global Crossing Ltd., 32 216–19

Global Engineering Company, **9** 266

Global Health Care Partners, **42** 68

Global Imaging Systems, Inc., 73 163–65

Global Industries, Ltd., 37 168–72

Global Information Solutions, **34** 257

Global Interactive Communications Corporation, **28** 242

Global Marine Inc., 9 266–67; 11 87

Global Motorsport Group, Inc. *See* Custom Chrome, Inc.

Global One, **52** 108

Global Outdoors, Inc., 49 173–76

Global Petroleum Albania S.A./Elda Petroleum Sh.P.K., **64** 177

Global Power Equipment Group Inc., 52 137–39

Global Switch International Ltd., **67** 104–05

Global TeleSystems, Inc. *See* Global Crossing Ltd.

Global Vacations Group. *See* Classic Vacation Group, Inc.

Global Van Lines. *See* Allied Worldwide, Inc.

GlobalCom Telecommunications, Inc., **24** 122

GlobaLex, **28** 141

Globalia, **53** 301

GlobalSantaFe Corporation, 48 187–92 (upd.)

Globalstar Telecommunications Limited, **54** 233

GLOBALT, Inc., **52** 339

Globe Business Furniture, **39** 207

Globe Feather & Down, **19** 304

Globe Newspaper Co., **7** 15

Globe Pequot Press, **36** 339, 341

INDEX TO INDUSTRIES

Index to Industries

CONSTRUCTION

ENTERTAINMENT & LEISURE

FINANCIAL SERVICES: BANKS

FOOD PRODUCTS

FOOD SERVICES & RETAILERS

HEALTH & PERSONAL CARE PRODUCTS

INSURANCE

MINING & METALS

REAL ESTATE

TEXTILES & APPAREL

WASTE SERVICES

GEOGRAPHIC INDEX

Geographic Index

Ghana

Greece

Hong Kong

NOTES ON CONTRIBUTORS ────────────────

Notes on Contributors

BRENNAN, Gerald E. California-based writer.

COHEN, M. L. Novelist and business writer living in Paris.

COVELL, Jeffrey L. Seattle-based writer.

DINGER, Ed. Bronx-based writer and editor.

GARIEPY, Jennifer. Editor and artist in Detroit, Michigan.

GREENLAND, Paul R. Illinois-based writer and researcher; author of two books and former senior editor of a national business magazine; contributor to *The Encyclopedia of Chicago History, The Encyclopedia of Religion,* and the *Encyclopedia of American Industries.*

HALASZ, Robert. Former editor in chief of *World Progress* and *Funk & Wagnalls New Encyclopedia Yearbook*; author, *The U.S. Marines* (Millbrook Press, 1993).

INGRAM, Frederick C. Utah-based business writer who has contributed to *GSA Business, Appalachian Trailway News,* the *Encyclopedia of Business,* the *Encyclopedia of Global Industries,* the *Encyclopedia of Consumer Brands,* and other regional and trade publications.

MONTGOMERY, Bruce. Curator and director of historical collection, University of Colorado at Boulder.

ROTHBURD, Carrie. Writer and editor specializing in corporate profiles, academic texts, and academic journal articles.

STANSELL, Christina M. Writer and editor based in Louisville, Kentucky.

UHLE, Frank. Ann Arbor-based writer; movie projectionist, disc jockey, and staff member of *Psychotronic Video* magazine.

WILOCH, Thomas. Author whose most recent title is *Crime: A Serious American Problem* (2005); regular contributor to *Rain Taxi Review of Books*; associate editor with *Sidereality.*